The CRB Commodity Yearbook 2016

Commodity Research Bureau

www.crbyearbook.com

For general information on our other products and services or for technical support, please contact our Customer Support Department within the United States at (800) 621-5271, outside the United States at (312) 554-8456 or fax (312) 939-4135.

ISBN 978-0-910418-00-3

Printed in the United States of America

10   9   8   7   6   5   4   3   2   1

Commodity Research Bureau
209 W. Jackson Blvd, 2nd Floor
Chicago, Illinois 60606
800.621.5271 or +1.312.554.8456
Fax: +1.312.939.4135
Website: www.crbyearbook.com
Email: info@crbyearbook.com

Table of Contents

The Commodity Price Trend

The Thomson Reuters Equal Weight Commodity Index (ticker symbol CCI), formerly known as the Reuters/Jefferies CRB Continuous Commodity Index, showed continued weakness in 2015, falling by another -15.2%. The CCI index since 2011 has now plunged by a total of -49% from the record high posted in April 2011 to the 7-year low posted in January 2016, giving back more of the 278% rally seen during the 2001-11 bull market, which was the largest rally in post-war history. The CCI index moved lower in 2015 due to (1) weak commodity demand tied to the soft global economy and the decline in China's 2015 GDP to a 25-year low of +6.9%, (2) the continued strength in the dollar index seen in 2015, (3) the general disinflationary trend seen in the developed world, and (4) the Federal Reserve's tighter monetary policy with the end of its third quantitative easing program in October 2014 and its first interest rate hike in December 2015.

All of the six CCI index sub-sectors closed lower in 2015. The ranked returns in 2015 were as follows: Softs -2.2%, Industrials -9.7%, Grains -14.8%, Metals -16.0%, Livestock -21.4%, and Energy -25.4%. These sub-sector changes are calculated by taking the average of the percentage changes of the constituents in each sub-sector.

Energy

The CCI Energy sub-sector, which is composed of Crude Oil, Heating Oil, and Natural Gas, accounts for 18% of the overall index. The constituents in the Energy sub-sector in 2015 closed down -25.4%, adding to the -41.5% plunge seen in 2014. On a nearest-futures basis, crude oil in 2015 closed down -30.5%, gasoline closed down -11.7%, heating oil closed down -40.4%, and natural gas closed down -19.1%. Crude oil prices plunged in 2014-2015 on over-production and a massive buildup of world crude oil inventories. Natural gas prices during 2015 closed sharply lower on ample supplies and a mild winter.

Grains

The CCI Grains and Oilseeds sub-sector, which is composed of Corn, Soybeans, and Wheat, accounts for 18% of the overall index. The constituents in the Grains and Oilseeds sub-sector closed down -14.8% in 2015, falling for the third consecutive year after a combined −33.4% decline in 2013-2014. On a nearest-futures basis, corn in 2015 fell -9.6%, soybeans fell -14.5%, and wheat fell -20.3%. Corn, soybeans and wheat prices were weak again in 2015 due to ample world supplies.

Industrials

The CCI Industrials sub-sector, which is composed of Copper and Cotton, accounts for 12% of the overall index. The constituents in the Industrials sub-sector showed a -9.7% decline in 2015, adding to the sharp -22.8% decline in 2014. Cotton in 2015 closed up +5.0% after the sharp -28.8% decline seen in 2014. Copper fell by -24.4% in 2015 due to the strong dollar and weak demand tied to slow global economic growth and especially to slower growth in China.

Livestock

The CCI Livestock sub-sector, which is composed of Live Cattle and Lean Hogs, accounts for 12% of the overall index. The constituents in the Livestock sub-sector closed down -21.4% in 2015, snapping the string of six consecutive annual gains. On a nearest-futures basis, live cattle futures in 2015 closed down -16.4% and lean hog futures closed down -26.4% for the third consecutive annual decline.

Precious Metals

The CCI Precious Metals sub-sector, which is composed of Gold, Platinum, and Silver, accounts for 17% of the overall index. The constituents in the Precious Metals sub-sector closed down -16.0% in 2015, adding to the sharp sell-offs of -11.0% in 2014 and -25.0% in 2013. Gold fell -10.5%, silver fell -11.3%, and platinum fell -26.2%. Precious metals prices showed continued weakness in 2015 due to the strength in the dollar, weak global economic growth, and world disinflation.

Softs

The CCI Softs sub-sector, which is composed of Cocoa, Coffee, Orange Juice, and Sugar #11, accounts for 23% of the overall index. The constituents in the Softs sub-sector in 2015 closed down -2.2% after rising by +12.3% in 2014. Coffee closed 2015 sharply lower by -23.9%, while frozen orange juice was unchanged, sugar rose +5.0% and cocoa rose +10.3%.

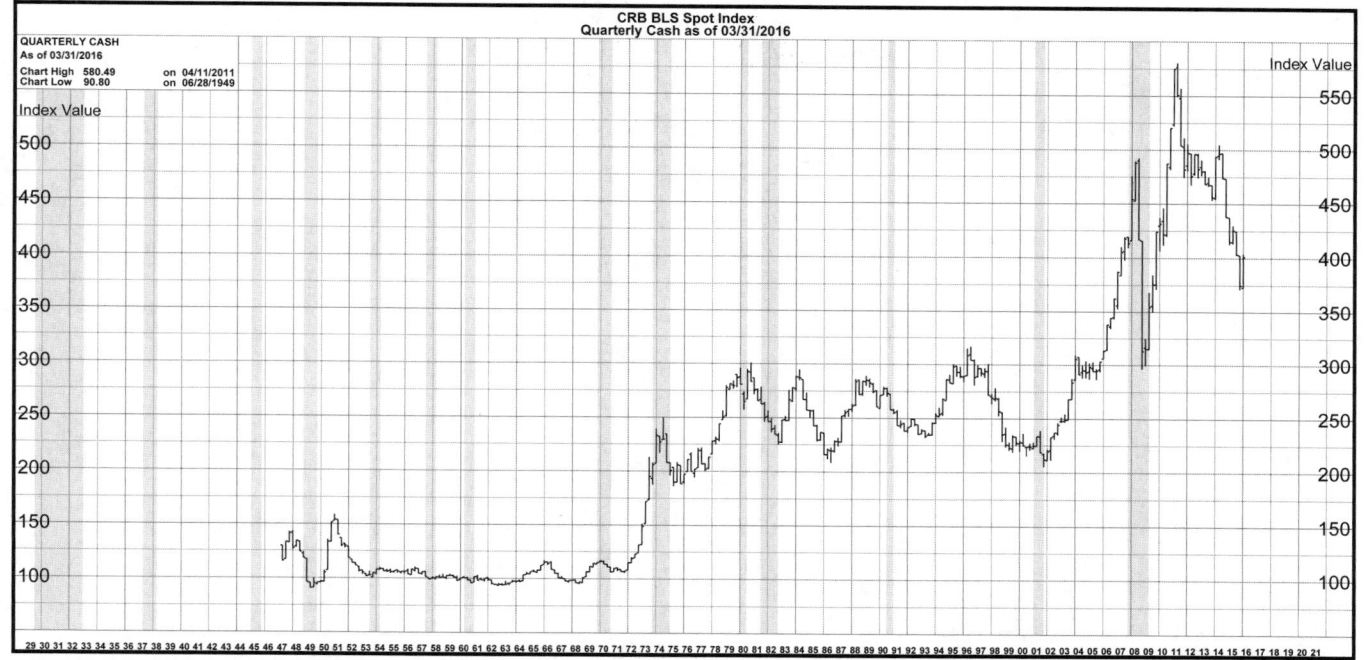

Unweighted Index of 23 Commodities: Hides, tallow, copper scrap, lead scrap, steel scrap, zinc, tin, burlap, cotton, print cloth, wool tops, rosin, rubber, hogs, steers, lard, butter, soybean oil, cocoa, corn, Kansas City wheat, Minneapolis wheat, and sugar.   Shaded areas indicate US recessions.

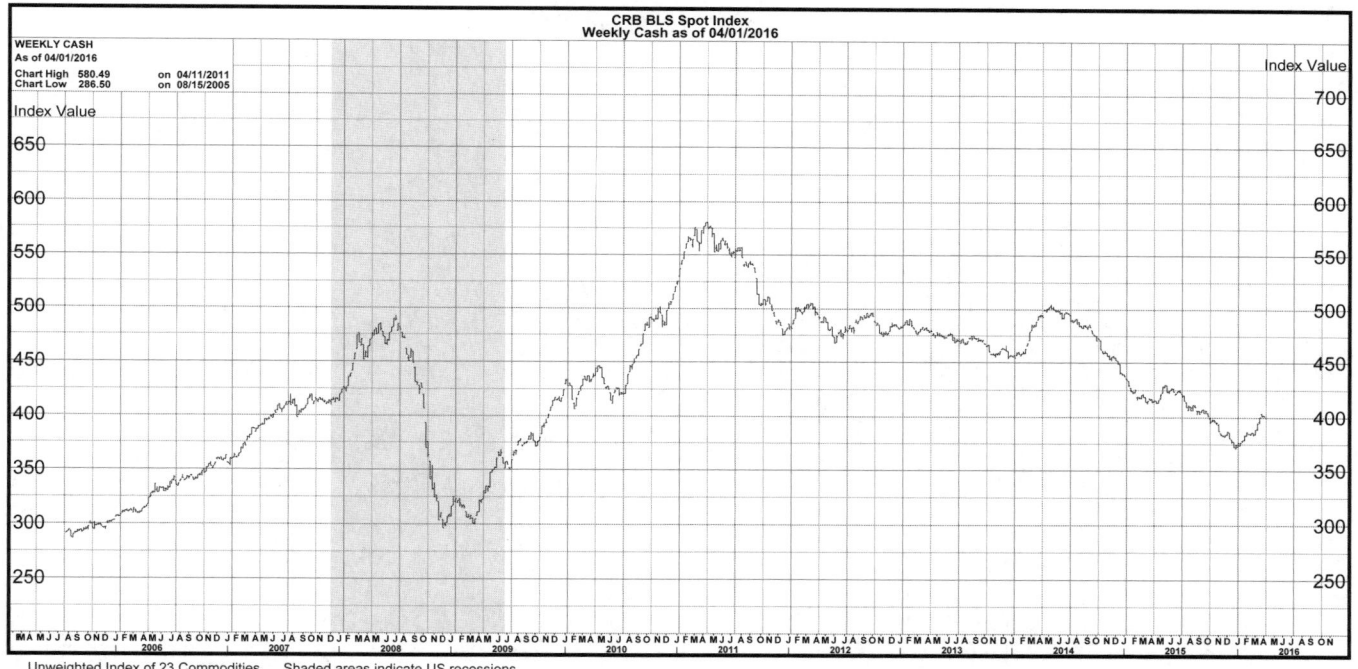

Unweighted Index of 23 Commodities.   Shaded areas indicate US recessions.

CRB Spot Sub-Index   (1967=100)

Year	Jan.	Feb.	Mar.	Apr.	May	June	July	Aug.	Sept.	Oct.	Nov.	Dec.	Average
2006	308.31	311.58	310.86	319.47	330.81	332.19	337.82	341.11	341.85	347.18	354.58	359.35	332.93
2007	358.84	366.47	381.36	388.90	396.79	405.08	410.71	405.97	410.96	414.11	412.79	413.88	397.16
2008	424.32	449.73	464.01	470.41	476.34	475.87	478.60	456.61	428.42	367.61	318.88	303.90	426.23
2009	320.03	312.26	305.91	326.11	347.44	359.84	358.67	374.28	378.72	381.73	403.44	416.74	357.10
2010	428.27	417.21	433.51	441.48	431.40	420.89	425.03	449.12	473.29	489.05	491.25	507.30	450.65
2011	538.09	562.60	566.40	575.61	559.14	557.32	553.30	543.59	527.83	506.85	496.08	480.93	538.98
2012	488.60	498.90	501.77	490.93	480.92	474.62	480.69	488.41	493.34	486.07	477.98	484.25	487.21
2013	485.62	481.97	481.13	477.55	474.67	474.05	469.75	471.23	470.60	462.25	458.57	459.56	472.25
2014	457.25	465.09	487.18	497.58	500.90	495.60	491.20	484.78	479.78	465.82	455.62	445.75	477.21
2015	429.10	420.06	416.96	415.41	425.99	424.32	416.08	408.18	405.50	397.38	385.58	379.17	410.31

Average.   *Source: Commodity Research Bureau*

CRB INDICIES

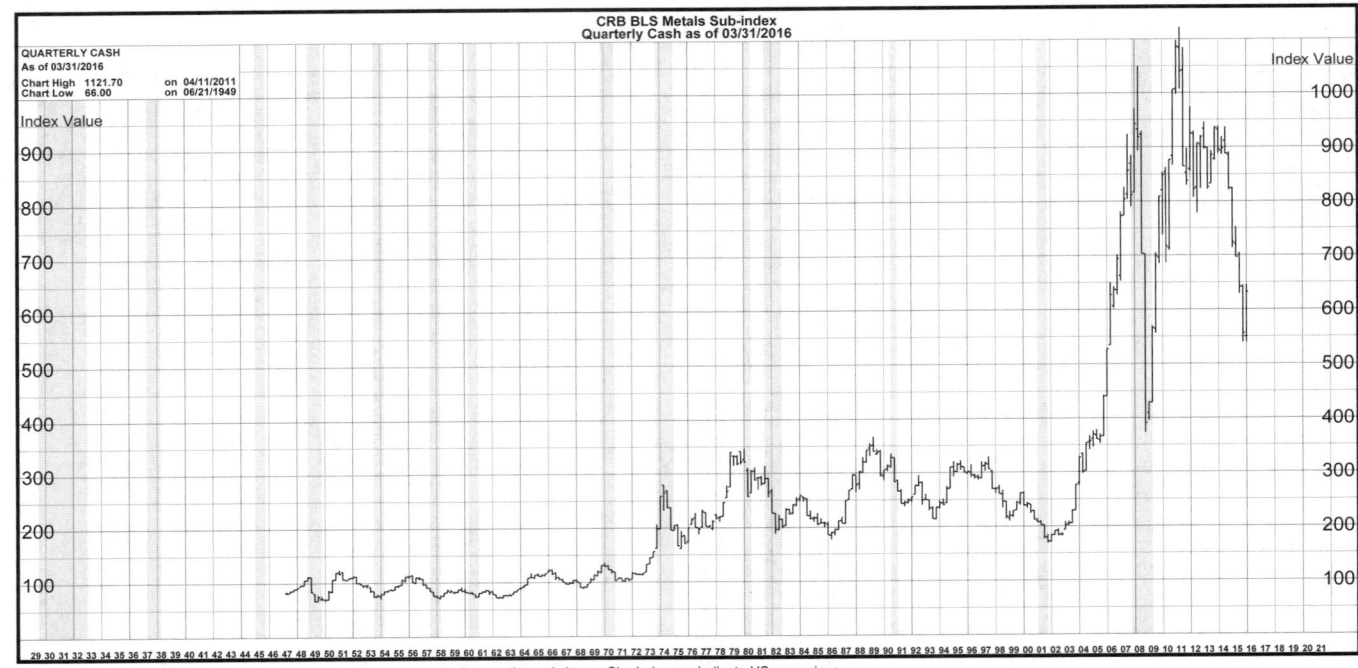

CRB BLS Metals Sub-index
Quarterly Cash as of 03/31/2016

QUARTERLY CASH
As of 03/31/2016
Chart High 1121.70 on 04/11/2011
Chart Low 66.00 on 06/21/1949

Index Value

Unweighted Index of 5 Commodities: Copper scrap, lead scrap, steel scrap, tin, and zinc.   Shaded areas indicate US recessions.

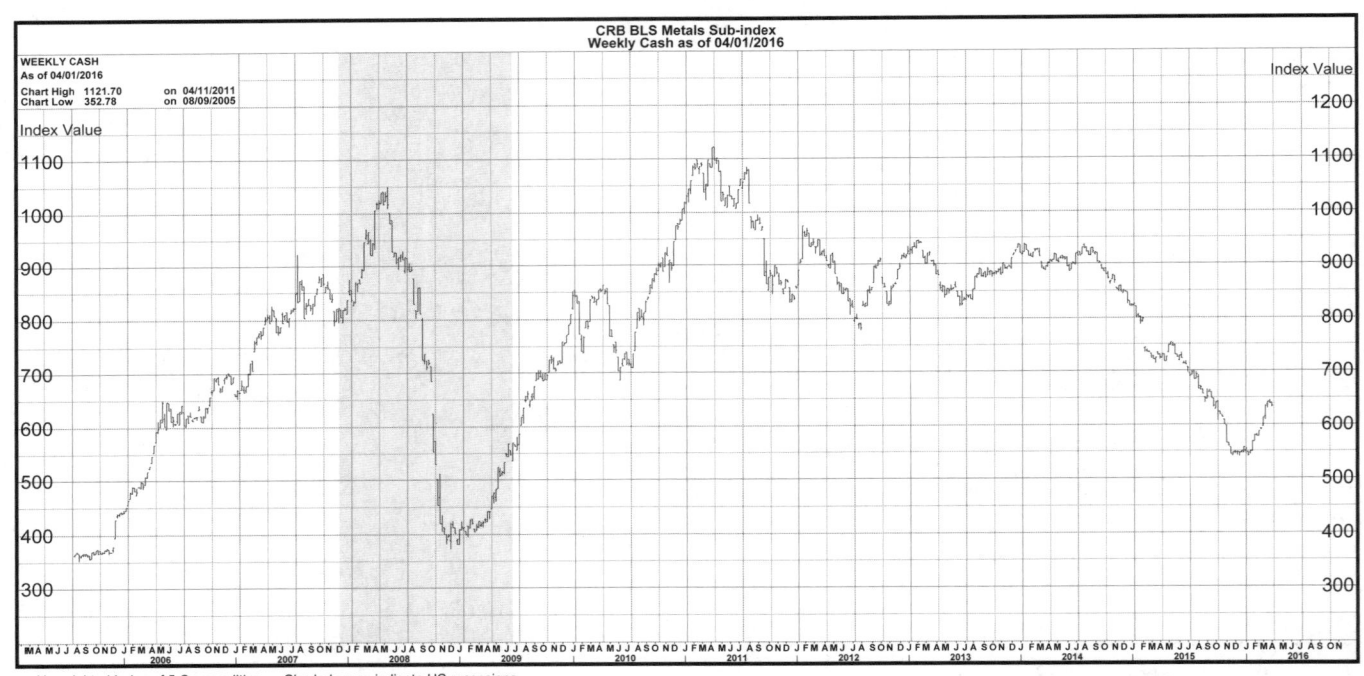

CRB BLS Metals Sub-index
Weekly Cash as of 04/01/2016

WEEKLY CASH
As of 04/01/2016
Chart High 1121.70 on 04/11/2011
Chart Low 352.78 on 08/09/2005

Index Value

Unweighted Index of 5 Commodities.   Shaded areas indicate US recessions.

CRB Spot Metals Sub-Index   (1967=100)

Year	Jan.	Feb.	Mar.	Apr.	May	June	July	Aug.	Sept.	Oct.	Nov.	Dec.	Average
2006	458.64	485.21	504.91	571.37	623.28	616.35	621.31	617.86	623.05	660.11	681.87	693.51	596.46
2007	668.94	691.71	761.81	798.96	798.65	803.29	834.00	840.13	835.06	868.19	828.50	812.12	795.11
2008	843.66	883.22	947.21	1,011.63	1,006.52	914.50	901.61	837.56	728.05	545.95	404.38	400.04	785.36
2009	409.17	416.80	421.44	455.21	410.21	552.61	591.59	651.17	688.67	704.55	716.43	767.81	565.47
2010	830.98	773.24	833.04	850.73	765.47	717.04	728.15	804.22	853.40	896.08	905.01	971.85	827.43
2011	1,029.49	1,085.28	1,066.15	1,096.80	1,033.85	1,023.86	1,063.60	994.80	942.14	874.77	868.19	849.37	994.03
2012	903.04	949.99	931.85	908.47	878.62	843.33	800.76	828.46	883.07	862.76	859.31	910.40	880.01
2013	929.61	930.76	908.99	870.31	850.59	841.39	838.54	875.10	881.56	883.73	891.08	919.04	885.06
2014	925.99	920.45	900.88	905.67	908.51	897.46	921.84	922.59	903.65	876.01	856.97	836.99	898.08
2015	808.63	753.27	725.64	726.61	741.70	717.50	693.73	662.74	649.72	619.91	560.90	546.74	683.92

Average.   *Source: Commodity Research Bureau*

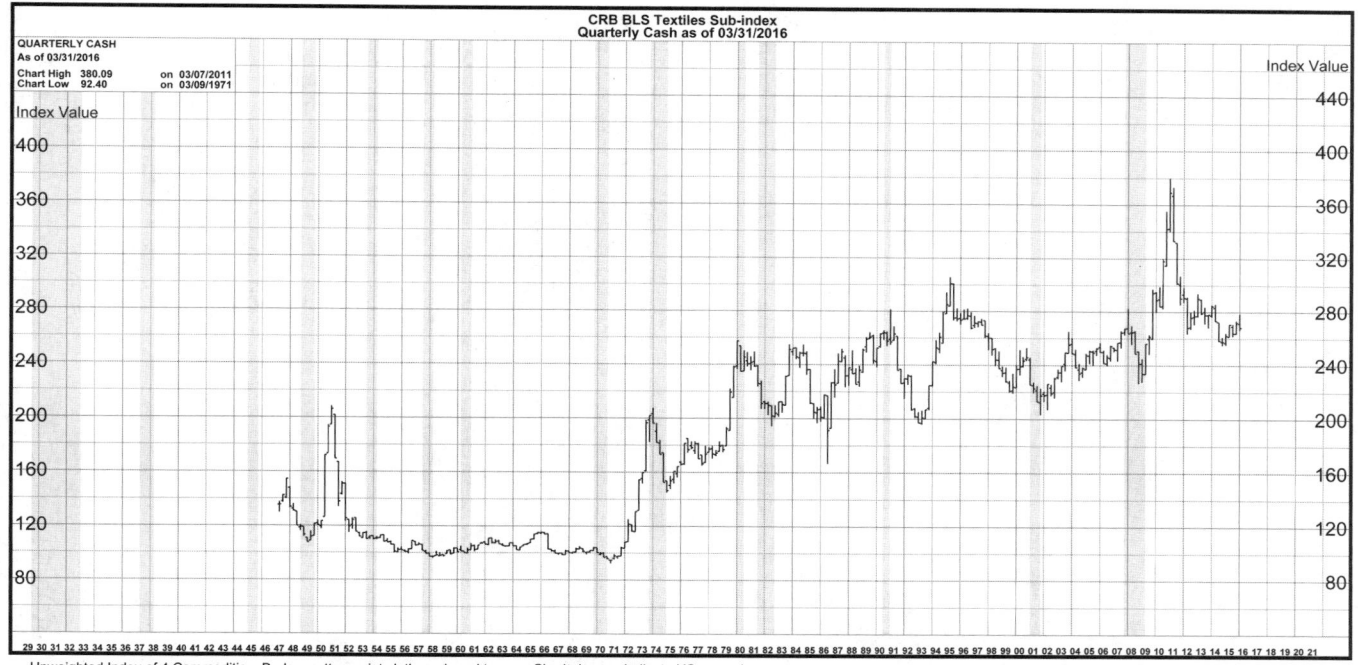

Unweighted Index of 4 Commodities: Burlap, cotton, print cloth, and wool tops.   Shaded areas indicate US recessions.

Unweighted Index of 4 Commodities.   Shaded areas indicate US recessions.

CRB Spot Textiles Sub-Index   (1967=100)

Year	Jan.	Feb.	Mar.	Apr.	May	June	July	Aug.	Sept.	Oct.	Nov.	Dec.	Average
2006	255.02	255.52	251.74	248.26	244.26	244.16	242.03	243.89	245.78	244.89	246.37	251.15	247.76
2007	252.50	251.35	251.91	248.99	245.40	250.72	260.09	256.51	261.58	264.79	265.79	265.28	256.24
2008	267.18	269.60	271.76	267.02	264.71	262.29	263.92	261.98	255.47	241.15	231.28	235.84	257.68
2009	241.13	237.01	229.83	240.05	252.00	253.03	258.94	253.52	257.42	265.67	280.85	293.96	255.28
2010	290.62	287.34	291.16	294.69	292.22	290.03	284.28	295.19	310.18	329.04	341.31	344.99	304.25
2011	347.26	365.82	372.19	365.44	352.18	344.70	319.66	310.92	310.19	303.37	299.19	289.50	331.70
2012	294.47	293.94	289.55	288.47	276.62	269.11	268.88	274.55	277.06	276.65	272.43	276.20	279.83
2013	279.44	283.14	289.79	286.96	286.20	283.33	278.59	278.23	275.03	274.73	269.70	275.78	280.08
2014	278.29	278.84	283.25	283.66	283.35	277.98	268.12	262.53	262.02	259.07	257.53	258.34	271.08
2015	257.16	260.85	261.80	265.21	265.95	267.24	267.42	267.46	263.78	266.74	268.72	271.68	265.33

Average.   *Source: Commodity Research Bureau*

CRB INDICIES

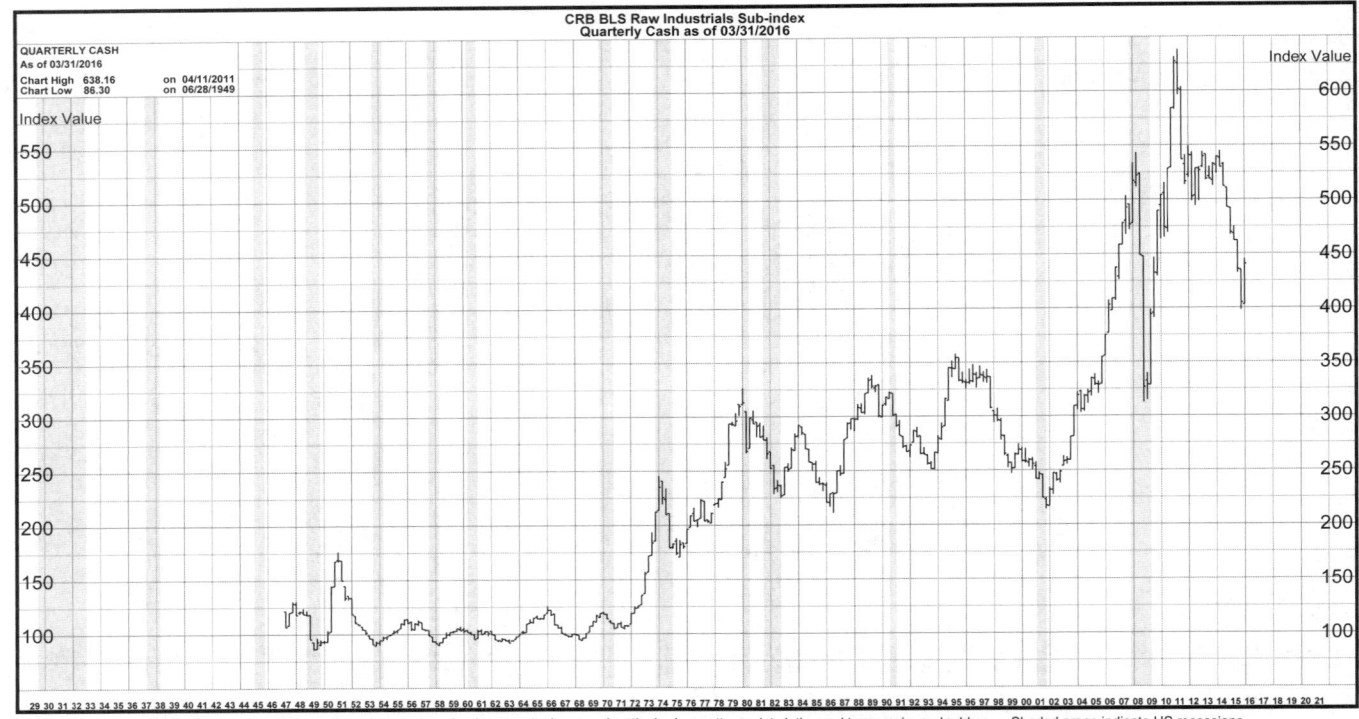

Unweighted Index of 13 Commodities: Hides, tallow, copper scrap, lead scrap, steel scrap, zinc, tin, burlap, cotton, print cloth, wool tops, rosin, and rubber.   Shaded areas indicate US recessions.

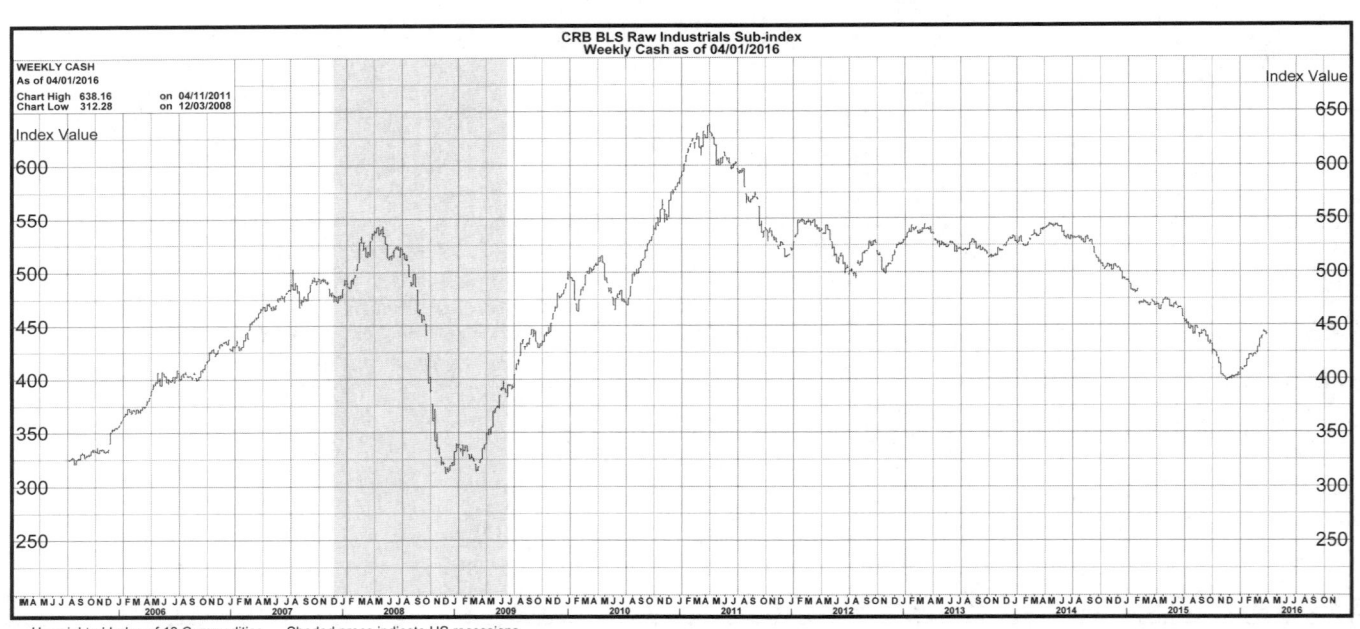

Unweighted Index of 13 Commodities.   Shaded areas indicate US recessions.

CRB Spot Raw Industrials Sub-Index   (1967=100)

Year	Jan.	Feb.	Mar.	Apr.	May	June	July	Aug.	Sept.	Oct.	Nov.	Dec.	Average
2006	363.05	371.00	372.08	385.69	400.62	399.97	403.50	403.90	403.19	415.76	426.67	434.25	398.31
2007	430.87	434.54	452.81	465.37	468.44	475.75	485.36	478.47	483.09	492.43	486.68	475.95	469.15
2008	487.92	502.29	522.98	534.29	532.30	517.02	517.29	495.17	460.96	392.49	329.86	317.83	467.53
2009	335.09	331.50	321.35	343.49	370.17	391.18	403.99	431.59	439.72	435.97	455.27	480.02	394.95
2010	492.93	476.13	499.63	510.22	489.56	476.07	474.97	498.86	518.04	539.43	555.01	574.70	508.80
2011	595.51	619.22	621.89	628.72	606.29	602.99	596.81	573.01	559.74	536.77	528.95	519.49	582.45
2012	531.91	546.88	544.73	538.46	526.82	510.28	500.22	510.14	524.29	515.30	506.62	523.72	523.28
2013	534.06	538.69	539.87	532.46	524.75	523.74	520.86	525.30	521.20	514.92	519.98	529.58	527.12
2014	528.48	527.92	535.44	541.50	542.77	534.33	532.02	529.81	520.65	506.18	504.60	497.80	525.13
2015	485.52	474.22	470.13	467.83	471.58	466.96	451.80	443.96	439.86	424.27	403.04	401.58	450.06

Average.   *Source: Commodity Research Bureau*

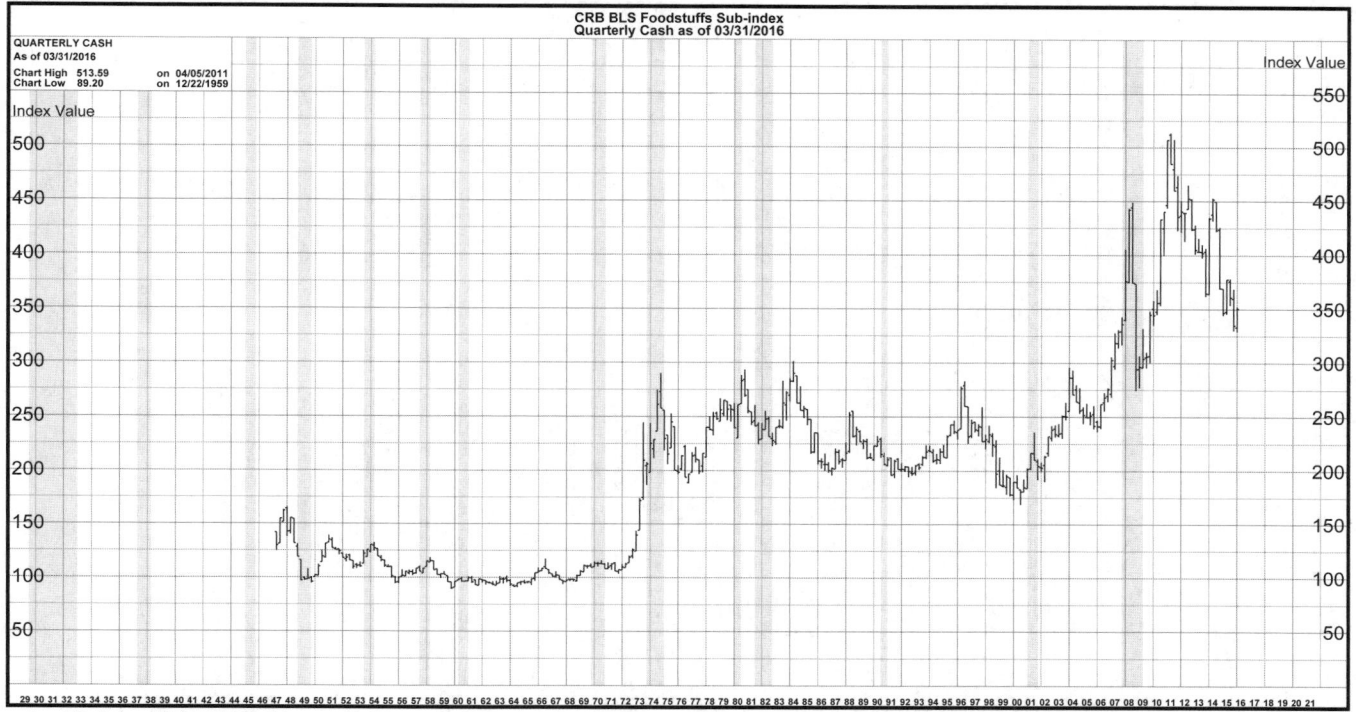

Unweighted Index of 10 Commodities: Hogs, steers, lard, butter, soybean oil, cocoa, corn, Kansas City wheat, Minneapolis wheat, and sugar.   Shaded areas indicate US recessions.

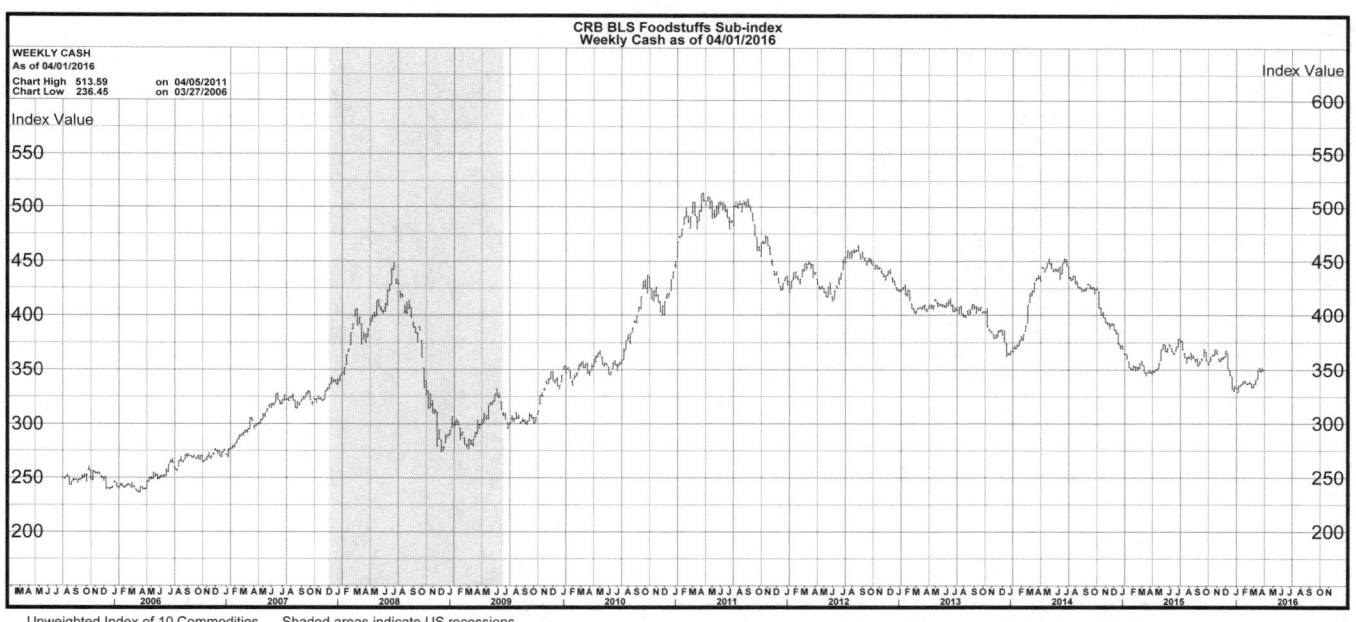

Unweighted Index of 10 Commodities.   Shaded areas indicate US recessions.

CRB Spot Foodstuffs Sub-Index   (1967=100)

Year	Jan.	Feb.	Mar.	Apr.	May	June	July	Aug.	Sept.	Oct.	Nov.	Dec.	Average
2006	243.31	241.95	239.60	243.17	250.70	253.86	261.17	267.04	269.14	267.52	271.19	273.16	256.82
2007	275.31	286.30	297.37	299.85	311.98	320.79	322.44	319.95	325.01	322.19	325.40	337.97	312.05
2008	346.56	383.11	390.10	391.07	405.44	421.87	427.47	405.89	385.15	334.27	303.48	284.65	373.26
2009	299.83	286.21	284.71	302.35	316.81	318.81	301.83	304.44	305.01	314.86	338.56	339.54	309.41
2010	349.28	344.48	352.89	357.94	359.11	352.01	361.74	385.62	415.09	424.20	411.58	423.33	378.11
2011	464.45	489.47	494.49	506.33	497.04	497.00	495.67	503.38	484.57	466.21	451.87	429.91	481.70
2012	431.88	436.61	445.29	429.26	421.32	427.19	453.49	458.33	451.49	446.42	439.14	432.15	439.38
2013	422.99	410.14	407.07	407.78	410.33	410.17	404.33	402.51	405.75	395.29	382.14	374.23	402.73
2014	370.69	387.03	424.76	440.01	445.70	444.24	437.38	426.08	426.02	412.87	392.84	379.75	415.61
2015	358.69	352.29	350.34	349.61	367.54	369.24	369.14	361.25	360.32	361.29	361.42	348.87	359.17

Average.   *Source: Commodity Research Bureau*

CRB INDICIES

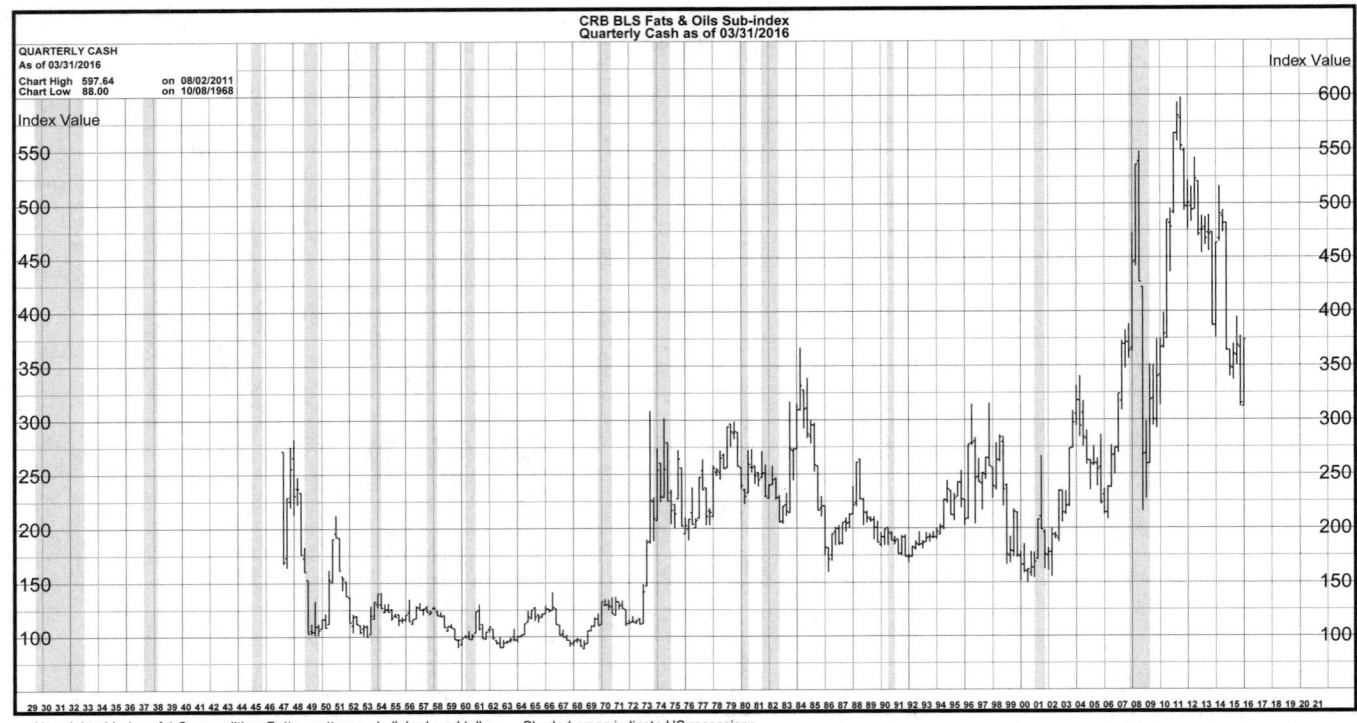

Unweighted Index of 4 Commodities: Butter, cottonseed oil, lard, and tallow.   Shaded areas indicate US recessions.

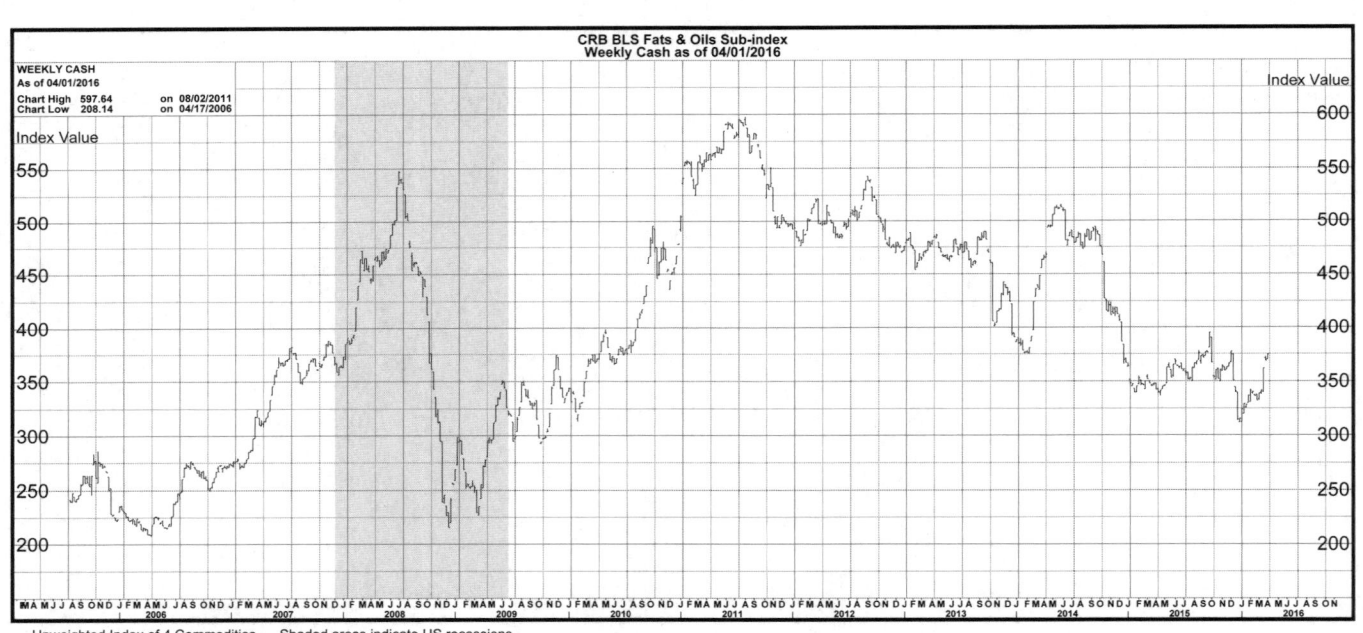

Unweighted Index of 4 Commodities.   Shaded areas indicate US recessions.

CRB Spot Fats and Oils Sub-Index   (1967=100)

Year	Jan.	Feb.	Mar.	Apr.	May	June	July	Aug.	Sept.	Oct.	Nov.	Dec.	Average
2006	231.10	221.46	217.14	214.75	222.03	221.97	247.09	271.97	267.18	257.29	264.75	270.94	242.31
2007	274.74	274.35	300.01	313.08	339.65	366.31	376.09	357.79	365.74	365.51	381.69	364.06	339.92
2008	381.95	418.92	459.52	457.65	467.23	498.89	526.26	467.08	443.38	366.91	283.76	238.42	417.50
2009	283.42	254.79	243.41	285.09	321.74	335.76	308.54	340.28	324.64	298.33	343.85	344.85	307.06
2010	337.27	329.26	366.69	378.35	381.68	374.59	379.27	399.57	444.83	471.40	463.11	458.65	398.72
2011	536.41	542.91	553.67	561.25	569.84	588.10	587.94	578.55	567.28	536.83	502.49	499.60	552.07
2012	488.60	489.04	512.32	501.11	495.37	490.44	506.48	516.93	532.05	501.87	478.36	474.48	498.92
2013	478.78	463.85	472.83	480.48	466.32	473.86	473.76	463.55	484.31	435.85	427.75	414.70	461.34
2014	383.34	388.71	444.35	482.96	511.46	492.95	483.40	482.99	488.24	444.49	416.67	383.76	450.28
2015	345.69	348.02	348.93	342.31	357.64	363.99	355.78	368.38	378.59	356.58	362.48	345.06	356.12

Average.   *Source: Commodity Research Bureau*

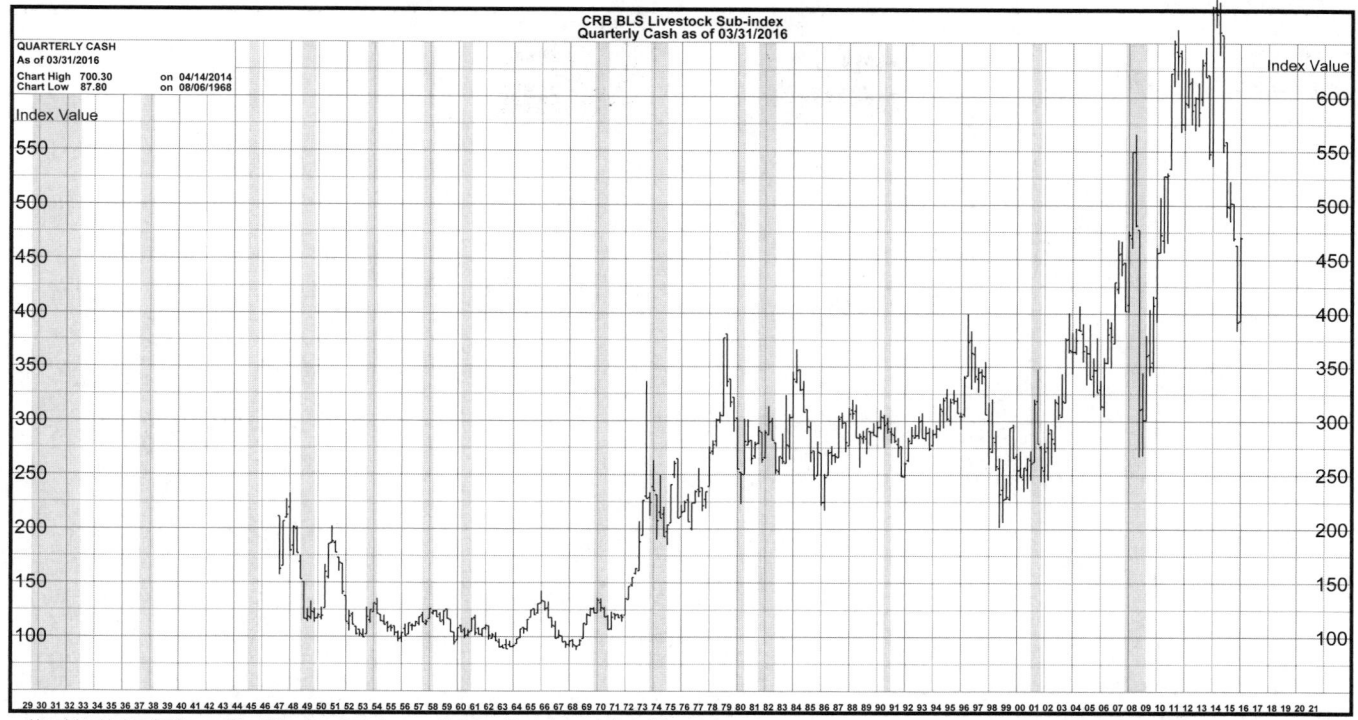

CRB BLS Livestock Sub-index
Quarterly Cash as of 03/31/2016

QUARTERLY CASH
As of 03/31/2016
Chart High 700.30 on 04/14/2014
Chart Low 87.80 on 08/06/1968

Unweighted Index of 5 Commodities: Hides, hogs, lard, steers, and tallow.   Shaded areas indicate US recessions.

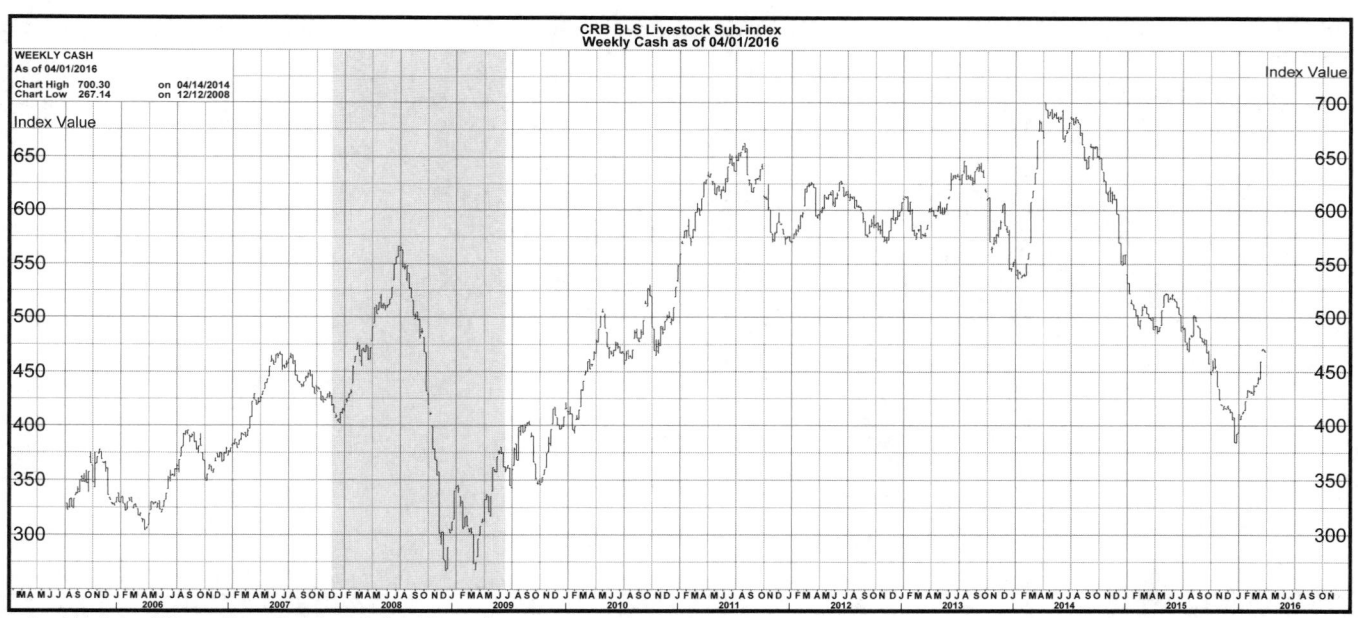

CRB BLS Livestock Sub-index
Weekly Cash as of 04/01/2016

WEEKLY CASH
As of 04/01/2016
Chart High 700.30 on 04/14/2014
Chart Low 267.14 on 12/12/2008

Unweighted Index of 5 Commodities.   Shaded areas indicate US recessions.

CRB Spot Livestock Sub-Index   (1967=100)

Year	Jan.	Feb.	Mar.	Apr.	May	June	July	Aug.	Sept.	Oct.	Nov.	Dec.	Average
2006	331.93	328.72	320.09	314.72	327.28	340.29	359.18	388.13	384.78	366.35	364.05	372.08	349.80
2007	379.93	388.03	407.19	425.25	449.92	462.39	459.18	445.81	444.91	434.88	425.72	412.45	427.97
2008	417.36	451.42	468.41	483.09	510.01	522.82	556.10	526.98	492.24	426.75	342.41	288.42	457.17
2009	333.60	310.58	288.18	321.58	347.01	368.85	362.91	393.37	389.53	350.90	386.75	403.06	354.69
2010	411.55	408.71	450.01	478.92	488.46	470.53	465.13	475.55	498.82	495.89	485.02	505.23	469.49
2011	561.16	577.76	601.55	629.36	618.46	635.68	646.41	644.21	626.64	618.26	580.65	580.02	610.01
2012	575.19	598.32	620.12	600.69	612.10	619.49	613.35	601.44	582.23	585.33	577.18	594.91	598.36
2013	606.27	584.54	580.26	598.17	601.26	626.31	634.54	630.72	637.72	591.03	583.70	571.43	603.83
2014	543.02	557.63	645.13	685.62	689.00	676.46	683.71	661.15	656.18	639.12	613.66	573.26	635.33
2015	523.85	500.96	503.91	491.27	517.22	513.03	484.28	490.90	477.86	452.68	419.99	404.96	481.74

Average.   *Source: Commodity Research Bureau*

CRB INDICIES

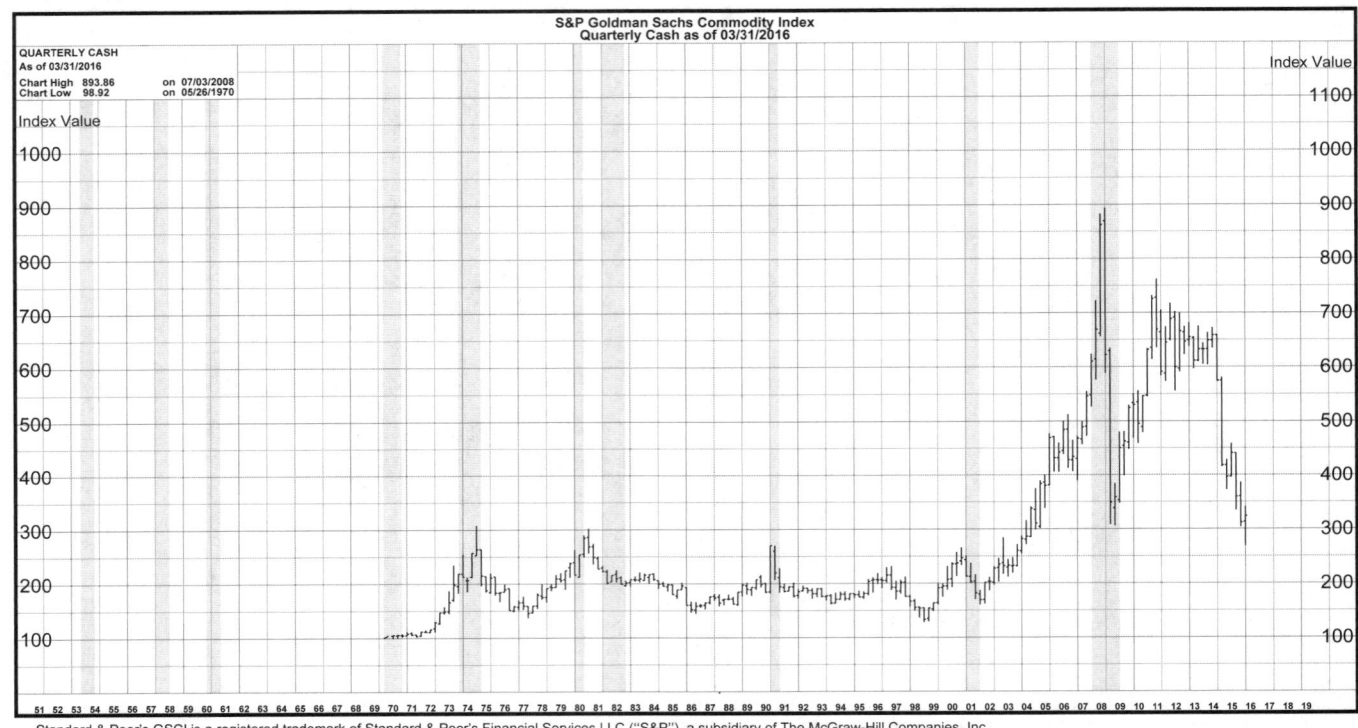

Standard & Poor's GSCI is a registered trademark of Standard & Poor's Financial Services LLC ("S&P"), a subsidiary of The McGraw-Hill Companies, Inc.
Currently the S&P GSCI includes 24 commodity nearby futures contracts.   Shaded areas indicate US recessions.

Standard & Poor's GSCI is a registered trademark of Standard & Poor's Financial Services LLC ("S&P"), a subsidiary of The McGraw-Hill Companies, Inc.
Currently the S&P GSCI includes 24 commodity nearby futures contracts.   Shaded areas indicate US recessions.

S&P Goldman Sachs Commodity Index (GSCI)   (12/31/1969=100)

Year	Jan.	Feb.	Mar.	Apr.	May	June	July	Aug.	Sept.	Oct.	Nov.	Dec.	Average
2006	442.12	422.49	427.47	469.73	477.93	471.65	490.32	485.65	434.56	431.13	442.05	444.62	453.31
2007	406.98	435.26	446.69	469.60	470.72	485.26	504.65	490.16	528.83	559.36	600.37	593.12	499.25
2008	606.71	638.88	689.26	717.94	778.15	832.31	818.90	716.84	644.00	496.05	405.96	338.27	640.27
2009	346.03	327.48	350.86	367.12	410.82	458.22	429.21	466.68	453.77	492.51	509.71	505.07	426.46
2010	520.05	503.83	523.07	543.90	499.87	497.00	503.57	517.41	526.98	561.66	579.86	614.79	532.67
2011	634.64	661.44	707.87	744.48	695.62	679.91	689.47	651.63	638.94	625.65	653.51	642.72	668.82
2012	661.12	685.83	701.92	681.61	637.66	579.93	627.42	661.68	670.25	654.57	639.84	640.09	653.49
2013	658.10	669.41	648.20	624.14	627.04	622.56	639.34	645.98	645.31	633.40	614.88	631.12	638.29
2014	617.20	640.25	645.88	653.19	652.42	657.64	636.14	609.55	588.76	548.78	521.86	449.57	601.77
2015	388.27	412.87	403.39	423.64	443.38	436.70	402.75	360.85	362.48	364.45	345.91	315.98	388.39

Average.   *Source: CME Group; Chicago Mercantile Ezchange*

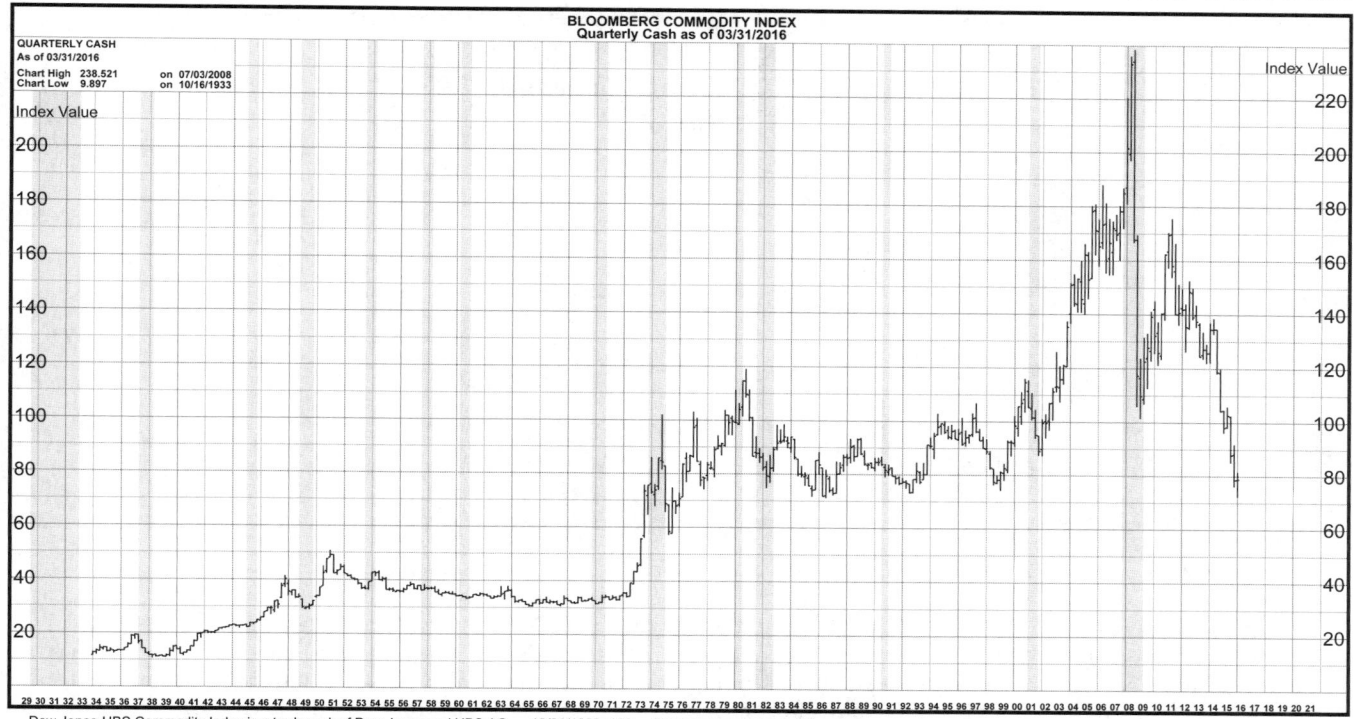

BLOOMBERG COMMODITY INDEX
Quarterly Cash as of 03/31/2016

QUARTERLY CASH
As of 03/31/2016
Chart High 238.521   on 07/03/2008
Chart Low   9.897   on 10/16/1933

Dow Jones-UBS Commodity Index is a trademark of Dow Jones and UBS AG.   12/31/1990=100   Shaded areas indicate US recessions.

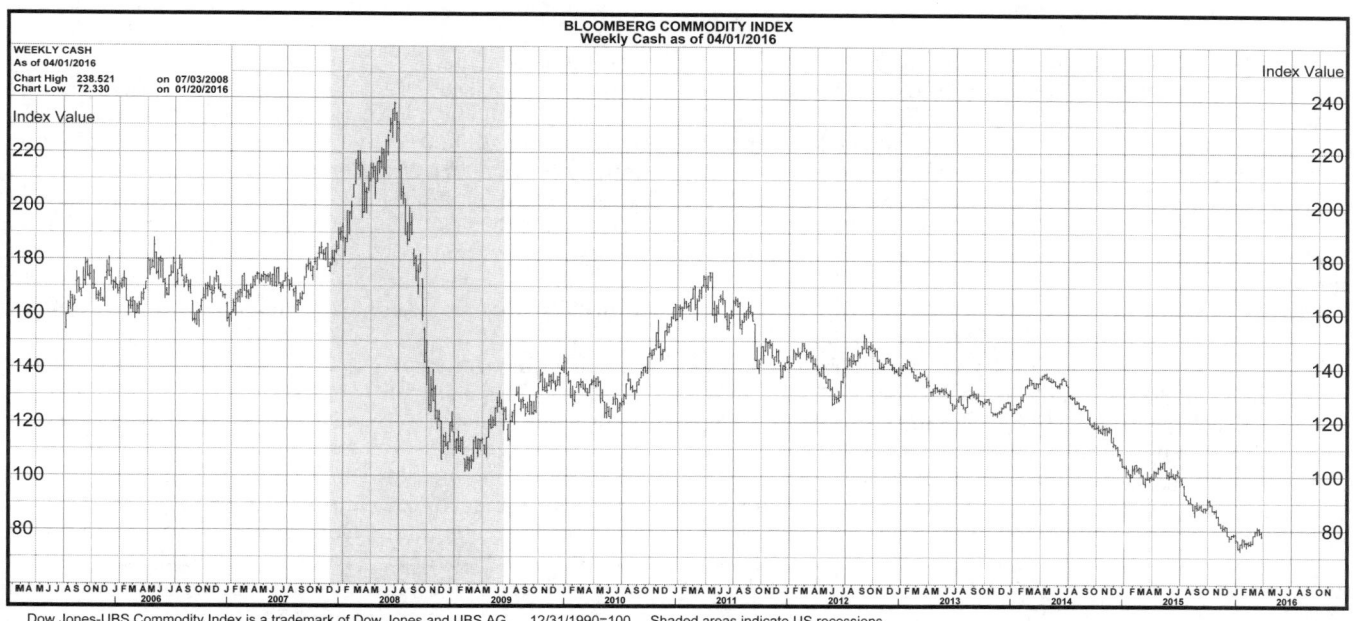

BLOOMBERG COMMODITY INDEX
Weekly Cash as of 04/01/2016

WEEKLY CASH
As of 04/01/2016
Chart High 238.521   on 07/03/2008
Chart Low   72.330   on 01/20/2016

Dow Jones-UBS Commodity Index is a trademark of Dow Jones and UBS AG.   12/31/1990=100   Shaded areas indicate US recessions.

Bloomberg Commodity Index   (12/31/1990=100)

Year	Jan.	Feb.	Mar.	Apr.	May	June	July	Aug.	Sept.	Oct.	Nov.	Dec.	Average
2006	169.96	165.06	162.42	172.83	179.22	170.50	174.84	173.39	161.59	164.26	169.68	168.39	169.35
2007	160.36	167.86	168.37	172.74	172.50	172.41	171.57	165.81	173.32	177.90	182.03	180.86	172.14
2008	188.93	202.02	210.29	209.98	214.57	225.51	218.94	192.70	176.00	141.46	125.23	112.57	184.85
2009	114.17	107.49	107.93	111.21	119.75	125.98	119.71	128.50	125.34	132.15	134.35	135.93	121.88
2010	137.76	131.70	132.79	134.85	127.45	125.94	127.89	132.81	137.28	144.46	148.49	156.14	136.46
2011	160.80	163.41	165.87	171.91	163.23	161.47	162.81	159.01	154.26	145.52	146.73	141.41	158.04
2012	143.34	146.45	144.63	139.84	134.79	129.46	141.40	143.91	147.64	146.02	142.06	140.45	141.67
2013	140.01	139.55	137.44	132.99	132.04	129.38	127.65	128.32	128.98	127.48	123.20	126.25	131.11
2014	125.24	130.97	134.71	136.56	135.81	134.75	130.44	126.39	121.57	117.97	116.95	109.39	126.73
2015	102.09	102.74	99.64	100.95	103.32	100.92	96.70	89.46	88.43	88.72	83.31	78.74	94.58

Average.   *Source: CME Group; Chicago Board of Trade*

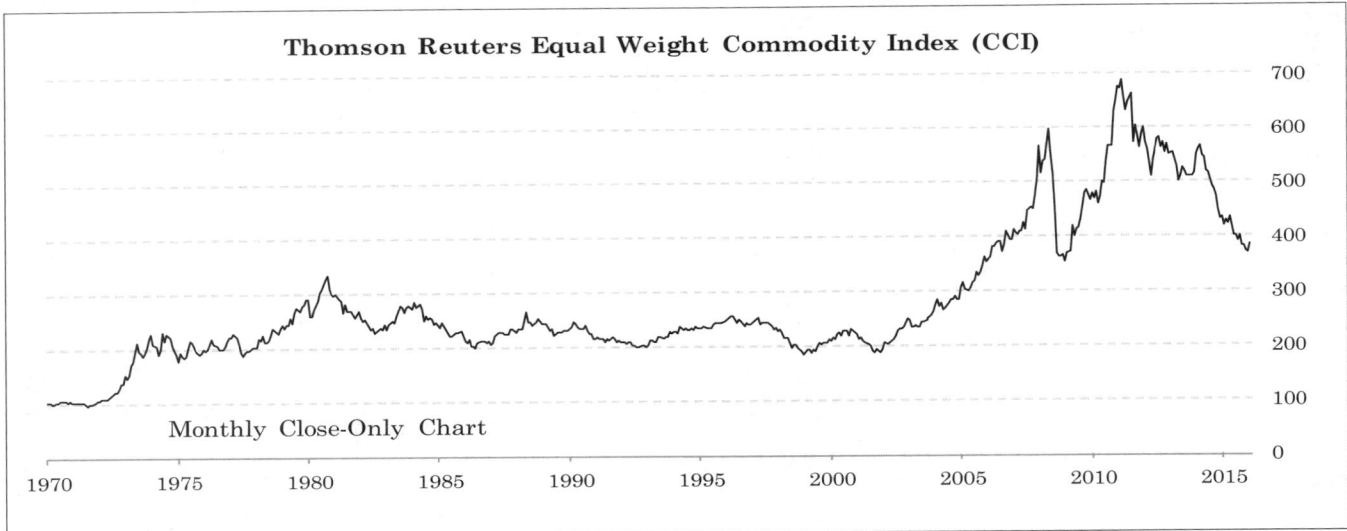

Thomson Reuters Equal Weight Commodity Index (CCI)

Monthly Close-Only Chart

The Thomson Reuters Equal Weight Commodity Index (CCI), formerly known as the Reuters/Jefferies Continuous Commodity Index, saw another weak year in 2015, falling by -15.2%. The CCI index since 2011 has now plunged by a total of -49% from the record high posted in April 2011 to the 7-year low posted in January 2016.

The CCI index continues to move lower after the extraordinary rally that began in 2001 reached a record high in April 2011 of 691.09. That decade-long rally of +278% is by far the largest commodity bull market in post-war history, exceeding even the rallies seen in the 1970s. The 1971-74 and 1977-80 commodity bull markets were separated by two years of consolidation in 1975-76. Even if those two rallies are counted as one large bull market, that bull market of 250% is less than the 2001-2011 bull market of 278%.

The 2001-11 commodity bull market was driven mainly by strong commodity demand from fast-growing emerging countries such as China, India, Brazil, and others. The fact that the rally was driven by demand, as opposed to a temporary supply disruption, accounts for its size and longevity. The commodity rallies in the 1970s, by contrast, were driven mainly by supply disruptions and inflation, not by demand. A rally caused by demand is typically much more durable.

Along with strong demand, the weak dollar was an important driver of the commodity bull market from 2001 through 2008. During that time frame, the dollar plunged and provided a powerful bullish factor for commodity prices. As the value of the dollar falls, the price of hard assets tends to rise to account for the lower value of the currency in which the hard assets are priced. From 2008 through mid-2014, however, the dollar had less impact on commodity prices because the dollar was in a sideways consolidation mode.

The commodity bull market received a new head of steam in 2009-2011 in the aftermath of the 2008-09 global financial crisis. Commodity prices were driven higher during 2009-2011 by extra liquidity from the Fed's extraordinarily easy monetary policy and by safe-haven buying of commodities as protection in the event that the Fed's extraordinarily easy monetary policy might eventually cause hyperinflation and a plunge in the dollar.

However, commodity prices topped out in early 2011 and have since been on a downward track. Commodity prices have been driven lower in the past five years by weaker physical demand for commodities due to below-par global economic growth. In addition, many investors have been forced to give up on any imminent arrival of hyperinflation stemming from the Fed's extraordinarily easy monetary policy. Indeed, the U.S. and global economies are still feeling the deflationary pressures seen during the post-crisis recovery period. The latest reading of +1.7% y/y for the Fed's preferred inflation measure, the core PCE deflator, is only +0.8 points above the record low

Ranked Commodity Bull Markets - Thomson-Reuters Equal Weight Commodity Index (CCI) (1960-2016[1])							
	-------- Low --------		-------- High --------		Percent Rally	Rally Duration Months	Avg CPI (yr-yr%)
2001-11	Oct-01	182.83	Apr-11	691.09	278.0%	114	2.4%
1971-74	Oct-71	96.40	Feb-74	237.80	146.7%	28	4.9%
1977-80	Aug-77	184.70	Nov-80	337.60	82.8%	39	10.2%
1986-88	Jul-86	196.16	Jun-88	272.19	38.8%	23	3.2%
1992-96	Aug-92	198.17	Apr-96	263.79	33.1%	44	2.8%
[1] Data as of February 2016.							

of +0.9% posted in July 2012 and remains below the Fed's +2.0% inflation target.

A big part of the reason behind the 5-year slump in commodity prices is the economic slowdown in China. It is no coincidence that the massive commodity bull market began in 2003 at the same time that the Chinese economy started to show double-digit growth. China's building and investment boom produced huge demand for various types of commodities. However, there is now excess supply and production in many commodity markets because Chinese GDP growth has downshifted to the 25-year low of +6.9% in 2015.

Commodity prices have also been pressured by the end of the Fed's quantitative easing programs in Oct 2014 and by the Fed's first interest rate hike in December 2015. The end of the Fed's QE programs and rising interest rates means there is less fuel for the commodities markets and a reduced risk of eventual hyperinflation.

Commodity prices also saw weakness due to the +27% surge in the dollar index seen from mid-2014 through spring 2015. That surge in the dollar index undercut the price of commodities in terms of appreciated dollars.

The nearby chart shows that the carnage was spread across all the major commodities in 2015 except for cocoa, cotton and sugar. The petroleum sector took a heavy hit, along with natural gas and industrial metals such as nickel, copper and aluminum. Crude oil prices fell sharply in 2015 on excess oil production and a record buildup in world inventories, along with Saudi Arabia's refusal to act as the world's swing producer as it switched its strategy to protecting its market share. Industrial metal demand took a heavy hit as China's construction and manufacturing sectors slowed. Agriculture markets also saw weakness in 2015 due to general commodity weakness along with supply overhang.

The weakness in commodity prices is likely to continue for some time since commodity suppliers need to cut production to meet lower demand levels and inventory levels need to be worked down. In addition, commodity prices are likely to see continued downward pressure

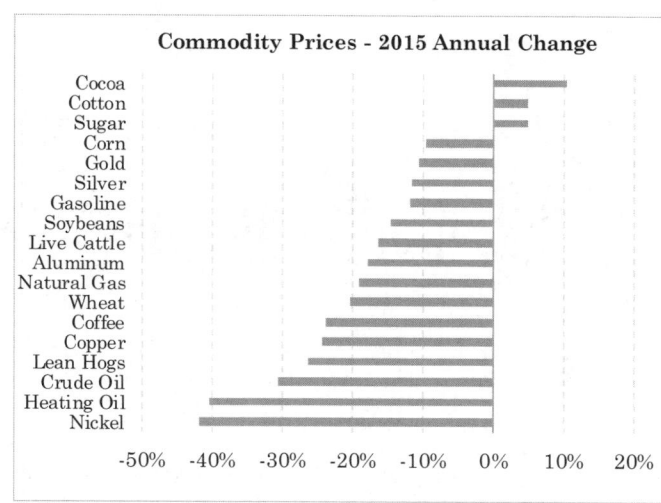

from weak demand, deflationary world conditions, and continued strength in the dollar index.

Yet commodity prices over the longer term will eventually find a bottom and start to recover once the world economy regains its balance and strong commodity demand reemerges from the developing world. The need in the developing world continues to be enormous for food, shelter and infrastructure, which are all sectors that utilize raw commodities. According to the World Bank's Development Indicators, 80% of the world's population lives on less than $10 per day. As these people are slowly integrated into the global economy in the coming years and decades, their food, shelter and transportation needs will expand and they will use more commodities. Commodity demand will also be driven higher over the long term by population growth. The United Nations forecasts that there will be a net 2.2 billion more people on earth by 2050, bringing the world's population to 9.0 billion from its current level near 6.8 billion.

The world economy has been through a harrowing experience since 2007 and has yet to get fully back onto its feet. Yet as the world economy slowly normalizes in coming years, commodity prices will eventually find a bottom and start to slowly recover.

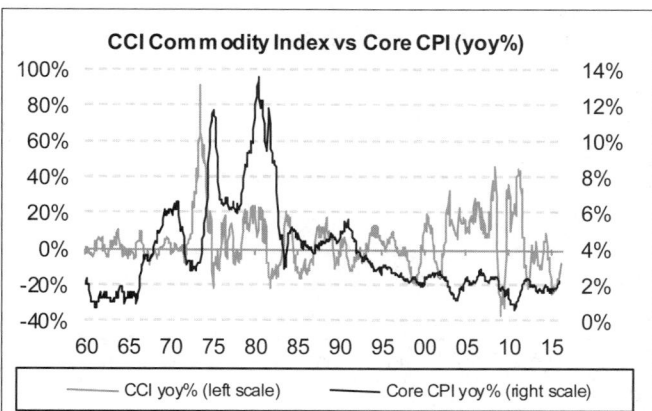

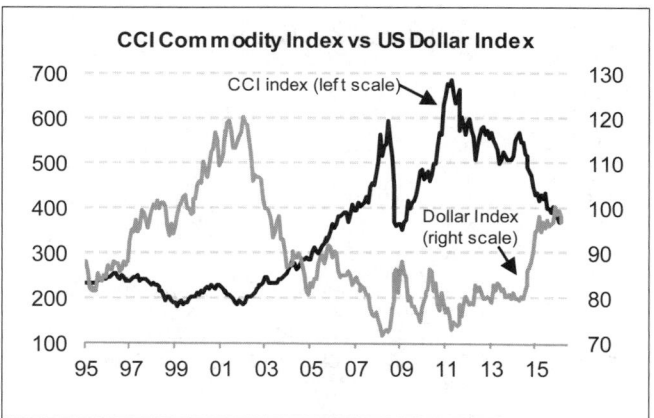

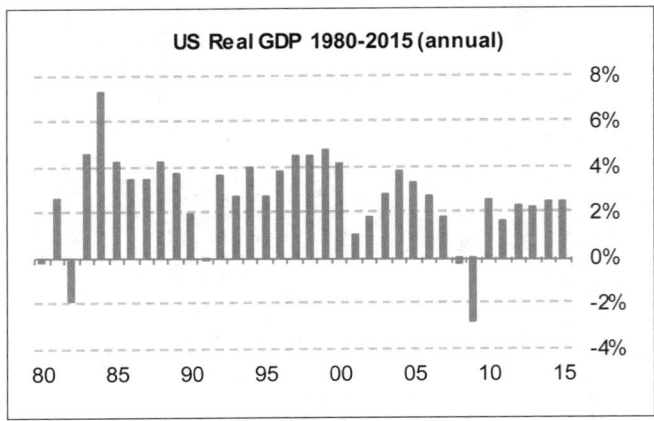

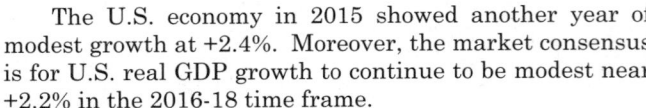

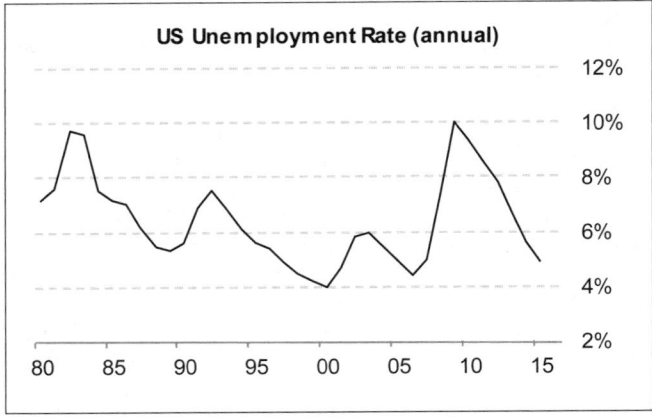

The U.S. economy in 2015 showed another year of modest growth at +2.4%. Moreover, the market consensus is for U.S. real GDP growth to continue to be modest near +2.2% in the 2016-18 time frame.

The U.S. economy in 2015 faced headwinds from the strong dollar, weak overseas economic growth, and the petroleum and mining sector recession caused by the plunge in crude oil and metals prices.

U.S. exports in 2015 fell by -6.9% y/y mainly because of the strong dollar, which made U.S. exports more expensive and less attractive overseas. U.S. exports were also hurt by weak overseas economic growth and low demand for U.S. exports in general.

The weakness in exports hurt the U.S. manufacturing sector, which showed growth of only +0.5% y/y in 2015 and teetered on the edge of a recession during the year. The only supportive factor for the U.S. manufacturing sector during 2015 was continued strong auto sales and production.

The ISM manufacturing index, which measures confidence in the manufacturing sector, fell sharply from 54.9 at the end of 2014 to post a 6-1/2 year low of 48.0 in December 2015, finally recovering by +1.5 points in early 2016 to 49.5. The ISM manufacturing index fell below the expansion-contraction level of 50.0 in October 2015 and remained below 50.0 through February 2016, indicating net pessimism among U.S. manufacturing executives.

Business investment faded during 2015 and by Q4-2015 made virtually no contribution to GDP. Government spending made little contribution to GDP during the year as Congress continued with relatively tight spending. There was an unwanted buildup of inventories early in 2015 and the inventory correction in the second half of the year subtracted from GDP. These various factors combined to produce a weak U.S. preliminary quarterly GDP growth rate of +1.0% by the fourth quarter of 2015.

On the brighter side, the U.S. economy during 2015 saw support from U.S. consumers, who were in a better spending mood thanks to rising income and a strengthening labor market. Personal income in 2015 rose by +4.0% y/y and personal spending rose by +3.2% y/y. The U.S. consumer sentiment index from the University of Michigan posted a 12-year high of 98.1 in January 2015 and returned to the previous levels seen in 2002-07 before the Great Recession emerged, indicating a fundamental recovery of consumer confidence.

The U.S. labor market in 2015 was strong with an average monthly increase in payroll jobs of +229,000, which was better than the pre-recession average (2004-2006) of +185,000. The unemployment rate during 2015 fell by -0.6 percentage points from 5.6% at the end of 2014 to 5.0% by the end of 2015. The unemployment rate in early 2016 then fell further to an 8-year low of 4.9%, which was only +0.2 points above the Federal Reserve's long-run forecast for a 4.7% unemployment rate through 2017-18. The U.S. labor market by early 2016 was close to getting to

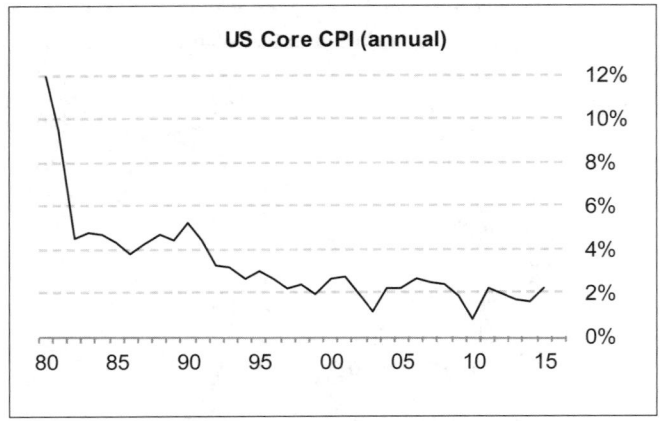

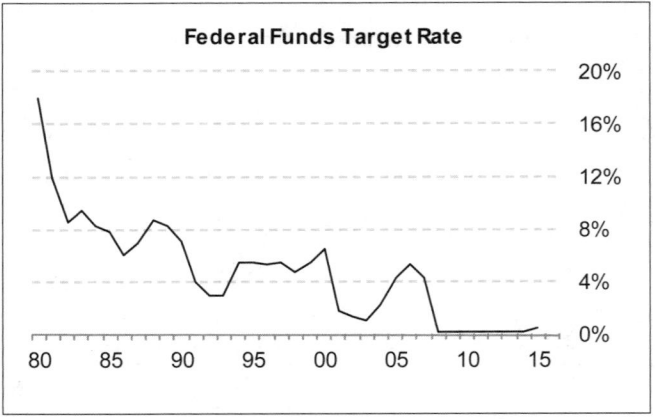

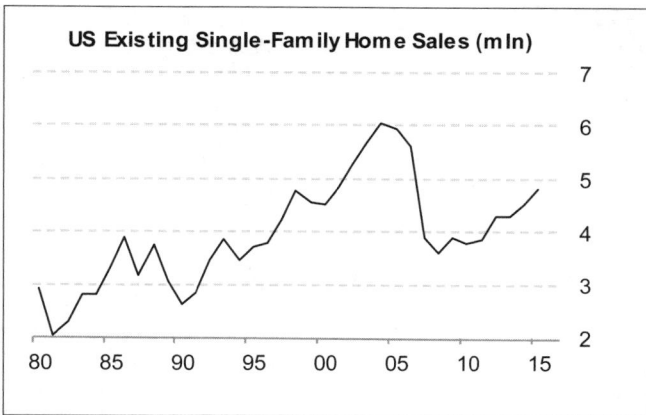

US Existing Single-Family Home Sales (mln)

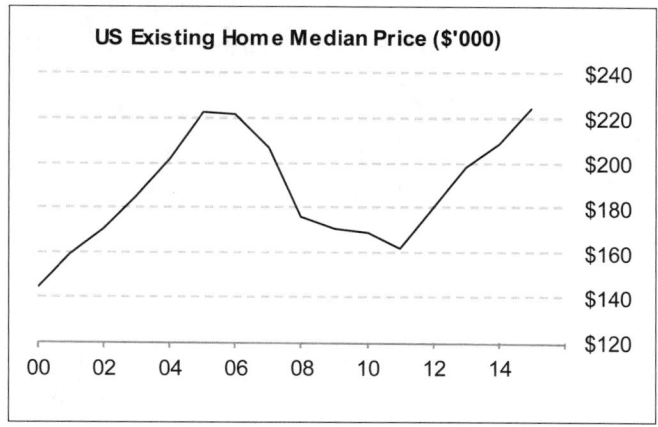

US Existing Home Median Price ($'000)

the Fed's idea of full employment even though there were still indications of long-term labor market problems such as a low number of people in the work force and continued high long-term unemployment.

The U.S. housing market continued to provide support for the overall U.S. economy in 2015. U.S. existing home sales posted an 8-3/4 year high of 5.48 million units in July and ended the year just below that level. Home sales in 2015 returned to the levels seen prior to the housing bust that started in 2006. U.S. single-family housing starts were strong during 2015, reaching an 8-year high of 786,000 in December 2015. In addition, U.S. home prices continue to rise steadily during 2015, The FHFA U.S. home price index rose by 6% in 2015, thus bringing the overall home price recovery to +27% from the housing bust low.

While the U.S. economy is expected to chug along near +2.2% over the next several years, there are still headwinds that the U.S. economy will have to navigate. Those headwinds include the slowing of the Chinese economy, weak overall world growth, a strong dollar, and the Fed's current intention to slowly raise interest rates over the next few years.

The 10-year T-note yield fell to a 2-year low of 1.64% in January 2015 but then rebounded and closed the year up +10 basis points at 2.27% from 2014. T-note prices saw downward pressure during 2015 from (1) the Fed's move to end its third quantitative easing (QE3) program in October 2014 and the Fed's first interest rate hike in

December 2015, and (2) steady 2015 GDP growth of +2.4% and the continued improvement in the U.S. labor market. However, T-note prices saw support during 2015 from (1) low inflation expectations with the plunge in crude oil and commodity prices, (2) weak global economic growth with China's GDP growth rate falling to a 25-year low of +6.9%, (3) safe-haven demand for Treasury securities given doubts about China and various geopolitical hot spots, and (4) the Fed's intention to only raise interest rates slowly.

The S&P 500 index topped out at a record high in May 2015 and then spent the rest of the year on the defensive. The S&P 500 index in early 2016 then fell to a 2-year low and corrected lower by -15% from the record high. The stock market in 2015 was undercut by (1) the Fed's first interest rate hike in December 2015 and expectations for further rate hikes, (2) the strong dollar, which hurt corporate earnings and U.S. exports, (3) negative carry-over from the plunge in crude oil prices which decimated the petroleum sector and caused a sharp drop in energy junk bond prices, (4) the plunge in the Chinese stock market in the second half of 2015 as its year-long bubble burst, (5) mildly high valuation levels, and (6) an earnings recession with negative S&P 500 earnings growth in the second half of 2015.

The U.S. stock market in 2016 may continue to struggle given tepid world economic growth, the strong dollar, expectations for negative earnings growth in the first half of 2015, and expectations for steady Fed rate hikes.

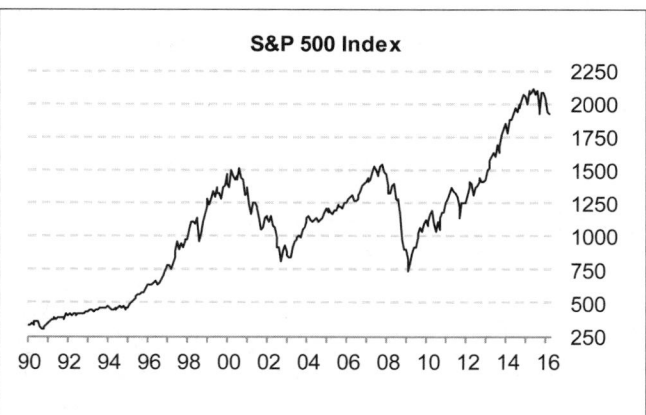

S&P 500 Index

10-year T-Note Yield

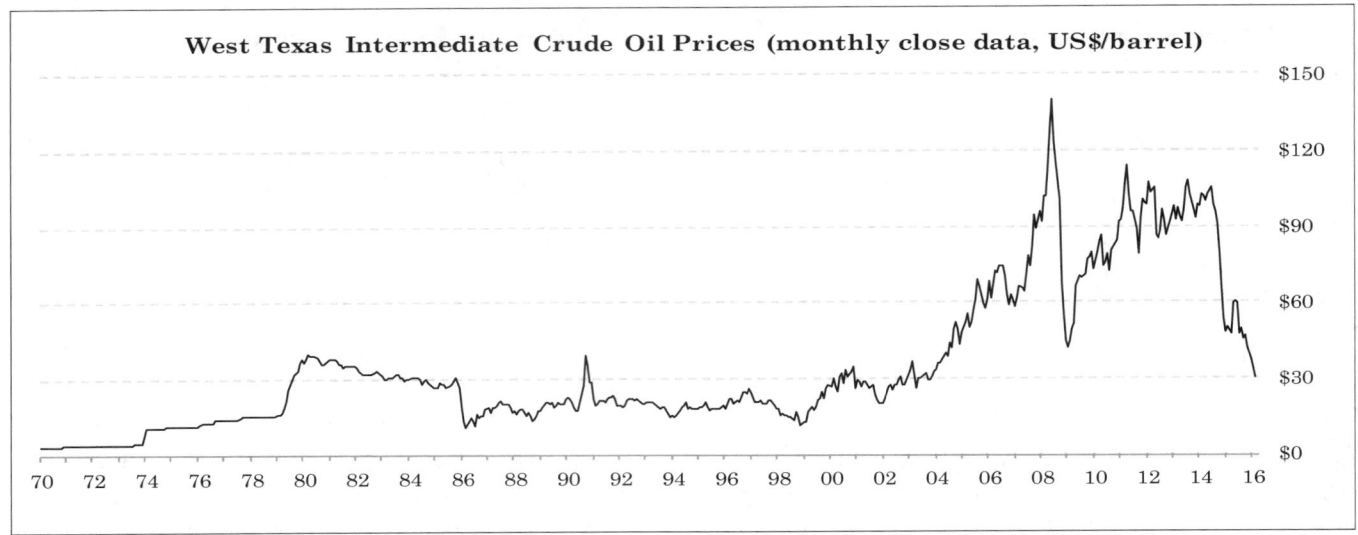

West Texas Intermediate Crude Oil Prices (monthly close data, US$/barrel)

Nymex West Texas Intermediate (WTI) crude oil futures prices in 2015 extended the plunge that began in the middle of 2014, closing the year down -30%. WTI crude oil futures prices plunged by a total of -76% from mid-2014 through the 13-year low of $26.05 per barrel posted in mid-February 2016, finally recovering moderately in late February and early March 2016.

The plunge in oil prices that began in the latter part of 2014 was driven in part by Saudi Arabia's announcement that it would not cut production in response to world oil oversupply and would instead maintain its current market share regardless of how far crude oil prices might drop. Saudi Arabia thereby relinquished its role as the world's swing producer and declared war on high-cost oil producers the world over. Saudi Arabia enjoys some of the lowest extraction costs in the world, which means that Saudi Arabia will be the last one standing in any oil price war.

Saudi Arabia's price war has so far had remarkably little effect in forcing high-cost producers to shut down production. In fact, world oil production in 2015 actually rose by +3.7% from 2014. Production rose because some producers had already locked in higher prices through hedging and others just kept producing to cover cash expenses amidst hopes for a quick rebound in oil prices.U.S. shale producers are a primary target of Saudi Arabia's price

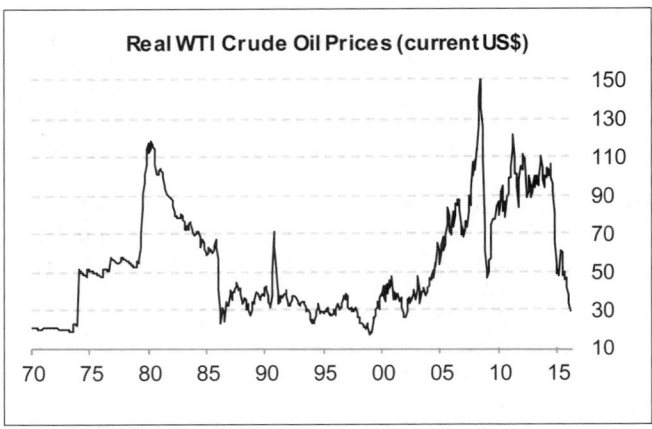

Real WTI Crude Oil Prices (current US$)

war. Due to new fracking technologies in shale formations, U.S. oil production in the space of just five years surged by 75% to the 43-year high of 9.61 million bpd in June 2015. From that high, U.S. oil production fell by only -6% through February 2016 despite a -76% plunge in the number of active U.S. oil wells as U.S. producers clung to hopes for a rebound in oil prices. Yet, U.S. oil production will fall more quickly in 2016 due to oil company bankruptcies and the roll-off of hedges.

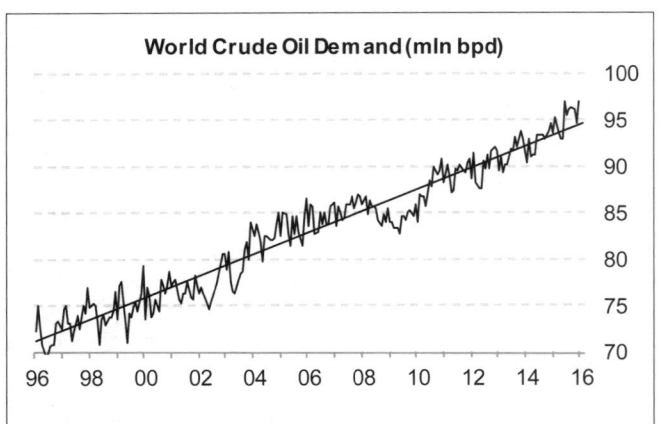

World Crude Oil Demand (mln bpd)

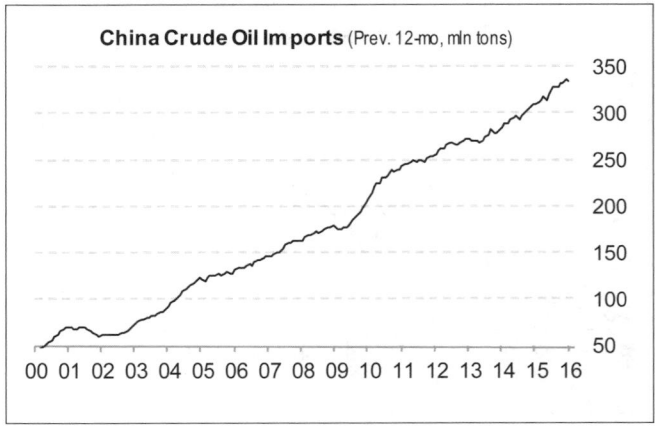

China Crude Oil Imports (Prev. 12-mo, mln tons)

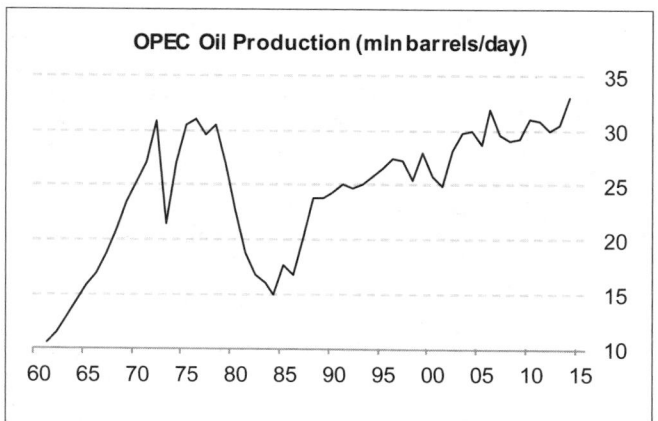

OPEC Oil Production (mln barrels/day)

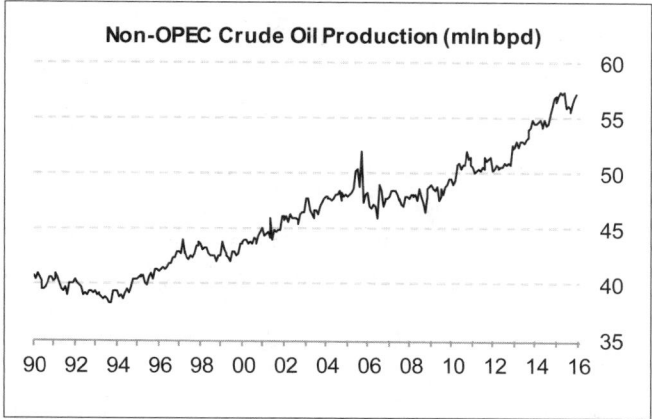

Non-OPEC Crude Oil Production (mln bpd)

The high level of world oil production relative to consumption caused a sharp buildup of inventories during 2014-15 and rising inventories are expected to continue through 2016-2017. The massive amount of world oil inventories residing in land and floating storage is keeping heavy downward pressure on oil prices.

The drop in oil prices into the high-$20's in early 2016 finally convinced Saudi Arabia and Russia to agree on at least a production freeze, an agreement that they hoped other producers would adopt as well. However, Saudi Arabia and Russia only agreed to freeze production since their production levels were already near record highs. Neither country has any apparent intention to actually cut production, which is what would be necessary to start bringing down world inventory levels. In fact, Saudi Arabia's oil minister remained as hawkish as ever and in early 2016 said that Saudi Arabia could coexist with $20 oil and that high-cost producers would either have to cut costs or liquidate.

Oil prices were also pressured in late 2015 and early 2016 after world sanctions on Iran were dropped as part of Iran's agreement to give up its nuclear program. Iran said it intends to boost production by 500,000 bpd within months and by 1 million bpd within a year. However, Iran faced unexpected delays in getting its production and exports quickly ramped up, which helped to produce the recovery in oil prices in late-Feb and early-March 2016. Yet Iranian oil is expected to flood the markets through 2016 without any offsetting cuts by other OPEC producers, thus producing even larger world oil inventories.U.S. Congress

in late 2015 approved a law that allows U.S. oil companies to export U.S. oil again, ending a 40-year ban. The end of the U.S. oil export embargo is not expected to have much impact on the global oil markets since the U.S. continues to be a large net oil importer. Still, the end of the embargo means that the U.S. will now be more efficient in its oil usage, exporting light sweet oil that U.S. refineries do not need and continuing to import the heavier grade oils that many U.S. refineries are set up to use.

The emergence of the new oil extraction technologies that caused the 2011-2015 surge in U.S. oil production has been a game-changer for the world oil markets. There is still the possibility of temporary upward oil spikes from supply disruptions caused by storms or wars. However, the long-term outlook is now for low to moderate oil prices for at least the next decade. Oil prices cannot trade at higher levels for long because that would attract higher-cost producers back into the market, thus boosting supply and pushing prices back down. OPEC, in short, has lost its grip on the world oil markets and technology has essentially succeeded in curbing oil prices.

The surge in U.S. oil and gas production and the plunge in oil prices is providing a major benefit for the U.S. economy since cheap energy gives U.S. industry a major competitive advantage. In addition, the decline in net U.S. oil imports and the increase in U.S. refined petroleum exports should also lead to a sustained decline in the U.S. trade deficit, which should be a supportive factor for the dollar.

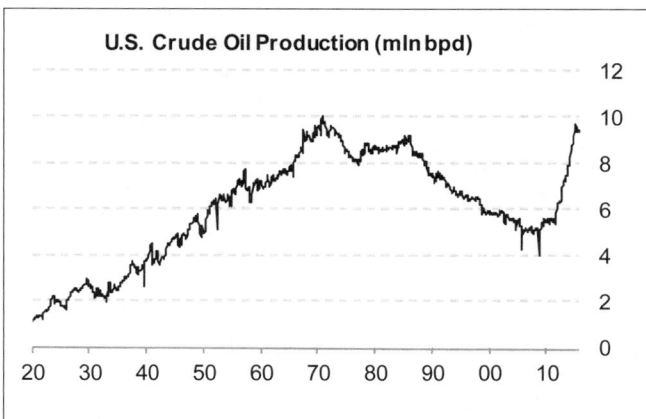

U.S. Crude Oil Production (mln bpd)

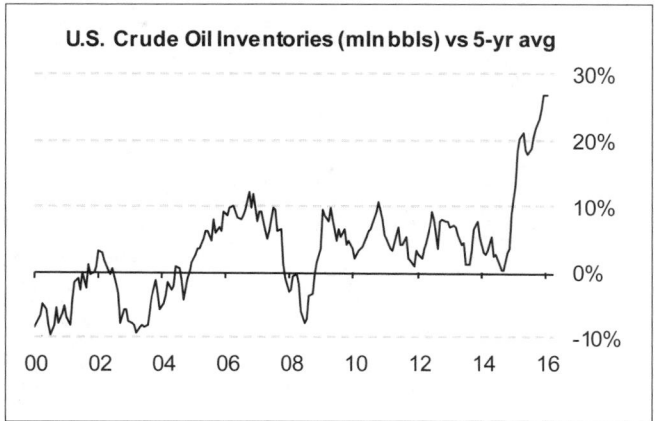

U.S. Crude Oil Inventories (mln bbls) vs 5-yr avg

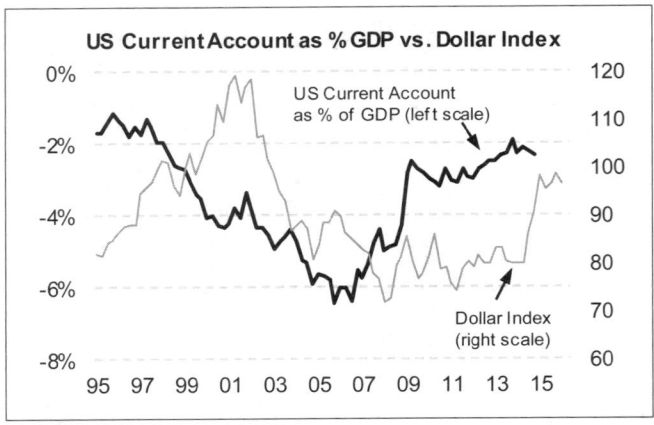

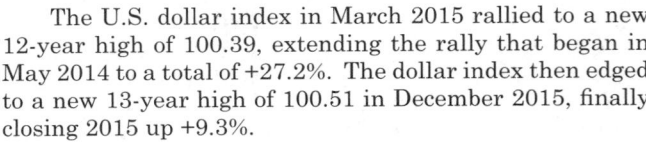

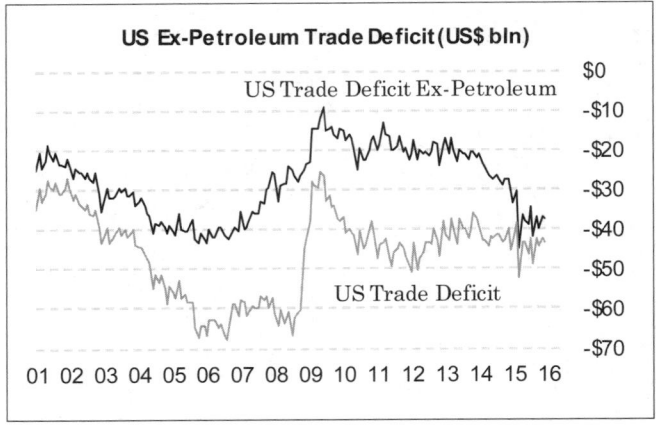

The U.S. dollar index in March 2015 rallied to a new 12-year high of 100.39, extending the rally that began in May 2014 to a total of +27.2%. The dollar index then edged to a new 13-year high of 100.51 in December 2015, finally closing 2015 up +9.3%.

The dollar index in 2014 finally broke out to the upside after trading roughly sideways in a wide range during 2009-2013. Before that 2009-2013 trading range emerged, the dollar index took a huge -41% hit during the 2002-2007 bear market when the dollar plunged on the Federal Reserve's easy monetary policy and the sharp widening of America's trade deficit.

The dollar index rallied sharply starting in the latter half of 2014 because of (1) the relative strength of the U.S. economy, (2) the end of the Fed's third quantitative easing (QE3) program in October 2014, and (3) expectations for the Fed to begin raising interest rates.

U.S. GDP growth in 2015 was only moderate at +2.4%. Still, the U.S. GDP performance was much better than the 2015 GDP growth rates of +1.6% in the Eurozone and +0.5% in Japan. In addition, the U.S. economy is expected to outperform again in 2016 with growth of +2.2%, much better than the consensus for 2016 GDP growth of +1.5% in the Eurozone and +0.7% in Japan.

The dollar rallied sharply starting in the latter half of 2014 when it became clear that the Fed would end its quantitative easing programs that started with the 2008/09

global financial crisis. The Fed's QE3 program, which lasted from Sep 2012 to Oct 2014, involved the purchase of $1.7 trillion of Treasury securities and mortgage-backed securities. That was larger than the QE2 program of $600 billion and the QE1 program of $1.425 trillion.

When QE3 ended in Dec 2014, the Fed's balance sheet totaled $4.5 trillion and the Fed had injected a net $3.6 trillion of excess liquidity into the U.S. financial system. Since ending QE3, the Fed has reinvested the proceeds from maturing securities into new securities, thus keeping its balance sheet constant near $4.5 trillion. In normal times, a central bank that engages in such a bond-buying program risks causing hyperinflation and a plunge in its currency. However, the Fed has been able to get away with this liquidity injection so far because (1) there are still heavy deflationary pressures that are bearing down on the U.S. and global economies, (2) other major central banks have also engaged in QE programs, and (3) global investors remain willing to hold dollars for safe-haven purposes.

The dollar's strength continued in 2015 as the market expected the Fed to start raising interest rates. There were several false starts, but the Fed in December 2015 finally implemented its first rate hike, raising its federal funds target by 25 basis points to 0.25-0.50% from the zero-0.25% range that prevailed since 2008. The Fed indicated its intention to steadily raise interest rates in coming years to push the funds rate target up to more normal levels.

While the Fed started its rate-hike regime in late

US Export Growth (yoy%)

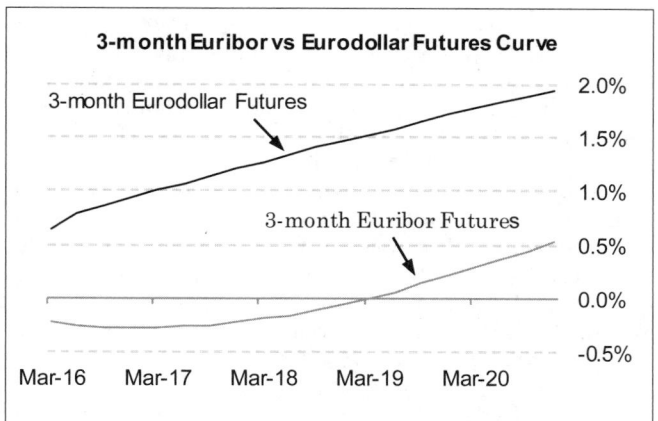

3-month Euribor vs Eurodollar Futures Curve

2015, the European Central Bank (ECB) and the Bank of Japan (BOJ) both remained in rate-cutting modes and implemented rate cuts in early 2016. The BOJ and ECB will not be raising interest rates for a matter of years while the Fed will likely be slowly raising its interest rates. Higher interest rates are supportive for a currency because those higher rates are anti-inflationary and also attract money inflows from global investors.

The dollar also continues to see support from safe-haven demand and from its status as the world's reserve currency. Global investors continue to be attracted to the dollar because they remain traumatized by the 2008/09 global financial crisis, the subsequent Eurozone sovereign debt crisis, the possibility of a hard-landing in China, and the seeming inability of the world to escape from deflationary forces. There are also various geopolitical hot spots where serious trouble could emerge. The dollar has the greatest depth of investment opportunities and is perceived to be the best place to park assets during times of stress.

The large U.S. current account deficit continues to be a bearish factor for the dollar. The U.S. current account deficit, which is the broadest measure of U.S. trade, was most recently reported at -$124 billion in Q3-2015. That means that a net $1.4 billion worth of dollars are flowing out of the U.S. each calendar day to pay for goods and services. That net dollar outflow puts downward pressure on the dollar since the recipients of those dollars sell them into the foreign exchange market if they do not want to hold them and invest them in dollar-denominated investments.

In terms of GDP, however, the U.S. trade position has improved substantially in recent years. The U.S. current account deficit has narrowed sharply to -2.7% of GDP from the peak of -6.2% of GDP seen in Q4-2005.

The ECB's stimulative monetary policy continues to be a major bearish factor for the euro (EUR/USD) and a bullish factor for the dollar index. The ECB first announced a quantitative easing (QE) program in January 2015 involving the purchase of 60 billion euros per month of securities. The ECB then announced an increase in the size of that QE program in March 2016 to 80 billion euros per month. The ECB implemented two rate cuts in 2014 and another -5 basis point cut in its refinancing rate to zero in March 2016. The ECB was forced to cut rates and implement a QE program in response to the weak Eurozone economy and increased deflation risks.

Meanwhile, the yen has fallen sharply against the dollar in the past several years. USD/JPY rallied by 67% from the record low of 75.57 yen in October 2011 to a 14-year high of 125.85 yen in June 2015. The yen fell against the dollar mainly because of the Bank of Japan's highly stimulative monetary policy and its explicit attempt to push inflation higher. This has been part of Prime Minister Shinzo Abe's pursuit of extraordinarily aggressive policies to boost the Japanese economy and shock the nation out of more than 15 years of deflation. The BOJ has been pursuing a massive QE program and announced a surprise cut in its policy rate to -0.10% in January 2016, implementing a negative interest rate for the first time ever.

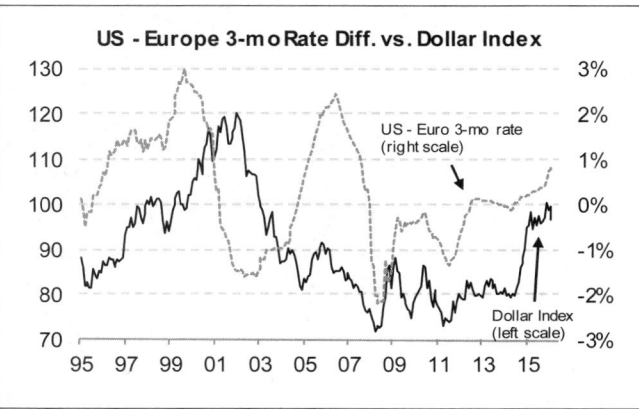

US - Europe 3-mo Rate Diff. vs. Dollar Index

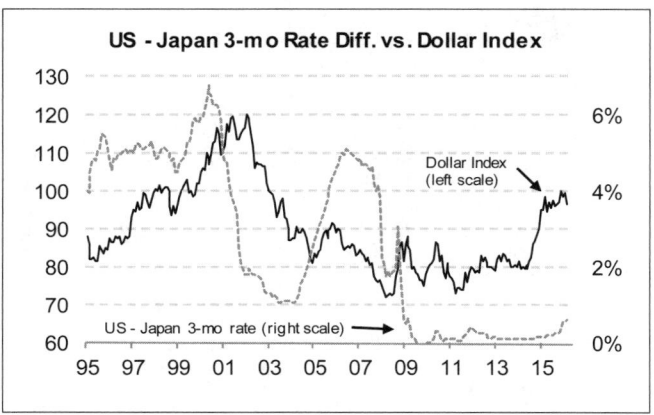

US - Japan 3-mo Rate Diff. vs. Dollar Index

The Federal Reserve is still pursuing a massively stimulative monetary policy even though it has now been almost ten years since the U.S. housing bubble started deflating in 2006 and nearly seven years since the U.S. 2007/09 recession officially ended in June 2009. The Fed has so far taken only one baby step towards normalizing monetary policy with a 25 basis point rate hike in December 2015. However, the Fed will not be able to fully normalize its monetary policy for many years considering the current low level of interest rates and the massive amount liquidity that the Fed injected in connection with the global financial crisis.

The Fed responded very aggressively to the financial crisis in 2008 with a wide range of measures. The Fed started cutting its federal funds rate target in October 2007 from 5.25% when the housing crisis started. By early 2009 the Fed had cut the funds rate to the target range of zero to 0.25%, which was the range that then prevailed until late 2015.

After the financial crisis erupted into global proportions in September 2008 with the bankruptcy of Lehman Brothers, the Fed began its so-called "quantitative easing" (QE) operations whereby it bought securities in the marketplace to permanently inject reserves into the banking system and boost liquidity.

The Fed began its first quantitative easing move (QE1) in March 2008, which eventually involved the purchase of $1.425 trillion of securities by the time it ended in March 2010. When the economy continued to struggle in the first half of 2010, the Fed launched its QE2 program of buying $600 billion worth of Treasury securities from November 2010 through June 2011.

The U.S. economy in the first half of 2011, however, started to falter again due to a confluence of negative events that included high gasoline prices, the Japanese earthquake/tsunami in March 2011, and the U.S. debt ceiling debacle in early summer 2011. In addition, the European debt crisis flared up in 2011 and the European banking system was near an all-out systemic crisis.

The Fed in September 2011, therefore, began a new program dubbed "Operation Twist" in which the Fed sold shorter-term Treasury securities from its portfolio and used the proceeds to buy longer-term securities. The purpose of this program was to keep long-term Treasury yields low, which in theory keeps other rates low such as mortgage rates and corporate bond yields.

The U.S. economy remained weak through 2012 as the European debt crisis continued to rage and as U.S. domestic demand remained weak. The Fed in September 2012 therefore began its QE3 program, which initially involved the purchase of $40 billion per month of mortgage securities. The Fed in December 2012 then announced that it would expand QE3 to $85 billion per month involving the purchase of $45 billion of longer-term Treasury securities and $40 billion of mortgage securities. The Fed starting in December 2013 cut its QE3 program by $10 billion per month at each successive FOMC meeting, making the final $15 billion cut at its Oct 28-29, 2014 meeting. The Fed's QE3 program lasted until October 2014 and ended up totaling $1.7 trillion.

At the end of QE3, the Fed announced that going forward it would roll over maturing securities in its portfolio by buying new securities, thus ensuring that its balance sheet level remained unchanged and did not start falling in a back-door type of tightening. The Fed said that it would continue to keep its balance sheet level unchanged until the normalization of interest rates is "well underway." Since QE3 ended in late 2014, the Fed has therefore kept its balance sheet roughly unchanged near $4.5 trillion, which represents $3.6 trillion of excess liquidity compared with pre-crisis levels.

The wisdom of the Fed's quantitative easing programs remains open to debate. The Fed's goals with its QE programs included (1) keeping banks fully supplied with excess reserves to reduce the chance of any liquidity squeeze and to provide plenty of reserves as a base for expanded lending, (2) keeping long-term Treasury yields relatively low in order to hold down private rates such as corporate bond yields and mortgage rates, and (3) providing a boost to asset prices and the stock market to increase household confidence and wealth. The Fed's QE measures were intended to prevent the U.S. economy from slipping into a deflationary trap such as the one seen in Japan in recent decades.

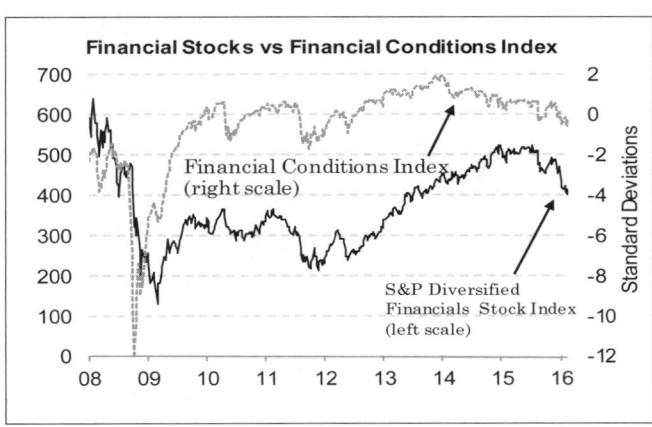

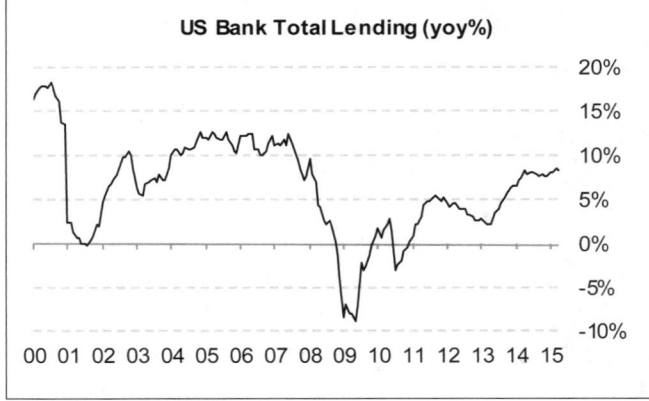

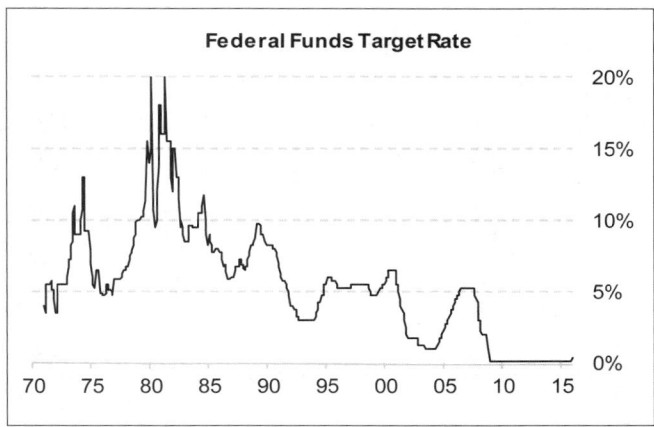

Federal Funds Target Rate

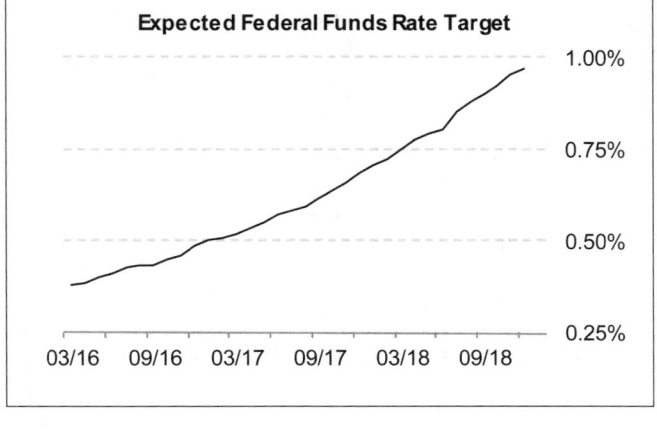

Expected Federal Funds Rate Target

Only time will tell whether the Fed made a huge mistake with its QE programs. The Fed has permanently injected a massive $3.6 trillion of liquidity into the U.S. financial system with its QE programs, which is equal to about 15% of U.S. GDP. In normal times, this high-powered liquidity could cause hyper-inflation. Indeed, there is still a small chance that the massive amount of liquidity in the banking system could yet cause an upward spike in inflation, which would force the Fed to raise interest rates sharply, undoubtedly causing a deep recession.

The U.S. economy in 2015 slowly gained traction and the labor market continued to recover with the unemployment rate falling to 5.0% by the end of 2015. After a long delay, the Fed in December 2015 finally announced its first interest rate hike in ten years, raising its federal funds target range by 25 basis points to 0.25%-0.50% from the post-crisis range of zero-0.25%.

After the Fed's first rate hike in December 2015, the markets were expecting at least two 25 bp rate hikes in 2016. However, there was substantial market turmoil in early 2016 that caused the markets to turn more dovish and expect only one rate hike by late 2016. In any case, the markets are expecting the Fed to raise interest rates slowly in coming years as it tries to get the federal funds rate back to a more normal spread above its 2% U.S. inflation target.

The U.S. economy is expected to show only modest growth in coming years near +2.2%. The U.S. economy

is expected to face ongoing headwinds from cautious consumers, weak overseas economic growth, and a strong dollar that hurts U.S. exports. In this environment, the Fed risks causing a recession if it raises interest rates too quickly. The Fed will have to take its time on raising interest rates as it waits to see whether the economy can absorb the last interest rate hike before it implements another rate hike. However, the Fed can afford to take its time on raising interest rates only if inflation remains low.

In addition to raising interest rates, the Fed at some point will have to take action to reduce the level of its balance sheet. As mentioned earlier, the Fed plans to maintain its policy of rolling over maturing securities until the process of normalizing interest rates is "well underway." When the Fed feels the economy is strong enough, its first step towards normalizing its balance sheet will be to announce that it will no longer roll over maturing securities, thus causing its balance sheet to slowly decline as securities mature. However, it remains to be seen whether the Fed will ever actually sell securities in its balance sheet, which would put upward pressure on long-term interest rates.

The Fed in any case faces a very tricky task over the next few years in trying to exit from its monetary largesse without either causing a recession or allowing an upward spike in inflation. The Fed's exit path could easily end up causing some major volatility for the economy and the markets over the next few years.

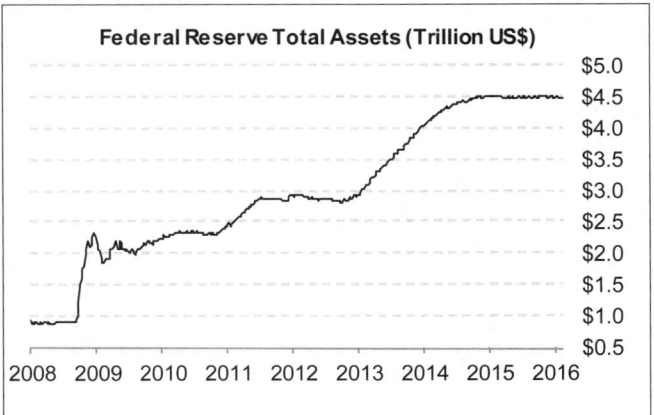

Federal Reserve Total Assets (Trillion US$)

U.S. 10-year Inflation Expectations

10-yr T-note minus TIPS

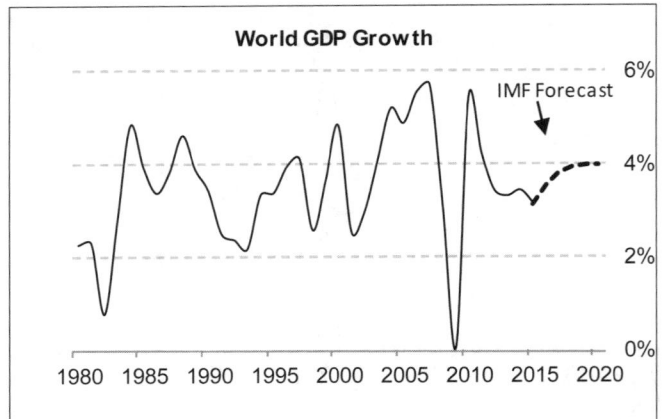

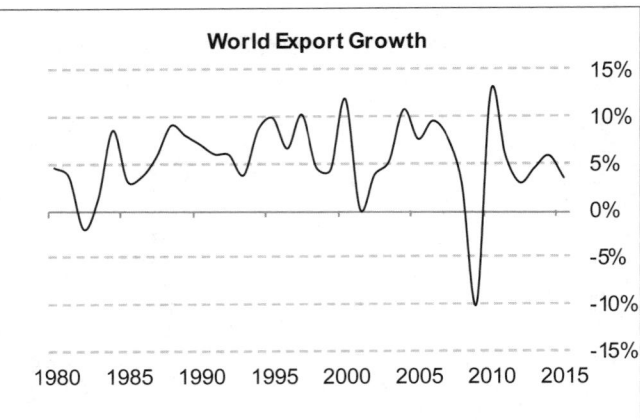

The global economy in 2015 continued to struggle. World GDP growth in 2015 edged downward to a 6-year low of +3.1% from +3.4% in 2014. World GDP growth has slowed ever since the world financial crisis ended the strong growth rates of above 5% seen in 2006-07. The world economy now faces weakness from the slowdown in China, low growth rates in the industrialized world, and slow growth in the developing world due to weak oil and commodity prices and the need to clamp down on inflation and support weak currencies.

The strongest GDP growth rates among for the world's ten largest countries belonged once again to China and India. Chinese GDP growth in 2015 slowed to a 25-year low of +6.9% but that was still far stronger than most other countries in the world. Meanwhile, India showed strong growth of +7.3% in 2015.

U.S. GDP growth in 2015 was moderate at +2.4% and was strong enough to help keep the world economy afloat. However, quarterly U.S. GDP growth eased to only +1.0% in Q4-2015 as consumer spending was the only major positive factor. U.S. GDP growth in Q4 suffered from negligible growth in business investment and government spending and from GDP subtractions from net exports and inventories. Still, the market consensus is that U.S. GDP growth will recover to +2.2% in early 2016.

The Eurozone economy in 2015 finally recovered to a growth rate of +1.6% from the very poor growth rates seen in the three previous years in 2012 (-0.9%), 2013 (-0.3%), and 2014 (+0.9%). The Eurozone economy finally shook off the Eurozone debt crisis, but continued to see weak consumer and export demand and austere government budgets. The market consensus is for Eurozone GDP growth to move sideways near +1.6% in 2016-18.

Japan's GDP in 2015 improved slightly to +0.5% from zero growth in 2014 but the economy continued to be weighed down by tax increases and weak exports. The market consensus is for Japan's GDP to remain weak at +0.9% in 2016 and +0.6% in 2017.

Meanwhile, Russia and Brazil saw recessions in 2015. Brazil's GDP fell by -3.8% in 2015 and is expected to fall by another -3.3% in 2016. Brazil's economy has been hurt by the sharp drop in commodity prices, high interest rates to battle a weak currency and high inflation, and a serious corruption and political scandal. Russia's GDP fell by -3.7% in 2015 and is expected to fall by another -1.5% in 2016. The Russian economy continues to be hurt by the plunge in oil and gas prices and by Western sanctions against Russia over Crimea and Ukraine.

Looking ahead, the IMF is predicting a slow improvement in global GDP through 2020 since global monetary policies remain very stimulative. The market consensus is for world GDP of +3.1% in 2016 and +3.4% in 2017. However, there are still plenty of risks that could derail the global economy once again.

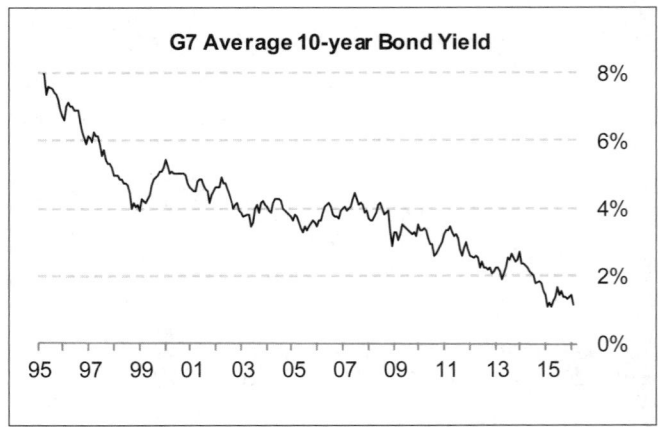

China is causing increasing trepidation in the global markets as it tries to navigate an inexorable decline in its GDP growth rate to a more sustainable long-term rate. China's real GDP growth in 2015 fell to a 25-year low of 6.9% from 7.3% in 2014. By contrast, China posted double-digit growth rates as recently as 2003-2007 before the world financial crisis halted China's upside momentum.

China in the past several decades has relied mainly on a very aggressive economic development model focused on exports and investment in infrastructure, real estate, and heavy industry. However, that model started to run out of steam when the global financial crisis decimated China's export customers and caused overcapacity in many of China's industries. China has ended up with overbuilt industries and property market, which has led to the need to downsize to weaker demand.

China now has no choice but to shift to a more modern consumer economy where the focus is more on goods and services for its consumers rather than on exports and investment. Yet China's middle class may not yet be large enough to support a world-class consumer economy.

China also faces the serious problem of trying to use a Communist political system to transition to a market economy. China still tries to direct its economy from the top levels of government, which results in numerous judgment mistakes and the misallocation of capital. Moreover, it remains an open question about how long the Chinese people will allow themselves to be governed by self-appointed Communist party officials and whether serious social unrest may eventually break out, particularly if the Chinese economy continues to slow.

For the Chinese government, the slowdown in the Chinese economy could be an existential threat since people without jobs or a future are ripe for political rebellion. The Chinese government therefore continues to pull out all the stops to stimulate the economy, even if the net effect will be even bigger problems down the road.

The Chinese economic data is also of suspicious quality as Chinese officials try meet targets and exude confidence. Yet the opaque nature of China's economic data means that it is very difficult to assess whether China will be able to engineer a soft landing or whether the economy will fall apart like a house of cards. If the world missed the fact that the U.S. banking system was a house of cards before the 2008/09 global financial crisis, it may also be missing the possibility that the entire Chinese economy could be a house of cards as well.

China responded to the 2008/2009 financial crisis with a very aggressive stimulus program that succeeded in limiting the drop in China's quarterly real GDP growth rate to +6.2% in Q1-2009 and then produced an upward rebound to as high as +12.2% a year later in Q1-2010.

However, that stimulus program came with collateral damage that is now undercutting the Chinese economy. The government stimulus program resulted in annual budget deficits that reached 2.3% of GDP by 2015 and that caused an increase in China's total government debt from 35% of GDP in 2007 to 43% by 2015. Moreover, the IMF is predicting that China's government total debt will continue to rise in coming years, hitting 50% of GDP by 2020.

More alarming than the government debt situation, however, is that the Chinese government caused Chinese banks to force-feed loans to Chinese businesses in order to stimulate the economy. The result has been a dangerous surge in Chinese corporate and household debt from 125% of GDP in 2008 to the current level of 210% of GDP. A large amount of that debt has turned into bad loans, thus raising questions about the stability of the Chinese financial system.

The People's Bank of China (PBOC), China's central bank, has so far cut its 1-year lending rate by 165 basis points to 4.35% from the 5.60% level seen in November 2014. However, the PBOC's ability to continue cutting interest rates to stimulate the economy is limited by the need to avoid causing further weakness in the Chinese yuan, which has dropped by -8% since early 2014. Further weakness in the yuan would fuel additional capital flight that has already been a problem since 2014.

The world markets are hoping for a soft-landing in China. However, there is still the outside chance of a hard-landing in China that could cause a world recession and sharp declines in the world's stock markets.

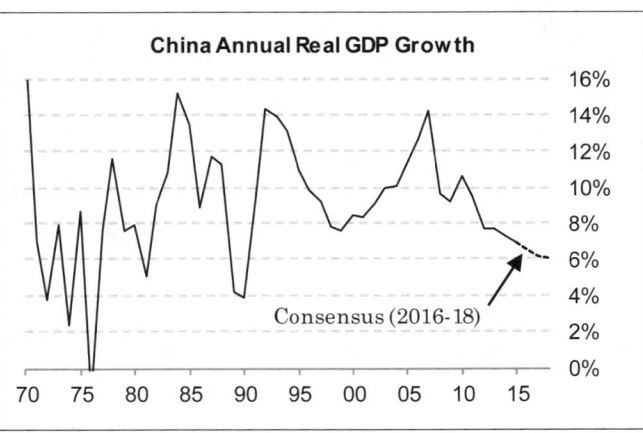

China Annual Real GDP Growth

Consensus (2016-18)

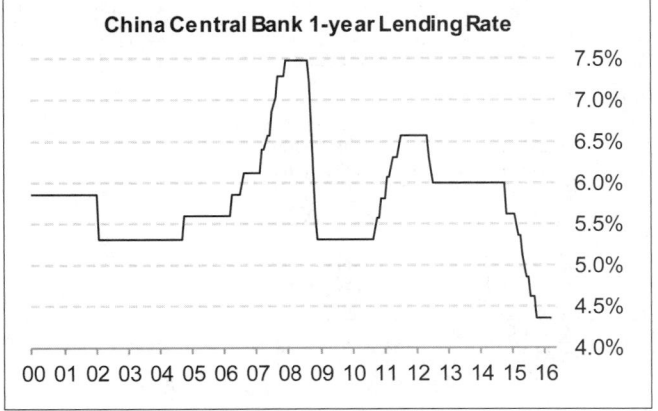

China Central Bank 1-year Lending Rate

Volume - U.S.

U.S. Futures Volume Highlights
2015 in Comparison with 2014

2015 Rank	Top 50 Contracts Traded in 2015	2015 Contracts	%	2014 Contracts	%	2014 Rank
1	Eurodollar, CME	586,913,126	21.23%	664,433,493	24.03%	1
2	E-mini S&P 500, CME	429,803,221	15.55%	425,020,210	15.37%	2
3	10 Year Treasury Note, CBOT	328,341,066	11.88%	340,485,319	12.32%	3
4	Crude Oil (CL), NYMEX	202,202,392	7.31%	145,147,334	5.25%	6
5	5 Year Treasury Note, CBOT	190,707,727	6.90%	196,429,135	7.10%	4
6	North American Natural Gas, ICE FUTURES U.S.	160,942,339	5.82%	180,868,570	6.54%	5
7	Corn, CBOT	83,094,271	3.01%	69,437,304	2.51%	11
8	2 Year Treasury Note, CBOT	83,040,660	3.00%	71,814,288	2.60%	10
9	Henry Hub Natural Gas (NG), NYMEX	81,772,492	2.96%	74,206,602	2.68%	9
10	30 Year Treasury Bond, CBOT	71,901,544	2.60%	93,189,109	3.37%	7
11	E-mini Nasdaq 100, CME	67,310,282	2.43%	75,483,720	2.73%	8
12	Euro FX, CME	65,356,062	2.36%	52,208,275	1.89%	12
13	Soybeans, CBOT	54,095,051	1.96%	49,169,361	1.78%	14
14	CBOE Volatility Index (VX), CFE	51,656,362	1.87%	50,531,366	1.83%	13
15	Gold (GC), NYMEX	41,847,338	1.51%	40,518,804	1.47%	15
16	Mini-sized $5 Dow Jones Industrial Index, CBOT	40,601,073	1.47%	39,053,744	1.41%	16
17	RBOB Gasoline Physical (RB), NYMEX	40,302,099	1.46%	34,421,866	1.25%	19
18	NY Harbor ULSD (HO), NYMEX	36,947,020	1.34%	33,946,420	1.23%	20
19	Japanese Yen, CME	36,180,466	1.31%	38,319,796	1.39%	17
20	Sugar #11, ICE FUTURES U.S.	34,394,482	1.24%	29,396,597	1.06%	21
21	Chicago Soft Red Winter Wheat, CBOT	31,102,037	1.12%	25,853,004	0.94%	23
22	Ultra T-Bond, CBOT	29,133,162	1.05%	25,427,616	0.92%	24
23	Soybean Oil, CBOT	28,897,275	1.05%	23,769,391	0.86%	26
24	Russell 2000 Mini Index, ICE FUTURES U.S.	28,367,406	1.03%	34,606,377	1.25%	18
25	North American Power, ICE FUTURES U.S.	28,325,682	1.02%	27,169,421	0.98%	22
26	Brent Last Day Financial (BZ), NYMEX	26,251,078	0.95%	18,493,384	0.67%	29
27	Soybean Meal, CBOT	24,315,276	0.88%	20,637,382	0.75%	28
28	British Pound, CME	24,144,659	0.87%	24,837,008	0.90%	25
29	Australian Dollar, CME	23,382,408	0.85%	22,728,891	0.82%	27
30	Federal Funds, CBOT	20,247,761	0.73%	7,894,868	0.29%	29
31	Canadian Dollar, CME	17,301,876	0.63%	15,096,546	0.55%	30
32	Copper (HG), NYMEX	16,986,055	0.61%	14,591,200	0.53%	31
33	Mini MSCI Emerging Markets, ICE FUTURES U.S.	14,135,268	0.51%	9,245,982	0.33%	38
34	Silver (SI), NYMEX	13,454,406	0.49%	13,696,961	0.50%	32
35	Live Cattle, CME	13,440,934	0.49%	13,599,292	0.49%	33
36	Nikkei 225 (Yen), CME	13,352,541	0.48%	12,184,838	0.44%	34
37	US Dollar Index, ICE FUTURES U.S.	12,106,494	0.44%	7,112,150	0.26%	40
38	Mexican Peso, CME	10,951,568	0.40%	10,484,059	0.38%	36
39	Lean Hogs, CME	9,575,882	0.35%	10,656,944	0.39%	35
40	Coffee C, ICE FUTURES U.S.	8,108,135	0.29%	7,052,230	0.26%	41
41	Cocoa, ICE FUTURES U.S.	7,913,036	0.29%	6,315,792	0.23%	43
42	KC Hard Red Winter Wheat, CBOT	7,359,985	0.27%	5,868,505	0.21%	44
43	Cotton #2, ICE FUTURES U.S.	6,725,842	0.24%	5,787,883	0.21%	45
44	Swiss Franc, CME	5,634,413	0.20%	9,638,920	0.35%	37
45	E-mini S&P Midcap 400, CME	5,381,033	0.19%	5,285,715	0.19%	46
46	Henry Hub Natural Gas Last Day Financial, NYMEX	5,330,807	0.19%	6,332,365	0.23%	42
47	New Zealand Dollar, CME	5,040,002	0.18%	4,108,009	0.15%	49
48	E-Micro EUR/USD, CME	4,325,807	0.16%	1,969,393	0.07%	
49	Mini MSCI EAFE Index, ICE FUTURES U.S.	4,302,898	0.16%	2,963,517	0.11%	
50	Nikkei 225 ($), CME	4,236,624	0.15%	4,815,946	0.17%	47
	Top 50 Contracts	3,137,239,423	97.62%	3,102,304,902	97.72%	
	Contracts Below the Top 50	76,460,983	2.38%	72,453,103	2.28%	
	TOTAL	**3,213,700,406**	**100.00%**	**3,174,758,005**	**100.00%**	

U.S. Futures Volume Highlights
2015 in Comparison with 2014

2015 Rank	EXCHANGE	2015 Contracts	%	2014 Contracts	%	2014 Rank
1	Chicago Mercantile Exchange (CME Group)	1,336,988,253	41.60%	1,404,178,272	44.23%	1
2	Chicago Board of Trade (CME Group)	996,141,892	31.00%	972,566,847	30.63%	2
3	New York Mercantile Exchange (CME Group)	505,584,026	15.73%	419,742,753	13.22%	3
4	ICE Futures U.S.	308,647,365	9.60%	314,104,173	9.89%	4
5	CBOE Futures Exchange	51,675,531	1.61%	50,615,305	1.59%	5
6	OneChicago	11,714,015	0.36%	10,907,977	0.34%	6
7	Minneapolis Grain Exchange	2,288,685	0.07%	2,153,373	0.07%	7
8	ERIS Exchange	660,462	0.02%	489,305	0.02%	8
9	ELX Futures	177	0.00%			
	Total Futures	**3,213,700,406**	**100.00%**	**3,174,758,005**	**100.00%**	

CBOE Futures Exchange (CFE)

FUTURE	2015	2014	2013	2012	2011
CBOE Brazil ETF Volume Index Security Futures	645	18,087	8,490	7,262	
CBOE Emerging Markets ETF Volatility Index	670	21,689	24,751	55,388	
CBOE Gold ETF Volatility Index (GVZ)	304	5,821	15,960	6,378	129
CBOE Mini-Volatility Index (VM)		230	18,198	17,057	8,388
CBOE Nasdaq 100 Volatility Index (VXN)	1,140	10,430	6,576	2,316	
CBOE Oil ETF Volatility Index Securities Futures	2,848	10,087	8,285	11,215	
CBOE Russell 2000 Volatility Index (RVX)	5,677	5,340	758		
CBOE S&P 500 Twelve-Month Variance (IIK)	5,011	2,308	166,287	6,550	
CBOE Short-Term Volatility Index (VXST)	2,721	9,933			
CBOE Volatility Index (VX)	51,656,362	50,531,366	39,944,022	23,785,831	12,031,528
CBOE/CBOT 10 Year US Treasury Note Volatility	153	14			
Total Futures	**51,675,531**	**50,615,305**	**40,193,447**	**23,892,203**	**12,040,074**

Chicago Board of Trade (CBT), division of the CME Group

FUTURE	2015	2014	2013	2012	2011
$10 Dow Jones Industrial Index	37,166	126,948	166,905	202,771	286,697
10-Year Treasury Notes	328,341,066	340,485,319	325,928,194	264,997,089	317,402,598
10-Year USD Deliverable Interest Rate Swap	756,375	784,215	681,577	12,246	
2-Year Treasury Notes	83,040,660	71,814,288	57,815,900	55,108,651	72,178,803
2-Year USD Deliverable Interest Rate Swap	38,436	110,791	75,017	4,475	
30-Year Treasury Bonds	71,901,544	93,189,109	97,963,266	91,745,232	92,338,638
30-Year USD Deliverable Interest Rate Swap	35,760	62,513	89,144	1,816	
5-Year Treasury Notes	190,707,727	196,429,135	175,328,163	133,342,429	170,563,052
5-Year USD Deliverable Interest Rate Swap	696,148	779,579	516,179	8,570	
7-Year USD Deliverable Interest Rate Swap	7,832				
Chicago Soft Red Winter Wheat	31,100,598	25,853,004	24,993,158	27,379,403	24,283,331
Corn	83,094,271	69,437,304	64,322,600	73,184,337	79,004,801
DJ UBS Commodity Index	369,468	255,563	192,673	132,339	140,479
DJ UBS Roll Select Commodity Index	8,018	4,072	1,787		
DJ US Real Estate	177,627	121,166	52,486	14,081	6
Ethanol	187,661	243,072	298,718	330,913	238,946
Federal Funds	20,247,761	7,894,868	4,649,878	6,425,956	12,306,131
Fertilizer Products	27,175	16,925	10,436	4,175	360
KC Hard Red Winter Wheat	7,359,752	5,868,505			
Mini Corn	132,596	172,411	206,491	267,428	363,832
Mini Soybeans	229,208	316,771	299,308	359,324	394,119
Mini Wheat	82,987	101,124	125,944	95,600	149,102
Mini-sized $5 Dow Jones Industrial Index	40,601,073	39,053,744	35,448,824	30,902,047	32,496,922
Oats	194,575	200,531	254,958	279,570	349,316
OTC Ethanol Forward Swap	9,329	16,245	44,452	355,943	632,211
Rough Rice	316,315	225,694	280,048	388,936	555,854
Soybean Meal	24,315,276	20,637,382	20,237,181	18,187,433	16,920,194
Soybean Oil	28,897,275	23,769,391	23,805,912	27,627,590	24,156,509
Soybeans	54,095,051	49,169,361	46,721,081	52,041,615	45,143,755
Ultra T-Bond	29,133,162	25,427,616	21,149,865	16,560,093	15,461,984
Total Futures	**996,141,892**	**972,566,847**	**901,909,220**	**800,706,309**	**906,707,754**

Chicago Mercantile Exchange (CME), division of the CME Group

FUTURE	2015	2014	2013	2012	2011
2 Year Eurodollar Bundle	595	2,153			
3 Year Eurodollar Bundle	168	971			
5 Year Eurodollar Bundle	38	140			
Australian Dollar	23,382,408	22,728,891	26,332,299	32,727,390	30,751,538
Australian Dollar / Canadian Dollar	234	1,022	1,179	1,503	1,694
Australian Dollar / Japanese Yen	49,242	70,201	31,712	24,811	26,857
Australian Dollar / New Zealand Dollar	605	2,200	672	532	438
Brazilian Real	703,676	648,815	353,333	168,852	260,730
British Pound	24,144,659	24,837,008	29,237,763	26,166,290	29,028,755
British Pound / Japanese Yen	15,468	51,224	31,209	31,925	36,105
British Pound / Swiss Franc	1,629	4,891	3,240	22,380	10,610
Butter	30,896	2,480	3,191	1,050	
Canadian Dollar	17,301,876	15,096,546	17,427,832	22,799,446	22,416,680
Canadian Dollar / Japanese Yen	261	1,214	1,205	1,591	624
Cash Settled Cheese	123,000	80,507	35,800	30,164	15,990
CDD Seasonal Weather Strips	1,404	100	3,550	2,121	3,150
CDD Weather	5,992	7,407	15,924	16,305	22,856
Chilean Peso	73				
Chinese Renimibi / Euro	13,267		6		
Chinese Renimibi / US Dollar	5,239	10,799	18,981	4,101	7,563
Class III Milk	275,539	358,659	293,941	294,497	368,614
Class IV Milk	12,071	24,447	20,115	2,755	10,744
CSI Housing Index	93	133	230	357	195
Dry Whey	21,482	17,790	11,457	11,904	10,601
E-micro AUD/USD	652,469	519,173	393,937	239,396	240,406
E-micro EUR/USD	4,325,807	1,969,393	2,014,893	1,653,362	1,532,755

Chicago Mercantile Exchange (CME), division of the CME Group (continued)

FUTURE	2015	2014	2013	2012	2011
E-micro GBP/USD	488,050	362,251	388,124	364,989	206,527
E-micro INR/USD	2,576				
E-micro USD/CAD	12	2	20	1,365	12,898
E-micro USD/CHF	9	6		750	19,911
E-micro USD/CNH	367				
E-micro USD/JPY	113	119	98	10,595	29,465
E-mini CNX Nifty Index	1,018	0		86	1,495
E-mini Euro FX	1,481,391	915,094	1,039,366	1,010,884	1,426,462
E-mini FTSE 100 Index	4,525				
E-mini Japanese Yen	212,810	176,328	334,137	123,064	129,518
E-mini NASDAQ 100 Index	67,310,282	75,483,720	59,393,053	63,530,758	75,165,277
E-mini Russell 1000 Growth Index	1,782				
E-mini Russell 1000 Index	2,913				
E-mini Russell 1000 Value Index	1,729				
E-mini S&P 500 Index	429,803,221	425,020,210	452,291,450	474,278,939	620,368,790
E-mini S&P Consumer Discretionary Sector	134,064	36,813	21,625	15,881	5,570
E-mini S&P Consumer Staples Sector	154,403	67,346	43,185	25,599	7,766
E-mini S&P Energy Sector	94,819	93,174	82,626	25,266	17,788
E-mini S&P Financial Sector	63,667	40,078	49,872	24,455	10,000
E-mini S&P Healthcare Sector	144,470	56,750	45,818	25,476	6,810
E-mini S&P Industrial Sector	43,235	37,218	23,630	27,956	15,953
E-mini S&P Materials Sector	41,622	29,985	22,769	20,928	16,133
E-mini S&P MidCap 400 Index	5,381,033	5,285,715	5,601,547	6,536,907	7,689,306
E-mini S&P SmallCap 600 Index	1	57	353	1,752	13,422
E-mini S&P Technology Sector	60,448	41,290	40,270	24,833	6,581
E-mini S&P Utilities Sector	138,316	88,427	50,600	25,018	8,197
Euro HDD Weather	50	1,750	3,800	5,675	4,664
Euro FX	65,356,062	52,208,275	61,285,617	67,407,741	84,236,825
Euro HDD Seasonal Strip Weather	100	6,250	1,000	2,050	1,028
Euro / Australian Dollar	24,807	16,076	12,193	9,527	4,816
Euro / British Pound	772,968	742,968	739,215	461,063	341,899
Euro / Canadian Dollar	31,904	40,530	9,508	8,502	4,049
Euro / Japanese Yen	555,285	559,039	904,294	368,161	369,522
Euro / Norwegian Krone	769	1,198	2,118	3,275	1,386
Euro / Swedish Krona	5,059	8,972	3,579	3,602	1,110
Euro / Swiss Franc	411,198	459,297	446,215	332,729	351,429
Euro / Turkish Lira	10	14,267	27,706	30,188	10,825
Eurodollar (3-month)	586,913,126	664,433,493	517,250,183	426,438,437	564,086,746
Feeder Cattle	2,493,051	2,116,262	1,669,284	1,796,592	1,580,387
HDD Seasonal Weather Strips	952	800	600	1,350	3,975
HDD Weather	8,427	7,039	23,636	14,843	28,491
Hungarian Forint	2	624	15,645	792	2,117
Ibovespa Index	5,090	4,431	28,968	3,397	
Indian Rupee	130,396	50,949	166,114		
Israeli Shekel	22	5,983	9,681	9,350	5,599
Japanese Yen	36,180,466	38,319,796	42,762,257	23,520,562	28,369,147
Korean Won	815	2,301	5,246	8,144	3,939
Lean Hogs	9,575,882	10,656,944	11,277,038	11,461,892	9,969,961
Live Cattle	13,440,934	13,599,292	12,463,043	13,985,374	13,532,554
Malaysian Palm Oil Calendar Swap	54,412	43,020	14,980		
Mexican Peso	10,951,568	10,484,059	10,374,701	11,482,886	9,203,730
Micro CAD/USD	158,108	177,522	59,749	45,460	24,582
Micro CHF/USD	28,110	48,379	61,530	45,582	59,900
Micro JPY/USD	150,355	164,072	177,033	46,755	68,499
NASDAQ 100 Index	91,150	252,932	234,032	332,288	472,587
NASDAQ Biotech	1,724	600			
New Zealand Dollar	5,040,002	4,108,009	3,618,319	3,655,690	2,077,277
Nikkei 225 ($)	4,236,624	4,815,946	4,680,898	1,690,244	2,766,559
Nikkei 225 (Yen)	13,352,541	12,184,838	11,792,392	5,738,629	7,670,282
Nonfat Dry Milk	50,714	28,461	12,015	5,355	6,372
Norwegian Krone/US Dollar	14,381	14,647	13,963	8,206	13,082
One Month Eurodollar	63,422	19,870	11,440	110,823	187,511
Euro / Polish Zloty	6,483	36,075	44,416	41,911	31,006
Polish Zloty	8,434	24,500	19,594	22,312	38,951
Random Lumber	201,352	160,497	224,351	304,928	319,333
Russian Ruble	399,570	372,359	244,995	313,867	687,845
S&P 500 Index	3,043,109	3,387,740	4,156,499	5,032,650	7,220,582
S&P Citigroup Growth	401	803	689	522	554
S&P Citigroup Value	6,105	1,609	733	522	697
Goldman Sachs Commodity Index	354,566	274,161	305,187	291,520	328,281
S&P GSCI Enhanced Excess Return Swap	104,576	80,586	18,548	4,732	
GSCI Excess Return Index	254,115	201,879	12,057	16,680	92,046
S&P Midcap 400 Index	6,922	21,223	20,744	24,182	42,724
South African Rand	216,350	122,259	141,518	164,012	143,544
Swedish Krona	15,398	12,163	13,438	4,306	3,217

Chicago Mercantile Exchange (CME), division of the CME Group (continued)

FUTURE	2015	2014	2013	2012	2011
Swiss Franc	5,634,413	9,638,920	9,061,770	9,911,325	10,238,684
Turkish Lira	126	20,215	45,418	39,286	13,729
US Dollar/South African Rand	580	1,476			
USD Crude Palm Oil	200		1,080	318	1,016
Total Futures	**1,336,988,253**	**1,404,178,272**	**1,290,230,093**	**1,215,594,457**	**1,535,793,841**

ELX Futures Exchange (ELX)

FUTURE	2015	2014	2013	2012	2011
Eurodollar (GEE)	177		907	185,710	3,888,256
Total Futures	**177**	**0**	**3,772**	**818,664**	**16,757,952**

ERIS Exchange

FUTURE	2015	2014	2013
10-Year Standards	286,612	164,539	79,027
2-Year Standards	37,500	44,965	96,619
30-Year Standards	2,769	2,196	2,400
5-Year Standards	289,268	162,162	54,020
7-Year Standards	25,761	34,953	10,122
Flexes	18,552	80,490	61,892
Total Futures	**660,462**	**489,305**	**304,080**

ICE Futures U.S. (ICE)

FUTURE	2015	2014	2013	2012	2011
100 oz. Gold	376	388	5,705	17,905	103,864
5,000 oz. Silver	209	118	2,795	7,065	45,694
Australian Dollar / Canadian Dollar	8,346	3,505	8,389	15,043	18,411
Australian Dollar / Japanese Yen	7,016	7,211	7,229	10,439	19,346
Australian Dollar / New Zealand Dollar	22,609	11,411	12,791	13,485	17,688
Australian Dollar / US Dollar (KAU)	10,312	4,172	3,579	2,303	4,219
British Pound / Australian Dollar	6,176	4,532	9,552	12,649	19,111
British Pound / Canadian Dollar	7,870	5,549	9,330	14,563	14,099
British Pound / Japanese Yen	42,001	33,124	20,751	33,868	82,549
British Pound / New Zealand Dollar	2,806	3,643	5,423	5,595	7,019
British Pound / Norwegian Krone	7,583	5,508	11,937	13,579	17,952
British Pound / South Africa Rand	714	1,020	1,240		
British Pound / Swedish Krona	645	980	410	2	
British Pound / Swiss franc	19,869	22,049	19,391	19,249	15,076
Canadian Dollar / Japanese Yen	6,931	5,729	7,847	13,362	17,562
Canadian Dollar / US Dollar (KSV)	14,943	9,222	14	844	178
Cocoa	7,913,036	6,315,792	6,583,746	5,999,813	4,948,052
Coffee 'C'	8,108,135	7,052,230	7,124,029	6,125,484	5,174,538
Cotton #2	6,725,842	5,787,883	6,155,024	6,130,352	5,288,454
Eris CDX HY Credit Index Future 5Y	905				
Eris CDX IG Credit Index Future 5Y	2,786				
Euro / Australian Dollar (KRA)	27,783	31,842	31,443	53,939	28,941
Euro / British Pound (KGB)	32,683	31,059	63,612	114,160	30,679
Euro / Canadian Dollar (KEP)	12,131	7,045	11,969	16,097	5,609
Euro / Czech Koruna	25,929	18,904	23,423	22,692	34,069
Euro / Hungarian Forint	50,989	34,564	35,207	54,051	42,289
Euro / Japanese Yen (KEJ)	26,269	54,032	118,255	98,906	31,351
Euro / Norwegian Krone (KOL)	13,683	48,624	47,570	61,363	17,743
Euro / South African Rand	693	1,624	1,329	393	183
Euro / Swedish Krona (KRK)	51,925	27,738	45,792	38,806	11,268
Euro / Swiss Franc (KRZ)	12,895	16,786	24,120	16,871	3,934
Euro / US Dollar (KEO)	230,182	221,758	113,818	101,583	79,547
Israeli Shekel / US Dollar	7,845				
Japanese Yen / US Dollar (KSN)	18,606	15,742	12	857	371
Mexican Peso / US Dollar	1,400	160	20		
Million Euro / British Pound	36	20			60
Mini Gold	280,497	495,869	1,065,347	1,105,993	1,955,899
Mini MSCI All Country World Index	2				
Mini MSCI Canada Index	152	64	527	623	
Mini MSCI EAFE Index	4,302,898	2,963,517	2,078,265	1,745,910	860,513
Mini MSCI Emerging Markets	14,135,268	9,245,982	6,102,827	3,044,608	1,148,430
Mini MSCI Emerging Markets Asia	316	108			
Mini MSCI Emerging Markets Latin America Index	10,749	3,152	4,716	2,808	4,989
Mini MSCI Europe Index	441,714	416,392			
Mini MSCI World Index	18,640	11,756	24,424	656	
Mini Pan Euro Index	57,306	141,076	79,310	48,937	51,297
Mini Silver	129,850	188,863	485,998	668,178	1,550,088
MSCI ACWI NTR	139,820	143,859			
MSCI Euro	1,242		10,481		
New Zealand Dollar / Japanese Yen	14,479	22,499	11,497	12,176	12,900
New Zealand Dollar / US Dollar (KZX)	4,143	3,327	6	364	191
North American Natural Gas	160,942,339	180,868,570	239,612,322	60,193,117	

ICE Futures U.S. (ICE) (continued)

FUTURE	2015	2014	2013	2012	2011
North American Natural Gas and Power	223,560	17,554			
North American Power	28,325,682	27,169,421	137,201,064	33,064,337	
Norwegian Krone / Japanese Yen	571	878	2,174	708	176
Norwegian Krone / Swedish Koruna	19,931	31,714	20,590	22,715	17,044
Orange Juice, Frozen Concentrate	398,567	398,529	505,019	586,775	627,610
Polish Zloty / Euro	26,182				
Polish Zloty / US Dollar	6,024				
Russell 1000 Growth Index Mini	106,399	150,113	190,268	72,078	120,758
Russell 1000 Mini Index	269,188	372,183	315,793	362,590	414,079
Russell 1000 Value Index Mini	139,083	182,675	138,772	109,958	129,021
Russell 2000 Growth Index Mini	21	1,844	54		
Russell 2000 Mini Index	28,367,406	34,606,377	28,837,712	33,044,716	43,594,169
Russell 2000 Value Index Mini	4	666	1,050		
Russian Ruble / US Dollar (KRU)	6	11,211	19,549	6,595	
Small British Pound / US Dollar	19,807	15,852	5,513	6,426	20,833
Sugar #11	34,394,482	29,396,597	29,813,680	27,126,728	24,629,369
Sugar #16	71,502	86,261	76,117	76,565	74,876
Swedish Krona / Japanese Yen	471	770	1,554		
Swiss Franc / Japanese Yen (KZY)	10,955	11,225	7,820	5,188	1,820
Swiss Franc / US Dollar (KMF)	8,194	2,714	52	262	137
Turkish Lira / Euro	2,161				
Turkish Lira / US Dollar	35,457				
U.S. Corn	443	294	103,000	153,577	
U.S. Soybean Meal	20	8	5,324	29,874	
U.S. Soybean Oil	20	123	9,071	46,442	
U.S. Soybeans	179	108	52,204	154,453	
U.S. Wheat	128	271	75,295	79,809	
US Dollar / Czech Koruna (Half Size)	18,306	10,043	19,142	20,729	32,584
US Dollar / Hungarian Forint (Half Size)	24,160	12,587	23,307	28,895	39,723
US Dollar / Norwegian Krone (Half Size)	19,344	39,626	52,755	59,163	80,993
US Dollar / South African Rand	112,509	124,300	117,262	94,907	102,942
US Dollar / Swedish Krona (Half Size)	37,791	34,290	65,457	84,331	70,409
US Dollar Index	12,106,494	7,112,150	8,050,966	6,321,418	7,751,270
World Cotton	744				
Total Futures	**308,647,365**	**314,104,173**	**475,694,217**	**187,400,477**	**99,827,775**

Minneapolis Grain Exchange (MGE)

FUTURE	2015	2014	2013	2012	2011
Apple Juice Concentrate	30	290	504	127	
Hard Red Spring Wheat	2,288,655	2,153,083	1,460,147	1,223,457	1,732,331
Total Futures	**2,288,685**	**2,153,373**	**1,460,651**	**1,223,584**	**1,732,331**

New York Mercantile Exchange (NYMEX), division of the CME Group

FUTURE	2015	2014	2013	2012	2011
1% Fuel Oil Cargoes CIF MED (Platts) Futures (1W)	264	246	257	401	875
1% Fuel Oil Cargoes CIF NWE (Platts) Futures (1X)	206	238	203	385	579
1% Fuel Oil Cargoes FOB MED (Platts) BALMO	62	47	10	44	
1% Fuel Oil Cargoes FOB NWE (Platts) Crack Spread	306	1,945	11,938	28,195	15,426
1% Fuel Oil Cargoes FOB NWE (Platts) vs. 3.5% Fuel	4,656	7,151	15,683	37,853	20,067
1% Fuel Oil Rdam vs 1% Fuel Oil NWE (Platts) Swap	618	1,128	1,421	3,154	2,212
1,000-oz. Silver Futures (SIL)	89,934	143,368	56,864		
1.0% Fuel Oil Cargoes FOB NWE (Platts) Crack	31	15	487	36	
3.5% Fuel Oil Barges FOB Rdam (Platts) Crack Spread	20,213	9,164	7,847	1,665	452
3.5% Fuel Oil Barges FOB Rdam (Platts) Crack Spread	3,082	3,042	1,857	1,976	
3.5% Fuel Oil Barges FOB Rdam (Platts) Crack Spread	44,483	49,990	192,036	311,707	130,348
3.5% Fuel Oil Cargoes FOB MED (Platts) vs. 3.5% Fuel	10,806	7,869	2,895	1,940	1,295
3.5% Fuel Oil CIF MED (Platts) BALMO Futures (8D)	153	100	2		
3.5% Fuel Oil CIF MED (Platts) Futures (7D)	896	1,094	132	30	29
3.5% Fuel Oil Rdam vs. 3.5% FOB MED Spread	1,245	1,619	1,101	322	742
Algonquin City-Gates Natural Gas (Platts IFERC)	1,419	7,934	6,126	10,705	9,891
Aluminium European Premium Metal Bulletin (25mt-	4,651				
Aluminum Futures (ALI)	4,044	5,991			
Aluminum MW U.S. Transaction Premium Platts	37,447	5,431	139		
ANR, Louisiana Natural Gas (Platts IFERC) Basis	2,996		183	2,122	5,140
ANR, Oklahoma Natural Gas (Platts IFERC) Basis	11,514	10,956	2,842	3,065	20,157
Argus Gasoline Eurobob Oxy Barges NWE Crack	456	130	34		30
Argus LLS vs. WTI (Argus) Trade Month Futures (E5)	98,118	64,272	93,158	43,898	35,595
Argus Propane (Saudi Aramco) Futures (9N)	7,128	10,193	11,231	10,737	8,313
Argus Propane Far East Index BALMO Swap (22)	401	290	462	460	637
Argus Propane Far East Index Futures (7E)	5,791	3,031	3,344	5,079	5,952
Argus Propane Far East Index vs European Propane	356	310	899	942	325
Argus Sour Crude Index vs WTI Diff Spread Calendar	300	150	150	309	800
Australian Coking Coal (Platts) Low Vol Futures	1,890	3,812	168	31	102
Brent CFD: Dated Brent (Platts) vs. Brent Second	950	6,075	1,395	6,070	7,753
Brent Crude Oil BALMO Futures (J9)	4,854	3,378	4,560	7,385	2,363

New York Mercantile Exchange (NYMEX), division of the CME Group (continued)

FUTURE	2015	2014	2013	2012	2011
Brent Crude Oil Futures (BB)	73,795	73,495	239,036	343,578	241,343
Brent Crude Oil vs. Dubai Crude Oil (Platts) Futures	12,540	4,467	16,689	28,014	51,835
Brent Financial Futures (CY)	59,242	89,889	113,912	223,213	221,197
Brent Last Day Financial (BZ)	26,251,078	18,493,384	9,214,951	1,161,113	787,768
Canadian Heavy Crude Oil Index (Net Energy)	63,522	61,456	68,497	46,461	18,615
Canadian Light Sweet Oil (Net Energy) Index	14,637	2,400	45		
Center Point Natural Gas Fixed Price (DAC)	32				
Chicago CBOB Gasoline (Platts) vs. RBOB Gasoline	345	238	1,220	425	61
Chicago Ethanol (Platts) (CU)	1,001,090	1,151,356	789,683	358,041	227,267
Chicago ULSD (Platts) vs. NY Harbor ULSD (5C)	4,402	5,166	4,810	1,437	971
CIG Rockies Natural Gas (Platts IFERC) Basis	47,921	11,071	4,900	7,467	21,569
Coal (API 5) fob Newcastle (Argus/McCloskey)	4,120	4,275			
Coal (API 8) cfr South China (Argus/McCloskey)	3,162	24,245	280		
Coal (API2) CIF ARA (ARGUS-McCloskey) (MTF)	2,131,742	1,559,529	989,486	260,219	2,592
Coal (API4) FOB Richards Bay (ARGUS-McCloskey)	283,926	393,262	278,396	64,790	1,140
Coal (QL)	2,651	18,957	84,710	81,015	95,330
Cocoa (CJ)	1,816	317	197	384	1,608
Coffee (KT)	635	427	332	356	1,077
Columbia Gas TCO (Platts Gas Daily/Platts IFERC)	3,904	3,656			240
Columbia Gas TCO (Platts IFERC) Basis Futures	39,379	166,413	2,146	1,348	11,872
COLUMBIA GULF NAT GAS FIXED PRICE (DCE)	488				
Columbia Gulf, Louisiana Natural Gas (Platts	4,622	17,183		16,425	1,476
Columbia Gulf, Mainline Natural Gas (Platts Gas	3,379	2,176		16,441	11,066
Columbia Gulf, Mainline Natural Gas (Platts IFERC)	25,715	48,877	1,774	5,682	21,690
Conway Natural Gasoline (OPIS) BALMO Futures	30			112	210
Conway Natural Gasoline (OPIS) Futures (8L)	1,032	589	115	1,341	3,890
Conway Normal Butane (OPIS) Futures (8M)	1,964	1,135	1,049	752	2,523
Conway Propane (OPIS) BALMO Futures (CPB)	506	628	270	243	229
Conway Propane (OPIS) Futures (8K)	55,695	45,438	8,648	18,089	13,514
Copper (HG)	16,986,055	14,591,200	17,127,383	16,158,815	12,491,517
Copper Financial Futures (HGS)	6,538	12,819	1,761	289	
Cotton Futures (TT)	585	737	572	365	2,949
Crude Oil (CL)	202,202,392	145,147,334	147,690,593	140,531,588	175,036,216
Crude Oil Financial Futures (WS)	201,068	117,285	306,513	406,087	313,463
CSX Coal (Platts OTC Broker Index) Futures (QX)	35,651	55,289	115,418	72,557	66,795
D4 Biodiesel RINS (Argus) 2014 Futures (D44)	34	1,163	50		
D4 Biodiesel RINs (Argus) 2015 Futures (D45)	58				
D6 Ethanol RINS (Argus) 2014 Futures (D64)	209	2,339	272		
D6 Ethanol RINs (Argus) 2015 Futures (D65)	140				
Daily European 3.5% Fuel Oil Barges FOB Rdam	840				
Daily European Naphtha CIF NWE (Platts) Futures	2,687	474	20		
Dated Brent (Platts) Daily Futures (7G)	23,657	4,160	1,262	8,865	11,816
Dated Brent (Platts) Financial Futures (UB)	39,030	29,055	13,324	41,226	45,517
Dated Brent (Platts) to Frontline Brent BALMO	235	100	775	2,190	2,792
Dated Brent (Platts) to Frontline Brent Futures (FY)	31,885	15,270	28,215	37,723	44,615
Demarc Natural Gas (Platts Gas Daily/Platts IFERC)	2,740	682			2,696
Demarc Natural Gas (Platts IFERC) Basis Futures	5,913	8,908		1,619	7,084
Diesel 10ppm Barges FOB Rdam (Platts) vs. Low	10	28	155	124	389
Dominion, South Point Natural Gas (Platts Gas	2,561		360	1,304	25,127
Dominion, South Point Natural Gas (Platts IFERC)	85,651	63,229	21,471	25,964	28,072
Dubai Crude Oil (Platts) BALMO Futures (BI)	2,525	252	200	1,150	1,975
Dubai Crude Oil (Platts) Financial Futures (DC)	43,926	22,191	22,614	123,003	207,050
East-West Fuel Oil Spread (Platts) BALMO Futures	25	27	75		
East-West Fuel Oil Spread (Platts) Futures (EW)	10,226	6,521	15,338	43,339	20,056
East-West Gasoline Spread (Platts-Argus) Futures	18	152	126		
East-West Naphtha: Japan C&F vs. Cargoes CIF	1,038	579	171	20	
EIA Flat Tax On-Highway Diesel Futures (A5)	9,618	8,943	7,221	5,317	3,929
EIA Flat Tax U.S. Retail Gasoline Futures (JE)	565	20	30	174	
Electric Financially Settled (47)	1,534			5,936	7,072
Electric MISO Peak (55)	2,036		767		
Electric NYISO Off-Peak (58)	37,600		14,008		
Electricity Off-Peak (4P)	11,680			82,357	52,992
E-Micro Gold Futures (MGC)	407,643	276,815	372,280	260,447	474,444
E-mini Copper Futures (QC)	9,171	11,304	18,025	20,717	23,655
E-mini Crude Oil (QM)	3,149,495	1,898,735	1,764,795	2,097,040	3,000,140
E-mini Natural Gas Futures (QG)	330,199	397,582	318,694	435,591	547,462
E-mini NY Harbor ULSD (QH)	98	119	167	205	289
E-mini RBOB Gasoline Futures (QU)	57	51	50	52	49
EMMISSIONS (CPL)	500				
Enable Natural Gas (Platts Gas Daily/Platts IFERC)	677	248			1,524
Enable Natural Gas (Platts IFERC) Basis Futures	22,747	11,549	4,521	12,988	19,409
ERCOT North 345 kV Hub 5 MW Off-Peak Futures	28,797	145,365	268,480	185,685	
ERCOT North 345 kV Hub 5 MW Peak Futures (I5)	3,051	9,719	16,530	19,933	4,233
ERCOT West 345 kV Hub 5 MW Off-Peak Futures	17,565	34,848	296,125	478,848	
ERCOT West 345 kV Hub 5 MW Peak Futures (N1)	1,170	1,828	11,395	19,117	

New York Mercantile Exchange (NYMEX), division of the CME Group (continued)

FUTURE	2015	2014	2013	2012	2011
Ethanol T2 FOB Rdam Including Duty (Platts)	29,375	21,891	19,555	9,327	6,149
EuroBob Gasoline 10 ppm Barges FOB Rdam (Platts)	40	25	15	6	19
European 1% Fuel Oil Barges FOB Rdam (Platts)	16		25	9	8
European 1% Fuel Oil Barges FOB Rdam (Platts)	166	260	680	521	2,092
European 1% Fuel Oil Cargoes FOB MED (Platts)	455	1,170	450	1,097	173
European 1% Fuel Oil Cargoes FOB MED vs.	703	1,524	1,038	730	100
European 1% Fuel Oil Cargoes FOB NWE (Platts)	131	287	690	597	258
European 1% Fuel Oil Cargoes FOB NWE (Platts)	1,920	1,970	5,100	9,471	12,576
European 3.5% Fuel Oil Barges FOB Rdam (Platts)	6,365	4,604	5,898	4,813	1,790
European 3.5% Fuel Oil Barges FOB Rdam (Platts)	98,474	97,311	103,960	178,569	89,321
European 3.5% Fuel Oil Cargoes FOB MED (Platts)	169	246	22	112	
European 3.5% Fuel Oil Cargoes FOB MED (Platts)	1,410	1,758	410	898	175
European Diesel 10 ppm Barges FOB Rdam (Platts)	14	7	398	87	508
European Diesel 10 ppm Barges FOB Rdam (Platts)	1,064	1,556	4,357	3,740	4,848
European Jet Kerosene Cargoes CIF NWE (Platts)	499	119	516	629	430
European Low Sulphur Gasoil (100mt) Bullet Futures	770,779	6,040	58,540	44,956	17,317
European Low Sulphur Gasoil Brent Crack Spread	38,850	28,118	96,363	91,366	97,917
European Low Sulphur Gasoil Financial Futures (GX)	263	472	1,643	5,217	10,202
European Naphtha (Platts) BALMO Futures (KZ)	986	2,792	2,649	2,594	1,423
European Naphtha (Platts) Crack Spread Futures	77,928	108,341	102,003	125,320	99,444
European Naphtha Cargoes CIF NWE (Platts)	14,968	21,344	30,109	34,187	27,807
European Propane CIF ARA (Argus) BALMO Swap	615	785	2,075	964	1,063
European Propane CIF ARA (Argus) Futures (PS)	4,938	4,437	8,481	11,214	12,819
European Propane CIF ARA (Argus) vs. Naphtha	580	1,061	2,859	3,475	1,659
FAME 0 Biodiesel FOB Rdam (Argus) (RED	121	15	70	200	
FAME 0 Biodiesel FOB Rdam (Argus) (RED	870	900	16,067	6,827	
Florida Gas, Zone 3 Natural Gas (Platts IFERC)	14,510	3,652		1,242	4,929
Freight Route Liquid Petroleum Gas (Baltic) Future	764				
Freight Route TC2 (Baltic) Futures (TM)	13	250	730	920	435
Freight Route TC5 (Platts) Futures (TH)	30	25	1,119	2,410	2,566
Gasoil 0.1 Barges FOB Rdam (Platts) Futures (VL)	40	90	51	212	517
Gasoil 0.1 Barges FOB Rdam (Platts) vs. Low Sulphur	10	10	75	43	60
Gasoil 0.1 Barges FOB Rdam (Platts) vs. Low Sulphur	180	893	3,561	5,403	10,455
Gasoil 0.1 Cargoes CIF MED (Platts) BALMO	5				
Gasoil 0.1 Cargoes CIF MED (Platts) Futures (Z4)	50			151	58
Gasoil 0.1 Cargoes CIF MED (Platts) vs. Low Sulphur	241	341	821	943	1,043
Gasoil 0.1 Cargoes CIF NWE (Platts) Futures (TW)	10	90	50	24	79
Gasoil 0.1 Cargoes CIF NWE (Platts) vs. Low Sulphur	10		15	30	14
Gasoil 0.1 Cargoes CIF NWE (Platts) vs. Low Sulphur	266	47	176	71	93
Gasoline Euro-bob Oxy NWE Barges (Argus) BALMO	3,148	5,551	7,602	6,260	3,615
Gasoline Euro-bob Oxy NWE Barges (Argus) Crack	2,181	6,943	2,929	2,013	1,996
Gasoline Euro-bob Oxy NWE Barges (Argus) Crack	205,698	277,461	248,729	218,455	140,943
Gasoline Euro-bob Oxy NWE Barges (Argus) Futures	80,515	80,573	99,668	92,156	73,570
Gold (GC)	41,847,338	40,518,804	47,294,551	43,893,311	49,175,593
Gold Kilo (GCK)	51,336				
Group Three Sub-octane Gasoline (Platts) vs. RBOB	18,787	17,903	3,287	11,935	1,695
Group Three ULSD (Platts) Futures (A7)	200	474	180	8,676	
Group Three ULSD (Platts) vs. NY Harbor ULSD	46,007	59,295	55,817	19,799	3,671
Gulf Coast 3.0% Fuel Oil (Platts) BALMO Futures	12,429	15,735	20,130	23,044	32,679
Gulf Coast CBOB Gasoline A2 (Platts) vs. RBOB	3,843	951	1,221	1,297	187
Gulf Coast Jet (Platts) Up-Down BALMO Futures	38,460	30,742	14,185	2,952	2,908
Gulf Coast Jet (Platts) Up-Down Futures (ME)	269,633	266,693	497,944	169,807	114,056
Gulf Coast Jet Fuel (Platts) Futures (GE)	3,668	3,689	12,881	16,248	870
Gulf Coast No. 2 (Platts) Up-Down Financial Futures	4,034	2,175	12,943	12,191	14,564
Gulf Coast No. 6 Fuel Oil (Platts) Crack Spread	100	240	1,263	1,027	695
Gulf Coast No. 6 Fuel Oil (Platts) Crack Spread	17,530	43,558	38,427	32,740	66,893
Gulf Coast No. 6 Fuel Oil 3.0% (Platts) Futures (MF)	811,531	602,488	755,088	714,705	854,111
Gulf Coast No. 6 Fuel Oil 3.0% (Platts) vs. European	1,158	1,750	475	978	1,162
Gulf Coast No. 6 Fuel Oil 3.0% (Platts) vs. European	134,083	139,985	183,614	171,446	159,564
Gulf Coast No.6 Fuel Oil 3.0% (Platts) Brent Crack	11,990	11,378	8,015	13,107	5,006
Gulf Coast ULSD (Platts) Crack Spread Futures (GY)	3,960	17,023	36,317	44,656	17,900
Gulf Coast ULSD (Platts) Futures (LY)	8,713	13,066	10,021	46,558	9,143
Gulf Coast ULSD (Platts) Up-Down BALMO Futures	45,366	19,937	30,520	26,059	20,681
Gulf Coast ULSD (Platts) Up-Down Futures (LT)	499,641	371,429	660,461	550,191	556,663
Gulf Coast Unl 87 (Platts) Up-Down BALMO Futures	6,145	3,700	6,332	5,520	4,234
Gulf Coast Unl 87 Gasoline M1 (Platts) Crack Spread	3,550	4,800	6,785	3,170	7,500
Gulf Coast Unl 87 Gasoline M1 (Platts) Futures (GS)	7,265	1,451	1,378	1,885	1,042
Gulf Coast Unl 87 Gasoline M1 (Platts) vs. RBOB	122,100	103,538	107,547	103,909	114,851
Gulf Coast Unl 87 Gasoline M2 (Platts) Crack Spread	700				
Gulf Coast Unl 87 Gasoline M2 (Platts) vs. RBOB	50	300			
Gulf Coast Unl 87 Gasoline M2 (Platts) vs. RBOB	6,306	5,770	2,415	1,700	4,490
HDPE High Density Polyethylene (PCW) Financial	58	347	360	1,028	546
Henry Hub Natural Gas (NG)	81,772,492	74,206,602	84,282,495	94,799,542	76,864,334
Henry Hub Natural Gas (Platts Gas Daily) Swing	1,200	1,046	1,200	1,704	4,074
Henry Hub Natural Gas (Platts Gas Daily/Platts	111,082	137,728	106,126	62,518	48,277

New York Mercantile Exchange (NYMEX), division of the CME Group (continued)

FUTURE	2015	2014	2013	2012	2011
Henry Hub Natural Gas (Platts IFERC) Basis	147,869	146,260	115,810	60,564	66,870
Henry Hub Natural Gas Last Day Financial (NN)	5,330,807	6,332,365	11,457,837	18,156,113	20,825,660
Henry Hub Penultimate NP (NP)	2,200,047	4,476,844	6,418,797	7,945,695	7,384,147
Houston Ship Channel Natural Gas (Platts Gas Daily/	180	372	200	643	2,139
Houston Ship Channel Natural Gas (Platts IFERC)	48,495	43,479	1,716	20,162	33,836
HUSTN SHIP CHNL PIPE SWP (XJ)	4,073				
In Delivery Month European Union Allowance (EUA)	104,603	122,156	402,555	158,501	14,167
Indonesian Coal (McCloskey sub-bituminous) Futures	1,805	14,715	7,190	1,450	195
Iron Ore 62% Fe, CFR China (TSI) Futures (TIO)	136,158	24,988	22,302	7,032	1,854
Iron Ore 62% Fe, CFR North China (Platts) Futures	2,613	120	60	75	
ISO New England Mass Hub 5 MW Peak Calendar-	20,388	17,633	29,060	35,662	42,914
ISO New England Mass Hub Day-Ahead Off-Peak	319,140	365,739	419,727	541,375	851,583
ISO New England Mass Hub Day-Ahead Peak	20	1,246	2,954	25,314	24,342
ISO New England North East Massachusetts Zone 5	1,385	630		12,488	8,104
ISO New England Rhode Island Zone 5 MW Off-Peak	109,503	365,366	69,830	18,990	294,247
ISO New England Rhode Island Zone 5 MW Peak	11,069	21,494	3,825	1,017	15,934
ISO New England West Central Massachusetts Zone	44,368	9,392	42,240	137,618	74,173
ISO New England West Central Massachusetts	1,700	508	2,310	8,554	5,290
Japan C&F Naphtha (Platts) BALMO Futures (E6)	505	845	958	565	312
Japan C&F Naphtha (Platts) Brent Crack Spread	3,237	1,488	270	1,997	
Japan C&F Naphtha (Platts) Futures (JA)	11,776	14,376	23,502	29,467	24,965
Jet Aviation Fuel Cargoes FOB MED (Platts) Futures	90	31	78	19	15
Jet Aviation Fuel Cargoes FOB MED (Platts) vs. Low	279	280	141	117	42
Jet Barges FOB Rdam (Platts) vs. Low Sulphur	15	15	74	64	145
Jet Cargoes CIF NWE (Platts) vs. Low Sulphur Gasoil	1,275	1,533	2,451	3,980	6,428
Jet Fuel Barges FOB Rdam (Platts) vs. Low Sulphur	40	15	18	5	12
Jet Fuel Cargoes CIF NWE (Platts) vs. Low Sulphur	47	77	55	88	504
LLDPE Linear Low Density Polyethylene (PCW)	76	82		292	1,038
LLS (Argus) vs. WTI Financial Futures (WJ)	110,156	115,106	211,157	33,463	36,158
LOOP Crude Oil Storage Futures (LPS)	30,548				
Los Angeles CARB Diesel (OPIS) Futures (LX)	234	141	378	586	291
Los Angeles CARB Diesel (OPIS) vs. NY Harbor	7,675	11,206	15,548	17,185	22,688
Los Angeles CARBOB Gasoline (OPIS) vs. RBOB	5,941	7,200	12,660	4,770	20,325
Los Angeles Jet (OPIS) vs. NY Harbor ULSD (JS)	10,820	6,950	10,985	11,450	21,548
Los Angeles Jet Fuel (Platts) vs. NY Harbor ULSD	540	1,705	2,776	900	1,260
Low Sulphur Gasoil Crack Spread (1000mt) Financial	674	602	1,632	1,139	820
Low Sulphur Gasoil Mini Financial Futures (QA)	3,321	6,113	1,673	3,441	14,106
Mars (Argus) vs. WTI Financial Futures (YX)	74,060	49,005	25,015	1,790	2,202
Mars (Argus) vs. WTI Trade Month Futures (YV)	17,008	670	1,560	6,826	3,699
MichCon Natural Gas (Platts IFERC) Basis Futures	6,554	3,021	2,950	6,482	11,495
Mini 1% Fuel Oil Cargoes FOB MED (Platts) Futures	907	1,156	224	169	
Mini 3.5% Fuel Oil Cargoes FOB MED (Platts)	1,939	851	310	773	
Mini Argus Propane (Saudi Aramco) Futures (MAS)	355	642	110		
Mini Argus Propane Far East Index Futures (MAE)	290	60	10		
Mini Brent Financial Futures (MBC)	1,114				
Mini Dated Brent (Platts) Financial Futures (MDB)	390				
Mini Dubai Crude Oil (Platts) Futures (DBL)	32,612	1,400			
Mini European 1% Fuel Oil Barges FOB Rdam	90	90			
Mini European 1% Fuel Oil Barges FOB Rdam	1,997	964	213	202	804
Mini European 1% Fuel Oil Cargoes FOB NWE	213	515	70		
Mini European 1% Fuel Oil Cargoes FOB NWE	1,074	3,285	1,257	124	60
Mini European 3.5% Fuel Oil Barges FOB Rdam	6,094	3,195	712	24	
Mini European 3.5% Fuel Oil Barges FOB Rdam	52,314	41,207	38,764	27,053	28,573
Mini European Diesel 10 ppm Barges FOB Rdam	957	1,716	658	744	
Mini European Jet Kero Barges FOB Rdam (Platts) vs.	10	0			
Mini European Jet Kero Cargoes CIF NWE (Platts) vs.	780	600	984	916	672
Mini European Naphtha (Platts) BALMO Futures	7,763	9,504	3,561	228	
Mini European Naphtha CIF NWE (Platts) Futures	50,904	60,494	33,522	4,870	2,369
Mini Gasoil 0.1 Barges FOB Rdam (Platts) vs. Low	434	253	54	31	
Mini Gasoil 0.1 Cargoes CIF NWE (Platts) vs. Low	86	150	24	10	
Mini Gasoline Euro-bob Oxy NWE Barges (Argus)	3,490	7,144	337		
Mini Gasoline Euro-bob Oxy NWE Barges (Argus)	100,465	112,317	78,260	5,323	
Mini Japan C&F Naphtha (Platts) BALMO Futures	862	870	1,178	148	
Mini Japan C&F Naphtha (Platts) Futures (MJN)	19,125	21,227	23,703	2,018	226
Mini RBOB Gasoline vs. Gasoline Euro-bob Oxy NWE	4,803	6,555	93		
Mini RBOB Gasoline vs. Gasoline Euro-bob Oxy NWE	8,766	5,468	130		
Mini Singapore Fuel Oil 180 cst (Platts) BALMO	1,345	1,893	1,345		
Mini Singapore Fuel Oil 180 cst (Platts) Futures (0F)	11,368	14,538	15,698	1,886	811
Mini Singapore Fuel Oil 380 cst (Platts) BALMO	1,460	1,898	784	78	55
Mini Singapore Fuel Oil 380 cst (Platts) Futures (MTS)	30,302	24,945	20,476	1,569	401
Mini Singapore Gasoil (Platts) Futures (MSG)	6,868	7,896	80		
Mini ULSD 10ppm Cargoes CIF MED (Platts) vs. Low	578	618	256		
Mini ULSD 10ppm Cargoes CIF NWE (Platts) vs.	1,903	1,052	673	268	
miNY Gold Futures (QO)	66,758	51,504	97,252	111,323	192,575
miNY Silver Futures (QI)	9,823	12,160	19,153	26,842	106,576

New York Mercantile Exchange (NYMEX), division of the CME Group (continued)

FUTURE	2015	2014	2013	2012	2011
MISO Indiana Hub (formerly Cinergy Hub) 5 Month	20,718	20,915	53,842	20,636	25,243
MISO Indiana Hub (formerly Cinergy Hub) Day-	178,560	448,064	331,736	263,776	571,672
MISO Indiana Hub (formerly Cinergy Hub) Day-	10,579	22,269	20,886	12,089	44,471
MISO Indiana Hub (formerly Cinergy Hub) Off-Peak	630	356	1,642	6,270	5,840
MISO Indiana Hub (formerly Cinergy Hub) Real-	787,752	410,704	924,760	392,008	171,600
MISO Indiana Hub (formerly Cinergy Hub) Real-	40	552	1,148	7,972	12,722
MISO Indiana Hub Day-Ahead Peak Calendar-Month	2,240	8,093	1,899	321	1,530
MISO Michigan Hub 5 MW Off-Peak Calendar-Month	121,440	308,784	102,840		
MISO Michigan Hub 5 MW Peak Calendar-Month	6,795	14,296	6,932	640	
Mont Belvieu Ethane (OPIS) BALMO Futures (8C)	2,765	1,605	35	1,105	920
Mont Belvieu Ethane (OPIS) Futures (C0)	92,745	55,129	18,578	21,193	
Mont Belvieu Ethylene (PCW) BALMO Futures	245	809		200	
Mont Belvieu Ethylene (PCW) Financial Futures	13,609	18,081	5,553	2,036	942
Mont Belvieu Iso-Butane (OPIS) Futures (8I)	5,223	3,027	5,414	1,780	3,761
Mont Belvieu LDH Iso-Butane (OPIS) Futures (MBL)	746	1,490	1,424	4,880	
Mont Belvieu LDH Propane (OPIS) BALMO Futures	7,879	8,767	3,676	3,155	5,009
Mont Belvieu LDH Propane (OPIS) Futures (B0)	616,592	424,193	115,047	139,722	114,417
Mont Belvieu Natural Gasoline (OPIS) BALMO	4,160	4,107	2,161	697	1,677
Mont Belvieu Natural Gasoline (OPIS) Futures (7Q)	64,931	86,123	26,436	37,653	58,523
Mont Belvieu Normal Butane (OPIS) BALMO	5,424	6,661	4,232	2,891	2,477
Mont Belvieu Normal Butane (OPIS) Futures (D0)	209,582	175,113	92,711	58,873	46,202
Mont Belvieu Normal Butane LDH (OPIS) Futures	15,956	14,978	19,859	23,594	10,871
Mont Belvieu Spot Ethylene In-Well Futures (MBE)	22,730	28,116	10,280	6,436	7,020
Naphtha Cargoes CIF NWE (Platts) Crack Spread	56	25	36	6	
Naphtha Cargoes CIF NWE (Platts) Crack Spread	2,396	1,357	1,373	1,036	136
Nat Gas Basis Swap (SGW)	40				
Natural Gas (Henry Hub) Last-day Financial (HH)	2,897,566	2,330,546	2,389,724	922,816	63,980
Natural Gas (Henry Hub) Penultimate Financial (HP)	1,067,919	678,445	217,114	81,777	27,786
Natural Gas Fixed Price Swap Futures (CFS)	3,416				
Natural Gas Fixed Price Swap Futures (DSF)	6,452				
Natural Gas Fixed Price Swap Futures (MFS)	1,464				
Natural Gas Fixed Price Swap Futures (PFS)	496				
Natural Gas Fixed Price Swap Futures (WFS)	572				
Natural Gas Fixed Price Swap Futures (Z5P)	448				
Natural Gas Fixed Price Swap Futures (ZTS)	84				
NEPOOL NE Mass 5MW Day Ahead Off Peak (P8)	3,920			201,513	107,570
New York Harbor 1.0% Fuel Oil (Platts) BALMO	531	1,001	4,451	3,294	7,927
New York Harbor Residual Fuel (Platts) Crack	100	450	1,160	335	1,070
New York Harbor Residual Fuel 1.0% (Platts) Futures	62,080	73,140	142,479	172,096	141,667
NGPL Mid-Con Natural Gas (Platts Gas Daily/Platts	300		60		542
NGPL Mid-Con Natural Gas (Platts IFERC) Basis	50,587	7,234	5,584	34,039	21,895
NGPL TexOk Natural Gas (Platts Gas Daily/Platts	1,146			248	1,838
NGPL TexOk Natural Gas (Platts IFERC) Basis	84,276	54,615	4,420	24,645	43,928
No. 11 Sugar Futures (YO)	1,570	760	793	1,030	3,516
Northwest Europe Fuel Oil High-Low Sulfur Spread	305	186	118	391	
NY 1% Fuel Oil (Platts) vs. Gulf Coast 3% Fuel Oil	200	830	895	686	1,917
NY 1% Fuel Oil (Platts) vs. Gulf Coast 3% Fuel Oil	27,649	52,582	77,742	81,710	70,946
NY 2.2% Fuel Oil (Platts) Futures (Y3)	980	1,358		120	1,927
NY 3.0% Fuel Oil (Platts) BALMO Futures (NYT)	25	365	519	739	558
NY 3.0% Fuel Oil (Platts) Futures (H1)	5,245	2,385	3,452	2,492	4,653
NY 3.0% Fuel Oil (Platts) vs. Gulf Coast No. 6 Fuel	8,150	3,678	4,576	3,985	637
NY Buckeye Jet Fuel (Platts) vs. NY Harbor ULSD	16,905				
NY Ethanol (Platts) Futures (EZ)	12,070	15,517	10,789	8,424	11,158
NY Fuel Oil 1.0% (Platts) vs. European 1% Fuel Oil	2,300	6,122	11,435	23,750	21,103
NY Harbor ULSD (HO)	36,947,020	33,946,420	32,749,553	36,087,707	31,838,626
NY Harbor ULSD BALMO Futures (1G)	1,814	525	680	43	62
NY Harbor ULSD Brent Crack Spread Futures (HOB)	38,784	14,554	7,643	11,237	1,345
NY Harbor ULSD Bullet Futures (BH)	2,146	670	48,452	40,449	44,784
NY Harbor ULSD Crack Spread Futures (HK)	31,218	45,901	66,551	26,098	63,503
NY Harbor ULSD Financial Futures (MP)	53,763	77,983	64,489	138,224	93,313
NY Harbor ULSD vs. Low Sulphur Gasoil (1,000bbl)	4,042	6,810			
NY Heating Oil (Platts) vs. NY Harbor ULSD (YH)	976	5,540	9,347		2,962
NY Jet Fuel (Platts) vs. NY Harbor ULSD (1U)	1,745	32,083	11,550	4,200	4,850
NY RBOB (Platts) vs. RBOB Gasoline Futures (RI)	92	63	697	11,400	
NY ULSD (Argus) vs. NY Harbor ULSD (7Y)	33,130	28,259	20,560	32,776	4,653
NY ULSD (Argus) vs. NY Harbor ULSD BALMO	1,550	490	4,345	1,225	
NY ULSD (Platts) vs. NY Harbor ULSD (UY)	1,188	839		2,401	782
NYISO NYC In-City Capacity Calendar-Month	3,723	1,134	648	408	125
NYISO Rest of the State Capacity Calendar-Month	5,170	1,917	790	1,007	56
NYISO Zone A Day-Ahead Off-Peak Calendar-Month	433,136	269,628	1,345,805	375,201	267,274
NYISO Zone A Day-Ahead Peak Calendar-Month 5	19,321	15,610	118,501	21,858	12,809
NYISO Zone A Off-Peak LBMP Futures (KB)	440	2,550	5,364	4,146	4,982
NYISO Zone A Peak LBMP Futures (KA)	982	7,490	16,929	10,952	9,728
NYISO Zone F 5 MW Off-Peak Calendar-Month Day-	5,796	23,520	75,963	28,080	122,528
NYISO Zone F 5 MW Peak Calendar-Month Day-	1,530	1,375	6,552	2,360	6,968

New York Mercantile Exchange (NYMEX), division of the CME Group (continued)

FUTURE	2015	2014	2013	2012	2011
NYISO Zone G Day-Ahead Off-Peak Calendar-Day 5	8,020			400	
NYISO Zone G Day-Ahead Off-Peak Calendar-Month	256,288	123,931	1,137,172	259,269	213,204
NYISO Zone G Day-Ahead Peak Calendar-Month 5	35,469	12,130	98,468	25,734	26,581
NYISO Zone G Off-Peak LBMP Futures (KH)	190	610	9,437	4,490	3,608
NYISO Zone G Peak LBMP Futures (KG)	471	1,586	9,474	9,570	7,814
NYISO Zone J Day-Ahead Off-Peak Calendar-Month	63,874	104,528	453,830	63,441	73,623
NYISO Zone J Day-Ahead Peak Calendar-Month 5	9,481	7,551	42,122	12,843	10,947
NYISO Zone J Off-Peak LBMP Futures (KK)	590	520	1,066	3,036	2,264
NYISO Zone J Peak LBMP Futures (KJ)	3,242	5,172	5,988	6,701	5,680
OneOk, Oklahoma Natural Gas (Platts IFERC) Basis	2,991	2,476	1,570	2,625	6,739
Ontario Off-Peak Calendar-Month Futures (OFM)	159,856	253,474	186,534	74,114	122,410
Ontario Peak Calendar-Day Futures (OPD)	355	439	885	630	965
Ontario Peak Calendar-Month Futures (OPM)	8,990	22,947	46,135	812	4,103
Palladium Futures (PA)	1,344,426	1,573,972	1,486,016	1,118,480	1,139,529
Panhandle Natural Gas (Platts Gas Daily/Platts	2,638	0	488	2,876	2,899
Panhandle Natural Gas (Platts IFERC) Basis Futures	131,807	43,650	22,481	35,642	121,303
Panhandle Natural Gas (Platts IFERC) Fixed Price	314	0	135		
Permian Natural Gas (Platts IFERC) Basis Futures	36,870	13,143	1,327	6,359	31,758
Petro European Naphtha Crack Spread BALMO	3,738	3,676	2,433	2,812	3,739
PGP Polymer Grade Propylene (PCW) Financial	10,575	6,493	4,135	3,797	1,722
PJM AECO Zone Peak Calendar-Month Day-Ahead	132	6,894	3,825	13,436	
PJM AEP Dayton Hub 5MW Peak Calendar-Month	111,974	115,264	99,141	28,646	51,695
PJM AEP Dayton Hub Day-Ahead LMP Peak	16,495	32,284	17,071	37,046	45,571
PJM AEP Dayton Hub Day-Ahead Off-Peak	238,308	565,222	246,892	508,893	640,076
PJM AEP Dayton Hub Off-Peak LMP Futures (VP)	942	1,082	3,782	14,921	17,979
PJM AEP Dayton Hub Real-Time Off-Peak Calendar-	1,661,753	1,989,829	2,056,995	789,550	853,031
PJM AEP Dayton Hub Real-Time Peak Calendar-	662	1,506	5,944	16,960	20,332
PJM ATSI Zone 5mw Off-Peak Calendar-Month Day-	23,400	0		11,056	
PJM ATSI Zone 5mw Peak Calendar-Month Day-	1,275	0		508	
PJM ComEd Zone 5 MW Off-Peak Calendar-Month	86,445	24,648	123,585	119,279	155,803
PJM ComEd Zone 5 MW Peak Calendar-Month Day-	7,150	1,362	6,490	7,048	8,559
PJM JCPL Zone Off-Peak Calendar-Month Day-	15,360	140,480	23,400	19,440	141,238
PJM JCPL Zone Peak Calendar-Month Day-Ahead	650	7,660	1,275	4,895	9,896
PJM Meted Zone Off Peak Cal Mth Day Ahead LMP	28,064	0		108,976	118,041
PJM Northern Illinois Hub 5 MW Peak Calendar-	69,427	27,630	80,710	35,494	65,570
PJM Northern Illinois Hub Day-Ahead LMP Peak	23,715	14,777	25,056	38,589	58,068
PJM Northern Illinois Hub Day-Ahead Off-Peak	506,843	236,798	408,282	400,759	1,057,271
PJM Northern Illinois Hub Off-Peak LMP Futures	102	140	2,892	16,620	18,323
PJM Northern Illinois Hub Real-Time Off-Peak	1,879,247	617,032	1,187,306	880,993	1,619,448
PJM Northern Illinois Hub Real-Time Peak Calendar-	70	1,106	3,560	11,247	16,542
PJM Off-Peak Calendar-Month LMP Futures (JP)	1,864	4,734	70,952	35,702	41,402
PJM PENELEC Zone Off-Peak Calendar-Month Day-	23,520				47,040
PJM PENELEC Zone Peak Calendar-Month Day-	1,275				2,550
PJM PEPCO Zone 5MW Peak Cal Mth Day Ahead	650			5,071	3,827
PJM PEPCO Zone Off-Peak Calendar-Month Day-	7,440			23,400	222,125
PJM PPL Zone Off-Peak Calendar-Month Day-Ahead	61,152		55,976	35,234	203,108
PJM PPL Zone Peak Calendar-Month Day-Ahead	3,315		3,597	1,540	10,729
PJM PSEG Zone Off-Peak Calendar-Month Day-	1,960		4,696	322,642	789,728
PJM PSEG Zone Peak Calendar-Month Day-Ahead	110		254	19,591	48,385
PJM Western Hub Day-Ahead Off-Peak Calendar-	807,716	1,241,519	758,040	783,668	1,671,911
PJM Western Hub Day-Ahead Peak Calendar-Month	42,139	70,693	33,946	57,013	115,898
PJM Western Hub Peak Calendar-Month Real-Time	251,063	220,143	145,354	56,375	83,776
PJM Western Hub Real-Time Off-Peak Calendar-	3,630,757	3,609,397	3,098,831	1,290,881	2,248,985
PJM Western Hub Real-Time Peak Calendar-Month	7,366	25,174	35,503	154,039	215,741
Platinum (PL)	3,641,144	3,235,941	3,262,775	2,621,704	1,993,263
Powder River Basin Coal (Platts OTC Broker Index)	26,220	35,735	74,721	74,015	19,145
Premium Unleaded Gasoline 10 ppm Barges FOB	84	38	45	23	52
Premium Unleaded Gasoline 10 ppm Barges FOB	340	358	616	1,418	467
Premium Unleaded Gasoline 10 ppm FOB MED	698	1,277	1,890	909	527
Premium Unleaded Gasoline 10 ppm FOB MED	3,391	4,876	5,376	5,756	2,987
Propane Non-LDH Mont Belvieu (OPIS) BALMO	2,513	480	817	1,670	399
Propane Non-LDH Mont Belvieu (OPIS) Futures (1R)	90,810	21,925	6,854	4,132	4,905
RBOB Gasoline BALMO Futures (1D)	13,121	9,281	12,816	14,522	4,891
RBOB Gasoline Brent Crack Spread Futures (RBB)	125,379	102,467	128,250	144,282	68,379
RBOB Gasoline Bullet Futures (RT)	18,062	9,369	89,192	74,124	45,008
RBOB Gasoline Crack Spread BALMO Futures (1E)	30	0	26	44	
RBOB Gasoline Crack Spread Futures (RM)	12,795	17,019	18,780	7,335	37,893
RBOB Gasoline Financial Futures (RL)	85,040	100,107	95,844	123,922	151,780
RBOB Gasoline Physical (RB)	40,302,099	34,421,866	34,470,288	36,603,841	31,129,256
RBOB Gasoline vs. Euro-bob Oxy NWE Barges (Argus)	13,510	13,702	15,778	13,791	1,051
RBOB Gasoline vs. Euro-bob Oxy NWE Barges (Argus)	90	50	900		
RBOB Gasoline vs. NY Harbor ULSD (RH)	12,265	6,025	300	14,286	13,450
RME Biodiesel FOB Rdam (Argus) (RED Compliant)	170	1,060	9,150	5,574	
Rockies Natural Gas (Platts Gas Daily/Platts IFERC)	1,880	0		480	67
Rockies Natural Gas (Platts IFERC) Basis Futures	135,936	18,072	5,349	16,953	23,587

New York Mercantile Exchange (NYMEX), division of the CME Group (continued)

FUTURE	2015	2014	2013	2012	2011
Rockies Natural Gas (Platts IFERC) Fixed Price	991	3,608	270		
San Juan Natural Gas (Platts IFERC) Basis Futures	29,833	2,632	1,332	6,979	13,109
Silver (SI)	13,454,406	13,696,961	14,475,593	13,315,679	19,608,557
Singapore Fuel Oil 180 cst (Platts) 6.35 Brent Crack	760	1,868	4,020	448	
Singapore Fuel Oil 180 cst (Platts) 6.35 Dubai (Platts)	318	295	5,623	4,364	750
Singapore Fuel Oil 180 cst (Platts) BALMO Futures	458	854	1,852	1,506	2,718
Singapore Fuel Oil 180 cst (Platts) Futures (UA)	22,208	51,466	98,722	99,854	105,335
Singapore Fuel Oil 180 cst (Platts) vs. 380 cst (Platts)	10	20	210	45	
Singapore Fuel Oil 180 cst (Platts) vs. 380 cst (Platts)	5,708	5,046	17,584	16,427	10,611
Singapore Fuel Oil 380 cst (Platts) 6.35 Dubai (Platts)	1,062	0	63	721	
Singapore Fuel Oil 380 cst (Platts) BALMO Futures	1,271	909	1,144	997	901
Singapore Fuel Oil 380 cst (Platts) Futures (SE)	63,496	37,549	46,652	21,239	17,417
Singapore Fuel Oil 380 cst (Platts) vs. European 3.5%	15	5			
Singapore Fuel Oil 380 cst (Platts) vs. European 3.5%	16,421	9,225	1,743		
Singapore Gasoil (Platts) BALMO Futures (VU)	1,316	8,976	7,035	13,807	19,196
Singapore Gasoil (Platts) Futures (SG)	28,055	89,154	144,385	143,251	192,079
Singapore Gasoil (Platts) vs. Low Sulphur Gasoil	6,000	41,284	52,945	76,211	35,079
Singapore Gasoil 10 ppm (Platts) BALMO Futures	150		150		75
Singapore Gasoil 10 ppm (Platts) vs. Singapore Gasoil	250	1,165	2,250	8,810	8,730
Singapore Jet Kerosene (Platts) BALMO Futures (BX)	550	270	1,028	2,057	1,921
Singapore Jet Kerosene (Platts) Dubai (Platts) Crack	390	300	1,700	700	
Singapore Jet Kerosene (Platts) Futures (KS)	16,364	51,766	74,257	67,208	48,422
Singapore Jet Kerosene (Platts) vs. Gasoil (Platts)	50	50	2,885	2,200	1,775
Singapore Jet Kerosene (Platts) vs. Gasoil (Platts)	3,640	18,226	27,884	54,044	31,603
Singapore Mogas 92 Unleaded (Platts) BALMO	3,618	7,124	7,368	7,918	3,438
Singapore Mogas 92 Unleaded (Platts) Brent Crack	20,131	29,903	24,989	5,758	260
Singapore Mogas 92 Unleaded (Platts) Dubai (Platts)	50		50		
Singapore Mogas 92 Unleaded (Platts) Futures (1N)	80,419	179,698	136,999	113,468	105,150
Singapore Mogas 95 Unleaded (Platts) Futures (V0)	2,876	2,700	2,635	850	750
Singapore Mogas 95 Unleaded (Platts) vs. Singapore	600	300		175	
Singapore Mogas 97 Unleaded (Platts) BALMO	100			100	
Singapore Mogas 97 Unleaded (Platts) Futures (X0)	698	294	468	50	516
Singapore Naphtha (Platts) Futures (SP)	1,175	1,675	2,757	2,562	3,504
SoCal Basis Swap (NS)	96			1,280	6,880
SoCal Natural Gas (Platts IFERC) Fixed Price	488	66	114	364	15,768
Southern Natural, Louisiana Natural Gas (Platts Gas	4,280				
Southern Natural, Louisiana Natural Gas (Platts	14,718	6,188		774	11,144
Southern Star, Tx.-Okla.-Kan. Natural Gas (Platts	7,255	765	2,390	4,647	12,698
Steel Billet FOB Black Sea (Platts) (FOB)	10	20			
SUMAS NAT GAS PLATTS FIXED PRICE (DVS)	2,893				
Sumas Natural Gas (Platts IFERC) Basis Futures	14,347	2,767	3,419	6,841	7,049
Tennessee 500 Leg Natural Gas (Platts IFERC) Basis	5,526	2,541		997	17,781
Tennessee 800 Leg Natural Gas (Platts Gas Daily/	3,192	124	6,939	5,774	35,017
Tennessee 800 Leg Natural Gas (Platts IFERC) Basis	3,908	2,568	6,457	4,472	47,179
Tennessee Zone 0 Natural Gas (Platts IFERC) Basis	1,032	224	1,406	2,488	5,448
TETCO ELA Natural Gas (Platts IFERC) Basis	1,360				2,268
TETCO M-3 Natural Gas (Platts Gas Daily/Platts	11,064	7,698		868	3,252
TETCO STX Natural Gas (Platts IFERC) Basis	4,669	62	96	1,628	4,528
Texas Eastern Zone M-3 Natural Gas (Platts IFERC)	25,107	42,981	23,212	2,856	28,924
Texas Gas, Zone 1 Natural Gas (Platts IFERC) Basis	16,156	6,632	2,420		492
Transco Zone 1 Natural Gas (Platts IFERC) Basis	368	122		96	304
Transco Zone 3 Natural Gas (Platts IFERC) Basis	6,975	4,646	7,300		2,619
Transco Zone 4 Natural Gas (Platts Gas Daily/Platts	1,240	372	720	58	5,000
Transco Zone 4 Natural Gas (Platts IFERC) Basis	75,885	13,138	3,890	2,957	4,761
Transco Zone 6 Natural Gas (Platts Gas Daily/Platts	76	875	112		
Transco Zone 6 Natural Gas (Platts IFERC) Basis	10,666	3,742	2,696	3,912	8,324
Transco Zone 6 Non-N.Y. Natural Gas (Platts IFERC)	5,234	7,676	8,978		
TRANSCO ZONE 6 PIPE SWAP (XZ4)	122				
U.S. Midwest Busheling Ferrous Scrap (AMM)	558	34	1,567	506	
U.S. Midwest Domestic Hot-Rolled Coil Steel (CRU)	58,817	48,230	53,793	43,867	31,738
ULSD 10ppm Cargoes CIF NWE (Platts) Futures (TY)	33	12	36	148	805
ULSD 10ppm Cargoes CIF NWE (Platts) vs. Low	25	94	113	425	347
ULSD 10ppm Cargoes CIF NWE (Platts) vs. Low	1,460	1,170	2,990	3,598	7,439
ULSD 10ppm CIF MED (Platts) vs. Low Sulphur	25	37	70	231	507
ULSD 10ppm CIF MED (Platts) vs. Low Sulphur	1,119	627	1,331	2,278	4,018
UxC Uranium U3O8 Futures (UX)	4,548	3,453	6,515	8,113	22,598
VENTURA NAT GAS PLATTS FIXED PRICE (DVA)	44				
Ventura Natural Gas (Platts IFERC) Basis Futures	5,722	7,759	1,763	11,827	36,903
Waha Natural Gas (Platts Gas Daily/Platts IFERC)	1,712	210		15,870	1,754
Waha Natural Gas (Platts IFERC) Basis Futures (NW)	40,876	27,932	3,694	41,141	41,601
WTI BALMO Swap (42)	12,032	9,736			
WTI Financial Futures (CS)	404,806	400,686	417,936	459,044	879,489
WTI Midland (Argus) vs. WTI Financial Futures (FF)	60,936	63,435	14,664	300	576
WTI Midland (Argus) vs. WTI Trade Month Futures	7,543				
WTI-Brent Financial Futures (BK)	277,619	267,854	348,918	83,466	99,413

New York Mercantile Exchange (NYMEX), division of the CME Group (continued)

FUTURE	2015	2014	2013	2012	2011
WTS (Argus) vs. WTI Trade Month Futures (FH)	19,453	12,470	11,113	2,826	7,414
Zinc Futures (ZNC)	386				
Total Futures	**505,584,026**	**419,742,753**	**441,373,921**	**435,672,648**	**458,412,470**

ONECHICAGO

FUTURE	2015	2014	2013	2012	2011
Exchange Traded Funds Futures	2,918,444	2,898,979	2,772,658	1,281,854	42,157
Single Stock Futures	8,795,571	8,008,998	6,742,536	5,150,363	3,599,917
Total Futures	**11,714,015**	**10,907,977**	**9,515,194**	**6,432,217**	**3,679,484**

Total Futures Volume

	2015	2014	2013	2012	2011
Total Futures	**3,213,700,406**	**3,174,758,005**	**3,169,781,022**	**2,689,760,818**	**3,056,541,757**
Precent Change	**1.23%**	**0.16%**	**17.85%**	**-12.00%**	**10.55%**

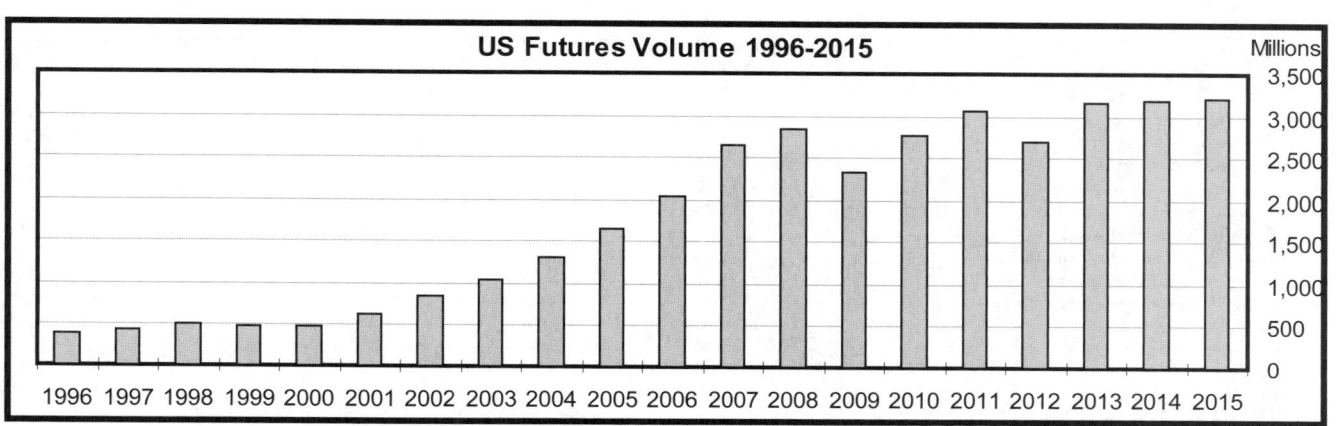

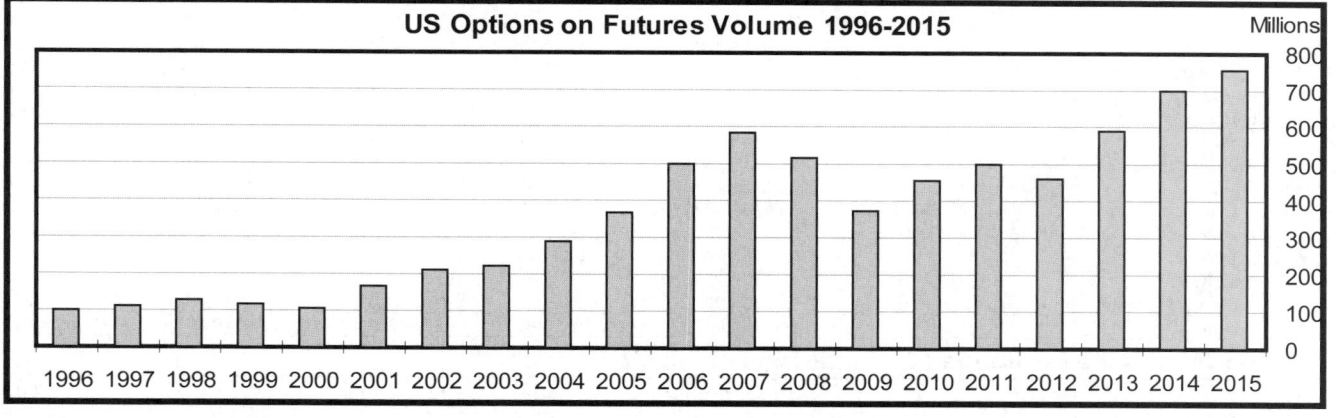

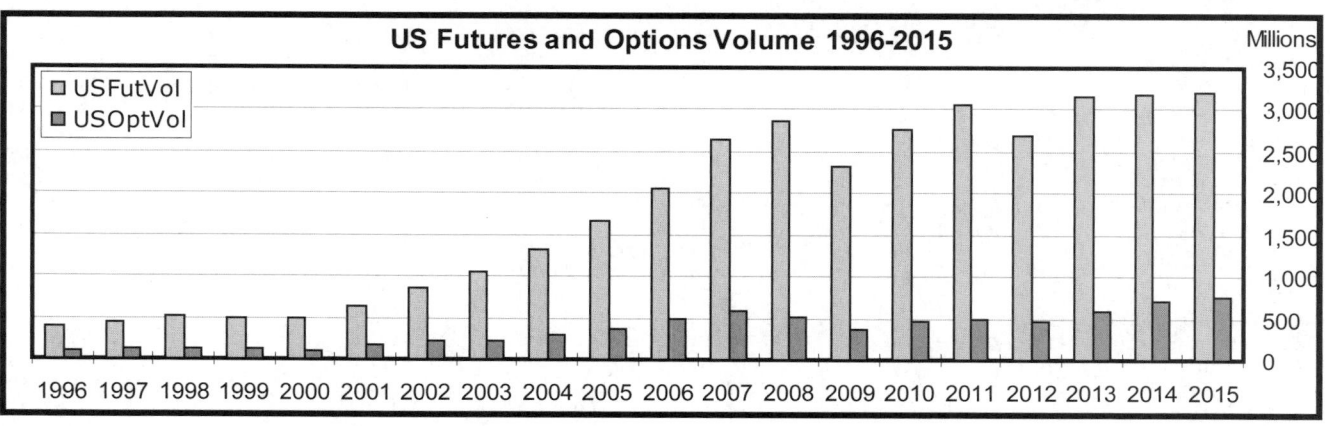

Options Traded on U.S. Futures Exchanges Volume Highlights
2015 in Comparison with 2014

2015 Rank	EXCHANGE	2015 Contracts	%	2014 Contracts	%	2014 Rank
1	Chicago Mercantile Exchange (CME Group)	412,622,695	54.60%	371,826,055	53.11%	1
2	Chicago Board of Trade (CME Group)	200,789,567	26.57%	198,920,909	28.41%	2
3	New York Mercantile Exchange (CME Group)	79,632,474	10.54%	75,536,148	10.79%	3
4	ICE Futures U.S.	56,785,985	7.51%	50,146,497	7.16%	4
5	North American Derivative Exchange	5,809,225	0.77%	3,691,287	0.53%	5
6	Minneapolis Grain Exchange	26,501	0.00%	24,367	0.00%	6
	Total Options	**755,666,447**	**100.00%**	**700,145,263**	**100.00%**	

Chicago Board of Trade (CBT), division of the CME Group

OPTION	2015	2014	2013	2012	2011
10-Year Treasury Notes	97,821,923	100,663,916	90,401,169	56,070,376	50,797,081
2-Year Treasury Notes	2,412,018	2,487,998	1,928,675	3,182,052	2,686,449
30-Year Treasury Bonds	21,046,810	16,405,485	19,125,728	17,668,681	12,849,585
5-Year Treasury Notes	22,776,553	28,561,850	24,336,555	10,291,773	10,849,707
Chicago Soft Red Winter Wheat	7,422,967	6,141,089	4,603,551	5,278,947	4,680,418
Chicago SRW Wheat-Corn Intercommodity Spread	20,400	15,310			
Corn	24,150,182	21,246,732	23,534,308	26,599,756	28,650,380
Corn Nearby + 2 Calendar Spread	52,620	89,104	157,010	70,606	41,790
Dec-Dec Corn Calendar Spread	4,240	2,787	2,239	4,933	1,926
Dec-July Corn Calendar Spread	10,070	1,010	562	2,478	400
Dec-July Wheat Calendar Spread	35	1,230		2,278	4,686
Dow Jones Industrial Index	32	524	4,472	1,325	1,948
Federal Funds	339,751	25,533	54,120	1,062,855	3,272,313
Intercommodity Spread	325				
July-Dec Corn Calendar Spread	36,161	89,967	93,045	104,046	64,105
July-Dec Soy Meal Calendar Spread	45	255			50
July-Dec Wheat Calendar Spread	15,671	6,116	7,351	5,756	1,375
July-Nov Soybean Calendar Spread	37,235	57,566	59,922	95,742	104,727
KC Hard Red Winter Wheat	461,670	437,286			
Mar-Dec Corn Calendar Spread	5,430	4,135	510		
Mar-July Corn Calendar Spread	2,769				
Mar-July Wheat Calendar Spread	12,076	435	185		
Mini $5 Dow Jones Industrial Index	138,575	150,742	182,259	97,994	107,389
Nov-July Soybean Calendar Spread	68	991	50	1,106	9,607
Nov-Nov Soybean Calendar Spread	272		587	52	16,105
Oats	20,935	25,010	31,378	22,546	19,727
Rough Rice	23,200	16,261	17,245	14,180	37,222
September-December Soybean Meal CSO	1,060				
Soy Oil Nearby + 2 Calendar Spread	75	2,496	2,129	3,236	4,380
Soybean Crush	2,712	2,984	3,224	1,260	1,016
Soybean Meal	2,909,760	2,588,548	2,044,056	1,675,979	946,723
Soybean Nearby + 2 Calendar Spread	280	8,463	10,319	865	18,973
Soybean Oil	2,159,102	1,739,640	1,428,088	2,212,857	2,360,836
Soybeans	18,663,389	17,916,675	14,760,704	18,402,208	13,236,367
Soymeal Nearby + 2 Calendar Spread	300	210	115		70
Ultra T-Bond	105,390	156,763	88,106	64,775	185,581
Wheat - Corn ICSO	175	375	1,778	195	1,109
Wheat Nearby + 2 Calendar Spread	135,291	63,961	34,528	46,068	43,257
Total Options	**200,789,567**	**198,920,909**	**182,915,946**	**143,010,967**	**131,039,321**

Chicago Mercantile Exchange (CME), division of the CME Group

OPTION	2015	2014	2013	2012	2011
Australian Dollar	1,534,672	1,563,533	1,737,747	1,203,772	946,663
Australian Dollar (European)	1,291	3,292	14,277	2,850	1,966
British Pound	2,570,095	3,033,414	1,841,943	659,792	735,630
British Pound (European)	7,684	9,717	29,267	9,139	6,845
Canadian Dollar	1,407,539	1,400,169	1,103,543	789,900	782,225
Canadian Dollar (European)	1,588	6,303	14,524	27,890	14,484
Cash Butter	12,220	12,020	15,145	5,839	2,310
Cash Settled Cheese	80,024	39,074	26,471	14,557	1,368
CAT Weather European	3,000	7,500			500
CDD Seasonal Strip Weather	67,000	34,480	39,060	35,800	67,600
CDD Weather	150	2,300	6,950	10,785	7,875
Class III Milk	265,414	361,945	260,071	273,517	304,232
Class IV Milk	8,446	20,734	24,943	3,201	4,667
Dry Whey	2,973	4,523	3,526	1,429	974
E-Mini NASDAQ 100 Index	1,535,576	3,154,154	889,508	758,987	923,266
E-Mini S&P 500 Index	77,768,004	74,080,842	56,641,470	35,726,356	36,130,942
E-Mini S&P MidCap 400 Index	37	926	1,436	457	581
EOM E-Mini S&P 500 Index	13,277,837	11,522,506	7,594,221	5,096,141	3,793,860
EOM S&P 500 Index	1,280,558	1,023,767	839,407	797,394	1,521,319
EOW1 E-mini S&P 500 Index	11,552,239	10,419,487	5,930,560	2,908,629	1,885,408

Chicago Mercantile Exchange (CME), division of the CME Group (continued)

OPTION	2015	2014	2013	2012	2011
EOW1 S&P 500 Index	381,560	530,588	339,834	83,907	212,794
EOW2 E-mini S&P 500 Index	12,558,487	10,554,604	5,800,851	3,517,143	1,961,040
EOW2 S&P 500 Index	952,275	933,010	540,683	197,960	382,127
EOW4 E-mini S&P 500 Index	11,744,931	9,137,555	5,837,467	2,988,624	1,973,286
Euro FX	12,366,261	7,630,825	6,462,404	6,083,870	5,684,036
Euro FX European	59,879	90,707	72,293	56,306	69,717
Euro HDD Seasonal Strip Weather	7,500	34,800	11,000	28,500	9,000
Eurodollar (3-month)	112,278,366	49,471,203	27,821,432	48,279,896	100,855,181
Eurodollar Mid-Curve	131,374,348	167,167,523	122,159,718	91,189,258	92,429,741
Feeder Cattle	437,202	375,384	215,072	219,142	153,216
HDD Seasonal Weather Strip	17,100	23,960	38,260	48,720	83,086
HDD Weather	2,800	6,125	5,366	12,750	27,220
HDD Weather European	3,000	1,800	1,500	1,000	20,000
Japanese Yen	2,897,094	3,009,287	3,684,829	1,540,799	1,292,246
Japanese Yen European	4,515	11,667	33,371	4,267	6,654
Lean Hogs	2,837,639	3,107,748	1,596,454	1,596,423	1,070,098
Live Cattle	3,974,324	4,041,314	2,737,051	3,006,744	3,012,718
Live Cattle Calendar ISO	81	572	856	2,778	135
Mexican Peso	17,624	9,809	2,843	750	
Mini BFP Milk	533	1,349	1,125	1,719	2,365
NASDAQ 100 Index	30	249	379	277	13,005
New Zealand Dollar	13	753	62	10	
Nonfat Dry Milk	46,112	16,339	6,400	3,078	177
Random Lumber	13,305	13,891	15,605	8,111	7,226
Russian Ruble	543	7,349	1,186	1,186	15,600
S&P 500 Index	9,099,788	8,647,971	6,985,661	6,966,596	11,718,229
Swiss Franc	171,038	296,944	175,718	67,608	306,134
Total Options	**412,622,695**	**371,826,055**	**261,572,433**	**214,258,946**	**268,518,626**

ICE Futures U.S. (ICE)

OPTION	2015	2014	2013	2012	2011
Cocoa	1,351,396	993,275	733,129	579,668	652,080
Coffee 'C'	1,817,282	2,726,981	1,691,629	2,498,884	2,624,667
Coffee 'C' 1-month	24,455	4,821			
Coffee 'C' 2-month	3,660	0			
Cotton #2	1,740,642	1,780,315	2,452,654	2,366,598	2,794,411
Cotton #2 1-month	1,200	4,443	3,707	1,335	
Cotton #2 2-month	5,425	287	1,885	3,481	
Cotton #2 Weekly Options	371	0		405	
North American Natural Gas and Power	45,436,400	39,458,277	54,587,428	14,789,230	
North American Power	101,570	26,000			
Orange Juice Frozen Concentrate	62,187	87,559	130,160	184,931	153,176
Russell 2000 Index Mini	29,374	73,624	65,132	67,774	155,824
Sugar #11	6,159,101	4,917,608	4,930,254	5,063,067	6,667,573
Sugar #11 1-month	36,793	46,678	73,296	41,105	
US Dollar Index	16,099	23,399	41,915	19,608	41,793
Weekly Coffee 'C' (KCW)	30	181			
Total Options	**56,785,985**	**50,146,497**	**64,736,820**	**25,680,667**	**13,180,700**

Minneapolis Grain Exchange (MGE)

OPTION	2015	2014	2013	2012	2011
Hard Red Spring Wheat - CSOs	301				
Hard Red Spring Wheat	26,200	24,127	18,971	16,157	43,315
Total Options	**26,501**	**24,367**	**23,006**	**16,157**	**43,315**

New York Mercantile Exchange (NYMEX), division of the CME Group

OPTION	2015	2014	2013	2012	2011
Brent Crude Oil Futures-Style Margin Option (BZO)	720				
Brent Financial Average Price Options (BA)	153,151	413,914	350,250	617,716	566,278
Brent Last Day Financial (European) Options (BE)	52,621	117,326	129,920	309,727	516,740
Brent Last Day Financial Options (OS)	55,192	228,871	269,125	171,509	139,652
Central Appalachian Coal Quarterly Strip Options	40	845	1,000	1,955	1,815
Chicago Ethanol (Platts) Average Price Options (CVR)	72,994	100,845	31,900	9,238	2,135
Coal (API 2) cif ARA (Argus/McCloskey) Calendar	66,223	4,455	485	160	
Coal (API 2) cif ARA (Argus/McCloskey) Options	8,995	26,945	10,775	2,685	
Coal (API 2) cif ARA (Argus/McCloskey) Quarterly	100,652	3,765	175	200	
Coal (API 2) cif ARA (Argus/McCloskey) Short Dated	151				
Coal (API 4) fob Richards Bay (Argus/McCloskey)	1,400	1,240	75		
Coal (API 4) fob Richards Bay (Argus/McCloskey)	1,875	6,540	2,730	1,500	
Coal (API 4) fob Richards Bay (Argus/McCloskey)	600	430		180	
Conway Propane (OPIS) Average Price Options (CPR)	14	265	588	119	300
Copper Options (HX)	27,111	21,022	36,172	5,689	6,897
Copper Weekly Options Wk 4 (H4E)	10				
Crude Oil (LO)	39,627,070	31,107,783	31,478,060	32,525,624	36,716,805
Crude Oil Weekly Options Wk 1 (LO1)	50,765	39,235			

VOLUME - U.S.

New York Mercantile Exchange (NYMEX), division of the CME Group (continued)

OPTION	2015	2014	2013	2012	2011
Crude Oil Weekly Options Wk 2 (LO2)	40,298	42,977			
Crude Oil Weekly Options Wk 3 (LO3)	24,850	27,747			
Crude Oil Weekly Options Wk 4 (LO4)	30,301	43,192			
Crude Oil Weekly Options Wk 5 (LO5)	15,318	11,322			
CSX Coal (Platts OTC Broker Index) Options (CPF)	730	995	265	90	
Daily Crude Oil Calendar Spread (1 Month) Options	8,000	37,900	14,600	100	3,350
Dated Brent (Platts) Average Price Option (DBP)	900	5,220	5,040	6,180	4,200
Dubai Crude Oil (Platts) Average Price Options (AH)	21,600	900	10,038	25,800	3,104
European 3.5% Fuel Oil Barges FOB Rdam (Platts)	615	5,401	13,818	15,487	12,047
European Low Sulphur Gasoil Calendar (1 month)	100				
European Naphtha Cargoes CIF NWE (Platts)	15	40	70	542	
European-Style Low Sulphur Gasoil Options (F8)	260			28	144
Gasoline Euro-bob Oxy NWE Barges (Argus) Crack	125	699			
Gold (OG)	7,534,527	8,415,139	10,587,160	9,454,650	10,080,754
Gold Weekly Options Wk 1 (OG1)	6,117	8,922			
Gold Weekly Options Wk 2 (OG2)	7,513	4,224			
Gold Weekly Options Wk 3 (OG3)	5,632	5,279			
Gold Weekly Options Wk 4 (OG4)	3,235	3,771			
Gold Weekly Options Wk 5 (OG5)	1,305	580			
Gulf Coast Jet Fuel (Platts) Average Price Options	3,934	18,390	40,861	900	
Iron Ore 62% Fe, CFR China (TSI) Average Price	73,556	13,482	5,896	24,599	6,633
Light Sweet Crude Oil (WTI) Daily Physical Options	17,900	23,850	16,675	47,170	113,280
Light Sweet Crude Oil (WTI) Financial 1 Month	1,845,556	1,451,107	826,639	81,250	21,350
Light Sweet Crude Oil European Financial Option	487,003	220,375	196,720	312,533	860,949
LLS (Argus) vs. WTI Crude Oil Average Price Option	4,080				
Low Sulphur Gasoil Average Price Options (F7)	1,462	268	916	2,813	12,826
Mont Belvieu Ethane (OPIS) Average Price Options	1,840	10,040	15,410	17,105	6,540
Mont Belvieu LDH Propane (OPIS) Average Price	13,341	22,579	23,746	17,080	7,318
Natural Gas (American) (ON)	3,029,693	3,369,085	3,480,049	2,778,387	2,064,055
Natural Gas (European) (LN)	19,594,491	20,936,070	21,053,064	24,260,726	23,773,183
Natural Gas (Henry Hub) Daily Options (KD)	271,330	254,700	264,701	483,564	466,319
Natural Gas (Henry Hub) Last-day Financial 1 Month	271,714	883,039	836,761	379,022	303,810
Natural Gas (Henry Hub) Last-day Financial 12	2,600				1,000
Natural Gas (Henry Hub) Last-day Financial 2 Month	4,950	2,100	3,400	5,800	7,800
Natural Gas (Henry Hub) Last-day Financial 3 Month	65,445	67,783	262,605	683,351	567,772
Natural Gas (Henry Hub) Last-day Financial 5 Month	2,700	650	5,000	500	
Natural Gas (Henry Hub) Last-day Financial 6 Month	46,900	41,678	95,038	198,550	109,575
Natural Gas (Henry Hub) Last-day Financial Options	23,660	65,737	64,590	17,292	27,294
Natural Gas Calendar Strip Options (6J)	13,020	14,066	18,636	27,585	98,055
Natural Gas Short-Term Options D01 (U01)	1,855	475	1,850	1,375	50
Natural Gas Short-Term Options D02 (U02)	6,013	2,175	600	1,100	100
Natural Gas Short-Term Options D03 (U03)	3,100	1,750	5,875	1,575	275
Natural Gas Short-Term Options D04 (U04)	2,330	1,200	3,200	500	50
Natural Gas Short-Term Options D05 (U05)	2,200	1,225	2,400	1,675	
Natural Gas Short-Term Options D06 (U06)	2,325	2,850	2,435	1,175	25
Natural Gas Short-Term Options D07 (U07)	2,920	825	3,675	450	200
Natural Gas Short-Term Options D08 (U08)	1,975	1,550	875	700	
Natural Gas Short-Term Options D09 (U09)	5,431	750	2,750	1,900	750
Natural Gas Short-Term Options D10 (U10)	3,750	1,900	3,225	1,250	
Natural Gas Short-Term Options D11 (U11)	3,510	2,350	3,550	475	100
Natural Gas Short-Term Options D12 (U12)	2,065	1,100	4,600	2,625	200
Natural Gas Short-Term Options D13 (U13)	2,535	2,125	4,525	1,750	
Natural Gas Short-Term Options D14 (U14)	1,675	1,100	4,600	2,700	50
Natural Gas Short-Term Options D15 (U15)	2,750	2,280	1,780	1,700	75
Natural Gas Short-Term Options D16 (U16)	3,025	675	2,015	975	
Natural Gas Short-Term Options D17 (U17)	1,985	1,925	1,525	300	175
Natural Gas Short-Term Options D18 (U18)	1,100	1,175	2,500	900	
Natural Gas Short-Term Options D19 (U19)	3,170	625	3,300	1,150	250
Natural Gas Short-Term Options D20 (U20)	1,730	405	1,300	1,500	
Natural Gas Short-Term Options D21 (U21)	2,350	950	5,150	1,000	
Natural Gas Short-Term Options D22 (U22)	1,560	3,150	3,750	950	400
Natural Gas Short-Term Options D23 (U23)	2,465	900	1,450	625	
Natural Gas Short-Term Options D24 (U24)	2,105	625	825	800	
Natural Gas Short-Term Options D25 (U25)	1,000	100	1,275	305	500
Natural Gas Short-Term Options D26 (U26)	1,075	425	955	500	
Natural Gas Short-Term Options D27 (U27)	1,225	175	2,175	325	100
Natural Gas Short-Term Options D28 (U28)	450	350	1,625	200	
Natural Gas Short-Term Options D29 (U29)	1,600	550	400	950	
Natural Gas Short-Term Options D30 (U30)	4,075	250	3,300	1,275	
Natural Gas Short-Term Options D31 (U31)	380	500	2,200	625	100
Natural Gas Weekly Options (American) Wk 5 (ON5)	25				
NY Harbor ULSD Average Price Option (AT)	165,910	287,936	220,389	331,398	423,583
NY Harbor ULSD Calendar Spread Option - 1 Month	3,500	21,960	12,875	31,075	25,785
NY Harbor ULSD European Financial Option (LB)	6,205	8,800	8,810	4,218	3,201
NY Harbor ULSD Option (OH)	606,659	785,306	564,974	755,394	889,524

New York Mercantile Exchange (NYMEX), division of the CME Group (continued)

OPTION	2015	2014	2013	2012	2011
NYISO Zone A Day-Ahead Peak Calendar-Month 5	2,540				
NYISO Zone G 5 MW Peak Calendar-Month Day-	550				26,640
Palladium Options (PAO)	42,981	137,511	134,120	66,307	37,389
Panhandle Natural Gas (Platts IFERC) "Pipe" Option	3,724		500	3,004	5,508
PJM 50 MW Calendar-Month LMP Option (PML)	39	1,425	2,983	12,920	34,087
PJM Electricity Option on Calendar Futures Strip	1,640	9,870	15,950	47,340	82,040
PJM WES HUB PEAK CAL MTH (6OA)	200				
Platinum Option (PO)	58,275	144,370	183,818	98,351	84,927
Powder River Basin Coal (Platts OTC Broker Index)	3,830	2,840	4,200	740	
RBOB Gasoline Average Price Options (RA)	21,649	98,941	87,514	58,290	28,167
RBOB Gasoline European Financial Option (RF)	5,440	12,090	6,645	1,599	165
RBOB Gasoline Physical Options (OB)	347,789	401,970	520,529	502,982	470,606
Rockies Natural Gas (Platts IFERC) "Pipe" Option	6,429	15,444	4,744	13,227	20,506
San Juan Natural Gas (Platts IFERC) "Pipe" Option	5,092	3,330	3,600	5,244	6,216
Silver Options (SO)	1,224,664	1,853,652	2,043,988	1,741,080	2,124,108
Silver Weekly Options Wk 1 (SO1)	428	1,538			
Silver Weekly Options Wk 2 (SO2)	190	1,508			
Silver Weekly Options Wk 3 (SO3)	194	1,298			
Silver Weekly Options Wk 4 (SO4)	141	1,174			
Silver Weekly Options Wk 5 (SO5)	203	381			
Singapore Fuel Oil 380 cst (Platts) Average Price	180	1,214	2,773	522	18
Singapore Gasoil (Platts) Average Price Options (M2)	300	150	200	9,882	1,200
Singapore Jet Kerosene (Platts) Average Price Options	1,500	2,875	17,588	30,352	6,060
WTI Average Price Options (AO)	722,701	889,225	742,805	1,549,657	2,488,882
WTI Crude Oil 1 Month Calendar Spread (WA)	2,359,207	2,061,821	2,281,455	2,873,842	2,886,427
WTI Crude Oil 12 Month Physical Spread Option (WZ)	2,000	88,141	15,150	10,500	15,575
WTI-Brent Crude Oil Spread Options (BV)	268,360	554,571	700,183	52,079	24,943
Total Options	**79,632,474**	**75,536,148**	**77,848,760**	**80,793,179**	**86,514,666**

North American Derivative Exchange (NADEX)

OPTION	2015	2014
AUD-JPY	60,357	46,350
AUD-USD	533,812	232,603
Bitcoin	32,504	1,463
China 50	12,776	
Copper	16,885	15,423
Corn	15,483	7,445
Crude Oil	207,378	184,372
EUR-GBP	71,969	32,313
EUR-JPY	141,546	114,282
EUR-USD	950,038	358,338
FTSE 100	33,421	26,294
GBP-JPY	149,463	49,932
GBP-USD	503,436	173,936
Germany 30	65,557	71,917
Gold	132,370	144,353
Japan 225	142,128	73,336
Natural Gas	57,115	18,299
Silver	51,300	35,684
Soybeans	14,996	3,926
US 500	889,096	753,877
US SmallCap 2000	170,568	162,169
US Tech 100	315,952	319,436
USD-CAD	112,833	83,313
USD-CHF	79,846	48,433
USD-JPY	628,743	414,544
Wall St. 30	419,653	319,249
Total Options	**5,809,225**	**3,691,287**

Total Volume

	2015	2014	2013	2012	2011
Total Options	**755,666,447**	**700,145,263**	**587,268,793**	**463,863,612**	**499,550,971**
Percent Change	**7.93%**	**19.22%**	**26.60%**	**-7.14%**	**9.23%**

Volume - Worldwide

ASX, Australia

	2015	2014	2013	2012	2011
All Futures on Individual Equities	5,862,951	6,703,662	6,117,166	5,407,123	3,460,934
S&P/ASX Index	12,968	238,602	257,098	258,989	270,236
Total Futures	**5,875,919**	**6,942,264**	**6,374,264**	**5,666,112**	**3,731,170**
All Options on Individual Equities	89,218,026	108,984,616	124,300,972	140,439,020	108,860,114
S&P / ASX Index	11,462,192	9,797,586	9,224,326	11,501,735	10,321,625
Total Options	**100,680,218**	**118,782,202**	**133,525,298**	**151,940,755**	**119,181,739**

ASX 24, Australia

(formerly Sydney Futures Exchange)	2015	2014	2013	2012	2011
10 Year Treasury Bonds	31,786,345	27,186,944	23,926,468	18,469,473	15,954,349
20 Year Bonds	191,600				
3 Year Treasury Bonds	49,308,108	48,517,655	48,978,355	44,003,411	41,662,349
30 Day Interbank Cash Rate	4,325,909	2,347,004	4,913,943	4,499,015	6,296,489
ASX Electricity Base Load $300 CAP Quarterly NSW	7,618	11,289	11,181	9,761	12,051
ASX Electricity Base Load $300 CAP Quarterly QLD	8,667	9,634	4,781	5,811	5,729
ASX Electricity Base Load $300 CAP Quarterly SA (GS)	1,722	2,159	2,402	1,871	1,185
ASX Electricity Base Load $300 CAP Quarterly VIC (GV)	7,535	10,342	10,281	10,150	9,837
ASX Electricity Base Load $300 Cap Strip Future (RN)	261				
ASX Electricity Base Load $300 Cap Strip Future (RQ)	215				
ASX Electricity Base Load $300 Cap Strip Future (RS)	5				
ASX Electricity Base Load $300 Cap Strip Future (RV)	165				
ASX Electricity Base Load Monthly Futures NSW (EN)	40		5		
ASX Electricity Base Load Monthly Futures QLD (EQ)	358	816	355		
ASX Electricity Base Load Quarterly NSW	40,785	56,033	34,962	47,572	64,143
ASX Electricity Base Load Quarterly QLD	44,392	46,800	27,587	31,722	49,345
ASX Electricity Base Load Quarterly SA	3,440	4,039	4,916	4,398	4,530
ASX Electricity Base Load Quarterly VIC	37,928	44,972	29,294	26,393	42,174
ASX Electricity Base Load Strip NSW	3,999	175			
ASX Electricity Base Load Strip QLD	4,137	211			
ASX Electricity Base Load Strip SA	157	18			
ASX Electricity Base Load Strip VIC	3,041	206			
ASX Electricity Peak Load Quarterly NSW	4,396	5,268	4,914	7,862	7,668
ASX Electricity Peak Load Quarterly QLD	979	1,188	1,865	3,223	1,819
ASX Electricity Peak Load Quarterly SA	134	110	203	457	319
ASX Electricity Peak Load Quarterly VIC	2,181	2,251	3,886	2,641	5,476
ASX Electricity Peak Load Strip Futures NSW (DN)	100				
ASX Electricity Peak Load Strip Futures QLD (DQ)	85				
ASX Electricity Peak Load Strip Futures VIC (DV)	38				
Australian Sorghum	432	4,412	9,530	12,467	1,690
Bank Bills 90 Day	28,492,027	26,392,134	29,020,415	21,382,203	22,391,055
Eastern Australia Feed Barley	4,546	15,773	28,490	49,128	8,558
Eastern Australia Wheat	100				
Mini-ASX SPI 200	9,752				
NSW Wheat	116,820	132,119	178,357	322,372	93,940
S&P/ASX 200 A-REIT Index	155,392	8,711			
S&P/ASX 200 Financials-x-A-REIT Index	1,514	969	1,286		
S&P/ASX 200 Resources Index	168	552	806		
S&P/ASX 200 Volatility Index	14	73	57		
SPI 200	11,039,188	10,011,422	10,239,412	10,025,717	12,130,237
WA Wheat	75	2,157	16,580	18,582	12,283
Total Futures	**125,604,368**	**114,816,294**	**117,456,259**	**98,957,493**	**98,767,181**
10 Year Treasury Bond	4,235	41,899	12,731	11,706	2,052
3 Year Bonds Intra-Day	732,605	1,245,326	1,711,088	1,096,285	1,249,257
3 Year Treasury Bond	273,988	370,759	423,077	526,889	509,638
ASX Electricity Base Load Quarterly NSW	5,206	2,393	175		
ASX Electricity Base Load Quarterly QLD	4,710	5,775	372		
ASX Electricity Base Load Quarterly SA	316	87	15		
ASX Electricity Base Load Quarterly VIC	4,258	2,593	740		
ASX Electricity Base Load Strip NSW	3,635	75			
ASX Electricity Base Load Strip QLD	4,645	325			
ASX Electricity Base Load Strip SA	135				
ASX Electricity Base Load Strip VIC	3,968	210			
NSW Wheat	3,457	5,841	1,250	14,930	160
Overnight 3 Year Treasury Bond	649,101	1,299,967	1,890,929	1,301,374	1,433,184
SPI 200	331,089	553,388	388,450	441,838	423,390
Total Options	**2,021,348**	**3,530,098**	**4,435,077**	**3,401,670**	**3,673,533**

Athens Derivatives Exchange S.A. (ADEX), Greece

	2015	2014	2013	2012	2011
All Futures on Individual Equities	12,410,089	6,969,083	6,666,992	24,861,696	7,553,643
FTSE/Athex Large Cap	2,134,904	3,572,231	2,322,341	2,903,594	2,482,713
Total Futures	**14,544,993**	**10,541,314**	**8,991,219**	**27,766,252**	**10,038,456**
All Options on Individual Equities	13,384	30,164	18,481	65,098	64,238
FTSE/Athex Large Cap	94,728	227,510	194,455	429,874	328,391
Total Options	**108,112**	**257,674**	**212,936**	**494,972**	**392,629**

Bolsa de Mercadorias & Futuros (BM&F), Brazil

	2015	2014	2013	2012	2011
Arabica Coffee	124,297	188,789	147,301	237,663	450,802
Arabica Coffee Rollover	11,154	13,942	9,858	9,656	8,002
Australian Dollar	51,707	86,940	73,569	111,648	138,216
Bovespa Mini Index	89,671,637	69,989,607	49,215,793	38,951,711	26,234,515
Bovespa Rollover	6,251,834	4,968,870	4,639,339	3,142,382	3,075,094
Bovespa Stock Index Futures	16,924,855	20,496,231	20,443,962	22,328,572	21,650,138
Canadian Dollar	18,531	41,038	37,047	116,360	74,623
Chilean Peso	8,381	24,004	3,515	872	
Corn Cash Settled	685,723	968,841	738,812	683,881	464,387
Cross Listing Mini-Sized Soybean CME	43,789	57,465	32,465	22	
DI x US Dollar Swap with reset	523,543	193,063			
E-mini S&P 500	260,013	343,009	243,120	51,848	
E-mini S&P 500 Rollover	42,292	37,046	19,576		
Euro	610,614	334,525	348,861	656,707	552,481
Forward Exchange Rate	17,521	86,381	9,841		2,205
Gold Spot (250g)	9,873	12,754	11,682	10,258	23,579
Hydrous Ethanol	36,424	44,602	43,030	66,610	81,725
IBrX-50	92,637	117,869			
ID x IPCA Spread Futures	1,805		23,725	4,495	4,425
ID x US Dollar FRA	66,957,541	53,344,699	36,458,503	34,986,267	33,933,356
ID x US Dollar Spread Futures	3,175,476	1,073,054	1,521,459	1,124,566	1,685,441
Interbank Deposits futures SELIC	2,432,536	2,310,699			
Interest Rate Swap	222,770	1,324,955	179,626	263,945	161,230
Interest Rate x Exchange Rate	3,517,095	308,742	158,613	461,109	193,759
Interest Rate x Price Index	353,513	782,445	1,148,801	1,238,285	1,646,628
Live Cattle	545,842	813,312	863,127	758,720	975,362
Mexican Peso	25,945	30,813	88,008	123,482	58,419
Mini Euro	11	464	75		
Mini US Dollar	38,287,575	6,983,457	2,393,580	1,821,820	2,259,014
New Zealand Dollar	4,715	6,708	1,245	1,955	260
Odd-lot gold spot (0.225g)	19,385				
Odd-lot gold spot (10g.)	13,839				
One Day Inter-Bank Deposit	309,308,981	286,125,664	394,055,420	340,800,485	320,821,062
Pound Sterling	34,188	65,337	58,972	16,236	42,771
Price Index x Exchange Rate Swap	2,393				
South African Rand	15,082	26,121	9,765	1,412	600
Soybean Cash Settled	4,598	43,748	56,913	52,034	37,465
Swiss Franc	5,772	12,471	29,977	19,487	6,468
Turkish Lira	9,170	25,269	1,825	1,270	2,032
US Dollar	77,490,315	82,365,540	83,426,499	84,049,097	86,167,955
US Dollar forward points	5,021,955	4,929,440	3,072,885	2,553,745	3,303,276
US Dollar Rollover	22,384,437	25,029,948	25,400,303	23,236,158	20,145,632
US T-Note	9,848	45,039	31,637	15,221	30,065
West Texas Intermediate (WTI)	7,519	3,738			
Yen	54,561	85,125	143,934	21,887	30,303
Yuan (CNY)	57	192	120	135	
Total Futures	**645,291,749**	**563,743,123**	**625,592,252**	**557,948,335**	**524,392,180**
Arabica Coffee	2,694	2,536	6,108	8,878	4,009
Bovespa Index	1,100,040	3,216,792	2,353,368	8,658,743	5,586,998
Corn Cash Settled	154,471	122,434	58,746	110,337	88,833
Flexible BOVA11 Index	1,600	2,080			
Flexible Bovespa Stock Index	120,600	103,579	68,150	154,236	191,537
Flexible Spot Interest Rate Index	206,937	269,799	155,764	70,150	514,642
Flexible US Dollar	371,643	166,743	615,515	2,125	53,402
Gold Spot (250g)	7,996				
IDI Index	31,762,121	48,454,406	40,626,100	107,961,438	95,790,772
Live Cattle on Futures	214,298	204,757	200,723	270,098	172,660
One Day Inter-Bank Deposit	6,191,959				
Soybean Cash Settled on Futures	2,884	1,423	2,715	13,664	33,174
US Dollar	7,154,790	8,419,449	8,609,024	9,422,497	11,136,468
US Dollar Volatility	142,420	235,510	357,155	331,030	597,785
Total Options	**47,434,453**	**66,641,600**	**67,114,261**	**146,139,337**	**135,084,822**

VOLUME - WORLDWIDE

Bolsa de Valores de Colombia (BCV), Colombia

	2015	2014	2013	2012	2011
All Futures on Individual Equities	291,360	347,522	113,053	53,959	32,563
COLCAP Index	933	1,005	851	611	563
Consumer Price Index	40		248	391	
IBR	6,072	59	256	161	
Mini US Dollar	90,697	61,570	125,757	165,149	198,216
Other Treasury Bonds	191,619	213,887	51,570		
US Dollar	467,478	299,721	218,756	272,587	389,693
Total Futures	**1,048,199**	**941,620**	**685,133**	**630,590**	**795,298**

BOVESPA, Brazil

	2015	2014	2013	2012	2011
All Options on Individual Equities	659,993,736	786,115,608	909,313,950	929,284,637	838,325,495
Exchange Traded Funds	4,809,002	2,352,231	597,500	1,540,039	2,018,403
Ibovespa Index	1,063,917	1,626,643	982,688	1,045,256	623,103
Total Options	**665,866,655**	**790,094,482**	**910,894,138**	**931,869,932**	**840,967,001**

Borsa Istanbul, Turkey

(formerly TurkDEX)	2015	2014	2013	2012	2011
All Futures on Individual Equities	2,739,426	194,377	24,073	6,291	
Base Load Electricity	23,647	26	152	928	32
BIST 30 Index	46,057,541	43,020,419	40,433,038	48,757,352	54,612,000
EUR/USD Cross Currency	888,551	400,627	1,127,698	1,339,713	1,453,964
FBIST ETF Futures	6,067				
Gold	989,478	929,006	26,567	48,941	165,729
TRY/EUR	2,336,850	434,442			
TRY/USD	32,986,013	12,929,674	8,927,709	10,503,364	16,028,342
USD/Ounce Gold	415,146	585,995	1,710,574	1,347,200	595,495
Total Futures	**86,442,719**	**58,494,568**	**53,117,987**	**62,480,755**	**74,287,630**
All Options on Individual Equities	847,500	88,919	45,806	2,710	
BIST 30 Index	266,425	94,484	8,572		
TRY/USD	1,323,524	25,494			
Total Options	**2,437,449**	**208,897**	**54,378**	**2,710**	

Borsa Italiana, Italy

	2015	2014	2013	2012	2011
All Futures on Individual Equities	3,772,920	605,592	845,333	4,300,831	11,194,546
Electricity	2,811	7,544	9,169	1,239,219	3,575
Mini S&P/MIB Index	4,920,082	4,204,244	2,785,314	2,881,040	3,202,721
S&P/MIB Index	9,563,659	8,493,311	6,537,910	5,943,504	6,134,326
Single Stock Dividend Futures	39,447	133,853	82,209		
Wheat	968	880	301		
Total Futures	**18,299,887**	**13,445,424**	**10,260,236**	**14,364,594**	**20,535,168**
All Options on Individual Equities	21,416,914	21,585,798	18,965,858	19,732,822	23,770,068
S&P/MIB Index	4,655,965	4,015,974	3,274,234	2,857,034	3,521,489
Total Options	**26,072,879**	**25,601,772**	**22,240,092**	**22,589,856**	**27,291,557**

Bombay Stock Exchange, India

	2015	2014	2013	2012	2011
91-day Government of India (GOI) Treasury Bill	5,063,460	1,076,089			
All Futures on Individual Equities	139,683	579,391	1,640,045	170,421	156,842
EUR/INR	778,180	328,954			
GBP/INR	311,114	338,174			
JPY/INR	247,796	599,336			
S&P BSE 100 Index (BSI)	59	85,590	1,201,058	406,970	
S&P Sensex Index (BSX)	498,367	1,271,330	914,349	8,326,789	2,467,231
US Dollar/Indian Rupee	258,083,484	171,642,176			
Total Futures	**265,122,143**	**175,921,040**	**3,755,484**	**9,142,734**	**2,624,073**
All Options on Individual Equities	7,071,245	2,012,537	750,426	45,908	
Bankex Index (BKX)	100				
S&P Sensex Index (BSX)	172,389,921	439,090,333	108,612,615	148,314,519	
US Dollar/Indian Rupee	170,311,114	32,110,966			
Total Options	**349,772,380**	**554,252,129**	**251,090,445**	**234,614,523**	

Budapest Stock Exchange (BSE), Hungary

	2015	2014	2013	2012	2011
1 month BUBOR	5,200				
6 month BUBOR	193,866				
All Futures on Individual Equities	498,528	567,669	686,028	609,797	806,061
AUD/CAD	400		4,600	2,500	850
AUD/CAD (1 week)	400	400	200	200	3,500
AUD/JPY (1 week)	200	600	12,000	800	200
AUD/USD	6,800	6,650	21,500	43,860	14,180
AUD/USD (1 week)	500	2,800	9,000	28,800	27,200
CAD/HUF	8,265	1,220	1,010	1,440	500
CHF/HUF	181,645	100,267	110,200	200,085	1,322,258

Budapest Stock Exchange (BSE), Hungary (continued)

	2015	2014	2013	2012	2011
CHF/JPY	4,200			200	100
EUR/AUD	2,600	1,000	7,650	9,370	1,000
EUR/AUD (1 week)	200	2,000	1,200		
EUR/CAD	1,700	1,900	1,200	3,520	100
EUR/CHF	60,650	90,790	138,370	100,150	196,790
EUR/CHF (1 week)	200	2,400	3,500	1,400	16,600
EUR/CZK	3,150		2,800	200	1,200
EUR/GBP	18,200	7,850	11,400	7,870	5,650
EUR/HUF	3,269,167	3,174,892	3,282,205	2,128,821	1,894,259
EUR/HUF (1 week)	4,600				
EUR/JPY (1 week)	1,200	26,200	26,600	17,400	15,000
EUR/NOK	15,500	6,750	14,650	100	3,700
EUR/PLN	5,620	3,700	5,100	5,150	26,000
EUR/RON	88,170	400	900	4,200	4,675
EUR/RSD	3,800				
EUR/SEK	300	1,100	1,300	800	
EUR/USD (1 week)	24,900	33,650	115,400	208,100	424,150
EURO/JPY	29,350	41,100	98,295	26,450	69,400
EURO/TRY	127,625	164,470	141,220	45,300	126,835
EURO/USD	1,103,722	786,835	611,104	340,190	365,652
Feed Barley	170	145	239	83	135
Feed Corn	1,900	1,920	2,911	3,165	3,352
Feed Corn Index	5	2		10	2
Feed Wheat	262	506	439	112	203
GBP/AUD	2,600	4,600	6,900	400	1,400
GBP/AUD (1 week)	6,600	17,600	19,000	2,600	7,700
GBP/CAD	1,300	3,200	5,800	700	2,600
GBP/CAD (1week)	6,400	16,400	18,100	2,400	9,800
GBP/CHF	300	450	1,000	300	4,250
GBP/HUF	269,558	256,972	210,272	137,950	16,350
GBP/HUF (1 week)	1,900				
GBP/JPY	2,600	1,800	5,300	4,400	8,300
GBP/JPY (1 week)	600	10,900	12,950	3,500	2,200
GBP/PLN	1,000	600	2,000		100
GBP/PLN (1 week)	3,200	4,400	3,800	1,000	800
GBP/TRY	300				
GBP/USD	10,200	37,060	46,960	11,200	12,300
GBP/USD (1 week)	2,600	7,500	31,300	16,000	25,500
JPY/HUF	188,314	3,045	16,440	9,350	17,900
Mill Wheat	29	82	200	408	298
Mill Wheat Index	43				
PLN/HUF	2,105	485	2,845	1,300	120
Rapeseed	265	290	178	352	377
Sunflower Seed	744	875	946	366	872
TRY/HUF	36,100	36,410	42,200	27,620	37,775
TRY/HUF (1 week)	17,000	36,900			
USD/BRL	8,640				
USD/CAD	10,730	14,390	4,040	8,000	5,600
USD/CHF	13,500	40,450	20,600	3,300	33,000
USD/HUF	2,154,428	1,281,715	1,056,745	755,858	1,086,439
USD/HUF (1 week)	8,300				
USD/JPY	98,010	114,680	171,910	49,440	99,300
USD/JPY (1 week)	5	2,200	2,500	400	4,400
USD/NOK	6,300	1,800	1,200		
USD/PLN	800	1,400	8,200	2,800	2,000
USD/PLN (1 week)	5,756	1,800	11,000	12,000	7,200
USD/RUB	100	100			
USD/SEK	5,900	4,000	1,100		
USD/TRY	40,400	22,150	49,850	21,250	12,750
Total Futures	**8,569,622**	**7,533,757**	**7,577,781**	**5,821,356**	**8,750,083**
All Options on Individual Equities	2				
BUX	2				
EUR/CHF	2,700	3,700	5,750	8,590	1,300
EUR/HUF	27,200				
EUR/USD	200	2,400	200	1,600	1,000
EURO/TRY	2,200	17,250	7,850	1,200	1,700
USD/HUF	2,600				
USD/TRY	300	400	2,500	1,800	3,900
Total Options	**35,204**	**29,300**	**34,800**	**58,300**	**36,697**

China Financial Futures Exchange (CFFE)

	2015	2014	2013	2012	2011
10 year Treasury Bond Futures	1,652,441				
5 Year Treasury Bond	4,612,100	**922,871**	**328,795**		
CSI 300 Index	267,007,814	216,658,274	193,220,516	105,061,825	50,411,860
Shanghai 50 Index	29,258,693				
Zhongzheng 500 Index Futures	19,059,875				
Total Futures	**321,590,923**	**217,581,145**	**193,549,311**	**105,061,825**	**50,411,860**

Dalian Commodity Exchange (DCE), China

	2015	2014	2013	2012	2011
Block Board	76,720	17,760,375	1,988,112		
Coke	14,361,543	63,688,294	115,306,637	32,915,885	1,512,734
Corn	41,583,905	9,329,939	13,313,633	37,824,356	26,849,738
Corn Starch	26,934,449	71,958			
Egg	13,353,228	35,188,187	1,951,323		
Fibre Board	38,103	15,354,378	2,374,759		
Hard Coking Coal	14,637,569	57,605,436	34,259,550		
Iron Ore	251,891,651	96,359,128	2,189,215		
Linear Low Density Polyethylene (LLDPE)	109,133,322	71,754,393	72,142,084	71,871,537	95,219,058
No. 1 Soybeans	17,658,839	27,197,413	10,993,500	45,475,425	25,239,532
No. 2 Soybeans	4,799	6,952	7,236	10,400	10,662
Polypropylene	101,043,188	24,781,150			
Polyvinyl Chloride (PVC)	1,424,323	1,471,673	1,787,233	6,900,153	9,438,431
RBD Palm Olein	107,506,542	79,996,388	82,495,230	43,310,013	22,593,961
Soybean Meal	266,541,153	204,988,746	265,357,592	325,876,653	50,170,334
Soybean Oil	87,878,200	64,082,631	96,334,673	68,858,554	58,012,550
Total Futures	**1,054,067,534**	**769,637,041**	**700,500,777**	**633,042,976**	**289,047,000**

EUREX, Frankfurt, Germany

	2015	2014	2013	2012	2011
2y Euro GMEX IRS CMF	24				
3 Month Euribor	376,042	160,355	275,098	66,360	125,557
3y Euro GMEX IRS CMF	29				
All Futures on Individual Equities	122,981,360	123,997,353	179,424,059	196,072,416	174,271,102
ATX	330,033	270,120	300,324	328,923	284,229
ATX five	17,384	38,068	50,205	32,799	42,764
Bloomberg Agriculture Subindex (FCAG)	129		2,683	1,126	6,481
Bloomberg Commodity IndexSM	4,695	28,669	64,036	61,544	54,974
Bloomberg Energy Sub-IndexSM	32,188	16,960	7,965	2,248	2,898
Bloomberg ex-Agriculture & Livestock Index	469	2,513			
Bloomberg ex-Industrial Metals Subindex	19				
Bloomberg Industrial Metals Sub-IndexSM	5,587	6,032	3,758	3,637	4,771
Bloomberg Livestock Subindex	30	150	2	1,044	937
Bloomberg Petroleum Sub-Index	177	741	867	1,333	2,337
Bloomberg Precious Metals Sub-Index	16,562	14,646	21,891	19,674	8,649
Bloomberg Softs Sub-Index		2,292	84	2,305	2,125
Butter	650	3,366			
Butter Future (FABT)	2,723		1,887	691	510
CECE EUR	12,594	6,179	8,029	9,916	15,109
Daily Futures auf TAIEX-Futures	195,275	58,619			
Dax	29,991,539	29,718,354	28,417,740	37,409,537	44,990,070
DivDAX	12,215	13,700	18,418	23,090	3,948
Euro Stoxx	270,114	250,923	30,389	24,457	2,663
Euro Stoxx 50 ex Financials Index	37,213	6,436	611	1,005	
Euro Stoxx 50 Index	341,824,375	293,837,558	268,495,189	315,179,597	408,860,002
Euro Stoxx 50 Index Dividend	4,922,323	4,548,195	3,676,120	3,543,392	4,232,260
Euro Stoxx Automobiles & Parts	65,743	47,282	56,758	111,429	58,072
Euro Stoxx Banks	24,155,819	19,744,140	10,074,089	9,565,474	5,229,347
Euro Stoxx Banks Index Dividend	11,899	7,900	7,370	1,000	
Euro Stoxx Basic Resources	27,018	23,870	28,293	33,644	32,098
Euro Stoxx Chemicals	17,876	13,803	11,844	21,950	29,076
Euro Stoxx Construction & Materials	26,411	37,712	44,408	41,537	39,676
Euro Stoxx Financial Services	5,367	8,356	7,765	15,467	8,502
Euro Stoxx Food and Beverage	26,051	43,727	42,175	32,292	24,402
Euro Stoxx Healthcare	15,894	18,065	22,372	52,490	49,145
Euro Stoxx Industrial Goods & Services	18,156	31,224	33,284	30,660	24,727
Euro Stoxx Insurance	281,044	158,282	288,511	378,492	220,847
Euro Stoxx Large	7,955	10,020	5,376	6,701	2,735
Euro Stoxx Media	14,320	11,567	22,705	25,771	25,575
Euro Stoxx Mid	23,644	5,482	16,744	17,185	9,699
Euro Stoxx Oil & Gas	412,583	254,357	242,109	123,732	67,219
Euro Stoxx Oil Gas Index Dividend	10,821		525		
Euro Stoxx Personal & Household Goods	11,106	28,487	13,002	24,088	15,058
Euro Stoxx Real Estate	38,583	8,539	2,072	4,670	4,706
Euro Stoxx Retail	8,524	9,073	12,986	12,440	41,504
Euro Stoxx Select Dividend 30 Index	246,961	140,887	98,978	95,555	92,084

EUREX, Frankfurt, Germany (continued)

	2015	2014	2013	2012	2011
Euro Stoxx Select Dividend 30 Index Dividend	16,658	650			
Euro Stoxx Small	108,962	75,857	48,792	50,057	22,009
Euro Stoxx Technology	19,157	37,800	27,856	51,724	44,757
Euro Stoxx Telecommunications	170,303	285,158	299,547	182,580	125,229
Euro Stoxx Telecommunications Index Dividend	450	450		320	
Euro Stoxx Travel & Leisure	22,710	16,800	12,053	34,628	19,914
Euro Stoxx Utilities	371,290	466,050	168,313	131,201	89,787
Euro-BOBL	118,963,514	113,554,369	129,530,977	107,645,238	142,309,151
Euro-BONO	40,273				
Euro-BTP	25,543,794	17,356,789	9,285,418	4,870,645	2,386,768
Euro-BUND	177,107,346	179,136,822	190,299,482	184,338,704	236,188,831
Euro-BUXL	9,314,084	6,428,189	3,987,038	2,465,158	1,806,195
Euro-OAT	21,562,432	17,372,490	11,734,475	4,342,912	
European Processing Potatoes	10,445	36,274			
European Processing Potatoes	39,019		53,947	50,382	52,918
European Whey Powder	231	639			
European Whey Powder	361		118	17	
Euro-SCHATZ	70,279,064	71,376,790	95,505,726	93,840,656	165,798,952
EURSecured Funding-Futures	235	2			
FX futures on EUR/USD	47	6			
FX futures on GBP/USD	10	11			
Gold	141	242	835	1,433	2,105
Hog Future (FAHG)	88		902	1,814	2,009
Hogs	71	420			
IPD UK Annual All Industrial Index	600	700			35
IPD UK Annual All Office Index	200	200			15
IPD UK Annual All Property Index	1,922	4,574	13,171	9,913	3,337
IPD UK Quarterly All Property Index Futures - Calendar	4,647				
IPD UK Quarterly Shopping Centre Index Futures	500				
MDAX	342,212	309,115	214,848	310,476	422,382
Mid Term Euro-OAT	50,932	138,687	350,965		
Mini-DAX Futures	608,835				
Mini-Futures auf VSTOXX	7,225,150	6,960,491	5,324,708	3,901,530	1,889,492
MSCI AC Asia Pacific ex Japan	11,974	3,694	537		
MSCI ACWI	10,290				
MSCI Australia (FMAU)	30				
MSCI Chile	3,866	166			
MSCI China Free	7,235	148			
MSCI Colombia	1,299	80			
MSCI Czech Rep (FMCZ)	21				
MSCI Egypt	55	219			
MSCI Emerging Markets	9,020	7,790	8,151		
MSCI Emerging Markets Asia	4,684	364			
MSCI Emerging Markets EMEA	2,576	14			
MSCI Emerging Markets Latin America	2,588	91	14		
MSCI Europe	450,068	232,605	115,939		
MSCI Europe (FMEF)	2,642				
MSCI Europe (FMEN)	19,055				
MSCI Europe (FMEP)	35,416				
MSCI Greece	15				
MSCI Hong Kong	134				
MSCI Hungary (FMHU)	105				
MSCI India (FMIN)	139				
MSCI Indonesia	1,003				
MSCI Japan Index	908	440	10,372	32,123	1,112
MSCI Kokusai (FMKG)	220				
MSCI Kokusai (FMKN)	216				
MSCI Malaysia	2,012	345	35		
MSCI Mexico	324	502	84		
MSCI New Zealand (FMNZ)	125				
MSCI Pacific ex Japan (FMPX)	181				
MSCI Philippines	954	88	20		
MSCI Poland	751	284			
MSCI Qatar	2,317	495			
MSCI Russia	6,886	7,468	824		
MSCI Russia Index	49,505	105,274	46,581	76,144	41,514
MSCI South Africa	305	121			
MSCI Thailand	229	368	100		
MSCI UAE	604	129			
MSCI UK	7,733				
MSCI USA (FMUS)	202				
MSCI World (FMWN)	437,739	28,737	24,952		
MSCI World (FMWO)	256,555	142,743			
MSCI World (FMWP)	700				
MSCI World Midcap (FMWM)	11,369	2,574			

EUREX, Frankfurt, Germany (continued)

	2015	2014	2013	2012	2011
OMX-Helsinki 25	169,775	103,876	66,326	134,950	255,060
Piglet Future (FAPG)	26		143	309	258
Piglets	11	38			
RDX EUR	290	2,986			
RDX USD Index	759,353	917,116	698,674	233,968	
Short Term Euro-BTP	5,584,445	3,706,784	1,961,926	814,408	575,349
Single Stock Dividend	2,456,657	3,145,117	2,330,137	2,078,118	938,950
Skimmed Milk Powder	288	1,272			
Skimmed Milk Powder Future (FASM)	3,363		392	200	7
SMI Index Dividend	1,795	2,096	4,464	10,544	14,375
Stoxx Europe 50 Index	901,275	686,507	914,717	1,050,022	1,330,841
Stoxx Europe 600	6,520,341	3,273,465	2,490,175	1,272,689	1,247,760
Stoxx Europe 600 Automobiles & Parts	477,859	492,680	334,787	320,017	303,586
Stoxx Europe 600 Banks	1,894,102	1,850,759	1,355,558	1,852,717	2,456,184
Stoxx Europe 600 Basic Resources	916,390	959,180	774,499	765,336	707,868
Stoxx Europe 600 Chemicals	57,366	61,840	69,926	82,899	114,697
Stoxx Europe 600 Construction & Materials	121,177	76,409	76,901	100,264	130,865
Stoxx Europe 600 Financial Services	65,563	29,359	35,442	30,022	38,373
Stoxx Europe 600 Food & Beverage	268,077	197,695	250,561	245,242	268,565
Stoxx Europe 600 Healthcare	265,689	252,262	220,028	267,426	411,857
Stoxx Europe 600 Industrial Goods & Services	199,465	235,237	282,456	420,605	577,074
Stoxx Europe 600 Insurance	601,403	359,704	323,586	454,975	757,845
Stoxx Europe 600 Media	98,076	105,441	128,112	153,951	254,493
Stoxx Europe 600 Oil & Gas	1,169,216	664,417	387,800	349,893	645,483
Stoxx Europe 600 Oil&Gas Index Dividend Futures	2,320				
Stoxx Europe 600 Personal & Household Goods	99,603	58,716	57,732	84,122	116,613
Stoxx Europe 600 Real Estate	117,008	20,904	39,066	13,942	24,520
Stoxx Europe 600 Retail	78,718	55,441	65,943	61,431	148,710
Stoxx Europe 600 Technology	123,685	103,823	101,429	147,659	172,508
Stoxx Europe 600 Telecom	314,938	418,363	359,203	439,407	346,960
Stoxx Europe 600 Travel & Leisure	96,038	65,674	94,692	62,227	138,866
Stoxx Europe 600 Utilities	473,537	341,489	250,923	270,383	361,392
Stoxx Europe Large 200	122,014	105,646	50,194	53,037	75,207
Stoxx Europe Mid 200	260,514	298,166	258,243	400,450	490,301
Stoxx Europe Small 200	623,605	460,064	284,290	278,232	428,524
STOXX Global Select Dividend 100 Index	480				
Swiss Government Bond (CONF)	104,041	115,674	141,272	150,484	181,740
Swiss Leader Index (SLI)	66,577	24,205	14,413	11,313	21,384
Swiss Market Index (SMI)	11,605,853	9,141,697	8,243,441	8,942,315	13,482,706
Swiss Market Index Mid-Cap (SMIM)	142,076	214,386	156,740	216,059	181,654
TA-25-Index	10	43			
Tecdax	115,937	109,249	80,485	90,248	203,962
Varianz-Futures auf den EURO STOXX 50 Index	1,683	1,697			
Total Futures	**996,487,896**	**916,533,113**	**962,201,303**	**987,761,500**	**1,217,635,185**
3-Month Euribor	278,361	337,164	89,500		100,003
All Options on Austrian Equities	513,706	398,383	382,695	255,359	559,998
All Options on Belgian Equities	565,356	682,907	497,785	454,324	309,027
All Options on Dutch Equities	10,123,724	9,966,922	7,033,679	5,150,348	6,552,069
All Options on Finnish Equities	11,001,476	14,285,048	24,308,008	18,161,501	24,569,269
All Options on French Equities	21,544,339	20,060,331	21,861,783	19,255,843	17,081,302
All Options on German Equities	89,548,522	82,968,214	99,551,563	119,585,110	156,521,894
All Options on Great Britain	260,699	294,190	224,736	107,168	121,109
All Options on Ireland	14,954	6,925	5,580	5,580	
All Options on Italian Equities	5,316,686	3,548,003	2,857,908	2,077,547	2,439,964
All Options on Russian Equities	187,557	125,092	69,585	90,211	44,789
All Options on Spanish Equities	6,280,385	6,065,820	4,681,837	4,958,061	2,160,580
All Options on Swedish Equities	5,263	1,021	714	827	1,500
All Options on Swiss Equities	41,045,258	38,002,420	41,338,189	44,817,876	64,969,435
ATX	28,249	7,418	11,278	20,044	23,338
ATX five	7,433	2,444	3,598	4,843	4,994
Bund Weekly - Week1 (OGB1)	272,071				
Bund Weekly - Week2 (OGB2)	214,920				
Bund Weekly - Week3 (OGB3)	124,112				
Bund Weekly - Week4 (OGB4)	35,159				
Bund Weekly - Week5 (OGB5)	62,748				
CECE EUR	750				
CS ETF (CH) on SMI	1				
Daily Futures auf TAIEX (OTX)	93,054	83,153			
Daily Futures auf TAIEX (OTX1)	34,521	22,976			
Daily Futures auf TAIEX (OTX2)	33,140	16,439			
Daily Futures auf TAIEX (OTX4)	31,097	25,568			
Daily Futures auf TAIEX (OTX5)	9,661	6,225			
DAX	42,130,864	39,792,092	42,288,248	51,558,088	67,616,997
DAX 1st Friday Weekly	707,439	981,896	974,314	571,327	603,610
DAX 2nd Friday Weekly	672,894	788,852	835,862	537,235	542,074

EUREX, Frankfurt, Germany (continued)

	2015	2014	2013	2012	2011
DAX 4th Friday Weekly	978,252	1,027,793	910,077	621,495	654,937
DAX 5th Friday Weekly	295,736	371,679	343,615	191,218	144,953
db x-trackers MSCI Emerg. Markets TRN	632				
DivDAX	201	8,792	10,990	760	
Euro STOXX 50 Index	299,881,600	241,254,907	225,105,846	280,610,954	369,241,952
Euro STOXX 50 Index - 1st Friday	4,313,199	4,595,091	3,593,745	1,750,970	792,380
Euro STOXX 50 Index - 2nd Friday	3,204,106	3,136,464	2,744,799	1,531,056	527,710
Euro STOXX 50 Index - 4th Friday	5,282,926	4,839,024	3,360,601	2,169,215	855,663
Euro STOXX 50 Index - 5th Friday	1,777,432	1,731,467	1,543,774	615,003	299,572
Euro Stoxx 50 Index Dividend	1,515,550	1,968,591	1,125,677	1,290,153	804,612
Euro Stoxx 600 Automobiles & Parts	240,192	217,780	129,041	146,946	33,677
Euro Stoxx 600 Banks	316,735	305,576	132,340	316,343	916,728
Euro Stoxx 600 Basic Resources	346,945	594,603	431,342	252,566	313,369
Euro Stoxx 600 Construction & Materials	6,641	11,013	60,879	177,681	9,535
Euro Stoxx 600 Financial Services	5,578	1,787	673		259
Euro Stoxx 600 Food & Beverage	12,585	14,558	5,363	10,028	8,070
Euro Stoxx 600 Healthcare	19,597	26,713	18,904	6,850	23,403
Euro Stoxx 600 Industrial Goods & Services	9,640	22,915	11,644	32,400	104,553
Euro Stoxx 600 Insurance	31,792	18,357	25,501	13,223	72,791
Euro Stoxx 600 Media	2,109	2,584	12,253		3,196
Euro Stoxx 600 Oil & Gas	309,696	159,504	73,256	24,659	163,125
Euro Stoxx 600 Personal & Household Goods	11,139	2,475	570	40	11,365
Euro Stoxx 600 Real Estate	600		960	895	
Euro Stoxx 600 Retail	556	8,662	16,933	3,726	12,747
Euro Stoxx 600 Technology	1	8,750	910	30	323
Euro Stoxx 600 Telecom	27,099	112,944	25,048	24,996	15,088
Euro Stoxx 600 Travel & Leisure	26,175	6,227	6,545	16,476	559
Euro Stoxx 600 Utilities	15,172	25,185	11,129	19,540	14,372
Euro Stoxx Automobiles & Parts	7,967	6,218	14,074	11,159	14,662
Euro Stoxx Banks	10,901,633	12,131,518	8,618,864	3,922,934	1,888,904
Euro Stoxx Banks 1st Friday	15,852	63,627			
Euro Stoxx Banks 2nd Friday	14,000	43,342			
Euro Stoxx Banks 4th Friday	31,793	7,104			
Euro Stoxx Banks 5th Friday	4,079	32,720			
Euro Stoxx Basic Resources	1,586	1,459	736		694
Euro Stoxx Chemicals	5,186	2,541	230		3,620
Euro Stoxx Construction & Materials	989	1,282	719		132
Euro Stoxx Financial Services	1,102	998	590		191
Euro Stoxx Food and Beverage	1,520		1,000	900	2,581
Euro Stoxx Healthcare	4,161	2,975	1,187	975	281
Euro Stoxx Industrial Goods & Services	1,738	1,002	3,537	800	24
Euro Stoxx Insurance	24,945	5,472	15,585	2,014	21,056
Euro Stoxx Oil & Gas	35,945	41,640	26,137	7,440	2,406
Euro Stoxx Personal & Household Goods	2,718		2,400		868
Euro Stoxx Select Dividend 30 Index	9,300	1,001			
Euro Stoxx Technology	5,588				80
Euro Stoxx Telecom	9,723	23,668	23,910	24,562	12,189
Euro Stoxx Travel & Leisure	255	2,698	151		577
Euro Stoxx Utilities	180,626	53,424	27,879	5,978	2,383
Euro-Bobl	14,979,787	8,242,904	14,790,234	11,378,443	16,188,346
Euro-Bund	45,385,172	33,679,659	35,220,103	39,924,387	38,154,098
Euro-Schatz	18,277,115	9,050,906	16,343,935	20,570,946	26,531,383
FX on EURCHF - European Style	2	3			
FX on EURGBP - European Style	13				
FX on EURUSD - European Style	12,895	3,871			
FX on GBPUSD - European Style	2,947	512			
FX on USDCHF - European Style	4,506	2,555			
Gold	484	613	9,311	13,664	14,543
iShares DAX® UCITS ETF (DE)	24,612				
iShares EURO STOXX50® UCITS ETF	16,002				
KOSPI 200	24,423,032	22,497,002	20,498,732	32,402,451	17,442,744
MDAX	11,292	19,352	10,145	6,066	44,866
MSCI EM (OMEF)	24,999				
MSCI EM (OMEN)	34,459	4,551			
MSCI Emerging Markets	83,844	75,816	21,681		
MSCI Emerging Markets Asia (OMEA)	4,155				
MSCI Emerging Markets EMEA	4,890				
MSCI Europe	19,500	34,866	130,178		
MSCI Europe OMEP	9,018	88,116			
MSCI World	52,530	25,730	16,154		
MSCI World (OMWN)	6,075				
OMX-Helsinki 25	25				
One year EURIBOR Mid-Curve	113,150	299,422			
RDX USD Index	567,629	996,854	1,081,541	542,989	
Stoxx Europe 50 Index	314	2,198	8,038	87,381	41,866

VOLUME - WORLDWIDE

EUREX, Frankfurt, Germany (continued)

	2015	2014	2013	2012	2011
Stoxx Europe 600	154,649	13,500	16,337	9,160	5,367
Stoxx Europe Mid 200	320	234,645	51,696	52,941	105,985
Stoxx Europe Small 200 Index	963				
Swiss Leader Index (SLI)	14,655	6,532	24,672	40,452	53,573
Swiss Market Index (SMI)	3,801,588	3,566,161	4,101,925	4,287,524	5,679,053
Swiss Market Index Mid-Cap (SMIM)	32,013	11,688	25,690	20,107	33,981
TecDAX	16,207	5,359	3,577	4,474	16,566
Three year EURIBOR Mid-Curve	45,000				
Two year EURIBOR Mid-Curve	375,000	304,000			
VSTOXX	6,633,704	2,986,319	2,010,663	1,437,759	553,463
Xetra-Gold	625	361	518	650	1,488
Total Options	**676,170,162**	**574,008,711**	**590,003,131**	**672,586,694**	**826,654,471**

Euronext Derivatives Market

	2015	2014	2013	2012	2011
AEX Mini	48,127	59,961	4,157		
AEX Stock Index (FTI)	10,657,589	9,458,794	9,038,280	10,476,310	12,602,311
AEX Weekly	406	38			
All Futures on Individual Equities	87,490	21,652	120,239,502	246,541,679	250,441,783
Bel 20 Index (BXF)	15,429	31,924	35,837	58,094	106,922
CAC 40	35,646,788	36,653,426	37,211,714	38,092,777	43,403,809
CAC 40 (WEEKLY)	526				
CAC 40 Dividend Index	88,106	207,561	15,700	13,382	20,643
CAC 40 Mini	14,973	23,082	1,491		
Corn	670,938	565,519	497,114	574,067	402,397
Euronext Southern European Banks Index	1	1			
FTSE EPRA Euro Zone	998	32	2,552	5,820	9,859
FTSE EPRA Europe	154,732	87,836	56,784	82,456	79,618
FTSEurofirst 80	1,402	1,610	47,891	51,577	52,345
Milling Wheat	9,073,162	8,444,694	6,471,781	7,472,845	5,687,888
Premium Milling Wheat No 3	3,040		117,266	135,037	162,683
PSI 20 Index	271,991	263,883	112,489	66,279	77,939
Rapeseed	2,143,032	1,775,676	1,864,450	1,973,468	1,908,310
Rapeseed Meal	19,171	155			
Rapeseed Oil	497	63			
Skimmed Milk Powder	38				9
Stock Dividend Futures	7,048				
Total Futures	**58,905,484**	**57,598,004**	**175,726,356**	**305,568,915**	**315,025,691**
AEX Daily	1,611,387	2,107,194			
AEX Mini	42,749	94,018			
AEX Weekly	1,659,125	2,066,600			
AEX-Index (AEX)	7,333,284	8,483,732	12,774,623	15,490,211	25,079,752
All Options on Individual Equities	60,094,108	66,791,184	98,697,280	112,840,693	150,562,241
Bel 20 (€10)	1,898	770	675	707	149
CAC 40 (€10)	3,348,106	4,427,108	4,400,084	4,996,392	5,281,378
Corn	92,099	82,086	57,348	38,789	43,794
Euro/US Dollar (EDX)	127,702	112,357	188,100	181,873	170,392
ISHARES EURO STOXX 50 UCITS ETF (DIST)	1,456				
ISHARES MSCI EMERGING MARKETS UCITS ETF	800				
ISHARES MSCI EUROPE UCITS ETF (DIST)	1,046				
ISHARES MSCI JAPAN EUR HEDGED UCITS ETF	48				
ISHARES MSCI WORLD UCITS ETF (DIST)	865				
ISHARES S&P 500 UCITS ETF (DIST)	1,699				
Milling Wheat	1,961,639	1,846,385	1,363,852	1,646,903	1,298,748
PREMIUM MILLING WHEAT NO 3	300		884	1,025	1,363
Rapeseed	331,888	176,618	290,353	443,698	408,554
Total Options	**76,610,199**	**86,460,872**	**117,773,659**	**135,642,845**	**182,865,548**

ICE Futures Canada (ICE), Canada

	2015	2014	2013	2012	2011
Barley	935	710	70	1,157	
Canola	5,559,469	5,553,922	5,491,687	4,870,261	4,653,153
Durum Wheat	10		5	234	
Total Futures	**5,491,767**	**4,872,500**	**4,653,582**	**4,121,060**	**3,406,632**
Canola 1 Month CSO	8,300	15,265	1,795		
Canola	151,319	106,438	194,733	166,660	68,375
Total Options	**159,619**	**121,703**	**196,528**	**166,660**	**68,375**

Hong Kong Futures Exchange (HKFE), Hong Kong

	2015	2014	2013	2012	2011
All Futures on Individual Equities	729,013	427,609	459,190	322,715	444,014
CES China 120 Index	27,427	40,283	50,213		
Hang Seng Index	21,239,775	17,067,247	19,580,330	20,353,069	23,085,833
HSCEI Dividend Point Index	205,269	240,572	156,496	184,786	53,054
H-Shares Index	33,379,310	21,984,297	20,871,257	15,923,813	15,003,870
HSI Dividend Point Index	9,573	15,658	11,214	20,793	11,196
HSI Volatility Index	464	475	978	1,526	
London Aluminium Mini Futures	11,554	1,644			
London Copper Mini Futures	27,388	4,318			
London Nickel Mini Futures	155				
London Tin Mini Futures	2				
London Zinc Mini Futures	16,654	2,828			
Mini Hang Seng Index	10,046,556	6,959,838	7,853,800	8,545,847	10,294,537
Mini H-Shares Index	7,506,543	3,429,393	2,252,621	1,560,515	1,845,116
One-Month Hibor	6		20	10	245
RMB Currency - USD/CNH	262,433	205,049	138,708	20,277	
Three-Month Hibor	90	35	2	150	414
Total Futures	**51,374,854**	**46,933,708**	**50,741,995**	**43,006,523**	**43,483,237**
All Options on Individual Equities	92,463,479	74,543,861	60,827,975	56,081,545	74,325,068
Flexible Hang Seng Index	5,300	36,621	9,197	14,183	9,260
Flexible H-shares Index	39,848		30,789	11,171	23,510
Hang Seng Index	7,515,466	7,518,710	8,601,509	9,230,145	10,667,426
H-shares Index	15,304,245	8,998,897	8,027,274	6,300,889	3,771,799
Mini Hang Seng Index	1,033,813	961,354	1,157,266	1,230,997	954,414
Total Options	**116,362,151**	**92,059,793**	**78,654,010**	**72,868,930**	**89,751,477**

ICE Futures Europe (ICE), United Kingdom

	2015	2014	2013	2012	2011
3-Month Euribor	110,151,762	127,427,642	238,493,786	178,762,097	241,950,875
3-Month Euroswiss	6,740,041	7,800,896	6,579,896	6,428,995	8,233,176
3-Month Short Sterling	146,337,942	149,357,479	144,279,092	114,915,025	115,586,702
All Futures on Individual Equities	61,752,480	97,858,715			
Belgian Power Futures	24,305	18,360			
CER Futures	79,766	200,254			
CFR South China Coal Futures	45	15			
Cocoa	6,430,848	5,671,277	5,125,146	4,106,182	4,079,975
Dutch Power	131,783	194,805			
Dutch TTF Gas	4,853,206	2,320,254			
ERIS Standard EUR 2 Year 0.00% Interest Rate Future	15				
ERIS Standard EUR 3 Year 0.25% Interest Rate Future	20				
ERIS Standard EUR 5 Year 0.50% Interest Rate Future	150				
ERIS Standard GBP 2 Year 1.00% Interest Rate Future	22				
ERIS Standard GBP 3 Year 1.25% Interest Rate Future	60				
ERIS Standard GBP 5 Year 1.50% Interest Rate Future	40				
ERU Futures	49	34,128	114,206	411,393	61,119
EUA Futures	5,195,957	7,008,526	7,260,390	6,465,262	5,444,050
EUA Phase 3 Daily	207,070	194,987			
EUA UK Auction	149,916	132,440			
EUAA Futures	5,732	1,630	1,450	230	
EUAA UK Auction	5,041	5,415			
Eurodollar	5,447	46,891			
FTSE 100 Declared Dividend	5,752	3,100			
FTSE 100 Dividend Index	368,186	659,120	941,252	692,288	447,151
FTSE 100 Equally Weighted TR Index	50,467	35,782			
FTSE 100 Index	33,170,416	33,522,718	33,529,120	32,619,662	39,283,942
FTSE 250 £2	288,889	233,513	46,872	57,439	81,345
gC Newcastle Coal	356,946	228,878	17,726	13,217	10,634
GCF Repo Mortgage Backed Securities Index	9,986				
GCF Repo US Treasury Index	175,709				
German Natural Gas Futures	1,215	2,234			
ICE Brent	183,853,174	160,425,461	159,093,303	147,385,858	132,045,563
ICE Gas Oil	63,239,874	52,800,084	63,964,827	63,503,591	65,774,151
ICE Global Oil Products	30,761,725	21,509,940	15,218,162	2,727,003	
ICE Heating Oil	4,244,432	4,502,749	4,147,790	2,571,293	876,937
ICE Natural Gas	11,772,115	10,600,335	3,057,320	3,114,820	2,788,240
ICE NYH (RBOB) Gasoline (Monthly)	5,807,503	5,006,982	4,094,627	2,100,786	664,784
ICE Richards Bay Coal	64,850	85,481	15,793	29,299	30,281
ICE Rotterdam Coal	742,948	523,591	34,342	64,101	40,976
ICE UK Electricity Futures Peak (1MWh)	15,225	2,015			
ICE WTI Crude	39,802,954	31,600,959	36,106,788	33,142,089	51,097,818
Italian PSV Natural Gas Futures	245				
Long Gilt	47,917,051	44,582,727	42,299,274	37,777,306	34,362,932
Medium Gilt	39,632	29,207	40,030	43,146	36,307
Mortgage Backed DTCC GCF Repo Index Futures	7,580	19,853	1,272,128	864,089	766,349
MSCI AC Asia Pacific Ex Japan Futures	42,442				

ICE Futures Europe (ICE), United Kingdom (continued)

	2015	2014	2013	2012	2011
MSCI AC Far East ex Japan Index Future	7,892				
MSCI All Countries Asia Ex Japan Index Futures	221,987				
MSCI Brazil Index Future	17,369				
MSCI BRIC Index Future	58				
MSCI Canada Index Futures	605				
MSCI Canada Net TR EUR Index Future	592				
MSCI EAFE Index Future	2,712				
MSCI EM Asia Index Future	9,908				
MSCI EM EMEA Index Future	124				
MSCI EM Lat Am Index Future	14,474				
MSCI Emerging Markets (EM) Index Future	560,936				
MSCI Emerging Markets Net TR EUR Index Future	83,436				
MSCI Europe Consumer Disc NTR EUR Index Future	7,235				
MSCI Europe Consumer Stap NTR EUR Index Futures	850				
MSCI Europe Ex UK Index Futures	3,647				
MSCI Europe Financials NTR EUR Index Future	6,150				
MSCI Europe Index Future	232,439				
MSCI Europe Materials NTR EUR Index	2,810				
MSCI Europe Net Total Return EUR Index Future	316,660		111,878	131,237	
MSCI Hong Kong Index Future	2,323				
MSCI India Index Futures	36,018				
MSCI India Index Futures (100 Point)	38,639				
MSCI Japan Index Futures	254				
MSCI KOKUSAI Net Total Return Index Futures (JPY)	45,199				
MSCI KOKUSAI Net TR USD Index Future	2,207				
MSCI Mexico Index Future	5,925				
MSCI Pacific ex Japan Index Futures	221,468				
MSCI USA Equal Weighted NTR USD Index Future	38,310				
MSCI USA Index Futures	31,547				
MSCI USA Net TR EUR Index Future	1,271				
MSCI World Consumer Disc NTR USD Index Futures	18,744				
MSCI World Consumer Stap NTR USD Index Futures	7,089				
MSCI World Energy Net TR USD Index Futures	9,261				
MSCI World Financials Net TR USD Index Futures	21,369				
MSCI World Health Care Net TR USD Index Futures	7,389				
MSCI World Index Future	645,825				
MSCI World Industrials Net TR USD Index Futures	979				
MSCI World IT Net TR USD Index Futures	12,835				
MSCI World Materials Net TR USD Index Futures	1,654				
MSCI World Min Volatility NTR USD Index	1,136				
MSCI World Net Total Return EUR Index Future	351,876				
MSCI World Telecom Net TR USD Index Futures	6,562				
MSCI World Utilities Net TR USD Index Futures	6,324				
Robusta Coffee - 10 Tonne	3,982,365	3,707,464	4,075,212	3,104,053	3,502,508
Russell UK MID 150 NTR Index	21,667	2,246			
Short Gilt	85,977	109,645	107,137	268,635	432,744
Swapnote € - 10 Yr	99,151	131,654	124,012	150,409	77,825
Swapnote € - 2 Yr	263,741	424,292	433,411	376,091	357,849
Swapnote € - 5 Yr	213,436	324,589	371,687	283,872	220,966
UK Feed Wheat	123,284	152,373			
Ultra Long Gilt	11,622	80,596			
US Coal Futures (1,000 tons)	1,575	11,574			
US Treasury DTCC GCF Repo Index Futures (Monthly)	98,083	863,027			
White Sugar	2,340,302	2,023,273	2,049,442	1,852,267	1,497,216
Total Futures	**775,056,304**	**775,279,517**	**778,296,337**	**651,896,083**	**715,820,168**
3 Month Euribor	15,984,090	20,455,410	50,888,649	70,671,111	126,535,338
3 Month Euribor 1 Year Mid Curve	6,234,485	8,565,948	29,825,751	10,504,341	16,617,712
3 Month Euribor 2 Year Mid Curve	7,157,550	7,263,456	24,345,916	8,445,744	131,056
3 Month Euribor 3 Year Mid Curve	2,492,075	3,309,290	13,409,662	3,089,075	
3 Month Sterling	15,542,252	21,352,762	9,916,727	8,982,932	21,575,685
3 Month Sterling 2 Year Mid Curve	3,135,867	7,540,691	7,064,627	4,441,041	94,370
3 Month Sterling 3 Year Mid Curve	177,470	542,504	480,911	33,800	
3 Month Sterling 4 Year Mid Curve	24,337	2			
3 Month Sterling Mid Curve	6,627,443	15,161,256	5,541,772	5,381,200	11,784,839
All Options on Individual Equities	25,911,090	26,367,076			
Cocoa	1,883,865	1,733,250	1,048,269	783,694	79,238
Dutch TTF Gas	339,080	105,240	13,560	3,600	
EUA	433,897	702,117	499,001	735,351	700,929
FTSE 100 Euro FLEX Index	21,418	704,914			
FTSE 100 (ESX)	16,804,267	19,928,232	23,427,928	17,146,155	20,341,926
FTSE 250 Index FLEX	6,010	9,180			
gC Newcastle Coal	105,550	38,505			
ICE Brent Crude Oil	13,594,212	13,285,768	9,675,876	8,908,862	2,191,733
ICE Gasoil	279,438	607,747	617,993	568,594	407,827
ICE Global Oil Products	1,668,712	3,473,601	2,191,790	623,323	

ICE Futures Europe (ICE), United Kingdom (continued)

	2015	2014	2013	2012	2011
ICE Natural Gas	2,032,675	1,336,920	543,665	530,090	204,195
ICE Richards Bay Coal	4,800	21,075			1,470
ICE Rotterdam Coal	559,574	459,801	11,484	24,084	1,560
ICE WTI Crude	4,942,451	3,998,924	3,535,888	1,959,493	829,972
Robusta Coffee 10 Tonne	633,806	742,481	877,076	770,343	898,109
UK Feed Wheat	1,583	3,673			
White Sugar	5,650	2,942	1,672	11,824	17,624
Total Options	**126,603,647**	**157,739,517**	**185,490,968**	**144,815,092**	**203,077,119**

Indonesia Commodity & Derivatives Exchange, Indonesia

	2015	2014	2013	2012	2011
Gold (GR)	117,276	66,707	84,477	6,443	12,873
Gold (ID)	1,451	949	606	4,867	7,063
Gold (UD)	295				
Olein	383	588	1,963	4,375	1,542
Palm Oil	439,635	603,168	795,296	817,123	771,981
PAMP Gold (GRID) (IDR)	2,040	3,578			
PAMP Gold (GUD) (UDS)	1,287	1,473			
Tin	13,496	11,373	3,658		
UBSG	33				
Total Futures	**575,896**	**691,238**	**934,685**	**946,828**	**872,825**

Japan Exchange, Japan

	2015	2014	2013	2012	2011
10 Year Japan Government Bond	8,677,576	8,791,553	9,053,623	8,769,717	6,802,032
CNX Nifty Index	3,950	1,130			
JPX-Nikkei Index 400 Futures	10,474,332	1,606,338			
Mini 10 Year Japan Government Bond	40,562	21,171	17,831	32,065	7,734
Mini-TOPIX Futures	4,314,181	4,743,111	3,156,452	2,148,039	621,569
Nikkei 225	27,678,234	25,917,773	30,907,691	19,523,347	19,294,064
Nikkei 225 Dividend Index	6,272	7,840	111,644	123,512	61,050
Nikkei 225 Mini	247,159,359	199,121,967	233,860,478	130,443,680	117,905,210
Nikkei VI Futures	218,280	206,536	38,496	12,959	
OSE DJIA	74,958	70,190	26,816	19,154	
REIT Index Futures	175,450	132,531	74,612	60,388	51,457
SL-JGB 20 Year Japan Government Bond	2,978	5,041			
TOPIX	22,303,956	20,877,250	22,714,121	15,192,439	14,608,165
TOPIX Banks Index	22,604	28,700	16,398	3,500	
TOPIX Core30	4,772	3,827	8,383	10,150	91,715
Total Futures	**321,157,464**	**263,257,676**	**305,644,874**	**182,585,710**	**169,995,408**
10 Year Japan Government Bond	1,142,738	1,133,723	1,692,752	2,283,839	1,853,672
All Options on Individual Equities (Combined)	834,886	1,062,389	22,978	120,545	1,231,796
Nikkei 225	37,806,896	43,958,283	57,269,727	48,763,723	45,192,519
Nikkei 225 Weekly	188,422				
TOPIX Index	329,529	320,313	386,231	22,683	21,342
Total Options	**40,302,471**	**46,474,708**	**60,501,046**	**51,624,392**	**48,900,485**

London Metal Exchange (LME), United Kingdom

	2015	2014	2013	2012	2011
Aluminium	59,880,649	65,439,689	63,767,903	59,123,583	59,558,330
Aluminium Alloy	217,503	275,957	521,980	606,102	610,935
Cobalt	8,668	12,162	13,827	13,291	6,578
Copper - Grade A	38,557,831	38,811,609	40,486,017	35,874,789	34,537,310
Molybdenum	356	382	512	461	513
North American Special Aluminum Alloy (NASAAC)	540,645	770,651	573,770	603,378	699,863
Primary Nickel	19,959,729	18,079,099	13,678,490	11,164,449	8,056,421
Special High Grade Zinc	28,751,185	30,323,897	30,270,370	29,559,338	21,984,302
Standard Lead	12,522,608	12,872,940	12,931,067	14,248,937	10,921,882
Steel Mediterranean Billet	28	1,404	71,752	144,724	219,163
Tin	1,463,139	2,111,938	2,061,899	1,846,814	1,891,633
Total Futures	**161,902,341**	**168,712,316**	**164,384,521**	**153,201,377**	**138,487,658**
Copper - Grade A	2,485,153	2,003,739	2,408,984	2,605,512	3,371,191
Copper Grade A TAPOs	5,625	19,689	50,219	16,649	24,309
High Grade Primary Aluminum	2,608,985	3,271,338	2,681,694	2,424,466	3,218,299
Lead TAPOs	1,552	852	6,920	4,764	6,806
Nickel TAPOs	13,643	43,712	7,250	3,157	2,091
North American Special Aluminum Alloy (NASAAC)	3,210	7,640	370	1,175	4,178
North American Special Aluminum Alloy (NASAAC)	2,500	750			
Primary Aluminium TAPOs	51,416	108,818	140,542	45,361	44,196
Primary Nickel	726,373	1,240,163	285,039	178,844	233,837
Special High Grade Zinc	1,284,521	1,453,349	826,821	952,958	913,771
Special High Grade Zinc TAPOs	1,333	61,845	64,234	11,239	74,938
Standard Lead	447,282	220,491		260,265	189,831
Tin	6,250	7,010	13,227	14,014	26,114
Total Options	**7,637,843**	**8,439,396**	**6,485,300**	**6,518,404**	**8,109,887**

VOLUME - WORLDWIDE

Korea Futures Exchange (KFE), Korea

	2015	2014	2013	2012	2011
10 Year Treasury Bond	11,794,685	9,970,610	11,992,729	13,045,101	3,503,677
3 Year Treasury Bond	25,997,164	21,519,203	29,291,859	29,728,075	34,140,210
All Futures on Individual Equities	165,104,827	96,365,483	95,870,157	100,490,960	59,966,166
Euro	970,127	759,008	306,023	93,939	205,395
Japanese yen	374,364	370,112	907,501	862,806	803,734
KOSDAQ 150 Futures	47,775				
KOSPI 200	39,515,553	38,056,972	49,970,933	62,430,640	87,274,461
Mini Gold	34,703	10,723	34,858	22,644	182,278
Mini KOSPI 200 Futures	2,276,951				
US Dollar	52,508,299	48,663,722	51,814,466	53,549,300	70,212,467
Yuan	1,735				
Total Futures	**298,626,183**	**215,715,833**	**240,188,609**	**260,223,478**	**256,294,408**
All Options on Individual Equities	719,582	28,962			
KOSPI 200	**488,009,055**	**462,010,885**	**580,460,364**	**1,575,394,249**	**3,671,662,258**
Mini KOSPI 200	**7,580,506**				
Total Options	**580,476,012**	**1,575,394,249**	**3,671,662,258**	**3,525,910,648**	**2,920,991,635**

Malaysia Derivatives Exchange, Malaysia

	2015	2014	2013	2012	2011
3 Month Klibor (FKB3)	1,271	13,150	16,791	50,946	101,979
5 Year Malaysian Government Securities (FMG5)	3,700				
Crude Palm Oil (FCPO)	10,984,549	10,088,131	7,966,096	7,443,143	5,871,587
Gold	39,974	111,844	24,253		
KLSE Composite Index (FKLI)	3,023,971	2,094,807	2,607,429	2,096,493	2,489,204
RBD Palm Olein (FPOL)	60	656			
Total Futures	**14,053,525**	**12,308,588**	**10,614,569**	**9,590,582**	**8,462,770**
Crude Palm Oil (OCPO)	2,300	714	2,020	821	
KLSE Composite Index (OKLI)	4,702	4,188	5,040	5,493	16
Total Options	**7,002**	**4,902**	**7,060**	**6,314**	**16**

MEFF Renta Variable (RV), Spain

	2015	2014	2013	2012	2011
10 Year Notional Bond (New)	8,012	5,347	13,667	45,238	
All Futures on Individual Equities	10,054,830	13,119,374	14,927,659	21,220,876	27,578,789
Ibex 35	7,384,896	6,930,104	5,578,607	4,745,067	5,281,218
Ibex 35 Dividend Impact	32,499	23,939	3,520	2,162	3,154
Mini Ibex 35	3,181,287	3,034,973	1,987,362	2,424,766	3,099,647
Single Stock Dividend Futures Plus	1,152				
Stock Dividend	291,688	236,151	66,650	25,000	
Total Futures	**20,954,364**	**23,349,888**	**22,577,465**	**28,463,109**	**35,962,808**
All Options on Individual Equities	21,420,685	25,635,035	26,944,611	34,507,360	29,410,340
IBEX 35 Plus Index	5,444,156	7,319,962	5,172,426	4,206,058	2,198,967
Total Options	**26,864,841**	**32,954,997**	**32,117,037**	**38,713,418**	**31,609,307**

Mercado a Termino de Buenos Aires (MATBA), Argentina

	2015	2014	2013	2012	2011
Barley	5	563	3,589	5,511	
Chicago Corn	3,719	5,936	5,594	950	
Chicago Soybean	5,314	10,664	10,365	2,920	
Chicago Wheat	2,880	5,387	5,352	596	
Corn	35,335	31,988	31,530	44,788	17,114
Sorghum	40	190	556	208	293
Soybean	153,351	128,156	142,322	186,399	116,719
Soybean 30 ton	10		4	301	
Sunflower	10	68	67	106	32
Wheat	14,699	18,749	19,536	29,406	22,810
Total Futures	**215,363**	**201,701**	**218,915**	**271,188**	**156,968**
Chicago Corn	4				
Chicago Soybean	8	484	1,147	4	
Corn	4,297	5,131	2,751	2,335	2,415
Soybean	24,566	26,348	27,954	66,788	45,431
Wheat	1,080	3,095	4,646	552	539
Total Options	**29,955**	**35,058**	**36,620**	**71,877**	**48,387**

Metropolitan Stock Exchange, India

	2015	2014	2013	2012	2011
EUR/Indian Rupee	2,154,619	4,509,383	14,409,559	10,496,445	29,403,759
GBP/Indian Rupee	1,699,872	5,121,278	9,027,201	4,414,631	7,305,618
JPY/Indian Rupee	570,706	2,157,102	9,706,316	4,624,969	5,859,837
US Dollar/Indian Rupee	53,568,902	112,458,175	496,230,881	551,326,121	807,559,846
Total Futures	**57,994,099**	**124,245,938**	**529,373,957**	**570,862,166**	**850,129,060**

Moscow Interbank Currency Exchange (MICEX), Russia

	2015	2014	2013	2012	2011
10 Year Federal Bond issued by Russian Federation	445,441	2,458,939	6,535,538	192,374	
15 Year Federal Bond issued by Russian Federation	988,591	3,496,494	4,382,830		
2-year Russian Federation Government Bond Futures	530,919	1,039,762	1,629,490	3,978,269	2,530,693
3 Month Moscow MosPrime Rate	48	1,498	42,743	16,927	141,858
4-year Russian Federation Government Bond Futures	417,033	1,439,202	2,668,125	6,326,067	4,645,995
6-year Russian Federation Government Bond Futures	228,409	626,275	2,152,683	10,741,890	159,000
All Futures on Individual Equities	307,107,435	343,151,338	302,635,507	242,630,281	355,374,012
AUD/USD Exchange Rate	486,061	569,862	2,138,081	883,238	1,228,766
Brent Oil	111,415,185	7,084,451	18,170,809	11,952,101	18,707,384
CNY/RUB Exchange Rate	28,158				
Copper	1,160	3,125	68,722	68,869	118,593
EUR/RUB	17,410,092	20,982,195	8,210,577	1,980,420	1,736,514
EUR/USD	59,826,374	26,179,646	66,436,523	33,632,175	45,657,240
FTSE/JSE Top 40	207	16	158	346	
GBP/USD Exchange Rate	685,154	1,892,645	4,370,140	471,425	1,361,481
Gold	10,784,533	11,519,763	15,892,846	8,156,949	13,018,359
Hang Seng Index	222	37	651	3,899	
IBOVESPA	224	248	1,312	8,317	
MICEX Index	3,995,588	1,728,304	1,511,962	1,045,857	663,411
MICEX Index (mini)	6,992,354				
Palladium	3,578	262	6,988	18,224	10,871
Platinum	128,311	97,461	144,356	211,431	379,285
Refined Silver	777,933	1,273,493	1,833,579	1,359,708	3,923,342
RTS Index	184,124,166	243,320,038	266,131,127	321,031,540	377,845,640
RTS Standard Index	76	82	136,796	709,342	1,197,521
Ruble Overnight Index Average (RUONIA)	124	16	2,705	1,800	7,953
Russian Eurobonds	10,705	87,676			
Russian Market Volatility	22,532	1,070			
Russian Volatility Index	18	658	3,641	12,719	47,244
Sensex Index	92	69	37	10	
Sugar (cash settled - SA)	821	66		50,090	605,513
US Dollar/Russian Ruble	903,374,140	656,476,373	373,466,315	373,108,731	206,820,695
USD/CAD exchange rate	128,779				
USD/CHF Exchange Rate	289,536	304,197	336,814		
USD/JPY Exchange Rate	777,702	763,907	1,471,045		
USD/TRY exchange rate	30,331				
USD/UAH Exchange Rate	7,806	28,290	2,950		
Total Futures	**1,611,019,838**	**1,324,551,013**	**1,080,609,808**	**1,019,741,152**	**1,054,106,253**
All Options on Individual Equities	5,866,674	4,059,807	7,414,191	5,865,454	8,411,748
Brent Crude Oil	126,593	47,493	37,901	33,971	45,911
EUR/RUB	61,665	103,972	28,721	750	
EUR/USD	22,394	99,915	32,742	43,041	24,332
Futures-style option on Transneft futures contract	1,553				
Gold	36,367	153,854	149,251	156,569	139,284
MICEX Index	173,230	64,512	78,664	41,425	6,195
MICEX Index (mini)	1,095,588				
Platinum	262	6,228	5,003	34,139	20,453
Refined Silver	7,572	10,785	17,091	47,559	40,481
RTS Index	18,650,221	40,884,039	42,233,069	33,915,936	35,389,828
USD/RUB	22,379,627	43,240,578	3,348,701	904,498	
Total Options	**48,421,746**	**88,671,183**	**53,867,450**	**42,094,752**	**44,931,599**

Mexican Derivatives Exchange (MEXDER), Mexico

	2015	2014	2013	2012	2011
10 Year Interest Rate Swap (Centrally Cleared)	1,200	1,600	3,200	3,860	6,434
All Futures on Individual Equities	19,252	38,550	66,870	35,839	63,711
DC18 Bond	33,200				
DC24 Bond	1,127,072	434,712			
IPC Stock Index	1,095,845	976,682	952,165	1,060,760	1,231,048
M10 Bond	204	74,454	383,867	1,686,335	2,917,800
M3 Bond	25,000	282,700	317,000	272,824	197,623
M30 Bond	22,630	29,422	229,480	327,252	396,078
Mexican Peso/Euro	74,685	69,394	24,919	14,411	24,397
Mexican Peso/US Dollar	7,949,772	19,855,606	13,535,162	9,827,086	7,189,846
Mini IPC Stock Index	431,151	93,179			
MY31 Bond	42,400	85,007			
NV42 Bond	32,850				
TIIE 28	5,693,368	7,030,428	9,609,597	25,408,966	26,906,390
Total Futures	**16,548,629**	**29,230,798**	**26,578,329**	**41,717,187**	**46,246,427**
All Options on Individual Equities	257,524	524,309	701,376	477,565	446,547
IPC Stock Index	92,938	53,822	54,853	42,653	65,631
Mexican Peso/US Dollar	74,995	27,756	18,075	1,673	422
Total Options	**439,059**	**683,174**	**779,903**	**913,471**	**512,602**

59T

VOLUME - WORLDWIDE

Montreal Exchange (ME), Canada

	2015	2014	2013	2012	2011
10 Year Government of Canada Bond (CGB)	17,913,516	14,956,206	13,824,451	9,951,321	7,788,218
2 Year Government of Canada Bond Futures (CGZ)	2,840	14,269	79,349	71,699	59,650
5 Year Canadian Gov't Bond (CGF)	176,269	301,026	276,610	153,598	105,580
Bankers Acceptance 3 Months (BAX)	21,746,698	24,640,229	22,578,143	20,804,167	20,865,769
FTSE Emerging Markets Index Futures (EMF)	2,626	3,308			
Gold Index (SXA)	20				
S&P/TSX 60 Index Mini Futures (SXM)	45,867	98,767	100,194	132,549	100,554
S&P/TSX 60 Index Standard Futures (SXF)	5,474,698	4,405,739	3,994,992	3,826,976	4,228,938
S&P/TSX Capped Energy Index (SXY)	189				
S&P/TSX Capped Utilities Index (SXU)	1,629				
S&P/TSX Composite Index Banks (Industry Group)	3,950				
S&P/TSX Composite Index Mini (SCF)	115	597	406	539	232
Total Futures	**45,368,417**	**44,420,141**	**40,854,145**	**34,940,999**	**33,148,941**
All Options on Individual Equities	21,456,144	20,674,540	21,335,465	24,200,766	24,211,857
ETFs	8,719,474	4,064,224	2,905,949	4,405,451	
10 Year Government of Canada Bond Futures (OGB)	3,677	5,130	4,669	4,767	8,775
Bankers Acceptance Futures 3 Months (OBX)	580,007	392,661	588,279	493,047	635,046
US Dollar (USX)	2,491	2,170	6,931	5,235	16,947
S&P Canada 60 Index (SXO) (incl. LEAPS)	541,759	428,590	511,384	314,631	93,151
S&P/TSX Composite Index Banks (Industry Group)	202				
Total Options	**31,303,754**	**25,567,315**	**25,352,677**	**29,423,897**	**28,832,465**

National Stock Exchange of India

	2015	2014	2013	2012	2011
All Futures on Individual Equities	257,370,023	211,004,887	157,885,578	153,122,207	160,878,260
Bank Nifty Index	36,040,824	30,415,661	26,253,848	21,741,473	17,131,900
CNX INFRA	91	92	144	389	1,072
CNX IT Index	130,845	174,048	63,462	43,015	71,672
CNX Nifty Index	128,656,346	74,236,766	74,863,943	80,061,861	123,144,880
CNX PSE	76	67	277	230	984
DIJA Index	96,400	123,089	195,252	408,998	230,828
EUR/Indian Rupee	18,041,680	12,482,953	16,984,993	5,770,205	18,065,186
FTSE 100	305	2,545	22,939	302,162	
GBP/Indian Rupee	12,977,847	11,654,280	10,259,534	2,591,566	5,569,204
INDIA VIX	474	28,428			
JPY/Indian Rupee	5,556,373	4,856,701	9,715,049	2,689,841	5,411,351
Nifty Midcap 50 Index	5,788	7,195	19,449	5,723	2,935
S&P 500 Index	74,438	65,659	81,970	257,093	135,323
US Dollar/Indian Rupee	358,801,689	294,069,368	566,399,936	620,215,043	697,825,411
Total Futures	**817,753,199**	**639,121,739**	**862,994,796**	**896,681,187**	**1,043,463,263**
All Options on Individual Equities	104,454,088	85,404,647	90,190,480	57,221,005	33,172,963
Bank Nifty Index	127,694,954	84,347,528	55,120,938	15,369,585	1,867,147
CNX IT Index	1,365	190	735	834	873
CNX Nifty Index	1,765,858,934	972,738,636	874,835,809	803,086,926	868,684,582
S&P 500 Index	8	110	479	12,815	31,023
Total Options	**2,214,139,585**	**1,241,241,993**	**1,272,642,661**	**1,113,812,300**	**1,156,903,387**

Nasdaq Exchanges Nordic Markets

	2015	2014	2013	2012	2011
10 Year Swedish Government Bond Forward (R10)	1,000,106	1,005,501	1,331,975	1,536,138	1,339,726
10 Year Swedish Government Bond Future (SGB10H)	52,429				
10 Year Swedish Government Bond Future (SGB10Z)	22				
2 Year Nordea Hypotek Bond Forward (NBHYP2)	91,887	146,131	188,646	218,544	175,208
2 Year Nordea Hypotek Bond Future (NDH2YH)	12,736				
2 Year Spintab Bond Foward (SPA2)	118,653	146,986	168,729	217,141	252,565
2 Year Spintab Bond Future (SWH2YH)	21,339				
2 Year Stadshypotek Bond Forward (ST2)	347,003	359,372	527,279	575,666	275,194
2 Year Stadshypotek Bond Future (STH2YH)	23,524				
2 Year Stadshypotek Bond Future (STH2YZ)	76				
2 Year Swedish Government Bond Forward (R2)	924,824	1,391,495	1,842,401	1,752,451	2,303,865
2 Year Swedish Government Bond Future (SGB2YH)	40,224				
5 Year Nordea Hypotek Bond Forward (NBHYP5)	107,492	142,460			
5 Year Nordea Hypotek Bond Future (NDH5YH)	10,396		124,877	99,917	216,357
5 Year SBC Bond Forward (SB5)	3,000				
5 Year SBC Bond Future (SCBC5H)	1,575				
5 Year Spintab Bond Foward (SPA5)	127,300	155,088	195,582	228,715	250,373
5 Year Spintab Bond Future (SWH5YH)	7,381				
5 Year Stadshypotek Bond Forward (ST5)	424,440	368,990	402,211	356,112	298,374
5 Year Stadshypotek Bond Future (STH5YH)	24,840				
5 Year Swedish Government Bond Forward (R5)	1,087,862	1,223,379	1,480,964	1,161,729	1,445,999
5 Year Swedish Government Bond Future (SGB5YH)	89,456				

Nasdaq Exchanges Nordic Markets (continued)

	2015	2014	2013	2012	2011
5 Year Swedish Government Bond Future (SGB5YZ)	3				
All Futures on Individual Equities	4,426,022	2,523,612	3,613,984	1,979,581	4,012,218
Danish Mortgage Bond Futures (20MBFZ)	950		2,950		
Danish Mortgage Bond Futures (3MBFZ)	100		9,700		
Danish Mortgage Bond Futures (3YMBFZ)	600		5,900		
Mortgage Bond Future (20MBFU)	400		2,500		
Mortgage Bond Future (3MBFH)	900	4,859	2,100		
Mortgage Bond Future (3MBFM)	3,450	1,312			
Mortgage Bond Future (3MBFU)	2,200		8,625		
Mortgage Bond Future (3YMBFH)	4,203	4,400	400		
Mortgage Bond Future (3YMBFM)	1,502	2,000			
Mortgage Bond Future (3YMBFU)	1,900				
NIBOR-FRA	412,503	580,820	342,500	511,600	638,600
OMX (Index)	39,853,871	32,935,776	30,898,519	32,637,547	37,462,177
Policy Rate (RIBA)	3,233,280	2,728,500	5,348,960	6,495,914	4,680,389
Stadshypotek Bond Forward (ST1576)	9,053				
STIBOR-FRA	8,444,508	9,544,148	15,394,749	19,118,953	19,872,815
Total Futures	**60,912,010**	**53,265,679**	**61,926,001**	**67,008,230**	**73,420,598**
10 Year Swedish Government Bond Forward (R10)	2,500	2,750	2,750	7,800	50
All Options on Individual Equities	29,078,684	29,058,264	27,476,014	27,500,926	29,836,598
NIBOR-FRA	36,000		61,000	28,000	32,500
OMX Index Options	9,911,654	9,276,282	7,987,697	9,625,030	12,485,788
STIBOR-FRA	50,000		888,000	707,500	1,312,800
Total Options	**39,078,838**	**38,533,796**	**36,461,961**	**37,896,006**	**43,686,686**

Rosario Futures Exchange (ROFEX), Argentina

	2015	2014	2013	2012	2011
Chicago Corn	86,693	43,981	76,601	16,324	
Chicago Soybean	140,560	80,624	140,041	73,192	4,698
Corn	2,031	1,341	7,616	4,663	4,635
Euro (EC)	250	1,600	122,714	112,087	132,020
Gold	19,446	17,117	68,023	63,891	139,207
Goverment Bonds - BODEN 15	31,563	72,936			
Goverment Bonds - BONAD 2016	1,555				
Goverment Bonds - BONAR 2024	17,798	3,922			
Goverment Bonds - BONAR X	22,102	43,219			
Goverment Bonds - DICA	304				
Merval Stock Index	5,500				
Oil Crude	33,244	34,168	18,198	18,664	9,928
Rosafe Soybean Index (ISR)	14,693	20,484	125,746	212,783	227,596
Soybeans	56,079	76,161	119,325	83,430	68,583
TVPP	110	39,000	72,535	21,045	
US Dollar	73,243,271	64,700,492	50,360,076	50,359,614	54,373,381
Wheat	1,460	1,785	4,551	5,881	3,074
Total Futures	**73,676,659**	**65,136,830**	**51,115,426**	**50,971,574**	**54,967,681**
Chicago Corn	15,921	15,145	4,318		
Chicago Soybeans	20,907	27,743	7,192	2,366	
Gold	8,280		2,000	51,504	2,444
Rosafe Soybean Index (ISR)	6,844	5,614	31,582	29,489	25,755
US Dollar (DLR)	142,305	2,540	16,032	10,872	4,048
Total Options	**194,257**	**51,102**	**61,124**	**99,653**	**32,360**

Shanghai Metal Exchange, China

	2015	2014	2013	2012	2011
Aluminum	22,900,691	13,926,276	3,305,575	3,942,680	9,953,918
Bitumen	32,397,823	650,169	3,134,301		
Copper	88,318,558	70,510,306	64,295,856	57,284,835	48,961,130
Fuel Oil	3,875	1,469	1,039	9,132	1,971,141
Gold	25,317,200	23,865,406	20,087,824	5,916,745	7,221,758
Hot Rolled Coil	2,012,366	1,255,424			
Lead	1,310,106	1,457,822	172,759	68,646	293,280
Nickel	63,590,118				
Rubber	83,067,547	88,631,586	72,438,058	75,176,266	104,286,399
Silver	144,786,451	193,487,650	173,222,611	21,264,954	
Steel Rebar	541,035,860	408,078,103	293,728,929	180,562,480	81,884,789
Tin	515,789				
Wire Rod	327	665	3,862	2,717	3,242
Zinc	45,237,435	40,429,347	12,083,166	21,100,924	53,663,483
Total Futures	**1,050,494,146**	**842,294,223**	**642,473,980**	**365,329,379**	**308,239,140**

VOLUME - WORLDWIDE

Singapore Exchange (SGX), Singapore

	2015	2014	2013	2012	2011
Euroyen Tibor	107	9	10,221	25,826	59,250
FTSE China A50 Index	95,845,784	41,346,887	21,906,479	10,022,496	3,071,428
Mini Japanese Government Bond	703,059	702,718	862,112	1,025,937	759,703
Mini Nikkei 225	8,168	5,709	12,080	6,124	68,298
MSCI India Index	491,130	2,488	82		
MSCI Indonesia Index	285,954	251,331	344,691	59,947	
MSCI Malaysia Index	1,601				
MSCI PSE Philippines Index	259	85	123		
MSCI Singapore Index	4,207,914	3,167,077	3,732,386	4,027,281	4,358,862
MSCI Taiwan Index	16,719,529	17,216,807	18,357,967	17,183,604	17,624,091
MSCI Thailand Index	3,936	4,298	1,266		
Nikkei 225 Index	25,542,958	27,179,349	39,087,816	27,994,913	29,022,284
Nikkei Stock Average Dividend Point Index	93,792	115,374	159,223	152,554	62,653
RSS3	61,233	35,490	17,267	13,196	22,454
SGX AUD/JPY	305	8,342	1,803		
SGX AUD/USD	192	3,781	1,202		
SGX CNX Nifty Index	21,434,975	18,356,984	16,079,671	14,719,166	14,678,520
SGX CNY/USD	3,976	1,370			
SGX EUR/CNH	60				
SGX INR/USD	3,832,462	597,738	5,819		
SGX KRW/USD	30,120	4,742	102		
SGX SGD/CNH	50				
SGX USD/CNH	247,065	29,824			
SGX USD/JPY (Standard)	321	2,022			
SGX USD/JPY (Titan)	78	112			
SGX USD/SGD	88,221	30,221	2,184		
Straits Times Index	295	148	253	570	229
TSR20 (FOB)	593,620	454,300	328,994	242,619	205,439
TWD_USD FX Futures	5				
USD Nikkei 225	3,674	394	3,601	1,341	2,695
Total Futures	**170,200,843**	**109,517,621**	**100,915,464**	**75,482,509**	**70,028,574**
MSCI Singapore Index	11,295	350		1,910	9,397
MSCI Taiwan Index	18,328	29,107	26,167	9,352	10,695
Nikkei 225 Index	5,474,250	7,744,469	10,184,676	4,393,629	2,070,984
SGX S&P CNX Nifty Index	246,677	144,204	290,588	323,217	
Total Options	**5,750,550**	**7,918,130**	**10,501,431**	**4,728,108**	**2,091,076**

Taiwan Futures Exchange, Taiwan

	2015	2014	2013	2012	2011
All Futures on Individual Equities	12,189,434	9,325,030	5,448,554	4,670,750	2,471,605
ETF Futures	2,129,871	183,440			
Gold Futures (GDF)	2	1	7	36	383
GreTai Securities Weighted Stock Index (GTF)	2,613	4,655	4,634	18,695	30,478
Mini Taiex Futures (MTX)	21,021,527	13,286,373	13,093,325	15,980,510	19,128,802
NT Dollar Gold (TGF)	58,014	45,069	67,341	62,418	105,458
Taiex (TX)	33,059,533	24,759,873	22,693,270	24,642,382	30,611,932
Taiwan 50 Futures (T5F)	261	134	231	445	2,503
Taiwan Stock Exch NonFin/NonElec SubIndx (XIF)	138,726	139,097	108,487	100,024	181,233
Taiwan Stock Exchange Electronic Sector Index Futures	1,221,577	1,227,119	931,196	1,036,915	1,552,291
Taiwan Stock Exchange Finance Sector Index Futures	1,060,748	1,086,554			
TOPIX Futures (TJF)	17,393				
USD/CHN FX (RHF)	106,938				
USD/CNT FX (RTF)	1,046,265				
Total Futures	**72,052,902**	**50,057,345**	**43,389,650**	**47,769,142**	**56,372,485**
All Options on Individual Equities	169,589	110,454	78,638	113,134	130,558
ETF Options (ETC)	8,626				
NTD-denominated Gold (TGO)	73,579	52,022	85,176	75,925	101,708
Taiex (TXO)	191,513,144	151,620,546	109,311,515	108,458,103	125,767,624
Taiwan Stock Exch NonFin/NonElec SubIndx (XIO)	337	1,111	979	801	46,334
Taiwan Stock Exchange Electronic Sector Index Options	297,571	238,646	113,279	105,009	187,576
Taiwan Stock Exchange Finance Sector Index Options	379,912	330,969	245,997	209,689	352,241
Total Options	**192,442,758**	**152,353,748**	**109,835,588**	**108,962,770**	**126,622,686**

Tel-Aviv Stock Exchange (TASE), Israel

	2015	2014	2013	2012	2011
TA-25 Index	17,398	52,945	60,237	48,172	35,429
TA-Banks Index	12,635	4,551	1,174	22,861	19,496
Total Futures	**30,033**	**57,496**	**61,411**	**92,186**	**188,734**
All Options on Individual Equities	1,525,235	1,794,563	1,078,697	480,087	827,357
Shekel-Dollar Rate	15,674,801	12,685,813	9,957,286	8,683,705	10,400,167
Shekel-Euro Rate Options	1,002,216	1,120,409	638,681	499,774	392,139
TA-100 index	41,939				
TA-25 Index	47,646,434	48,264,048	48,764,430	57,396,506	87,133,824
TA-Banks Index	133,909	130,167	13,926	27,102	22,489
Total Options	**66,024,534**	**63,995,000**	**60,453,020**	**67,087,609**	**98,776,425**

Thailand Futures Exchange, Thailand

	2015	2014	2013	2012	2011
10 Baht Gold	1,328,932	1,303,151	1,655,381	2,597,235	2,171,795
50 Baht Gold	132,604	238,544	551,887	1,045,370	1,817,483
All Futures on Individual Equities	19,708,113	19,624,561	7,915,967	2,168,037	1,578,092
Brent Crude Oil	25,970	32,530	46,496	147,823	3,320
SET50	26,764,395	14,403,574	5,688,404	4,034,460	4,316,437
US Dollar	271,754	309,926	239,345	396,138	
Total Futures	**48,231,768**	**35,912,295**	**16,098,717**	**10,403,871**	**9,919,123**
SET 50	307,131	108,855	65,409	54,057	107,993
Total Options	**307,131**	**108,855**	**65,409**	**54,057**	**107,993**

Tokyo Commodity Exchange (TOCOM), Japan

	2015	2014	2013	2012	2011
Chukyo Gasoline	15,070	22,214	33,409	61,919	65,225
Chukyo Kerosene	8,150	9,705	14,607	38,232	52,213
Corn	469,557	423,597	325,518		
Crude Oil	3,651,528	840,192	1,166,495	1,285,388	1,297,512
Gas Oil	200	58,011	4,644	9,787	11,314
Gasoline	1,685,518	1,869,868	2,257,935	2,390,679	2,462,261
Gold	7,927,825	8,744,990	12,224,611	11,895,357	16,075,145
Gold (Daily Futures)	2,075,048				
Gold Mini	1,269,045	1,414,905	2,475,797	2,814,289	3,312,107
Kerosene	418,314	689,541	925,421	746,163	900,700
Palladium	62,574	76,823	79,352	59,934	110,163
Platinum	3,853,480	4,593,224	4,278,478	3,489,874	3,455,529
Platinum Mini	307,921	418,695	420,524	314,882	287,322
Red Beans	21,355	20,823	24,764		
Rubber	2,411,306	2,440,391	2,329,414	2,251,817	3,259,984
Silver	62,575	85,963	96,374	120,436	373,445
Soybeans	159,602	147,071	187,170		
Total Futures	**24,399,068**	**21,856,063**	**26,845,712**	**25,479,111**	**31,670,031**

Tokyo International Financial Futures Exchange (TIFFE), Japan

	2015	2014	2013	2012	2011
3 Month Euroyen	2,000,289	2,708,318	5,044,236	4,734,503	7,201,901
Australian Dollar/Japanese Yen	4,572,137	5,478,496	10,256,158	16,500,368	41,589,199
Australian Dollar/Japanese Yen (Large)	2,828				
Australian Dollar/US Dollar	563,014	500,322	799,275	1,216,523	2,369,321
British Pound/Australian Dollar	148,347	150,456	226,661	154,758	233,642
British Pound/Japanese Yen	2,291,868	2,522,602	3,387,074	3,969,313	11,782,185
British Pound/Japanese Yen (Large)	829				
British Pound/Swiss Franc	22,186	25,563	56,602	56,633	186,041
British Pound/US Dollar	212,126	193,658	281,851	288,047	772,999
Canadian Dollar/Japanese Yen	273,991	271,873	303,776	397,062	1,156,599
DAX Margin	291,958	204,069	88,219	83,266	100,509
Euro/Australian Dollar	255,196	297,823	470,198	526,204	355,969
Euro/British Pound	73,122	46,566	55,076	49,537	157,660
Euro/Japanese Yen	3,348,524	2,968,883	11,291,735	16,927,476	26,769,174
Euro/Japanese Yen (Large)	1,721				
Euro/Swiss Franc	58,628	19,213	67,457	80,461	522,352
Euro/US Dollar	3,056,292	752,951	1,083,008	3,628,083	8,246,516
Euro/US Dollar (Large)	1,541				
FTSE 100 Margin	166,485	173,047	39,709	21,353	80,189
Hong Kong Dollar/Japanese Yen	36,030	33,123	29,498	12,764	42,391
New Zealand Dollar/Japanese Yen	2,467,301	1,878,175	2,369,064	3,337,884	5,781,332
New Zealand Dollar/US Dollar	249,845	205,664	204,479	150,176	195,778
Nikkei 225 Margin	7,840,578	5,065,037	5,153,821	1,609,751	812,346
Norway Krone/Japanese Yen	86,261	51,076	86,320	68,347	80,369
Polish Zloty/Japanese Yen	346,273	794,226	700,069	709,891	259,632
South African Rand/Japanese Yen	4,031,856	3,746,597	2,650,993	2,191,285	2,138,750
Sweden Krona/Japanese Yen	36,832	29,463	72,398	40,082	56,304
Swiss Franc/Japanese Yen	353,886	140,575	337,848	489,095	1,631,739
Turkish Lira /Japanese Yen	3,074,957				
US Dollar/Canadian Dollar	108,986	58,245	61,444	68,262	178,483
US Dollar/Japanese Yen	12,919,505	12,550,958	20,120,943	9,212,876	31,441,164
US Dollar/Japanese Yen (Large)	4,135				
US Dollar/Swiss Franc	88,915	30,212	75,880	144,767	497,869
Total Futures	**48,986,442**	**40,900,423**	**65,527,790**	**66,924,393**	**144,866,413**

VOLUME - WORLDWIDE

Turquoise Derivatives, London

(Formerly EDX)	2015	2014	2013	2012	2011
IOB DR Futures on Individual Equities	111,916	923,860	272,227	104,757	648,800
Norwegian Futures on Individual Equities	205,533	46,242	428,969	410,351	170,000
OBX Index	1,193,117	1,100,864	995,644	1,027,366	1,456,874
Total Futures	**1,510,566**	**2,080,134**	**1,787,700**	**1,755,963**	**2,520,530**
IOB DR Options on Individual Equities	1,237,534	7,646,176	14,948,193	28,351,903	34,060,682
Norwegian Options on Individual Equities	1,483,813	1,366,368	874,146	1,203,051	1,551,337
OBX Index	274,064	351,897	269,462	212,804	206,763
UK Options on Individual Equities	500				
Total Options	**2,995,911**	**9,365,361**	**16,096,173**	**29,874,347**	**35,938,246**

Warsaw Stock Exchange, Poland

	2015	2014	2013	2012	2011
1 Month WIBOR	43	276	208		
3 Month WIBOR	1,675	2,699	1,200		
All Futures on Individual Equities	1,033,300	580,185	613,563	540,330	737,742
CHFPLN	170,108	64,268	95,672	28,343	73,155
EURPLN	254,653	174,644	215,902	110,832	21,885
Long Term Bond	222	809	610		
Medium Term Bond	160	582	723		
Short Term Bond	198	1,385	206		
USDPLN	1,742,842	2,016,605	2,538,358	821,760	104,450
WIG20 Index	4,443,040	6,038,355	8,259,066	9,077,040	13,642,282
WIG40 Index	120,650	120,803	81,468	14,048	29,439
Total Futures	**7,766,891**	**9,001,819**	**11,806,976**	**10,592,353**	**14,608,953**
WIG20 Index	438,206	479,020	808,360	715,364	897,801
Total Options	**438,206**	**479,020**	**808,360**	**715,364**	**897,801**

Zhengzhou Commodity Exchange (ZCE), China

	2015	2014	2013	2012	2011
Common Wheat (PM)	1,175	1,203	1,894	6,262	
Cotton No. 1 (CF)	22,613,311	31,782,665	7,452,748	21,033,646	139,044,152
Early Rice (RI)	3,571	332,910	515,471	1,287	
Ferrosilicon	39,406	767,619			
Flat Glass (FG)	41,548,298	78,725,549	186,105,091	16,136,920	
Japonica Rice (JR)	99	10,005	40,480		
Late Rice (LR)	1,063	52,116			
Methanol (MA)	314,357,813	14,048,540			
Methanol (ME)	392,811	10,566,232	3,497,720	3,797,412	316,107
PTA (TA)	231,578,021	117,865,244	76,283,987	121,263,913	120,528,824
Rapeseed (RS)	45,703	17,219	1,174,626	137,084	
Rapeseed Meal (RM)	261,487,209	303,515,966	160,100,378	421,207	
Rapeseed Oil (OI)	7,780,455	13,897,650	11,853,858	2,021	
Silicon Manganese	50,439	361,462			
Strong Gluten Wheat (WH)	460,729	1,025,946	1,871,991	10,262	
Thermal Coal (TC)	1,671,337	5,646,295	4,357,384		
Thermal Coal (ZC)	980,710				
White Sugar (SR)	187,323,456	97,726,662	69,794,046	148,290,190	128,193,356
Total Futures	**1,070,335,606**	**676,343,283**	**525,299,023**	**347,091,533**	**406,390,664**

Total Worldwide Volume

	2015	2014	2013	2012	2011
Total Futures	**11,203,953,277**	**8,965,682,686**	**9,048,066,041**	**8,383,947,627**	**9,101,990,067**
Percent Change	**23.81%**	**-19.98%**	**7.92%**	**-7.89%**	**6.59%**
Total Options	**5,396,546,760**	**4,726,908,336**	**4,726,796,145**	**5,648,591,935**	**7,759,707,692**
Percent Change	**14.17%**	**-12.41%**	**-16.32%**	**-27.21%**	**14.57%**
Total Futures and Options	**16,600,500,037**	**13,692,591,022**	**13,774,862,186**	**14,032,539,562**	**16,861,697,759**
Percent Change	**20.50%**	**-17.52%**	**-1.84%**	**-16.78%**	**10.12%**

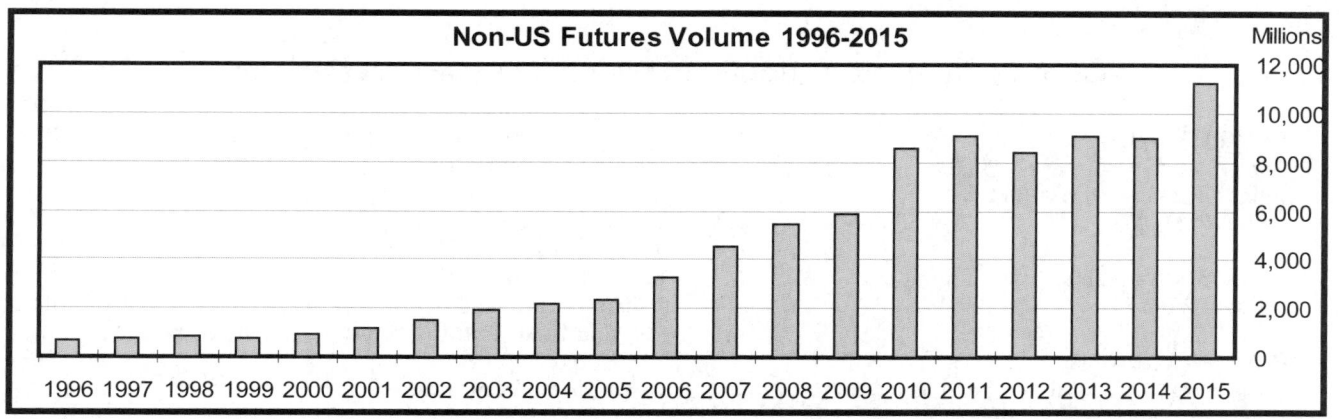

Non-US Futures Volume 1996-2015

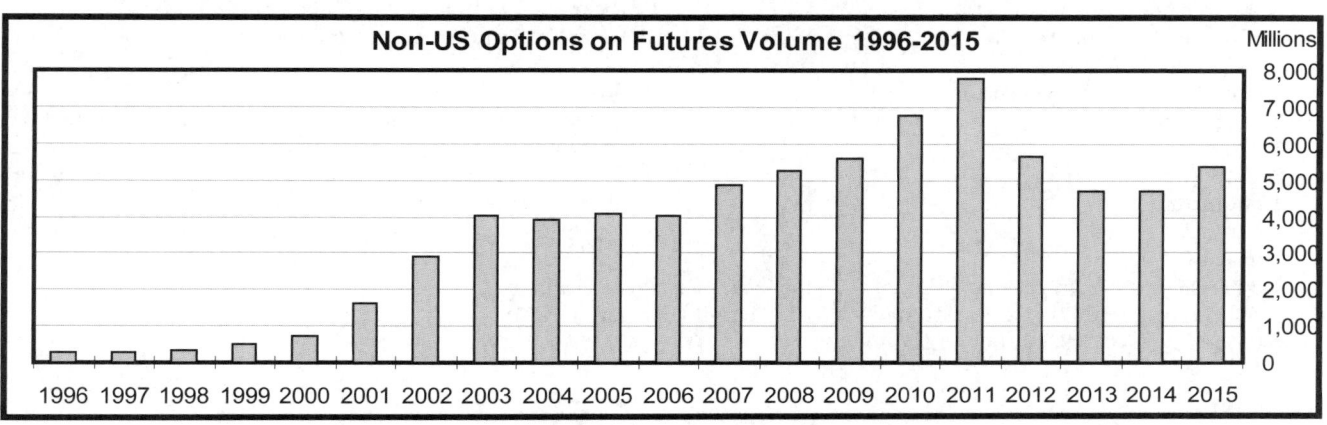

Non-US Options on Futures Volume 1996-2015

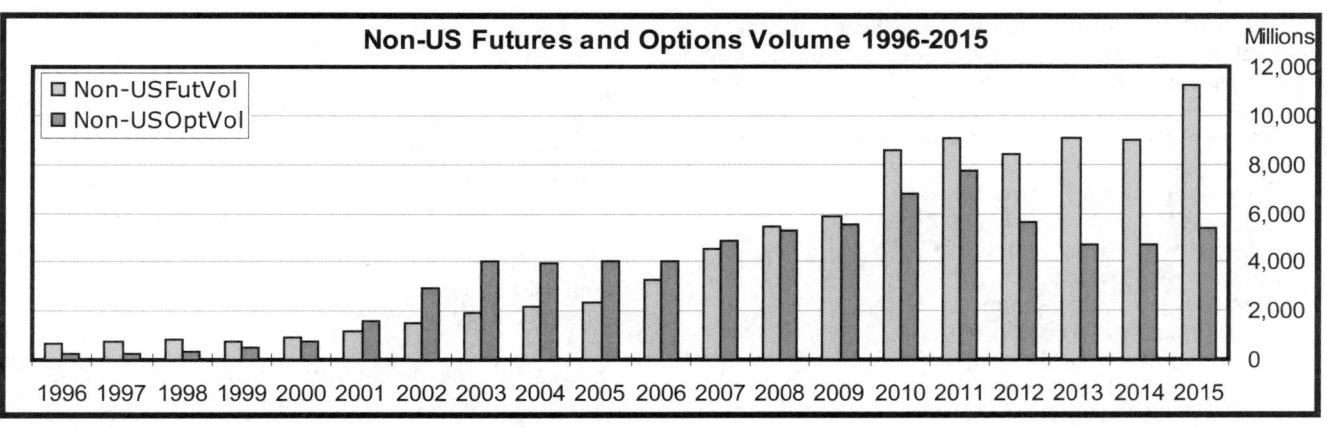

Non-US Futures and Options Volume 1996-2015

□ Non-USFutVol
■ Non-USOptVol

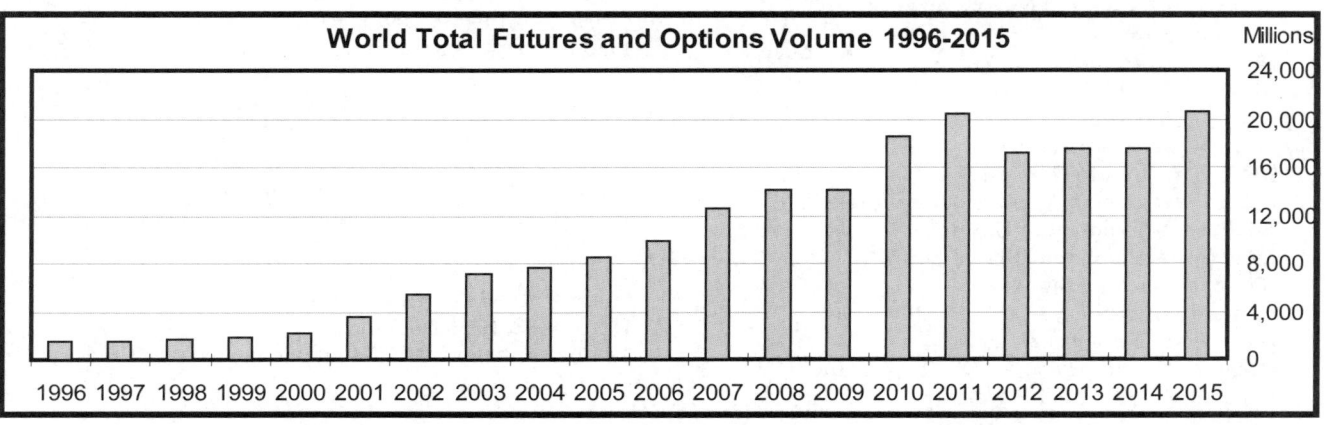

World Total Futures and Options Volume 1996-2015

Conversion Factors

Commonly Used Agricultural Weights and Measurements

Bushel Weights:
Corn, Sorghum and Rye = 56 lbs.
Wheat and Soybeans = 60 lbs.
Canola = 50 lbs.
Barley Grain = 48 lbs.
Barley Malt = 34 lbs.
Oats = 32 lbs.

Bushels to tonnes:
Corn, Sorghum and Rye = bushels x 0.0254
Wheat and Soybeans = bushels x 0.027216
Barley Grain = bushels x 0.021772
Oats = bushels x 0.014515

1 tonne (metric ton) equals:
2204.622 lbs.
1,000 kilograms
22.046 hundredweight
10 quintals

Ethanol
1 bushel Corn = 2.75 gallons Ethanol = 18 lbs Dried Distillers Grain
1 tonne Corn = 101.0 gallons Ethanol = 661 lbs Dried Distillers Grain
1 tonne Sugar = 149.3 gallons Ethanol

1 tonne (metric ton) equals:
39.3679 bushels of Corn, Sorghum or Rye
36.7437 bushels of Wheat or Soybeans
22.046 hundredweight
45.9296 bushels of Barley Grain
68.8944 bushels of Oats
4.5929 Cotton bales (the statistical bale used by the USDA and ICAC contains a net weight of 480 pounds of lint)

Area Measurements:
1 acre = 43,560 square feet = 0.040694 hectare
1 hectare = 2.4710 acres = 10,000 square meters
640 acres = 1 square mile = 259 hectares

Yields:
Rye, Corn: bushels per acre x 0.6277 = quintals per hectare
Wheat: bushels per acre x 0.6725 = quintals per hectare
Barley Grain: bushels per acre x 0.538 = quintals per hectare
Oats: bushels per acre x 0.3587 = quintals per hectare

Commonly Used Weights

The troy, avoirdupois and apothecaries' grains are identical in U.S. and British weight systems, equal to 0.0648 gram in the metric system. One avoirdupois ounce equals 437.5 grains. The troy and apothecaries' ounces equal 480 grains, and their pounds contain 12 ounces.

Troy weights and conversions:
24 grains = 1 pennyweigh
20 pennyweights = 1 ounce
12 ounces = 1 pound
1 troy ounce = 31.103 grams
1 troy ounce = 0.0311033 kilogram
1 troy pound = 0.37224 kilogram
1 kilogram = 32.1507 troy ounces
1 tonne = 32,151 troy ounces

Avoirdupois weights and conversions:
27 11/32 grains = 1 dram
16 drams = 1 ounce
16 ounces = 1 lb.
1 lb. = 7,000 grains
14 lbs. = 1 stone (British)
100 lbs. = 1 hundredweight (U.S.)
112 lbs. = 8 stone = 1 hundredweight (British)
2,000 lbs. = 1 short ton (U.S. ton)
2,240 lbs. = 1 long ton (British ton)
160 stone = 1 long ton
20 hundredweight = 1 ton
1 lb. = 0.4536 kilogram
1 hundredweight (cwt.) = 45.359 kilograms
1 short ton = 907.18 kilograms
1 long ton = 1,016.05 kilograms

Metric weights and conversions:
1,000 grams = 1 kilogram
100 kilograms = 1 quintal
1 tonne = 1,000 kilograms = 10 quintals
1 kilogram = 2.204622 lbs.
1 quintal = 220.462 lbs.
1 tonne = 2204.6 lbs.
1 tonne = 1.102 short tons
1 tonne = 0.9842 long ton

U.S. dry volumes and conversions:
1 pint = 33.6 cubic inches = 0.5506 liter
2 pints = 1 quart = 1.1012 liters
8 quarts = 1 peck = 8.8098 liters
4 pecks = 1 bushel = 35.2391 liters
1 cubic foot = 28.3169 liters

U.S. liquid volumes and conversions:
1 ounce = 1.8047 cubic inches = 29.6 milliliters
1 cup = 8 ounces = 0.24 liter = 237 milliliters
1 pint = 16 ounces = 0.48 liter = 473 milliliters
1 quart = 2 pints = 0.946 liter = 946 milliliters
1 gallon = 4 quarts = 231 cubic inches = 3.785 liters
1 milliliter = 0.033815 fluid ounce
1 liter = 1.0567 quarts = 1,000 milliliters
1 liter = 33.815 fluid ounces
1 imperial gallon = 277.42 cubic inches = 1.2 U.S. gallons = 4.546 liters

Energy Conversion Factors

U.S. Crude OIl (average gravity)
1 U.S. barrel = 42 U.S. gallons
1 short ton = 6.65 barrels
1 tonne = 7.33 barrels

Barrels per tonne for various origins

Abu Dhabi	7.624
Algeria	7.661
Angola	7.206
Australia	7.775
Bahrain	7.335
Brunei	7.334
Canada	7.428
Dubai	7.295
Ecuador	7.580
Gabon	7.245
Indonesia	7.348
Iran	7.370
Iraq	7.453
Kuwait	7.261
Libya	7.615
Mexico	7.104
Neutral Zone	6.825
Nigeria	7.410
Norway	7.444
Oman	7.390
Qatar	7.573
Romania	7.453
Saudi Arabia	7.338
Trinidad	6.989
Tunisia	7.709
United Arab Emirates	7.522
United Kingdom	7.279
United States	7.418
Former Soviet Union	7.350
Venezuela	7.005
Zaire	7.206

Barrels per tonne of refined products:

aviation gasoline	8.90
motor gasoline	8.50
kerosene	7.75
jet fuel	8.00
distillate, including diesel	7.46

(continued above)

residual fuel oil	6.45
lubricating oil	7.00
grease	6.30
white spirits	8.50
paraffin oil	7.14
paraffin wax	7.87
petrolatum	7.87
asphalt and road oil	6.06
petroleum coke	5.50
bitumen	6.06
LPG	11.6

Approximate heat content of refined products:

(Million Btu per barrel, 1 British thermal unit is the amount of heat required to raise the temperature of 1 pound of water 1 degree F.)

Petroleum Product	Heat Content
asphalt	6.636
aviation gasoline	5.048
butane	4.326
distillate fuel oil	5.825
ethane	3.082
isobutane	3.974
jet fuel, kerosene	5.670
jet fuel, naptha	5.355
kerosene	5.670
lubricants	6.065
motor gasoline	5.253
natural gasoline	4.620
pentanes plus	4.620

Petrochemical feedstocks:

naptha less than 401*F	5.248
other oils equal to or greater than 401*F	5.825
still gas	6.000
petroleum coke	6.024
plant condensate	5.418
propane	3.836
residual fuel oil	6.287
special napthas	5.248
unfinished oils	5.825
unfractionated steam	5.418
waxes	5.537

Source: U.S. Department of Energy

Natural Gas Conversions

Although there are approximately 1,031 Btu in a cubic foot of gas, for most applications, the following conversions are sufficient:

Cubic Feet			MMBtu		
1,000	(one thousand cubic feet)	=	1 Mcf	=	1
1,000,000	(one million cubic feet)	=	1 MMcf	=	1,000
10,000,000	(ten million cubic feet)	=	10 MMcf	=	10,000
1,000,000,000	(one billion cubic feet)	=	1 Bcf	=	1,000,000
1,000,000,000,000	(one trillion cubic feet)	=	1 Tcf	=	1,000,000,000

Acknowledgments

The editors wish to thank the following for source material:

Agricultural Marketing Service (AMS)

Agricultural Research Service (ARS)

American Bureau of Metal Statistics, Inc. (ABMS)

American Iron and Steel Institute (AISI)

American Metal Market (AMM)

Bureau of the Census

Bureau of Economic Analysis (BEA)

Bureau of Labor Statistics (BLS)

Chicago Board of Trade (CBT)

Chicago Mercantile Exchange (CME / IMM / IOM)

Commodity Credit Corporation (CCC)

Commodity Futures Trading Commision (CFTC)

The Conference Board

Economic Research Service (ERS)

Edison Electric Institute (EEI)

Farm Service Agency (FSA)

Federal Reserve Bank of St. Louis

Food and Agriculture Organization of the United Nations (FAO)

Foreign Agricultural Service (FAS)

Futures Industry Association (FIA)

ICE Futures U.S, Canada, Europe (ICE)

International Cotton Advisory Committee (ICAC)

International Cocoa Organization (ICCO)

Johnson Matthey

Kansas City Board of Trade (KCBT)

Leather Industries of America

Minneapolis Grain Exchange (MGEX)

National Agricultural Statistics Service (NASS)

New York Mercantile Exchange (NYMEX)

Oil World

The Organisation for Economic Co-Operation and Development (OECD)

The Silver Institute

The Society of the Plastics Industry, Inc. (SPI)

United Nations (UN)

United States Department of Agriculture (USDA)

Wall Street Journal (WSJ)

Aluminum

Aluminum (symbol Al) is a silvery, lightweight metal that is the most abundant metallic element in the earth's crust. Aluminum was first isolated in 1825 by a Danish chemist, Hans Christian Oersted, using a chemical process involving a potassium amalgam. A German chemist, Friedrich Woehler, improved Oersted's process by using metallic potassium in 1827. He was the first to show aluminum's lightness. In France, Henri Sainte-Claire Deville isolated the metal by reducing aluminum chloride with sodium and established a large-scale experimental plant in 1854. He displayed pure aluminum at the Paris Exposition of 1855. In 1886, Charles Martin Hall in the U.S. and Paul L.T. Heroult in France simultaneously discovered the first practical method for producing aluminum through electrolytic reduction, which is still the primary method of aluminum production today.

By volume, aluminum weighs less than a third as much as steel. This high strength-to-weight ratio makes aluminum a good choice for construction of aircraft, railroad cars, and automobiles. Aluminum is used in cooking utensils and the pistons of internal-combustion engines because of its high heat conductivity. Aluminum foil, siding, and storm windows make excellent insulators. Because it absorbs relatively few neutrons, aluminum is used in low-temperature nuclear reactors. Aluminum is also useful in boat hulls and various marine devices due to its resistance to corrosion in salt water.

Futures and options on Primary Aluminum and Aluminum Alloy are traded on the London Metal Exchange (LME). Aluminum futures are traded on the Multi Commodity Exchange of India (MCX), the Singapore Exchange (SGX), and the Shanghai Futures Exchange (SHFE). The London Metals Exchange aluminum futures contracts are priced in terms of dollars per metric ton.

Prices – The London Metals Exchange aluminum futures contract on the nearest futures chart fell fairly steadily during 2015 to post a 6-1/2 year low and finally close the year down -17.9% yr/yr at $1505.50 per metric ton.

Supply – World production of aluminum in 2015 rose by +15.4% to a new record high of 58.3 million metric tons. The world's largest producers of aluminum are China with 54.9% of world production in 2015, Russia (6.0%), Canada (5.0%), Australia (2.8%), and the U.S. (2/7%). U.S. production of primary aluminum in 2015 fell -6.5% yr/yr to 1.600 million metric tons.

Demand – U.S. consumption of aluminum in 2015 rose +6.1% yr/yr to 5.390 million metric tons, up from the 3-decade low of 3.320 million metric tons in 2009.

Trade – U.S. exports in 2015 fell -6.5% yr/yr to 3.020 million metric tons, further below the 2012 record high of 3.480 million metric tons. U.S. imports of aluminum in 2015 rose +9.6% yr/yr to 4.700 million metric tons, but still below the 2005 record high of 4.850 million metric tons. The U.S. was a net importer in 2015 and relied on imports for 40% of its consumption.

World Production of Primary Aluminum   In Thousands of Metric Tons

Year	Australia	Brazil	Canada	China	France	Germany	Norway	Russia[3]	Spain	United Kingdom	United States	Vene-zuela	World Total
2006	1,932	1,605	3,051	9,360	442	516	1,331	3,718	349	360	2,284	610	33,900
2007	1,957	1,655	3,083	12,600	428	551	1,357	3,955	408	365	2,554	610	37,900
2008	1,974	1,661	3,120	13,200	389	606	1,358	4,190	408	326	2,658	608	39,700
2009	1,943	1,536	3,030	12,900	345	292	1,139	3,815	360	253	1,727	561	37,200
2010	1,928	1,536	2,963	16,200	356	402	1,543	3,947	340	186	1,726	335	41,800
2011	1,945	1,440	2,988	18,100	334	432	1,530	3,993	365	213	1,986	380	44,900
2012	1,864	1,436	2,781	20,300	349	410	1,395	3,924	230	60	2,070	200	46,100
2013	1,778	1,304	2,969	22,100	346	492	1,338	3,724	235	44	1,946	160	47,800
2014[1]	1,704	962	2,858	24,380	360	580	1,331	3,488	230	42	1,710	140	50,500
2015[2]	1,650	780	2,900	32,000			1,320	3,500			1,600		58,300

[1] Preliminary.   [2] Estimate.   Source: U.S. Geological Survey (USGS)

Production of Primary Aluminum (Domestic and Foreign Ores) in the U.S.   In Thousands of Metric Tons

Year	Jan.	Feb.	Mar.	Apr.	May	June	July	Aug.	Sept.	Oct.	Nov.	Dec.	Total
2006	197	179	198	190	197	189	192	185	183	190	188	197	2,285
2007	202	185	217	209	210	209	219	220	216	224	220	225	2,556
2008	233	219	234	228	236	224	225	222	214	217	202	204	2,658
2009	193	149	154	145	147	132	135	133	129	137	133	140	1,727
2010	142	130	146	142	148	141	146	146	143	148	144	148	1,726
2011	152	140	162	162	170	167	171	172	169	175	171	177	1,986
2012	178	167	179	174	179	173	177	171	164	170	166	171	2,070
2013	171	155	172	167	171	165	168	163	157	154	149	154	1,946
2014	153	139	153	143	147	140	143	143	136	137	134	141	1,710
2015[1]	142	130	143	138	142	133	134	135	128	128	121	113	1,587

[1] Preliminary.   Source: U.S. Geological Survey (USGS)

ALUMINUM

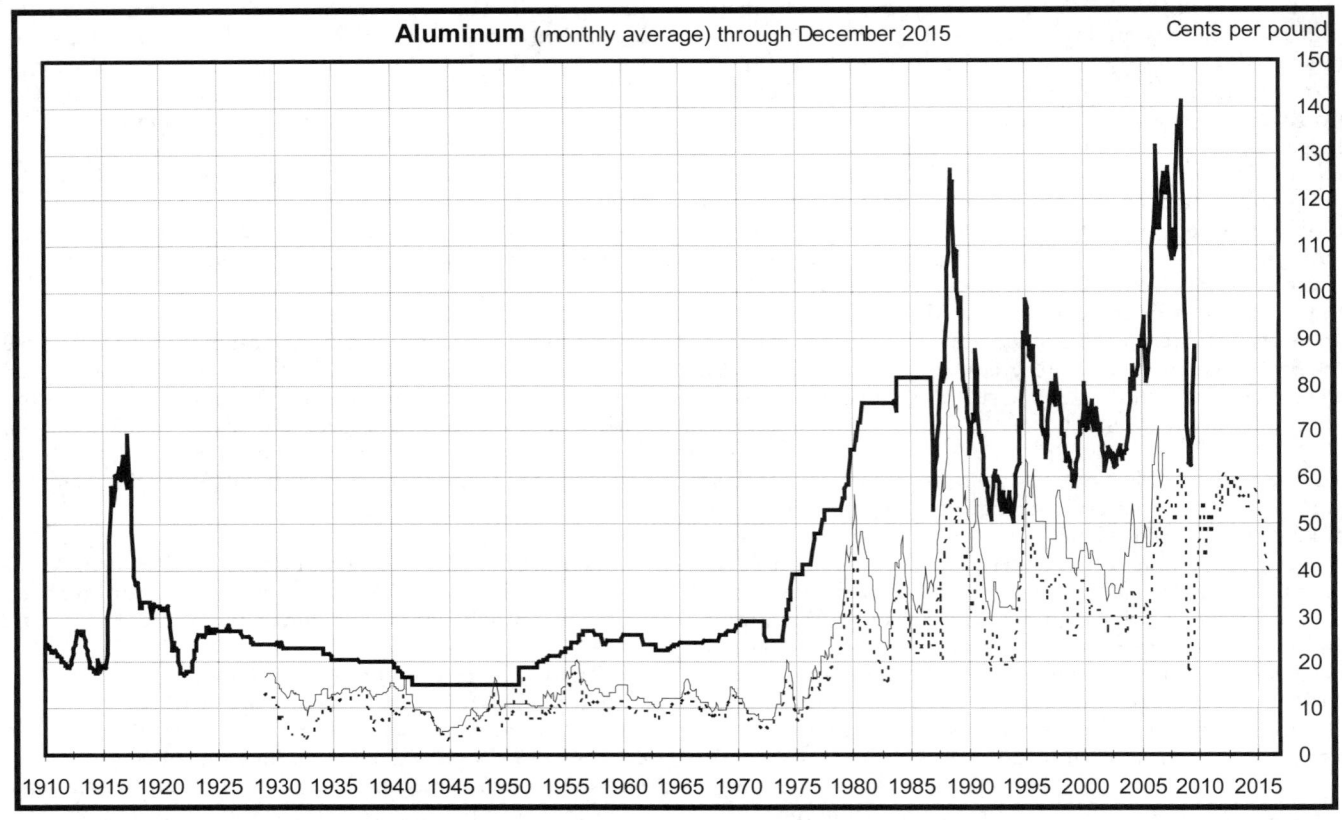

Aluminum (monthly average) through December 2015 — Cents per pound

Salient Statistics of Aluminum in the United States   In Thousands of Metric Tons

Year	Net Import Reliance as a % of Apparent Consump	Production Primary	Production Second ary	Primary Ship-ments	Recovery from Scrap Old	Recovery from Scrap New	Apparent Con-sumption	Wrought Products Plate, Sheet, Foil	Wrought Products Rolled Structural Shapes[3]	Wrought Products Ex-truded Shapes[4]	Wrought Products All	Castings Perma-nent Mold	Castings Die	Castings Sand	Castings All	Total All Net Ship-ments
2005	41	2,481	3,030	10,461	1,080	1,950	6,530	5,330	1,080	2,090	8,500	785	1,110	289	2,290	10,790
2006	31	2,284	3,540	10,500	1,580	2,800	5,700	4,690	608	192	5,490	754	1,170	335	2,310	7,800
2007	18	2,554	4,120	9,730	1,660	2,450	5,170	5,000	888	1,580	7,468	615	1,260	315	2,230	9,698
2008	E	2,658	3,630	8,570	1,500	2,130	3,940	4,770	789	1,380	6,939	570	1,030	255	1,900	8,839
2009	10	1,727	2,820	6,810	1,260	1,570	3,320	4,050	632	1,070	5,752	377	691	160	1,230	6,982
2010	14	1,726	2,790	7,720	1,250	1,540	3,460	4,450	703	1,530	6,683	475	949	147	1,580	8,263
2011	3	1,986	3,120	8,520	1,470	1,640	3,570	4,000	537	1,700	6,237	494	1,010	178	1,690	7,927
2012	11	2,070	3,270	9,670	1,440	1,830	3,950	4,770	915	2,130	7,815	589	1,110	127	1,860	9,675
2013	21	1,946	3,480	9,920	1,630	1,850	4,530	4,820	914	2,190	7,924	604	1,240	132	2,000	9,924
2014[1]	33	1,710	3,640	10,400	1,700	1,930	5,080	5,020	884	2,350	8,254	563	1,330	214	2,120	10,374

[1] Preliminary.   [2] To domestic industry.   [3] Also rod, bar & wire.   [4] Also rod, bar, tube, blooms & tubing.   [5] Consists of total shipments less shipments to other mills for further fabrication.   *Source: U.S. Geological Survey (USGS)*

Supply and Distribution of Aluminum in the United States   In Thousands of Metric Tons

Year	Apparent Con-sumption	Production Primary	Production From Old Scrap	Imports	Exports	Inventories - December 31 - Private	Inventories Govern-ment[2]	Year	Apparent Con-sumption	Production Primary	Production From Old Scrap	Imports	Exports	Inventories - December 31 - Private	Inventories Govern-ment[2]
2004	6,570	2,516	1,160	4,720	1,820	1,470	----	2010	3,460	1,726	1,250	3,610	3,040	1,010	----
2005	6,530	2,481	1,080	4,850	2,370	1,430	----	2011	3,570	1,986	1,470	3,710	3,420	1,060	----
2006	5,700	2,284	1,580	4,660	2,820	1,410	----	2012	3,950	2,070	1,440	3,760	3,480	1,140	----
2007	5,170	2,554	1,660	4,020	2,840	1,400	----	2013	4,530	1,946	1,630	4,160	3,390	1,130	----
2008	3,940	2,658	1,500	3,710	3,280	1,220	----	2014[1]	5,080	1,710	1,700	4,290	3,230	1,280	----
2009	3,320	1,727	1,260	3,680	2,710	937	----	2015[2]	5,390	1,600	1,640	4,700	3,020	1,350	----

[1] Preliminary.   [2] Estimate.   [3] National Defense Stockpile.   *Source: U.S. Geological Survey (USGS)*

Aluminum Products Distribution of End-Use Shipments in the United States   In Thousands of Metric Tons

Year	Building & Construction	Consumer Durables	Containers and Packaging	Electrical	Exports	Machinery and Equipment	Trans-portation	Other	Total
2005	1,671	708	2,320	746	1,125	741	3,939	336	11,586
2006	1,650	746	2,320	774	1,270	762	3,930	330	11,800
2007	1,410	664	2,230	762	1,450	736	3,580	359	11,200
2008	1,180	607	2,240	700	1,490	688	2,830	334	10,100
2009	964	458	2,150	593	1,280	475	1,910	254	8,090
2010	1,030	547	2,200	668	1,460	564	2,390	318	9,180
2011	1,110	631	2,160	798	1,700	682	2,820	322	10,200
2012	1,180	672	2,110	861	1,690	696	3,220	343	10,800
2013	1,310	700	2,090	867	1,720	726	3,430	332	11,200
2014[1]	1,390	748	2,090	809	1,620	770	3,810	337	11,600

[1] Preliminary.   Source: U.S. Geological Survey (USGS)

World Consumption of Primary Aluminum   In Thousands of Metric Tons

Year	Brazil	Canada	China	France	Germany	India	Italy	Japan	Korea, South	Russia	United Kingdom	United States	World Total
1992	377.1	420.4	1,253.8	730.5	1,457.1	414.3	660.0	2,271.6	397.0	1,242.0	550.0	4,616.9	18,529.5
1993	378.9	492.5	1,339.9	667.2	1,150.7	475.3	554.0	2,138.3	524.8	657.0	540.0	4,877.1	18,122.6
1994	414.1	559.0	1,500.1	736.3	1,370.3	475.0	660.0	2,344.8	603.9	470.0	570.0	5,407.1	19,670.8
1995	500.6	611.9	1,941.6	743.8	1,491.3	581.0	665.4	2,335.6	675.4	476.0	620.0	5,054.8	20,480.9
1996	497.0	619.9	2,135.3	671.7	1,355.4	584.8	585.1	2,392.6	674.3	443.8	571.0	5,348.0	20,596.4
1997	478.6	628.2	2,260.3	724.2	1,558.4	553.4	671.0	2,434.3	666.3	469.2	583.0	5,390.0	21,721.8
1998	521.4	720.6	2,425.4	733.8	1,519.0	566.5	675.4	2,082.0	505.7	489.2	579.0	5,813.6	21,797.2
1999	463.1	777.2	2,925.9	774.2	1,438.6	569.5	735.3	2,112.3	814.0	562.8	496.8	6,203.3	23,323.0
2000	513.8	798.7	3,499.1	780.4	1,490.3	602.4	780.3	2,224.9	822.6	748.4	575.5	6,079.5	24,811.4
2001[1]	550.8	759.6	3,545.4	772.9	1,590.9	558.0	770.4	2,014.0	849.6	786.2	433.3	5,117.0	23,612.8

[1] Preliminary.   Source: American Metal Market (AMM)

Salient Statistics of Recycling Aluminum in the United States

Year	Percent Recycled	New Scrap[1]	Old Scrap[2]	Recycled Metal[3]	Apparent Supply	New Scrap[1]	Old Scrap[2]	Recycled Metal[3]	Apparent Supply
		In Thousands of Metric Tons				Value in Millions of Dollars			
2004	33	1,870	1,160	3,030	9,080	3,460	2,140	5,600	16,800
2005	33	1,950	1,080	3,030	9,220	3,910	2,160	6,070	18,500
2006	52	2,800	1,580	4,380	8,500	7,490	4,220	11,700	22,700
2007	56	2,450	1,660	4,120	7,320	6,610	4,480	11,100	19,700
2008	60	2,130	1,500	3,630	6,070	5,660	3,970	9,640	16,100
2009	58	1,570	1,260	2,820	4,890	2,740	2,200	4,940	8,550
2010	56	1,540	1,250	2,790	5,000	3,550	2,880	6,430	11,500
2011	60	1,640	1,470	3,120	5,210	4,200	3,770	7,980	13,300
2012	57	1,830	1,440	3,270	5,780	4,080	3,210	7,290	12,900
2013	55	1,850	1,630	3,480	6,380	3,840	3,390	7,230	13,200

[1] Scrap that results from the manufacturing process.   [2] Scrap that results from consumer products.   [3] Metal recovered from new plus old scrap.
Source: U.S. Geological Survey (USGS)

Producer Prices for Aluminum Used Beverage Can Scrap   In Cents Per Pound

Year	Jan.	Feb.	Mar.	Apr.	May	June	July	Aug.	Sept.	Oct.	Nov.	Dec.	Average
2006	81.03	85.76	85.13	91.08	99.41	83.50	83.40	82.74	80.70	79.66	83.90	85.00	85.11
2007	89.05	89.58	90.18	93.14	93.16	87.86	85.90	80.39	76.37	79.57	82.98	79.68	85.66
2008	82.81	90.35	100.19	100.09	97.52	98.88	98.75	88.83	79.38	63.43	55.67	46.33	83.52
2009	43.70	41.42	41.91	44.00	46.80	50.64	54.27	61.62	58.00	61.43	64.42	71.16	53.28
2010	73.95	68.05	75.48	78.77	69.10	65.77	67.43	72.45	74.76	82.57	79.38	82.26	74.16
2011	86.78	89.11	90.98	96.08	94.72	94.05	90.95	86.54	83.69	78.07	75.25	73.18	86.62
2012	77.30	79.83	79.87	75.67	74.27	69.76	70.81	70.35	77.82	75.72	74.33	80.09	75.49
2013	79.03	79.19	75.69	76.25	75.18	73.08	71.02	72.27	68.95	69.74	68.16	68.76	73.11
2014	73.24	76.75	77.52	82.43	79.62	80.41	83.80	85.33	85.93	85.92	91.17	88.64	82.56
2015	83.85	81.13	75.14	71.00	61.70	56.09	57.86	58.00	60.24	59.30	56.84	59.89	65.09

Source: American Metal Market (AMM)

ALUMINUM

Average Price of Cast Aluminum Scrap (Crank Cases) in Chicago[1]   In Cents Per Pound

Year	Jan.	Feb.	Mar.	Apr.	May	June	July	Aug.	Sept.	Oct.	Nov.	Dec.	Average
2006	42.50	42.50	43.80	47.50	47.50	55.91	46.48	45.46	44.50	46.45	51.15	51.10	47.07
2007	52.50	52.50	54.00	55.50	55.50	53.07	52.50	52.50	51.34	50.50	50.50	50.50	52.58
2008	50.50	52.00	58.50	62.09	60.12	57.50	60.00	60.60	53.69	35.76	26.94	18.45	49.68
2009	17.50	17.50	22.27	22.50	22.50	22.50	24.55	27.50	37.50	37.50	37.50	42.24	27.63
2010	45.39	47.50	48.80	55.23	51.50	43.41	42.50	47.27	47.50	51.31	52.50	47.50	48.37
2011	48.75	52.50	52.50	52.50	52.50	52.50	56.00	57.50	56.93	54.50	54.70	52.45	53.61
2012	55.05	59.60	61.50	60.93	59.23	55.93	55.50	55.50	58.55	59.50	57.00	58.67	58.08
2013	60.50	60.45	59.50	59.00	58.50	58.35	55.50	56.00	55.90	55.54	55.55	54.50	57.44
2014	54.50	53.50	53.50	55.00	56.50	56.50	56.50	56.55	57.40	56.50	56.50	55.45	55.70
2015	53.40	52.50	51.32	50.50	51.00	46.50	46.41	43.88	42.45	41.41	38.97	38.64	46.42

[1] Dealer buying prices.   Source: American Metal Market (AMM)

Aluminum Exports of Crude Metal and Alloys from the United States   In Thousands of Metric Tons

Year	Jan.	Feb.	Mar.	Apr.	May	June	July	Aug.	Sept.	Oct.	Nov.	Dec.	Total
2006	40.0	26.0	30.5	29.4	38.8	25.3	23.7	32.0	26.1	25.8	27.0	22.0	346.6
2007	32.1	27.1	27.0	28.6	33.8	31.1	26.4	30.3	28.5	29.9	29.6	24.5	348.9
2008	30.8	26.8	26.4	30.4	28.4	27.6	25.9	26.4	27.4	25.3	17.3	15.6	308.3
2009	15.9	15.9	12.7	14.8	24.7	24.9	24.6	24.7	24.4	28.0	26.4	25.1	262.1
2010	20.2	22.0	22.4	16.8	20.5	25.6	22.8	24.5	35.2	24.4	26.0	23.5	283.9
2011	25.5	24.2	30.2	34.6	26.1	23.1	25.7	23.2	23.2	24.3	29.5	24.4	314.0
2012	30.8	29.5	32.0	29.9	31.0	30.6	31.6	32.2	24.3	24.3	33.0	24.5	353.7
2013	27.5	29.4	31.1	32.9	30.0	29.8	26.5	33.7	31.0	32.3	32.3	25.9	362.4
2014	31.1	25.6	30.5	30.7	33.0	31.0	28.7	31.5	30.0	33.7	26.9	28.2	360.9
2015[1]	26.5	26.0	25.2	25.0	26.9	29.5	26.7	27.2	25.2	26.1	22.9	22.8	310.0

[1] Preliminary.   Source: U.S. Geological Survey (USGS)

Aluminum General Imports of Crude Metal and Alloys into the United States   In Thousands of Metric Tons

Year	Jan.	Feb.	Mar.	Apr.	May	June	July	Aug.	Sept.	Oct.	Nov.	Dec.	Total
2006	348.0	247.0	289.0	353.0	315.0	298.0	249.0	315.0	289.0	259.0	233.0	241.0	3,436.0
2007	251.0	258.0	238.0	259.0	220.0	254.0	236.0	266.0	268.0	244.0	238.0	215.0	2,947.0
2008	240.0	208.0	247.0	238.0	237.0	263.0	227.0	204.0	229.0	249.0	219.0	233.0	2,794.0
2009	270.0	204.0	333.0	233.0	292.0	200.0	299.0	216.0	212.0	207.0	211.0	217.0	2,894.0
2010	238.0	209.0	230.0	257.0	233.0	232.0	223.0	207.0	224.0	203.0	209.0	179.0	2,644.0
2011	211.0	212.0	232.0	220.0	285.0	263.0	220.0	241.0	263.0	243.0	192.0	245.0	2,827.0
2012	281.0	284.0	248.0	231.0	293.0	240.0	233.0	234.0	214.0	204.0	196.0	244.0	2,902.0
2013	248.0	220.0	283.0	457.0	314.0	267.0	273.0	271.0	242.0	219.0	299.0	220.0	3,313.0
2014	253.0	221.0	439.0	291.0	290.0	294.0	237.0	270.0	253.0	271.0	213.0	270.0	3,302.0
2015[1]	273.0	245.0	312.0	322.0	299.0	301.0	301.0	251.0	283.0	270.0	267.0	259.0	3,383.0

[1] Preliminary.   Source: U.S. Geological Survey (USGS)

Average Open Interest of Aluminum Futures in New York   In Contracts

Year	Jan.	Feb.	Mar.	Apr.	May	June	July	Aug.	Sept.	Oct.	Nov.	Dec.
2002	3,277	2,744	2,738	2,250	2,397	2,902	3,903	4,618	4,643	5,139	8,057	10,479
2003	9,573	9,163	6,960	7,190	7,686	8,529	8,402	8,445	7,655	7,283	8,434	9,427
2004	8,815	7,384	9,666	10,575	10,363	10,370	9,626	10,287	10,292	10,035	9,706	8,879
2005	8,183	8,487	7,464	6,612	5,654	5,061	4,359	3,223	3,225	2,676	2,232	1,670
2006	1,066	708	482	1,110	948	816	1,068	1,125	1,116	865	994	950
2007	608	614	491	450	415	368	329	276	237	194	156	132
2008	0	0	0	0	0	0	0	0	0	0	0	0

Source: CME Group; New York Mercantile Exchange (NYMEX)

Volume of Trading of Aluminum Futures in New York   In Contracts

Year	Jan.	Feb.	Mar.	Apr.	May	June	July	Aug.	Sept.	Oct.	Nov.	Dec.	Total
2002	2,774	4,635	4,924	2,593	5,388	5,389	8,953	4,194	2,571	7,328	16,185	9,066	74,000
2003	12,565	9,625	8,163	5,440	10,567	8,463	11,797	9,451	5,119	6,222	8,536	11,542	107,490
2004	9,425	9,621	9,548	9,770	5,438	5,453	5,280	2,063	5,533	4,822	2,525	2,691	72,169
2005	5,294	2,829	3,244	2,627	2,613	1,832	1,247	902	1,625	623	3,135	2,520	28,491
2006	633	245	1,343	1,558	210	471	1,046	1,546	662	323	842	270	9,149
2007	94	332	82	28	2	56	84	19	25	0	1	0	723
2008	0	0	0	0	0	0	0	0	0	0	0	0	0

Source: CME Group; New York Mercantile Exchange (NYMEX)

Antimony

Antimony (atomic symbol Sb) is a lustrous, extremely brittle and hard crystalline semi-metal that is silvery white in its most common allotropic form. Antimony is a poor conductor of heat and electricity. In nature, antimony has a strong affinity for sulfur and for such metals as lead, silver, and copper. Antimony is primarily a byproduct of the mining, smelting and refining of lead, silver, and copper ores. There is no longer any mine production of antimony in the U.S.

The most common use of antimony is in antimony trioxide, a chemical that is used as a flame retardant in textiles, plastics, adhesives and building materials. Antimony trioxide is also used in battery components, ceramics, bearings, chemicals, glass, and ammunition.

Prices – Antimony prices in 2015 fell by -22.7% to 331.13 cents per pound, remaining well below the 2011 record high of 671.10 cents per pound. However, antimony prices in 2015 were still far above the 35-year low price of 66.05 cents per pound posted in 1999.

Supply – World mine production of antimony in 2015 fell -5.1% yr/yr to 150,000 metric tons, remaining below the 2008 record high of 182,000 metric tons. China accounted for 76.7% of world antimony production in 2015. After China, the only significant producers were Russia (6.0% of world production), Australia (3.7%), and Bolivia (3.3%). U.S. secondary production of antimony in 2015 fell by -5.4% yr/yr to 4,000 metric tons.

Demand – U.S. industrial consumption of antimony in 2013 (latest data available) rose +7.1% yr/yr to 8,620 metric tons. Of the consumption in the U.S. in 2013, 42% was used for non-metal products, 32% was used for flame-retardants, and 26% was used for metal products.

Trade –The total U.S. gross weight of imports of antimony ore in 2013 (latest data available) fell -5.5% yr/yr to 494 metric tons. The antimony content of that ore fell by -10.0% to 342 metric tons. The gross weight of U.S. imports of antimony oxide in 2013 rose+5.8% to 21,900 metric tons. U.S. exports of antimony oxide in 2015 fell by -4.3% to 3,100 metric tons.

World Mine Production of Antimony (Content of Ore)   In Metric Tons

Year	Australia	Bolivia	Canada	China	Kyrgyzstan	Russia	South Africa	Tajikistan	Turkey	World Total
2012	2,481	5,088	6,000	136,000	1,200	7,300	3,066	4,248	7,300	180,000
2013	3,275	5,081	76	120,000	1,200	8,700	2,400	4,675	4,600	159,000
2014[1]	5,800	5,500		120,000		9,000	1,600	4,700	4,500	158,000
2015[2]	5,500	5,000		115,000		9,000		4,700	4,500	150,000

[1] Preliminary.   [2] Estimate.   [3] Includes antimony content of miscellaneous smelter products.   [4] Recoverable.
Source: U.S. Geological Survey (USGS)

Salient Statistics of Antimony in the United States   In Metric Tons

Year	Avg. Price Cents/lb. C.i.f. U.S. Ports	Primary[2] Mine	Primary[2] Smelter	Secondary (Alloys)[2]	Imports for Consumption: Ore Gross Weight	Imports for Consumption: Ore Antimony Content	Imports for Consumption: Oxide (Gross Weight)	Exports (Oxide)	Industry Stocks, December 31[3] Metallic	Industry Stocks Oxide	Industry Stocks Sulfide	Industry Stocks Other	Industry Stocks Total
2012	564.51	----	W	3,050	523	380	20,700	4,710	117	886	----	431	1,430
2013	462.63	----	W	4,400	494	342	21,900	3,980	261	789	----	424	1,470
2014[1]	425.00	----	W	4,230		365		3,240					1,400
2015[2]	344.00	----	W	4,000				3,100					1,400

[1] Preliminary.   [2] Estimate.   [3] Antimony content.   [4] Including primary antimony residues & slag.   W = Withheld proprietary data.
Source: U.S. Geological Survey (USGS)

Industrial Consumption of Primary Antimony in the United States   In Metric Tons (Antimony Content)

Year	Metal Products: Ammunition	Metal Products: Antimonial Lead[3]	Metal Products: Sheet & Pipe[4]	Metal Products: Bearing Metal & Bearings	Metal Products: Solder	Metal Products: Products	Flame Retardants: Plastics	Flame Retardants: Total	Non-Metal Products: Ceramics & Glass	Non-Metal Products: Pigments	Non-Metal Products: Plastics	Non-Metal Products: Total	Grand Total
2010	W	W	W	26	34	2,130	2,610	3,190	W	399	W	3,540	8,860
2011	W	W	W	20	34	3,040	3,000	3,430	W	393	W	3,720	10,200
2012	W	W	W	13	46	2,270	2,210	2,520	W	369	W	3,270	8,050
2013[1]	W	W	W	21	54	2,210	2,350	2,780	W	1,050	W	3,630	8,620

[1] Preliminary.   [2] Estimated coverage based on 77% of the industry.   W = Withheld proprietary data.   *Source: U.S. Geological Survey (USGS)*

Average Price of Antimony[1] in the United States   In Cents Per Pound

Year	Jan.	Feb.	Mar.	Apr.	May	June	July	Aug.	Sept.	Oct.	Nov.	Dec.	Average
2012	558.83	581.28	585.96	585.68	634.62	626.94	602.20	568.77	567.71	572.22	560.42	544.57	582.43
2013	511.16	501.22	501.22	480.61	471.23	460.51	427.00	450.50	474.58	476.77	450.55	427.04	469.37
2014	439.77	445.66	442.85	434.58	434.27	437.72	434.94	425.73	419.04	415.53	409.75	401.22	428.42
2015	368.32	354.52	378.08	397.36	400.64	374.53	334.38	313.63	288.95	278.34	252.23	232.62	331.13

[1] Prices are for antimony metal (99.65%) merchants, minimum 18-ton containers, c.i.f. U.S. Ports.   *Source: American Metal Market (AMM)*

Apples

The apple tree is the common name of trees from the rose family, Rosaceae, and the fruit that comes from them. The apple tree is a deciduous plant and grows mainly in the temperate areas of the world. The apple tree is believed to have originated in the Caspian and Black Sea area. Apples were the favorite fruit of the ancient Greeks and Romans. The early settlers brought apple seeds with them and introduced them to America. John Champman, also known as Johnny Appleseed, was responsible for extensive planting of apple trees in the Midwestern United States.

Prices – The average monthly price of apples received by growers in the U.S. in 2014, the last full reporting year, fell by -15.9% yr/yr to 31.5 cents per pound.

Supply – World apple production in the 2015-16 marketing year rose 0.74% yr/yr to 77.018 million metric tons. The world's largest apple producers in 2015-16 were China (with 55.8% of world production), the European Union (15.9%), the U.S. (5.9%), and Turkey (3.6%). U.S. apple production in 2015-16 fell -10.1% to 4.561 million metric tons, but still far above the 2-decade low of 3.798 million metric tons posted in 2002-03.

Demand – The utilization breakdown of the 2014 (latest data available) apple crop showed that 69.5% of apples were for fresh consumption, 12.8% for juice and cider, 9.8% for canning, 2.0% for frozen apples, and 1.6% for dried apples. U.S. per capita apple consumption in 2012 (latest data available) was 16.0 pounds.

World Production of Apples[3], Fresh (Dessert & Cooking)   In Thousands of Metric Tons

Year	Argen-tina	Brazil	Chile	China	European Union	India	Japan	Russia	South Africa	Turkey	Ukraine	United States	World Total
2008-09	933	1,223	1,280	29,800	12,703	1,985	846	1,115	747	2,600	853	4,324	63,349
2009-10	830	1,279	1,370	31,681	12,096	1,777	787	1,230	781	2,750	897	4,280	64,384
2010-11	1,060	1,339	1,431	33,263	10,981	2,891	655	910	767	2,500	954	4,175	65,538
2011-12	860	1,340	1,360	35,985	12,338	2,203	794	1,124	813	2,700	1,127	4,231	69,648
2012-13	860	1,231	1,420	38,500	12,207	1,915	742	1,264	908	2,900	1,211	4,049	71,624
2013-14	630	1,377	1,310	39,680	11,865	2,200	742	1,417	793	2,930	1,211	4,690	73,815
2014-15[1]	640	1,266	1,350	40,920	13,619	2,200	742	1,409	860	2,289	1,211	5,075	76,452
2015-16[2]	720	1,240	1,350	43,000	12,220	2,200	742	1,390	865	2,740	1,211	4,561	77,019

[1] Preliminary.   [2] Estimate.   NA = Not available.   *Source: Foreign Agricultural Service, U.S. Department of Agriculture (FAS-USDA)*

Salient Statistics of Apples[2] in the United States

	-- Production --		- Growers Prices -		----------- Utilization of Quantities Sold ------------						Avg. Farm	----- Foreign Trade[4] ------			Fresh Per Capita
						--------------- Processed[5] ---------------					Price	--- Domestic ---			
			Fresh Cents/ lb.	Pro-cessing $/ton	Fresh	Canned	Dried	Frozen	Juice & Cider	Other[3]	Cents/ lb.	Farm Value Million $	Exports Fresh	Dried[5]	Imports Fresh & Dried[5]	Con-sump-tion
Year	Total	Utilized	------------------------------- Millions of Pounds -------------------------------										----- Metric Tons -----			Lbs.
2007	9,089	9,045	38.3	190.0	6,077	1,091	204	258	1,257	60	28.8	2,608.2	680.6	31.7	238.3	16.4
2008	9,633	9,540	30.1	198.0	6,274	1,253	213	211	1,349	112	23.2	2,599.5	811.0	26.8	206.7	15.9
2009	9,705	9,453	31.4	132.0	6,314	1,158	161	236	1,389	55	23.1	2,187.0	748.1	22.1	225.7	16.3
2010	9,292	9,213	32.6	187.0	6,257	1,088	176	206	1,266	74	25.1	2,313.6	817.0	26.8	184.5	15.3
2011	9,425	9,318	39.4	226.0	6,302	1,124	184	191	1,208	71	30.3	2,823.4	856.8	28.8	219.3	15.4
2012	8,992	8,927	45.3	281.0	6,595	749	223	67	1,112	53	37.1	3,315.0	908.2	23.0	243.1	16.0
2013	10,432	10,340	40.5	197.0	6,895	1,264	161	239	1,519	72	30.3	3,132.9				
2014[1]	11,431	11,188	32.5	168.0	7,947	1,123	181	223	1,463	60	25.5	2,855.8				

[1] Preliminary.   [2] Commercial crop.   [3] Mostly crushed for vinegar, jam, etc.   [4] Year beginning July.   [5] Fresh weight basis.
NA = Not available.   *Source: Economic Research Service, U.S. Department of Agriculture (ERS-USDA)*

Price of Apples Received by Growers (for Fresh Use) in the United States   In Cents Per Pound

Year	Jan.	Feb.	Mar.	Apr.	May	June	July	Aug.	Sept.	Oct.	Nov.	Dec.	Average
2008	35.5	34.8	34.4	33.8	36.2	41.2	44.6	53.7	50.6	42.5	36.0	29.3	39.4
2009	27.2	23.7	21.5	20.4	18.7	18.1	17.2	23.8	35.7	31.2	33.3	27.5	24.9
2010	29.0	28.9	29.5	29.7	30.9	30.8	29.9	29.1	36.5	35.7	35.3	29.3	31.2
2011	30.0	28.0	28.2	26.6	25.6	26.3	35.8	45.8	42.1	43.1	34.4	30.2	33.0
2012	32.0	30.6	33.2	30.0	30.0	38.4	41.9	49.3	58.7	52.2	51.9	45.4	41.1
2013	43.8	41.6	39.5	NQ	NQ	NQ	NQ	NQ	NQ	NQ	NQ	NQ	41.6
2014	NQ	NQ	NQ	39.2	37.2	34.4	33.2	38.8	46.9	40.2	35.8	31.8	37.5
2015[1]	31.6	29.2	27.8	25.9	24.3	20.5	18.4	30.7	43.0	41.2	40.3	45.4	31.5

[1] Preliminary.   NQ = No quote.   *Source: Economic Research Service, U.S. Department of Agriculture (ERS-USDA)*

Arsenic

Arsenic (atomic symbol As) is a silver-gray, extremely poisonous, semi-metallic element. Arsenic, which is odorless and flavorless, has been known since ancient times, but it wasn't until the Middle Ages that its poisonous characteristics first became known. Metallic arsenic was first produced in the 17th century by heating arsenic with potash and soap. Arsenic is rarely found in nature in its elemental form and is generally recovered as a by-product of ore processing. Recently, small doses of arsenic have been found to put some forms of cancer into remission. It can also help thin blood. Homoeopathists have successfully used undetectable amounts of arsenic to cure stomach cramps.

The U.S. does not produce any arsenic and instead imports all its consumption needs for arsenic metals and compounds. More than 95 percent of the arsenic consumed in the U.S. is in compound form, mostly as arsenic trioxide, which in turn is converted into arsenic acid. Production of chromated copper arsenate, a wood preservative, accounts for about 90% of the domestic consumption of arsenic trioxide. Three companies in the U.S. manufacture chromate copper arsenate. Another company used arsenic acid to produce an arsenical herbicide. Arsenic metal is used to produce nonferrous alloys, primarily for lead-acid batteries.

One area where there is increased consumption of arsenic is in the semiconductor industry. Very high-purity arsenic is used in the production of gallium arsenide. High-speed and high-frequency integrated circuits that use gallium arsenide have better signal reception and lower power consumption. An estimated 30 metric tons per year of high-purity arsenic is used in the production of semiconductor materials.

In the early 2000's, as much as 88% of U.S. arsenic production was used for wood preservative treatments, so the demand for arsenic was closely tied to new home construction, home renovation, and deck construction. However, the total demand for arsenic in 2004 dropped by 69% from 2003, and due to arsenic's toxicity and tighter environmental regulation; only 65% of that much smaller amount was used for wood preservative treatments. Since then the specific percentage used for wood preservative treatments is no longer available.

Supply –World production of white arsenic (arsenic trioxide) in 2015 fell by -1.1% to 36,000 metric tons. The world's largest producer is China with about 69% of world production, followed by Morocco with 24% of world production, Russia with 4%, and Belgium with 3%. China's production of arsenic use to be fairly constant at about 40,000 metric tons per year but that has dropped to about 25,000 in the last nine years. The U.S. supply of arsenic in 2015 rose by +14.3% to 6,800 metric tons.

Demand – U.S. demand for arsenic in 2015 rose by +14.5% to 6,800 metric tons. The use for arsenic is no longer available but in 2004 (latest data) about 65% was for wood preservatives, 10% was for non-ferrous alloys and electric usage, 10% was for glass, and 3% was for other uses.

Trade – U.S. imports of trioxide arsenic in 2014 (latest data available) fell by -16.5% to 6.940 metric tons, above the 2010 record low of 5,920 metric tons. U.S. exports of trioxide arsenic in 2015 fell -35.6% 1,900 metric tons, well below the record high of 3,270 metric tons in 2005.

World Production of White Arsenic (Arsenic Trioxide)   In Metric Tons

Year	Belgium	Bolivia	Chile	China	Japan	Mexico	Morocco	Peru	Morocco	Peru	Portugal	Russia	World Total
2008	1,000	74	10,000	25,000	40	513	8,800	4,822	15	1,500	50,500	1,500	60,900
2009	1,000	115	11,000	25,000	40	500	8,655	301	15	1,500	47,600	1,500	53,900
2010	1,000	155	11,000	25,000	40	----	13,731	----	15	1,500	41,400	1,500	50,500
2011	1,000	99	11,000	25,000	45	----	8,154	----	15	1,500	35,800	1,500	47,600
2012	1,000	104	10,000	26,000	45	----	8,820	----	15	1,500	37,500	1,500	52,400
2013	1,000	120	10,000	25,000	45	----	8,968	----	----	1,500	36,600	1,500	45,800
2014[1]	1,000	52	10,000	25,000	45	----	8,800	----	----	1,500	36,400	1,500	46,700
2015[2]	1,000	50	----	25,000	45	----	8,500	----	----	1,500	36,000	1,500	45,000

[1] Preliminary.   [2] Estimate.   [3] Output of Tsumeb Corp. Ltd. only.   [4] Includes low-grade dusts that were exported to the U.S. for further refining.
Source: U.S. Geological Survey (USGS)

Salient Statistics of Arsenic in the United States   (In Metric Tons -- Arsenic Content)

	Supply			Distribution		Estimated Demand Pattern						Average Price			
	Imports		Industry			Agricul-tural		Wood	Non-Ferrous			Trioxide	Metal		
	Metal	Com-pounds	Stocks Jan. 1	Total	Apparent Demand	Industry Stocks Dec. 31	Chem-icals	Glass	Preserv-atives	Alloys & lectric	Other	Total	Mexican	Chinese	Imports Trioxide[3]	Exports
Year													-- Cents/Pound --		
2008	376	4,810	----	5,186	4,130	----	----	----	----	----	----	4,130	----	125	6,320	1,050
2009	438	4,660	----	5,098	5,100	----	----	----	----	----	----	5,100	----	121	6,130	354
2010	769	4,530	----	5,299	5,300	----	----	----	----	----	----	5,300	----	72	5,920	481
2011	628	4,990	----	5,618	5,620	----	----	----	----	----	----	5,620	----	74	6,570	705
2012	883	5,740	----	6,623	6,620	----	----	----	----	----	----	6,620	----	75	7,550	439
2013	514	6,290	----	6,804	6,810	----	----	----	----	----	----	6,810	----	72	8,310	1,630
2014[1]	688	5,260	----	5,948	5,940	----	----	----	----	----	----	5,940	----	75	6,940	2,950
2015[2]	600	6,200	----	6,800	6,800	----	----	----	----	----	----	6,800	----	80	----	1,900

[1] Preliminary.   [2] Estimate.   [3] For Consumption.   *Source: U.S. Geological Survey (USGS)*

Barley

Barley is the common name for the genus of cereal grass and is native to Asia and Ethiopia. Barley is an ancient crop and was grown by the Egyptians, Greek, Romans and Chinese. Barley is now the world's fourth largest grain crop, after wheat, rice, and corn. Barley is planted in the spring in most of Europe, Canada and the United States. The U.S. barley crop year begins June 1. It is planted in the autumn in parts of California, Arizona and along the Mediterranean Sea. Barley is hardy and drought resistant and can be grown on marginal cropland. Salt-resistant strains are being developed for use in coastal regions. Barley grain, along with hay, straw, and several by-products are used for animal feed. Barley is used for malt beverages and in cooking. Barley, like other cereals, contains a large proportion of carbohydrate (67%) and protein (12.8%).

Barley futures and options are traded on the Mercado a Termino de Buenos Aires (MTBA), the NYSE LIFFE European Derivatives Market and the Sydney Futures Exchange (SFE). Barley futures are traded on the Budapest Stock Exchange (BSE), ICE Futures Canada, the Multi Commodity Exchange of India (MCX), and the National Commodity & Derivatives Exchange (NCDEX).

Prices – The monthly average price for all barley received by U.S. farmers in the 2015-16 marketing year rose by +5.1% yr/yr to $5.48 per bushel.

Supply – World barley production in the 2015-16 marketing year rose by +3.5% yr/yr to 146.159 million metric tons. The world's largest barley crop of 179.038 million metric tons occurred in 1990-91. The world's largest barley producers are the European Union with 41.7% of world production in 2015-16, Russia (11.7%), Ukraine (6.0%), Australia (5.9%), Canada (5.6%), and Turkey (5.1%).

U.S. barley production in the 2015-16 marketing year rose by +18.0% yr/yr to 214.297 million bushels and that is less than 50% of the record U.S. barley crop of 608.532 million bushels seen in 1986-87. U.S. farmers harvested 24.5% yr/yr more acres in 2015-16 at 3.109 million acres, above the 2006-07 level of 2.951 million acres which was the lowest acreage since 1885. Barley yield in 2015-16 fell -5.2% yr/yr to 68.9 bushels per acre, down from the 2010-11 record high yield of 73.1 bushels per acre. Ending stocks for the 2015-16 marketing year rose +20.7% yr/yr to 94.88 million bushels.

Demand – U.S. total barley disappearance in 2015-16 rose +3.0% yr/yr to 215.0 million bushels.
About 72% of barley is used for food and alcoholic beverages, 25% for animal feed, and 3% for seed.

Trade – World exports of barley in 2015-16 fell -5.6% yr/yr to 27.436 million metric tons. The largest world exporters of barley in 2015-16 were the European Union with 31.4% of world exports, Australia with 21.9%, Argentina with 7.7%, and Canada with 4.9%. The single largest importer of barley is Saudi Arabia with 8.500 million metric tons of imports in 2015-16, which is about 34% of total world imports.

World Production of Barley   In Thousands of Metric Tons

Year	Argen-tina	Australia	Canada	Ethiopia	European Union	Iran	Kazakh-stan	Morocco	Russia	Turkey	Ukraine	United States	World Total
2006-07	4,000	2,000	10,182	4,300	55,943	3,400	2,500	16,400	7,010	7,300	6,300	4,596	143,316
2007-08	3,100	2,000	7,842	3,800	54,450	3,600	1,800	15,050	7,430	6,100	5,000	4,324	133,904
2008-09	4,000	2,200	8,949	4,300	57,270	3,550	1,700	17,100	7,425	5,700	5,900	5,102	143,182
2009-10	4,500	2,200	8,717	4,500	56,770	3,700	2,900	16,650	7,525	5,900	5,600	4,589	144,807
2010-11	4,200	2,000	7,464	4,050	56,610	3,900	3,050	9,500	6,325	6,000	6,000	4,536	134,340
2011-12	3,300	2,100	6,916	3,800	51,200	4,100	3,100	14,300	7,225	6,750	6,300	4,170	135,245
2012-13	3,000	2,000	6,809	4,000	51,000	4,300	1,900	12,100	8,325	6,200	5,100	4,638	131,515
2013-14	2,800	1,800	7,720	6,300	53,400	4,500	2,300	12,700	8,625	6,950	5,000	4,775	141,041
2014-15[1]	2,600	2,100	6,472	11,600	51,000	4,600	2,700	14,100	8,125	5,350	4,500	4,234	141,609
2015-16[2]	2,600	2,200	6,600	8,800	53,100	4,800	3,000	13,900	8,525	6,900	4,500	4,421	143,917

[1] Preliminary.   [2] Estimate.   *Source: Foreign Agricultural Service, U.S. Department of Agriculture (FAS-USDA)*

World Exports of Barley   In Thousands of Metric Tons

Year	Argen-tina	Australia	Canada	European Union	India	Kazak-stan	Russia	Serbia	Turkey	Ukraine	United States	Uruguay	World Total
2006-07	531	1,851	1,232	3,394	----	609	1,547	9	345	5,103	441	118	15,354
2007-08	911	3,386	3,046	3,760	348	792	1,046	4	----	1,044	902	21	15,433
2008-09	1,018	3,234	1,483	3,569	167	291	3,444	7	3	6,371	288	----	19,998
2009-10	482	3,915	1,309	1,123	51	358	2,657	21	801	6,232	123	----	17,140
2010-11	1,614	4,664	1,207	4,873	11	233	267	11	1	2,794	165	----	15,916
2011-12	3,616	5,376	1,299	3,008	46	704	3,544	9	103	2,462	193	----	20,392
2012-13	3,581	4,482	1,434	4,939	266	164	2,236	17	----	2,134	193	107	19,602
2013-14	2,891	6,216	1,559	5,741	441	416	2,681	28	6	2,476	311	34	22,824
2014-15[1]	1,600	5,219	1,516	9,547	431	483	5,336	7	9	4,456	312	50	29,052
2015-16[2]	2,100	6,000	1,350	8,600	200	600	3,700	25	25	4,500	261	25	27,436

[1] Preliminary.   [2] Estimate.   *Source: Foreign Agricultural Service, U.S. Department of Agriculture (FAS-USDA)*

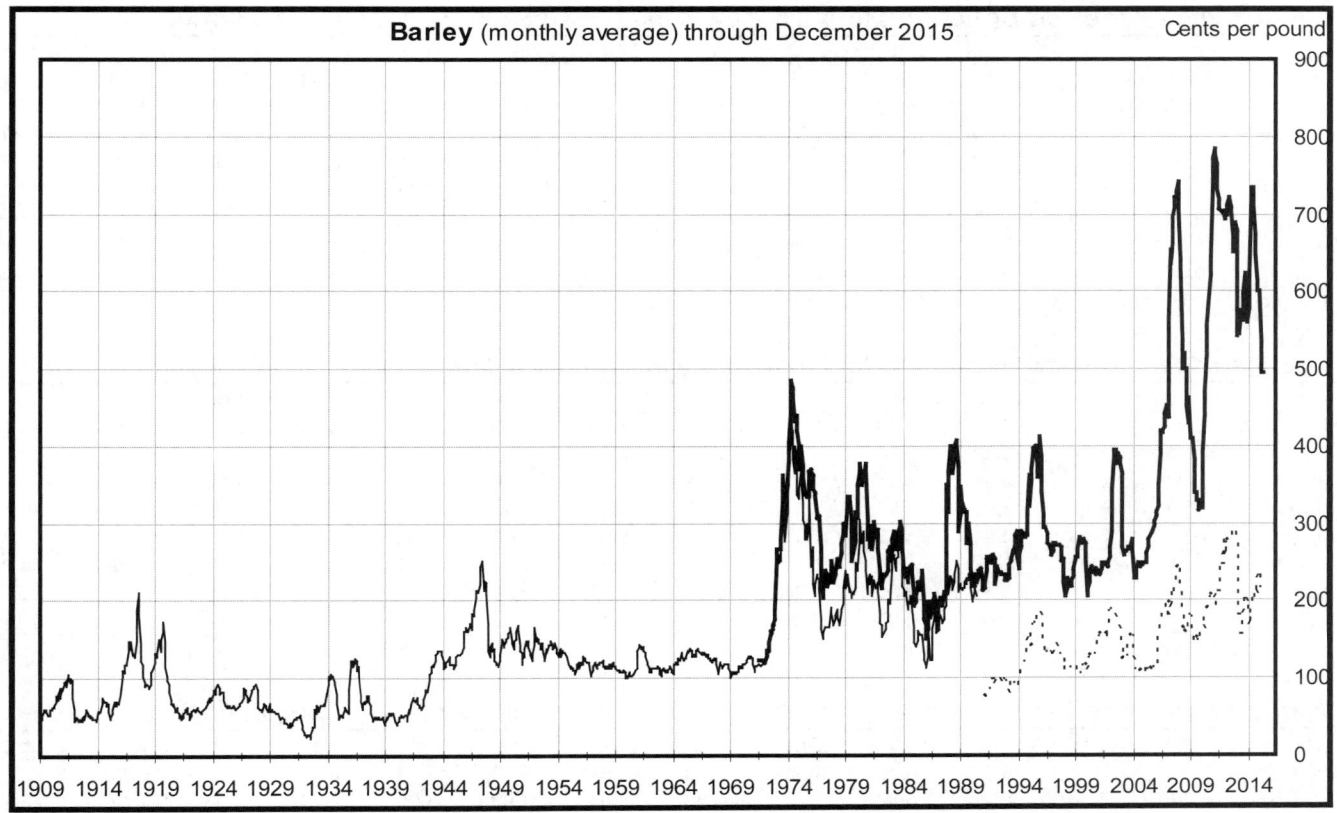

Barley (monthly average) through December 2015 — Cents per pound

Barley Acreage and Prices in the United States

Crop Year Beginning June 1	Acreage ------- 1,000 Acres ------ Planted	Harvested for Gain	Yield Per Harvested Acre -- Bushels --	Seasonal Prices ------- Received by Farmers[3] ------- All	Feed[4]	Malting[4]	Portland No. 2 Western	Government Price Support Operations National Average Loan Rate	Target Price	Put Under Support (mil. Bu.)	Percent of Production
				------------------- Dollars per Bushel -----------------------------							
2008-09	4,246	3,779	63.6	5.23	3.61	5.56	5.29	1.85	2.24	6.7	2.8
2009-10	3,567	3,113	73.0	4.58	2.62	4.95	----	1.85	2.24	12.7	5.6
2010-11	2,872	2,465	73.1	3.90	3.40	4.06	----	1.95	2.63	6.4	3.6
2011-12	2,559	2,239	69.6	5.37	4.88	5.46	----	1.95	2.63	2.8	1.8
2012-13	3,660	3,274	66.9	6.36	5.62	6.50	----	1.95	2.63	3.1	1.4
2013-14	3,528	3,040	71.3	6.06	4.22	6.49	----	1.95	2.63	4.2	1.9
2014-15[1]	3,031	2,497	72.7	5.21	3.20	5.76	----				
2015-16[2]	3,558	3,109	68.9	5.47	3.13	5.79	----				

[1] Preliminary. [2] Estimate. [3] Excludes support payments. *Source: Economic Research Service, U.S. Department of Agriculture (ERS-USDA)*

Salient Statistics of Barley in the United States   In Millions of Bushels

Crop Year Beginning June 1	Supply Beginning Stocks	Pro- duction	Imports	Total Supply	Disappearance Domestic Use Food & Alcohol Beverage	Seed	Feed & Residual	Total	Exports	Total Disap- pearance	Ending Stocks Gov't Owned	Privately Owned	Total Stocks
2008-09	68.2	240.2	29.0	337.4	163.0	5.9	66.6	235.5	13.2	248.7	----	88.7	88.7
2009-10	88.7	227.3	16.6	332.7	158.7	5.0	47.8	211.5	5.7	217.2	----	115.5	115.5
2010-11	115.5	180.3	9.5	305.2	153.7	4.8	49.8	208.3	7.6	215.9	----	89.4	89.4
2011-12	89.4	155.8	16.3	260.4	149.0	6.0	36.6	191.6	8.8	200.4	----	60.0	60.0
2012-13	60.0	219.0	23.3	302.3	141.0	5.8	66.2	213.0	8.9	221.9	----	80.4	80.4
2013-14	80.4	216.7	18.7	315.9	148.3	4.9	66.1	219.4	14.3	233.6	----	82.3	82.3
2014-15[1]	82.3	181.5	23.6	287.4	145.9	5.5	43.1	194.5	14.3	208.8	----	78.6	78.6
2015-16[2]	78.6	214.3	20.0	312.9	147.0	6.0	50.0	203.0	14.0	217.0	----	95.9	95.9

[1] Preliminary. [2] Estimate. [3] Uncommitted inventory. [4] Includes quantity under loan & farmer-owned reserve. [5] Included in Food & Alcohol.
Source: Economic Research Service, U.S. Department of Agriculture (ERS-USDA)

BARLEY

Average Price Received by Farmers for All Barley in the United States   In Dollars Per Bushel

Year	June	July	Aug.	Sept.	Oct.	Nov.	Dec.	Jan.	Feb.	Mar.	Apr.	May	Average
2008-09	4.78	5.12	5.46	5.97	5.73	5.44	5.49	5.34	4.99	5.03	4.84	4.59	5.23
2009-10	4.70	5.09	5.17	4.78	4.41	4.46	4.54	4.68	4.53	4.22	4.08	4.25	4.58
2010-11	3.64	3.79	3.69	3.61	3.73	3.86	3.86	3.86	3.95	4.29	4.41	4.15	3.90
2011-12	4.65	5.07	5.27	5.45	5.51	5.44	5.46	5.44	5.41	5.34	5.69	5.72	5.37
2012-13	5.52	6.25	6.54	6.42	6.49	6.49	6.44	6.41	6.48	6.49	6.30	6.45	6.36
2013-14	6.35	6.38	6.15	5.88	5.94	6.20	6.11	6.04	5.94	5.94	5.90	5.94	6.06
2014-15	6.01	5.62	5.60	5.31	5.24	5.09	5.16	4.86	5.21	4.78	4.94	4.75	5.21
2015-16[1]	5.04	5.19	5.59	5.49	5.54	5.59	5.89	5.46					5.47

[1] Preliminary.   *Source: National Agricultural Statistical Service, U.S. Department of Agriculture (NASS-USDA)*

Average Price Received by Farmers for Feed Barley in the United States   In Dollars Per Bushel

Year	June	July	Aug.	Sept.	Oct.	Nov.	Dec.	Jan.	Feb.	Mar.	Apr.	May	Average
2008-09	5.49	4.72	4.54	4.46	3.82	3.43	3.00	2.90	2.63	2.73	2.65	2.99	3.61
2009-10	3.16	2.94	2.49	2.14	2.29	2.50	2.63	2.63	3.11	2.66	2.40	2.49	2.62
2010-11	2.24	2.40	2.39	2.89	3.38	3.34	3.40	3.46	3.56	4.26	4.89	4.61	3.40
2011-12	4.74	5.04	4.91	5.07	4.76	4.85	4.88	4.81	4.74	4.76	5.10	4.89	4.88
2012-13	5.46	5.53	5.61	5.58	5.72	5.67	5.53	5.60	5.91	5.61	5.55	5.68	5.62
2013-14	5.75	5.17	4.42	4.25	4.10	3.63	3.65	4.21	3.77	3.81	3.77	4.15	4.22
2014-15	4.32	3.85	3.31	2.97	3.13	2.84	2.99	2.99	2.94	3.05	3.05	2.90	3.20
2015-16[1]	3.55	2.98	3.00	3.25	2.98	3.03	3.12	3.14					3.13

[1] Preliminary.   *Source: National Agricultural Statistical Service, U.S. Department of Agriculture (NASS-USDA)*

Average Price Received by Farmers for Malting Barley in the United States   In Dollars Per Bushel

Year	June	July	Aug.	Sept.	Oct.	Nov.	Dec.	Jan.	Feb.	Mar.	Apr.	May	Average
2008-09	4.51	5.23	5.67	6.40	6.20	5.63	5.91	5.62	5.54	5.50	5.33	5.17	5.56
2009-10	5.38	5.48	5.47	5.32	4.94	4.88	4.84	4.87	4.70	4.43	4.55	4.51	4.95
2010-11	4.24	4.14	3.94	3.96	3.88	3.98	3.97	3.97	4.06	4.29	4.22	4.04	4.06
2011-12	4.60	5.09	5.31	5.57	5.69	5.57	5.55	5.54	5.50	5.43	5.87	5.84	5.46
2012-13	5.54	6.43	6.68	6.70	6.65	6.65	6.57	6.49	6.56	6.64	6.48	6.55	6.50
2013-14	6.68	6.56	6.56	6.44	6.49	6.61	6.52	6.52	6.43	6.30	6.45	6.37	6.49
2014-15	6.30	5.90	6.11	5.91	5.76	5.69	5.63	5.47	5.67	5.33	5.75	5.62	5.76
2015-16[1]	5.68	5.72	5.90	5.73	5.78	5.83	5.99	5.67					5.79

[1] Preliminary.   *Source: National Agricultural Statistical Service, U.S. Department of Agriculture (NASS-USDA)*

Stocks of Barley in the United States   In Thousands of Bushels

Year	On Farms Mar. 1	On Farms June 1	On Farms Sept. 1	On Farms Dec. 1	Off Farms Mar. 1	Off Farms June 1	Off Farms Sept. 1	Off Farms Dec. 1	Total Stocks Mar. 1	Total Stocks June 1	Total Stocks Sept. 1	Total Stocks Dec. 1
2008	28,270	9,950	127,750	77,050	82,154	58,273	81,669	95,766	110,424	68,223	209,419	172,816
2009	44,310	27,010	154,050	114,630	84,791	61,723	85,414	91,759	129,101	88,733	239,464	206,389
2010	67,370	40,440	125,070	91,660	89,985	75,059	98,818	88,720	157,355	115,499	223,888	180,380
2011	57,700	26,040	93,050	55,320	80,424	63,311	82,007	83,621	138,124	89,351	175,057	138,941
2012	26,480	9,670	111,550	72,580	67,248	50,317	85,226	85,473	93,728	59,987	196,776	158,053
2013	35,180	15,840	105,620	81,340	81,897	64,557	90,470	88,063	117,077	80,397	196,090	169,403
2014	43,830	19,110	97,820	74,510	77,734	63,145	81,997	81,625	121,564	82,255	179,817	156,135
2015[1]	41,990	20,940	135,840	96,650	76,247	57,639	83,132	84,474	118,237	78,579	218,972	181,124

[1] Preliminary.   *Source: National Agricultural Statistics Service, U.S. Department of Agriculture (NASS-USDA)*

Production of Barley in the United States, by State   In Thousands of Bushels

Year	Arizona	California	Colorado	Idaho	Minnesota	Montana	North Dakota	Oregon	Pennsylvania	Virginia	Washington	Wyoming	U.S. Total
2008	4,800	3,300	8,640	49,880	7,150	37,740	86,240	2,100	4,125	3,060	11,115	6,900	240,193
2009	5,175	2,970	10,395	48,450	4,880	41,040	79,100	1,920	3,375	3,182	6,208	6,720	227,323
2010	5,500	4,350	8,379	43,240	4,340	38,440	43,550	2,960	3,375	3,216	5,832	6,076	180,268
2011	8,000	4,725	7,938	46,500	3,060	31,000	16,450	2,400	3,575	6,160	8,510	6,111	155,780
2012	4,935	4,400	6,710	54,000	6,270	40,290	60,600	3,816	3,604	2,870	12,425	6,141	218,990
2013	8,142	3,150	7,714	57,660	5,175	43,160	46,080	3,500	4,080	3,608	14,040	6,052	216,745
2014	4,000	1,825	6,696	51,700	3,120	44,660	35,845	1,900	3,550	2,212	6,300	7,276	181,542
2015[1]	1,920	1,375	8,190	53,350	9,240	44,200	67,200	1,924	2,600	1,200	4,800	8,170	214,297

[1] Preliminary.   *Source: National Agricultural Statistics Service, U.S. Department of Agriculture (NASS-USDA)*

Weekly Outstanding Export Sales and Cumulative Exports of U.S. Barley   In Thousands of Metric Tons

Marketing Year 2014/2015 Week Ending	Weekly Exports	Accumu-lated Exports	Net Sales	Out-standing Sales	Marketing Year 2015/2016 Week Ending	Weekly Exports	Accumu-lated Exports	Net Sales	Out-standing Sales
Jun 05, 2014	12,788	12,788	13,650	6,423	Jun 04, 2015	353	353	3,942	8,030
Jun 12, 2014	562	13,350	2,880	8,741	Jun 11, 2015	341	694		7,689
Jun 19, 2014	1,272	14,622	-62	7,407	Jun 18, 2015	494	1,188	54	7,249
Jun 26, 2014	541	15,163	1,100	7,966	Jun 25, 2015	489	1,677	40	6,800
Jul 03, 2014	599	15,762	700	8,067	Jul 02, 2015	905	2,582	296	6,191
Jul 10, 2014	300	16,062	500	8,267	Jul 09, 2015	350	2,932	-75	5,766
Jul 17, 2014		16,062		8,267	Jul 16, 2015		2,932		5,766
Jul 24, 2014	21	16,083	513	8,759	Jul 23, 2015		2,932	100	5,866
Jul 31, 2014	422	16,505	383	8,720	Jul 30, 2015		2,932		5,866
Aug 07, 2014	734	17,239	12,000	19,986	Aug 06, 2015	262	3,194		5,604
Aug 14, 2014	267	17,506		19,719	Aug 13, 2015	140	3,334	15,000	20,464
Aug 21, 2014	3,187	20,693	560	17,092	Aug 20, 2015	242	3,576		20,222
Aug 28, 2014	253	20,946	750	17,589	Aug 27, 2015	363	3,939	513	20,372
Sep 04, 2014	646	21,592	500	17,443	Sep 03, 2015	13,860	17,799	-1,020	5,492
Sep 11, 2014	878	22,470	42,600	59,165	Sep 10, 2015		17,799		5,492
Sep 18, 2014	495	22,965		58,670	Sep 17, 2015		17,799		5,492
Sep 25, 2014	408	23,373	500	58,762	Sep 24, 2015	552	18,351	52	4,992
Oct 02, 2014	28,042	51,415	32,499	63,219	Oct 01, 2015		18,351	530	5,522
Oct 09, 2014	589	52,004	-28,601	34,029	Oct 08, 2015	63	18,414		5,459
Oct 16, 2014	75	52,079	346	34,300	Oct 15, 2015		18,414	-44	5,415
Oct 23, 2014		52,079	-112	34,188	Oct 22, 2015	411	18,825	674	5,678
Oct 30, 2014	536	52,615	416	34,068	Oct 29, 2015	137	18,962	3,145	8,686
Nov 06, 2014	414	53,029	457	34,111	Nov 05, 2015	296	19,258		8,390
Nov 13, 2014		53,029	4,251	38,362	Nov 12, 2015	1,279	20,537	-1,500	5,611
Nov 20, 2014	193	53,222	14,000	52,169	Nov 19, 2015	120	20,657		5,491
Nov 27, 2014	34,595	87,817	2,424	19,998	Nov 26, 2015	148	20,805	-1	5,342
Dec 04, 2014	460	88,277	15,000	34,538	Dec 03, 2015	87	20,892		5,255
Dec 11, 2014	618	88,895	11,496	45,416	Dec 10, 2015	433	21,325	2	4,824
Dec 18, 2014	584	89,479	-2	44,830	Dec 17, 2015	439	21,764		4,385
Dec 25, 2014	489	89,968		44,341	Dec 24, 2015		21,764		4,385
Jan 01, 2015	152	90,120		44,189	Dec 31, 2015	462	22,226		3,923
Jan 08, 2015	371	90,491		43,818	Jan 07, 2016	175	22,401		3,748
Jan 15, 2015	16,588	107,079	2,360	29,590	Jan 14, 2016	219	22,620		3,529
Jan 22, 2015	68	107,147	-36	29,486	Jan 21, 2016		22,620		3,529
Jan 29, 2015	219	107,366	1,000	30,267	Jan 28, 2016		22,620		3,529
Feb 05, 2015	165	107,531	140	30,242	Feb 04, 2016	362	22,982	2	3,169
Feb 12, 2015	15,743	123,274	528	15,027	Feb 11, 2016	175	23,157		2,994
Feb 19, 2015		123,274		15,027	Feb 18, 2016		23,157		2,994
Feb 26, 2015		123,274	1,344	16,371	Feb 25, 2016		23,157	1,000	3,994
Mar 05, 2015	174	123,448	2,960	19,157	Mar 03, 2016	172	23,329	23	3,845
Mar 12, 2015	303	123,751	-3,100	15,754	Mar 10, 2016		23,329		3,845
Mar 19, 2015	1,312	125,063	534	14,976	Mar 17, 2016	192	23,521		3,653
Mar 26, 2015	436	125,499	40	14,580	Mar 24, 2016				
Apr 02, 2015	252	125,751	68	14,396	Mar 31, 2016				
Apr 09, 2015	29	125,780	16	14,383	Apr 07, 2016				
Apr 16, 2015	333	126,113		14,050	Apr 14, 2016				
Apr 23, 2015	143	126,256	6,003	19,910	Apr 21, 2016				
Apr 30, 2015	936	127,192	2,580	21,554	Apr 28, 2016				
May 07, 2015	528	127,720	-17	21,009	May 05, 2016				
May 14, 2015	243	127,963		20,766	May 12, 2016				
May 21, 2015	139	128,102		20,627	May 19, 2016				
May 28, 2015	15,894	143,996	-133	4,600	May 26, 2016				
Jun 04, 2015	679	144,675	21	3,942					

Source: Foreign Agricultural Service, U.S. Department of Agriculture (FAS-USDA)

Bauxite

Bauxite is a naturally occurring, heterogeneous material comprised of one or more aluminum hydroxide minerals plus various mixtures of silica, iron oxide, titanium, alumina-silicates, and other impurities in trace amounts. Bauxite is an important ore of aluminum and forms by the rapid weathering of granite rocks in warm, humid climates. It is easily purified and can be converted directly into either alum or metallic aluminum. It is a soft mineral with hardness varying from 1 to 3, and specific gravity from 2 to 2.55. Bauxite is dull in appearance and may vary in color from white to brown. It usually occurs in aggregates in pea-sized lumps.

Bauxite is the only raw material used in the production of alumina on a commercial scale in the United States. Bauxite is classified according to the intended commercial application, such as abrasive, cement, chemical, metallurgical, and refractory. Of all the bauxite mined, about 95 percent is converted to alumina for the production of aluminum metal with some smaller amounts going to nonmetal uses as various forms of specialty alumina. Small amounts are used in non-metallurgical bauxite applications. Bauxite is also used to produce aluminum chemicals and is used in the steel industry.

Supply – World production of bauxite in 2015 rose +11.8% yr/yr to 274.000 million metric tons. The world's

largest producer of bauxite is Australia with 29.2% of the world's production in 2015, followed by China (21.9%), Brazil (12.8%), India (7.0%), Guinea (6.5%), , and Jamaica (3.9%). Chinese production of bauxite has almost quadrupled in the past 10 years. India's bauxite production has also risen rapidly and is about triple the amount seen 15 years ago.

Demand – U.S. consumption of bauxite in 2015 fell by -8.0% yr/yr to 9.000 million metric tons, well below the record high of 15.962 million metric tons seen in 1980. The alumina industry took about 96% of bauxite production in 2013, or 9.810 million metric tons. According to 2004 data (the latest data available) the refractory industry usually takes about 1.4% of the U.S. bauxite supply, the abrasive industry takes about 0.2%, and the chemical industry takes the rest.

Trade – The U.S. relies on imports for almost 100% of its consumption needs. Domestic ore, which provides less than 1 percent of the U.S. requirement for bauxite, is mined by one company from surface mines in the states of Alabama and Georgia. U.S. imports of bauxite rose +9.9% yr/yr to 10.800 million metric tons in 2014, but still well below the record of 14.976 million metric tons seen in 1974. U.S. exports of bauxite in 2014 were negligible at only 3,460 metric tons and down -20.5% yr/yr.

World Production of Bauxite   In Thousands of Metric Tons

Year	Australia	Brazil	China	Greece	Guinea	Guyana[3]	Hungary	India	Jamaica[3]	Russia[3]	Sierra Leone	Suriname	World Total
2006	61,780	23,236	27,000	2,163	18,784	1,479	538	13,940	14,865	6,300	1,071	4,924	193,000
2007	62,398	25,461	30,000	2,126	18,519	2,239	546	20,343	14,568	5,775	1,169	5,054	221,000
2008	64,038	28,098	35,000	2,176	16,000	2,109	511	21,210	14,636	5,675	954	5,333	227,000
2009	65,231	26,074	40,000	1,935	13,600	1,485	267	16,000	7,817	5,775	757	3,388	209,000
2010	68,414	32,028	44,000	1,902	15,300	1,083	307	18,000	8,540	5,690	1,089	3,104	239,000
2011	69,976	33,625	45,000	1,900	15,300	1,818	278	19,000	10,189	5,943	1,300	3,236	260,000
2012	76,282	34,956	47,000	2,100	16,041	2,214	250	19,000	9,339	5,166	776	3,400	259,000
2013	76,282	32,481	46,000	2,100	18,763	1,713	290	15,400	9,435	5,322	616	2,700	283,000
2014[1]	78,600	34,800	55,000	1,900	17,300	1,600		16,500	9,680	5,590		3,000	245,000
2015[2]	80,000	35,000	60,000	1,900	17,700	1,700		19,200	10,700	6,600		2,200	274,000

[1] Preliminary.   [2] Estimate.   [3] Dry Bauxite equivalent of ore processed.   *Source: U.S. Geological Survey (USGS)*

Salient Statistics of Bauxite in the United States   In Thousands of Metric Tons

Year	Net Import Reliance as a % of Apparent Consump	Average Price F.O.B. Mine $ per Ton	Consumption by Industry Total	Alumina	Abrasive	Chemical	Refractoty	Dry Equivalent Imports[4]	Exports[3]	Consumption	Stocks, December 31 Producers & Consumers	Gov't Owned	Total
2005	100	26	12,400	11,900	W	W	W	11,800	34	12,400	W	----	W
2006	100	28	12,300	11,800	W	W	W	11,600	20	12,300	W	----	W
2007	100	31	10,200	9,830	W	W	W	9,840	15	10,200	W	----	W
2008	100	26	9,550	9,310	W	W	W	10,500	14	9,550	W	----	W
2009	100	30	5,490	5,330	W	W	W	6,970	9	4,960	W	----	W
2010	100	29	8,180	8,050	W	W	W	8,120	21	8,180	W	----	W
2011	100	39	8,820	8,670	----	----	----	9,540	22	8,820	W	----	W
2012	100	36	9,560	9,330	----	----	----	10,300	11	9,560	W	----	W
2013[1]	100		10,200	9,810	----	----	----	9,830	4	10,200	W	----	W
2014[2]	100		9,780		----	----	----	10,800	3				

[1] Preliminary.   [2] Estimate.   [3] Including concentrates.   [4] For consumption.   W = Withheld.   *Source: U.S. Geological Survey (USGS)*

Bismuth

Bismuth (symbol Bi) is a rare metallic element with a pinkish tinge. Bismuth has been known since ancient times, but it was confused with lead, tin, and zinc until the middle of the 18th century. Among the elements in the earth's crust, bismuth is ranked about 73rd in natural abundance. This makes bismuth about as rare as silver. Most industrial bismuth is obtained as a by-product of ore extraction.

Bismuth is useful for castings because of the unusual way that it expands after solidifying. Some of bismuth's alloys have unusually low melting points. Bismuth is one of the most difficult of all substances to magnetize. It tends to turn at right angles to a magnetic field. Because of this property, it is used in instruments for measuring the strength of magnetic fields.

Bismuth finds a wide variety of uses such as pharmaceutical compounds, ceramic glazes, crystal ware, and chemicals and pigments. Bismuth is found in household pharmaceuticals and is used to treat stomach ulcers. Bismuth is opaque to X-rays and can be used in fluoroscopy. Bismuth has also found new use as a nontoxic substitute for lead in various applications such as brass plumbing fixtures, crystal ware, lubricating greases, pigments, and solders. There has been environmental interest in the use of bismuth as a replacement for lead used in shot for waterfowl hunting and in fishing sinkers. Another use has been for galvanizing to improve drainage characteristics of galvanizing alloys. Zinc-bismuth alloys have the same drainage properties as zinc-lead without being as hazardous.

Prices – The average price of bismuth (99.99% pure) in the U.S. in 2015 fell by -40.8% to $6.47 per pound, well below the 2007 record high of $13.32 per pound. Up until 2007, bismuth prices were much lower in the range of $3.00 to $5.00 per pound.

Supply – World mine production of bismuth in 2015 fell -2.2% to 13,300 metric tons, down from the 2014 record high of 13,600 metric tons. The world's largest producer in 2015 was China with 56.4% of world production, followed by Mexico with 5.3%. Regarding production of the refined metal in 2013 (latest data), China had 91.2% of production, Mexico had 4.8%, Japan had 2.9%, and Kazakhstan had 0.9%. The U.S. does not have any significant domestic refinery production of bismuth.

Demand – U.S. consumption of bismuth in 2015 rose by +23.8% to 900 metric tons, but still well below the record high of 2,630 metric tons in 2007. In 2013 (latest data) the consumed uses of bismuth were 70.9% for chemicals and 8.1% for fusible alloys.

Trade – U.S. imports of bismuth in 2015 fell -3.1% to 2,200 metric tons, well below the 2007 record high of 3,070 metric tons. Of U.S. imports in 2015, 13.3% came from Belgium. U.S. exports of bismuth and alloys in 2015 rose + 5.8% yr/yr to 600 metric tons, but still well below the 2010 record high of 1,040 metric tons.

World Production of Bismuth   In Metric Tons (Mine Output=Metal Content)

| | Mine Output, Metal Content | | | | | | Refined Metal | | | | | | |
Year	Canada	China	Japan	Mexico	Peru	World Total	Belgium	China	Japan	Kazak-hastan[3]	Mexico	Peru	World Total
2009	86	6,000	----	854	423	7,500	----	12,300	423	90	854	423	14,000
2010	91	6,500	----	952	----	7,700	----	14,000	454	150	952	----	16,000
2011	92	7,000	----	935	----	8,100	----	15,000	460	150	935	----	17,000
2012	121	6,000	----	800	----	7,000	----	15,000	470	150	800	----	17,000
2013	35	7,500	----	824	----	8,400	----	15,500	500	150	824	----	17,000
2014[1]	3	7,600	----	948	----	13,600							
2015[2]	3	7,500	----	700	----	13,300							

[1] Preliminary.   [2] Estimate.   *Source U.S. Geological Survey (USGS)*

Salient Statistics of Bismuth in the United States   In Metric Tons

| | Bismuth Consumed, By Uses | | | | | | | Imports from | | | | Dealer Price $ Per Pound |
| | Metal-lurgical Additives | Other Alloys & Uses | Fusible Alloys | Chem-icals[3] | Total Consumption | Consumer Stocks Dec. 31 | Exports of Metal & Alloys | Metallic Bismuth from | | | | |
Year								Belgium	Mexico	Preu	Total	
2008	375	38	75	597	1,210	228	375	509.0	40.0	55.7	1,930	12.73
2009	232	2	58	528	812	134	397	450.0	59.4	29.4	1,250	7.84
2010	231	4	62	589	636	133	1,040	674.0	0.4	0.5	1,620	8.76
2011	W	W	68	492	696	138	628	713.0	0.1	----	1,750	11.47
2012	W	W	52	434	647	134	764	505.0	----	----	1,700	10.10
2013[1]	W	W	62	549	774	50	816	389.0	----	144.0	1,710	8.71
2014[2]					727	329	567	303.0	----	71.6	2,270	11.14

[1] Preliminary.   [2] Estimate.   [3] Includes pharmaceuticals.   *Source: U.S. Geological Survey (USGS)*

Average Price of Bismuth (99.99%) in the United States   In Dollars Per Pound

Year	Jan.	Feb.	Mar.	Apr.	May	June	July	Aug.	Sept.	Oct.	Nov.	Dec.	Average
2012	10.58	10.86	10.74	10.45	10.59	10.39	10.21	9.59	9.36	9.78	9.20	8.64	10.03
2013	8.73	8.81	9.12	9.16	8.92	8.75	8.12	7.86	8.42	8.89	9.03	8.99	8.73
2014	9.25	9.99	10.50	10.45	10.45	10.50	10.65	11.51	12.39	12.41	11.96	11.03	10.92
2015	10.06	8.42	7.65	7.09	6.90	6.68	6.08	5.33	5.18	5.11	4.72	4.43	6.47

Source: American Metal Market (AMM)

Broilers

Broiler chickens are raised for meat rather than for eggs. The broiler industry was started in the late 1950's when chickens were selectively bred for meat production. Broiler chickens are housed in massive flocks mainly between 20,000 and 50,000 birds, with some flocks reaching over 100,000 birds. Broiler chicken farmers usually rear five or six batches of chickens per year.

After just six or seven weeks, broiler chickens are slaughtered (a chicken's natural lifespan is around seven years). Chickens marketed as pouissons, or spring chickens, are slaughtered after four weeks. A few are kept longer than seven weeks to be sold as the larger roasting chickens.

Prices – The average monthly price received by farmers for broilers (live weight) fell in 2015 by -17.2% yr/yr to 52.9 cents per pound. The average monthly price for wholesale broilers (ready-to-cook) in 2015 fell -13.8% to 90.39 cents per pound, below last year's record high of 104.88 cents per pound.

Supply – Total production of broilers in 2015 rose +2.2% yr/yr to 40.925 billion pounds. The number of broilers raised for commercial production in 2014 was up +0.1% yr/yr to 8.544 billion birds, down from the 2008 record high of 9.009 billion birds. The average live-weight per bird rose +1.3% to 6.01 pounds, which was a new record high and was about 50% heavier than the average bird weight of 3.62 pounds seen in 1970, attesting to the increased efficiency of the industry.

Demand – U.S. per capita consumption of broilers in 2015 rose by +0.9% to 89.1 pounds (ready-to-cook) per person per year, a new record high. U.S. consumption of chicken has nearly doubled in the past two decades, up from 47.0 pounds in 1980, as consumers have increased their consumption of chicken because of the focus on low-carb diets and because chicken is a leaner and healthier meat than either beef or pork.

Broiler Supply and Prices in the United States

Years and Quarters	Number (Million)	Average Weight (Pounds)	Liveweight Pounds (Mil. Lbs.)	Certified RTC[3] Weight (Mil. Lbs.)	Total Production RTC[3] (Mil. Lbs.)	Per Capita Consumption RTC[3] Basis (Mil. Lbs.)	Farm Cents per Pound	Georgia Dock[4] Cents per Pound
2010	8,649	5.70	49,313	36,909	36,911	82.3	49.08	85.25
2011	8,532	5.80	49,520	37,178	37,201	82.9	46.67	86.37
2012	8,429	5.86	49,349	37,035	37,039	80.4	51.42	93.60
2013[1]	8,505	5.92	50,353	37,826	37,830	81.9	60.25	103.26
2014[1]	8,522	6.01	50,839	38,550	38,550	83.3	63.92	109.71
2015[2]	8,688	6.12	53,165	40,046	40,042	88.9	52.92	113.83
I	2,120	6.09	12,918	9,717	9,717	21.4	57.67	112.31
II	2,177	6.11	13,292	10,020	10,020	22.1	63.67	114.16
III	2,252	6.12	13,767	10,373	10,373	23.3	47.00	114.76
IV	2,138	6.17	13,188	9,935	9,932	22.2	43.33	114.09

[1] Preliminary.　[2] Estimate.　[3] Total production equals federal inspected slaughter plus other slaughter minus cut-up & further processing condemnation.
[4] Ready-to-cook basis.　*Source: Economic Research Service, U.S. Department of Agriculture (ERS-USDA)*

Salient Statistics of Broilers in the United States

Year	Commercial Production Number (Mil. Lbs.)	Commercial Production Liveweight (Mil. Lbs.)	Average Liveweight Per Bird (Mil. Lbs.)	Average Price (cents Lb.)	Value of Production (Mil. $)	Federally Inspected	Other Chickens	Total	Storage Stocks January 1	Exports	Broiler Feed Ratio (pounds)	Consumption Total (Mil. Lbs.)	Consumption Per Capita[4] (Pounds)
2008	9,009	50,442	5.60	45.8	23,203	36,906	395	37,301	719	6,961	3.7	29,619	83.54
2009	8,550	47,752	5.58	45.2	21,823	35,511	380	35,891	745	6,818	4.1	28,540	79.79
2010	8,624	49,153	5.70	49.1	23,692	36,910	395	37,305	616	6,762	4.5	29,693	82.36
2011	8,608	50,082	5.82	46.7	22,988	37,202	398	37,601	773	6,978	3.1	30,102	82.92
2012	8,463	49,656	5.87	51.4	24,828	37,039	396	37,435	590	7,274	3.1	29,413	80.39
2013[1]	8,534	50,678	5.94	60.3	30,762				651	7,345	3.7	30,166	81.90
2014[2]	8,544	51,373	6.01	63.9	32,725				669	7,304	5.0	30,939	83.40

[1] Preliminary.　[2] Estimate.　[3] Ready-to-cook.　[4] Retail weight basis.　Source: Economic Research Service, U.S. Department of Agriculture (ERS-USDA)

Average Wholesale Broiler[2] Prices RTC (Ready-to-Cook)　In Cents Per Pound

Year	Jan.	Feb.	Mar.	Apr.	May	June	July	Aug.	Sept.	Oct.	Nov.	Dec.	Average
2009	81.90	80.17	77.01	76.39	82.96	86.22	82.95	74.50	72.81	71.00	71.76	73.56	77.60
2010	81.57	81.07	84.00	82.12	86.35	86.63	86.12	83.25	84.04	80.42	81.12	78.38	82.92
2011	76.28	75.43	81.97	82.12	83.38	82.44	79.97	80.89	75.42	73.71	76.46	80.28	79.03
2012	81.76	86.59	93.23	85.01	87.26	85.41	82.62	84.40	82.68	84.05	95.42	97.81	87.19
2013	101.48	101.80	107.27	107.10	110.40	108.28	99.04	91.12	91.51	90.02	93.72	94.60	99.70
2014	96.45	92.45	106.26	110.11	117.59	113.40	107.16	99.69	107.05	106.68	103.68	98.07	104.88
2015[1]	99.62	92.56	98.88	104.79	106.71	101.17	91.01	82.61	77.40	74.09	75.37	82.05	90.52

[1] Preliminary.　[2] 12-city composite wholesale price.　*Source: Economic Research Service, U.S. Department of Agriculture (ERS-USDA)*

Butter

Butter is a dairy product produced by churning the fat from milk, usually cow's milk, until it solidifies. In some parts of the world, butter is also made from the milk of goats, sheep, and even horses. Butter has been in use since at least 2,000 BC. Today butter is used principally as a food item, but in ancient times it was used more as an ointment, medicine, or illuminating oil. Butter was first churned in skin pouches thrown back and forth over the backs of trotting horses.

It takes about 10 quarts of milk to produce 1 pound of butter. The manufacture of butter is the third largest use of milk in the U.S. California is generally the largest producing state, followed closely by Wisconsin, with Washington as a distant third. Commercially finished butter is comprised of milk fat (80% to 85%), water (12% to 16%), and salt (about 2%). Although the price of butter is highly correlated with the price of milk, it also has its own supply and demand dynamics.

The consumption of butter has dropped in recent decades because pure butter has a high level of animal fat and cholesterol that have been linked to obesity and heart disease. The primary substitute for butter is margarine, which is produced from vegetable oil rather than milk fat. U.S. per capita consumption of margarine has risen from 2.6 pounds in 1930 to recent levels near 8.3 pounds, much higher than U.S. butter consumption.

Futures on butter are traded at the Chicago Mercantile Exchange (CME). The CME's butter futures contract calls for the delivery of 40,000 pounds of Grade AA butter and is priced in cents per pound.

Prices – The average monthly price of butter at the CME in 2015 fell -15.1% yr/yr to 2183.86 cents/pound, below last year's record high of 216.43 cents/pound.

Supply – World production of butter in 2016 is expected to rise +2.2% yr/yr to 10.062 million metric tons, a new record high. The world's largest producers of butter will be India with 51.7% of the world production in 2016, the European Union with 23.3%, the United States with 8.5%, New Zealand with 5.5%, and Russia with 2.6%. Production of creamery butter by U.S. factories in 2015 fell -0.4% yr/yr to 1.848 billion pounds, below the 2013 record high of 1.862 billion pounds.

Demand – Total commercial use of creamery butter in the U.S fell by -7.0% yr/yr to 1.633 million pounds in 2015. That is about one-third higher that the commercial use of butter back in the 1950's. Cold storage stocks of creamery butter in the U.S. on December 1, 2015 rose +23.4% yr/yr to 132.702 million pounds.

Trade – World imports of butter are expected to fall -2.9% yr/yr to 270,000 metric tons in 2016. U.S. imports of butter are expected to fall by -24.5% yr/yr to 40,000 metric tons in 2016. World exports of butter in 2016 are expected to rise by +5.2% yr/yr to 945,000 metric tons. U.S exports in 2016 are expected to rise +50.0% yr/yr to 33,000 metric tons, which would still be well below the 1993 record high of 145,000 metric tons.

Supply and Distribution of Butter in the United States   In Millions of Pounds

	---------------- Supply ----------------				-------------------------- Distribution --------------------------						------- 93 Score --------	
		Cold Storage				-- Domestic Disappearance --			-- Department of Agriculture --				AA Wholesale Price	
Year	Production	Stocks[3] Jan. 1	Imports	Total Supply	Total	Per Capita (Pounds)	Exports	Stocks[4] Jan. 1	Stocks[4] Dec 31	Removed by USDA Programs	Total Use	----- $ per Pound -----	
2007	1,533	108,605	39.683	1,680	1,437	4.7	88	----	----	----	1,526	----	1.3682
2008	1,651	155,162	35.274	1,834	1,519	5.0	196	----	----	----	1,715	----	1.4631
2009	1,572	118,962	37.478	1,728	1,530	5.0	66	----	----	----	1,596	----	1.2427
2010	1,564	133,022	22.046	1,717	1,506	4.9	130	----	----	----	1,636	----	1.7280
2011	1,810	81,695	26.455	1,918	1,669	5.4	143	----	----	----	1,812	----	1.9618
2012	1,860	106,856	37.478	2,002	1,746	5.5	104	----	----	----	1,850	----	1.6029
2013	1,863	153,027	26.455	2,041	1,724		205	----	----	----	1,929	----	
2014[1]	1,856	112,467	48.501	2,017	1,750		163	----	----	----	1,914	----	
2015[2]	1,845	104,728	116.844	2,050	1,858		49	----	----	----	1,907	----	

[1] Preliminary.   [2] Estimates.   [3] Includes butter-equivalent.   [4] Includes butteroil.   [5] Includes stocks held by USDA.
Source: Economic Research Service, U.S. Department of Agriculture (ERS-USDA)

Quarterly Commercial Disappearance of Creamery Butter in the United States   In Millions of Pounds

Year	First Quarter	Second Quarter	Third Quarter	Fourth Quarter	Total	Year	First Quarter	Second Quarter	Third Quarter	Fourth Quarter	Total
2004	283.8	296.3	335.5	410.3	1,325.9	2010	362.6	353.0	365.1	443.5	1,524.1
2005	283.8	300.0	347.7	414.2	1,345.7	2011	387.0	372.0	426.3	494.5	1,679.7
2006	294.5	288.5	356.5	459.8	1,399.4	2012	402.5	403.6	435.6	491.3	1,733.0
2007	337.8	284.3	349.2	459.2	1,430.5	2013	412.3	372.2	434.2	517.8	1,736.5
2008	350.1	321.4	369.0	477.0	1,517.5	2014	380.9	433.5	433.6	508.5	1,756.4
2009	371.0	352.3	343.2	457.9	1,524.6	2015[1]	417.3	403.2	468.4	509.5	1,798.4

[1] Preliminary.   *Source: Economic Research Service, U.S. Department of Agriculture (ERS-USDA)*

BUTTER

World Production of Butter[3]   In Thousands of Metric Tons

Year	Argentina	Australia	Brazil	Canada	European Union	India	Japan	Mexico	New Zealand	Russia	Ukraine	United States	World Total
2009	51	118	76	86	2,030	3,910	81	171	482	246	75	713	8,155
2010	55	132	78	80	1,980	4,162	74	182	441	207	79	709	8,278
2011	63	121	79	85	2,055	4,330	63	187	487	217	76	821	8,688
2012	58	119	81	98	2,100	4,525	69	190	527	216	88	843	9,027
2013	60	117	83	95	2,100	4,745	68	190	535	219	93	845	9,249
2014	55	125	85	88	2,250	4,887	61	192	580	252	115	842	9,637
2015[1]	54	122	87	91	2,310	5,035	64	195	570	265	105	830	9,848
2016[2]	56	125	88	93	2,340	5,200	63	197	550	265	100	850	10,062

[1] Preliminary.   [2] Forecast.   [3] Factory (including creameries and dairies) & farm.   NA = Not available.
Source: Foreign Agricultural Service, U.S. Department of Agriculture (FAS-USDA)

Production of Creamery Butter in Factories in the United States   In Millions of Pounds

Year	Jan.	Feb.	Mar.	Apr.	May	June	July	Aug.	Sept.	Oct.	Nov.	Dec.	Total
2008	168.8	146.8	151.9	150.1	142.6	119.8	114.2	115.7	121.0	130.0	133.7	156.3	1,651.1
2009	176.7	147.2	147.0	141.7	139.2	125.3	114.4	101.0	94.7	113.1	120.9	151.3	1,572.5
2010	162.4	140.2	139.3	133.1	131.9	117.1	111.2	101.5	113.8	122.2	133.5	157.8	1,564.0
2011	167.1	150.1	165.4	158.7	155.9	141.3	135.5	133.7	137.9	145.7	152.8	165.9	1,809.8
2012	181.6	170.6	176.3	169.9	164.1	137.0	133.6	129.5	136.3	144.5	142.9	173.1	1,859.5
2013	188.0	173.3	181.4	166.7	163.8	140.1	132.7	134.4	132.2	145.9	142.2	161.7	1,862.5
2014	184.0	166.1	166.6	167.7	166.3	140.4	137.8	130.2	132.8	150.2	144.5	169.8	1,856.3
2015[1]	179.6	156.3	164.3	164.2	169.8	142.1	133.3	128.5	134.9	147.5	151.3	172.9	1,844.8

[1] Preliminary.   *Source: Economic Research Service, U.S. Department of Agriculture (ERS-USDA)*

Cold Storage Holdings of Creamery Butter in the United States, on First of Month   In Millions of Pounds

Year	Jan.	Feb.	Mar.	Apr.	May	June	July	Aug.	Sept.	Oct.	Nov.	Dec.
2008	155,162	188,072	210,422	224,804	251,533	269,474	258,360	246,132	213,744	186,878	149,391	119,946
2009	118,962	176,526	204,927	212,477	240,044	253,310	262,854	262,782	259,578	227,924	190,624	142,661
2010	133,022	168,092	202,896	195,888	206,291	212,488	197,601	193,506	155,253	129,956	108,809	69,932
2011	81,695	118,784	138,672	144,244	141,728	170,095	190,310	187,796	165,698	150,979	130,684	93,523
2012	106,856	170,348	205,172	208,253	254,184	261,586	243,235	234,352	201,135	195,819	145,098	127,282
2013	153,027	207,075	238,342	254,991	309,719	321,954	318,893	295,751	263,928	233,031	181,799	121,627
2014	112,467	143,890	171,773	191,755	186,914	209,430	199,248	180,834	172,789	152,361	147,956	107,566
2015[1]	104,728	148,885	179,003	184,373	232,372	264,801	256,000	254,340	212,189	187,528	178,834	132,740

[1] Preliminary.   *Source: Agricultural Statistics Board, U.S. Department of Agriculture (ASB-USDA)*

Average Price of Butter at Chicago Mercantile Exchange   In Cents Per Pound

Year	Jan.	Feb.	Mar.	Apr.	May	June	July	Aug.	Sept.	Oct.	Nov.	Dec.	Average
2008	1.2246	1.2088	1.3454	1.3905	1.4750	1.5001	1.5385	1.6279	1.6973	1.7320	1.6165	1.2007	1.4631
2009	1.1096	1.1097	1.1770	1.2042	1.2526	1.2235	1.2349	1.2005	1.2199	1.2830	1.5008	1.3968	1.2427
2010	1.3950	1.3561	1.4641	1.5460	1.5896	1.6380	1.7787	1.9900	2.2262	2.1895	1.9295	1.6327	1.7280
2011	2.0345	2.0622	2.0863	1.9970	2.0724	2.1077	2.0443	2.0882	1.8724	1.8295	1.7356	1.6119	1.9618
2012	1.5831	1.4273	1.4895	1.4136	1.3531	1.4774	1.5831	1.7687	1.8803	1.9086	1.7910	1.5590	1.6029
2013	1.4933	1.5713	1.6421	1.7197	1.5997	1.5105	1.4751	1.4013	1.5233	1.5267	1.6126	1.5963	1.5560
2014	1.7756	1.8047	1.9145	1.9357	2.1713	2.2630	2.4624	2.5913	2.9740	2.3184	1.9968	1.7633	2.1643
2015	1.5714	1.7293	1.7166	1.7937	1.9309	1.9065	1.9056	2.1542	2.6690	2.4757	2.8779	2.3318	2.0886

Source: Economic Research Service, U.S. Department of Agriculture (ERS-USDA)

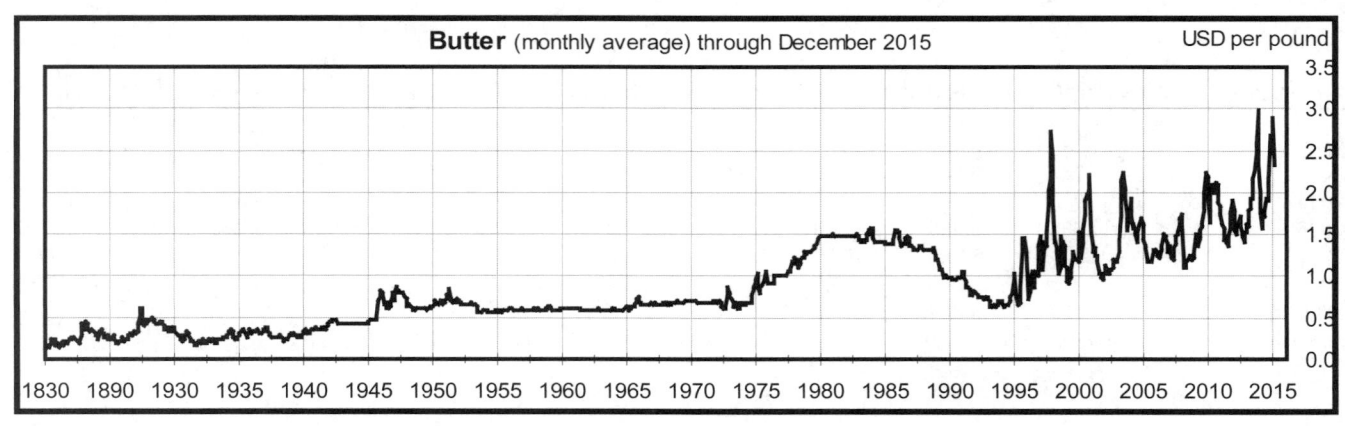

Butter (monthly average) through December 2015

Cadmium

Cadmium (atomic symbol Cd) is a soft, bluish-white, metallic element that can easily be shaped and cut with a knife. Cadmium melts at 321 degrees Celsius and boils at 765 degrees Celsius. Cadmium burns brightly in air when heated, forming the oxide CdO. In 1871, the German chemist Friedrich Stromeyer discovered cadmium in incrustations in zinc furnaces.

Rare greenockite is the only mineral bearing cadmium. Cadmium occurs most often in small quantities associated with zinc ores, such as sphalerite. Electrolysis or fractional distillation is used to separate the cadmium and zinc. About 80% of world cadmium output is a by-product from zinc refining. The remaining 20% comes from secondary sources and recycling of cadmium products. Cadmium recycling is practical only from nickel-cadmium batteries and from some alloys and dust from electric-arc furnaces.

Cadmium is used primarily for metal plating and coating operations in transportation equipment, machinery, baking enamels, photography, and television phosphors. It is also used in solar modules, pigments and lasers, and in nickel-cadmium and solar batteries.

Prices – Cadmium prices for the 8 years up through 2004 were at severely depressed levels, reflecting the decreased demand for the substance. However, cadmium prices then rallied sharply during 2005-07 and posted a record high of $334.28 per pound in 2007. Cadmium prices have since trended lower. In 2015, the average cadmium price moved lower by -38.5% to $50.25 per pound.

Supply – World cadmium production in 2015 rose by +8.0% yr/yr to a new record high of 24,200 metric tons. The largest producer was China with 33.4% of total world production followed by Republic of Korea with 17.6%, Japan with 8.1%, and Canada with 6.1%. U.S. production in 2010 (latest data) fell by -0.6% to 637 metric tons, which was just above the 2009 record low of 633 metric tons.

Demand – U.S. cadmium consumption in 2010 (latest available data) rose by +139.7% yr/yr to 477 metric tons. Of the total apparent consumption, generally about 75% is used for batteries, 12% for pigments, 8% for coatings and plating, 4% for nonferrous alloys, and 1% for other uses.

Trade – The U.S. has been a net exporter of cadmium since 2004. In 2015 the U.S. imported 370 metric tons which was up +166.2% from 2014. U.S. exports of cadmium in 2015 rose +51.9% yr/yr to 410 metric tons, way below the 2009 17-year high of 661 metric tons.

World Refinery Production of Cadmium   In Metric Tons

Year	Australia	Canada	China	Germany	India	Japan	Kazakh-stan	Korea, South	Mexico	Nether-lands	Russia	United States[3]	World Total
2008	350	1,409	6,960	420	599	2,126	1,100	3,090	1,550	530	800	777	21,600
2009	370	1,299	7,050	278	553	1,824	1,300	2,500	1,510	490	1,100	633	20,800
2010	350	1,357	7,360	290	550	2,142	1,400	4,166	1,464	560	1,200	637	23,400
2011	390	1,240	6,670	300	449	1,755	1,300	3,005	1,485	570	1,600	W	21,000
2012	380	1,286	7,000	300	450	1,855	1,200	3,904	1,624	560	1,500	W	22,300
2013	380	1,400	7,000	300	450	1,826	1,200	4,000	1,489	560	1,200	W	22,000
2014[1]	350	1,310	7,000		380	1,830	1,200	4,010	1,410	640	1,200	W	22,400
2015[2]	380	1,480	8,090		460	1,970	1,190	4,250	1,460	640	1,170	W	24,200

[1] Preliminary.   [2] Estimate.   [3] Primary and secondary metal.   *Source: U.S. Geological Survey (USGS)*

Salient Statistics of Cadmium in the United States   In Metric Tons of Contained Cadmium

Year	Net import Reliance As a % of Apparent Consumption	Production (Metal)	Producer Shipments	Cadmium Sulfide Production	Production Other Compounds	Imports of Cadmium Metal[3]	Exports[4]	Apparent Consumption	Industry Stocks Dec. 31[5]	New York Dealer Price $ Per Lb.
2009	E	633	737	----	----	122	661	199	1,450	1.30
2010	9	637	563	----	----	221	306	477	W	1.77
2011	E	W	W	----	----	211	271	W	W	1.25
2012	E	W	W	----	----	192	631	W	W	.92
2013	E	W	W	----	----	388	417	W	W	.87
2014[1]	E	W	W	----	----	139	270	W	W	.88
2015[2]	E	W	W	----	----	370	410	W	W	.48

[1] Preliminary.   [2] Estimate.   [3] For consumption.   [4] Cadmium metal, alloys, dross, flue dust.   [5] Metallic, Compounds, Distributors.   [6] Sticks & Balls in 1 to 5 short ton lots of metal (99.95%).   E = Net exporter.   *Source: U.S. Geological Survey (USGS)*

Average Price of Cadmium (99.95%) in the United States   In Dollars Per Pound

Year	Jan.	Feb.	Mar.	Apr.	May	June	July	Aug.	Sept.	Oct.	Nov.	Dec.	Average
2011	161.38	144.61	140.00	140.00	140.00	140.00	140.00	140.00	125.71	125.00	121.63	116.18	136.21
2012	104.00	91.75	91.25	87.50	87.50	85.95	84.05	80.22	80.00	84.78	86.13	85.00	87.34
2013	85.54	88.68	89.43	94.77	103.41	101.50	94.21	88.87	88.50	90.00	90.00	86.26	91.76
2014	82.98	82.50	80.71	80.00	80.00	80.00	80.00	81.90	85.00	85.00	83.06	80.00	81.76
2015	79.90	73.82	64.61	54.91	50.25	44.66	41.97	39.16	35.50	36.11	39.33	42.83	50.25

Source: American Metal Market (AMM)

Canola (Rapeseed)

Canola is a genetic variation of rapeseed that was developed by Canadian plant breeders specifically for its nutritional qualities and its low level of saturated fat. The term Canola is a contraction of "Canadian oil." The history of canola oil begins with the rapeseed plant, a member of the mustard family. The rape plant is grown both as feed for livestock and birdfeed. For 4,000 years, the oil from the rapeseed was used in China and India for cooking and as lamp oil. During World War II, rapeseed oil was used as a marine and industrial lubricant. After the war, the market for rapeseed oil plummeted. Rapeseed growers needed other uses for their crop, and that stimulated the research that led to the development of canola. In 1974, Canadian plant breeders from the University of Manitoba produced canola by genetically altering rapeseed. Each canola plant produces yellow flowers, which then produce pods. The tiny round seeds within each pod are crushed to produce canola oil. Each canola seed contains approximately 40% oil. Canola oil is the world's third largest source of vegetable oil accounting for 13% of world vegetable oils, following soybean oil at 32%, and palm oil at 28%. The rest of the seed is processed into canola meal, which is used as high protein livestock feed.

The climate in Canada is especially suitable for canola plant growth. Today, over 13 million acres of Canadian soil are dedicated to canola production. Canola oil is Canada's leading vegetable oil. Due to strong demand from the U.S. for canola oil, approximately 70% of Canada's canola oil is exported to the U.S. Canola oil is used as a salad oil, cooking oil, and for margarine as well as in the manufacture of inks, biodegradable greases, pharmaceuticals, fuel, soap, and cosmetics.

Canola futures and options are traded at ICE Futures Canada. The futures contract calls for the delivery of 20 metric tons of canola and 5 contracts are together called a "1 board lot." The futures contract is priced in Canadian dollars per metric ton.

Prices – Winnipeg canola prices on the nearest-futures chart (Barchart.com symbol code RS) in 2015 rallied to a 2-1/2 year high during mid-year, but then sold off again and closed the year up by only +5.4% at CD$476.50 per metric ton.

The average monthly wholesale price of canola oil in the Midwest in 2015 fell -13.6% yr/yr to 36.70 cents per pound. The average monthly wholesale price of canola meal (delivery Pacific Northwest) in the 2015-16 crop year fell -17.3% to $249.10 per short ton.

Supply – World canola production in the 2015-16 marketing year fell -6.2% yr/yr to 67.678 million metric tons, below last year's record high of 72.120 million metric tons. The world's largest canola producers were the European Union with 32.2% of world production in 2015-16, Canada (25.4%), China (20.8%), and India (8.9%). U.S. production of canola and canola oil in 2015-16 rose by +14.4% yr/yr to 1.305 million metric tons. Regarding canola products, world production of canola oil in 2015-16 fell -3.5% to 26.300 million metric tons, below last year's record high of 27.262 million metric tons. U.S. production of canola oil in 2015-16 fell -5.5% to 665,000 metric tons, below the 2013-14 record high of 709,000 metric tons. World production of canola meal in 2015-16 fell -3.7% to 38.883 million metric tons, below last year's record high of 40.386 million metric tons.

Demand – World crush demand for canola in 2015-16 fell -3.7% yr/yr to 65.975 million metric tons. World consumption of canola oil in 2015-16 fell -0.6% yr/yr to 26.732 million metric tons. World consumption of canola meal in 2015-16 fell by -3.0% to 38.883 million metric tons.

Trade – World canola exports in 2015-16 fell -9.9% to 13.487 million metric tons, world canola oil exports rose +5.0% to 4.265 million metric tons, and world canola meal exports fell -5.1% yr/yr to 5.541 million metric tons. World canola imports in 2015-16 fell -7.0% to 13.127 million metric tons, world canola oil imports rose +7.0% to 4.177 million metric tons, and world canola meal imports fell -3.3% to 5.405 million metric tons. Regarding U.S. canola trade, U.S. canola imports in 2015-16 fell -35.5% to 501,000 metric tons and U.S. exports fell -12.3% to 136,000 metric tons.

World Production of Canola (Rapeseed)   In Thousands of Metric Tons

Year	Australia	Bangla-desh	Belarus	Canada	China	European Union	India	Kazakh-stan	Pakistan	Russia	Ukraine	United States	World Total
2006-07	573	189	115	9,000	10,966	16,112	5,800	63	221	523	606	633	45,039
2007-08	1,214	228	240	9,611	10,573	18,397	5,450	118	185	630	1,047	650	48,644
2008-09	1,844	203	514	12,644	12,102	19,062	6,700	83	199	752	2,873	656	57,891
2009-10	1,907	223	611	12,898	13,657	21,633	6,400	107	162	667	1,873	665	61,029
2010-11	2,359	246	374	12,789	13,082	20,782	7,100	109	192	670	1,470	1,112	60,606
2011-12	3,427	262	379	14,608	13,426	19,240	6,200	148	179	1,050	1,437	694	61,457
2012-13	4,142	294	705	13,869	14,007	19,560	6,800	117	220	1,035	1,300	1,087	63,616
2013-14[1]	3,832	230	676	18,551	14,458	21,304	7,300	242	190	1,393	2,352	1,004	71,958
2014-15[2]	3,464	230	730	16,410	14,772	24,450	6,310	241	220	1,464	2,200	1,141	72,120
2015-16[3]	3,100	230	300	17,200	14,100	21,800	6,000	138	160	1,125	1,750	1,305	67,678

[1] Preliminary.   [2] Estimate.   [3] Forecast.   *Source: Economic Research Service, U.S. Department of Agriculture (ERS-USDA); The Oil World*

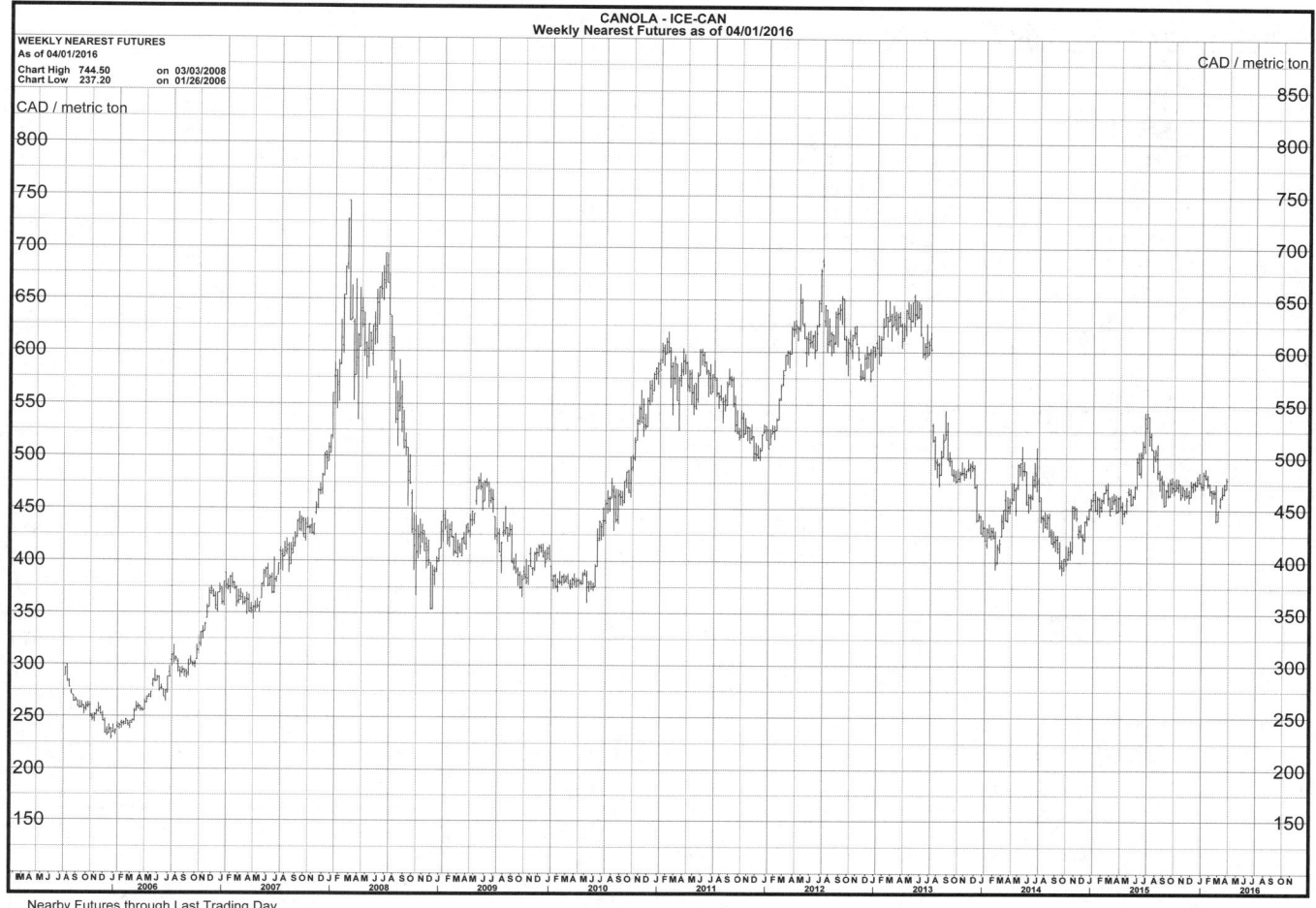

CANOLA - ICE-CAN
Weekly Nearest Futures as of 04/01/2016

WEEKLY NEAREST FUTURES
As of 04/01/2016

Chart High 744.50   on 03/03/2008
Chart Low 237.20   on 01/26/2006

CAD / metric ton

Nearby Futures through Last Trading Day.

Volume of Trading of Canola Futures in Winnipeg   In 20 Metric Ton Units

Year	Jan.	Feb.	Mar.	Apr.	May	June	July	Aug.	Sept.	Oct.	Nov.	Dec.	Total
2006	195,189	240,070	237,537	229,470	211,688	238,967	129,433	145,133	212,164	284,033	191,676	291,994	2,607,354
2007	204,893	309,278	198,589	273,755	281,240	321,022	160,846	181,145	212,288	396,852	268,743	360,531	3,169,182
2008	368,963	388,180	307,536	318,641	209,631	290,152	172,089	170,596	220,479	293,978	126,273	265,670	3,132,188
2009	265,415	345,108	267,276	358,030	286,069	326,924	161,569	188,651	268,629	340,368	211,160	332,594	3,351,793
2010	239,347	349,512	283,156	415,932	232,711	534,781	200,250	277,736	351,663	500,943	284,703	447,694	4,118,428
2011	345,505	483,744	342,887	417,453	326,805	436,050	268,144	331,289	490,065	443,909	361,250	406,052	4,653,153
2012	375,738	588,006	536,743	535,291	367,014	399,329	299,775	279,962	332,661	487,242	279,767	388,733	4,870,261
2013	413,545	558,269	295,056	489,741	355,341	347,609	276,608	381,094	523,431	654,471	479,983	716,539	5,491,687
2014	536,669	570,465	454,015	552,959	369,170	424,087	331,748	298,308	486,457	615,158	346,000	568,886	5,553,922
2015	489,637	486,854	400,209	447,467	327,911	644,971	335,432	365,804	447,279	624,741	403,539	585,625	5,559,469

Contract size = 20 tonnes.   *Source: ICE Futures Canada (ICE)*

Average Open Interest of Canola Futures in Winnipeg   In 20 Metric Ton Units

Year	Jan.	Feb.	Mar.	Apr.	May	June	July	Aug.	Sept.	Oct.	Nov.	Dec.
2006	82,651	88,576	84,828	88,970	84,710	81,561	81,243	77,356	81,597	80,800	90,694	102,651
2007	103,317	103,250	94,001	102,050	114,244	124,321	117,967	111,470	121,589	122,965	146,879	156,698
2008	164,326	172,229	165,282	135,226	111,687	102,353	91,891	82,272	90,075	90,062	91,459	88,373
2009	88,487	100,072	97,016	104,423	111,922	109,921	94,574	104,426	95,168	99,968	93,108	99,736
2010	112,406	125,895	122,112	133,172	134,768	159,949	154,881	150,209	155,712	181,660	199,487	193,948
2011	204,715	207,186	188,138	176,678	166,554	166,105	150,624	166,066	188,592	166,852	160,276	140,345
2012	151,192	181,837	200,941	228,092	242,231	224,287	220,919	224,646	233,085	198,147	157,664	147,883
2013	155,134	189,913	178,763	164,200	143,013	129,283	118,115	145,257	186,811	177,248	200,975	226,220
2014	230,796	224,847	230,852	219,844	168,705	165,651	147,462	165,501	173,282	159,986	142,371	139,732
2015	170,492	217,729	205,075	168,204	151,739	189,500	180,410	173,734	172,828	186,334	174,098	187,855

Contract size = 20 tonnes.   *Source: ICE Futures Canada (ICE)*

CANOLA

World Supply and Distribution of Canola and Products   In Thousands of Metric Tons

| | Canola | | | | Canola Meal | | | | | Canola oil | | | | |
Year	Pro-duction	Exports	Imports	Crush	Ending Stocks	Pro-duction	Exports	Imports	Con-sumption	Ending Stocks	Pro-duction	Exports	Imports	Con-sumption	Ending Stocks
2008-09	57,891	12,126	12,114	52,032	7,297	30,696	3,587	3,563	30,729	245	20,592	2,441	2,442	20,474	952
2009-10	61,029	10,842	10,744	56,626	8,900	33,414	3,598	3,625	33,234	452	22,514	2,741	2,923	22,303	1,345
2010-11	60,606	10,867	10,099	57,926	8,356	34,051	5,188	4,921	33,724	512	23,045	3,423	3,333	23,024	1,276
2011-12	61,457	12,915	13,181	60,468	6,568	35,626	5,439	5,143	35,256	586	24,037	3,970	4,011	23,536	1,818
2012-13	63,616	12,450	12,659	62,571	4,778	36,987	5,535	5,183	36,846	375	24,892	3,944	3,872	23,674	2,964
2013-14/1	71,958	14,965	15,258	66,651	7,521	39,350	6,072	5,924	39,160	417	26,450	3,821	3,776	25,339	4,030
2014-15/2	72,120	14,973	14,109	68,508	6,897	40,386	5,838	5,588	40,071	482	27,262	4,063	3,915	26,901	4,243
2015-16/3	67,678	13,487	13,127	65,975	4,846	38,883	5,541	5,405	38,883	346	26,300	4,265	4,177	26,732	3,723

[1] Preliminary.   [2] Estimate.   [3] Forecast.   *Source: Economic Research Service, U.S. Department of Agriculture (ERS-USDA); The Oil World*

Salient Statistics of Canola and Canola Oil in the United States   In Thousands of Metric Tons

| | Canola | | | | | | | Canola Oil | | | | | | |
| | Supply | | | | Disappearance | | | Supply | | | | Disappearance | | |
Year	Stocks June 1	Pro-duction	Imports	Total Supply	Crush	Exports	Total[3]	Stocks Oct. 1	Pro-duction	Imports	Total Supply	Domestic	Exports	Total
2008-09	158	656	825	1,639	191	1,218	1,639	60	501	1,050	1,611	249	1,284	1,611
2009-10	203	665	568	1,436	177	1,112	1,436	78	487	1,067	1,632	251	1,293	1,632
2010-11	122	1,112	482	1,716	294	1,292	1,716	88	516	1,421	2,025	232	1,657	2,025
2011-12	102	694	622	1,418	153	1,168	1,418	136	499	1,492	2,127	301	1,741	2,127
2012-13	70	1,087	394	1,551	177	1,266	1,551	85	578	1,252	1,915	215	1,636	1,915
2013-14	81	1,004	927	2,012	159	1,689	2,012	64	709	1,538	2,311	119	2,067	2,311
2014-15[1]	129	1,141	777	2,047	155	1,736	2,047	125	704	1,672	2,501	109	2,347	2,501
2015-16[2]	118	1,305	501	1,924	136	1,633	1,924	45	665	1,773	2,483	122	2,298	2,483

[1] Preliminary.   [2] Forecast.   [3] Includes planting seed and residual.   *Source: Economic Research Service, U.S. Department of Agriculture (ERS-USDA)*

Wholesale Price of Canola Oil in Midwest   In Cents Per Pound

Year	Jan.	Feb.	Mar.	Apr.	May	June	July	Aug.	Sept.	Oct.	Nov.	Dec.	Average
2008	64.94	71.80	70.56	71.38	73.05	76.69	74.13	61.05	54.88	42.85	39.81	37.19	61.53
2009	38.80	35.66	35.38	39.75	41.50	42.38	39.80	42.00	39.31	41.55	44.38	42.90	40.28
2010	40.56	41.88	42.50	42.20	40.00	40.00	44.00	47.19	47.38	51.45	53.63	58.25	45.75
2011	59.50	60.13	60.25	62.05	60.19	59.56	60.70	60.00	58.45	56.81	56.13	55.40	59.10
2012	55.06	56.94	59.10	60.94	55.88	54.10	57.44	58.75	59.75	57.50	58.20	57.13	57.57
2013	57.19	59.38	58.95	60.44	60.45	57.50	53.25	48.05	46.00	44.88	45.05	42.63	52.81
2014	39.75	42.56	45.75	47.63	47.50	46.00	43.63	40.10	38.94	39.45	38.94	39.25	42.46
2015[1]	38.80	38.94	35.69	37.19	38.55	40.19	38.30	35.13	33.31	34.20	33.63	36.50	36.70

[1] Preliminary.   *Source: Economic Research Service, U.S. Department of Agriculture (ERS-USDA)*

Average Price of Canola in Vancouver   In Canadian Dollars Per Metric Ton

Year	Jan.	Feb.	Mar.	Apr.	May	June	July	Aug.	Sept.	Oct.	Nov.	Dec.	Average
2008	519.88	608.92	618.85	594.74	578.47	616.27	601.79	517.00	457.86	391.62	399.41	371.48	523.02
2009	413.77	416.13	409.67	428.95	459.08	461.29	422.69	429.38	394.03	377.19	377.74	389.42	414.95
2010	376.26	373.42	374.40	377.22	372.83	400.29	439.34	443.06	453.22	481.16	514.84	542.25	429.02
2011	567.16	577.71	558.19	569.44	555.48	574.44	563.30	547.52	528.64	509.52	513.06	502.88	547.28
2012	512.75	539.92	591.55	626.52	624.60	629.57	657.26	632.65	644.75	627.09	594.75	601.67	606.92
2013	613.04	636.36	635.99	641.70	643.47	626.04	571.91	513.54	473.76	457.25	461.44	418.96	557.79
2014	386.37	380.71	412.23	435.66	459.42	453.37	446.33	430.27	397.71	404.23	423.82	419.92	420.84
2015	432.04	437.63	444.39	443.37	448.45	488.36	514.22	475.87	457.49	460.78	454.54	460.90	459.84

Source: ICE Futures Canada (ICE)

Average Wholesale Price of Canola Meal, 36% Pacific Northwest   In Dollars Per Short Ton

Year	Oct.	Nov.	Dec.	Jan.	Feb.	Mar.	Apr.	May	June	July	Aug.	Sept.	Average
2008-09	192.55	217.99	228.62	279.23	243.30	217.02	230.06	287.99	325.48	261.55	277.30	224.74	248.82
2009-10	220.90	177.69	NA	248.63	218.18	214.11	226.95	222.28	224.56	245.18	244.44	231.20	224.92
2010-11	251.03	257.73	265.54	275.80	261.20	260.32	254.68	267.82	263.45	277.55	271.04	257.34	263.63
2011-12	238.70	235.20	NA	253.98	257.63	277.83	313.38	333.69	335.26	378.86	388.13	370.79	307.59
2012-13	354.49	334.46	349.55	347.22	359.23	356.74	340.42	362.51	376.19	374.89	340.44	354.55	354.22
2013-14	334.95	342.86	373.60	365.48	384.21	383.68	398.39	407.14	387.65	317.81	303.74	316.94	359.70
2014-15	301.75	356.31	349.31	311.56	296.21	279.54	261.35	274.60	305.85	328.03	285.83	264.01	301.20
2015-16[1]	257.69	248.98	240.64	231.76	224.34								240.68

[1] Preliminary.   *Source: Economic Research Service, U.S. Department of Agriculture (ERS-USDA)*

Cattle and Calves

The beef cycle begins with the cow-calf operation, which breeds the new calves. Most ranchers breed their herds of cows in summer, thus producing the new crop of calves in spring (the gestation period is about nine months). This allows the calves to be born during the milder weather of spring and provides the calves with ample forage through the summer and early autumn. The calves are weaned from the mother after 6-8 months and most are then moved into the "stocker" operation. The calves usually spend 6-10 months in the stocker operation, growing to near full-sized by foraging for summer grass or winter wheat. When the cattle reach 600-800 pounds, they are typically sent to a feedlot and become "feeder cattle." In the feedlot, the cattle are fed a special food mix to encourage rapid weight gain. The mix includes grain (corn, milo, or wheat), a protein supplement (soybean, cottonseed, or linseed meal), and roughage (alfalfa, silage, prairie hay, or an agricultural by-product such as sugar beet pulp). The animal is considered "finished" when it reaches full weight and is ready for slaughter, typically at around 1,200 pounds, which produces a dressed carcass of around 745 pounds. After reaching full weight, the cattle are sold for slaughter to a meat packing plant. Futures and options on live cattle and feeder cattle are traded at the CME Group. Both the live and feeder cattle futures contracts trade in terms of cents per pound.

Prices – CME live cattle futures prices (Barchart.com electronic symbol LE) began 2015 on a weak note as they continued to retreat from the Oct 2014 record high $1.71975 a pound, the highest since cattle futures trading began in 1964. The USDA's Jan 2015 bi-annual Cattle inventory report pressured cattle prices as it showed an unexpected +1.4% y/y increase in the U.S. cattle herd on Jan 1 to 89.8 million head. Cattle prices traded sideways until spring when the Mar USDA Cold Storage report showed total frozen beef supplies in February surged +20.2% y/y to 492.116 million pounds, the most for a February since the

USDA began tracking the data in 1957. Cattle prices then sold-off the rest of the year and posted a 3-1/2 year low of $1.16975 in December. High beef prices took their toll on domestic demand as wholesale beef prices sank to a 2-1/2 year low in December, while supplies were robust as USDA slaughter data showed the average weight of cattle sold to beef processors in November 2015 was a record 1,393 pounds (data from 1974). Foreign demand weakened as well after 2015 U.S. beef exports tumbled -11.9% y/y to 2.266 billion pounds. With the increased supplies, ranchers were trying to limit their herd sizes as the December Cattle on Feed report showed cattle placements, or cattle place on feed in November, fell -10.8% y/y to 1.601 million head, the lowest for a November since the data series began in 1996. Cattle prices finished 2015 down -18% yr/yr at $1.35800 a pound.

Supply – The world's number of cattle as of January 1, 2016 rose +0.7% to 971.482 million head. As of January 1, 2016, the number of cattle on Brazilian farms rose by +2.8% to 219.093 million head. As of January 1, 2016 the number of cattle and calves on U.S. farms rose by +3.2% to 91.988 million head. The USDA is forecasting that U.S. commercial production of beef in 2016 will rise by +4.9% to 24.960 billion pounds.

Demand – The federally-inspected slaughter of cattle in the U.S., a measure of cattle consumption, fell by -4.7% to a 5-decade low of 28.295 million head in 2015.

Trade – U.S. imports of live cattle in 2015 fell by -14.6% to 2.014 million head. U.S. exports of live cattle in 2015 fell by -38% to an estimated 67,362 head, down sharply from 193,908 posted as recently as 2011. U.S. imports of beef in 2016 are projected to fall -11.4% to 3.045 billion pounds. U.S. exports of beef in 2016 are projected to rise +6.3% to 2.425 billion pounds, remaining well below the 2011 record high of 2.785 billion pounds.

World Cattle and Buffalo Numbers as of January 1　In Thousands of Head

Year	Argentina	Australia	Brazil	Canada	China	European Union	India	Mexico	New Zealand	Russia	United States	Uruguay	World Total
2007	55,664	28,393	173,830	14,135	104,651	89,329	298,000	23,316	9,610	21,562	96,573	11,915	1,023,135
2008	55,662	28,037	175,437	13,755	105,948	89,899	304,418	22,850	9,730	21,546	96,035	11,869	1,025,297
2009	54,260	27,321	179,540	13,030	105,760	90,408	306,000	22,666	9,715	21,040	94,721	11,950	1,017,167
2010	49,057	27,906	185,159	12,670	107,265	89,829	304,500	22,192	9,917	20,677	94,081	11,828	998,143
2011	48,156	27,550	190,925	12,155	106,264	87,831	302,500	21,456	9,864	19,970	92,887	11,241	990,958
2012	49,597	28,506	197,550	12,245	103,605	87,054	300,000	20,090	10,021	20,134	91,160	11,232	989,237
2013	51,095	29,000	203,273	12,305	103,434	87,106	299,606	18,521	10,180	19,930	90,095	11,384	991,850
2014	51,545	29,290	207,959	12,220	103,000	87,619	300,600	17,760	10,183	19,564	88,526	11,903	994,038
2015[1]	51,545	27,600	213,035	11,920	100,450	88,388	301,100	17,120	10,368	19,152	89,800	12,053	964,450
2016[2]	51,995	26,150	219,093	11,930	100,250	88,600	301,600	16,450	10,283	18,665	92,900	12,063	971,482

[1] Preliminary.　[2] Forecast.　*Source: Foreign Agricultural Service, U.S. Department of Agriculture (FAS-USDA)*

CATTLE AND CALVES

Cattle Supply and Distribution in the United States   In Thousands of Head

Year	Cattle & Calves on Farms Jan. 1	Imports	Calves Born	Total Supply	Livestock Slaughter - Cattle and Calves — Commercial — Federally Inspected	Other[3]	All Commercial	Farm	Total Slaughter	Deaths on Farms	Exports	Total Disappearance
2006	96,342	2,289	37,016	135,646	33,844	566	34,410	187	34,597	4,167	50	38,813
2007	96,573	2,495	36,759	135,827	34,465	557	35,022	187	35,209	4,251	66	39,526
2008	96,035	2,284	36,153	134,471	34,747	574	35,322	186	35,507	4,074	107	39,688
2009	94,521	2,002	35,939	132,462	33,696	587	34,283	185	34,468	4,064	58	38,590
2010	94,081	2,284	35,740	132,105	34,566	561	35,128	197	35,325	4,001	91	39,417
2011	92,887	2,107	35,357	130,352	34,394	546	34,939	169	35,108	4,017	194	39,319
2012	91,160	2,284	34,469	127,914	33,185	538	33,723	151	33,874	3,881	191	37,947
2013	90,095	2,037	33,730	125,862	32,698	526	33,224	128	33,353	3,870	161	37,384
2014[1]	88,526	2,360	33,522	124,408	30,242	495	30,737	124	30,861	3,850	108	34,818
2015[2]	89,143	1,985	34,302	125,430	28,742						72	

[1] Preliminary.   [2] Estimate.   [3] Wholesale and retail.   *Source: Economic Research Service, U.S. Department of Agriculture (ERS-USDA)*

Beef Supply and Utilization in the United States

Years and Quarters	Beginning Stocks	Production Commercial	Total	Imports	Total Supply	Exports	Ending Stocks	Total Disappearance	Per Capita Disappearance - Carcass Weight	Per Capita Disappearance - Retail Weight Total
2012	----	25,913	25,913	2,220	28,133	2,452	----	----	----	57.4
I	----	6,282	6,282	582	6,864	558	----	----	----	14.0
II	----	6,473	6,473	669	7,142	624	----	----	----	14.7
III	----	6,586	6,586	516	7,102	650	----	----	----	14.5
IV	----	6,572	6,572	453	7,025	620	----	----	----	14.2
2013	----	25,720	25,720	2,250	27,970	2,590	----	----	----	56.3
I	----	6,175	6,175	590	6,765	557	----	----	----	13.7
II	----	6,513	6,513	629	7,142	637	----	----	----	14.5
III	----	6,609	6,609	515	7,124	716	----	----	----	14.3
IV	----	6,423	6,423	516	6,939	680	----	----	----	13.9
2014	----	24,252	24,252	2,947	27,199	2,573	----	----	----	54.1
I	----	5,868	5,868	596	6,464	583	----	----	----	13.1
II	----	6,184	6,184	768	6,952	667	----	----	----	13.9
III	----	6,179	6,179	764	6,943	679	----	----	----	13.7
IV	----	6,021	6,021	818	6,839	643	----	----	----	13.4
2015[1]	----	23,690	23,690	3,370	27,060	2,266	----	----	----	53.9
I	----	5,664	5,664	876	6,540	526	----	----	----	13.1
II	----	5,855	5,855	991	6,846	606	----	----	----	13.6
III	----	6,066	6,066	890	6,956	541	----	----	----	13.9
IV	----	6,105	6,105	613	6,718	593	----	----	----	13.3
2016[2]	----	24,580	24,580	2,845	27,425	2,475	----	----	----	54.3
I	----	5,885	5,885	760	6,645	545	----	----	----	13.4
II	----	6,115	6,115	790	6,905	635	----	----	----	13.6
III	----	6,365	6,365	675	7,040	660	----	----	----	13.8
IV	----	6,215	6,215	620	6,835	635	----	----	----	13.5

[1] Preliminary.   [2] Forecast.   *Source: Economic Research Service, U.S. Department of Agriculture (ERS-USDA)*

United States Cattle on Feed in 13 States   In Thousands of Head

Year	Number on Feed[3]	Placed on Feed	Marketings	Other Disappearance	Year	Number on Feed[3]	Placed on Feed	Marketings	Other Disappearance
2012	11,861	22,254	22,028	915	2014[1]	10,523	21,470	20,464	903
I	11,861	5,353	5,489	243	I	10,523	5,473	4,997	207
II	11,482	5,269	5,797	244	II	10,792	5,000	5,490	259
III	10,710	5,933	5,466	188	III	10,043	5,298	5,162	194
IV	10,989	5,699	5,276	240	IV	9,985	5,699	4,815	243
2013	11,172	21,860	21,618	849	2015[2]	10,626	20,427	19,660	818
I	11,172	5,191	5,219	220	I	10,626	5,149	4,772	206
II	10,924	5,326	5,643	232	II	10,797	4,748	5,097	212
III	10,375	5,444	5,533	176	III	10,236	5,110	4,955	173
IV	10,110	5,899	5,223	221	IV	10,218	5,420	4,836	227

[1] Preliminary.   [2] Estimate.   [3] Beginning of period.   *Source: Economic Research Service, U.S. Department of Agriculture (ERS-USDA)*

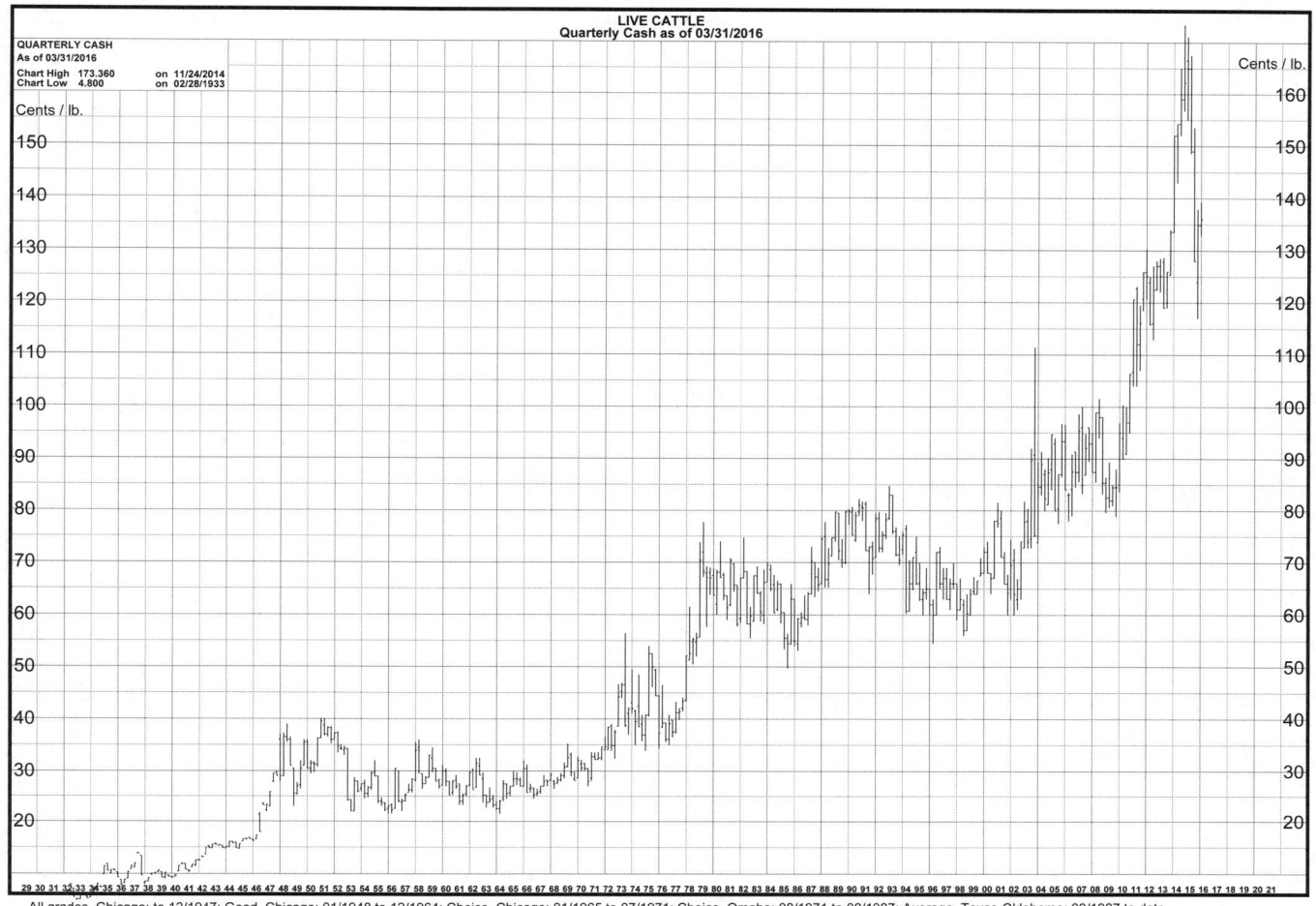

LIVE CATTLE
Quarterly Cash as of 03/31/2016

QUARTERLY CASH
As of 03/31/2016
Chart High   173.360   on 11/24/2014
Chart Low   4.800   on 02/28/1933

Cents / lb.

All grades, Chicago: to 12/1947; Good, Chicago: 01/1948 to 12/1964; Choice, Chicago: 01/1965 to 07/1971; Choice, Omaha: 08/1971 to 08/1987; Average, Texas-Oklahoma: 09/1987 to date.

United States Cattle on Feed, 1000+ Capacity Feedlots, on First of Month   In Thousands of Head

Year	Jan.	Feb.	Mar.	Apr.	May	June	July	Aug.	Sept.	Oct.	Nov.	Dec.
2006	11,804	12,110	12,023	11,812	11,559	11,187	10,872	10,822	10,986	11,385	11,969	11,973
2007	11,974	11,726	11,599	11,644	11,297	11,272	10,737	10,299	10,302	10,967	11,769	12,099
2008	12,092	11,966	11,853	11,684	11,135	10,815	10,295	9,869	9,997	10,415	10,972	11,346
2009	11,234	11,288	11,228	11,162	10,822	10,407	9,752	9,637	9,900	10,474	11,134	11,277
2010	10,983	10,959	10,849	10,742	10,428	10,495	10,071	9,880	10,181	10,788	11,497	11,620
2011	11,513	11,571	11,386	11,257	11,175	10,902	10,433	10,579	10,700	11,282	11,889	12,055
2012	11,861	11,811	11,677	11,482	11,110	11,077	10,710	10,656	10,647	10,989	11,254	11,348
2013	11,172	11,070	10,845	10,924	10,760	10,767	10,375	10,025	9,876	10,110	10,585	10,724
2014	10,523	10,678	10,716	10,792	10,554	10,497	10,043	9,752	9,719	9,985	10,571	10,816
2015[1]	10,626	10,713	10,688	10,797	10,640	10,571	10,236	10,002	9,986	10,218	10,799	10,800

[1] Preliminary.   *Source: Economic Research Service, U.S. Department of Agriculture (ERS-USDA)*

United States Cattle Placed on Feed, 1000+ Capacity Feedlots   In Thousands of Head

Year	Jan.	Feb.	Mar.	Apr.	May	June	July	Aug.	Sept.	Oct.	Nov.	Dec.	Total
2006	2,199	1,588	1,837	1,619	1,903	1,946	1,958	2,290	2,227	2,430	1,884	1,714	23,595
2007	1,690	1,659	1,960	1,568	2,159	1,657	1,622	2,119	2,415	2,725	2,125	1,701	23,400
2008	1,787	1,723	1,736	1,536	1,900	1,518	1,656	2,061	2,281	2,438	2,016	1,647	22,299
2009	1,858	1,678	1,808	1,600	1,638	1,391	1,863	2,119	2,388	2,474	1,844	1,526	22,187
2010	1,822	1,674	1,856	1,634	2,030	1,628	1,758	2,271	2,463	2,505	1,959	1,789	23,389
2011	1,889	1,667	1,914	1,785	1,810	1,695	2,135	2,246	2,469	2,492	2,037	1,673	23,812
2012	1,847	1,714	1,792	1,521	2,084	1,664	1,922	2,007	2,004	2,180	1,943	1,576	22,254
2013	1,869	1,438	1,884	1,720	2,055	1,551	1,684	1,772	1,988	2,378	1,867	1,654	21,860
2014	2,014	1,658	1,801	1,623	1,909	1,468	1,559	1,725	2,014	2,368	1,794	1,537	21,470
2015[1]	1,789	1,551	1,809	1,548	1,719	1,481	1,547	1,632	1,931	2,286	1,607	1,527	20,427

[1] Preliminary.   *Source: Economic Research Service, U.S. Department of Agriculture (ERS-USDA)*

CATTLE AND CALVES

CATTLE, LIVE - CME
Weekly Selected Futures as of 04/01/2016

WEEKLY SELECTED FUTURES
As of 04/01/2016
Chart High 171.975 on 10/31/2014
Chart Low 73.450 on 05/01/2006

Nearby Futures through Last Trading Day.

United States Cattle Marketings, 1000+ Capacity Feedlots[2]   In Thousands of Head

Year	Jan.	Feb.	Mar.	Apr.	May	June	July	Aug.	Sept.	Oct.	Nov.	Dec.	Total
2006	1,810	1,602	1,958	1,785	2,160	2,198	1,950	2,067	1,760	1,765	1,797	1,625	22,477
2007	1,841	1,711	1,843	1,816	2,085	2,140	1,999	2,066	1,696	1,876	1,738	1,650	22,461
2008	1,853	1,776	1,842	2,010	2,140	1,978	2,037	1,884	1,812	1,814	1,575	1,683	22,404
2009	1,737	1,682	1,824	1,871	1,952	1,989	1,935	1,800	1,767	1,755	1,635	1,745	21,692
2010	1,776	1,716	1,903	1,857	1,865	1,997	1,901	1,923	1,802	1,734	1,774	1,830	22,078
2011	1,774	1,791	1,990	1,807	2,002	2,092	1,918	2,053	1,813	1,787	1,774	1,776	22,577
2012	1,816	1,755	1,918	1,815	2,017	1,965	1,913	1,955	1,598	1,837	1,761	1,678	22,028
2013	1,892	1,603	1,724	1,815	1,948	1,880	1,970	1,871	1,692	1,827	1,660	1,736	21,618
2014	1,788	1,549	1,660	1,778	1,865	1,847	1,787	1,692	1,683	1,685	1,475	1,655	20,464
2015[1]	1,625	1,516	1,631	1,639	1,711	1,747	1,725	1,588	1,642	1,630	1,532	1,674	19,660

[1] Preliminary.   *Source: Economic Research Service, U.S. Department of Agriculture (ERS-USDA)*

Quarterly Trade of Live Cattle in the United States   In Head

| | ---------- Imports ---------- | | | | ---------- Exports ---------- | | | |
Year	First Quarter	Second Quarter	Third Quarter	Fourth Quarter	Total	First Quarter	Second Quarter	Third Quarter	Fourth Quarter	Total
2006	708,680	470,176	418,117	691,870	2,288,843	8,721	12,473	10,249	18,235	49,678
2007	629,157	518,173	462,359	885,276	2,494,965	13,723	15,112	10,441	27,107	66,383
2008	682,174	562,566	405,199	634,054	2,283,993	38,319	30,581	15,175	23,417	107,492
2009	612,188	423,742	342,988	622,956	2,001,874	6,903	18,153	16,354	16,613	58,023
2010	598,853	596,339	406,926	681,767	2,283,885	15,526	20,853	17,552	37,159	91,090
2011	580,696	488,356	376,602	661,649	2,107,303	35,446	41,142	45,749	71,571	193,908
2012	672,937	650,291	326,659	634,438	2,284,325	41,420	45,955	36,497	67,300	191,172
2013	596,206	475,719	310,746	654,448	2,037,119	30,803	50,571	38,304	41,268	160,946
2014	600,806	562,996	415,352	780,587	2,359,741	27,561	25,994	25,818	28,342	107,715
2015[1]	564,336	533,942	413,448	473,352	1,985,078	12,576	23,606	15,605	20,700	72,487

[1] Preliminary.   *Source: Economic Research Service, U.S. Department of Agriculture (ERS-USDA)*

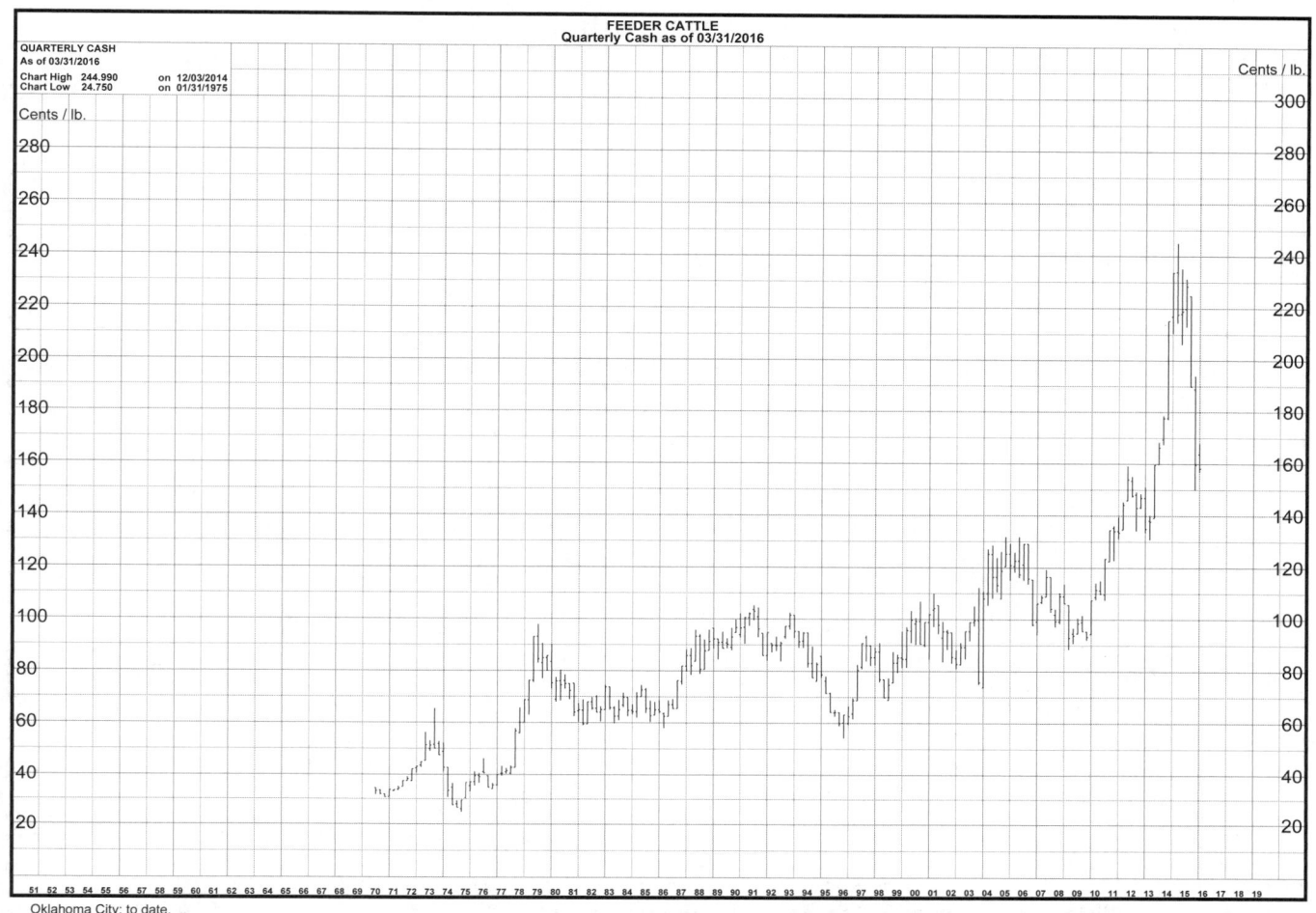

FEEDER CATTLE
Quarterly Cash as of 03/31/2016

QUARTERLY CASH
As of 03/31/2016

| Chart High | 244.990 | on 12/03/2014 |
| Chart Low | 24.750 | on 01/31/1975 |

Cents / lb.

Oklahoma City: to date.

Average Slaughter Steer Price, Choice 2-4, Nebraska Direct (1100-1300 Lb.)   In Dollars Per 100 Pounds

Year	Jan.	Feb.	Mar.	Apr.	May	June	July	Aug.	Sept.	Oct.	Nov.	Dec.	Average
2009	81.60	79.68	81.66	87.02	85.27	81.31	82.72	82.48	83.13	83.53	83.43	80.34	82.68
2010	83.46	87.41	92.93	99.58	97.93	92.25	93.12	96.42	97.22	97.85	99.89	102.30	95.03
2011	105.12	109.50	116.81	119.80	111.42	109.00	110.87	114.17	117.17	121.25	124.76	122.80	115.22
2012	123.73	125.74	127.16	122.26	122.07	119.27	114.95	119.50	125.14	125.61	125.75	125.65	123.07
2013	124.33	125.47	126.33	128.08	126.48	121.70	120.41	123.78	124.23	130.09	132.23	131.18	126.19
2014	143.33	146.45	151.93	149.01	146.19	149.55	158.57	158.35	159.86	164.91	170.04	163.09	155.11
2015	165.13	160.29	163.42	162.98	160.76	151.13	149.17	149.06	136.28	132.88	126.90	125.00	148.58

Source: Economic Research Service, U.S. Department of Agriculture (ERS-USDA)

Average Price of Feeder Steers in Oklahoma City   In Dollars Per 100 Pounds

Year	Jan.	Feb.	Mar.	Apr.	May	June	July	Aug.	Sept.	Oct.	Nov.	Dec.	Average
2009	95.57	93.19	92.47	98.05	99.58	97.74	100.65	100.39	97.75	93.56	93.33	93.29	96.30
2010	96.25	100.06	103.82	112.43	111.44	109.75	112.68	113.53	111.92	109.65	112.58	119.32	109.45
2011	125.33	127.22	130.02	133.94	128.32	126.90	136.72	134.25	132.02	137.54	142.47	144.22	133.25
2012	150.15	155.24	155.34	150.24	149.53	152.85	140.49	138.43	142.56	144.22	144.25	147.32	147.55
2013	147.99	142.75	136.98	136.75	133.75	135.73	144.26	152.68	156.92	161.92	165.05	166.20	148.41
2014	170.98	170.61	174.43	178.55	185.49	201.90	216.19	221.28	228.15	239.59	240.37	233.67	205.10
2015	224.57	210.18	212.80	218.29	219.14	226.34	219.98	215.14	200.97	188.55	181.41	159.43	206.40

Source: Economic Research Service, U.S. Department of Agriculture (ERS-USDA)

Federally Inspected Slaughter of Cattle in the United States   In Thousands of Head

Year	Jan.	Feb.	Mar.	Apr.	May	June	July	Aug.	Sept.	Oct.	Nov.	Dec.	Total
2009	2,668	2,479	2,681	2,724	2,806	2,936	2,878	2,738	2,766	2,829	2,556	2,704	32,765
2010	2,657	2,503	2,864	2,802	2,743	3,004	2,860	2,912	2,851	2,809	2,830	2,868	33,702
2011	2,687	2,580	2,913	2,678	2,778	3,058	2,728	3,053	2,830	2,804	2,739	2,706	33,555
2012	2,666	2,515	2,713	2,528	2,836	2,826	2,755	2,952	2,497	2,897	2,740	2,500	32,425
2013	2,785	2,315	2,545	2,689	2,823	2,693	2,856	2,778	2,568	2,851	2,527	2,518	31,947
2014	2,634	2,204	2,413	2,556	2,597	2,568	2,562	2,463	2,490	2,591	2,210	2,398	29,684
2015[1]	2,377	2,135	2,342	2,346	2,345	2,430	2,459	2,288	2,435	2,469	2,258	2,414	28,296

[1] Preliminary.   *Source: National Agricultural Statistics Service, U.S. Department of Agriculture (NASS-USDA)*

CATTLE AND CALVES

CATTLE, FEEDER - CME
Weekly Nearest Futures as of 04/01/2016

WEEKLY NEAREST FUTURES
As of 04/01/2016
Chart High 245.200 on 10/09/2014
Chart Low 85.450 on 12/05/2008

Nearby Futures through Last Trading Day using Selected contract months: February, April, June, August, October and December.

Volume of Trading of Live Cattle Futures Chicago   In Thousands of Contracts

Year	Jan.	Feb.	Mar.	Apr.	May	June	July	Aug.	Sept.	Oct.	Nov.	Dec.	Total
2006	783.0	498.8	849.5	570.0	817.5	709.7	718.8	670.4	698.3	631.9	757.8	504.0	8,209.7
2007	907.2	663.1	1,046.7	575.8	814.4	513.7	849.1	634.5	724.5	638.9	761.9	458.3	8,588.0
2008	982.6	596.4	954.2	724.4	936.2	731.3	1,006.4	738.2	998.2	801.1	773.9	558.4	9,801.4
2009	819.5	616.8	789.3	641.3	721.5	617.8	855.4	657.9	854.6	739.7	844.3	638.9	8,797.0
2010	901.0	782.9	1,167.2	863.2	1,204.5	785.8	923.8	868.3	1,158.8	827.1	1,066.3	783.9	11,332.7
2011	1,181.8	910.9	1,531.6	928.4	1,293.3	1,097.4	1,148.8	1,034.4	1,325.4	1,067.2	1,136.1	877.4	13,532.6
2012	1,179.7	1,078.3	1,516.9	1,180.1	1,399.6	1,022.4	1,293.1	1,097.1	1,185.9	977.2	1,090.4	964.8	13,985.4
2013	1,484.1	1,069.5	1,249.3	977.9	1,189.7	831.3	1,020.8	884.5	972.5	1,040.2	986.9	756.2	12,463.0
2014	1,381.4	970.0	1,270.2	847.7	1,139.3	1,126.6	1,503.5	1,023.5	1,303.4	1,061.5	962.5	1,009.6	13,599.3
2015	1,282.2	918.7	1,163.5	959.6	1,139.1	955.3	1,166.5	901.6	1,344.2	1,222.5	1,213.9	1,173.9	13,440.9

Contract size = 40,000 lbs.   *Source: CME Group; Chicago Mercantile Exchange (CME)*

Average Open Interest of Live Cattle Futures in Chicago   In Contracts

Year	Jan.	Feb.	Mar.	Apr.	May	June	July	Aug.	Sept.	Oct.	Nov.	Dec.
2006	225,313	220,947	220,042	240,567	261,496	235,783	231,914	213,918	214,583	205,776	211,814	224,501
2007	257,373	273,121	296,235	281,239	261,866	240,526	235,110	212,154	234,754	234,584	240,710	241,614
2008	252,555	273,397	276,043	285,956	298,370	298,937	300,862	278,808	265,436	227,860	215,054	211,836
2009	207,768	203,912	207,221	206,462	204,424	211,978	222,562	233,578	251,083	260,285	266,293	262,738
2010	276,265	294,225	343,951	362,939	362,895	327,910	323,477	339,349	344,298	317,349	321,039	332,858
2011	344,671	358,852	366,250	380,138	346,614	326,592	322,313	309,147	324,714	336,225	325,195	315,700
2012	333,921	350,623	358,333	351,179	337,579	318,041	305,336	290,534	294,356	289,303	327,964	331,211
2013	329,529	330,784	335,436	325,462	315,201	290,113	275,925	289,980	295,826	314,058	333,154	323,189
2014	354,327	371,310	369,611	352,639	345,372	352,223	343,096	313,046	315,722	313,134	317,289	286,556
2015	261,167	243,091	259,858	273,309	296,935	287,815	241,553	236,485	258,984	258,122	271,979	256,669

Contract size = 40,000 lbs.   *Source: CME Group; Chicago Mercantile Exchange (CME)*

Beef Steer-Corn Price Ratio[1] in the United States

Year	Jan.	Feb.	Mar.	Apr.	May	June	July	Aug.	Sept.	Oct.	Nov.	Dec.	Average
2006	51.0	48.3	45.0	42.3	39.8	41.2	42.1	43.8	43.3	36.7	31.3	29.6	41.2
2007	29.4	26.6	28.5	29.4	28.1	26.4	28.0	29.4	30.0	29.4	27.9	25.3	28.2
2008	23.5	20.8	19.8	17.9	18.2	17.6	19.0	19.0	19.8	21.3	21.3	20.9	19.9
2009	19.7	21.7	21.8	22.9	22.1	21.2	23.7	25.6	26.3	23.4	23.4	23.3	22.9
2010	23.9	25.5	27.0	29.6	28.6	27.8	27.5	26.9	24.4	22.9	22.2	21.6	25.7
2011	22.3	19.6	21.3	19.2	18.2	17.2	18.2	16.6	18.3	21.3	21.6	21.5	19.6
2012	21.4	20.9	20.8	20.2	19.7	19.5	16.4	15.7	18.1	18.7	18.3	18.6	19.0
2013	18.7	17.8	17.8	18.2	18.2	17.8	17.8	19.6	23.0	27.6	30.2	29.9	21.4
2014	31.7	33.3	33.2	31.8	31.2	32.9	38.7	43.8	45.3	45.7	46.9	43.8	38.2
2015[1]	43.5	42.5	42.5	43.7	44.5	43.6	39.5	40.5	38.0	35.1	36.4	33.7	40.3

[1] Bushels of corn equal in value to 100 pounds of steers and heifers.   [2] Preliminary.   *Source: Economic Research Service, U.S. Department of Agriculture*

Average Price Received by Farmers for Beef Cattle in the United States   In Dollars Per 100 Pounds

Year	Jan.	Feb.	Mar.	Apr.	May	June	July	Aug.	Sept.	Oct.	Nov.	Dec.	Average
2006	95.10	92.40	87.90	84.80	82.20	84.00	85.80	87.20	90.00	88.20	84.40	83.10	87.09
2007	84.30	86.10	91.60	93.70	92.80	88.80	89.00	91.40	93.10	90.90	89.90	89.20	90.07
2008	87.30	89.00	87.80	86.80	91.30	91.90	95.00	95.80	94.20	87.40	84.30	79.70	89.21
2009	80.10	78.90	79.10	83.80	83.20	80.10	80.90	80.40	80.50	79.20	79.60	78.50	80.36
2010	82.10	85.70	90.40	95.60	94.70	90.40	91.70	93.50	94.10	93.10	94.00	98.10	91.95
2011	107.00	108.00	115.00	119.00	112.00	107.00	111.00	111.00	112.00	117.00	120.00	120.00	113.25
2012	125.00	127.00	128.00	124.00	122.00	121.00	114.00	117.00	121.00	123.00	123.00	124.00	122.42
2013	126.00	123.00	125.00	125.00	126.00	122.00	120.00	121.00	122.00	127.00	130.00	130.00	124.75
2014	138.00	144.00	148.00	148.00	146.00	147.00	156.00	158.00	157.00	161.00	167.00	164.00	152.83
2015[1]	164.00	159.00	160.00	162.00	160.00	155.00	149.00	148.00	139.00	128.00	129.00	122.00	147.92

[1] Preliminary.   *Source: National Agricultural Statistics Service, U.S. Department of Agriculture (NASS-USDA)*

Average Price Received by Farmers for Calves in the United States   In Dollars Per 100 Pounds

Year	Jan.	Feb.	Mar.	Apr.	May	June	July	Aug.	Sept.	Oct.	Nov.	Dec.	Average
2006	141.00	143.00	139.00	137.00	134.00	135.00	137.00	136.00	136.00	128.00	119.00	116.00	133.42
2007	115.00	114.00	122.00	125.00	124.00	124.00	126.00	127.00	126.00	123.00	122.00	120.00	122.33
2008	117.00	120.00	118.00	116.00	120.00	118.00	114.00	117.00	113.00	106.00	105.00	98.90	113.58
2009	106.00	104.00	106.00	109.00	111.00	109.00	108.00	108.00	105.00	103.00	104.00	105.00	106.50
2010	109.00	113.00	117.00	124.00	124.00	122.00	122.00	123.00	118.00	121.00	125.00	130.00	120.67
2011	136.00	139.00	148.00	147.00	137.00	133.00	138.00	134.00	132.00	145.00	153.00	157.00	141.58
2012	169.00	184.00	184.00	178.00	176.00	166.00	144.00	155.00	162.00	164.00	161.00	163.00	167.17
2013	168.00	170.00	163.00	159.00	157.00	152.00	162.00	178.00	200.00	190.00	192.00	197.00	174.00
2014	208.00	209.00	216.00	222.00	229.00	249.00	257.00	271.00	279.00	307.00	305.00	303.00	254.58
2015[1]	288.00	277.00	290.00	288.00	288.00	292.00	275.00	273.00	241.00	234.00	217.00	193.00	263.00

[1] Preliminary.   *Source: National Agricultural Statistics Board, U.S. Department of Agriculture (NASS-USDA)*

Federally Inspected Slaughter of Calves and Vealers in the United States   In Thousands of Head

Year	Jan.	Feb.	Mar.	Apr.	May	June	July	Aug.	Sept.	Oct.	Nov.	Dec.	Total
2006	54.3	51.6	57.9	46.7	55.9	57.8	57.0	65.8	56.5	62.3	65.6	67.2	698.6
2007	73.3	65.6	69.6	55.8	58.0	60.3	61.7	64.5	54.8	63.7	57.5	59.9	744.7
2008	70.4	67.9	69.9	72.2	70.0	74.2	86.7	78.1	86.1	93.9	79.7	92.8	941.9
2009	83.6	73.0	78.8	67.1	64.2	76.0	78.9	75.6	79.9	82.2	80.0	91.1	930.4
2010	81.6	72.9	78.8	67.4	59.1	67.3	74.1	74.8	70.0	70.0	71.7	76.6	864.3
2011	70.8	67.9	71.8	57.9	60.0	71.5	72.4	78.9	72.5	71.5	71.9	71.8	838.9
2012	66.6	59.3	58.5	55.4	58.2	55.0	66.5	71.6	63.2	71.6	69.4	64.5	759.8
2013	69.9	58.7	61.6	57.7	57.6	56.7	69.1	63.5	62.0	68.5	59.7	65.8	750.8
2014	62.0	51.5	52.9	48.0	45.9	44.6	47.8	43.0	41.8	42.6	35.2	42.2	557.5
2015[1]	39.3	36.1	39.2	34.7	32.7	34.5	36.0	33.9	36.8	39.6	38.2	44.5	445.5

[1] Preliminary.   *Source: Crop Reporting Board, U.S. Department of Agriculture (CRB-USDA)*

Cement

Cement is made in a wide variety of compositions and is used in many different ways. The best-known cement is *Portland cement*, which is bound with sand and gravel to create concrete. Concrete is used to unite the surfaces of various materials and to coat surfaces to protect them from various chemicals. Portland cement is almost universally used for structural concrete. It is manufactured from lime-bearing materials, usually limestone, together with clays, blast-furnace slag containing alumina and silica or shale. The combination is usually approximately 60 percent lime, 19 percent silica, 8 percent alumina, 5 percent iron, 5 percent magnesia, and 3 percent sulfur trioxide. To slow the hardening process, gypsum is often added. In 1924, the name "Portland cement" was coined by Joseph Aspdin, a British cement maker, because of the resemblance between concrete made from his cement and Portland stone. The United States did not start producing Portland cement in any great quantity until the 20th century. Hydraulic cements are those that set and harden in water. Clinker cement is an intermediate product in cement manufacture. The production and consumption of cement is directly related to the level of activity in the construction industry.

Prices – The average value (F.O.B. mill) of Portland cement in 2015 rose by +5.0% yr/yr to $105.50 per ton, posting a new record high.

Supply – World production of hydraulic cement in 2015 fell by -1.9% yr/yr to 4.100 billion tons from the record high of 4.180 billion tons posted in 2014. The world's largest hydraulic cement producers were China with 57.3% of world production in 2014, India (6.6%), U.S. (2.0%), and Brazil (1.8%).

U.S. production of cement in 2015 rose +0.2% yr/yr to 82.800 million metric tons, far below the 2005 record high of 99.319 million metric tons. U.S. shipments of cement from mills in the U.S. in 2015 rose +2.9% to 92.700 million metric tons, but remained below the 2005 record high of 128.000 million metric tons.

Demand – U.S. consumption of cement in 2015 rose +4.3% to 93.000 million metric tons, but was still far below the 2005 record high of 128.260 million metric tons.

Trade – The U.S. relied on imports for 10% of its cement consumption in 2015. The two main suppliers of cement to the U.S. were Canada and Mexico. U.S. exports of cement in 2015 fell -6.9% yr/yr to 1.300 million metric tons.

World Production of Hydraulic Cement   In Thousands of Short Tons

Year	Brazil	China	France	Germany	India	Italy	Japan	Korea, South	Russia	Spain	Turkey	United States	World Total
2008	51,884	1,400,000	20,895	33,581	185,000	43,030	62,810	51,653	53,548	42,088	51,432	87,610	2,850,000
2009	51,748	1,644,000	17,974	29,974	205,000	36,317	54,800	50,126	44,266	29,505	53,973	64,843	3,050,000
2010	59,118	1,822,000	17,733	29,203	220,000	34,408	51,526	47,420	50,400	26,217	62,737	67,202	3,290,000
2011	64,093	2,099,000	19,270	32,779	250,000	33,120	51,291	48,249	56,200	22,178	63,405	68,639	3,650,000
2012	69,323	2,210,000	17,810	31,956	270,000	26,200	54,737	47,087	61,700	15,939	63,879	74,934	3,820,000
2013	69,975	2,416,000	18,018	31,308	280,000	22,000	57,400	47,291	66,400	13,600	71,337	77,415	4,070,000
2014[1]	72,000	2,480,000		32,000	260,000	22,000	53,800	63,200	68,400		75,000	83,200	4,180,000
2015[2]	72,000	2,350,000		32,000	270,000	23,000	55,000	63,000	69,000		77,000	83,400	4,100,000

[1] Preliminary.   [2] Estimate.   *Source: U.S. Geological Survey (USGS)*

Salient Statistics of Cement in the United States

Year	Net Import Reliance as a % of Apparent Consump	Production (1,000 Metric tons) Portland	Production Other[3]	Production Total	Capacity Used at Portland Mills %	Shipments From Mills Total (Mil. MT)	Shipments From Mills Value[4] (Mil. $)	Average Value (F.O.B. Mill) $ per MT	Stocks at Mills Dec. 31	Exports	Apparent Consumption	Imports for Consumption[5] by Country (1,000 Metric Tons) Canada	Japan	Mexico	Spain	Total
2008	11	83,283	3,027	86,310	70.9	97,322	9,990	103.50	8,360	823	96,760	4,104	6	1,071	1	11,365
2009	8	61,939	1,990	63,929	49.9	71,489	7,020	99.00	6,080	884	71,510	3,426	1	366	----	6,767
2010	8	64,520	1,927	66,447	53.0	71,169	6,490	92.00	6,180	1,178	71,180	3,410	28	370	----	6,626
2011	7	66,136	1,759	67,895	54.1	73,402	6,440	89.50	6,270	1,414	72,200	3,416	1	354	[6]	6,418
2012	7	72,222	1,929	74,151	59.9	79,951	7,020	89.50	6,900	1,749	77,900	3,709	1	300	38	6,893
2013[1]	7	74,689	2,115	76,804	62.2	83,187	7,760	95.00	6,570	1,670	81,700	3,615	2	308	[6]	7,095
2014[2]	8			82,600		90,047		100.50	6,150	1,397	89,200					8,304
2015[2]	10			82,800		92,700		105.50	4,800	1,300	93,000					10,900

[1] Preliminary.   [2] Estimate.   [3] Masonry, natural & pozzolan (slag-line).   [4] Value received F.O.B. mill, excluding cost of containers.   [5] Hydraulic & clinker cement for consumption.   [6] Less than 1/2 unit.   *Source: U.S. Geological Survey (USGS)*

Shipments of Finished Portland Cement from Mills in the United States   In Thousands of Metric Tons

Year	Jan.	Feb.	Mar.	Apr.	May	June	July	Aug.	Sept.	Oct.	Nov.	Dec.	Total
2009	4,021.7	4,242.1	4,908.2	5,539.5	5,727.3	6,507.7	6,614.6	6,305.6	6,167.0	5,623.7	5,215.4	3,545.3	64,418.2
2010	3,165.4	3,132.6	5,008.8	6,051.5	5,778.6	6,458.9	6,143.8	6,673.1	6,221.5	6,460.9	5,410.5	3,852.7	64,358.1
2011	3,407.0	3,388.7	4,971.5	5,249.7	5,934.6	6,683.6	6,271.3	7,290.4	6,548.9	6,743.7	5,653.5	4,479.6	66,622.3
2012	4,256.6	4,375.9	5,565.9	6,172.8	6,858.9	6,984.9	6,709.5	7,455.3	6,340.6	7,371.7	6,094.6	4,341.5	72,528.2
2013	4,413.4	4,290.4	5,344.9	6,098.7	7,022.2	6,954.2	7,422.6	7,856.7	7,287.9	7,965.3	6,025.7	4,708.3	75,390.3
2014	4,405.2	4,336.7	5,644.2	6,786.1	7,503.4	7,598.1	8,240.1	7,970.4	8,187.0	8,742.4	5,905.7	5,685.6	81,004.8
2015[1]	4,878.8	4,292.3	5,701.8	6,894.7	6,919.6	7,977.7	8,296.5	8,161.6	8,038.0	8,303.0	6,535.0		82,908.1

[1] Preliminary.   *Source: U.S. Geological Survey (USGS)*

Cheese

Since prehistoric times, humans have been making and eating cheese. Dating back as far as 6,000 BC, archaeologists have discovered that cheese had been made from cow and goat milk and stored in tall jars. The Romans turned cheese making into a culinary art, mixing sheep and goat milk and adding herbs and spices for flavoring. By 300 AD, cheese was being exported regularly to countries along the Mediterranean coast.

Cheese is made from the milk of cows and other mammals such as sheep, goats, buffalo, reindeer, camels, yaks, and mares. More than 400 varieties of cheese exist. There are three basic steps common to all cheese making. First, proteins in milk are transformed into curds, or solid lumps. Second, the curds are separated from the milky liquid (or whey) and shaped or pressed into molds. Finally, the shaped curds are ripened according to a variety of aging and curing techniques. Cheeses are usually grouped according to their moisture content into fresh, soft, semi-soft, hard, and very hard. Many classifications overlap due to texture changes with aging.

Cheese is a multi-billion-dollar a year industry in the U.S. Cheddar cheese is the most common natural cheese produced in the U.S., accounting for 35% of U.S. production. Cheeses originating in America include Colby, cream cheese, and Monterey Jack. Varieties other than American cheeses, mostly Italian, now have had a combined level of production that easily exceeds American cheeses.

Prices – Average monthly cheese prices at the CME Group in 2015 fell -23.5% yr/yr to 161.43 cents per pound, below last year's record high of 210.94 cents per pound.

Supply – World production of cheese in 2016 is expected to rise +0.7% yr/yr to 18.931 million metric tons, well below the 2007 record high of 21.440 million metric tons. The European Union is the world's largest producer of cheese with 51.1% of the total world production in 2015. The U.S. production was the next largest with 28.2% of the total. U.S. production of cheese in 2013 (latest data available) rose +1.9% to 11.102 billion pounds, which was a new record high.

World Production of Cheese   In Thousands of Metric Tons

Year	Argentina	Australia	Brazil	Canada	European Union	Japan	Korea, South	Mexico	New Zealand	Russia	Ukraine	United States	World Total
2007	520	345	580	371	8,674	43	24	184	331	817	244	4,435	17,181
2008	525	344	607	370	8,717	47	25	188	288	804	249	4,496	16,807
2009	530	321	614	378	8,739	45	23	242	308	840	228	4,570	16,993
2010	540	319	648	383	8,959	48	27	264	268	776	212	4,737	17,348
2011	572	339	679	378	8,981	45	25	270	300	753	185	4,806	17,482
2012	564	330	700	386	9,287	47	23	264	328	790	145	4,938	17,957
2013	556	320	722	388	9,368	49	22	270	311	713	140	5,036	18,037
2014	564	320	736	396	9,560	46	24	275	325	760	104	5,194	18,476
2015[1]	570	330	751	400	9,610	42	24	282	347	850	100	5,299	18,797
2016[2]	580	340	766	400	9,635	42	24	287	310	860	100	5,375	18,931

[1] Preliminary.   [2] Forecast.   NA = Not available.   *Source: Foreign Agricultural Service, U.S. Department of Agriculture (FAS-USDA)*

Production of Cheese in the United States   In Millions of Pounds

Year	American Whole Milk	American Part Skim	American Total	Swiss, Including Block	Munster	Brick	Lim-burger	Crean & Neufchatel Cheese	Italian Varieties	Blue Mond	All Other Varieties	Total of All Cheese[2]	Cottage Cheese Lowfat	Cottage Cheese Curd[3]	Cottage Cheese Cream-ed[4]
2006	3,913	----	3,913	314.5	95.5	8.6	.8	756.2	3,972.9	[5]	281.5	9,525	409.2	459.0	368.8
2007	3,877	----	3,877	313.7	103.6	7.4	.7	772.8	4,198.8	[5]	311.9	9,777	425.4	458.5	348.6
2008	4,109	----	4,109	294.0	117.2	6.9	.6	763.6	4,120.8	[5]	307.5	9,913	389.2	428.1	325.0
2009	4,203	----	4,203	322.3	115.5	9.4	[5]	766.9	4,180.6	[5]	270.0	10,074	389.0	432.3	342.4
2010	4,289	----	4,289	336.5	117.6	6.7	[5]	744.9	4,415.7	[5]	136.7	10,443	387.7	432.9	331.3
2011	4,227	----	4,227	329.1	146.6	11.4	[5]	714.6	4,585.3	[5]	147.5	10,595	381.5	423.7	322.1
2012	4,358	----	4,358	320.6	152.6	12.5	[5]	807.7	4,633.6	[5]	146.6	10,890	386.1	424.1	323.2
2013	4,420	----	4,420	294.5	163.2	9.3	[5]	842.3	4,733.5	[5]	151.9	11,102	370.3	389.4	307.4
2014[1]	4,534	----	4,534	297.8	163.7	2.9	[5]	851.7	4,949.6		154.2	11,450	366.6	382.6	304.0
2015[1]	4,641	----	4,641					848.4	5,069.6			11,730			

[1] Preliminary.   [2] Excludes full-skim cheddar and cottage cheese.   [3] Includes cottage, pot, and baker's cheese with a butterfat content of less than 4%.
[4] Includes cheese with a butterfat content of 4 to 19 %.   [5] Included in All Other Varieties.   NA = Not available.
Source: Economic Research Service, U.S. Department of Agriculture ERS-USDA)

CHEESE

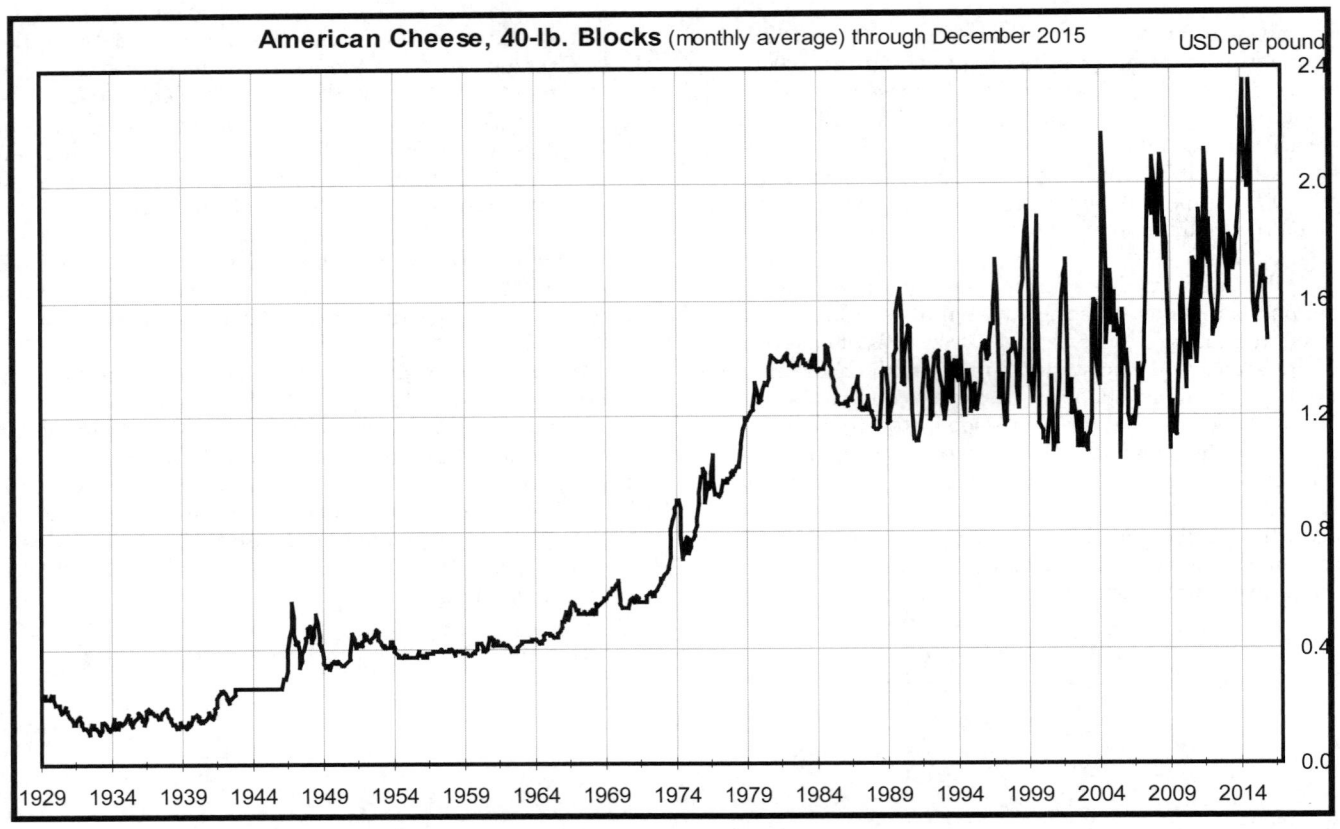

American Cheese, 40-lb. Blocks (monthly average) through December 2015   USD per pound

Average Price of Cheese, 40-lb. Blocks, Chicago Mercantile Exchange   In Dollars Per Pound

Year	Jan.	Feb.	Mar.	Apr.	May	June	July	Aug.	Sept.	Oct.	Nov.	Dec.	Average
2006	1.3335	1.1989	1.1638	1.1651	1.1855	1.1924	1.1630	1.2345	1.2933	1.2347	1.3745	1.3223	1.2385
2007	1.3180	1.3408	1.3823	1.4628	1.7211	2.0100	1.9138	1.9554	1.9929	1.8957	2.0926	2.0083	1.7578
2008	1.8257	2.0023	1.8234	1.8826	2.0976	2.0350	1.9673	1.7398	1.8762	1.7963	1.7099	1.5132	1.8558
2009	1.0833	1.2171	1.2455	1.2045	1.1394	1.1353	1.1516	1.3474	1.3294	1.4709	1.5788	1.6503	1.2961
2010	1.4536	1.4526	1.2976	1.4182	1.4420	1.3961	1.5549	1.6367	1.7374	1.7246	1.4619	1.3807	1.4964
2011	1.5140	1.9064	1.8125	1.6036	1.6858	2.0995	2.1150	1.9725	1.7561	1.7231	1.8716	1.6170	1.8064
2012	1.5546	1.4793	1.5193	1.5039	1.5234	1.6313	1.6855	1.8262	1.9245	2.0757	1.9073	1.7448	1.6980
2013	1.6965	1.6420	1.6240	1.8225	1.8052	1.7140	1.7072	1.7493	1.7956	1.8236	1.8478	1.9431	1.7642
2014	2.2227	2.1945	2.3554	2.2439	2.0155	2.0237	1.9870	2.1820	2.3499	2.1932	1.9513	1.5938	2.1094
2015[1]	1.5218	1.5382	1.5549	1.5890	1.6308	1.7052	1.6659	1.7111	1.6605	1.6674	1.6176	1.4616	1.6103

[1] Preliminary.   *Source: Economic Research Service, U.S. Department of Agriculture (ERS-USDA)*

Average Price of American Cheese, Barrels, Chicago Mercantile Exchange   In Dollars Per Pound

Year	Jan.	Feb.	Mar.	Apr.	May	June	July	Aug.	Sept.	Oct.	Nov.	Dec.	Average
2006	1.3009	1.1742	1.1237	1.1295	1.1674	1.1818	1.1271	1.2223	1.2899	1.2430	1.3813	1.2860	1.2189
2007	1.3310	1.3374	1.3840	1.4490	1.6894	1.9887	1.8927	1.9107	1.9901	1.8830	2.0223	2.0147	1.7411
2008	1.8774	1.9560	1.7980	1.8010	2.0708	2.0562	1.8890	1.6983	1.8517	1.8025	1.6975	1.5295	1.8357
2009	1.0832	1.1993	1.2738	1.1506	1.0763	1.0884	1.1349	1.3271	1.3035	1.4499	1.4825	1.4520	1.2518
2010	1.4684	1.4182	1.2782	1.3854	1.4195	1.3647	1.5161	1.6006	1.7114	1.7120	1.4520	1.3751	1.4751
2011	1.4876	1.8680	4.8049	1.5756	1.6902	2.0483	2.1124	1.9571	1.7010	1.7192	1.8963	1.5839	2.0370
2012	1.5358	1.4823	1.5152	1.4524	1.4701	1.5871	1.6826	1.7889	1.8780	2.0240	1.8388	1.6634	1.6599
2013	1.6388	1.5880	1.5920	1.7124	1.7251	1.7184	1.6919	1.7425	1.7688	1.7714	1.7833	1.8651	1.7165
2014	2.1727	2.1757	2.2790	2.1842	1.9985	1.9856	1.9970	2.1961	2.3663	2.0782	1.9326	1.5305	2.0747
2015[1]	1.4995	1.4849	1.5290	1.6135	1.6250	1.6690	1.6313	1.6689	1.5840	1.6072	1.5305	1.4638	1.5756

[1] Preliminary.   *Source: Economic Research Service, U.S. Department of Agriculture (ERS-USDA)*

Production of Cheese[2] in the United States In Millions of Pounds

Year	Jan.	Feb.	Mar.	Apr.	May	June	July	Aug.	Sept.	Oct.	Nov.	Dec.	Total
2006	782.7	720.5	820.8	793.6	820.0	796.1	775.4	795.1	788.6	812.3	798.1	831.1	9,534
2007	822.9	754.1	840.5	803.8	824.6	792.6	799.5	797.0	777.2	825.8	815.2	847.3	9,700
2008	812.7	784.6	834.7	810.2	831.8	809.4	813.2	820.7	796.5	843.5	824.0	859.0	9,840
2009	826.9	768.0	870.5	847.6	856.1	838.1	842.8	850.7	842.5	862.8	839.5	863.9	10,109
2010	842.5	779.0	895.3	864.6	881.0	883.3	878.0	871.2	873.2	882.2	884.5	908.5	10,443
2011	883.5	804.6	912.2	883.3	912.3	889.0	854.9	861.9	867.9	899.1	895.6	930.6	10,595
2012	911.8	860.6	955.6	898.5	918.2	901.2	882.6	891.2	870.6	930.4	914.3	951.2	10,886
2013	931.7	848.7	954.3	929.8	943.9	912.1	893.9	931.7	899.2	954.8	922.5	979.3	11,102
2014	957.8	854.4	970.2	961.1	971.0	945.1	958.5	941.9	933.9	976.4	970.1	1,009.7	11,450
2015[1]	977.4	887.3	996.2	969.8	989.2	964.0	991.0	978.6	954.6	997.4	994.0	1,030.1	11,730

[1] Preliminary. [2] Excludes cottage cheese. *Source: National Agricultural Statistics Service, U.S. Department of Agriculture (NASS-USDA)*

Production of American Cheese[2] in the United States In Millions of Pounds

Year	Jan.	Feb.	Mar.	Apr.	May	June	July	Aug.	Sept.	Oct.	Nov.	Dec.	Total
2006	325.6	299.0	336.1	337.3	346.2	331.4	327.5	318.1	320.1	320.9	312.2	338.2	3,912.6
2007	339.6	306.2	339.4	325.9	332.5	315.5	324.7	311.9	299.6	321.3	324.7	336.4	3,877.8
2008	334.0	319.3	339.1	337.4	351.3	335.2	341.4	338.5	317.2	343.1	339.1	359.5	4,055.1
2009	357.2	323.4	364.4	354.8	368.0	356.9	354.7	347.1	342.9	349.4	331.6	352.2	4,202.5
2010	350.8	322.3	365.4	361.4	372.5	371.2	368.9	351.8	353.2	357.9	346.6	367.5	4,289.3
2011	357.0	327.3	363.5	355.8	369.1	362.1	349.0	337.5	337.5	351.7	348.3	367.9	4,226.7
2012	366.5	343.8	378.1	363.3	367.6	360.4	356.2	353.2	347.5	370.1	364.5	384.1	4,355.3
2013	377.3	347.3	384.8	376.9	387.6	363.0	345.7	381.1	347.4	371.1	356.2	381.5	4,419.8
2014	383.5	341.0	382.1	380.4	394.3	369.7	380.3	375.7	365.4	388.2	378.5	394.9	4,534.1
2015[1]	396.7	351.1	390.3	391.1	401.2	384.0	392.3	390.8	375.8	391.4	377.6	399.1	4,641.4

[1] Preliminary. [2] Includes Cheddar, Colby, Monterey, and Jack. *Source: National Agricultural Statistics Service, U.S. Department of Agriculture*

Production of Cheddar Cheese in the United States In Millions of Pounds

Year	Jan.	Feb.	Mar.	Apr.	May	June	July	Aug.	Sept.	Oct.	Nov.	Dec.	Total
2006	265.8	241.5	267.8	271.7	274.2	263.4	266.0	250.4	254.2	249.4	247.2	273.1	3,125
2007	272.3	249.2	271.0	257.6	265.7	251.3	255.3	240.5	230.1	245.2	253.2	265.8	3,057
2008	262.4	251.3	265.3	268.0	273.7	259.3	264.9	256.0	235.4	255.3	258.0	283.9	3,133
2009	278.2	244.4	279.3	272.7	287.4	276.6	269.5	264.7	259.0	263.4	249.0	263.1	3,207
2010	268.8	245.1	283.7	272.4	287.7	286.2	275.6	261.4	257.2	265.5	256.6	274.8	3,235
2011	270.8	239.5	262.7	260.5	279.6	266.3	256.7	243.3	247.3	247.6	251.8	270.4	3,096
2012	271.8	252.2	274.4	263.8	268.5	260.3	258.5	250.7	242.9	262.6	259.1	278.7	3,143
2013	280.9	252.0	284.1	279.1	281.3	259.6	246.8	269.7	241.7	268.5	252.2	273.8	3,190
2014	278.7	249.7	278.5	285.8	289.0	269.5	269.3	265.4	257.8	272.8	261.0	285.6	3,263
2015[1]	291.8	256.3	281.8	282.3	291.2	282.4	282.4	275.3	267.9	279.6	266.6	291.7	3,349

[1] Preliminary. *Source: National Agricultural Statistics Service, U.S. Department of Agriculture (NASS-USDA)*

Production of Mozzarella Cheese in the United States In Millions of Pounds

Year	Jan.	Feb.	Mar.	Apr.	May	June	July	Aug.	Sept.	Oct.	Nov.	Dec.	Total
2006	259.9	240.5	273.4	262.3	265.8	260.9	255.3	261.2	258.7	266.3	259.1	281.0	3,144.6
2007	281.8	259.7	287.2	276.6	280.7	274.9	271.6	266.2	266.6	276.1	273.5	288.3	3,303.3
2008	281.2	265.3	285.7	273.8	270.9	260.0	259.5	258.0	258.3	263.9	260.1	278.0	3,214.6
2009	267.3	246.4	280.0	270.6	271.4	268.9	273.8	272.6	270.3	278.1	279.1	288.8	3,267.3
2010	283.0	258.4	299.4	287.4	293.1	289.7	290.2	290.5	290.3	291.2	298.6	307.9	3,479.4
2011	308.0	273.6	310.4	300.1	308.9	298.1	287.4	286.7	286.4	296.9	296.6	321.4	3,574.4
2012	311.9	291.4	318.7	302.6	306.3	299.7	291.9	286.2	286.4	297.1	297.7	324.8	3,614.8
2013	311.8	278.5	323.2	302.6	307.1	308.0	307.9	296.4	302.0	319.0	307.5	336.0	3,700.0
2014	333.4	300.5	335.2	332.1	331.1	328.7	327.4	318.8	315.9	320.7	336.4	343.4	3,923.5
2015[1]	335.7	310.1	339.7	327.2	340.0	327.5	334.6	323.1	313.4	323.8	346.4	359.0	3,980.5

[1] Preliminary. *Source: National Agricultural Statistics Service, U.S. Department of Agriculture (NASS-USDA)*

CHEESE

Cold Storage of All Varieties of Cheese in the United States, on First of Month — In Millions of Pounds

Year	Jan.	Feb.	Mar.	Apr.	May	June	July	Aug.	Sept.	Oct.	Nov.	Dec.
2006	758.2	765.0	782.8	810.7	832.8	863.3	876.0	898.9	862.3	843.1	810.2	784.8
2007	817.4	850.0	875.7	892.9	894.3	898.9	891.2	886.0	846.2	820.4	810.6	805.9
2008	798.3	781.4	801.0	824.3	855.9	881.3	902.5	902.8	880.3	834.2	829.0	818.6
2009	852.0	882.4	892.5	915.2	938.9	970.3	987.4	1,000.2	997.6	983.9	969.2	961.7
2010	966.8	981.6	995.9	1,004.8	1,018.6	1,026.8	1,037.8	1,070.1	1,059.0	1,060.6	1,057.8	1,026.1
2011	1,047.9	1,052.4	1,035.3	1,029.5	1,040.1	1,049.2	1,051.4	1,084.9	1,065.4	1,046.0	1,017.6	977.8
2012	991.6	1,020.1	1,026.4	1,045.5	1,072.1	1,069.1	1,095.0	1,092.6	1,049.5	1,040.0	995.4	985.9
2013	1,023.1	1,032.2	1,068.8	1,105.7	1,121.3	1,150.0	1,149.4	1,146.1	1,100.4	1,070.7	1,019.7	996.6
2014	1,009.4	1,015.1	1,010.1	1,018.3	1,037.6	1,065.5	1,055.4	1,054.9	1,041.4	1,013.8	995.7	1,017.2
2015[1]	1,017.9	1,048.2	1,067.1	1,065.3	1,085.9	1,111.9	1,142.2	1,162.1	1,167.4	1,152.4	1,146.2	1,146.6

Quantities are given in "net weight."   [1] Preliminary.   *Source: National Agricultural Statistics Service, U.S. Department of Agriculture (NASS-USDA)*

Cold Storage of Natural American Cheese in the United States, on First of Month — In Millions of Pounds

Year	Jan.	Feb.	Mar.	Apr.	May	June	July	Aug.	Sept.	Oct.	Nov.	Dec.
2006	536.9	541.9	553.8	569.5	580.4	601.4	603.7	601.8	580.6	562.9	533.9	519.7
2007	534.2	546.7	565.1	571.9	586.2	576.7	565.9	563.9	548.8	540.4	524.1	518.0
2008	508.7	494.4	513.1	526.0	543.1	568.4	581.8	577.6	567.7	549.6	540.1	526.9
2009	538.1	533.4	541.7	548.6	577.4	586.1	602.0	605.0	598.7	596.2	579.8	583.1
2010	585.0	588.2	599.2	602.1	609.6	614.9	627.1	639.5	633.6	636.9	639.0	625.3
2011	630.8	637.9	621.0	611.2	622.1	622.7	619.1	648.8	647.3	639.2	619.4	584.0
2012	611.0	642.2	634.6	651.0	663.5	652.1	662.4	670.7	649.4	641.7	610.9	611.7
2013	635.6	643.2	661.0	684.7	698.7	714.6	710.6	702.0	668.4	661.0	626.2	614.0
2014	618.3	630.8	628.7	639.1	648.9	656.4	655.2	660.4	648.8	631.3	623.3	635.8
2015[1]	627.8	636.0	645.7	631.6	644.1	669.5	685.7	698.1	709.0	698.8	696.8	698.3

Quantities are given in "net weight."   [1] Preliminary.   *Source: National Agricultural Statistics Service, U.S. Department of Agriculture (NASS-USDA)*

Cold Storage of Other Natural American Cheese in the United States, on First of Month — In Millions of Pounds

Year	Jan.	Feb.	Mar.	Apr.	May	June	July	Aug.	Sept.	Oct.	Nov.	Dec.
2006	195.2	195.1	199.9	211.0	219.8	228.8	236.8	262.9	251.8	250.6	246.9	236.2
2007	254.1	272.9	278.6	286.8	277.0	292.0	291.9	289.5	269.3	253.3	257.9	260.5
2008	265.5	259.0	262.0	273.8	288.4	285.9	295.4	300.4	287.5	260.4	266.8	269.0
2009	291.3	325.8	327.5	343.4	338.7	362.2	362.3	371.9	375.5	364.6	365.8	354.4
2010	357.0	367.2	369.4	375.7	382.3	384.5	383.8	402.9	397.0	396.0	390.2	371.9
2011	385.6	378.1	379.7	385.7	386.6	392.8	397.9	401.9	384.5	375.5	366.0	354.9
2012	353.0	351.9	364.7	365.6	379.8	387.5	402.2	391.3	371.3	369.4	354.4	343.3
2013	355.8	358.6	377.6	390.5	394.1	406.4	407.4	411.5	400.0	379.7	365.6	356.5
2014	366.4	358.8	354.5	351.8	360.4	378.6	372.2	369.9	365.5	356.8	346.7	357.0
2015[1]	368.9	389.8	397.0	409.1	417.8	421.0	435.7	442.5	436.2	431.5	428.0	425.6

Quantities are given in "net weight."   [1] Preliminary.   *Source: National Agricultural Statistics Service, U.S. Department of Agriculture (NASS-USDA)*

Cold Storage of Swiss Cheese in the United States, on First of Month — In Millions of Pounds

Year	Jan.	Feb.	Mar.	Apr.	May	June	July	Aug.	Sept.	Oct.	Nov.	Dec.
2006	26.0	27.9	29.1	30.2	32.6	33.0	35.5	34.3	29.9	29.6	29.4	29.0
2007	29.1	30.4	32.0	34.2	31.2	30.5	33.3	32.6	28.1	26.7	28.6	27.4
2008	24.2	27.9	25.9	24.5	24.4	26.9	25.3	24.7	25.1	24.1	22.0	22.7
2009	22.6	23.1	23.3	23.2	22.9	22.1	23.1	23.3	23.4	23.1	23.5	24.3
2010	24.8	26.2	27.4	27.0	26.8	27.3	27.0	27.7	28.4	27.7	28.6	28.9
2011	31.5	36.3	34.6	32.6	31.4	33.7	34.4	34.2	33.6	31.3	32.2	30.1
2012	27.6	25.9	27.0	28.9	28.8	29.6	30.4	30.6	28.8	28.9	30.0	30.9
2013	31.7	30.4	30.1	30.6	28.5	29.1	31.3	32.7	32.0	30.0	27.9	26.1
2014	24.7	25.4	26.9	27.4	28.3	30.5	28.0	24.6	27.1	25.7	25.6	24.4
2015[1]	21.3	22.4	23.6	24.6	24.0	21.4	20.8	21.6	22.2	22.0	21.4	22.7

Quantities are given in "net weight."   [1] Preliminary.   *Source: National Agricultural Statistics Service, U.S. Department of Agriculture (NASS-USDA)*

Chromium

Chromium (atomic symbol Cr) is a steel-gray, hard, and brittle, metallic element that can take on a high polish. Chromium and its compounds are toxic. Discovered in 1797 by Louis Vauquelin, chromium is named after the Greek word for color, *khroma*. Vauquelin also discovered that an emerald's green color is due to the presence of chromium. Many precious stones owe their color to the presence of chromium compounds.

Chromium is primarily found in chromite ore. The primary use of chromium is to form alloys with iron, nickel, or cobalt. Chromium improves hardness and resistance to corrosion and oxidation in iron, steel, and nonferrous alloys. It is a critical alloying ingredient in the production of stainless steel, making up 10% or more of the final composition. More than half of the chromium consumed is used in metallic products, and about one-third is used in refractories. Chromium is also used as a lustrous decorative plating agent, in pigments, leather processing, plating of metals, and catalysts.

Supply – World production of chromium in 2014 (latest data available) rose +0.7% yr/yr to 29.000 million metric tons, a new record high. The world's largest producers of chromium in 2014 were South Africa with 51.7% of world production, India with 10.3%, and Kazakhstan with 13.8%. India has emerged as a major producer of chromium in the past two decades. India's 2014 production level of 3.000 million metric tons was more than ten times the level of 360,000 metric tons seen 20 years earlier. South Africa's production in 2014 was up +9.5% yr/yr to a record high of 15.0 million metric tons and that is more than double the levels seen as recently as the early 1990s. Kazakhstan's production in 2014 was up +8.1% yr/yr to 4.000 million metric tons, a new record high.

Trade – The U.S. relied on imports for 66% of its chromium consumption in 2015. That is well below the record high of 91% posted back in the 1970s. U.S. chromium imports in 2012 (latest available data) rose +3.7% yr/yr to 413,980 metric tons. U.S. exports of chromium in 2012 (latest available data) rose +8.3% yr/yr to 27,700 metric tons.

World Mine Production of Chromite   In Thousands of Metric Tons (Gross Weight)

Year	Albania	Brazil	Cuba	Finland	India	Iran	Kazakhstan	Madagascar	Philippines	South Africa	Turkey	Zimbabwe	World Total[1]
2006	213	563	28	549	3,600	245	3,366	132	47	7,418	1,060	713	19,700
2007	200	628	----	556	3,320	186	3,687	78	32	9,647	1,679	664	22,500
2008	225	664	----	614	3,900	269	3,552	113	15	9,683	1,886	443	23,800
2009	284	365	----	247	3,760	269	3,544	133	14	7,561	1,574	194	19,500
2010	328	520	----	598	3,800	45	3,760	135	15	10,871	1,904	510	24,400
2011	331	543	----	693	3,850	100	3,800	67	23	10,721	2,901	599	25,800
2012	330	543	----	425	3,900	100	4,000	67	24	11,000	2,500	550	25,600
2013			----		2,950		3,700			13,700	3,300		28,800
2014[1]			----		3,540		3,700			12,000	2,600		26,400
2015[2]			----		3,500		3,800			15,000	3,600		31,000

[1] Preliminary.   [2] Estimate.   *Source: U.S. Geological Survey (USGS)*

Salient Statistics of Chromite in the United States   In Thousands of Metric Tons (Gross Weight)

Year	Net Import Reliance as a % of Apparent Consumpn	Production of Ferro-chromium	Exports	Imports for Con-sumption	Reexports	Consumption by -- Primary Consumer Group -- Total	Metal-lurgical & Chemical	Refractory	- Government[5] Stocks, Dec. 31 - Metal-lurgical & Chemical	Refractory	Total Stocks	--- $/Metric Ton --- South Africa[3]	Turkish[4]
2006	70	W	56	342	----	W	W	W	----	1	1	NA	NA
2007	67	W	60	328	----	W	W	W	----	----	----	NA	NA
2008	66	W	36	402	----	W	W	W	----	----	----	NA	NA
2009	12	W	17	181	----	W	W	W	----	----	----	NA	NA
2010	63	W	28	367	----	W	W	W	----	----	----	NA	NA
2011	67	W	26	399	----	W	W	W	----	----	----	NA	NA
2012	69	W	28	414	----	W	W	W	----	----	----	NA	NA
2013	63	W			----	W	W	W	----	----	----	NA	NA
2014[1]	72	W			----	W	W	W	----	----	----	NA	NA
2015[2]	66	W			----	W	W	W	----	----	----	NA	NA

[1] Preliminary.   [2] Estimate.   [3] Cr_2O_3, 44% (Transvaal).   [4] 48% Cr_2O_3.   [5] Data through 1999 are for Consumer.   W = Withheld.
Source: U.S. Geological Survey (USGS)

Coal

Coal is a sedimentary rock composed primarily of carbon, hydrogen, and oxygen. Coal is a fossil fuel formed from ancient plants buried deep in the Earth's crust over 300 million years ago. Historians believe coal was first used commercially in China for smelting copper and for casting coins around 1,000 BC. Almost 92% of all coal consumed in the U.S. is burned by electric power plants, and coal accounts for about 55% of total electricity output. Coal is also used in the manufacture of steel. The steel industry first converts coal into coke, then combines the coke with iron ore and limestone, and finally heats the mixture to produce iron. Other industries use coal to make fertilizers, solvents, medicine, pesticides, and synthetic fuels.

There are four types of mined coal: anthracite (used in high-grade steel production), bituminous (used for electricity generation and for making coke), sub-bituminous, and lignite (both used primarily for electricity generation).

Coal futures trade at the CME Group. The contract trades in units of 1,550 tons and is priced in terms of dollars and cents per short ton.

Supply – U.S. production of bituminous coal in 2015 fell -8.8% yr/yr to 910.252 million tons, above last year's 20-year low of 984.842 million tons, but well below the 2008 record high of 1.172 billion tons.

Demand – U.S. consumption of coal in 2014 (latest data available) fell -0.8% to 916.854 million tons, below the 2007 record high of 1.128 billion tons.

Trade – U.S. exports of coal in 2014 (latest data available) fell -17.3% yr/yr to 97.335 million short tons, below the 2012 record high of 1.257 billion short tons. U.S. imports rose +27.0% yr/yr to 11.310 million tons, well below the 2007 record high of 36.347 million tons. The major exporting destinations for the U.S. are Canada and Europe.

World Production of Primary Coal   In Thousands of Short Tons

Year	Australia	China	Colom-bia	Germany	India	Indonesia	Kazakh-stan	Poland	Russia	South Africa	Turkey	United States	World Total
2003	376,619	1,951,928	55,147	229,102	420,525	129,089	93,820	179,213	283,271	263,784	53,532	1,071,753	5,739,700
2004	388,231	2,132,343	59,186	232,673	446,683	158,418	95,912	178,260	285,437	267,666	51,122	1,112,099	6,043,692
2005	410,675	2,477,879	65,107	226,993	473,266	187,989	96,118	174,988	311,823	270,051	64,309	1,131,498	6,526,927
2006	425,313	2,647,755	72,307	220,554	500,193	257,187	106,555	171,135	313,680	269,817	70,829	1,162,750	6,865,647
2007	441,696	2,844,311	77,054	225,526	531,521	274,290	107,837	159,773	318,591	273,005	83,075	1,146,635	7,134,922
2008	432,383	3,099,061	81,022	214,268	570,010	274,218	122,436	157,993	336,163	278,017	87,526	1,171,809	7,470,959
2009	449,631	3,301,803	80,256	202,410	614,918	321,045	111,173	148,356	304,228	275,015	87,633	1,074,923	7,601,609
2010	467,823	3,560,635	81,957	200,955	619,843	358,251	122,278	146,257	354,615	280,562	80,909	1,084,368	7,999,455
2011[1]	443,390	3,878,012	94,582	207,853	633,774	397,202	128,364	152,680	354,869	278,617	83,904	1,095,628	8,443,803
2012[2]	463,783	4,025,377	98,603	217,144	649,644	488,112	138,918	158,197	390,152	285,832	76,622	1,016,458	8,694,754

[1] Preliminary.   [2] Estimate.   NA = Not available.   *Source: United Nations*

Production of Bituminous & Lignite Coal in the United States   In Thousands of Short Tons

Year	Alabama	Colorado	Illinois	Indiana	Kentucky	Montana	Ohio	Pennsyl-vania	Texas	West Virginia	Virginia	Wyoming	U.S. Total
2005	21,453	38,510	32,014	34,457	120,029	40,354	24,718	65,852	45,939	27,964	153,655	404,319	1,129,794
2006	18,830	36,322	32,729	35,119	120,848	41,823	22,722	64,500	45,548	29,740	152,374	446,742	1,162,750
2007	19,522	36,384	32,857	35,003	115,530	43,390	22,575	63,621	41,948	25,462	153,522	453,568	1,145,067
2008	20,611	32,028	32,918	35,893	120,323	44,786	26,251	65,414	39,017	24,712	157,778	467,644	1,171,809
2009	18,796	28,267	33,748	35,655	107,338	39,486	27,501	57,979	35,093	21,019	137,127	431,107	1,074,923
2010	19,915	25,163	33,241	34,950	104,960	44,732	26,707	58,593	40,982	22,385	135,220	442,522	1,084,368
2011	19,071	26,890	37,770	37,426	108,766	42,008	28,166	57,051	45,904	22,523	134,662	438,673	1,095,628
2012	19,321	28,566	48,486	36,720	90,862	36,694	26,328	52,384	44,178	18,965	120,425	401,442	1,016,458
2013[1]	18,620	24,236	52,147	39,102	80,380	42,231	25,113	54,009	42,851	16,619	112,786	387,924	984,842
2014[2]	16,388	24,007	57,924	39,270	77,412	44,562	22,252	60,953	43,654	14,993	111,898	395,620	999,651

[1] Preliminary.   [2] Estimate.   *Source: Energy Information Administration, U.S. Department of Energy (EIA-DOE)*

Production[2] of Bituminous Coal in the United States   In Thousands of Short Tons

Year	Jan.	Feb.	Mar.	Apr.	May	June	July	Aug.	Sept.	Oct.	Nov.	Dec.	Total
2006	98,621	89,033	101,490	95,413	99,843	97,160	94,994	100,654	94,144	98,808	96,526	96,063	1,162,750
2007	99,784	88,580	97,677	93,084	97,038	95,566	93,003	100,627	92,404	98,825	96,910	93,138	1,146,635
2008	98,587	93,525	96,903	97,287	96,725	90,319	99,132	100,428	99,351	104,390	95,405	99,758	1,171,809
2009	97,022	89,688	96,062	89,072	85,236	88,708	90,847	90,308	88,185	88,002	85,564	86,229	1,074,923
2010	85,711	83,087	96,904	90,960	85,401	88,621	90,795	93,350	93,360	91,831	91,558	92,791	1,084,368
2011	91,355	85,575	96,548	88,563	86,850	88,878	85,498	95,495	94,013	94,643	94,109	94,101	1,095,628
2012	95,102	85,914	85,849	77,514	81,717	81,816	86,321	90,816	81,818	85,239	84,147	80,205	1,016,458
2013	82,529	77,414	84,381	78,724	83,075	80,841	84,344	90,013	82,707	80,435	80,408	77,827	982,699
2014	82,835	75,177	86,794	82,835	83,645	78,929	84,275	87,167	83,410	85,286	81,587	86,163	998,102
2015[1]	86,378	72,068	81,270	74,521	69,771	66,322	76,618	82,777	77,868	75,455	68,431	62,903	894,381

[1] Preliminary.   [2] Includes small amount of lignite.   *Source: Energy Information Administration, U.S. Department of Energy (EIA-DOE)*

Production[2] of Pennsylvania Anthracite Coal   In Thousands of Short Tons

Year	Jan.	Feb.	Mar.	Apr.	May	June	July	Aug.	Sept.	Oct.	Nov.	Dec.	Total
2006	138	121	147	110	121	118	124	140	115	133	125	122	1,514
2007	141	125	139	125	133	134	120	135	116	134	141	128	1,568
2008	131	126	127	160	162	103	147	146	148	168	140	154	1,712
2009	150	141	153	153	139	154	172	168	171	176	168	177	1,921
2010	129	128	156	158	140	151	161	169	168	131	140	143	1,776
2011	163	156	176	177	180	186	185	218	205	191	199	198	2,235
2012	198	185	193	205	213	206	210	224	195	186	179	174	2,368
2013	183	172	187	186	196	191	174	186	171	168	168	163	2,143
2014	157	143	165	147	148	140	174	180	172	176	168	177	1,947
2015[1]	170	142	160	182	171	162							1,976

[1] Preliminary.   [2] Represents production in Pennsylvania only.   Source: Energy Information Administration, U.S. Department of Energy (EIA-DOE)

Salient Statistics of Coal in the United States   In Thousands of Short Tons

| | | | | ------- Exports ------- | | | | | Total Ending | Losses & Unaccounted |
Year	Production	Imports	Consumption	Brazil	Canada	Europe	Asia	Total	Stocks[2]	For[3]
2005	1,131,498	30,460	1,125,978	4,199	19,466	18,825	5,082	49,942	144,304	9,092
2006	1,162,750	36,246	1,112,292	4,534	19,889	20,805	2,008	49,647	186,946	8,824
2007	1,146,635	36,347	1,127,998	6,512	18,389	27,119	1,202	59,163	192,758	4,085
2008	1,171,809	34,208	1,120,548	6,380	22,979	40,306	5,269	81,519	205,112	5,740
2009	1,074,923	22,639	997,478	7,416	10,599	30,073	6,483	59,097	244,780	14,985
2010	1,084,368	19,353	1,048,514	7,925	11,400	38,208	17,896	81,716	231,740	182
2011	1,095,628	13,088	1,002,948	8,680	6,845	53,942	27,533	107,259	231,951	11,506
2012	1,016,458	9,159	889,185	7,954	7,211	66,399	32,512	125,746	238,853	14,980
2013	984,842	8,906	924,442	8,610	7,110	60,755	27,245	117,659	200,335	1,444
2014[1]	999,651	11,310	916,854	7,987	6,715	52,511	19,541	97,335	203,200	5,090

[1] Preliminary.   [2] Producer & distributor and consumer stocks, excludes stocks held by retail dealers for consumption by the residential and commercial sector.   [3] Equals production plus imports minus the change in producer & distributor and consumer stocks minus consumption minus exports.
Source: Energy Information Administraion, U.S. Department of Energy (EIA-DOE)

Consumption and Stocks of Coal in the United States   In Thousands of Short Tons

| | ------- Consumption ------- | | | | | | | | ------- Stocks, Dec. 31 ------- | | | |
| | --- Electric Utilities --- | | | | ---- Industrial ---- | | Residential and | | ---- Consumer ---- | | | Producers and |
Year	Anthracite	Bituminous	Lignite	Total	Coke Plants	Other Industrial[2]	Commercial	Total	Electric Utilities	Coke Plants	Other Industrials	Distributors
2005	----	----	----	1,037,485	23,434	60,340	4,720	1,125,978	101,237	2,615	5,582	34,971
2006	----	----	----	1,026,636	22,957	59,472	3,226	1,112,292	140,964	2,928	6,506	36,548
2007	----	----	----	1,045,141	22,715	56,615	3,526	1,127,998	151,221	1,936	5,624	33,977
2008	----	----	----	1,040,580	22,070	54,393	3,506	1,120,548	161,589	2,331	6,007	34,688
2009	----	----	----	933,627	15,326	45,314	3,210	997,478	189,467	1,957	5,109	47,718
2010	----	----	----	975,052	21,092	49,289	3,081	1,048,514	174,917	1,925	4,525	49,820
2011	----	----	----	932,484	21,434	46,238	2,793	1,002,948	172,387	2,610	4,455	51,897
2012	----	----	----	823,551	20,751	42,838	2,045	889,185	185,116	2,522	4,475	46,157
2013	----	----	----	857,962	21,474	43,055	1,951	924,442	147,884	2,200	4,097	45,659
2014[1]	----	----	----	851,428	20,400	42,815	2,212	916,854	151,362	1,853	4,801	44,750

[1] Preliminary.   [2] Including transportation.   [3] Excludes stocks held at retail dealers for consumption by the residential and commercial sector.
Source: Energy Information Administration, U.S. Department of Energy (EIA-DOE)

Average Prices of Coal in the United States   In Dollars Per Short Ton

| | ----- End-Use Sector ----- | | | | ---- Exports ---- | | | ----- End-Use Sector ----- | | | | ---- Exports ---- | |
Year	Electric Utilities	Coke Plants	Other Industrial[2]	Imports[3]	Steam	Metal-lurgical	Total Average[3]	Year	Electric Utilities	Coke Plants	Other Industrial[2]	Imports[3]	Steam	Metal-lurgical	Total Average[3]
2005	31.22	83.79	47.63	46.71	47.64	81.56	67.10	2010	----	153.59	64.38	71.77	65.54	145.44	120.41
2006	34.26	92.87	51.67	49.10	46.25	90.81	70.93	2011	----	184.44	70.62	103.32	80.42	185.99	148.86
2007	NA	94.97	54.42	47.64	47.90	88.99	70.25	2012	----	190.55	70.33	96.78	76.16	152.23	118.43
2008	NA	118.09	63.44	59.83	57.35	134.62	97.68	2013	----	156.99	69.32	83.35	69.23	115.50	95.06
2009	----	143.01	64.87	63.91	73.63	117.73	101.44	2014[1]	----		80.83	68.30	98.12		87.62

[1] Preliminary.   [2] Manufacturing plants only.   [3] Based on the free alongside ship (F.A.S.) value.
Source: Energy Information Administration, U.S. Department of Energy (EIA-DOE)

COAL

Trends in Bituminous Coal, Lignite and Pennsylvania Anthracite in the United States   In Thousands of Short Tons

| | ---------------------------- Bituminous Coal and Lignite ---------------------------- | | | | ------- Labor Productivity ------- | | | ------------- Pennsylvania Anthracite ------------- | | | | | All Mines |
| | ------------------ Production ------------------ | | | | Under- | | | | | | | Labor Productivity | Labor Productivity |
Year	Under-Ground	Surface	Total	Miners[1] Employd	Ground	Surface	Average	Under-Ground	Surface	Total	Miners[1] Employed	Short Tons Miner/Hr.	Short Tons Miner/Hr.
					-Short Tons Per Miner Per Hour-								
2005	368,612	762,190	1,131,498	79,283	3.62	10.04	6.36	264	1,296	1,560	891	.95	6.36
2006	359,022	802,976	1,161,998	82,959	3.37	10.19	6.26	239	1,132	1,371	869	.95	6.26
2007	351,790	793,690	1,145,480	81,278	3.34	10.25	6.27	224	1,199	1,423	910	.89	6.27
2008	357,079	813,322	1,170,401	86,859	3.15	9.82	5.96	227	2,455	2,682	929	.91	5.96
2009	332,062	740,174	1,072,236	87,592	2.99	9.22	5.61	176	1,555	1,731	941	.95	5.61
2010	337,155	745,357	1,082,512	86,057	2.89	9.47	5.55	139	1,566	1,705	928	.98	5.55
2011	345,606	748,372	1,093,978	91,482	2.72	8.97	5.19	166	1,965	2,131	952	1.11	5.19
2012	342,387	672,748	1,015,135	89,838	2.84	8.97	5.19	120	2,215	2,335	1,146	1.02	5.19
2013	341,685	641,191	982,876	80,396	3.07	9.69	5.53	95	1,965	2,060	1,095	1.01	5.53
2014	354,704	643,721	998,425	74,931	3.35	10.42	5.95	----	1,474	1,474	956	.54	3.36

[1] Excludes miners employed at mines producing less than 10,000 tons.
Source: Energy Information Administration, U.S. Department of Energy (EIA-DOE)

Average Mine Prices of Coal in the United States   In Dollars Per Short Ton

| | ---- Average Mine Prices by Method ----- | | | ---------- Average Mine Prices by Rank ---------- | | | | Bituminous & Lignite FOB Mines[2] | Anthracite FOB Mines[2] | All Coal CIF[3] Electric Utility Plants |
Year	Under-ground	Surface	Total	Lignite	Sub-bituminous	Bituminous	Anthracite[1]			
2005	36.42	17.37	23.59	13.49	8.68	36.80	41.00	36.80	41.00	31.22
2006	38.28	18.88	25.16	14.00	9.95	39.32	43.61	39.32	43.61	34.26
2007	40.29	19.41	26.20	14.89	10.69	40.80	52.24	40.80	52.24	36.06
2008	51.35	22.35	31.25	16.50	12.31	51.40	60.76	51.40	60.76	41.32
2009	55.77	23.24	33.24	17.26	13.35	55.44	57.10	55.44	57.10	44.47
2010	60.73	24.13	35.61	18.76	14.11	60.88	59.61	60.88	59.61	44.27
2011	70.47	27.00	41.01	18.77	14.07	68.50	75.70	68.50	75.70	46.29
2012	66.56	26.43	39.95	19.60	15.34	66.04	80.21	66.04	80.21	45.77
2013	60.98	24.50	37.24	19.96	14.86	60.61	87.82	60.61	87.82	45.03
2014	56.97	22.83	34.83	19.44	14.72	55.99	90.98	55.99	90.98	45.66

[1] Produced in Pennsylvania.   [2] FOB = free on board.   [3] CIF = cost, insurance and freight.   W = Withheld data.
Source: Energy Information Adminstration, U.S. Department of Energy (EIA-DOE)

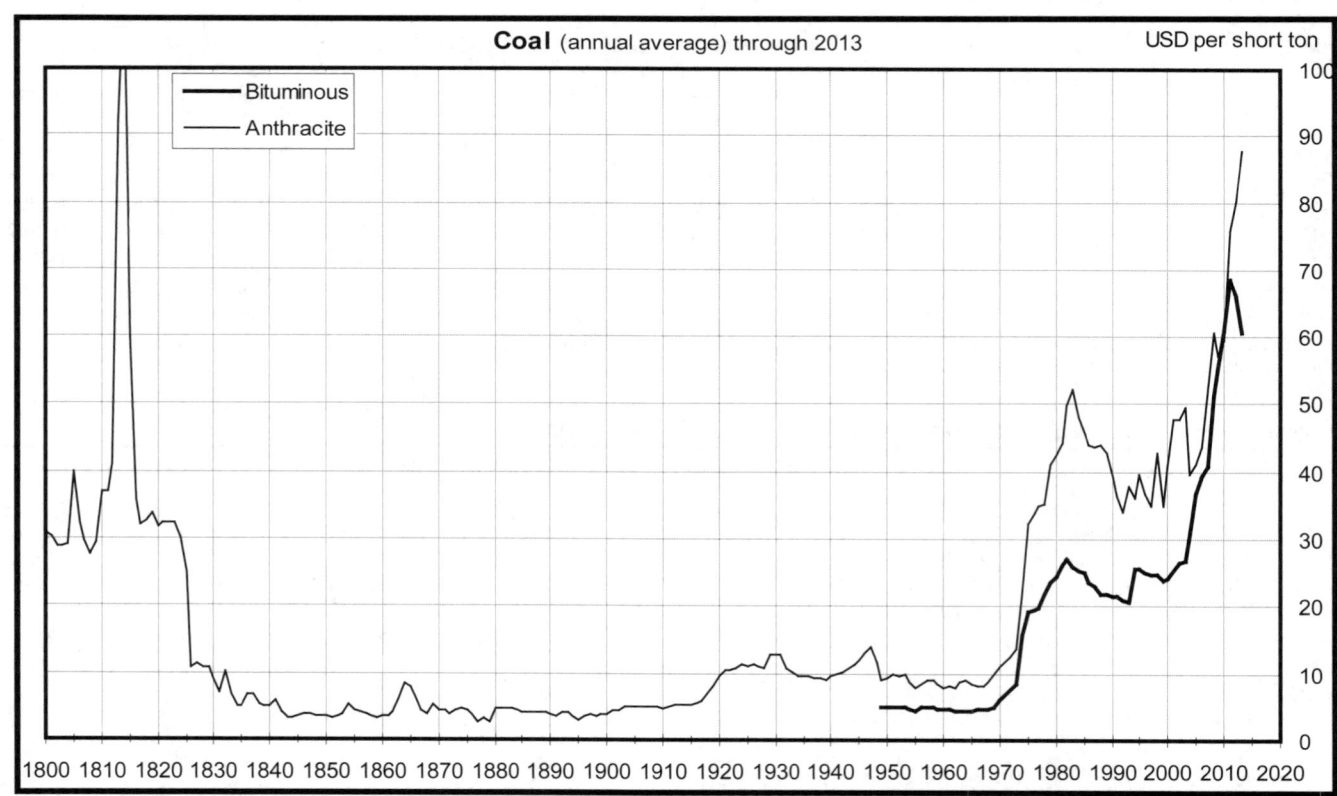

36

Cobalt

Cobalt (atomic symbol Co) is a lustrous, silvery-white, magnetic, metallic element used chiefly for making alloys. Cobalt was known in ancient times and used by the Persians in 2250 BC to color glass. The name *cobalt* comes from the German word **kobalt** or **kobold**, meaning evil spirit. Miners gave cobalt its name because it was poisonous and troublesome since it polluted and degraded other mined elements, like nickel. In the 1730s, George Brandt first isolated metallic cobalt and was able to show that cobalt was the source of the blue color in glasses. In 1780, it was recognized as an element. Cobalt is generally not found in nature as a free metal and is instead found in ores. Cobalt is generally produced as a by-product of nickel and copper mining.

Cobalt is used in a variety of applications: high temperature steel alloys; fasteners in gas turbine engines; magnets and magnetic recording media; drying agents for paints and pigments; and steel-belted radial tires. Cobalt-60, an important radioactive tracer and cancer-treatment agent, is an artificially produced radioactive isotope of cobalt.

Prices – The price of cobalt in 2015 fell by -6.8% to $13.50 per pound, well below the 2008 record high of $39.01 per pound, but almost double the 20-year low of $6.91 per pound in 2002.

Supply – World production of cobalt in 2015 rose by +0.8% to a record high of 124,000 metric tons. The world's largest cobalt mine producers in 2014 were the Congo with 50.8% of world production, China (5.8%), Canada (5.1%), Russia (5.1$), and Australia (4.8%).

The U.S. does not specifically mine or refine cobalt although some cobalt is produced as a by-product of other mining operations. Imports, stock releases, and secondary materials comprise the U.S. cobalt supply. Secondary production includes extraction from super-alloy scrap, cemented carbide scrap, and spent catalysts. In the U.S. there are two domestic producers of extra-fine cobalt powder. One company produces the powder from imported primary metal and the other from recycled materials. There are only about seven companies that produce cobalt compounds. U.S. secondary production of cobalt in 2015 rose +13.6% yr/yr to 2,500 metric tons, but still well below the record high of 3,080 metric tons seen in 1998.

Demand – U.S. consumption of cobalt in 2015 rose by +12.1% yr/yr to 10,000 metric tons, but still below the 2005 record high of 11,800 metric tons. The largest use of cobalt by far was for super-alloys 38.9% of consumption in 2014 consumption. Other smaller-scaled applications for cobalt include cutting and wear-resistant materials (8.1%) and magnetic alloys (3.3%). Demand for some other uses is not available as proprietary information.

Trade – U.S. imports of cobalt in 2015 rose +4.5% to 11,908 metric tons, a new record high. In 2015 the U.S. relied on imports for 75% of its cobalt consumption, which is down from the 99% level seen in the early 1970s.

World Mine Production of Cobalt — In Metric Tons (Cobalt Content)

Year	Australia	Botswana	Brazil	Canada	China	Congo[3] (Kinshasa)	Cuba	Indonesia	Morocco	New Caledonia	Russia	Zambia	World Total
2006	5,130	303	1,100	7,115	1,840	27,100	5,602	1,600	2,600	1,629	6,300	8,000	70,000
2007	4,730	242	2,725	8,692	6,100	25,400	4,540	1,600	1,800	2,250	6,300	7,500	73,700
2008	4,785	337	2,631	8,953	6,630	32,300	4,000	1,300	1,700	2,110	6,200	7,000	79,900
2009	4,345	342	2,075	3,919	6,000	40,000	4,600	1,200	2,610	2,000	6,100	4,900	80,200
2010	3,852	272	3,139	4,636	6,380	60,000	4,800	1,600	3,110	2,850	6,200	6,200	107,000
2011	3,848	149	3,623	6,836	6,800	59,000	5,100	1,600	2,160	3,100	6,100	5,400	108,000
2012	5,870	195	2,900	6,676	7,000	50,000	4,900	1,700	2,000	2,670	6,300	4,200	101,000
2013	6,398	248	3,000	6,916	7,200	54,000	4,200	1,700	2,000	3,190	6,300	5,200	110,000
2014[1]	5,980		2,600	6,570	7,200	63,000	3,700			4,040	6,300	5,500	123,000
2015[2]	6,000		2,600	6,300	7,200	63,000	4,200			3,300	6,300	5,500	124,000

[1] Preliminary. [2] Estimate. [3] Formerly Zaire.   *Source: U.S. Geological Survey (USGS)*

Salient Statistics of Cobalt in the United States — In Metric Tons (Cobalt Content)

Year	Net Import Reliance As a % of Apparent Consump	Cobalt Secondary Production	Processor and Consumer Stocks Dec. 31	Imports for Consumption	Ground Coat Frit	Stainless & Heat Resisting	Catalysts	Super-alloys	Tool Steel	Magnetic Alloys	Pigments	Drier in Paints, etc	Cutting & Wear-Resistant Material	Welding Materials	Total Apparent Uses	Price $ Per Pound[4]
2006	82	2,010	1,180	11,600	W	W	W	4,170	W	386	W	W	808	224	11,000	17.22
2007	80	1,930	1,310	10,300	W	W	W	4,410	W	385	W	W	726	225	9,630	30.55
2008	81	1,930	1,160	10,700	W	W	W	4,320	W	368	W	W	827	226	10,100	39.01
2009	76	1,790	780	7,680	W	W	W	3,570	W	287	W	W	503	331	7,470	17.86
2010	81	2,000	880	11,100	W	W	W	3,740	W	357	W	W	696	364	8,030	20.85
2011	76	2,210	1,040	10,600	W	W	W	4,650	W	313	W	W	773	438	9,230	17.99
2012	77	2,160	980	11,100	W	W	W	4,190	W	285	W	W	774	414	9,510	14.07
2013	75	2,160	1,080	10,500	W	W	W	3,770	W	303	W	W	705	397	8,670	12.89
2014[1]	75	2,200	1,240	11,400	W	W	W	3,560	W	294	W	W	720	W	8,920	14.48
2015[2]	75	2,500	1,190	11,908											10,000	13.50

[1] Preliminary. [2] Estimate. [3] Or related usage. [4] Annual spot for cathodes. W = Withheld.   *Source: U.S. Geological Survey (USGS)*

Cocoa

Cocoa is the common name for a powder derived from the fruit seeds of the cacao tree. The Spanish called cocoa "the food of the gods" when they found it in South America 500 years ago. Today, it remains a valued commodity. Dating back to the time of the Aztecs, cocoa was mainly used as a beverage. The processing of the cacao seeds, also known as cocoa beans, begins when the harvested fruit is fermented or cured into a pulpy state for three to nine days. The cocoa beans are then dried in the sun and cleaned in special machines before they are roasted to bring out the chocolate flavor. After roasting, they are put into a crushing machine and ground into cocoa powder. Cocoa has a high food value because it contains as much as 20 percent protein, 40 percent carbohydrate, and 40 percent fat. It is also mildly stimulating because of the presence of theobromine, an alkaloid that is closely related to caffeine. Roughly two-thirds of cocoa bean production is used to make chocolate and one-third to make cocoa powder.

Four major West African cocoa producers, the Ivory Coast, Ghana, Nigeria and Cameroon, together account for about two-thirds of world cocoa production. Outside of West Africa, the major producers of cocoa are Indonesia, Brazil, Malaysia, Ecuador, and the Dominican Republic. Cocoa producers like Ghana and Indonesia have been making efforts to increase cocoa production while producers like Malaysia have been switching to other crops. Ghana has had an ongoing problem with black pod disease and with smuggling of the crop into neighboring Ivory Coast. Brazil was once one of the largest producers of cocoa but has had problems with witches' broom disease. In West Africa, the main crop harvest starts in the September-October period and can be extended into the January-March period. Cocoa trees reach maturity in 5-6 years but can live to be 50 years old or more. During the course of a growing season, the cocoa tree will produce thousands of flowers but only a few will develop into cocoa pods.

Cocoa futures and options are traded at ICE Futures U.S. and on the NYSE LIFFE European Derivatives Market. The futures contracts call for the delivery of 10 metric tons of cocoa and the contract is priced in US dollars per metric ton.

Prices – ICE cocoa futures prices (Barchart.com symbol CC) moved lower to start off 2015 and dropped to the low for the year, and also a 2-year low, in February at $2,669 per metric ton. Weak global demand undercut cocoa prices after Q4 2014 Asian cocoa processing sank -17% y/y, Q4 North American cocoa grindings unexpectedly fell -2.0% y/y, and Q4 European cocoa processing slid -7.3% y/y, the lowest for a Q4 in 9 years. Cocoa prices traded sideways until late spring when they ratcheted higher on crop concerns in Ghana, the world's second biggest cocoa producer. Drought decimated Ghana's 2015 cocoa crop which fell to a 5-year low of 696,000 MT. The Ghana Meteorological Agency said that Ghana had its driest Q3 in 2015 in 35 years and that the seasonal Harmattan winds were "severe" and added to the low quality of Ghana's cocoa crop. The decline in Ghana's cocoa harvest prompted the International Cocoa Organization (ICCO) to cut its 2014/15 global cocoa production estimate to 4.168 MMT from a 4.23 MMT forecast in February and to project that the 2015/16 global cocoa deficit will widen to -96,000 MT from a -15,000 MT deficit forecast for 2014/15. Cocoa prices fell back slightly from their best levels in December and finished 2015 at $3,211 per metric ton, up +10.3% for the year.

Supply – The world production of cocoa beans in the 2013-14 crop year fell by -12.8% to 4.365 million metric tons. The world's largest cocoa producer by far is the Ivory Coast with 40.0% of total world production in 2013-14. The Ivory Coast's production in 2013-14, rose +5.5 yr/yr to 1.741 million metric tons. After the Ivory Coast the major producers are Ghana with 20.6% of total world production in 2013-14, Indonesia with 9.3%, Nigeria with 5.7%, and Brazil with 5.2%, Cameroon with 4.8%. Closing stocks of cocoa in the 2013-14 crop year rose +3.3% yr/yr to 1.659 metric tons.

Demand – World seasonal grindings of cocoa in 2013-14 rose +3.4% yr/yr to 4.268 million metric tons, a new record high. Europe is by far the largest global consumer of cocoa, consuming about 34% of the global crop.

Trade – U.S. imports of cocoa and cocoa products in 2014 (annualized through November) rose +1.3% yr/yr to 1.316 million metric tons, a new record high.

World Supply and Demand Cocoa   In Thousands of Metric Tons

Crop Year Beginning Oct. 1	Stocks Oct. 1	Net World Production[4]	Total Availability	Seasona Grindings	Closing Stocks	Stock Change	Stock/Consumption Ratio %
2006-07	1,892	3,430	5,322	3,675	1,613	-279	43.9
2007-08	1,613	3,737	5,350	3,775	1,538	-75	40.7
2008-09	1,538	3,592	5,130	3,537	1,557	19	44.0
2009-10	1,557	3,634	5,191	3,737	1,418	-139	37.9
2010-11	1,418	4,309	5,727	3,938	1,746	328	44.3
2011-12	1,746	4,095	5,841	3,972	1,828	82	46.0
2012-13	1,828	3,943	5,771	4,173	1,559	-269	37.4
2013-14[1]	1,559	4,372	5,931	4,322	1,565	6	36.2
2014-15[2]	1,565	4,230	5,795	4,146	1,607	42	38.8
2015-16[3]	1,607	4,154	5,761	4,225	1,494	-113	35.4

[1] Preliminary. [2] Estimate. [3] Forecast. [4] Obtained by adjusting the gross world crop for a one percent loss in weight.
Source: International Cocoa Organization (ICO

World Production of Cocoa Beans   In Metric Tons

Crop Year Beginning Oct. 1	Brazil	Cameroon	Colombia	Côte d'Ivoire	Dominican Republic	Ecuador	Ghana	Indonesia	Malaysia	Mexico	Nigeria	Papau New Guinea	World Total
2006-07	212,270	164,553	35,258	1,408,854	47,020	87,561	734,000	769,386	31,937	38,151	485,000	51,100	4,301,335
2007-08	201,651	212,619	39,904	1,229,908	43,322	85,891	614,500	740,006	35,180	40,000	360,570	49,300	3,897,965
2008-09	202,030	229,203	44,740	1,382,441	45,518	94,300	680,781	803,593	27,955	50,000	367,020	51,500	4,263,272
2009-10	218,487	235,500	44,740	1,223,153	54,994	120,582	710,638	809,583	18,152	60,000	363,510	59,400	4,206,746
2010-11	235,389	264,077	39,534	1,301,347	58,334	132,100	632,037	844,626	15,654	61,000	399,200	39,400	4,339,064
2011-12	248,524	239,000	44,241	1,559,441	54,279	224,163	700,020	712,200	4,605	83,000	391,000	47,600	4,679,108
2012-13	253,211	256,000	49,509	1,650,000	72,225	133,323	879,348	936,300	3,645	83,000	383,000	38,700	5,003,211
2013-14[1]	228,200	211,000	48,800	1,746,200	70,000	234,000	896,900	375,000	6,000	30,000	248,000	36,200	4,371,600
2014-15[2]	230,000	232,300	51,000	1,795,900	82,000	250,000	740,300	325,000	6,500	28,000	195,000	35,900	4,229,600
2015-16[3]	210,000	230,000	53,000	1,690,000	72,000	230,000	840,000	300,000	6,500	30,000	200,000	36,000	4,154,100

[1] Preliminary.   [2] Estimate.   [3] Forecast.   *Source: Food and Agricultural Organization of the United Nations (FAO)*

World Consumption of Cocoa[4]   In Thousands of Metric Tons

Crop Year Beginning Oct. 1	Canada	Côte d'Ivoire	Brazil	European Union	Ghana	Indonesia	Japan	Malaysia	Singapore	Turkey	United States	Russia	World Total
2006-07	66	360	226	1,390	121	140	50	301	87	64	418	65	3,675
2007-08	59	374	232	1,439	123	160	42	331	89	60	391	65	3,775
2008-09	55	419	216	1,357	133	120	41	278	80	57	361	54	3,537
2009-10	59	411	226	1,409	212	130	42	298	83	68	382	52	3,737
2010-11	62	361	239	1,492	230	190	40	305	83	70	401	61	3,938
2011-12	60	431	243	1,383	212	270	40	297	83	75	387	63	3,972
2012-13	64	471	241	1,443	225	290	40	293	77	75	429	71	4,173
2013-14[1]	67	519	240	1,461	234	340	44	259	79	88	446	62	4,322
2014-15[2]	62	559	224	1,435	234	335	45	195	80	86	398	46	4,146
2015-16[3]	60	575	230	1,461	235	370	46	190	80	90	395	48	4,225

[1] Preliminary.   [2] Estimate.   [3] Forecast.   [4] Figures represent the "grindings" of cocoa beans in each country.
Source: International Cocoa Organization (ICO)

Imports of Cocoa Butter in Selected Countries   In Metric Tons

Year	Australia	Austria	Belgium	Canada	France	Germany	Italy	Japan	Netherlands	Sweden	Switzerland	United Kingdom	United States
2006	19,172	4,729	68,173	23,803	75,572	82,726	16,285	25,603	82,864	5,774	25,725	48,447	96,455
2007	15,845	4,367	75,283	31,301	78,858	85,113	20,973	24,417	70,598	3,441	27,265	48,911	86,258
2008	14,970	4,847	64,782	23,516	69,153	85,605	21,706	23,368	72,786	3,993	27,193	42,879	102,868
2009	13,110	3,856	70,155	20,759	64,495	84,939	21,735	22,038	72,609	3,699	24,820	42,921	84,498
2010	15,024	4,929	65,336	20,885	57,639	88,713	22,439	19,365	70,529	6,416	26,462	50,639	102,878
2011	15,081	5,155	75,003	22,463	61,948	89,511	21,988	19,475	91,297	6,010	26,813	43,440	92,572
2012	15,971	5,090	75,402	24,090	71,043	92,370	25,999	26,566	72,416	6,219	26,430	51,541	72,085
2013	17,900	5,425	75,585	25,929	65,205	109,853	30,310	24,260	92,547	6,192	28,795	50,789	80,676
2014	16,074	4,912	79,049	26,250	68,073	124,839	28,364	27,351	82,319	6,400	28,767	47,171	97,774
2015[1]	18,054	3,328	74,574	23,780	55,886	81,042	26,772	21,528	60,782	6,494	25,466	56,968	94,118

[1] Preliminary.   *Sources: Food and Agricultural Organization of the United Nations (FAO)*

Imports of Cocoa Liquor and Cocoa Powder in Selected Countries   In Metric Tons

| | ---- Cocoa Liquor ---- | | | | | | ---- Cocoa Powder ---- | | | | | | |
Year	France	Germany	Japan	Netherlands	United Kingdom	United States	Denmark	France	Germany	Italy	Japan	Netherlands	United States
2006	79,593	41,900	5,190	44,442	5,960	33,803	3,053	39,833	41,050	22,485	15,831	34,770	145,820
2007	79,733	48,038	14,126	44,044	6,740	20,180	3,106	41,030	47,480	28,241	16,218	35,979	158,132
2008	58,304	51,712	7,952	49,399	6,494	23,652	3,046	45,652	47,232	28,576	18,050	24,364	156,028
2009	59,017	64,206	7,515	44,915	6,635	19,367	2,530	42,022	49,689	26,708	15,613	35,034	163,874
2010	59,205	94,860	6,006	60,067	10,073	29,709	2,549	53,861	54,056	26,161	18,765	45,047	172,904
2011	84,704	79,039	9,358	82,633	12,108	22,996	2,532	58,723	54,215	27,717	17,361	53,899	162,723
2012	83,905	82,605	9,351	74,125	14,907	20,461	2,200	53,499	52,762	25,370	17,201	45,494	161,081
2013	96,205	81,726	8,487	98,497	9,934	18,379	2,368	65,479	59,576	26,630	15,897	49,255	150,266
2014	94,219	77,645	9,829	112,010	9,238	22,302	2,115	59,356	69,838	28,444	17,705	56,878	154,294
2015[1]	68,878	67,956	11,690	81,036	7,332	16,202	2,116	57,448	67,642	32,910	18,094	39,020	143,138

[1] Preliminary.   *Source: Food and Agricultural Organization of the United Nations (FAO)*

COCOA

Imports of Cocoa and Products in the United States   In Thousands of Metric Tons

Year	Jan.	Feb.	Mar.	Apr.	May	June	July	Aug.	Sept.	Oct.	Nov.	Dec.	Total
2006	114.1	104.0	109.1	93.7	91.7	86.4	108.5	139.8	102.5	90.7	90.4	123.6	1,254.7
2007	110.9	120.6	109.9	101.8	82.0	76.5	83.4	83.3	83.8	95.1	76.2	106.1	1,129.6
2008	108.0	115.1	108.5	87.1	79.8	65.2	87.8	81.9	79.0	89.7	83.7	128.5	1,114.3
2009	113.5	98.0	87.6	95.1	82.5	98.6	80.0	88.0	103.2	103.3	94.2	125.7	1,169.7
2010	153.8	99.7	133.9	85.4	94.2	78.1	79.6	84.4	109.6	88.5	100.4	114.7	1,222.4
2011	132.3	144.1	88.2	89.8	92.0	138.0	125.2	121.6	93.8	97.7	90.1	100.5	1,313.3
2012	147.3	152.5	115.0	99.2	82.9	90.6	91.5	95.6	83.1	91.7	88.4	99.9	1,237.8
2013	118.1	125.9	119.3	106.9	136.4	88.1	112.1	95.0	93.6	91.9	90.0	126.7	1,303.9
2014	105.7	141.2	165.4	133.9	95.6	94.8	104.6	98.2	91.0	93.5	80.5	91.7	1,296.0
2015[1]	109.7	121.6	132.2	138.9	115.8	124.7	107.9	88.5	101.4	105.5	87.7	105.5	1,339.3

[1] Preliminary.   Source: Foreign Agricultural Service, U.S. Department of Agriculture (FAS-USDA)

Visible Stocks of Cocoa in Port of Hampton Road Warehouses[1], at End of Month   In Thousands of Bags

Year	Jan.	Feb.	Mar.	Apr.	May	June	July	Aug.	Sept.	Oct.	Nov.	Dec.
2006	18.3	17.9	17.3	17.3	17.3	17.3	17.3	17.3	17.1	17.1	17.1	17.1
2007	16.8	16.8	16.8	16.8	16.8	16.8	16.8	15.6	15.6	15.6	15.6	15.6
2008	15.6	15.6	15.6	15.6	15.8	15.8	15.8	15.8	15.8	15.6	15.6	15.6
2009	14.9	14.9	14.9	14.9	14.9	14.9	13.7	13.7	13.7	13.7	13.7	13.7
2010	13.3	12.3	12.3	12.3	12.3	12.3	12.3	12.3	12.3	12.3	12.3	12.3
2011	10.4	12.3	12.3	12.3	12.3	12.3	12.3	12.3	11.6	11.6	11.6	11.6
2012	11.6	11.6	11.6	11.6	11.6	11.6	11.6	11.6	11.6	11.3	11.3	11.3
2013	11.3	11.3	11.3	9.6	9.6	9.6	10.5	10.5	5.1	9.6	9.5	9.6
2014	9.6	9.6	9.6	9.6	9.6	9.6	9.6	9.6	9.6	9.6	9.6	9.6
2015	9.6	9.6	9.6	9.6	9.6	7.2	7.2	7.2	7.2	7.2	7.2	7.2

[1] Licensed warehouses approved by ICE.   Source: ICE Futures U.S. (ICE)

Visible Stocks of Cocoa in Philadelphia (Del. River) Warehouses[1], at End of Month   In Thousands of Bags

Year	Jan.	Feb.	Mar.	Apr.	May	June	July	Aug.	Sept.	Oct.	Nov.	Dec.
2006	2,888.5	2,828.9	3,013.5	3,246.1	3,111.0	2,913.8	2,754.7	3,404.0	3,382.1	3,307.2	3,085.7	3,293.0
2007	3,488.8	4,113.3	4,326.8	4,324.0	4,226.5	3,860.3	3,437.9	3,106.8	2,883.0	2,660.0	2,327.4	2,334.5
2008	2,431.0	2,679.8	2,920.4	2,787.6	2,733.9	2,486.3	2,223.6	2,110.8	1,717.5	1,571.2	1,390.4	1,533.4
2009	2,062.7	2,339.1	2,292.6	2,530.2	2,456.1	2,405.8	2,137.2	2,059.1	1,938.5	1,931.4	2,105.8	2,196.4
2010	2,699.9	3,217.3	3,442.6	3,400.3	3,317.0	3,128.8	2,935.7	2,602.8	2,491.2	2,159.6	1,985.2	2,197.6
2011	2,551.7	2,900.4	2,856.1	2,633.1	2,546.0	2,971.6	3,388.2	3,089.4	3,055.1	2,758.3	2,559.1	2,856.1
2012	3,210.7	3,538.5	4,156.0	4,123.5	3,985.5	3,815.8	3,792.4	3,655.2	3,442.7	3,204.1	2,895.2	2,956.3
2013	3,070.3	3,690.7	3,924.4	3,884.4	4,110.6	4,035.9	3,945.1	3,897.9	3,583.0	3,170.0	2,921.9	3,050.1
2014	3,215.1	3,687.7	4,395.1	4,862.6	4,647.1	4,354.2	4,167.4	3,909.4	3,569.5	3,168.6	2,816.0	2,494.7
2015	2,640.6	2,953.7	3,044.0	3,700.4	3,780.4	4,166.1	4,013.1	3,788.7	3,568.2	3,286.3	3,146.1	2,956.1

[1] Licensed warehouses approved by ICE.   Source: ICE Futures U.S. (ICE)

Visible Stocks of Cocoa in New York Warehouses[1], at End of Month   In Thousands of Bags

Year	Jan.	Feb.	Mar.	Apr.	May	June	July	Aug.	Sept.	Oct.	Nov.	Dec.
2006	758.4	971.5	869.7	820.6	758.3	691.8	634.1	685.8	654.2	649.1	532.3	502.8
2007	532.2	460.2	632.6	667.1	611.9	605.4	577.7	530.5	496.8	442.2	394.8	343.2
2008	408.9	411.1	574.4	618.7	614.0	554.4	527.9	434.6	396.1	375.6	323.1	242.5
2009	291.7	413.2	423.9	472.0	501.5	557.3	672.2	664.2	653.9	726.0	714.6	722.3
2010	831.4	1,005.7	1,099.3	1,042.0	954.2	825.2	730.7	662.7	618.4	572.3	524.9	487.3
2011	499.4	604.9	701.2	711.1	639.3	661.5	719.8	734.1	807.6	884.8	875.5	857.6
2012	845.1	881.2	1,031.7	1,016.7	962.8	944.4	862.3	928.4	877.0	829.7	752.3	716.5
2013	679.9	619.6	621.1	708.3	779.6	779.6	717.2	660.4	589.3	529.2	451.3	475.6
2014	391.0	386.7	364.5	482.6	619.3	566.5	505.4	435.9	419.3	380.9	317.1	308.3
2015	276.6	266.0	245.3	260.4	286.9	366.0	342.2	314.5	284.7	277.7	278.0	287.8

[1] Licensed warehouses approved by ICE.   Source: ICE Futures U.S. (ICE)

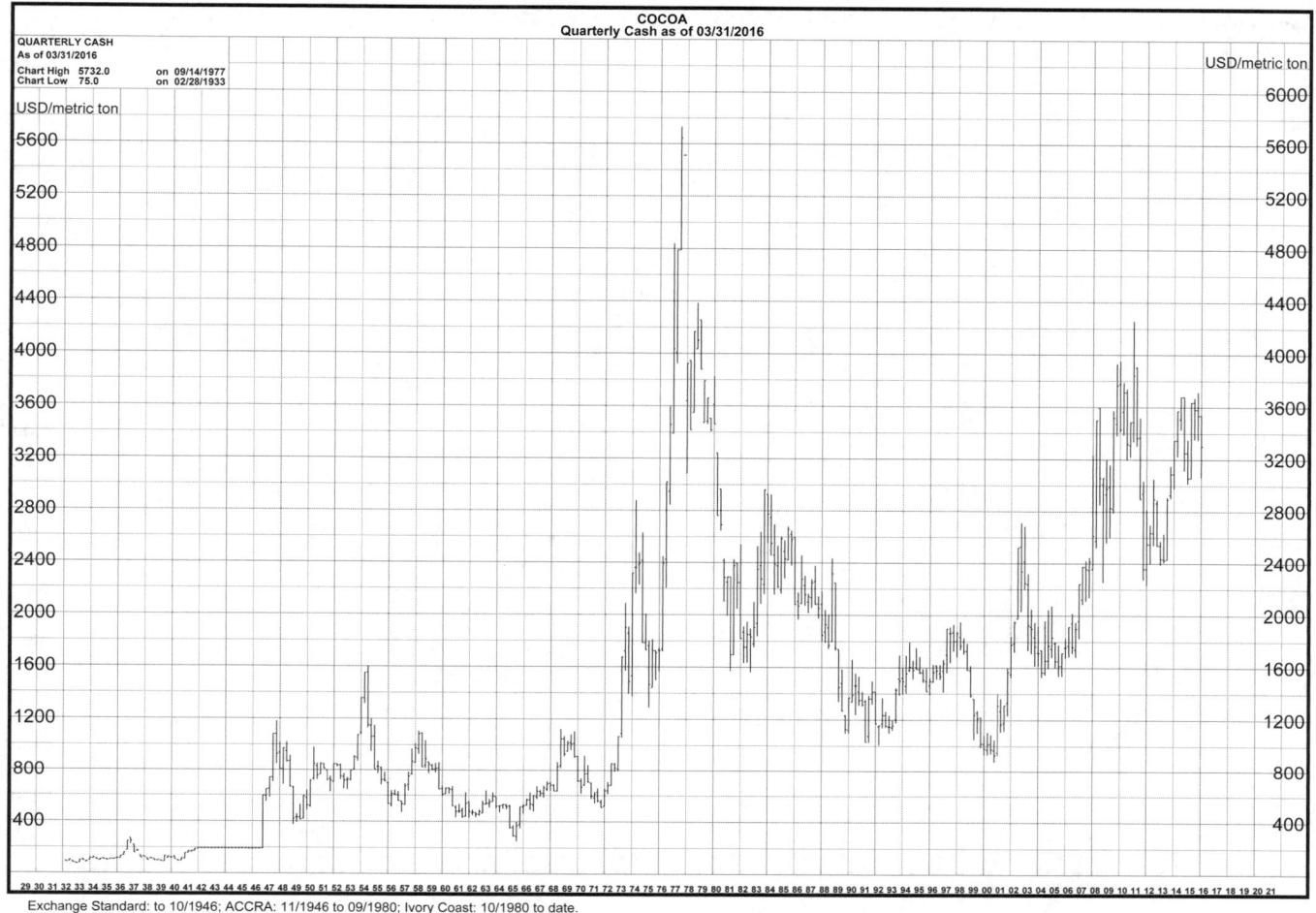

QUARTERLY CASH
As of 03/31/2016
Chart High 5732.0 on 09/14/1977
Chart Low 75.0 on 02/28/1933

COCOA
Quarterly Cash as of 03/31/2016

Exchange Standard: to 10/1946; ACCRA: 11/1946 to 09/1980; Ivory Coast: 10/1980 to date.

Average Cash Price of Cocoa, Ivory Coast in New York   In Dollars Per Metric Ton

Year	Jan.	Feb.	Mar.	Apr.	May	June	July	Aug.	Sept.	Oct.	Nov.	Dec.	Average
2006	1,752	1,729	1,739	1,749	1,806	1,794	1,862	1,795	1,764	1,725	1,773	1,897	1,782
2007	1,883	1,996	2,120	2,169	2,214	2,225	2,361	2,185	2,242	2,198	2,251	2,396	2,187
2008	2,486	2,806	2,922	2,867	2,971	3,307	3,248	3,078	2,972	2,533	2,371	2,837	2,867
2009	2,985	2,977	2,781	2,830	2,699	2,892	3,047	3,186	3,427	3,634	3,596	3,782	3,153
2010	3,851	3,611	3,452	3,580	3,535	3,539	3,602	3,455	3,269	3,314	3,279	3,354	3,487
2011	3,507	3,937	3,992	3,697	3,565	3,360	3,422	3,312	3,199	2,949	2,831	2,396	3,347
2012	2,448	2,621	2,647	2,553	2,605	2,506	2,595	2,759	2,956	2,787	2,745	2,724	2,662
2013	2,519	2,455	2,428	2,492	2,566	2,494	2,521	2,672	2,819	2,988	2,996	3,099	2,671
2014	3,068	3,281	3,325	3,340	3,287	3,476	3,494	3,591	3,523	3,455	3,176	3,191	3,351
2015	3,170	3,181	3,181	3,129	3,331	3,493	3,590	3,424	3,546	3,434	3,630	3,632	3,395

Source: Economic Research Service, U.S. Department of Agriculture (ERS-USDA)

Total Visible Stocks of Cocoa in Warehouses[1], at End of Month   In Thousands of Bags

Year	Jan.	Feb.	Mar.	Apr.	May	June	July	Aug.	Sept.	Oct.	Nov.	Dec.
2006	3,665.1	3,818.4	3,900.5	4,249.5	4,021.8	3,737.7	3,512.1	4,375.5	4,271.5	4,166.7	3,811.4	4,194.0
2007	4,366.4	4,882.7	5,251.1	5,260.8	5,155.3	4,821.1	4,327.5	3,897.1	3,604.0	3,297.4	2,867.8	2,832.9
2008	3,140.9	3,453.9	3,917.9	3,757.7	3,648.4	3,322.8	3,003.3	2,771.8	2,322.7	2,114.2	1,875.9	1,950.5
2009	2,557.4	2,996.2	2,956.5	3,266.2	3,179.4	3,166.2	3,000.9	2,909.0	2,751.1	2,783.3	2,932.8	3,027.8
2010	3,639.8	4,330.1	4,727.3	4,636.9	4,477.2	4,170.8	3,901.1	3,492.1	3,318.1	2,884.6	2,645.7	2,801.8
2011	3,158.1	3,611.9	3,757.3	3,520.8	3,324.1	3,729.7	4,185.3	3,892.5	3,928.4	3,704.4	3,491.6	3,767.1
2012	4,108.5	4,627.0	5,393.6	5,343.0	5,149.2	4,947.6	4,834.9	4,758.7	4,483.8	4,161.4	3,753.2	3,763.1
2013	3,814.6	4,416.3	4,653.7	4,690.9	4,987.5	4,966.3	4,745.1	4,632.7	4,232.5	3,754.5	3,436.3	3,574.1
2014	3,648.9	4,117.1	4,800.1	5,384.4	5,305.6	4,960.0	4,711.8	4,384.1	4,027.5	3,588.3	3,171.9	2,824.9
2015	2,939.1	3,241.1	3,310.7	3,978.6	4,085.2	4,546.7	4,369.9	4,117.8	3,867.5	3,578.7	3,438.3	3,255.3

[1] Licensed warehouses approved by ICE.   *Source: ICE Futures U.S. (ICE)*

COCOA

Nearby Futures through Last Trading Day.

Volume of Trading of Cocoa Futures in New York   In Contracts

Year	Jan.	Feb.	Mar.	Apr.	May	June	July	Aug.	Sept.	Oct.	Nov.	Dec.	Total
2006	235,410	264,557	201,604	295,814	244,032	333,275	331,108	313,591	174,246	264,490	308,782	202,293	3,169,202
2007	239,568	338,998	273,605	333,551	212,318	328,646	242,710	378,897	213,143	265,018	273,419	235,410	3,335,283
2008	322,864	434,965	316,509	328,981	293,874	353,593	280,275	345,973	197,765	313,220	228,699	175,550	3,592,268
2009	265,308	282,200	242,110	279,621	214,640	303,030	216,046	292,552	188,138	289,133	338,296	175,892	3,086,966
2010	255,025	361,068	282,222	372,997	290,545	366,645	253,289	425,322	247,749	284,483	404,682	253,652	3,797,679
2011	395,349	401,740	390,590	423,879	357,282	454,217	328,156	571,410	335,481	388,486	554,320	347,142	4,948,052
2012	395,832	586,013	474,613	605,217	459,683	620,166	457,510	627,854	346,794	467,949	651,655	306,527	5,999,813
2013	505,589	598,270	425,547	752,332	541,022	792,100	504,933	646,114	379,515	484,417	621,749	332,158	6,583,746
2014	571,906	588,461	453,219	593,071	454,372	625,401	551,959	541,132	478,549	617,492	508,452	331,778	6,315,792
2015	586,564	679,362	694,091	739,813	520,024	710,582	531,381	801,763	602,091	770,424	775,633	501,308	7,913,036

Source: ICE Futures U.S. (ICE)

Average Open Interest of Cocoa Futures in New York   In Contracts

Year	Jan.	Feb.	Mar.	Apr.	May	June	July	Aug.	Sept.	Oct.	Nov.	Dec.
2006	131,527	127,471	129,426	129,814	131,035	138,004	154,163	134,942	139,544	153,485	136,329	140,099
2007	145,503	152,358	172,846	157,373	154,649	148,608	167,565	134,823	123,171	133,362	137,208	165,522
2008	188,039	182,389	166,939	136,591	146,759	160,366	151,896	134,715	127,674	122,381	113,422	113,240
2009	119,496	118,145	114,051	111,859	117,027	114,792	112,079	112,935	121,226	133,635	129,171	129,296
2010	137,675	127,994	129,562	128,298	130,258	119,074	124,335	119,070	127,315	138,385	136,708	137,345
2011	148,426	158,965	163,700	159,411	157,851	162,945	172,670	166,766	176,524	191,211	168,734	167,339
2012	171,138	165,555	170,143	178,362	183,549	174,848	186,439	190,328	202,142	202,142	189,765	193,643
2013	197,848	192,704	200,696	199,773	220,741	196,543	176,618	183,556	201,739	219,812	212,717	213,685
2014	210,130	216,867	215,297	206,091	204,253	216,264	214,879	213,149	208,448	199,236	177,425	186,443
2015	200,884	193,672	211,199	199,675	208,637	215,736	219,497	182,777	200,200	216,932	232,054	234,884

Source: ICE Futures U.S. (ICE)

Coconut Oil and Copra

Coconut oil and copra come from the fruit of the coconut palm tree, which originated in Southeast Asia. Coconut oil has been used for thousands of years as cooking oil, and is still a staple in the diets of many people living in tropical areas. Until shortages of imported oil developed during WWII, Americans also used coconut oil for cooking.

Copra is the meaty inner lining of the coconut. It is an oil-rich pulp with a light, slightly sweet, nutty flavor. Copra is used mainly as a source of coconut oil and is also used shredded for baking. High-quality copra contains about 65% to 72% oil, and oil made from the copra is called crude coconut oil. Crude coconut oil is processed from copra by expeller press and solvent extraction. It is not considered fit for human consumption until it has been refined, which consists of neutralizing, bleaching and deodorizing it at high heat with a vacuum. The remaining oil cake obtained as a by-product is used for livestock feed.

Premium grade coconut oil, also called virgin coconut oil, is oil made from the first pressing without the addition of any chemicals. Premium grade coconut oil is more expensive than refined or crude oil because the producers use only selected raw materials and there is a lower production yield due to only one pressing.

Coconut oil accounts for approximately 20% of all vegetable oils used worldwide. Coconut oil is used in margarines, vegetable shortening, salad oils, confections, and in sports drinks to boost energy and enhance athletic performance. It is also used in the manufacture of soaps, detergents, shampoos, cosmetics, candles, glycerin and synthetic rubber. Coconut oil is very healthy, unless it is hydrogenated, and is easily digested.

Supply – World production of copra in 2015 fell -0.3% yr/yr to 4.890 million metric tons, remaining below the record high of 5.662 million metric tons posted in 2001. The world's largest producers of copra are the Philippines with 35.8% of world production, Indonesia with 30.7%, India with 13.1%, and Mexico with 4.2%. World production of coconut oil in the 2014-15 marketing year fell -3.3% yr/yr to 2.968 million metric tons.

Demand – Virtually all of world production of copra goes for crushing into coconut meal and oil (over 99%). World consumption of coconut oil in 2014-15 fell by -6.0% yr/yr to 2.920 million metric tons, below the 2009-10 record high of 3.588 million metric tons.

Trade – Copra is generally crushed in the country of origin, meaning that less than 4% of copra itself is exported; the rest is exported in the form of coconut oil. World exports of coconut oil in 2014-15 fell by -1.4% yr/yr to 1.848 million metric tons, below the 2009-10 record high of 2.374 million metric tons.

World Production of Copra   In Thousands of Metric Tons

Year	India	Indonesia	Ivory Coast	Malaysia	Mexico	Mozam-bique	Papua New Guinea	Philip-pines	Sri Lanka	Thailand	Vanuatu	Vietnam	World Total
2006	680	1,370	45	51	187	48	94	2,100	65	65	30	51	5,110
2007	670	1,570	45	49	217	46	97	1,880	69	68	30	54	5,121
2008	680	1,435	46	52	226	48	123	1,910	73	68	32	55	5,076
2009	680	1,520	46	54	228	48	100	2,040	89	69	31	55	5,284
2010	690	1,440	46	53	211	48	102	2,680	85	48	32	57	5,816
2011	680	1,400	46	51	209	48	115	1,700	87	44	32	57	4,791
2012	670	1,550	46	58	216	49	85	2,030	90	48	32	57	5,247
2013[1]	640	1,460	46	79	207	50	80	2,270	90	49	25	57	5,374
2014[2]	670	1,530	46	62	203	52	72	1,740	80	49	25	57	4,906
2015[3]	640	1,500	46	76	203	54	92	1,750	85	49	18	57	4,890

[1] Preliminary.   [2] Estimate.   [3] Forecast.   *Source: The Oil World*

World Supply and Distribution of Coconut Oil   In Thousands of Metric Tons

	Production							Consumption						Ending Stocks		
Year	India	Indo-nesia	Malay-sia	Philip-pines	World Total	World Exports	World Imports	European Union	India	Indo-nesia	Philip-pines	United States	World Total	Philip-pines	United States	World Total
2005-06	409	789	45	1,450	3,240	2,189	2,176	768	437	180	253	494	3,223	66	101	405
2006-07	402	960	47	1,220	3,178	1,924	1,909	704	417	187	351	435	3,173	105	58	396
2007-08	401	887	44	1,346	3,248	2,001	2,030	685	417	179	428	506	3,271	85	82	402
2008-09	396	851	44	1,239	3,099	1,766	1,795	632	411	181	441	419	3,087	145	83	442
2009-10	400	890	45	1,732	3,621	2,406	2,374	794	404	179	445	587	3,574	55	84	457
2010-11	398	847	50	1,240	3,090	1,948	1,973	730	409	153	336	474	3,237	70	62	336
2011-12	393	914	47	1,208	3,123	1,908	1,907	594	402	143	375	487	3,075	110	77	381
2012-13[1]	380	850	51	1,624	3,451	2,079	2,075	716	381	193	533	521	3,405	80	80	423
2013-14[2]	390	933	51	1,165	3,070	1,874	1,878	646	391	161	375	513	3,108	68	73	389
2014-15[3]	381	899	55	1,097	2,968	1,848	1,840	540	388	187	268	527	2,920	87	81	429

[1] Preliminary.   [2] Estimate.   [3] Forecast.   *Source: The Oil World*

COCONUT OIL AND COPRA

Supply and Distribution of Coconut Oil in the United States   In Millions of Pounds

| | --- Rotterdam --- | | | | | | -------- Disapearance -------- | | | ------ Production of Coconut Oil (Refined) ------ | | | | |
| | Copra Tonne | Coconut Oil, CIF | Imports For Con- | Stocks | Total | | Total | Edible | Inedible | | Oct.- | Jan.- | April- | July- |
Year	------ $ U.S. ------		sumption	Oct. 1	Supply	Exports	Domestic	Products	Products	Total	Dec.	Mar.	June	Sept.
2005-06	387	583	1,127	242	1,369	58	1,323	366	270	599.9	141.9	156.2	160.5	141.4
2006-07	537	812	892	222	1,114	26	1,443	339	309	654.6	162.6	152.2	165.4	174.4
2007-08	867	1,306	1,196	128	1,325	28	1,383	373	447	627.4	139.9	165.9	161.1	160.5
2008-09	487	735	961	181	1,143	37	1,293	364	394	586.6	147.6	131.1	122.8	185.2
2009-10	613	921	1,338	183	1,521	41	1,836	441	W	833.0	190.1	214.9	211.2	216.8
2010-11	1,188	1,772	1,080	186	1,266	85	1,045	467	W	808.8	202.2	NA	NA	NA
2011-12	829	1,244	1,165	137	1,302	60	1,073	NA	NA	NA	NA	NA	NA	NA
2012-13	570	858	1,214	169	1,382	56	1,149	NA	NA	NA	NA	NA	NA	NA
2013-14[1]	854	1,278	1,179	176	1,356	64	1,131	----	----	----	----	----	----	----
2014-15[2]	767	1,153	1,257	161	1,418	77	1,162	----	----	----	----	----	----	----

[1] Preliminary.   [2] Forecast.   *Source: Bureau of Census, U.S. Department of Commerce*

Consumption of Coconut Oil in End Products (Edible and Inedible) in the United States   In Millions of Pounds

Year	Jan.	Feb.	Mar.	Apr.	May	June	July	Aug.	Sept.	Oct.	Nov.	Dec.	Total
2002	55.4	41.3	50.8	59.3	53.9	46.4	50.7	51.8	45.9	54.3	56.1	49.4	615.4
2003	51.2	49.3	56.8	50.6	52.3	46.7	48.9	49.6	50.3	47.8	41.8	38.5	583.7
2004	50.0	51.7	58.5	54.6	48.5	55.6	52.9	55.1	48.9	48.2	64.3	51.7	640.0
2005	46.7	52.0	47.9	48.8	51.4	55.5	47.2	58.1	49.2	52.8	53.4	58.1	621.1
2006	70.4	62.7	50.4	47.5	50.7	51.6	43.1	51.6	43.8	49.6	44.4	40.8	606.4
2007	49.8	48.5	47.0	51.2	53.7	60.3	60.3	74.2	67.5	71.8	71.3	62.7	718.3
2008	63.6	72.1	64.8	74.4	69.7	70.4	65.8	67.6	65.8	63.0	63.6	53.6	794.5
2009	67.9	62.8	60.2	66.9	66.9	27.6	36.5	28.1	29.4	32.8	32.1	30.6	541.8
2010	41.0	36.6	45.3	34.9	39.8	38.6	37.2	40.4	32.1	41.4	39.9	70.8	498.0
2011[1]	34.6	37.0	40.6	38.0	39.0	37.0	26.7	NA	NA	NA	NA	NA	433.5

[1] Preliminary.   *Source: Bureau of Census, U.S. Department of Commerce*

Stocks of Coconut Oil (Crude and Refined) in the United States, on First of Month   In Millions of Pounds

Year	Jan.	Feb.	Mar.	Apr.	May	June	July	Aug.	Sept.	Oct.	Nov.	Dec.
2002	245.9	238.8	249.6	251.3	233.5	231.6	303.3	301.6	245.8	226.5	273.8	264.1
2003	195.2	194.0	214.3	224.9	223.7	187.8	162.2	202.9	195.6	218.9	184.6	186.1
2004	167.2	160.3	192.6	181.7	131.4	108.7	90.6	132.8	149.2	131.3	147.7	182.5
2005	225.9	163.7	188.4	191.0	170.6	187.7	263.5	250.4	253.7	242.1	252.3	273.3
2006	268.3	236.9	224.5	227.3	260.2	229.1	213.8	214.4	204.7	224.5	179.2	180.2
2007	214.4	228.5	261.5	223.1	191.8	157.9	171.2	154.4	127.7	128.4	142.5	212.6
2008	205.6	192.9	180.9	191.9	223.9	203.9	187.8	181.5	180.4	182.2	163.3	174.6
2009	164.1	183.7	215.6	167.2	143.9	138.0	134.8	133.2	102.3	182.3	159.0	154.7
2010	220.2	204.5	172.1	144.6	119.3	120.3	172.2	179.3	197.1	185.8	166.7	167.2
2011[1]	181.5	150.2	162.7	154.6	150.0	157.6	158.4	190.9	NA	NA	NA	NA

[1] Preliminary.   *Source: Bureau of Census, U.S. Department of Commerce*

Average Price of Coconut Oil (Crude) Tank Cars in New York   In Cents Per Pound

Year	Jan.	Feb.	Mar.	Apr.	May	June	July	Aug.	Sept.	Oct.	Nov.	Dec.	Average
2005	31.05	31.00	32.67	35.00	34.67	34.00	33.00	33.00	33.00	35.00	29.13	27.75	32.44
2006	27.75	27.75	27.75	27.75	27.75	27.75	27.75	27.75	29.25	30.75	32.25	34.95	29.10
2007	35.75	36.00	36.00	37.50	40.13	45.75	48.00	NA	42.50	45.16	45.38	46.32	41.68
2008	58.02	62.33	70.98	67.38	67.38	71.73	70.33	59.62	55.82	47.73	37.46	35.51	58.69
2009	35.25	33.14	30.07	31.58	37.84	37.34	32.78	35.00	35.75	35.75	35.75	35.53	34.65
2010	36.20	35.75	37.88	41.99	43.60	44.00	46.49	54.31	55.94	63.65	69.00	79.50	50.69
2011	87.00	92.50	85.00	91.80	95.50	96.50	87.00	81.75	74.40	57.75	57.00	61.00	80.60
2012	68.25	68.00	64.90	63.63	59.25	54.00	52.75	50.30	47.75	43.75	41.40	38.88	54.40
2013	39.38	41.25	39.30	38.00	38.20	40.75	41.50	41.50	46.00	45.00	59.30	61.00	44.26
2014[1]	59.70	63.00	65.38	62.75	65.70	65.31	62.88	56.60	55.31	53.75	55.69	56.50	60.21

[1] Preliminary.   *Source: Economic Research Service, U.S. Department of Agriculture (ERS-USDA)*

Coffee

Coffee is one of the world's most important cash commodities. Coffee is the common name for any type of tree in the genus madder family. It is actually a tropical evergreen shrub that has the potential to grow 100 feet tall. The coffee tree grows in tropical regions between the Tropics of Cancer and Capricorn in areas with abundant rainfall, year-round warm temperatures averaging about 70 degrees Fahrenheit, and no frost. In the U.S., the only areas that produce any significant amount of coffee are Puerto Rico and Hawaii. The coffee plant will produce its first full crop of beans at about 5 years old and then be productive for about 15 years. The average coffee tree produces enough beans to make about 1 to 1 ½ pounds of roasted coffee per year. It takes approximately 4,000 handpicked green coffee beans to make a pound of coffee. Wine was actually the first drink made from the coffee tree using the coffee cherries, honey, and water. In the 17th century, the first coffee house, also known as a "penny university" because of the price per cup, opened in London. The London Stock Exchange grew from one of these first coffee houses.

Coffee is generally classified into two types of beans: arabica and robusta. The most widely produced coffee is arabica, which makes up about 70 percent of total production. It grows mostly at high altitudes of 600 to 2,000 meters, with Brazil and Colombia being the largest producers. Arabic coffee is traded at the Intercontinental Exchange (ICE). The stronger of the two types is robusta. It is grown at lower altitudes with the largest producers being Indonesia, West Africa, Brazil, and Vietnam. Robusta coffee is traded on the LIFFE exchange.

Ninety percent of the world coffee trade is in green (unroasted) coffee beans. Seasonal factors have a significant influence on the price of coffee. There is no extreme peak in world production at any one time of the year, although coffee consumption declines by 12 percent or more below the year's average in the warm summer months. Therefore, coffee imports and roasts both tend to decline in spring and summer and pick up again in fall and winter.

The very low prices for coffee in 2000-03 created serious problems for coffee producers. When prices fall below the costs of production, there is little or no economic incentive to produce coffee. The result is that coffee trees are neglected or completely abandoned. When prices are low, producers cannot afford to hire the labor needed to maintain the trees and pick the crop at harvest. The result is that trees yield less due to reduced use of fertilizer and fewer employed coffee workers. One effect is a decline in the quality of the coffee that is produced. Higher quality Arabica coffee is often produced at higher altitudes, which entails higher costs. It is this coffee that is often abandoned. Although the pressure on producers can be severe, the market eventually comes back into balance as supply declines in response to low prices.

Coffee prices are subject to upward spikes in June, July and August due to possible freeze scares in Brazil during the winter months in the Southern Hemisphere. The Brazilian coffee crop is harvested starting in May and extending for several weeks into what are the winter months in Brazil. A major freeze in Brazil occurs roughly every five years on average.

Coffee futures and options are traded on ICE Futures U.S., the Bolsa de Mercadorias & Futuros (BM&F), and the NYSE-LIFFE European Derivatives Market. Coffee futures are traded on the CME Group, the Singapore Exchange, and the Tokyo Grain Exchange (TGE).

Prices – ICE Arabica coffee futures prices (Barchart.com symbol KC) posted the high for 2015 in January at 184.90 cents per pound on concern that Brazil's coffee output may drop in 2015 for a third year, the first 3-year output decline since 1965. However, coffee prices turned lower after researcher Volcafe forecast that global 2015/16 coffee production would climb +7.5% y/y to 152.8 million bags and that the global 2015/16 coffee deficit would shrink to -1.4 million bags from 2014/15's 9-year-high-deficit of -5.1 million bags. Also, the sharp plunge in the Brazilian real to a record low against the dollar gave Brazilian coffee producers incentive to boost more-profitable exports as Brazil's 2015 coffee exports rose +1.2% y/y to a record 33.3 million bags. That boosted supplies worldwide as Green Coffee Association (GCA) data showed U.S. green coffee inventories rose to 6.123 million bags in August, a 12-year high. Robust coffee supplies weighed on prices throughout the year and in November coffee prices posted a 2-year low at 111.60 cents per pound. Further losses were contained after Conab projected 2015 Brazil coffee output at 42.15 million bags, down -7% y/y and a 6-year low, and after the ICO reported global Arabica coffee exports in the 12-months through October 2015 fell 1.3% y/y to 68.48 million bags. Coffee finished 2015 down 23.9% for the year at 126.70 cents per pound.

Supply – World coffee production in the 2014-15 marketing year (July-June) fell -1.8% yr/yr to 149.801 million bags (1 bag equals 60 kilograms or 132.3 pounds), below the 2012-13 record high of 154.816 million bags. Coffee ending stocks in the 2014-1 marketing year fell -9.0% to 36.495 million bags.

Brazil is the world's largest coffee producer by far with 51.200 million bags of production in 2014-15, which was 34.2% of total world production. Other key producers include Vietnam with 19.6% of the world's production Columbia with 8.3%, and Indonesia with 5.9%. Brazil's coffee production in 2014-15 fell -6.1% yr/yr to 51.200 million bags. Vietnam has become a major coffee producer in recent years, boosting its production to 29.350 million bags in 2014-15, up from less than a million bags in 1990.

Demand – U.S. coffee consumption in 2013 (latest data) rose +3.4% to 25.684 million bags, a new record high.

Trade – World coffee exports in 2014-15 rose +0.7% yr/yr to 119.919 million bags, a new record high. The world's largest exporters of coffee in 2014-15 were Brazil with 28.0% of world exports, Vietnam with 22.2%, and Columbia with 9.9%. U.S. coffee imports in 2014 rose +3.0% yr/yr from the previous year to 26.463 million bags, a new record high. The key countries from which the U.S. imported coffee in 2013 (latest data) were Brazil (which accounted for 23.7% of U.S. imports), Columbia (16.5%), Mexico (7.5%), and Guatemala (6.6%).

COFFEE

World Supply and Distribution of Coffee for Producing Countries   In Thousands of 60 Kilogram Bags

Year	Beginning Stocks	Production	Imports	Total Supply	Total Exports	Bean Exports	Rst/Grn Exports	Soluble Exports	Domestic Use	Ending Stocks
2006-07	32,601	133,622	99,396	265,619	106,388	95,544	1,818	9,026	123,525	35,706
2007-08	35,706	123,955	100,208	259,869	100,110	88,021	2,244	9,845	128,351	31,408
2008-09	31,408	136,196	100,107	267,711	102,931	91,241	2,260	9,430	125,184	39,596
2009-10	39,596	128,601	103,510	271,707	104,813	91,746	2,183	10,884	138,049	28,845
2010-11	28,845	140,417	109,084	278,346	115,319	99,881	2,141	13,297	134,387	28,640
2011-12	28,640	143,882	111,793	284,315	116,402	100,592	2,360	13,450	142,220	25,693
2012-13	25,693	154,933	116,024	296,520	119,074	102,387	2,641	14,046	142,216	35,230
2013-14[1]	35,230	155,671	116,324	307,225	123,553	106,442	3,060	14,051	142,753	40,919
2014-15[2]	40,919	149,535	116,897	307,351	119,296	101,108	3,474	14,714	145,521	42,534
2015-16[3]	42,534	150,122	117,418	310,074	125,115	106,505	3,598	15,012	148,267	36,692

[1] Preliminary.   [2] Estimate.   [3] Forecast.   132.276 Lbs. Per Bag   *Source: Foreign Agricultural Service, U.S. Department of Agriculture (FAS-USDA)*

World Production of Green Coffee   In Thousands of 60 Kilogram Bags

Crop Year	Brazil	Colombia	Costa Rica	Cote d'Ivoire	El Salvador	Ethiopia	Guatemala	India	Indonesia	Mexico	Uganda	Vietnam	World Total
2006-07	46,700	12,164	1,782	2,447	1,400	5,000	4,050	4,800	7,500	4,500	2,905	19,500	133,622
2007-08	39,100	12,515	1,867	2,098	1,650	5,000	4,110	4,365	8,000	4,350	3,490	18,000	123,955
2008-09	53,300	8,664	1,580	1,853	1,550	5,500	3,980	4,375	10,000	4,550	3,260	16,980	136,196
2009-10	44,800	8,100	1,475	2,350	1,300	6,000	4,010	4,825	10,500	4,150	2,870	18,500	128,601
2010-11	54,500	8,525	1,575	1,600	1,860	6,125	3,960	5,035	9,325	4,000	3,212	19,415	140,417
2011-12	49,200	7,655	1,775	1,600	1,200	6,320	4,410	5,230	8,300	4,300	3,075	26,000	143,882
2012-13	57,600	9,927	1,675	1,750	1,250	6,325	4,010	5,303	10,500	4,650	3,600	26,500	154,933
2013-14[1]	57,200	12,075	1,450	1,675	550	6,345	3,515	5,075	9,500	3,950	3,850	29,833	155,671
2014-15[2]	54,300	13,300	1,400	1,400	700	6,475	3,365	5,440	8,800	3,300	3,550	27,400	149,535
2015-16[3]	49,400	13,400	1,350	1,325	700	6,500	3,315	5,300	10,605	3,400	3,800	29,300	150,122

[1] Preliminary.   [2] Estimate.   [3] Forecast.   132.276 Lbs. Per Bag   *Source: Foreign Agricultural Service, U.S. Department of Agriculture (FAS-USDA)*

World Exportable[4] Production of Green Coffee   In Thousands of 60 Kilogram Bags

Crop Year	Brazil	Colombia	Cote d'Ivoire	Ethiopia	Guatemala	Honduras	India	Indonesia	Mexico	Peru	Uganda	Vietnam	World Total
2006-07	29,260	11,155	2,095	3,000	3,980	3,370	3,660	6,490	2,865	4,200	2,700	18,840	106,388
2007-08	27,290	11,525	1,890	2,800	3,915	3,440	3,660	6,360	2,610	2,660	3,210	15,735	100,110
2008-09	31,475	8,935	1,555	3,000	3,815	3,050	2,950	7,700	2,735	3,830	3,050	15,565	102,931
2009-10	29,780	7,435	2,045	3,250	3,890	3,200	4,265	8,750	2,480	3,150	2,670	18,670	104,813
2010-11	35,010	8,385	985	3,235	3,725	3,900	5,515	9,720	2,460	3,880	3,150	18,640	115,319
2011-12	29,843	7,360	1,620	3,140	3,840	5,290	5,223	7,450	3,365	5,140	3,000	24,495	116,402
2012-13	30,660	8,855	1,680	3,280	3,770	4,480	4,858	8,900	3,616	4,100	3,575	24,643	119,074
2013-14[1]	34,146	11,040	1,570	3,285	3,175	3,940	4,983	7,800	2,725	4,100	3,600	28,289	123,553
2014-15[2]	36,570	12,125	1,350	3,500	3,070	4,700	4,700	7,040	2,535	2,750	3,400	22,072	119,296
2015-16[3]	33,330	12,230	1,250	3,520	3,020	5,600	5,000	8,080	2,450	2,800	3,500	28,717	125,115

[1] Preliminary.   [2] Estimate.   [3] Forecast.   [4] Marketing year begins in October in some countries and April or July in others. Exportable production represents total harvested production minus estimated domestic consumption.   132.276 Lbs. Per Bag
Source: Foreign Agricultural Service, U.S. Department of Agriculture (FAS-USDA)

Coffee[2] Imports in the United States   In Thousands of 60 Kilogram Bags

Year	Brazil	Colombia	Costa Rica	Republic	Ecuador	El Salvador	Ethiopia	Guatemala	Indonesia	Mexico	Peru	Venezuela	World Total
2006	4,795	3,904	751	60	147	435	250	1,654	1,677	1,528	850	2	22,659
2007	4,968	4,064	823	35	123	565	234	1,815	1,122	1,495	919	25	23,216
2008	4,970	4,245	953	35	40	657	348	1,901	1,351	1,427	963	93	23,217
2009	5,642	3,425	750	56	65	463	202	1,739	1,318	1,642	854	7	22,465
2010	6,302	3,017	715	6	56	366	306	1,311	1,352	1,371	882	7	23,165
2011	6,971	3,552	707	26	73	657	283	1,576	990	1,639	1,051	0	24,912
2012	5,582	3,009	749	77	45	397	207	1,787	1,328	1,989	863	0	24,841
2013	6,090	4,241	762	34	54	427	268	1,696	1,344	1,923	869	4	25,683
2014	7,326	4,610	671	23	71	205	293	1,390	1,117	1,393	873		26,213
2015[1]	7,818	5,378	586	4	54	287	366	1,190	1,218	1,231	777		26,410

[1] Preliminary.   132.276 Lbs. Per Bag   *Source: Bureau of Census, U.S. Department of Commerce*

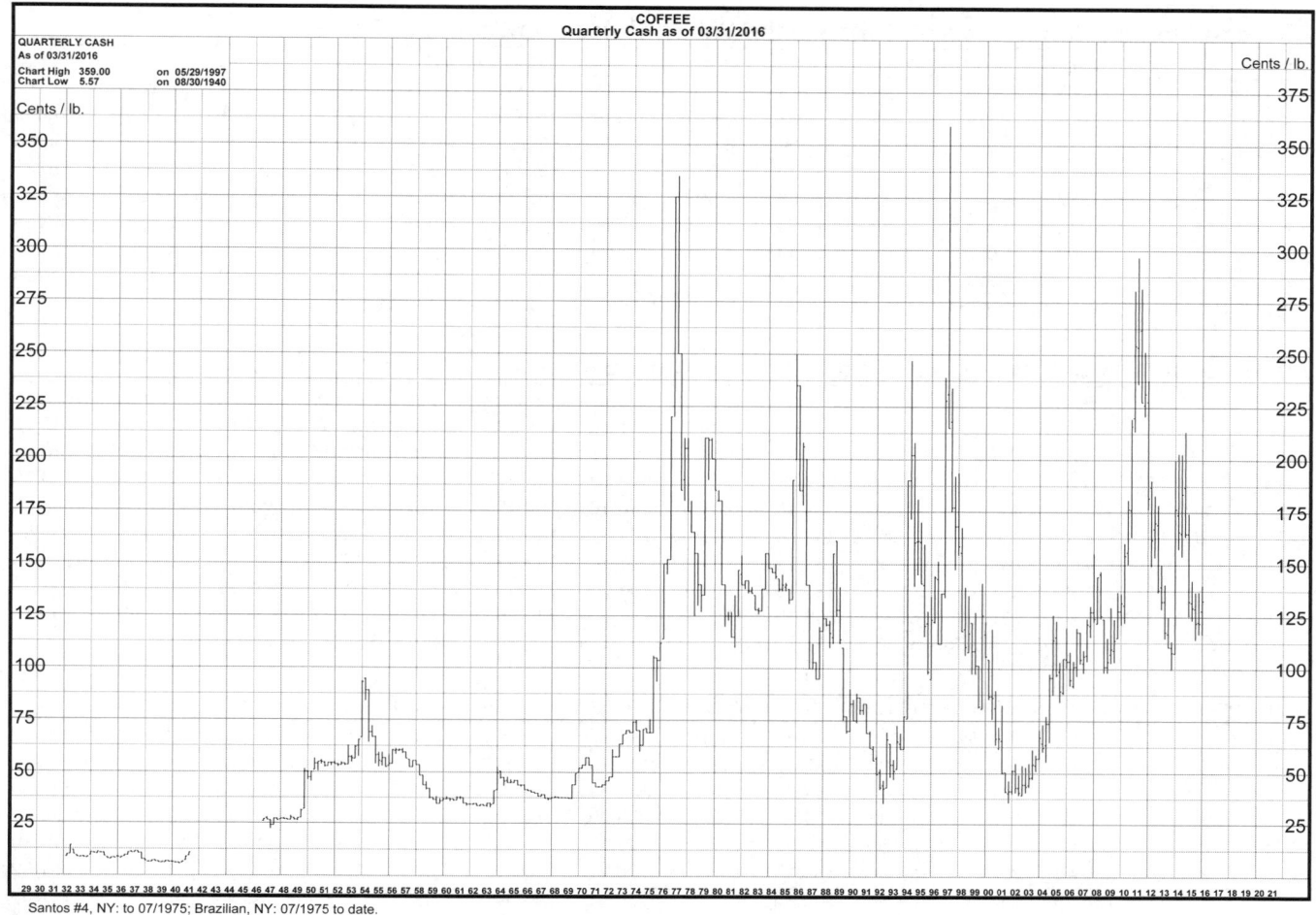

COFFEE
Quarterly Cash as of 03/31/2016

QUARTERLY CASH
As of 03/31/2016
Chart High   359.00   on 05/29/1997
Chart Low   5.57   on 08/30/1940

Cents / lb.

Santos #4, NY: to 07/1975; Brazilian, NY: 07/1975 to date.

Monthly Coffee Imports in the United States   In Thousands of 60 Kilogram Bags (132.276 Lbs. Per Bag)

Year	Jan.	Feb.	Mar.	Apr.	May	June	July	Aug.	Sept.	Oct.	Nov.	Dec.	Total
2006	1,853	1,647	2,043	1,672	2,007	1,916	1,780	2,091	2,089	1,894	1,834	1,833	22,659
2007	2,167	1,760	1,992	2,016	1,888	1,743	2,005	2,249	2,037	2,038	1,712	1,608	23,216
2008	1,985	1,867	2,119	2,073	2,034	1,913	1,980	1,856	1,973	1,863	1,542	2,012	23,217
2009	1,872	1,680	1,998	1,978	2,042	2,197	2,357	1,895	1,661	1,605	1,389	1,793	22,465
2010	1,705	1,696	1,989	1,989	2,036	1,988	1,870	2,095	1,863	1,826	2,054	2,053	23,165
2011	2,058	1,913	2,389	2,187	2,105	2,092	2,050	1,830	1,871	2,013	2,138	2,267	24,912
2012	2,376	1,891	2,186	1,945	2,172	2,081	2,269	2,246	2,055	1,803	1,893	1,923	24,841
2013	2,200	1,933	2,090	2,154	2,629	2,283	2,459	2,184	1,875	1,933	1,828	2,115	25,683
2014	1,919	1,895	2,407	2,489	2,545	2,468	2,356	2,357	2,174	2,019	1,640	1,943	26,213
2015[1]	1,780	1,708	2,430	2,255	2,489	2,407	2,338	2,265	2,269	2,120	2,154	2,194	26,410

[1] Preliminary.   *Source: Bureau of the Census, U.S. Department of Commerce*

Average Price of Brazilian[1] Coffee in New York   In Cents Per Pound

Year	Jan.	Feb.	Mar.	Apr.	May	June	July	Aug.	Sept.	Oct.	Nov.	Dec.	Average
2006	115.89	109.51	103.52	105.89	99.00	91.26	91.01	98.90	97.36	97.39	109.34	115.60	102.89
2007	111.99	109.78	102.34	100.84	99.66	105.89	105.25	112.47	116.43	120.95	118.99	124.06	110.72
2008	126.26	142.25	130.45	123.15	125.18	130.52	131.10	131.85	126.82	104.57	102.74	95.22	122.51
2009	101.43	100.45	97.48	101.46	113.13	109.81	104.55	114.01	114.12	122.84	126.21	131.23	111.39
2010	128.11	121.61	125.28	124.94	121.66	136.18	146.74	152.91	162.02	163.86	179.16	186.05	145.71
2011	209.26	237.43	257.24	271.39	266.02	247.19	242.66	251.78	251.70	230.62	233.13	225.59	243.67
2012	222.41	211.95	188.15	177.20	170.39	151.55	171.69	158.75	162.59	155.77	146.35	138.80	171.30
2013	139.36	133.37	129.74	130.11	129.82	116.91	114.89	111.97	106.33	103.58	98.82	100.48	117.95
2014	107.49	142.75	174.89	182.89	170.89	154.02	154.00	171.99	168.11	181.58	169.10	157.87	161.30
2015	151.21	143.32	127.81	136.70	130.38	130.51	123.64	127.24	117.83	127.47	115.03	114.63	128.81

[1] And other Arabicas.   *Source: Foreign Agricultural Service, U.S. Department of Agriculture (FAS-USDA)*

COFFEE

Average Monthly Retail[1] Price of Coffee in the United States   In Cents Per Pound

Year	Jan.	Feb.	Mar.	Apr.	May	June	July	Aug.	Sept.	Oct.	Nov.	Dec.	Average
2008	NA	NA	NA	NA	NA	NA	NA	NA	NA	NA	NA	NA	NA
2009	NA	NA	NA	NA	NA	NA	NA	NA	NA	NA	NA	3.669	3.669
2010	3.811	3.736	3.565	3.641	3.664	3.697	3.857	3.935	4.174	4.175	4.467	4.146	3.906
2011	4.417	4.218	4.642	5.101	5.129	5.234	5.547	5.766	5.651	5.511	5.636	5.437	5.191
2012	5.497	5.382	5.558	5.513	5.596	5.582	5.723	5.693	5.693	5.888	6.066	5.921	5.676
2013	5.902	5.742	6.014	5.674	5.678	5.588	5.394	5.214	5.091	5.149	5.040	4.948	5.453
2014	5.025	5.002	5.005	5.204	5.153	4.670	5.099	5.167	5.215	5.032	4.713	4.590	4.990
2015	4.738	4.910	4.827	4.990	4.715	4.686	4.790	4.808	4.669	4.609	4.412	4.486	4.720

[1] Roasted in 13.1 to 20 ounce cans.   *Source: Foreign Agricultural Service, U.S. Department of Agriculture (FAS-USDA)*

Average Price of Colombian Mild Arabicas[1] in the United States   In Cents Per Pound

Year	Jan.	Feb.	Mar.	Apr.	May	June	July	Aug.	Sept.	Oct.	Nov.	Dec.	Average
2008	143.37	161.30	151.48	142.41	143.51	150.60	151.56	154.23	150.20	133.37	133.40	134.72	145.85
2009	148.88	149.58	162.00	190.94	225.58	195.27	192.11	181.61	169.90	175.16	180.08	199.38	180.87
2010	214.55	208.36	206.37	195.18	197.76	229.06	230.88	241.77	239.26	225.83	239.59	256.52	223.76
2011	280.05	289.49	300.93	314.26	301.48	290.19	286.46	288.43	283.51	256.86	259.74	254.41	283.82
2012	258.70	248.09	224.69	215.85	207.66	184.45	203.31	189.27	191.54	182.73	172.55	167.67	203.88
2013	170.64	164.74	163.46	164.52	161.14	148.56	147.70	142.47	135.93	130.14	123.92	125.82	148.25
2014	133.51	173.96	213.63	223.79	213.45	196.14	194.91	210.42	202.77	219.27	203.71	191.53	198.09
2015	182.32	171.68	151.94	157.06	150.19	152.02	144.52	146.96	135.55	143.10	138.63	139.89	151.16

[1] ICO monthly and composite indicator prices on the New York Market, 1979 ICA Agreement basis.   *Source: Foreign Agricultural Service, U.S. Department of Agriculture (FAS-USDA)*

Average Price of Other Mild Arabicas[1] in the United States   In Cents Per Pound

Year	Jan.	Feb.	Mar.	Apr.	May	June	July	Aug.	Sept.	Oct.	Nov.	Dec.	Average
2008	139.10	158.03	148.07	138.06	139.32	144.90	145.13	146.03	141.50	122.04	120.76	116.87	138.32
2009	128.03	128.63	127.76	134.44	147.34	145.17	137.87	146.87	145.67	151.95	150.23	155.86	141.65
2010	154.40	155.92	162.13	171.32	174.21	193.52	205.25	212.80	222.10	215.84	227.96	237.33	194.40
2011	262.94	288.08	294.48	303.59	293.06	277.78	269.18	273.54	274.38	248.49	249.50	243.40	273.20
2012	239.43	225.49	201.85	193.35	186.35	169.79	190.77	175.97	179.60	172.37	160.64	154.65	187.52
2013	158.27	153.00	152.96	152.96	151.43	138.86	138.44	135.63	132.78	128.83	122.75	127.05	141.08
2014	135.03	176.28	216.06	226.99	215.24	198.91	198.59	214.50	212.01	227.06	212.93	200.59	202.85
2015	190.90	179.94	160.02	164.00	158.48	159.76	154.45	156.92	146.15	153.25	147.98	148.66	160.04

[1] ICO monthly and composite indicator prices on the New York Market, 1979 ICA Agreement basis.   *Source: Foreign Agricultural Service, U.S. Department of Agriculture (FAS-USDA)*

Average Price of Robustas 1976[1] in the United States   In Cents Per Pound

Year	Jan.	Feb.	Mar.	Apr.	May	June	July	Aug.	Sept.	Oct.	Nov.	Dec.	Average
2008	100.68	117.10	122.44	112.06	109.58	112.16	115.09	113.48	106.67	89.69	92.81	83.99	106.31
2009	85.77	81.66	77.48	76.50	77.00	75.88	74.83	75.04	77.31	76.68	73.08	74.68	77.16
2010	75.09	73.49	72.53	76.26	76.21	82.51	89.95	89.06	87.11	90.57	97.94	98.32	84.09
2011	106.03	114.62	122.46	121.55	126.30	122.15	116.58	119.00	113.47	107.34	108.18	114.23	115.99
2012	109.40	111.25	113.60	111.71	116.01	113.34	113.37	113.01	110.87	109.89	102.94	102.26	110.64
2013	105.79	109.70	112.47	107.58	105.76	97.05	102.41	100.73	93.48	90.01	85.67	95.30	100.50
2014	92.93	101.14	111.90	110.68	108.35	104.63	107.23	105.07	105.57	109.39	106.81	103.51	105.60
2015	102.33	103.74	98.07	92.06	87.56	90.25	87.12	85.78	81.50	82.78	81.74	79.28	89.35

[1] ICO monthly and composite indicator prices on the New York Market, 1979 ICA Agreement basis.   *Source: Foreign Agricultural Service, U.S. Department of Agriculture (FAS-USDA)*

Average Price of Composite 1979[1] in the United States   In Cents Per Pound

Year	Jan.	Feb.	Mar.	Apr.	May	June	July	Aug.	Sept.	Oct.	Nov.	Dec.	Average
2008	122.33	138.82	136.17	126.55	126.76	130.51	132.78	131.14	126.69	108.31	107.88	103.07	124.25
2009	108.39	107.60	105.87	111.61	123.05	119.05	112.90	117.45	116.40	121.09	119.67	124.96	115.67
2010	126.85	123.37	125.30	126.89	128.10	142.20	153.41	157.46	163.61	161.56	173.90	184.26	147.24
2011	197.35	216.03	224.33	231.24	227.97	215.58	210.36	212.19	213.04	193.90	193.66	189.02	210.39
2012	188.90	182.29	167.77	160.46	157.68	145.31	159.07	148.50	151.28	147.12	136.35	131.31	156.34
2013	135.38	131.51	131.38	129.55	126.96	117.58	118.93	116.45	111.82	107.03	100.99	106.56	119.51
2014	110.75	137.81	165.03	170.58	163.94	151.92	152.50	163.08	161.79	172.88	162.17	150.66	155.26
2015	148.24	141.10	127.04	129.02	123.49	124.97	119.77	121.21	113.14	118.43	122.95	123.73	126.09

[1] ICO monthly and composite indicator prices on the New York Market, 1979 ICA Agreement basis.   *Source: Foreign Agricultural Service, U.S. Department of Agriculture (FAS-USDA)*

Nearby Futures through Last Trading Day.

Volume of Trading of Coffee "C" Futures in New York   In Contracts

Year	Jan.	Feb.	Mar.	Apr.	May	June	July	Aug.	Sept.	Oct.	Nov.	Dec.	Total
2006	357,994	416,964	326,256	429,249	322,932	476,542	289,027	481,870	238,953	313,459	492,904	261,362	4,407,512
2007	334,593	468,712	383,506	474,542	373,291	600,122	361,467	596,622	373,925	484,038	468,987	208,818	5,128,623
2008	419,096	729,397	515,528	556,002	354,887	642,074	317,917	512,002	381,241	384,451	383,346	250,575	5,446,516
2009	309,386	406,786	328,940	404,635	305,326	435,239	244,504	388,567	244,371	332,043	535,063	300,489	4,235,349
2010	336,188	544,197	388,468	586,602	372,641	791,873	384,464	601,583	336,930	370,233	519,808	255,209	5,488,196
2011	390,345	471,890	408,416	516,121	388,052	555,238	332,701	577,095	391,134	420,084	483,740	239,722	5,174,538
2012	401,399	578,415	541,098	628,814	494,615	642,772	466,738	581,141	406,023	503,577	603,866	277,026	6,125,484
2013	555,032	758,665	468,082	904,549	609,068	742,238	590,940	703,755	347,915	423,480	700,471	319,834	7,124,029
2014	567,574	1,140,881	596,963	736,494	458,676	596,745	404,407	619,641	394,952	583,259	610,793	341,845	7,052,230
2015	586,593	795,022	615,139	786,626	596,214	847,139	540,970	964,634	490,262	633,066	864,055	388,415	8,108,135

Contract size = 37,500 lbs.   *Source: ICE Futures U.S. (ICE)*

Average Open Interest of Coffee "C" Futures in New York   In Contracts

Year	Jan.	Feb.	Mar.	Apr.	May	June	July	Aug.	Sept.	Oct.	Nov.	Dec.
2006	102,195	102,614	99,982	102,882	104,230	120,907	120,007	107,928	105,175	111,392	117,469	123,259
2007	128,158	132,849	141,033	146,723	159,011	157,086	168,019	163,288	162,445	173,426	158,146	160,331
2008	176,128	193,555	179,957	160,544	150,017	146,166	147,056	133,178	126,573	132,112	116,643	118,223
2009	129,577	130,101	135,143	134,290	134,827	127,263	107,711	100,880	97,935	114,065	118,016	123,699
2010	129,749	126,850	124,238	133,961	136,711	151,959	169,669	156,086	143,454	139,801	138,738	134,477
2011	139,619	133,869	123,270	120,639	113,874	109,539	108,411	108,089	114,318	119,559	107,527	102,687
2012	113,404	131,880	149,533	151,527	148,352	147,775	137,737	137,322	141,421	147,434	141,940	141,395
2013	151,087	161,116	170,696	168,341	164,440	167,032	153,493	151,666	154,791	160,797	159,934	146,729
2014	146,800	162,005	169,201	160,266	162,103	163,163	161,218	156,931	154,752	168,847	156,410	155,382
2015	166,609	172,443	195,176	190,207	190,814	183,516	186,782	178,827	187,577	188,355	188,664	169,129

Contract size = 37,500 lbs.   *Source: ICE Futures U.S. (ICE)*

Coke

Coke is the hard and porous residue left after certain types of bituminous coals are heated to high temperatures (up to 2,000 degrees Fahrenheit) for about 17 hours. It is blackish-gray and has a metallic luster. The residue is mostly carbon. Coke is used as a reducing agent in the smelting of pig iron and the production of steel. Petroleum coke is made from the heavy tar-like residue of the petroleum refining process. It is used primarily to generate electricity.

Supply – Production of petroleum coke in the U.S. in 2015 (annualized through April) fell -1.2% yr/yr to 316.727 million barrels, a three-decade high but well below the U.S. production record of 369.305 million barrels posted back in 1957. U.S. stocks of coke at coke plants (Dec 31) in 2013 (latest data available) rose +43.9% yr/yr to 872,000 short tons.

Trade – U.S. coke exports in 2014 (latest data available) rose +12.6% yr/yr to 945.885 tons, and over a third of those exports went to Canada. U.S. coke imports in 2014 fell -45.1% yr/yr to 75.567 thousand short tons. About 82% of the imports were from Canada, 14% from Columbia, and 3% from Japan.

Salient Statistics of Coke in the United States   In Thousands of Short Tons

| | Coke and Breeze Production at Coke Plants | | | | | | | Producer and Distributor | | Exports | | Imports | |
| | By Census Division | | | | | | | | | | | | |
Year	Middle Atlantic	East North Central	East South Central	Other	Total	Coke Total	Breeze Total	Con-sumption[2]	Stocks Dec. 31	Canada	Total	Japan	Total
2008	W	7,578	W	9,153	16,731	15,646	1,085	17,006	916	758	1,959	604	3,603
2009	W	5,972	W	5,796	11,768	11,143	625	10,323	776	419	1,307	46	347
2010	W	8,385	W	7,803	16,188	15,022	1,166	14,847	702	400	1,463	245	1,214
2011	W	8,907	W	7,624	16,531	15,420	1,110	15,825	745	407	970	141	1,418
2012	W	9,355	W	6,784	16,139	15,172	967	15,472	606	404	974	50	1,135
2013[1]	W	8,864	W	7,362	16,226	15,320	906	14,351	872	278	840	1	138

[1] Preliminary.   [2] Equal to production plus imports minus the change in producer and distributor stocks minus exports.
W = Withheld.   *Source: Energy Information Administration, U.S. Department of Energy (EIA-DOE)*

Production of Petroleum Coke in the United States   In Thousands of Barrels

Year	Jan.	Feb.	Mar.	Apr.	May	June	July	Aug.	Sept.	Oct.	Nov.	Dec.	Total
2009	25,902	21,991	25,071	24,741	24,402	25,339	25,205	24,862	24,364	23,823	22,490	23,857	292,047
2010	23,127	20,913	24,490	23,911	25,878	25,618	26,761	26,089	23,986	24,674	24,394	26,437	296,278
2011	25,976	20,975	24,952	23,904	25,635	25,745	27,115	27,363	25,962	26,460	26,271	26,882	307,240
2012	25,427	23,451	24,656	24,774	26,408	25,602	26,785	26,670	25,385	26,477	26,303	28,543	310,481
2013	26,197	22,792	25,535	25,051	26,308	27,314	28,718	28,243	26,440	26,890	26,215	28,168	317,871
2014	26,979	23,225	26,073	26,851	26,716	26,020	29,087	28,017	26,498	26,383	26,383	28,485	320,717
2015[1]	27,131	23,655	26,744	25,434	26,722	26,531	28,090	27,341	25,749	25,858	27,078		316,727

[1] Preliminary.   *Source: Energy Information Administration, U.S. Department of Energy (EIA-DOE)*

Coal Receipts and Average Prices at Coke Plants in the United States

| | Coal Receipts at Coke Plants | | | | | Average Price of Coal Receipts at Coke Plants | | | | |
| | By Census Division, in Thousands of Short Tons | | | | | By Census Division, In Dollars per Short Ton | | | | |
Year	Middle Atlantic	East North Central	East South Central	Other	Total	Middle Atlantic	East North Central	East South Central	Other	Total
2009	W	7,772	W	7,333	15,105	W	150.93	W	W	143.01
2010	W	11,081	W	10,000	21,081	W	164.08	W	W	153.59
2011	W	12,251	W	9,822	22,073	W	195.13	W	W	184.44
2012	W	12,157	W	8,705	20,862	W	198.78	W	W	190.55
2013	W	11,815	W	9,295	21,110	W	157.52	W	W	156.99
2014[1]	NA	NA	NA	NA	NA	NA	NA	NA	NA	NA

[1] Preliminary.   W = Withheld.   *Source: Energy Information Administration, U.S. Department of Energy (EIA-DOE)*

Coal Carbonized and Coke and Breeze Stocks at Coke Plants in the United States   In Thousands of Short Tons

| | Coal Carbonized at Coke Plants | | | | | Stocks at Coke Plants, Dec. 31 | | | | | | |
| | By Census Division | | | | | By Census Division | | | | | | |
Year	Middle Atlantic	East North Central	East South Central	Other	Total	Middle Atlantic	East North Central	East South Central	Other	Total	Coke Total	Breeze Total
2009	W	7,849	W	7,477	15,326	W	538	W	320	858	776	82
2010	W	10,952	2,068	8,072	21,092	W	545	W	240	785	702	83
2011	W	11,673	W	9,761	21,434	W	571	W	236	807	745	62
2012	W	12,125	W	8,626	20,751	W	513	W	194	707	606	101
2013	W	11,948	W	9,526	21,474	W	739	W	344	1,083	872	211
2014[1]	NA	NA	NA	NA	NA	NA	NA	NA	NA	NA	NA	NA

[1] Preliminary.   W = Withheld.   *Source: Energy Information Administration, U.S. Department of Energy (EIA-DOE)*

Copper

The word *copper* comes from name of the Mediterranean island Cyprus that was a primary source of the metal. Dating back more than 10,000 years, copper is the oldest metal used by humans. From the Pyramid of Cheops in Egypt, archeologists recovered a portion of a water plumbing system whose copper tubing was found in serviceable condition after more than 5,000 years.

Copper is one of the most widely used industrial metals because it is an excellent conductor of electricity, has strong corrosion-resistance properties, and is very ductile. It is also used to produce the alloys of brass (a copper-zinc alloy) and bronze (a copper-tin alloy), both of which are far harder and stronger than pure copper. Electrical uses of copper account for about 75% of total copper usage, and building construction is the single largest market (the average U.S. home contains 400 pounds of copper). Copper is biostatic, meaning that bacteria will not grow on its surface, and it is therefore used in air-conditioning systems, food processing surfaces, and doorknobs to prevent the spread of disease.

Copper futures and options are traded at the CME Group, and the London Metal Exchange (LME). Copper futures are traded on the Moscow Exchange, the Shanghai Futures Exchange (SHFE), the Singapore Exchange (SGX), and the Singapore Mercantile Exchange (SMX). The CME copper futures contract calls for the delivery of 25,000 pounds of Grade 1 electrolyte copper and is priced in terms of cents per pound.

Prices – CME copper futures prices (Barchart.com symbol HG) began 2015 on a weak note and posted a 5-1/2 year low in January at $2.42 per pound after the dollar index soared to an 11-year high and after the IMF cut its 2015 global GDP forecast to 3.5% from 3.8%. Prices rebounded in Q2-2015 and posted the high for the year in May at $2.9610 per pound on optimism Chinese copper demand would strengthen after China cut interest rates for the third time in six months. However, prices fell back and sold-off to a 6-1/2 year low in November at $2.0015 per pound. Weak Chinese demand was a major bearish factor for copper prices after China 2015 unwrought copper imports fell -0.3% y/y to 4.81 MMT. Copper prices finished 2015 down -25% at $2.1255 per pound.

Supply – World production of copper in 2014 rose by +2.2% yr/yr to 18.700 million metric tons, which was a new record high. The largest producer of copper was Chile with 31.0% of the world's production, followed by China with 8.7%, Peru with 7.5%, the U.S. with 7.3%, and Australia with 5.4%. U.S. production of refined copper in 2014 rose +7.8% yr/yr to 1.070 million short tons, which was far below the record U.S. production level of 2.490 million short tons seen in 1998.

Demand – U.S. consumption of copper in 2012 (latest data) rose +1.1% to 1.780 million metric tons. The primary users of copper in the U.S. by class of consumer are wire rod mills with about 72% of usage, brass mills with 24% of usage, and nominal use of 2% or less by each of foundries, ingot makers, and chemical plants.

Trade – U.S. exports of refined copper in 2014 fell -7.8% to 104,544 metric tons, below the 17-year high of 159,950 metric tons seen in 2012. U.S. imports of copper in 2014 fell -15.7% yr/yr to 618,720 metric tons, below the record high of 1.1 million metric tons in 2006.

World Mine Production of Copper (Content of Ore)　In Thousands of Metric Tons

Year	Australia	Canada[3]	Chile	China	Indonesia	Mexico	Peru	Poland	Russia	South Africa	United States[3]	Zambia	World Total[2]
2006	858.8	603.3	5,360.8	889	818.0	327.5	1,048.5	497.0	725	89.5	1,197	474.0	15,080
2007	870.0	596.2	5,557.0	946	796.9	335.5	1,190.3	452.0	740	97.0	1,169	509.0	15,510
2008	886.0	607.0	5,327.6	1090	632.6	246.5	1,267.9	429.0	750	108.7	1,309	533.5	15,570
2009	854.0	485.6	5,394.4	1065	998.5	241.0	1,276.2	439.0	666	107.6	1,181	698.0	15,980
2010	870.4	523.0	5,418.9	1195	878.4	270.1	1,247.1	425.4	703	102.6	1,109	686.0	16,150
2011	957.9	569.8	5,262.8	1305	534.9	444.0	1,235.3	426.7	713	96.6	1,113	668.0	16,160
2012	958.0	579.5	5,433.9	1580	394.0	500.0	1,298.7	427.1	720	81.0	1,167	690.0	16,890
2013	990.0	631.9	5,776.0	1600	504.0	480.0	1,375.6	429.3	802	74.0	1,249	760.0	18,260
2014[1]	970.0	696.0	5,750.0	1760	400.0	515.0	1,380.0	425.0	742		1,360	708.0	18,500
2015[2]	960.0	695.0	5,700.0	1750		550.0	1,600.0		740		1,250	600.0	18,700

[1] Preliminary.　[2] Estimate.　[3] Recoverable.　*Source: U.S. Geological Survey (USGS)*

Commodity Exchange Inc. Warehouse Stocks of Copper, on First of Month　In Thousands of Short Tons

Year	Jan.	Feb.	Mar.	Apr.	May	June	July	Aug.	Sept.	Oct.	Nov.	Dec.
2006	6.8	11.7	30.4	20.7	16.7	9.5	7.9	6.8	12.4	22.3	23.2	31.3
2007	34.0	36.2	37.0	36.4	33.7	27.2	22.1	21.8	20.7	20.1	19.0	18.0
2008	14.1	14.0	13.1	11.9	10.8	11.1	11.0	5.4	5.4	9.9	9.9	24.5
2009	NA	40.2	45.3	46.5	54.1	56.8	59.8	54.1	53.5	55.0	55.0	70.7
2010	94.5	94.5	94.5	102.0	101.2	101.9	101.9	100.4	95.3	84.9	74.3	70.8
2011	65.0	73.2	82.9	84.7	82.5	80.7	80.7	82.8	85.8	88.5	89.9	87.7
2012	90.1	89.7	91.2	86.5	75.1	59.1	53.3	48.1	49.8	50.3	56.6	63.6
2013	70.7	74.1	75.0	76.2	85.6	79.8	71.7	64.6	36.5	31.1	26.3	19.1
2014	13.0	19.2	13.6	20.0	18.3	16.4	19.7	23.9	28.0	34.2	29.8	28.1
2015	26.2	21.3	18.0	26.9	23.3	22.5	30.1	37.3	36.9	40.2	53.5	72.7

Source: CME Group; New York Mercantile Exchange (NYMEX)

COPPER

Salient Statistics of Copper in the United States   In Thousands of Metric Tons

Year	New Copper Produced - From Domestic Ores - Mines	Smelters	Refineries	From Foreign Ores	Total New	Secondary Re-covery	Imports[5] Unmanu-factured	Refined	Exports Ore, Concentrate[6]	Refined[7]	COMEX	Primary Producers (Refined)	Blister & Material in Solution	Apparent Consumption Refined Copper (Reported)	Primary & Old Copper[8]
2006	1,200	501	531	144	1,210	151	1,320	1,070	108	106	31	194	19	2,110	2,200
2007	1,170	617	702	62	1,270	158	1,100	829	134	51	14	130	26	2,140	2,270
2008	1,310	574	603	109	1,220	156	934	724	301	37	31	199	24	2,020	1,990
2009	1,180	597	588	48	1,110	138	788	664	151	81	90	434	16	1,650	1,580
2010	1,110	601	606	21	1,060	143	760	605	137	78	59	384	21	1,760	1,760
2011	1,110	538	545	----	992	153	----	670	252	40	80	409	13	1,760	1,730
2012	1,170	485	491	----	962	164	----	630	301	169	64	236	12	1,760	1,760
2013	1,250	516	518	----	993	166	----	734	348	111	15	258	13	1,830	1,760
2014[1]	1,360			----	1,050	171	----	620	410	127				1,750	1,780
2015[2]	1,250			----	1,000	160	----	770	380	120				1,800	1,780

[1] Preliminary.   [2] Estimate.   [3] Also from matte, etc., refinery reports.   [4] From old scrap only.   [5] For consumption.   [6] Blister (copper content).   [7] Ingots, bars, etc.   [8] Old scrap only.   W = Withheld.   *Source: U.S. Geological Survey (USGS)*

Consumption of Refined Copper[3] in the United States   In Thousands of Metric Tons

Year	By-Products Cathodes	Wire Bars	Ingots and Ingot Bars	Cakes & Slabs	Billets	Other[4]	By Class of Consumer Wire Rod Mills	Brass Mills	Chemical Plants	Ingot Makers	Foundries	Miscel-laneous[5]	Total Con-sumption
2004	2,160.0	W	21.4	57.0	W	173.0	1,780.0	573.0	1.2	4.6	21.0	35.2	2,410.0
2005	2,040.0	W	28.8	35.3	W	167.0	1,680.0	528.0	1.2	4.5	20.2	39.3	2,270.0
2006	1,910.0	W	30.8	37.1	W	135.0	1,570.0	490.0	1.0	4.5	21.4	24.1	2,110.0
2007	1,930.0	W	28.8	42.7	W	135.0	1,610.0	476.0	1.0	4.5	19.4	25.7	2,140.0
2008	1,820.0	W	28.6	45.0	W	130.0	1,490.0	479.0	0.3	4.5	20.4	24.7	2,020.0
2009	1,450.0	W	27.4	43.6	W	125.0	1,140.0	454.0	0.4	4.5	19.1	30.1	1,650.0
2010	1,570.0	W	22.5	44.1	W	127.0	1,250.0	459.0	0.4	4.5	18.2	34.6	1,760.0
2011	1,580.0	W	2.5	43.8	W	136.0	1,270.0	430.0	1.5	5.0	17.7	37.5	1,760.0
2012[1]	1,610.0	W	2.3	42.8	W	102.0	1,280.0	424.0	0.3	4.5	19.9	34.3	1,760.0
2013[2]	1,680.0	W	2.1	43.5	W	103.0	1,310.0	457.0	0.2	4.5	18.5	36.3	1,830.0

[1] Preliminary.   [2] Estimate.   [3] Primary & secondary.   [4] Includes Wirebars and Billets.   [5] Includes iron and steel plants, primary smelters producing alloys other than copper, consumers of copper powder and copper shot, and other manufacturers.   W = Withheld.
Source: U.S. Geological Survey (USGS)

Salient Statistics of Recycling Copper in the United States

Year	New Scrap[1]	Old Scrap[2]	Recycled Metal[3]	Apparent Supply	Percent Recycled	New Scrap[1]	Old Scrap[2]	Recycled Metal[3]	Apparent Supply
	In Thousands of Metric Tons					Value in Millions of Dollars			
2004	774	191	965	3,330	29.0	2,290	565	2,850	9,830
2005	769	183	953	3,190	30.0	2,940	701	3,640	12,200
2006	819	150	968	3,010	32.1	5,680	1,040	6,720	20,900
2007	772	162	933	3,050	30.6	5,580	1,170	6,750	22,000
2008	700	159	859	2,700	31.8	4,930	1,120	6,050	18,900
2009	639	138	777	2,220	35.0	3,400	734	4,130	11,800
2010	642	143	785	2,400	32.7	4,930	1,100	6,030	18,400
2011	649	153	802	2,380	33.7	5,810	1,370	7,180	21,300
2012	642	164	806	2,410	33.0	5,200	1,330	6,530	19,500
2013	630	166	796	2,410	33.0	4,720	1,250	5,970	18,100

[1] Scrap that results from the manufacturing process.   [2] Scrap that results from consumer products.   [3] Metal recovered from new plus old scrap.
Source: U.S. Geological Survey (USGS)

Copper Refined from Scrap in the United States   In Thousands of Metric Tons

Year	Jan.	Feb.	Mar.	Apr.	May	June	July	Aug.	Sept.	Oct.	Nov.	Dec.	Total
2006	3.8	3.7	3.8	3.7	3.7	3.7	3.7	3.7	3.8	3.7	3.7	3.8	44.8
2007	3.9	3.9	3.4	3.5	3.4	3.4	3.4	3.4	3.5	3.4	3.6	3.5	46.0
2008	4.1	4.2	4.1	4.3	4.6	5.0	4.3	4.5	4.3	4.6	4.6	4.6	53.8
2009	5.4	4.8	4.4	4.4	4.0	4.2	4.1	2.9	3.0	3.0	3.0	3.2	46.4
2010	2.9	3.2	2.8	3.3	3.0	3.3	3.2	3.5	3.3	3.2	3.2	2.9	37.7
2011	3.8	3.0	3.2	3.0	3.2	3.1	3.0	3.2	3.0	3.1	3.0	2.6	37.3
2012	3.1	3.4	3.0	3.0	2.9	3.0	2.8	2.8	3.1	4.5	4.0	3.9	39.5
2013	3.9	3.7	4.6	4.8	4.9	4.9	4.7	3.8	3.8	4.0	4.0	4.5	46.9
2014	3.9	3.9	3.8	4.0	3.8	3.9	3.9	3.4	4.2	3.9	3.8	3.6	46.0
2015[1]	4.0	3.8	4.2	4.2	4.4	3.3	3.6	3.9	4.2	5.0	4.3		48.8

[1] Preliminary.   *Source: U.S. Geological Survey (USGS)*

Imports of Refined Copper into the United States   In Thousands of Metric Tons

Year	Jan.	Feb.	Mar.	Apr.	May	June	July	Aug.	Sept.	Oct.	Nov.	Dec.	Total
2006	138.0	108.0	80.1	69.1	100.0	94.1	91.4	101.0	106.0	96.4	58.3	56.5	1,070.0
2007	87.3	76.4	68.4	65.8	80.1	58.9	66.6	77.7	68.5	66.9	54.5	NA	829.0
2008	58.6	57.8	53.6	59.8	63.6	48.9	77.5	86.9	54.5	49.7	51.0	61.7	724.0
2009	76.4	67.7	80.0	53.9	52.6	35.7	54.2	36.4	56.0	39.9	55.2	55.5	664.0
2010	60.3	61.3	46.2	46.7	46.7	61.6	66.0	37.7	35.3	45.6	34.4	63.3	605.0
2011	57.4	50.5	66.2	73.1	65.5	45.5	69.5	32.3	64.3	46.7	50.3	48.9	670.0
2012	37.8	51.1	47.1	51.6	52.4	57.2	53.4	49.5	46.2	52.7	64.7	86.8	630.0
2013	86.8	64.6	88.2	55.6	83.6	69.2	70.0	50.2	42.8	40.3	33.9	48.5	734.0
2014	42.9	36.2	45.1	56.2	54.1	53.0	62.9	46.7	59.9	58.6	46.0	58.5	620.0
2015[1]	70.9	50.3	68.7	60.5	56.1	64.5	78.5	47.4	47.8	51.7	44.2		698.8

[1] Preliminary.   *Source: U.S. Geological Survey (USGS)*

Exports of Refined Copper from the United States   In Thousands of Metric Tons

Year	Jan.	Feb.	Mar.	Apr.	May	June	July	Aug.	Sept.	Oct.	Nov.	Dec.	Total
2006	5.6	7.3	6.8	9.6	6.3	13.1	6.0	9.6	9.3	13.7	6.2	12.6	106.0
2007	3.1	2.7	5.1	3.6	3.9	6.6	3.6	3.4	5.4	7.1	3.0	NA	51.1
2008	6.0	5.7	6.3	3.2	1.9	1.4	2.0	2.0	1.5	3.2	1.7	1.6	36.5
2009	.9	1.7	3.8	6.5	21.4	19.2	8.9	6.3	4.0	2.1	3.0	3.2	80.8
2010	6.2	13.9	13.6	10.4	4.7	4.5	4.2	5.3	7.0	1.5	1.2	5.7	78.3
2011	1.6	5.0	3.1	2.1	3.5	1.9	1.9	5.1	2.1	2.4	6.9	4.7	40.4
2012	9.6	18.3	26.0	37.9	33.0	10.2	4.9	5.7	4.3	3.2	3.3	3.5	159.0
2013	3.5	5.3	5.1	5.4	5.7	4.9	8.3	17.1	14.9	10.3	15.2	17.7	113.0
2014	9.4	9.0	8.6	5.5	7.7	6.3	10.2	8.4	11.0	11.1	17.3	22.9	127.0
2015[1]	5.9	8.5	10.1	6.6	7.2	9.4	5.9	6.4	4.5	6.1	8.7		86.5

[1] Preliminary.   *Source: U.S. Geological Survey (USGS)*

Production of Refined Copper in the United States   In Thousands of Short Tons

Year	Jan.	Feb.	Mar.	Apr.	May	June	July	Aug.	Sept.	Oct.	Nov.	Dec.	Total
2006	99.9	101.0	117.0	109.0	113.0	114.0	100.0	101.0	102.0	89.8	94.4	108.0	1,249
2007	101.0	97.1	116.0	113.0	116.0	112.0	116.0	117.0	108.0	120.0	91.5	103.0	1,311
2008	109.0	107.0	108.0	102.0	107.0	102.0	98.7	107.0	108.0	110.0	107.0	113.0	1,279
2009	105.0	96.7	95.9	93.7	91.8	90.3	94.4	97.6	94.3	101.0	98.0	101.0	1,160
2010	96.2	91.3	95.2	89.5	85.4	89.3	95.6	94.4	94.2	90.1	84.1	89.2	1,090
2011	86.8	76.3	84.9	79.7	82.9	86.4	79.2	79.7	93.6	89.6	95.1	96.5	1,030
2012	88.5	82.4	78.4	74.4	78.2	68.3	82.6	87.9	82.4	94.1	92.9	91.3	1,000
2013	89.3	76.2	85.7	88.5	83.0	80.3	83.8	85.3	81.1	94.8	92.8	99.2	1,040
2014	96.6	87.3	88.4	95.5	99.6	98.4	103.0	101.0	91.6	80.9	70.0	82.3	1,090
2015[1]	83.7	85.5	93.9	90.7	86.7	91.0	94.4	93.0	97.6	104.0	107.0		1,121

Recoverable Copper Content.   [1] Preliminary.   *Source: U.S. Geological Survey (USGS)*

Mine Production of Recoverable Copper in the United States   In Thousands of Metric Tons

Year	Recoverable Copper			Contained Copper		
	Arizona	Others[2]	Total	Electrowon	Concentrates[3]	Total
2006	712.2	485.1	1,197.5	530.3	690.1	1,219.0
2007	731.4	437.6	1,168.8	504.1	690.0	1,193.3
2008	836.2	472.0	1,307.7	507.8	826.4	1,335.1
2009	711.4	470.3	1,181.8	476.4	727.6	1,203.9
2010	703.2	406.0	1,109.2	428.3	700.9	1,128.9
2011	751.3	361.0	1,112.5	448.9	689.7	1,138.4
2012	763.3	404.1	1,167.9	471.0	724.0	1,196.4
2013	795.0	453.0	1,250.0	475.0	804.0	1,280.0
2014	893.0	464.0	1,360.0	514.0	871.0	1,380.0
2015[1]	955.3	417.2	1,372.4	581.7	825.5	1,407.3

[1] Preliminary.   [2] Includes production from Alaska, Idaho, Missouri, Montana, Nevada, New Mexico, and Utah.   [3] Includes copper content of precipitates and other metal concentrates.   *Source: U.S. Geological Survey (USGS)*

COPPER

Production of Recoverable Copper in Arizona   In Thousands of Short Tons

Year	Jan.	Feb.	Mar.	Apr.	May	June	July	Aug.	Sept.	Oct.	Nov.	Dec.	Total
2006	55.9	52.7	60.8	58.9	62.0	60.5	60.4	59.9	59.3	59.7	60.8	61.3	712.2
2007	57.6	52.2	58.9	60.2	63.5	63.0	65.5	66.3	62.8	62.1	60.1	59.2	731.4
2008	63.0	57.9	64.7	68.0	68.7	67.9	71.2	74.7	72.9	78.4	73.1	75.7	836.2
2009	65.8	57.3	57.8	53.7	58.7	59.0	62.7	58.2	56.5	60.7	59.0	62.0	711.4
2010	62.6	53.1	56.6	56.6	61.5	58.6	59.1	56.2	57.7	60.0	57.6	63.6	703.2
2011	57.3	53.0	60.8	59.3	66.5	63.9	61.9	65.0	64.4	66.5	67.1	65.6	751.3
2012	62.8	64.5	65.7	64.6	65.2	56.7	60.7	66.2	60.9	64.0	67.5	64.5	763.3
2013	65.7	57.7	66.5	64.1	70.7	64.6	68.2	65.1	66.6	68.5	65.9	71.3	795.0
2014	69.7	66.6	75.1	70.3	68.6	73.1	75.8	76.2	73.3	82.3	72.1	85.6	893.0
2015[1]	78.4	70.5	80.5	75.9	76.5	77.2	81.3	84.1	82.4	85.7	83.2		955.3

[1] Preliminary.   Source: U.S. Geological Survey (USGS)

Copper Stocks in the United States at Yearend   In Metric Tons

Year	Crude Copper[2]	Refined Copper						Total Refined
		Refineries[3]	Wire-rod Mills[3]	Brass Mills[3]	Other[4]	Comex	LME[5]	
2005	44.3	8.2	21.3	24.6	5.8	6.2	0.8	66.8
2006	18.8	28.1	21.5	34.5	5.8	30.9	75.6	196.0
2007	26.3	21.8	20.6	10.4	5.8	13.5	60.6	133.0
2008	19.8	15.7	22.6	8.3	5.8	31.3	106.0	190.0
2009	15.5	23.7	25.3	7.6	3.2	90.0	283.0	433.0
2010	21.1	10.3	19.7	6.4	4.3	58.6	284.0	384.0
2011	13.0	8.4	24.0	6.9	4.4	79.8	286.0	409.0
2012	12.3	12.9	28.1	6.5	4.3	64.1	120.0	236.0
2013	12.7	15.0	32.6	6.7	4.2	15.0	185.0	258.0
2014[1]	9.9	9.5	42.0	6.4	4.4	24.2	102.0	189.0

[1] Preliminary.   [2] Copper content of blister and anode.   [3] Stocks of refined copper as reported; no estimates are made for nonrespondents.   [4] Monthly estimates based on reported and 2011 annual data, comprising stocks at ingot makers, chemical plants, foundries, and miscellaneous manufacturers. [5] London Metal Exchange Ltd., U.S. warehouses.   Source: U.S. Geological Survey (USGS)

Stocks of Crude Copper[2] in the United States, at End of Month   In Thousands of Metric Tons

Year	Jan.	Feb.	Mar.	Apr.	May	June	July	Aug.	Sept.	Oct.	Nov.	Dec.
2006	17.3	21.7	15.2	18.8	40.6	18.6	23.9	20.5	27.3	24.3	19.0	18.8
2007	24.7	22.3	24.4	26.0	27.0	33.5	29.9	30.1	28.9	21.5	22.3	26.3
2008	29.0	21.1	15.7	15.1	14.3	30.5	16.0	10.8	11.8	14.1	16.3	19.8
2009	24.7	16.0	21.3	25.2	22.5	23.8	26.1	32.5	27.1	28.9	28.2	15.5
2010	25.8	25.2	25.5	24.4	23.8	18.1	23.7	22.4	19.9	17.6	23.4	21.1
2011	25.2	24.8	24.7	24.9	27.2	20.1	20.1	13.0	14.3	18.5	14.5	13.0
2012	10.9	14.2	16.5	19.2	15.0	12.6	12.3	12.5	16.7	19.7	18.6	12.3
2013	8.6	20.1	17.9	21.8	28.7	11.5	12.8	10.7	11.2	14.2	15.3	12.7
2014	13.4	13.8	18.4	15.1	22.2	14.7	10.3	15.9	15.7	11.3	9.7	9.9
2015[1]	14.2	11.3	11.3	11.3	16.6	15.4	13.2	14.3	21.2	17.9	13.5	

[1] Preliminary.   [2] Copper content of blister and anode.   Source: U.S. Geological Survey (USGS)

Total Stocks of Refined Copper in the United States, at End of Month   In Thousands of Metric Tons

Year	Jan.	Feb.	Mar.	Apr.	May	June	July	Aug.	Sept.	Oct.	Nov.	Dec.
2006	82.1	106.0	109.0	90.2	86.4	75.6	84.3	89.5	102.0	111.0	157.0	196.0
2007	198.0	193.0	174.0	148.0	116.0	105.0	104.0	103.0	102.0	106.0	113.0	133.0
2008	100.0	90.1	71.1	62.7	62.1	61.6	69.7	91.1	109.0	118.0	146.0	190.0
2009	258.0	289.0	337.0	337.0	312.0	284.0	293.0	298.0	323.0	339.0	379.0	433.0
2010	467.0	487.0	467.0	455.0	434.0	431.0	422.0	407.0	381.0	364.0	356.0	384.0
2011	282.0	383.0	372.0	366.0	365.0	359.0	368.0	370.0	377.0	383.0	387.0	409.0
2012	393.0	358.0	309.0	268.0	235.0	210.0	199.0	192.0	187.0	194.0	203.0	236.0
2013	261.0	275.0	308.0	325.0	318.0	314.0	306.0	292.0	273.0	260.0	250.0	258.0
2014	246.0	239.0	258.0	246.0	222.0	201.0	198.0	202.0	215.0	210.0	193.0	189.0
2015[1]	182.0	186.0	191.0	192.0	173.0	167.0	161.0	181.0	183.0	189.0	196.0	

[1] Preliminary.   Source: U.S. Geological Survey (USGS)

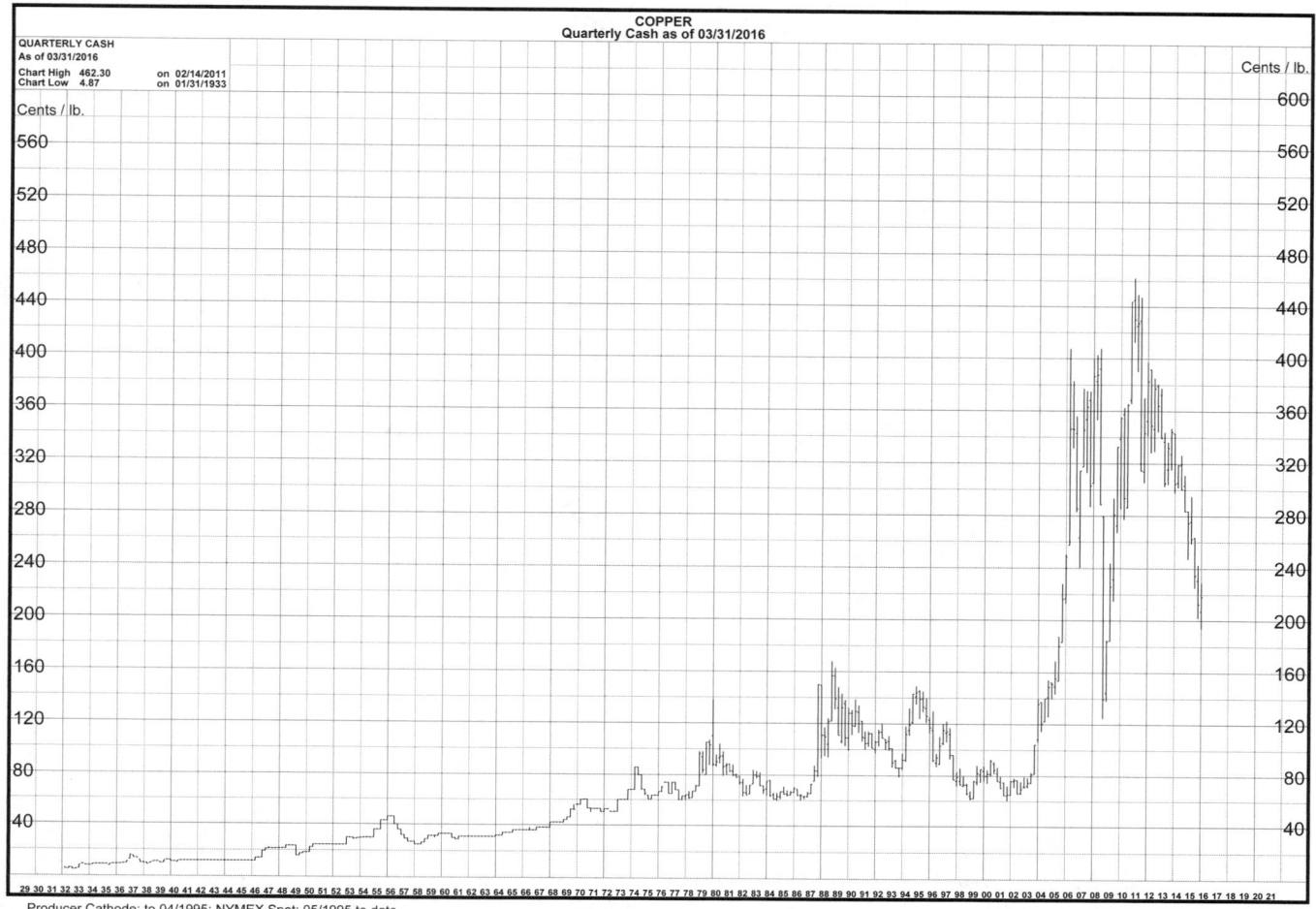

COPPER
Quarterly Cash as of 03/31/2016

QUARTERLY CASH
As of 03/31/2016
Chart High 462.30   on 02/14/2011
Chart Low   4.87   on 01/31/1933

Producer Cathode: to 04/1995; NYMEX Spot: 05/1995 to date.

Producers' Price of Electrolytic (Wirebar) Copper, Delivered to U.S. Destinations   In Cents Per Pound

Year	Jan.	Feb.	Mar.	Apr.	May	June	July	Aug.	Sept.	Oct.	Nov.	Dec.	Average
2006	225.07	230.74	238.31	302.74	382.65	346.65	368.49	359.91	353.01	345.83	322.45	307.00	315.24
2007	263.89	265.67	298.65	356.76	355.24	346.59	370.42	343.65	351.87	364.48	318.93	306.74	328.57
2008	325.53	364.78	385.98	399.96	383.39	375.08	382.31	349.89	320.54	224.32	174.59	145.09	319.29
2009	153.55	155.38	176.45	209.36	215.36	233.23	243.36	285.81	285.91	292.24	307.45	320.57	239.89
2010	337.71	315.88	343.54	356.46	315.33	299.00	312.18	337.50	357.31	382.81	390.16	419.69	347.30
2011	439.85	454.13	436.70	435.63	410.49	415.91	445.11	412.86	378.78	339.15	349.89	348.73	405.60
2012	371.87	389.59	389.13	377.51	362.32	340.76	349.95	348.05	378.12	374.24	356.44	368.84	367.24
2013	372.47	371.83	351.31	332.72	337.45	325.95	321.50	335.18	334.13	334.93	328.07	339.43	340.41
2014	342.10	334.93	315.05	313.99	320.45	317.04	329.34	322.01	315.28	309.62	308.64	296.45	318.74
2015	271.73	268.95	277.04	281.50	295.59	273.57	254.27	239.79	243.31	243.04	222.34	214.01	257.10

Source: American Metal Market (AMM)

Dealers' Buying Price of No. 2 Heavy Copper Scrap in Chicago   In Cents Per Pound

Year	Jan.	Feb.	Mar.	Apr.	May	June	July	Aug.	Sept.	Oct.	Nov.	Dec.	Average
2006	137.50	137.50	139.46	145.00	145.00	171.36	175.25	185.89	184.10	192.09	192.85	183.30	165.78
2007	155.83	153.92	164.32	197.83	210.09	203.60	216.83	219.89	213.97	224.72	210.20	191.87	196.92
2008	198.21	210.00	238.21	246.82	247.02	237.50	240.00	233.93	226.07	141.85	97.50	87.02	200.34
2009	80.00	92.24	104.32	124.40	134.00	155.23	166.59	182.02	192.50	194.40	203.55	224.61	154.49
2010	245.13	220.92	258.37	275.68	244.50	214.32	214.64	255.68	260.36	273.93	277.50	268.29	250.78
2011	285.00	292.50	299.13	295.00	290.72	295.23	315.00	311.41	293.69	241.55	261.50	256.97	286.48
2012	262.50	287.75	292.50	283.93	280.00	259.64	262.50	262.50	275.39	282.50	270.25	281.39	275.07
2013	287.74	292.24	287.02	272.50	263.18	269.00	255.23	260.55	265.00	274.63	272.76	277.76	273.13
2014	287.02	277.50	266.55	262.73	270.36	269.07	270.64	268.26	262.64	257.24	255.50	240.31	265.65
2015	220.60	205.08	215.50	218.86	232.50	219.77	212.86	195.79	195.12	193.91	184.97	165.64	205.05

Source: American Metal Market (AMM)

COPPER

COPPER, HIGH GRADE - COMEX
Weekly Selected Futures as of 04/01/2016

WEEKLY SELECTED FUTURES
As of 04/01/2016

Chart High 464.95 on 02/15/2011
Chart Low 124.75 on 12/24/2008

Nearby Futures through Last Trading Day using selected contract months: March, May, July, September and December.

Volume of Trading of Copper Futures in New York   In Thousands of Contracts

Year	Jan.	Feb.	Mar.	Apr.	May	June	July	Aug.	Sept.	Oct.	Nov.	Dec.	Total
2006	234.3	401.4	284.5	407.0	260.4	321.6	182.2	310.0	189.4	216.4	320.8	153.4	3,281.3
2007	241.3	334.0	264.5	402.8	292.4	367.2	272.4	451.6	225.6	289.3	412.9	199.1	3,753.2
2008	345.5	459.5	298.5	466.5	344.5	462.0	382.1	463.2	349.5	403.8	414.4	228.4	4,618.1
2009	343.5	446.0	361.0	592.9	373.6	661.9	499.5	746.2	511.2	599.7	809.3	454.0	6,399.0
2010	645.5	996.3	772.6	1,049.0	894.7	1,051.1	724.9	980.5	604.4	822.3	1,132.3	631.8	10,305.7
2011	777.6	1,079.7	931.9	1,079.4	915.2	1,170.7	765.9	1,312.5	1,142.5	1,268.8	1,234.6	812.7	12,491.5
2012	1,131.5	1,572.7	1,222.8	1,768.1	1,491.4	1,790.3	1,163.1	1,478.0	1,084.8	1,137.7	1,469.8	848.6	16,158.8
2013	1,163.8	1,547.7	1,199.1	2,262.6	1,646.6	1,760.9	1,307.1	1,696.7	913.6	1,265.4	1,443.0	920.9	17,127.4
2014	1,049.9	1,236.2	1,401.8	1,422.9	933.0	1,434.3	1,081.3	1,276.8	1,089.7	1,269.0	1,459.4	927.7	14,582.2
2015	1,376.3	1,513.4	1,327.0	1,570.8	1,078.6	1,638.6	1,410.3	1,753.1	1,197.7	1,227.4	1,843.6	1,049.2	16,986.1

Source: CME Group; New York Mercantile Exchange (NYMEX)

Average Open Interest of Copper Futures in New York   In Contracts

Year	Jan.	Feb.	Mar.	Apr.	May	June	July	Aug.	Sept.	Oct.	Nov.	Dec.
2006	102,227	93,813	93,069	97,283	83,758	75,841	74,471	72,158	69,004	72,023	72,517	68,402
2007	69,972	70,373	69,324	78,919	80,834	79,257	88,691	78,113	72,469	86,909	78,385	71,626
2008	81,778	94,021	101,503	105,050	98,787	103,055	109,591	96,254	76,523	80,961	76,869	71,809
2009	82,402	85,831	90,636	103,517	106,511	111,555	111,849	118,935	117,782	127,204	146,612	149,621
2010	147,311	126,659	131,619	151,712	132,069	134,323	132,119	140,543	142,628	160,288	156,869	162,683
2011	162,325	157,918	138,261	134,959	122,036	128,861	148,876	130,312	120,015	126,973	124,770	115,634
2012	134,294	159,589	152,255	154,073	147,975	149,350	138,220	148,201	147,632	153,484	148,322	148,754
2013	160,188	174,428	166,007	179,530	162,279	180,744	165,350	160,513	149,129	150,400	162,528	160,424
2014	160,638	155,280	153,880	153,104	148,544	148,751	171,388	153,255	146,669	170,902	167,274	155,661
2015	175,389	178,359	165,403	163,159	173,340	174,453	165,716	180,019	153,941	160,277	181,603	175,301

Source: CME Group; New York Mercantile Exchange (NYMEX)

Corn

Corn is a member of the grass family of plants and is a native grain of the American continents. Fossils of corn pollen that are over 80,000 years old have been found in lake sediment under Mexico City. Archaeological discoveries show that cultivated corn existed in the southwestern U.S. for at least 3,000 years, indicating that the indigenous people of the region cultivated corn as a food crop long before the Europeans reached the New World. Corn is a hardy plant that grows in many different areas of the world. It can grow at altitudes as low as sea level and as high as 12,000 feet in the South American Andes Mountains. Corn can also grow in tropical climates that receive up to 400 inches of rainfall per year, or in areas that receive only 12 inches of rainfall per year. Corn is used primarily as livestock feed in the United States and the rest of the world. Other uses for corn are alcohol additives for gasoline, adhesives, corn oil for cooking and margarine, sweeteners, and as food for humans. Corn is the largest crop in the U.S., both in terms of the value of the crop and of the acres planted.

The largest futures and options market for corn is at the CME Group. Corn futures and options also trade at ICE Futures U.S., the Bolsa de Mercadorias & Futuros (BM&F), the JSE Securities Exchange, the Mercado a Termino de Buenos Aires (MTBA), and the NYSE LIFFE European Derivatives Market. Corn futures are traded on the Budapest Stock Exchange (BSE), the Dalian Commodity Exchange (DCE), the Kansai Commodities Exchange, the Moscow Exchange, Rosario Futures Exchange, and the Tokyo Grain Exchange (TGE). The CME futures contract calls for the delivery of 5000 bushels of No. 2 yellow corn at par contract price, No. 1 yellow at 1-1/2 cents per bushel over the contract price, or No. 3 yellow at 1-1/2 cents per bushel below the contract price.

Prices – CME corn futures prices (Barchart.com electronic symbol code ZC) traded sideways to lower the first half of 2015 on signs of ample supplies as the USDA projected a record global corn crop of 999.45 MMT and record high global ending stocks of 197.01 MMT. Corn prices came under further pressure in June after the EPA lowered the mandate for corn ethanol levels. The EPA cut the ethanol levels for 2015 to 13.4 billion gallons and to 14 billion gallons for 2016 from 15 billion gallons, which reduced corn demand from ethanol producers. Corn prices rallied late June into early July and posted a 1-1/2 year high in July at $4.3875 a bushel that was also the high for 2015. Excessive early summer rains flooded Midwest fields and raised crop concerns after an early-July USDA Crop Progress report showed the U.S. corn crop in 69% good-to-excellent condition, down -7 points y/y. Corn prices retreated, however, as the USDA hiked its 2014/15 global corn production estimate to a record 1006.24 MMT and raised its global corn ending stocks estimate to a record 197.42 MMT. That helped to push corn prices down to a 1-year low, and the low for 2015, in August at $3.465 a bushel. Corn traded sideways into Q4 of 2015 on ample supplies amid weak demand. In the Nov 10 WASDE report the USDA raised its U.S. 2015/16 corn crop estimate to 13.654 billion bushels, the third-largest U.S. crop on record, and hiked its global 2015/16 corn ending stocks estimate to a record 211.91 MMT. The surge in the dollar index to a 12-year high in 2015 curbed U.S. corn export prospects and prompted the USDA in the December 9 WASDE report to cut its U.S. 2015/16 corn export estimate to 1.75 billion bushels from 1.80 billion bushels, and to raise its U.S. 2015/16 ending stocks estimate to a 10-year high of 1.785 billion bushels. Another negative for corn prices in 2015 was the plunge in crude oil to a 12-year low, which undercut ethanol prices and reduced corn demand from ethanol producers who were forced to cut production. Corn prices finished 2015 down 9.6% at $3.5875 a bushel.

Supply – World production of corn in the 2014-15 marketing year rose +0.1% to 988.077 million metric tons, a new record high. The world's largest corn producers are the U.S. with 36.5% of world production, China (21.8%), and Brazil (7.6%). Corn production in both China and Brazil has nearly tripled since 1980. Production in the U.S. over that same time frame has risen by about 50%. The world area harvested with corn in 2014-15 fell -1.6% yr/yr to 317.2 million hectares, below last year's 14-year high of 322.4 million hectares. World ending stocks of corn and coarse grains in 2014-15 rose +7.7% to 226.0 million metric tons.

U.S. corn production estimates for the 2014-15 marketing year (Sep-Aug) rose by +2.8% yr/yr to 14.215 billion bushels. U.S. farmers harvested 83.136 million acres of corn for grain usage in 2014-15, which was down -4.9% yr/yr. U.S. corn yield in 2014-15 rose +8.2% to 171.0 bushels per acre. U.S. 2014-15 ending stocks rose by +68.4% to 2.080 billion bushels. The largest corn producing states in the U.S. in 2014 were Iowa with 16.7% of U.S. production, Illinois (16.5%), Nebraska (11.3%), Minnesota (8.3%), and Indiana (7.6%). The value of the U.S. corn crop in 2013-14 (latest data) was $62.716 billion.

Demand – World consumption of corn and rough grains in 2014-15 rose +1.5% yr/yr to 1.256 billion metric tons, a new record high. The U.S. distribution tables for corn show that in 2014-15 the largest category of usage, aside from animal feed, is for ethanol production (alcohol fuel) with 5.125 billion bushels, which is 78.5% of total non-feed usage. That was down -0.1% yr/yr. Corn usage for ethanol is more than seven times the usage in 2000. After ethanol, the largest non-feed usage categories are for high fructose corn syrup (HFCS) with 7.5% of U.S. usage, glucose and dextrose sugars (4.5%), corn starch (3.8%), cereal and other corn products (3.1%), and alcoholic beverages (2.2%).

Trade – U.S. exports of corn in 2014-15 fell -4.2% to 1.983 billion bushels. The largest destination countries for U.S. corn exports are Japan, which accounted for 36% of U.S. corn exports, Mexico (27%), and Venezuela (6%).

CORN

World Production of Corn or Maize   In Thousands of Metric Tons

Crop Year Beginning Oct. 1	Argentina	Brazil	Canada	China	European Union	India	Indonesia	Mexico	Russia	South Africa	Ukraine	United States	World Total
2006-07	22,500	51,000	8,990	151,600	55,629	15,097	7,850	22,350	3,510	7,300	6,426	267,503	716,318
2007-08	22,017	58,600	11,649	152,300	49,355	18,955	8,500	23,600	3,798	13,164	7,421	331,177	795,528
2008-09	15,500	51,000	10,643	165,914	64,821	19,731	8,700	24,226	6,682	12,567	11,447	305,911	799,765
2009-10	25,000	56,100	9,796	163,974	59,151	16,719	6,900	20,374	3,963	13,420	10,486	331,921	824,848
2010-11	25,200	57,400	12,043	177,245	58,272	21,726	6,800	21,058	3,075	10,924	11,919	315,618	835,529
2011-12	21,000	73,000	11,359	192,780	68,123	21,759	8,850	18,726	6,962	12,759	22,838	312,789	889,772
2012-13	27,000	81,500	13,060	205,614	58,896	22,258	8,500	21,591	8,213	12,365	20,922	273,192	869,503
2013-14[1]	26,000	80,000	14,194	218,490	64,635	24,259	9,100	22,880	11,635	14,925	30,900	351,272	991,380
2014-15[2]	27,000	85,000	11,487	215,646	75,793	23,670	8,800	25,480	11,325	10,800	28,450	361,091	1,008,994
2015-16[3]	27,000	84,000	13,600	224,580	57,751	21,000	9,100	23,500	13,000	7,000	23,300	345,486	970,080

[1] Preliminary.   [2] Estimate.   [3] Forecast.   *Source: Foreign Agricultural Service, U.S. Department of Agriculture (FAS-USDA)*

World Supply and Demand of Coarse Grains   In Millions of Metric Tons/Hectares

Crop Year Beginning Oct. 1	Area Harvested	Yield	Production	World Trade	Total Consumption	Ending Stocks	Stocks as % of Consumption[3]
2006-07	306.8	3.20	988.0	114.5	1,013.6	139.5	13.8
2007-08	317.5	3.40	1,080.0	128.7	1,058.2	161.3	15.2
2008-09	315.3	3.50	1,107.9	110.4	1,078.9	190.3	17.6
2009-10	307.9	3.60	1,116.7	118.8	1,114.8	192.2	17.2
2010-11	306.5	3.60	1,098.2	116.0	1,129.6	160.8	14.2
2011-12	317.0	3.60	1,156.5	133.4	1,155.5	161.9	14.0
2012-13	316.5	3.60	1,136.2	132.2	1,134.5	163.5	14.4
2013-14	321.6	4.00	1,281.0	164.6	1,233.4	211.2	17.1
2014-15[1]	322.3	4.00	1,297.5	173.2	1,266.6	242.0	19.1
2015-16[2]	320.6	3.90	1,264.3	170.1	1,261.1	245.2	19.4

[1] Preliminary.   [2] Estimate.   [3] Represents the ratio of marketing year ending stocks to total consumption.   *Source: Foreign Agricultural Service, U.S. Department of Agriculture (FAS-USDA)*

Acreage and Supply of Corn in the United States   In Millions of Bushels

Crop Year Beginning Sept. 1	Planted	Harvested For Grain	Harvested For Silage	Yield Per Harvested Acre Bushels	Carry-over, Sept. 1 On Farms	Carry-over, Sept. 1 Off Farms	Supply Beginning Stocks	Supply Production	Supply Imports	Total Supply
	In Thousands of Acres									
2006-07	78,327	70,648	6,477	149.1	749.5	1,217.7	1,967	10,531	12	12,510
2007-08	93,527	86,520	6,060	150.7	460.1	843.5	1,304	13,038	20	14,362
2008-09	85,982	78,570	5,965	153.9	500.0	1,124.2	1,624	12,092	14	13,729
2009-10	86,382	79,490	5,605	164.7	607.5	1,065.8	1,673	13,110	8	14,774
2010-11	88,192	81,446	5,567	152.8	485.1	1,222.7	1,708	12,447	28	14,161
2011-12	91,936	83,989	5,935	147.2	315.0	812.7	1,128	12,360	29	13,471
2012-13	97,291	87,365	7,419	123.1	313.7	675.3	989	10,755	160	11,904
2013-14	95,365	87,451	6,281	158.1	275.0	546.2	821	13,829	36	14,686
2014-15[1]	90,597	83,136	6,371	171.0	462.0	769.9	1,232	14,216	32	15,479
2015-16[2]	87,999	80,749	6,221	168.4	593.0	1,138.2	1,731	13,601	40	15,372

[1] Preliminary.   [2] Estimate.   *Source: Economic Research Service, U.S. Department of Agriculture (ERS-USDA)*

Production of Corn (For Grain) in the United States, by State   In Millions of Bushels

Year	Illinois	Indiana	Iowa	Kansas	Michigan	Minnesota	Missouri	Nebraska	Ohio	South Dakota	Texas	Wisconsin	US Total
2006	1,817.5	844.7	2,050.1	345.0	286.7	1,102.9	362.9	1,178.0	470.6	312.3	175.5	400.4	10,531.1
2007	2,283.8	981.0	2,376.9	507.8	287.8	1,146.1	457.8	1,472.0	541.5	542.1	291.6	442.8	13,037.9
2008	2,130.1	873.6	2,188.8	486.4	295.3	1,180.8	381.6	1,393.7	421.2	585.2	253.8	394.6	12,091.6
2009	2,053.2	933.7	2,420.6	598.3	309.3	1,244.1	446.8	1,575.3	546.4	706.7	254.8	448.3	13,110.1
2010	1,946.8	898.0	2,153.3	581.3	315.0	1,292.1	369.0	1,469.1	533.0	569.7	301.6	502.2	12,446.9
2011	1,946.8	839.5	2,356.4	449.4	335.1	1,201.2	350.0	1,536.0	508.8	653.4	136.7	517.9	12,359.6
2012	1,286.3	597.0	1,876.9	375.3	314.2	1,374.5	247.5	1,292.2	438.0	535.3	200.0	396.0	10,755.1
2013	2,100.4	1,031.9	2,140.2	504.0	345.7	1,294.3	435.2	1,614.0	649.0	802.8	265.2	439.4	13,829.0
2014	2,350.0	1,084.8	2,367.4	566.2	355.8	1,177.8	628.7	1,602.1	610.7	787.4	294.5	485.2	14,215.5
2015[1]	2,012.5	822.0	2,505.6	580.2	335.3	1,428.8	437.4	1,692.8	498.8	799.8	266.0	492.0	13,601.2

[1] Preliminary.   *Source: National Agricultural Statistics Service, U.S. Department of Agriculture (NASS-USDA)*

Quarterly Supply and Disappearance of Corn in the United States   In Millions of Bushels

Crop Year Beginning Sept. 1	Supply Beginning Stocks	Pro-duction	Imports[3]	Total Supply	Disappearance Domestic Use Food & Alcohol	Seed	Feed & Residual	Total	Exports[3]	Total Disap-pearance	Ending Stocks Gov't Owned[4]	Privately Owned[5]	Total Stocks
2011-12	1,128	12,314	29.4	13,471	6,400	24.5	4,519	10,943	1,539	12,482	----	----	989
Sept.-Nov.	1,128	12,314	4.1	13,446	1,611	----	1,782	3,393	406	3,799	----	----	9,647
Dec.-Feb.	9,647	----	3.9	9,651	1,637	----	1,546	3,183	444	3,627	----	----	6,023
Mar.-May	6,023	----	10.7	6,034	1,602	23.6	862	2,488	398	2,886	----	----	3,148
June-Aug.	3,148	----	10.7	3,159	1,550	1.0	328	1,879	291	2,170	----	----	989
2012-13	989	10,755	159.9	11,904	6,013	24.6	4,315	10,353	730	11,083	----	----	821
Sept.-Nov.	989	10,755	34.8	11,779	1,466	----	2,060	3,525	221	3,746	----	----	8,033
Dec.-Feb.	8,033	----	45.4	8,078	1,430	----	1,087	2,517	161	2,678	----	----	5,400
Mar.-May	5,400	----	40.2	5,440	1,545	22.4	921	2,488	186	2,674	----	----	2,766
June-Aug.	2,766	----	39.6	2,806	1,573	2.2	247	1,822	162	1,985	----	----	821
2013-14/1	821	13,829	35.8	14,686	6,471	22.9	5,040	11,534	1,920	13,454	----	----	1,232
Sept.-Nov.	821	13,829	14.5	14,665	1,550	----	2,312	3,862	350	4,212	----	----	10,453
Dec.-Feb.	10,453	----	6.6	10,459	1,602	----	1,459	3,061	390	3,451	----	----	7,008
Mar.-May	7,008	----	8.6	7,017	1,642	21.7	865	2,529	636	3,165	----	----	3,852
June-Aug.	3,852	----	6.1	3,858	1,676	1.2	404	2,081	544	2,626	----	----	1,232
2014-15[2]	1,232	14,216	31.7	15,479	6,537	22.5	5,324	11,883	1,864	13,748	----	----	1,731
Sept.-Nov.	1,232	14,216	5.0	15,452	1,615	----	2,225	3,840	401	4,241	----	----	11,211
Dec.-Feb.	11,211	----	5.9	11,217	1,622	----	1,441	3,063	404	3,467	----	----	7,750
Mar.-May	7,750	----	10.0	7,760	1,634	21.4	1,115	2,771	536	3,307	----	----	4,453
June-Aug.	4,453	----	10.8	4,464	1,667	1.1	542	2,210	523	2,733	----	----	1,731
2015-16[2]	1,731	13,601	50.0	15,382	6,572	22.9	5,300	11,895	1,650	13,545	----	----	1,837
Sept.-Nov.	1,731	13,601	12.9	15,345	1,631	----	2,199	3,830	303	4,134	----	----	11,212

[1] Preliminary.   [2] Estimate.   [3] Uncommitted inventory.   [4] Includes quantity under loan and farmer-owned reserve.   *Source: Economic Research Service, U.S. Department of Agriculture (ERS-USDA)*

Corn Production Estimates and Cash Price in the United States

Year	Corn for Grain Production Estimates Aug. 1	Sept. 1	Oct. 1	Nov. 1	Final	St. Louis No. 2 Yellow	Omaha No. 2 Yellow	Gulf Ports No. 2 Yellow	Kansas City No. 2 White	Chicago No. 2 Yellow	Average Farm Price[2]	Value of Pro-duction (Mil. $)
	In Thousands of Bushels					Dollars Per Bushel						
2006-07	10,975,740	11,113,766	10,905,194	10,744,806	10,531,123	3.60	3.33	3.94	4.18	3.46	3.13	32,083
2007-08	13,053,617	13,307,999	13,318,102	13,167,741	13,037,875	5.05	4.84	5.53	5.19	4.98	4.45	54,667
2008-09	12,287,875	12,072,365	12,199,908	12,019,894	12,091,648	3.88	3.80	4.39	4.13	3.89	4.05	49,313
2009-10	12,760,986	12,954,500	13,018,058	12,920,928	13,110,062	3.69	3.49	4.14	3.71	3.64	3.53	46,734
2010-11	13,365,225	13,159,700	12,663,949	12,539,646	12,446,865	6.50	6.29	7.04	6.55	6.38	5.51	64,643
2011-12	12,914,085	12,497,070	12,432,910	12,309,936	12,359,612	6.95	6.65	7.22	7.37	6.73	6.36	76,940
2012-13	10,778,589	10,727,364	10,705,729	10,725,191	10,755,111	6.94	7.20	7.58	7.52	7.17	6.88	74,155
2013-14	13,763,025	13,843,320	NA	13,988,720	13,828,964	4.91	4.35	5.16	4.63	4.47	4.48	61,928
2014-15	14,031,915	14,395,350	14,474,920	14,407,420	14,215,532	3.82	3.60	4.35	3.75	3.76	3.69	52,952
2015-16[1]	13,686,063	13,584,945	13,554,923	13,653,507	13,601,198	3.77	3.55	4.18	3.84	3.79	3.65	49,039

[1] Preliminary.   [2] Season-average price based on monthly prices weigthed by monthly marketings.
Source: Economic Research Service, U.S. Department of Agriculture (ERS-USDA)

Distribution of Corn in the United States   In Millions of Bushels

Crop Year Beginning Sept. 1	Food, Seed and Industrial Use HFCS	Glucose & Dextrose	Starch	Alcohol Fuel	Bev-rage[3]	Seed	Cereal & Other Products	Total	Livestock Feed[4]	Exports (Including Grain Equiv. of Products)	Domestic Disap-pearance	Total Utilization
2006-07	510	239	272	2,117	136	23.8	190	3,464	5,591	2,125.4	9,081	11,207
2007-08	490	236	262	3,049	135	21.8	192	4,387	5,858	2,437.4	10,300	12,737
2008-09	489	245	234	3,709	134	21.9	192	5,025	5,133	1,848.9	10,159	12,008
2009-10	512	257	250	4,591	134	22.3	194	5,961	5,101	1,979.0	11,062	13,041
2010-11	521	272	258	5,019	135	23.0	197	6,426	4,777	1,830.9	11,202	13,033
2011-12	513	297	254	5,000	137	24.5	203	6,428	4,519	1,539.2	10,943	12,482
2012-13	493	291	249	4,641	140	24.6	199	6,039	4,315	730.1	10,353	11,083
2013-14	478	308	219	5,124	142	22.9	201	6,494	5,041	1,920.5	11,534	13,454
2014-15[1]	478	300	216	5,209	142	22.5	201	6,568	5,300	1,875.0	11,870	13,745
2015-16[2]	470	300	230	5,200	144	22.9	203	6,570	5,275	1,850.0	11,905	13,755

[1] Preliminary.   [2] Estimate.   [3] Also includes nonfuel industrial alcohol.   [4] Feed and waste (residual, mostly feed).
Source: Economic Research Service, U.S. Department of Agriculture (ERS-USDA)

CORN

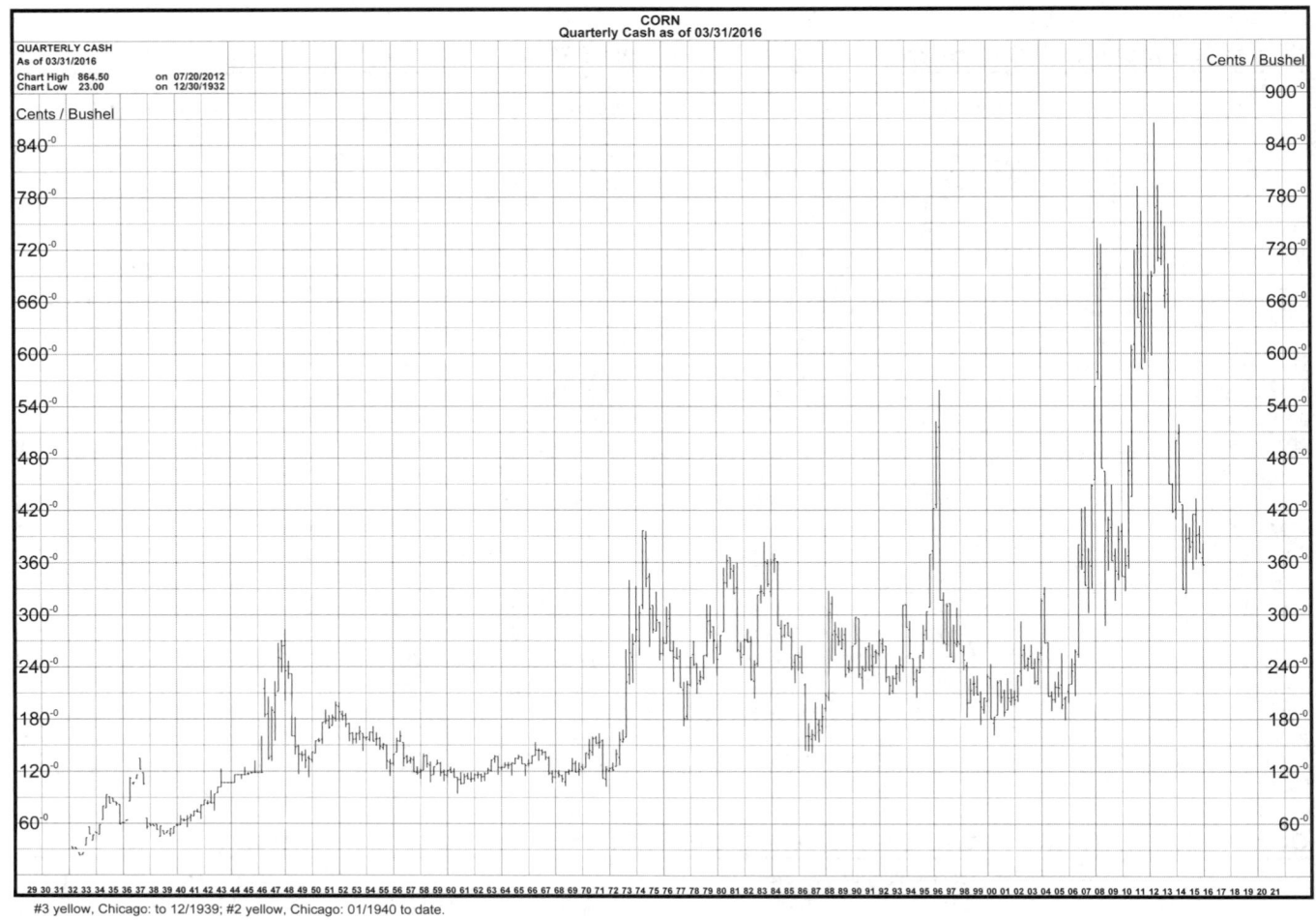

QUARTERLY CASH
As of 03/31/2016
Chart High 864.50 on 07/20/2012
Chart Low 23.00 on 12/30/1932

Cents / Bushel

#3 yellow, Chicago: to 12/1939; #2 yellow, Chicago: 01/1940 to date.

Average Cash Price of Corn, No. 2 Yellow in Central Illinois   In Dollars Per Bushel

Year	Sept.	Oct.	Nov.	Dec.	Jan.	Feb.	Mar.	Apr.	May	June	July	Aug.	Average
2006-07	2.21	2.82	3.43	3.53	3.66	3.90	3.76	3.36	3.52	3.68	3.03	3.08	3.33
2007-08	3.15	3.28	3.66	4.03	4.55	4.91	5.15	5.59	5.58	6.55	5.97	5.04	4.79
2008-09	5.00	3.69	3.42	3.33	3.61	3.46	3.60	3.69	3.98	3.97	3.22	3.21	3.68
2009-10	3.10	3.52	3.62	3.59	3.52	3.39	3.40	3.36	3.43	3.24	3.49	3.77	3.45
2010-11	4.51	5.19	5.33	5.65	6.10	6.69	6.59	7.33	7.08	7.17	6.96	7.30	6.33
2011-12	6.77	6.23	6.26	5.96	6.25	6.41	6.46	6.34	6.27	6.30	7.85	8.15	6.60
2012-13	7.70	7.48	7.39	7.23	7.17	7.15	7.33	6.57	6.83	6.94	6.61	5.98	7.03
2013-14	4.78	4.20	4.10	4.13	4.13	4.33	4.64	4.98	4.72	4.37	3.74	3.59	4.31
2014-15	3.16	3.09	3.45	3.75	3.67	3.65	3.66	3.59	3.49	3.52	3.85	3.51	3.53
2015-16[1]	3.55	3.67	3.62	3.62	3.55	3.56							3.60

[1] Preliminary.   *Source: Economic Research Service, U.S. Department of Agriculture (ERS-USDA)*

Average Cash Price of Corn, No. 2 Yellow at Gulf Ports[2]   In Dollars Per Bushel

Year	Sept.	Oct.	Nov.	Dec.	Jan.	Feb.	Mar.	Apr.	May	June	July	Aug.	Average
2006-07	3.05	3.82	4.17	4.08	4.19	4.50	3.81	3.88	4.07	4.20	3.73	3.84	3.94
2007-08	4.05	4.17	4.35	4.58	5.25	5.59	5.95	6.26	6.19	7.29	6.74	5.97	5.53
2008-09	5.94	4.65	4.18	4.02	4.39	4.15	4.18	4.29	4.58	4.56	3.86	3.87	4.39
2009-10	3.82	4.25	4.36	4.18	4.25	4.11	4.04	3.99	4.15	3.88	4.15	4.46	4.14
2010-11	5.23	5.99	6.05	6.36	6.73	7.44	7.38	8.11	7.82	7.89	7.64	7.88	7.04
2011-12	7.50	6.98	6.97	6.57	6.94	7.10	7.13	6.96	6.84	6.79	8.46	8.44	7.22
2012-13	8.15	8.16	8.18	7.85	7.70	7.70	7.85	7.11	7.50	7.58	7.10	6.07	7.58
2013-14	5.27	5.13	5.06	5.06	5.03	5.32	5.65	5.65	5.51	5.14	4.64	4.48	5.16
2014-15	4.14	4.15	4.54	4.55	4.44	4.41	4.43	4.38	4.23	4.24	4.56	4.14	4.35
2015-16[1]	4.22	4.36	4.22	4.17	4.09	4.06							4.18

[1] Preliminary.   [2] Barge delivered to Louisiana Gulf.   *Source: Economic Research Service, U.S. Department of Agriculture (ERS-USDA)*

Weekly Outstanding Export Sales and Cumulative Exports of U.S. Corn   In Thousands of Metric Tons

Marketing Year 2014/2015 Week Ending	Weekly Exports	Accumu- lated Exports	Net Sales	Out- standing Sales	Marketing Year 2015/2016 Week Ending	Weekly Exports	Accumu- lated Exports	Net Sales	Out- standing Sales
Sep 04, 2014	695,470	695,470	1,904,615	11,684,066	Sep 03, 2015	267,430	267,430	1,838,271	8,538,831
Sep 11, 2014	722,401	1,417,871	659,665	11,621,330	Sep 10, 2015	806,649	1,074,079	533,038	8,265,220
Sep 18, 2014	1,038,629	2,456,500	836,379	11,419,080	Sep 17, 2015	795,357	1,869,436	426,299	7,896,162
Sep 25, 2014	620,444	3,076,944	638,016	11,436,652	Sep 24, 2015	813,809	2,683,245	748,175	7,830,528
Oct 02, 2014	978,110	4,055,054	784,772	11,243,314	Oct 01, 2015	489,874	3,173,119	519,685	7,860,339
Oct 09, 2014	901,691	4,956,745	1,922,827	12,264,450	Oct 08, 2015	606,942	3,780,061	598,416	7,851,813
Oct 16, 2014	676,683	5,633,428	1,031,197	12,618,964	Oct 15, 2015	409,753	4,189,814	248,017	7,690,077
Oct 23, 2014	829,506	6,462,934	489,820	12,279,278	Oct 22, 2015	433,288	4,623,102	708,787	7,965,576
Oct 30, 2014	443,994	6,906,928	478,163	12,313,447	Oct 29, 2015	492,708	5,115,810	556,037	8,028,905
Nov 06, 2014	600,780	7,507,708	505,348	12,218,015	Nov 05, 2015	270,852	5,386,662	618,627	8,376,680
Nov 13, 2014	386,944	7,894,652	908,689	12,739,760	Nov 12, 2015	388,962	5,775,624	779,801	8,767,519
Nov 20, 2014	616,403	8,511,055	944,914	13,068,271	Nov 19, 2015	531,688	6,307,312	2,036,323	10,272,154
Nov 27, 2014	746,431	9,257,486	1,170,654	13,492,494	Nov 26, 2015	373,842	6,681,154	499,368	10,397,680
Dec 04, 2014	678,339	9,935,825	962,778	13,776,933	Dec 03, 2015	486,849	7,168,003	1,032,328	10,943,159
Dec 11, 2014	754,018	10,689,843	693,460	13,716,375	Dec 10, 2015	495,044	7,663,047	579,449	11,027,564
Dec 18, 2014	746,913	11,436,756	1,653,124	14,622,586	Dec 17, 2015	823,584	8,486,631	803,626	11,007,606
Dec 25, 2014	667,828	12,104,584	895,059	14,849,817	Dec 24, 2015	556,412	9,043,043	705,165	11,156,359
Jan 01, 2015	510,397	12,614,981	387,648	14,727,068	Dec 31, 2015	357,820	9,400,863	252,921	11,051,460
Jan 08, 2015	400,204	13,015,185	818,809	15,145,673	Jan 07, 2016	638,230	10,039,093	669,231	11,082,461
Jan 15, 2015	762,448	13,777,633	2,185,432	16,568,657	Jan 14, 2016	571,590	10,610,683	1,157,741	11,668,612
Jan 22, 2015	831,085	14,608,718	956,705	16,694,277	Jan 21, 2016	648,744	11,259,427	817,002	11,836,870
Jan 29, 2015	714,792	15,323,510	844,892	16,824,377	Jan 28, 2016	660,652	11,920,079	1,129,100	12,305,318
Feb 05, 2015	618,536	15,942,046	1,002,761	17,208,602	Feb 04, 2016	528,652	12,448,731	404,963	12,181,629
Feb 12, 2015	696,217	16,638,263	932,164	17,444,549	Feb 11, 2016	728,938	13,177,669	1,050,675	12,503,366
Feb 19, 2015	865,138	17,503,401	715,847	17,295,258	Feb 18, 2016	807,570	13,985,239	871,350	12,567,146
Feb 26, 2015	1,378,760	18,882,161	828,056	16,744,554	Feb 25, 2016	789,807	14,775,046	1,097,634	12,874,973
Mar 05, 2015	1,165,270	20,047,431	417,969	15,997,253	Mar 03, 2016	1,052,478	15,827,524	1,172,311	12,994,806
Mar 12, 2015	692,712	20,740,143	502,288	15,806,829	Mar 10, 2016	873,901	16,701,425	1,227,047	13,347,952
Mar 19, 2015	1,065,894	21,806,037	434,953	15,175,888	Mar 17, 2016	997,525	17,698,950	803,228	13,153,655
Mar 26, 2015	683,400	22,489,437	406,630	14,899,118	Mar 24, 2016				
Apr 02, 2015	1,171,149	23,660,586	639,602	14,367,571	Mar 31, 2016				
Apr 09, 2015	870,902	24,531,488	588,175	14,084,844	Apr 07, 2016				
Apr 16, 2015	1,041,063	25,572,551	867,901	13,911,682	Apr 14, 2016				
Apr 23, 2015	1,269,284	26,841,835	832,542	13,474,940	Apr 21, 2016				
Apr 30, 2015	1,135,203	27,977,038	841,848	13,181,585	Apr 28, 2016				
May 07, 2015	1,109,320	29,086,358	370,030	12,442,295	May 05, 2016				
May 14, 2015	1,079,459	30,165,817	812,594	12,175,430	May 12, 2016				
May 21, 2015	1,070,813	31,236,630	654,600	11,759,217	May 19, 2016				
May 28, 2015	957,249	32,193,879	464,771	11,266,739	May 26, 2016				
Jun 04, 2015	826,098	33,019,977	495,581	10,936,222	Jun 02, 2016				
Jun 11, 2015	1,044,859	34,064,836	627,185	10,518,548	Jun 09, 2016				
Jun 18, 2015	1,125,975	35,190,811	496,798	9,889,371	Jun 16, 2016				
Jun 25, 2015	1,024,895	36,215,706	594,343	9,458,819	Jun 23, 2016				
Jul 02, 2015	966,205	37,181,911	535,236	9,027,850	Jun 30, 2016				
Jul 09, 2015	1,131,659	38,313,570	331,058	8,227,249	Jul 07, 2016				
Jul 16, 2015	1,156,817	39,470,387	223,447	7,293,879	Jul 14, 2016				
Jul 23, 2015	1,072,723	40,543,110	364,945	6,586,101	Jul 21, 2016				
Jul 30, 2015	1,004,954	41,548,064	-2,666	5,578,481	Jul 28, 2016				
Aug 06, 2015	840,608	42,388,672	29,239	4,767,112	Aug 04, 2016				
Aug 13, 2015	918,068	43,306,740	282,747	4,131,791	Aug 11, 2016				
Aug 20, 2015	820,621	44,127,361	-131,776	3,179,394	Aug 18, 2016				
Aug 27, 2015	1,077,218	45,204,579	112,674	2,214,850	Aug 25, 2016				
Sep 03, 2015	640,909	45,845,488	-146,860	1,427,081					

Source: Foreign Agricultural Service, U.S. Department of Agriculture (FAS-USDA)

CORN

Average Price Received by Farmers for Corn in the United States   In Dollars Per Bushel

Year	Sept.	Oct.	Nov.	Dec.	Jan.	Feb.	Mar.	Apr.	May	June	July	Aug.	Average
2006-07	2.20	2.55	2.88	3.01	3.05	3.44	3.43	3.39	3.49	3.53	3.32	3.26	3.13
2007-08	3.28	3.29	3.44	3.77	3.98	4.54	4.70	5.14	5.27	5.47	5.25	5.26	4.45
2008-09	5.01	4.37	4.26	4.11	4.36	3.87	3.85	3.85	3.96	4.01	3.60	3.33	4.05
2009-10	3.25	3.61	3.65	3.60	3.66	3.55	3.55	3.41	3.48	3.41	3.49	3.65	3.53
2010-11	4.08	4.32	4.55	4.82	4.94	5.65	5.53	6.36	6.32	6.38	6.33	6.88	5.51
2011-12	6.38	5.73	5.83	5.86	6.07	6.28	6.35	6.34	6.34	6.37	7.14	7.63	6.36
2012-13	6.89	6.78	7.01	6.87	6.96	7.04	7.13	6.97	6.97	6.97	6.79	6.21	6.88
2013-14	5.40	4.63	4.37	4.41	4.42	4.35	4.52	4.71	4.71	4.50	4.06	3.63	4.48
2014-15	3.49	3.57	3.60	3.79	3.82	3.79	3.81	3.75	3.62	3.58	3.80	3.68	3.69
2015-16[1]	3.68	3.67	3.60	3.65	3.66								3.65

[1] Preliminary.   *Source: Economic Research Service, U.S. Department of Agriculture (ERS-USDA)*

Corn Price Support Data in the United States

Crop Year Beginning Sept. 1	National Average Loan Rate[3] --- Dollars Per Bushel -----	Target Price	Placed Under Loan	% of Production	Acquired by CCC	Owned by CCC Aug. 31	CCC Inventory ----- As of Dec. 31 ----- CCC Owned	Under CCC Loan	Quantity Pledged (Thousands of Bushels)	Face Amount (Thousands of Dollars)
2004-05	1.95	2.63	1,366	11.6	25	0	12	----	40,814	87,053
2005-06	1.95	2.63	1,064	9.6	2	2	12	----	47,595	99,406
2006-07	1.95	2.63	1,108	10.5	0	0	1	----	31,873	65,968
2007-08	1.95	2.63	1,217	9.3	0	0	1	----	1,217,822	2,332,929
2008-09	1.95	2.63	1,074	8.9	0	0	30	----	1,078,175	2,025,300
2009-10	1.95	2.63	934	7.1	0	0	9	----	940,474	1,707,092
2010-11	1.95	2.63	801	6.4	0	0	0	----	38,062	76,121
2011-12	1.95	2.63	574	4.6	0	0	0	----		
2012-13[1]	1.95	2.63	368	3.4	0	0	0	----		
2013-14[2]	1.95	2.63	460	3.3	0	0	0	----		

[1] Preliminary.   [2] Estimate.   [3] Findley or announced loan rate.   NA = Not available.
Source: National Agricultural Statistics Service, U.S. Department of Agriculture (NASS-USDA)

U.S. Exports[1] of Corn (Including Seed), By Country of Destination   In Thousands of Metric Tons

Crop Year Beginning Oct. 1	Algeria	Canada	Egypt	Israel	Japan	Mexico	Korea, South	Russia	Saudi Arabia	Spain	Taiwan	Vene-zuela	Total
2005-06	1,255	1,901	4,156	725	16,361	6,755	5,866	15	619	8	4,519	133	56,038
2006-07	940	2,142	3,522	844	14,840	8,886	3,873	9	540	3	4,213	514	54,159
2007-08	898	3,051	2,971	1,207	15,043	9,526	8,380	7	985	10	3,792	1,085	60,593
2008-09	95	1,810	2,445	138	15,491	7,710	5,735		440	3	3,713	1,145	47,658
2009-10	64	1,935	2,961	330	14,616	8,243	6,795		706	3	3,012	1,121	49,642
2010-11		962	2,939	679	13,762	7,476	6,059		574	330	2,731	852	45,109
2011-12		718	298	29	11,703	9,878	3,189		361	1	1,500	1,398	38,282
2012-13		451		0	6,511	4,861	296		345	9	514	1,079	18,176
2013-14	76	604	2,874	469	12,379	10,895	5,312	1	1,030	693	1,751	1,058	50,571
2014-15[2]	239	1,442	1,127	27	11,911	11,149	3,655		1,184	66	1,840	806	46,699

[1] Excludes exports of corn by-products.   [2] Preliminary.   *Source: Foreign Agricultural Service, U.S. Department of Agriculture (FAS-USDA)*

Stocks of Corn (Shelled and Ear) in the United States   In Millions of Bushels

Year	On Farms Mar. 1	June 1	Sept. 1	Dec. 1	Off Farms Mar. 1	June 1	Sept. 1	Dec. 1	Total Stocks Mar. 1	June 1	Sept. 1	Dec. 1
2006	4,055.0	2,350.5	749.5	5,627.0	2,932.3	2,011.2	1,217.7	3,305.7	6,987.3	4,361.7	1,967.2	8,932.7
2007	3,330.0	1,826.6	460.1	6,530.0	2,738.3	1,706.8	843.5	3,748.1	6,068.3	3,533.4	1,303.6	10,278.1
2008	3,780.0	1,970.9	500.0	6,482.0	3,078.7	2,057.1	1,124.2	3,590.1	6,858.7	4,028.0	1,624.2	10,072.1
2009	4,085.0	2,205.4	607.5	7,405.0	2,869.1	2,056.0	1,065.8	3,497.5	6,954.1	4,261.4	1,673.3	10,902.5
2010	4,548.0	2,131.4	485.1	6,302.0	3,145.8	2,178.7	1,222.7	3,754.8	7,693.8	4,310.1	1,707.8	10,056.8
2011	3,384.0	1,681.5	315.0	6,175.0	3,139.2	1,988.3	812.7	3,472.5	6,523.2	3,669.8	1,127.6	9,647.5
2012	3,192.0	1,482.0	313.7	4,586.0	2,831.4	1,666.2	675.3	3,446.7	6,023.4	3,148.2	989.0	8,032.7
2013	2,669.2	1,260.1	275.0	6,380.0	2,730.7	1,506.1	546.2	4,072.5	5,399.9	2,766.2	821.2	10,452.5
2014	3,860.5	1,863.2	462.0	7,087.0	3,147.6	1,988.5	769.9	4,124.4	7,008.1	3,851.7	1,231.9	11,211.4
2015[1]	4,380.0	2,275.0	593.0	6,829.0	3,369.8	2,178.0	1,138.2	4,382.6	7,749.8	4,453.0	1,731.2	11,211.6

[1] Preliminary.   *Source: National Agricultural Statistics Service, U.S. Department of Agriculture (NASS-USDA)*

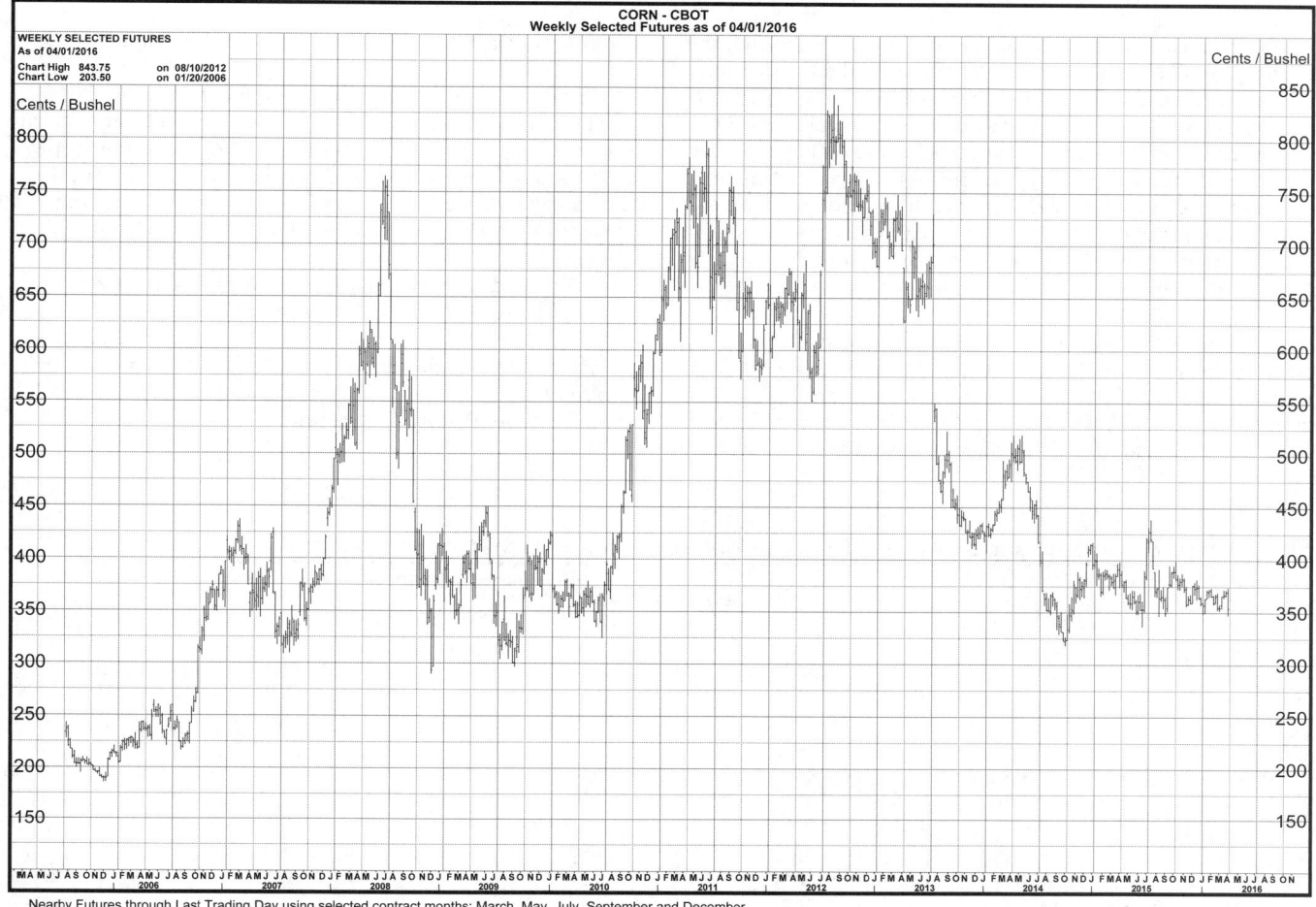

CORN - CBOT
Weekly Selected Futures as of 04/01/2016

WEEKLY SELECTED FUTURES
As of 04/01/2016

Chart High 843.75 on 08/10/2012
Chart Low 203.50 on 01/20/2006

Cents / Bushel

Nearby Futures through Last Trading Day using selected contract months: March, May, July, September and December.

Volume of Trading of Corn Futures in Chicago   In Thousands of Contracts

Year	Jan.	Feb.	Mar.	Apr.	May	June	July	Aug.	Sept.	Oct.	Nov.	Dec.	Total
2006	2,494.6	3,599.1	3,041.0	3,507.5	3,773.1	4,693.4	3,743.6	4,226.9	3,760.5	5,300.2	6,279.4	2,820.6	47,239.9
2007	5,166.5	5,111.6	4,959.0	6,095.4	4,519.9	6,090.9	4,035.7	4,344.1	3,128.9	3,306.5	4,615.6	3,145.9	54,520.2
2008	4,213.2	5,808.2	4,350.8	6,501.1	4,876.9	7,593.8	5,402.2	4,989.1	3,934.7	4,572.5	4,448.6	3,266.2	59,957.1
2009	3,041.3	4,487.1	3,684.9	4,567.6	4,151.8	5,636.8	4,765.8	4,441.8	3,153.8	4,374.0	5,509.1	3,134.9	50,948.8
2010	4,025.9	5,217.5	3,935.4	6,466.0	4,240.6	6,207.8	4,863.8	6,899.6	7,033.7	7,501.1	9,169.7	4,280.4	69,841.4
2011	5,981.0	7,473.1	7,552.4	8,715.1	5,676.9	8,639.5	5,119.3	6,834.9	5,385.7	5,568.2	8,003.4	4,055.2	79,004.8
2012	6,194.8	7,388.6	6,538.5	7,418.0	6,162.5	8,027.0	6,825.3	6,003.0	4,164.7	4,701.6	6,406.8	3,353.5	73,184.3
2013	5,151.4	6,347.6	4,929.5	7,089.9	4,937.7	5,823.6	4,824.9	6,128.2	3,436.3	4,919.5	7,695.2	3,039.0	64,322.6
2014	5,790.8	7,614.4	5,772.2	6,996.2	4,613.5	6,677.8	4,938.4	5,781.3	3,784.4	5,875.4	7,439.7	4,153.1	69,437.3
2015	5,468.9	6,810.9	6,111.2	7,860.2	5,957.5	10,795.4	8,553.2	7,835.9	4,880.3	5,708.6	8,736.5	4,375.5	83,094.3

Contract size = 5,000 bu.   Source: CME Group; Chicago Board of Trade (CBT)

Average Open Interest of Corn Futures in Chicago   In Thousands of Contracts

Year	Jan.	Feb.	Mar.	Apr.	May	June	July	Aug.	Sept.	Oct.	Nov.	Dec.
2006	875.3	1,048.8	1,066.0	1,176.0	1,288.2	1,327.8	1,360.2	1,347.2	1,302.1	1,312.6	1,405.7	1,381.5
2007	1,448.2	1,498.8	1,427.3	1,345.9	1,257.6	1,244.1	1,213.4	1,132.8	1,108.5	1,161.7	1,202.6	1,211.5
2008	1,383.2	1,463.1	1,421.8	1,445.3	1,409.2	1,396.1	1,279.9	1,170.4	1,050.9	995.5	967.6	820.5
2009	806.7	801.1	767.8	823.3	860.6	971.7	894.1	862.6	850.1	923.9	1,002.9	969.2
2010	1,105.4	1,149.6	1,124.2	1,169.6	1,196.2	1,204.5	1,161.3	1,324.5	1,405.8	1,509.8	1,629.6	1,511.5
2011	1,595.6	1,697.7	1,598.8	1,617.6	1,439.8	1,406.3	1,196.7	1,244.3	1,214.8	1,220.0	1,268.5	1,156.4
2012	1,209.5	1,289.9	1,312.4	1,330.4	1,212.9	1,125.0	1,138.0	1,211.6	1,175.6	1,247.8	1,282.1	1,168.4
2013	1,187.9	1,275.3	1,264.8	1,270.8	1,160.8	1,196.6	1,135.7	1,166.2	1,114.6	1,252.2	1,335.0	1,193.8
2014	1,284.5	1,343.4	1,318.8	1,396.1	1,338.9	1,370.7	1,332.4	1,316.6	1,254.5	1,289.5	1,298.1	1,216.6
2015	1,291.3	1,332.4	1,296.8	1,360.9	1,370.6	1,428.7	1,350.7	1,346.0	1,253.1	1,309.6	1,365.9	1,291.4

Contract size = 5,000 bu.   Source: CME Group; Chicago Board of Trade (CBT)

Corn Oil

Corn oil is a bland, odorless oil produced by refining the crude corn oil that is mechanically extracted from the germ of the plant seed. High-oil corn, the most common type of corn used to make corn oil, typically has an oil content of 7% or higher compared to about 4% for normal corn. Corn oil is widely used as cooking oil, for making margarine and mayonnaise, and for making inedible products such as soap, paints, inks, varnishes, and cosmetics. For humans, studies have shown that no vegetable oil is more effective than corn oil in lowering blood cholesterol levels.

Prices –The average Prices –The average monthly price of corn oil (wet mill price in Chicago) in the 2015-16 marketing year (Oct-Sep) fell into the range of 37.5-40.5 cents per pound, still well below the 2007-08 record high of 69.37 cents per pound. Seasonally, prices tend to be highest around March/April and lowest late in the calendar year.

Supply – U.S. corn oil production in the 2014-15 marketing year fell -1.1% yr/yr to 4.450 billion pounds, a new record high. Seasonally, production tends to peak around December and March and reaches a low in July. U.S. stocks in the 2014-15 marketing year (beginning Oct 1) remained unchanged at 165.0 million pounds.

Demand – U.S. usage (domestic disappearance) in 2014-15 rose +4.2% to 3.690 billion pounds.

Exports – U.S. corn oil exports in 2014-15 fell -20.0% to 800 billion pounds. U.S. corn oil imports in 2014-15 fell by -4.9% to 40.000 million pounds.

Supply and Disappearance of Corn Oil in the United States   In Millions of Pounds

	Supply			Baking and Frying Fats	Salad and Cooking Oil	Marg- arine	Total Edible Products	Domestic Disap- pearance	Exports	Total Disap- pearance
Year	Stocks Oct. 1	Pro- duction	Imports	Total Supply							
2005-06	156	2,483	45.0	2,683	W	1,407	W	1,607	1,685	799	2,483
2006-07	200	2,560	43.1	2,803	W	1,335	W	1,735	1,832	793	2,625
2007-08	179	2,507	45.2	2,731	W	1,722	W	1,606	1,756	769	2,525
2008-09	205	2,418	43.5	2,667	W	1,722	W	1,591	1,568	814	2,382
2009-10	286	2,485	37.0	2,808	W	1,930	W	1,589	1,895	774	2,669
2010-11	139	3,850	47.6	4,036	W	2,375	W	1,691	3,005	792	3,796
2011-12	240	4,225	45.8	4,511	NA	NA	NA	NA	3,342	1,003	4,346
2012-13	165	4,125	60.0	4,350	----	----	----	----	3,160	1,025	4,185
2013-14[1]	165	4,500	42.1	4,707	----	----	----	----	3,543	1,000	4,542
2014-15[2]	165	4,450	40.0	4,655	----	----	----	----	3,690	800	4,490

[1] Preliminary.   [2] Estimate.   W = Withheld.   *Source: Economic Research Service, U.S. Department of Agriculture (ERS-USDA)*

Production[2] of Crude Corn Oil in the United States   In Millions of Pounds

Year	Oct.	Nov.	Dec.	Jan.	Feb.	Mar.	Apr.	May	June	July	Aug.	Sept.	Total
2004-05	208.8	187.1	191.0	205.2	182.5	206.6	217.2	188.2	211.5	206.7	198.5	189.0	2,392
2005-06	207.5	199.9	200.3	209.2	184.8	217.6	191.7	218.7	206.7	215.3	222.0	209.0	2,483
2006-07	228.7	216.0	226.1	224.7	187.9	216.4	194.1	214.4	212.7	219.8	209.5	209.4	2,560
2007-08	213.5	213.0	214.0	205.4	193.7	222.5	190.7	220.9	193.7	214.9	217.3	207.3	2,507
2008-09	206.3	210.6	198.7	200.3	199.8	218.8	189.4	202.5	189.0	186.0	201.4	215.8	2,419
2009-10	212.9	205.2	203.2	197.9	188.1	212.4	214.7	205.4	214.7	216.8	213.6	200.1	2,485
2010-11[1]	205.1	211.2	198.9	220.9	199.4	218.1	203.1	215.0	216.3	205.7			2,512

[1] Preliminary.   [2] Not seasonally adjusted.   *Source: Bureau of the Census, U.S. Department of Commerce*

Average Corn Oil Price, Wet Mill in Chicago   In Cents Per Pound

Year	Oct.	Nov.	Dec.	Jan.	Feb.	Mar.	Apr.	May	June	July	Aug.	Sept.	Average
2006-07	24.70	26.47	28.05	28.05	28.66	29.08	29.93	31.56	34.71	37.25	39.61	43.61	31.81
2007-08	52.50	56.32	59.47	63.67	74.89	83.55	87.09	87.29	82.33	76.64	60.00	48.71	69.37
2008-09	34.76	31.06	26.88	25.19	29.05	29.64	31.31	37.23	39.57	36.30	35.23	36.83	32.75
2009-10	37.59	38.12	40.02	40.34	37.54	38.37	38.50	38.50	38.93	39.29	41.48	42.85	39.29
2010-11	47.50	51.96	54.71	57.91	63.39	67.72	68.89	68.33	66.70	62.00	62.00	57.95	60.76
2011-12	54.24	53.98	53.36	54.00	56.30	59.31	60.75	58.05	52.90	54.76	57.26	58.21	56.09
2012-13	54.75	51.93	50.63	52.06	51.71	47.76	47.06	45.23	42.50	38.91	38.93	38.46	46.66
2013-14	37.85	38.79	38.31	38.79	41.07	43.19	41.94	41.02	40.01	39.02	38.00	35.17	39.43
2014-15	34.50	33.96	33.68	34.86	36.13	37.73	39.27	39.50	40.34	41.49	40.75	37.55	37.48
2015-16[1]	36.60	36.43	38.25	39.93	40.29								38.30

[1] Preliminary.   *Source: Economic Research Service, U.S. Department of Agriculture (ERS-USDA)*

Cotton

Cotton is a natural vegetable fiber that comes from small trees and shrubs of a genus belonging to the mallow family, one of which is the common American Upland cotton plant. Cotton has been used in India for at least the last 5,000 years and probably much longer, and was also used by the ancient Chinese, Egyptians, and North and South Americans. Cotton was one of the earliest crops grown by European settlers in the U.S.

Cotton requires a long growing season, plenty of sunshine and water during the growing season, and then dry weather for harvesting. In the United States, the Cotton Belt stretches from northern Florida to North Carolina and westward to California. In the U.S., planting time varies from the beginning of February in Southern Texas to the beginning of June in the northern sections of the Cotton Belt. The flower bud of the plant blossoms and develops into an oval boll that splits open at maturity. At maturity, cotton is most vulnerable to damage from wind and rain. Approximately 95% of the cotton in the U.S. is now harvested mechanically with spindle-type pickers or strippers and then sent off to cotton gins for processing. There it is dried, cleaned, separated, and packed into bales.

Cotton is used in a wide range of products from clothing to home furnishings to medical products. The value of cotton is determined according to the staple, grade, and character of each bale. Staple refers to short, medium, long, or extra-long fiber length, with medium staple accounting for about 70% of all U.S. cotton. Grade refers to the color, brightness, and amount of foreign matter and is established by the U.S. Department of Agriculture. Character refers to the fiber's diameter, strength, body, maturity (ratio of mature to immature fibers), uniformity, and smoothness. Cotton is the fifth leading cash crop in the U.S. and is one of the nation's principal agricultural exports. The weight of cotton is typically measured in terms of a "bale," which is deemed to equal 480 pounds.

Cotton futures and options are traded on ICE Futures U.S. Cotton futures are also traded on the CME Group, Moscow Exchange, Multi Commodity Exchange of India (MCX), National Commodity & Derivatives Exchange (NCDEX), Turkish Derivatives Exchange, and the Zhengzhou Commodity Exchange. The ICE futures contract calls for the delivery of 50,000 pounds net weight (approximately 100 bales) of No. 2 cotton with a quality rating of Strict Low Middling and a staple length of 1-and-2/32 inch. Delivery points include Texas (Galveston and Houston), New Orleans, Memphis, and Greenville/Spartanburg in South Carolina.

Prices – ICE cotton futures prices (Barchart.com symbol CT) began 2015 on a weak note and tumbled to a 5-1/4 year low in January at 57.05 cents a pound. Global economic concerns and weak Chinese demand conspired to push cotton prices lower as the IMF joined the World Bank in lowering their 2015 global GDP forecasts, and Chinese cotton demand slumped as China's 2014 cotton imports plunged -41% y/y to 2.4 MMT. Cotton prices recovered slightly and moved sideways into Q3-2015 when they pushed upward in August and posted a 1-year high at 68.30 cents a pound. Cotton prices found support in the August WASDE report when the USDA cut its 2015/16 global cotton production estimate to a 6-year low of 108.99 million bales. Prices then moved sideways with an upward bias into year-end as weak Chinese demand was offset by shrinking supplies. The USDA projected that China 2015/16 cotton imports would fall -31% y/y to 1.25 MMT, the lowest since China joined the WTO in 2001, and that U.S. 2015/16 cotton exports would drop 11% to a 15-year low of 10 million bales. However, prices moved higher after the USDA in the December WASDE report cut its 2015/16 global cotton production forecast to a 6-year low of 103.71 million bales. Cotton prices finished 2015 up +5% at 63.28 cents a pound.

Supply – World cotton production in 2014-15 fell -1.1% yr/yr to 118.978 million bales (480 pounds per bale), below 2011-12 record high of 127.280 million bales. The world's largest cotton producers were China with 25.2% of world production in 2014-15, India with 26.1%, the U.S. with 13.4%, and Pakistan with 8.2%. World beginning stocks in 2013-14 (latest data) rose +21.6% yr/yr to 89.157 million bales, a new record high.

The U.S. cotton crop in 2014-15 rose +24.6% yr/yr to 16.084 million bales, which was well below the 2005-06 record high of 23.890 million bales. U.S. farmers harvested 9.707 million acres of cotton in 2014-15, up +28.7% yr/yr. The U.S. cotton yield in 2014-15 fell -3.2% to 795 pounds per acre, not far behind the 2007-08 record high of 879 pounds per acre. The leading U.S. producing states of Upland cotton are Texas with 37.4% of U.S. production in 2014, Georgia (15.5%), Mississippi (6.4%), Arkansas (5.1%), California (4.7%), Alabama (4.1%), and Missouri (3.5%). U.S. production of cotton cloth has fallen sharply by almost half in the past decade due to the movement of the textile industry out of the U.S. to low-wage foreign countries.

Demand – World consumption of cotton in 2014-15 rose +3.7% yr/yr to 112.500 million bales, but still below the 2006-07 record high of 121.986. Consumption of cotton continues to move toward countries with low wages, where the raw cotton is utilized to produce textiles and other cotton products. The largest consumers of cotton in 2014-15 were China (32.9% of world total), India (21.3%), and Pakistan (9.4%). U.S. consumption of cotton by mills in 2014-15 rose +7.0% yr/yr to 3.800 million bales, and accounted for 27.5% of U.S. production. The remaining 72.5% of U.S. cotton production went for exports.

Trade – World exports of cotton in 2014-15 fell -15.9% yr/yr to 34.288 million bales, which was below the 2005-06 record high of 44.854 million bales. The U.S. is the world's largest cotton exporter by far and accounts for 29.2% of world cotton exports. Key world cotton importers include China with 20.4% of total world imports in 2014-15, Bangladesh with 13.0%, Turkey and Vietnam each with 10.5%, and Indonesia with 9.1%. U.S. cotton exports in 2013-14 (latest data) rose by +21.9% yr/yr to 10.412 million bales. The main destinations for U.S. exports in 2013-14 were China (25.4%), Mexico (9.7%), Indonesia (6.7%), South Korea and Thailand each with (4.4%).

COTTON

Supply and Distribution of All Cotton in the United States — In Thousands of 480-Pound Bales

Crop Year Beginning Aug. 1	Acre Planted 1,000 Acres	Acre Harvested 1,000 Acres	Yield Lbs./Acre	Supply Beginning Stocks[3]	Supply Pro-duction[4]	Supply Imports	Supply Total	Mill Use	Exports	Total	Unac-counted	Ending Stocks	Farm Price[5]	"A" Index Price[6]	Value of Pro-duction Million USD
2006-07	15,274	12,732	814	6,069	21,588	19	27,676	4,935	12,959	17,894	-303	9,479	48.4	59.22	5,013.2
2007-08	10,827	10,489	879	9,479	19,207	12	28,698	4,584	13,634	18,218	-429	10,051	61.3	73.02	5,652.9
2008-09	9,471	7,569	813	10,051	12,815	0	22,876	3,541	13,261	16,802	263	6,337	49.1	61.10	3,021.5
2009-10	9,150	7,529	776	6,337	12,188	0	18,520	3,550	12,037	15,587	14	2,947	64.8	78.13	3,788.0
2010-11	10,974	10,699	812	2,947	18,104	9	21,058	3,900	14,376	18,276	-182	2,600	84.6	164.29	7,348.1
2011-12	14,735	9,461	790	2,600	15,573	19	18,192	3,300	11,714	15,014	172	3,350	93.5		6,986.0
2012-13	12,264	9,322	892	3,350	17,314	10	20,674	3,500	13,026	16,526	-348	3,800	75.7		6,291.8
2013-14	10,407	7,544	821	3,800	12,909	13	16,722	3,550	10,530	14,080	-192	2,450	82.5		5,191.5
2014-15[1]	11,037	9,347	838	2,350	16,319	12	18,681	3,550	11,200	13,800	43	5,100	59-67		5,147.2
2015-16[2]	8,581	8,077	769	3,700	12,943	10	16,792	3,700	10,000						3,862.4

[1] Preliminary. [2] Estimate. [3] Excludes preseason ginnings (adjusted to 480-lb. bale net weight basis). [4] Includes preseason ginnings. [5] Marketing year average price. [6] Average of 5 cheapest types of SLM 1 3/32" staple length cotton offered on the European market.
Source: Economic Research Service, U.S. Department of Agriculture (ERS-USDA)

World Production of All Cotton — In Thousands of 480-Pound Bales

Crop Year Beginning Aug. 1	Australia	Brazil	Burkina	China	Greece	India	Mexico	Pakistan	Turkey	Turkmen-istan	United States	Uzbek-istan	World Total
2006-07	1,350	7,000	1,300	35,500	1,550	22,500	650	9,580	3,800	1,400	21,588	5,350	123,013
2007-08	625	7,360	675	37,000	1,550	24,700	620	8,550	3,100	1,350	19,207	5,350	120,577
2008-09	1,525	5,480	850	36,700	1,150	23,300	567	8,540	1,930	1,550	12,825	4,600	108,300
2009-10	1,775	5,450	695	32,000	940	24,500	475	9,240	1,750	1,470	12,183	3,900	103,359
2010-11	4,200	9,000	645	30,500	940	27,200	732	8,640	2,110	1,750	18,102	4,200	117,630
2011-12	5,500	8,700	795	34,000	1,330	29,000	1,180	10,600	3,440	1,525	15,573	4,000	127,420
2012-13	4,600	6,000	1,215	35,000	1,194	28,500	1,036	9,300	2,650	1,700	17,314	4,600	123,875
2013-14	4,100	8,000	1,250	32,750	1,369	31,000	933	9,500	2,300	1,550	12,909	4,100	120,406
2014-15[1]	2,300	7,000	1,350	30,000	1,286	29,500	1,366	10,600	3,200	1,525	16,319	3,900	119,151
2015-16[2]	2,400	6,700	1,200	23,800	950	27,800	950	7,200	2,650	1,300	12,943	3,700	101,384

[1] Preliminary. [2] Estimate. *Source: Foreign Agricultural Service, U.S. Department of Agriculture (FAS-USDA)*

World Consumption of Cotton — In Thousands of 480-Pound Bales

Crop Year Beginning Aug. 1	Bangla-desh	Brazil	China	India	Indonesia	Mexico	Pakistan	Thailand	Turkey	United States	Uzbek-istan	Vietnam	World Total
2006-07	3,210	4,423	48,000	18,100	2,425	2,125	12,025	1,975	7,300	5,238	900	975	122,548
2007-08	3,510	4,450	48,500	18,600	2,650	2,025	12,025	1,975	6,100	5,013	1,000	1,200	121,688
2008-09	3,710	4,050	42,750	17,750	2,400	1,875	11,125	1,625	4,950	3,278	1,000	1,250	108,843
2009-10	4,010	4,250	50,000	19,750	2,650	1,925	10,425	1,800	5,900	3,536	1,100	1,600	119,526
2010-11	4,210	4,150	46,000	20,550	2,650	1,725	9,925	1,725	5,600	4,082	1,250	1,625	115,518
2011-12	3,710	3,850	38,000	19,450	2,450	1,725	10,025	1,325	5,600	3,128	1,350	1,675	103,734
2012-13	4,710	3,950	36,000	20,750	3,050	1,825	10,775	1,525	6,050	3,848	1,450	2,250	107,584
2013-14	5,310	4,050	34,500	22,750	3,050	1,875	10,425	1,550	6,300	3,842	1,500	3,200	109,541
2014-15[1]	5,510	3,350	33,000	24,500	3,250	1,875	10,625	1,500	6,400	3,735	1,550	4,100	110,393
2015-16[2]	5,860	3,050	32,000	24,500	3,150	1,925	9,825	1,475	6,400	3,553	1,575	5,100	109,447

[1] Preliminary. [2] Estimate. *Source: Foreign Agricultural Service, U.S. Department of Agriculture (FAS-USDA)*

World Ending Stocks of Cotton — In Thousands of 480-Pound Bales

Crop Year Beginning Aug. 1	Argen-tina	Australia	Bangla-desh	Brazil	China	India	Mexico	Pakistan	Turkey	Turkmen-istan	United States	Uzbek-istan	World Total
2006-07	743	1,269	591	5,408	20,536	7,829	1,027	4,240	1,851	799	9,479	1,198	63,309
2007-08	779	725	716	6,251	20,504	7,029	932	4,403	1,748	959	10,051	1,348	62,768
2008-09	641	1,104	848	4,992	21,366	11,019	764	3,378	1,511	1,434	6,337	1,948	62,720
2009-10	878	852	888	4,353	14,246	9,699	617	3,042	1,605	1,329	2,947	948	47,782
2010-11	1,156	2,762	992	7,906	10,603	11,549	595	2,520	1,319	1,804	2,600	1,248	51,336
2011-12	1,021	3,807	768	7,993	31,081	10,619	710	2,835	1,241	2,029	3,350	1,398	74,416
2012-13	839	2,399	1,166	5,801	50,361	11,795	646	2,710	1,315	2,279	3,800	1,348	91,741
2013-14	1,222	1,807	1,271	7,668	62,707	11,459	584	2,475	1,357	1,529	2,350	1,248	103,072
2014-15[1]	1,297	1,779	1,281	7,432	67,920	13,486	740	2,835	1,596	854	3,700	1,148	112,166
2015-16[2]	1,292	1,494	1,296	6,932	64,520	11,986	590	2,260	1,396	429	3,600	973	104,080

[1] Preliminary. [2] Estimate. *Source: Foreign Agricultural Service, U.S. Department of Agriculture (FAS-USDA)*

World Exports of Cotton   In Thousands of 480-Pound Bales

Crop Year Beginning Aug. 1	Australia	Benin	Brazil	Burkina	Cote d'Ivoire	Greece	India	Malaysia	Mali	Turkmenistan	United States	Uzbekistan	World Total
2006-07	2,129	475	1,300	1,350	385	1,250	4,875	----	850	800	12,959	4,500	37,401
2007-08	1,219	500	2,231	775	275	1,299	7,500	2	500	750	13,634	4,200	38,893
2008-09	1,201	375	2,739	800	175	800	2,360	10	325	650	13,261	3,000	30,102
2009-10	2,112	400	1,990	775	325	875	6,550	43	440	1,150	12,037	3,800	35,689
2010-11	2,500	300	2,000	675	250	750	5,000	80	450	725	14,376	2,650	34,821
2011-12	4,640	275	4,792	650	425	1,100	11,080	1,023	625	700	11,714	2,500	46,064
2012-13	6,168	400	4,307	1,200	575	1,100	7,761	739	900	800	13,026	3,200	46,530
2013-14	4,852	525	2,230	1,250	725	1,285	9,261	150	800	1,625	10,530	2,700	40,813
2014-15[1]	2,393	675	3,910	1,125	850	1,168	4,199	81	750	1,500	11,246	2,450	35,376
2015-16[2]	2,750	700	4,200	1,300	800	900	5,700	50	1,200	1,000	9,500	2,300	35,107

[1] Preliminary.   [2] Estimate.   *Source: Foreign Agricultural Service, U.S. Department of Agriculture (FAS-USDA)*

World Imports of Cotton   In Thousands of 480-Pound Bales

Crop Year Beginning Aug. 1	Bangladesh	China	India	Indonesia	Korea, South	Malaysia	Mexico	Pakistan	Taiwan	Thailand	Turkey	Vietnam	World Total
2006-07	3,250	10,588	465	2,400	1,068	153	1,353	2,305	1,160	1,905	4,029	978	38,305
2007-08	3,600	11,530	600	2,700	975	198	1,530	3,907	964	1,928	3,267	1,208	39,463
2008-09	3,800	6,996	800	2,400	988	222	1,315	1,917	787	1,602	2,919	1,251	30,597
2009-10	4,000	10,903	480	2,700	1,010	271	1,393	1,574	1,016	1,806	4,394	1,695	36,918
2010-11	4,250	11,979	200	2,500	1,038	290	1,196	1,443	803	1,752	3,350	1,569	36,263
2011-12	3,400	24,533	600	2,500	1,170	1,125	1,000	900	863	1,263	2,382	1,625	45,458
2012-13	5,000	20,327	1,187	3,137	1,314	800	950	1,800	941	1,511	3,692	2,410	47,564
2013-14	5,300	14,122	675	2,989	1,286	400	1,040	1,200	857	1,546	4,246	3,200	41,279
2014-15[1]	5,400	8,284	1,226	3,345	1,321	365	830	835	873	1,475	3,675	4,300	35,712
2015-16[2]	5,750	5,000	900	3,100	1,300	250	975	2,300	875	1,475	3,800	5,200	35,084

[1] Preliminary.   [2] Estimate.   *Source: Foreign Agricultural Service, U.S. Department of Agriculture (FAS-USDA)*

Average Spot Cotton, 1-3/32", Price (SLM) at Designated U.S. Markets[2]   In Cents Per Pound (Net Weight)

Year	Aug.	Sept.	Oct.	Nov.	Dec.	Jan.	Feb.	Mar.	Apr.	May	June	July	Average
2006-07	53.80	51.95	50.20	51.13	54.71	54.75	53.66	54.05	51.59	49.12	54.71	61.59	53.44
2007-08	57.53	61.15	63.08	63.71	63.50	67.22	69.73	72.68	67.25	63.99	66.67	66.17	65.22
2008-09	64.25	60.01	50.52	43.76	45.95	48.76	45.67	42.40	49.02	56.81	54.70	57.94	51.65
2009-10	57.77	59.82	64.58	69.23	72.59	70.45	72.47	79.02	79.81	78.99	79.37	80.30	72.03
2010-11	87.38	95.48	112.06	130.62	139.68	148.24	181.61	199.76	185.94	155.89	148.73	117.00	141.87
2011-12	106.41	105.50	100.97	97.13	89.53	94.10	89.52	87.76	88.07	77.26	72.12	70.91	89.94
2012-13	74.76	74.19	72.87	72.06	75.42	77.99	81.37	87.28	85.39	84.29	86.63	86.07	79.86
2013-14	87.80	85.65	83.66	78.84	83.15	85.69	87.45	90.94	89.71	87.41	82.74	73.89	84.74
2014-15	68.94	68.70	67.32	63.40	63.13	62.12	66.02	64.89	67.33	67.30	67.09	66.60	66.07
2015-16[1]	66.09	63.93	65.06	65.17	66.47	64.76	62.05						64.79

[1] Preliminary.   *Source: Agricultural Marketing Service, U.S. Department of Agriculture (AMS-USDA)*

Average Producer Price Index of Gray Cotton Broadwovens   Index 1982 = 100

Year	Jan.	Feb.	Mar.	Apr.	May	June	July	Aug.	Sept.	Oct.	Nov.	Dec.	Average
2006	111.1	110.5	109.9	109.9	110.1	110.1	110.1	110.1	110.1	110.0	110.0	109.9	110.2
2007	110.0	109.9	109.9	110.1	109.8	109.9	109.9	109.9	109.9	110.0	109.9	109.9	109.9
2008	110.1	110.1	110.1	110.1	110.0	109.9	110.2	111.7	111.7	111.7	111.6	111.4	110.7
2009	111.0	111.0	111.0	107.2	107.2	107.2	107.2	107.5	107.5	107.5	108.9	108.9	108.5
2010	109.8	113.7	113.7	113.7	114.9	116.6	119.0	118.8	118.8	118.8	119.1	119.1	116.3
2011	144.8	145.4	147.0	153.5	154.3	154.3	162.1	162.0	161.3	148.5	148.5	141.1	151.9
2012	139.1	139.2	139.2	135.0	135.0	135.2	126.1	126.1	126.1	124.7	123.6	122.7	131.0
2013	122.6	122.3	123.3	126.9	126.4	126.4	126.4	126.4	126.4	127.7	127.7	127.7	125.9
2014	124.5	124.5	121.8	124.7	124.7	124.7	124.8	124.8	124.8	123.3	123.3	123.3	124.1
2015[1]	118.2	121.2	121.2	121.5	121.5	121.5	123.7	123.7	123.7	123.5		123.5	122.1

[1] Preliminary.   *Source: Bureau of Labor Statistics (0337-01), U.S. Department of Commerce*

COTTON

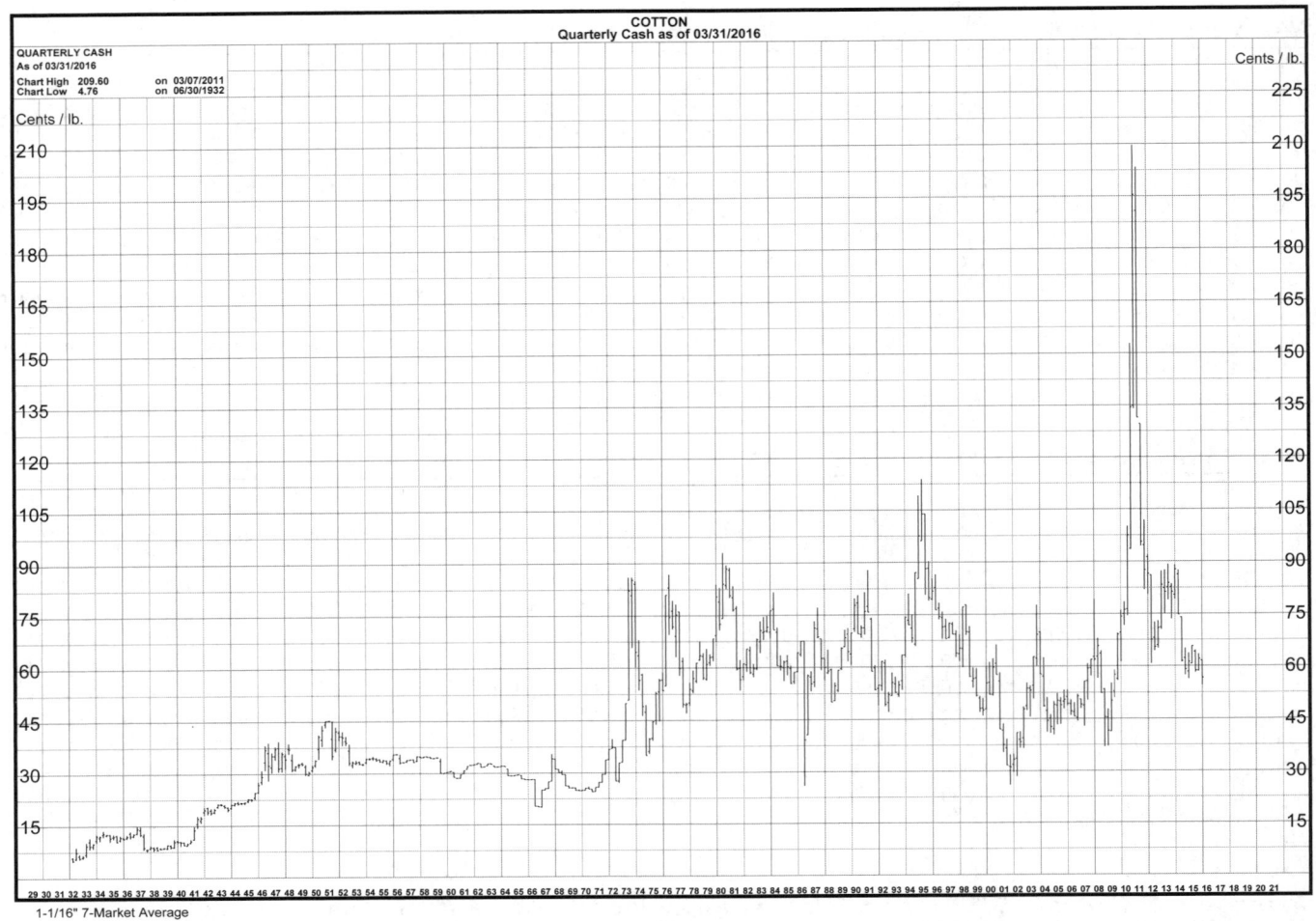

Average Price of SLM 1-1/16", Cotton/5 at Designated U.S. Markets — In Cents Per Pound (Net Weight)

Year	Aug.	Sept.	Oct.	Nov.	Dec.	Jan.	Feb.	Mar.	Apr.	May	June	July	Average
2006-07	48.65	46.80	45.15	46.32	49.85	49.90	48.77	49.21	46.97	44.62	50.35	57.50	48.67
2007-08	53.46	57.08	59.06	59.59	59.44	63.34	65.92	69.27	63.91	60.67	63.34	62.85	61.49
2008-09	60.93	56.72	46.90	39.83	42.07	44.87	41.81	38.53	45.11	52.92	50.80	53.98	47.87
2009-10	53.77	55.78	60.44	64.90	68.11	65.93	68.08	74.54	75.46	74.70	75.19	76.16	67.76
2010-11	81.16	91.53	108.26	126.62	135.46	144.79	177.65	195.79	181.98	151.93	144.77	113.03	137.75
2011-12	102.89	102.06	97.63	93.59	85.99	89.83	85.17	83.14	83.37	72.51	67.35	66.14	85.81
2012-13	69.97	69.38	68.03	67.34	70.61	73.33	76.87	82.80	80.94	79.84	82.18	81.62	75.24
2013-14	83.36	81.25	77.37	74.43	78.75	81.43	83.21	86.70	85.48	83.20	78.54	69.63	80.28
2014-15	64.99	64.83	63.51	59.64	59.38	58.19	61.74	60.65	63.08	63.06	62.86	62.36	62.02
2015-16[1]	61.85	59.70	60.83	60.99	62.32	60.69	58.06						60.63

[1] Preliminary.   [2] Grade 41, leaf 4, staple 34, mike 35-36 and 43-49 , strength 23.5-26.4.   *Source: Agricultural Marketing Service, U.S. Department of Agriculture (AMS-USDA)*

Average Price[1] Received by Farmers for Upland Cotton in the United States — In Cents Per Pound

Year	Aug.	Sept.	Oct.	Nov.	Dec.	Jan.	Feb.	Mar.	Apr.	May	June	July	Average
2006-07	45.8	47.3	45.9	47.4	49.0	49.4	47.4	46.4	46.3	44.0	45.4	45.2	46.6
2007-08	44.9	52.0	55.5	57.4	59.6	61.5	63.0	63.0	65.5	64.6	64.0	66.2	59.8
2008-09	58.5	61.1	58.8	54.8	53.3	46.0	41.2	40.4	44.7	44.9	45.0	43.6	49.4
2009-10	47.7	55.0	58.5	59.5	63.4	60.8	65.0	65.0	66.7	66.6	68.5	68.5	62.1
2010-11	77.2	74.7	77.3	81.5	81.2	82.1	92.9	84.4	86.7	83.2	83.3	82.5	82.3
2011-12	94.0	93.5	92.2	92.6	88.9	90.1	92.3	90.0	90.4	84.4	77.1	76.6	88.5
2012-13	71.4	70.7	69.8	69.2	71.8	72.9	76.9	77.5	78.4	78.3	79.3	80.9	74.8
2013-14	76.9	74.6	77.8	75.9	77.2	77.5	80.2	81.7	82.7	81.7	83.9	84.7	79.6
2014-15	70.5	68.9	64.5	62.7	60.8	59.1	57.4	59.9	62.4	64.1	65.1	66.1	63.5
2015-16[2]	58.0	60.3	57.8	59.1	59.9	58.0							58.9

[1] Weighted average by sales.   [2] Preliminary.   *Source: Agricultural Marketing Service, U.S. Department of Agriculture (AMS-USDA)*

Purchases Reported by Exchanges in Designated U.S. Spot Markets[1]   In Running Bales

Crop Year Beginning Aug. 1	Aug.	Sept.	Oct.	Nov.	Dec.	Jan.	Feb.	Mar.	Apr.	May	June	July	Market Total
2006-07	87,527	58,849	111,619	112,634	214,384	174,852	140,273	125,562	207,478	310,748	168,730	137,204	1,849,860
2007-08	85,183	133,709	126,008	149,748	197,651	359,180	303,523	95,053	104,513	64,281	119,022	46,555	1,784,426
2008-09	79,487	75,191	89,246	92,960	113,117	149,362	106,701	175,099	265,718	92,969	66,390	77,746	1,383,986
2009-10	34,279	54,457	57,362	179,007	199,006	75,580	175,053	69,900	34,523	9,790	13,412	1,732	904,101
2010-11	1,431	5,498	69,122	126,009	153,780	130,932	59,520	27,102	10,609	27,288	33,804	7,581	652,676
2011-12	9,762	31,213	95,360	122,388	131,642	227,089	115,427	119,698	25,990	20,764	20,687	36,712	956,732
2012-13	38,533	55,227	81,437	408,050	417,927	382,992	112,442	62,556	65,991	27,923	25,573	12,135	1,690,786
2013-14	20,398	26,066	52,042	198,579	433,317	345,007	141,663	57,669	24,792	24,878	7,569	6,815	1,338,795
2014-15	21,486	35,934	141,203	200,756	593,113	425,345	404,710	121,097	117,746	26,509	19,259	20,128	2,127,286
2015-16	18,634	24,429	56,127	220,807	424,830	297,380	196,419						2,117,213

[1] Seven markets.   Source: Agricultural Marketing Service, U.S. Department of Agriculture (AMS-USDA)

Production of Cotton (Upland and American-Pima) in the United States   In Thousands of 480-Pound Bales

	--- Upland ---												Total American-Pima
Year	Alabama	Arizona	Arkansas	California	Georgia	Louisiana	Mississippi	Missouri	North Carolina	South Carolina	Tennessee	Texas	
2006	675	556	2,525	779	2,334	1,241	2,107	985	1,285	433	1,368	5,800	765.4
2007	416	514	1,896	650	1,660	699	1,318	764	783	160	600	8,250	851.8
2008	469	405	1,296	367	1,600	281	683	698	755	246	530	4,450	430.8
2009	345	443	852	240	1,860	349	415	502	763	207	492	4,620	399.9
2010	480	610	1,176	380	2,250	437	848	685	951	376	681	7,840	504.1
2011	685	800	1,277	556	2,465	511	1,200	741	1,026	519	813	3,500	851.2
2012	745	605	1,297	508	2,910	478	993	731	1,225	593	743	5,000	779.8
2013	590	480	720	333	2,320	326	719	496	766	360	414	4,170	633.9
2014[1]	653	490	787	214	2,570	404	1,078	570	995	528	494	6,175	566.4
2015[2]	550	285	475	165	2,300	190	670	405	522	150	302	5,750	435.0

[1] Preliminary.   [2] Forecast.   Source: Agricultural Statistics Board, U.S. Department of Agriculture (ASB-USDA)

Cotton Production and Yield Estimates in the United States

	--------- Forecasts of Production (1,000 Bales of 480 Lbs.[1]) ---------						Actual	---- Forecasts of Yield (Lbs. Per Harvested Acre) ----						Actual
Year	Aug.1	Sept.1	Oct. 1	Nov. 1	Dec. 1	Jan. 1	Crop	Aug.1	Sept.1	Oct. 1	Nov. 1	Dec. 1	Jan. 1	Yield
2006	20,431	20,345	20,659	21,299	21,297	----	21,588	765	762	774	798	798	----	814
2007	17,346	17,812	18,154	18,862	18,987	----	19,207	783	811	826	859	864	----	879
2008	13,767	13,846	13,711	13,528	13,613	----	12,815	842	849	849	837	843	----	813
2009	13,207	13,438	12,998	12,496	12,592	----	12,188	816	816	807	776	782	----	776
2010	18,534	18,841	18,873	18,418	18,268	----	18,104	837	839	841	821	814	----	812
2011	16,554	16,556	16,608	16,300	15,827	----	15,573	822	807	809	794	771	----	790
2012	17,651	17,109	17,287	17,447	17,257	----	17,314	784	786	795	802	793	----	892
2013	13,053	12,899	NA	13,105	13,069	----	12,909	813	796	NA	808	806	----	821
2014	17,502	16,538	16,255	16,397	15,923	----	16,319	820	803	790	797	773	----	838
2015	13,082	13,428	13,338	13,281	13,031	----	12,943	795	789	784	782	768	----	769

[1] Net weight bales.   Source: Agricultural Statistics Board, U.S. Department of Agriculture (ASB-USDA)

Supply and Distribution of Upland Cotton in the United States   In Thousands of 480-Pound Bales

Crop Year Beginning Aug. 1	-------------- Area --------------			-------------------- Supply --------------------				-------------- Disappearance --------------				Farm Price[5] Cents/ Lb.
	Planted	Harvested	Yield	Beginning Stocks[3]	Pro-duction	Imports	Total Supply	Mill Use	Exports	Total	Ending Stocks	
	----- 1,000 Acres -----		Lbs./Acre									
2006-07	14,948	12,408	806	5,991	20,823	10	26,824	4,896	12,324	17,220	9,291	46.6
2007-08	10,535	10,201	864	9,291	18,355	6	27,652	4,548	12,801	17,349	9,895	59.8
2008-09	9,297	7,400	803	9,895	12,395		22,289	3,512	13,029	16,541	6,032	49.4
2009-10	9,008	7,391	766	6,032	11,783		17,815	3,529	11,343	14,872	2,929	62.1
2010-11	10,770	10,497	805	2,929	17,598	2	20,529	3,874	13,881	17,755	2,572	82.3
2011-12	14,428	9,156	772	2,572	14,722	13	17,307	3,278	11,120	14,398	3,081	88.5
2012-13	12,026	9,085	874	3,081	16,534	6	19,621	3,478	12,182	15,660	3,613	74.8
2013-14	10,206	7,345	802	3,613	12,275	6	15,894	3,527	9,850	13,377	2,325	79.6
2014-15[1]	10,845	9,157	826	2,325	15,753	5	18,149	3,775	9,450	13,225	4,967	63.5
2015-16[2]	8,398	7,995	770		12,830							

[1] Preliminary.   [2] Estimate.   [3] Excludes preseason ginnings (adjusted to 480-lb. bale net weight basis).   [4] Includes preseason ginnings.
[5] Marketing year average price.   Source: Economic Research Service, U.S. Department of Agriculture (ERS-USDA)

COTTON

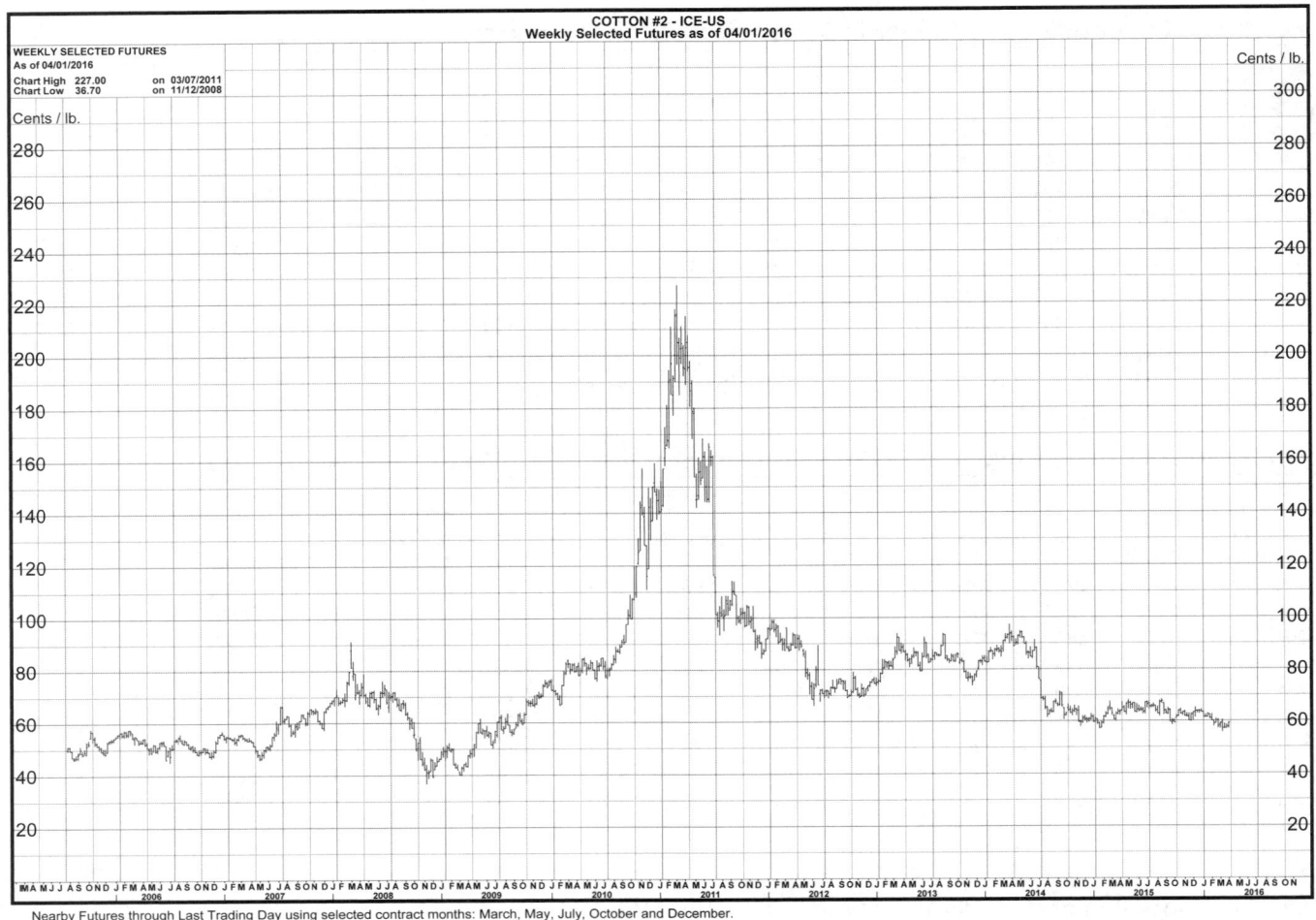

COTTON #2 - ICE-US
Weekly Selected Futures as of 04/01/2016

WEEKLY SELECTED FUTURES
As of 04/01/2016

Chart High 227.00 on 03/07/2011
Chart Low   36.70   on 11/12/2008

Nearby Futures through Last Trading Day using selected contract months: March, May, July, October and December.

Volume of Trading of Cotton #2 Futures in New York   In Contracts

Year	Jan.	Feb.	Mar.	Apr.	May	June	July	Aug.	Sept.	Oct.	Nov.	Dec.	Total
2006	311,926	495,729	375,624	515,709	330,785	601,971	184,482	259,259	268,847	308,584	587,710	249,781	4,490,407
2007	366,579	713,894	375,964	765,244	439,838	745,901	428,059	445,099	435,529	520,221	759,829	338,822	6,334,979
2008	684,489	971,319	730,160	651,281	427,731	690,183	281,522	306,004	418,279	401,064	426,785	174,146	6,162,963
2009	276,977	326,853	272,091	373,379	274,983	372,124	187,347	177,989	228,815	347,989	509,375	227,073	3,574,995
2010	321,331	570,117	344,389	567,774	365,998	550,206	327,296	331,579	440,411	600,977	887,594	425,234	5,732,906
2011	457,454	719,075	590,294	602,903	325,606	536,555	293,608	290,265	307,617	350,452	598,711	215,914	5,288,454
2012	471,729	605,161	499,276	660,539	564,011	826,818	308,028	339,672	349,649	584,358	632,610	288,501	6,130,352
2013	599,171	738,954	474,475	725,015	494,848	729,167	282,565	464,074	273,354	487,233	588,624	297,544	6,155,024
2014	544,180	602,542	446,810	568,063	399,736	611,785	362,461	338,548	460,119	477,742	625,593	350,304	5,787,883
2015	474,061	764,365	532,511	774,667	504,552	748,679	391,137	541,234	378,522	492,136	718,549	405,429	6,725,842

Contract size = 50,000 lbs.   *Source: ICE Futures U.S. (ICE)*

Average Open Interest of Cotton #2 Futures in New York   In Contracts

Year	Jan.	Feb.	Mar.	Apr.	May	June	July	Aug.	Sept.	Oct.	Nov.	Dec.
2006	118,234	129,108	129,728	141,156	165,386	170,190	161,719	166,806	178,539	184,002	170,275	164,797
2007	177,495	199,342	214,628	225,473	223,839	212,296	214,893	206,042	215,820	239,217	229,629	219,185
2008	264,235	279,240	286,505	259,800	258,309	239,935	219,979	216,387	211,933	177,277	146,431	127,380
2009	130,049	120,331	128,054	128,973	134,079	120,861	122,153	127,019	136,585	165,683	180,594	182,489
2010	178,305	166,475	185,608	190,458	184,193	171,459	160,118	201,962	231,513	235,834	217,587	201,510
2011	204,871	198,798	176,675	180,626	150,430	148,695	138,168	144,300	150,834	155,592	149,292	146,219
2012	156,940	180,632	183,618	186,859	188,255	185,629	171,383	180,207	183,282	199,026	179,969	165,382
2013	185,106	201,378	205,753	188,311	181,012	173,729	162,260	191,013	178,447	203,972	172,006	164,247
2014	180,149	171,213	178,245	178,514	190,808	169,165	152,321	167,437	181,359	190,436	181,192	175,349
2015	197,949	192,586	182,898	180,941	191,700	175,835	177,911	185,267	180,786	192,945	184,447	188,025

Contract size = 50,000 lbs.   *Source: ICE Futures U.S. (ICE)*

Average Spot Prices of U.S. Cotton,² Base Quality (SLM) at Designated Markets   In Cents Per Pound

Crop Year Beginning Aug. 1	Dallas (EastTex.-Okl.)	Fresno (San Joaquin Valley)	Greenville (South-east)	Greenwood (South Delta)	Lubbock (West Texas)	Memphis (North Delta)	Phoenix Desert (Southwest)	Average
2006-07	48.17	48.58	49.90	49.46	48.06	49.46	47.08	48.67
2007-08	60.89	60.57	63.95	62.67	60.64	62.67	59.07	61.50
2008-09	47.08	49.10	48.97	47.99	46.93	47.99	47.03	47.87
2009-10	66.57	67.20	70.13	69.30	66.38	69.30	65.40	67.76
2010-11	135.51	138.91	139.70	139.10	135.11	139.02	137.91	137.88
2011-12	83.30	86.74	87.75	86.95	83.31	86.91	85.73	85.81
2012-13	77.50	76.56	76.56	73.79	73.68	73.89	74.74	75.24
2013-14	82.74	81.85	81.85	79.27	79.14	78.23	78.88	80.28
2014-15	63.55	62.64	62.64	69.08	60.71	61.57	62.32	62.02
2015-16[1]	62.79	61.77	61.77	59.31	59.06	59.33	60.41	60.63

[1] Preliminary.   [2] Prices are for mixed lots, net weight, uncompressed in warehouse.
Source: Agricultural Marketing Service, U.S. Department of Agriculture (AMS-USDA)

Cotton Ginnings[1] in the United States To: In Thousands of Running Bales

Crop Year	Aug. 1	Sept. 1	Sept. 15	Oct. 1	Oct. 15	Nov. 1	Nov. 15	Dec. 1	Dec. 15	Jan. 1	Jan. 15	Feb. 1	Total Crop
2006-07	23	406	996	2,572	5,039	8,604	11,833	15,139	17,657	19,212	20,062	20,559	20,998
2007-08	W	182	375	1,566	3,793	7,072	10,099	12,593	14,341	15,700	16,690	17,585	18,713
2008-09	13	335	476	797	2,027	4,358	6,800	8,928	10,463	11,572	12,094	12,370	12,462
2009-10	5	110	175	234	552	2,189	4,957	7,873	9,728	10,812	11,383	11,706	11,832
2010-11	W	287	747	2,284	4,716	7,947	10,576	13,170	15,126	16,442	17,138	17,518	17,643
2011-12	203	822	1,095	1,734	3,467	6,440	9,214	11,668	13,064	13,949	14,458	14,805	15,153
2012-13	60	473	756	1,552	2,943	6,307	9,394	12,263	14,194	15,327	16,029	16,547	16,834
2013-14	W	132	274	486	1,101	3,038	5,723	8,260	10,459	11,402	12,053	12,391	12,521
2014-15	1	367	696	1,154	2,108	4,807	7,530	10,246	12,601	14,214	15,030	15,538	15,876
2015-16[2]	----	105	293	635	1,448	3,686	5,738	7,961	9,832	11,094	11,739	12,257	

[1] Excluding linters.   [2] Preliminary.   W = Withheld.   *Source: National Agricultural Statistics Service, U.S. Department of Agriculture (NASS-USDA)*

Exports of All Cotton² from the United States   In Thousands of Running Bales

Year	Aug.	Sept.	Oct.	Nov.	Dec.	Jan.	Feb.	Mar.	Apr.	May	June	July	Total
2006-07	688	412	487	599	812	683	824	1,266	1,269	1,385	2,174	1,745	12,342
2007-08	1,116	1,337	883	977	781	981	945	955	1,096	1,360	1,292	1,427	13,150
2008-09	994	983	1,159	923	747	733	813	1,128	1,442	1,475	1,266	1,106	13,179
2009-10	885	809	664	570	778	942	1,174	1,447	1,175	1,354	1,344	1,373	12,515
2010-11	1,023	467	449	1,141	1,688	2,057	1,839	2,085	1,561	1,163	706	533	14,714
2011-12	302	303	422	776	930	1,284	1,583	1,672	1,322	1,241	942	785	11,561
2012-13	743	743	494	731	1,098	1,549	1,796	1,730	1,445	1,394	913	694	13,330
2013-14	767	533	414	606	975	1,417	1,345	1,347	1,087	873	607	446	10,418
2014-15	499	380	354	572	1,024	1,126	1,430	1,596	1,418	1,369	945	769	11,482
2015-16[1]	559	406	366	398	643								5,691

[1] Preliminary.   *Source: Foreign Agricultural Service, U.S. Department of Agriculture (FAS-USDA)*

U.S. Exports of American Cotton to Countries of Destination   In Thousands of 480-Pound Bales

Crop Year Beginning Aug. 1	Canada	China	Hong Kong	Indo-nesia	Italy	Japan	Korea, South	Mexico	Philip-pines	Taiwan	Thailand	United Kingdom	Total
2004-05	305	4,085	274	1,138	75	301	643	1,589	110	846	711	60	14,436
2005-06	178	9,095	280	933	33	265	431	1,511	46	660	530	23	18,039
2006-07	101	3,641	238	928	36	265	307	1,200	39	429	456	0	12,219
2007-08	40	4,491	177	1,261	62	376	361	1,432	26	390	838	0	13,972
2008-09	19	3,770	184	1,057	23	158	302	1,320	52	436	615	----	13,179
2009-10	9	3,886	69	660	21	150	353	1,490	51	424	605	----	12,515
2010-11	10	4,863	47	889	53	186	513	1,245	37	357	712	1	14,714
2011-12	3	6,279	45	329	15	97	329	956	16	271	275	0	11,564
2012-13[1]	2	5,615	105	533	8	120	355	979	31	419	353	0	13,330
2013-14[2]	2	2,642	13	698	9	115	461	1,009	39	296	458	0	10,412

[1] Preliminary.   [2] Estimate.   *Source: Foreign Agricultural Service, U.S. Department of Agriculture (FAS-USDA)*

Cotton[1] Government Loan Program in the United States

Crop Year Beginning Aug. 1	Support Price --- Cents Per Lb. ---	Target Price	Put Under Support Ths Bales	% of Production	Acquired ----- Ths. Bales -----	Owned July 31	Crop Year Beginning Aug. 1	Support Price --- Cents Per Lb. ---	Target Price	Put Under Support Ths Bales	% of Production	Acquired ----- Ths. Bales -----	Owned July 31
2004-05	52.00	72.4	17,092	73.5	8	0	2009-10	52.00	71.3	8,278	67.9	0	0
2005-06	52.00	72.4	17,783	74.4	181	11	2010-11	52.00	71.3	11,403	63.0	0	0
2006-07	52.00	72.4	17,839	82.6	79	0	2011-12	52.00	71.3	7,268	46.7	1	0
2007-08	52.00	72.4	14,636	76.2	169	0	2012-13	52.00	71.3	8,347	48.2	0	0
2008-09	52.00	71.3	10,005	78.1	4	0	2013-14[1]	52.00	71.3	3,731	28.9	0	0

[1] Upland.   [2] Preliminary.   NA = Not applicable.   *Source: Economic Research Service, U.S. Department of Agriculture (ERS-USDA)*

Weekly Outstanding Export Sales and Cumulative Exports of U.S. Cotton   In Running Bales

Marketing Year 2014/2015 Week Ending	Weekly Exports	Accumulated Exports	Net Sales	Outstanding Sales	Marketing Year 2015/2016 Week Ending	Weekly Exports	Accumulated Exports	Net Sales	Outstanding Sales
Aug 07, 2014	94,460	94,460	176,363	4,466,792	Aug 06, 2015	99,587	99,587	536,184	2,429,002
Aug 14, 2014	105,653	200,113	155,602	4,516,741	Aug 13, 2015	110,561	210,148	52,827	2,371,268
Aug 21, 2014	96,680	296,793	247,699	4,667,760	Aug 20, 2015	102,457	312,605	61,097	2,329,908
Aug 28, 2014	103,995	400,788	82,727	4,646,492	Aug 27, 2015	153,096	465,701	66,475	2,243,287
Sep 04, 2014	83,558	484,346	-34,219	4,528,715	Sep 03, 2015	137,134	602,835	83,414	2,189,567
Sep 11, 2014	104,491	588,837	74,977	4,499,201	Sep 10, 2015	59,388	662,223	96,584	2,226,763
Sep 18, 2014	87,903	676,740	155,722	4,567,020	Sep 17, 2015	109,276	771,499	90,750	2,208,237
Sep 25, 2014	77,597	754,337	226,395	4,715,818	Sep 24, 2015	70,452	841,951	117,300	2,255,085
Oct 02, 2014	81,275	835,612	68,499	4,703,042	Oct 01, 2015	126,556	968,507	206,882	2,335,411
Oct 09, 2014	65,948	901,560	6,995	4,644,089	Oct 08, 2015	67,402	1,035,909	67,296	2,335,305
Oct 16, 2014	98,129	999,689	78,764	4,624,724	Oct 15, 2015	61,166	1,097,075	96,931	2,371,070
Oct 23, 2014	70,841	1,070,530	185,433	4,739,316	Oct 22, 2015	67,361	1,164,436	76,061	2,379,770
Oct 30, 2014	64,960	1,135,490	65,024	4,739,380	Oct 29, 2015	164,326	1,328,762	147,235	2,362,679
Nov 06, 2014	88,562	1,224,052	158,293	4,809,111	Nov 05, 2015	71,101	1,399,863	127,937	2,419,515
Nov 13, 2014	62,648	1,286,700	172,039	4,918,502	Nov 12, 2015	53,759	1,453,622	194,434	2,560,190
Nov 20, 2014	107,568	1,394,268	305,663	5,116,597	Nov 19, 2015	90,806	1,544,428	267,586	2,736,970
Nov 27, 2014	106,573	1,500,841	167,023	5,177,047	Nov 26, 2015	80,566	1,624,994	287,137	2,943,541
Dec 04, 2014	193,155	1,693,996	199,189	5,183,081	Dec 03, 2015	111,816	1,736,810	78,703	2,910,428
Dec 11, 2014	174,485	1,868,481	89,458	5,098,054	Dec 10, 2015	91,856	1,828,666	99,539	2,918,111
Dec 18, 2014	202,516	2,070,997	314,312	5,209,850	Dec 17, 2015	127,555	1,956,221	118,241	2,908,797
Dec 25, 2014	169,608	2,240,605	89,358	5,129,600	Dec 24, 2015	158,608	2,114,829	106,663	2,856,852
Jan 01, 2015	205,787	2,446,392	149,894	5,073,707	Dec 31, 2015	161,669	2,276,498	82,809	2,777,992
Jan 08, 2015	227,847	2,674,239	441,767	5,287,627	Jan 07, 2016	79,374	2,355,872	170,986	2,869,604
Jan 15, 2015	226,224	2,900,463	470,282	5,531,685	Jan 14, 2016	135,978	2,491,850	194,559	2,928,185
Jan 22, 2015	274,843	3,175,306	546,174	5,803,016	Jan 21, 2016	157,142	2,648,992	128,338	2,899,381
Jan 29, 2015	281,731	3,457,037	422,765	5,944,050	Jan 28, 2016	233,531	2,882,523	251,560	2,917,410
Feb 05, 2015	289,705	3,746,742	52,179	5,706,524	Feb 04, 2016	180,464	3,062,987	227,668	2,964,614
Feb 12, 2015	288,465	4,035,207	-69,734	5,348,325	Feb 11, 2016	163,784	3,226,771	308,764	3,109,594
Feb 19, 2015	192,914	4,228,121	71,413	5,226,824	Feb 18, 2016	171,458	3,398,229	110,626	3,048,762
Feb 26, 2015	360,812	4,588,933	-62,498	4,803,514	Feb 25, 2016	197,103	3,595,332	173,918	3,025,577
Mar 05, 2015	307,773	4,896,706	36,786	4,532,527	Mar 03, 2016	252,072	3,847,404	185,144	2,958,649
Mar 12, 2015	295,963	5,192,669	238,567	4,475,131	Mar 10, 2016	175,799	4,023,203	224,898	3,007,748
Mar 19, 2015	290,328	5,482,997	177,617	4,362,420	Mar 17, 2016	214,878	4,238,081	84,438	2,877,308
Mar 26, 2015	325,276	5,808,273	61,201	4,098,345	Mar 24, 2016				
Apr 02, 2015	433,760	6,242,033	45,748	3,710,333	Mar 31, 2016				
Apr 09, 2015	201,454	6,443,487	-21,816	3,487,063	Apr 07, 2016				
Apr 16, 2015	324,159	6,767,646	144,933	3,307,837	Apr 14, 2016				
Apr 23, 2015	285,251	7,052,897	124,191	3,146,777	Apr 21, 2016				
Apr 30, 2015	412,503	7,465,400	19,816	2,754,090	Apr 28, 2016				
May 07, 2015	233,430	7,698,830	48,802	2,569,462	May 05, 2016				
May 14, 2015	343,335	8,042,165	59,319	2,285,446	May 12, 2016				
May 21, 2015	339,167	8,381,332	117,452	2,063,731	May 19, 2016				
May 28, 2015	300,478	8,681,810	106,578	1,869,831	May 26, 2016				
Jun 04, 2015	312,110	8,993,920	43,485	1,601,206	Jun 02, 2016				
Jun 11, 2015	208,982	9,202,902	52,614	1,444,838	Jun 09, 2016				
Jun 18, 2015	187,605	9,390,507	60,544	1,317,777	Jun 16, 2016				
Jun 25, 2015	230,401	9,620,908	80,485	1,167,861	Jun 23, 2016				
Jul 02, 2015	211,108	9,832,016	30,398	987,151	Jun 30, 2016				
Jul 09, 2015	136,181	9,968,197	51,243	902,213	Jul 07, 2016				
Jul 16, 2015	173,437	10,141,634	91,504	820,280	Jul 14, 2016				
Jul 23, 2015	168,522	10,310,156	23,251	675,009	Jul 21, 2016				
Jul 30, 2015	186,576	10,496,732	-14,248	474,185	Jul 28, 2016				
Aug 06, 2015	38,337	10,535,069	3,407	439,255					

Source: Foreign Agricultural Service, U.S. Department of Agriculture (FAS-USDA)

Cottonseed and Products

Cottonseed is crushed to produce both oil and meal. Cottonseed oil is typically used for cooking oil and cottonseed meal is fed to livestock. Before the cottonseed is crushed for oil and meal, it is de-linted of its linters. Linters are used for padding in furniture, absorbent cotton swabs, and for the manufacture of many cellulose products. The sediment left by cottonseed oil refining, called foots, provides fatty acids for industrial products. The value of cottonseeds represents a substantial 18% of a cotton producer's income.

Prices – The average monthly price of cottonseed oil in 2015 fell by -22.1% yr/yr to 47.01 cents per pound, still below the 2008 record high of 68.09 cents per pound. The average monthly price of cottonseed meal in 2015 fell by -20.8% yr/yr to $292.45 per short ton, a new record high.

Supply – World production of cottonseed in the 2014-

15 marketing year rose +0.5% yr/yr to 44.653 million metric tons, below the 2011-12 record high of 45.570. The world's largest cottonseed producers are India with 27.5%, China with 24.0% of world production, the U.S. with 10.8%, and Pakistan with 10.2%. U.S. production of cottonseed in the 2015-16 marketing year fell by -19.0% yr/yr to 4.153 million tons. U.S. production of cottonseed oil in 2015-16 fell by -13.1% yr/yr to 530 million pounds, but still below the 12-year high of 957 million pounds posted in 2004-05.

Demand – U.S. cottonseed crushed (consumed) in the U.S. in the 2015-16 marketing year fell by -13.2% to 1.650 million tons, which was still far below the levels of over 4 million tons seen in the 1970s.

Trade – U.S. exports of cottonseed in 2015-16 fell -56.1% to 100,000 short tons. U.S. imports in 2014-15 (latest data) were down -70.2% yr/yr to 59,000 short tons.

World Production of Cottonseed   In Thousands of Metric Ton

Crop Year Beginning Oct. 1	Argentina	Australia	Brazil	China	Egypt	Greece	India	Mexico	Pakistan	Turkey	United States	Former USSR	World Total
2006-07	300	330	2,498	13,409	372	520	9,300	249	4,065	1,477	6,666	3,100	45,866
2007-08	271	180	2,422	13,571	389	500	10,400	209	3,695	1,321	5,977	3,158	45,248
2008-09	214	466	1,785	13,330	185	420	9,800	201	3,760	1,077	3,901	3,070	41,132
2009-10	374	547	1,786	11,351	145	449	9,800	151	4,138	1,021	3,764	2,772	39,147
2010-11	568	1,269	3,084	10,610	187	310	10,800	239	3,665	1,273	5,530	2,680	43,292
2011-12	390	1,694	3,028	11,744	219	490	11,800	410	4,347	1,527	4,872	2,815	47,158
2012-13	299	1,439	2,076	12,168	155	425	11,500	355	4,000	1,373	5,140	2,830	45,570
2013-14[1]	520	1,252	2,615	11,212	140	507	12,500	280	4,071	1,287	3,813	2,744	44,441
2014-15[2]	460	680	2,340	10,700	200	470	12,300	400	4,550	1,391	4,821	2,712	44,653

[1] Preliminary.   [2] Estimate.   *Source: The Oil World*

Salient Statistics of Cottonseed in the United States   In Thousands of Short Tons

Crop Year Beginning Aug. 1	Stocks	Production	Total Supply	Crush	Exports	Other	Total	Farm Price USD/Ton	Value of Production Mil. USD	Products Produced	Total
		Supply			Disappearance					Products Produced	
2007-08	489	6,589	7,080	2,706	599	3,132	6,437	162	1,069.8	856	1,262
2008-09	643	4,300	4,943	2,240	190	1,999	4,429	223	962.7	669	938
2009-10	514	4,149	4,687	1,901	296	2,149	4,345	158	670.0	617	883
2010-11	342	6,098	6,440	2,563	275	2,984	5,822	161	988.7	835	1,163
2011-12	618	5,370	6,059	2,400	133	3,096	5,629	260	1,413.3	755	1,090
2012-13	430	5,666	6,278	2,500	191	3,094	5,786	252	1,456.2	800	1,125
2013-14	492	4,203	4,893	2,000	219	2,250	4,468	246	1,054.0	630	900
2014-15[1]	425	5,125	5,609	1,900	228	3,044	5,172	194	1,055.4	610	855
2015-16[2]	437	4,153	4,590	1,500	60	2,638	4,198	210-250		467	705

[1] Preliminary.   [2] Estimate.   *Source: Economic Research Service, U.S. Department of Agriculture (ERS-USDA)*

Average Wholesale Price of Cottonseed Meal (41% Solvent)[2] in Memphis   In Dollars Per Short Ton

Year	Jan.	Feb.	Mar.	Apr.	May	June	July	Aug.	Sept.	Oct.	Nov.	Dec.	Average
2007	161.00	174.75	185.50	148.25	137.00	131.25	137.50	144.75	167.50	183.40	176.25	196.67	161.99
2008	273.60	292.00	245.00	230.00	240.50	293.25	333.00	290.00	292.00	238.75	225.00	229.50	265.22
2009	237.50	236.25	213.00	212.50	236.25	306.00	305.00	315.00	308.00	250.00	260.00	283.75	263.60
2010	286.25	253.75	213.00	175.00	171.25	176.00	183.75	198.00	200.00	225.31	235.00	240.63	213.16
2011	245.63	258.75	256.50	240.00	275.50	307.50	313.13	342.50	345.63	255.63	240.50	220.63	275.16
2012	213.00	190.00	225.00	240.63	270.00	294.38	350.50	407.50	393.75	343.00	376.88	345.00	304.14
2013	327.50	279.38	301.88	314.50	311.88	329.38	344.50	330.00	374.38	355.00	345.00	401.88	334.60
2014	378.34	388.75	401.25	405.50	416.88	412.50	359.50	310.00	360.63	346.88	313.13	334.38	368.98
2015[1]	313.75	302.50	310.50	288.13	274.38	281.00	299.38	295.63	293.50	292.50	291.88	267.50	292.55

[1] Preliminary.   *Source: Economic Research Service, U.S. Department of Agriculture (ERS-USDA)*

COTTONSEED AND PRODUCTS

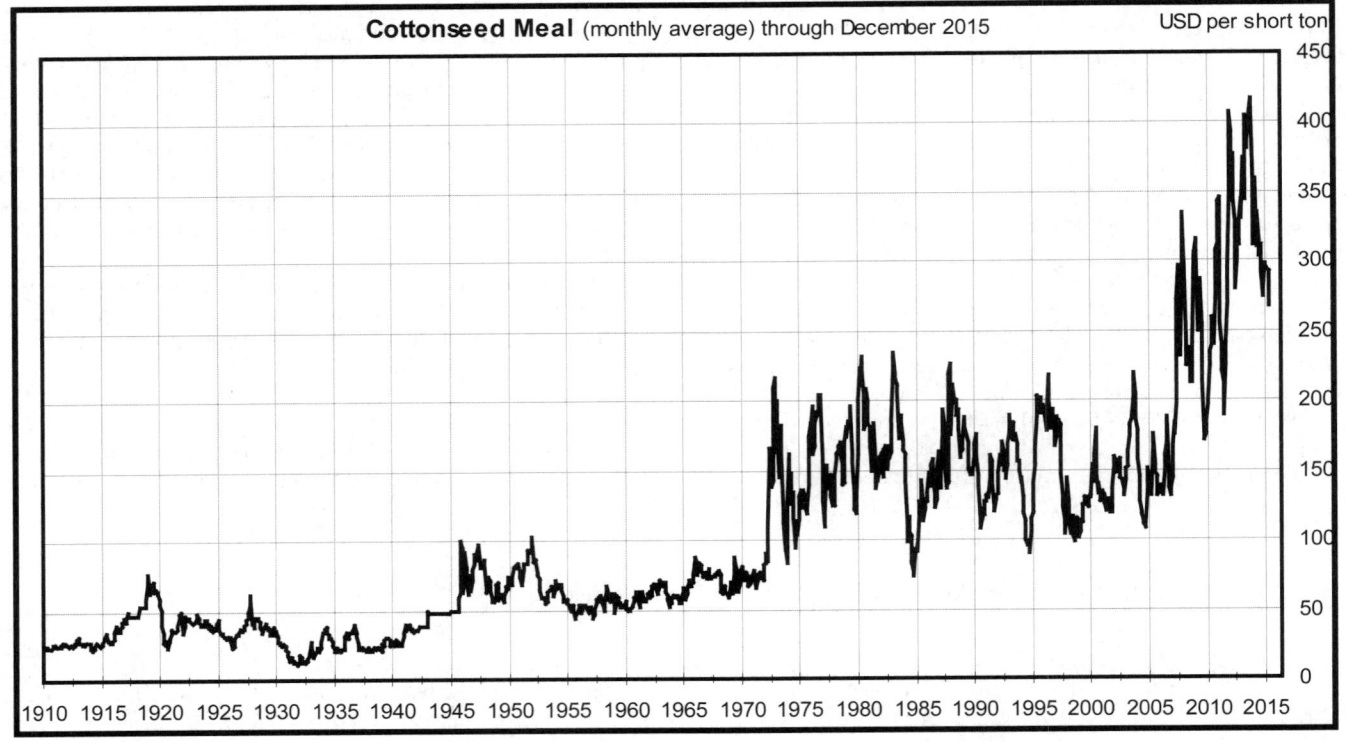

Cottonseed Meal (monthly average) through December 2015 — USD per short ton

Supply and Distribution of Cottonseed Oil in the United States   In Millions of Pounds

Crop Year Beginning Oct. 1	Supply				Disappearance			Per Capita Consumption of Salad & Cooking Oils --- In Lbs. ---	Utilization Food Uses			Prices	
	Stocks	Pro-duction	Imports	Total Supply	Domestic	Exports	Total		Short-ening	Salad & Cooking Oils	Total	U.S.[3] (Crude) --- $/Metric Ton ---	Rott[4] (Cif)
2006-07	101	849	1.0	951	714	138	852	45	162	547	709	787	804
2007-08	99	856	0	956	623	186	809	50	166	567	733	1,622	1,648
2008-09	147	669	0	815	502	192	694	54	W	638	638	820	829
2009-10	121	617	0	738	551	94	646	51	W	509	509	888	895
2010-11	93	835	0	928	599	164	763	54	123	521	644	1,201	1,258
2011-12	165	755	10.0	930	572	259	830	NA	NA	NA	NA	1,173	1,188
2012-13	100	800	20.0	920	599	221	820	----	----	----	----	1,071	1,121
2013-14	100	630	32.0	762	514	148	662	----	----	----	----	1,337	
2014-15[1]	100	610	17.0	727	551	118	669	----	----	----	----	1,008	
2015-16[2]	58	467	20.0	545	420	75	495	----	----	----	----	1,013	

[1] Preliminary.   [2] Estimate.   [3] Valley Points FOB; Tank Cars.   [4] Rotterdam; US, PBSY, fob gulf.   W = Withheld.
Source: Economic Research Service, U.S. Department of Agriculture (ERS-USDA)

Exports of Cottonseed Oil (Crude and Refined) from the United States   In Thousands of Pounds

Year	Jan.	Feb.	Mar.	Apr.	May	June	July	Aug.	Sept.	Oct.	Nov.	Dec.	Total
2006	5,084	5,724	5,410	7,738	5,519	6,640	7,539	6,608	5,755	8,827	9,377	14,365	88,586
2007	7,461	17,932	9,732	14,573	10,676	10,647	11,768	10,404	12,055	12,697	17,137	11,420	146,503
2008	11,089	21,546	25,577	11,565	12,436	17,019	17,441	11,300	17,263	22,083	20,819	18,611	206,747
2009	14,423	20,981	15,258	19,313	12,296	14,087	12,070	10,915	11,370	8,506	14,923	8,455	162,597
2010	6,767	9,348	7,075	6,728	6,189	4,234	3,539	5,523	12,740	19,988	16,878	7,038	106,046
2011	8,142	11,103	19,150	17,085	15,053	9,531	11,479	14,273	13,515	25,841	31,753	18,691	195,617
2012	18,551	12,596	31,375	19,626	20,622	24,030	17,908	21,019	16,715	21,956	17,805	15,878	238,080
2013	19,609	20,389	16,582	21,550	21,218	19,340	15,042	15,886	15,406	15,674	13,338	11,094	205,128
2014	13,667	19,061	18,084	20,029	8,709	7,165	2,999	5,895	12,687	12,384	11,780	14,205	146,664
2015[1]	19,843	8,117	10,559	11,852	6,246	6,162	4,005	8,573	4,379	8,700	4,634	6,080	99,149

[1] Preliminary.   *Source: Economic Research Service, U.S. Department of Agriculture (ERS-USDA)*

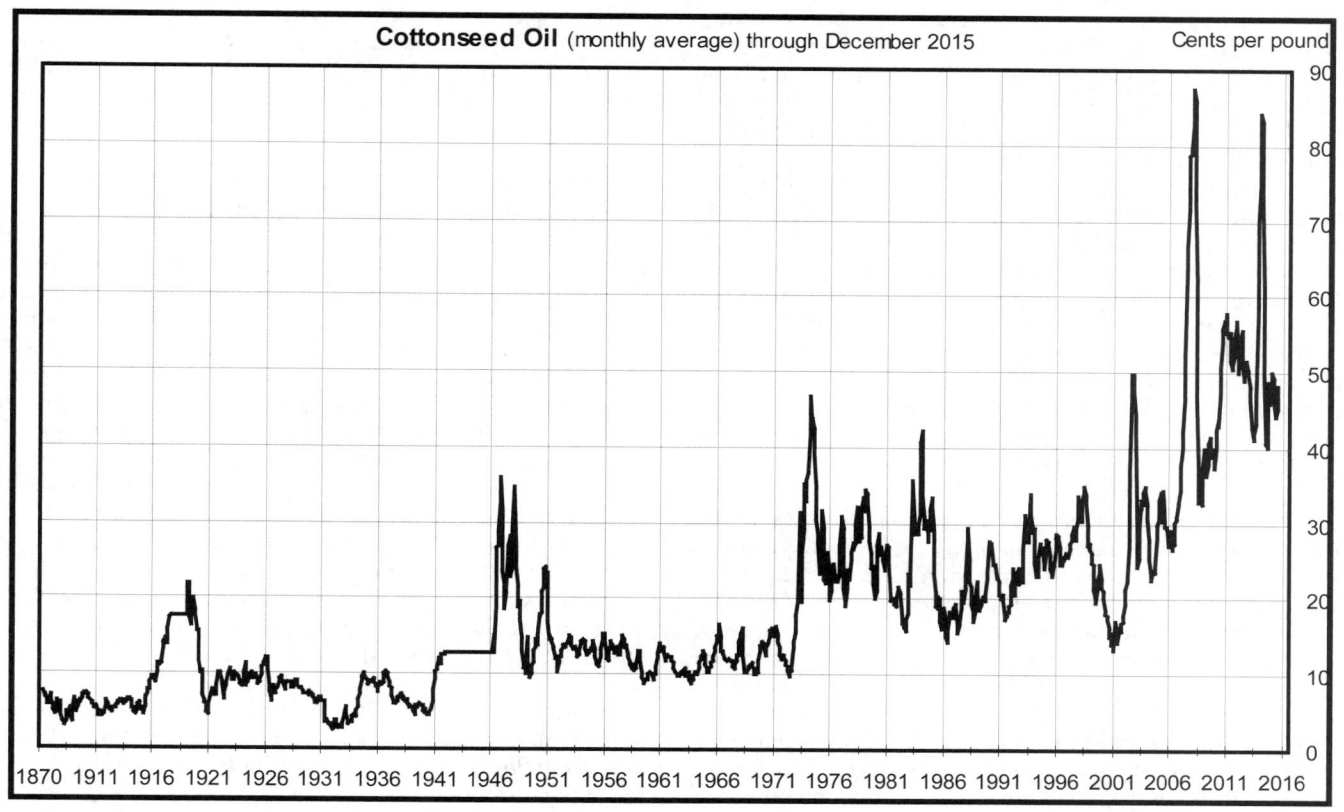

Cottonseed Oil (monthly average) through December 2015 — Cents per pound

Average Price of Crude Cottonseed Oil, PBSY, Greenwood, MS.[1] in Tank Cars   In Cents Per Pound

Year	Jan.	Feb.	Mar.	Apr.	May	June	July	Aug.	Sept.	Oct.	Nov.	Dec.	Average
2006	29.63	29.50	29.75	27.05	28.06	27.25	29.20	26.69	27.13	27.44	30.25	30.75	28.56
2007	31.00	32.69	33.00	34.38	37.75	40.00	42.44	42.15	46.56	52.20	63.60	66.63	43.53
2008	71.69	78.60	78.94	79.75	82.75	87.56	86.06	72.55	62.44	46.45	37.38	32.88	68.09
2009	35.70	33.19	32.63	37.38	39.90	38.75	36.55	39.13	36.44	37.90	40.69	41.40	37.47
2010	39.00	39.13	39.88	38.75	37.38	40.00	42.45	43.69	43.00	47.20	50.75	54.00	42.94
2011	55.92	56.75	55.50	57.70	56.06	55.25	54.75	54.75	55.35	51.56	50.50	51.10	54.60
2012	52.19	54.56	55.95	56.88	52.00	50.05	53.75	54.65	55.50	51.31	49.05	50.06	53.00
2013	50.94	51.56	50.20	49.94	49.75	48.25	46.19	43.10	42.81	41.19	42.05	43.19	46.60
2014	47.10	57.81	69.94	75.00	84.25	83.31	73.15	61.25	49.63	41.45	40.75	40.31	60.33
2015[1]	44.95	48.81	46.06	48.19	48.90	49.94	49.15	46.25	44.13	44.25	45.19	48.35	47.01

[1] Preliminary.   Source: Economic Research Service, U.S. Department of Agriculture (ERS-USDA)

Exports of Cottonseed Oil to Important Countries from the United States   In Thousands of Metric Tons

Year	Canada	Dominican Republic	Egypt	Guate-mala	Japan	Mexico	Nether-lands	El Salvador	Korea, South	Turkey	Venez-uela	Total
2006	10.0	.0	0	.0	1.3	14.1	11.2	0	0	0	.1	40.2
2007	24.0	.1	0	0	7.1	17.3	11.6	0	0	0	.0	66.5
2008	40.8	.1	0	0	9.0	14.5	22.3	0	0	0	0	93.8
2009	37.0	0	0	0	2.6	8.7	18.1	.1	.2	0	0	73.8
2010	17.6	0	0	0	1.4	.9	26.0	0	0	0	0	48.1
2011	39.8	.0	0	0	0	.9	45.8	0	0	.0	0	88.7
2012	30.7	.0	0	0	.5	0	73.9	.2	0	.0	0	108.0
2013	22.3	0	0	0	.2	.0	63.5	1.2	0	.3	0	93.0
2014	11.8	0	0	0	2.1	0	36.4	.9	0	.3	0	66.5
2015[1]	12.3	0	0	.1	.9	.5	24.8	.5	0	.1	0	45.0

[1] Preliminary.   Source: Foreign Agricultural Service, U.S. Department of Agriculture (FAS-USDA)

Currencies

A "currency" rate involves the price of the base currency (e.g., the dollar) quoted in terms of another currency (e.g., the yen), or in terms of a basket of currencies (e.g., the dollar index). The world's major currencies have traded in a floating exchange rate regime ever since the Bretton-Woods international payments system broke down in 1971 when President Nixon broke the dollar's peg to gold. The two key factors affecting a currency's value are central bank monetary policy and the trade balance. An easy monetary policy (low interest rates) is bearish for a currency because the central bank is aggressively pumping new currency reserves into the marketplace and because foreign investors are not attracted to the low interest rate returns available in the country. By contrast, a tight monetary policy (high interest rates) is bullish for a currency because of the tight supply of new currency reserves and attractive interest rate returns for foreign investors.

The other key factor driving currency values is the nation's current account balance. A current account surplus is bullish for a currency due to the net inflow of the currency, while a current account deficit is bearish for a currency due to the net outflow of the currency. Currency values are also affected by economic growth and investment opportunities in the country. A country with a strong economy and lucrative investment opportunities will typically have a strong currency because global companies and investors want to buy into that country's investment opportunities. Futures on major currencies and on cross-currency rates are traded primarily at the CME Group.

Dollar – The U.S. Dollar Index (Barchart.com symbol DXY00) extended the sharp rally that began in mid-2014 to post a new 12-year high in early 2015, bringing the 2014-15 rally to a total of +27.2%. The dollar index briefly edged to a new 13-year high in December 2015 but then fell back to close the year up +9.3%. The dollar remained strong during 2015 after the Fed ended its third quantitative easing program (QE3) in Oct 2014 and stopped expanding its balance sheet. The dollar also remained strong as the market during 2015 anticipated the Fed's first rate hike, which finally took place in December 2015 when the Fed raised its federal funds rate target by 25 basis points to 0.25-0.50% from the former target of zero to 0.25% that prevailed since the 2008/09 financial crisis. The dollar index should see continued support going forward since the Fed is expected to continue slowly raising its federal funds rate target over at least the next two years, in contrast to the European Central (ECB) and Bank of Japan (BOJ), which are not likely to raise interest rates for at least several years.

Euro – EUR/USD (Barchart.com symbol ^EURUSD) showed a sharp sell-off totaling -25.2% from mid-2014 though early-2015, posting a 13-year low of $1.0461 in March 2015. EUR/USD then consolidated mildly above that low for the remainder of 2015, finally closing the year down -10.3% at $1.0854 per euro. EUR/USD plunged in the latter half of 2014 when the U.S. Federal Reserve was winding down its third quantitative easing program while the ECB was coming under increasing pressure to implement its first true quantitative easing (QE) program. The ECB in January 2015 finally did announce a large-scale QE program involving the purchase of 60 billion euros of securities per month, a program that was increased in size to 80 billion euros per month in March 2016. The ECB in March 2016 also cut its deposit rate by -10 basis points to -0.40% and cut its refinancing rate by -5 bp to zero. The sharp divergence in monetary policies between the Fed and the ECB has been a highly bearish factor for the euro.

Yen – USD/JPY (Barchart.com symbol ^USDJPY) rallied very sharply by +67% from the record low of 75.57 yen per dollar in October 2011 to the 14-year high of 125.85 yen posted in June 2015. USD/JPY then fell back late in 2015 to close the year just slightly higher by +0.4%. USD/JPY then fell further in early 2016 as the market shook off the BOJ's move to negative interest rates and the yen instead saw safe-haven demand tied to early-2016 weakness in the world's stock markets. The yen in general remains weak as the Fed has started what is likely to be a long series of interest rate hikes while the Bank of Japan (BOJ) pursues a massive quantitative easing program and is still cutting interest rates. The BOJ surprised the markets in late January 2016 by announcing a cut in its policy rate to -0.10%. The BOJ's move to negative rates was softened somewhat by the fact that the BOJ has a tiered deposit rate system than shields some of bank deposits from the negative rate. Nevertheless, the yen is likely to see ongoing weakness due to the divergent monetary policies between the U.S. and Japan and because the Japanese economy is expected to show continued weak growth in 2016-18.

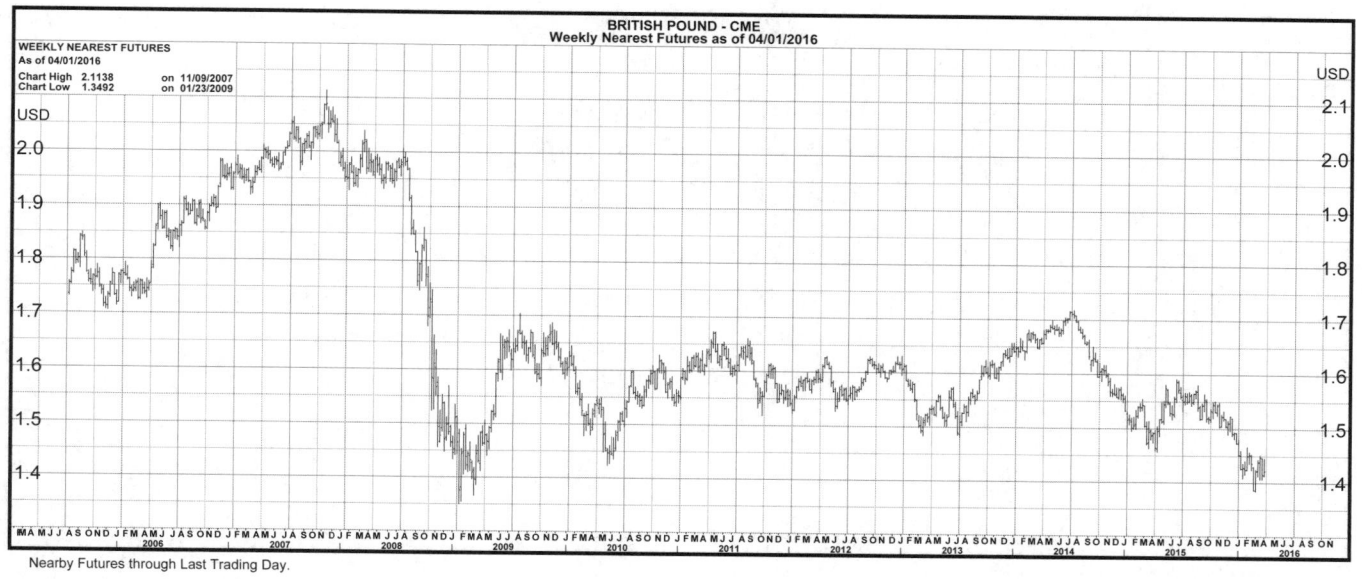

BRITISH POUND - CME
Weekly Nearest Futures as of 04/01/2016

WEEKLY NEAREST FUTURES
As of 04/01/2016
Chart High 2.1138   on 11/09/2007
Chart Low   1.3492   on 01/23/2009

Nearby Futures through Last Trading Day.

U.S. Dollars per British Pound

Year	Jan.	Feb.	Mar.	Apr.	May	June	July	Aug.	Sept.	Oct.	Nov.	Dec.	Average
2006	1.7665	1.7478	1.7446	1.7690	1.8693	1.8435	1.8451	1.8934	1.8858	1.8766	1.9124	1.9634	1.8431
2007	1.9585	1.9586	1.9479	1.9874	1.9834	1.9870	2.0344	2.0112	2.0202	2.0453	2.0709	2.0168	2.0018
2008	1.9692	1.9640	2.0012	1.9815	1.9662	1.9675	1.9897	1.8870	1.7997	1.6899	1.5290	1.4869	1.8526
2009	1.4484	1.4417	1.4197	1.4727	1.5460	1.6379	1.6387	1.6532	1.6312	1.6196	1.6610	1.6230	1.5661
2010	1.6160	1.5621	1.5059	1.5337	1.4658	1.4758	1.5302	1.5652	1.5575	1.5858	1.5953	1.5599	1.5461
2011	1.5789	1.6137	1.6158	1.6385	1.6338	1.6219	1.6150	1.6359	1.5776	1.5773	1.5799	1.5587	1.6039
2012	1.5522	1.5806	1.5829	1.6009	1.5909	1.5556	1.5598	1.5718	1.6113	1.6073	1.5964	1.6144	1.5854
2013	1.5961	1.5468	1.5083	1.5309	1.5287	1.5498	1.5184	1.5505	1.5875	1.6089	1.6112	1.6383	1.5646
2014	1.6468	1.6566	1.6617	1.6747	1.6841	1.6916	1.7075	1.6700	1.6303	1.6077	1.5773	1.5631	1.6476
2015	1.5139	1.5334	1.4969	1.4960	1.5454	1.5586	1.5558	1.5581	1.5334	1.5335	1.5193	1.4984	1.5286

Average.   *Source: FOREX*

Volume of Trading of British Pound Futures in Chicago   In Thousands of Contracts

Year	Jan.	Feb.	Mar.	Apr.	May	June	July	Aug.	Sept.	Oct.	Nov.	Dec.	Total
2006	1,013.7	1,012.0	1,479.2	1,207.6	1,465.1	1,262.1	963.1	1,262.2	1,486.2	1,387.1	1,563.9	1,997.4	16,099.5
2007	1,639.3	1,485.2	2,151.4	1,330.1	1,705.8	2,066.0	1,946.6	1,964.1	1,668.3	1,729.8	1,793.9	1,319.3	20,799.8
2008	1,541.0	1,442.5	1,886.1	1,979.0	1,633.7	2,058.8	1,896.4	1,805.7	2,151.8	1,584.1	1,240.3	1,278.1	20,497.4
2009	1,446.3	1,457.1	1,721.8	1,509.2	1,736.4	2,609.0	2,127.0	2,126.5	2,644.3	2,864.8	2,389.1	2,222.4	24,853.8
2010	2,258.4	2,538.3	3,253.0	2,367.8	3,139.4	2,906.1	2,170.7	2,349.4	2,541.7	2,305.1	2,299.2	2,091.1	30,220.2
2011	2,520.0	2,519.3	2,933.2	2,170.3	2,578.2	2,683.0	2,159.4	2,348.8	2,732.7	2,313.8	2,015.5	2,054.4	29,028.8
2012	1,688.5	2,010.0	2,445.6	2,058.2	2,510.7	2,495.4	2,189.7	2,168.2	2,372.3	2,133.3	1,941.9	2,152.6	26,166.3
2013	2,460.2	2,647.5	2,948.2	2,172.0	2,678.5	3,067.9	2,504.8	2,298.1	2,348.2	2,002.0	1,936.9	2,173.5	29,237.8
2014	2,123.0	2,139.8	2,315.4	1,415.6	1,592.2	2,547.6	1,728.8	1,781.2	3,181.2	2,283.2	1,740.6	1,988.2	24,837.0
2015	2,024.6	1,677.7	2,854.7	1,918.6	2,234.4	2,374.3	1,744.8	2,048.9	2,139.5	1,635.5	1,506.4	1,985.3	24,144.7

Contract size = 62,500 GBP.   *Source: CME Group; Chicago Mercantile Exchange (CME)*

Average Open Interest of British Pound Futures in Chicago   In Contracts

Year	Jan.	Feb.	Mar.	Apr.	May	June	July	Aug.	Sept.	Oct.	Nov.	Dec.
2006	83,051	97,226	83,641	83,275	106,555	98,417	91,563	129,334	120,737	106,288	145,026	157,837
2007	147,183	152,892	135,618	130,611	130,861	145,405	157,336	124,948	110,905	118,737	128,761	96,974
2008	87,465	94,154	98,154	109,464	158,836	126,688	100,775	105,857	112,717	110,761	113,147	93,313
2009	81,141	84,191	88,354	82,933	91,683	92,365	90,994	98,358	88,658	104,344	96,882	83,847
2010	86,016	116,480	136,357	122,843	145,514	136,099	126,486	138,872	97,056	89,011	95,465	80,042
2011	92,434	118,770	118,434	114,166	111,901	103,047	106,501	100,953	142,668	174,087	162,814	206,391
2012	198,201	190,107	167,722	159,541	191,394	150,584	115,951	115,580	166,427	165,761	156,794	188,125
2013	165,256	184,350	248,526	201,357	202,681	172,212	145,625	145,596	167,475	181,110	186,634	226,964
2014	207,609	232,142	231,703	226,479	236,374	262,034	246,579	231,599	184,224	135,955	160,534	165,669
2015	178,585	173,893	187,709	180,094	179,361	174,693	167,418	168,889	163,232	155,414	169,080	191,263

Contract size = 62,500 GBP.   *Source: CME Group; Chicago Mercantile Exchange (CME)*

CURRENCIES

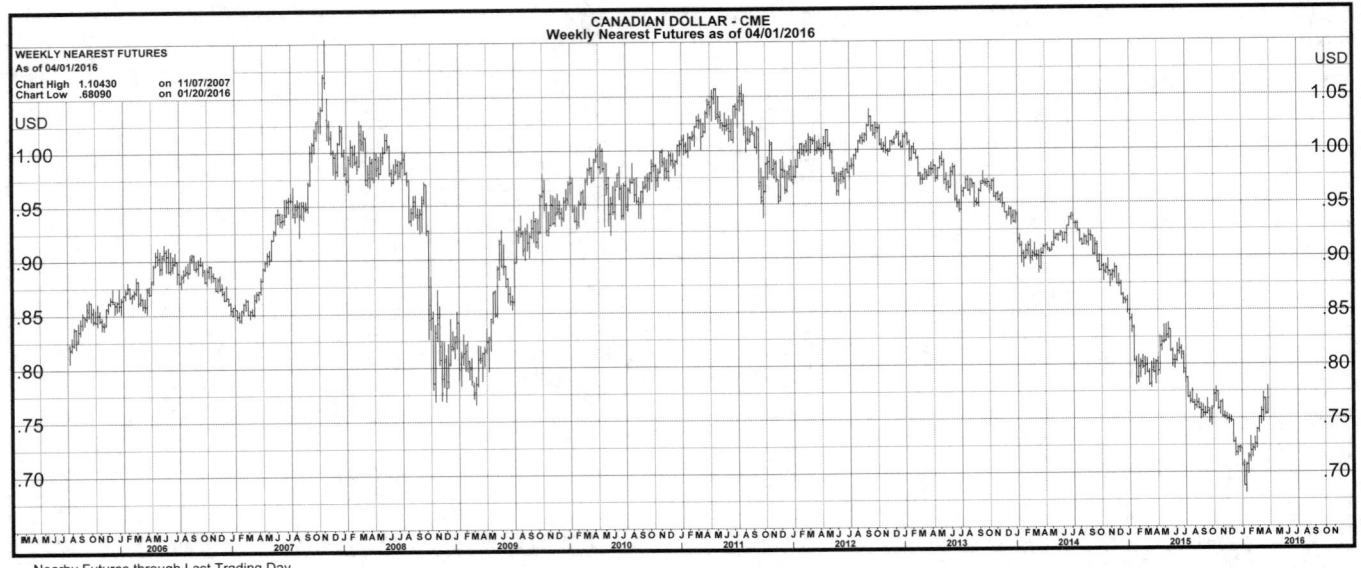

CANADIAN DOLLAR - CME
Weekly Nearest Futures as of 04/01/2016

Nearby Futures through Last Trading Day.

Canadian Dollars per U.S. Dollar

Year	Jan.	Feb.	Mar.	Apr.	May	June	July	Aug.	Sept.	Oct.	Nov.	Dec.	Average
2006	1.1573	1.1488	1.1571	1.1440	1.1094	1.1139	1.1287	1.1191	1.1161	1.1281	1.1365	1.1531	1.1343
2007	1.1757	1.1708	1.1687	1.1351	1.0948	1.0655	1.0512	1.0585	1.0260	0.9752	0.9680	1.0021	1.0743
2008	1.0114	1.0001	1.0031	1.0130	0.9999	1.0170	1.0133	1.0539	1.0582	1.1797	1.2204	1.2337	1.0670
2009	1.2244	1.2449	1.2638	1.2244	1.1502	1.1274	1.1225	1.0878	1.0812	1.0547	1.0587	1.0558	1.1413
2010	1.0435	1.0561	1.0233	1.0052	1.0415	1.0397	1.0433	1.0408	1.0335	1.0180	1.0128	1.0081	1.0305
2011	0.9939	0.9875	0.9767	0.9574	0.9682	0.9771	0.9558	0.9814	1.0023	1.0201	1.0253	1.0238	0.9891
2012	1.0132	0.9970	0.9934	0.9929	1.0106	1.0275	1.0137	0.9930	0.9788	0.9872	0.9969	0.9899	0.9995
2013	0.9919	1.0094	1.0240	1.0185	1.0206	1.0315	1.0404	1.0404	1.0354	1.0367	1.0488	1.0637	1.0301
2014	1.0947	1.1054	1.1106	1.0992	1.0890	1.0825	1.0734	1.0922	1.1007	1.1214	1.1332	1.1542	1.1047
2015	1.2128	1.2500	1.2610	1.2338	1.2183	1.2354	1.2851	1.3144	1.3270	1.3071	1.3275	1.3710	1.2786

Average.　Source: FOREX

Volume of Trading of Canadian Dollar Futures in Chicago　In Thousands of Contracts

Year	Jan.	Feb.	Mar.	Apr.	May	June	July	Aug.	Sept.	Oct.	Nov.	Dec.	Total
2006	695.1	648.6	1,040.9	654.9	816.6	1,043.4	658.3	811.0	1,073.7	805.8	960.8	1,070.4	10,279.6
2007	795.9	724.5	1,089.4	749.9	949.9	1,348.4	1,101.2	1,015.5	1,226.6	1,054.0	1,238.3	931.2	12,224.8
2008	960.2	957.8	1,202.2	948.1	958.2	1,151.9	932.0	966.4	1,240.9	812.9	601.8	645.8	11,378.0
2009	625.5	685.7	1,040.2	964.4	1,222.0	1,691.7	1,318.6	1,319.2	1,644.8	1,626.3	1,569.5	1,773.2	15,481.2
2010	1,391.4	1,623.9	1,989.7	1,742.0	2,329.7	2,120.7	1,774.7	1,839.7	1,905.7	1,841.7	1,889.4	1,635.3	22,083.8
2011	1,477.5	1,505.0	2,143.4	1,403.3	1,943.9	2,213.2	1,557.3	2,545.8	2,479.4	2,000.8	1,624.9	1,522.3	22,416.7
2012	1,441.3	1,790.3	2,203.3	1,812.6	2,260.5	2,546.9	1,947.1	1,871.8	2,213.3	1,713.8	1,467.8	1,530.9	22,799.4
2013	1,472.2	1,439.5	1,815.4	1,502.0	1,770.9	1,891.0	1,434.3	1,327.6	1,256.7	1,077.0	986.0	1,455.2	17,427.8
2014	1,495.5	1,064.6	1,572.7	903.8	917.2	1,253.6	1,064.6	1,057.9	1,612.2	1,569.7	1,191.6	1,393.1	15,096.5
2015	1,371.7	1,298.8	1,881.8	1,394.8	1,170.1	1,595.7	1,447.1	1,477.1	1,710.6	1,283.7	1,040.4	1,630.2	17,301.9

Contract size = 100,000 CAD.　Source: CME Group; Chicago Mercantile Exchange (CME)

Average Open Interest of Canadian Dollar Futures in Chicago　In Contracts

Year	Jan.	Feb.	Mar.	Apr.	May	June	July	Aug.	Sept.	Oct.	Nov.	Dec.
2006	103,427	118,978	103,066	92,541	114,587	107,605	89,443	91,591	112,788	99,209	121,729	146,474
2007	151,511	144,025	140,775	119,430	163,570	180,961	147,966	132,910	136,952	145,923	120,912	99,261
2008	86,448	99,650	109,567	103,486	115,665	103,145	95,618	120,175	116,163	103,135	94,297	66,313
2009	59,962	70,940	70,863	63,119	83,214	88,873	87,203	98,521	91,989	97,587	89,022	94,758
2010	106,475	92,349	143,969	148,414	125,802	102,117	87,121	100,655	101,319	113,964	116,126	110,800
2011	123,984	139,328	141,949	141,548	124,951	108,081	118,209	111,898	102,180	118,239	127,296	143,821
2012	119,930	126,823	147,325	128,867	141,093	120,545	101,536	134,628	225,238	185,312	168,662	167,449
2013	142,358	161,037	216,418	167,325	145,528	128,346	126,955	115,698	127,754	114,266	121,783	158,005
2014	159,815	152,844	144,262	119,310	123,899	117,918	125,230	111,259	91,900	100,526	106,812	106,069
2015	108,171	115,078	124,649	120,477	120,938	101,560	143,112	167,447	148,706	121,352	137,170	164,083

Contract size = 100,000 CAD.　Source: CME Group; Chicago Mercantile Exchange (CME)

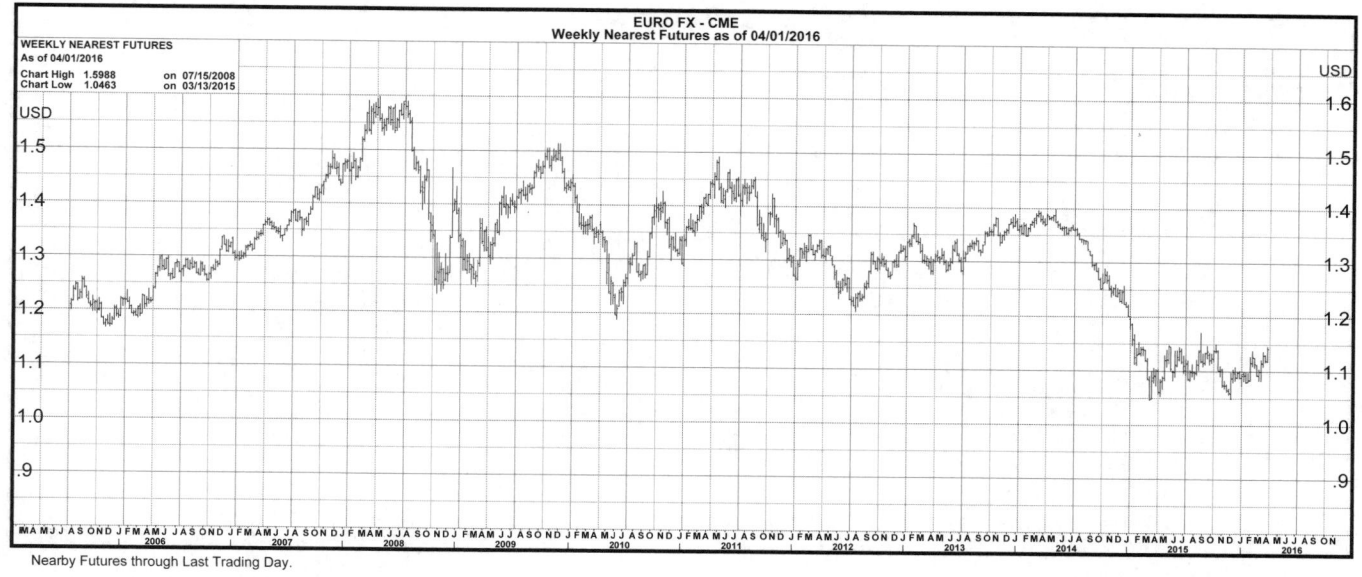

EURO FX - CME
Weekly Nearest Futures as of 04/01/2016

WEEKLY NEAREST FUTURES
As of 04/01/2016

| Chart High | 1.5988 | on 07/15/2008 |
| Chart Low | 1.0463 | on 03/13/2015 |

Nearby Futures through Last Trading Day.

Euro per U.S. Dollar

Year	Jan.	Feb.	Mar.	Apr.	May	June	July	Aug.	Sept.	Oct.	Nov.	Dec.	Average
2006	1.2121	1.1940	1.2033	1.2282	1.2773	1.2665	1.2693	1.2811	1.2734	1.2623	1.2893	1.3200	1.2564
2007	1.2989	1.3087	1.3249	1.3512	1.3511	1.3422	1.3720	1.3620	1.3918	1.4234	1.4681	1.4561	1.3709
2008	1.4722	1.4759	1.5527	1.5760	1.5560	1.5569	1.5765	1.4954	1.4367	1.3286	1.2723	1.3518	1.4709
2009	1.3253	1.2805	1.3074	1.3207	1.3675	1.4014	1.4087	1.4267	1.4565	1.4817	1.4926	1.4577	1.3939
2010	1.4270	1.3681	1.3574	1.3427	1.2536	1.2212	1.2803	1.2899	1.3092	1.3899	1.3640	1.3227	1.3272
2011	1.3374	1.3661	1.4018	1.4472	1.4324	1.4400	1.4289	1.4339	1.3754	1.3727	1.3551	1.3148	1.3921
2012	1.2910	1.3238	1.3213	1.3164	1.2788	1.2546	1.2293	1.2403	1.2873	1.2969	1.2837	1.3124	1.2863
2013	1.3306	1.3340	1.2956	1.3025	1.2978	1.3202	1.3090	1.3320	1.3362	1.3638	1.3496	1.3704	1.3285
2014	1.3616	1.3669	1.3827	1.3811	1.3733	1.3600	1.3538	1.3315	1.2895	1.2680	1.2474	1.2307	1.3289
2015	1.1605	1.1352	1.0830	1.0817	1.1157	1.1237	1.0997	1.1144	1.1236	1.1218	1.0728	1.0896	1.1101

Average.   *Source: FOREX*

Volume of Trading of Euro FX Futures in Chicago   In Thousands of Contracts

Year	Jan.	Feb.	Mar.	Apr.	May	June	July	Aug.	Sept.	Oct.	Nov.	Dec.	Total
2006	2,956.0	2,563.9	3,411.2	2,984.4	4,496.3	3,765.7	2,789.0	3,229.5	3,364.0	3,123.5	3,790.4	4,316.6	40,790.4
2007	3,701.9	3,032.1	4,427.3	2,979.1	3,337.4	3,877.6	3,560.5	4,074.2	3,286.6	3,831.5	3,793.1	3,161.6	43,063.1
2008	3,669.9	3,327.5	4,709.2	4,596.3	4,537.8	5,312.0	4,661.3	5,009.7	6,216.8	4,556.3	3,607.9	3,447.8	53,652.6
2009	3,574.5	3,903.4	4,564.5	3,155.7	3,758.9	5,261.4	4,675.6	4,220.4	5,123.9	5,429.9	5,419.9	5,305.7	54,393.6
2010	5,407.6	6,439.6	7,562.4	7,157.1	9,578.8	7,913.1	6,006.4	6,418.2	7,294.2	7,476.0	8,241.8	6,737.2	86,232.4
2011	7,402.8	6,451.9	7,437.7	5,453.1	7,657.0	7,504.8	6,906.8	8,061.0	8,376.7	7,008.3	6,638.4	5,338.4	84,236.8
2012	5,611.6	5,984.0	6,055.0	4,864.4	6,510.0	7,165.7	5,311.9	5,059.1	5,927.6	5,197.0	5,281.1	4,440.5	67,407.7
2013	5,675.6	6,088.9	6,391.7	5,480.1	6,055.8	5,970.9	5,093.7	4,390.9	4,120.9	3,988.5	4,047.7	3,981.0	61,285.6
2014	4,422.1	3,733.1	4,781.4	3,046.6	3,338.3	4,261.9	3,048.4	3,507.4	6,106.3	5,900.3	4,564.9	5,497.7	52,208.3
2015	5,560.3	3,639.7	7,724.4	5,745.4	5,549.4	6,980.8	4,666.0	5,245.6	5,468.3	4,455.2	4,243.0	6,077.9	65,356.1

Contract size = 125,000 EUR.   *Source: CME Group; Chicago Mercantile Exchange (CME)*

Average Open Interest of Euro FX Futures in Chicago   In Contracts

Year	Jan.	Feb.	Mar.	Apr.	May	June	July	Aug.	Sept.	Oct.	Nov.	Dec.
2006	133,092	150,085	152,674	166,920	196,057	177,700	155,865	173,151	155,567	152,410	182,079	214,241
2007	173,989	196,963	205,366	217,899	222,019	204,945	218,401	221,095	221,268	207,644	221,736	204,536
2008	179,767	206,661	200,084	178,993	211,068	193,878	170,675	153,423	163,948	180,955	169,315	144,926
2009	127,134	156,321	141,863	110,261	124,438	130,793	129,062	133,469	156,493	168,629	169,331	155,488
2010	169,083	199,832	211,780	216,500	285,206	251,763	226,656	242,448	198,817	203,635	198,138	172,703
2011	190,755	202,950	225,190	244,014	257,695	222,331	184,688	178,500	231,100	228,018	251,778	297,070
2012	301,627	288,301	275,581	277,812	349,794	369,192	321,319	318,368	276,124	220,770	225,676	217,375
2013	214,230	236,476	211,778	220,576	242,334	232,139	217,712	237,132	250,358	270,275	239,030	258,190
2014	251,507	285,722	289,786	266,980	270,902	302,019	322,167	390,128	429,750	434,763	467,267	427,194
2015	430,963	443,172	477,046	453,055	436,488	388,813	358,550	366,585	340,638	357,347	432,251	432,591

Contract size = 125,000 EUR.   *Source: CME Group; Chicago Mercantile Exchange (CME)*

CURRENCIES

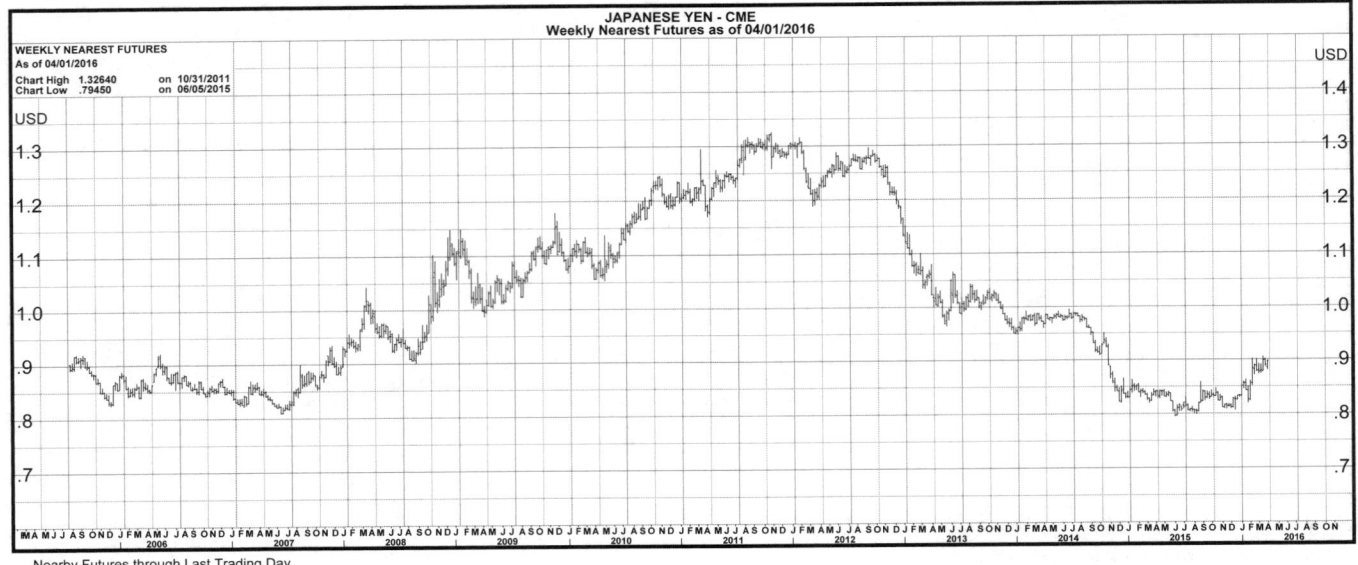

Nearby Futures through Last Trading Day.

Japanese Yen per U.S. Dollar

Year	Jan.	Feb.	Mar.	Apr.	May	June	July	Aug.	Sept.	Oct.	Nov.	Dec.	Average
2006	115.53	117.92	117.31	116.97	111.77	114.65	115.69	115.95	117.14	118.61	117.28	117.43	116.35
2007	120.45	120.40	117.33	118.96	120.82	122.65	121.47	116.78	115.08	115.92	110.92	112.37	117.76
2008	107.71	107.11	100.80	102.69	104.33	106.88	106.87	109.41	106.62	100.15	96.80	91.13	103.37
2009	90.33	92.86	97.74	98.94	96.49	96.67	94.46	94.90	91.40	90.32	89.12	89.99	93.60
2010	91.13	90.17	90.71	93.49	91.88	90.81	87.56	85.38	84.38	81.79	82.58	83.23	87.76
2011	82.61	82.57	81.65	83.18	81.14	80.47	79.29	77.05	76.88	76.68	77.54	77.83	79.74
2012	76.93	78.60	82.54	81.28	79.69	79.36	78.98	78.68	78.16	79.00	81.04	83.86	79.84
2013	89.19	93.11	94.88	97.75	100.97	97.30	99.64	97.80	99.18	97.85	100.12	103.55	97.61
2014	103.80	102.12	102.34	102.51	101.83	102.07	101.75	102.97	107.37	108.03	116.37	119.42	105.88
2015	118.27	118.75	120.36	119.52	120.85	123.67	123.31	123.04	120.08	120.15	122.63	121.63	121.02

Average.   *Source: FOREX*

Volume of Trading of Japanese Yen Futures in Chicago   In Thousands of Contracts

Year	Jan.	Feb.	Mar.	Apr.	May	June	July	Aug.	Sept.	Oct.	Nov.	Dec.	Total
2006	1,221.1	1,128.7	1,950.5	1,385.9	1,890.9	1,905.3	1,317.9	1,395.9	1,965.8	1,525.1	1,852.8	2,137.5	19,677.4
2007	1,602.2	2,006.6	3,286.7	1,771.1	1,802.4	2,777.8	3,083.8	3,954.2	2,860.7	2,493.1	3,125.2	2,056.6	30,820.4
2008	3,013.2	2,558.7	3,384.5	2,632.6	2,502.9	3,193.9	2,898.0	2,428.9	3,446.2	3,117.8	1,937.5	1,730.2	32,844.4
2009	1,644.2	1,802.9	1,796.0	1,469.3	1,600.9	1,932.6	2,061.8	1,924.0	2,260.9	2,157.6	1,916.7	2,182.7	22,749.6
2010	2,321.3	2,382.1	2,664.8	2,397.2	3,481.7	3,094.9	2,712.4	2,591.6	3,065.3	2,171.1	2,484.6	2,495.8	31,862.8
2011	2,542.6	2,572.2	3,764.0	2,438.4	2,297.9	2,563.3	2,023.5	2,701.8	2,393.6	2,135.9	1,425.0	1,510.9	28,369.1
2012	1,445.7	1,772.5	2,609.4	1,752.1	1,820.9	2,037.7	1,397.4	1,721.5	2,223.2	1,912.0	2,189.4	2,638.8	23,520.6
2013	3,831.3	4,175.7	3,820.2	4,510.5	4,431.7	5,387.8	2,849.1	2,885.5	3,045.1	2,564.9	2,379.8	2,880.5	42,762.3
2014	3,335.1	2,865.2	3,324.4	2,335.1	2,285.1	2,615.9	2,143.3	2,335.6	3,904.6	4,728.3	3,791.3	4,655.9	38,319.8
2015	4,041.9	2,593.2	3,160.9	2,462.5	2,548.1	3,539.0	2,236.0	3,410.2	3,926.7	2,985.0	2,201.2	3,075.8	36,180.5

Contract size = 12,500,000 JPY.   *Source: CME Group; Chicago Mercantile Exchange (CME)*

Average Open Interest of Japanese Yen Futures in Chicago   In Contracts

Year	Jan.	Feb.	Mar.	Apr.	May	June	July	Aug.	Sept.	Oct.	Nov.	Dec.
2006	168,309	198,855	203,450	201,459	210,578	197,160	191,480	218,893	239,426	258,509	242,216	265,490
2007	312,252	338,933	246,715	234,352	303,537	347,031	302,278	272,937	227,242	225,047	202,361	195,324
2008	197,886	233,558	224,932	176,577	171,298	171,516	185,657	207,309	168,119	142,938	128,891	130,118
2009	112,194	108,893	90,828	79,142	86,624	81,378	95,456	80,087	119,014	118,478	123,821	110,809
2010	116,578	121,216	117,096	131,315	143,384	111,812	129,460	135,623	130,539	142,646	133,612	111,840
2011	112,265	119,793	118,104	123,251	102,290	101,702	121,491	128,615	135,195	151,744	147,224	168,945
2012	162,827	160,215	161,521	145,491	143,219	151,494	127,493	147,320	152,104	136,446	176,769	226,165
2013	203,930	217,961	246,456	211,493	222,136	199,960	182,942	168,128	184,355	160,423	204,490	251,937
2014	217,565	201,386	190,296	174,544	163,960	170,679	163,460	202,088	234,084	205,740	233,431	252,694
2015	218,141	204,791	206,382	190,770	217,291	275,725	249,546	259,312	213,125	181,162	237,763	217,541

Contract size = 12,500,000 JPY.   *Source: CME Group; Chicago Mercantile Exchange (CME)*

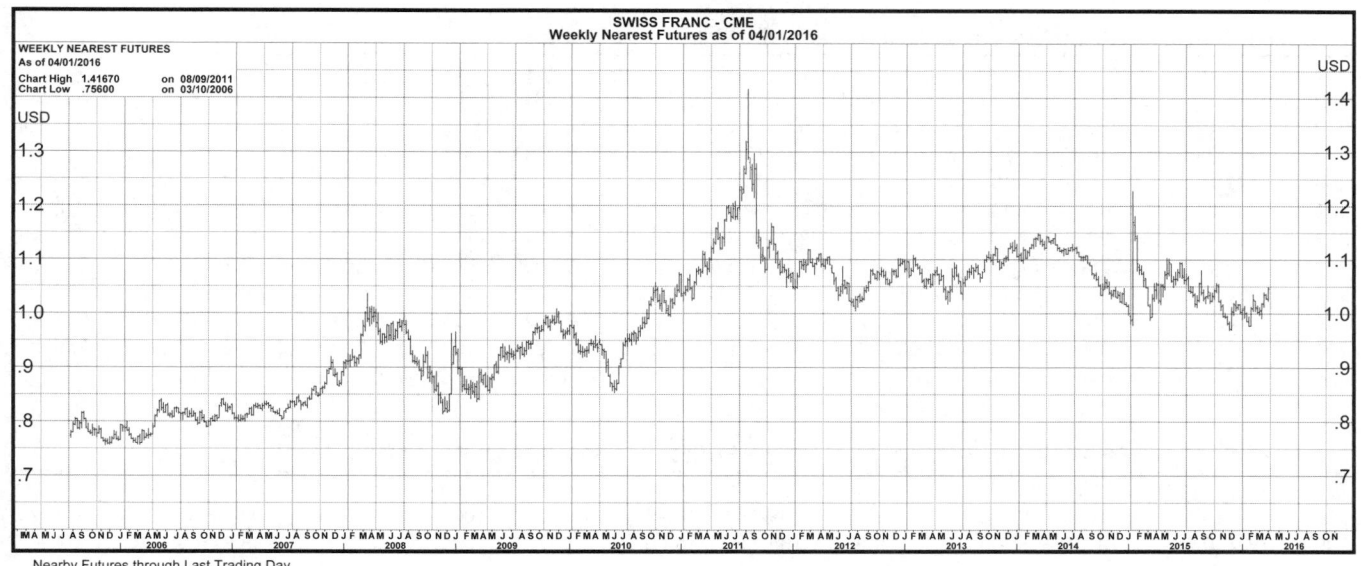

SWISS FRANC - CME
Weekly Nearest Futures as of 04/01/2016

WEEKLY NEAREST FUTURES
As of 04/01/2016
Chart High 1.41670   on 08/09/2011
Chart Low   .75600   on 03/10/2006

Nearby Futures through Last Trading Day.

Swiss Francs per U.S. Dollar

Year	Jan.	Feb.	Mar.	Apr.	May	June	July	Aug.	Sept.	Oct.	Nov.	Dec.	Average
2006	1.2781	1.3056	1.3044	1.2822	1.2185	1.2319	1.2362	1.2319	1.2440	1.2597	1.2351	1.2102	1.2532
2007	1.2438	1.2385	1.2179	1.2128	1.2217	1.2329	1.2076	1.2034	1.1847	1.1743	1.1229	1.1397	1.2000
2008	1.1001	1.0894	1.0116	1.0141	1.0443	1.0363	1.0278	1.0843	1.1091	1.1429	1.1923	1.1393	1.0826
2009	1.1280	1.1635	1.1540	1.1472	1.1057	1.0810	1.0784	1.0677	1.0399	1.0218	1.0117	1.0304	1.0858
2010	1.0341	1.0719	1.0660	1.0682	1.1325	1.1263	1.0531	1.0392	1.0012	0.9688	0.9852	0.9671	1.0428
2011	0.9567	0.9495	0.9187	0.8964	0.8733	0.8404	0.8221	0.7810	0.8734	0.8963	0.9086	0.9335	0.8875
2012	0.9377	0.9119	0.9129	0.9131	0.9397	0.9574	0.9771	0.9685	0.9394	0.9327	0.9388	0.9212	0.9375
2013	0.9243	0.9215	0.9465	0.9368	0.9564	0.9330	0.9446	0.9255	0.9232	0.9032	0.9126	0.8937	0.9268
2014	0.9039	0.8934	0.8805	0.8830	0.8888	0.8955	0.8977	0.9100	0.9367	0.9526	0.9641	0.9769	0.9152
2015	0.9412	0.9361	0.9796	0.9602	0.9325	0.9309	0.9544	0.9685	0.9723	0.9697	1.0099	0.9938	0.9624

Average.   *Source: FOREX*

Volume of Trading of Swiss Franc Futures in Chicago   In Thousands of Contracts

Year	Jan.	Feb.	Mar.	Apr.	May	June	July	Aug.	Sept.	Oct.	Nov.	Dec.	Total
2006	803.5	745.9	1,129.0	837.5	1,011.3	993.3	771.2	1,014.8	1,046.8	919.6	1,078.1	1,118.9	11,470.0
2007	994.4	998.5	1,418.5	959.4	1,100.0	1,507.0	1,660.0	1,588.2	1,113.7	1,129.8	1,067.3	941.8	14,478.7
2008	1,090.5	1,082.4	1,311.8	1,350.7	1,362.8	1,789.1	1,650.0	1,330.3	1,578.9	1,042.4	574.0	651.3	14,814.2
2009	677.7	624.5	813.9	641.5	731.2	1,094.1	844.8	727.0	1,015.2	1,098.5	1,206.6	1,143.5	10,618.6
2010	1,046.8	954.5	1,218.2	1,105.8	1,299.4	1,066.8	813.5	806.1	997.7	847.7	940.4	914.3	12,011.2
2011	848.8	1,025.6	1,266.4	827.0	928.5	1,074.6	936.2	1,098.0	643.1	539.6	489.5	561.4	10,238.7
2012	552.9	773.9	1,034.3	865.2	1,140.5	1,163.6	870.0	855.3	827.8	623.8	599.5	604.6	9,911.3
2013	767.5	643.9	850.4	696.4	1,085.0	938.7	665.1	677.3	688.4	711.0	632.6	705.7	9,061.8
2014	714.1	552.0	819.7	535.8	607.3	792.8	721.4	758.5	1,121.3	1,026.6	834.4	1,154.9	9,638.9
2015	752.0	244.8	537.2	472.1	421.0	513.2	379.8	433.0	433.6	381.7	458.4	607.8	5,634.4

Contract size = 125,000 CHF.   *Source: CME Group; Chicago Mercantile Exchange (CME)*

Average Open Interest of Swiss Franc Futures in Chicago   In Contracts

Year	Jan.	Feb.	Mar.	Apr.	May	June	July	Aug.	Sept.	Oct.	Nov.	Dec.
2006	80,904	107,509	101,445	82,280	98,416	89,254	67,127	69,406	83,545	97,034	89,039	74,522
2007	83,176	103,073	70,627	66,246	89,737	121,557	108,394	118,597	100,948	73,433	81,366	73,025
2008	67,993	67,786	71,972	60,528	65,029	58,511	56,337	61,521	53,448	39,448	42,315	31,420
2009	26,083	32,701	33,518	28,613	34,585	40,027	35,918	39,324	49,537	51,736	52,912	41,890
2010	36,523	41,531	36,834	38,093	49,842	48,989	52,203	55,870	58,484	53,703	45,087	44,460
2011	42,658	46,656	62,300	65,373	70,315	61,349	50,716	20,516	33,972	25,587	29,848	44,100
2012	40,696	48,122	50,263	40,932	59,311	68,970	60,351	56,214	47,686	36,825	43,328	47,914
2013	42,982	44,119	58,519	49,385	59,413	47,741	36,890	38,631	39,298	51,347	45,586	53,657
2014	42,329	48,122	56,682	47,081	49,564	42,368	38,273	52,798	61,701	58,348	60,929	63,108
2015	54,230	35,769	42,525	32,785	32,615	26,518	26,717	40,075	40,143	37,866	64,828	62,677

Contract size = 125,000 CHF.   *Source: CME Group; Chicago Mercantile Exchange (CME)*

CURRENCIES

United States Merchandise Trade Balance[2]   In Millions of Dollars

Year	Jan.	Feb.	Mar.	Apr.	May	June	July	Aug.	Sept.	Oct.	Nov.	Dec.	Total
2006	-72,871	-67,493	-68,017	-68,707	-71,283	-69,728	-72,687	-74,214	-71,279	-65,954	-65,796	-69,259	-837,288
2007	-65,776	-66,380	-70,644	-68,670	-67,895	-68,735	-69,198	-67,060	-67,714	-68,299	-71,741	-69,084	-821,196
2008	-71,650	-74,110	-70,917	-74,315	-73,868	-72,286	-77,628	-71,541	-70,455	-70,138	-53,601	-51,983	-832,492
2009	-47,164	-37,359	-38,976	-39,544	-35,595	-36,844	-42,838	-41,816	-45,296	-45,350	-49,072	-49,840	-509,694
2010	-48,966	-51,997	-51,498	-52,540	-53,634	-59,026	-53,171	-58,069	-57,546	-54,054	-52,393	-55,783	-648,677
2011	-62,494	-59,400	-59,642	-57,913	-63,202	-65,602	-61,880	-61,972	-59,455	-60,906	-62,890	-65,289	-740,645
2012	-66,689	-60,139	-67,148	-63,977	-62,817	-60,389	-59,566	-60,980	-57,410	-60,633	-64,722	-56,700	-741,170
2013	-60,517	-61,647	-56,233	-58,039	-62,257	-55,869	-58,200	-58,804	-61,409	-58,316	-54,523	-56,774	-702,588
2014	-59,968	-61,292	-63,050	-64,321	-62,091	-61,700	-60,177	-60,824	-62,075	-61,917	-59,331	-64,716	-741,462
2015[1]	-62,978	-58,069	-71,192	-62,027	-62,105	-65,143	-61,475	-67,884	-61,153	-63,189	-61,492	-62,600	-759,307

[1] Preliminary.   [2] Not seasonally adjusted.   *Source: Bureau of Economic Analysis, U.S. Department of Commerce (BEA)*

Index of Real Trade-Weighted Dollar Exchange Rates for Total Agriculture[3] (U.S. Markets)   (2000 = 100)

Year	Jan.	Feb.	Mar.	Apr.	May	June	July	Aug.	Sept.	Oct.	Nov.	Dec.
2007	110.3	110.3	110.4	109.7	109.0	108.7	107.4	107.3	105.9	103.7	102.7	102.9
2008	102.4	101.3	100.1	99.9	100.3	100.8	100.2	101.3	102.9	108.3	108.6	106.9
2009	108.2	111.1	112.7	109.3	106.4	106.3	105.6	104.3	103.6	102.0	101.5	101.2
2010	101.1	101.7	100.7	100.0	102.3	102.6	101.2	100.2	99.3	96.8	96.6	97.1
2011	96.6	96.2	95.9	95.0	95.1	95.1	94.1	94.8	96.8	97.4	97.3	97.6
2012	97.1	95.7	96.6	96.7	97.9	99.0	97.9	97.4	96.5	96.0	96.2	95.5
2013	96.0	97.4	98.2	97.8	98.3	99.2	99.6	99.5	99.4	98.1	98.4	98.8
2014	99.9	100.1	100.1	99.4	99.1	99.2	99.0	99.2	100.3	101.1	102.2	103.7
2015[1]	105.1	106.6	108.3	107.5	107.2	108.6	110.2	112.2	112.7	111.2	111.9	113.1
2016[2]	114.7	115.2	115.4	115.4	115.7	116.0	116.4	116.6	116.8	117.0	117.3	117.6

[1] Preliminary.   [2] Forecast.   [3] Real indexes adjust nominal exchange rates for differences in rates of inflation, to avoid the distortion caused by high-inflation countries. A higher value means the dollar has appreciated. Federal Reserve Board Index of trade-weighted value of the U.S. dollar against 10 major currencies. Weights are based on relative importance in world financial markets.
Source: Bureau of Economic Analysis, U.S. Department of Commerce (BEA)

Index of Real Trade-Weighted Dollar Exchange Rates for Total Agriculture[3] (U.S. Competitors)   (2000 = 100)

Year	Jan.	Feb.	Mar.	Apr.	May	June	July	Aug.	Sept.	Oct.	Nov.	Dec.
2007	107.3	106.9	106.5	104.8	104.5	104.5	102.6	103.6	101.9	99.1	97.3	97.4
2008	96.9	95.9	93.2	92.5	93.1	93.3	92.5	95.2	99.1	106.6	109.5	105.8
2009	107.9	111.4	111.0	108.1	104.5	102.7	102.0	100.4	98.9	96.9	96.1	97.0
2010	97.9	100.3	99.7	99.5	103.9	105.5	102.3	101.1	99.7	95.7	96.3	97.7
2011	97.1	95.8	94.7	92.5	93.1	92.8	92.7	93.0	96.6	97.1	97.6	99.0
2012	99.7	97.2	98.0	98.4	101.0	102.8	102.8	102.2	100.3	99.5	99.9	98.3
2013	97.6	97.8	99.4	98.8	99.5	100.4	101.2	101.2	100.9	98.8	99.8	99.7
2014	101.2	101.5	100.6	100.0	100.4	101.0	100.8	101.9	104.2	105.7	106.6	107.9
2015[1]	111.5	113.8	117.9	117.3	115.7	116.6	118.6	119.9	121.2	120.1	122.5	123.0
2016[2]	125.5	126.4	126.9	127.2	127.5	127.9	128.3	128.5	128.9	129.1	129.4	129.7

[1] Preliminary.   [2] Forecast.   [3] Real indexes adjust nominal exchange rates for differences in rates of inflation, to avoid the distortion caused by high-inflation countries. A higher value means the dollar has appreciated. Federal Reserve Board Index of trade-weighted value of the U.S. dollar against 10 major currencies. Weights are based on relative importance in world financial markets.
Source: Bureau of Economic Analysis, U.S. Department of Commerce (BEA)

Merchandise Trade and Current Account Balances[3]   In Billions of Dollars

	Merchanise Trade Balance					Current Account Balance				
Year	Canada	Germany	Japan	Switzerland	United Kingdom	Canada	Germany	Japan	Switzerland	United Kingdom
2007	30.5	231.2	73.6	54.2	-81.4	11.2	233.8	213.1	47.4	-81.4
2008	28.3	224.1	8.2	59.2	-83.9	3.6	208.5	142.1	12.3	-104.5
2009	-20.2	169.2	18.8	41.8	-43.8	-40.3	195.1	146.1	39.6	-63.7
2010	-30.6	173.8	68.9	62.9	-57.3	-56.6	184.7	220.8	81.8	-62.8
2011	-21.6	178.4	-50.8	58.8	-38.2	-47.8	226.7	127.7	47.0	-43.2
2012	-33.9	209.0	-114.8	69.3	-54.6	-60.0	243.1	61.9	66.2	-98.2
2013	-29.3	219.5	-139.2	83.0	-52.9	-54.6	248.1	39.6	73.2	-120.2
2014	-16.0	249.6	-144.3	84.9	-55.8	-39.2	300.9	22.9	49.1	-161.5
2015[1]	-39.5	235.1	-47.6	96.7	-57.9	-59.2	287.1	115.7	70.0	-143.9
2016[2]	-32.2	237.6	-40.2	101.4	-59.4	-51.7	291.2	129.8	75.2	-132.8

[1] Estimate.   [2] Projection.   [3] Not seasonally adjusted.   *Source: Organization for Economic Cooperation and Development (OECD)*

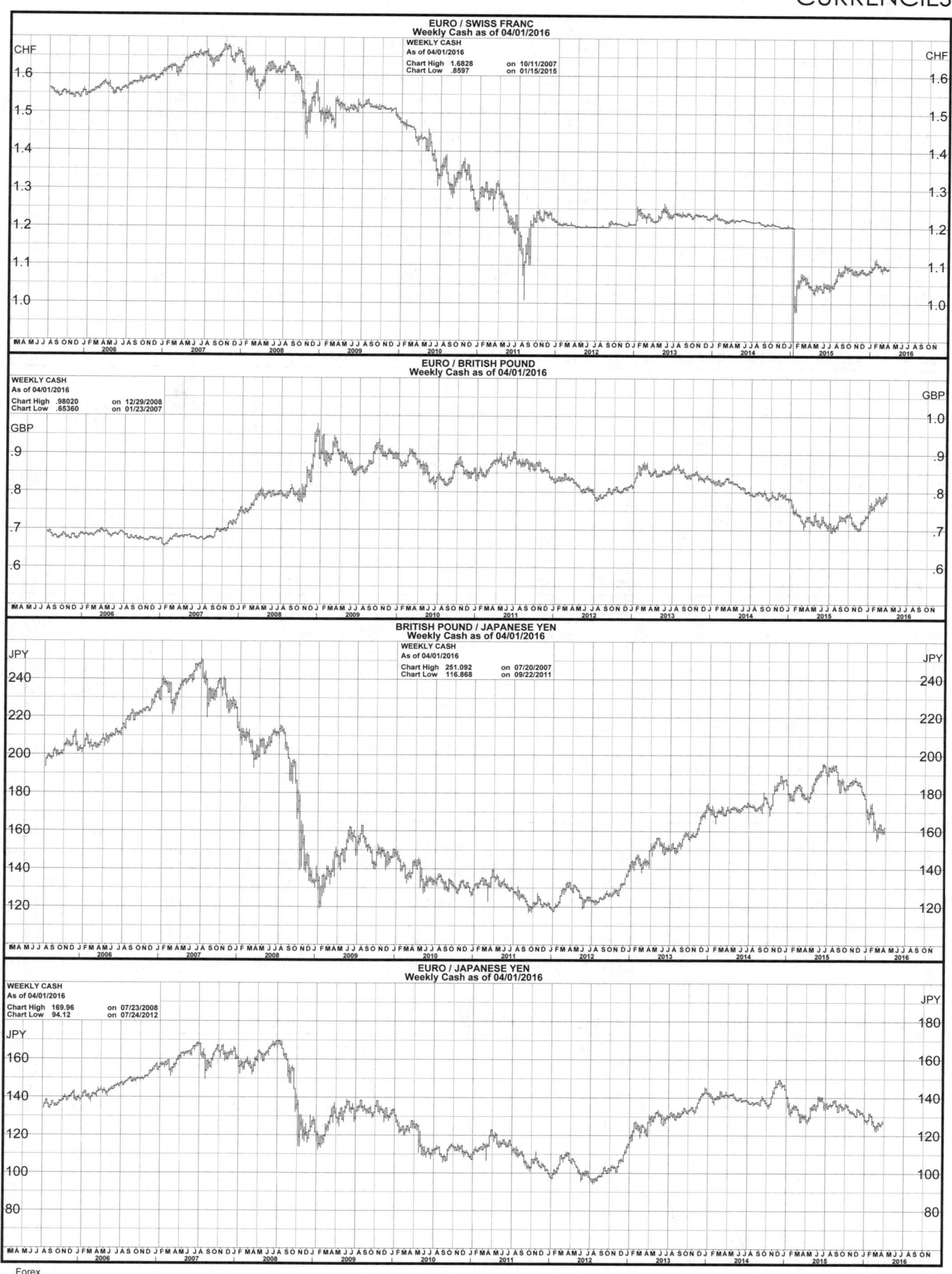

EURO / SWISS FRANC
Weekly Cash as of 04/01/2016

WEEKLY CASH
As of 04/01/2016

Chart High 1.6828 on 10/11/2007
Chart Low .8597 on 01/15/2015

EURO / BRITISH POUND
Weekly Cash as of 04/01/2016

WEEKLY CASH
As of 04/01/2016

Chart High .98020 on 12/29/2008
Chart Low .65360 on 01/23/2007

BRITISH POUND / JAPANESE YEN
Weekly Cash as of 04/01/2016

WEEKLY CASH
As of 04/01/2016

Chart High 251.092 on 07/20/2007
Chart Low 116.868 on 09/22/2011

EURO / JAPANESE YEN
Weekly Cash as of 04/01/2016

WEEKLY CASH
As of 04/01/2016

Chart High 169.96 on 07/23/2008
Chart Low 94.12 on 07/24/2012

Forex.

Diamonds

The diamond, which is the mineral form of carbon, is the hardest, strongest natural material known on earth. The name *diamond* is derived from *adamas*, the ancient Greek term meaning "invincible." Diamonds form deep within the Earth's crust and are typically billions of years old. Diamonds have also have been found in and near meteorites and their craters. Diamonds are considered precious gemstones but lower grade diamonds are used for industrial applications such as drilling, cutting, grinding and polishing.

Supply – World production of natural gem diamonds in 2013 (latest data available) rose by +5.7% yr/yr to 70.600 million carats, well below the 2008 record high of 114.000 million carats (one carat equals 1/5 gram or 200 milligrams). The world's largest producers of natural gem diamonds are Russia with 30.0% of world production in 2013, Botswana with 22.9%, Angola with 11.9%, and South Africa with 9.2%. World production of natural industrial diamonds in 2013 (latest data available) fell -2.1% yr/yr to 59.900 million carats. The main producer of natural industrial diamonds in 2013 was Russia with 27.9% of world production. World production of synthetic diamonds in 2011 remained the same yr/yr at 4.380 million carats. The main producer of synthetic diamonds was China with 91.3% of world production.

Trade – The U.S. in 2015 imported 1.35 million carats of natural diamonds and relied on imports for 84% of its consumption.

World Production of Natural Gem Diamonds   In Thousands of Carats

Year	Angola	Australia	Botswana	Brazil, unspec- ified	Central African Republic	China, unspec- ified	Congo (Kinshasa)	Ghana, unspec- ified	Namibia	Russia	Sierra Leone	South Africa	World Total
2008	8,020	149	22,600	80	302	69	33,402	643	2,435	21,900	223	5,160	114,000
2009	8,310	312	12,400	21	249	46	4,260	376	1,190	19,500	241	4,910	63,800
2010	7,530	200	15,400	25	241	17	4,030	334	1,690	19,500	263	7,090	69,900
2011	7,500	157	16,000	46	259	5	3,850	302	1,260	19,700	214	5,640	67,200
2012[1]	7,500	184	14,400	46	293	2	4,300	233	1,630	19,600	406	5,660	66,800
2013[2]	8,420	235	16,200	49	200	1	3,140	169	1,690	21,200	457	6,510	70,600

[1] Preliminary.   [2] Estimate.   [3] Less than 1/2 unit.   *Source: U.S. Geological Survey (USGS)*

World Production of Natural Industrial Diamonds[4]   In Thousands of Carats

Year	Angola	Australia	Botswana	Brazil	Central African Republic	China	Congo (Kinshasa)	Ghana	Russia	Sierra Leone	South Africa	Vene- zuela	World Total
2008	891	14,800	9,680	600	75	1,000	88	120	15,000	149	7,740	6	49,100
2009	924	15,300	5,320	600	62	1,000	17,000	75	15,300	160	1,230	5	56,400
2010	836	9,800	6,610	600	60	1,000	16,100	67	15,300	175	1,770	1	58,400
2011	833	7,700	6,870	600	65	1,000	15,400	67	15,500	143	1,410	----	55,600
2012[1]	833	9,000	6,170	----	73	----	17,200	----	15,400	135	1,420	----	61,200
2013[2]	936	11,500	6,960	----	----	----	12,500		16,700	152	1,630	----	59,900

[1] Preliminary.   [2] Estimate.   [3] Formerly Zaire.   *Source: U.S. Geological Survey (USGS)*

World Production of Synthetic Diamonds   In Thousands of Carats

Year	Belarus	China	France	Ireland	Japan	Russia	South Africa	Sweden	Ukraine	United States	World Total
2006	25,000	3,900,000	3,000	60,000	34,000	80,000	60,000	20,000	8,000	128,000	4,320,000
2007	25,000	4,000,000	3,000	60,000	34,000	80,000	60,000	20,000	8,000	130,000	4,420,000
2008	25,000	4,000,000	3,000	60,000	34,000	80,000	60,000	20,000	4,000	131,000	4,420,000
2009	25,000	4,000,000	3,000	60,000	34,000	80,000	60,000	20,000	NA	91,000	4,370,000
2010[1]	25,000	4,000,000	3,000	60,000	34,000	80,000	60,000	20,000	NA	93,000	4,380,000
2011[2]	25,000	4,000,000	3,000	60,000	34,000	80,000	60,000	20,000	NA	98,200	4,380,000

[1] Preliminary.   [2] Estimate.   *Source: U.S. Geological Survey (USGS)*

Salient Statistics of Industrial Diamonds in the United States   In Millions of Carats

	Bort, Grit & Powder & Dust Natural and Synthetic							Stones (Natural)						Net Import Reliance
	Production													
Year	Manu- factured Diamond	Secon- dary	Imports for Con- sumption	Exports & Reexports	In Manu- factured Products	Gov't Sales	Apparent Con- sumption	Price Value of Imports $/Carat	Secon- dary Pro- duction	Imports for Con- sumption	Exports & Reexports	Gov't Sales	Apparent Con- sumption	Price Value of Imports $/Carat	% of Con- sumption
2010	NA	33.4	596.0	113.0	----	----	556.0	.14	----	1.7	----	----	3.0	18.78	87
2011	NA	34.7	726.0	148.0	----	----	654.0	.13	----	2.5	----	----	4.0	19.67	88
2012	NA	36.5	595.0	155.0	----	----	520.0	.13	----	2.3	----	----	4.0	15.30	85
2013	NA	38.1	728.0	149.0	----	----	663.0	.11	----	1.9	----	----		15.50	87
2014[1]	NA	43.7	682.0	163.0	----	----	615.0	.11	----	2.2	----	----		14.40	84
2015[2]	NA	37.8	550.0	143.0	----	----	484.0	.13	----	1.4	----	----		15.50	84

[1] Preliminary.   [2] Estimate.   [3] Less than 1/2 unit.   *Source: U.S. Geological Survey (USGS)*

Eggs

Eggs are a low-priced protein source and are consumed worldwide. Each commercial chicken lays between 265-280 eggs per year. In the United States, the grade and size of eggs are regulated under the federal Egg Products Inspection Act (1970). The grades of eggs are AA, A, and B, and must have sound, whole shells and must be clean. The difference among the grades of eggs is internal and mostly reflects the freshness of the egg. Table eggs vary in color and can be determined by the color of the chicken's earlobe. For example, chickens with white earlobes lay white eggs and chickens with reddish-brown earlobes lay brown eggs. In the U.S., egg size is determined by the weight of a dozen eggs, not individual eggs, and range from Peewee to Jumbo. Store-bought eggs in the shell stay fresh for 3 to 5 weeks in a home refrigerator, according to the USDA.

Eggs are primarily used as a source of food, although eggs are also widely used for medical purposes. Fertile eggs, as a source of purified proteins, are used to produce many vaccines. Flu vaccines are produced by growing single strains of the flu virus in eggs, which are then extracted to make the vaccine. Eggs are also used in biotechnology to create new drugs. The hen's genetic make-up can be altered so the whites of the eggs are rich in tailored proteins that form the basis of medicines to fight cancer and other diseases. The U.S. biotech company Viragen and the Roslin Institute in Edinburgh have produced eggs with 100 mg or more of the easily-extracted proteins used in new drugs to treat various illnesses including ovarian and breast cancers.

Prices – The average monthly price of all eggs received by farmers in the U.S. in 2015 rose by +31.1% yr/yr to 164.8 cents per dozen, a new record high.

Supply – World egg production in 2013 (latest data available) was 1.284 billion eggs, up +2.6% yr/yr. The world's largest egg producers at that time were China with 38.6% of world production, the U.S. with 7.4%, Mexico with 3.9%, Japan with 3.3%, Russia and Brazil each with 3.2%. U.S. egg production in 2015 fell -5.3% to 94.750 billion eggs, below last year's record high of 100.010 billion eggs. The average number of hens and pullets on U.S. farms in 2014 (latest data available) rose by +1.7% yr/yr to 360.873 million, a new record high.

Demand – U.S. consumption of eggs in 2013 (latest data available) rose +1.1% yr/yr to 6.729 billion dozen eggs, a new record high. U.S. consumption of eggs is up sharply by about 20% from ten years earlier, reflecting the increased popularity of eggs in American diets. U.S. per capita egg consumption in 2016 is forecasted to rise +1.7% yr/yr to 252.6 eggs per year per person. Per capita egg consumption was at a high of 277.2 eggs in 1970, then fell sharply in the 1990s to a low of 174.9 in 1995, and then began rebounding in 1997 to current levels of about 250 eggs per year.

Trade – U.S. imports of eggs in 2013 (latest data available) fell -8.6% yr/yr to 16.9 million dozen eggs. U.S. exports of eggs in 2013 rose +23.3% yr/yr to 371.9 million dozen eggs, a new record high.

World Production of Eggs   In Millions of Eggs

Year	Brazil	China	France	Germany	Italy	Japan	Mexico	Russia	Spain	Ukraine	United Kingdom	United States	World Total
2005	33,499	414,480	15,502	12,028	12,896	41,377	40,494	36,691	13,122	12,955	10,608	90,027	1,066,202
2006	35,207	412,080	15,138	12,137	12,123	41,611	45,801	37,651	13,122	14,122	10,224	91,800	1,087,906
2007	35,584	429,980	14,640	11,974	12,929	43,050	45,817	37,889	13,095	13,978	9,972	91,044	1,120,299
2008	36,893	465,484	13,355	12,103	13,393	42,567	46,744	37,804	12,896	14,809	10,404	90,012	1,162,404
2009	38,438	472,671	14,601	10,754	14,509	41,750	47,206	39,188	13,166	15,303	10,319	90,408	1,183,797
2010	38,961	476,403	15,094	10,191	13,157	41,900	47,623	40,392	12,896	16,865	11,274	91,482	1,206,342
2011	40,731	484,633	14,088	12,035	13,482	41,377	49,170	40,778	12,995	18,428	11,201	91,855	1,229,055
2012[1]	41,676	493,184	14,155	12,800	13,661	41,780	46,361	41,548	11,409	18,919	10,806	92,275	1,251,373
2013[2]	43,431	495,754	15,750	13,736	13,839	42,033	50,317	40,779	11,787	19,419	11,517	95,176	1,284,449

[1] Preliminary.   [2] Forecast.   [3] Selected countries.   *Source: Food and Agricultural Organization of the United Nations (FAO)*

Salient Statistics of Eggs in the United States

	Hens & Pullets		Rate of Lay	Eggs			Total				Consumption	
Year	On Farm Dec. 1[3]	Average Number During Year	Per Layer During Year[4]	Total Produced	Price in cents Per Dozen	Value of Production[5]	Egg Production	Imports[6]	Exports[6]	Used for Hatching	Total	Per Capita Eggs[6]
	----- Thousands -----		(Number)	----- Millions -----		Million USD	------------------ Million Dozen ------------------					Number
2007	344,492	346,498	263	91,101	88.5	6,719	7,588	28.2	250.3	1,016.3	6,351	251.7
2008	339,643	339,131	266	90,239	109.0	8,239	7,501	27.6	206.3	996.3	6,320	248.3
2009	339,526	337,848	268	90,737	82.1	6,191	7,547	19.5	242.2	955.3	6,368	248.2
2010	341,551	340,335	269	91,811	86.5	6,553	7,656	21.8	258.4	982.2	6,436	247.9
2011	338,472	338,475	271	92,450	97.7	7,356	7,755	20.9	276.5	950.1	6,501	250.0
2012	346,965	341,052	274	94,364	100.1	7,929	7,930	18.5	301.7	941.4	6,666	254.6
2013	356,923	354,844	275	97,555	108.8	8,679	8,186	16.9	371.8	964.8	6,827	258.4
2014[1]	370,637	364,707	277	100,879	125.8	10,166	8,489	34.7	393.8	980.7	7,091	263.0
2015[2]	343,523	349,565	276	96,437	164.8		8,124	123.3	317.6	995.4	6,780	250.1

[1] Preliminary.   [2] Forecast.   [3] All layers of laying age.   [4] Number of eggs produced during the year divided by the average number of all layers of laying age on hand during the year.   [5] Value of sales plus value of eggs consumed in households of producers. 6/ Shell-egg equivalent of eggs and egg products.
Source: National Agricultural Statistics Service, U.S. Department of Agriculture (NASS-USDA)

EGGS

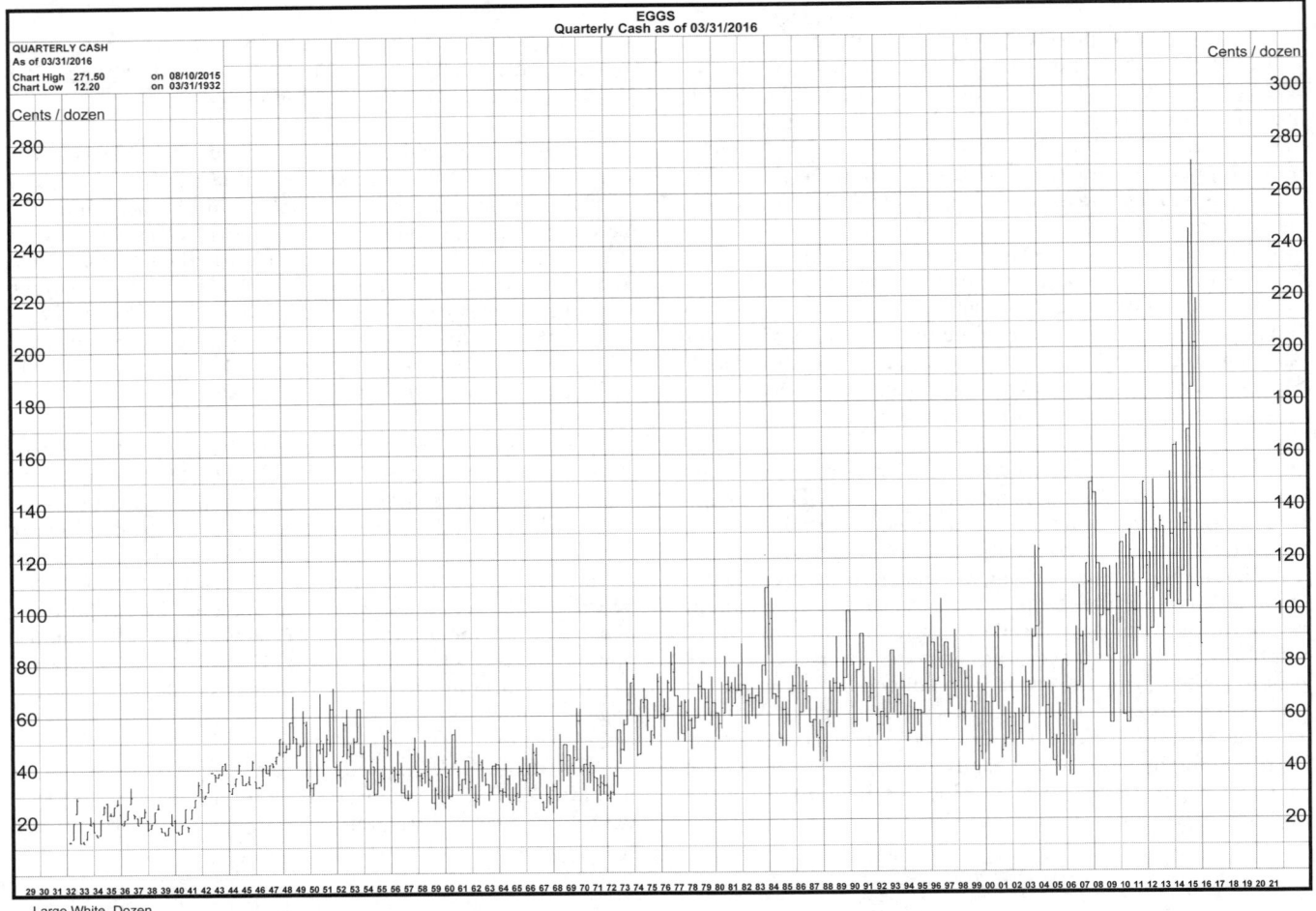

EGGS
Quarterly Cash as of 03/31/2016

QUARTERLY CASH
As of 03/31/2016
Chart High 271.50 on 08/10/2015
Chart Low 12.20 on 03/31/1932

Cents / dozen

Large White, Dozen

Average Price Received by Farmers for All Eggs in the United States   In Cents Per Dozen

Year	Jan.	Feb.	Mar.	Apr.	May	June	July	Aug.	Sept.	Oct.	Nov.	Dec.	Average
2006	61.0	49.5	67.0	51.2	42.7	54.7	43.5	55.0	53.4	54.1	81.2	80.7	57.8
2007	91.5	78.1	82.8	72.9	78.0	73.4	94.5	86.6	107.0	93.5	126.0	136.0	93.4
2008	129.0	131.0	138.0	103.0	86.8	106.0	84.1	96.3	99.6	102.0	102.0	99.9	106.5
2009	103.0	80.9	81.6	92.0	61.7	59.4	70.8	75.8	74.4	80.0	101.0	105.0	82.1
2010	103.0	91.7	116.0	79.4	63.3	61.9	70.9	78.9	68.4	83.6	113.0	108.0	86.5
2011	85.0	95.4	84.9	105.0	82.2	88.6	88.0	115.0	102.0	102.0	102.0	122.0	97.7
2012	87.9	88.5	99.5	86.5	82.8	90.7	96.9	113.0	122.0	102.0	118.0	113.0	100.1
2013	106.0	99.3	115.0	88.5	117.0	93.0	104.0	108.0	103.0	104.0	132.0	136.0	108.8
2014	112.0	140.0	124.0	127.0	117.0	109.0	124.0	108.0	105.0	114.0	152.0	177.0	125.8
2015[1]	125.0	129.0	155.0	108.0	173.0	201.0	190.0	239.0	190.0	144.0	200.0	124.0	164.8

[1] Preliminary.   *Source: Economic Research Service, U.S. Department of Agriculture (ERS-USDA)*

Average Wholesale Price of Shell Eggs (Large) Delivered, Chicago   In Cents Per Dozen

Year	Jan.	Feb.	Mar.	Apr.	May	June	July	Aug.	Sept.	Oct.	Nov.	Dec.	Average
2006	65.40	46.08	65.11	57.11	41.32	56.14	40.30	57.46	54.97	55.64	84.38	87.65	59.30
2007	91.75	92.71	89.23	80.00	83.55	69.60	99.95	97.37	117.50	101.89	128.93	147.70	100.02
2008	144.55	142.70	150.15	115.23	90.64	107.33	95.43	100.07	108.98	103.85	110.50	109.50	114.91
2009	113.40	92.29	85.64	99.26	64.55	72.41	73.55	85.69	80.17	86.14	110.75	114.41	89.86
2010	111.50	107.55	116.80	84.81	64.15	69.68	73.74	88.73	83.17	76.88	124.79	124.73	93.88
2011	100.20	99.08	86.37	106.05	87.31	86.95	92.70	114.07	105.93	111.79	112.50	130.07	102.75
2012	106.25	91.47	98.59	96.10	76.55	92.50	105.45	131.33	119.50	114.28	123.93	123.90	106.65
2013	112.93	112.92	114.30	97.86	105.45	89.75	104.77	106.82	106.50	106.41	133.60	150.21	111.79
2014	113.10	135.97	133.93	145.98	116.21	115.83	122.16	116.02	111.93	117.11	143.18	194.45	130.49
2015[1]	111.10	133.50	149.18	113.10	136.20	223.82	206.55	260.40	217.02	161.95	192.55	157.14	171.88

[1] Preliminary.   *Source: National Agricultural Statistics Service, U.S. Department of Agriculture (NASS-USDA)*

Total Egg Production in the United States   In Millions of Eggs

Year	Jan.	Feb.	Mar.	Apr.	May	June	July	Aug.	Sept.	Oct.	Nov.	Dec.	Total
2006	7,727	6,980	7,843	7,543	7,637	7,401	7,645	7,647	7,430	7,678	7,549	7,815	90,895
2007	7,675	6,951	7,806	7,472	7,622	7,380	7,599	7,594	7,393	7,726	7,542	7,808	90,568
2008	7,646	7,114	7,675	7,373	7,564	7,367	7,599	7,551	7,339	7,625	7,490	7,778	90,121
2009	7,678	6,903	7,737	7,472	7,607	7,360	7,590	7,593	7,376	7,696	7,569	7,853	90,434
2010	7,724	6,935	7,839	7,578	7,716	7,484	7,719	7,765	7,514	7,698	7,573	7,927	91,472
2011	7,833	7,013	7,840	7,617	7,773	7,503	7,732	7,719	7,503	7,783	7,612	7,987	91,915
2012	7,892	7,283	7,916	7,653	7,850	7,582	7,798	7,869	7,625	7,965	7,874	8,226	93,533
2013	8,125	7,321	8,195	7,929	8,139	7,857	8,082	8,178	7,969	8,267	8,098	8,538	96,698
2014	8,490	7,636	8,522	8,298	8,523	8,242	8,597	8,591	8,289	8,632	8,521	8,829	101,170
2015[1]	8,613	7,688	8,635	8,294	8,083	7,512	7,778	7,802	7,565	7,874	7,764	8,119	95,727

[1] Preliminary.   Source: National Agricultural Statistics Service, U.S. Department of Agriculture (NASS-USDA)

Per Capita Disappearance of Eggs[4] in the United States   In Number of Eggs

Year	First Quarter	Second Quarter	Third Quarter	Fourth Quarter	Total	Year	First Quarter	Second Quarter	Third Quarter	Fourth Quarter	Total
2005	63.4	63.0	63.5	65.0	257.2	2011	61.3	61.5	62.8	64.3	250.0
2006	64.1	63.7	63.9	64.7	259.7	2012	63.3	62.3	63.3	65.6	254.6
2007	62.2	61.7	62.4	63.8	251.7	2013	64.3	63.4	64.7	66.0	258.4
2008	61.8	61.3	62.0	63.8	248.3	2014[1]	64.7	65.3	66.3	66.7	263.0
2009	62.0	61.5	61.4	62.9	248.2	2015[2]	64.4	61.5	60.4	63.9	250.1
2010	61.5	61.4	62.2	62.8	247.9	2016[3]	64.5	64.0	64.0	65.9	258.3

[1] Preliminary.   [2] Estimate.   [3] Forecast.   Source: Economic Research Service, U.S. Department of Agriculture (ERS-USDA)

Egg-Feed Ratio[1] in the United States

Year	Jan.	Feb.	Mar.	Apr.	May	June	July	Aug.	Sept.	Oct.	Nov.	Dec.	Average
2006	8.5	5.9	9.8	6.3	4.2	7.1	4.6	7.5	6.9	6.4	10.6	10.1	7.3
2007	11.7	8.4	9.1	7.6	8.1	6.4	10.7	9.5	12.3	10.2	13.9	13.9	10.2
2008	12.7	11.1	11.8	7.4	5.8	7.3	5.4	6.6	7.7	8.9	9.4	9.2	8.6
2009	9.0	7.0	7.2	8.4	4.3	3.8	5.6	6.5	6.8	7.3	10.0	10.3	7.2
2010	10.1	8.9	12.2	7.0	5.1	5.0	6.0	6.9	4.6	6.5	9.5	8.1	7.5
2011	5.8	6.0	5.1	6.4	4.5	4.9	4.9	6.7	6.3	6.8	6.8	8.7	6.1
2012	5.1	5.0	5.7	4.5	5.0	4.8	4.8	5.6	7.0	5.6	6.6	6.3	5.5
2013	5.6	5.0	6.1	4.2	6.3	4.4	5.3	6.1	6.4	7.3	10.4	10.7	6.5
2014	8.0	10.9	8.9	8.9	7.9	7.3	9.6	8.6	9.0	10.5	15.1	17.7	10.2
2015[1]	11.4	12.2	15.3	9.6	18.2	22.0	19.6	26.5	20.7	14.7	22.9	12.2	17.1

[1] Pounds of laying feed equivalent in value to one dozen eggs.   [2] Preliminary.   Source: Economic Research Service, U.S. Department of Agriculture (ERS-USDA)

Hens and Pullets of Laying Age (Layers) in the United States, on First of Month   In Thousands

Year	Jan.	Feb.	Mar.	Apr.	May	June	July	Aug.	Sept.	Oct.	Nov.	Dec.
2006	349,763	349,930	350,452	350,453	346,809	343,596	341,733	340,728	342,309	343,946	345,090	348,719
2007	349,192	348,563	349,081	347,280	343,835	341,057	339,373	340,648	340,604	341,322	343,909	344,492
2008	345,535	343,891	342,666	341,320	340,318	339,867	337,416	335,094	335,396	333,534	336,301	339,643
2009	341,373	341,388	340,716	341,067	339,239	334,953	333,064	332,371	332,808	334,917	336,671	339,526
2010	341,411	339,747	341,191	342,969	339,635	339,018	340,442	339,384	340,749	336,691	337,300	341,551
2011	344,255	340,247	339,296	342,237	339,520	336,232	336,559	334,997	335,794	334,826	336,909	338,472
2012	340,522	339,826	340,926	343,073	341,885	341,486	338,416	337,525	339,302	341,076	345,269	346,965
2013	344,920	344,916	347,025	348,468	344,363	345,740	343,944	349,862	351,870	349,950	352,971	356,923
2014	363,828	362,628	363,000	364,610	364,840	363,604	363,572	365,799	365,748	366,306	366,329	370,637
2015[1]	368,380	364,996	365,857	362,455	354,344	328,911	328,368	329,580	332,124	334,948	337,404	343,523

[1] Preliminary.   Source: National Agricultural Statistics Service, U.S. Department of Agriculture (NASS-USDA)

EGGS

Eggs Laid Per Hundred Layers in the United States   In Number of Eggs

Year	Jan.	Feb.	Mar.	Apr.	May	June	July	Aug.	Sept.	Oct.	Nov.	Dec.	Average
2006	2,210	1,994	2,238	2,164	2,212	2,160	2,240	2,239	2,165	2,228	2,176	2,234	2,188
2007	2,200	1,993	2,242	2,162	2,226	2,169	2,235	2,229	2,168	2,255	2,191	2,255	2,194
2008	2,218	2,072	2,244	2,163	2,224	2,175	2,260	2,252	2,194	2,277	2,216	2,283	2,215
2009	2,249	2,024	2,269	2,197	2,256	2,203	2,281	2,283	2,209	2,292	2,239	2,303	2,234
2010	2,267	2,036	2,291	2,220	2,273	2,203	2,271	2,283	2,218	2,284	2,231	2,311	2,241
2011	2,289	2,064	2,301	2,234	2,300	2,230	2,303	2,301	2,238	2,317	2,254	2,351	2,265
2012	2,320	2,140	2,315	2,234	2,297	2,229	2,307	2,325	2,241	2,321	2,275	2,347	2,279
2013	2,327	2,090	2,326	2,259	2,329	2,249	2,315	2,331	2,271	2,352	2,281	2,354	2,290
2014	2,337	2,105	2,342	2,275	2,340	2,267	2,357	2,349	2,265	2,356	2,312	2,389	2,308
2015[1]	2,349	2,104	2,360	2,291	2,341	2,258	2,334	2,332	2,247	2,320	2,260	2,334	2,294

[1] Preliminary.   Source: National Agricultural Statistics Service, U.S. Department of Agriculture (NASS-USDA)

Egg-Type Chicks Hatched by Commercial Hatcheries in the United States   In Thousands

Year	Jan.	Feb.	Mar.	Apr.	May	June	July	Aug.	Sept.	Oct.	Nov.	Dec.	Total
2006	35,230	33,473	38,910	35,549	39,827	37,475	32,860	35,779	37,048	36,345	31,623	33,254	427,373
2007	36,176	37,071	38,672	39,634	37,744	40,421	35,927	36,969	35,386	36,310	36,219	36,033	446,562
2008	40,156	38,429	42,189	42,329	41,829	40,704	37,234	35,594	37,179	40,288	34,247	37,585	467,763
2009	37,826	36,809	41,752	42,808	40,772	41,980	36,227	38,078	40,310	37,392	34,525	39,502	467,981
2010	39,815	38,854	44,189	47,132	44,039	41,474	38,831	37,172	39,761	41,965	38,794	38,367	490,393
2011	40,587	37,412	43,600	42,956	42,946	38,918	36,948	41,428	39,803	37,616	37,503	38,889	478,606
2012	41,290	40,523	43,101	43,202	44,564	38,829	35,968	42,269	38,319	37,901	36,492	40,985	483,443
2013	43,454	41,840	43,600	45,423	49,468	41,584	39,225	38,231	41,668	42,406	41,750	41,144	509,793
2014	44,458	40,986	44,233	45,703	49,146	44,006	42,297	39,803	43,722	44,468	36,544	42,980	518,346
2015[1]	44,174	43,091	50,077	49,595	47,652	46,868	42,582	46,863	48,972	49,953	46,038	47,103	562,968

[1] Preliminary.   Source: National Agricultural Statistics Service, U.S. Department of Agriculture (NASS-USDA)

Cold Storage Holdings of Frozen Eggs in the United States, on First of Month   In Thousands of Pounds[2]

Year	Jan.	Feb.	Mar.	Apr.	May	June	July	Aug.	Sept.	Oct.	Nov.	Dec.
2006	21,018	22,452	24,468	20,757	23,259	21,013	22,063	23,596	21,560	19,038	16,262	17,057
2007	16,478	17,207	15,693	14,632	14,318	15,165	17,411	17,495	18,485	17,696	17,556	15,184
2008	14,652	12,007	16,732	16,302	16,034	12,443	16,139	21,097	20,800	21,890	22,358	21,261
2009	22,638	22,558	22,065	20,343	18,241	21,714	21,655	22,578	22,558	21,590	22,912	21,158
2010	23,644	24,340	24,106	21,623	22,388	22,419	25,010	24,684	24,688	26,054	25,552	22,910
2011	25,357	26,788	28,143	27,287	27,681	29,025	33,813	33,924	31,009	31,889	33,895	32,967
2012	36,491	37,415	36,326	33,669	32,528	34,498	40,191	38,654	35,856	31,375	28,971	27,251
2013	27,376	29,659	28,620	27,138	29,339	28,856	30,591	26,118	30,144	33,577	33,832	29,754
2014	30,350	34,687	34,631	29,044	27,430	28,300	30,142	31,453	29,820	31,126	31,960	30,349
2015	30,718	34,670	35,648	31,978	31,260	28,092	26,890	27,407	30,572	32,324	37,486	36,013

[1] Preliminary.   [2] Converted on basis 39.5 pounds frozen eggs equals 1 case.   Source: National Agricultural Statistics Service, U.S. Department of Agriculture (NASS-USDA)

Electric Power Production by Electric Utilities in the United States   In Millions of Kilowatt Hours

Year	Jan.	Feb.	Mar.	Apr.	May	June	July	Aug.	Sept.	Oct.	Nov.	Dec.	Total
2005	212,654	185,283	196,136	178,408	197,082	221,116	239,381	238,790	211,139	193,687	188,255	212,914	2,474,845
2006	204,976	192,304	197,249	184,803	204,107	223,950	243,526	242,624	200,655	193,321	189,435	206,705	2,483,655
2007	218,288	197,329	197,229	184,017	202,783	218,554	234,728	246,147	209,641	197,285	189,498	208,631	2,504,130
2008	220,229	197,368	194,959	185,415	201,811	225,775	239,383	230,563	201,631	186,930	184,192	207,111	2,475,367
2009	216,218	179,859	184,963	174,130	189,695	213,482	221,545	222,452	193,720	184,019	179,276	213,417	2,372,776
2010	222,362	195,895	188,491	172,441	199,835	228,551	243,756	240,185	203,521	178,917	179,858	217,820	2,471,632
2011	220,900	188,700	195,148	183,567	196,994	225,535	253,142	242,540	199,144	181,359	176,515	197,306	2,460,850
2012	196,498	176,554	175,331	169,095	194,593	210,514	242,595	229,579	191,871	178,825	178,834	194,884	2,339,173
2013	204,308	178,510	187,573	172,366	188,659	210,788	230,218	226,603	196,318	180,417	179,433	205,119	2,360,312
2014[1]	222,427	190,724	193,861	170,037	192,471	212,588	227,208	225,079	193,157	176,012	180,173		2,382,259

[1] Preliminary.   Source: Energy Information Administration, U.S. Department of Energy (EIA-DOE)

Electric Power

The modern electric utility industry began in the 1800s. In 1807, Humphry Davy constructed a practical battery and demonstrated both incandescent and arc light. In 1831, Michael Faraday built the first electric generator proving that rotary mechanical power could be converted into electric power. In 1879, Thomas Edison perfected a practical incandescent light bulb. The electric utility industry evolved from gas and electric carbon-arc commercial and street lighting systems. In 1882, in New York City, Thomas Edison's Pearl Street electricity generating station established the industry by displaying the four key elements of a modern electric utility system: reliable central generation, efficient distribution, successful end use, and a competitive price.

Electricity is measured in units called watts and watt-hours. Electricity must be used when it is generated and cannot be stored to any significant degree. That means the power utilities must match the level of electricity generation to the level of demand in order to avoid wasteful over-production. The power industry has been deregulated to some degree in the past decade and now major utility companies sell power back and forth across major national grids in order to meet supply and demand needs. The rapid changes in the supply-demand situation mean that the cost of electricity can be very volatile.

Electricity futures trade at the CME Group. The futures contract is a financially settled contract, which is priced based on electricity prices in the PJM western hub at 111 delivery points, mainly on the utility transmission systems of Pennsylvania Electric Co. and the Potomac Electric Co. The contract is priced in dollars and cents per megawatt hours.

Supply – U.S. electricity production in 2015 (annualized through August) rose +1.1% yr/yr to 2.407 trillion kilowatt-hours. That was well below the record high of 3.212 trillion kilowatt-hours in 1998 and indicated that recent electricity production has been reduced mainly because of more efficient production and distribution systems, and to some extent by conservation of electricity by both business and residential consumers.

U.S. electricity generation in 2015 required the use of 10.067 billion cubic feet of natural gas (+17.8% yr/yr), 754 million tons of coal (-11.7% yr/yr), and 51 million barrels of fuel oil (-4.5% yr/yr).

In terms of kilowatt-hours, coal is the most widely used source of electricity production in the U.S. accounting for 40.3% of electricity production in 2013 (latest data available), followed by natural gas (26.2%), nuclear (20.2%), hydro (6.8%), and fuel oil (0.6%). Alternative sources of fuel for electricity generation that are gaining favor include geothermal, biomass, solar, wind, etc. but so far they only account for 5.7% of total electricity production in the U.S.

Demand – Residential use of electricity accounts for the largest single category of electricity demand with usage of 1.374 trillion kilowatt hours in 2012 (latest data available) accounting for 37.2% of overall usage. Business users in total use more electricity than residential users, but business users are broken into the categories of commercial with 35.9% of usage and industrial with 26.7% of usage.

World Net Generation of Electricity   In Billions of Kilowatt Hours

Year	Brazil	Canada	China	France	Germany	India	Japan	Korea, South	Russia	Spain	United Kingdom	United States	World Total
2003	358.9	572.3	1,810.3	533.7	567.5	599.7	982.1	323.9	866.5	244.2	372.6	3,883.2	15,904.2
2004	381.2	582.3	2,103.5	540.6	579.2	644.8	1,010.2	345.7	883.7	259.4	368.7	3,970.6	16,691.9
2005	395.7	606.3	2,370.1	544.9	576.9	675.7	1,020.2	363.9	899.3	268.9	370.6	4,055.4	17,330.0
2006	411.9	592.6	2,714.8	542.8	593.5	727.4	1,038.5	379.1	939.9	280.0	368.4	4,064.7	18,032.9
2007	437.2	612.9	3,087.3	538.5	597.9	775.9	1,077.8	402.4	958.4	286.5	367.6	4,156.7	18,866.7
2008	454.5	614.6	3,280.7	544.0	595.2	796.1	1,012.9	419.1	982.5	295.6	360.4	4,119.4	19,157.2
2009	458.6	595.0	3,507.5	507.3	556.7	856.1	985.6	426.0	937.8	278.3	348.9	3,950.3	19,093.3
2010	506.8	585.8	4,051.9	540.3	591.2	912.3	1,044.2	468.3	980.9	285.4	354.8	4,125.1	20,437.0
2011[1]	530.4	626.6	4,547.1	531.6	572.3	1,006.3	1,032.2	489.7	996.8	278.1	341.5	4,100.1	21,182.4
2012[2]	537.6	616.2	4,768.3	533.3	585.2	1,052.5	966.4	499.7	1,012.5	280.0	335.7	4,047.8	21,531.7

[1] Preliminary.   [2] Estimate.   NA = Not avaliable.   *Source: Energy Information Administration, U.S. Department of Energy (EIA-DOE)*

World Consumption of Electricity   In Billions of Kilowatt Hours

Year	Brazil	Canada	China	France	Germany	India	Italy	Japan	Korea, South	Russia	United Kingdom	United States	World Total
2003	336.9	528.2	1,676.8	435.5	537.2	427.4	295.0	932.4	312.9	742.6	342.7	3,662.0	14,452.3
2004	353.3	534.1	1,955.4	447.0	548.4	471.0	302.1	961.3	332.9	763.5	343.0	3,715.9	15,135.9
2005	367.9	547.8	2,193.3	452.3	543.0	497.1	306.7	969.8	350.2	774.3	351.0	3,811.0	15,719.7
2006	382.5	534.0	2,522.0	447.6	548.1	547.1	313.8	988.3	364.5	816.5	348.4	3,816.8	16,400.8
2007	404.2	561.5	2,870.8	450.1	552.0	593.3	314.7	1,026.9	387.0	840.7	345.0	3,890.2	17,181.2
2008	419.6	561.6	3,054.1	462.5	545.0	621.3	314.6	961.6	403.0	855.6	343.3	3,865.2	17,453.4
2009	418.4	523.8	3,270.3	446.5	519.4	669.2	297.4	935.1	409.2	816.1	323.6	3,723.8	17,388.1
2010	455.7	526.3	3,781.5	474.2	547.2	725.5	306.8	994.8	450.2	858.5	330.9	3,886.4	18,679.9
2011[1]	478.8	543.7	4,264.3	442.7	543.7	803.0	311.3	983.2	472.3	869.3	320.2	3,882.6	19,396.6
2012[2]	483.5	524.8	4,467.9	451.1	540.1	864.7	303.1	921.0	482.4	889.3	319.1	3,832.3	19,710.4

[1] Preliminary.   [2] Estimate.   NA = Not avaliable.   *Source: Energy Information Administration, U.S. Department of Energy (EIA-DOE)*

ELECTRIC POWER

World Installed Capacity of Electricity   In Billions of Kilowatt Hours

Year	Brazil	Canada	China	France	Germany	India	Italy	Japan	Russia	Spain	United Kingdom	United States	World Total
2003	86.4	119.0	397.6	116.7	124.3	131.5	78.1	268.7	215.3	71.8	77.8	948.4	3,843.9
2004	90.7	119.7	448.8	116.9	126.7	139.0	81.3	273.4	216.9	69.7	79.8	962.9	3,983.6
2005	93.3	122.5	524.2	115.8	128.1	147.2	85.5	275.3	218.1	76.6	82.4	978.0	4,123.0
2006	96.8	124.2	631.0	115.7	132.2	155.4	89.5	276.8	220.6	81.3	83.6	986.2	4,303.4
2007	100.2	125.3	725.4	116.6	136.2	168.9	93.6	277.2	223.2	88.8	83.5	994.9	4,478.5
2008	103.5	126.4	806.4	117.7	142.7	176.8	98.6	279.9	222.8	93.7	84.8	1,010.2	4,650.1
2009	105.4	131.6	890.4	119.2	150.9	189.2	101.4	282.5	224.1	96.7	86.7	1,025.4	4,853.0
2010	113.6	132.2	987.3	124.4	162.5	207.7	106.5	284.9	228.1	91.8	92.9	1,039.1	5,081.4
2011[1]	119.1	132.8	1,084.7	127.4	167.6	237.9	118.5	287.3	231.6	101.4	92.0	1,051.3	5,314.5
2012[2]	121.7	135.0	1,174.3	129.3	177.1	254.7	124.2	293.3	234.4	105.3	93.8	1,063.0	5,549.6

[1] Preliminary.   [2] Estimate.   NA = Not avaliable.   *Source: Energy Information Administration, U.S. Department of Energy (EIA-DOE)*

Electricity in the United States   In Billions of Kilowatt Hours

	Net Generation				Trade			T&D Losses[6] and Unaccounted for[7]	End Use		
Year	Electric Power Sector[2]	Commercial Sector[3]	Industrial Sector[4]	Total	Imports[5]	Exports[5]	Net Imports[5]		Retail Sales[8]	Direct Use[9]	Total
2006	3,908.1	8.4	148.3	4,064.7	42.7	24.3	18.4	266.3	3,669.9	146.9	3,816.8
2007	4,005.3	8.3	143.1	4,156.7	51.4	20.1	31.3	297.8	3,764.6	125.7	3,890.2
2008	3,974.3	7.9	137.1	4,119.4	57.0	24.2	32.8	287.1	3,733.0	132.2	3,865.2
2009	3,809.8	8.2	132.3	3,950.3	52.2	18.1	34.1	260.6	3,596.9	126.9	3,723.8
2010	3,972.4	8.6	144.1	4,125.1	45.1	19.1	26.0	264.6	3,754.5	131.9	3,886.4
2011	3,948.2	10.1	141.9	4,100.1	52.3	15.0	37.3	254.8	3,749.8	132.8	3,882.6
2012	3,890.4	11.3	146.1	4,047.8	59.3	12.0	47.3	262.7	3,694.7	137.7	3,832.3
2013	3,903.7	12.2	150.0	4,066.0	70.4	11.4	59.0	256.6	3,724.9	143.5	3,868.3
2014	3,937.0	12.5	144.1	4,093.6	61.6	13.5	48.1	238.6	3,764.7	138.5	3,903.2
2015[1]	3,930.6	13.0	143.8	4,087.4	75.6	9.1	66.5	290.6	3,724.5	138.7	3,863.3

[1] Preliminary.   [2] Electricity-only and combined-heat-and-power (CHP) plants within the NAICS 22 category whose primary business is to sell electricity, or electricity and heat, to the public.   [3] Commercial combined-heat-and-power (CHP) and commercial electricity-only plants.   [4] Industrial combined-heat-and-power (CHP) and industrial electricity-only plants.   [5] Electricity transmitted across U.S. borders. Net imports equal imports minus exports.   [6] Transmission and distribution losses.   [7] Data collection frame differences and nonsampling error.   [8] Electricity retail sales to ultimate customers by electric utilities and other energy service providers.   [9] Use of electricity that is 1) self-generated, 2) produced by either the same entity that consumes the power or an affiliate, and 3) used in direct support of a service or industrial process located within the same facility or group of facilities that house the generating equipment. Direct use is exclusive of station use.   *Source: U.S. Geological Survey (USGS)*

Electricity Net Generation in the United States by Sector   In Millions of Kilowatt Hours

	Fossil Fuels						Renewable Energy						
Year	Coal[2]	Petro-leum[3]	Natural Gas[4]	Other Gases[5]	Nuclear electric power	Hydro-electric Pumped Storage[6]	Conven-tional Hydro-electric Power	Biomass: Wood[7]	Biomass: Waste[8]	Geo-thermal	Solar/ PV[9]	Wind	Total
2005	2,012,873	122,225	760,960	13,464	781,986	-6,558	270,321	38,856	15,420	14,692	550	17,811	4,055,423
2006	1,990,511	64,166	816,441	14,177	787,219	-6,558	289,246	38,762	16,099	14,568	508	26,589	4,064,702
2007	2,016,456	65,739	896,590	13,453	806,425	-6,896	247,510	39,014	16,525	14,637	612	34,450	4,156,745
2008	1,985,801	46,243	882,981	11,707	806,208	-6,288	254,831	37,300	17,734	14,840	864	55,363	4,119,388
2009	1,755,904	38,937	920,979	10,632	798,855	-4,627	273,445	36,050	18,443	15,009	891	73,886	3,950,331
2010	1,847,290	37,061	987,697	11,313	806,968	-5,501	260,203	37,172	18,917	15,219	1,212	94,652	4,125,060
2011	1,733,430	30,182	1,013,689	11,566	790,204	-6,421	319,355	37,449	19,222	15,316	1,818	120,177	4,100,141
2012	1,514,043	23,190	1,225,894	11,898	769,331	-4,950	276,240	37,799	19,823	15,562	4,327	140,822	4,047,765
2013	1,585,998	26,863	1,113,665	12,271	789,017	-4,424	269,136	39,937	19,957	16,517	9,252	167,665	4,058,209
2014[1]	1,612,515	31,736	1,129,725	11,404	790,278	-5,780	261,198	42,134	19,403	16,252	19,167	177,656	4,117,768

[1] Preliminary.   [2] Anthracite, bituminous coal, subbituminous coal, lignite, waste coal, and coal synfuel.   [3] Distillate fuel oil, residual fuel oil, petroleum coke, jet fuel, kerosene, other petroleum, waste oil, and propane.   [4] Natural gas, plus a small amount of supplemental gaseous fuels.   [5] Blast furnace gas, and other manufactured and waste gases derived from fossil fuels.   [6] Pumped storage facility production minus energy used for pumping.   [7] Wood and wood-derived fuels.   [8] Municipal solid waste from biogenic sources, landfill gas, sludge waste, agricultural byproducts, and other biomass.   [9] Solar thermal and photovoltaic (PV) energy.   *Source: U.S. Geological Survey (USGS)*

Total Electricity Net Generation in the United States   In Billions of Kilowatt Hours

Year	Jan.	Feb.	Mar.	Apr.	May	June	July	Aug.	Sept.	Oct.	Nov.	Dec.	Total
2006	328.7	307.3	318.7	297.9	330.6	364.3	410.4	407.8	332.1	321.6	309.2	336.3	4,064.7
2007	353.5	323.2	320.5	303.1	330.2	362.8	393.2	421.8	355.4	332.6	314.1	346.3	4,156.7
2008	363.0	325.1	324.6	305.9	325.2	373.1	402.9	389.0	338.1	318.5	310.0	343.9	4,119.4
2009	355.0	300.9	310.6	289.5	311.3	347.7	372.5	381.2	327.4	307.0	296.6	350.5	3,950.3
2010	361.0	319.7	312.2	287.8	327.9	375.8	409.7	408.9	346.0	307.9	306.0	362.1	4,125.1
2011	362.9	313.1	318.7	302.4	323.6	367.7	418.7	406.5	337.9	308.7	304.1	335.7	4,100.1
2012	339.5	309.4	309.1	295.2	336.5	360.8	414.6	395.7	334.6	311.7	306.0	334.6	4,047.8
2013	349.0	309.7	325.4	299.3	322.2	356.8	394.8	385.3	340.9	314.9	314.5	353.0	4,066.0
2014	377.3	324.3	331.8	297.6	324.7	357.8	385.8	384.3	339.9	314.5	317.5	338.0	4,093.6
2015[1]	361.6	335.6	324.7	294.2	322.9	362.9	401.5	393.7	351.0	313.0	301.6	324.4	4,087.4

[1] Preliminary.   *Source: Energy Information Administration, U.S. Department of Energy (EIA-DOE)*

Imports[2] of Electricity in the United States   In Billions of Kilowatt Hours

Year	Jan.	Feb.	Mar.	Apr.	May	June	July	Aug.	Sept.	Oct.	Nov.	Dec.	Total
2006	3.9	3.4	3.7	3.4	3.7	3.8	4.7	4.7	2.2	2.7	2.9	3.7	42.7
2007	3.5	4.2	3.9	4.0	4.6	4.5	5.5	5.4	3.8	3.6	4.3	4.1	51.4
2008	5.0	4.6	4.8	4.1	5.3	6.1	6.0	5.8	4.9	3.6	3.3	3.5	57.0
2009	4.3	3.9	2.9	3.3	4.1	4.7	5.5	5.8	4.5	4.7	3.8	4.6	52.2
2010	5.3	4.4	4.4	3.9	3.1	4.1	4.3	3.6	2.9	2.5	2.7	4.0	45.1
2011	4.3	3.7	4.0	3.8	4.9	4.5	6.0	5.6	4.0	3.7	3.5	4.3	52.3
2012	4.1	3.6	4.2	5.0	5.5	5.4	6.7	6.3	4.9	4.4	4.7	4.4	59.3
2013	5.8	5.3	5.8	5.0	5.9	6.0	6.7	6.9	5.6	5.6	6.0	5.9	70.4
2014	5.0	4.0	5.1	4.3	4.9	4.9	5.8	6.2	5.5	4.9	5.6	5.4	61.6
2015[1]	6.0	5.6	6.6	6.5	6.6	6.7	6.9	7.2	6.6	5.2	5.8	5.9	75.6

[1] Preliminary.   [2] Electricity transmitted across U.S. borders. Net imports equal imports minus exports.   *Source: Energy Information Administration, U.S. Department of Energy (EIA-DOE)*

Exports[2] of Electricity in the United States   In Billions of Kilowatt Hours

Year	Jan.	Feb.	Mar.	Apr.	May	June	July	Aug.	Sept.	Oct.	Nov.	Dec.	Total
2006	2.4	1.8	2.0	2.0	2.3	2.4	1.6	1.6	2.2	2.3	2.2	1.4	24.3
2007	1.6	1.4	2.1	1.2	1.2	1.3	1.7	1.9	2.5	1.6	1.8	2.0	20.1
2008	1.8	1.5	2.7	1.3	3.0	3.4	1.7	1.5	1.8	2.0	2.1	1.4	24.2
2009	2.3	1.5	1.7	1.5	1.4	1.6	1.4	1.4	1.4	1.4	1.3	1.4	18.1
2010	1.2	1.0	1.3	1.3	1.7	1.6	1.5	1.8	2.4	2.1	1.9	1.4	19.1
2011	1.6	1.5	1.5	1.6	1.3	1.3	1.3	1.0	1.0	0.9	1.1	0.9	15.0
2012	0.9	0.9	1.2	1.3	1.2	1.2	1.0	0.9	0.9	0.7	0.8	1.1	12.0
2013	1.0	0.8	0.9	1.2	1.0	0.8	1.0	0.9	0.7	1.0	0.9	1.1	11.4
2014	1.3	1.3	1.9	1.3	0.8	1.1	1.1	0.9	0.8	1.0	0.9	1.1	13.5
2015[1]	0.8	1.4	0.9	0.6	0.6	0.6	0.7	0.7	0.7	0.7	0.7	0.8	9.1

[1] Preliminary.   [2] Electricity transmitted across U.S. borders. Net imports equal imports minus exports.   *Source: Energy Information Administration, U.S. Department of Energy (EIA-DOE)*

Total End Use of Electricity in the United States   In Billions of Kilowatt Hours

Year	Jan.	Feb.	Mar.	Apr.	May	June	July	Aug.	Sept.	Oct.	Nov.	Dec.	Total
2006	317.4	292.3	301.9	279.5	299.5	333.9	375.7	381.9	329.4	303.7	289.0	312.6	3,816.8
2007	326.4	310.8	301.7	285.2	303.1	333.3	363.7	384.9	348.1	318.4	296.4	318.2	3,890.2
2008	338.3	315.8	305.8	288.7	299.1	339.6	372.6	364.1	332.5	302.5	287.9	318.3	3,865.2
2009	331.7	296.5	294.0	275.3	285.0	315.5	349.5	356.9	322.1	298.1	278.4	320.8	3,723.8
2010	342.9	308.6	303.4	277.1	294.3	341.9	380.7	384.0	338.9	298.4	285.4	330.7	3,886.4
2011	345.3	306.9	302.4	285.6	298.7	339.9	382.8	385.0	337.5	298.6	286.1	313.6	3,882.6
2012	322.6	298.0	294.7	281.3	308.3	336.6	383.5	377.2	329.5	301.9	289.5	309.2	3,832.3
2013	333.0	302.6	309.2	288.9	301.0	332.2	371.7	366.3	335.2	306.0	293.2	329.1	3,868.3
2014	353.1	319.5	313.7	286.5	302.5	334.0	363.7	364.1	338.4	307.7	296.6	323.4	3,903.2
2015[1]	338.6	315.3	313.7	283.0	296.4	335.0	372.5	371.4	341.8	304.5	284.8	306.2	3,863.3

[1] Preliminary.   *Source: Energy Information Administration, U.S. Department of Energy (EIA-DOE)*

Ethanol

World Production of Fuel Ethanol   In Thousands of Barrels per Day

Year	Australia	Brazil	Canada	China	Colombia	France	Germany	India	Jamaica	Spain	Thailand	United States	World Total
2003	----	249.4	4.0	13.8	----	1.7	----	3.3	2.6	3.0	----	182.9	465.3
2004	----	251.7	4.0	17.2	----	1.7	0.4	3.5	2.0	4.0	0.1	221.5	510.9
2005	0.4	276.4	4.4	20.7	0.5	2.5	2.8	3.7	2.2	5.0	1.2	254.7	585.0
2006	1.3	306.1	4.4	28.0	4.6	5.0	7.4	4.1	5.2	7.0	2.2	318.6	715.9
2007	1.4	388.7	13.8	28.7	4.7	9.3	6.8	4.5	4.9	7.0	3.0	425.4	924.5
2008	2.5	466.3	15.0	34.4	4.4	16.0	10.0	5.0	6.4	6.0	5.7	605.6	1,215.2
2009	3.5	449.8	20.0	37.5	5.6	17.0	13.0	1.7	6.9	8.0	7.2	713.5	1,323.2
2010	4.7	486.0	24.0	36.7	4.8	18.0	13.0	0.9	2.0	8.0	7.8	867.4	1,521.0
2011[1]	5.5	392.0	30.0	38.9	6.0	17.4	13.3	6.3	3.0	8.0	8.4	908.6	1,490.5
2012[2]	5.3	402.5	32.7	43.2	8.5	17.0	13.4	5.3	----	7.9	8.1	875.6	1,470.1

[1] Preliminary.   [2] Estimate.   *Source: Renewable Fuels Association*

Salient Statistics of Ethanol in the United States

Year	Ethanol Plants	Ethanol Production Capacity (mgy)	Plants Under Con-struction	Capacity Under Construction (mgy)	Farmer Owned Plants	Farmer Owned Capacity (mgy)	Percent of Total Capacity Farmer	Farmer Owned UC Plants	Farmers Owned UC Capacity	Percent of Total UC Capacity	States with Ethanol Plants
2006	95	4,336.4	31	1,778.0	46	1,677.1	39	4	187	11	20
2007	110	5,493.4	76	5,635.5	46	1,677.1	39	4	187	11	21
2008	139	7,888.4	61	5,536.0	49	1,948.6	28	13	771	12	21
2009	170	12,475.4	24	2,066.0	NA	NA	NA	NA	NA	NA	26
2010	189	13,028.4	15	1,432.0	----	----	----	----	----	----	26
2011	204	14,071.4	10	560.0	----	----	----	----	----	----	29
2012	209	14,906.9	2	140.0	----	----	----	----	----	----	29
2013	211	14,837.4	2	50.0	----	----	----	----	----	----	28
2014[1]	210	14,879.5	7	167.0	----	----	----	----	----	----	28
2015[2]	213	15,077.0	3	100.0	----	----	----	----	----	----	29

[1] Preliminary.   [2] Estimate.   *Source: Renewable Fuels Association*

Production of Fuel Ethanol in the United States   In Thousands of Barrels

Year	Jan.	Feb.	Mar.	Apr.	May	June	July	Aug.	Sept.	Oct.	Nov.	Dec.	Total
2006	8,935	8,463	9,333	8,663	9,086	9,531	9,791	10,235	10,088	10,512	10,442	11,215	116,294
2007	11,621	10,795	11,892	11,716	12,573	12,553	13,083	13,581	13,402	14,221	14,568	15,258	155,263
2008	16,058	15,527	17,527	17,152	18,756	17,651	19,040	20,059	19,338	20,048	20,139	20,342	221,637
2009	19,561	18,255	20,121	19,374	21,024	21,125	22,887	23,136	22,218	23,467	24,122	25,134	260,424
2010	25,625	23,802	26,486	25,384	26,244	25,632	26,584	26,964	26,221	27,471	27,747	28,457	316,617
2011	28,467	25,300	28,178	26,538	27,720	27,224	27,541	27,976	26,588	28,013	28,383	29,718	331,646
2012	29,038	26,647	27,548	26,346	27,616	26,513	25,236	26,092	24,376	24,976	24,744	25,582	314,714
2013	24,778	22,494	25,620	25,601	27,197	26,722	26,923	26,279	25,564	27,995	27,915	29,405	316,493
2014	28,194	25,269	28,120	27,733	28,888	28,629	29,413	28,665	27,807	28,644	28,588	30,831	340,781
2015[1]	29,755	26,788	29,489	27,910	29,666	29,684	30,256	29,621	28,543	30,139	29,594		350,667

[1] Preliminary.   *Source: Energy Information Administration, U.S. Department of Energy (EIA-DOE)*

Stocks of Fuel Ethanol in the United States   In Thousands of Barrels

Year	Jan.	Feb.	Mar.	Apr.	May	June	July	Aug.	Sept.	Oct.	Nov.	Dec.
2006	6,099	7,268	8,626	8,990	7,767	6,675	7,706	9,133	9,725	9,723	9,232	8,760
2007	8,656	8,765	8,539	8,807	8,966	9,171	9,866	11,011	11,555	11,449	11,218	10,535
2008	11,383	11,173	12,288	12,572	13,297	13,323	13,448	14,771	16,110	15,214	15,286	14,226
2009	14,514	15,834	16,411	15,322	14,173	13,974	14,223	14,671	15,283	14,933	15,578	16,594
2010	18,251	19,297	20,222	20,042	19,851	18,565	17,809	17,380	17,437	17,278	18,150	17,941
2011	20,826	21,016	21,593	21,065	20,609	19,217	18,788	18,123	18,465	18,038	18,308	18,238
2012	21,475	22,393	22,583	22,050	21,635	21,239	20,224	19,180	19,921	18,626	19,992	20,350
2013	19,894	19,009	18,410	17,370	16,804	16,428	17,072	16,945	15,986	15,750	15,569	16,424
2014	17,153	16,865	17,310	17,610	18,330	18,785	18,696	18,218	18,724	17,341	17,035	18,739
2015[1]	20,543	20,979	20,865	20,787	20,120	20,029	19,594	19,259	18,904	18,889	19,945	

[1] Preliminary.   *Source: Energy Information Administration, U.S. Department of Energy (EIA-DOE)*

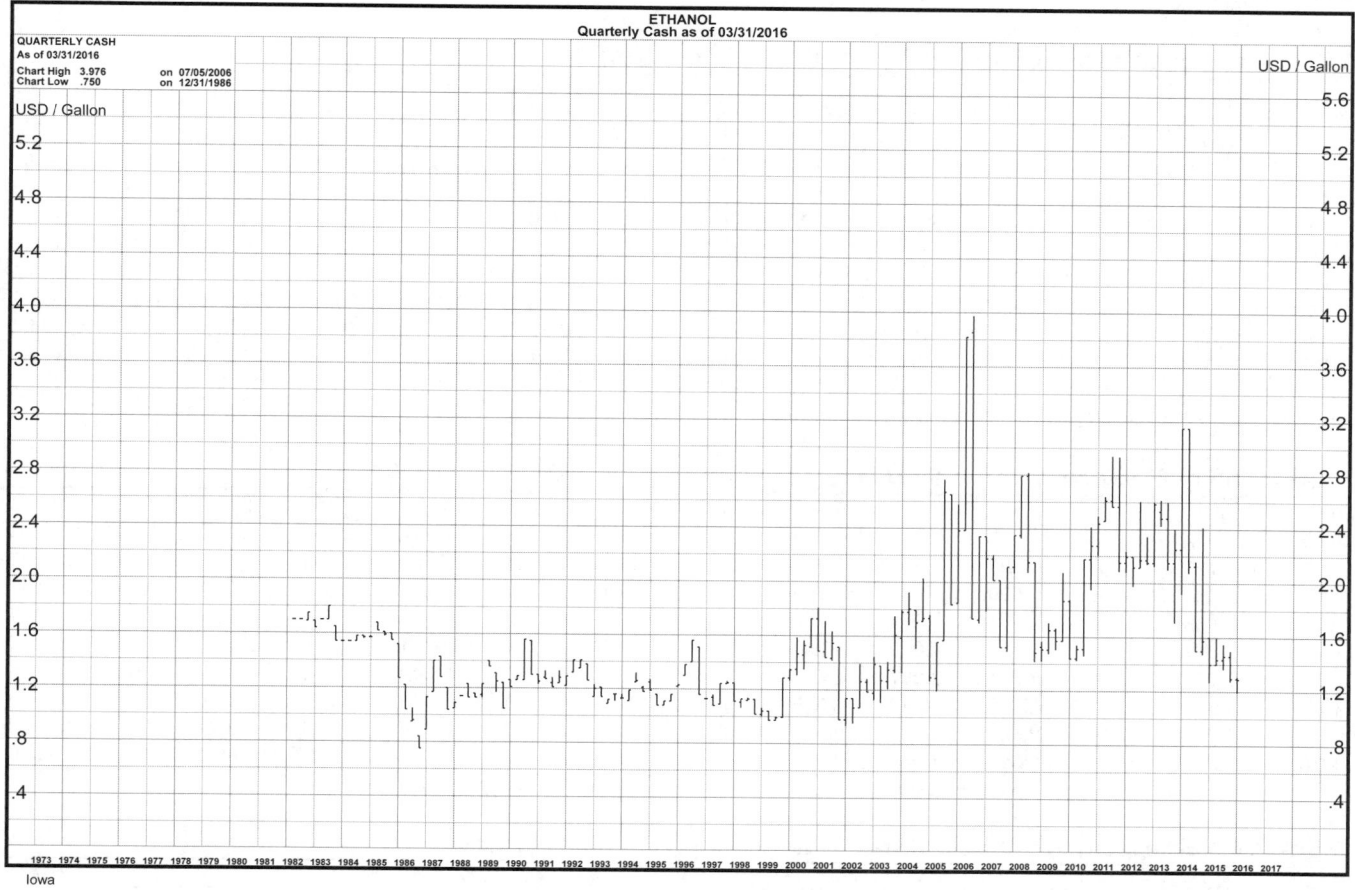

ETHANOL
Quarterly Cash as of 03/31/2016

QUARTERLY CASH
As of 03/31/2016

Chart High 3.976 on 07/05/2006
Chart Low .750 on 12/31/1986

USD / Gallon

USD / Gallon

Iowa

Average Price of Ethanol in the United States[1]   In Dollars Per Gallon

Year	Jan.	Feb.	Mar.	Apr.	May	June	July	Aug.	Sept.	Oct.	Nov.	Dec.	Average
2008	2.188	2.129	2.316	2.455	2.485	2.535	2.642	2.224	2.150	1.846	1.648	1.493	2.176
2009	1.518	1.488	1.461	1.497	1.553	1.673	1.585	1.535	1.540	1.798	1.984	1.962	1.633
2010	1.817	1.689	1.515	1.439	1.508	1.523	1.507	1.692	2.012	2.120	2.331	2.108	1.772
2011	2.268	2.292	2.435	2.564	2.546	2.600	2.718	2.830	2.745	2.596	2.825	2.324	2.562
2012	2.128	2.089	2.177	2.152	2.107	2.002	2.399	2.532	2.397	2.296	2.301	2.265	2.237
2013	2.197	2.331	2.473	2.478	2.553	2.571	2.430	2.287	2.346	2.096	1.942	2.314	2.335
2014	2.073	1.946	2.478	2.800	2.237	2.225	2.100	2.096	1.827	1.561	2.019	1.995	2.113
2015	1.382	1.313	1.386	1.479	1.568	1.440	1.493	1.418	1.408	1.472	1.425	1.347	1.428

[1] Northeast and Northwest Iowa.   *Source: Agricultural Marketing Service, U.S. Department of Agriculture (AMS-USDA)*

Volume of Trading of Ethanol Futures in Chicago   In Contracts

Year	Jan.	Feb.	Mar.	Apr.	May	June	July	Aug.	Sept.	Oct.	Nov.	Dec.	Total
2010	9,629	9,887	19,404	12,659	12,794	17,809	15,406	15,073	13,694	13,176	11,952	11,242	162,725
2011	12,857	15,589	18,387	16,665	21,406	25,489	22,550	22,026	22,766	21,370	19,710	20,131	238,946
2012	19,054	17,458	25,690	26,004	38,420	41,795	35,450	23,875	23,434	26,077	26,094	27,562	330,913
2013	29,052	31,990	37,290	40,033	30,116	30,695	27,053	22,140	16,027	13,413	11,025	9,884	298,718
2014	18,334	20,874	20,547	24,319	20,168	24,842	18,015	17,399	20,134	22,580	19,087	16,773	243,072
2015	24,040	13,103	17,508	20,055	20,013	17,466	17,981	11,506	10,947	10,938	11,211	12,893	187,661

Contract size = 29,000 US gallons.   *Source: CME Group; Chicago Board of Trade (CBT)*

Month-End Open Interest of Ethanol Futures in Chicago   In Contracts

Year	Jan.	Feb.	Mar.	Apr.	May	June	July	Aug.	Sept.	Oct.	Nov.	Dec.
2010	6,876	8,076	8,211	8,472	9,337	11,294	11,917	10,996	9,790	9,168	7,973	7,276
2011	7,724	7,791	7,932	7,467	8,081	9,138	9,041	9,812	10,010	10,103	10,795	9,994
2012	10,210	11,135	11,278	11,850	12,504	11,202	11,914	12,065	11,336	10,496	11,214	9,344
2013	9,090	9,812	11,152	10,792	10,018	9,985	9,137	7,796	6,382	4,724	3,798	3,278
2014	3,944	5,403	5,556	6,826	7,137	6,617	6,381	6,252	6,519	6,796	5,810	5,548
2015	6,518	6,892	7,296	6,781	7,978	7,336	6,511	5,381	4,905	5,167	5,098	4,253

Contract size = 29,000 US gallons.   *Source: CME Group; Chicago Board of Trade (CBT)*

ETHANOL

World Production of Biodiesel   In Thousands of Barrels per Day

Year	Argentina	Austria	Belgium	Brazil	China	France	Germany	Indonesia	Italy	Spain	Thailand	United States	World Total
2003	0.2	0.6	----	----	0.1	7.3	14.0	----	5.3	2.0	----	0.9	34.1
2004	0.2	1.1	----	----	0.1	7.7	20.0	----	6.2	2.2	----	1.8	43.8
2005	0.2	1.6	----	----	0.8	8.4	33.0	0.2	7.7	3.2	0.4	5.9	71.2
2006	0.6	2.4	0.5	1.2	4.0	11.6	52.0	0.4	11.6	1.2	0.4	16.3	124.6
2007	3.6	5.2	3.2	7.0	2.0	18.7	57.0	1.0	9.2	3.5	1.2	32.0	178.8
2008	13.9	4.2	5.4	20.1	5.0	34.4	55.0	2.0	13.1	4.3	7.7	44.1	262.1
2009	23.1	6.1	8.1	27.7	10.2	41.0	45.0	5.7	15.6	13.0	10.5	34.0	311.7
2010	36.0	5.7	8.5	41.1	9.8	37.0	49.0	12.8	14.5	16.0	11.4	22.0	345.4
2011[1]	47.3	6.2	8.7	46.1	14.7	34.0	57.2	31.0	11.2	11.0	10.9	63.0	425.3
2012[2]	47.9	7.0	8.7	46.7	15.7	32.7	54.7	37.9	9.8	8.7	15.5	64.0	431.3

[1] Preliminary.   [2] Estimate.   *Source: Renewable Fuels Association*

Production of Biodiesel in the United States   In Thousands of Barrels (mbbl)

Year	Jan.	Feb.	Mar.	Apr.	May	June	July	Aug.	Sept.	Oct.	Nov.	Dec.	Average
2007	692	564	775	765	958	943	1,237	1,298	1,224	1,188	993	1,026	11,662
2008	1,197	1,074	1,188	1,268	1,292	1,445	1,604	1,623	1,501	1,465	1,438	1,052	16,145
2009	1,011	780	599	624	689	761	1,030	1,070	1,158	1,364	1,511	1,455	12,281
2010	633	696	804	814	760	644	657	653	723	676	528	588	8,177
2011	842	961	1,419	1,692	1,838	1,938	2,183	2,273	2,284	2,508	2,494	2,604	23,035
2012	1,751	1,887	2,251	2,237	2,428	2,223	2,127	2,176	1,949	1,792	1,363	1,406	23,588
2013	1,640	1,672	2,412	2,548	2,645	2,699	3,072	3,086	3,025	3,272	3,080	3,217	32,368
2014	1,727	1,801	2,361	2,223	2,531	2,645	2,926	2,987	2,754	2,928	2,610	2,958	30,452
2015[1]	1,706	1,827	2,323	2,565	2,755	2,897	2,875	2,933	2,553	2,537	2,521		29,990

[1] Preliminary.   *Source: Energy Information Administration, U.S. Department of Energy (EIA-DOE)*

Stocks of Biodiesel in the United States   In Thousands of Barrels (Mbbl)

Year	Jan.	Feb.	Mar.	Apr.	May	June	July	Aug.	Sept.	Oct.	Nov.	Dec.
2009	664	424	665	632	600	581	511	511	527	553	531	711
2010	1,049	1,039	1,057	1,009	1,016	968	830	771	682	650	676	672
2011	1,016	1,217	1,381	1,408	1,576	1,524	1,748	1,834	1,617	1,938	1,866	2,005
2012	2,503	2,888	2,886	2,773	2,710	2,348	2,262	2,011	2,049	2,176	1,862	1,984
2013	2,002	2,026	2,390	2,507	2,460	2,485	2,683	2,549	2,509	2,483	3,360	3,810
2014	3,708	3,726	3,604	3,402	3,135	2,798	3,082	2,786	2,293	2,641	3,084	3,131
2015[1]	3,713	3,827	3,996	3,950	3,464	2,948	3,284	3,227	2,948	2,981	3,458	

[1] Preliminary.   *Source: Energy Information Administration, U.S. Department of Energy (EIA-DOE)*

Imports of Biodiesel in the United States   In Thousands of Barrels (mbbl)

Year	Jan.	Feb.	Mar.	Apr.	May	June	July	Aug.	Sept.	Oct.	Nov.	Dec.	Average
2008	598	838	274	688	513	512	526	907	908	721	612	404	7,755
2009	261	158	383	52	117	138	58	126	123	159	105	165	1,906
2010	42	32	62	46	83	56	33	54	71	19	31	35	564
2011	50	39	55	54	49	50	64	67	67	85	69	241	890
2012	48	72	25	32	75	132	166	55	108	60	9	71	853
2013	38	88	439	372	410	698	358	385	781	1,177	1,641	1,765	8,152
2014	222	161	240	135	133	235	493	571	352	507	989	540	4,578
2015[1]	372	416	311	294	307	673	1,157	858	927	863	701		7,504

[1] Preliminary.   *Source: Energy Information Administration, U.S. Department of Energy (EIA-DOE)*

Exports of Biodiesel in the United States   In Thousands of Barrels (mbbl)

Year	Jan.	Feb.	Mar.	Apr.	May	June	July	Aug.	Sept.	Oct.	Nov.	Dec.	Average
2008	1,100	1,384	1,172	1,592	1,364	1,758	1,421	1,606	1,452	1,333	1,181	766	16,673
2009	1,150	1,166	203	154	417	366	581	397	224	424	819	431	6,546
2010	306	144	448	234	260	314	206	233	135	137	59	113	2,588
2011	224	91	204	229	198	120	147	74	199	136	135	40	1,799
2012	258	125	189	230	320	392	426	403	295	209	65	143	3,056
2013	16	37	176	371	563	587	429	687	511	415	408	476	4,675
2014	134	141	91	261	208	263	320	264	136	40	65	51	1,974
2015[1]	22	23	190	240	255	263	255	275	200	161	76		2,138

[1] Preliminary.   *Source: Energy Information Administration, U.S. Department of Energy (EIA-DOE)*

Fertilizer

Fertilizer is a natural or synthetic chemical substance, or mixture, that enriches soil to promote plant growth. The three primary nutrients that fertilizers provide are nitrogen, potassium, and phosphorus. In ancient times, and still today, many commonly used fertilizers contain one or more of the three primary ingredients: manure (containing nitrogen), bones (containing small amounts of nitrogen and large quantities of phosphorus), and potash (containing potassium).

At least fourteen different nutrients have been found essential for crops. These include three organic nutrients (carbon, hydrogen, and oxygen, which are taken directly from air and water), three primary chemical nutrients (nitrogen, phosphorus, and potassium), and three secondary chemical nutrients (magnesium, calcium, and sulfur). The others are micronutrients or trace elements and include iron, manganese, copper, zinc, boron, and molybdenum.

Prices – The average price of ammonia (Gulf Coast delivery), a key source of ingredients for fertilizers, fell by -11.3% yr/yr in 2015 to $470 per metric ton, below the 2008 record high of $590 per metric ton. The average price of potash in the U.S. in 2015 rose by +9.5% yr/yr to $635.00 per metric ton, below the 2009 record high of $800.00 per metric ton.

Supply – World production of ammonia (as contained in nitrogen) in 2015 rose +0.7% to 146.000 million metric tons, a new record high. The world's largest producers of nitrogen in 2015 were China with 32.9% of world production, Russia (8.2%), India (7.5%), and the U.S.

(6.4%). U.S. nitrogen production in 2015 rose +0.8% to 9.400 million metric tons.

World production of phosphate rock, basic slag and guano in 2015 rose +2.3% yr/yr to 223.000 million metric tons. The world's largest producers of phosphate rock in 2015 were China (with 44.8% of world production), Morocco (13.5%), U.S. (12.4%), and Russia (5.6%). U.S. production in 2015 rose +9.1% y/y to 27.600 million metric tons.

World production of marketable potash in 2015 was unchanged yr/yr to 38.800 million metric tons. The world's largest producers of potash in 2015 were Canada with 28.4% of world production, Russia (19.1%), Belarus (16.8%), and China (10.8%). U.S. production of potash in 2015 fell -9.4% yr/yr to 770,000 metric tons.

Demand –U.S. consumption of phosphate rock in 2015 fell -2.7% yr/yr to 28.300 million metric tons. U.S. consumption of potash in 2015 fell by -19.0% yr/yr to 4.700 million metric tons. U.S. consumption of nitrogen in 2013 (latest data available) fell -2.4% yr/yr to 12.000 million metric tons.

Trade – U.S. imports of nitrogen in 2015 rose +9.2% yr/yr to 4.530 million metric tons and the U.S. relied on imports for 29% of consumption. U.S. imports of phosphate rock in 2015 fell -20.5% yr/yr to 1.900 million metric tons. U.S. imports of potash in 2015 fell -19.5% to 4.000 million metric tons, but was still higher than the 4-decade low of 2.400 million metric tons posted in 2009. Imports accounted for 84% of U.S. consumption.

World Production of Ammonia — In Thousands of Metric Tons of Contained Nitrogen

Year	Canada	China	France	Germany	India	Indonesia	Japan	Mexico	Nether-lands	Poland	Russia	United States	Total
2007	3,688	42,480	800	2,746	11,000	4,400	1,114	714	1,800	1,995	10,500	8,540	130,000
2008	3,920	41,140	800	2,819	11,100	4,500	1,244	737	----	2,000	10,425	7,870	123,000
2009	3,611	42,290	2,970	2,363	11,200	4,600	1,021	861	1,800	1,697	10,441	7,700	127,000
2010	3,620	40,870	3,517	2,677	11,500	4,800	1,178	824	1,800	1,700	10,902	8,290	133,000
2011	3,946	43,250	3,500	2,821	11,800	5,000	1,211	766	1,800	1,918	11,418	9,350	140,000
2012	3,942	45,520	2,644	2,823	12,000	5,100	1,055	880	1,800	2,026	11,418	8,730	142,000
2013	3,942	47,310	2,600	2,757	12,000	5,000	1,007	879	1,800	2,100	11,345	9,170	144,000
2014[1]	3,940	47,300	2,600	2,800	11,000	5,000	1,200		1,800	2,100	11,836	9,330	145,000
2015[2]	3,900	48,000	2,600	2,800	11,000	5,000			1,800	2,100	11,800	9,400	146,000

[1] Preliminary. [2] Estimate. *Source: U.S. Geological Survey (USGS)*

Salient Statistics of Nitrogen[3] (Ammonia) in the United States — In Thousands of Metric Tons

Year	Net Import Reliance As a % of Apparent Consumption	Production[3] (Fixed) Fertilizer	Non-fertilizer	Total	Imprts[4] (Fixed)	Exports	Nitrogen[5] Compounds Pro-duced	Con-sumption	Stocks, Dec. 31 Am-monia	Fixed Nitrogen Com-pounds	Ammonia Con-sumption (Apparent)	Average Price ($/Metric Ton) Urea FOB Gulf[6]	FOB Corn Belt	Ammonium Nitrate: FOB Corn Belt	Ammonia FOB Gulf Coast
2007	43	7,610	930	8,540	6,530	145	9,485	12,000	157	407	15,000	435-445	465-490	590-620	307
2008	42	6,730	1,140	7,870	6,020	192	8,605	11,500	302	794	13,500	190-210	270-330	450-650	590
2009	38	6,470	1,240	7,700	4,530	16	8,071	10,500	167	364	12,300	307-315	350-360	340-390	251
2010	40	7,130	1,160	8,290	5,540	36	8,597	11,200	165	328	13,800	370-380	415-440	640-685	396
2011	37	8,170	1,180	9,350	5,600	26	8,759	11,600	178	NA	14,900	360-375	410-450	670-710	531
2012	37	7,600	1,140	8,730	5,170	31	8,579	12,300	180	NA	13,900	393-410	440-480	760-820	579
2013	34	8,070	1,100	9,170	4,960	196	8,759	12,000	240	NA	13,900	325-342	370-380	510-550	541
2014[1]	30			9,330	4,150	111			280		14,300				530
2015[2]	29			9,400	4,530	640			300						470

[1] Preliminary. [2] Estimate. [3] Anhydrous ammonia, synthetic. [4] For consumption. [5] Major downstream nitrogen compounds. [6] Granular.
Source: U.S. Geological Survey (USGS)

FERTILIZER

World Production of Phosphate Rock, Basic Slag & Guano   In Thousands of Metric Tons (Gross Weight)

Year	Brazil	China	Egypt	Israel	Jordan	Morocco	Russia	Senegal	Syria	Togo	Tunisia	United States	World Total
2006	5,932	38,600	2,177	2,949	5,805	27,400	11,000	584	3,664	1,650	7,801	30,100	151,000
2007	6,185	45,400	3,890	3,069	5,552	27,800	11,400	691	3,678	750	8,005	29,700	160,000
2008	6,727	50,700	5,523	3,088	6,266	24,861	10,400	645	2,629	842	7,692	30,200	166,000
2009	6,084	60,200	6,227	2,697	5,282	18,307	9,500	949	2,128	726	7,409	26,400	161,000
2010	6,192	68,000	3,435	3,135	6,529	26,603	11,000	1,079	3,167	695	8,149	25,800	184,000
2011	6,738	81,000	4,746	3,105	7,594	28,052	11,000	1,411	3,541	866	2,479	28,100	199,000
2012	6,740	95,300	6,236	3,514	6,383	27,060	12,500	1,381	1,534	1,110	2,762	30,100	217,000
2013	6,000	108,000	5,922	3,578	5,399	26,400	10,000	800	1,000	1,110	3,283	31,200	224,000
2014[1]	6,040	100,000	5,500	3,360	7,140	30,000	11,000	900	1,230	1,200	3,780	25,300	218,000
2015[2]	6,700	100,000	5,500	3,300	7,500	30,000	12,500	1,000	750	1,000	4,000	27,600	223,000

[1] Preliminary.   [2] Estimate.   *Source: U.S. Geological Survey (USGS)*

Salient Statistics of Phosphate Rock in the United States   In Thousands of Metric Tons

Year	Mine Production	Marketable Production	Value Million Dollars	Imports for Consumption	Exports	Apparent Consumption	Producer Stocks, Dec. 31	Avg. Price FOB Mine $/Metric Ton	Avg. Price of Florida & N. Carolina - $/Met. Ton - FOB Mine (-60% to +74%) - Domestic	Export	Average
2006	111,000	30,100	919	2,420	----	32,600	7,070	30.49	W	----	30.52
2007	126,000	29,700	1,520	2,670	----	33,800	4,970	51.10	----	----	51.36
2008	124,000	30,200	2,320	2,750	----	31,600	6,340	76.76	----	----	76.64
2009	107,000	26,400	3,360	2,000	----	27,500	8,120	127.19	----	----	NA
2010	106,000	25,800	1,980	2,400	----	30,500	5,620	76.69	----	----	----
2011	129,000	28,100	2,720	3,750	----	32,000	4,580	96.64	----	----	----
2012	150,000	30,100	3,080	3,570	----	30,400	6,700	102.54	----	----	----
2013	139,000	31,200	2,850	3,170	----	31,300	9,000	91.11	----	----	----
2014[1]		25,300		2,390	----	29,100	5,880	78.59	----	----	----
2015[2]		27,600		1,900	----	28,300	6,500	80.00	----	----	----

[1] Preliminary.   [2] Estimate.   *Source: U.S. Geological Survey (USGS)*

World Production of Marketable Potash   In Thousands of Metric Tons (K_2O Equivalent)

Year	Belarus	Brazil	Canada	Chile	China	Germany	Israel	Jordan	Russia	Spain	United Kingdom	United States	World Total
2006	4,605	403	8,518	496	1,800	3,625	2,187	1,036	5,740	435	420	1,100	30,400
2007	4,972	424	11,085	515	2,600	3,637	2,182	1,096	6,430	435	427	1,100	34,900
2008	4,968	383	10,455	559	2,750	3,280	2,170	1,223	5,992	435	411	1,100	33,700
2009	2,485	453	4,297	691	3,200	1,825	1,900	683	3,727	400	411	715	20,800
2010	5,223	448	9,700	964	3,600	3,024	2,080	1,185	6,283	415	427	930	34,300
2011	5,306	424	10,686	861	3,800	3,215	1,820	1,378	6,498	420	470	1,000	35,900
2012	4,840	425	8,976	1,053	4,100	3,149	2,100	1,092	5,563	420	470	900	33,100
2013	4,243	430	10,140	1,050	4,300	3,200	2,100	1,080	6,100	420	470	960	34,500
2014[1]	6,290	311	11,000	1,200	4,400	3,000	1,770	1,260	7,380	715	610	850	38,800
2015[2]	6,500	311	11,000	1,200	4,200	3,000	1,800	1,250	7,400	700	610	770	38,800

[1] Preliminary.   [2] Estimate.   *Source: U.S. Geological Survey (USGS)*

Salient Statistics of Potash in the United States   In Thousands of Metric Tons (K_2O Equivalent)

Year	Net Import Reliance As a % of Apparent Consump	Production	Sales by Producers	Value Million Dollars	Imports for Consumption	Exports	Apparent Consumption	Producer Stocks Dec. 31	Avg Value of Product	Avg Value of K_2O Equiv	Avg. Price[3] (Metric Ton)
2006	79	1,100	1,100	410.0	4,470	332	5,200	----	170.00	375.00	290.00
2007	81	1,100	1,200	480.0	4,970	199	5,900	----	185.00	400.00	400.00
2008	84	1,100	1,100	740.0	5,800	222	6,700	----	305.00	675.00	700.00
2009	73	720	630	500.0	2,220	303	2,500	----	330.00	800.00	800.00
2010	83	930	1,000	660.0	4,760	297	5,500	----	275.00	630.00	605.00
2011	83	1,000	990	740.0	4,980	202	5,800	----	320.00	745.00	730.00
2012	82	900	980	750.0	4,240	234	5,000	----	340.00	765.00	710.00
2013	82	960	880	630.0	4,650	289	5,200	----		720.00	640.00
2014[1]	85	850	930		4,970	118	5,800	----		730.00	580.00
2015[2]	84	770	760		4,000	30	4,700				635.00

[1] Preliminary.   [2] Estimate.   [3] Unit of K_2O, standard 60% muriate F.O.B. mine.   *Source: U.S. Geological Survey (USGS)*

Fish

Fish are the primary source of protein for a large portion of the world's population. The worldwide yearly harvest of all sea fish (including aquaculture) is between 85 and 130 million metric tons. There are approximately 20,000 species of fish, of which 9,000 are regularly caught. Only 22 fish species are harvested in large amounts. Ground-fish, which are fish that live near or on the ocean floor, account for about 10% of the world's fishery harvest, and include cod, haddock, pollock, flounder, halibut and sole. Large pelagic fish such as tuna, swordfish, marlin, and mahi-mahi, account for about 5% of world harvest. The fish eaten most often in the United States is canned tuna.

Rising global demand for fish has increased the pressure to harvest more fish to the point where all 17 of the world's major fishing areas have either reached or exceeded their limits. Atlantic stocks of cod, haddock and blue-fin tuna are all seriously depleted, while in the Pacific, anchovies, salmon and halibut are all over-fished. Aquaculture, or fish farming, reduces pressure on wild stocks and now accounts for nearly 20% of world harvest.

Supply – The U.S. grand total of fishery products in 2014 (latest data) rose +0.3% to 21.049 billion pounds, a new record high. The U.S. total domestic catch in 2014 fell -3.9% to 9.485 billion pounds, and that comprised 45.1% of total U.S. supply. Of the U.S. total domestic catch in 2014, 69.4% of the catch was finfish for human consumption, 17.5% of the catch was a variety of fish for industrial use, and 13.1% was shellfish for human consumption. The principal species of U.S. fishery landings in 2014 were Pollock (with 3.155 billion pounds landed), Menhaden (1.256 billion pounds), Pacific Salmon (720 million pounds), Flounder (713 million pounds), and Sea Herring (308 million pounds).

About 30% of the fish harvested in the world are processed directly into fishmeal and fish oil. Fishmeal is used primarily in animal feed. Fish oil is used in both animal feed and human food products. World fishmeal production in the 2014-15 marketing year fell by -7.8% to 4.330 million metric tons. World production of fish oil in 2014-15 fell -13.4% to 819.000 thousand metric tons. Peru and Chile are by far the world's largest producers of fishmeal and fish oil.

Trade – U.S. imports of fishery products in 2014 (latest data) rose +4.0% yr/yr to 11.563 billion pounds, a new record high, comprising 54.9% of total U.S. supply.

Year	Grand Total	- For Human Food - Finfish	- For Human Food - Shellfish[3]	For Industrial Use[4]	Domestic Catch Total	Percent of Grand Total	- For Human Food - Finfish	- For Human Food - Shellfish[3]	For Industrial Use[4]	Imports Total	Percent of Grand Total	- For Human Food - Finfish	- For Human Food - Shellfish[3]	For Industrial Use[4]
2008	19,200	12,295	4,742	2,163	8,326	43.4	5,590	1,043	1,692	10,874	56.6	6,705	3,699	471
2009	18,899	11,700	4,936	2,262	8,031	42.5	4,930	1,268	1,833	10,868	57.5	6,771	3,668	430
2010	19,748	12,505	5,055	2,188	8,231	41.7	5,216	1,310	1,705	11,517	58.3	7,288	3,746	483
2011	21,106	13,644	5,088	2,374	9,858	46.7	6,540	1,369	1,949	11,248	53.3	7,104	3,719	425
2012	20,757	13,159	4,907	2,692	9,634	46.4	6,163	1,314	2,157	11,123	53.6	6,996	3,592	535
2013[1]	20,988	13,787	4,786	2,416	9,870	47.0	6,777	1,266	1,827	11,118	53.0	7,009	3,520	589
2014[1]	21,050	13,680	5,053	2,317	9,486	45.1	6,588	1,240	1,658	11,564	54.9	7,092	3,813	659

[1] Preliminary. [2] Live weight, except percent. [3] For univalue and bivalues mollusks (conchs, clams, oysters, scallops, etc.) the weight of meats, excluding the shell is reported. [4] Fish meal and sea herring. *Source: Fisheries Statistics Division, U.S. Department of Commerce*

Fisheries -- Landings of Principal Species in the United States   In Millions of Pounds

Year	Cod, Atlantic	Flounder	Halibut	Herring, Sea	Man-haden	Pollock	Salmon, Pacific	Tuna	Whiting	Clams (Meats)	Crabs	Lobsters American	Oysters (Meats)	Scallops (Meats)	Shrimp
2008	19	663	67	259	1,341	2,298	658	48	14	108	325	82	30	54	257
2009	20	575	60	313	1,568	1,883	705	49	17	101	326	97	36	58	301
2010	18	624	56	253	1,472	1,959	788	48	18	89	350	115	28	58	259
2011	18	707	43	276	1,875	2,827	780	50	17	86	369	126	29	59	313
2012	11	703	34	270	1,771	2,887	636	60	16	91	367	150	33	57	303
2013	5	717	30	298	1,467	3,014	1,069	56	14	91	332	149	35	41	283
2014[1]	5	714	23	309	1,256	3,156	720	59	16	91	295	148	34	34	295

[1] Preliminary. *Source: National Marine Fisheries Service, U.S. Department of Commerce*

U.S. Fisheries: Quantity & Value of Domestic Catch & Consumption & World Fish Oil Production

Year	Fresh & Frozen	Canned	Cured	For Meal, Oil, etc.	Total	For Human Food	For Industrial Products	Ex-vessel Value[3] Million $	Average Price Cents /Lb.	Fish Per Capita Consumption Pounds	World[2] Fish Oil Production 1,000 Tons
2008	6,538	336	138	1,313	8,325	6,633	1,692	4,383	52.6	16.0	1,075
2009	6,204	392	103	1,332	8,031	6,198	1,833	3,891		16.0	1,040
2010	6,515	373	102	1,241	8,231	6,526	1,705	4,520		15.8	897
2011	7,817	371	52	1,618	9,858	7,909	1,949	5,289			1,078
2012	7,541	299	82	1,712	9,634	7,477	2,157	5,103			934
2013	7,009	365	45	1,451	9,870	8,043	1,827	5,466			930
2014[1]	7,916	196	63	1,311	9,486	7,828	1,658	5,448			899

Disposition ----- Millions of Pounds

[1] Preliminary. [2] Crop years on a marketing year basis. [3] At the Dock Prices. Source: Fisheries Statistics Division, U.S. Department of Commerce

FISH

Imports of Seafood Products into the United States   In Thousands of Pounds

Year	Trout, fresh and frozen	Atlantic salmon, fresh	Pacific salmon, fresh[2]	Atlantic salmon, frozen	Pacific salmon, frozen[2]	Atlantic salmon, canned fillets	Salmon, canned and pre-pared[3]	Tilapia[4]	Shrimp, frozen	Shrimp, fresh and prepared[5]	Oysters[6]	Mussels[6]	Clams[6]	Scallops[6]
2008	9,137	182,929	12,843	6,219	52,407	250,282	28,468	395,559	943,989	304,907	20,544	54,261	33,143	57,800
2009	12,021	198,260	12,278	7,844	61,750	220,550	32,444	404,132	896,045	321,372	20,503	57,062	37,657	56,262
2010	16,326	203,913	18,956	6,058	80,859	178,871	27,222	474,967	914,925	321,800	23,802	56,921	40,145	51,865
2011	11,082	192,231	19,704	5,694	85,406	201,601	25,167	433,162	948,460	323,579	26,779	63,813	44,832	56,804
2012	19,616	222,313	9,770	4,828	65,491	276,703	27,539	503,644	922,877	253,456	18,566	75,384	45,518	34,021
2013	18,713	190,427	12,153	5,604	71,480	317,981	37,106	504,698	865,133	248,756	19,830	70,916	48,705	60,429
2014	19,154	172,155	11,070	6,853	76,134	360,239	32,329	508,483	988,270	265,140	21,337	74,635	50,644	60,039
2015[1]	26,689	236,428	10,049	6,112	79,040	371,698	32,309	496,095	1,000,382	292,725	24,496	70,605	52,789	48,388

[1] Preliminary.   [2] Includes salmon with no specific species noted.   [3] Includes smoked and cured salmon.   [4] Frozen whole fish plus fresh and frozen fillets.   [5] Canned, breaded or otherwise prepared.   [6] Fresh or prepared.   *Source: Bureau of the Census, U.S. Department of Commerce*

Exports of Seafood Products From the United States   In Thousands of Pounds

Year	Trout, fresh and frozen	Atlantic salmon, fresh	Pacific salmon, fresh[2]	Atlantic salmon, frozen	Pacific salmon, frozen[2]	Salmon, canned and prepared[3]	Shrimp, frozen	Shrimp, fresh and prepared[4]	Oysters[5]	Mussels[5]	Clams[5]	Scallops[5]
2008	1,107	17,705	16,198	247	277,331	138,048	7,902	17,684	7,241	1,855	14,366	24,694
2009	978	14,039	11,661	173	263,564	115,974	7,841	12,842	6,396	1,498	12,907	26,183
2010	667	20,958	18,128	205	316,240	112,952	6,155	11,269	7,658	1,069	12,789	24,615
2011	503	7,537	20,881	667	337,058	137,878	9,980	16,449	10,376	1,141	13,526	32,136
2012	1,779	17,234	20,934	380	222,933	92,838	14,951	9,260	7,781	931	14,056	28,756
2013	2,148	15,574	24,129	223	359,834	101,469	14,760	7,897	7,624	1,043	18,114	21,206
2014	2,232	11,865	17,704	295	310,517	94,793	15,251	12,975	8,229	1,275	17,482	20,022
2015[1]	1,271	9,428	23,711	335	413,321	87,663	25,725	11,933	8,305	1,207	18,851	16,807

[1] Preliminary.   [2] Includes salmon with no specific species noted.   [3] Includes smoked and cured salmon.   [4] Canned, breaded, or prepared.   [5] Fresh or prepared.   *Source: Bureau of the Census, U.S. Department of Commerce*

World Production of Fish Meal   In Thousands of Metric Tons

Year	Chile	Denmark	European Union	Iceland	Japan	Norway	Peru	Russia	South Africa	Spain	Thailand	United States	World Total
2007-08	740.8	161.9	375.6	140.0	202.0	141.3	1,426.9	70.3	80.7	35.0	421.0	223.9	5,028.8
2008-09	685.9	177.5	389.5	106.3	209.2	119.9	1,442.6	74.9	69.8	33.0	436.0	222.6	4,953.0
2009-10	470.1	182.5	394.6	89.3	200.9	160.6	1,189.6	84.7	84.8	31.2	488.0	201.7	4,737.3
2010-11	564.1	176.2	394.0	96.6	185.7	113.0	1,286.0	82.8	90.0	30.4	503.0	277.4	5,043.9
2011-12	464.5	90.0	307.2	130.3	189.8	86.0	1,413.8	82.2	96.2	30.0	489.0	278.6	5,046.6
2012-13[1]	336.6	140.4	368.2	123.0	207.0	101.0	775.0	84.2	28.4	30.5	462.5	236.7	4,320.9
2013-14[2]	395.9	161.8	392.3	82.0	201.0	111.7	1,071.1	85.0	74.8	30.1	460.0	219.9	4,694.0
2014-15[3]	283.1	141.7	375.8	160.0	203.0	111.0	698.4	86.0	77.0	30.4	430.0	230.0	4,330.0

[1] Preliminary.   [2] Estimate.   [3] Forecast.   *Source: The Oil World*

World Production of Fish Oil   In Thousands of Metric Tons

Year	Canada	Chile	China	Denmark	Iceland	Japan	Norway	Peru	Africa	Russia	United States	World Total	Fish Oil CIF[4] $ Per Tonne
2007-08	5.4	181.5	12.5	63.5	72.1	64.3	42.9	298.6	4.0	4.0	81.7	1,077.0	1,612
2008-09	5.5	178.4	14.0	67.5	71.5	63.6	38.8	302.1	4.2	4.0	80.7	1,061.3	855
2009-10	5.6	107.4	15.4	67.1	44.0	62.0	49.8	238.4	6.4	4.1	54.1	958.2	994
2010-11	5.7	131.6	16.7	61.8	53.1	55.7	49.3	237.9	5.0	4.2	69.1	963.7	1,502
2011-12	6.0	117.5	17.8	35.2	59.9	56.2	36.0	307.4	5.8	4.3	56.5	1,045.4	1,718
2012-13[1]	6.2	91.1	18.7	46.8	57.0	58.4	36.0	137.6	2.2	4.4	78.1	890.3	2,190
2013-14[2]	6.0	137.9	20.0	50.1	42.9	60.0	37.0	174.4	4.8	4.5	68.2	946.6	1,791
2014-15[3]	6.1	95.3	20.2	41.7	45.0	59.0	34.0	80.0	5.0	4.6	75.0	819.6	2,052

[1] Preliminary.   [2] Estimate.   [3] Forecast.   [4] Any origin, N.W. Europe.   *Source: The Oil World*

Monthly Production of Catfish--Round Weight Processed--in the United States   In Thousands of Pounds (Live Weight)

Year	Jan.	Feb.	Mar.	Apr.	May	June	July	Aug.	Sept.	Oct.	Nov.	Dec.	Total
2007	46,079	44,083	45,477	37,954	38,867	37,275	39,168	42,626	39,519	45,890	40,307	39,001	496,246
2008	45,992	47,634	47,908	45,018	44,326	43,265	42,583	40,985	39,057	43,344	36,869	32,616	509,597
2009	36,406	37,702	44,912	40,768	39,925	39,370	40,966	39,490	36,408	40,191	36,211	33,751	466,100
2010	40,042	40,977	46,650	37,111	38,244	38,656	39,302	39,231	39,494	40,455	36,683	34,838	471,683
2011	35,076	27,782	30,372	23,605	24,749	24,337	26,595	30,680	30,271	32,446	25,814	22,598	334,325
2012	25,843	26,950	28,098	22,463	25,009	23,938	25,056	24,886	24,535	28,596	22,124	22,653	300,151
2013	29,458	29,959	NA	NA	NA	NA	NA	NA	NA	NA	NA	NA	356,502
2014[1]	NA	NA	NA	NA	NA	NA	NA	NA	NA	NA	NA	NA	NA

[1] Preliminary.   NA = Not available.   *Source: Economic Research Service, U.S. Department of Agriculture ERS-USDA)*

Average Price Paid to Producers for Farm-Raised Catfish in the United States   In Cents Per Pound (Live Weight)

Year	Jan.	Feb.	Mar.	Apr.	May	June	July	Aug.	Sept.	Oct.	Nov.	Dec.	Average
2007	83.7	83.8	83.8	84.1	84.0	81.7	76.2	73.1	69.7	68.2	66.6	65.0	76.7
2008	65.8	68.8	74.3	75.7	77.6	79.4	81.8	82.7	82.7	82.5	82.3	82.1	78.0
2009	81.0	77.0	77.3	76.3	76.2	76.3	77.1	76.9	77.2	76.8	76.5	76.3	77.1
2010	76.4	76.5	78.5	80.4	79.6	78.6	78.8	79.0	81.6	83.2	84.1	86.1	80.2
2011	93.1	100.3	107.5	114.1	116.9	123.1	125.2	127.7	127.5	126.2	125.7	125.1	117.7
2012	124.8	122.9	120.1	116.7	103.8	93.4	84.3	79.8	79.3	80.3	82.2	83.0	97.6
2013	81.9	82.2	NA	NA	NA	NA	NA	NA	NA	NA	NA	NA	82.1
2014[1]	NA	NA	NA	NA	NA	NA	NA	NA	NA	NA	NA	NA	NA

[1] Preliminary.   NA = Not available.   *Source: Economic Research Service, U.S. Department of Agriculture (ERS-USDA)*

Sales of Fresh Catfish in the United States   In Thousands of Pounds

Year	Jan.	Feb.	Mar.	Apr.	May	June	July	Aug.	Sept.	Oct.	Nov.	Dec.	Total
Whole
2008	3,338	3,585	3,194	2,908	2,868	2,612	2,552	2,605	2,227	2,830	2,302	2,517	33,538
2009	2,537	2,752	3,137	2,733	2,551	2,546	2,582	2,332	2,321	2,830	2,352	2,461	31,134
2010	2,811	3,156	3,743	3,046	2,844	2,730	2,277	2,582	2,518	2,863	2,297	2,434	33,301
2011	2,488	2,046	2,614	2,259	2,061	2,025	1,484	1,701	1,635	2,024	2,021	1,878	24,236
2012	2,219	2,323	2,353	2,004	2,107	2,097	2,206	2,076	2,086	2,546	2,204	2,295	26,516
2013[1]	2,859	2,480	NA	NA	NA	NA	NA	NA	NA	NA	NA	NA	32,034
Fillets[2]
2008	4,489	4,922	4,823	4,145	4,000	4,761	3,943	3,803	3,503	3,723	3,083	3,075	48,270
2009	3,795	3,732	4,196	3,894	3,864	3,621	3,649	3,554	3,444	3,495	2,989	3,038	43,271
2010	3,607	4,221	3,905	3,495	3,720	3,475	3,411	3,606	3,456	3,343	2,791	3,045	42,075
2011	3,220	2,650	2,880	2,351	2,199	2,105	2,227	2,199	2,047	2,173	1,892	1,877	27,820
2012	2,231	2,349	2,399	2,150	2,234	2,148	2,218	2,474	2,433	2,400	1,913	1,934	26,883
2013[1]	2,372	2,543	NA	NA	NA	NA	NA	NA	NA	NA	NA	NA	29,490
Other[3]
2008	913	819	755	786	736	704	653	665	642	713	717	568	8,671
2009	709	810	797	684	751	783	646	709	644	685	616	611	8,445
2010	695	735	807	668	713	641	631	650	647	621	516	564	7,888
2011	615	535	556	551	485	461	456	462	444	476	423	420	5,884
2012	473	515	529	475	497	445	459	476	449	479	422	425	5,644
2013[1]	530	566	NA	NA	NA	NA	NA	NA	NA	NA	NA	NA	6,576

[1] Preliminary.   [2] Includes regular, shank and strip fillets; excludes breaded products.   [3] Includes steaks, nuggets and all other products not reported.
NA = Not available.   *Source: Economic Research Service, U.S. Department of Agriculture (ERS-USDA)*

Prices of Fresh Catfish in the United States   In Dollars Per Pound

Year	Jan.	Feb.	Mar.	Apr.	May	June	July	Aug.	Sept.	Oct.	Nov.	Dec.	Average
Whole
2008	1.49	1.50	1.56	1.59	1.60	1.68	1.68	1.76	1.73	1.71	1.72	1.66	1.64
2009	1.72	1.67	1.65	1.68	1.70	1.64	1.66	1.69	1.66	1.59	1.57	1.57	1.65
2010	1.55	1.49	1.50	1.55	1.55	1.58	1.67	1.58	1.63	1.57	1.61	1.71	1.58
2011	1.90	2.06	2.17	2.28	2.40	2.49	2.64	2.61	2.65	2.54	2.42	2.45	2.38
2012	2.44	2.44	2.42	2.35	2.25	2.12	2.04	1.95	1.89	1.84	1.81	1.78	2.11
2013[1]	1.81	1.83	NA	NA	NA	NA	NA	NA	NA	NA	NA	NA	1.82
Fillets[2]
2008	2.90	2.88	2.96	3.03	3.10	3.08	3.25	3.33	3.33	3.31	3.30	3.31	3.15
2009	3.30	3.24	3.24	3.23	3.23	3.22	3.21	3.21	3.20	3.19	3.18	3.19	3.22
2010	3.16	3.10	3.18	3.22	3.25	3.26	3.25	3.22	3.24	3.29	3.32	3.32	3.23
2011	3.47	3.75	4.18	4.43	4.55	4.60	4.84	4.77	4.88	4.86	4.84	4.78	4.50
2012	4.73	4.68	4.68	4.57	4.35	4.09	3.87	3.76	3.72	3.74	3.73	3.73	4.14
2013[1]	3.70	3.68	NA	NA	NA	NA	NA	NA	NA	NA	NA	NA	3.69
Other[3]
2008	1.46	1.51	1.57	1.61	1.65	1.80	1.81	1.77	1.76	1.73	1.68	1.62	1.66
2009	1.64	1.52	1.61	1.75	1.60	1.68	1.64	1.64	1.67	1.64	1.66	1.67	1.64
2010	1.66	1.60	1.65	1.81	1.76	1.71	1.72	1.72	1.69	1.68	1.74	1.75	1.71
2011	1.77	1.95	2.07	2.14	2.24	2.29	2.17	2.26	2.29	2.25	2.23	2.20	2.16
2012	2.15	2.11	2.10	2.14	1.91	1.97	1.87	1.84	1.85	1.85	1.80	1.80	1.95
2013[1]	1.82	1.78	NA	NA	NA	NA	NA	NA	NA	NA	NA	NA	1.80

[1] Preliminary.   [2] Includes regular, shank and strip fillets; excludes breaded products.   [3] Includes steaks, nuggets and all other products not reported.
NA = Not available.   *Source: Economic Research Service, U.S. Department of Agriculture (ERS-USDA)*

Flaxseed and Linseed Oil

Flaxseed, also called linseed, is an ancient crop that was cultivated by the Babylonians around 3,000 BC. Flaxseed is used for fiber in textiles and to produce oil. Flaxseeds contain approximately 35% oil, of which 60% is omega-3 fatty acid. Flaxseed or linseed oil is obtained through either the expeller extraction or solvent extraction method. Manufacturers filter the processed oil to remove some impurities and then sell it as unrefined. Unrefined oil retains its full flavor, aroma, color, and naturally occurring nutrients. Flaxseed oil is used for cooking and as a dietary supplement as well as for animal feed. Industrial linseed oil is not for internal consumption due to possible poisonous additives and is used for making putty, sealants, linoleum, wood preservation, varnishes, and oil paints.

Prices – The average monthly price received by U.S. farmers for flaxseed in the 2015-16 marketing year (through January 2016) fell by -22.5% yr/yr to $9.28 per bushel, below the record high of $14.08 per bushel posted in the 2012-13 marketing year.

Supply – World production of flaxseed in the 2014-15 (latest data available) marketing year rose by +8.3% yr/yr to 2.494 million metric tons, still well below the 9-year high of 2.864 million metric tons in 2005-06. The world's largest producer of flaxseed is the former USSR with 29.5% of world production in 2014-15, followed by Canada (34.0%), China (14.0%), the U.S. (6.5%), and India (4.4%). U.S. production of flaxseed in 2015-16 rose +58.5% to 10.095 million bushels, up from the 2011-12 record low of 2.791 million bushels. North Dakota is by far the largest producing state for flaxseed and accounted for 92.3% of flaxseed production in 2015, followed by Montana 4.5% and South Dakota with 2.9% of production.

World production of linseed oil in 2014-15 (latest data available) rose by +6.7% yr/yr to 659.700 million metric tons. The world's largest producers of linseed oil are China (with 29.6% of world production in 2014-15), Belgium (18.2%), the U.S. (15.7%), and Germany (7.0%). U.S. production of linseed oil in 2014-15 rose by +34.7% yr/yr to 229.000 million pounds.

Demand – U.S. distribution of flaxseed in 2014-15 rose by +30.4% yr/yr to 13.231 million bushels. The breakdown was 88.8% for crushing into meal and oil, 4.7% for residual, 4.6% for exports and 1.9% for seed.

Trade – U.S. exports of flaxseed in 2014-15 rose by +1.1% yr/yr to 605,000 thousand bushels. U.S. imports of flaxseed in 2014-15 rose by +20.7% yr/yr to 8.000 million bushels.

World Production of Flaxseed   In Thousands of Metric Tons

Crop Year	Argen-tina	Australia	Bang-ladesh	Canada	China	Egypt	France	Hungary	India	Romania	United States	Former USSR	World Total
2005-06	54	10	3	1,150	475	28	25	3	210	----	480	105	2,870
2006-07	38	7	9	1,040	480	27	43	2	200	----	280	157	2,551
2007-08	13	8	8	660	480	12	34	2	190	----	150	135	1,942
2008-09	19	8	8	861	475	12	15	1	150	----	145	145	2,098
2009-10	52	8	7	930	318	8	21	1	154	1	189	206	2,163
2010-11	32	7	7	419	353	12	36	----	147	2	230	326	1,806
2011-12	21	7	7	399	359	5	31	1	152	3	71	802	2,136
2012-13[1]	17	7	6	489	391	5	26	----	149	4	147	571	2,053
2013-14[2]	20	6	6	724	399	7	16	1	140	4	85	648	2,302
2014-15[3]	18	6	7	847	350	10	23	1	110	3	162	735	2,494

[1] Preliminary.   [2] Estimate.   [3] Forecast.   *Source: The Oil World*

Supply and Distribution of Flaxseed in the United States   In Thousands of Bushels

Crop Year Beginning June 1	Planted	Harvested	Yield Per Acre (Bushels)	Beginning Stocks	Pro-duction	Imports	Total Supply	Seed	Crush	Exports	Residual	Total
	---- 1,000 Acres ----			------------------- Supply -------------------				------------------------ Distribution ------------------------				
2006-07	813	767	14.4	3,535	11,019	5,464	20,018	287	14,900	1,788	599	17,574
2007-08	354	349	16.9	2,444	5,896	8,019	16,359	287	11,700	2,221	640	14,847
2008-09	354	340	16.8	1,512	5,716	4,794	12,022	257	8,150	432	631	9,470
2009-10	317	314	23.6	2,552	7,423	6,283	16,258	341	12,000	1,752	608	14,701
2010-11	421	418	21.7	1,557	9,056	6,040	16,653	144	11,635	2,130	573	14,483
2011-12	178	173	16.1	2,170	2,791	8,286	13,247	279	10,500	654	694	12,127
2012-13	349	336	17.3	1,120	5,798	6,928	13,846	147	11,000	1,020	755	12,922
2013-14[1]	181	172	19.5	924	3,356	6,630	10,910	252	8,700	599	597	10,147
2014-15[2]	311	302	21.1	763	6,368	8,000	15,131	256	11,750	605	620	13,231
2015-16[3]	463	456	22.1		10,095							

[1] Preliminary.   [2] Estimate.   [3] Forecast.   NA = not avaliable.   *Source: Economic Research Service, U.S. Department of Agriculture (ERS-USDA)*

Supply and Distribution of Linseed Meal in the United States   In Millions of Pounds

Crop Year Beginning June 1	Stocks June 1	Production	Imports	Total Supply	Domestic Disappear-ance	Exports	Total Disappear-ance	Ending Stocks	Average Price at Minneapolis (34% Protein) Cents/Lb.
2005-06	5	295	18	318	269	44	313	5	124.69
2006-07	5	268	17	290	275	10	285	5	124.61
2007-08	5	211	9	225	210	10	220	5	191.54
2008-09	5	147	10	162	130	28	157	5	227.66
2009-10	5	216	3	224	210	10	219	5	217.24
2010-11	5	209	7	221	208	7	216	5	223.23
2011-12	5	189	8	202	194	3	197	5	238.35
2012-13	5	198	6	209	199	5	204	5	320.13
2013-14[1]	5	157	1	163	152	6	158	5	359.42
2014-15[2]	5	212	2	219	209	5	214	5	240-280

[1] Preliminary.   [2] Forecast.   Source: Economic Research Service, U.S. Department of Agriculture (ERS-USDA)

Supply and Distribution of Linseed Oil in the United States   In Millions of Pounds

Crop Year Beginning June 1	Stocks June 1	Production	Total Supply	Exports	Domestic Disappearance	Total Disappearance	Average Price at Minneapolis Cents/Lb.
2005-06	45	320	375	98	248	346	54.0
2006-07	29	291	328	76	202	278	44.4
2007-08	51	228	291	74	191	265	70.3
2008-09	26	159	191	66	52	118	86.5
2009-10	73	234	312	103	172	275	67.5
2010-11	37	227	270	101	131	232	NA
2011-12	38	205	248	89	124	213	NA
2012-13	35	215	255	94	126	220	NA
2013-14[1]	35	170	210	58	117	175	NA
2014-15[2]	35	229	269	55	179	234	NA

[1] Preliminary.   [2] Forecast.   Source: Economic Research Service, U.S. Department of Agriculture (ERS-USDA)

World Production and Price of Linseed Oil   In Thousands of Metric Tons

Year	Argen-tina	Bang-ladesh	Belgium	China	Egypt	Germany	India	Japan	United Kingdom	United States	Former USSR	World Total	Rotterdam Ex-Tank USD $/Tonne
2005-06	13.1	2.6	97.9	137.6	14.8	65.2	63.7	5.7	3.5	147.7	16.2	695.0	686
2006-07	5.0	4.3	118.9	146.6	11.2	59.3	52.0	6.2	5.3	140.3	15.8	693.9	809
2007-08	2.8	2.8	114.6	87.3	8.5	53.6	48.2	4.6	2.8	98.1	18.1	574.5	1,635
2008-09	2.1	2.3	77.4	121.3	6.4	37.7	47.9	2.6	3.2	84.8	14.2	524.3	975
2009-10	1.7	2.1	96.9	159.2	5.2	34.5	45.2	2.0	2.6	115.7	21.9	587.7	1,114
2010-11	1.9	2.0	107.2	120.4	4.3	40.9	41.4	1.6	5.9	108.0	27.3	546.0	1,451
2011-12	1.1	2.3	108.8	144.5	4.3	49.5	41.1	1.6	5.6	105.5	30.9	621.5	1,267
2012-13	1.6	2.0	107.2	150.5	2.9	44.8	38.6	2.0	4.9	99.2	27.9	601.3	1,217
2013-14[1]	----	----	110.4	182.1	3.4	48.7	35.3	1.5	6.0	86.2	30.7	618.2	1,191
2014-15[2]	----	----	120.0	195.6	4.5	46.2	29.4	2.6	4.2	103.7	36.0	659.7	1,202

[1] Preliminary.   [2] Forecast.   Source: The Oil World

Production of Flaxseed in the United States, by States   In Thousands of Bushels

Year	Minnesota	Montana	North Dakota	South Dakota	U.S. Total
2006	126	297	10,368	228	11,019
2007	72	180	5,548	96	5,896
2008	69	72	5,491	84	5,716
2009	63	160	7,032	168	7,423
2010	56	255	8,536	209	9,056
2011	45	208	2,426	112	2,791
2012	45	156	5,478	119	5,798
2013	76	240	2,920	120	3,356
2014	48	425	5,805	90	6,368
2015[1]	42	450	9,315	288	10,095

[1] Preliminary.   Source: National Agricultural Statistics Service, U.S. Department of Agriculture (NASS-USDA)

FLAXSEED AND LINSEED OIL

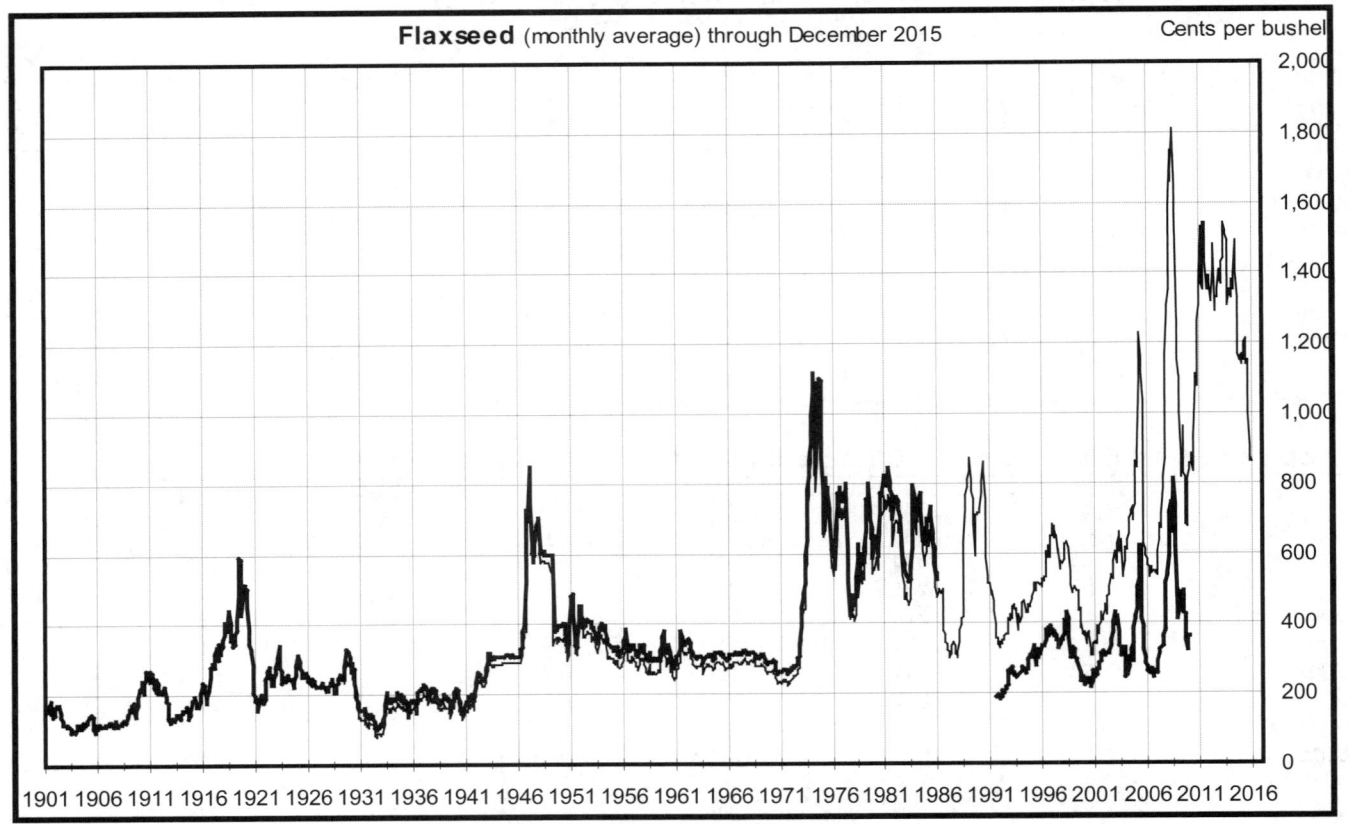

Flaxseed (monthly average) through December 2015   Cents per bushel

Average Price Received by Farmers for Flaxseed in the United States   In Dollars Per Bushel

Year	July	Aug.	Sept.	Oct.	Nov.	Dec.	Jan.	Feb.	Mar.	Apr.	May	June	Average
2006-07	5.47	5.50	5.46	5.41	5.38	5.73	6.03	6.39	6.79	6.72	7.08	7.81	6.15
2007-08	8.14	8.64	9.55	11.60	12.90	13.10	13.50	16.00	17.50	16.60	16.90	18.00	13.54
2008-09	18.10	16.50	15.60	12.60	12.60	11.50	11.00	9.98	8.84	8.13	8.96	9.59	11.95
2009-10	8.28	8.14	6.79	6.78	8.12	8.40	8.53	8.57	8.82	8.53	8.34	9.26	8.21
2010-11	10.70	11.10	10.80	11.90	12.60	13.10	13.80	15.30	13.70	13.50	14.20	15.40	13.01
2011-12	15.40	14.30	13.50	13.90	13.90	13.50	13.70	13.20	13.30	14.10	14.80	12.90	13.88
2012-13	13.30	13.30	13.30	13.50	14.10	13.80	13.70	14.30	14.40	14.90	15.40	15.20	14.10
2013-14	15.10	14.90	13.10	13.50	13.40	13.40	13.30	13.80	13.50	13.90	14.90	14.40	13.93
2014-15	14.00	13.30	11.70	11.50	11.60	11.40	11.70	11.50	11.50	12.00	12.10	11.40	11.98
2015-16[1]	11.50	10.00	9.07	8.59	8.71	8.62	8.45	8.10					9.13

[1] Preliminary.   *Source: National Agricultural Statistics Service, U.S. Department of Agriculture (NASS-USDA)*

Average Price of Linseed Meal (34% protein) at Minneapolis   In Dollars Per Ton

Year	July	Aug.	Sept.	Oct.	Nov.	Dec.	Jan.	Feb.	Mar.	Apr.	May	June	Average
2006-07	111.50	101.10	92.80	100.80	118.10	123.30	134.20	156.40	156.30	149.00	135.10	132.00	125.88
2007-08	135.80	123.90	131.40	170.20	184.60	186.80	242.70	250.00	247.10	253.70	240.30	265.40	202.66
2008-09	273.70	231.30	200.00	160.80	164.00	189.60	248.80	270.00	231.90	233.50	263.10	250.00	226.39
2009-10	226.90	217.00	195.20	185.00	220.00	256.50	228.75	222.50	201.50	200.83	202.75	189.50	212.20
2010-11	199.38	204.00	200.00	208.75	237.50	234.38	255.00	256.25	236.50	225.63	231.88	254.38	228.64
2011-12	260.63	247.50	239.38	243.75	239.00	221.25	209.00	193.75	216.25	256.25	279.00	287.50	241.11
2012-13	343.00	358.75	340.63	334.00	297.50	335.83	296.00	303.75	303.75	309.00	331.88	340.00	324.51
2013-14	382.50	317.50	400.00	363.75	316.25	328.75	330.00	377.50	413.75	388.00	355.00	323.75	358.06
2014-15	295.00	252.50	302.50	214.38	283.75	287.50	250.00	230.63	230.50	239.38	256.88	258.00	258.42
2015-16[1]	284.38	287.50	256.00	215.00	209.80	200.00	195.00	197.50					230.65

[1] Preliminary.   *Source: Economic Research Service, U.S. Department of Agriculture (ERS-USDA)*

Fruits

A fruit is any seed-bearing structure produced from a flowering plant. A widely used classification system divides fruit into fleshy or dry types. Fleshy fruits are juicy and include peaches, mangos, apples, and blueberries. Dry fruits include tree nuts such as almonds, walnuts, and pecans. Some foods that are commonly called vegetables, such as tomatoes, squash, peppers and eggplant, are technically fruits because they develop from the ovary of a flower.

Worldwide, over 430 million tons of fruit are produced each year and are grown everywhere except the Arctic and the Antarctic. The tropics, because of their abundant moisture and warm temperatures, produce the most diverse and abundant fruits. Mexico and Chile produce more than half of all the fresh and frozen fruit imported into the U.S. In the U.S., the top three fruits produced are oranges, grapes, and apples. Virtually all U.S. production of almonds, pistachios, and walnuts occurs in California, which leads the U.S. in tree nut production.

Prices – Overall fruit prices were fairly strong in 2014 (latest data available) with the fresh fruit Consumer Price Index (CPI) rising +4.8% to 359.7 and the processed fruit CPI index falling -0.3% to 154.0. Individual fruit prices, however, were mixed in 2014: Red Delicious Apples (-14.7% to $1.182 per pound), Bananas (-2.0% to 59.0 cents per pound), Anjou pears (-11.1% to $1.253 per pound),

Thompson seedless grapes (-10.2% to $2.639 per pound), Lemons (+24.4% to $1.968 per pound), Grapefruit (+5.8% to $1.109 per pound), Navel oranges (+14.6% to $1.319 cents per pound), and Valencia oranges (+2.3% to $1.032 per pound).

Supply – U.S. commercial production of selected fruits in 2014 (latest data) fell -6.7% to 28.044 million short tons. By weight, grapes accounted for 27.7% of that U.S. fruit production figure, followed by oranges at 24.1%, and apples at 20.4%. The value of U.S. fruit production in 2014 fell-0.4% yr/yr to $29.735 billion.

Demand – U.S. per capita fresh fruit consumption in 2014 (latest data) rose +1.7% to 113.10 pounds per year, a new record high. The highest per capita consumption categories for non-citrus fruits in 2014 were bananas (27.90 pounds) and apples (18.80 pounds).

Per capital consumption of citrus fruits were oranges (9.43 pounds), tangerines & tangelos (5.06 pounds), lemons (3.42 pounds), and grapefruit (2.43 pounds). The utilization breakdown for 2014 shows that total U.S. non-citrus fruit was used for fresh fruit (43.7%), wine (23.8%), dried fruit (10.9%), juice (8.5%), canned fruit (6.3%), and frozen fruit (4.4%). The value of utilized non-citrus fruit production in 2014 rose +0.7%yr/yr to $16.329 billion.

Commercial Production for Selected Fruits in the United States — In Thousands of Short Tons

Year	Apples	Cherries[2]	Cran-berries	Grapes	Grape-fruit	Lemons	Nect-arines	Oranges	Peach-es	Pears	Pine-apple[3]	Prunes & Plums	Straw-berries	Tang-elos	Tang-erines	Total All Fruits
2008	4,817	355	393	7,319	1,548	619	303	10,076	1,135	870	W	544	1,266	68	527	30,105
2009	4,853	623	346	7,307	1,304	912	220	9,128	1,104	957	W	627	1,401	52	443	29,712
2010	4,646	408	340	7,471	1,238	882	233	8,243	1,150	814	----	543	1,426	41	596	28,356
2011	4,713	450	386	7,448	1,264	920	225	8,905	1,072	966	----	617	1,451	52	657	29,555
2012	4,496	467	402	7,531	1,153	850	189	8,982	968	851	----	564	1,526	52	644	28,832
2013	5,216	479	448	8,632	1,204	912	162	8,268	904	877	----	364	1,524	45	682	30,071
2014[1]	5,716	516	420	7,772	1,047	824	205	6,768	853	832	----	440	1,511	40	732	28,045

[1] Preliminary. [2] Sweet and tart. [3] Utilized production. *Source: Economic Research Service, U.S. Department of Agriculture (ERS-USDA)*

Utilized Production for Selected Fruits in the United States — In Thousands of Short Tons

	Utilized Production				Value of Production			
Year	Citrus[2]	Noncitrus	Tree nuts[3]	Total	Citrus[2]	Noncitrus	Tree nuts[3]	Total
	In Thousands of Short Tons				In Thousands of Dollars			
2008	12,838	17,558	2,144	32,541	3,240,263	11,547,473	3,828,207	18,615,943
2009	11,839	18,021	2,014	31,874	2,741,963	12,232,459	4,172,838	19,147,260
2010	11,000	17,835	2,374	31,209	2,965,231	12,751,568	5,862,688	21,579,487
2011	11,798	18,111	2,584	32,493	3,240,896	13,886,156	7,007,694	24,134,746
2012	11,681	17,635	2,636	31,952	3,712,817	15,611,441	8,337,036	27,661,294
2013	11,111	19,433	2,659	33,203	3,170,508	16,220,752	10,462,270	29,853,530
2014[1]	9,411	19,035	2,564	31,010	3,392,988	16,329,920	10,012,641	29,735,549

[1] Preliminary. [2] Year harvest was completed. [3] Tree nuts on an in-shell equivalent.
Source: Economic Research Service, U.S. Department of Agriculture (ERS-USDA)

Annual Average Retail Prices for Selected Fruits in the United States — In Dollars Per Pound

Year	Red Delicious Apples	Bananas	Anjou Pears	Thompson Seedless Grapes	Lemons	Grapefruit	Oranges Navel	Oranges Valencias
2008	1.319	.609	1.331	2.212	2.006	.966	1.116	1.016
2009	1.182	.611	1.305	2.109	1.520	.903	1.050	.956
2010	1.220	.580	1.287	2.181	1.634	.927	1.062	1.017
2011	1.350	.610	1.409	2.386	1.581	.976	1.096	1.009
2012	1.377	.602	1.253	2.488	1.565	1.078	1.053	----
2013	1.386	.600	----	2.940	1.582	1.078	1.151	1.032
2014[1]	1.182	.588	----	2.639	1.968	1.109	1.319	----

[1] Estimate. *Source: Economic Research Service, U.S. Department of Agriculture (ERS-USDA)*

FRUITS

Utilization of Noncitrus Fruit Production, and Value in the United States — 1,000 Short Tons (Fresh Equivalent)

Year	Utilized Production	Fresh	Canned	Dried	Juice	Frozen	Wine	Other Processed	Value of Utilized Production $1,000
2005	18,272	7,188	1,575	2,101	1,555	712	4,551	277	9,805,757
2006	16,816	6,930	1,400	2,219	1,256	710	3,726	235	10,510,417
2007	17,048	7,013	1,453	2,030	1,277	748	3,921	278	11,436,449
2008	17,558	7,203	1,406	2,413	1,228	682	3,944	289	11,547,473
2009	18,021	7,514	1,394	2,148	1,235	742	4,373	269	12,232,459
2010	17,835	7,414	1,386	2,318	1,103	706	4,271	298	12,751,568
2011	18,111	7,666	1,301	2,399	1,153	737	4,155	316	13,886,156
2012	17,635	7,443	1,100	2,091	1,213	707	4,707	374	15,611,441
2013	19,433	7,718	1,373	2,321	1,631	876	5,068	448	16,220,752
2014[1]	19,035	8,325	1,202	2,076	1,609	841	4,522	460	16,329,920

[1] Preliminary. Source: Economic Research Service, U.S. Department of Agriculture (ERS-USDA)

Average Price Indexes for Fruits in the United States

Year	Index of all Fruit & Nut Prices Received by Growers (1990-92=100)	Producer Price Index Fresh Fruit	Dried Fruit	Canned Fruits and Juices	Frozen Fruits and Juices	Consumer Price Index Fresh Fruit	Processed Fruit
		1982 = 100				1982-84 = 100	
2005	77.0	102.8	NA	148.1	112.4	297.4	118.4
2006	92.0	111.0	----	153.0	119.7	315.2	121.5
2007	95.0	123.4	----	169.3	138.5	329.5	125.2
2008	89.0	122.9	----	179.0	146.7	345.4	135.6
2009	84.0	110.4	----	186.9	150.5	324.4	142.8
2010	86.6	123.8	----	187.3	148.7	322.3	141.0
2011	100.0	117.7	----	195.4	160.0	333.1	146.0
2012	113.0	119.0	----	203.8	168.9	336.6	150.4
2013	115.0	121.2	----	206.4	170.3	343.2	154.5
2014[1]	133.0	124.5	----	208.7	172.7	359.7	154.0

[1] Estimate.   NA = Not availavle.   Source: Economic Research Service, U.S. Department of Agriculture (ERS-USDA)

Fresh Fruit: Per Capita Consumption[1] in the United States — In Pounds

Year	Oranges	Citrus Fruit Tangerines & Tangelos	Lemons	Limes	Grape-fruit	U.S. Total	Apples	Apricots	Noncitrus Fruit Avocados	Bananas	Blue-berries	Cherries	Cran-berries
2005	11.42	2.50	2.95	2.09	2.65	21.60	16.66	.13	3.46	25.18	.44	.87	.09
2006	10.25	2.69	4.15	2.26	2.31	21.64	17.73	.08	3.50	25.11	.56	1.06	.09
2007	7.46	2.57	2.81	2.27	2.84	17.94	16.39	.16	3.50	25.95	.59	1.22	.10
2008	9.93	3.08	1.97	2.48	3.16	20.62	15.88	.13	3.83	25.04	.80	1.00	.10
2009	9.06	3.16	3.12	2.55	2.80	20.69	16.20	.14	4.25	22.01	.96	1.56	.09
2010	9.68	3.76	2.79	2.57	2.76	21.57	15.29	.12	4.00	25.61	1.12	1.31	.06
2011	9.97	4.13	3.46	2.50	2.71	22.77	15.44	.12	5.10	25.53	1.29	1.30	.06
2012	10.54	4.17	3.94	2.57	2.37	23.59	16.01	.10	5.61	26.97	1.33	1.50	.07
2013	10.45	4.44	3.48	2.96	2.63	23.96	17.32	.11	6.11	28.05	1.38	.98	.08
2014[1]	9.43	5.06	3.42	3.06	2.43	23.40	18.80	.12	6.47	27.90	1.54	1.19	.07

[1] All data on calendar-year basis except for citrus fruits; apples, August; grapes and pears, July; grapefruit, September; lemons, August of prior year; all other citrus, November.   [2] Preliminary.   Source: Economic Research Service, U.S. Department of Agriculture (ERS-USDA)

Fresh Fruit: Per Capita Consumption[1] in the United States — In Pounds

Year	Grapes	Kiwifruit	Mangos	Peaches & Nectarines	Pears	Pineapples	Papaya	Prunes	Straw-berries	Total Noncitrus	Total Fruit
2005	8.60	.45	1.88	4.83	2.91	4.90	.94	1.11	5.83	78.27	99.88
2006	7.59	.47	2.10	4.58	3.19	5.20	1.04	1.02	6.14	79.46	101.11
2007	8.01	.44	2.10	4.46	3.09	5.02	1.08	1.01	6.26	79.37	97.32
2008	8.26	.46	2.10	5.08	3.11	5.07	.98	.92	6.45	79.23	99.84
2009	7.66	.50	2.02	4.41	3.19	5.09	1.20	.73	7.17	77.17	97.85
2010	7.93	.50	2.24	4.73	2.90	5.70	1.17	.78	7.23	80.66	102.23
2011	7.35	.58	2.53	4.46	3.21	5.72	1.05	.87	7.36	81.97	104.74
2012	7.57	.54	2.49	3.86	2.76	6.42	.97	.62	7.97	84.79	108.38
2013	7.74	.46	2.87	3.00	2.83	6.73	1.12	.51	7.99	87.29	111.25
2014[1]	7.66	.51	2.50	3.26	2.85	7.18	1.14	.58	7.95	89.71	113.10

[1] All data on calendar-year basis except for citrus fruits; apples, August; grapes and pears, July; grapefruit, September; lemons, August of prior year; all other citrus, November.   [2] Preliminary.   Source: Economic Research Service, U.S. Department of Agriculture (ERS-USDA)

Average Price Received by Growers for Grapefruit in the United States   In Dollars Per Box

Year	Jan.	Feb.	Mar.	Apr.	May	June	July	Aug.	Sept.	Oct.	Nov.	Dec.	Average
2006	11.06	9.92	8.18	8.12	11.41	10.98	11.16	9.42	11.38	11.17	8.34	7.98	9.93
2007	5.66	4.02	2.91	2.10	4.49	9.89	8.95	7.53	8.55	10.06	9.93	5.97	6.67
2008	4.67	3.30	2.70	2.89	4.94	6.61	5.59	4.58	5.50	10.64	5.49	4.52	5.12
2009	4.19	3.74	3.61	2.99	6.21	8.23	7.15	6.15	6.55	16.41	10.78	8.82	7.07
2010	8.86	7.10	5.93	4.19	4.05	5.40	1.30	0.50	4.70	7.62	12.06	8.06	5.81
2011	6.94	6.31	5.69	5.27	7.55	9.50	8.20	7.10	9.50	8.67	7.90	7.18	7.48
2012	6.83	6.79	6.91	10.20	9.62	15.43	13.23	10.33	10.13	12.49	7.68	6.87	9.71
2013	7.19	5.71	4.29	4.33	8.26	8.76	6.66	6.36	8.76	7.96	8.54	7.51	7.03
2014	7.30	5.78	5.60	5.34	7.89	7.69	7.19	8.05	13.40	12.33	9.82	8.92	8.28
2015[1]	7.03	4.83	4.87	5.32	6.68	9.12	9.33	5.71	7.64	13.79	13.42	10.79	8.21

On-tree equivalent.   [1]Preliminary.   *Source: National Agricultural Statistics Service, U.S. Department of Agriculture (NASS-USDA)*

Average Price Received by Growers for Lemons in the United States   In Dollars Per Box

Year	Jan.	Feb.	Mar.	Apr.	May	June	July	Aug.	Sept.	Oct.	Nov.	Dec.	Average
2006	3.78	9.42	9.44	13.50	15.09	16.98	18.88	21.19	27.80	28.83	20.71	12.98	16.55
2007	11.50	27.69	8.68	9.18	8.14	13.04	13.64	31.67	33.08	37.98	29.80	23.89	20.69
2008	23.90	29.41	23.67	22.13	20.54	27.04	24.17	24.64	21.33	11.08	10.40	7.86	20.51
2009	5.90	2.62	1.80	4.26	5.68	11.34	12.21	20.79	17.60	15.59	14.60	11.81	10.35
2010	9.88	8.48	8.68	10.06	9.13	11.24	12.59	16.60	19.72	19.92	18.51	9.51	12.86
2011	8.84	3.91	5.70	8.54	10.26	12.32	16.16	21.99	17.98	12.87	14.10	14.29	12.25
2012	12.97	11.38	12.51	15.55	17.19	16.10	17.29	11.89	14.94	16.38	13.96	11.60	14.31
2013	10.65	7.28	7.08	9.18	14.77	16.35	18.98	28.45	27.85	32.77	26.65	23.52	18.63
2014	21.17	21.69	21.31	22.39	24.54	29.91	40.05	33.68	37.40	38.47	29.54	21.15	28.44
2015[1]	18.53	13.44	16.20	22.76	32.59	38.51	37.34	34.95	31.02	36.18	30.46	24.02	28.00

On-tree equivalent.   [1]Preliminary.   *Source: National Agricultural Statistics Service, U.S. Department of Agriculture (NASS-USDA)*

Average Price Received by Growers for Tangelos in the United States   In Dollars Per Box

Year	Jan.	Feb.	Mar.	Apr.	May	June	July	Aug.	Sept.	Oct.	Nov.	Dec.	Average
2006	4.81	2.70	1.00	NQ	NQ	NQ	NQ	NQ	NQ	NQ	6.69	8.19	4.68
2007	8.52	9.01	NQ	NQ	NQ	NQ	NQ	NQ	NQ	NQ	5.08	2.78	6.35
2008	2.18	1.87	NQ	NQ	NQ	NQ	NQ	NQ	NQ	NQ	4.71	2.92	2.92
2009	1.28	-0.40	NQ	NQ	NQ	NQ	NQ	NQ	NQ	NQ	6.68	4.49	3.01
2010	3.83	4.00	NQ	NQ	NQ	NQ	NQ	NQ	NQ	NQ	NQ	5.56	4.46
2011	5.70	5.75	NQ	NQ	NQ	NQ	NQ	NQ	NQ	NQ	6.53	6.63	6.15
2012	13.79	10.67	NQ	NQ	NQ	NQ	NQ	NQ	NQ	NQ	7.44	12.89	11.20
2013	9.02	NQ	NQ	NQ	NQ	NQ	NQ	NQ	NQ	NQ	10.34	8.74	9.37
2014	7.85	NQ	NQ	NQ	NQ	NQ	NQ	NQ	NQ	NQ	8.76	9.43	8.68
2015[1]	14.29	8.06	NQ	NQ	NQ	NQ	NQ	NQ	NQ	NQ	12.19	10.30	11.21

On-tree equivalent.   [1]Preliminary.   NQ = No quote.   *Source: National Agricultural Statistics Service, U.S. Department of Agriculture (NASS-USDA)*

Average Price Received by Growers for Tangerines in the United States   In Dollars Per Box

Year	Jan.	Feb.	Mar.	Apr.	May	June	July	Aug.	Sept.	Oct.	Nov.	Dec.	Average
2006	10.39	10.21	7.96	6.52	5.88	NQ	NQ	NQ	12.62	10.39	16.25	14.81	10.56
2007	14.05	14.19	12.98	14.68	17.01	NQ	NQ	NQ	NQ	12.75	20.06	18.63	15.54
2008	12.19	13.72	11.70	7.95	4.13	NQ	NQ	NQ	NQ	14.16	17.47	12.31	11.70
2009	13.71	18.37	14.38	14.91	NQ	NQ	NQ	NQ	NQ	9.87	18.61	19.56	15.63
2010	15.25	8.12	12.07	15.91	NQ	NQ	NQ	NQ	NQ	10.38	27.06	21.53	15.76
2011	16.93	14.68	13.23	13.53	NQ	NQ	NQ	NQ	NQ	8.35	15.74	20.11	14.65
2012	14.73	18.68	24.11	NQ	NQ	NQ	NQ	NQ	NQ	12.70	18.60	21.86	18.45
2013	19.94	20.57	25.04	NQ	NQ	NQ	NQ	NQ	NQ	NQ	NQ	24.41	22.49
2014	22.15	24.88	26.29	NQ	NQ	NQ	NQ	NQ	NQ	NQ	NQ	NQ	24.44
2015[1]	14.49	NQ	NQ	NQ	NQ	NQ	NQ	NQ	NQ	NQ	NQ	NQ	14.49

On-tree equivalent.   [1]Preliminary.   NQ = No quote.   *Source: National Agricultural Statistics Service, U.S. Department of Agriculture (NASS-USDA)*

FRUITS

Average Price Received by Growers for Grapes in the United States   In Dollars Per Box

Year	Jan.	Feb.	Mar.	Apr.	May	June	July	Aug.	Sept.	Oct.	Nov.	Dec.	Average
2006	NQ	NQ	NQ	NQ	NQ	2,400	1,030	880	910	830	930	1,320	1,186
2007	NQ	NQ	NQ	NQ	NQ	770	660	680	790	940	1,200	1,710	964
2008	NQ	NQ	NQ	NQ	420	590	660	530	480	370	360	300	464
2009	NQ	NQ	NQ	NQ	1,380	1,120	610	310	470	630	630	1,220	796
2010	NQ	NQ	NQ	NQ	NQ	650	460	430	420	430	500	750	520
2011	NQ	NQ	NQ	NQ	NQ	1,080	1,480	960	820	790	980	1,040	1,021
2012	NQ	NQ	NQ	NQ	NQ	1,410	1,030	980	1,130	1,540	1,770	1,780	1,377
2013	NQ	NQ	NQ	NQ	NQ	NQ	NQ	NQ	NQ	NQ	NQ	NQ	NQ
2014	NQ	NQ	NQ	NQ	NQ	1,870	1,550	1,360	1,350	1,530	1,660	1,680	1,571
2015[1]	NQ	NQ	NQ	NQ	2,330	1,690	1,340	1,470	1,490	1,590	1,810	2,070	1,724

Fresh.   [1]Preliminary.   NQ = No quote.   *Source: National Agricultural Statistics Service, U.S. Department of Agriculture (NASS-USDA)*

Average Price Received by Growers for Peaches in the United States   In Dollars Per Box

Year	Jan.	Feb.	Mar.	Apr.	May	June	July	Aug.	Sept.	Oct.	Nov.	Dec.	Average
2006	NQ	NQ	NQ	NQ	NQ	809	721	746	589	NQ	NQ	NQ	716
2007	NQ	NQ	NQ	NQ	937	562	579	593	563	NQ	NQ	NQ	647
2008	NQ	NQ	NQ	NQ	960	537	485	510	468	NQ	NQ	NQ	592
2009	NQ	NQ	NQ	NQ	846	794	644	676	655	NQ	NQ	NQ	723
2010	NQ	NQ	NQ	NQ	1,080	587	573	568	506	NQ	NQ	NQ	663
2011	NQ	NQ	NQ	NQ	1,290	705	666	704	564	NQ	NQ	NQ	786
2012	NQ	NQ	NQ	NQ	1,100	836	780	737	689	NQ	NQ	NQ	828
2013	NQ	NQ	NQ	NQ	NQ	NQ	NQ	NQ	NQ	NQ	NQ	NQ	NQ
2014	NQ	NQ	NQ	NQ	NQ	1,270	1,180	1,070	954	NQ	NQ	NQ	1,119
2015[1]	NQ	NQ	NQ	NQ	1,480	1,110	933	1,010	828	NQ	NQ	NQ	1,072

Fresh.   [1]Preliminary.   NQ = No quote.   *Source: National Agricultural Statistics Service, U.S. Department of Agriculture (NASS-USDA)*

Average Price Received by Growers for Pears in the United States   In Dollars Per Box

Year	Jan.	Feb.	Mar.	Apr.	May	June	July	Aug.	Sept.	Oct.	Nov.	Dec.	Average
2006	404	392	339	356	419	596	759	286	283	568	570	563	461
2007	541	517	544	597	651	714	584	374	380	526	514	557	542
2008	560	552	537	527	525	654	638	546	543	628	582	574	572
2009	539	473	452	462	518	642	537	424	383	481	449	398	480
2010	381	368	350	426	533	640	598	496	485	622	548	587	503
2011	639	636	625	599	571	565	561	576	490	533	512	474	565
2012	428	386	301	286	353	594	673	583	601	692	686	713	525
2013	774	778	753	NQ	NQ	NQ	NQ	NQ	NQ	NQ	NQ	NQ	768
2014	NQ	NQ	NQ	592	686	893	695	531	631	696	692	702	680
2015[1]	725	729	652	607	619	633	706	700	708	744	778	813	701

Fresh.   [1]Preliminary.   NA = Not available.   *Source: National Agricultural Statistics Service, U.S. Department of Agriculture (NASS-USDA)*

Average Price Received by Growers for Strawberries in the United States   In Dollars Per Box

Year	Jan.	Feb.	Mar.	Apr.	May	June	July	Aug.	Sept.	Oct.	Nov.	Dec.	Average
2006	142.00	99.90	68.80	61.10	61.80	51.40	64.00	63.70	77.60	72.90	96.10	189.00	87.36
2007	131.00	147.00	88.90	64.90	68.60	66.10	53.00	79.30	57.40	80.00	116.00	171.00	93.60
2008	194.00	131.00	95.30	65.50	83.30	61.90	65.90	91.00	70.10	72.00	87.60	208.00	102.13
2009	116.00	128.00	91.10	78.90	76.10	62.80	74.80	73.50	75.00	108.00	87.60	210.00	98.48
2010	218.00	179.00	116.00	75.70	78.90	67.70	62.00	81.70	73.30	87.60	139.00	285.00	121.99
2011	217.00	126.00	99.20	93.50	80.80	72.70	89.20	78.80	87.60	66.90	84.40	153.00	104.09
2012	137.00	113.00	103.00	94.40	82.70	74.40	74.00	85.00	87.60	90.10	139.00	222.00	108.52
2013	109.00	123.00	117.00	NA	NA	NA	NA	NA	NA	NA	NA	NA	116.33
2014	NA	NA	NA	87.60	96.10	91.80	89.30	92.70	133.00	112.00	152.00	209.00	118.17
2015[1]	135.00	101.00	63.60	76.80	72.60	61.50	60.20	86.70	71.30	100.00	190.00	193.00	100.98

Fresh.   [1]Preliminary.   NA = Not available..   *Source: National Agricultural Statistics Service, U.S. Department of Agriculture (NASS-USDA)*

Cold Storage Stocks of Frozen Blackberries[2] in the United States, on First of Month In Thousands of Pounds

Year	Jan.	Feb.	Mar.	Apr.	May	June	July	Aug.	Sept.	Oct.	Nov.	Dec.
2006	25,677	25,365	25,417	19,575	18,023	15,825	14,397	31,908	32,164	31,326	30,528	28,310
2007	26,743	25,604	24,726	22,748	20,937	18,456	18,641	43,124	46,102	44,603	42,769	36,000
2008	32,000	27,355	25,578	22,673	19,206	16,257	15,989	36,058	40,136	39,871	35,328	31,335
2009	26,148	22,370	20,797	17,505	15,256	13,742	11,081	39,708	40,099	37,329	34,855	32,393
2010	27,630	25,010	23,056	21,793	19,425	16,174	12,879	26,312	31,930	32,384	28,823	26,794
2011	23,857	18,649	14,941	14,603	13,864	13,113	11,946	20,833	36,913	38,718	37,111	33,876
2012	31,909	26,925	24,149	21,359	19,248	18,076	15,138	40,692	40,867	39,689	37,508	36,152
2013	35,272	33,021	25,975	24,247	21,792	17,887	18,727	40,606	39,237	37,880	33,468	32,048
2014	30,066	28,823	27,183	22,994	21,110	21,107	22,053	42,581	40,339	37,494	34,756	32,368
2015[1]	30,925	28,843	25,499	23,071	20,892	19,931	25,158	34,001	35,240	33,078	30,553	28,366

[1] Preliminary.   [2] Includes IQF, Pails and Tubs, Barrels (400lbs net), and Concentrate.   *Source: Economic Research Service, U.S. Department of Agriculture (ERS-USDA)*

Cold Storage Stocks of Frozen Blueberries in the United States, on First of Month In Thousands of Pounds

Year	Jan.	Feb.	Mar.	Apr.	May	June	July	Aug.	Sept.	Oct.	Nov.	Dec.
2006	77,360	68,466	58,454	47,039	36,613	28,909	26,785	62,220	123,072	114,351	110,139	99,826
2007	98,719	83,196	75,709	65,398	56,362	45,921	37,700	84,342	154,880	147,570	134,715	125,577
2008	114,114	100,696	94,652	78,106	66,604	58,282	51,960	69,783	172,145	182,478	174,334	164,703
2009	153,445	141,089	130,964	115,615	100,820	87,790	81,404	106,327	189,893	189,628	173,849	154,647
2010	141,883	123,579	109,095	93,342	75,482	61,331	57,332	100,100	163,387	155,105	140,707	129,877
2011	116,485	104,091	93,103	80,016	65,583	50,865	57,467	76,551	167,015	174,805	160,156	147,757
2012	136,966	124,003	114,066	96,723	85,700	73,717	82,218	148,315	238,510	234,207	215,588	196,702
2013	171,296	165,932	152,187	137,358	119,814	100,876	103,559	166,382	260,094	251,279	235,007	217,393
2014	201,834	172,718	150,626	130,825	117,065	98,716	102,012	171,661	269,537	265,303	240,830	229,225
2015[1]	208,324	187,523	166,469	152,745	133,836	119,328	132,732	236,357	273,635	280,085	259,198	245,754

[1] Preliminary.   *Source: Economic Research Service, U.S. Department of Agriculture (ERS-USDA)*

Cold Storage Stocks of Frozen Cherries[2] in the United States, on First of Month In Thousands of Pounds

Year	Jan.	Feb.	Mar.	Apr.	May	June	July	Aug.	Sept.	Oct.	Nov.	Dec.
2006	110,359	102,319	92,935	78,660	71,560	61,316	47,806	137,736	143,082	133,717	123,486	112,606
2007	110,361	97,425	88,896	76,170	66,958	58,337	48,989	168,436	158,643	153,812	142,039	132,845
2008	126,646	117,609	109,423	100,479	87,495	75,690	63,055	118,790	137,994	120,386	113,867	108,046
2009	101,892	96,533	90,052	79,608	69,139	59,714	53,206	128,571	193,312	185,263	179,608	167,716
2010	156,136	145,923	136,313	124,138	113,941	103,008	96,431	161,826	150,298	136,233	128,236	118,223
2011	110,166	97,223	87,153	71,167	62,380	50,776	40,803	96,444	124,645	108,842	98,395	90,339
2012	83,622	73,371	65,185	54,211	44,684	32,532	26,924	59,120	51,815	50,514	49,966	56,135
2013	51,161	44,651	38,315	33,746	26,644	19,127	14,227	114,938	150,224	139,064	128,171	114,676
2014	112,101	99,639	91,631	82,926	71,746	58,869	50,181	103,362	178,542	164,429	153,521	144,280
2015[1]	134,908	129,319	120,870	105,707	98,519	85,866	79,028	146,251	158,170	159,154	141,734	132,880

[1] Preliminary.   [2] Tart (ripe tart pitted).   *Source: Economic Research Service, U.S. Department of Agriculture (ERS-USDA)*

Cold Storage Stocks of Frozen Peaches in the United States, on First of Month In Thousands of Pounds

Year	Jan.	Feb.	Mar.	Apr.	May	June	July	Aug.	Sept.	Oct.	Nov.	Dec.
2006	61,937	41,079	36,253	34,552	32,246	29,955	21,848	21,197	38,302	61,098	74,673	70,200
2007	73,133	68,955	62,954	60,635	52,576	35,415	29,501	35,881	63,129	89,711	84,584	77,439
2008	75,780	68,716	62,681	52,331	41,348	34,291	27,422	37,217	54,995	87,006	87,140	82,656
2009	76,356	69,001	59,525	45,757	40,755	34,667	29,049	32,155	48,217	59,280	56,959	57,070
2010	52,278	48,051	48,298	44,625	41,204	40,744	31,570	30,403	52,904	64,624	63,093	60,595
2011	56,317	52,137	46,376	39,799	35,267	31,398	27,005	28,034	56,462	77,798	73,554	73,053
2012	66,344	60,950	60,096	48,374	44,074	39,734	35,430	36,517	59,775	70,173	67,100	55,085
2013	50,717	45,535	40,062	33,489	28,880	22,290	19,137	36,193	59,642	72,610	73,147	65,548
2014	61,092	53,367	47,862	39,621	32,936	25,714	19,497	34,001	54,810	63,033	57,543	52,384
2015[1]	47,465	44,353	38,646	35,803	30,722	27,605	26,877	41,492	63,364	78,572	75,817	75,253

[1] Preliminary.   *Source: Economic Research Service, U.S. Department of Agriculture (ERS-USDA)*

FRUITS

Cold Storage Stocks of Frozen Raspberries[2] in the United States, on First of Month — In Thousands of Pounds

Year	Jan.	Feb.	Mar.	Apr.	May	June	July	Aug.	Sept.	Oct.	Nov.	Dec.
2006	55,801	50,804	46,381	39,472	34,752	30,989	36,572	85,911	78,993	64,459	60,612	56,486
2007	52,208	45,239	39,593	34,686	33,569	30,317	27,572	72,044	60,685	52,212	44,626	39,369
2008	33,681	27,326	25,349	19,566	15,043	12,548	10,744	49,092	55,382	49,094	45,873	41,861
2009	34,083	29,155	25,817	24,155	20,797	18,742	15,963	75,263	65,422	59,133	52,459	48,339
2010	41,572	38,012	30,972	28,317	25,137	20,192	19,296	67,816	63,950	59,331	53,098	46,875
2011	42,151	37,949	33,062	28,151	27,424	23,199	21,531	66,893	73,113	71,489	65,330	62,067
2012	56,868	51,127	45,651	38,328	34,302	31,284	26,663	77,169	73,056	68,773	61,981	56,825
2013	53,505	44,526	39,815	32,916	31,666	26,920	25,369	72,447	82,984	79,479	72,788	65,095
2014	62,102	52,730	45,071	38,418	33,673	31,353	30,226	87,492	81,541	74,858	67,095	62,337
2015[1]	57,298	52,133	47,260	42,776	37,243	32,435	40,185	76,650	70,585	69,798	63,343	61,126

[1] Preliminary . [2] Red: Includes IQF, Pails and Tubs, Barrels (400 lbs net), and Concentrate. *Source: Economic Research Service, U.S. Department of Agriculture (ERS-USDA)*

Cold Storage Stocks of Frozen Strawberries[2] in the United States, on First of Month — In Thousands of Pounds

Year	Jan.	Feb.	Mar.	Apr.	May	June	July	Aug.	Sept.	Oct.	Nov.	Dec.
2006	218,762	193,324	159,547	127,657	148,933	227,983	382,403	400,725	357,189	294,710	260,489	232,352
2007	202,475	185,241	166,281	150,460	250,998	306,734	443,993	476,180	436,899	401,274	349,491	308,867
2008	280,186	256,852	236,353	182,162	205,462	258,745	331,009	379,197	347,910	329,502	296,064	271,843
2009	235,241	198,713	182,112	151,904	212,641	281,133	390,580	423,878	412,766	389,377	364,611	342,063
2010	322,452	289,623	269,111	236,089	273,591	274,438	358,348	421,410	385,612	355,255	322,577	297,494
2011	263,147	233,644	203,393	177,108	180,773	244,433	333,190	384,184	367,425	350,563	348,285	323,160
2012	291,697	259,308	224,105	199,485	206,876	305,961	399,764	424,417	414,358	399,632	381,561	343,201
2013	302,987	265,250	240,083	218,149	334,359	397,352	421,128	463,698	428,160	392,032	345,152	320,036
2014	279,977	240,382	215,168	211,064	233,147	257,783	357,526	362,127	330,666	294,969	270,553	236,828
2015[1]	206,841	175,520	163,599	186,817	199,290	237,849	341,295	360,062	328,776	314,350	278,860	253,146

[1] Preliminary. [2] Includes IQF and Poly, Pails and Tubs, Barrels and Drums, and Juice Stock. *Source: Economic Research Service, U.S. Department of Agriculture (ERS-USDA)*

Cold Storage Stocks of Other Frozen Fruit in the United States, on First of Month — In Thousands of Pounds

Year	Jan.	Feb.	Mar.	Apr.	May	June	July	Aug.	Sept.	Oct.	Nov.	Dec.
2006	421,491	399,423	353,776	301,890	274,713	249,472	224,001	212,044	160,851	172,959	424,987	495,447
2007	458,222	396,189	371,397	319,167	276,074	254,816	232,344	215,691	196,806	209,121	451,052	498,790
2008	464,609	425,313	402,895	350,167	312,823	269,330	251,309	234,242	206,201	219,247	537,319	527,876
2009	509,807	467,363	414,907	360,587	343,101	311,835	286,675	246,058	215,985	198,200	551,910	530,591
2010	486,760	449,112	399,408	355,773	318,497	289,097	246,690	209,745	174,476	225,587	502,560	473,224
2011	439,996	404,540	367,245	345,131	294,806	254,167	217,588	189,747	150,499	160,415	452,421	452,416
2012	423,367	388,229	360,867	331,923	294,833	256,890	220,723	194,871	170,723	224,022	525,515	510,323
2013	493,200	444,506	417,678	382,611	355,428	316,247	284,810	277,685	238,619	224,171	470,098	589,226
2014	575,025	528,790	475,527	440,532	389,071	341,283	305,249	286,727	264,490	293,231	542,534	576,843
2015[1]	535,775	482,436	434,463	384,732	348,299	321,547	297,358	309,243	309,356	354,983	620,103	665,020

[1] Preliminary. *Source: Economic Research Service, U.S. Department of Agriculture (ERS-USDA)*

Cold Storage Stocks of Total Frozen Fruit in the United States, on First of Month — In Millions of Pounds

Year	Jan.	Feb.	Mar.	Apr.	May	June	July	Aug.	Sept.	Oct.	Nov.	Dec.
2006	1,067.1	972.0	863.5	747.0	710.9	740.3	849.1	1,057.4	1,027.2	963.3	1,179.7	1,192.4
2007	1,136.5	1,019.9	950.7	853.6	882.8	866.8	949.6	1,218.4	1,226.8	1,200.0	1,352.4	1,319.9
2008	1,239.5	1,140.3	1,068.7	920.5	866.2	839.8	864.1	1,043.1	1,125.7	1,130.7	1,393.6	1,337.5
2009	1,245.6	1,134.2	1,038.1	911.0	916.8	910.6	973.2	1,154.3	1,257.8	1,200.7	1,501.1	1,428.2
2010	1,328.6	1,226.0	1,125.9	1,014.5	971.8	902.7	921.1	1,124.3	1,118.5	1,113.1	1,335.7	1,259.8
2011	1,165.1	1,060.7	950.9	847.7	770.1	750.6	785.5	953.4	1,058.5	1,063.6	1,317.2	1,269.3
2012	1,189.3	1,082.2	989.1	881.4	813.3	835.1	889.5	1,077.5	1,145.4	1,178.0	1,425.6	1,342.3
2013	1,246.6	1,123.5	1,030.1	934.9	985.0	962.6	954.1	1,251.3	1,335.0	1,270.0	1,431.1	1,489.0
2014	1,405.6	1,261.1	1,140.4	1,052.0	981.1	912.1	972.2	1,176.0	1,317.9	1,286.1	1,461.4	1,426.8
2015[1]	1,315.4	1,191.8	1,084.2	1,015.6	948.7	921.4	1,028.1	1,294.3	1,322.6	1,363.0	1,541.1	1,535.4

[1] Preliminary. *Source: Economic Research Service, U.S. Department of Agriculture (ERS-USDA)*

Gas

Natural gas is a fossil fuel that is colorless, shapeless, and odorless in its pure form. It is a mixture of hydrocarbon gases formed primarily of methane, but it can also include ethane, propane, butane, and pentane. Natural gas is combustible, clean burning, and gives off a great deal of energy. Around 500 BC, the Chinese discovered that the energy in natural gas could be harnessed. They passed it through crude bamboo-shoot pipes and then burned it to boil sea water to create potable fresh water. Around 1785, Britain became the first country to commercially use natural gas produced from coal for streetlights and indoor lights. In 1821, William Hart dug the first well specifically intended to obtain natural gas and he is generally regarded as the "father of natural gas" in America. There is a vast amount of natural gas estimated to still be in the ground in the U.S. Natural gas as a source of energy is significantly less expensive than electricity per Btu.

Natural gas futures and options are traded at the CME Group. The CME natural gas futures contract calls for the delivery of natural gas representing 10,000 million British thermal units (mmBtu) at the Henry Hub in Louisiana, which is the nexus of 16 intra-state and inter-state pipelines. The contract is priced in terms of dollars per mmBtu. CME also has basic swap futures contracts available for 30 different natural gas pricing locations versus the benchmark Henry Hub location. Natural gas futures are also listed on the ICE Futures Europe exchange.

Prices – CME natural gas futures (Barchart.com symbol code NG) on the nearest-futures chart fell to a new 17-year low in December 2015 and closed 2015 down -19.1% at $2.337 per mmBtu.

Supply – U.S. recovery of natural gas in 2014 (latest data available) rose +6.2% to a record high of 31.346 billion cubic feet. The top U.S. producing states for natural gas were Texas with 29.1% of U.S. production in 2014, Louisiana with 7.2%, Wyoming with 6.6%, Oklahoma with 8.5%, and New Mexico with 4.3%. In 2015 the world's largest natural gas producers were the U.S. with 2,439,678 Tera joules and Russia with 1,688,694 Tera joules of production.

Demand – U.S. total delivered consumption of natural gas in 2014 rose +2.2% yr/yr to 24.362 billion cubic feet, of which about 33.4% was delivered to electrical utility plants, 31.3% to industrial establishments, 20.9% to residences, and 14.2% to commercial establishments.

Trade – U.S. imports of natural gas (consumed) in 2013 (latest data) fell -8.1% yr/yr to 2.883 billion cubic feet, down from the 2007 record high of 4,608 billion cubic feet. U.S. exports of natural gas in 2013 (latest data) fell -2.9% yr/yr to 1,572 billion cubic feet, below 2012's record high of 1,619 billion cubic feet.

World Dry Natural Gas Production   In Billion Cubic Feet

Year	Algeria	Canada	China	Indonesia	Iran	Nether-lands	Norway	Qatar	Russia	Saudi Arabia	United States	Uzbek-istan	World Total
2004	2,830	6,483	1,439	2,028	2,963	3,035	2,948	1,383	20,991	2,319	18,591	2,114	95,642
2005	3,151	6,561	1,763	2,001	3,655	2,773	3,072	1,617	21,224	2,516	18,051	2,108	98,395
2006	3,079	6,548	2,067	2,199	3,836	2,730	3,094	1,790	21,736	2,594	18,504	2,216	101,588
2007	2,996	6,416	2,446	2,422	3,952	2,687	3,168	2,232	21,595	2,628	19,266	2,302	104,143
2008	3,055	6,046	2,685	2,472	4,107	2,957	3,503	2,719	21,515	2,841	20,159	2,387	107,761
2009	2,876	5,634	2,975	2,557	4,986	2,786	3,664	3,154	19,303	2,770	20,624	2,169	105,179
2010	2,988	5,390	3,334	2,841	5,161	3,131	3,756	4,166	21,536	3,096	21,316	2,123	112,574
2011	2,923	5,218	3,629	2,693	5,361	2,851	3,580	5,198	22,213	3,258	22,902	2,226	116,255
2012[1]	3,053	5,070	3,666	2,559	5,649	2,843	4,156	5,523	21,764	3,508	24,058	2,222	118,910
2013[2]		5,129	4,135			3,052	3,840		21,359	3,637	24,282		

[1] Preliminary.   [2] Estimate.   *Source: Energy Information Administration, U.S. Department of Energy (EIA-DOE)*

Marketed Production of Natural Gas in the United States, by States   In Million Cubic Feet

Year	Alaska	Arkansas	California	Colorado	Kansas	Louisiana	New Mexico	Oklahoma	Pennsyl-vania	Texas	Wyoming	Total
2005	487,282	190,533	317,637	1,133,086	377,229	1,296,048	1,645,166	1,639,310	168,501	5,276,401	1,639,317	18,927,095
2006	444,724	270,293	315,209	1,202,821	371,044	1,361,119	1,609,223	1,688,985	175,950	5,548,022	1,816,201	19,409,674
2007	433,485	269,886	307,160	1,242,571	365,877	1,365,333	1,517,922	1,783,682	182,277	6,123,180	2,047,882	20,196,346
2008	398,442	446,457	296,469	1,389,399	374,310	1,377,969	1,446,204	1,886,710	198,295	6,960,693	2,274,850	21,112,053
2009	397,077	679,952	276,575	1,499,070	354,440	1,548,607	1,383,004	1,901,556	273,869	6,818,973	2,335,328	21,647,936
2010	374,226	926,639	286,841	1,578,379	324,720	2,210,099	1,292,185	1,827,328	572,902	6,715,294	2,305,525	22,381,873
2011	356,225	1,072,212	250,177	1,637,576	309,124	3,029,206	1,237,303	1,888,870	1,310,592	7,112,863	2,159,422	24,036,352
2012	351,259	1,146,168	246,822	1,709,376	296,299	2,955,437	1,215,773	2,023,461	2,256,696	7,475,495	2,022,275	25,283,278
2013	338,182	1,139,654	252,310	1,604,860	292,467	2,360,202	1,171,640	1,993,754	3,259,042	7,633,618	1,858,207	25,562,232
2014[1]	345,331	1,123,678	252,718	1,631,390	286,080	1,980,287	1,180,808	2,310,114	4,214,643	7,953,343	1,791,235	27,336,644

[1] Preliminary.   *Source: Energy Information Administration, U.S. Department of Energy (EIA-DOE)*

GAS

World Production of Natural Gas Plant Liquids   Thousand Barrels per Day

Year	Algeria	Canada	Mexico	Saudi Arabia	Russia	United States	Persian Gulf[2]	OAPEC[3]	OPEC-12[4]	OPEC-11[4]	World
2006	270	685	338	472	1,860	1,739	2,722	2,554	3,292	3,270	8,178
2007	260	726	328	486	1,940	1,783	2,813	2,582	3,407	3,383	8,394
2008	250	677	318	500	2,080	1,784	2,985	2,592	3,550	3,540	8,514
2009	325	640	326	539	1,980	1,910	2,922	2,744	3,562	3,552	8,641
2010	340	597	332	574	1,920	2,074	2,935	2,972	3,592	3,582	8,901
2011	322	591	334	611	1,920	2,216	3,102	2,958	3,637	3,627	9,130
2012	342	611	318	647	1,920	2,408	3,152	3,164	3,786	3,776	9,502
2013	300	639	320	684	1,920	2,606	3,141		3,685	3,673	9,636
2014[1]	300	665	320	720	1,800	2,964	3,117		3,644	3,629	10,013

Average.   [1] Preliminary.   [2] Bahrain, Iran, Iraq, Kuwait, Qatar, Saudi Arabia, and the United Arab Emirates.   [3] Organization of Arab Petroleum Exporting Countriess: Algeria, Iraq, Kuwait, Libya, Qatar, Saudi Arabia, and the United Arab Emirates.   [4] OPEC-12: Organization of the Petroleum Exporting Countries: Algeria, Angola, Indonesia, Iran, Iraq, Kuwait, Libya, Nigeria, Qatar, Saudi Arabia, the United Arab Emirates, and Venezuela. OPEC-11 does not include Angola.   *Source: Energy Information Administration, U.S. Department of Energy (EIA-DOE)*

Recoverable Reserves and Deliveries of Natural Gas in the United States   In Billions of Cubic Feet

Year	Gross Withdrawals	Recoverable Reserves of Natural Gas Dec. 31[2]	Residential	Commercial	Electric Utility Plants[3]	Industrial	Total	Lease & Plant Fuel	Used as Pipeline Fuel	Heating Value BTU per Cubic Foot
2006	23,535	211,085	4,368	2,832	6,222	6,512	21,685	1,142	584	1,028
2007	24,664	237,726	4,722	3,013	6,655	6,655	21,256	1,226	621	1,027
2008	25,636	244,656	4,892	3,153	6,686	6,670	21,409	1,220	648	1,027
2009	26,057	272,509	4,779	3,119	6,873	6,167	20,965	1,275	670	1,025
2010	26,816	304,625	4,782	3,103	7,387	6,826	22,127	1,286	674	1,023
2011	28,479	334,067	4,714	3,155	7,574	6,994	22,467	1,323	688	1,022
2012	29,542	308,036	4,150	2,895	9,111	7,226	23,411	1,396	731	1,024
2013	29,523	338,264	4,897	3,295	8,191	7,425	23,839	1,483	833	1,027
2014[1]	31,346	368,704	5,087	3,467	8,149	7,624	24,362	1,500	836	1,030

[1] Preliminary.   [2] Estimated proved recoverable reserves of dry natural gas.   [3] Figures include gas other than natural (impossible to segregate); therefore, shown separately from other consumption.   *Source: Energy Information Administration, U.S. Department of Energy (EIA-DOE)*

Gas Utility Sales in the United States by Types and Class of Service   In Trillions of BTUs

Year	Total Utility Sales	Number of Customers (Millions)	Residential	Commercial	Industrial	Electric Generation	Other	Total	Residential	Commercial	Industrial	Electric Generation	Other
			Class of Service					Revenue - Million $ From Sales to Customers					
2000	9,232	61.3	4,741	2,077	1,698	709	6	59,243	35,828	13,338	7,432	2,612	33
2001	8,667	61.4	4,525	2,053	1,461	620	8	69,150	42,454	16,848	7,513	2,286	49
2002	8,864	62.0	4,589	2,055	1,748	459	13	57,112	35,062	13,512	6,840	1,639	59
2003	8,927	62.6	4,722	2,125	1,672	397	11	72,606	43,664	17,349	9,478	2,048	68
2004	8,766	63.3	4,566	2,075	1,763	351	12	79,929	47,275	18,689	11,230	2,653	83
2005	8,848	64.4	4,516	2,056	1,654	610	12	96,909	55,680	22,653	13,751	4,718	107
2006	8,222	65.0	4,117	1,861	1,576	606	62	91,928	53,961	21,557	12,006	3,921	484
2007[1]	8,565	65.4	4,418	1,943	1,522	626	57	92,131	55,027	21,248	11,323	4,076	457
2008[2]	8,594	65.5	4,541	2,009	1,410	614	21	102,641	60,195	23,592	13,205	5,406	243

[1] Preliminary.   [2] Estimate.   *Source: American Gas Association (AGA)*

Salient Statistics of Natural Gas in the United States

Year	Marketed Production	Extraction Loss	Dry Production	Storage Withdrawals	Imports (Consumed)	Total Supply	Consumption	Exports	Added to Storage	Total Disposition	Wellhead Price	Imports	Exports	Residential	Commercial	Industrial	Electric Utilities
	Supply — In Billions of Cubic Feet						Disposition				Average Price Delivered to Customers — Dollars Per Thousand Cubic Feet						
2006	19,410	906	18,504	2,493	4,186	26,089	21,685	724	2,924	25,333	6.39	6.88	6.83	13.73	12.00	7.87	7.11
2007	20,196	930	19,266	3,325	4,608	28,129	23,104	822	3,133	27,059	6.25	6.87	6.92	13.08	11.34	7.68	7.31
2008	21,112	953	20,159	3,374	3,984	28,470	23,277	963	3,340	27,581	7.97	8.70	8.58	13.89	12.23	9.65	9.26
2009	21,648	1,024	20,624	2,966	3,751	28,366	22,910	1,072	3,315	27,297	3.67	4.19	4.47	12.14	10.06	5.33	4.93
2010	22,382	1,066	21,316	3,274	3,741	29,397	24,087	1,137	3,291	28,515	4.48	4.52	5.02	11.39	9.47	5.49	5.27
2011	24,036	1,134	22,902	3,074	3,469	30,579	24,477	1,506	3,422	29,405	3.95	4.24	4.64	11.03	8.91	5.13	4.89
2012	25,283	1,250	24,033	2,818	3,138	31,239	25,538	1,619	2,854	30,011	2.75	2.88	3.25	10.65	8.10	3.88	3.54
2013[1]	25,691	1,357	24,334	3,702	2,883	32,276	26,131	1,572	3,156	30,859	3.73	3.83	4.08	10.32	8.08	4.64	4.49
2014[2]	27,260	1,553	25,707	3,586	2,442	33,288	24,096	1,370	3,839	29,305	4.37	5.49	5.53	10.97	8.90	5.53	5.19

[1] Preliminary.   [2] Estimate.   *Source: Energy Information Administration, U.S. Department of Energy (EIA-DOE)*

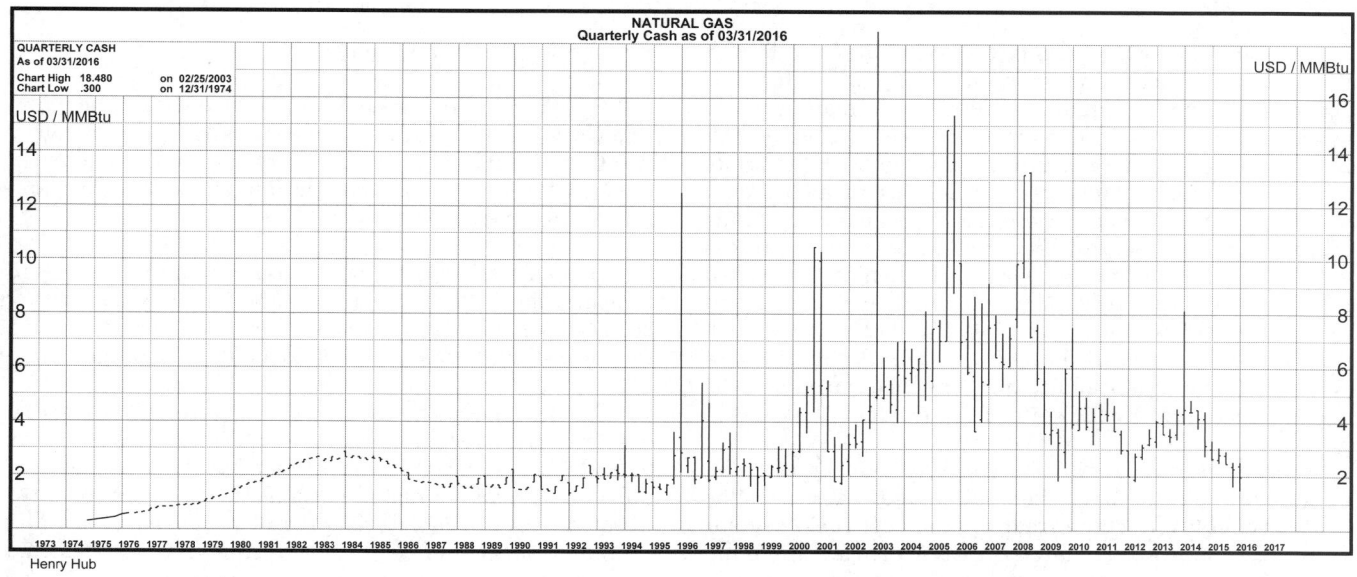

Henry Hub

Average Price of Natural Gas at Henry Hub   In Dollars Per MMBtu

Year	Jan.	Feb.	Mar.	Apr.	May	June	July	Aug.	Sept.	Oct.	Nov.	Dec.	Average
2006	8.69	7.54	6.89	7.16	6.25	6.21	6.17	7.14	4.90	5.85	7.41	6.73	6.74
2007	6.55	8.00	7.11	7.60	7.64	7.35	6.22	6.22	6.08	6.74	7.10	7.11	6.98
2008	7.99	8.54	9.41	10.18	11.27	12.69	11.09	8.26	7.67	6.74	6.68	5.82	8.86
2009	5.24	4.52	3.96	3.50	3.83	3.80	3.38	3.14	2.99	4.01	3.66	5.35	3.95
2010	5.83	5.32	4.29	4.03	4.14	4.80	4.63	4.32	3.89	3.43	3.71	4.25	4.39
2011	4.49	4.09	3.97	4.24	4.31	4.54	4.42	4.06	3.90	3.57	3.24	3.17	4.00
2012	2.67	2.51	2.17	1.95	2.43	2.46	2.95	2.84	2.85	3.32	3.54	3.34	2.75
2013	3.33	3.33	3.81	4.17	4.04	3.83	3.62	3.43	3.62	3.68	3.64	4.24	3.73
2014	4.71	6.00	4.90	4.66	4.58	4.59	4.05	3.91	3.92	3.78	4.12	3.48	4.39
2015	3.00	2.88	2.83	2.61	2.85	2.78	2.84	2.77	2.66	2.34	2.09	1.94	2.63

Source: Energy Information Administration, U.S. Department of Energy (EIA-DOE)

Volume of Trading of Natural Gas Futures in New York   In Thousands of Contracts

Year	Jan.	Feb.	Mar.	Apr.	May	June	July	Aug.	Sept.	Oct.	Nov.	Dec.	Total
2006	1,609.9	1,833.9	1,682.2	1,911.6	2,272.5	1,920.6	1,786.2	2,428.7	2,017.7	1,935.1	1,799.6	1,832.0	23,030.0
2007	2,597.6	2,417.5	1,922.6	2,163.2	2,266.2	2,683.7	2,346.7	3,049.9	2,468.5	3,044.3	2,452.0	2,374.2	29,786.3
2008	2,921.9	3,330.7	2,983.6	3,382.9	3,168.0	3,379.1	4,274.0	3,756.1	3,458.5	3,151.7	2,539.9	2,384.3	38,730.5
2009	2,343.7	2,780.6	2,989.9	2,493.1	3,479.0	4,486.6	3,979.4	4,445.9	5,597.7	5,594.7	4,413.7	5,347.2	47,951.4
2010	4,501.7	4,557.7	4,690.9	5,740.4	4,729.9	5,911.9	5,267.7	5,791.0	5,428.1	5,920.0	5,780.8	6,002.9	64,323.1
2011	6,468.6	6,123.2	7,284.0	6,432.0	6,015.2	6,759.5	5,317.9	6,904.9	6,363.8	7,199.9	6,117.1	5,878.3	76,864.3
2012	9,328.0	8,723.2	6,798.8	7,488.9	8,660.3	8,639.0	7,412.7	8,579.0	7,272.7	9,259.2	6,262.3	6,375.6	94,799.5
2013	7,329.4	6,910.3	8,343.9	9,484.9	6,796.2	6,271.5	5,626.2	6,944.2	5,741.2	6,991.3	5,618.2	8,225.0	84,282.5
2014	8,872.0	8,301.5	4,804.4	5,114.8	5,031.3	5,425.1	5,022.7	5,374.9	5,623.7	6,087.8	7,980.1	6,568.4	74,206.6
2015	7,617.0	7,014.7	6,255.0	6,141.5	6,663.2	7,705.9	6,403.9	6,458.0	5,714.9	7,578.3	6,236.2	7,984.0	81,772.5

Contract size = 10,000 MMBtu.   *Source: CME Group; New York Mercantile Exchange (NYMEX)*

Average Open Interest of Natural Gas Futures in New York   In Thousands of Contracts

Year	Jan.	Feb.	Mar.	Apr.	May	June	July	Aug.	Sept.	Oct.	Nov.	Dec.
2006	545.2	582.2	634.1	700.6	795.4	851.7	883.5	938.0	940.3	931.9	903.4	889.8
2007	905.4	839.1	761.7	747.7	752.6	787.1	823.1	776.7	778.5	749.5	789.4	843.4
2008	881.8	942.1	906.5	875.5	885.2	946.7	964.0	922.5	915.6	859.3	744.8	702.9
2009	693.3	709.0	652.4	649.9	678.4	709.2	737.5	731.6	713.8	710.0	713.6	719.6
2010	762.0	786.4	839.2	855.4	860.8	817.7	783.9	819.2	812.4	800.8	783.7	774.4
2011	820.8	917.0	922.1	948.1	956.5	980.4	977.0	990.3	952.1	969.6	977.2	981.2
2012	1,122.7	1,241.6	1,226.2	1,271.3	1,221.7	1,177.7	1,120.4	1,089.0	1,106.9	1,184.3	1,166.7	1,157.0
2013	1,172.0	1,196.1	1,315.3	1,539.1	1,511.7	1,434.8	1,389.5	1,356.6	1,306.4	1,263.8	1,271.2	1,302.4
2014	1,278.0	1,246.6	1,160.8	1,104.7	1,021.9	1,032.9	1,017.1	962.3	970.3	914.8	952.5	939.1
2015	991.0	1,004.6	979.6	1,016.3	1,015.3	1,038.6	1,001.3	957.0	918.7	977.8	1,011.8	1,007.1

Contract size = 10,000 MMBtu.   *Source: CME Group; New York Mercantile Exchange (NYMEX)*

Gasoline

Gasoline is a complex mixture of hundreds of lighter liquid hydrocarbons and is used chiefly as a fuel for internal-combustion engines. Petroleum crude, or crude oil, is still the most economical source of gasoline with refineries turning more than half of every barrel of crude oil into gasoline. The three basic steps to all refining operations are the separation process (separating crude oil into various chemical components), conversion process (breaking the chemicals down into molecules called hydrocarbons), and treatment process (transforming and combining hydrocarbon molecules and other additives). Another process, called *hydro treating*, removes a significant amount of sulfur from finished gasoline as is currently required by the state of California.

Octane is a measure of a gasoline's ability to resist pinging or knocking noise from an engine. Most gasoline stations offer three octane grades of unleaded fuel—regular at 87 (R+M)/2, mid-grade at 89 (R+M)/2, and premium at 93 (R+M)/2. Additional refining steps are needed to increase the octane, which increases the retail price. This does not make the gasoline any cleaner or better, but yields a different blend of hydrocarbons that burn more slowly.

In an attempt to improve air quality and reduce harmful emissions from internal combustion engines, Congress in 1990 amended the Clean Air Act to mandate the addition of ethanol to gasoline. Some 2 billion gallons of ethanol are now added to gasoline each year in the U.S. The most common blend is E10, which contains 10% ethanol and 90% gasoline. Auto manufacturers have approved that mixture for use in all U.S. vehicles. Ethanol is an alcohol-based fuel produced by fermenting and distilling crops such as corn, barley, wheat and sugar.

Gasoline futures and options trade at the CME Group. The CME gasoline futures contract calls for the delivery of 1,000 barrels (42,000 gallons) of unleaded gasoline in the New York harbor and is priced in terms of dollars and cents per gallon.

Prices – CME gasoline futures prices (Barchart.com symbol code RB) rallied in early 2015 to retrace some of 2014's sharp decline, but gasoline prices then resumed the decline to close 2015 down -13.7% at $1.2710 per gallon.

The average monthly retail price of regular unleaded gasoline in 2015 (through November) fell -27.3% yr/yr to $2.45 per gallon. The average monthly retail price of unleaded premium motor gasoline in the U.S. in 2015 (through November) fell -22.8% to $2.87 per gallon. The average monthly refiner price of finished aviation gasoline to end users in 2014 (through September) rose +4.6% yr/yr to $4.14 per gallon.

Supply – U.S. production of gasoline in 2015 (through November, annualized) rose +1.5% yr/yr to 9.762 million barrels per day. Gasoline stocks in November of 2015 were 27.805 million barrels, down from 29.532 million barrels in November of 2014.

Demand – U.S. consumption of finished motor gasoline in 2015 (through November, annualized) rose +2.5% yr/yr to 9.147 million barrels per day, below 2007's record high of 9.284 million barrels per day.

World Production of Motor Gasoline   In Thousands of Barrels Per Day

Year	Brazil	Canada	China	France	Germany	India	Italy	Japan	Mexico	Russia	United Kingdom	United States	World Total
2004	337.8	772.4	1,219.4	391.3	612.1	256.8	478.8	999.6	442.2	710.9	567.7	8,265.4	21,032.6
2005	348.5	756.7	1,269.7	379.5	636.7	245.4	488.0	1,009.1	436.1	748.1	523.7	8,317.5	21,364.0
2006	369.9	724.4	1,304.0	401.9	626.9	293.0	455.3	998.0	435.0	803.2	496.4	8,363.7	21,281.5
2007	393.9	763.4	1,378.7	389.2	608.1	331.1	480.6	1,004.6	436.7	820.2	493.4	8,357.8	21,281.4
2008	364.1	703.8	1,483.3	386.8	584.7	374.4	460.4	974.1	430.0	832.0	471.0	8,548.3	21,418.2
2009	373.6	717.8	1,710.8	365.8	559.9	527.1	434.0	980.0	454.5	837.3	473.0	8,785.6	22,251.6
2010	399.0	719.2	1,720.1	316.7	499.2	604.8	438.0	1,012.4	407.7	839.6	466.0	9,058.6	22,303.8
2011	425.2	670.4	1,850.4	303.5	499.3	627.4	405.3	943.4	387.2	857.3	461.0	9,057.6	22,289.2
2012[1]	461.6	687.4	2,097.7	276.0	478.7	703.9	395.7	919.9	404.5	893.5	406.9	8,926.3	22,456.5
2013[2]		675.3		250.7	473.3		357.8	934.0	422.8		433.7	9,234.1	

[1] Preliminary.   [2] Estimate.   *Source: Energy Information Administration, U.S. Department of Energy (EIA-DOE)*

World Imports of Motor Gasoline   In Thousands of Barrels Per Day

Year	Australia	Canada	Indonesia	Iran	Malaysia	Mexico	Netherlands	Nigeria	Saudi Arabia	Singapore	United Kingdom	United States	World Total
2004	59.6	65.0	99.7	142.6	54.7	161.7	181.3	136.9	----	161.6	50.2	496.4	2,891.4
2005	57.5	81.7	125.2	156.0	66.3	214.2	212.2	128.1	41.1	166.6	55.1	602.7	3,242.9
2006	56.1	98.8	128.9	172.9	76.3	245.5	242.4	126.4	79.2	172.4	87.8	475.2	3,212.4
2007	46.8	75.3	145.3	119.8	73.3	284.7	170.7	135.4	75.2	200.0	75.6	412.6	3,040.0
2008	70.7	94.2	94.8	130.0	78.1	307.1	225.2	107.4	108.0	230.3	53.7	301.6	3,030.0
2009	77.1	89.1	199.3	132.5	74.0	307.6	234.1	140.0	102.9	20.2	77.8	223.4	2,943.9
2010	47.3	79.9	219.0	93.9	97.1	354.4	217.2	162.7	86.2	324.9	85.3	134.3	3,366.9
2011	57.2	90.4	268.8	31.1	104.6	386.8	240.5	142.0	51.9	323.3	88.0	104.8	3,508.0
2012[1]	57.3	62.2	307.9	9.6	134.9	374.9	276.2	137.3	92.2	305.7	111.5	44.1	3,628.2
2013[2]	63.6	54.7				319.4	225.1				108.7	45.0	

[1] Preliminary.   [2] Estimate.   *Source: Energy Information Administration, U.S. Department of Energy (EIA-DOE)*

World Exports of Motor Gasoline In Thousands of Barrels Per Day

Year	Canada	France	Germany	India	Italy	Nether-lands	Russia	Singa-pore	United Kingdom	United States	Vene-zuela	Virgin Islands	World Total
2004	156.2	161.7	121.5	67.5	127.6	340.4	98.3	240.4	169.3	124.3	178.0	158.9	3,358.6
2005	161.4	179.1	132.1	53.1	161.3	376.4	138.4	332.0	152.5	135.5	172.0	159.3	3,655.9
2006	138.8	160.0	128.6	86.4	161.3	400.4	147.4	330.2	161.5	141.8	132.0	131.6	3,669.6
2007	147.4	147.0	125.4	105.3	208.7	297.6	140.4	376.5	169.7	127.0	115.1	140.1	3,562.2
2008	129.3	182.6	132.2	126.8	196.6	357.1	104.3	428.7	162.6	171.7	117.0	131.9	3,635.9
2009	136.5	148.4	125.5	228.1	166.8	376.0	105.2	216.8	177.2	195.4	127.5	115.8	3,564.1
2010	149.7	133.2	112.1	318.9	192.7	382.9	69.2	525.4	208.4	295.8	9.5	107.9	3,887.4
2011	130.7	118.5	109.6	329.1	187.2	348.7	90.3	535.7	214.3	478.8	27.9	102.3	4,052.4
2012[1]	138.4	107.9	114.9	336.8	201.8	448.9	74.9	530.9	196.5	408.9	8.7	18.0	4,020.3
2013[2]	143.2	85.8	115.4		180.4	409.3			238.5	373.0			

[1] Preliminary. [2] Estimate. Source: Energy Information Administration, U.S. Department of Energy (EIA-DOE)

Production of Finished Motor Gasoline in the United States In Thousand Barrels per Day

Year	Jan.	Feb.	Mar.	Apr.	May	June	July	Aug.	Sept.	Oct.	Nov.	Dec.	Average
2006	8,189	7,969	7,765	8,032	8,613	8,957	8,624	8,610	8,465	8,210	8,335	8,567	8,361
2007	8,348	8,012	8,101	8,122	8,491	8,686	8,504	8,547	8,320	8,276	8,353	8,501	8,355
2008	8,516	8,495	8,373	8,560	8,700	8,564	8,523	8,513	7,855	8,889	8,722	8,850	8,547
2009	8,445	8,408	8,646	8,724	8,793	9,068	8,952	8,856	8,829	8,770	8,905	9,006	8,784
2010	8,348	8,510	8,913	9,062	9,113	9,211	9,500	9,426	9,143	9,049	9,134	9,252	9,055
2011	8,714	8,866	8,908	8,978	9,157	9,289	9,166	9,264	9,140	8,932	9,141	9,128	9,057
2012	8,385	8,606	8,705	8,720	8,950	9,157	9,073	9,237	8,888	9,176	9,156	9,051	8,925
2013	8,718	8,926	8,971	9,042	9,299	9,472	9,374	9,340	9,190	9,484	9,476	9,495	9,232
2014	8,999	9,259	9,533	9,733	9,823	9,890	10,052	9,734	9,418	9,541	9,603	9,891	9,623
2015[1]	9,321	9,546	9,571	9,787	9,811	9,894	10,037	9,993	9,866	9,926	9,794	9,606	9,763

[1] Preliminary. Source: Energy Information Administration, U.S. Department of Energy (EIA-DOE)

Disposition of Finished Motor Gasoline, Total Product Supplied in the United States In Thousand Barrels per Day

Year	Jan.	Feb.	Mar.	Apr.	May	June	July	Aug.	Sept.	Oct.	Nov.	Dec.	Average
2006	8,839	8,911	9,054	9,154	9,308	9,478	9,607	9,564	9,236	9,267	9,244	9,338	9,250
2007	8,886	9,006	9,178	9,215	9,434	9,491	9,640	9,582	9,254	9,236	9,229	9,251	9,284
2008	8,810	8,866	9,066	9,112	9,251	9,110	9,150	9,134	8,497	9,024	8,904	8,927	8,988
2009	8,623	8,836	8,903	9,029	9,084	9,180	9,260	9,295	8,911	8,986	8,906	8,931	8,995
2010	8,520	8,579	8,793	9,108	9,162	9,311	9,301	9,255	9,112	9,016	8,816	8,911	8,990
2011	8,370	8,604	8,799	8,796	8,817	9,067	9,031	8,925	8,744	8,649	8,537	8,683	8,752
2012	8,190	8,598	8,582	8,741	8,979	8,996	8,810	9,154	8,561	8,701	8,483	8,389	8,682
2013	8,331	8,395	8,641	8,855	9,033	9,078	9,146	9,124	8,946	8,944	8,923	8,670	8,841
2014	8,206	8,699	8,684	8,979	9,016	9,034	9,220	9,287	8,775	9,196	8,930	9,023	8,921
2015[1]	8,718	8,650	9,055	9,139	9,251	9,391	9,438	9,467	9,275	9,250	9,109	9,031	9,148

[1] Preliminary. Source: Energy Information Administration, U.S. Department of Energy (EIA-DOE)

Stocks of Finished Gasoline[2] on Hand in the United States, at End of Month In Thousands of Barrels

Year	Jan.	Feb.	Mar.	Apr.	May	June	July	Aug.	Sept.	Oct.	Nov.	Dec.
2006	142,175	137,882	124,152	115,411	121,471	119,148	117,930	116,560	120,495	112,819	113,798	116,097
2007	124,256	115,992	109,169	108,493	114,519	116,639	114,241	110,623	113,215	108,773	110,535	111,426
2008	117,418	119,915	110,601	106,202	106,001	107,316	102,257	97,765	92,594	95,868	96,850	98,314
2009	95,266	86,907	85,864	86,034	83,542	88,643	86,143	86,729	84,658	79,383	83,016	84,927
2010	87,152	83,618	81,941	78,134	75,189	71,787	71,882	72,412	70,207	65,103	65,537	63,257
2011	69,617	67,835	61,206	54,636	56,353	55,521	53,335	54,546	56,308	55,052	57,573	60,631
2012	61,550	58,671	54,112	50,538	49,986	51,896	51,952	48,294	47,788	49,668	52,626	55,211
2013	55,228	53,143	47,327	45,108	46,376	48,634	49,726	47,655	39,780	37,595	37,548	38,976
2014	39,790	37,687	34,274	30,710	31,057	28,854	28,320	27,514	28,773	27,432	29,532	30,615
2015[1]	29,923	30,558	26,891	25,898	26,580	25,678	24,418	26,048	29,028	27,638	27,805	28,453

[1] Preliminary. [2] Includes oxygenated and other finished. Source: Energy Information Administration, U.S. Department of Energy (EIA-DOE)

GASOLINE

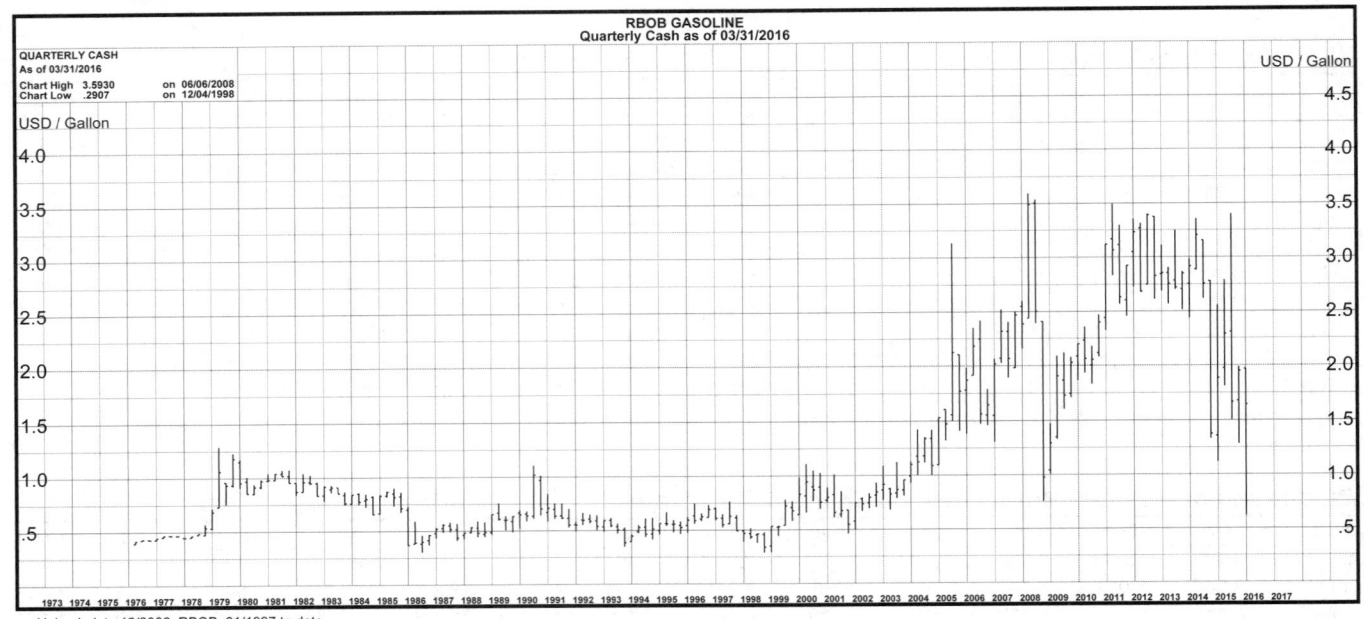

RBOB GASOLINE
Quarterly Cash as of 03/31/2016

QUARTERLY CASH
As of 03/31/2016
Chart High 3.5930 on 06/06/2008
Chart Low   .2907   on 12/04/1998

USD / Gallon   USD / Gallon

Unleaded: to 12/2006; RBOB: 01/1997 to date.

Average Spot Price of Unleaded Gasoline in New York   In Dollars Per Gallon

Year	Jan.	Feb.	Mar.	Apr.	May	June	July	Aug.	Sept.	Oct.	Nov.	Dec. Average
2006	1.7339	1.4998	1.7587	2.1462	2.0468	2.0650	2.2399	2.0323	1.5842	1.5200	1.5871	1.6670	1.8234
2007	1.4163	1.6455	1.9358	2.1005	2.2409	2.1830	2.1351	1.9983	2.0972	2.1693	2.4233	2.3269	2.0560
2008	2.3309	2.3837	2.4909	2.7745	3.0923	3.2979	3.1586	2.9020	2.8069	1.9084	1.2929	0.9718	2.4509
2009	1.1511	1.2166	1.2884	1.3777	1.6979	1.9079	1.7474	1.9301	1.7843	1.9230	1.9863	1.9200	1.6609
2010	2.0428	1.9938	2.1486	2.2210	2.0135	2.0113	2.0038	1.9501	1.9747	2.1607	2.2431	2.3874	2.0959
2011	2.4461	2.5295	2.8348	3.1655	3.0277	2.8341	3.0240	2.8205	2.8144	2.7653	2.6311	2.6319	2.7937
2012	2.8187	3.0235	3.1595	3.2096	2.8724	2.6217	2.7567	3.0271	3.2656	2.9681	2.8434	2.7256	2.9410
2013	2.8604	3.0547	2.9121	2.7268	2.7446	2.7454	2.9178	2.9330	2.6038	2.4887	2.4511	2.5201	2.7465
2014	2.5477	2.6772	2.7144	2.8008	2.7826	2.8958	2.7245	2.6314	2.6050	2.1793	1.9375	1.4235	2.4933
2015	1.2714	1.6027	1.6798	1.7337	1.8844	1.9451	1.8538	1.5743	1.3520	1.3070	1.2459	1.1814	1.5526

Source: Energy Information Administration, U.S. Department of Energy (EIA-DOE)

Average Refiner Price of Finished Motor Gasoline to End Users[2] in the United States   In Dollars Per Gallon

Year	Jan.	Feb.	Mar.	Apr.	May	June	July	Aug.	Sept.	Oct.	Nov.	Dec. Average
2006	1.872	1.833	1.983	2.331	2.458	2.436	2.528	2.486	2.076	1.789	1.788	1.868	2.128
2007	1.791	1.842	2.138	2.405	2.669	2.569	2.488	2.320	2.337	2.350	2.614	2.552	2.345
2008	2.571	2.566	2.783	2.984	3.316	3.580	3.568	3.279	3.207	2.537	1.617	1.219	2.775
2009	1.358	1.468	1.503	1.601	1.856	2.187	2.067	2.157	2.086	2.104	2.173	2.144	1.888
2010	2.240	2.173	2.301	2.370	2.353	2.251	2.247	2.250	2.219	2.319	2.378	2.514	2.301
2011	2.615	2.712	3.072	3.340	3.419	3.184	3.172	3.134	3.090	2.980	2.922	2.808	3.050
2012	2.914	3.087	3.389	3.405	3.289	3.061	2.981	3.248	3.357	3.261	2.994	2.828	3.154
2013	2.850	3.221	3.233	3.102	3.188	3.184	3.146	3.097	3.059	2.893	2.759	2.759	3.041
2014	2.816	2.913	3.104	3.214	3.245	3.265	3.128	3.016	2.936	2.670	2.406	2.013	2.894
2015[1]	1.673	1.858	2.054	2.058	2.322	2.374	2.338	2.218	1.920	1.849	1.711	1.603	1.998

[1] Preliminary.   [2] Excludes aviation and taxes.   *Source: Energy Information Administration, U.S. Department of Energy (EIA-DOE)*

Average Retail Price of All-Types[2] Motor Gasoline[3] in the United States   In Dollars Per Gallon

Year	Jan.	Feb.	Mar.	Apr.	May	June	July	Aug.	Sept.	Oct.	Nov.	Dec. Average
2006	2.359	2.354	2.444	2.801	2.993	2.963	3.046	3.033	2.637	2.319	2.287	2.380	2.635
2007	2.321	2.333	2.639	2.909	3.176	3.100	3.013	2.833	2.839	2.843	3.118	3.069	2.849
2008	3.096	3.083	3.307	3.491	3.813	4.115	4.142	3.838	3.749	3.225	2.208	1.742	3.317
2009	1.838	1.979	2.000	2.107	2.314	2.681	2.594	2.677	2.626	2.613	2.709	2.671	2.401
2010	2.779	2.709	2.829	2.906	2.915	2.783	2.783	2.795	2.754	2.843	2.899	3.031	2.836
2011	3.139	3.215	3.594	3.863	3.982	3.753	3.703	3.680	3.664	3.521	3.475	3.329	3.577
2012	3.447	3.622	3.918	3.976	3.839	3.602	3.502	3.759	3.908	3.839	3.542	3.386	3.695
2013	3.407	3.748	3.792	3.647	3.682	3.693	3.687	3.658	3.616	3.434	3.310	3.333	3.584
2014	3.378	3.422	3.590	3.717	3.745	3.750	3.690	3.540	3.463	3.241	2.945	2.618	3.425
2015[1]	2.170	2.308	2.544	2.545	2.832	2.889	2.893	2.745	2.463	2.357	2.249	2.125	2.510

[1] Preliminary.   [2] Also includes types of motor oil not shown separately.   [3] Including taxes   *Source: Energy Information Administration, U.S. Department of Energy (EIA-DOE)*

114

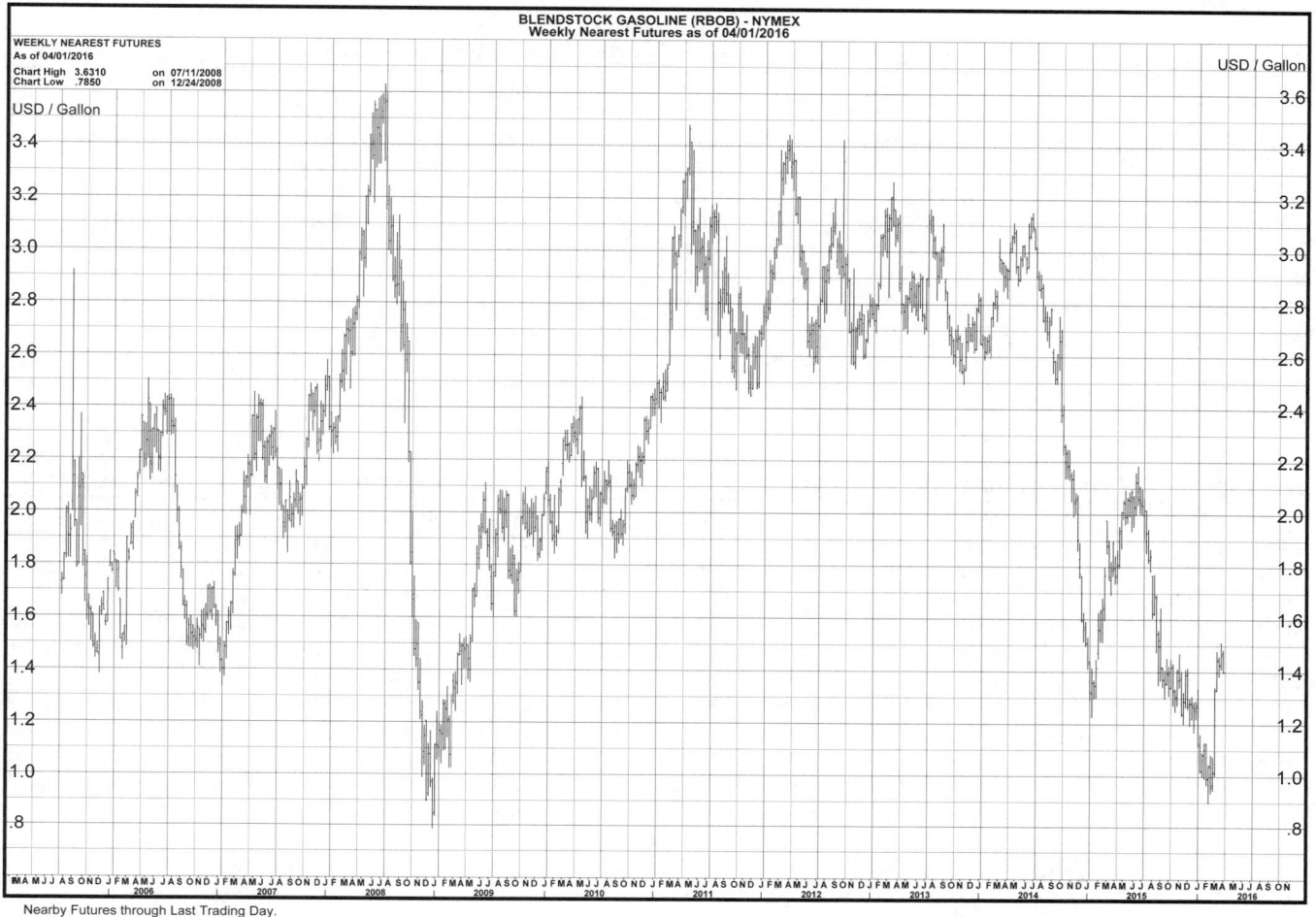

BLENDSTOCK GASOLINE (RBOB) - NYMEX
Weekly Nearest Futures as of 04/01/2016

WEEKLY NEAREST FUTURES
As of 04/01/2016

Chart High 3.6310 on 07/11/2008
Chart Low .7850 on 12/24/2008

Nearby Futures through Last Trading Day.

Volume of Trading of Gasoline, RBOB[1] Futures in New York — In Thousands of Contracts

Year	Jan.	Feb.	Mar.	Apr.	May	June	July	Aug.	Sept.	Oct.	Nov.	Dec.	Total
2006	1,149.6	1,233.0	1,259.1	1,079.6	1,122.7	1,039.8	939.8	1,145.5	891.4	839.6	838.1	966.0	12,504.2
2007	1,172.9	1,272.2	1,722.5	1,826.7	2,134.5	1,811.8	1,770.2	1,872.8	1,627.3	1,706.1	1,531.3	1,343.2	19,791.4
2008	1,660.6	1,887.5	2,111.9	1,986.3	1,917.6	1,854.4	1,621.6	1,667.7	1,862.1	1,452.9	1,193.4	1,306.4	20,522.6
2009	1,597.7	1,592.3	1,594.4	1,612.9	1,841.8	2,060.8	1,748.6	1,773.9	1,600.3	2,082.5	1,908.8	1,746.5	21,160.5
2010	1,979.2	1,978.8	2,318.0	2,829.9	2,537.8	2,186.6	1,946.1	2,402.3	2,325.4	2,614.0	2,529.1	2,251.3	27,898.7
2011	2,315.2	2,274.1	2,342.8	2,592.4	3,390.6	2,720.4	2,078.4	2,874.5	2,745.1	2,791.8	2,780.3	2,223.6	31,129.3
2012	2,899.2	2,844.2	3,480.0	3,789.4	3,257.2	3,107.9	2,844.9	3,043.1	3,015.4	3,298.3	2,674.1	2,350.2	36,603.8
2013	2,981.2	3,000.0	3,079.8	3,578.7	3,090.8	2,566.9	3,105.3	2,810.5	2,516.6	2,664.8	2,777.1	2,298.6	34,470.3
2014	2,470.9	2,417.0	2,562.7	3,316.9	3,240.6	2,679.3	3,001.7	2,894.1	3,173.3	3,170.5	2,713.5	2,781.4	34,421.9
2015	3,070.7	3,387.9	3,396.1	3,449.5	3,113.9	3,869.0	3,621.4	3,736.9	2,961.2	3,158.0	3,171.9	3,365.6	40,302.1

[1] Data thru September 2005 are Unleaded, October 2005 thru December 2006 are Unleaded and RBOB.
Contract size = 42,000 US gallons.   *Source: CME Group; New York Mercantile Exchange (NYMEX)*

Average Open Interest of Gasoline, RBOB[1] Futures in New York — In Contracts

Year	Jan.	Feb.	Mar.	Apr.	May	June	July	Aug.	Sept.	Oct.	Nov.	Dec.
2006	157,562	173,978	168,067	165,233	150,913	138,578	146,173	135,367	131,771	124,963	128,906	135,085
2007	161,557	161,335	166,936	170,675	172,870	183,443	189,084	184,342	188,954	196,730	206,392	208,238
2008	230,032	253,303	241,781	250,852	264,988	256,220	238,170	219,229	198,263	162,480	172,267	194,234
2009	192,691	187,748	199,423	204,956	220,450	215,256	200,537	217,625	205,517	219,883	256,151	238,789
2010	262,247	258,312	304,437	320,529	275,659	245,923	239,242	246,901	241,014	270,830	282,949	273,638
2011	280,084	274,277	275,857	293,452	280,369	251,349	245,309	250,244	268,974	273,495	280,706	275,994
2012	312,848	345,884	374,449	348,606	306,453	293,802	258,931	273,299	290,070	279,312	276,945	282,942
2013	312,415	328,903	318,974	301,346	283,215	277,107	270,359	271,797	264,119	232,420	240,735	246,590
2014	252,519	274,087	283,756	310,549	332,460	314,754	307,808	274,978	283,206	310,119	334,015	349,589
2015	366,741	362,191	372,013	383,705	383,960	372,487	367,208	378,562	371,326	345,971	360,109	365,200

[1] Data thru September 2005 are Unleaded, October 2005 thru December 2006 are Unleaded and RBOB.
Contract size = 42,000 US gallons.   *Source: CME Group; New York Mercantile Exchange (NYMEX)*

GASOLINE

Average Retail Price of Unleaded Premium Motor Gasoline[2] in the United States   In Dollars per Gallon

Year	Jan.	Feb.	Mar.	Apr.	May	June	July	Aug.	Sept.	Oct.	Nov.	Dec.	Average
2006	2.521	2.519	2.603	2.967	3.169	3.139	3.219	3.207	2.819	2.493	2.459	2.550	2.805
2007	2.501	2.509	2.818	3.093	3.348	3.281	3.200	3.018	3.021	3.037	3.307	3.264	3.033
2008	3.291	3.272	3.502	3.690	4.003	4.319	4.350	4.045	3.940	3.432	2.433	1.951	3.519
2009	2.036	2.182	2.197	2.309	2.511	2.883	2.806	2.887	2.845	2.826	2.917	2.882	2.607
2010	2.987	2.922	3.035	3.113	3.124	3.000	2.997	3.015	2.968	3.055	3.109	3.234	3.047
2011	3.345	3.424	3.807	4.074	4.192	3.972	3.915	3.893	3.887	3.745	3.700	3.553	3.792
2012	3.663	3.840	4.138	4.194	4.062	3.825	3.726	3.991	4.140	4.079	3.782	3.626	3.922
2013	3.646	3.990	4.038	3.901	3.936	3.957	3.951	3.919	3.881	3.702	3.585	3.604	3.843
2014	3.651	3.694	3.858	3.986	4.020	4.027	3.976	3.835	3.758	3.547	3.262	2.940	3.713
2015[1]	2.497	2.621	2.867	2.868	3.166	3.218	3.252	3.120	2.860	2.749	2.640	2.532	2.866

[1] Preliminary.   [2] Including taxes.   *Source: Energy Information Administration, U.S. Department of Energy (EIA-DOE)*

Average Retail Price of Unleaded Regular Motor Gasoline[2] in the United States   In Dollars per Gallon

Year	Jan.	Feb.	Mar.	Apr.	May	June	July	Aug.	Sept.	Oct.	Nov.	Dec.	Average
2006	2.315	2.310	2.401	2.757	2.947	2.917	2.999	2.985	2.589	2.272	2.241	2.334	2.589
2007	2.274	2.285	2.592	2.860	3.130	3.052	2.961	2.782	2.789	2.793	3.069	3.020	2.801
2008	3.047	3.033	3.258	3.441	3.764	4.065	4.090	3.786	3.698	3.173	2.151	1.689	3.266
2009	1.787	1.928	1.949	2.056	2.265	2.631	2.543	2.627	2.574	2.561	2.660	2.621	2.350
2010	2.731	2.659	2.780	2.858	2.869	2.736	2.736	2.745	2.704	2.795	2.852	2.985	2.788
2011	3.091	3.167	3.546	3.816	3.933	3.702	3.654	3.630	3.612	3.468	3.423	3.278	3.527
2012	3.399	3.572	3.868	3.927	3.792	3.552	3.451	3.707	3.856	3.786	3.488	3.331	3.644
2013	3.351	3.693	3.735	3.590	3.623	3.633	3.628	3.600	3.556	3.375	3.251	3.277	3.526
2014	3.320	3.364	3.532	3.659	3.691	3.695	3.633	3.481	3.403	3.182	2.887	2.560	3.367
2015[1]	2.110	2.249	2.483	2.485	2.775	2.832	2.832	2.679	2.394	2.289	2.185	2.060	2.448

[1] Preliminary.   [2] Including taxes.   *Source: Energy Information Administration, U.S. Department of Energy (EIA-DOE)*

Average Retail Price of All-Types[2] Motor Gasoline[3] in the United States   In Dollars per Gallon

Year	Jan.	Feb.	Mar.	Apr.	May	June	July	Aug.	Sept.	Oct.	Nov.	Dec.	Average
2006	2.359	2.354	2.444	2.801	2.993	2.963	3.046	3.033	2.637	2.319	2.287	2.380	2.635
2007	2.321	2.333	2.639	2.909	3.176	3.100	3.013	2.833	2.839	2.843	3.118	3.069	2.849
2008	3.096	3.083	3.307	3.491	3.813	4.115	4.142	3.838	3.749	3.225	2.208	1.742	3.317
2009	1.838	1.979	2.000	2.107	2.314	2.681	2.594	2.677	2.626	2.613	2.709	2.671	2.401
2010	2.779	2.709	2.829	2.906	2.915	2.783	2.783	2.795	2.754	2.843	2.899	3.031	2.836
2011	3.139	3.215	3.594	3.863	3.982	3.753	3.703	3.680	3.664	3.521	3.475	3.329	3.577
2012	3.447	3.622	3.918	3.976	3.839	3.602	3.502	3.759	3.908	3.839	3.542	3.386	3.695
2013	3.407	3.748	3.792	3.647	3.682	3.693	3.687	3.658	3.616	3.434	3.310	3.333	3.584
2014	3.378	3.422	3.590	3.717	3.745	3.750	3.690	3.540	3.463	3.241	2.945	2.618	3.425
2015[1]	2.170	2.308	2.544	2.545	2.832	2.889	2.893	2.745	2.463	2.357	2.249	2.125	2.510

[1] Preliminary.   [2] Also includes types of motor oil not shown separately.   [3] Including taxes.   *Source: Energy Information Administration, U.S. Department of Energy (EIA-DOE)*

Average Refiner Price of Finished Aviation Gasoline to End Users[2] in the United States   In Dollars per Gallon

Year	Jan.	Feb.	Mar.	Apr.	May	June	July	Aug.	Sept.	Oct.	Nov.	Dec.	Average
2006	2.391	2.324	2.473	2.869	3.013	3.057	3.103	3.058	2.532	2.385	2.353	2.349	2.682
2007	2.179	2.285	2.627	2.969	3.096	2.978	3.053	2.823	2.900	2.855	3.067	2.975	2.849
2008	2.987	2.954	3.296	3.358	3.615	3.965	3.929	3.792	3.837	2.975	2.230	1.814	3.273
2009	1.857	1.974	1.977	2.150	2.423	2.707	2.607	2.764	2.684	2.693	2.845	2.799	2.442
2010	2.914	2.855	3.103	3.201	3.129	2.981	3.028	2.967	2.893	3.000	3.095	3.218	3.028
2011	3.323	3.374	3.767	4.132	4.091	3.913	4.027	3.920	3.915	3.697	3.620	W	3.803
2012	3.732	W	4.133	4.313	W	W	W	4.091	4.262	4.064	3.561	3.599	3.971
2013	W	4.060	4.022	3.860	3.900	4.191	4.224	4.298	3.982	3.653	3.673	3.678	3.932
2014	W	4.142	W	W	W	W	W	W	W	W	W	W	3.986
2015[1]	W	W	W	W	W	W	W	W	W	W	W	W	W

[1] Preliminary.   [2] Excluding taxes.   NA = Not available.   W = Withheld proprietary data.   *Source: Energy Information Administration, U.S. Department Energy (EIA-DOE)*

Gold

Gold is a dense, bright yellow metallic element with a high luster. Gold is an inactive substance and is unaffected by air, heat, moisture, and most solvents. Gold has been coveted for centuries for its unique blend of rarity, beauty, and near indestructibility. The Egyptians mined gold before 2,000 BC. The first known, pure gold coin was made on the orders of King Croesus of Lydia in the sixth century BC.

Gold is found in nature in quartz veins and secondary alluvial deposits as a free metal. Gold is produced from mines on every continent with the exception of Antarctica, where mining is forbidden. Because it is virtually indestructible, much of the gold that has ever been mined still exists above ground in one form or another. The largest producer of gold in the U.S. by far is the state of Nevada, with Alaska and California running a distant second and third.

Gold is a vital industrial commodity. Pure gold is one of the most malleable and ductile of all the metals. It is a good conductor of heat and electricity. The prime industrial use of gold is in electronics. Another important sector is dental gold where it has been used for almost 3,000 years. Other applications for gold include decorative gold leaf, reflective glass, and jewelry.

In 1792, the United States first assigned a formal monetary role for gold when Congress put the nation's currency on a bimetallic standard, backing it with gold and silver. Under the gold standard, the U.S. government was willing to exchange its paper currency for a set amount of gold, meaning the paper currency was backed by a physical asset with real value. However, President Nixon in 1971 severed the convertibility between the U.S. dollar and gold, which led to the breakdown of the Bretton Woods international payments system. Since then, the prices of gold and of paper currencies have floated freely. U.S. and other central banks now hold physical gold reserves primarily as a store of wealth.

Gold futures and options are traded at the CME Group, NYSE-LIFFE U.S., the Bolsa de Mercado & Futuros (BM&F), EUREX, JSE Securities Exchange, and the Moscow Exchange. Gold futures are traded on the Hong Kong Exchanges & Clearing, the Indonesia Commodity & Derivatives Exchange (ICDX), the Multi Commodity Exchange of India (MCX), the Korea Exchange, Shanghai Futures Exchange (SHFE), and the Singapore Exchange (SGX). The CME gold futures contract calls for the delivery of 100 troy ounces of gold (0.995 fineness), and the contract trades in terms of dollars and cents per troy ounce.

Prices – CME gold futures prices (Barchart.com symbol GC) began 2015 very strong as they rallied up to the high for the year in January at $1,307 an ounce. Global economic concerns pushed gold higher after the actions by the IMF and World Bank to cut their 2015 global GDP forecasts bolstered speculation that world central banks would continue their overly easy monetary policies. Gold prices traded sideways to lower the rest of the year after a Greek bailout agreement and an Iranian nuclear agreement dried up safe-haven demand for gold. Also, a lack of global inflation reduced demand for gold as an inflation hedge as U.S. inflation expectations plunged when the 10-yeat T-note breakeven inflation rate sank to a 6-1/2 year low in October. A lack of bullish reasons to own gold then fostered fund selling as long gold positions in ETFs tumbled to a 6-1/2 year low. The Fed's 25 bp rate hike in December sent the dollar soaring to a 12-1/2 year high, which further undercut gold prices. Gold sank to a 6-year low of $1,046 an ounce in December and finished 2015 down -10.5% at $1,060 an ounce.

Supply – World mine production of gold rose +2.1% yr/yr to 2.860 million kilograms in 2014, a new record high (1 kilogram = 32.1507 troy ounces). The world's largest producers of gold in 2014 were China with 15.7% of world production, followed by Australia (9.4%), Russia (8.6%), the U.S (7.4%), and Peru and South Africa each with (5.2%).

Gold mine production has been moving lower in most major gold-producing countries such as South Africa, Australia, and the U.S. For example, South Africa's production of 150,000 kilograms in 2014 was down -6.3% yr/yr and that was about one-third the production levels of more than 600,000 kilograms seen in the 1980s and early 1990s. On the other hand, China's gold production in 2014 rose +4.7% to a record 450,000 kilograms. U.S. gold mine production in 2014 fell -8.3% yr/yr to 211,000 kilograms, just above 2009 production level which was the lowest production since 1988. U.S. refinery production of gold from domestic and foreign ore sources in 2014 fell -10.3% yr/yr to 200,000 kilograms. U.S. refinery production of gold from secondary scrap sources in 2014 fell -4.8% yr/yr to 200,000 kilograms.

Demand – U.S. consumption of gold in 2014 rose +3.1% yr/yr to 165,000 kilograms. The most recent data available from the early 1990s showed that 71% of that gold demand came from jewelry and the arts, 22% from industrial uses, and 7% from dental uses.

Trade – U.S. exports of gold (excluding coinage) in 2014 fell -37.8% yr/yr to 430,000 kilograms, below the 2012 record high of 695,000 kilograms. U.S. imports of gold for consumption in 2014 remained unchanged yr/yr at 315,000 kilograms, below the 2012 record high of 326,000 kilograms.

World Mine Production of Gold   In Kilograms (1 Kilogram = 32.1507 Troy Ounces)

Year	Australia	Brazil	Canada	China	Ghana	Indonesia	Papua New Guinea	Peru	Russia	South Africa	United States	Uzbekistan	World Total
2007	247,000	49,613	102,211	275,000	83,558	117,851	57,549	170,236	156,975	252,598	238,000	85,000	2,350,000
2008	215,000	54,666	94,909	285,000	73,819	64,390	67,463	179,870	172,031	212,571	233,000	85,000	2,300,000
2009	224,000	60,330	97,235	320,000	67,818	140,488	63,600	183,995	192,832	197,628	223,000	90,000	2,490,000
2010	261,000	62,047	102,693	345,000	72,441	119,726	62,900	164,084	189,000	188,702	231,000	90,000	2,590,000
2011	260,000	65,209	102,624	362,000	82,919	68,220	61,760	166,187	199,642	180,293	234,000	91,000	2,630,000
2012	252,000	66,773	105,270	405,000	86,699	69,291	52,100	161,545	217,800	154,178	235,000	93,000	2,710,000
2013	265,000	71,000	124,054	430,000	90,000	61,357	56,700	151,486	229,982	159,542	230,000	98,000	2,800,000
2014[1]	274,000	80,000	152,000	450,000	91,000	69,000	53,000	140,000	247,000	152,000	210,000	100,000	2,990,000
2015[2]	300,000	80,000	150,000	490,000	85,000	75,000	50,000	150,000	242,000	140,000	200,000	103,000	3,000,000

[1] Preliminary.   [2] Estimate.   *Source: U.S. Geological Survey (USGS)*

GOLD

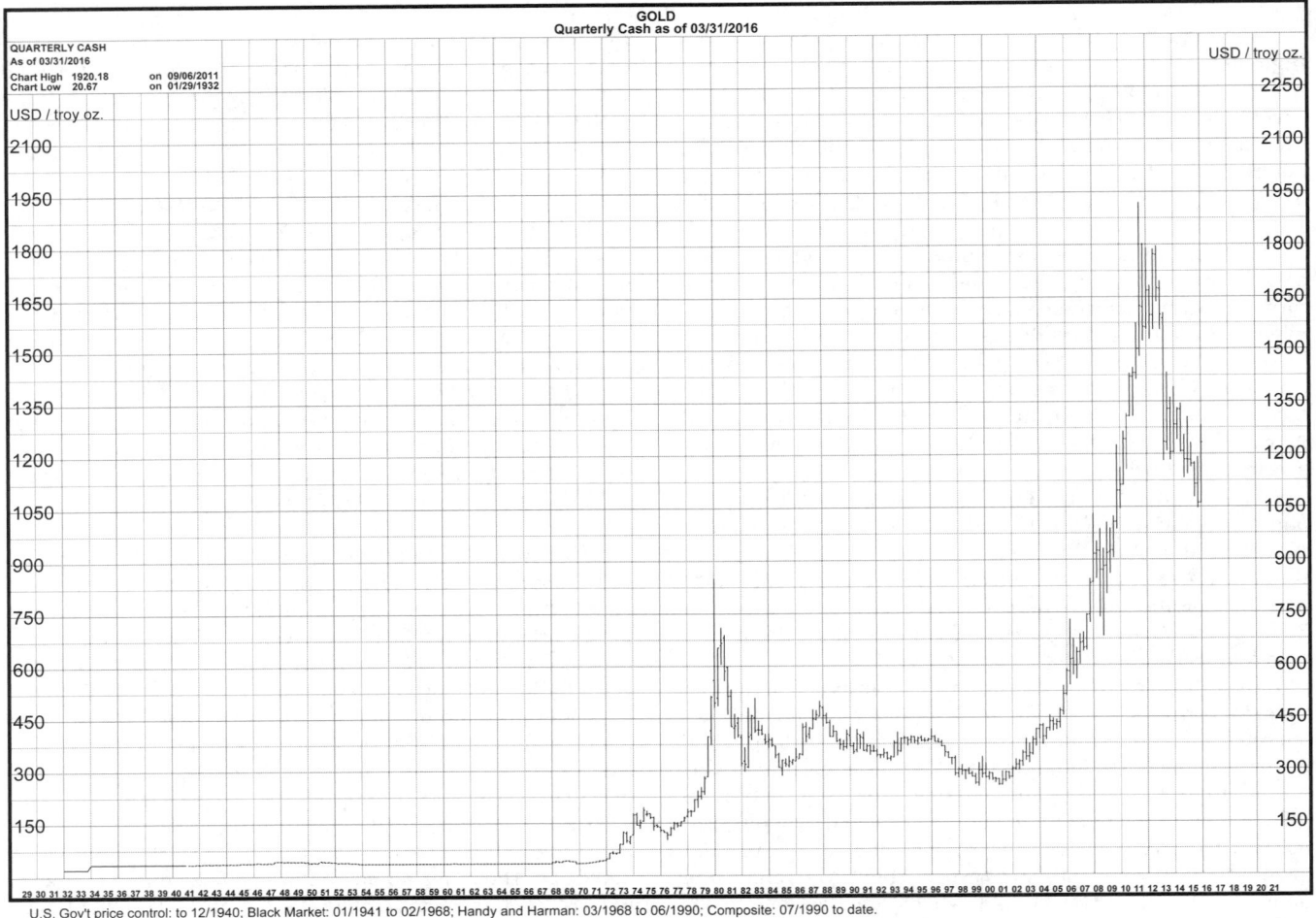

QUARTERLY CASH
As of 03/31/2016
Chart High 1920.18 on 09/06/2011
Chart Low 20.67 on 01/29/1932

USD / troy oz.

USD / troy oz.

U.S. Gov't price control: to 12/1940; Black Market: 01/1941 to 02/1968; Handy and Harman: 03/1968 to 06/1990; Composite: 07/1990 to date.

Salient Statistics of Gold in the United States   In Kilograms (1 Kilogram = 32.1507 Troy Ounces)

			- Refinery Production -				-------- Stocks, Dec. 31 ---------			---------- Consumption -----------				
	Mine		Domestic		Exports,	Imports	Treasury			Official				
	Pro-	Value	& Foreign	Secondary	Excluding	for Con-	Depart-	Futures		World		Indus-	Jewelry	
Year	duction	Million $	Ores	(Old Scrap)	Coinage	sumption	ment[3]	Exchange	Industry	Reserves[4]	Dental	trial[5]	& Arts	Total
2006	252,000	4,910.0	181,000	89,100	389,000	263,000	8,140,000	234,000	2,000	30,400	----	----	----	185,000
2007	238,000	5,350.0	176,000	135,000	519,000	170,000	8,140,000	229,000	1,140	29,900	----	----	----	180,000
2008	233,000	6,550.0	168,000	181,000	567,000	231,000	8,140,000	265,000	W	28,700	----	----	----	176,000
2009	223,000	7,000.0	170,000	189,000	381,000	320,000	8,140,000	305,000	9,200	30,400	----	----	----	173,000
2010	231,000	9,130.0	175,000	198,000	383,000	616,000	8,140,000	361,000	6,810	30,700	----	----	----	180,000
2011	234,000	11,800.0	220,000	263,000	664,000	550,000	8,140,000	353,000	6,470	31,100	----	----	----	168,000
2012	235,000	12,600.0	222,000	215,000	695,000	326,000	8,140,000	344,000	4,070	31,700	----	----	----	147,000
2013	230,000	10,400.0	223,000	210,000	691,000	315,000	8,140,000	243,000	5,940	31,900	----	----	----	160,000
2014[1]	210,000		203,000	161,000	500,000	308,000	8,140,000				----	----	----	150,000
2015[2]	200,000		200,000	140,000	500,000	265,000	8,140,000				----	----	----	150,000

[1] Preliminary.   [2] Estimate.   [3] Includes gold in Exchange Stabilization Fund.   [4] Held by market economy country central banks and governments and international monetary orgainzations.   [5] Including space and defense.   NA = Not available.   *Source: U.S. Geological Survey (USGS)*

Monthly Average Gold Price (Handy & Harman) in New York   Dollars Per Troy Ounce

Year	Jan.	Feb.	Mar.	Apr.	May	June	July	Aug.	Sept.	Oct.	Nov.	Dec.	Average
2006	549.27	555.02	557.09	610.41	673.97	596.15	634.89	632.10	596.76	585.78	627.12	629.38	604.00
2007	630.97	664.43	655.30	679.20	667.86	655.40	665.83	665.21	714.79	749.73	806.68	803.20	696.55
2008	890.47	923.25	966.30	909.70	886.29	889.49	940.16	838.30	830.30	806.62	754.95	816.09	870.99
2009	859.98	943.20	924.27	890.50	927.34	945.67	934.31	949.34	996.76	1,043.16	1,122.03	1,212.50	979.09
2010	1,116.74	1,095.26	1,114.36	1,147.70	1,204.50	1,232.92	1,192.25	1,217.11	1,272.02	1,342.02	1,370.46	1,389.70	1,224.59
2011	1,359.39	1,371.13	1,424.01	1,478.55	1,511.63	1,528.66	1,576.70	1,757.21	1,765.99	1,665.36	1,743.83	1,645.50	1,569.00
2012	1,656.88	1,743.10	1,673.77	1,649.72	1,588.34	1,598.98	1,592.98	1,627.97	1,747.24	1,748.69	1,719.98	1,684.18	1,669.32
2013	1,670.17	1,628.47	1,592.85	1,490.22	1,415.91	1,342.36	1,288.31	1,349.30	1,346.63	1,316.19	1,276.94	1,220.65	1,411.50
2014	1,244.53	1,300.60	1,336.08	1,298.45	1,288.74	1,279.10	1,310.59	1,295.13	1,236.14	1,222.49	1,175.33	1,200.62	1,265.65
2015	1,250.75	1,227.08	1,178.63	1,198.93	1,198.63	1,181.50	1,128.31	1,117.93	1,124.88	1,159.25	1,086.44	1,068.25	1,160.05

Source: U.S. Geological Survey (USGS)

GOLD - COMEX
Weekly Selected Futures as of 04/01/2016

WEEKLY SELECTED FUTURES
As of 04/01/2016
Chart High 1920.80 on 09/06/2011
Chart Low 534.50 on 03/10/2006

USD / troy oz.

Nearby Futures through Last Trading Day using selected contract months: February, April, June, August, October and December.

Volume of Trading of Gold Futures in New York (COMEX)   In Thousands of Contracts

Year	Jan.	Feb.	Mar.	Apr.	May	June	July	Aug.	Sept.	Oct.	Nov.	Dec.	Total
2006	2,018.8	1,162.7	2,052.7	1,302.9	2,071.0	1,148.6	1,487.2	804.5	884.7	857.1	1,284.7	842.7	15,917.6
2007	1,929.8	1,455.9	2,195.9	1,405.2	2,336.6	1,610.8	2,292.2	1,710.7	2,024.6	2,584.4	3,837.1	1,677.2	25,060.4
2008	4,041.7	2,617.6	3,901.8	2,765.5	3,328.0	2,624.0	4,269.9	3,066.1	4,109.4	3,045.1	2,687.1	1,921.1	38,377.4
2009	3,073.0	2,444.2	3,385.0	1,808.4	2,766.7	2,305.0	2,846.2	1,815.6	2,831.4	3,216.7	4,564.3	4,083.1	35,139.5
2010	4,574.3	3,616.1	4,385.6	2,932.3	4,824.1	3,024.7	4,097.3	2,184.9	2,732.1	3,858.8	5,530.4	2,969.7	44,730.3
2011	4,724.6	2,740.4	4,512.3	3,145.2	4,955.3	3,078.9	4,278.2	6,406.6	5,300.5	3,026.4	4,105.3	2,901.9	49,175.6
2012	4,146.5	3,506.7	4,860.6	2,834.8	4,913.7	3,479.4	3,732.7	2,793.5	3,460.8	3,147.0	4,380.3	2,637.3	43,893.3
2013	4,221.1	3,632.3	3,906.6	5,218.8	5,312.3	3,744.7	4,647.2	3,466.7	3,331.9	3,458.2	3,577.1	2,777.7	47,294.6
2014	3,754.8	2,607.5	4,200.3	2,692.9	3,631.1	2,508.1	3,848.3	2,381.8	3,205.8	3,703.7	4,676.7	3,307.7	40,518.8
2015	4,507.9	2,558.8	4,403.4	3,057.0	3,721.5	2,856.0	4,554.8	3,431.6	2,917.1	3,070.1	4,034.0	2,735.2	41,847.3

Contract size = 100 oz.   *Source: CME Group; New York Mercantile Exchange (NYMEX)*

Average Open Interest of Gold in New York (COMEX)   In Contracts

Year	Jan.	Feb.	Mar.	Apr.	May	June	July	Aug.	Sept.	Oct.	Nov.	Dec.
2006	348,949	338,851	331,223	350,380	336,735	288,309	316,969	309,186	320,850	330,152	346,141	335,204
2007	350,958	387,321	372,781	377,094	405,645	401,337	379,066	339,923	394,400	479,735	530,775	500,409
2008	556,302	487,373	471,320	418,693	435,847	401,914	460,178	382,302	378,216	321,545	290,706	280,402
2009	331,891	359,420	376,201	341,491	366,468	382,960	380,301	383,826	454,286	493,909	522,556	504,102
2010	512,723	469,214	489,600	521,976	574,107	579,416	561,781	541,408	595,118	619,536	626,630	589,823
2011	556,448	479,014	507,118	522,520	513,744	504,841	522,091	517,064	494,932	438,488	453,477	424,014
2012	426,896	445,515	434,210	402,740	423,294	417,783	424,790	400,896	471,946	469,628	461,382	430,717
2013	442,707	435,425	437,300	416,489	431,460	383,314	424,302	388,278	380,768	382,216	395,583	383,980
2014	397,700	381,045	404,828	369,755	395,313	385,660	400,977	365,066	381,961	400,455	433,102	372,432
2015	415,408	399,097	415,894	397,632	411,656	417,416	451,224	430,894	416,389	448,795	425,138	398,843

Contract size = 100 oz.   *Source: CME Group; New York Mercantile Exchange (NYMEX)*

GOLD

Commodity Exchange, Inc. (COMEX) Depository Warehouse Stocks of Gold   In Thousands of Troy Ounces

Year	Jan. 1	Feb. 1	Mar. 1	Apr. 1	May 1	June 1	July 1	Aug. 1	Sept. 1	Oct. 1	Nov. 1	Dec. 1
2006	6,657.7	7,320.9	7,518.9	7,426.6	7,334.4	7,796.0	8,031.2	8,199.0	7,980.8	7,695.2	7,565.8	7,491.1
2007	7,534.5	7,459.2	7,487.2	7,302.5	7,624.8	7,633.1	7,276.1	7,130.5	7,077.1	7,211.9	7,346.7	7,366.1
2008	7,492.5	7,588.0	7,371.3	7,623.1	7,760.4	7,588.9	7,611.6	8,266.0	8,442.8	8,594.9	8,171.8	8,540.3
2009	8,548.5	8,556.8	8,635.9	8,508.6	8,322.6	8,725.8	8,893.4	9,144.6	9,173.0	9,316.2	9,316.2	9,508.9
2010	9,679.4	9,679.4	9,679.4	10,022.9	10,184.3	10,736.8	10,923.5	11,112.1	10,816.9	10,896.7	11,311.9	11,488.4
2011	11,694.3	11,401.9	11,075.3	11,033.0	11,140.8	11,310.3	11,439.7	11,431.5	11,559.8	11,246.8	11,236.9	11,301.8
2012	11,469.4	11,434.6	11,405.2	11,350.5	10,895.2	10,978.4	10,831.7	10,806.6	10,844.5	11,009.3	11,243.3	11,151.0
2013	11,058.7	11,009.3	10,289.3	9,279.4	8,129.2	8,054.9	7,534.5	6,991.4	7,013.2	6,862.8	7,153.7	7,247.9
2014	7,828.1	7,081.3	7,177.1	7,740.8	7,935.6	8,262.7	8,298.5	8,684.3	9,927.3	9,127.3	8,056.0	7,928.7
2015	7,932.1	7,983.9	8,321.5	8,010.7	7,718.4	7,871.5	8,043.6	7,572.3	7,221.1	6,852.5	6,700.8	6,377.6

Source: CME Group; New York Mercantile Exchange (NYMEX)

Central Gold Bank Reserves   In Millions of Troy Ounces

Year	Bel-gium	Can-ada	France	Ger-many	Italy	Japan	Nether-lands	Switzer-land	United Kingdom	United States	Industrial Total	Deve-loping Oil	Deve-loping Non-Oil	IMF[2]	Bank for Int'l Settle-ments	World Total
2006	7.3	0.1	87.4	110.0	78.8	24.6	20.6	41.5	10.0	261.5	----	----	----	----	----	979.7
2007	7.3	0.1	83.7	109.9	78.8	24.6	20.0	36.8	10.0	261.5	----	----	----	----	----	963.5
2008	7.3	0.1	80.1	109.7	78.8	24.6	19.7	33.4	10.0	261.5	----	----	----	----	----	964.1
2009	7.3	0.1	78.3	109.5	78.8	24.6	19.7	33.4	10.0	261.5	----	----	----	----	----	980.9
2010	7.3	0.1	78.3	109.3	78.8	24.6	19.7	33.4	10.0	261.5	----	----	----	----	----	991.5
2011	7.3	0.1	78.3	109.2	78.8	24.6	19.7	33.4	10.0	261.5	----	----	----	----	----	1,003.3
2012	7.3	0.1	78.3	109.0	78.8	24.6	19.7	33.4	10.0	261.5	----	----	----	----	----	1,018.6
2013	7.3	0.1	78.3	108.9	78.8	24.6	19.7	33.4	10.0	261.5	----	----	----	----	----	1,024.1
2014	7.3	0.1	78.3	108.8	78.8	24.6	19.7	33.4	10.0	261.5	----	----	----	----	----	1,029.8
2015[1]	7.3	0.1	78.3	108.7	78.8	24.6	19.7	33.4	10.0	261.5	----	----	----	----	----	

[1] Preliminary.   [2] International Monetary Fund.   *Source: American Metal Market (AMM)*

Mine Production of Recoverable Gold in the United States   In Kilograms

Year	Alaska	Arizona	California	Colorado	Idaho	Montana	Nevada	New Mexico	South Dakota	Utah	Washington	Other States	Total
2006	W	W	W	W	W	W	206,000	W	W	W	W	45,800	252,000
2007	W	W	W	W	W	W	186,000	W	W	W	W	52,400	238,000
2008	W	W	W	W	W	W	178,000	W	W	W	W	55,400	233,000
2009	W	W	W	W	W	W	161,000	W	W	W	W	62,500	223,000
2010	28,100	W	W	W	W	W	166,000	W	W	W	W	36,900	231,000
2011	25,800	W	W	W	W	W	172,000	W	W	W	W	36,100	234,000
2012	27,700	W	W	W	W	W	175,000	W	W	W	W	31,400	235,000
2013	32,200	W	W	W	W	W	170,000	W	W	W	W	27,800	230,000
2014	31,400	W	W	W	W	W	151,000	W	W	W	W	27,800	210,000
2015/1	28,636	W	W	W	W	W	159,491	W	W	W	W	24,316	212,509

[1] Preliminary.   W = Withheld proprietary data, included in "Other States."   *Source: U.S. Geological Survey (USGS)*

U.S. Exports of Gold   In Kilograms

Year	Australia	Canada	China	Germany	Hong Kong	India	Mexico	South Africa	Switzer-land	Thailand	United Arab Emirates	United Kingdom	Total
2004	5,250	18,100	45	77	30	10	12,500	14	174,000	23	7,910	29,300	257,000
2005	1,980	738	49	1,940	6,270	2,500	5,980	----	197,000	5,980	22,200	64,900	324,000
2006	6,010	1,530	3	124	2,320	67	7,430	----	213,000	505	10,200	145,000	389,000
2007	2,470	9,210	10	664	1,170	17,000	5,890	----	266,000	1,330	20,000	191,000	519,000
2008	12,300	11,800	219	305	4,280	18,800	4,660	5,270	296,000	8,510	20,700	181,000	568,000
2009	26,700	3,110	51	832	844	21,000	3,120	----	103,000	----	147	220,000	381,000
2010	14,200	8,750	558	1,390	18,400	30,900	2,270	9,510	113,000	5,000	3,080	170,000	383,000
2011	18,200	1,460	5,150	1,440	111,000	15,500	5,160	11,900	105,000	21,200	10,300	161,000	474,000
2012	5,140	18,400	1,200	2,230	133,000	66,900	7,040	8,260	280,000	9,280	64,200	137,000	692,000
2013	5,200	18,900	14,400	941	217,000	32,500	947	19,600	284,000	27,000	34,300	29,000	691,000

[1] Less than 1/2 unit.   *Source: U.S. Geological Survey (USGS)*

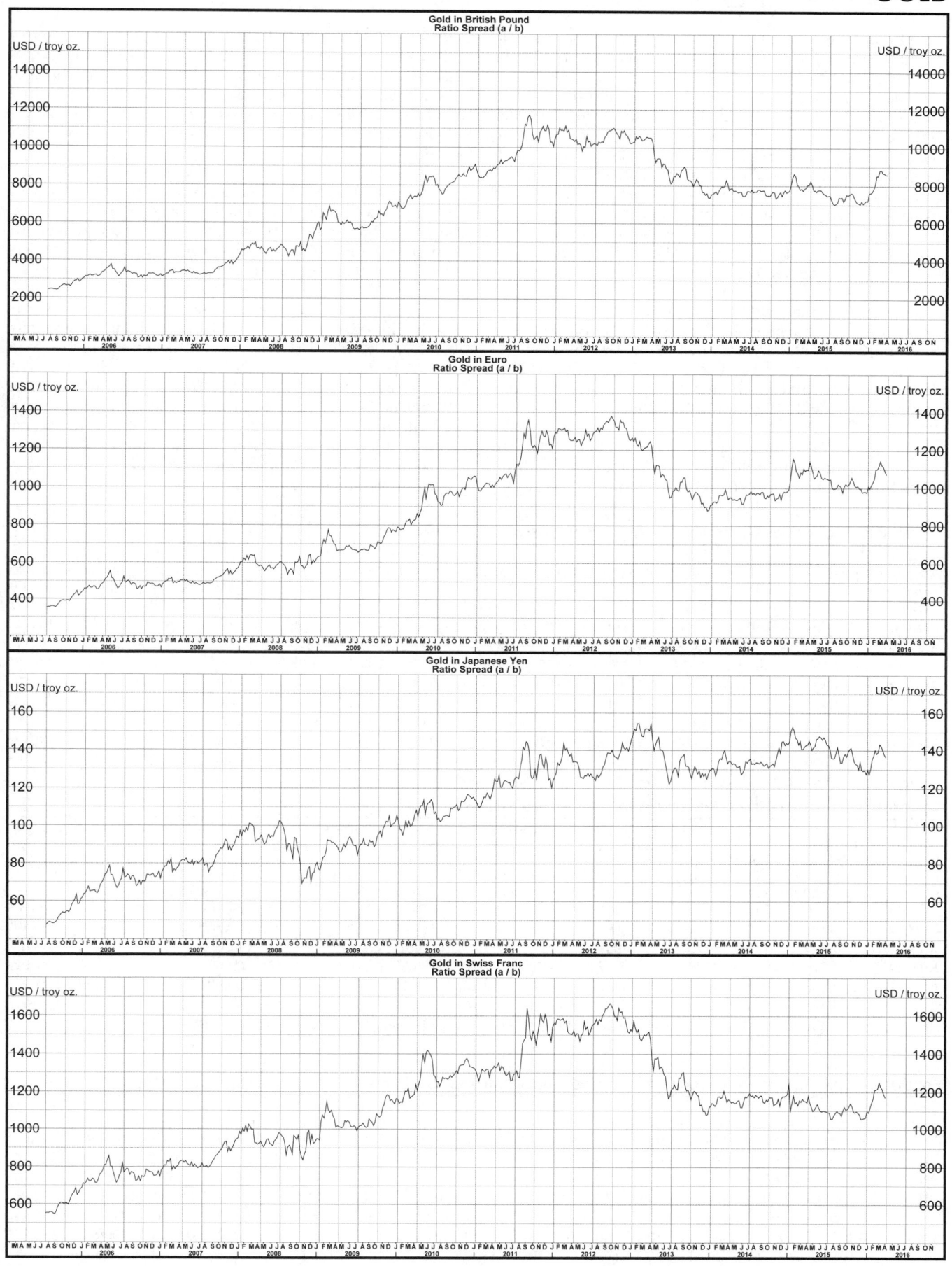

Gold in British Pound
Ratio Spread (a / b)

Gold in Euro
Ratio Spread (a / b)

Gold in Japanese Yen
Ratio Spread (a / b)

Gold in Swiss Franc
Ratio Spread (a / b)

Grain Sorghum

Grain sorghums include milo, kafir, durra, feterita, and kaoliang. Grain sorghums are tolerant of drought by going into dormancy during dry and hot conditions and then resuming growth as conditions improve. Grain sorghums are a staple food in China, India, and Africa but in the U.S. they are mainly used as livestock feed. The two key U.S. producing states are Texas and Kansas, each with about one-third of total U.S. production. U.S. sorghum production has become more popular with the breeding of dwarf grain sorghum hybrids which are only about 3 feet tall (versus up to 10 feet tall for wild sorghum) and are easier to harvest with a combine. The U.S. sorghum crop year begins September 1.

Prices – The monthly average price for sorghum grain received by U.S. farmers in the 2015-16 marketing year (Sep-Aug) fell by -9.3% yr/yr to $6.29 per hundred pounds (annualized through December 2015). The value of U.S. grain sorghum production in the 2014-15 (latest data) marketing year fell -2.7% to $1.670 billion.

Supply – World production of sorghum in the 2015-16 marketing year rose +6.5% to 67.608 million metric tons, below the 13-year high of 65.909 million metric tons posted in 2007-08. U.S. grain sorghum production in 2015-16 rose +38.0% yr/yr to 596.751 million bushels. Sorghum acreage harvested in 2015-16 is forecasted to rose +22.7% to 7.851 million acres, above the 2006-07 figure of 4.937 acres which was the smallest sorghum acreage since the late 1930s. Yield in 2015-16 was 76.0 bushels per acre, a new record high.

Demand – World utilization (consumption) of grain sorghum in the 2015-16 marketing year rose +2.1% to 65.719 million metric tons. The biggest consumers are China utilizing 15.2% of the world supply and Mexico utilizing 11.0% of the world supply.

Trade – World exports of sorghum in the 2015-16 marketing year fell -12.7% to 10.720 million metric tons, below last year's record high of 12.273 million metric tons. U.S. exports in 2015-16 fell -7.9% yr/yr to 8.255 million metric tons, accounting for 77.0% of total world exports. Argentina is the world's other major exporter with 1.000 million metric tons of exports in 2015-16, accounting for 9.3% of total world exports. World imports of sorghum in 2015-16 fell -22.4% yr/yr to 9.532 million metric tons. Major world importers are China and Japan.

World Production of Grain Sorghum   In Thousands of Metric Tons

Crop Year	Argentina	Australia	Brazil	Burkina	China	Ethiopia	India	Mali	Mexico	Nigeria	Sudan	United States	World Total
2006-07	2,795	1,283	1,497	1,516	2,183	2,316	7,151	770	5,810	10,500	4,327	7,032	56,964
2007-08	2,937	3,790	1,986	1,507	1,920	2,659	7,926	901	6,200	10,000	4,999	12,636	67,429
2008-09	1,660	2,692	1,935	1,875	1,837	2,619	7,246	1,027	7,067	11,000	3,869	12,087	65,212
2009-10	3,629	1,508	1,624	1,522	1,677	2,971	6,698	1,466	6,250	6,600	4,192	9,693	57,170
2010-11	4,400	1,935	2,314	1,990	2,456	3,960	7,003	1,257	7,385	6,750	2,630	8,775	61,126
2011-12	4,200	2,239	2,222	1,500	2,051	3,951	5,979	1,191	6,425	6,900	4,605	5,410	57,209
2012-13	4,700	2,230	2,102	1,924	2,556	3,604	5,281	1,212	6,174	5,943	4,524	6,293	57,684
2013-14[1]	4,400	1,282	1,890	1,880	2,892	4,114	5,542	820	8,500	6,592	2,249	9,966	61,254
2014-15[2]	3,500	2,104	2,000	1,836	2,885	4,000	5,050	1,300	6,270	6,700	6,281	10,988	63,488
2015-16[3]	3,900	2,200	2,000	1,900	2,900	3,800	5,500	1,300	6,600	6,150	5,500	15,158	67,608

[1] Preliminary.   [2] Estimate.   [3] Forecast.   Source: Foreign Agricultural Service, U.S. Department of Agriculture (FAS-USDA)

Salient Statistics of Grain Sorghum in the United States

Crop Year Beginning Sept. 1	Acreage Planted[4] for All Purposes	Acreage Harvested	Production (1,000 Bushels)	Yield Per Harvested Acre (Bushels)	Price in Cents Per Bushel	Value of Production (Million $)	Acreage Harvested (1,000 Acres)	Production (1,000 Tons)	Yield Per Harvested Acre (Tons)	On Farms Dec. 1	Off Farms Dec. 1	On Farms June 1	Off Farms June 1
	-- 1,000 Acres --									----------- 1,000 Bushels -----------			
2010-11	5,404	4,813	345,625	71.8	502	1,617.9	268	3,370	12.6	30,500	207,168	3,140	76,894
2011-12	5,481	3,929	214,443	54.6	599	1,268.5	224	2,298	10.3	27,850	123,101	4,120	54,405
2012-13	6,259	4,995	247,742	49.6	633	1,606.2	353	4,196	11.9	17,600	122,247	2,710	38,398
2013-14[1]	8,076	6,585	392,331	59.6	428	1,716.9	380	5,420	14.3	32,950	198,441	4,500	87,924
2014-15[2]	7,138	6,401	432,575	67.6	400	1,721.3	315	4,123	13.1	30,500	192,094	2,960	31,329
2015-16[3]	8,459	7,851	596,751	76.0	365-435	2,080.6	306	4,475	14.6	51,500	262,628		

[1] Preliminary.   [2] Estimate.   [3] Forecast.   Source: Foreign Agricultural Service, U.S. Department of Agriculture (FAS-USDA)

Production of All Sorghum for Grain in the United States, by States   In Thousands of Bushels

Year	Arkansas	Colorado	Illinois	Kansas	Louis-iana	Miss-issippi	Missouri	Nebraska	New Mexico	Okla-homa	South Dakota	Texas	Total
2010	2,695	7,520	3,168	171,000	7,410	650	2,574	6,750	4,488	13,000	5,270	119,000	345,625
2011	6,480	4,900	1,820	110,000	10,788	3,700	2,376	6,580	1,344	1,680	6,600	56,350	214,443
2012	11,340	3,000	1,620	81,900	12,300	3,864	3,190	3,540	798	4,940	5,880	112,100	247,742
2013	12,750	5,760	1,880	168,150	12,091	5,828	4,920	9,715	2,312	14,850	22,000	128,800	392,331
2014	16,005	8,400	2,226	199,800	8,928	8,400	7,373	13,120	2,520	17,360	9,450	137,250	432,575
2015[1]	43,120	22,000	3,196	281,600	6,290	9,085	13,160	23,040	4,230	21,320	18,260	149,450	596,751

[1] Preliminary.   Source: National Agricultural Statistics Service, U.S. Department of Agriculture (NASS-USDA)

Quarterly Supply and Disappearance of Grain Sorghum in the United States   In Millions of Bushels

Crop Year Beginning Sept. 1	Beginning Stocks	Pro- duction	Imports[3]	Total Supply	Food & Alcohol	Seed	Feed & Residual	Total	Exports[3]	Total Disap- pearance	Gov't Owned[4]	Privately Owned[5]	Total Stocks
2012-13	23.0	247.7	9.6	280.3	94.3	1.0	93.5	188.8	76.3	265.1	----	----	23.0
Sept.-Nov.	23.0	247.7	1.1	271.8	24.9	0	79.7	104.6	27.3	131.9	----	----	151.0
Dec.-Feb.	139.8	----	.1	139.9	24.9	0	4.3	29.2	19.1	48.4	----	----	108.1
Mar.-May	91.5	----	5.5	97.1	25.4	.5	16.5	42.4	13.6	55.9	----	----	58.5
June-Aug.	41.1	----	2.9	44.0	19.1	.5	-7.0	12.6	16.2	28.9	----	----	23.0
2013-14	15.2	392.3	.1	407.6	69.0	.9	92.6	162.4	211.1	373.5	----	----	15.2
Sept.-Nov.	15.2	392.3	.0	407.5	45.0	0	97.7	142.7	33.4	176.1	----	----	139.8
Dec.-Feb.	231.4	----	.0	231.4	10.0	0	4.2	14.2	41.5	55.7	----	----	91.5
Mar.-May	175.7	----	.0	175.7	11.5	.5	2.6	14.6	68.7	83.3	----	----	41.1
June-Aug.	92.4	----	.1	92.5	2.5	.4	-11.9	-9.0	67.5	58.5	----	----	15.2
2014-15[1]	34.0	432.6	.4	467.0	14.1	1.1	80.4	95.6	352.9	448.6	----	----	34.0
Sept.-Nov.	34.0	432.6	.2	466.8	10.4	0	150.2	160.6	83.6	244.2	----	----	231.4
Dec.-Feb.	222.6	----	.1	222.7	2.9	0	2.6	5.5	97.4	102.9	----	----	175.7
Mar.-May	119.9	----	.0	119.9	.5	.5	-17.1	-16.1	101.6	85.6	----	----	92.4
June-Aug.	34.3	----	.0	34.3	.4	.6	-55.3	-54.4	70.3	15.9	----	----	34.0
2015-16[2]	18.4	596.8	5.0	620.2	99.1	.9	130.0	230.0	325.0	555.0	----	----	31.8
Sept.-Nov.	18.4	596.8	3.6	618.8	22.0	0	169.5	191.5	113.1	304.6	----	----	229.1

[1] Preliminary.   [2] Estimate.   [3] Uncommitted inventory.   [4] Includes quantity under loan and farmer-owned reserve.   *Source: Economic Research Service, U.S. Department of Agriculture (ERS-USDA)*

Average Price of Sorghum Grain, No. 2, Yellow in Kansas City   In Dollars Per Hundred Pounds (Cwt.)

Year	Sept.	Oct.	Nov.	Dec.	Jan.	Feb.	Mar.	Apr.	May	June	July	Aug.	Average
2008-09	8.43	5.92	5.49	5.19	5.67	5.48	5.51	5.76	6.37	6.29	4.66	4.75	5.79
2009-10	4.81	5.49	5.72	6.44	5.81	5.58	5.69	5.64	5.77	5.50	6.03	6.59	5.75
2010-11	8.23	9.10	9.40	9.91	10.62	11.62	11.37	12.64	12.08	12.21	12.27	12.97	11.04
2011-12	11.79	10.90	11.30	10.91	11.27	11.36	11.14	10.61	10.04	9.90	12.96	13.46	11.30
2012-13	12.74	12.65	12.88	12.74	12.74	12.59	12.63	11.38	11.82	11.97	11.00	8.61	11.98
2013-14	8.15	7.57	7.40	7.52	7.62	8.08	8.64	8.89	8.74	7.98	6.79	6.05	7.79
2014-15	5.31	5.67	6.71	7.25	6.93	6.85	8.16	7.92	6.79	7.23	7.76	6.65	6.94
2015-16[1]	6.09	6.31	6.22	6.53									6.29

[1] Preliminary.   *Source: Economic Research Service, U.S. Department of Agriculture (ERS-USDA)*

Exports of Grain Sorghum, by Country of Destination from the United States   In Metric Tons

Year	Canada	Ecuador	Eritrea (Ethiopia)	Israel	Japan	Jordan	Mexico	South Africa	Spain	Sudan	Turkey	World Total
2008-09	4,987	----	28,170	----	313,179	----	2,476,004	41,000	----	268,160	----	3,585,632
2009-10	3,928	----	----	20,681	818,807	----	2,475,084	21,000	----	344,283	----	4,015,978
2010-11	3,704	----	----	134,990	327,689	----	2,364,880	23,039	482,697	191,658	----	3,803,830
2011-12	2,379	----	----	----	127,396	----	1,153,494	20,000	295	108,480	----	1,529,460
2012-13	3,347	----	----	----	220,070	----	1,336,805	38,720	35,500	178,240	813	2,099,421
2013-14[1]	5,368	----	----	----	254,692	----	135,236	27,363	18,910	155,813	----	5,667,392
2014-15[2]	6,053	----	----	----	74,961	----	12,515	10,000	----	179,450	----	9,222,984

[1] Preliminary.   [2] Estimate.   *Source: Economic Research Service, U.S. Department of Agriculture (ERS-USDA)*

Grain Sorghum Price Support Program and Market Prices in the United States

	Price Support Operations								No. 2 Yellow ($ Per Cwt.)			
	Price Support		Aquired by CCC	Owned by CCC at Year End	Basic Loan Rate	Target Price	Findley Loan Rate	Effective Base[3] (Million Acres)	Partici- pation Rate[4] % of Base	Kansas City	Texas High Plains	Los Angeles	Gulf Ports
Year	Quantity	% of Pro- duction											
	Million Cwt.				Dollars Per Bushel								
2007-08	1.8	.7	0	0	3.48	4.59	1.95	11.7	----	8.38	8.49	----	9.81
2008-09	4.5	1.7	0	0	3.48	4.59	1.95	11.5	----	5.79	5.44	----	7.18
2009-10	1.8	.8	0	0	3.48	4.59	1.95	----	----	5.75	5.73	----	7.74
2010-11	.5	.3	0	0	3.48	4.70	1.95	----	----	11.04	10.61	----	11.92
2011-12	.2	.2	0	0	3.48	4.70	1.95	----	----	11.30	10.92	----	12.33
2012-13[1]	.2	.1	0	0	3.48	4.70	1.95	----	----	11.98	----	----	12.66
2013-14[2]	.3	.1	0	0	3.48	4.70	1.95	----	----	7.79	----	----	9.53

[1] Preliminary.   [2] Estimate.   [3] National effective crop acreage base as determined by ASCS.   [4] Percentage of effective base acres enrolled in acreage reduction programs.   5/ Beginning with the 1996-7 marketing year, target prices are no longer applicable.   *Source: Economic Research Service, U.S. Department of Agriculture (ERS-USDA)*

Hay

Hay is a catchall term for forage plants, typically grasses such as timothy and Sudan-grass, and legumes such as alfalfa and clover. Alfalfa and alfalfa mixtures account for nearly half of all hay production. Hay is generally used to make cured feed for livestock. Curing, which is the proper drying of hay, is necessary to prevent spoilage. Hay, when properly cured, contains about 20% moisture. If hay is dried excessively, however, there is a loss of protein, which makes it less effective as livestock feed. Hay is harvested in virtually all of the lower 48 states.

Prices – The average monthly price of hay received by U.S. farmers in the first eight months of the 2015-16 marketing year (May/April) through December 2015 fell by -11.9% yr/yr to $151.63 per ton, down from the record high of $189.67 per ton seen in 2012-13. The farm production value of hay produced in 2014-15 (latest data) was $19.185 million.

Supply – U.S. hay production in 2015-16 fell -4.0% yr/yr to 134.388 million tons. U.S. farmers harvested 54.437 million acres of hay in 2015-16, down -4.6% yr/yr. The yield in 2015-16 was 2.47 tons per acre, below the 2004-05 record high of 2.55. U.S. carryover (May 1) in 2015-16 rose +27.9% to 24.517 million tons.

The largest hay producing states in the U.S. for 2015 were Texas, (with 7.2% of U.S. hay production), California (5.0%), South Dakota (4.9%), Missouri (4.8%), Nebraska (4.7%), Oklahoma (4.4%), and North Dakota (3.7%).

Salient Statistics of All Hay in the United States

Crop Year Beginning May 1	Acres Harvested (1,000 Acres)	Yield Per Acre (Tons)	Production	Carry-over May 1	Disappearance	Supply	Disappearance	Animal Units Fed[3] (Millions)	Farm Price ($ Per Ton)	Farm Production Value Million $	Alfalfa (Certified)	Timothy	Red Clover	Sudan-grass
			Millions of Tons			Per Animal Unit In Tons					Retail Price Paid by Farmers for Seed, April 15 Dollars Per Cwt.			
2010-11	59,872	2.43	145.6	20.9	143.9	2.40	2.08	69.3	116.1	14,656	379.00	135.00	213.00	73.60
2011-12	55,633	2.36	131.1	22.2		2.26	1.95	67.9	176.7	18,251				
2012-13	54,653	2.14	117.1	21.4		2.10	1.89	67.2	189.7	18,613				
2013-14	57,897	2.33	135.0	14.2		2.24		67.1	177.9	19,815				
2014-15[1]	57,062	2.45	139.9	19.2					171.8	19,099				
2015-16[2]	54,437	2.47	134.4	24.5					148.6	16,840				

[1] Preliminary. [2] Estimate. [3] Roughage-consuming animal units fed annually. NA = Not available.
Source: Economic Research Service, U.S. Department of Agriculture (ERS-USDA)

Production of All Hay in the United States, by States In Thousands of Tons

Year	California	Idaho	Iowa	Minnesota	Missouri	New York	North Dakota	Ohio	Oklahoma	South Dakota	Texas	Wisconsin	Total
2010	8,304	5,460	3,760	5,400	7,512	6,349	5,321	2,871	5,953	7,335	10,800	4,526	145,624
2011	7,980	5,070	3,460	5,530	6,250	5,624	5,224	2,772	2,330	8,625	4,440	4,075	131,144
2012	8,130	4,730	2,780	3,995	5,580	4,457	3,156	2,214	3,880	3,740	9,460	3,350	117,072
2013	7,646	4,976	3,377	3,895	7,921	4,935	5,090	2,495	4,981	5,905	8,880	3,760	135,002
2014	7,513	4,881	3,675	4,486	7,100	6,028	5,460	2,710	6,121	6,665	11,746	4,866	139,923
2015[1]	6,777	4,860	3,939	3,979	6,398	6,360	4,975	2,532	5,914	6,580	9,720	4,073	134,388

[1] Preliminary. *Source: Agricultural Statistics Board, U.S. Department of Agriculture (ASB-USDA)*

Hay Production and Farm Stocks in the United States In Thousands of Short Tons

Year	Production: Alfalfa & Mixtures	All Others	All Hay	Corn for Silage[1]	Sorghum Silage[1]	Farm Stocks: May 1	Dec. 1
2010	67,971	77,653	145,624	107,314	3,370	20,931	102,134
2011	65,332	65,812	131,144	108,926	2,298	22,217	90,726
2012	50,600	66,472	117,072	116,148	4,196	21,381	76,547
2013	57,217	77,785	135,002	118,296	5,420	14,156	89,304
2014	61,451	78,472	139,923	128,048	4,123	19,176	92,052
2015[2]	58,974	75,414	134,388	126,894	4,475	24,517	94,993

[1] Not included in all tame hay. [2] Preliminary. *Source: Agricultural Statistics Board, U.S. Department of Agriculture (ASB-USDA)*

Mid-Month Price Received by Farmers for All Hay (Baled) in the United States In Dollars Per Ton

Year	May	June	July	Aug.	Sept.	Oct.	Nov.	Dec.	Jan.	Feb.	Mar.	Apr.	Average
2010-11	116.0	114.0	112.0	110.0	112.0	111.0	110.0	111.0	112.0	116.0	126.0	143.0	116.1
2011-12	171.0	163.0	170.0	179.0	180.0	185.0	174.0	174.0	172.0	177.0	183.0	192.0	176.7
2012-13	201.0	183.0	184.0	183.0	185.0	191.0	190.0	189.0	188.0	192.0	195.0	195.0	189.7
2013-14	203.0	199.0	190.0	177.0	174.0	174.0	168.0	163.0	162.0	167.0	170.0	188.0	177.9
2014-15	202.0	197.0	185.0	181.0	172.0	171.0	162.0	156.0	149.0	153.0	160.0	173.0	171.8
2015-16[1]	175.0	162.0	156.0	145.0	145.0	146.0	142.0	142.0	137.0	136.0			148.6

[1] Preliminary. [2] Marketing year average. *Source: Economic Research Service, U.S. Department of Agriculture (ERS-USDA)*

Heating Oil

Heating oil is a heavy fuel oil that is derived from crude oil. Heating oil is also known as No. 2 fuel oil and accounts for about 25% of the yield from a barrel of crude oil. That is the second largest "cut" after gasoline. The price to consumers of home heating oil is generally comprised of 42% for crude oil, 12% for refining costs, and 46% for marketing and distribution costs (Source: EIA's Petroleum Marketing Monthly, 2001). Generally, a $1 increase in the price of crude oil translates into a 2.5-cent per gallon rise in heating oil. Because of this, heating oil prices are highly correlated with crude oil prices, although heating oil prices are also subject to swift supply and demand shifts due to weather changes or refinery shutdowns.

The primary use for heating oil is for residential heating. In the U.S., approximately 8.1 million households use heating oil as their main heating fuel. Most of the demand for heating oil occurs from October through March. The Northeast region, which includes the New England and the Central Atlantic States, is most reliant on heating oil. This region consumes approximately 70% of U.S. heating oil. However, demand for heating oil has been dropping as households switch to a more convenient heating source like natural gas. In fact, demand for heating oil is down by about 10 billion gallons/year from its peak use in 1976 (Source: American Petroleum Institute).

Refineries produce approximately 85% of U.S. heating oil as part of the "distillate fuel oil" product family, which includes heating oil and diesel fuel. The remainder of U.S. heating oil is imported from Canada, the Virgin Islands, and Venezuela.

Recently, a team of Purdue University researchers developed a way to make home heating oil from a mixture of soybean oil and conventional fuel oil. The oil blend is made by replacing 20% of the fuel oil with soybean oil, potentially saving 1.3 billion gallons of fuel oil per year. This soybean heating oil can be used in conventional furnaces without altering existing equipment. The soybean heating oil is relatively easy to produce and creates no sulfur emissions.

The "crack-spread" is the processing margin earned when refiners buy crude oil and refine it into heating oil and gasoline. The crack-spread ratio commonly used in the industry is the 3-2-1, which involves buying 1 heating oil contract and 2 gasoline futures contracts, and then selling 3 crude oil contracts. As long as the crack spread is positive, it is profitable for refiners to buy crude oil and refine it into products.

Heating oil futures and options trade at the CME Group. The heating oil futures contract calls for the delivery of 1,000 barrels of fungible No. 2 heating oil in the New York harbor. In London, heating oil and gas/oil futures and options are traded on ICE Futures Europe. Futures are also traded on the Multi Commodity Exchange of India (MCX).

Prices – CME heating oil futures prices (Barchart. com symbol code HO) on the nearest-futures chart traded sideways in early 2015 but then resumed 2014's decline and closed 2015 down -38.7% at $1.1239 per gallon.

Supply – U.S. production of distillate fuel oil in 2015 (through November, annualized) rose by +1.2% yr/yr to 4.970 million barrels per day, a new record high. Stocks of distillate fuel oil in November 2015 were 156.666 million barrels. U.S. production of residual fuel in 2015 (through November, annualized) fell by -4.1% yr/yr to an average of 417,000 barrels per day, which was less than half the production level of over 1 million barrels per day produced in the 1970s. U.S. stocks of residual fuel oil as of January 1, 2015 fell -6.9% to 34.267 million barrels, down from the 2007 record of 42.329 million barrels.

Demand – U.S. usage of distillate fuel oil in 2015 (through November, annualized) fell -15.8% yr/yr to 3.955 million barrels per day, down from the 2005 high of 4.198 million barrels a day.

Trade – U.S. imports of distillate fuel oil in 2015 (through November, annualized) rose +2.2% to an average of 199,000 barrels per day, down from the 2006 record high of 365,000 barrels per day. U.S. exports of distillate fuel oil in 2007 (latest data available) rose by +2.7% yr/yr to a 13-year high average of 221 barrels per day. U.S. imports of residual fuel oil in 2014 (latest data) fell -23.6% yr/yr to 172,000 barrels per day, which was less than a third of the levels of over 1 million barrels per day seen back in the 1970s.

World Production of Distillate Fuel Oil   In Thousands of Barrels Per Day

Year	Brazil	Canada	China	France	Germany	India	Italy	Japan	Korea, South	Russia	Saudi Arabia	United States	World Total
2004	674.6	631.0	2,070.5	708.5	1,015.8	967.2	795.2	1,172.1	591.9	1,129.8	641.8	3,814.3	23,048.4
2005	684.8	618.3	2,267.9	695.8	1,079.9	991.7	818.6	1,182.6	643.7	1,227.1	647.6	3,954.4	23,935.5
2006	663.0	614.9	2,398.9	701.5	1,060.0	1,081.6	804.1	1,130.2	664.9	1,312.3	694.6	4,040.4	24,222.9
2007	673.6	623.6	2,520.2	711.1	1,035.4	1,206.5	838.4	1,119.4	707.6	1,260.1	653.4	4,133.0	24,354.1
2008	705.2	616.6	2,740.6	753.8	1,019.1	1,297.7	817.9	1,135.3	730.9	1,407.8	677.9	4,293.8	25,435.1
2009	731.7	602.3	2,921.9	676.6	969.3	1,507.5	773.6	1,036.1	726.0	1,375.1	623.8	4,048.0	24,931.4
2010	755.1	618.3	3,052.0	616.3	918.1	1,578.6	809.3	1,020.2	744.0	1,431.2	633.4	4,223.3	25,387.4
2011	785.1	604.3	3,208.5	626.9	911.4	1,691.8	776.6	961.5	810.6	1,437.7	628.5	4,492.1	25,999.2
2012[1]	829.8	627.2	3,464.9	533.7	937.9	1,869.8	737.6	924.7	854.3	1,420.2	641.4	4,549.9	26,621.0
2013[2]		612.8		524.1	921.1		658.3	978.8	822.4			4,732.9	

[1] Preliminary.   [2] Estimate.   *Source: Energy Information Administration, U.S. Department of Energy (EIA-DOE)*

HEATING OIL

World Imports of Distillate Fuel Oil In Thousands of Barrels Per Day

Year	Australia	Belgium	France	Germany	Indonesia	Nether-lands	Singa-pore	Spain	Turkey	United Kingdom	United States	Vietnam	World Total
2004	63.0	164.7	322.3	265.8	130.1	203.0	112.5	230.1	77.8	81.8	325.5	111.6	4,268.5
2005	81.7	198.1	380.7	277.6	170.2	196.2	78.9	263.4	84.7	98.6	328.8	120.4	4,499.6
2006	105.7	166.1	317.3	332.0	176.1	278.0	125.2	264.9	130.9	158.3	364.7	110.8	4,906.3
2007	105.2	148.9	271.6	187.8	229.7	188.4	127.0	286.6	162.3	159.0	304.1	132.5	5,090.9
2008	147.8	156.4	292.1	317.2	211.6	250.9	178.6	246.3	169.8	152.6	212.9	132.6	5,466.6
2009	144.0	124.6	380.2	297.0	146.7	333.5	155.0	234.1	186.2	127.5	225.1	132.9	5,485.7
2010	141.7	111.8	414.0	318.9	259.0	385.2	393.5	220.7	197.9	193.0	228.4	100.5	6,318.7
2011	176.6	161.7	408.0	278.9	244.3	375.1	383.0	174.1	207.5	191.4	178.7	108.5	6,444.8
2012[1]	202.0	128.3	469.9	276.1	290.2	384.2	279.2	136.4	226.1	218.6	126.2	113.6	6,523.9
2013[2]	226.8	246.5	478.1	322.7		378.6		95.2	245.5	217.2	154.7		

[1] Preliminary.   [2] Estimate.   *Source: Energy Information Administration, U.S. Department of Energy (EIA-DOE)*

World Exports of Distillate Fuel Oil In Thousands of Barrels Per Day

Year	Belgium	Germany	India	Italy	Japan	Korea, South	Kuwait	Nether-lands	Russia	Singa-pore	Taiwan	United States	World Total
2004	167.0	166.1	148.5	187.3	29.4	185.8	225.3	411.2	614.3	294.0	119.9	109.6	4,692.3
2005	182.3	204.4	173.0	179.8	64.1	234.3	221.2	430.4	649.2	300.0	149.2	138.4	5,038.9
2006	162.1	223.0	238.0	160.2	70.5	250.6	185.5	495.9	752.6	341.3	150.0	215.1	5,394.9
2007	177.9	250.6	292.4	183.5	137.2	281.9	194.0	420.4	751.9	359.3	176.5	267.7	5,268.0
2008	171.7	203.2	300.2	170.2	220.5	357.6	190.2	464.7	767.8	406.8	181.1	528.3	5,830.8
2009	140.2	181.8	377.3	168.2	215.7	343.6	152.8	562.3	812.9	346.3	206.6	587.4	6,153.4
2010	142.4	138.8	376.5	189.1	197.4	358.0	143.8	636.1	851.0	540.0	177.2	656.0	6,209.9
2011	156.2	132.2	430.5	153.6	160.0	436.8	143.8	631.1	807.8	553.7	157.5	854.1	6,404.8
2012[1]	160.7	128.9	459.1	178.8	120.2	481.8	153.0	608.5	840.9	469.8	191.7	1,007.2	6,781.3
2013[2]	226.4	135.0		142.8	167.6	446.6		604.1				1,133.9	

[1] Preliminary.   [2] Estimate.   *Source: Energy Information Administration, U.S. Department of Energy (EIA-DOE)*

Production of Distillate Fuel Oil in the United States In Thousand Barrels per Day

Year	Jan.	Feb.	Mar.	Apr.	May	June	July	Aug.	Sept.	Oct.	Nov.	Dec.	Average
2006	3,840.2	3,940.9	3,735.9	3,832.7	4,104.8	4,107.4	4,064.9	4,233.9	4,300.1	4,090.5	4,069.8	4,158.8	4,040.0
2007	4,026.7	3,883.3	4,008.8	4,102.2	4,142.3	4,049.5	4,145.3	4,244.2	4,158.1	4,208.0	4,278.2	4,326.5	4,131.1
2008	4,129.8	3,979.7	3,952.6	4,287.4	4,459.1	4,587.5	4,523.2	4,465.6	3,681.5	4,435.1	4,488.6	4,511.3	4,291.8
2009	4,283.5	4,231.3	3,938.7	4,131.8	4,092.9	4,047.5	3,928.9	3,964.8	4,098.8	3,983.6	4,018.5	3,877.2	4,049.8
2010	3,551.3	3,658.1	3,835.0	4,156.5	4,374.8	4,407.8	4,424.7	4,403.9	4,341.4	4,315.3	4,502.9	4,669.7	4,220.1
2011	4,303.3	4,033.2	4,326.0	4,188.8	4,283.3	4,470.8	4,656.4	4,667.7	4,576.5	4,538.7	4,902.4	4,918.8	4,488.8
2012	4,500.4	4,407.7	4,262.8	4,351.7	4,547.3	4,631.8	4,660.1	4,599.7	4,565.5	4,509.8	4,668.8	4,884.4	4,549.2
2013	4,479.8	4,280.5	4,283.8	4,416.4	4,767.1	4,791.5	4,933.8	4,930.0	4,888.4	4,814.8	5,049.7	5,121.6	4,729.8
2014	4,685.3	4,594.5	4,779.7	4,987.9	5,026.1	4,896.0	5,021.2	5,042.5	4,939.8	4,662.0	5,011.6	5,322.9	4,914.1
2015[1]	4,827.9	4,745.7	4,882.3	4,980.7	4,974.0	5,020.8	5,091.0	5,107.5	5,053.2	4,815.1	5,143.5	5,010.0	4,971.0

[1] Preliminary.   *Source: Energy Information Administration; U.S. Department of Energy (EIA-DOE)*

Stocks of Distillate Fuel in the United States, on First of Month In Thousands of Barrels

Year	Jan.	Feb.	Mar.	Apr.	May	June	July	Aug.	Sept.	Oct.	Nov.	Dec.
2006	139,426	135,635	120,544	116,491	123,952	129,912	137,506	145,083	149,308	142,843	140,626	143,651
2007	139,608	123,723	120,007	121,311	125,083	123,800	130,297	134,569	134,236	134,431	134,800	133,944
2008	130,963	117,636	107,784	107,051	113,941	121,710	130,906	132,973	127,679	127,595	135,876	146,013
2009	143,730	148,105	145,301	150,058	156,706	162,723	165,940	168,649	172,731	171,164	171,125	165,964
2010	163,527	155,333	146,817	144,802	150,041	157,944	166,628	170,334	166,735	161,510	161,991	164,306
2011	163,086	154,077	149,239	142,919	144,847	143,870	154,455	155,064	153,399	142,327	143,857	149,212
2012	147,210	139,289	133,697	124,665	121,445	119,890	126,454	127,309	127,384	118,653	117,993	134,809
2013	131,268	121,963	118,737	118,791	122,132	122,463	126,020	129,060	129,326	118,035	121,118	127,543
2014	114,534	112,897	115,337	116,827	121,757	121,674	125,559	128,132	131,289	120,093	126,085	136,065
2015[1]	131,992	123,137	128,294	129,022	134,028	139,437	142,144	152,145	148,846	143,317	156,666	160,741

[1] Preliminary.   *Source: Energy Information Administration; U.S. Department of Energy (EIA-DOE)*

Imports of Distillate Fuel Oil in the United States   In Thousand of Barrels per Day

Year	Jan.	Feb.	Mar.	Apr.	May	June	July	Aug.	Sept.	Oct.	Nov.	Dec.	Average
2006	552	388	292	297	437	297	361	363	438	307	288	355	365
2007	352	334	360	323	274	273	335	354	270	288	245	241	304
2008	309	249	249	266	188	180	181	109	195	166	203	262	213
2009	368	327	269	166	206	245	191	166	205	177	164	224	225
2010	462	293	179	220	189	237	170	246	189	163	178	219	229
2011	337	206	190	191	170	127	157	148	179	128	138	175	179
2012	157	142	137	98	113	87	117	112	86	88	188	190	126
2013	213	174	146	238	168	121	107	123	132	128	145	164	155
2014	283	337	324	181	198	121	129	143	126	120	136	245	195
2015[1]	349	391	324	234	191	132	143	140	103	101	150	137	200

[1] Preliminary.   *Source: Energy Information Administration, U.S. Department of Energy (EIA-DOE)*

Disposition of Distillate Fuel Oil, Total Product Supplied in the United States   In Thousand of Barrels per Day

Year	Jan.	Feb.	Mar.	Apr.	May	June	July	Aug.	Sept.	Oct.	Nov.	Dec.	Average
2006	4,159.2	4,307.9	4,394.6	4,065.0	4,072.3	4,019.3	3,949.5	4,162.4	4,141.3	4,315.2	4,179.9	4,267.6	4,169.5
2007	4,256.2	4,582.1	4,333.7	4,214.0	4,068.0	4,114.3	4,026.2	4,145.7	4,160.6	4,212.9	4,074.3	4,193.1	4,198.4
2008	4,192.2	4,281.3	4,160.9	4,105.6	3,930.8	3,762.7	3,688.1	3,659.1	3,739.9	4,181.8	3,871.6	3,783.1	3,946.4
2009	4,078.6	3,863.6	3,743.6	3,455.0	3,436.3	3,513.0	3,394.6	3,426.2	3,560.3	3,654.1	3,595.8	3,861.5	3,631.9
2010	3,700.5	3,854.5	3,834.6	3,758.6	3,638.6	3,742.7	3,544.0	3,829.5	3,886.2	3,772.9	3,873.3	4,175.5	3,800.9
2011	3,958.0	3,913.5	4,045.1	3,754.5	3,699.4	3,947.4	3,563.7	4,008.9	3,936.0	4,003.4	4,109.4	3,853.2	3,899.4
2012	3,860.9	3,922.9	3,714.8	3,718.9	3,756.3	3,732.5	3,556.6	3,743.0	3,674.3	3,852.4	3,847.6	3,528.8	3,742.4
2013	4,061.8	3,984.4	3,769.1	3,854.4	3,749.0	3,662.9	3,621.0	3,693.2	3,724.6	4,038.8	3,893.2	3,886.8	3,828.3
2014	4,340.0	4,160.3	4,066.2	3,989.8	3,951.6	3,901.6	3,866.7	3,874.5	3,933.4	4,266.3	3,917.2	4,178.2	4,037.1
2015[1]	4,235.1	4,535.5	4,054.4	3,998.3	3,792.8	3,854.3	3,877.5	3,888.3	4,015.5	3,992.6	3,702.7	3,519.0	3,955.5

[1] Preliminary.   *Source: Energy Information Administration, U.S. Department of Energy (EIA-DOE)*

World Production of Residual Fuel Oil   In Thousands of Barrels Per Day

Year	Brazil	China	India	Iran	Italy	Japan	Korea, South	Mexico	Russia	Saudi Arabia	United States	Venezuela	World Total
2004	323.4	461.7	407.8	470.2	308.9	576.1	544.4	369.7	1,114.1	472.1	655.5	278.0	11,304.0
2005	335.5	403.1	407.4	480.2	330.5	576.6	571.2	352.2	1,193.3	487.6	627.6	265.7	11,506.2
2006	332.0	408.1	408.7	480.8	306.5	552.9	560.8	325.9	1,238.1	495.9	635.3	279.1	11,336.4
2007	265.2	358.9	459.9	459.2	307.0	526.0	496.5	302.1	1,235.1	477.8	672.7	267.3	10,745.3
2008	298.7	317.0	322.7	486.4	259.0	512.8	405.4	289.3	1,260.9	477.8	619.9	280.2	10,323.7
2009	289.3	351.1	375.0	478.6	233.0	423.2	336.6	316.8	1,332.1	497.6	598.2	312.5	10,102.5
2010	256.0	385.9	368.0	480.5	197.4	388.1	341.2	322.9	1,435.7	445.4	598.2	312.5	9,855.0
2011	241.0	321.2	347.9	484.2	159.8	398.4	336.6	308.0	1,412.1	416.9	584.9	272.6	9,540.2
2012[1]	248.3	284.7	274.7	502.6	172.7	461.2	281.3	273.9	1,439.8	461.3	537.4	300.2	9,392.2
2013[2]					109.4	382.7	215.6	269.4			500.6	283.7	

[1] Preliminary.   [2] Estimate.   *Source: Energy Information Administration, U.S. Department of Energy (EIA-DOE)*

Supply and Disposition of Residual Fuel Oil in the United States

	Supply		Disposition				Ending Stocks (Million Barrels)	Average Sales to End Users[3] (Cents per Gallon)
Year	Total Production	Imports	Stock Change	Exports	Product Supplied			
	In Tousands of Barrels Per Day							
2005	628	530	-14	251	920		37	104.8
2006	635	350	14	283	689		42	121.8
2007	673	372	-13	309	723		39	137.4
2008	620	349	NA	NA	622		36	196.4
2009	598	331	NA	NA	511		37	134.1
2010	585	366	----	----	535		41	171.3
2011	537	328	----	----	461		34	240.1
2012	501	256	----	----	369		34	259.2
2013	467	225	----	----	319		38	248.2
2014[1]	436	172	----	----	257		34	232.5

[1] Preliminary.   [2] Less than +500 barrels per day and greater than -500 barrels per day.   [3] Refiner price excluding taxes.
Source: Energy Information Administration, U.S. Department of Energy (EIA-DOE)

HEATING OIL

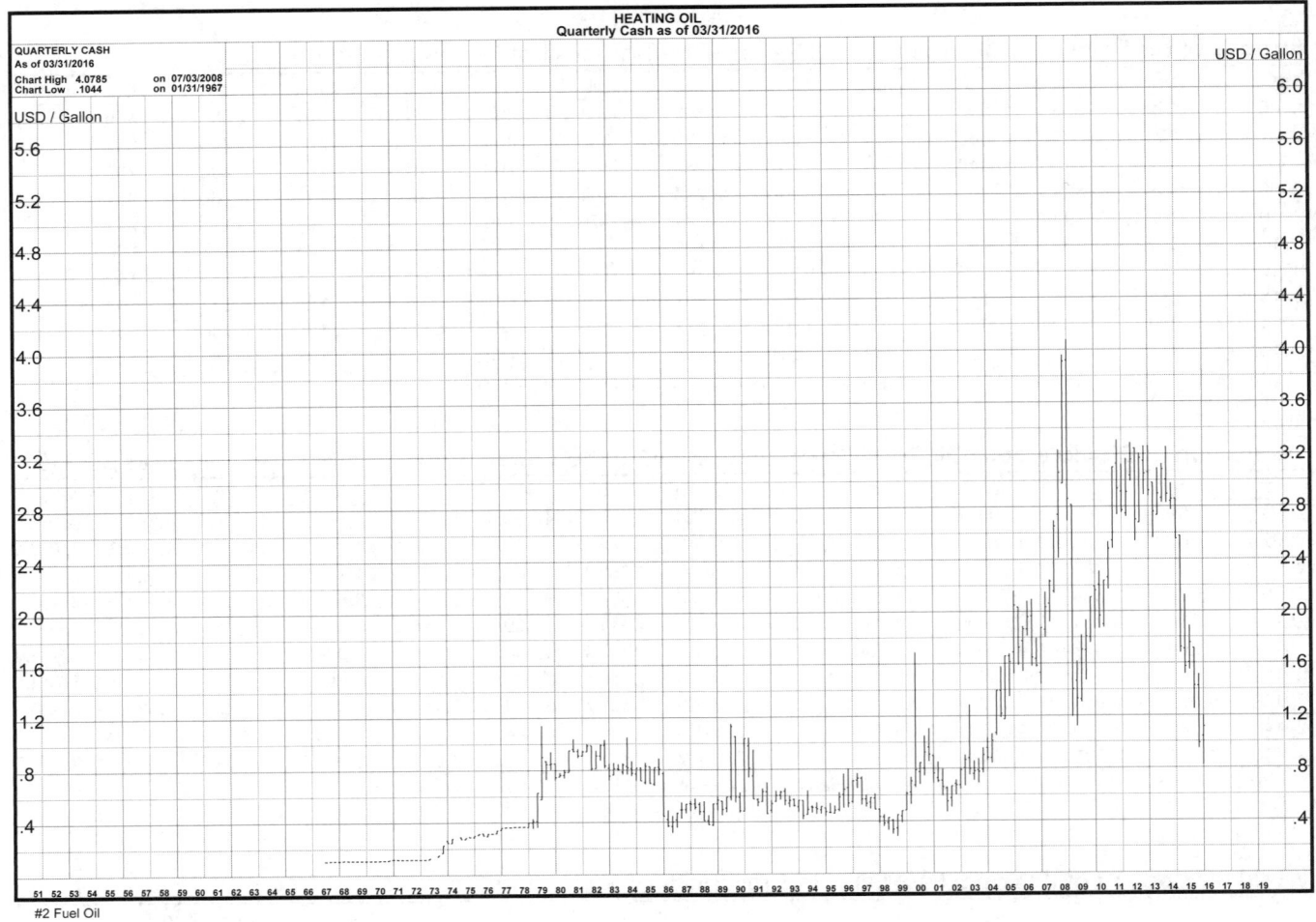

QUARTERLY CASH
As of 03/31/2016
Chart High 4.0785   on 07/03/2008
Chart Low   .1044   on 01/31/1967

USD / Gallon

USD / Gallon

#2 Fuel Oil

Production of Residual Fuel Oil in the United States   In Thousands of Barrels per Day

Year	Jan.	Feb.	Mar.	Apr.	May	June	July	Aug.	Sept.	Oct.	Nov.	Dec.	Average
2006	670.4	635.0	643.5	643.4	580.4	645.2	657.9	651.9	619.0	596.6	624.4	655.7	635.3
2007	667.0	649.5	655.5	657.9	647.4	627.9	708.0	697.7	698.4	689.4	694.3	676.3	672.4
2008	588.4	642.8	661.7	709.7	734.4	694.5	584.4	578.6	485.4	574.7	587.6	597.5	620.0
2009	584.6	571.3	583.1	474.9	604.9	613.1	586.0	631.1	604.5	671.6	624.4	623.7	597.8
2010	633.1	631.8	581.3	597.5	615.0	558.9	575.8	553.6	588.3	528.4	563.7	595.2	585.2
2011	552.5	529.4	525.7	534.3	538.2	553.5	562.6	604.0	516.1	529.8	515.7	485.9	537.3
2012	499.8	547.8	577.3	524.9	508.6	538.2	486.0	495.1	507.7	480.5	457.5	387.7	500.9
2013	395.4	504.1	569.4	508.2	488.1	469.0	481.4	416.9	433.8	420.3	466.2	454.8	467.3
2014	476.3	427.5	460.8	420.4	454.3	454.7	402.1	438.7	409.8	415.6	462.0	401.2	435.3
2015[1]	376.7	421.4	478.3	468.5	435.5	413.3	426.1	403.7	414.2	419.3	386.2	364.0	417.3

[1] Preliminary.   Source: Energy Information Administration, U.S. Department of Energy (EIA-DOE)

Average Price of Heating Oil #2   In Dollars Per Gallon

Year	Jan.	Feb.	Mar.	Apr.	May	June	July	Aug.	Sept.	Oct.	Nov.	Dec.	Average
2006	1.7499	1.6368	1.7770	1.9827	1.9717	1.9176	1.9230	1.9825	1.6917	1.5453	1.6500	1.6785	1.7922
2007	1.5199	1.6948	1.7405	1.8630	1.8847	2.0031	2.0699	1.9836	2.1806	2.2832	2.5879	2.5754	2.0322
2008	2.5564	2.6417	3.0680	3.2296	3.6164	3.7999	3.7567	3.1716	2.9076	2.2244	1.8515	1.3893	2.8511
2009	1.4643	1.2778	1.2830	1.3595	1.4787	1.7472	1.6318	1.8659	1.7305	1.9334	1.9848	1.9722	1.6441
2010	2.0523	1.9752	2.0847	2.2126	2.0378	2.0344	1.9775	2.0224	2.0948	2.2423	2.3174	2.4643	2.1263
2011	2.6035	2.7638	3.0339	3.1956	2.9514	2.9651	3.0692	2.9427	2.9199	2.9500	3.0524	2.8875	2.9446
2012	3.0452	3.1941	3.2146	3.1472	2.9123	2.6201	2.8200	3.0459	3.1295	3.1383	3.0107	2.9591	3.0198
2013	3.0720	3.1669	2.9468	2.7278	2.6882	2.7424	2.8863	2.9581	2.9613	2.9422	2.9228	3.0325	2.9206
2014	3.0633	3.0656	2.9124	2.8878	2.8603	2.8822	2.7758	2.7535	2.6332	2.4237	2.2493	1.8555	2.6969
2015	1.6163	1.8727	1.6315	1.7404	1.8317	1.7680	1.5505	1.3875	1.4311	1.4042	1.3198	1.0392	1.5494

Source: Energy Information Administration, U.S. Department of Energy (EIA-DOE)

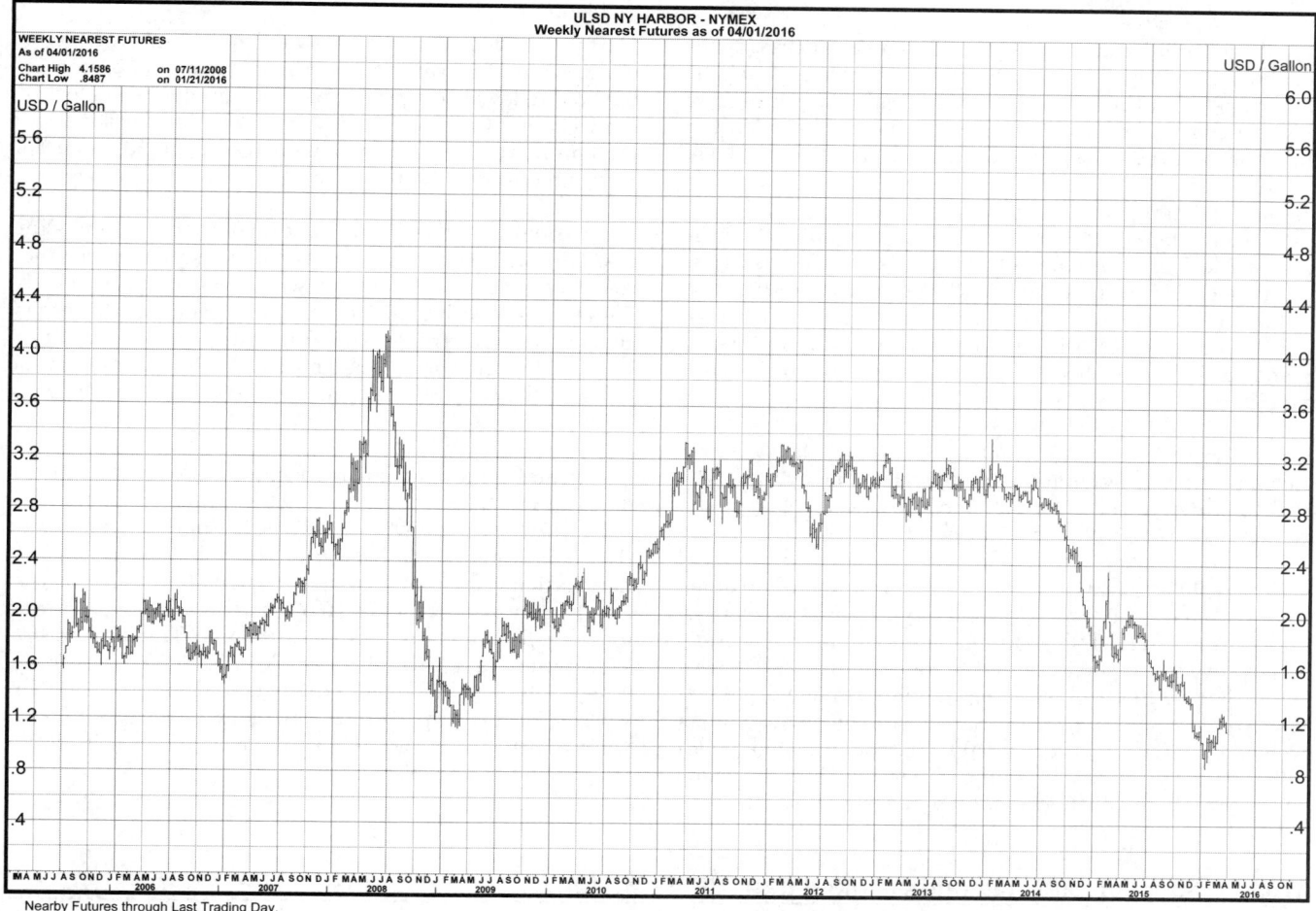

ULSD NY HARBOR - NYMEX
Weekly Nearest Futures as of 04/01/2016

WEEKLY NEAREST FUTURES
As of 04/01/2016

Chart High 4.1586   on 07/11/2008
Chart Low   .8487   on 01/21/2016

USD / Gallon

Nearby Futures through Last Trading Day.

Volume of Trading of Heating Oil #2 Futures in New York   In Thousands of Contracts

Year	Jan.	Feb.	Mar.	Apr.	May	June	July	Aug.	Sept.	Oct.	Nov.	Dec.	Total
2006	1,157.5	1,131.2	1,121.7	974.8	1,185.1	1,114.0	1,027.1	1,166.1	1,235.9	1,291.1	1,228.6	1,357.5	13,990.6
2007	1,655.6	1,507.5	1,370.3	1,326.0	1,462.2	1,605.8	1,478.9	1,579.8	1,394.7	1,687.2	1,544.1	1,467.0	18,079.0
2008	1,611.7	1,726.3	1,763.3	1,639.2	1,825.3	1,651.9	1,571.3	1,641.9	1,578.0	1,646.4	1,297.3	1,630.4	19,583.1
2009	1,789.0	1,512.9	1,670.1	1,633.3	1,644.5	1,809.7	2,004.2	1,652.6	1,777.3	1,975.9	1,921.9	2,035.1	21,426.5
2010	2,096.3	1,872.5	2,230.6	2,459.2	2,493.3	2,305.2	1,963.7	2,409.5	2,548.9	2,230.9	2,165.8	2,194.1	26,970.1
2011	2,545.9	2,600.7	2,805.0	2,206.5	2,645.6	2,624.9	2,022.6	2,843.7	2,889.1	2,964.2	3,071.0	2,619.4	31,838.6
2012	3,149.6	3,203.3	2,953.3	2,693.2	2,913.9	3,172.8	2,875.1	3,071.6	2,812.8	3,887.9	2,913.4	2,440.8	36,087.7
2013	3,122.0	2,801.6	2,900.0	3,057.7	2,852.8	2,540.0	2,700.0	2,490.4	2,384.5	2,932.3	2,608.5	2,359.7	32,749.6
2014	3,400.6	2,893.3	2,533.8	2,209.6	2,253.3	2,483.3	2,857.3	2,719.9	2,875.9	3,409.5	3,126.2	3,183.6	33,946.4
2015	3,247.1	3,451.1	3,022.4	2,733.6	2,616.5	2,981.7	3,024.6	3,254.2	2,906.7	3,473.0	2,765.9	3,470.1	36,947.0

Contract size = 42,000 US gallons.   *Source: CME Group; New York Mercantile Exchange (NYMEX)*

Average Open Interest of Heating Oil #2 Futures in New York   In Contracts

Year	Jan.	Feb.	Mar.	Apr.	May	June	July	Aug.	Sept.	Oct.	Nov.	Dec.
2006	170,094	165,627	168,415	170,955	171,732	169,123	179,773	185,648	208,848	221,942	228,152	216,033
2007	219,690	219,715	209,805	208,829	210,128	224,289	239,109	218,913	235,403	232,165	224,475	209,578
2008	202,976	220,716	230,646	227,140	224,480	218,004	223,645	221,733	212,561	212,981	224,465	224,359
2009	237,894	252,753	261,552	259,008	260,646	283,068	294,270	308,022	311,296	312,653	322,505	309,113
2010	317,506	306,607	319,389	310,085	311,994	313,624	304,866	305,549	325,342	327,588	319,732	308,661
2011	306,262	312,145	305,872	310,288	310,053	316,026	306,360	307,607	323,485	303,460	291,931	274,679
2012	273,761	299,758	286,319	296,190	314,645	323,256	313,376	320,011	332,853	316,594	303,742	280,933
2013	297,517	316,763	297,280	304,306	307,574	291,583	287,422	290,885	284,372	280,863	298,480	292,422
2014	281,102	294,144	280,719	263,461	269,766	285,931	313,266	353,133	373,004	390,505	391,923	355,367
2015	375,870	384,974	375,278	361,933	360,017	362,447	388,442	425,342	399,488	382,414	367,273	348,763

Contract size = 42,000 US gallons.   *Source: CME Group; New York Mercantile Exchange (NYMEX)*

Hides and Leather

Hides and leather have been used since ancient times for boots, clothing, shields, armor, tents, bottles, buckets, and cups. Leather is produced through the tanning of hides, pelts, and skins of animals. The remains of leather have been found in the Middle East dating back at least 7,000 years.

Today, most leather is made of cowhide but it is also made from the hides of lamb, deer, ostrich, snakes, crocodiles, and even stingray. Cattle hides are the most valuable byproduct of the meat packing industry. U.S. exports of cowhides bring more than $1 billion in foreign trade, and U.S. finished leather production is worth about $4 billion.

Prices – The average monthly price of wholesale cattle hides (packer heavy native steers FOB Chicago) in 2015 fell -21.7% yr/yr to 86.29 cents per pound, below last year's record high of 110.19 cents per pound.

Supply – World production of cattle and buffalo hides in 2013 (latest data) rose by +1.4% yr/yr to 9.078, down from 2009's record high of 9.135 million metric tons. The world's largest producers of cattle and buffalo hides in 2013 were the U.S. with 12.4% of world production, Brazil with 9.9%, and Argentina with 4.2%. U.S. new supply of cattle hides from domestic slaughter in 2009 (latest data available) fell 3.0% yr/yr to 33.338 million hides, which is far below the record high of 43.582 million hides posted in 1976.

U.S. production of leather footwear has been dropping off sharply in recent years due to the movement of production offshore to lower cost producers. U.S. production of leather footwear in 2003 (latest data available) fell -46% yr/yr to 22.3 million pairs and was a mere 4% of the 562.3 million pairs produced in 1970.

Demand – World consumption of cowhides and skins in 2000, the last reporting year for the series, rose +1.4% to 4,774 metric tons, which was a record high for the data series, which goes back to 1984. The world's largest consumers of cowhides and skins in 2000 were the U.S. with 13.0% of world consumption, Italy (10.6%), Brazil (8.9%), Mexico, (6.0%), Argentina (6.0%), and South Korea (5.9%).

Trade – U.S. net exports of cattle hides in 2013 (latest data) rose +34.9% yr/yr to 25.898 million hides, a new record high. The total value of U.S. leather exports in 2004 (latest data) rose +16.8% yr/yr to $1.344 billion. The largest destinations for U.S. exports in 2013 (latest data) were South Korea (which took 16.0% of U.S. exports), Taiwan (6.7%), Mexico (5.4%), Italy (1.5%), and Thailand (1.1%). World imports of cowhides and skins in 2000 (latest data) rose +2.8% yr/yr to a record high of 2,058 metric tons. The world's largest importers of cowhides and skins in 2000 were South Korea (with 13% of world imports in 2000), Italy (11%) and Taiwan (7%).

World Production of Cattle and Buffalo Hides   In Metric Tons

Year	Argentina	Australia	Brazil	Canada	Colom-bia	France	Germany	Italy	Mexico	Russia	United Kingdom	United States	World Total
2004	428,874	243,000	792,000	110,960	79,860	149,877	144,900	128,386	191,300	222,740	66,000	1,009,394	8,300,257
2005	427,551	245,000	850,000	111,860	85,800	147,563	132,000	125,839	191,700	202,772	67,500	1,015,986	8,401,720
2006	402,565	233,000	886,000	103,875	85,467	142,813	135,000	124,139	196,500	183,154	74,000	1,076,440	8,585,029
2007	448,670	251,550	914,200	95,510	87,604	142,296	132,000	121,558	199,200	180,139	74,500	1,085,784	8,757,386
2008	439,809	239,000	873,500	96,098	93,500	143,148	135,000	115,315	201,900	182,363	73,700	1,104,271	8,801,379
2009	481,591	235,900	856,400	92,630	84,169	144,432	134,500	115,304	206,900	178,557	70,350	1,102,973	8,907,858
2010	356,481	230,000	855,000	93,640	79,721	144,562	134,500	115,450	212,900	177,054	75,900	1,130,384	8,915,811
2011	325,951	230,000	848,500	84,848	85,809	145,236	132,000	116,198	219,900	162,732	79,450	1,123,459	8,904,854
2012[1]	342,864	230,000	872,400	77,763	90,742	138,628	129,700	118,060	222,900	163,078	79,450	1,123,459	8,949,143
2013[2]	378,759	230,000	902,500	76,660	89,231	130,396	129,700	116,258	219,900	162,821	79,450	1,123,459	9,078,146

[1] Preliminary.   [2] Forecast.   *Source: Food and Agricultural Organization of the United Nations (FAO-UN)*

Salient Statistics of Hides and Leather in the United States   In Thousands of Equivalent Hides

Year	New Supply of Cattle hides — Domestic Slaughter — Federally Inspected	Unin-spected[4]	Total Production	Net Exports	Wholesale Prices - Cents Per Pound - Heavy Native Cows[2]	Heavy Native[3] Steers	Production — All U.S. Tanning	Cattle-hide	Value of Leather Exports ($1,000)	Wholesale Leather Indicies (1982 = 100) Men	Women	Footwear Pro-duction[5] Million Pairs	Exports
2001	34,771	599	35,370	21,750	85.52	85.8	14,212	13,779	1,221,131	158.4	133.8	55,600	19,472
2002	35,120	614	35,735	19,484	85.73	82.3		16,403	1,161,944	158.8	133.5	41,100	21,582
2003	34,907	587	35,493	18,177	88.34	83.8		17,470	1,150,212	161.4	132.1	22,300	21,319
2004	32,156	573	32,728	17,388	57.07	67.1		15,492	1,344,017	161.7	129.2		21,464
2005	31,832	556	32,388		57.89	65.6				163.5	132.1		
2006	33,145	553	33,698		60.30	68.9				164.6	134.2		
2007	33,721	543	34,264	24,394	65.70	72.0				167.0	137.0		
2008	33,805	560	34,365	22,213	58.35	63.9				173.7	139.7		
2009[1]	32,765	573	33,338	22,126	29.00	45.3				177.6	139.9		
2010[1]				23,378	63.44	71.9				180.9	141.0		

[1] Preliminary.   [2] Central U.S., heifers.   [3] F.O.B. Chicago.   [4] Includes farm slaughter; diseased & condemned animals & hides taken off fallen animals.
[5] Other than rubber.   *Sources: Leather Industries of America (LIA); Bureau of Labor Statistics, U.S. Department of Commerce (BLS)*

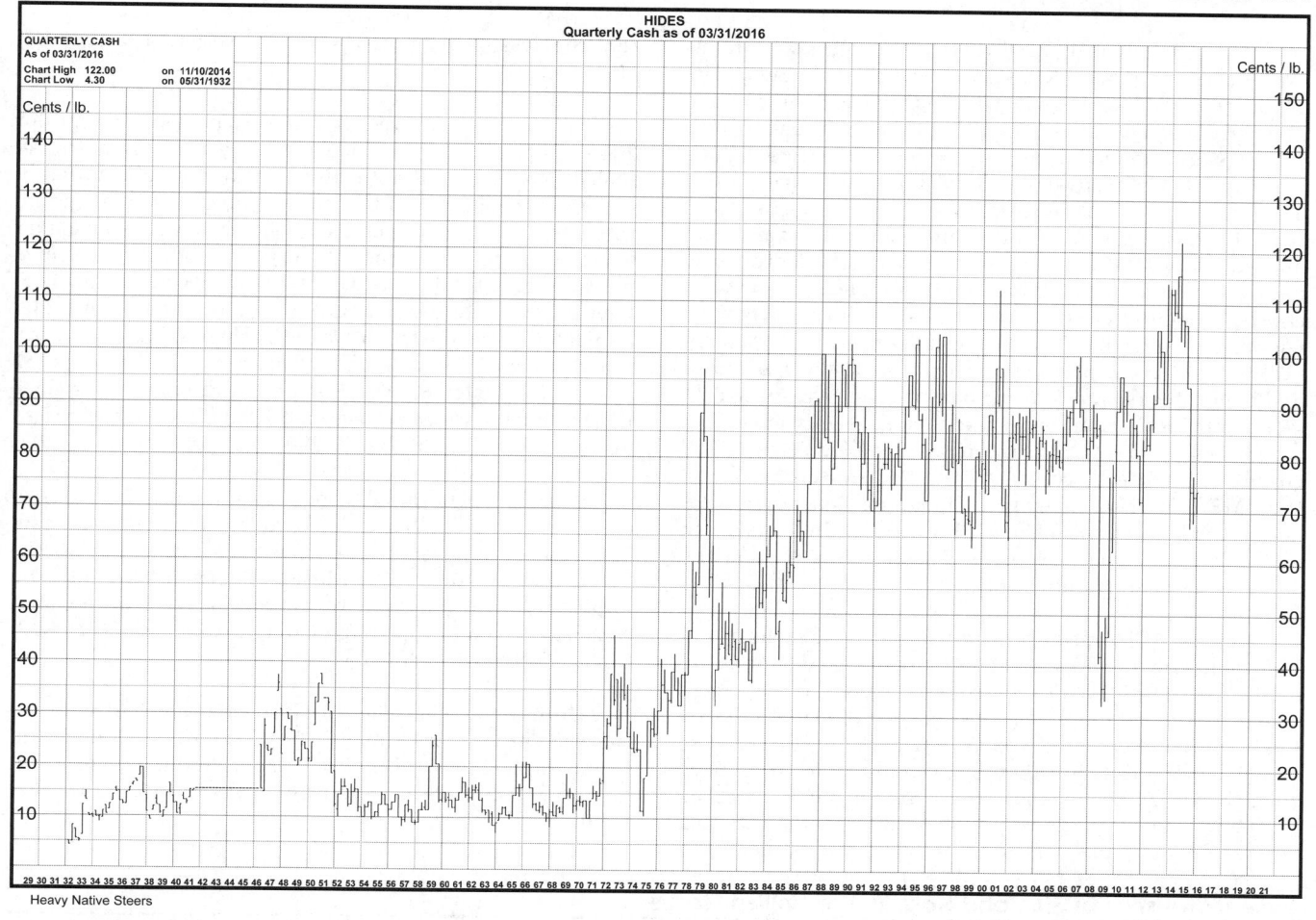

HIDES
Quarterly Cash as of 03/31/2016

QUARTERLY CASH
As of 03/31/2016
Chart High 122.00 on 11/10/2014
Chart Low 4.30 on 05/31/1932

Cents / lb.

Heavy Native Steers

Imports and Exports of All Cattle Hides in the United States   In Thousands of Hides

	----- Imports -----		------------------------------ U.S. Exports - by Country of Destination ------------------------------										
Year	Canada	Total	Canada	Italy	Japan	Korea, South	Mexico	Portugal	Romania	Spain	Taiwan	Thailand	Total
2004	6,171	9,000	346	417	468	4,218	1,419	4	0	16	1,842	684	18,795
2005	2,897	4,517	141	568	334	4,048	1,288	2	0	8	1,730	652	19,231
2006	1,786	2,491	57	523	277	3,455	1,225	5	0	41	1,902	441	20,059
2007	1,243	1,986	91	191	234	2,867	1,243	3	0	44	1,260	724	17,687
2008	1,182	1,863	113	265	175	2,346	1,135		0	99	795	453	16,015
2009	975	1,475	345	407	189	2,379	1,510	11	0	62	1,249	574	16,661
2010	1,064	1,388	193	1,010	148	2,042	1,423	1	0	90	1,446	460	15,440
2011	932	1,306	179	1,703	347	3,000	1,062	5	0	51	1,194	382	18,799
2012	1,209	1,610	97	547	211	3,473	1,264	2	0	3	983	400	19,204
2013[1]	1,008	1,622	62	378	237	4,148	1,408	17	0	18	1,753	272	25,899

[1] Preliminary.   Source: Leather Industries of America

Wholesale Price of Hides (Packer Heavy Native Steers) F.O.B. Chicago   In Cents Per Pound

Year	Jan.	Feb.	Mar.	Apr.	May	June	July	Aug.	Sept.	Oct.	Nov.	Dec.	Average
2006	79.28	81.01	83.86	84.95	87.76	88.07	87.93	87.15	88.29	88.08	88.81	90.50	86.31
2007	93.75	95.85	95.66	98.13	97.68	93.19	87.36	86.95	86.14	83.08	84.72	83.83	90.53
2008	79.55	79.43	82.79	85.58	85.82	87.01	87.55	87.49	85.10	85.31	78.38	44.98	80.75
2009	43.75	43.09	34.55	36.22	38.33	46.84	53.76	73.02	68.86	65.35	74.23	77.51	54.63
2010	79.31	78.31	83.78	91.83	93.38	93.69	92.86	91.36	88.90	90.68	90.44	90.90	88.79
2011	78.24	81.78	85.20	88.18	84.12	86.26	85.60	85.66	82.40	79.54	76.76	72.10	82.15
2012	72.19	78.90	83.55	84.32	85.95	83.71	84.10	85.89	83.66	86.48	88.52	91.10	84.03
2013	91.45	97.00	96.81	103.14	99.66	98.93	99.32	95.39	91.50	94.39	106.00	105.38	98.25
2014	104.76	107.00	110.62	112.00	108.90	108.14	108.59	112.00	114.43	114.37	114.29	107.16	110.19
2015	104.20	103.24	103.68	98.57	95.90	94.00	73.86	71.86	75.90	73.64	68.95	71.64	86.29

Source: National Agricultural Statistics Service, U.S. Department of Agriculture (NASS-USDA)

Hogs

Hogs are generally bred twice a year in a continuous cycle designed to provide a steady flow of production. The gestation period for hogs is 3-1/2 months and the average litter size is 9 pigs. The pigs are weaned at 3-4 weeks of age. The pigs are then fed so as to maximize weight gain. The feed consists primarily of grains such as corn, barley, milo, oats, and wheat. Protein is added from oilseed meals. Hogs typically gain 3.1 pounds per pound of feed. The time from birth to slaughter is typically 6 months. Hogs are ready for slaughter at about 254 pounds, producing a dressed carcass weight of around 190 pounds and an average 88.6 pounds of lean meat. The lean meat consists of 21% ham, 20% loin, 14% belly, 3% spareribs, 7% Boston butt roast and blade steaks, and 10% picnic, with the remaining 25% going into jowl, lean trim, fat, miscellaneous cuts, and trimmings. Futures on lean hogs are traded at the CME Group. The futures contract is settled in cash based on the CME Lean Hog Index price, meaning that no physical delivery of hogs occurs. The CME Lean Hog Index is based on the 2-day average net price of slaughtered hogs at the average lean percentage level.

Prices – CME lean hog futures prices (Barchart.com electronic symbol HE) sold off to begin 2015 and slumped to a 5-1/3 year low of 57.775 cents per pound in March. Signs of oversupply hammered hog prices after the USDA March Cold Storage report showed frozen pork in storage rose +4.8% y/y to 686.145 million lbs, the most for a February since the USDA began tracking the data in 1957. Also, the USDA Q1 Hogs & Pigs report showed the total U.S. hog herd on March 1 rose +7.2% y/y to 65.93 million hogs and that the average pigs per litter in Q1 rose to a record high 10.17 piglets.

Hog prices recovered and in May posted the high for 2015 at 85.125 cents per pound after a Bird-Flu outbreak fueled speculation that poultry demand would suffer in favor of cheaper pork. Hog prices then turned down and ratcheted lower and posted a 6-year low in November at 51.80 cents per pound. U.S. pork production ramped up throughout 2015 as the USDA reported that U.S. September pork output climbed +9% y/y to a record 2.04 billion lbs. Also, the Q3-2015 USDA Hogs & Pigs Inventory report showed the total U.S. hog herd on September 1 rose +2.7% y/y to 68.395 million hogs, the most hogs since USDA quarterly records began in 1988. Hog futures prices ended 2015 down -26% at 59.800 cents per pound.

Supply – The number of hogs on world farms as of January 1, 2016 fell by -5.6% to 750.940 million head. The number of hogs in the U.S. as of January 1, 2016 rose by +0.4% to 68.025 million head. The countries with the largest number of hogs as of January 1, 2016 were China with 56.0%, the European Union with 19.6%, the U.S. with 9.1%, and Brazil with 5.3%.

Demand – The federally-inspected hog slaughter in the U.S. in 2015 rose by +8.0% to 114.615 million head, below the 2008 record high of 115.421 million head. U.S. hog marketings in 2014 fell by -4.2% to 148.342 million head.

Salient Statistics of Pigs and Hogs in the United States

	Pig Crop						Value of Hogs on Farms, Dec. 1		Hog Mar-ketings (1,000 Head)	Quantity Pro-duced (Live Wt.) (Mil. Lbs)	Value of Pro-duction (Million$)	Hogs Slaughtered, Thousand Head --- Commercial				
	Spring[3]			Fall[4]												
Year	Sows Farrowed Pig Crop --- 1,000 Head ---		Pigs Per Litter	Sows Farrowed Pig Crop --- 1,000 Head ---		Pigs Per Litter	$ Per Head	Total Million $				Federally Inspected	Other	Total	Farm	Total
2006	5,768	52,242	9.06	5,862	53,376	9.11	90.0	5,599	132,262	28,149	12,702	103,689	1,048	104,737	105	104,842
2007	5,935	54,266	9.14	6,312	58,608	9.28	73.0	4,986	137,519	29,606	13,468	108,138	1,034	109,172	106	109,278
2008	6,123	57,019	9.31	6,103	58,011	9.51	89.0	5,958	148,986	31,411	14,457	115,421	1,026	116,446	106	116,553
2009	6,029	57,564	9.55	5,874	56,978	9.70	83.0	5,417	150,107	31,359	12,590	112,612	1,001	113,614	114	113,727
2010	5,801	56,326	9.71	5,824	57,359	9.85	106.0	6,899	144,486	30,437	16,095	109,315	948	110,263	107	110,370
2011	5,760	57,118	9.92	5,857	58,720	10.03	----	----	145,665	31,066	20,176	109,956	904	110,860	96	110,957
2012	5,759	57,749	10.03	5,810	58,906	10.14	----	----	151,353	31,961	20,224	112,265	896	113,162	83	113,245
2013	5,595	57,020	10.19	5,670	58,115	10.25	----	----	154,923	32,620	21,666	111,248	833	112,081	84	112,164
2014[1]	5,573	53,821	9.66	5,985	61,035	10.20	----	----	148,342	32,012	24,153	106,122	755	106,877	82	106,959
2015[2]	5,749	59,219	10.30	5,892	61,614	10.46	----	----				114,616	799	115,414		115,414

[1] Preliminary. [2] Estimate. [3] December-May. [4] June-November. *Source: Economic Research Service, U.S. Department of Agriculture (ERS-USDA)*

World Hog Numbers in Specified Countries as of January 1   In Thousands of Head

Year	Australia	Belarus	Brazil	Canada	China	European Union	Japan	Korea, South	Mexico	Russia	Ukraine	United States	World Total
2007	2,733	3,642	33,147	14,980	418,504	163,039	9,759	8,518	9,021	16,185	8,055	62,516	801,621
2008	2,605	3,598	32,947	14,080	439,895	160,918	9,745	8,742	9,401	16,340	7,020	68,177	775,866
2009	2,412	3,704	33,892	12,700	462,913	153,707	9,899	8,223	9,310	16,165	6,526	67,048	786,499
2010	2,302	3,782	35,122	12,465	469,960	152,780	10,000	8,721	8,979	17,236	7,577	64,687	793,611
2011	2,289	3,887	36,652	12,615	464,600	152,361	9,768	8,449	9,007	17,231	7,960	64,725	789,544
2012	2,285	3,989	38,336	12,625	468,627	149,809	9,735	8,171	9,276	17,258	7,373	66,259	793,743
2013	2,138	4,243	38,577	12,610	475,922	146,982	9,685	9,916	9,510	18,816	7,577	66,224	802,200
2014	2,098	3,267	38,844	12,940	474,113	146,172	9,537	9,912	9,775	19,081	7,922	64,775	798,436
2015[1]	2,308	2,924	39,395	13,165	465,830	148,310	9,440	10,090	9,700	19,405	7,513	67,776	795,856
2016[2]	2,300	2,650	40,150	13,300	420,200	147,500	9,590	10,200	9,600	20,125	7,300	68,025	750,940

[1] Preliminary.   [2] Forecast.   *Source: Foreign Agricultural Service, U.S. Department of Agriculture (FAS-USDA)*

Hogs and Pigs on Farms in the United States on December 1   In Thousands of Head

Year	Georgia	Illinois	Indiana	Iowa	Kansas	Minne-sota	Missouri	Nebraska	North Carolina	Ohio	South Dakota	Wisconsin	Total
2006	245	4,200	3,350	17,300	1,840	6,900	2,800	3,050	9,500	1,690	1,270	450	62,490
2007	265	4,350	3,700	19,400	1,880	7,700	3,150	3,350	10,200	1,830	1,460	440	68,177
2008	235	4,350	3,550	19,900	1,740	7,500	3,150	3,350	9,700	1,940	1,280	360	67,148
2009	195	4,250	3,600	19,000	1,810	7,200	3,100	3,100	9,600	2,010	1,190	350	64,887
2010	160	4,400	3,650	19,100	1,820	7,700	2,900	3,150	9,000	2,040	1,290	340	64,925
2011	155	4,650	3,800	20,000	1,890	7,800	2,750	3,150	8,900	2,200	1,400	340	66,361
2012	155	4,600	3,800	20,600	1,900	7,650	2,750	3,000	9,000	2,050	1,200	320	66,374
2013	141	4,550	3,650	20,200	1,750	7,800	2,750	3,050	8,500	2,200	1,200	295	64,775
2014	155	4,700	3,700	21,300	1,840	8,100	2,850	3,200	8,800	2,230	1,270	310	67,776
2015[1]	160	5,050	3,750	20,800	1,930	7,950	3,000	3,300	8,800	2,470	1,360	320	68,299

[1] Preliminary.   Source: National Agricultural Statistics Service, U.S. Department of Agriculture (NASS-USDA)

Cold Storage Holdings of Frozen Pork[2] in the United States, on First of Month   In Thousands of Pounds

Year	Jan.	Feb.	Mar.	Apr.	May	June	July	Aug.	Sept.	Oct.	Nov.	Dec.
2006	421,311	527,677	528,025	504,978	520,022	477,005	412,622	417,769	415,563	458,359	488,409	468,476
2007	442,501	484,302	483,200	494,761	528,527	491,950	467,949	455,854	458,252	484,934	494,751	474,571
2008	458,665	574,929	611,830	657,344	663,443	579,403	530,123	505,269	502,669	526,168	528,031	526,680
2009	555,642	606,936	624,477	594,127	612,290	584,544	577,914	539,700	530,148	528,681	516,300	482,816
2010	471,125	492,287	515,911	513,066	483,710	446,049	412,983	391,193	388,292	424,322	481,653	467,950
2011	475,829	538,754	574,236	574,398	549,279	548,322	495,064	454,337	442,903	491,910	488,721	495,117
2012	484,497	585,307	622,673	610,318	659,726	636,017	592,880	549,621	585,796	630,446	603,502	558,688
2013	551,510	606,425	633,399	647,784	700,977	658,947	565,063	543,668	548,975	567,827	565,020	546,238
2014	554,328	618,746	654,712	575,539	583,891	575,818	537,447	533,259	543,666	550,622	533,076	492,752
2015[1]	503,792	595,673	686,063	672,431	701,083	654,771	634,525	633,214	656,351	655,517	603,454	560,915

[1] Preliminary.   [2] Excludes lard.   Source: Economic Research Service, U.S. Department of Agriculture (ERS-USDA)

Cold Storage Holdings of Frozen Pork Belly in the United States, on First of Month   In Thousands of Pounds

Year	Jan.	Feb.	Mar.	Apr.	May	June	July	Aug.	Sept.	Oct.	Nov.	Dec.
2006	40,707	54,902	58,861	61,628	62,665	58,803	46,056	30,506	11,962	10,199	15,597	30,553
2007	41,917	46,227	46,643	55,160	61,796	57,294	47,214	31,619	21,410	17,050	20,356	34,328
2008	54,746	70,647	79,282	98,896	100,189	87,428	74,372	57,964	31,878	21,270	21,696	33,490
2009	51,593	69,166	75,668	72,940	79,543	78,801	76,333	60,238	48,958	38,481	37,127	44,638
2010	56,764	53,584	55,552	58,762	49,656	44,201	35,369	21,380	7,202	4,817	23,248	37,696
2011	50,677	51,326	50,900	52,487	53,185	57,123	48,645	29,503	15,162	9,297	8,734	26,599
2012	41,469	53,685	61,577	66,031	74,927	65,648	49,034	27,962	14,210	15,668	18,720	23,837
2013	36,037	36,425	42,976	51,473	56,352	54,829	42,033	28,177	19,335	15,668	18,720	23,837
2014	80,367	87,171	87,675	79,721	83,579	85,888	83,936	64,644	45,562	34,311	29,006	35,894
2015[1]	47,455	53,507	67,794	68,297	70,412	64,805	44,432	23,634	13,679	10,872	17,853	41,160

[1] Preliminary.   Source: National Agricultural Statistics Service, U.S. Department of Agriculture (NASS-USDA)

Hog-Corn Price Ratio[2] in the United States

Year	Jan.	Feb.	Mar.	Apr.	May	June	July	Aug.	Sept.	Oct.	Nov.	Dec.	Average
2006	20.4	21.1	20.8	19.6	22.2	25.1	23.5	24.7	22.2	18.2	15.6	14.5	20.7
2007	14.0	13.8	13.1	14.0	15.2	15.4	15.7	15.7	14.3	12.9	11.0	10.5	13.8
2008	9.3	9.3	8.6	8.6	10.5	9.8	10.3	11.5	10.5	11.1	9.6	10.2	9.9
2009	9.8	11.3	11.4	11.4	11.3	10.8	12.0	11.2	11.6	10.5	11.0	12.5	11.2
2010	13.2	13.8	14.7	16.6	17.9	17.1	16.8	16.8	15.0	12.3	10.5	10.9	14.6
2011	11.3	10.9	11.4	10.7	10.9	10.9	11.3	11.0	10.5	12.0	11.0	10.8	11.1
2012	10.5	10.4	10.3	9.9	9.9	11.0	10.1	8.8	8.1	9.1	8.7	9.9	9.7
2013	9.2	9.2	8.3	8.9	9.8	10.7	11.2	11.9	13.1	14.8	14.6	13.9	11.3
2014	13.8	15.1	18.1	18.9	17.6	18.8	23.0	22.9	21.7	21.6	18.5	17.0	18.9
2015[1]	15.0	13.3	13.2	13.1	16.3	16.7	15.4	16.0	14.8	15.1	12.8	11.7	14.5

[1] Preliminary.   [2] Bushels of corn equal in value to 100 pounds of hog, live weight.   Source: Economic Research Service, U.S. Department of Agriculture (ERS-USDA)

HOGS

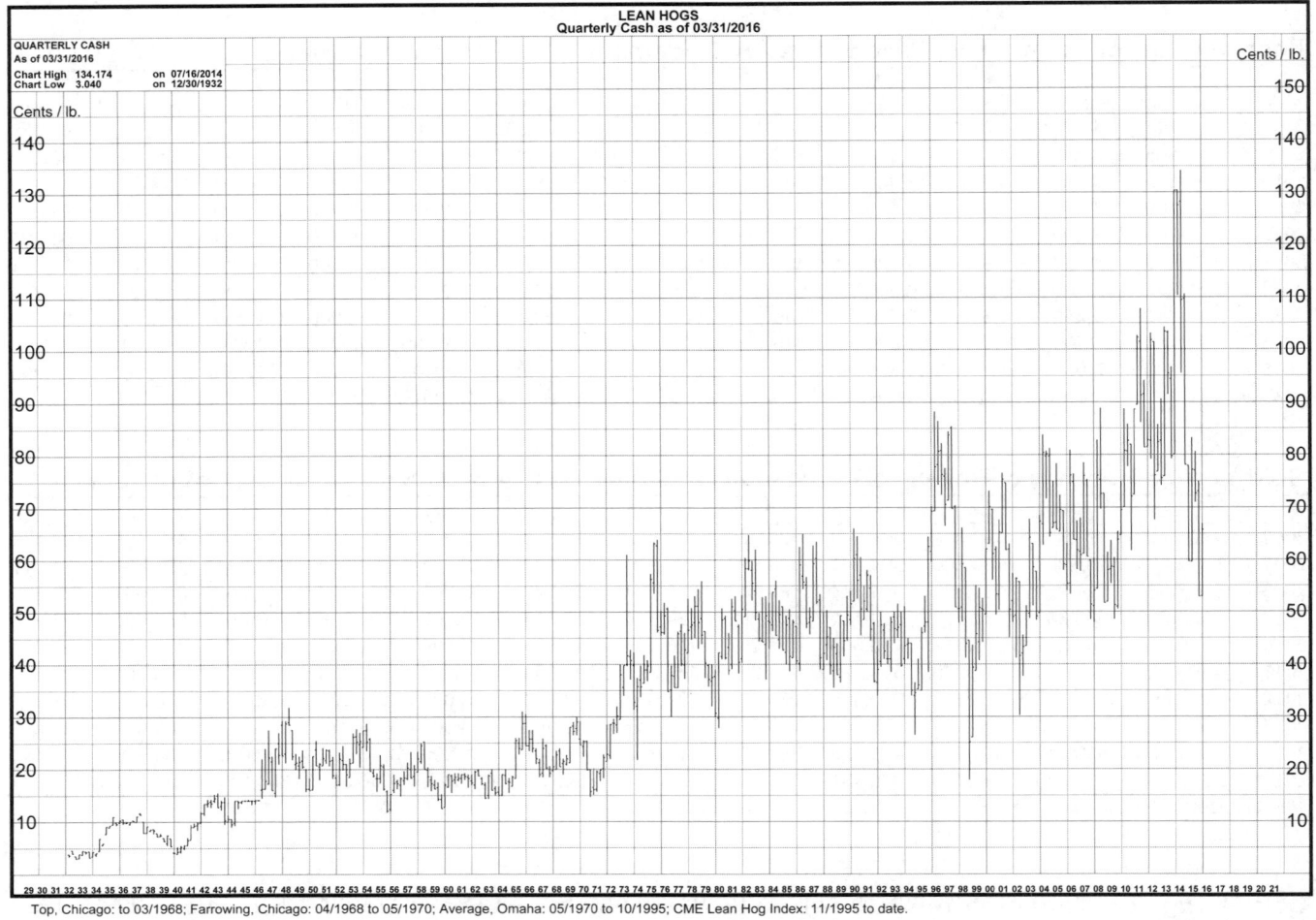

LEAN HOGS
Quarterly Cash as of 03/31/2016

QUARTERLY CASH
As of 03/31/2016
Chart High 134.174   on 07/16/2014
Chart Low   3.040   on 12/30/1932

Cents / lb.

Cents / lb.

Top, Chicago: to 03/1968; Farrowing, Chicago: 04/1968 to 05/1970; Average, Omaha: 05/1970 to 10/1995; CME Lean Hog Index: 11/1995 to date.

Average Price of Hogs, National Base 51-52% lean   In Dollars Per Hundred Pounds (Cwt.)

Year	Jan.	Feb.	Mar.	Apr.	May	June	July	Aug.	Sept.	Oct.	Nov.	Dec.	Average
2006	41.37	43.17	43.34	41.45	49.00	54.90	51.89	53.32	50.28	47.57	45.97	44.84	47.26
2007	44.04	48.60	45.47	48.43	54.40	54.82	52.39	52.01	46.61	41.96	36.95	39.40	47.09
2008	36.77	42.74	39.40	45.06	57.75	54.71	56.48	62.56	52.76	47.06	38.90	39.80	47.83
2009	41.43	42.43	42.47	42.83	43.18	42.21	42.74	36.56	37.41	37.65	40.12	45.82	41.24
2010	49.81	48.98	52.43	57.43	63.13	58.23	58.25	61.49	60.64	52.41	47.00	50.92	55.06
2011	55.56	61.62	62.63	68.10	68.41	69.88	71.65	76.09	65.45	68.44	63.40	62.14	66.11
2012	62.18	63.94	61.86	58.99	58.51	67.87	69.93	65.00	50.85	59.06	57.67	59.16	61.25
2013	61.22	61.59	54.28	57.71	66.03	72.65	72.88	71.03	67.84	64.95	60.21	58.16	64.05
2014	58.36	63.88	83.82	89.09	81.76	85.35	57.00	80.39	74.36	75.24	63.76	61.24	72.85
2015[1]	61.24	61.24	45.61	45.13	57.23	57.25	56.21	55.91	51.64	52.68	42.01	39.30	52.12

[1] Preliminary.   Source: Economic Research Service, U.S. Department of Agriculture (ERS-USDA)

Average Price Received by Farmers for Hogs in the United States   In Cents Per Pound

Year	Jan.	Feb.	Mar.	Apr.	May	June	July	Aug.	Sept.	Oct.	Nov.	Dec.	Average
2006	40.7	42.6	42.8	41.3	48.2	53.8	50.2	51.6	48.9	46.5	44.9	43.5	46.3
2007	42.7	47.5	44.9	47.3	53.1	54.3	52.2	51.3	46.8	42.4	37.9	39.6	46.7
2008	37.2	42.2	40.3	44.4	55.3	53.4	54.3	60.7	52.6	48.5	40.7	41.9	47.6
2009	42.8	43.8	43.9	44.0	44.6	43.3	43.3	37.3	37.7	37.8	40.3	45.0	42.0
2010	48.4	48.9	52.1	56.5	62.2	58.2	58.5	58.2	61.0	53.3	47.8	52.3	54.8
2011	55.8	61.4	62.9	67.8	68.6	69.7	71.7	75.8	67.1	68.7	64.4	63.5	66.5
2012	63.5	65.5	65.2	62.8	62.8	70.2	72.1	66.9	55.7	62.0	61.1	62.4	64.2
2013	63.8	64.5	59.2	61.8	68.6	74.4	75.8	74.2	70.7	68.5	63.6	61.5	67.2
2014	61.2	65.5	81.9	88.8	82.8	84.8	93.3	83.2	75.7	77.0	66.7	64.3	77.1
2015[1]	57.4	50.4	50.3	49.0	58.9	59.9	58.7	59.0	54.5	55.5	45.9	42.8	53.5

[1] Preliminary.   Source: Economic Research Service, U.S. Department of Agriculture (ERS-USDA)

Quarterly Hogs and Pigs Report in the United States, 10 States   In Thousands of Head

Year[2]	Inventory[3]	Breeding[3]	Market[3]	Farrowings	Pig Crop	Year[2]	Inventory[3]	Breeding[3]	Market[3]	Farrowings	Pig Crop
2006	61,449	6,011	55,438	11,629	105,618	2011	64,625	5,778	59,147	11,616	115,838
I	61,449	6,011	55,438	2,841	25,662	I	64,625	5,778	59,147	2,843	27,866
II	60,326	6,025	54,301	2,927	26,580	II	63,684	5,788	57,896	2,917	29,252
III	61,687	6,060	55,627	2,912	26,519	III	65,320	5,803	59,517	2,927	29,355
IV	62,914	6,079	56,835	2,949	26,857	IV	67,234	5,806	61,428	2,929	29,365
2007	62,490	6,087	56,402	12,248	112,873	2012	66,361	5,803	60,558	11,567	116,655
I	62,490	6,087	56,402	2,905	26,395	I	66,361	5,803	60,558	2,813	28,037
II	61,896	6,149	55,746	3,030	27,870	II	64,787	5,820	58,967	2,945	29,712
III	63,947	6,169	57,777	3,133	29,095	III	66,609	5,862	60,747	2,921	29,587
IV	67,275	6,208	66,708	3,180	29,513	IV	68,172	5,788	62,384	2,888	29,319
2008	68,177	6,233	61,944	12,226	115,030	2013	66,374	5,819	60,555	11,264	115,135
I	68,177	6,233	61,944	3,071	28,388	I	66,374	5,819	60,555	2,788	28,099
II	67,218	6,200	61,018	3,052	28,631	II	65,071	5,834	59,237	2,806	28,921
III	67,400	6,131	61,269	3,075	29,240	III	65,188	5,884	59,304	2,890	29,862
IV	68,196	6,061	62,135	3,028	28,771	IV	66,906	5,816	61,090	2,780	28,253
2009	67,148	6,062	61,087	11,903	114,542	2014	64,775	5,757	59,018	11,558	114,856
I	67,148	6,062	61,087	3,011	28,552	I	64,775	5,757	59,018	2,763	26,326
II	65,819	5,992	59,828	3,018	29,012	II	61,494	5,851	55,643	2,810	27,495
III	66,809	5,968	60,842	2,959	28,718	III	61,568	5,855	55,713	2,991	30,402
IV	66,716	5,875	60,842	2,915	28,260	IV	65,979	5,920	60,059	2,994	30,633
2010	64,887	5,850	59,037	11,626	113,685	2015[1]	67,776	5,939	61,838	11,641	120,834
I	64,887	5,850	59,037	2,872	27,596	I	67,776	5,939	61,838	2,895	29,627
II	63,568	5,760	57,808	2,929	28,730	II	67,399	5,982	61,418	2,854	29,593
III	64,650	5,788	58,862	2,944	28,871	III	67,165	5,926	61,240	3,017	31,343
IV	65,971	5,770	60,201	2,881	28,488	IV	69,185	5,986	63,200	2,875	30,271

[1] Preliminary.   [2] Quarters are Dec. preceding year-Feb.(I), Mar.-May(II), June-Aug.(III) and Sept.-Nov.(IV).
[3] Beginning of period.   *Source: National Agricultural Statistics Service, U.S. Department of Agriculture (NASS-USDA)*

Federally Inspected Hog Slaughter in the United States   In Thousands of Head

Year	Jan.	Feb.	Mar.	Apr.	May	June	July	Aug.	Sept.	Oct.	Nov.	Dec.	Total
2006	8,834	7,978	9,148	7,884	8,450	8,256	7,805	8,991	8,738	9,541	9,276	8,788	103,689
2007	9,281	8,040	9,119	8,389	8,680	8,218	8,312	9,296	8,683	9,541	9,964	9,601	108,138
2008	10,474	9,297	9,579	9,911	8,981	8,801	9,373	9,170	9,878	10,555	9,964	9,601	108,138
2009	9,846	8,840	9,574	9,353	8,379	9,101	9,062	9,250	9,848	10,654	9,250	10,053	115,421
2010	8,838	8,619	9,947	8,980	7,897	8,968	8,396	9,030	9,257	9,651	9,895	9,838	112,612
2011	9,036	8,440	9,795	8,559	8,470	8,866	8,089	9,440	9,603	9,822	9,968	9,868	109,315
2012	9,467	8,975	9,454	8,757	9,212	8,481	8,493	9,858	9,376	10,770	10,030	9,393	109,956
2013	9,885	8,526	9,252	9,292	9,147	8,132	9,003	9,474	8,952	10,341	9,579	9,665	112,265
2014	9,726	8,609	8,614	8,794	8,561	8,040	8,394	8,199	8,762	9,880	8,754	9,788	111,248
2015[1]	9,698	9,018	9,818	9,612	8,686	9,364	9,332	9,272	9,652	10,173	9,700	10,292	114,616

[1] Preliminary. *Source: National Agricultural Statistics Service, U.S. Department of Agriculture (NASS-USDA)*

Average Live Weight of all Hogs Slaughtered Under Federal Inspection   In Pounds Per Head

Year	Jan.	Feb.	Mar.	Apr.	May	June	July	Aug.	Sept.	Oct.	Nov.	Dec.	Average
2006	273	272	272	272	271	267	264	262	267	269	272	271	269
2007	271	270	271	270	269	267	265	264	267	270	273	272	269
2008	273	271	271	270	268	266	263	261	266	270	271	271	268
2009	272	272	272	272	272	270	268	268	270	272	272	270	271
2010	272	271	272	273	273	271	269	267	271	276	278	278	273
2011	278	278	278	277	276	273	268	266	271	276	279	278	275
2012	279	278	279	279	277	274	269	269	271	274	276	276	275
2013	277	277	277	277	276	274	271	271	273	279	283	283	277
2014	284	283	285	287	287	285	284	283	283	286	287	287	285
2015[1]	287	285	285	285	284	282	280	278	280	284	286	285	283

[1] Preliminary. *Source: National Agricultural Statistics Service, U.S. Department of Agriculture (NASS-USDA)*

HOGS

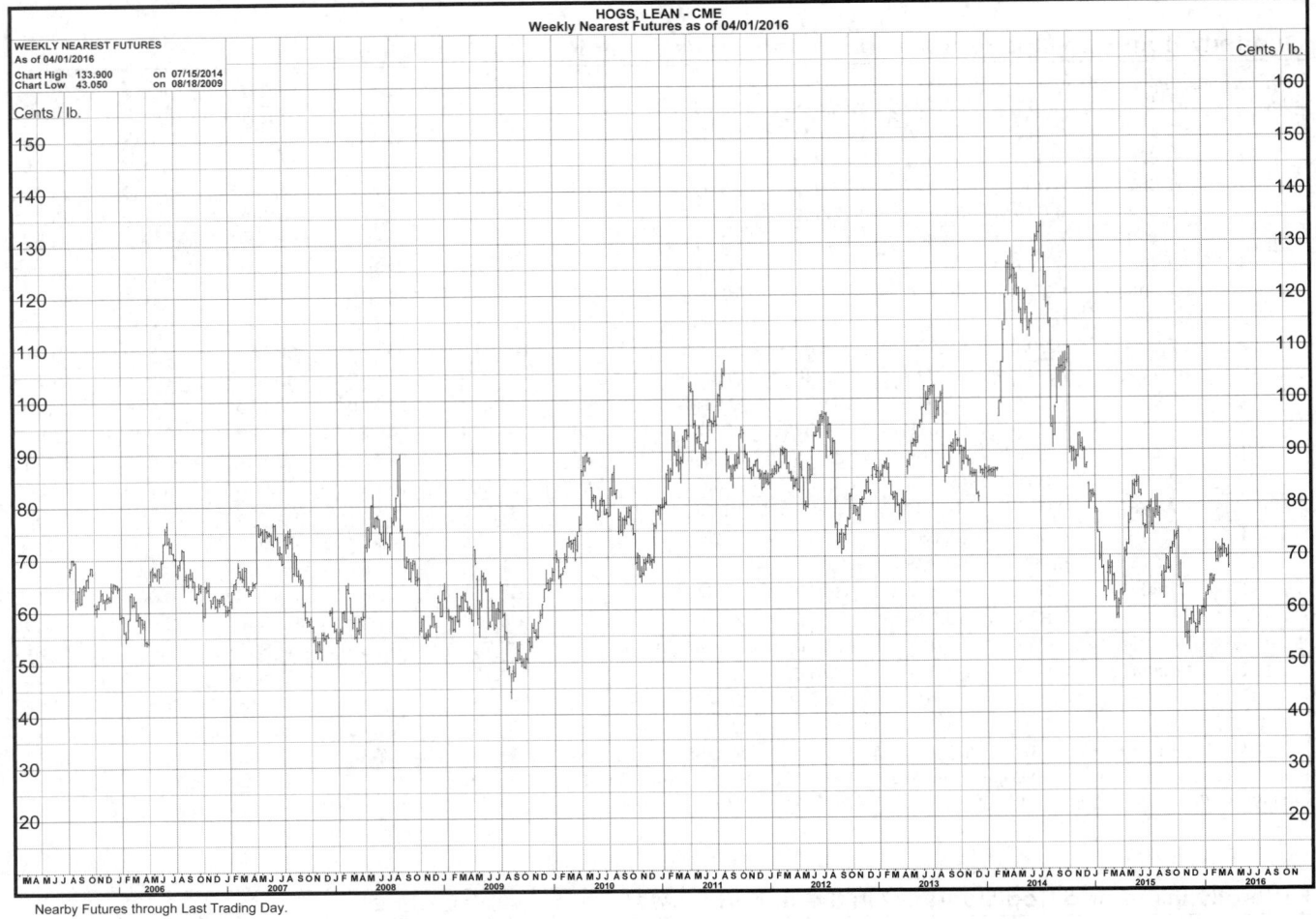

Nearby Futures through Last Trading Day.

Volume of Trading of Lean Hog Futures in Chicago   In Thousands of Contracts

Year	Jan.	Feb.	Mar.	Apr.	May	June	July	Aug.	Sept.	Oct.	Nov.	Dec.	Total
2006	561.2	319.8	597.9	357.0	659.0	826.3	578.7	478.8	577.4	533.5	649.3	342.2	6,481.0
2007	687.6	449.6	721.0	423.2	621.0	744.8	865.4	559.1	591.6	485.1	730.0	386.4	7,264.8
2008	800.6	527.1	809.7	736.4	796.7	938.7	968.4	617.9	781.6	506.8	576.3	445.1	8,505.1
2009	614.9	390.1	593.6	503.2	620.3	727.6	644.1	510.7	657.8	540.6	590.1	426.2	6,819.1
2010	672.2	464.9	706.3	567.4	740.5	803.0	763.6	627.9	808.6	683.5	753.5	485.3	8,076.5
2011	879.9	660.3	925.1	661.0	881.2	991.4	901.0	770.6	1,047.8	785.7	857.7	608.4	9,970.0
2012	908.4	715.1	1,093.7	882.7	1,312.9	1,189.3	1,082.5	819.3	979.4	869.2	949.2	660.3	11,461.9
2013	999.0	808.0	1,017.5	832.9	1,100.6	1,151.0	1,076.2	778.1	1,155.6	861.5	833.8	662.8	11,277.0
2014	940.1	880.1	1,402.3	760.6	893.0	937.5	1,046.6	818.8	1,000.4	674.1	708.0	595.5	10,656.9
2015	883.0	743.3	961.8	716.4	830.1	962.1	971.2	640.8	745.3	717.5	836.7	567.7	9,575.9

Contract size = 40,000 lbs.   *Source: Chicago Mercantile Exchange (CME)*

Average Open Interest of Lean Hog Futures in Chicago   In Contracts

Year	Jan.	Feb.	Mar.	Apr.	May	June	July	Aug.	Sept.	Oct.	Nov.	Dec.
2006	133,258	144,506	145,020	144,250	157,259	158,276	157,899	165,781	176,336	174,971	188,965	179,057
2007	174,424	182,146	178,296	174,233	176,897	177,274	174,144	176,425	175,093	179,402	204,475	206,458
2008	212,644	227,377	219,938	232,309	252,497	242,588	238,162	231,283	206,602	171,506	168,129	159,600
2009	137,693	122,594	126,377	134,363	143,493	135,606	131,683	130,844	143,952	152,820	164,819	174,739
2010	194,351	179,300	197,407	217,304	217,779	190,933	197,940	214,535	230,240	209,159	198,160	200,932
2011	218,818	243,878	226,344	233,168	222,193	221,633	242,921	253,224	247,476	273,568	257,632	246,758
2012	243,120	256,724	262,970	259,367	268,655	258,585	231,982	224,131	237,138	219,733	230,592	242,093
2013	244,228	226,691	235,834	229,097	247,125	279,932	297,930	306,652	326,192	302,314	282,782	263,509
2014	266,366	282,321	288,484	265,981	256,474	248,869	248,878	234,967	237,877	236,417	230,578	216,735
2015	208,643	192,716	208,128	216,998	219,669	221,626	210,767	196,682	196,033	198,965	204,049	173,053

Contract size = 40,000 lbs.   *Source: Chicago Mercantile Exchange (CME)*

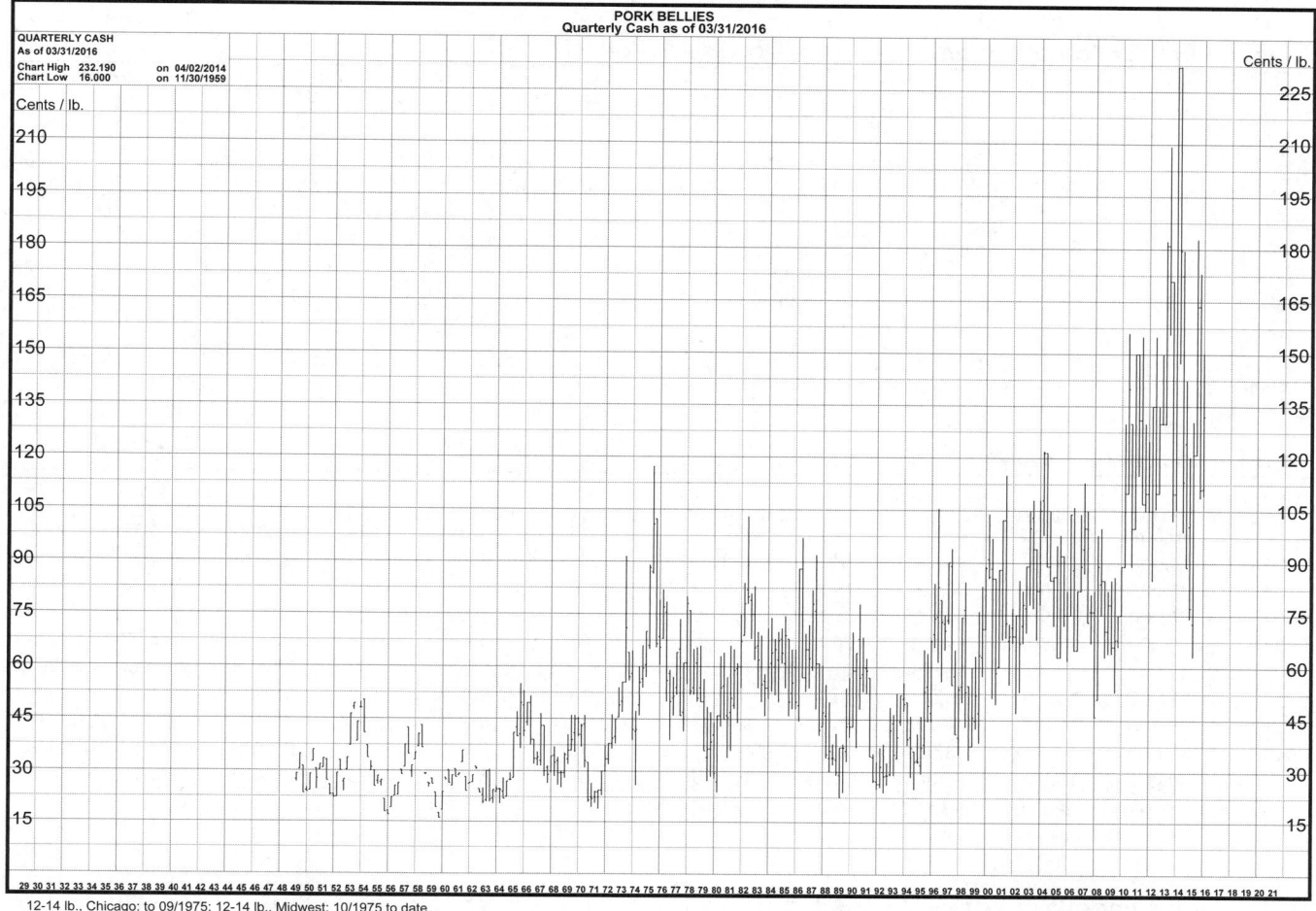

PORK BELLIES
Quarterly Cash as of 03/31/2016

QUARTERLY CASH
As of 03/31/2016
Chart High 232.190 on 04/02/2014
Chart Low   16.000   on 11/30/1959

12-14 lb., Chicago: to 09/1975; 12-14 lb., Midwest: 10/1975 to date.

Average Price of Pork Bellies (12-14 lbs.), Central, U.S.   In Cents Per Pound

Year	Jan.	Feb.	Mar.	Apr.	May	June	July	Aug.	Sept.	Oct.	Nov.	Dec.	Average
2006	75.00	71.83	78.67	78.83	87.00	101.25	94.29	90.67	82.56	75.44	78.64	79.50	82.81
2007	86.25	96.08	93.25	93.47	106.30	101.06	99.83	86.58	80.42	71.58	75.69	77.08	88.97
2008	75.56	78.94	67.26	61.08	79.00	64.54	78.75	74.17	63.50	77.00	57.25	61.25	69.86
2009	69.88	71.00	65.25	77.50	57.00	50.00	80.36	42.25	45.83	47.33	60.50	64.00	60.91
2010	82.00	73.50	89.00	NA	NA	NA	73.50	122.50	88.00	76.67	143.00	94.50	93.63
2011	110.00	NA	143.00	147.00	143.00	119.00	121.00	135.09	133.00	111.00	91.33	NA	125.34
2012	96.50	NA	90.00	80.00	NA	NA	NA	146.00	NA	NA	NA	123.50	107.20
2013	NA	NA	NA	151.44	161.60	175.55	163.12	177.24	149.62	134.99	128.41	127.35	152.15
2014	124.07	137.58	176.77	191.73	156.63	173.03	174.29	139.46	120.57	127.81	111.33	105.57	144.90
2015[1]	122.30	102.97	81.14	75.33	82.51	108.15	107.00	184.67	166.82	165.54	127.35	114.96	119.90

[1] Preliminary.   *Source: Economic Research Service, U.S. Department of Agriculture (ERS-USDA)*

Average Price of Pork Loins (12-14 lbs.)[2], Central, U.S.   In Cents Per Pound

Year	Jan.	Feb.	Mar.	Apr.	May	June	July	Aug.	Sept.	Oct.	Nov.	Dec.	Average
2006	95.00	96.21	101.31	107.25	112.77	124.61	114.95	109.35	99.58	99.27	92.02	101.15	104.46
2007	100.96	112.08	101.04	108.99	121.61	113.58	111.78	111.66	100.18	93.41	88.25	86.46	104.17
2008	87.70	90.22	90.33	108.10	130.43	115.19	117.11	128.86	114.54	111.10	92.88	93.10	106.63
2009	94.96	94.83	90.46	92.10	97.73	91.58	101.03	90.33	89.08	85.98	82.63	103.03	92.81
2010	110.94	104.08	108.14	122.64	137.62	114.17	118.47	132.73	120.09	110.36	104.06	108.22	115.96
2011	119.02	119.98	123.08	131.20	138.84	136.21	139.57	149.33	131.78	131.07	116.40	117.61	129.51
2012	116.21	118.22	123.09	119.81	128.27	149.14	127.43	119.00	108.86	117.45	105.20	105.56	119.85
2013	107.12	111.73	108.86	106.77	120.28	138.64	129.84	128.96	116.92	115.78	107.25	106.24	116.53
2014	115.27	128.19	165.28	147.55	135.39	153.75	167.79	150.01	153.69	152.92	117.50	115.82	141.93
2015[1]	108.25	99.88	100.25	101.55	124.08	112.35	111.13	107.61	102.46	103.50	88.44	85.76	103.77

[1] Preliminary.   *Source: Economic Research Service, U.S. Department of Agriculture (ERS-USDA)*

HOGS

Average Retail Price of Bacon, Sliced   In Dollars Per Pound

Year	Jan.	Feb.	Mar.	Apr.	May	June	July	Aug.	Sept.	Oct.	Nov.	Dec.	Average
2006	3.36	3.39	3.40	3.34	3.31	3.40	3.51	3.56	3.55	3.61	3.44	3.46	3.44
2007	3.51	3.57	3.46	3.50	3.65	3.66	3.72	3.80	3.78	3.88	3.66	3.69	3.66
2008	3.65	3.62	3.62	3.55	3.64	3.66	3.61	3.84	3.73	3.75	3.60	3.67	3.66
2009	3.73	3.62	3.59	3.58	3.66	3.62	3.64	3.59	3.59	3.60	3.50	3.57	3.61
2010	3.63	3.64	3.67	3.64	3.86	4.05	4.21	4.35	4.57	4.77	4.70	4.16	4.11
2011	4.25	4.37	4.54	4.66	4.77	4.84	4.76	4.77	4.82	4.59	4.64	4.55	4.63
2012	4.57	4.66	4.60	4.53	4.39	4.33	4.37	4.61	4.69	4.66	4.64	4.64	4.56
2013	4.72	4.83	4.91	4.89	5.09	5.33	5.49	5.62	5.68	5.71	5.62	5.54	5.29
2014	5.56	5.46	5.55	5.69	6.05	6.11	6.01	6.07	5.95	5.76	5.57	5.53	5.78
2015[1]	5.59	5.47	5.37	5.21	4.94	5.06	5.18	5.41	5.73	5.90	5.85	5.73	5.45

[1] Preliminary.   Source: Economic Research Service, U.S. Department of Agriculture (ERS-USDA)

World Production of Honey   In Metric Tons

Year	Argentina	Australia	Brazil	Canada	China	Germany	Japan	Mexico	Russia	United States	World Total
2004	80,000	14,632	32,290	34,241	293,000	25,575	3,585	56,917	52,666	83,272	1,365,213
2005	110,000	15,335	33,750	36,109	293,200	21,232	3,290	50,631	52,123	72,927	1,417,859
2006	105,000	17,500	36,194	48,353	332,600	25,199	3,133	55,970	55,678	70,238	1,505,353
2007	81,000	18,000	34,747	31,489	354,000	18,266	3,373	55,459	53,655	67,286	1,461,918
2008	72,000	17,600	37,792	29,440	400,000	15,727	3,384	55,271	57,440	74,293	1,520,956
2009	62,000	16,595	38,974	31,920	402,000	16,460	2,656	56,071	53,598	66,413	1,510,323
2010	59,000	16,150	38,073	33,710	409,149	23,178	2,639	55,684	51,535	80,042	1,546,710
2011	76,000	10,000	41,793	35,520	446,089	25,831	2,684	57,783	60,010	67,294	1,614,020
2012	80,000	10,500	33,932	41,113	462,203	15,699	2,763	58,602	64,898	64,544	1,616,820
2013[1]	80,000	10,500	35,365	34,640	466,300	15,700	2,800	56,907	68,446	67,812	1,663,800

[1] Preliminary.   Source: Food and Agricultural Organization of the United Nations (FAO)

United States Imports of Honey   In Metric Tons

Year	Argentina	Brazil	Canada	India	Mexico	New Zealand	Taiwan	Thailand	Turkey	Ukraine	Uruguay	Vietnam	World Total
2005	22,776	3,783	10,252	7,632	1,452	247	2,408	518	225	337	4,010	13,582	105,677
2006	28,878	10,806	11,576	11,090	2,580	195	311	1,795	57	1,134	1,525	13,263	125,939
2007	20,379	12,103	13,961	7,671	3,192	355	753	790	167	502	1,893	15,707	105,676
2008	10,043	13,598	17,305	13,648	1,411	650	3,983	956	54	84	227	19,378	104,984
2009	10,899	17,709	8,302	13,137	1,625	1,022	5,576	1,847	73	635	19	17,430	95,475
2010	17,414	10,036	11,053	18,462	3,325	1,048	1,755	1,699	37	440	852	20,738	113,930
2011	33,502	14,981	7,148	26,912	2,846	965	903	1,637	183	453	7,083	27,826	130,764
2012	42,482	11,303	15,971	21,454	6,179	966	1,324	258	1,073	1,302	10,877	20,700	141,016
2013	44,221	11,677	9,385	25,867	5,648	1,234	1,827	846	1,897	3,308	8,710	33,586	153,079
2014[1]	36,887	19,230	5,613	20,290	7,254	1,550	2,523	3,458	2,581	8,876	5,362	47,009	165,584

[1] Preliminary.   Source: Foreign Agricultural Service, U.S. Department of Agriculture (FAS-USDA)

Production of Honey in the United States   In Thousands of Pounds

Year	California	Florida	Georgia	Idaho	Louisiana	Michigan	Minnesota	Montana	North Dakota	South Dakota	Texas	Wisconsin	U.S. Total
2006	19,760	13,770	4,662	4,180	2,700	3,960	10,000	10,427	25,900	10,575	5,740	5,952	154,907
2007	13,600	11,360	3,480	3,772	2,581	4,608	8,840	9,180	31,080	13,260	8,610	5,040	148,341
2008	18,360	11,850	4,615	3,600	3,080	5,186	9,516	9,380	36,000	21,375	4,928	4,640	163,789
2009	11,715	11,560	2,665	4,738	3,811	3,960	7,930	10,220	34,650	17,820	5,607	3,780	146,416
2010	27,470	13,800	2,530	2,619	2,880	4,118	8,448	11,618	46,410	15,370	7,200	4,096	176,462
2011	17,760	10,980	2,795	3,132	2,772	4,736	6,360	13,340	32,660	16,500	4,524	3,591	148,357
2012	11,550	12,352	3,009	2,944	3,526	4,161	8,375	7,540	33,120	16,380	4,784	4,140	142,296
2013	10,890	13,420	3,350	2,656	4,900	4,675	7,540	14,946	33,120	14,840	6,254	3,540	149,499
2014	12,480	14,700	4,526	3,400	4,032	5,733	7,920	14,256	42,140	24,360	9,048	2,862	178,270
2015[1]	8,250	11,880	2,760	2,848	4,356	5,220	8,296	12,118	36,260	19,140	8,316	3,484	156,544

[1] Preliminary.   Source: National Agricultural Statistics Service, U.S. Department of Agriculture (NASS-USDA)

Honey

Honey is the thick, supersaturated sugar solution produced by bees to feed their larvae. It is composed of fructose, glucose and water in varying proportions and also contains several enzymes and oils. The color of honey varies due to the source of nectar and age of the honey. Light colored honeys are usually of higher quality than darker honeys. The average honeybee colony can produce more than 700 pounds of honey per year but only 10 percent is usually harvested by the beekeeper. The rest of the honey is consumed by the colony during the year. American per capita honey consumption is 1 pound per person per year. Honey is said to be humanity's oldest sweet, and beeswax the first plastic.

Honey is used in many ways, including direct human consumption, baking, and medicine. Honey has several healing properties. Its high sugar content nourishes injured tissues, thus enhancing faster healing time. Honey's phytochemicals create a form of hydrogen peroxide that cleans out the wound, and the thick consistency protects the wound from contact with air. Honey has also proven superior to antibiotic ointments for reducing rates of infection in people with burns.

Prices – U.S. average domestic honey prices in 2014 (latest data) rose by +1.0% to a record high of 216.1 cents per pound. The value of U.S. honey production in 2014 rose +20.4% to $385.24 million, a new record high.

Supply – World production of honey in 2013 (latest data) rose +2.9% to 1.663 million metric tons, a new record high. The major producer of honey by far is China with 466.300 metric tons in 2013 which is 28.0% of total world production. Other major producers in 2013 were the U.S. with 67,812 metric tons, Russia with 68,446, Argentina with 80,000 metric tons, and Mexico with 56,907 metric tons.

U.S. production of honey in 2014 rose +19.2% to 178.270 million pounds, remaining well below the 14-year high of 220.339 million pounds posted in 2000. Stocks rose by +7.9% to 41.190 million pounds in 2014 (Jan 1), which is a down from 2000's decade high of 220.339 million pounds. Yield per colony in 2014 rose +15.0% to 65.1 pounds per colony. The number of colonies in 2014 rose +3.8% to 2.740, a new decade record high.

Trade – U.S. imports of honey in 2013 (latest data) rose by +8.5% to 323.6 million pounds, a new record high. U.S. exports of honey are generally small and in 2013 they totaled only 11.9 million pounds, which was only 2.3% of U.S. production.

Salient Statistics of Honey in the United States   In Millions of Pounds

Year	Number of Colonies (1,000)	Yield Per Colony (Pounds)	Stocks Jan. 1	Total U.S. Production	Imports for Consumption	Domestic Disappearance	Exports	Total Supply	Placed Under Loan	CCC Take Over	Net Gov't. Expenditure[3] (Million $)	Domestic Avg. Price All Honey - Cents Per Pound -	National Avg. Price Support	Per Capita Consumption (Pounds)
2006	2,393	64.7	60.5	154.9	277.6	----	7.0	493.0	103.6	160.5	----	142.1	----	----
2007	2,443	60.7	52.6	148.3	232.9	----	8.3	433.9	107.7	159.8	----	147.3	----	----
2008	2,342	69.9	51.2	163.8	231.4	----	10.1	446.3	142.1	232.7	----	147.3	----	----
2009	2,498	58.6	37.5	146.4	210.4	----	9.7	394.4	147.3	215.7	----	147.3	----	----
2010	2,692	65.6	45.0	176.5	251.1	----	9.5	472.6	161.9	285.7	----	147.3	----	----
2011	2,491	59.6	36.8	148.4	288.2	----	11.9	473.3	176.5	261.9	----	147.3	----	----
2012	2,539	56.0	31.8	142.3	310.8	----	12.3	484.9	199.2	283.5	----	161.9	----	----
2013	2,640	56.6	38.2	149.5	337.4	----	11.9	525.0	214.1	320.1	----	176.5	----	----
2014[1]	2,740	65.1	41.2	178.3	364.9	----	10.9	584.4	217.3	387.4	----	199.2	----	----
2015[2]	2,660	58.9	42.2	156.5		----			209.0	327.2	----	212.1	----	----

[1] Preliminary.   [2] Forecast.   [3] Fiscal year.   *Source: Economic Research Service, U.S. Department of Agriculture (ERS-USDA)*

Average Price of Honey, by Color Class in the United States   In Cents Per Pound

	Co-op and Private					Retail					All				
Year	Water White, Extra White	Extra Light Amber	Light Amber, Amber, Dark Amber	All Other Honey, Area Specialties	All Honey	Water White, Extra White	Extra Light Amber	Light Amber, Amber, Dark Amber	All Other Honey, Area Specialties	All Honey	Water White, Extra White	Extra Light Amber	Light Amber, Amber, Dark Amber	All Other Honey, Area Specialties	All Honey
2006	97.0	94.0	86.7	114.0	94.0	175.6	176.0	201.7	231.9	192.0	99.9	104.0	106.3	163.2	103.6
2007	103.0	97.5	93.8	132.7	99.9	172.8	188.0	218.3	291.1	204.6	104.6	106.4	112.5	175.6	107.7
2008	138.9	135.2	127.4	143.3	135.4	195.0	209.7	240.5	326.8	224.7	141.2	140.7	142.0	205.9	142.1
2009	142.6	144.5	135.1	179.8	141.5	252.6	252.5	291.4	414.3	283.7	144.0	150.4	148.2	247.9	147.3
2010	157.5	151.1	148.9	172.1	154.1	297.1	266.3	330.5	471.4	311.6	159.8	157.6	167.0	208.1	161.9
2011	170.1	164.4	165.7	182.6	167.7	274.1	307.1	315.4	461.0	314.7	172.9	171.1	183.4	225.2	176.5
2012	192.3	195.4	183.0	213.4	191.3	323.9	303.5	352.4	519.5	348.0	194.2	200.2	205.8	281.6	199.2
2013	210.9	204.0	197.3	222.4	205.8	340.9	330.6	405.1	492.5	382.4	212.9	209.0	219.2	248.9	214.1
2014	204.6	209.6	208.8	255.4	207.1	328.5	392.2	417.1	535.2	405.4	206.2	218.3	234.2	318.2	217.3
2015[1]	189.0	204.0	198.8	238.3	195.5	354.2	411.8	398.4	647.0	409.6	191.0	215.4	230.5	330.3	209.0

[1] Preliminary.   *Source: National Agricultural Statistics Service, U.S. Department of Agriculture (NASS-USDA)*

Interest Rates - U.S.

U.S. interest rates can be characterized in two main ways, by credit quality and by maturity. Credit quality refers to the level of risk associated with a particular borrower. U.S. Treasury securities, for example, carry the lowest risk. Maturity refers to the time at which the security matures and must be repaid. Treasury securities carry the full spectrum of maturities, from short-term cash management bills, to T-bills (4-weeks, 3-months, 6-months), T-notes (2-year, 3-year, 5-year, 7-year, and 10-year), and 30-year T-bonds. The most active futures markets are the 10-year T-note futures, 30-year T-bond futures, and Eurodollar futures, all of which are traded at the CME Group.

Prices – CME 10-year T-note futures prices (Barchart. com electronic symbol ZN) in early 2015 edged to a new 2-1/2 year high but then fell back and traded basically sideways in a choppy range during the remainder of 2015, finally closing the year mildly lower by -28/32 points at 125-29/32. The U.S. 10-year T-note yield fell to a 2-1/2 year low of 1.64% in January 2015 but then rebounded higher to close the year at 2.27%, up 10 basis points from the 2014 close of 2.17%.

10-year T-note prices during 2015 saw support from modest U.S. economic growth and low inflation tied in part to the plunge in crude oil and commodity prices. The U.S. economy during 2015 showed modest growth of +2.4% for the year and ended the year on a weak note with a quarterly preliminary GDP growth rate in Q4-2015 of only +1.0%. The economy in the second half of 2015 was hurt by weakness in business investment and exports and also by an inventory correction after the unwanted inventory buildup seen in the first half of the year.

The 76% plunge in crude oil prices from mid-2014 through early 2016 was a very bullish factor for T-note prices due to reduced inflation expectations. The 10-year breakeven inflation expectations rate, which measures the difference between nominal and inflation-adjusted TIPS T-notes, fell to a 7-year low of 1.39% in late 2015, helping to boost nominal T-bond prices. The plunge in crude oil prices pushed the headline U.S. inflation indexes lower and also put downward pressure on the core inflation indexes because fuel prices are such a key cost for a wide variety of products and services.

Fed policy offered a less bullish factor for T-notes during 2015 after the Fed concluded its third quantitative easing program (QE3) in October 2014. However, the Fed continued to roll over maturing securities in its portfolio, meaning it was still buying new securities with the proceeds from maturing securities, thus preventing its balance sheet from declining.

The Fed's 25 basis point rate hike in December 2015 was a mildly bearish factor, although it had already been fully factored into the market by the time it occurred. Expectations for the Fed to slowly raise interest rates in coming years is also a mildly bearish factor for T-note prices.

U.S. interest rates continue to trade at extraordinarily low levels due to the Fed's zero interest rate policy, low inflation, and weak global economic growth. However, the question is whether long-term interest rates will slowly rise in coming years if the world economy starts to normalize and if the Fed moves ahead with its intent to slowly raise short-term interest rates.

U.S. Producer Price Index[2] for All Commodities   1982 = 100

Year	Jan.	Feb.	Mar.	Apr.	May	June	July	Aug.	Sept.	Oct.	Nov.	Dec.	Average
2006	164.3	161.8	162.2	164.3	165.8	166.1	166.8	167.9	165.4	162.2	164.6	165.6	164.8
2007	164.0	166.8	169.3	171.4	173.3	173.8	175.1	172.4	173.5	174.7	179.0	178.6	172.7
2008	181.0	182.7	187.9	190.9	196.6	200.5	205.5	199.0	196.9	186.4	176.8	170.9	189.6
2009	171.2	169.3	168.1	169.1	170.8	174.1	172.5	175.0	174.1	175.2	177.4	178.1	172.9
2010	181.9	181.0	183.3	184.4	184.8	183.5	184.1	184.9	184.9	186.6	187.7	189.7	184.7
2011	192.7	195.8	199.2	203.1	204.1	203.9	204.6	203.2	203.7	201.1	201.4	199.8	201.1
2012	200.7	201.6	204.2	203.7	201.9	199.8	200.1	202.7	204.4	203.5	201.8	201.5	202.2
2013	202.5	204.3	204.0	203.5	204.1	204.3	204.4	204.2	203.9	202.5	201.2	202.0	203.4
2014	203.8	205.7	207.0	208.3	208.0	208.3	208.0	207.0	206.4	203.4	200.9	197.0	205.3
2015[1]	192.0	191.1	191.5	190.9	193.4	194.8	193.9	191.9	189.1	187.5	185.9	183.8	190.5

[1] Preliminary.   [2] Not seasonally adjusted.   *Source: Bureau of Labor Statistics, U.S. Department of Commerce (BLS)*

U.S. Consumer Price Index[2] for All Urban Consumers   1982-84 = 100

Year	Jan.	Feb.	Mar.	Apr.	May	June	July	Aug.	Sept.	Oct.	Nov.	Dec.	Average
2006	198.3	198.7	199.8	201.5	202.5	202.9	203.5	203.9	202.9	201.8	201.5	201.8	201.6
2007	202.4	203.5	205.4	206.7	207.9	208.4	208.3	207.9	208.5	208.9	210.2	210.0	207.3
2008	211.1	211.7	213.5	214.8	216.6	218.8	220.0	219.1	218.8	216.6	212.4	210.2	215.3
2009	211.1	212.2	212.7	213.2	213.9	215.7	215.4	215.8	216.0	216.2	216.3	215.9	214.5
2010	216.7	216.7	217.6	218.0	218.2	218.0	218.0	218.3	218.4	218.7	218.8	219.2	218.1
2011	220.2	221.3	223.5	224.9	226.0	225.7	225.9	226.5	226.9	226.4	226.2	225.7	224.9
2012	226.7	227.7	229.4	230.1	229.8	229.5	229.1	230.4	231.4	231.3	230.2	229.6	229.6
2013	230.3	232.2	232.8	232.5	232.9	233.5	233.6	233.9	234.1	233.5	233.1	233.0	233.0
2014	233.9	234.8	236.3	237.1	237.9	238.3	238.3	237.9	238.0	237.4	236.2	234.8	236.7
2015[1]	233.7	234.7	236.1	236.6	237.8	238.6	238.7	238.3	237.9	237.8	237.3	236.5	237.0

[1] Preliminary.   [2] Not seasonally adjusted.   *Source: Bureau of Labor Statistics, U.S. Department of Commerce (BLS)*

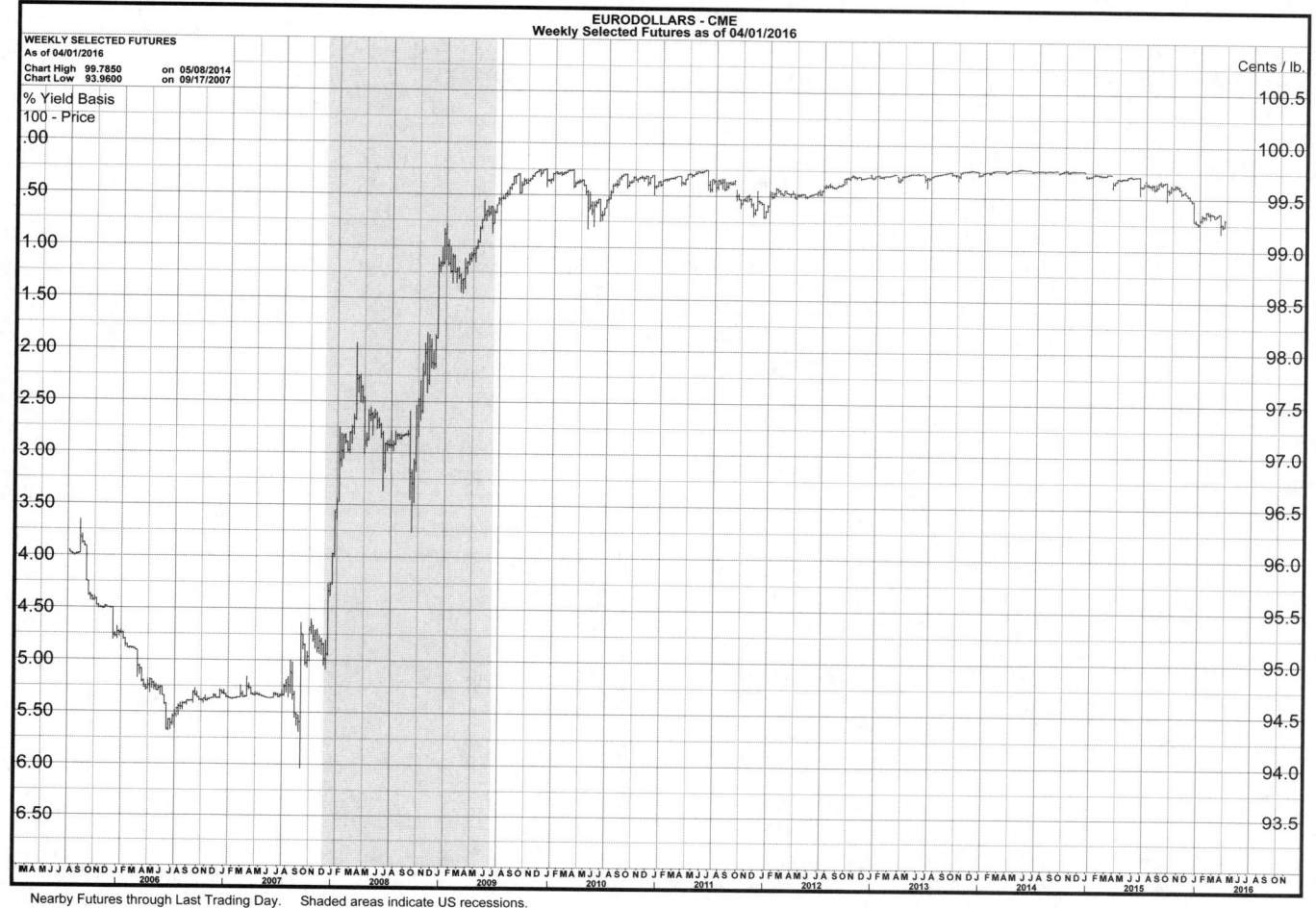

EURODOLLARS - CME
Weekly Selected Futures as of 04/01/2016

WEEKLY SELECTED FUTURES
As of 04/01/2016
Chart High 99.7850   on 05/08/2014
Chart Low   93.9600   on 09/17/2007

% Yield Basis
100 - Price

Cents / lb.

Nearby Futures through Last Trading Day.   Shaded areas indicate US recessions.

Volume of Trading of 3-month Eurodollar Futures in Chicago   In Thousands of Contracts

Year	Jan.	Feb.	Mar.	Apr.	May	June	July	Aug.	Sept.	Oct.	Nov.	Dec.	Total
2006	35,602.4	34,218.0	47,463.8	37,752.2	44,154.6	45,443.4	36,794.1	45,126.7	45,180.3	46,453.5	42,700.7	41,187.7	502,077
2007	43,204.2	46,365.8	63,154.7	39,567.7	50,305.2	58,372.0	53,290.3	77,539.0	49,528.8	45,862.8	53,795.1	40,484.5	621,470
2008	70,787.1	59,378.2	60,956.1	56,371.5	48,683.4	60,086.5	54,178.8	36,521.6	58,497.7	40,508.5	24,515.5	26,489.2	596,974
2009	31,370.9	29,422.6	35,280.3	29,706.4	34,665.5	51,021.4	40,062.0	36,483.1	39,604.4	40,397.6	32,914.4	36,656.6	437,585
2010	36,569.3	37,746.7	47,459.2	52,132.3	57,806.8	36,986.7	32,120.3	34,582.2	38,196.5	34,205.0	55,512.9	47,637.1	510,955
2011	42,213.1	51,117.3	62,877.0	49,748.5	46,199.0	62,516.2	46,462.8	61,739.9	38,864.4	34,186.8	39,340.0	28,821.7	564,087
2012	41,620.4	38,145.0	46,496.1	32,895.5	40,756.4	38,105.8	28,199.5	34,119.2	37,238.4	35,652.7	26,998.6	26,210.8	426,438
2013	40,800.6	32,152.3	37,526.2	30,235.7	51,371.9	69,283.3	41,177.9	38,851.4	51,413.1	43,321.9	39,422.5	41,693.4	517,250
2014	54,761.3	38,750.1	57,945.4	46,118.3	54,063.9	55,196.8	57,448.5	47,862.5	67,835.8	86,823.2	34,561.1	63,066.5	664,433
2015	60,557.7	53,474.6	56,886.5	39,486.9	46,358.9	55,022.2	45,717.3	51,075.2	47,750.9	44,983.2	39,937.9	45,661.9	586,913

Contract size = $1,000,000.   *Source: CME Group; International Monetary Market (IOM), division of the Chicago Mercantile Exchange (CME)*

Average Open Interest of 3-month Eurodollar Futures in Chicago   In Thousands of Contracts

Year	Jan.	Feb.	Mar.	Apr.	May	June	July	Aug.	Sept.	Oct.	Nov.	Dec.
2006	8,833.5	9,574.0	9,586.0	9,679.6	10,126.2	9,995.4	9,572.4	10,153.9	9,949.4	9,809.8	10,345.5	10,201.1
2007	9,682.3	10,400.5	10,847.9	10,827.1	11,895.5	11,285.2	11,166.9	11,416.3	10,782.6	10,019.4	10,631.2	10,515.5
2008	11,033.0	11,206.7	10,356.6	9,225.3	9,282.5	9,266.0	9,589.0	9,882.1	8,953.0	8,141.7	8,286.9	7,389.1
2009	6,772.8	6,857.6	6,371.3	6,055.5	6,480.5	6,383.2	6,540.1	6,748.5	6,659.5	6,937.8	7,382.3	6,876.4
2010	6,957.6	7,607.2	7,643.6	7,850.9	7,728.4	7,297.3	7,652.9	7,876.1	7,528.6	7,953.2	8,245.8	7,433.0
2011	7,675.5	8,820.5	9,086.9	9,494.8	10,101.6	10,117.4	10,018.2	9,997.3	9,011.2	8,239.0	8,624.3	8,123.4
2012	7,787.5	8,387.6	8,508.1	8,593.1	8,776.6	8,213.4	7,889.8	7,858.5	8,210.5	8,269.0	8,508.1	8,292.0
2013	8,320.7	8,898.0	9,261.8	9,350.3	9,681.0	9,020.2	8,685.1	9,291.6	9,141.1	9,420.5	10,163.4	10,422.3
2014	10,142.7	10,022.8	10,453.9	10,875.2	11,635.9	11,593.8	12,101.1	12,734.0	13,139.9	11,819.9	11,685.4	10,902.1
2015	10,860.6	11,099.2	10,806.9	10,972.8	11,415.8	11,292.4	11,483.9	12,050.4	11,528.6	11,072.0	11,202.6	10,704.9

Contract size = $1,000,000.   *Source: CME Group; International Monetary Market (IOM), division of the Chicago Mercantile Exchange (CME)*

INTEREST RATES - U.S.

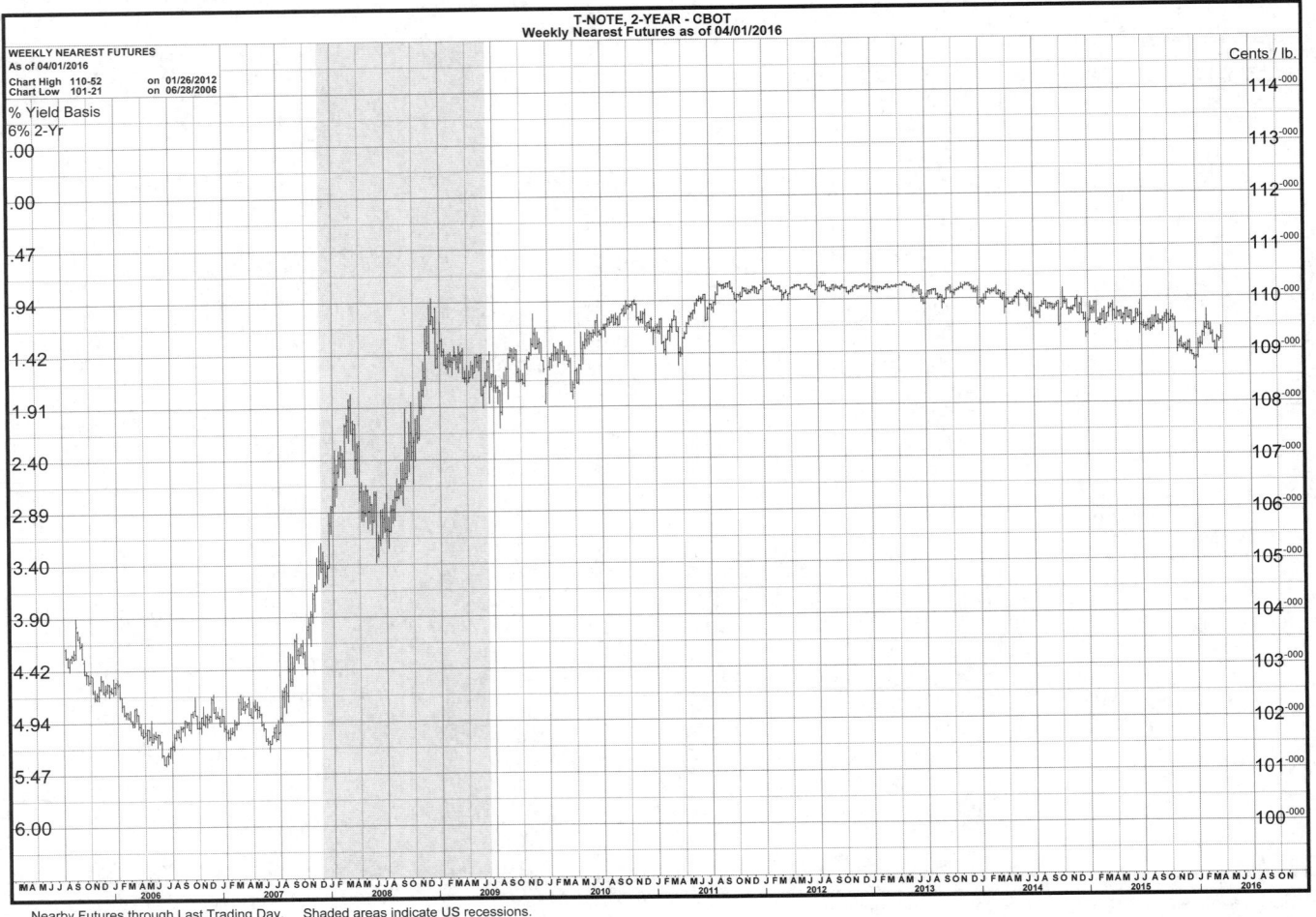

T-NOTE, 2-YEAR - CBOT
Weekly Nearest Futures as of 04/01/2016

WEEKLY NEAREST FUTURES
As of 04/01/2016
Chart High 110-52 on 01/26/2012
Chart Low 101-21 on 06/28/2006

% Yield Basis
6% 2-Yr

Cents / lb.

Nearby Futures through Last Trading Day.   Shaded areas indicate US recessions.

Volume of Trading of 2-Year U.S. Treasury Note Futures in Chicago   In Thousands of Contracts

Year	Jan.	Feb.	Mar.	Apr.	May	June	July	Aug.	Sept.	Oct.	Nov.	Dec.	Total
2006	2,053.3	3,223.3	3,206.5	2,090.0	4,690.9	2,837.1	2,525.1	4,461.0	2,768.3	2,422.9	4,826.4	2,862.0	37,967
2007	2,892.6	5,666.6	5,321.4	3,128.3	7,197.4	5,495.7	4,793.7	10,567.2	4,788.1	4,771.2	8,849.7	5,138.5	68,610
2008	7,526.1	10,092.8	7,515.4	5,102.6	8,195.6	7,207.2	6,366.1	7,529.6	8,126.5	5,355.3	4,067.9	2,225.8	79,311
2009	2,117.4	3,797.2	2,486.1	2,219.7	4,409.0	3,818.7	3,094.7	5,931.9	3,915.7	5,012.4	7,205.5	4,150.6	48,159
2010	4,487.2	8,143.4	6,164.3	6,164.1	9,494.2	4,398.8	4,083.6	6,491.7	3,719.2	3,189.8	6,849.9	3,791.0	66,977
2011	4,172.3	9,276.8	7,161.9	5,363.7	8,520.4	6,814.1	5,166.5	9,198.7	3,990.7	3,743.3	6,105.9	2,664.6	72,179
2012	3,162.6	6,083.1	4,858.3	3,568.9	6,748.6	3,626.2	3,831.4	6,593.6	3,575.3	3,318.0	6,615.1	3,127.6	55,109
2013	4,249.9	7,408.8	3,786.5	3,169.7	8,812.1	4,703.0	3,008.5	6,380.5	4,134.8	3,133.0	5,982.2	3,046.9	57,816
2014	4,004.9	4,637.1	4,670.2	4,402.3	8,206.8	4,404.6	3,913.5	9,120.7	6,155.0	6,801.9	8,643.1	5,054.2	70,014
2015	5,113.2	11,269.7	6,108.6	4,349.9	10,776.5	6,555.7	4,983.7	10,933.2	5,556.6	4,681.9	7,946.4	4,765.3	83,041

Contract size = $200,000.   *Source: CME Group; Chicago Board of Trade (CBT)*

Average Open Interest of 2-Year U.S. Treasury Note Futures in Chicago   In Thousands of Contracts

Year	Jan.	Feb.	Mar.	Apr.	May	June	July	Aug.	Sept.	Oct.	Nov.	Dec.
2006	437.8	489.3	469.0	489.5	607.6	541.1	595.1	701.4	683.6	680.7	698.4	716.0
2007	764.5	826.7	896.3	1,003.3	1,125.5	965.1	1,016.8	985.4	902.3	993.1	1,043.6	997.3
2008	1,101.2	1,313.0	1,187.3	1,110.0	1,166.8	972.5	895.4	922.6	783.7	735.0	648.0	503.4
2009	505.7	495.1	473.4	487.5	514.2	535.3	627.8	741.6	772.4	935.2	1,052.2	911.8
2010	885.7	982.1	891.3	1,001.7	1,022.3	900.3	847.1	805.6	708.2	734.8	710.8	664.9
2011	711.7	900.2	892.0	1,031.0	1,066.2	1,030.5	1,012.9	976.2	772.3	714.5	748.0	698.8
2012	781.4	904.4	842.3	835.7	975.7	928.1	953.8	1,012.6	963.5	942.0	1,030.2	1,015.8
2013	998.1	1,046.5	989.2	916.5	945.3	816.8	791.7	864.5	863.5	925.2	978.2	866.6
2014	858.0	934.8	942.0	1,077.5	1,153.4	1,051.2	1,164.8	1,400.5	1,546.2	1,425.6	1,432.8	1,292.8
2015	1,269.4	1,462.5	1,346.2	1,378.7	1,363.1	1,183.6	1,274.7	1,356.3	1,143.8	1,117.1	1,091.9	989.4

Contract size = $200,000.   *Source: CME Group; Chicago Board of Trade (CBT)*

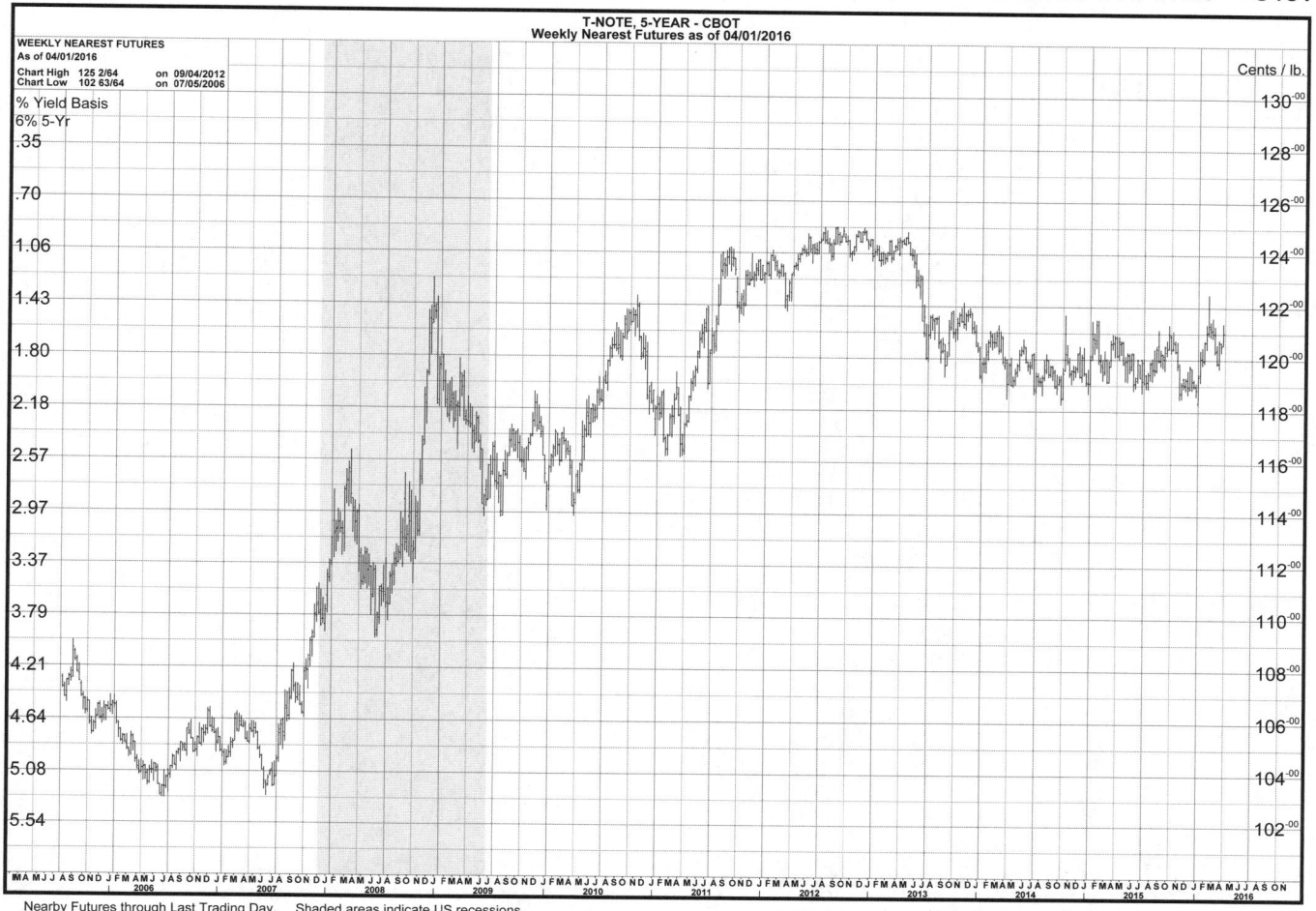

T-NOTE, 5-YEAR - CBOT
Weekly Nearest Futures as of 04/01/2016

WEEKLY NEAREST FUTURES
As of 04/01/2016

Chart High 125 2/64 on 09/04/2012
Chart Low 102 63/64 on 07/05/2006

% Yield Basis
6% 5-Yr

Nearby Futures through Last Trading Day.   Shaded areas indicate US recessions.

Volume of Trading of 5-Year U.S. Treasury Note Futures in Chicago   In Thousands of Contracts

Year	Jan.	Feb.	Mar.	Apr.	May	June	July	Aug.	Sept.	Oct.	Nov.	Dec.	Total
2006	9,388.4	12,141.7	11,865.2	7,869.8	12,971.9	9,368.7	8,102.0	13,347.5	9,369.3	8,730.9	13,423.5	8,291.5	124,870
2007	9,208.6	14,410.2	14,156.0	8,372.3	15,673.4	13,243.1	13,001.7	22,354.8	11,376.0	12,495.6	21,271.6	10,644.1	166,207
2008	15,479.7	20,790.4	17,424.0	12,474.7	17,616.2	14,904.3	14,514.1	15,085.6	16,979.1	10,079.8	8,057.9	4,721.7	168,127
2009	4,821.3	8,349.9	7,388.4	5,837.7	9,658.3	8,314.8	8,034.1	10,588.0	8,259.3	9,242.9	10,231.8	7,664.7	98,391
2010	7,434.9	11,815.6	10,096.3	9,631.3	16,093.0	10,212.4	9,662.0	13,062.2	9,627.7	9,404.1	14,828.5	10,282.0	132,150
2011	10,654.1	16,398.4	16,604.1	11,371.9	17,958.8	16,524.9	13,314.4	21,004.3	12,074.6	11,607.0	15,320.7	7,729.7	170,563
2012	9,260.0	14,543.1	12,251.9	8,980.8	14,647.3	10,565.4	7,291.7	13,493.4	10,510.3	9,281.0	13,968.6	8,549.0	133,342
2013	12,206.3	18,750.5	11,971.1	11,023.9	23,914.4	17,072.7	11,763.4	18,021.9	13,464.8	10,198.2	16,397.4	10,543.6	175,328
2014	13,081.6	18,022.0	16,060.6	14,088.2	20,473.5	13,605.3	14,182.4	20,546.3	16,596.0	20,858.3	15,933.0	12,982.0	196,429
2015	14,739.3	20,925.8	14,020.7	11,619.5	20,929.9	15,289.6	12,668.2	22,856.6	12,974.5	12,321.4	20,512.7	11,849.6	190,708

Contract size = $100,000.   *Source: CME Group; Chicago Board of Trade (CBT)*

Average Open Interest of 5-Year U.S. Treasury Note Futures in Chicago   In Thousands of Contracts

Year	Jan.	Feb.	Mar.	Apr.	May	June	July	Aug.	Sept.	Oct.	Nov.	Dec.
2006	1,105.1	1,404.8	1,238.0	1,257.2	1,326.0	1,264.7	1,258.3	1,409.8	1,341.3	1,413.8	1,484.4	1,423.8
2007	1,468.1	1,499.6	1,481.0	1,614.9	1,763.5	1,601.5	1,586.9	1,648.0	1,564.9	1,666.1	1,932.4	1,841.2
2008	1,940.6	2,101.2	1,923.8	1,850.9	1,851.0	1,669.6	1,574.5	1,600.7	1,483.4	1,378.1	1,267.1	1,057.8
2009	965.5	964.7	897.8	812.7	860.8	774.2	761.1	831.9	800.3	770.9	854.0	831.6
2010	805.1	939.1	942.4	937.2	1,045.8	932.2	940.4	1,095.6	925.0	1,012.8	1,136.6	1,010.9
2011	1,075.8	1,293.9	1,223.4	1,364.8	1,524.6	1,576.9	1,513.4	1,435.6	1,326.7	1,200.4	1,277.5	1,261.2
2012	1,398.3	1,444.8	1,390.1	1,306.6	1,384.1	1,144.6	1,145.8	1,236.3	1,330.2	1,399.5	1,461.6	1,506.2
2013	1,532.5	1,653.7	1,733.6	1,847.6	1,842.2	1,535.0	1,584.4	1,641.0	1,668.5	1,745.1	1,968.7	1,865.1
2014	1,939.7	2,002.5	1,959.1	2,036.7	2,126.3	2,070.6	2,130.6	2,190.1	2,130.5	1,992.7	1,993.5	1,844.4
2015	1,837.5	1,983.8	1,992.9	2,016.3	2,038.9	2,096.2	2,200.8	2,398.5	2,352.1	2,422.1	2,469.2	2,371.4

Contract size = $100,000.   *Source: CME Group; Chicago Board of Trade (CBT)*

INTEREST RATES - U.S.

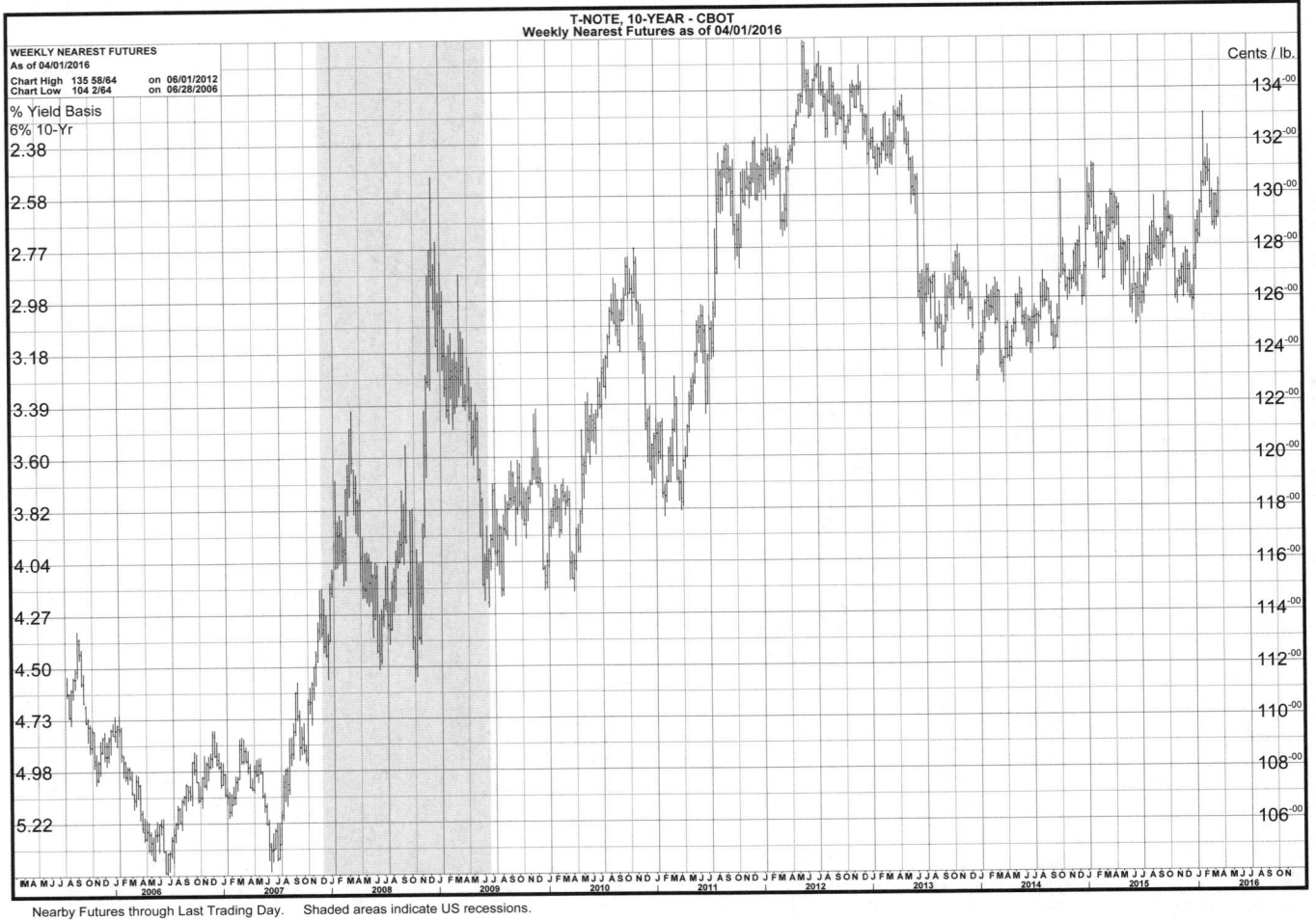

T-NOTE, 10-YEAR - CBOT
Weekly Nearest Futures as of 04/01/2016

WEEKLY NEAREST FUTURES
As of 04/01/2016
Chart High 135 58/64 on 06/01/2012
Chart Low 104 2/64 on 06/28/2006

% Yield Basis
6% 10-Yr

Cents / lb.

Nearby Futures through Last Trading Day.   Shaded areas indicate US recessions.

Volume of Trading of 10-year U.S. Treasury Note Futures in Chicago   In Thousands of Contracts

Year	Jan.	Feb.	Mar.	Apr.	May	June	July	Aug.	Sept.	Oct.	Nov.	Dec.	Total
2006	17,188.6	21,262.7	22,739.9	17,241.5	26,174.6	20,311.2	16,645.2	24,796.6	22,125.2	20,602.6	28,413.8	18,070.1	255,572
2007	21,492.5	30,367.2	30,210.2	18,529.8	34,343.9	37,171.0	32,361.3	38,785.6	24,375.6	25,280.4	36,890.7	19,421.3	349,229
2008	28,924.8	33,426.2	23,331.5	19,043.9	27,414.0	22,591.8	22,903.0	21,069.7	23,265.1	15,101.1	11,826.6	7,873.1	256,771
2009	9,778.0	14,548.1	15,116.1	11,893.7	17,309.8	16,994.6	16,420.7	19,292.8	16,099.0	19,268.8	19,037.2	14,093.3	189,852
2010	16,865.3	23,588.6	19,582.2	22,070.6	35,156.5	24,198.2	22,294.5	30,744.0	26,070.6	22,947.9	29,360.3	20,840.2	293,719
2011	22,260.8	27,531.8	29,500.1	20,162.8	31,149.4	31,897.7	25,851.1	39,911.1	24,612.4	23,559.8	26,614.2	14,351.4	317,403
2012	19,336.4	26,546.0	24,188.9	20,706.8	32,255.6	24,036.4	16,688.1	25,178.8	18,527.4	18,740.5	23,319.0	15,473.1	264,997
2013	24,720.9	33,572.4	24,606.7	23,859.0	43,005.7	32,912.7	21,673.6	31,715.3	23,332.3	21,265.7	27,463.8	17,800.2	325,928
2014	23,218.1	29,772.2	27,675.3	25,202.1	34,569.3	24,098.5	23,402.1	34,087.3	28,122.5	39,126.2	28,205.8	23,005.8	340,485
2015	27,499.2	33,705.2	24,770.7	22,343.8	38,005.7	29,805.4	23,574.7	34,287.1	22,586.7	23,505.9	28,612.5	19,644.2	328,341

Contract size = $100,000.   *Source: CME Group; Chicago Board of Trade (CBT)*

Average Open Interest of 10-year U.S. Treasury Note Futures in Chicago   In Thousands of Contracts

Year	Jan.	Feb.	Mar.	Apr.	May	June	July	Aug.	Sept.	Oct.	Nov.	Dec.
2006	1,700.0	1,990.4	2,048.7	2,259.7	2,321.0	2,054.2	2,087.1	2,265.3	2,271.5	2,408.2	2,398.2	2,236.0
2007	2,343.6	2,367.3	2,294.0	2,586.9	2,878.3	2,853.9	2,871.5	2,820.5	2,269.5	2,497.2	2,661.6	2,313.2
2008	2,431.2	2,517.6	2,179.8	2,073.7	2,144.6	1,978.8	1,802.6	1,835.2	1,658.2	1,385.2	1,226.4	1,074.2
2009	1,034.9	1,027.6	1,007.0	1,010.0	1,132.3	1,070.9	1,056.2	1,139.7	1,120.2	1,239.1	1,327.5	1,203.9
2010	1,292.9	1,420.4	1,423.8	1,632.0	1,838.8	1,756.8	1,802.2	1,973.0	1,686.3	1,617.2	1,527.4	1,335.3
2011	1,360.1	1,521.3	1,563.5	1,643.4	1,854.0	1,834.0	1,843.5	1,937.7	1,627.4	1,504.3	1,505.7	1,460.6
2012	1,647.6	1,847.4	1,796.4	1,804.4	1,949.8	1,806.5	1,787.3	1,640.5	1,593.8	1,685.3	1,783.4	1,674.9
2013	1,815.9	2,089.8	2,125.6	2,230.3	2,331.8	2,132.2	2,199.4	2,308.6	2,031.6	2,079.2	2,341.3	2,261.2
2014	2,260.5	2,426.0	2,433.4	2,526.5	2,720.3	2,591.6	2,679.0	2,853.2	2,705.4	2,776.0	2,855.5	2,652.6
2015	2,684.1	2,610.3	2,690.8	2,822.7	2,884.8	2,730.7	2,751.9	2,941.1	2,729.8	2,776.5	2,680.6	2,594.4

Contract size = $100,000.   *Source: CME Group; Chicago Board of Trade (CBT)*

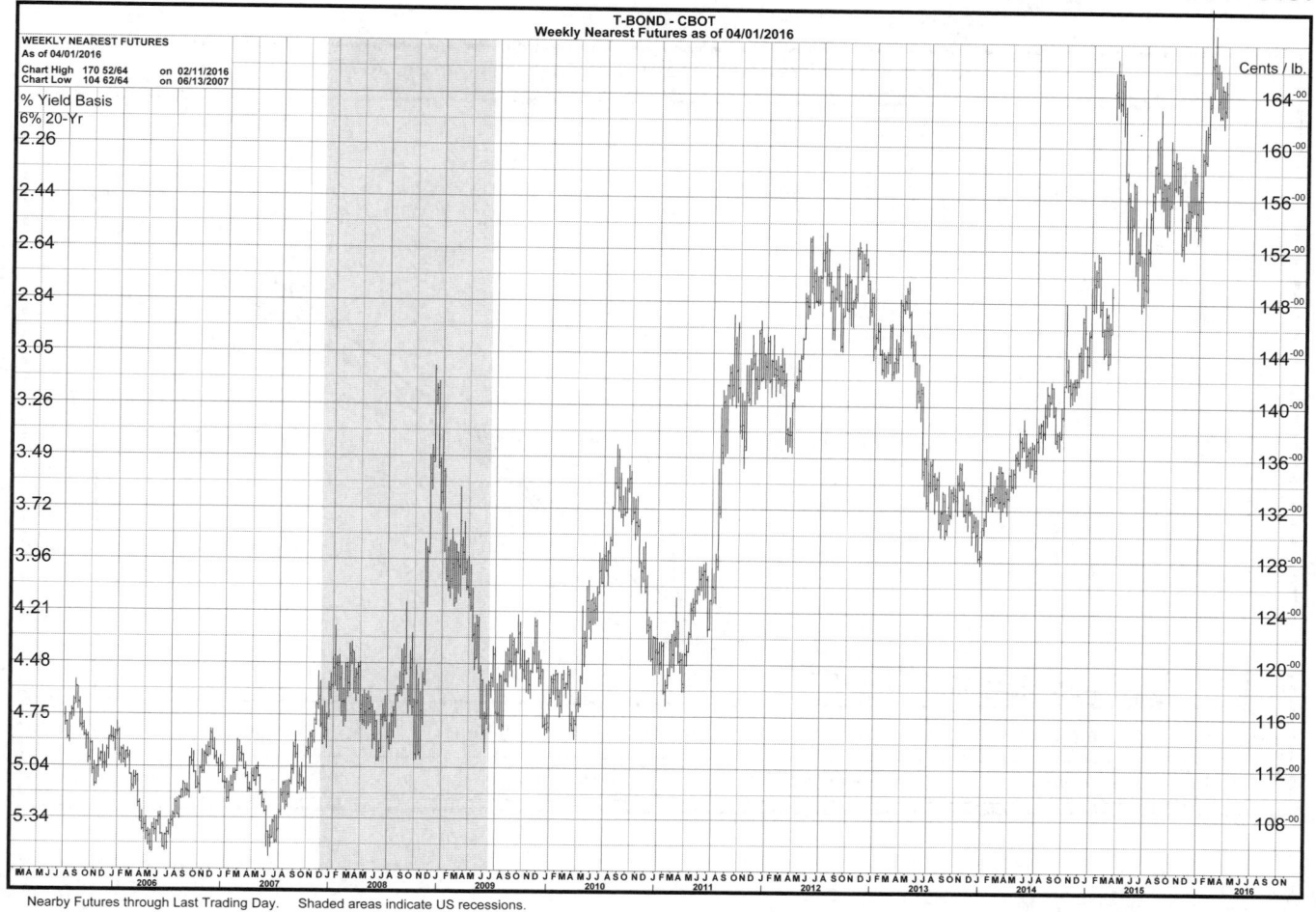

T-BOND - CBOT
Weekly Nearest Futures as of 04/01/2016

Nearby Futures through Last Trading Day.   Shaded areas indicate US recessions.

Volume of Trading of 30-year U.S. Treasury Bond Futures in Chicago   In Thousands of Contracts

Year	Jan.	Feb.	Mar.	Apr.	May	June	July	Aug.	Sept.	Oct.	Nov.	Dec.	Total
2006	7,044.8	8,511.6	8,980.6	6,969.2	10,354.4	7,564.5	5,854.2	8,736.7	7,553.9	6,375.1	9,461.6	6,348.2	93,755
2007	7,108.8	10,060.2	10,338.3	6,108.4	10,578.5	11,338.4	9,452.1	11,439.3	6,864.4	7,232.1	11,146.2	5,963.6	107,630
2008	9,667.3	11,646.2	8,739.1	5,835.3	9,173.4	7,176.8	7,429.4	7,521.6	7,830.0	5,559.1	5,267.6	3,618.7	89,465
2009	3,805.9	6,062.7	4,525.5	3,224.8	6,465.1	5,192.0	4,995.2	7,238.3	4,297.6	5,133.4	6,978.4	4,313.9	62,233
2010	4,617.8	7,345.1	5,748.7	6,033.7	10,457.5	5,899.4	5,711.8	9,165.6	6,774.8	6,806.7	9,379.5	5,569.2	83,510
2011	6,272.2	8,551.9	7,823.2	5,528.4	9,231.3	8,358.3	6,471.5	11,892.5	7,487.1	6,694.3	9,057.7	4,969.9	92,339
2012	6,143.3	8,623.0	7,335.2	5,890.8	11,326.7	9,060.1	6,493.7	8,685.7	6,680.1	6,866.2	8,530.8	6,109.6	91,745
2013	7,892.2	10,758.6	7,691.9	8,269.7	13,337.5	9,601.6	5,788.0	8,792.7	6,759.6	6,193.9	7,712.2	5,165.3	97,963
2014	5,871.1	8,211.2	6,867.7	6,259.9	9,648.8	7,044.9	6,719.0	9,948.4	7,678.1	10,370.2	7,827.0	6,742.1	93,188
2015	7,956.2	8,611.4	5,183.2	4,747.5	6,832.7	5,708.3	5,453.9	7,438.7	4,884.1	4,927.9	5,625.7	4,531.9	71,902

Contract size = $100,000.   *Source: CME Group; Chicago Board of Trade (CBT)*

Average Open Interest of 30-year U.S. Treasury Bond Futures in Chicago   In Contracts

Year	Jan.	Feb.	Mar.	Apr.	May	June	July	Aug.	Sept.	Oct.	Nov.	Dec.
2006	601,094	662,314	622,927	739,601	858,812	760,240	760,749	813,905	763,092	737,070	810,426	803,020
2007	816,747	903,121	852,305	875,810	949,173	980,004	988,995	991,513	915,693	948,940	1,022,623	947,588
2008	1,033,106	1,041,505	979,695	893,308	941,317	879,149	891,111	880,157	877,623	756,790	731,186	754,687
2009	726,062	733,323	712,813	708,243	724,577	706,818	696,641	727,674	749,290	739,723	777,241	704,259
2010	656,438	676,778	648,845	663,991	740,180	663,330	682,310	738,206	669,950	683,476	654,901	563,632
2011	552,937	613,356	609,003	573,206	702,197	668,848	628,174	661,826	647,168	618,884	634,941	597,183
2012	612,937	615,616	583,579	576,419	661,058	664,479	636,745	610,065	570,346	564,706	623,227	586,502
2013	551,333	632,060	630,148	681,045	667,210	568,046	574,724	626,392	630,549	644,843	696,333	656,867
2014	666,663	716,926	712,174	722,390	780,781	738,607	758,214	870,115	860,417	870,759	850,561	889,272
2015	829,094	640,877	414,934	437,101	478,017	484,216	500,019	533,913	505,812	501,845	491,806	519,574

Contract size = $100,000.   *Source: CME Group; Chicago Board of Trade (CBT)*

INTEREST RATES - U.S.

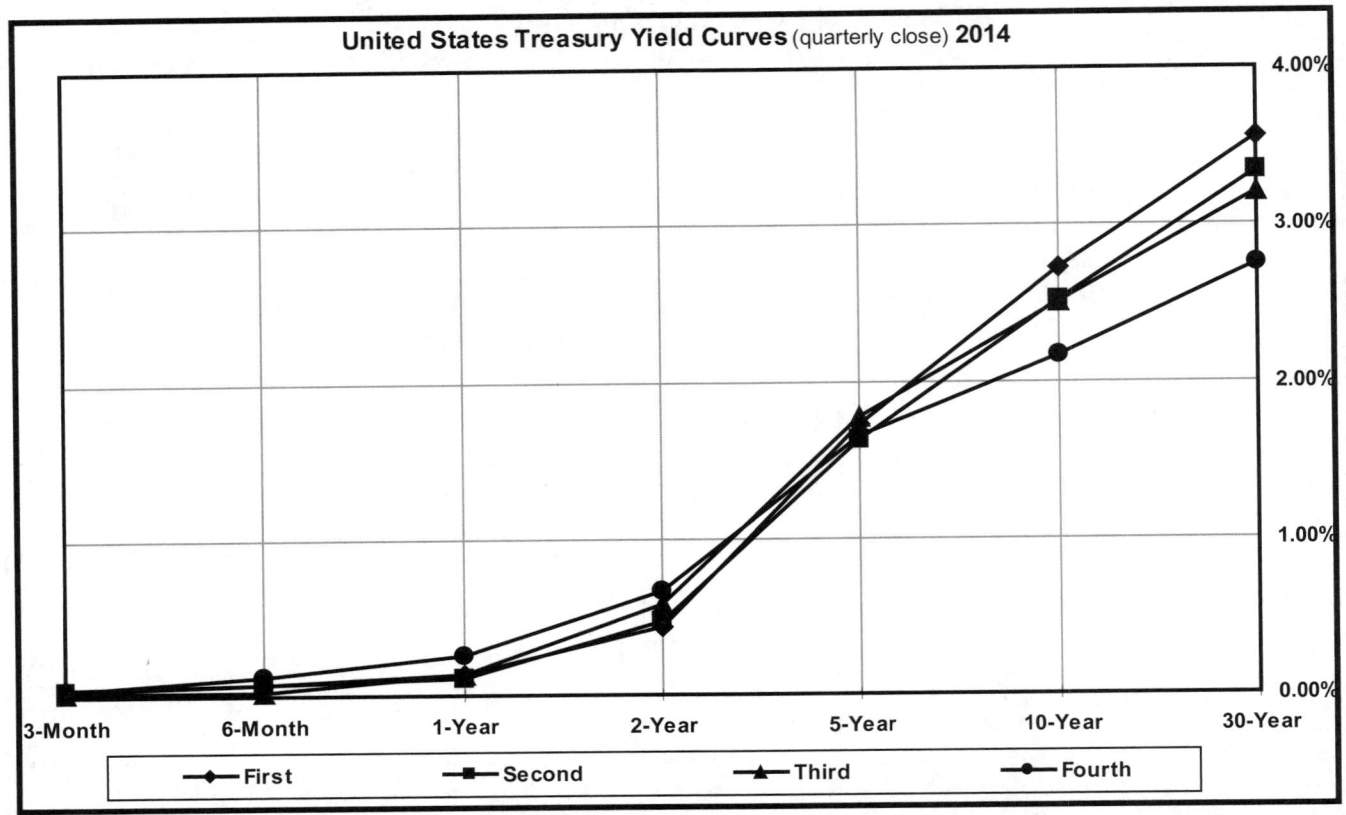

United States Treasury Yield Curves (quarterly close) **2014**

U.S. Federal Funds Rate   In Percent

Year	Jan.	Feb.	Mar.	Apr.	May	June	July	Aug.	Sept.	Oct.	Nov.	Dec.	Average
2006	4.29	4.49	4.59	4.79	4.94	4.99	5.24	5.25	5.25	5.25	5.25	5.24	4.96
2007	5.25	5.26	5.26	5.25	5.25	5.25	5.26	5.02	4.94	4.76	4.49	4.24	5.02
2008	3.94	2.98	2.61	2.28	1.98	2.00	2.01	2.00	1.81	0.97	0.39	0.16	1.93
2009	0.15	0.22	0.18	0.15	0.18	0.21	0.16	0.16	0.15	0.12	0.12	0.12	0.16
2010	0.11	0.13	0.16	0.20	0.20	0.18	0.18	0.19	0.19	0.19	0.19	0.18	0.18
2011	0.17	0.16	0.14	0.10	0.09	0.09	0.07	0.10	0.08	0.07	0.08	0.07	0.10
2012	0.08	0.10	0.13	0.14	0.16	0.16	0.16	0.13	0.14	0.16	0.16	0.16	0.14
2013	0.14	0.15	0.14	0.15	0.11	0.09	0.09	0.08	0.08	0.09	0.08	0.09	0.11
2014	0.07	0.07	0.08	0.09	0.09	0.10	0.09	0.09	0.09	0.09	0.09	0.12	0.09
2015	0.11	0.11	0.11	0.12	0.12	0.13	0.13	0.14	0.14	0.12	0.12	0.24	0.13

Source: Bureau of Economic Analysis, U.S. Department of Commerce (BEA)

U.S. Municipal Bond Yield[1]   In Percent

Year	Jan.	Feb.	Mar.	Apr.	May	June	July	Aug.	Sept.	Oct.	Nov.	Dec.	Average
2006	4.37	4.41	4.44	4.58	4.59	4.60	4.61	4.39	4.27	4.30	4.14	4.11	4.40
2007	4.23	4.22	4.15	4.26	4.31	4.60	4.56	4.64	4.51	4.39	4.46	4.42	4.40
2008	4.27	4.64	4.93	4.70	4.58	4.69	4.68	4.69	4.86	5.50	5.23	5.56	4.86
2009	5.07	4.90	4.99	4.78	4.56	4.81	4.72	4.60	4.24	4.20	4.37	4.21	4.62
2010	4.33	4.36	4.36	4.41	4.29	4.36	4.32	4.03	3.87	3.87	4.40	4.92	4.29
2011	5.28	5.15	4.92	4.99	4.59	4.51	4.52	4.02	4.01	4.13	4.05	3.95	4.51
2012	3.68	3.66	3.91	3.95	3.77	3.94	3.78	3.74	3.73	3.65	3.46	3.48	3.73
2013	3.60	3.72	3.96	3.92	3.72	4.27	4.56	4.82	4.79	4.56	4.60	4.73	4.27
2014	4.59	4.44	4.46	4.35	4.29	4.35	4.33	4.23	4.13	3.96	3.96	3.70	4.23
2015	3.40	3.58	3.59	3.51	3.76	3.82	3.79	3.74	3.78	3.67	3.68	3.57	3.66

[1] 20-bond average.   *Source: Bureau of Economic Analysis, U.S. Department of Commerce (BEA)*

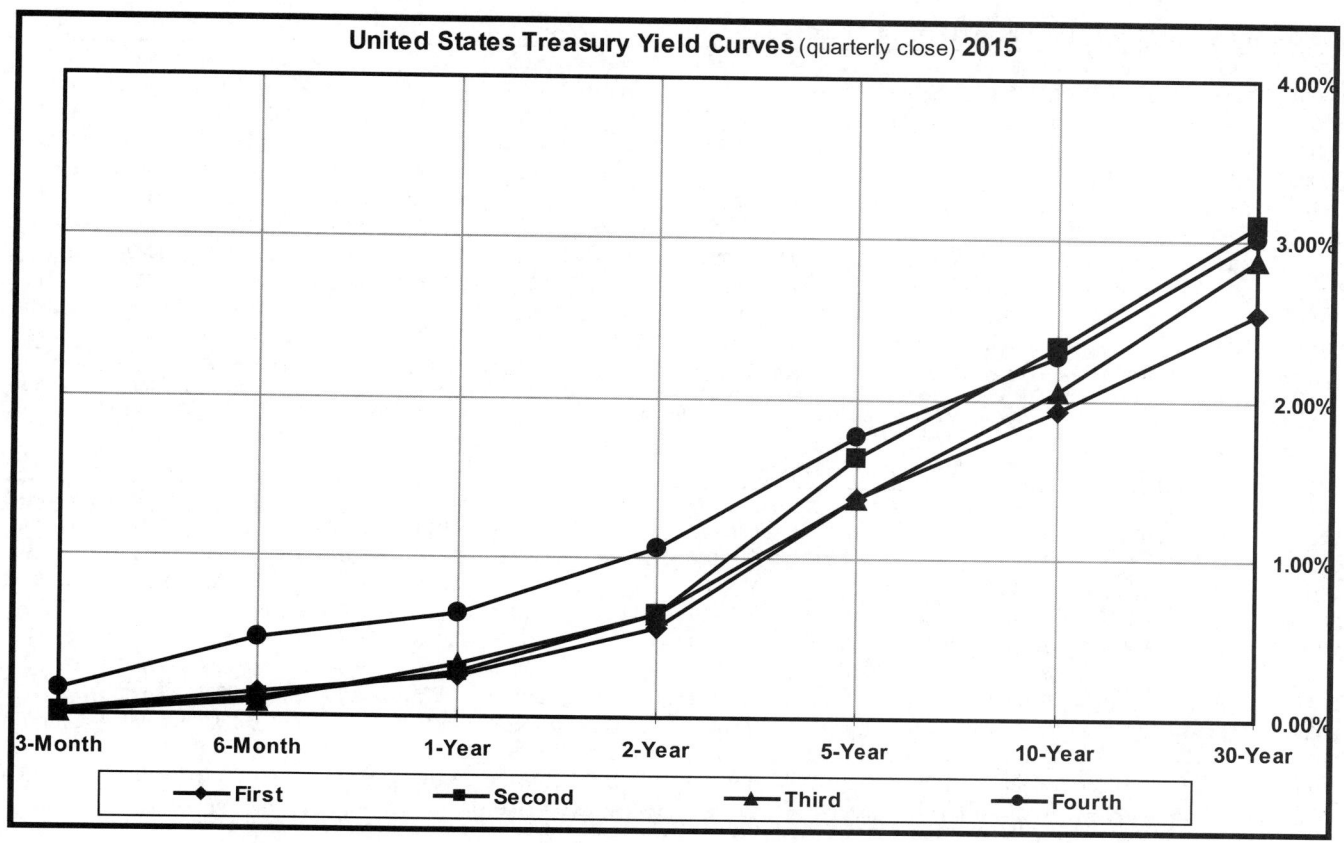

United States Treasury Yield Curves (quarterly close) **2015**

Legend: First, Second, Third, Fourth

U.S. Industrial Production Index[1]   1997 = 100

Year	Jan.	Feb.	Mar.	Apr.	May	June	July	Aug.	Sept.	Oct.	Nov.	Dec.	Average
2006	101.0	101.0	101.3	101.7	101.5	101.9	101.9	102.3	102.1	102.1	102.0	103.0	101.8
2007	102.5	103.6	103.8	104.5	104.6	104.6	104.5	104.7	105.1	104.5	105.2	105.1	104.4
2008	104.9	104.6	104.3	103.5	103.1	102.8	102.3	100.8	96.5	97.4	96.1	93.4	100.8
2009	91.2	90.6	89.2	88.5	87.6	87.2	88.2	89.1	89.8	90.2	90.4	90.8	89.4
2010	91.8	92.1	92.7	93.1	94.5	94.7	95.2	95.5	95.7	95.5	95.5	96.4	94.4
2011	96.4	95.9	96.7	96.3	96.5	96.8	97.2	97.8	97.8	98.4	98.3	98.8	97.2
2012	99.5	99.7	99.1	99.9	100.1	100.0	100.3	99.8	99.9	100.2	100.6	100.9	100.0
2013	100.9	101.3	101.6	101.5	101.5	101.7	101.3	102.0	102.6	102.7	102.9	103.2	101.9
2014	103.0	103.8	104.7	104.9	105.2	105.7	106.1	106.1	106.7	106.8	107.8	107.9	105.7
2015[1]	107.6	107.4	107.2	107.1	106.7	106.7	107.5	107.5	107.5	107.3	106.5	106.0	107.1

[1] Total Index of the Federal Reserve Index of Quantity Output, seasonally adjusted.   [2] Preliminary.   *Source: Bureau of Economic Analysis, U.S. Department of Commerce (BEA)*

U.S. Gross National Product, National Income, and Personal Income   In Billions of Constant Dollars[1]

	Gross Domestic Product					National Income					Personal Income				
Year	First Quarter	Second Quarter	Third Quarter	Fourth Quarter	Total	First Quarter	Second Quarter	Third Quarter	Fourth Quarter	Total	First Quarter	Second Quarter	Third Quarter	Fourth Quarter	Total
2006	13,650	13,803	13,911	14,068	13,858	11,865	11,956	12,062	12,139	12,006	11,206	11,326	11,436	11,591	11,390
2007	14,235	14,425	14,572	14,690	14,480	12,227	12,324	12,329	12,410	12,322	11,816	11,944	12,043	12,180	11,996
2008	14,673	14,817	14,844	14,547	14,720	12,476	12,516	12,545	12,187	12,431	12,362	12,513	12,474	12,374	12,431
2009	14,381	14,342	14,384	14,564	14,418	12,007	11,996	12,122	12,374	12,125	12,039	12,099	12,057	12,134	12,082
2010	14,681	14,889	15,058	15,230	14,964	12,457	12,621	12,869	13,012	12,740	12,235	12,413	12,544	12,716	12,477
2011	15,238	15,461	15,587	15,785	15,518	13,091	13,256	13,455	13,607	13,352	13,078	13,195	13,347	13,398	13,255
2012	15,974	16,122	16,228	16,297	16,155	13,943	13,997	14,062	14,246	14,062	13,662	13,814	13,867	14,317	13,915
2013	16,441	16,527	16,728	16,958	16,663	14,258	14,416	14,501	14,659	14,458	13,891	14,025	14,136	14,221	14,068
2014	16,984	17,270	17,522	17,616	17,348	14,710	14,981	15,257	15,358	15,077	14,434	14,613	14,775	14,956	14,694
2015[1]	17,649	17,914	18,060	18,148	17,943	15,336	15,520	15,616		15,491	15,080	15,277	15,444	15,567	15,342

[1] Seasonally adjusted at annual rates.   [2] Preliminary.   *Source: Bureau of Economic Analysis, U.S. Department of Commerce (BEA)*

INTEREST RATES - U.S.

U.S. Money Supply M1[2]   In Billions of Dollars

Year	Jan.	Feb.	Mar.	Apr.	May	June	July	Aug.	Sept.	Oct.	Nov.	Dec.	Average
2006	1,380.0	1,378.7	1,383.1	1,380.8	1,386.3	1,372.7	1,370.5	1,372.8	1,364.0	1,370.9	1,370.7	1,367.5	1,374.8
2007	1,372.6	1,363.1	1,366.2	1,377.4	1,379.6	1,364.6	1,368.8	1,377.2	1,375.2	1,380.4	1,371.2	1,374.9	1,372.6
2008	1,378.4	1,380.2	1,388.5	1,390.6	1,392.1	1,400.2	1,418.4	1,408.5	1,462.1	1,475.2	1,514.0	1,603.7	1,434.3
2009	1,583.8	1,566.9	1,578.5	1,610.9	1,615.7	1,653.2	1,660.5	1,662.4	1,664.8	1,678.9	1,681.9	1,693.9	1,637.6
2010	1,680.1	1,702.2	1,712.2	1,697.4	1,706.2	1,722.2	1,719.3	1,746.1	1,764.6	1,778.9	1,835.5	1,842.6	1,742.3
2011	1,858.5	1,874.1	1,890.6	1,898.2	1,932.9	1,945.9	1,997.9	2,110.7	2,128.7	2,139.5	2,175.1	2,170.0	2,010.2
2012	2,205.4	2,209.8	2,227.2	2,244.2	2,249.9	2,262.0	2,310.6	2,341.3	2,388.3	2,419.4	2,426.6	2,461.5	2,312.2
2013	2,469.8	2,465.3	2,473.3	2,508.3	2,522.4	2,519.9	2,541.6	2,550.5	2,586.9	2,625.2	2,625.3	2,660.5	2,545.8
2014	2,688.4	2,712.9	2,746.1	2,770.9	2,790.5	2,820.8	2,836.8	2,807.4	2,869.6	2,874.0	2,884.7	2,927.3	2,810.8
2015[1]	2,937.9	2,985.1	2,990.2	2,995.6	2,989.8	3,015.3	3,034.6	3,041.9	3,057.2	3,038.1	3,087.2	3,082.0	3,021.2

[1] Preliminary.   [2] M1 -- The sum of currency held outside the vaults of depository institutions, Federal Reserve Banks, and the U.S. Treasury; travelers checks; and demand and other checkable deposits issued by financial institutions (except demand deposits due to the Treasury and depository institutions), minus cash items in process of collection and Federal Reserve float. Seasonally adjusted.   *Source: Board of Governors of the Federal Reserve System*

U.S. Money Supply M2[2]   In Billions of Dollars

Year	Jan.	Feb.	Mar.	Apr.	May	June	July	Aug.	Sept.	Oct.	Nov.	Dec.	Average
2006	6,695.0	6,719.6	6,734.7	6,771.2	6,778.3	6,815.8	6,857.2	6,887.5	6,914.1	6,962.9	6,998.4	7,041.8	6,848.0
2007	7,079.9	7,096.2	7,131.0	7,203.0	7,218.1	7,250.7	7,280.6	7,357.2	7,375.3	7,387.8	7,414.0	7,445.5	7,269.9
2008	7,480.0	7,565.8	7,633.5	7,676.8	7,688.9	7,705.4	7,750.2	7,764.0	7,832.3	7,938.6	7,990.2	8,168.5	7,766.2
2009	8,250.9	8,281.9	8,349.7	8,353.5	8,411.1	8,418.5	8,421.0	8,419.3	8,414.5	8,440.7	8,474.5	8,472.5	8,392.3
2010	8,428.6	8,474.9	8,468.6	8,499.9	8,552.3	8,570.3	8,579.9	8,630.5	8,660.3	8,710.5	8,739.2	8,772.2	8,590.6
2011	8,807.5	8,849.1	8,892.6	8,955.1	9,005.4	9,089.5	9,278.0	9,491.4	9,515.3	9,547.5	9,591.7	9,629.8	9,221.1
2012	9,707.2	9,742.7	9,790.8	9,844.3	9,874.6	9,945.2	10,020.0	10,092.5	10,175.1	10,236.3	10,295.8	10,420.3	10,012.1
2013	10,444.9	10,430.7	10,509.5	10,545.5	10,581.7	10,637.8	10,696.6	10,758.1	10,811.1	10,920.5	10,928.0	10,985.4	10,687.5
2014	11,033.8	11,098.9	11,153.5	11,212.3	11,281.8	11,335.3	11,402.0	11,438.7	11,476.6	11,528.6	11,566.7	11,636.4	11,347.1
2015[1]	11,703.5	11,800.1	11,835.1	11,888.0	11,923.9	11,970.6	12,032.5	12,097.8	12,157.5	12,177.9	12,257.2	12,299.4	12,012.0

[1] Preliminary.   [2] M2 -- M1 plus savings deposits (including money market deposit accounts) and small-denomination (less than $100,000) time deposits issued by financial institutions; and shares in retail money market mutual funds (funds with initial investments of less than $50,000), net of retirement accounts. Seasonally adjusted.   *Source: Board of Governors of the Federal Reserve System*

U.S. Money Supply MZM[2]   In Billions of Dollars

Year	Jan.	Feb.	Mar.	Apr.	May	June	July	Aug.	Sept.	Oct.	Nov.	Dec.	Average
2006	6,874.5	6,883.1	6,888.8	6,919.6	6,923.4	6,963.0	7,000.0	7,026.2	7,053.6	7,108.9	7,152.0	7,227.3	7,001.7
2007	7,245.9	7,265.6	7,323.5	7,416.9	7,465.0	7,528.5	7,599.8	7,750.7	7,868.7	7,968.1	8,060.0	8,130.9	7,635.3
2008	8,179.6	8,395.3	8,556.7	8,643.0	8,684.4	8,734.0	8,782.1	8,790.0	8,793.2	8,829.6	8,946.9	9,170.1	8,708.7
2009	9,325.3	9,399.0	9,500.4	9,532.3	9,621.4	9,635.0	9,643.4	9,614.8	9,590.7	9,575.9	9,576.6	9,539.5	9,546.2
2010	9,493.0	9,499.5	9,440.7	9,406.9	9,432.3	9,443.3	9,474.8	9,553.2	9,606.4	9,668.4	9,716.5	9,742.5	9,539.8
2011	9,745.1	9,780.7	9,862.4	9,968.0	10,053.3	10,128.9	10,295.7	10,433.2	10,485.9	10,526.8	10,574.1	10,626.5	10,206.7
2012	10,706.1	10,744.0	10,813.5	10,872.5	10,912.7	10,984.9	11,069.5	11,164.0	11,256.2	11,317.5	11,380.8	11,529.3	11,062.6
2013	11,584.6	11,581.8	11,652.8	11,707.1	11,747.4	11,820.1	11,891.8	11,958.5	12,039.0	12,142.5	12,156.2	12,207.2	11,874.1
2014	12,259.2	12,328.0	12,383.9	12,428.3	12,502.2	12,551.6	12,621.4	12,655.2	12,702.2	12,777.5	12,833.5	12,934.9	12,581.5
2015[1]	12,996.0	13,093.3	13,158.1	13,208.2	13,262.7	13,330.3	13,426.0	13,530.6	13,569.7	13,617.7	13,697.6	13,729.2	13,385.0

[1] Preliminary.   [2] MZM (money, zero maturity): M2 minus small-denomination time deposits, plus institutional money market mutual funds (that is, those included in M3 but excluded from M2). The label MZM was coined by William Poole (1991); the aggregate itself was proposed earlier by Motley (1988). Seasonally adjusted.   *Source: Board of Governors of the Federal Reserve System*

U.S. Money Supply M3[2]   In Billions of Dollars

Year	Jan.	Feb.	Mar.	Apr.	May	June	July	Aug.	Sept.	Oct.	Nov.	Dec.	Average
1997	5,013.2	5,041.7	5,080.2	5,119.8	5,147.1	5,177.4	5,235.8	5,291.4	5,332.3	5,376.3	5,417.1	5,460.5	5,224.4
1998	5,508.8	5,541.3	5,611.5	5,647.3	5,686.9	5,728.4	5,750.0	5,815.0	5,882.0	5,953.7	6,010.1	6,051.9	5,765.6
1999	6,080.7	6,129.5	6,133.6	6,172.3	6,201.0	6,237.7	6,269.0	6,299.1	6,323.0	6,378.4	6,464.1	6,551.8	6,270.0
2000	6,605.5	6,642.2	6,704.0	6,767.3	6,776.9	6,823.6	6,875.2	6,945.0	7,003.5	7,027.0	7,038.3	7,117.6	6,860.5
2001	7,237.2	7,308.5	7,372.0	7,507.8	7,564.1	7,644.7	7,691.9	7,696.3	7,853.2	7,897.8	7,973.0	8,035.4	7,648.5
2002	8,063.9	8,109.3	8,117.3	8,142.6	8,175.1	8,190.8	8,244.2	8,298.1	8,331.5	8,368.9	8,498.8	8,568.0	8,259.0
2003	8,588.1	8,628.7	8,648.8	8,686.0	8,741.9	8,791.6	8,888.7	8,918.2	8,906.5	8,896.8	8,880.3	8,872.3	8,787.3
2004	8,930.2	9,000.3	9,080.7	9,149.6	9,243.8	9,275.7	9,282.7	9,314.4	9,351.8	9,359.4	9,395.1	9,433.0	9,234.7
2005	9,487.2	9,531.6	9,565.3	9,620.9	9,665.0	9,725.3	9,762.4	9,864.6	9,950.8	10,032.0	10,078.5	10,154.0	9,786.5
2006[1]	10,242.8	10,298.7	Discontinued										10,270.8

[1] Preliminary.   [2] M3 -- M2 plus large-denomination ($100,000 or more) time deposits; repurchase agreements issued by depository institutions; Eurodollar deposits, specifically, dollar-denominated deposits due to nonbank U.S. addresses held at foreign offices of U.S. banks worldwide and all banking offices in Canada and the United Kingdom; and institutional money market mutual funds (funds with initial investments of $50,000 or more). Seasonally adjusted. *Source: Board of Governors of the Federal Reserve System*

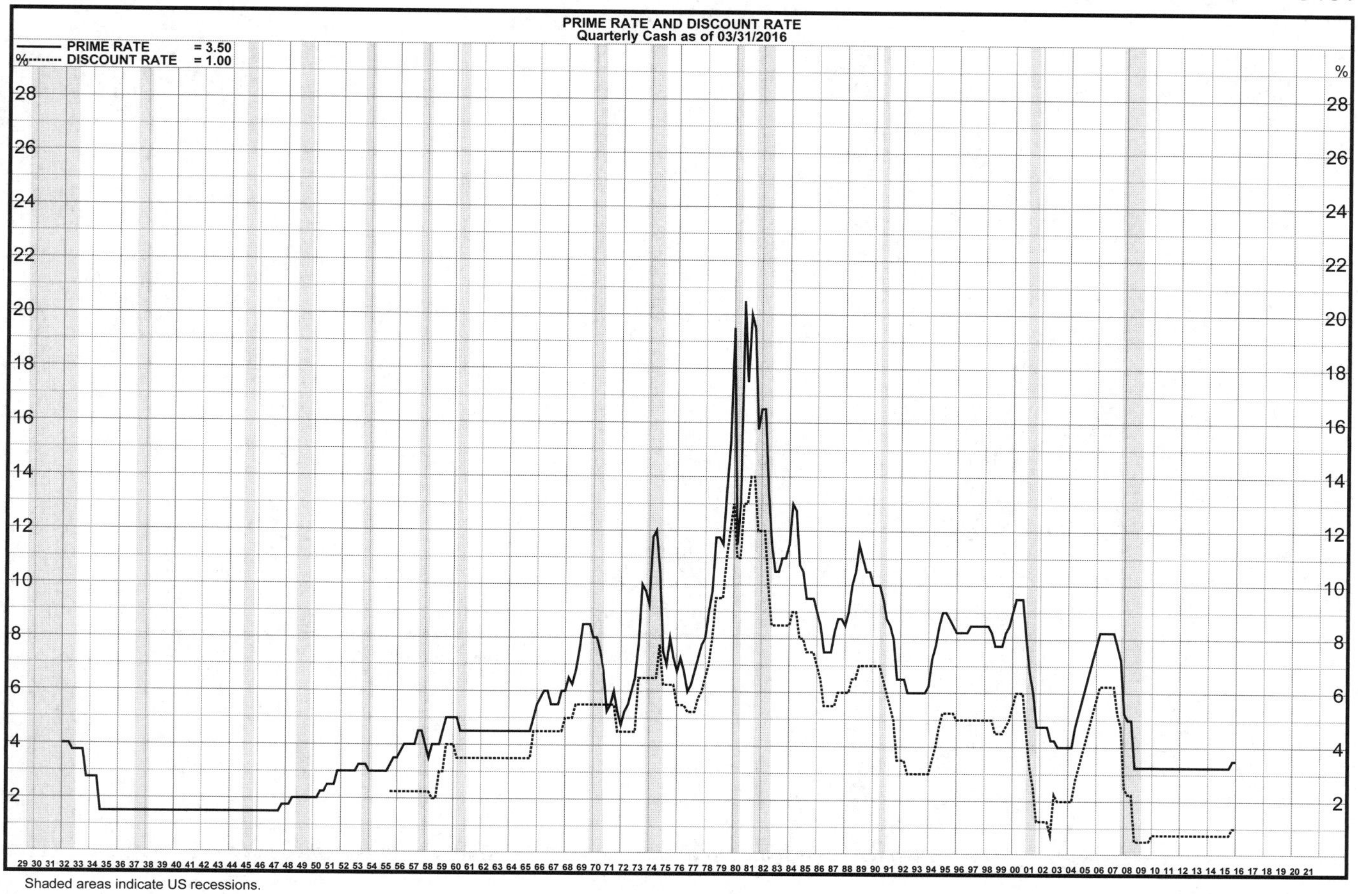

PRIME RATE AND DISCOUNT RATE
Quarterly Cash as of 03/31/2016

PRIME RATE	= 3.50
DISCOUNT RATE	= 1.00

Shaded areas indicate US recessions.

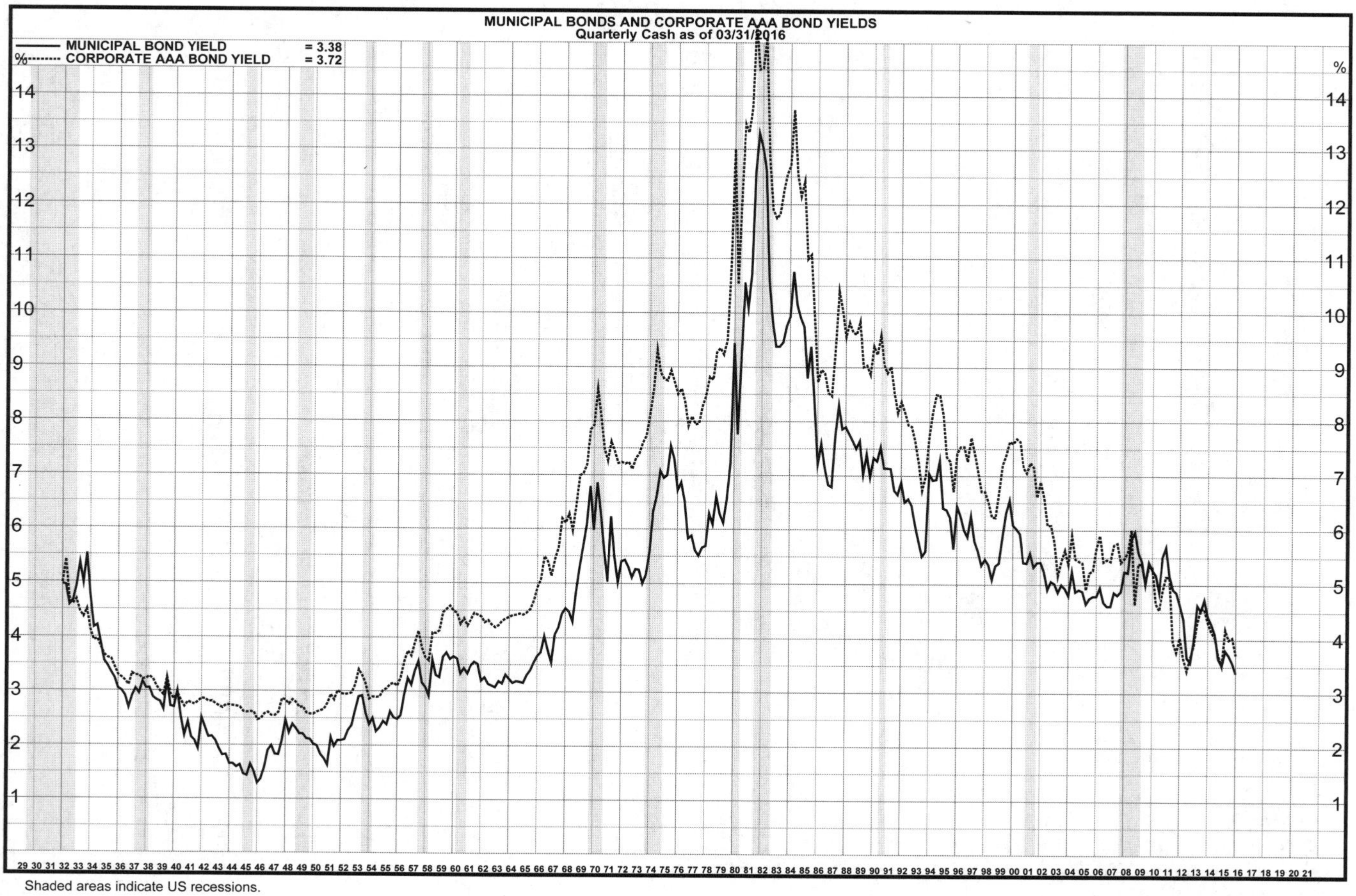

MUNICIPAL BONDS AND CORPORATE AAA BOND YIELDS
Quarterly Cash as of 03/31/2016

MUNICIPAL BOND YIELD	= 3.38
CORPORATE AAA BOND YIELD	= 3.72

Shaded areas indicate US recessions.

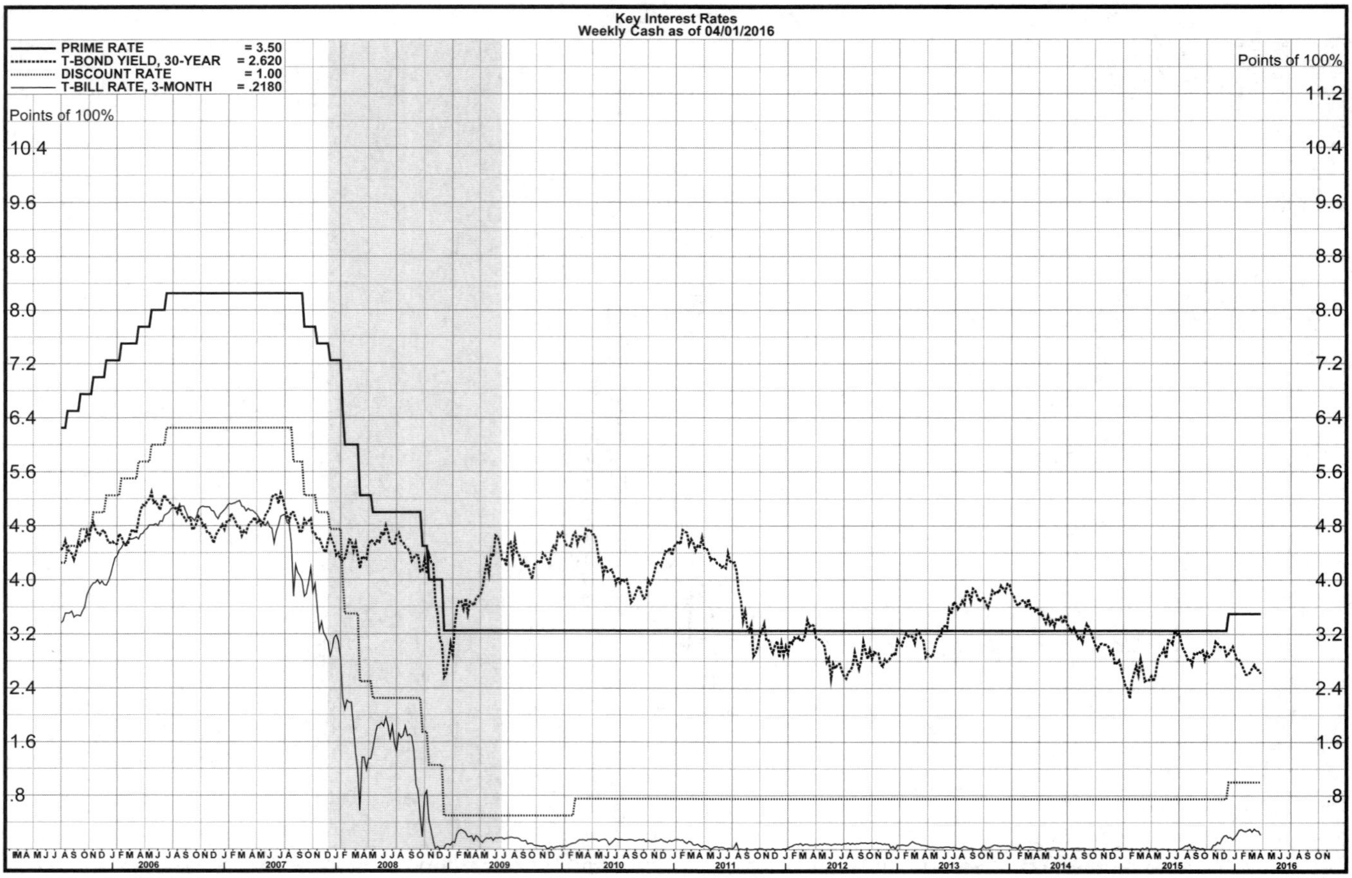

INTEREST RATES - U.S.

Key Interest Rates
Weekly Cash as of 04/01/2016

PRIME RATE = 3.50
T-BOND YIELD, 30-YEAR = 2.620
DISCOUNT RATE = 1.00
T-BILL RATE, 3-MONTH = .2180

Points of 100%

Points of 100%

Shaded areas indicate US recessions.

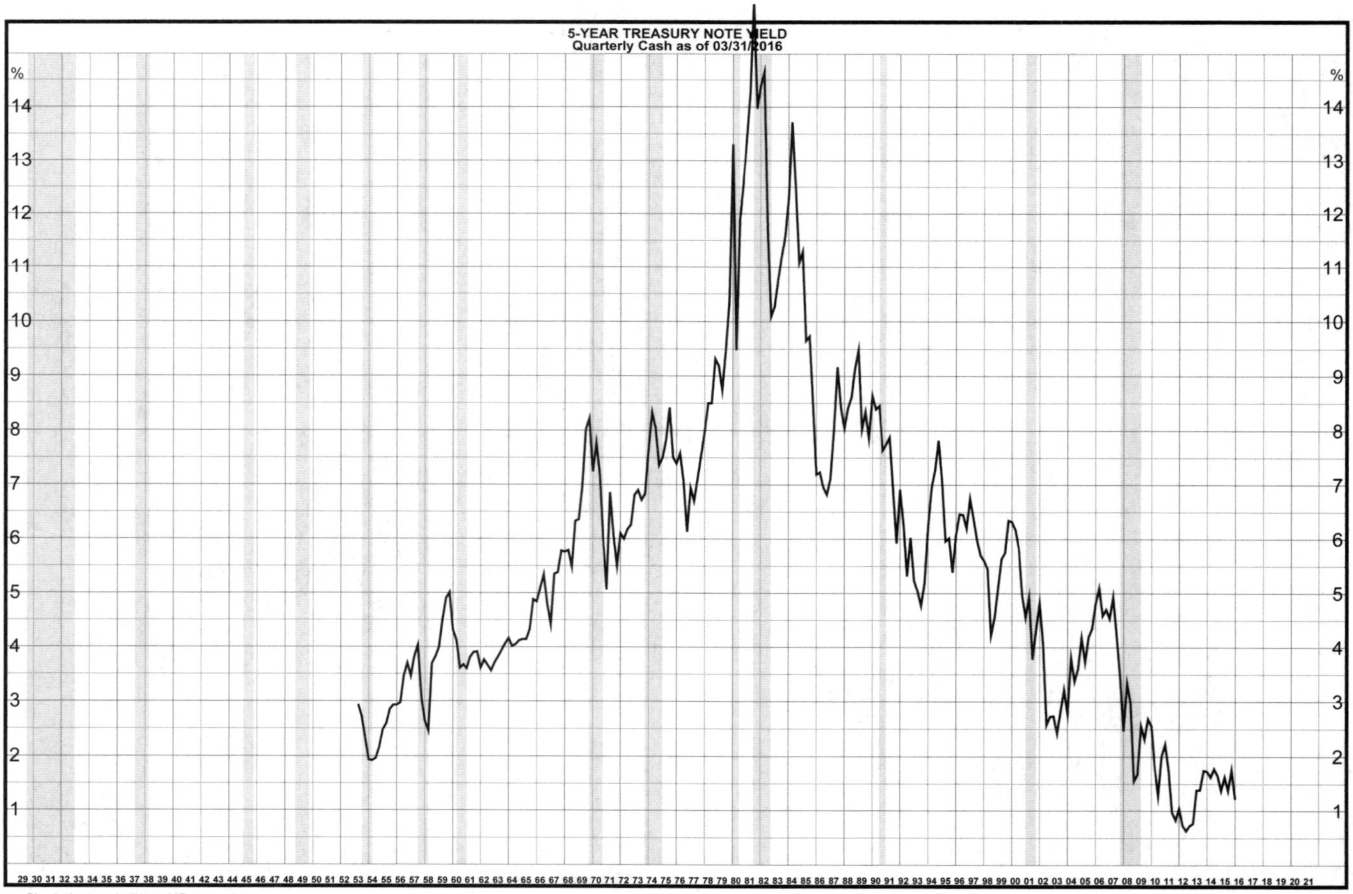

5-YEAR TREASURY NOTE YIELD
Quarterly Cash as of 03/31/2016

Shaded areas indicate US recessions.

Interest Rates - Worldwide

Interest rate futures contracts are widely traded throughout the world. The most popular futures contracts are generally the 10-year government bond and the 3-month interest rate contracts. In Europe, futures on German interest rates are traded at the Eurex Exchange. Futures on UK interest rates are traded at the Liffe Exchange in London. Futures on Canadian interest rates are traded at the Montreal Exchange. Futures on Japanese interest rates are traded at the Singapore Exchange (SGX) and at the Tokyo Stock Exchange. A variety of other interest rate futures contracts are traded throughout the rest of the world (please see the front of this Yearbook for a complete list).

Euro-Zone – The Eurex German 10-year Euro Bund futures contract (Barchart.com symbol GG) in 2015 showed some weakness during mid-year but then resumed its rally and closed 2015 up +2.05 points at 157.92. Bunds then rallied to a new record high in February 2016 of 166.63, bringing the extraordinary 7-1/2 year rally to a total of about 55 points. The Eurex French 10-year OAT bond futures contract (Barchart.com symbol FN) also showed weakness in mid-2015 but then resumed the rally and closed the year at up +2.83 points at 150.05. The Eurex Italy Euro BTP 10-year bond futures contract (Barchart.com symbol II) followed a similar pattern, showing weakness in mid-2015 but then resuming the rally to close the year up +2.32 points at 137.92.

The German 10-year bund yield during 2015 fell to a new record low of 0.08% in early 2015 but then rebounded higher to close the year up by +0.09 percentage points at 0.63%. Other Eurozone 10-year government bond yields in 2015 closed as follows: France +0.16 percentage points at 0.99%, Italy -0.29 percentage points at 1.60%, Spain +0.16 percentage points at 1.77%, Portugal -0.17 percentage points at 2.52%, Ireland -0.10 percentage points at 1.15%, and Greece -1.45 percentage points at 8.29%.

European 10-year bond yields in 2015 remained extremely low due to (1) lackluster Eurozone economic growth, (2) weak overall world economic growth, (3) the European Central Bank's (ECB) extremely easy monetary policy, and (4) low inflation. The Eurozone CPI in 2015 fell as low as -0.1% y/y in September 2015 and ended the year at only +0.2% y/y. The Eurozone core CPI fell as low at 0.6% y/y in early 2015 and ended the year at 0.9% y/y, which was well below the ECB's inflation target of "below, but close to" +2%.

The ECB in 2015 did not make any changes to its refinancing rate but in March 2016 the ECB cut the rate by another -5 basis points to zero. The ECB in December 2015 cut its deposit rate by -10 basis points to -0.30% and then cut the deposit rate by another -10 basis points to -0.40% in March 2016. The ECB in March 2015 began its quantitative easing (QE) program of buying 60 billion euros per month of securities. The ECB raised the size of that program to 80 billion euros in March 2016, which will produce an overall purchase size of about 1.7 trillion euros when the program is currently due to end in March 2017.

UK – The Liffe U.K. 10-year Gilt futures contract (Barchart.com symbol G) in January 2015 extended the 2014 rally to post a new 4-year high but then fell back through mid-year and ended up closing 2015 down -0.90 points at 116.77. The 10-year gilt yield in January 2015 fell to a new record low of 1.33% but then rebounded higher and finally closed 2015 up +0.20 percentage points at 1.96%. The U.K. gilt yield in 2015 remained low due to weak global growth, low inflation, and a stimulative U.K. monetary policy. The Bank of England left its monetary policy unchanged during 2015 for the second straight year. Specifically, the BOE during 2015 left its official base rate unchanged at 0.50% where it has been since early 2009. The BOE did not engage in bond purchases during 2015 and left its asset purchase target unchanged at 375 billion pounds. UK GDP growth in 2015 fell back to +2.2% from +2.9% in 2014 and is expected to remain steady in 2016-18 near the same level of +2.2%. The UK CPI fell to a record low of -0.1% y/y during 2015 and closed the year at +0.2% y/y due in part to sharply lower crude oil prices. However, the UK core CPI was also weak and fell to a record low of +0.8% y/y in mid-2015, rebounding higher to +1.4% y/y by year-end.

Canada – The Montreal Exchange's Canadian 10-year government note futures contract (Barchart.com symbol CG) in early 2015 extended the 2014 rally to post a new record high but then fell back and closed the year up +2.47 points at 140.99. The Canadian 10-year government bond yield posted a record low of 1.23% in early 2015 and then moved mostly sideways the remainder the year, closing 2015 down -0.40 percentage points at 1.39%. The Bank of Canada (BOC) during 2015 cut its overnight lending rate twice, the first cut by 25 basis points to 0.75% in January and the second cut by another 25 basis points to 0.50% in July 2015. Those rate cuts were designed to address the hit to inflation and GDP growth caused by the plunge in oil prices. Canada's GDP in 2015 weakened to +1.2% from 2.5% in 2014 and is expected to remain weak at +1.5% in 2016. Canada's CPI rate fell to a 2-year low of +0.8% y/y in mid-2015 but then rebounded higher to +1.6% y/y by the end of 2015.

Japan – The SGX Japan 10-year JGB futures contract (Barchart.com symbol JX) in the first half of 2015 traded sideways but the post-2007 rally resumed in the latter part of 2015 to produce a new record high and close the year up +1.22 points at 149.06. Japan's 10-year government bond (JGB) yield fell to what was then a record low of 0.20% in January 2015 and then moved sideways the remainder of the year, finally closing the year down -7 basis points at 0.26%. However, the 10-year JGB yield then fell further in February 2016 to a new record low of -0.10%. The Bank of Japan (BOJ) left its policy rate unchanged at 0.10% during 2015 but then announced a -20 basis point cut to -0.10% in January 2016. The BOJ in 2015 left its massive quantitative easing (QE) program in place in an effort to boost inflation and stimulate the economy. Japan's CPI in 2015 fell to zero from as high as +3.7% y/y in 2014, sparking the new stimulus measures by the BOJ. Japan's GDP growth in 2015 improved slightly to +0.5% from unchanged in 2014 but remained weak.

INTEREST RATES - WORLDWIDE

GILT, LONG - ICE-LIFF
Weekly Nearest Futures as of 04/01/2016

Points of 100%

% Yield Basis
6% 10-Yr

% Yield Basis	Points of 100%
1.30	148
1.65	144
2.01	140
2.38	136
2.77	132
3.18	128
3.60	124
	120
4.04	116
4.50	112
4.98	108
5.48	104
6.00	100
6.55	96

MA M J J A S O N D J F M A M J J A S O N D J F M A M J J A S O N D J F M A M J J A S O N D J F M A M J J A S O N D J F M A M J J A S O N D J F M A M J J A S O N D J F M A M J J A S O N D J F M A M J J A S O N D J F M A M J J A S O N D J F M A M J J A S O N
2006 2007 2008 2009 2010 2011 2012 2013 2014 2015 2016

Nearby Futures through Last Trading Day.

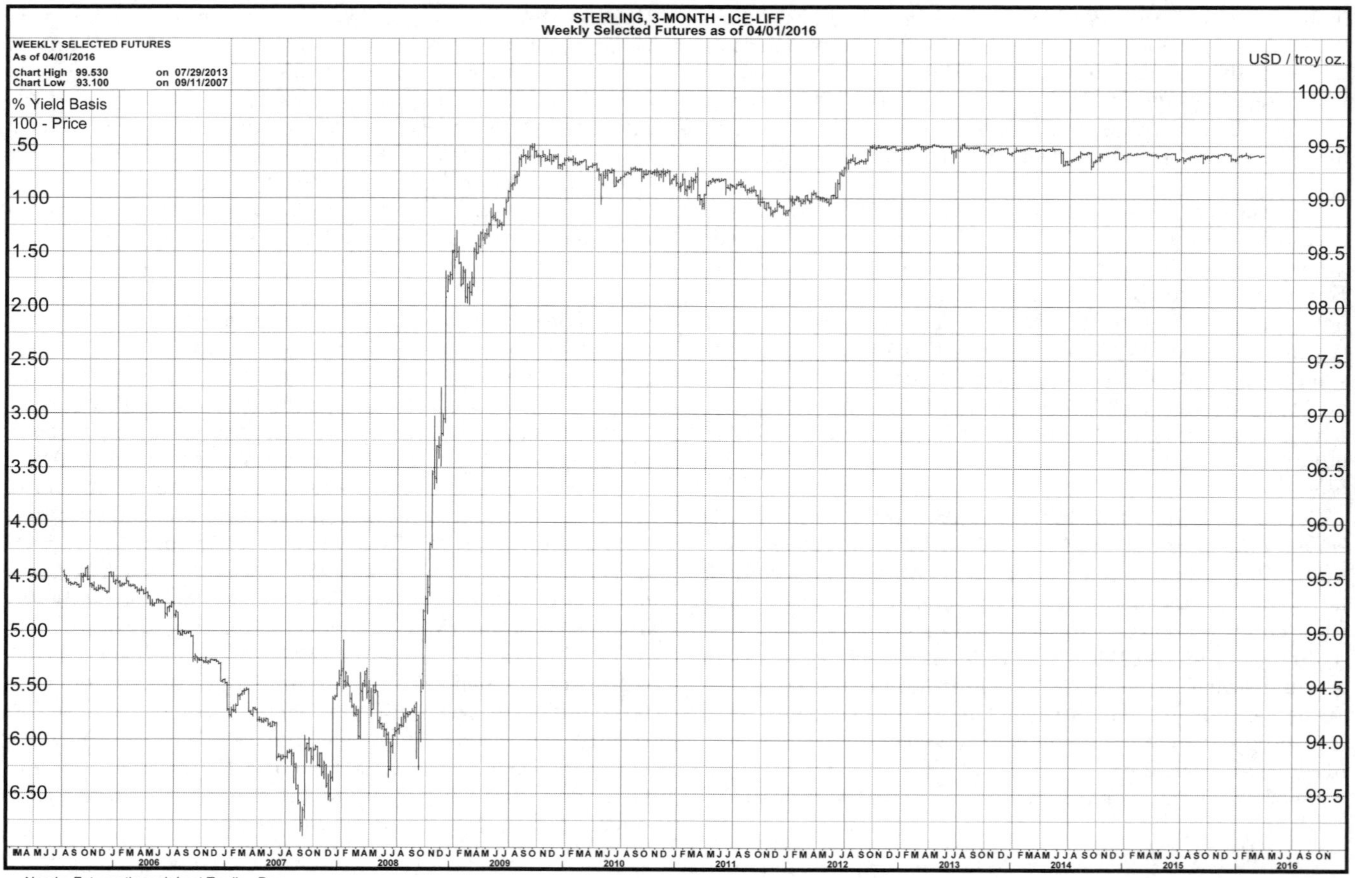

STERLING, 3-MONTH - ICE-LIFF
Weekly Selected Futures as of 04/01/2016

USD / troy oz.

% Yield Basis
100 - Price

% Yield Basis	USD / troy oz.
	100.0
.50	99.5
1.00	99.0
1.50	98.5
2.00	98.0
2.50	97.5
3.00	97.0
3.50	96.5
4.00	96.0
4.50	95.5
5.00	95.0
5.50	94.5
6.00	94.0
6.50	93.5

MA M J J A S O N D J F M A M J J A S O N D J F M A M J J A S O N D J F M A M J J A S O N D J F M A M J J A S O N D J F M A M J J A S O N D J F M A M J J A S O N D J F M A M J J A S O N D J F M A M J J A S O N D J F M A M J J A S O N D J F M A M J J A S O N
2006 2007 2008 2009 2010 2011 2012 2013 2014 2015 2016

Nearby Futures through Last Trading Day.

JAPANESE GOVT BOND, 10-YEAR - JPX
Weekly Nearest Futures as of 04/01/2016

WEEKLY NEAREST FUTURES
As of 04/01/2016

Chart High 152.48   on 02/10/2016
Chart Low   130.76   on 06/13/2007

Points of 100%

% Yield Basis
6% 10-Yr

% Yield Basis	Points of 100%
.79	152
.96	150
1.12	148
1.30	146
1.47	144
1.65	142
1.83	140
2.01	138
2.20	136
2.38	134
2.58	132
2.77	130
2.98	128
	126

Nearby Futures through Last Trading Day.

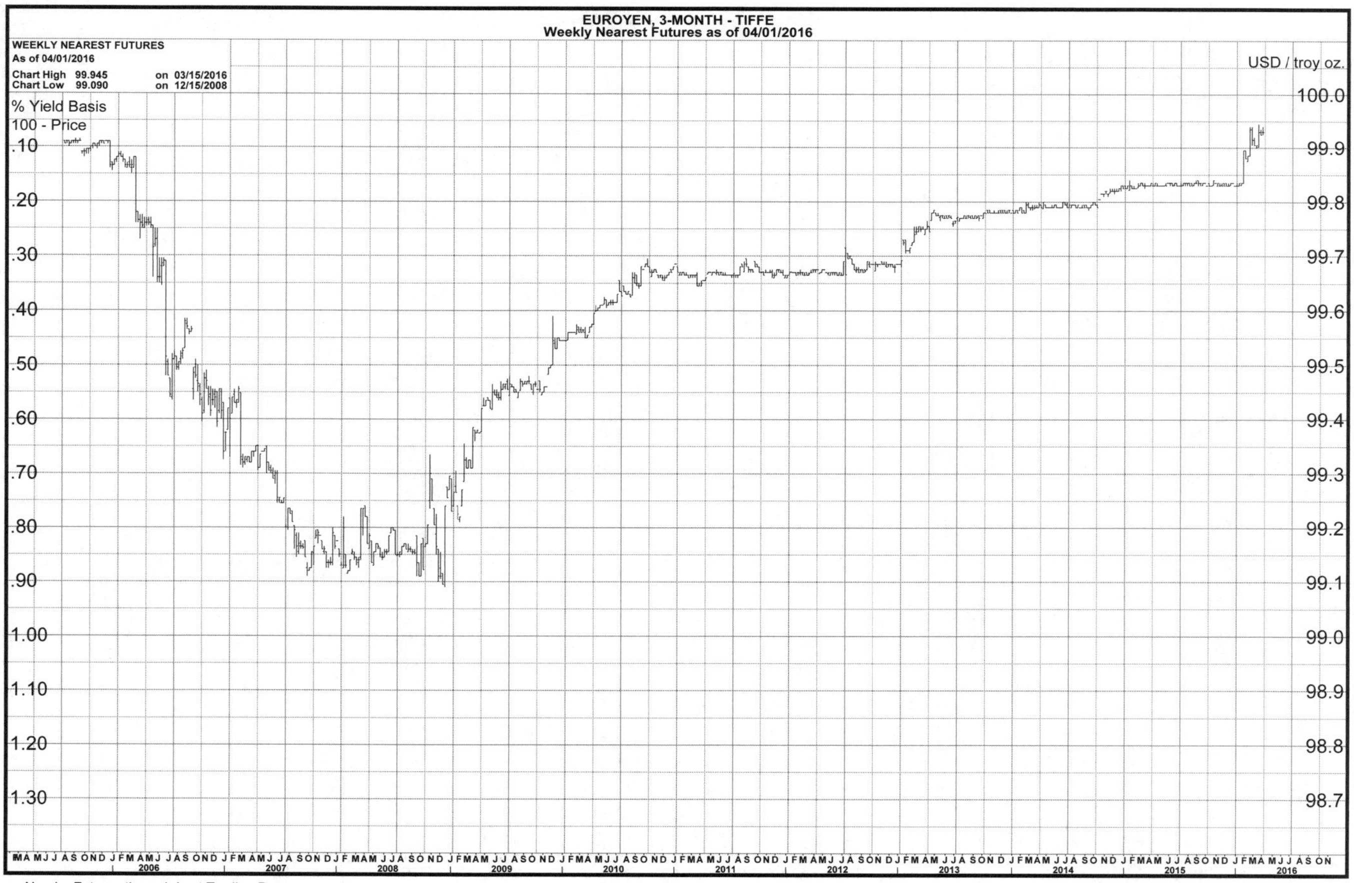

EUROYEN, 3-MONTH - TIFFE
Weekly Nearest Futures as of 04/01/2016

WEEKLY NEAREST FUTURES
As of 04/01/2016

Chart High 99.945   on 03/15/2016
Chart Low   99.090   on 12/15/2008

USD / troy oz.

% Yield Basis
100 - Price

% Yield Basis	USD / troy oz.
.10	100.0
.20	99.9
.30	99.8
.40	99.7
.50	99.6
.60	99.5
.70	99.4
.80	99.3
.90	99.2
1.00	99.1
1.10	99.0
1.20	98.9
1.30	98.8
	98.7

Nearby Futures through Last Trading Day.

INTEREST RATES - WORLDWIDE

CANADIAN GOVT BOND, 10-YR - MNTRL
Weekly Nearest Futures as of 04/01/2016

WEEKLY NEAREST FUTURES
As of 04/01/2016

Chart High 146.580   on 02/11/2016
Chart Low 108.830   on 06/12/2007

% Yield Basis
6% 10-Yr

Points of 100%

Yield	Points
.96	152
1.30	148
1.65	144
2.01	140
2.38	136
2.77	132
3.18	128
3.60	124
4.04	120
4.50	116
4.98	112
5.48	108
6.00	104
	100

MA MJ J A S O N D J F M A M J J A S O N D J F M A M J J A S O N D J F M A M J J A S O N D J F M A M J J A S O N D J F M A M J J A S O N D J F M A M J J A S O N D J F M A M J J A S O N D J F M A M J J A S O N D J F M A M J J A S O N
2006   2007   2008   2009   2010   2011   2012   2013   2014   2015   2016

Nearby Futures through Last Trading Day.

CAN. BANKERS' ACCEPTANCE, 3-MO - MNTRL
Weekly Selected Futures as of 04/01/2016

WEEKLY SELECTED FUTURES
As of 04/01/2016

Chart High 99.640   on 05/21/2009
Chart Low 94.895   on 09/12/2007

% Yield Basis
100 - Price

USD / troy oz.

Yield	Price
	100.0
.50	99.5
1.00	99.0
1.50	98.5
2.00	98.0
2.50	97.5
3.00	97.0
3.50	96.5
4.00	96.0
4.50	95.5
5.00	95.0
5.50	94.5
6.00	94.0
6.50	93.5

MA MJ J A S O N D J F M A M J J A S O N D J F M A M J J A S O N D J F M A M J J A S O N D J F M A M J J A S O N D J F M A M J J A S O N D J F M A M J J A S O N D J F M A M J J A S O N D J F M A M J J A S O N D J F M A M J J A S O N
2006   2007   2008   2009   2010   2011   2012   2013   2014   2015   2016

Nearby Futures through Last Trading Day.

154

Australia -- Economic Statistics   Percentage Change from Previous Period

Year	Real GDP	Nominal GDP	Real Private Consumption	Real Public Consumption	Grossed Fixed Investment	Real Total Domestic Demand	Real Exports of Goods & Services	Real Imports of Goods & Services	Consumer Prices[3]	Unemployment Rate
2008	2.5	9.1	1.9	4.3	7.8	3.5	3.5	10.5	4.3	4.2
2009	1.6	1.7	.8	1.6	-1.4	-.3	2.5	-8.8	1.8	5.6
2010	2.3	8.0	3.3	3.4	4.3	3.8	5.4	15.3	2.9	5.2
2011	2.6	7.1	3.1	3.6	7.0	4.7	-.2	10.7	3.3	5.1
2012	3.7	3.3	2.5	2.3	9.0	4.1	6.5	6.3	1.8	5.2
2013	2.0	3.3	1.7	.8	-2.2	.0	6.2	-1.9	2.4	5.7
2014	2.7	3.1	2.5	2.0	-2.0	1.2	6.7	-1.8	2.6	6.1
2015[1]	2.3	1.9	2.7	1.3	-1.3	1.4	5.7	-.3	2.3	6.2
2016[2]	2.9	4.9	3.0	1.6	.7	2.1	6.2	2.7	2.6	5.9

[1] Estimate.   [2] Projection.   [3] National accounts implicit private consumption deflator.   *Source: Organization for Economic Co-operation and Development (OECD)*

Canada -- Economic Statistics   Percentage Change from Previous Period

Year	Real GDP	Nominal GDP	Real Private Consumption	Real Public Consumption	Grossed Fixed Investment	Real Total Domestic Demand	Real Exports of Goods & Services	Real Imports of Goods & Services	Consumer Prices[3]	Unemployment Rate
2008	1.2	5.1	2.9	4.6	1.6	2.9	-4.5	.8	2.4	6.1
2009	-2.7	-4.8	.4	3.3	-11.5	-2.8	-13.1	-12.4	.3	8.3
2010	3.4	6.1	3.4	2.7	11.5	5.4	6.9	13.6	1.8	8.0
2011	3.0	6.5	2.3	.8	4.8	2.4	4.6	5.7	2.9	7.5
2012	1.9	3.5	1.9	1.2	4.8	2.2	2.6	3.7	1.5	7.3
2013	2.0	3.4	2.5	.4	.4	1.9	2.0	1.3	1.0	7.1
2014	2.4	4.3	2.7	.2	.3	1.4	5.4	1.7	2.0	6.9
2015[1]	1.5	1.2	2.1	.1	-1.5	1.1	3.4	2.0	1.6	6.5
2016[2]	2.3	4.1	2.3	1.0	.9	1.7	6.9	4.8	1.9	6.3

[1] Estimate.   [2] Projection.   [3] National accounts implicit private consumption deflator.   *Source: Organization for Economic Co-operation and Development (OECD)*

France -- Economic Statistics   Percentage Change from Previous Period

Year	Real GDP	Nominal GDP	Real Private Consumption	Real Public Consumption	Grossed Fixed Investment	Real Total Domestic Demand	Real Exports of Goods & Services	Real Imports of Goods & Services	Consumer Prices[3]	Unemployment Rate
2008	.1	2.5	.4	1.1	.7	.4	.0	1.1	3.2	7.1
2009	-2.9	-2.8	.3	2.5	-9.0	-2.5	-11.0	-9.3	.1	8.8
2010	1.9	3.0	1.8	1.2	1.9	2.0	8.6	8.5	1.7	8.9
2011	2.1	3.1	.4	1.1	2.1	2.0	7.1	6.5	2.3	8.8
2012	.2	1.4	-.2	1.6	.3	-.3	2.6	.8	2.2	9.4
2013	.7	1.5	.5	1.7	-.4	.8	1.8	1.8	1.0	9.9
2014	.2	.7	.7	1.5	-1.2	.7	2.4	3.9	.6	9.9
2015[1]	1.1	2.1	1.6	1.2	-.6	1.3	4.9	5.5	.5	10.1
2016[2]	1.7	2.5	1.7	.3	1.8	1.3	5.3	4.2	.9	10.0

[1] Estimate.   [2] Projection.   [3] National accounts implicit private consumption deflator.   *Source: Organization for Economic Co-operation and Development (OECD)*

Germany -- Economic Statistics   Percentage Change from Previous Period

Year	Real GDP	Nominal GDP	Real Private Consumption	Real Public Consumption	Grossed Fixed Investment	Real Total Domestic Demand	Real Exports of Goods & Services	Real Imports of Goods & Services	Consumer Prices[3]	Unemployment Rate
2008	.8	1.6	.4	3.4	.6	.9	1.3	1.8	2.8	7.5
2009	-5.6	-3.9	.2	3.0	-9.9	-3.1	-14.3	-9.6	.2	7.8
2010	3.9	4.7	.5	1.3	4.6	2.9	14.2	12.6	1.2	7.1
2011	3.7	4.8	2.3	.7	7.5	3.1	8.2	7.3	2.5	6.0
2012	.6	2.1	.6	1.2	.0	-.8	3.5	.4	2.1	5.5
2013	.2	2.3	.9	.7	-.4	.8	1.7	3.2	1.6	5.3
2014	1.6	3.3	1.2	1.2	3.3	1.3	3.7	3.4	.9	5.1
2015[1]	1.6	3.4	2.3	2.2	2.5	2.0	3.9	5.4	1.2	5.1
2016[2]	2.3	3.8	2.0	1.8	4.3	2.5	5.2	6.0	1.7	5.1

[1] Estimate.   [2] Projection.   [3] National accounts implicit private consumption deflator.   *Source: Organization for Economic Co-operation and Development (OECD)*

Italy -- Economic Statistics   Percentage Change from Previous Period

Year	Real GDP	Nominal GDP	Real Private Consumption	Real Public Consumption	Grossed Fixed Investment	Real Total Domestic Demand	Real Exports of Goods & Services	Real Imports of Goods & Services	Consumer Prices[3]	Unemployment Rate
2008	-1.1	1.4	-1.1	1.0	-3.2	-1.3	-3.3	-4.0	3.5	6.8
2009	-5.5	-3.7	-1.5	.4	-10.0	-4.2	-17.9	-12.7	.8	7.8
2010	1.7	2.0	1.2	.6	-.6	1.9	11.3	12.1	1.6	8.4
2011	.7	2.2	.0	-1.8	-1.7	-.5	6.1	1.2	2.9	8.4
2012	-2.8	-1.5	-4.0	-1.2	-9.4	-5.7	2.0	-8.3	3.3	10.7
2013	-1.7	-.4	-2.8	-.3	-5.8	-2.5	.7	-2.2	1.3	12.2
2014	-.4	.5	.3	-.9	-3.2	-.6	2.4	1.6	.1	12.4
2015[1]	.6	1.1	.4	-.5	1.6	.4	3.4	2.9	.0	12.3
2016[2]	1.5	2.4	1.1	-.9	1.9	.9	5.1	3.3	.6	12.1

[1] Estimate.   [2] Projection.   [3] National accounts implicit private consumption deflator.   *Source: Organization for Economic Co-operation and Development (OECD)*

Japan -- Economic Statistics   Percentage Change from Previous Period

Year	Real GDP	Nominal GDP	Real Private Consumption	Real Public Consumption	Grossed Fixed Investment	Real Total Domestic Demand	Real Exports of Goods & Services	Real Imports of Goods & Services	Consumer Prices[3]	Unemployment Rate
2008	-1.0	-2.3	-.9	-.1	-4.1	-1.3	1.4	.3	1.4	4.0
2009	-5.5	-6.0	-.7	2.3	-10.6	-4.0	-24.2	-15.7	-1.4	5.0
2010	4.7	2.4	2.8	1.9	-.2	2.9	24.8	11.1	-.7	5.0
2011	-.5	-2.3	.3	1.2	1.4	.4	-.4	5.9	-.3	4.6
2012	1.7	.8	2.3	1.7	3.4	2.6	-.2	5.3	.0	4.3
2013	1.6	1.0	2.1	1.9	3.2	1.9	1.2	3.1	.4	4.0
2014	-.1	1.6	-1.3	.3	2.6	-.1	8.4	7.4	2.9	3.6
2015[1]	.7	3.0	.3	.9	-.6	.5	7.2	4.9	1.8	3.5
2016[2]	1.4	2.5	2.0	.1	.1	1.2	5.8	4.6	1.6	3.5

[1] Estimate.   [2] Projection.   [3] National accounts implicit private consumption deflator.   *Source: Organization for Economic Co-operation and Development (OECD)*

Switzerland -- Economic Statistics   Percentage Change from Previous Period

Year	Real GDP	Nominal GDP	Real Private Consumption	Real Public Consumption	Grossed Fixed Investment	Real Total Domestic Demand	Real Exports of Goods & Services	Real Imports of Goods & Services	Consumer Prices[3]	Unemployment Rate
2008	2.3	4.2	1.5	-1.9	.7	2.7	3.9	4.9	2.4	3.3
2009	-2.1	-1.7	1.3	3.5	-7.5	2.5	-10.0	-3.8	-.5	4.3
2010	3.0	3.3	1.6	.2	4.4	-.5	12.8	8.1	.7	4.5
2011	1.8	2.0	.8	2.1	4.3	4.0	4.9	9.2	.2	4.0
2012	1.1	1.0	2.8	2.9	2.4	-1.2	.8	-2.8	-.7	4.1
2013	1.9	1.7	2.2	1.4	1.7	-.7	15.3	13.5	-.2	4.3
2014	2.0	2.0	1.0	1.1	1.5	1.8	-7.1	-9.4	.0	4.6
2015[1]	.8	.2	1.6	2.5	.9	-1.4	1.9	-1.2	.0	4.4
2016[2]	1.7	2.1	1.5	2.2	.9	1.5	2.0	1.8	.3	4.3

[1] Estimate.   [2] Projection.   [3] National accounts implicit private consumption deflator.   *Source: Organization for Economic Co-operation and Development (OECD)*

United Kingdom -- Economic Statistics   Percentage Change from Previous Period

Year	Real GDP	Nominal GDP	Real Private Consumption	Real Public Consumption	Grossed Fixed Investment	Real Total Domestic Demand	Real Exports of Goods & Services	Real Imports of Goods & Services	Consumer Prices[3]	Unemployment Rate
2008	-.3	2.5	-.5	2.0	-4.7	-1.2	1.6	-1.8	3.6	5.7
2009	-4.3	-2.4	-3.1	1.2	-14.4	-4.8	-8.2	-9.8	2.2	7.6
2010	1.9	5.1	.4	.0	5.9	2.7	6.2	8.7	3.3	7.9
2011	1.6	3.8	.1	.0	2.3	.4	5.6	1.0	4.5	8.1
2012	.7	2.3	1.1	2.3	.7	1.5	.7	3.1	2.8	8.0
2013	1.7	3.5	1.7	-.3	3.4	1.8	1.5	1.4	2.6	7.6
2014	2.8	4.6	2.5	1.7	7.8	3.4	.6	2.2	1.6	6.2
2015[1]	2.4	2.8	2.5	1.3	4.7	2.8	3.8	4.8	1.8	5.6
2016[2]	2.3	3.5	2.3	-.7	6.2	2.4	3.0	3.1	2.1	5.4

[1] Estimate.   [2] Projection.   [3] National accounts implicit private consumption deflator.   *Source: Organization for Economic Co-operation and Development (OECD)*

Iron and Steel

Iron (atomic symbol Fe) is a soft, malleable, and ductile metallic element. Next to aluminum, iron is the most abundant of all metals. Pure iron melts at about 1535 degrees Celsius and boils at 2750 degrees Celsius. Archaeologists in Egypt discovered the earliest iron implements dating back to about 3000 BC, and iron ornaments were used even earlier.

Steel is an alloy of iron and carbon, often with an admixture of other elements. The physical properties of various types of steel and steel alloys depend primarily on the amount of carbon present and how it is distributed in the iron. Steel is marketed in a variety of sizes and shapes, such as rods, pipes, railroad rails, tees, channels, and I-beams. Steel mills roll and form heated ingots into the required shapes. The working of steel improves the quality of the steel by refining its crystalline structure and making the metal tougher. There are five classifications of steel: carbon steels, alloy steels, high-strength low-alloy steels, stainless steel, and tool steels.

Iron Ore futures are traded at the CME Group and the Multi Commodity Exchange of India (MCX).

Prices – In 2015 the average wholesale price for No. 1 heavy-melting steel scrap in Chicago fell +40.4% to $217.84 per metric ton. In January 2015, the price was $323.60 per metric ton but then moved lower the rest of the year.

Supply – World production of iron ore in 2014 (latest data available) rose by +3.5% to 3.220 billion metric tons, which was a new record high. The world's largest producers

of iron ore are China with 46.6% of world production, Australia with 20.5%, and Brazil with 9.9%. The U.S. accounted for only 1.8% of world iron ore production in 2014. World production of raw steel (ingots and castings) in 2015 fell -0.6 % yr/yr to 1,640 million metric tons, with the largest producers being China with 50.1% of world production, Japan with 6.8%, and Russia with 4.3%.

U.S. production of steel ingots in 2015 fell by -8.0% to 81.0 million metric tons, but still up from the 2009 record low of 59.400 million metric tons. U.S. production of pig iron (excluding ferro-alloys) in 2015 (annualized through October) fell -7.4% to 30.204 million short tons.

Demand – U.S. consumption of ferrous scrap and pig iron fell -6.2% yr/yr in 2013 (latest data) to 97.590 million metric tons, but still above the record low of 84.660 million metric tons seen in 2009. The largest consumers of ferrous scrap and pig iron were the manufacturers of pig iron and steel ingots and castings with 90.6% of consumption at 88.390 million metric tons in 2013. Iron foundries and miscellaneous users accounted for 8.1% of consumption and manufacturers of steel castings (scrap) accounted for 1.2% of consumption.

Trade – The U.S. imported 5.100 million metric tons of iron ore in 2014, up +60.0% yr/yr from 3.170 million metric tons in 2011. The bulk of U.S. iron ore imports came from Canada (56.1% with 2.860 million metric tons), Brazil (33.9% with 1.730 metric tons), and Sweden (3.0% with 154,000 metric tons).

World Production of Raw Steel (Ingots and Castings)   In Thousands of Metric Tons

Year	Brazil	Canada	China	France	Germany	Italy	Japan	Rep. of Korea	Russia	Ukraine	United Kindom	United States	World Total
2006	30,901	15,493	419,150	19,857	47,224	31,550	116,266	48,455	70,816	40,899	13,931	98,200	1,250,000
2007	33,782	15,572	489,290	19,252	48,550	31,990	120,203	51,517	72,389	42,830	14,300	98,100	1,350,000
2008	33,726	14,845	500,490	17,874	45,833	30,477	118,739	53,322	68,700	37,279	13,538	91,900	1,330,000
2009	26,506	9,245	572,180	12,836	32,671	19,737	87,534	48,752	59,800	29,855	10,079	59,400	1,230,000
2010	33,033	13,003	637,230	15,416	43,830	25,751	109,599	58,914	66,800	33,559	9,709	80,500	1,430,000
2011	35,200	12,891	685,280	15,800	44,284	28,700	107,601	68,519	68,100	35,332	9,478	86,400	1,520,000
2012	34,682	13,507	716,540	15,607	42,661	27,227	107,232	39,321	68,500	32,912	9,819	88,700	1,520,000
2013	34,700	12,400	779,040	15,685	42,641	24,058	110,571	81,213	69,400	33,160	11,855	86,900	1,620,000
2014[1]	34,000		823,000	16,000	43,000		111,000	71,000	71,000	27,000	12,000	88,000	1,650,000
2015[2]	34,000		822,000	17,000	44,000		111,000	72,000	71,000	27,000	12,000	81,000	1,640,000

[1] Preliminary.   [2] Estimate.   *Source: U.S. Geological Survey (USGS)*

Average Wholesale Prices of Iron and Steel in the United States

	No. 1 Heavy Melting Steel Scrap			Sheet Bars		Pittsburg Prices				Rail Road	Used
Year	Pittsburg	Chicago	Hot Rolled	Hot Rolled	Cold Finished	Hot Rolled Strip	Carbon Steel Plates	Cold Rolled Strip	Galvanized Sheets	Steel Scrap[2]	Used Steel Cans[3]
	----- $ Per Gross Ton ----				Cents Per Pound					---- $ Per Gross Ton ----	
2002	101.06	89.92	16.46	----	23.26	----	----	----	22.00	NA	66.71
2003	128.32	113.82	14.80	----	25.15	----	----	----	20.08		116.21
2004	221.05	220.13	30.84	----	38.67	----	----	----	36.69	----	192.80
2005	199.10	196.75	27.83	----	44.96	----	----	----	33.77	----	172.00
2006	222.39	225.21	29.78	----	44.02	----	----	----	38.09	----	212.63
2007	250.98	262.80	26.89	----	45.26	----	----	----	38.25	----	244.65
2008	365.62	357.88	44.56	----	61.67	----	----	----	54.91	----	314.63
2009	204.21	206.14	24.60	----	42.10	----	----	----	34.23	----	121.84
2010	339.54	334.48	31.65	----	50.82	----	----	----	41.72	----	296.91
2011[1]	408.64	417.00	38.02	----	63.63	----	----	----	48.45	----	391.50

[1] Preliminary.   [2] Specialties scrap.   [3] Consumer buying prices.   NA = Not available.   *Source: American Metal Market (AMM)*

IRON AND STEEL

Salient Statistics of Steel in the United States   In Thousands of Short Tons

Year	Pig Iron Production	Producer Price Index for Steel Mill Products (1982=100)	Raw Steel Production							Net Shipments Steel Mill Products	Total Steel Products	
			By Type of Furnace								Exports	Imports
			Basic Oxygen	Open Hearth	Electric[2]	Stainless	Carbon	Alloy	Total			
2005	40,036	159.7	45,231	----	57,599	1,903	96,636	4,935	102,830	103,474	9,393	32,108
2006	37,900	174.1	39,298	----	50,346	2,712	98,656	6,823	108,246	99,300	8,830	41,100
2007	36,300	182.9	36,147	----	53,161	2,392	98,987	6,768	108,136	96,500	10,100	30,200
2008	33,700	220.6	41,336	----	58,532	2,127	92,703	6,404	101,301	89,400	12,200	29,000
2009	19,000	165.2	21,274	----	39,793	1,786	60,847	2,888	65,477	56,400	8,420	14,700
2010	26,800	191.7	30,975	----	54,343	2,425	81,129	5,159	88,735	75,700	11,000	21,700
2011	30,200	216.2	34,943	----	57,430	2,282	87,192	5,754	95,239	83,300	12,200	25,900
2012	30,100	208.0	36,817	----	57,761	2,183	90,278	5,258	97,774	87,000	12,500	30,400
2013	30,300	195.0								86,600	11,500	29,200
2014[1]	29,000	200.1								89,000	11,000	39,000

[1] Preliminary.   [2] Includes crucible steels.   *Sources: American Iron & Steel Institute (AISI); U.S. Geological Survey (USGS)*

Production of Steel Ingots, Rate of Capability Utilization[1] in the United States   In Percent

Year	Jan.	Feb.	Mar.	Apr.	May	June	July	Aug.	Sept.	Oct.	Nov.	Dec.	Average
2006	85.6	89.5	92.8	91.4	92.5	92.1	88.7	88.7	91.2	86.2	81.5	75.0	87.9
2007	78.2	87.8	86.3	85.0	88.4	88.6	87.0	87.7	86.5	88.5	88.5	88.1	86.7
2008	90.3	91.6	89.7	90.3	91.1	90.3	88.8	90.4	84.5	70.5	50.7	40.9	80.8
2009	42.6	45.5	42.9	40.8	42.8	46.9	52.4	57.7	62.1	62.3	61.4	60.9	51.5
2010	64.2	71.1	73.2	74.0	74.8	75.4	69.6	68.1	70.2	67.3	68.3	68.4	70.4
2011	73.2	75.4	75.0	74.2	72.7	76.2	75.0	75.7	76.1	71.9	73.0	75.2	74.5
2012	77.6	80.7	79.6	80.9	79.2	74.8	73.3	76.3	70.4	68.0	70.1	71.7	75.2
2013	76.5	78.3	76.2	76.7	76.5	76.1	77.3	77.6	78.3	76.5	76.2	74.0	76.7
2014	75.8	77.9	77.7	76.6	77.3	78.5	79.6	80.2	78.1	76.5	77.2	74.6	77.5
2015[2]	76.4	72.1	67.7	69.8	72.1	74.4	73.2	72.2	70.5	68.1			71.7

[1] Based on tonnage capability to produce raw steel for a full order book.   [2] Preliminary.   *Sources: American Iron and Steel Institute (AISI); U.S. Geological Survey (USGS)*

Production of Steel Ingots in the United States   In Thousands of Short Tons

Year	Jan.	Feb.	Mar.	Apr.	May	June	July	Aug.	Sept.	Oct.	Nov.	Dec.	Total
1997	8,735	8,266	9,175	8,882	9,048	8,662	8,692	8,818	9,006	9,128	9,116	9,071	107,488
1998	9,510	9,087	9,839	9,524	9,483	8,863	8,832	9,194	8,548	8,681	7,710	8,013	107,643
1999	8,422	7,837	8,854	8,643	8,914	8,413	8,619	8,993	8,650	9,574	9,357	9,604	105,882
2000	9,838	9,170	10,009	9,843	10,097	9,592	9,411	9,213	8,830	8,978	8,054	7,982	111,015
2001	8,475	8,122	8,932	8,685	8,832	8,550	8,459	8,525	8,263	8,125	7,226	6,695	98,889
2002	8,050	7,609	8,261	8,214	8,401	8,414	8,510	8,918	8,916	9,015	8,340	8,329	100,976
2003	8,617	8,175	8,817	8,692	8,047	8,534	8,163	8,096	8,026	8,514	8,347	8,414	100,442
2004	8,656	8,400	9,268	8,901	9,163	9,006	9,164	9,314	9,234	9,551	8,989	8,660	108,305
2005	9,123	8,419	9,028	8,757	8,543	7,837	7,896	8,330	8,562	9,032	8,629	8,599	102,754
2006[1]	8,918	8,506	9,770	9,382	9,811	9,458	9,324	9,320	9,282	8,922	8,169	7,760	108,621

[1] Preliminary.   *Source: American Iron and Steel Institute (AISI)*

Shipments of Steel Products[1] by Market Classifications in the United States   In Thousands of Short Tons

Year	Appliances Utensils & Cutlery	Automotive	Containers, Packaging & Shipping Materials	Construction Including Maint.	Contactors Products	Electrical Equipment	Export	Machinery, Industrial Equip. & Tools	Oil and Gas	Rail Transportation	Steel for Converting & Processing[2]	Steel Service Center & Distributors	All Other[3]	Total Shipments
1997	1,635	15,251	4,163	15,885	[5]	2,434	2,610	2,355	3,811	1,410	11,263	27,800	17,241	105,858
1998	1,729	15,842	3,829	15,289	[5]	2,255	2,556	2,147	2,649	1,657	9,975	27,751	16,741	102,420
1999	1,712	15,639	3,768	14,685	[5]	2,260	2,292	1,547	1,544	876	7,599	21,439	32,840	106,201
2000	1,530	14,697	3,684	14,763	[5]	2,039	2,752	1,513	2,268	994	7,753	22,537	35,093	109,624
2001	1,675	12,767	3,193	16,339	[5]	1,694	2,281	1,210	2,134	720	7,462	23,887	26,086	99,448
2002	1,734	12,562	3,251	15,729	[5]	1,336	1,844	1,137	1,658	751	7,201	22,828	29,160	99,191
2003	1,891	11,937	2,949	14,403	[5]	1,200	2,572	1,108	1,800	799	6,798	24,266	35,905	105,628
2004	1,919	12,527	2,978	15,114	[5]	1,139	2,426	1,332	2,043	957	7,295	25,385	38,969	112,085
2005	1,895	13,031	2,504	15,858	[5]	1,088	2,592	1,300	2,056	1,019	7,559	23,213	31,359	103,474
2006[4]	1,781	14,003	2,535	17,544	[5]	1,228	3,068	1,360	2,459	1,242	8,531	23,706	31,153	108,609

[1] All grades including carbon, alloy and stainless steel.   [2] Net total after deducting shipments to reporting companines for conversion or resale.
[3] Includes agricultural; bolts, nuts rivets & screws; forgings (other than automotive); shipbuilding & marine equipment; aircraft; mining, quarrying & lumbering; other domestic & commercial equipment machinery; ordnance & other direct military; and shipments of non-reporting companies.
[4] Preliminary.   [5] Included in Construction.   *Source: American Iron and Steel Institute (AISI)*

Net Shipments of Steel Products[2] in the United States   In Thousands of Short Tons

Year	Cold Finished Bars	Rails & Accessories	Wire Drawn	Tin Mill Products	Plates Cut & Coils	Sheet & Strip[3] Galv, Hot Dipped	Hot Rolled Bars	Pipe & Tubing	Structural Shapes & Steel Piling	Rein-forcing Bars	Hot Rolled Sheets	Cold Rolled Sheets	Carbon	Alloy	Stainless
1997	1,809	875	619	4,057	8,855	12,439	8,153	6,548	6,029	6,188	18,221	13,322	97,509	6,282	2,067
1998	1,780	938	725	3,714	8,864	13,481	8,189	5,409	5,595	5,909	15,715	13,185	94,536	5,847	2,037
1999	1,775	646	611	3,771	8,200	14,870	8,078	4,772	5,995	6,183	17,740	13,874	98,694	5,421	2,086
2000	1,756	783	579	3,742	8,898	14,917	7,901	5,385	7,402	6,893	19,236	14,802	102,141	5,379	2,104
2001	1,369	630	481	3,202	8,349	14,310	7,032	5,377	6,789	6,976	18,866	12,352	92,314	4,789	1,837
2002	1,404	789	733	3,419	8,769	14,944	6,581	4,809	6,729	6,359	19,243	12,673	92,518	4,779	1,894
2003	1,426	739	684	3,513	9,230	15,221	6,486	4,597	7,437	7,970	22,218	13,485	98,772	4,901	1,952
2004	1,520	843	428	3,247	10,740	16,306	7,181	5,328	7,812	8,274	23,106	14,762	105,161	4,851	2,073
2005	1,495	920	560	2,874	10,274	15,249	6,674	5,096	8,070	7,464	20,569	12,793	97,884	5,183	1,903
2006[1]	1,487	1,016	603	2,880	10,827	16,358	7,595	5,426	8,652	7,419	20,862	13,281	101,572	4,956	2,081

[1] Preliminary.   [2] All grades, including carbon, alloy and stainless steel.   *Source: American Iron and Steel Institute (AISI)*

World Production of Pig Iron (Excludes Ferro-Alloys)   In Thousands of Metric Tons

Year	Belgium	Brazil	China	France	Germany	India	Italy	Japan	Russia	Ukraine	United Kingdom	United States	World Total
2006	7,516	32,452	412,450	13,013	30,360	28,300	11,497	84,270	51,683	32,926	10,736	37,900	939,000
2007	6,576	35,571	476,520	12,426	31,149	28,800	11,100	86,771	51,523	35,647	10,960	36,300	1,020,000
2008	7,125	34,871	470,670	11,372	29,111	29,000	10,373	86,171	48,300	30,982	10,137	33,700	998,000
2009	3,087	25,135	552,830	8,105	20,104	38,233	5,719	66,943	43,930	25,682	7,674	19,000	984,000
2010	4,688	30,955	597,330	10,137	28,560	39,560	8,549	82,283	48,000	27,361	7,235	26,800	1,110,000
2011	4,725	33,319	640,510	9,700	27,943	43,624	9,800	81,028	48,000	28,881	6,600	30,200	1,180,000
2012	4,072	27,000	657,900	9,531	27,048	47,969	9,418	81,405	50,500	28,514	7,252	32,100	1,190,000
2013	4,343	26,207	708,970	10,276	26,910	50,256	6,935	83,849	51,000	29,089	9,512	30,300	1,240,000
2014[1]		27,000	712,000	11,000	27,000	55,000		84,000	51,000	25,000	10,000	29,000	1,170,000
2015[2]		30,000	710,000	11,000	28,000	54,000		84,000	51,000	25,000	9,000	26,000	1,180,000

[1] Preliminary.   [2] Estimate.   *Source: U.S. Geological Survey (USGS)*

Production of Pig Iron (Excludes Ferro-Alloys) in the United States   In Thousands of Short Tons

Year	Jan.	Feb.	Mar.	Apr.	May	June	July	Aug.	Sept.	Oct.	Nov.	Dec.	Total
2006	3,519	3,421	3,765	3,612	3,816	3,667	3,540	3,525	3,544	3,403	3,059	2,909	41,780
2007	2,850	2,610	3,040	3,010	3,130	3,120	3,080	3,010	3,010	3,200	2,940	3,160	36,160
2008	2,900	3,110	3,280	3,240	3,210	3,020	3,090	3,290	2,900	2,770	2,040	1,690	34,540
2009	1,450	1,510	1,630	1,410	1,370	1,380	1,840	2,090	1,930	2,510	2,240	2,410	21,770
2010	2,350	2,530	2,870	2,030	2,830	2,800	2,450	2,490	2,600	2,150	2,470	2,340	29,910
2011	2,400	2,490	2,790	2,550	2,870	2,820	2,520	2,610	2,540	3,010	2,990	3,190	32,780
2012	3,080	3,050	3,430	2,920	3,320	2,970	2,930	2,860	2,440	2,260	2,820	2,900	34,980
2013	3,060	2,760	3,040	2,800	2,880	2,760	2,760	2,890	2,880	2,870	2,760	2,780	34,240
2014	2,430	2,450	2,820	2,580	2,710	2,760	2,930	2,920	2,740	2,690	2,740	2,860	32,630
2015[1]	2,760	2,310	2,390	2,330	2,530	2,670	2,830	2,690	2,390	2,270	2,120		29,771

[1] Preliminary.   *Source: American Iron and Steel Institute*

Salient Statistics of Ferrous Scrap and Pig Iron in the United States   In Thousands of Metric Tons

	Mfg. of Pig Iron & Steel Ingots & Castings			Iron Foundries & Misc. Users			Mfg. of Steel Castings (Scrap)	All Uses			Imports of Scrap[2]	Exports of Scrap[3]	Stocks, Dec. 31 Ferrous Scrap & Pig Iron at Consumers	
Year	Scrap	Pig Iron	Total	Scrap	Pig Iron	Total		Ferrous Scrap	Pig Iron	Grand Total				Total
2004	57,100	38,000	96,590	8,490	1,020	9,514	1,330	66,500	39,100	107,100	4,660	11,800	5,400	721	6,121
2005	54,600	36,900	93,240	9,010	1,090	10,103	1,810	65,400	38,000	105,150	3,840	13,000	4,970	664	5,897
2006	54,500	36,700	92,730	9,370	857	10,232	1,640	65,600	37,600	104,740	4,820	14,900	4,210	787	5,309
2007	54,600	36,500	93,140	9,080	1,290	10,374	1,380	65,000	37,800	104,850	3,700	16,500	4,140	771	5,275
2008	56,600	33,500	92,050	7,760	844	8,608	2,070	66,400	34,400	102,760	3,600	21,500	4,340	885	5,660
2009	47,600	28,300	77,240	838	17	859	838	53,100	30,200	84,660	2,990	22,400	3,070	506	3,810
2010	53,100	34,100	88,690	5,180	1,910	7,093	1,810	60,100	36,000	97,590	3,780	20,500	3,330	418	3,909
2011	56,400	34,900	92,920	5,960	1,970	7,933	756	63,100	36,900	101,620	4,010	24,300	3,980	423	4,529
2012	55,800	35,400	94,780	6,710	1,980	8,693	639	63,100	37,400	104,080	3,720	21,400	4,170	405	4,722
2013[1]	52,100	31,800	88,390	5,660	2,260	7,923	1,180	59,000	34,100	97,590	3,930	18,500	4,190	449	4,746

Consumption: Ferrous Scrap & Pig Iron Charged To

[1] Preliminary.   [2] Includes tinplate and terneplate.   [3] Excludes used rails for rerolling and other uses and ships, boats, and other vessels for scrapping.
Source: U.S. Geological Survey (USGS)

IRON AND STEEL

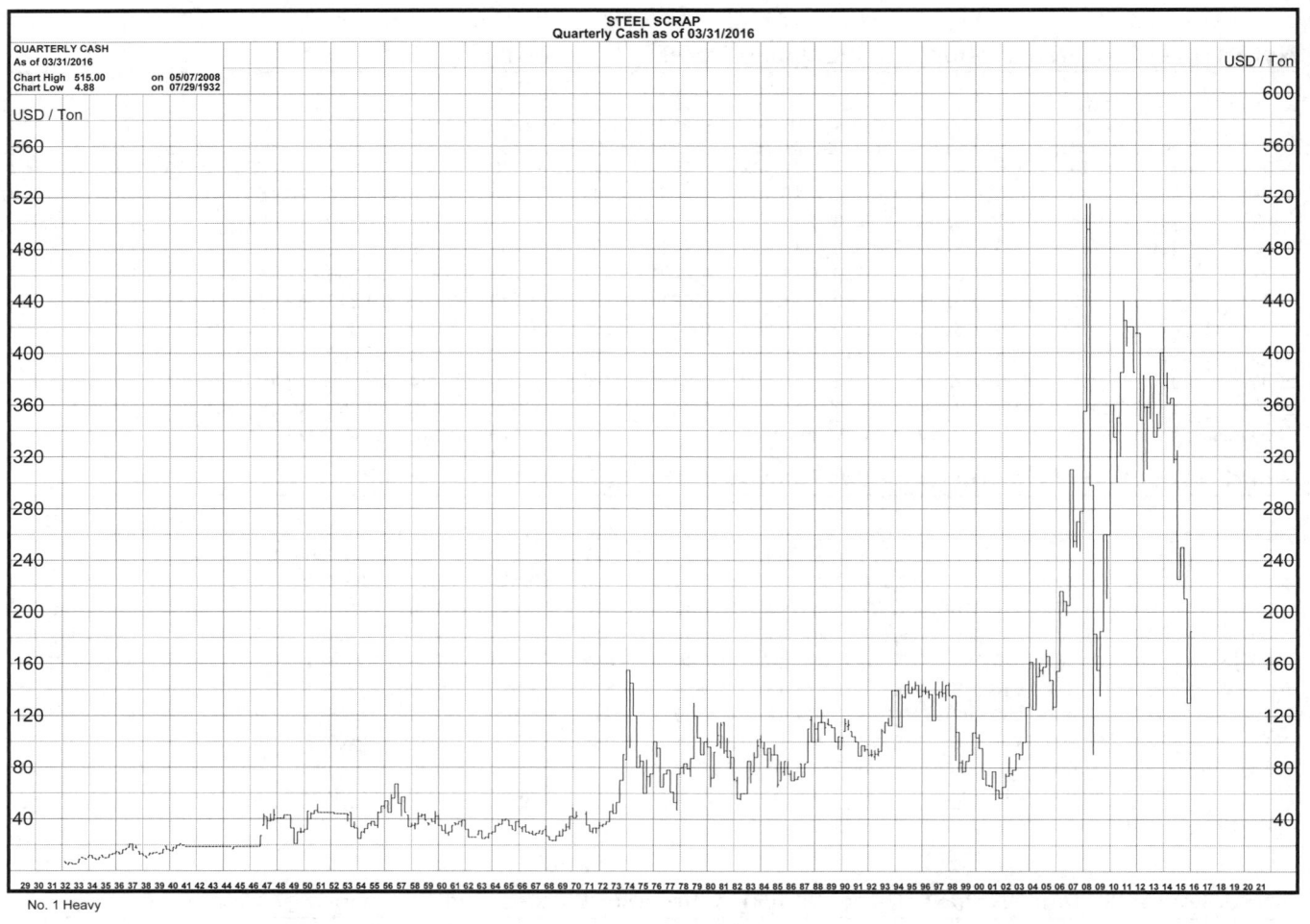

STEEL SCRAP
Quarterly Cash as of 03/31/2016

QUARTERLY CASH
As of 03/31/2016

Chart High 515.00 on 05/07/2008
Chart Low 4.88 on 07/29/1932

USD / Ton

No. 1 Heavy

Consumption of Pig Iron in the United States, by Type of Furance or Equipment — In Thousands of Metric Tons

Year	Open Hearth	Electric	Cupola	Basic Oxygen Process	Air & Other Furnace	Direct Casting	Total
2004	----	3,030	354	35,700	W	36	39,100
2005	----	3,040	528	34,400	W	36	38,000
2006	----	3,380	435	33,800	W	36	37,600
2007	----	3,980	401	33,400	8	36	37,800
2008	----	3,350	401	30,600	5	36	33,600
2009	----	4,140	148	25,900	----	36	30,200
2010	----	4,740	55	31,200	----	16	36,000
2011	----	5,410	76	31,300	12	36	36,900
2012	----	5,790	57	31,500	10	36	37,400
2013[1]	----	4,150	345	29,600	----	----	34,100

[1] Preliminary.   W = Withheld.   *Source: U.S. Geological Survey (USGS)*

Wholesale Price of No. 1 Heavy Melting Steel Scrap in Chicago — In Dollars Per Metric Ton

Year	Jan.	Feb.	Mar.	Apr.	May	June	July	Aug.	Sept.	Oct.	Nov.	Dec.	Average
2006	222.70	237.76	237.07	245.00	249.23	249.23	245.25	204.41	207.25	202.55	197.90	203.55	225.16
2007	225.24	252.37	305.00	291.90	255.36	254.71	250.71	257.04	268.74	265.65	252.10	273.42	262.69
2008	334.00	338.70	352.57	482.73	513.10	498.10	510.45	466.43	313.62	188.00	91.67	169.29	354.89
2009	183.00	176.68	157.73	150.00	179.25	185.00	230.00	244.29	257.86	244.76	216.32	251.05	206.33
2010	297.63	305.00	352.83	360.00	338.75	335.00	305.00	325.91	347.14	324.29	338.00	380.00	334.13
2011	429.00	427.37	425.00	425.00	407.86	419.32	420.00	420.00	420.00	411.43	388.75	408.68	416.87
2012	436.25	417.50	415.00	406.43	405.00	358.86	310.05	372.30	361.95	320.43	349.20	358.17	375.93
2013	358.00	350.89	375.71	363.86	342.82	336.20	351.36	351.18	343.35	344.61	370.26	395.16	356.95
2014	414.29	396.00	378.10	383.64	373.67	362.90	362.55	363.00	364.71	350.13	322.11	317.43	365.71
2015	323.60	250.00	225.91	225.00	229.00	246.36	242.27	222.86	211.43	171.36	136.32	130.00	217.84

Source: American Metal Market (AMM)

World Production of Iron Ore[3] In Thousands of Metric Tons (Gross Weight)

Year	Australia	Brazil	Canada	China	India	Maur-itania	Russia	South Africa	Sweden	Ukraine	United States	Venezula	World Total
2006	275,000	317,800	33,543	601,000	177,000	10,658	102,000	41,326	23,300	74,000	52,700	22,100	1,830,000
2007	299,000	354,674	32,744	707,000	207,000	11,817	105,000	42,083	24,700	77,900	52,500	20,700	2,040,000
2008	342,000	350,707	32,102	824,000	213,033	11,296	99,900	48,983	27,713	72,688	53,600	20,650	2,210,000
2009	394,000	298,528	31,704	880,000	217,155	10,524	92,000	55,313	20,389	66,476	26,700	13,801	2,230,000
2010	433,000	372,120	37,001	1,070,000	210,006	11,534	95,900	58,709	27,917	78,171	49,900	14,004	2,590,000
2011	488,000	398,131	33,573	1,330,000	177,256	11,160	104,000	58,057	22,968	80,581	54,700	17,037	2,930,000
2012	521,000	400,822	39,427	1,330,000	142,710	11,200	104,000	67,100	26,039	81,966	54,000	15,124	2,930,000
2013	609,000	386,270	42,800	1,450,000	150,000	13,000	105,000	71,534	26,000	82,000	53,000	10,583	3,110,000
2014[1]	774,000	411,000	44,000	309,000	129,000		102,000	81,000	37,000	68,000	55,900		2,220,000
2015[2]	824,000	428,000	39,000	264,000	129,000		112,000	80,000	37,000	68,000	42,500		2,210,000

[1] Preliminary.   [2] Estimate.   [3] Iron ore, iron ore concentrates and iron ore agglomerates.   *Source: U.S. Geological Survey (USGS)*

Salient Statistics of Iron Ore[3] in the United States   In Thousands of Metric Tons

Year	Net Import Reliance As a % of Apparent Consump	Production Total	Lake Superior	Other Regions	Ship-ments	Value Million $ (at Mine)	Average Value $ at Mine Per Ton	Stock, Dec. 31 Mines	Con-suming Plants	Lake Erie Docks	Imports	Exports	Con-sumption	Total
2006	8	52,700	NA	NA	52,700	2,840.0	53.88	1,650	----	----	11,500	8,270	58,200	611.0
2007	E	52,500	NA	NA	50,900	3,040.0	59.64	2,090	----	----	9,400	9,310	54,700	543.0
2008	E	53,600	NA	NA	53,600	3,770.0	70.43	4,070	----	----	9,250	11,100	51,900	918.0
2009	E	26,700	NA	NA	27,600	2,560.0	92.76	5,060	----	----	3,870	3,920	31,000	376.0
2010	E	49,900	----	----	50,600	5,000.0	98.79	3,470	----	----	6,420	10,000	42,300	703.0
2011	E	54,700	----	----	55,600	5,530.0	99.45	3,260	----	----	5,300	11,100	49,100	841.0
2012	E	54,000	----	----	52,900	5,190.0	98.16	3,110	----	----	5,200	11,200	48,100	759.0
2013	E	52,000	----	----	52,700	5,110.0	96.88	2,290	----	----	3,200	11,000	45,000	426.0
2014[1]	E	55,900	----	----	55,900		92.78	5,340	----	----	5,100	12,100	45,900	
2015[2]	E	42,500	----	----	44,900		84.00	4,500	----	----	4,200	8,100	39,400	

[1] Preliminary.   [2] Estimate.   [3] Usable iron ore exclusive of ore containing 5% or more manganese and includes byproduct ore.
NA = Not available.   *Source: U.S. Geological Survey (USGS)*

U.S. Imports (for Consumption) of Iron Ore[2]   In Thousands of Metric Tons

Year	Australia	Brazil	Canada	Chile	Mauritania	Peru	Sweden	Venezuela	Total
2005	1	4,180	7,510	270	----	33	133	148	13,000
2006	8	4,530	6,240	283	----	52	[3]	23	11,500
2007	----	3,210	5,520	279	----	140	141	58	9,400
2008	----	2,620	5,900	215	----	59	88	68	9,250
2009	----	188	3,140	203	----	34	31	21	3,870
2010	----	506	4,490	131	----	14	54	251	6,420
2011	----	562	3,910	165	----	14	81	279	5,270
2012	----	739	3,820	104	----	44	72	75	5,160
2013	----	630	2,090	152	----	12	49	----	3,250
2014[1]	----	1,730	2,860		----	35	154		5,100

[1] Preliminary.   [2] Including agglomerates.   [3] Less than 1/2 unit.   *Source: U.S. Geological Survey (USGS)*

Iron Ore Stocks in the United States, at End of Month   In Thousands of Metric Tons

Year	Jan.	Feb.	Mar.	Apr.	May	June	July	Aug.	Sept.	Oct.	Nov.	Dec.
2006	6,750	9,620	11,900	11,100	10,800	10,100	9,353	8,760	8,090	8,120	7,590	5,880
2007	7,330	10,100	11,800	11,000	10,300	9,870	9,340	8,700	7,950	7,660	7,110	6,490
2008	6,930	9,820	12,400	11,300	9,950	9,370	8,170	6,910	6,110	5,800	5,830	6,630
2009	8,680	10,900	12,500	12,300	10,600	9,010	7,410	5,990	5,430	5,130	3,900	3,120
2010	3,760	6,080	7,040	6,070	5,400	4,160	3,730	3,240	3,150	3,410	3,320	2,860
2011	4,250	7,470	9,750	9,250	8,970	8,200	7,060	6,380	5,140	4,660	4,250	3,390
2012	3,200	6,750	8,910	7,730	6,410	5,340	3,850	2,980	2,660	2,970	3,020	2,200
2013	3,290	6,580	8,960	7,830	6,350	5,390	4,130	3,320	2,770	2,110	2,470	3,690
2014	6,530	9,240	12,400	13,600	12,500	11,300	9,770	8,190	7,320	6,600	6,290	5,430
2015[1]	6,640	10,600	14,500	14,800	13,100	11,500	9,740	8,040	7,460	7,070	7,550	

[1] Preliminary.   *Source: U.S. Geological Survey (USGS)*

Lard

Lard is the layer of fat found along the back and underneath the skin of a hog. The hog's fat is purified by washing it with water, melting it under constant heat, and straining it several times. Lard is an important byproduct of the meatpacking industry. It is valued highly as cooking oil because there is very little smoke when it is heated. However, demand for lard in cooking is declining because of the trend toward healthier eating. Lard is also used for medicinal purposes such as ointments, plasters, liniments, and occasionally as a laxative for children. Lard production is directly proportional to commercial hog production, meaning the largest producers of hogs are the largest producers of lard.

Prices – The average monthly wholesale price of lard in 2015 fell by -30.1% to 30.30 per pound, well below the 2011 record high of 54.55 per pound.

Supply – World production of lard in the 2014-15 marketing year rose by +2.0% yr/yr to 8.596 million metric tons, which was a new record high. The world's largest lard producers were China (with 44.2% of world production), the U.S (7.2%), Germany (6.6%), the former USSR (6.3%), Brazil (5.3%), Spain (3.6%), and Poland (2.7%). U.S. production of lard in 2013-14 fell -0.9% yr/yr to 1.308 billion pounds.

Demand – U.S. consumption of lard in 2011 (latest data) fell -4.9% to 348.654 million pounds, down from 2008 record high of 490.602 million pounds. The current level of consumption is less than 20% of the consumption of 1.574 billion pounds in 1971.

Exports – U.S. exports of lard in 2013-14 (latest data) fell by -27.0% to 47.4 million pounds, and accounted for only 3.6% of U.S. production.

World Production of Lard   In Thousands of Metric Tons

Year	Brazil	Canada	China	France	Germany	Italy	Japan	Poland	Romania	Spain	United States	Ex-USSR	World Total
2006-07	382.5	126.1	3,181.3	152.2	501.2	207.7	54.2	270.9	76.2	300.5	552.7	369.5	7,636.8
2007-08	386.0	123.7	3,192.7	153.0	520.1	208.7	54.7	249.9	75.0	308.5	605.3	385.1	7,733.1
2008-09	404.9	120.4	3,280.9	140.6	532.9	207.9	52.9	208.9	72.1	297.8	597.3	383.6	7,694.2
2009-10	411.4	122.7	3,402.7	136.5	554.9	210.4	52.6	220.4	71.9	287.2	576.7	423.4	7,893.7
2010-11	429.5	125.0	3,468.0	136.6	566.7	208.4	51.0	234.3	76.2	302.2	586.9	448.3	8,060.6
2011-12	443.0	126.4	3,560.8	133.2	561.5	208.4	51.4	222.7	75.4	309.3	599.7	466.2	8,192.6
2012-13[1]	449.3	125.4	3,627.5	132.1	562.3	213.0	51.3	213.9	73.7	301.3	598.7	498.7	8,314.8
2013-14[2]	453.7	126.0	3,708.2	132.1	558.0	186.3	51.7	231.5	74.3	306.5	593.4	520.1	8,424.4
2014-15[3]	459.4	127.4	3,802.5	133.3	563.8	185.9	51.9	230.8	74.4	310.4	615.6	537.9	8,596.4

[1] Preliminary.   [2] Estimate.   [3] Forecast.   *Source: The Oil World*

Supply and Distribution of Lard in the United States   In Millions of Pounds

	Supply			Disappearance						
Year	Production	Stocks Oct. 1	Total Supply	Domestic	Baking or Frying Fats	Margarine[3]	Exports	Total Disappearance	Direct Use	Per Capita (Lbs.)
2005-06	1,193.3	13.8	1,207.1	694.8	W	3.0	93.8	788.6	459.7	1.5
2006-07	1,218.5	9.4	1,227.9	718.5	W	W	71.9	790.4	498.6	1.7
2007-08	1,334.4	14.2	1,348.6	756.8	W	W	72.9	829.7	486.7	1.6
2008-09	1,316.8	13.9	1,330.7	800.9	W	W	81.4	882.3	310.3	1.0
2009-10	1,271.4	17.5	1,288.9	775.8	W	W	71.6	847.4	479.8	1.5
2010-11	1,293.9	25.6	1,319.5	794.2	W	W	76.6	870.8	NA	NA
2011-12	1,322.1	20.0	1,342.1	830.1	W	W	54.8	884.9	NA	NA
2012-13[1]	1,319.9	20.0	1,339.9	816.3	W	W	64.9	881.2	NA	NA
2013-14[2]	1,308.2	20.0	1,328.2	820.9	W	W	47.4	868.3	NA	NA

[1] Preliminary.   [2] Forecast.   [3] Includes edible tallow.   W = Withheld.
Source: Economic Research Service, U.S. Department of Agriculture (ERS-USDA)

Consumption of Lard (Edible and Inedible) in the United States   In Millions of Pounds

Year	Jan.	Feb.	Mar.	Apr.	May	June	July	Aug.	Sept.	Oct.	Nov.	Dec.	Total
2002	26.4	26.1	21.8	26.7	24.8	21.2	22.9	26.4	23.6	26.4	28.1	28.7	303.2
2003	22.6	22.3	23.4	21.4	23.3	24.0	23.0	21.4	22.5	24.3	20.2	21.0	269.5
2004	22.9	25.8	25.9	23.9	23.5	22.0	19.1	19.7	21.3	22.4	21.9	19.9	268.1
2005	19.0	15.4	21.4	18.7	19.9	20.4	18.9	19.5	20.1	19.7	22.2	17.9	233.1
2006	15.7	16.4	20.6	21.4	20.2	16.7	14.9	17.7	17.8	18.9	22.3	20.9	223.4
2007	21.6	16.2	22.2	19.7	20.5	20.8	22.8	23.9	22.8	31.1	29.7	31.4	282.8
2008	34.8	32.2	44.6	50.7	50.8	44.4	47.8	39.7	44.0	37.5	31.7	32.2	490.6
2009	23.4	17.3	26.8	26.0	26.3	25.8	21.3	20.5	25.4	32.4	29.9	27.0	302.3
2010	22.2	W	38.8	W	30.4	30.8	30.4	32.4	30.1	31.1	30.4	28.8	366.6
2011[1]	22.2	26.3	36.0	W	28.8	29.6	31.4	W	W	W	W	W	348.7

[1] Preliminary.   *Source: Bureau of the Census, U.S. Department of Commerce*

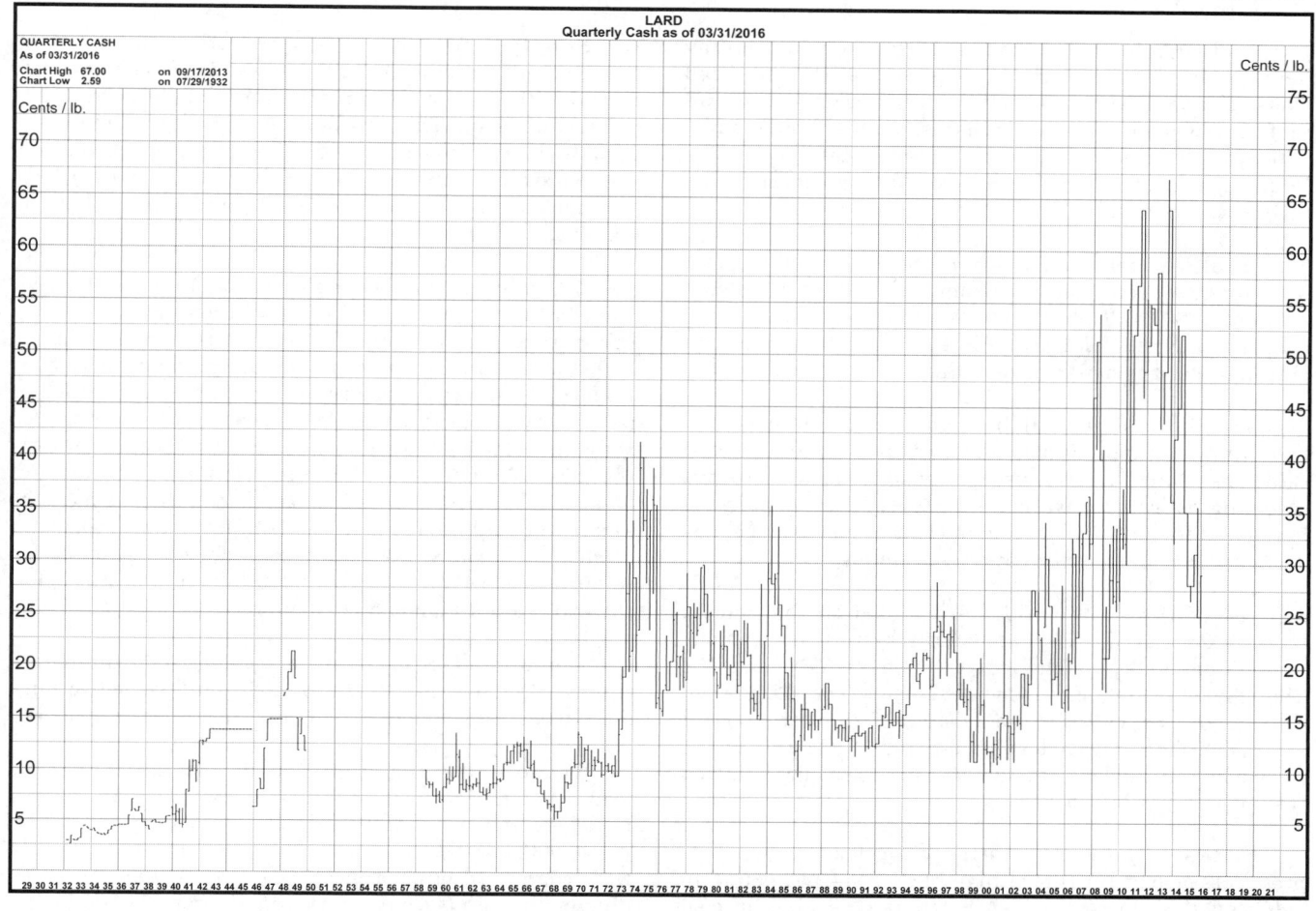

Average Wholesale Price of Lard--Loose, Tank Cars, in Chicago   In Cents Per Pound

Year	Jan.	Feb.	Mar.	Apr.	May	June	July	Aug.	Sept.	Oct.	Nov.	Dec.	Average
2006	17.16	16.44	16.82	18.00	17.13	17.63	22.21	29.91	31.86	23.55	20.78	22.58	21.17
2007	23.00	23.82	30.75	27.71	28.60	32.64	36.00	35.77	36.00	35.09	33.78	32.66	31.32
2008	33.01	38.33	46.00	43.04	42.27	44.93	52.82	46.50	41.73	37.07	26.40	20.00	39.34
2009	25.36	20.31	19.49	23.36	29.00	30.06	27.63	32.20	29.73	25.75	30.07	28.75	26.81
2010	28.60	28.25	32.95	33.95	34.24	32.98	31.42	33.33	43.59	46.64	37.32	38.30	35.13
2011	48.50	49.60	52.00	51.50	54.31	56.75	63.00	58.96	61.33	61.10	48.86	48.71	54.55
2012	NA	52.55	54.60	52.59	54.82	54.83	53.00	NA	NA	51.60	57.00	NA	53.87
2013	52.45	45.56	NA	43.50	44.50	48.50	53.25	56.89	64.78	43.00	48.00	41.50	49.27
2014	33.00	38.00	40.67	53.00	NA	45.00	NA	46.50	50.67	48.00	42.81	35.91	43.36
2015	29.50	28.00	NA	26.64	28.00	NA	31.00	31.00	NA	34.23	35.50	28.80	30.30

Source: Economic Research Service, U.S. Department of Agriculture (ERS-USDA)

Cold Storage Holdings of all Lard[1] in the United States, on First of Month   In Millions of Pounds

Year	Jan.	Feb.	Mar.	Apr.	May	June	July	Aug.	Sept.	Oct.	Nov.	Dec.
2002	13.2	18.0	16.4	16.5	20.3	22.4	18.9	18.3	12.0	10.5	14.6	11.3
2003	10.5	14.0	19.6	18.7	16.5	13.5	11.9	9.7	8.4	9.3	10.1	12.4
2004	13.3	19.8	18.6	20.3	20.5	15.0	12.9	10.8	10.3	11.8	11.4	13.2
2005	13.7	14.6	20.6	19.0	17.8	12.3	12.0	12.3	12.5	13.0	12.2	14.7
2006	9.6	11.5	13.7	13.6	9.3	9.9	13.0	12.4	13.0	11.5	16.1	16.0
2007	16.4	14.9	13.3	18.5	10.9	14.6	11.3	12.8	11.0	9.2	14.6	18.8
2008	14.0	22.4	20.4	22.9	23.0	19.5	22.7	13.6	18.0	17.8	16.1	20.4
2009	12.1	13.6	15.4	16.2	14.5	18.8	17.3	21.6	20.5	26.7	18.5	15.4
2010	13.9	14.5	21.0	22.9	26.1	15.7	19.4	17.9	14.1	13.8	15.6	15.5
2011[2]	17.5	20.5	25.3	20.9	26.2	19.9	23.4	23.9	NA	NA	NA	NA

[1] Stocks in factories and warehouses (except that in hands of retailers).   [2] Preliminary.   *Source: Bureau of the Census, U.S. Department of Commerce*

Lead

Lead (atomic symbol Pb) is a dense, toxic, bluish-gray metallic element, and is the heaviest stable element. Lead was one of the first known metals. The ancients used lead in face powders, rouges, mascaras, paints, condiments, wine preservatives, and water supply plumbing. The Romans were slowly poisoned from lead because of its diverse daily usage.

Lead is usually found in ore with zinc, silver, and most often copper. The most common lead ore is galena, containing 86.6% lead. Cerussite and angleside are other common varieties of lead. More than half of the lead currently used comes from recycling.

Lead is used in building construction, bullets and shot, tank and pipe lining, storage batteries, and electric cable sheathing. Lead is used extensively as a protective shielding for radioactive material (e.g., X-ray apparatus) because of its high density and nuclear properties. Lead is also part of solder, pewter, and fusible alloys.

Lead futures and options are traded on the London Metal Exchange (LME). Lead futures are traded on the Multi Commodity Exchange of India (MCX), and the Shanghai Futures Exchange (SHFE). The LME lead futures contract calls for the delivery of 25 metric tons of at least 99.970% purity lead ingots (pigs). The contract is priced in U.S. dollars per metric ton. Lead first started trading on the LME in 1903.

Prices – The average price of pig lead among U.S. producers reached a record high of $1.2474 per pound in 2007 but has since remained below that level. Pig lead prices in 2015 closed the year down -13.3% at $0.9358 per pound.

Supply – World smelter production of lead (both primary and secondary) in 2013 (latest data) rose +1.0% yr/yr to 10.500 million metric tons to post a new record high production level. The world's largest smelter producers of lead (both primary and secondary) are China with 45.5% of world production in 2013, followed by the U.S. with 12.0%, Germany and Mexico each with 3.8%, and with the UK and Canada, each with about 3%.

U.S. mine production of recoverable lead fell -1.5% yr/yr to 331,000 metric tons in 2013 (latest data available). Missouri was responsible for 94% of U.S. production in 2009 (latest data), with the remainder produced mainly by Idaho and Montana. Lead recovered from scrap in the U.S. (secondary production fell -0.9% yr/yr in 2015 (annualized through October) to 1.119 million metric tons, down from the 2008 record high of 1.220 metric tons. The amount of lead recovered from scrap is almost three times the amount of lead produced in the U.S. from mines (primary production). The value of U.S. secondary lead production in 2013 rose +4.3% yr/yr to $2.910 billion, but still below the 2007 record high of $3.040 billion.

Demand – U.S. lead consumption in 2015 (annualized through October) fell -9.1% to 1.572 million metric tons, down from last year's record high 1.730 million metric tons.

Trade – The U.S. relied on imports for 30% of its lead consumption in 2014 (latest data). U.S. imports of lead pigs and bars in 2013 (latest data) rose +43.3% yr/yr to 500,000 metric tons. U.S. lead exports in 2013 were comprised of ore concentrate (215,000 metric tons), unwrought lead (41,600 metric tons), scrap (34,900 metric tons), and wrought lead (6,610 metric tons).

World Smelter (Primary and Secondary) Production of Lead — In Thousands of Metric Tons

Year	Australia[3]	Belgium[4]	Canada[3]	China[2]	France	Germany	Italy	Japan	Mexico[3]	Spain	United Kingdom[3]	United States	World Total
2005	263.0	83.4	230.2	2,390.0	105.0	417.7	211.5	274.6	226.5	110.0	304.4	1,300	7,660
2006	233.0	101.4	250.5	2,720.0	100.2	379.0	190.5	280.0	212.5	129.0	318.7	1,310	8,100
2007	229.0	117.2	236.7	2,790.0	100.2	405.1	210.0	276.3	212.0	128.0	263.0	1,303	8,320
2008	248.0	109.0	259.1	3,200.0	88.0	415.1	211.8	279.5	243.8	125.0	283.0	1,275	8,730
2009	229.0	109.0	258.9	3,710.0	82.0	390.6	149.0	192.4	239.4	138.0	279.0	1,213	8,850
2010	204.0	105.0	272.9	4,200.0	71.0	404.0	150.0	215.8	286.0	165.0	295.0	1,255	9,520
2011	213.0	88.1	282.6	4,600.0	80.0	429.0	149.5	218.0	317.7	177.0	269.0	1,248	10,200
2012[1]	184.0	88.0	278.1	4,700.0	83.0	430.0	138.4	209.0	415.4	160.0	312.0	1,221	10,400
2013[2]	201.0	87.9	288.3	4,780.0	71.0	400.0	180.0	210.0	400.0	157.0	292.0	1,264	10,500

[1] Preliminary.   [2] Estimate.   [3] Refinded & bullion.   [4] Includes scrap.   *Source: U.S. Geological Survey (USGS)*

Consumption of Lead in the United States, by Products — In Metric Tons

Year	Ammunition	Bearing Metals	Pipes, Traps & Bends[2]	Cable Covering	Calking Lead	Casting Metals	Other Metal Products[3]	Total Other Oxides[4]	Sheet Lead	Storage Battery - Solder	Storage Battery - Grids, Post, etc.	Storage Battery - Oxides	Brass and Bronze	Total Consumption
2005	61,300	1,180	1,220	W	W	30,400	22,200	14,100	29,100	8,370	579,000	705,000	2,100	1,490,000
2006	65,700	1,240	1,440	W	W	29,900	23,400	16,000	28,400	7,280	586,000	710,000	3,130	1,490,000
2007	69,400	1,410	1,230	W	W	31,500	23,600	15,800	28,600	7,220	640,000	738,000	2,870	1,570,000
2008	67,400	1,250	1,190	W	W	20,100	7,670	10,700	26,400	6,610	575,000	715,000	2,460	1,440,000
2009	67,900	1,100	1,130	W	W	15,900	5,790	10,100	25,400	6,450	389,000	750,000	1,370	1,290,000
2010	65,700	1,230	990	W	W	16,400	8,800	9,760	23,400	6,420	478,000	806,000	1,410	1,430,000
2011	75,100	1,150	6,110	W	W	16,000	23,100	9,760	7,170	6,170	417,000	837,000	1,620	1,410,000
2012	73,900	1,090	6,240	W	W	16,700	18,500	9,740	7,390	6,280	449,000	745,000	1,120	1,350,000
2013[1]	84,800	1,110	7,000	W	W	20,400	33,000	9,740	4,870	8,200	464,000	734,000	1,420	1,390,000

[1] Preliminary.   [2] Including building.   [3] Including terne metal, type metal, and lead consumed in foil, collapsible tubes, annealing, plating, galvanizing and fishing weights.   [4] Includes paints, glass and ceramic products, and other pigments and chemicals.   W = Withheld.
Source: U.S. Geological Survey (USGS)

Salient Statistics of Lead in the United States   In Thousands of Metric Tons

Year	Net Import Reliance as a % of Apparent Consump	Production of Refined Lead From Domestic Ores[3]	Foreighn Ores[3]	Total Primary	Total Value of Refined Million $	Secondary Lead Recovered As Soft Lead	In Anti-monial Lead	In Other Alloys	Total	Total Value of Secondary Million USD	Stocks, Dec. 31 Primary	Con-sumer[4]	Average Price Cents Per Pound New York	London
2005	E	143	W	143	----	869	271	4.5	1,150	1,550	W	46.8	61.03	44.23
2006	E	153	W	153	----	948	200	12.4	1,160	1,980	W	54.8	77.40	58.00
2007	E	123	W	123	----	1,020	160	2.4	1,180	3,220	W	51.6	123.84	117.00
2008	E	135	W	135	----	1,000	140	2.4	1,140	3,040	W	72.5	120.33	94.79
2009	13	103	W	103	----	960	151	----	1,110	2,130	W	63.3	86.87	77.95
2010	13	115	W	115	----	968	174	----	1,140	2,740	W	64.8	108.91	97.42
2011	19	118	W	118	----	966	167	----	1,130	3,040	W	46.6	121.70	108.92
2012	18	111	W	111	----	873	236	----	1,110	2,790	W	72.0	114.00	93.50
2013[1]	26	114	W	114	----			----	1,150		W	70.0	114.00	97.20
2014[2]	30	1	W	1	----			----	1,150		W	60.0	----	86.00

[1] Preliminary.   [2] Estimate.   [3] And base bullion.   [4] Also at secondary smelters.   W = Withheld.   E = Net exporter.
Source: U.S. Geological Survey (USGS)

U.S. Foreign Trade of Lead   In Thousands of Metric Tons

Year	Exports Ore Con-centrate	Un-wrought Lead[3]	Wrought Lead[4]	Scrap	Ash & Re-sidues[5]	Imports for Consumption Ores, Flue Dust or Fume & Mattes	Base Bullion	Pigs & Bars	Re-claimed Scrap, Etc.	Value Million $	General Import From: Ore, Flue, Dust & Matte Aus-tralia	Can-ada	Peru	Pigs & Bars Can-ada	Mexico	Peru
2004	292.0	58.6	23.8	56.3	----	----	----	197.0	4.8	235.3	----	----	----	166.0	8.8	7.3
2005	390.2	45.5	19.0	67.3	----	----	----	298.0	3.3	334.8	----	----	----	190.0	15.2	23.9
2006	297.6	52.7	15.8	120.9	----	----	0.5	331.0	1.6	450.8	----	----	----	222.0	15.8	34.6
2007	300.0	51.8	4.6	129.0	----	----	2.0	263.0	2.4	591.4	----	----	----	208.0	35.6	16.5
2008	277.0	68.1	6.2	175.0	----	----	2.7	309.0	1.3	681.6	----	----	----	219.0	58.1	10.6
2009	287.0	77.6	4.3	140.0	----	----	0.8	251.0	1.3	418.8	----	----	----	205.0	41.1	1.0
2010	299.0	77.7	5.6	43.5	----	----	0.6	271.0	3.7	575.9	----	----	----	237.0	29.4	----
2011	223.0	40.1	7.0	31.1	----	----	0.4	313.0	2.4	718.4	----	----	----	250.0	56.0	0.1
2012[1]	214.0	47.0	6.3	25.9	----	1.5	1.0	349.0	2.9	715.9	----	----	----	240.0	56.1	0.0
2013[2]	210.0	48.0		34.9	----	0.0	1.9	500.0								

[1] Preliminary.   [2] Estimate.   [3] And lead alloys.   [4] Blocks, pigs, etc.   [5] Less than 1/2 unit.   Source: U.S. Geological Survey (USGS)

Annual Mine Production of Recoverable Lead in the United States   In Metric Tons

Year	Total	Idaho	Missouri	Montana	Other States	Missouri's % of Total
2004	430,000	W	407,000	W	23,400	95%
2005	426,000	W	397,000	W	29,500	93%
2006	419,000	W	393,000	W	26,100	94%
2007	434,000	W	400,000	W	34,200	92%
2008	399,000	W	360,000	W	38,600	90%
2009	395,000	W	370,000	W	24,900	94%
2010	356,000	W	W	W	W	W
2011	334,000	W	W	W	W	W
2012[1]	336,000	----	----	----	----	----
2013[2]	331,000	----	----	----	----	----

[1] Preliminary.   [2] Estimate.   W = Withheld, included in Other States.   Source: U.S. Geological Survey (USGS)

Mine Production of Recoverable Lead in the United States   In Thousands of Metric Tons

Year	Jan.	Feb.	Mar.	Apr.	May	June	July	Aug.	Sept.	Oct.	Nov.	Dec.	Total
2006	36.7	33.3	38.1	33.6	33.4	33.9	36.6	36.3	37.0	38.0	35.0	29.6	421.5
2007	38.1	33.9	36.7	31.6	36.9	34.5	38.7	41.3	34.6	39.4	31.5	37.1	434.3
2008	38.0	36.9	36.1	33.0	31.0	34.4	37.8	34.2	33.8	29.1	27.8	33.7	405.8
2009	33.8	30.5	32.8	34.7	33.6	33.7	29.9	35.7	35.6	36.9	28.5	32.8	398.5
2010	31.8	28.6	32.7	31.5	29.7	26.5	29.5	26.9	30.1	31.3	27.8	30.0	356.4
2011	30.4	25.1	29.5	32.5	27.4	27.2	29.3	24.4	29.2	25.2	28.1	30.7	339.0
2012	28.7	27.9	27.6	27.3	27.6	28.1	27.5	29.7	27.0	27.5	27.7	29.1	335.7
2013	27.0	25.7	26.0	28.6	28.9	28.0	28.5	28.7	29.6	27.2	25.7	28.6	332.5
2014	30.3	26.6	28.8	31.3	32.8	29.6	30.5	30.4	31.2	32.0	32.7	34.5	370.7
2015[1]	28.2	30.1	35.7	32.1	31.3	28.9	31.2	31.5	26.1	27.1			362.6

[1] Preliminary.   Source: U.S. Geological Survey (USGS)

LEAD

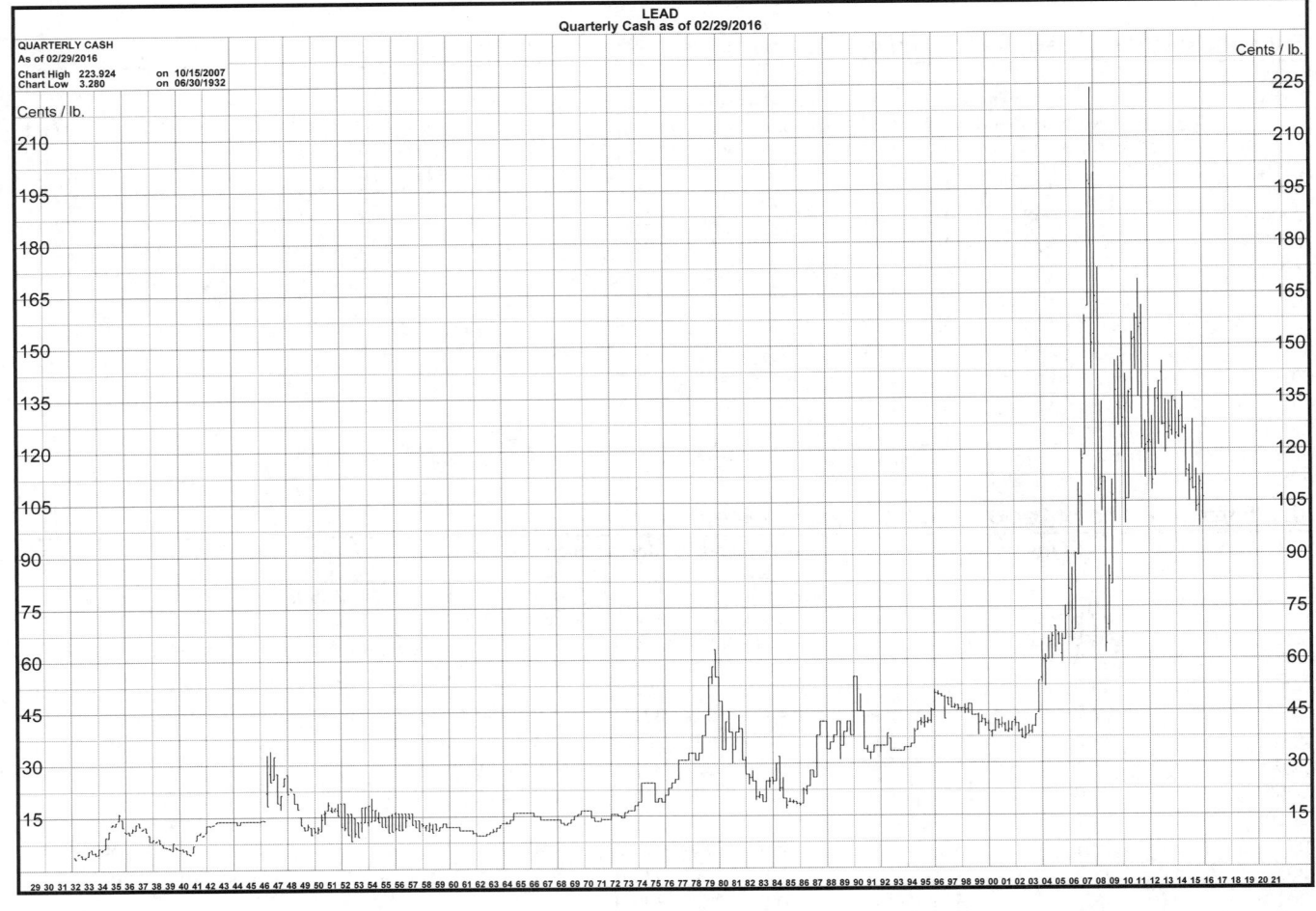

Average Price of Pig Lead, U.S. Primary Producers (Common Corroding)[1]   In Cents Per Pound

Year	Jan.	Feb.	Mar.	Apr.	May	June	July	Aug.	Sept.	Oct.	Nov.	Dec.	Average
2006	66.16	67.16	63.28	61.58	61.16	51.92	56.07	61.48	69.24	77.64	82.09	86.22	67.00
2007	83.62	88.42	94.72	98.73	103.14	117.95	148.17	148.47	153.50	175.59	159.80	124.81	124.74
2008	125.37	146.72	141.77	134.92	106.42	88.93	93.68	92.49	90.49	73.02	65.52	49.58	100.74
2009	57.27	55.74	61.81	67.86	70.02	80.87	81.05	91.57	104.06	105.75	109.61	110.96	83.05
2010	113.15	102.18	104.73	108.78	92.43	83.23	89.48	99.29	104.31	113.11	113.59	114.22	103.21
2011	123.37	122.83	124.67	130.68	117.43	121.38	129.14	116.63	111.36	95.84	97.61	100.19	115.93
2012	103.68	105.11	101.81	100.71	98.42	91.70	92.52	93.54	106.29	112.62	113.81	117.08	103.11
2013	120.19	121.68	112.79	106.17	105.82	109.38	106.18	111.56	107.53	108.72	107.97	109.40	110.62
2014	110.40	108.69	106.23	107.71	107.99	108.35	112.31	114.44	108.97	105.16	104.11	100.29	107.89
2015	95.45	94.25	93.41	102.60	103.12	94.25	92.01	93.72	91.66	88.54	84.72	89.21	93.58

[1] New York Delivery.   *Source: American Metal Market*

Refiners Production[1] of Lead in the United States   In Metric Tons

Year	Jan.	Feb.	Mar.	Apr.	May	June	July	Aug.	Sept.	Oct.	Nov.	Dec.	Total
2001	NA	NA	NA	NA	NA	NA	NA	NA	NA	NA	NA	NA	290,000
2002	NA	NA	NA	NA	NA	NA	NA	NA	NA	NA	NA	NA	262,000
2003	NA	NA	NA	NA	NA	NA	NA	NA	NA	NA	NA	NA	245,000
2004	NA	NA	NA	NA	NA	NA	NA	NA	NA	NA	NA	NA	NA
2005	NA	NA	NA	NA	NA	NA	NA	NA	NA	NA	NA	NA	143,000
2006	NA	NA	NA	NA	NA	NA	NA	NA	NA	NA	NA	NA	143,000
2007	NA	NA	NA	NA	NA	NA	NA	NA	NA	NA	NA	NA	NA
2008	NA	NA	NA	NA	NA	NA	NA	NA	NA	NA	NA	NA	NA
2009	NA	NA	NA	NA	NA	NA	NA	NA	NA	NA	NA	NA	NA
2010[2]	NA	NA	NA	NA	NA	NA	NA	NA	NA	NA	NA	NA	NA

[1] Represents refined lead produced from domestic ores by primary smelters plus small amounts of secondary material passing through these smelters.
Includes GSA metal purchased for remelt.   [2] Preliminary.   NA = Not available.   *Source: U.S. Geological Survey (USGS)*

Total Stocks of Lead[1] in the United States at Refiners, at End of Month   In Metric Tons

Year	Jan.	Feb.	Mar.	Apr.	May	June	July	Aug.	Sept.	Oct.	Nov.	Dec.
2006	59,300	59,700	59,800	60,100	61,500	60,100	49,000	48,000	47,900	48,900	49,900	50,900
2007	50,000	49,000	49,000	49,300	37,900	46,800	54,300	54,100	58,700	56,400	59,100	63,100
2008	53,100	50,800	53,600	50,900	51,600	49,900	46,100	52,500	52,300	55,500	69,100	69,900
2009	70,600	70,100	77,900	68,100	70,200	65,600	56,300	53,800	54,500	55,200	59,100	61,700
2010	60,200	60,200	55,700	50,700	55,500	57,200	57,600	59,100	59,800	58,700	67,700	67,400
2011	67,100	53,000	53,200	61,100	62,600	61,500	62,800	60,500	58,800	56,300	53,500	54,800
2012	58,700	63,300	54,800	54,000	51,800	56,600	62,600	65,700	63,400	63,800	56,000	57,500
2013	69,900	76,200	83,100	94,300	98,000	93,400	83,600	81,400	77,400	69,300	65,100	69,400
2014	68,100	63,600	65,400	65,700	64,000	66,600	62,500	62,080	63,300	63,100	66,300	66,300
2015[1]	64,900	63,800	63,600	64,100	62,700	62,400	60,800	66,900	69,500	81,800		

[1] Preliminary.   [2] Secondary smelters and consumers.   Source: U.S. Geological Survey (USGS)

Total[2] Lead Consumption in the United States   In Thousands of Metric Tons

Year	Jan.	Feb.	Mar.	Apr.	May	June	July	Aug.	Sept.	Oct.	Nov.	Dec.	Total
2006	124.0	130.0	129.0	128.0	128.0	128.0	125.0	126.0	127.0	128.0	126.0	126.0	1,525
2007	130.0	128.0	129.0	128.0	131.0	139.0	131.0	134.0	132.0	137.0	132.0	127.0	1,578
2008	140.0	136.0	130.0	135.0	135.0	141.0	134.0	129.0	134.0	136.0	127.0	126.0	1,603
2009	123.0	119.0	116.0	124.0	116.0	117.0	116.0	115.0	118.0	122.0	121.0	117.0	1,424
2010	120.0	118.0	114.0	115.0	117.0	118.0	116.0	117.0	118.0	117.0	118.0	117.0	1,405
2011	131.0	118.0	118.0	133.0	132.0	133.0	132.0	133.0	132.0	132.0	132.0	131.0	1,557
2012	122.0	130.0	135.0	123.0	121.0	122.0	120.0	122.0	121.0	122.0	122.0	123.0	1,483
2013	146.0	123.0	118.0	117.0	117.0	117.0	116.0	118.0	117.0	119.0	115.0	134.0	1,457
2014	159.0	159.0	148.0	153.0	148.0	146.0	131.0	155.3	128.0	134.0	131.0	138.0	1,730
2015[1]	132.0	121.0	135.0	151.0	130.0	135.0	128.0	125.0	121.0	132.0			1,572

[1] Preliminary.   [1] Represents total consumption of primary & secondary lead as metal, in chemicals, or in alloys.   Source: U.S. Geological Survey (USGS)

Lead Recovered from Scrap in the United States   In Thousands of Metric Tons (Lead Content)

Year	Jan.	Feb.	Mar.	Apr.	May	June	July	Aug.	Sept.	Oct.	Nov.	Dec.	Total
2006	90.2	96.7	97.4	98.2	99.5	95.7	94.9	97.0	95.6	98.4	98.4	95.9	1,157.9
2007	99.0	96.5	98.6	93.5	94.5	100.0	103.0	103.0	101.0	104.0	104.0	94.6	1,191.7
2008	104.0	98.2	102.0	100.0	105.0	102.0	92.0	102.0	91.7	100.0	122.0	101.0	1,219.9
2009	97.3	99.0	101.0	90.2	91.6	93.8	97.0	97.2	90.9	96.3	98.0	98.0	1,150.3
2010	96.2	95.2	92.1	86.3	89.8	92.9	94.2	98.0	95.6	101.0	100.0	96.3	1,137.6
2011	104.0	96.2	95.5	104.0	101.0	100.0	102.0	103.0	95.4	95.9	98.8	99.6	1,195.4
2012	102.0	101.0	97.8	98.0	99.4	102.0	100.0	98.0	97.3	100.0	100.0	99.2	1,194.7
2013	104.0	96.7	100.0	97.3	100.0	98.1	97.2	100.0	99.5	104.0	102.0	95.0	1,193.8
2014	92.7	91.1	97.3	96.3	94.5	94.5	96.9	93.8	94.8	94.4	88.6	94.8	1,129.7
2015[1]	88.6	88.9	92.2	94.6	93.6	92.9	92.5	95.4	96.3	97.5			1,119.0

[1] Preliminary.   Source: U.S. Geological Survey (USGS)

Domestic Shipments[1] of Lead in the United States, by Refiners   In Thousands of Short Tons

Year	Jan.	Feb.	Mar.	Apr.	May	June	July	Aug.	Sept.	Oct.	Nov.	Dec.	Total
1989	29.3	28.5	32.2	35.7	45.1	36.4	32.8	41.5	40.0	44.2	40.2	31.1	437.1
1990	39.3	33.9	39.1	33.5	38.4	32.9	32.6	38.9	36.6	38.9	37.9	31.7	433.7
1991	35.4	33.8	34.3	39.8	33.9	26.0	31.8	37.9	35.1	35.7	28.7	26.7	399.2
1992	31.3	23.9	30.4	26.3	25.6	27.2	27.3	28.7	26.3	28.5	26.3	21.7	323.5
1993	24.6	23.6	32.5	30.0	31.3	35.1	28.9	34.0	35.5	35.5	31.7	33.5	376.2
1994	35.9	32.8	35.2	32.7	34.7	36.7	31.6	33.4	34.8	34.3	34.0	33.3	409.3
1995	36.5	30.3	35.1	31.1	33.7	31.9	28.6	40.3	34.9	40.9	33.2	29.8	406.4
1996	37.2	32.4	29.5	30.2	29.4	26.7	27.7	33.5	30.1	33.5	28.1	27.6	366.0
1997[2]	31.5	27.8	24.7	35.2	39.2	36.1	33.4	29.4	26.4	31.5	30.4	28.1	377.8
1998[2]	Data no longer available.												

[1] Includes GSA metal.   [2] Preliminary.   Source: American Metal Market (AMM)

Lumber and Plywood

Humans have utilized lumber for construction for thousands of years, but due to the heaviness of timber and the manual methods of harvesting, large-scale lumbering didn't occur until the mechanical advances of the Industrial Revolution. Lumber is produced from both hardwood and softwood. Hardwood lumber comes from deciduous trees that have broad leaves. Most hardwood lumber is used for miscellaneous industrial applications, primarily wood pallets, and includes oak, gum, maple, and ash. Hardwood species with beautiful colors and patterns are used for such high-grade products as furniture, flooring, paneling, and cabinets and include black walnut, black cherry, and red oak. Wood from cone-bearing trees is called softwood, regardless of its actual hardness. Most lumber from the U.S. is softwood. Softwoods, such as southern yellow pine, Douglas fir, ponderosa pine, and true firs, are primarily used as structural lumber such as 2x4s and 2x6s, poles, paper and cardboard.

Plywood consists of several thin layers of veneer bonded together with adhesives. The veneer sheets are layered so that the grain of one sheet is perpendicular to that of the next, which makes plywood exceptionally strong for its weight. Most plywood has from three to nine layers of wood. Plywood manufacturers use both hard and soft woods, although hardwoods serve primarily for appearance and are not as strong as those made from softwoods. Plywood is primarily used in construction, particularly for floors, roofs, walls, and doors. Homebuilding and remodeling account for two-thirds of U.S. lumber consumption. The price of lumber and plywood is highly correlated with the strength of the U.S. home-building market.

The forest and wood products industry is dominated by Weyerhaeuser Company (ticker symbol WY), which has about $20 billion in annual sales. Weyerhaeuser is a forest products conglomerate that engages not only in growing and harvesting timber, but also in the production and distribution of forest products, real estate development, and construction of single-family homes. Forest products include wood products, pulp and paper, and containerboard. The timberland segment of the business manages 7.2 million acres of company-owned land and 800,000 acres of leased commercial forestlands in North America. The company's Canadian division has renewable, long-term licenses on about 35 million acres of forestland in five Canadian provinces. In order to maximize its long-term yield from its acreage, Weyerhaeuser engages in a number of forest management activities such as extensive planting, suppression of non-merchantable species, thinning, fertilization, and operational pruning.

Lumber futures and options are traded at the CME Group. The CME's lumber futures contract calls for the delivery of 111,000 board feet (one 73 foot rail car) of random length 8 to 12 foot 2 x 4s, the type used in construction. The contract is priced in terms of dollars per thousand board feet.

Prices – CME lumber futures prices (Barchart.com electronic symbol code LS) on the nearest-futures chart in 2015 sold off sharply early in the year to post a 4-year low in September but then rebounded through year-end to close the year down -22.2% yr/yr at $257.60 per thousand board feet.

Supply – The U.S. led the world in the production of industrial round wood and in 2014 (latest data) production rose +0.5% yr/yr to 356.812 million cubic meters, followed by Russia with 188.300 million cubic meters (+4.4% yr/yr) and Canada with 149.934 cubic meters (+1.5% yr/yr). The U.S. also led the world in the production of plywood with 9.452 million cubic meters of production in 2014 (-2.4% yr/yr), followed by Russia with 3.513 million cubic meters (+6.4% yr/yr), and then Japan with 2.902 million cubic meters (+5.1% yr/yr). U.S. softwood lumber production in latest data from the series of 2006 (latest data annualized through November) fell -4.4% yr/yr to 38.503 billion board feet.

Trade – World exports of plywood in 2014 (latest data) rose by +8.9% yr/yr to 29.164 million cubic meters. The world's largest exporter of plywood is Russia with a 6.5% share of world plywood exports in 2014, followed by Finland (3.4%) and Belgium (1.3%). U.S. exports of plywood accounted for 2.8% of world exports in 2014 and fell by -6.8% yr/yr to 828,000 cubic meters.

World exports of industrial roundwood in 2014 (latest data) rose by +4.6% yr/yr to 131.916 million cubic meters. Russia was the world's largest exporter of roundwood in 2014 with a 15.8% share of world exports, followed by the U.S. with an 10.6% share, and Canada with a 5.5% share. Russian exports of industrial roundwood in 2014 rose by +9.7% yr/yr to 20.899 million cubic meters. U.S. exports of industrial roundwood in 2014 fell by -5.0% yr/yr to 13.962 million cubic meters.

World Production of Industrial Roundwood by Selected Countries   In Thousands of Cubic Meters

Year	Austria	Canada	Czech Republic	Finland	France	Germany	Poland	Romania	Russia	Spain	Sweden	Turkey	United States
2005	12,786	200,247	47,116	27,944	50,905	14,285	28,531	11,542	167,580	13,351	92,300	11,202	423,456
2006	14,430	181,010	45,521	28,592	54,000	16,333	28,767	9,454	175,500	14,109	58,700	12,253	412,134
2007	16,521	161,390	51,406	29,817	68,029	16,738	32,461	11,572	189,770	12,546	72,300	13,674	378,771
2008	16,772	136,096	45,965	27,724	46,806	14,307	30,470	9,517	149,256	14,427	64,900	14,462	336,895
2009	12,144	113,306	36,701	29,081	38,987	13,769	30,475	8,587	146,310	11,900	59,200	14,252	292,091
2010	13,281	138,802	45,977	29,634	45,388	14,771	31,343	10,548	161,595	10,969	66,300	15,695	336,135
2011	13,631	146,735	45,526	28,387	45,358	13,467	32,200	10,344	175,625	11,528	66,000	16,423	354,704
2012	12,831	146,741	44,614	24,945	42,863	13,041	32,972	11,050	177,455	11,627	63,599	17,701	347,076
2013[1]	12,433	147,751	49,331	24,451	42,052	13,149	33,795	10,091	180,379	12,323	63,700	16,762	354,937
2014[2]	12,030	149,934	49,202	25,832	43,243	13,365	35,425	10,484	188,300	12,323	64,200	18,535	356,812

[1] Preliminary.   [2] Estimate.   *Source: Food and Agriculture Organization of the United Nations (FAO)*

Imports of Industrial Roundwood by Selected Countries   In Thousands of Cubic Meters

Year	Austria	Belgium	Canada	Finland	France	Germany	Italy	Norway	Poland	Portugal	Spain	Sweden	United States
2005	8,629	3,188	6,274	16,031	2,344	3,005	4,755	3,145	2,009	362	3,640	8,686	3,569
2006	9,102	3,284	5,787	14,655	2,601	3,669	4,486	2,333	1,814	335	3,841	6,664	2,922
2007	8,722	4,094	5,100	12,942	3,181	4,692	4,299	2,539	2,088	746	3,965	7,364	2,242
2008	7,550	3,669	4,608	13,371	2,358	5,758	3,478	1,808	1,868	521	2,860	6,781	1,430
2009	8,036	3,031	4,636	3,761	1,503	4,534	2,703	933	1,874	473	1,868	4,676	696
2010	8,041	4,193	4,745	6,256	1,690	7,656	3,198	1,288	2,289	855	1,839	6,276	816
2011	7,427	4,326	4,275	5,736	1,454	7,005	3,328	1,355	3,419	1,717	2,135	6,724	959
2012	7,319	4,338	4,495	5,457	1,368	6,567	2,802	940	2,469	1,644	1,727	6,855	1,167
2013[1]	8,214	4,507	4,872	6,694	1,244	8,442	2,691	661	2,270	2,320	2,047	7,532	926
2014[2]	7,260	4,507	4,261	6,256	1,503	8,317	2,911	447	3,256	2,485	2,047	8,127	909

[1] Preliminary.   [2] Estimate.   *Source: Food and Agricultural Organization of the United Nations (FAO)*

Exports of Industrial Roundwood by Selected Countries   In Thousands of Cubic Meters

Year	Canada	Czech Republic	Estonia	France	Germany	Hungary	Latvia	Lithuania	Russia	Slovakia	Sweden	Switzerland	United States
2005	5,592	2,942	1,806	3,862	6,819	871	3,919	1,131	48,020	1,691	3,095	1,416	9,815
2006	4,640	2,679	1,606	3,695	7,557	1,095	3,419	1,061	50,900	1,218	3,004	1,667	9,638
2007	3,560	2,384	1,502	3,966	7,674	1,054	3,690	1,671	49,100	1,457	3,808	2,005	9,949
2008	2,839	1,906	1,469	3,547	7,037	661	3,193	1,171	36,784	2,192	2,349	1,155	10,200
2009	2,723	2,596	1,080	5,047	3,857	684	2,503	673	21,700	2,538	1,177	575	9,619
2010	4,019	1,743	2,250	6,665	3,726	873	4,158	1,329	20,983	2,434	1,217	796	9,641
2011	5,706	3,487	2,610	6,380	3,658	881	4,401	1,844	20,429	2,533	846	926	9,405
2012	6,094	3,912	2,392	4,571	3,398	858	4,107	1,464	17,652	2,048	794	801	14,169
2013[1]	7,023	4,292	2,747	4,740	3,316	1,072	3,737	1,809	19,045	2,641	756	740	14,700
2014[2]	7,235	4,931	2,758	4,397	3,278	1,072	3,837	1,708	20,899	2,926	630	740	13,962

[1] Preliminary.   [2] Estimate.   *Source: Food and Agricultural Organization of the United Nations (FAO)*

U.S. Housing Starts: Seasonally Adjusted Annual Rate   In Thousands

Year	Jan.	Feb.	Mar.	Apr.	May	June	July	Aug.	Sept.	Oct.	Nov.	Dec.	Average
2006	2,273	2,119	1,969	1,821	1,942	1,802	1,737	1,650	1,720	1,491	1,570	1,649	1,812
2007	1,409	1,480	1,495	1,490	1,415	1,448	1,354	1,330	1,183	1,264	1,197	1,037	1,342
2008	1,084	1,103	1,005	1,013	973	1,046	923	844	820	777	652	560	900
2009	490	582	505	478	540	585	594	586	585	534	588	581	554
2010	614	604	636	687	583	536	546	599	594	543	545	539	586
2011	630	517	600	554	561	608	623	585	650	610	711	694	612
2012	723	704	695	753	708	757	740	754	847	915	833	976	784
2013	896	951	994	848	915	831	898	885	863	936	1,105	1,034	930
2014	888	951	963	1,039	986	927	1,095	966	1,026	1,079	1,007	1,080	1,001
2015[1]	1,080	900	954	1,190	1,072	1,211	1,152	1,116	1,207	1,071	1,176	1,143	1,106

[1] Preliminary.   Total Privately owned.   *Source: Bureau of the Census, U.S. Department of Commerce*

LUMBER AND PLYWOOD

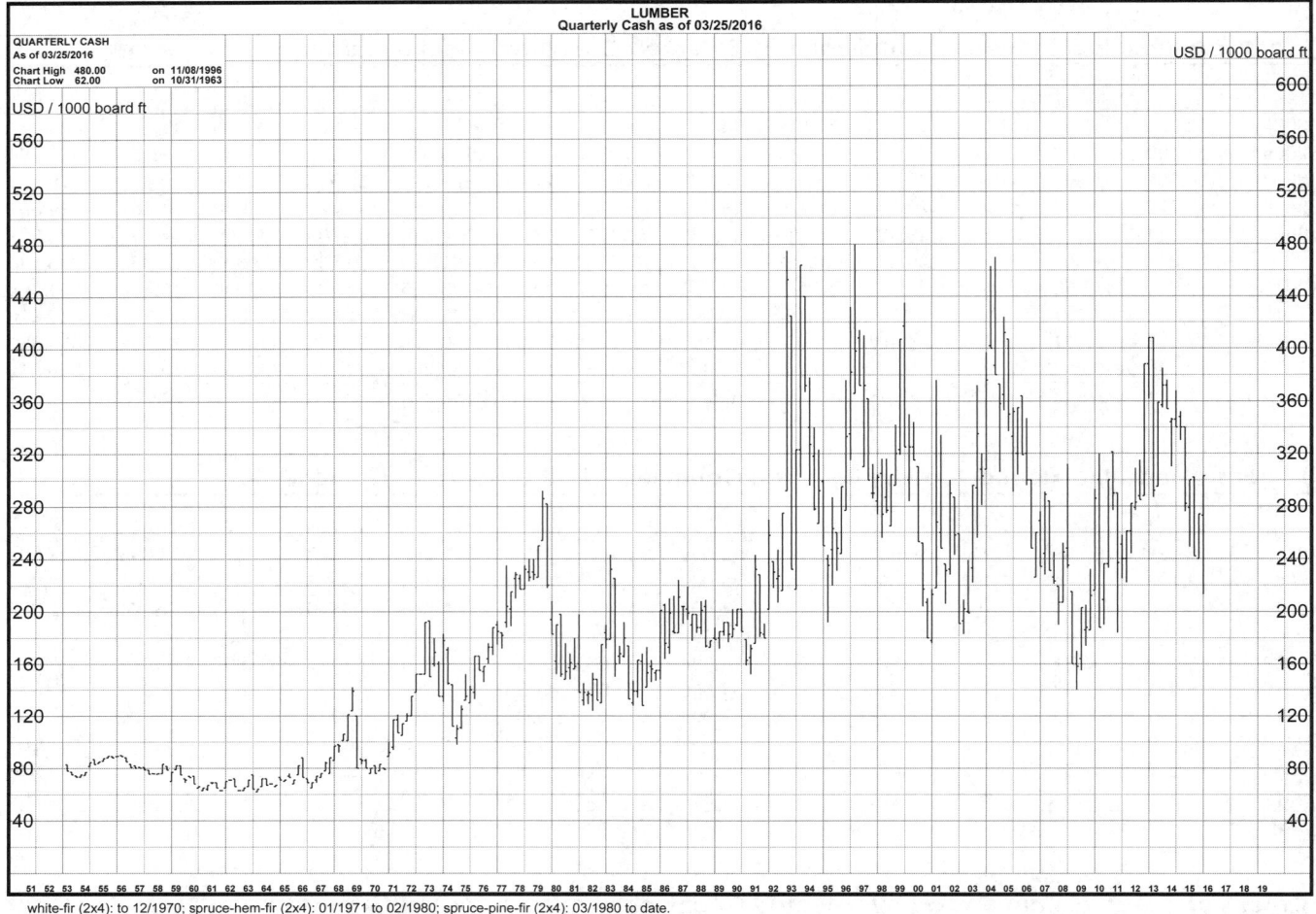

LUMBER
Quarterly Cash as of 03/25/2016

QUARTERLY CASH
As of 03/25/2016

Chart High 480.00 on 11/08/1996
Chart Low 62.00 on 10/31/1963

USD / 1000 board ft

USD / 1000 board ft

white-fir (2x4): to 12/1970; spruce-hem-fir (2x4): 01/1971 to 02/1980; spruce-pine-fir (2x4): 03/1980 to date.

Average Price of Lumber in the United States   In Dollars per Thousand Board Feet

Year	Jan.	Feb.	Mar.	Apr.	May	June	July	Aug.	Sept.	Oct.	Nov.	Dec.	Average
2006	357.00	344.50	329.40	332.50	320.75	298.60	291.75	271.25	271.60	238.00	242.75	251.60	295.81
2007	259.25	255.00	243.20	242.00	246.25	282.00	273.50	265.60	239.00	223.75	240.20	226.50	249.69
2008	206.50	203.00	200.50	214.25	238.20	244.00	259.50	283.40	247.25	194.40	180.75	164.50	219.69
2009	150.60	158.00	154.75	166.00	161.80	193.00	185.00	200.25	186.25	191.00	210.00	223.67	181.69
2010	238.50	287.00	281.50	312.00	272.50	207.50	203.40	219.75	231.75	245.80	275.33	283.80	254.90
2011	307.25	286.25	294.25	269.50	227.25	222.75	254.50	231.75	250.80	236.50	230.25	248.00	254.92
2012	253.50	262.67	280.75	281.25	305.50	300.00	294.25	310.20	292.33	298.00	339.50	370.00	299.00
2013	382.25	377.33	401.50	386.60	325.50	298.40	312.25	326.00	346.75	360.25	381.80	364.25	355.24
2014	373.20	364.00	362.75	339.00	342.00	323.75	351.50	361.00	355.25	347.00	333.75	337.75	349.25
2015	326.00	313.50	283.75	261.50	256.40	292.25	294.25	267.75	246.00	259.20	259.75	267.25	277.30

Source: National Agricultural Statistics Service, U.S. Department of Agriculture (NASS-USDA)

Average Price of Plywood in the United States   In Dollars per Thousand Board Feet

Year	Jan.	Feb.	Mar.	Apr.	May	June	July	Aug.	Sept.	Oct.	Nov.	Dec.	Average
2006	304.25	277.50	275.20	258.00	236.75	221.80	185.75	179.75	138.39	169.00	171.50	158.80	214.72
2007	145.50	148.00	141.40	149.75	148.25	169.00	191.00	176.20	164.25	165.50	177.60	149.00	160.45
2008	139.25	132.20	141.50	143.25	185.60	204.75	189.50	212.80	197.50	177.60	173.25	158.75	171.33
2009	151.00	163.00	150.75	148.00	140.80	153.75	174.00	186.00	176.50	158.00	171.25	186.33	163.28
2010	191.50	220.00	233.00	353.75	330.00	206.25	217.20	171.25	164.50	183.00	189.33	196.40	221.35
2011	210.75	196.75	189.25	178.25	167.25	180.25	171.25	192.25	188.60	190.75	185.00	192.00	186.86
2012	201.00	194.67	213.25	212.50	233.75	252.00	257.50	331.00	343.33	300.00	343.75	354.50	269.77
2013	401.50	412.67	430.00	410.00	354.33	279.25	256.25	254.40	244.75	263.00	244.00	227.75	314.83
2014	226.60	215.00	214.50	210.33	233.00	210.25	212.25	215.40	222.00	222.00	219.00	204.00	217.03
2015	200.80	194.25	183.50	177.50	194.00	207.25	194.00	200.50	218.33	239.20	257.00	233.50	208.32

Source: National Agricultural Statistics Service, U.S. Department of Agriculture (NASS-USDA)

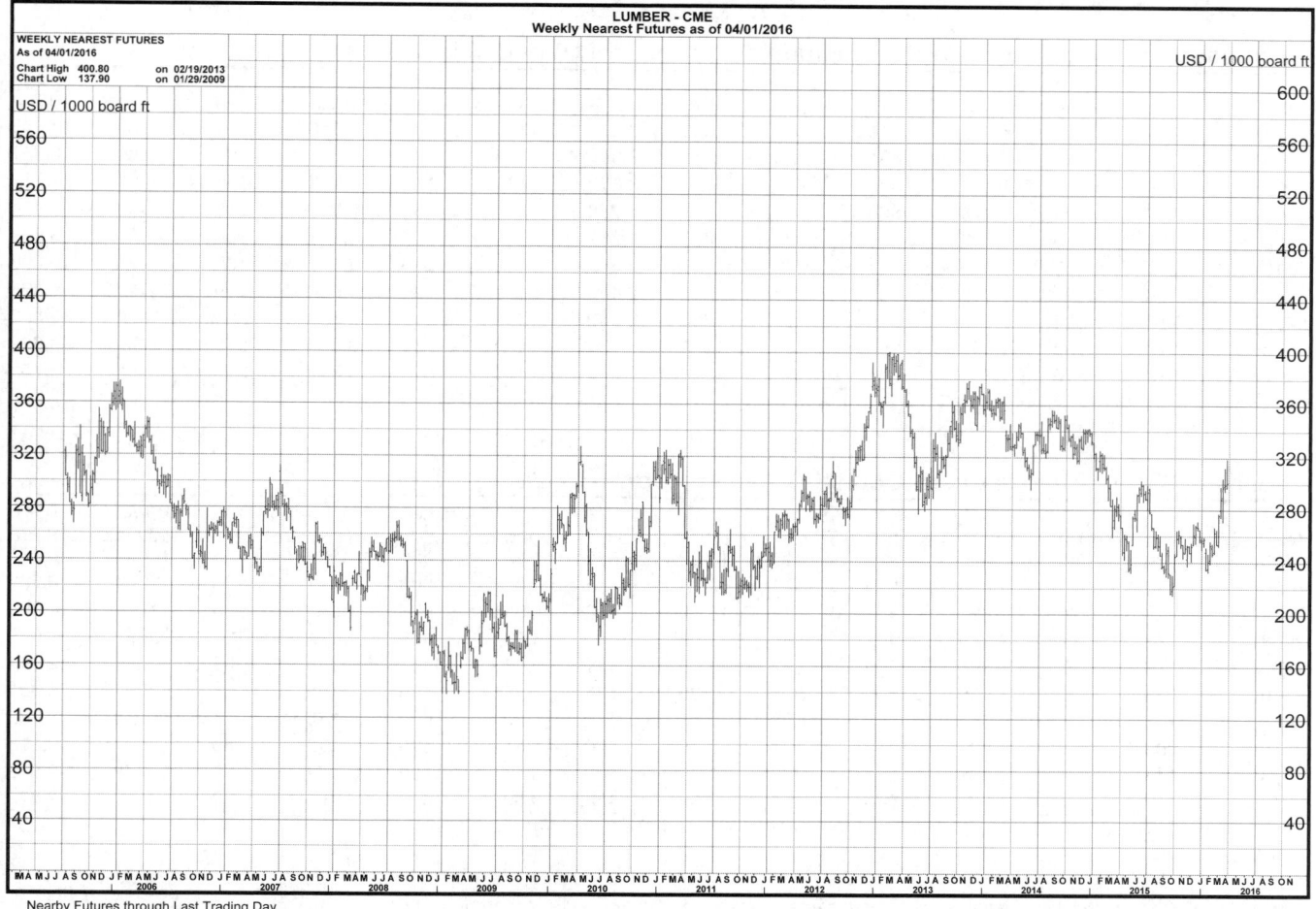

LUMBER - CME
Weekly Nearest Futures as of 04/01/2016

WEEKLY NEAREST FUTURES
As of 04/01/2016

Chart High 400.80 on 02/19/2013
Chart Low 137.90 on 01/29/2009

USD / 1000 board ft

USD / 1000 board ft

Nearby Futures through Last Trading Day.

Volume of Trading of Random Lumber Futures in Chicago   In Contracts

Year	Jan.	Feb.	Mar.	Apr.	May	June	July	Aug.	Sept.	Oct.	Nov.	Dec.	Total
2006	26,803	19,152	18,504	21,358	21,619	23,959	21,568	23,800	22,618	24,804	22,385	24,454	271,024
2007	26,214	28,328	24,741	26,433	31,540	28,545	23,462	28,610	24,841	33,876	29,738	28,361	334,689
2008	31,401	43,338	37,899	50,586	37,909	38,362	41,612	40,693	32,155	36,226	20,277	27,155	437,613
2009	18,478	29,930	22,193	25,349	24,351	34,027	24,340	29,548	22,271	33,768	21,817	31,155	317,227
2010	25,483	26,365	20,928	32,393	24,763	29,446	18,360	24,660	26,107	31,689	23,662	28,046	311,902
2011	22,691	25,642	25,141	32,161	20,134	30,740	18,440	32,615	28,562	26,650	22,589	33,968	319,333
2012	20,678	33,593	25,208	30,526	24,563	26,638	23,663	32,211	19,595	31,797	24,513	31,538	324,523
2013	26,219	29,842	18,671	26,472	23,349	19,914	18,572	18,118	19,271	17,021	11,100	15,073	243,622
2014	13,001	14,025	12,632	14,563	13,365	17,276	10,119	14,977	11,766	16,481	8,959	13,333	160,497
2015	13,744	16,696	14,710	21,116	16,757	19,374	14,253	20,509	15,592	21,061	11,475	16,065	201,352

Contract size = 110,000 board feet.   *Source: CME Group; Chicago Mercantile Exchange (CME)*

Average Open Interest of Random Lumber Futures in Chicago   In Contracts

Year	Jan.	Feb.	Mar.	Apr.	May	June	July	Aug.	Sept.	Oct.	Nov.	Dec.
2006	5,893	5,144	4,084	4,959	4,586	5,449	5,317	6,429	5,912	6,351	6,121	7,018
2007	6,466	7,807	7,684	8,680	7,726	8,206	7,130	7,666	6,493	9,356	8,960	9,731
2008	9,827	13,134	13,385	14,637	14,801	14,275	14,417	14,016	12,110	9,466	7,744	8,084
2009	7,912	7,937	6,852	7,732	7,815	9,039	7,910	8,873	9,248	9,593	10,174	9,557
2010	9,674	10,231	9,538	10,571	8,358	9,402	8,675	9,498	8,812	9,707	9,620	10,018
2011	11,235	10,223	9,471	9,813	10,090	10,408	9,233	10,170	9,465	10,314	9,663	10,768
2012	9,261	10,228	10,192	9,962	9,226	7,885	7,666	9,259	8,153	8,275	10,713	10,624
2013	9,354	8,222	8,609	7,345	5,872	6,726	5,816	5,539	5,699	4,816	4,672	4,086
2014	3,945	4,602	4,618	5,020	4,422	5,013	4,080	4,419	3,751	3,698	4,610	4,289
2015	4,831	5,256	6,336	6,860	6,379	4,660	4,389	6,151	6,104	5,553	3,974	4,158

Contract size = 110,000 board feet.   *Source: CME Group; Chicago Mercantile Exchange (CME)*

LUMBER AND PLYWOOD

Production of Plywood by Selected Countries   In Thousands of Cubic Meters

Year	Austria	Canada	Finland	France	Germany	Italy	Japan	Poland	Romania	Russia	Spain	Sweden	United States
2005	195	2,322	1,305	415	236	390	3,212	361	126	2,556	557	92	14,449
2006	178	2,252	1,415	431	235	334	3,314	385	188	2,614	468	92	13,651
2007	258	2,639	1,410	378	229	420	3,073	440	107	2,777	450	72	12,402
2008	268	2,225	1,273	360	174	421	2,586	391	152	2,592	250	56	10,376
2009	163	1,810	800	265	193	337	2,287	312	212	2,107	233	65	8,934
2010	273	2,005	980	271	232	310	2,645	402	266	2,689	267	60	9,397
2011	216	1,794	1,010	258	218	310	2,486	411	331	3,040	299	84	9,365
2012	216	1,824	1,020	324	178	280	2,549	388	472	3,150	255	54	9,493
2013[1]	216	1,792	1,090	255	135	225	2,761	430	665	3,303	275	53	9,680
2014[2]	216	1,810	1,160	245	148	266	2,902	485	670	3,513	275	53	9,452

[1] Preliminary.   [2] Estimate.   *Source: Food and Agricultural Organization of the United Nations (FAO)*

Imports of Plywood by Selected Countries   In Thousands of Cubic Meters

Year	Austria	Belgium	Canada	Denmark	France	Germany	Italy	Japan	Netherlands	Sweden	Switzerland	United Kingdom	United States
2005	140	521	690	371	411	1,142	532	4,732	526	189	145	1,456	6,181
2006	140	610	685	280	445	1,314	575	5,046	603	197	128	1,497	6,393
2007	172	672	1,827	358	459	1,516	588	4,064	608	240	126	1,624	4,397
2008	133	633	2,149	402	581	1,459	530	3,583	635	192	131	1,486	3,059
2009	116	527	861	229	397	1,066	417	2,948	457	144	53	1,164	2,647
2010	155	544	1,909	219	544	1,288	485	3,255	495	152	68	1,264	2,551
2011	196	593	1,554	262	492	1,423	463	3,809	620	185	74	1,330	2,632
2012	209	533	1,621	270	374	1,336	420	3,645	476	173	86	1,285	3,113
2013[1]	145	537	1,469	266	368	1,338	428	3,765	399	155	99	1,370	2,829
2014[2]	158	537	1,585	266	404	1,352	453	3,597	399	163	99	1,399	2,872

[1] Preliminary.   [2] Estimate.   *Source: Food and Agricultural Organization of the United Nations (FAO)*

Exports of Plywood by Selected Countries   In Thousands of Cubic Meters

Year	Austria	Baltic States	Belgium	Canada	Finland	France	Germany	Italy	Netherlands	Poland	Russia	Spain	United States
2005	287	253	423	1,118	1,173	196	287	146	40	177	1,527	117	503
2006	311	282	470	950	1,250	225	321	239	60	137	1,577	124	492
2007	285	318	386	964	1,229	227	368	295	55	148	1,503	162	443
2008	278	197	470	583	1,083	275	342	184	51	133	1,326	213	506
2009	278	211	374	306	683	162	277	148	49	117	1,334	122	529
2010	304	289	440	301	833	163	337	218	50	133	1,512	141	871
2011	353	302	437	359	863	127	355	228	63	141	1,600	165	837
2012	334	310	368	287	855	143	298	201	89	169	2,448	152	914
2013[1]	339	312	369	426	920	141	297	192	71	181	1,758	169	888
2014[2]	344	302	369	482	998	143	308	210	71	198	1,906	169	828

[1] Preliminary.   [2] Estimate.   *Source: Food and Agricultural Organization of the United Nations (FAO)*

Magnesium

Magnesium (atomic symbol Mg) is a silvery-white, light, and fairly tough, metallic element and is relatively stable. Magnesium is one of the alkaline earth metals. Magnesium is the eighth most abundant element in the earth's crust and the third most plentiful element found in seawater. Magnesium is ductile and malleable when heated, and with the exception of beryllium, is the lightest metal that remains stable under ordinary conditions. First isolated by the British chemist Sir Humphrey Davy in 1808, magnesium today is obtained mainly by electrolysis of fused magnesium chloride.

Magnesium compounds, primarily magnesium oxide, are used in the refractory material that line the furnaces used to produce iron and steel, nonferrous metals, glass, and cement. Magnesium oxide and other compounds are also used in the chemical, agricultural, and construction industries. Magnesium's principal use is as an alloying addition for aluminum. These aluminum-magnesium alloys are used primarily in beverage cans. Due to their lightness and considerable tensile strength, the alloys are also used in structural components in airplanes and automobiles.

Prices – The average price of magnesium in 2015 fell -6.7% to $1.90 per pound, well below the 2008 record high of $3.38 per pound.

Supply – World primary production of magnesium in 2015 fell -6.5% yr/yr to 910,000 metric tons, down from last year's record high of 973,000 metric tons. The current level of magnesium production has more than tripled since the mid-1970s when 1976's production was 249,367 metric tons.

The world's largest primary producers of magnesium in 2015 was China with 800,000 metric tons, which is 87.9% of the world's total production. Russia produced 30,000 metric tons and Israel produced 25,000 metric tons. The U.S. production amount is not available because it is considered proprietary data but is probably less than about 50,000 metric tons. China's production increased from 70,500 metric tons in 1998 to their new record high of 874,000 metric tons in 2014, but for 2015 China's production is down -8.5%.

Demand – Total U.S. consumption of primary magnesium in 2014 (latest data) fell -4.1% to 65,700. U.S. consumption of magnesium for all structural products fell -8.3% yr/yr to 11,978 metric tons. Of the structural product consumption category, 81.0% was for castings and the remaining 19% was for wrought products. U.S. consumption of magnesium for aluminum alloys fell -8.2% yr/yr to 22,400 metric tons. The consumption of magnesium for other uses fell -4.1% yr/yr to 43,300 metric tons.

Trade – U.S. exports of magnesium in 2015 fell -5.9% yr/yr to 16,000 metric tons, but still well above the 2005 record low of 9,650 metric tons. U.S. imports of magnesium in 2015 fell -9.6% yr/yr to 47,000 metric tons.

World Production of Magnesium (Primary)   In Metric Tons

Year	Brazil	Canada	China	Israel	Kazakhstan	Russia	Serbia	Ukraine	United States	Total
2010	16,000	----	654,000	23,309	15,000	29,000	1,100	7,000	W	737,000
2011	16,000	----	675,000	26,284	21,000	29,000	1,250	8,300	W	766,000
2012	16,000	----	698,000	27,292	21,000	20,000	1,600	10,500	W	795,000
2013	16,000	----	770,000	27,399	23,000	32,000	1,500	9,500	W	873,000
2014[1]	16,000	----	874,000	26,000	26,000	28,000	1,500	7,300	W	973,000
2015[2]	16,000	----	800,000	25,000	20,000	30,000	2,000	9,000	W	910,000

[1] Preliminary.   [2] Estimate.   W = Withheld.   *Source: U.S. Geological Survey (USGS)*

Salient Statistics of Magnesium in the United States   In Metric Tons

	Production							Price	Domestic Consumption of Primary Magnesium					
		Secondary				Imports			Structural Products					
Year	Primary (Ingot)	New Scrap	Old Scrap	Total	Total Exports[3]	for Consumption	Stocks Dec. 31[4]	Price $ Per Pound[5]	Castings	Wrought	Total	Aluminum Alloys	Other Uses	Total
2010	W	51,300	20,500	72,000	14,800	52,700	W	2.43	20,187	2,120	22,307	23,800	9,600	33,400
2011	W	43,100	24,100	67,200	12,300	48,400	W	2.13	23,191	3,720	26,911	25,400	28,300	53,700
2012	W	52,000	25,200	77,100	18,300	50,800	W	2.20	10,761	1,920	12,681	23,500	35,700	59,200
2013	W	54,200	25,000	79,100	16,100	45,900	W	2.13	10,829	2,240	13,069	24,400	44,100	68,500
2014[1]	W	54,100	24,500	79,000	17,000	52,000	W	2.15	9,638	2,340	11,978	22,400	43,300	65,700
2015[2]	W			80,000	16,000	47,000	W	2.15						

[1] Preliminary.   [2] Estimate.   [3] Metal & alloys in crude form & scrap.   [4] Estimate of Industry Stocks, metal.   [5] Magnesium ingots (99.8%), f.o.b. Valasco, Texas.   [6] Distributive or sacrificial purposes.   W = Withheld proprietary data.   *Source: U.S. Geological Survey (USGS)*

Average Price of Magnesium   In Dollars Per Pound

Year	Jan.	Feb.	Mar.	Apr.	May	June	July	Aug.	Sept.	Oct.	Nov.	Dec.	Average
2011	2.55	2.53	2.53	2.53	2.53	2.58	2.42	2.40	2.40	2.22	2.19	2.20	2.42
2012	2.14	2.13	2.13	2.13	2.15	2.15	2.15	2.15	2.15	2.15	2.15	2.15	2.14
2013	2.13	2.13	2.13	2.07	2.05	2.07	2.07	2.03	2.05	2.08	2.08	2.08	2.08
2014	2.08	2.06	2.05	2.05	2.05	2.03	2.02	2.02	2.02	2.02	2.02	2.02	2.04
2015	1.96	1.92	1.90	1.90	1.92	1.92	1.92	1.92	1.92	1.92	1.87	1.74	1.90

Source: American Metal Market (AMM)

Manganese

Manganese (atomic symbol Mn) is a silvery-white, very brittle, metallic element used primarily in making alloys. Manganese was first distinguished as an element and isolated in 1774 by Johan Gottlieb Gahn. Manganese dissolves in acid and corrodes in moist air.

Manganese is found in the earth's crust in the form of ores such as rhodochrosite, franklinite, psilomelane, and manganite. Pyrolusite is the principal ore of manganese. Pure manganese is produced by igniting pyrolusite with aluminum powder or by electrolyzing manganese sulfate.

Manganese is used primarily in the steel industry for creating alloys, the most important ones being ferromanganese and spiegeleisen. In steel, manganese improves forging and rolling qualities, strength, toughness, stiffness, wear resistance, and hardness. Manganese is also used in plant fertilizers, animal feed, pigments, and dry cell batteries.

Prices – The average monthly price of ferromanganese (high carbon, FOB plant) in 2015 fell by -13.7% yr/yr to $914.49 per gross ton, well below the 2008 record high of $2,953.84 per gross ton. The 2015 price, however, is still about two times the 25-year low price of $447.44 per gross ton posted as recently as 2001.

Supply – World production of manganese ore in 2013 (latest data available) rose by +8.7% to a record high of 51.300 million metric tons. The world's largest producers of manganese ore are China with 29.2% of world production in 2013, South Africa with 21.4%, Australia with 14.5%, Gabon with 8.4%, and the India with 4.4%. China's production in 2013 rose by +3.4% yr/yr to 15.000 million metric tons.

Demand – U.S. consumption of manganese ore in 2015 fell -3.8% to 530,000 metric tons. U.S. consumption of ferromanganese in 2015 fell -8.3% yr/yr to 330,000 metric tons, down from the 2012 record high of 382,000 metric tons. The 2015 figure is about 25% of the U.S. consumption back in the early 1970s.

Trade – The U.S. still relies on imports for 100% of its manganese consumption, as it has since 1985. U.S. imports of manganese ore for consumption in 2015 rose +8.6% yr/yr to 430,000 metric tons, up from 2009's 20-year low of 269,000 metric tons. U.S. imports of ferromanganese for consumption in 2015 fell -9.3% yr/yr to 330,000 metric tons. U.S. imports of silico-manganese in 2015 fell -23.4% yr/yr to 340,000 metric tons, but still up from 2009's 27-year low of 130,000 metric tons. The primary sources of U.S. imports of manganese ore in 2013 (latest data) were Gabon with 73.0% imports and Australia with 11.1%.

World Production of Manganese Ore   In Thousands of Metric Tons (Gross Weight)

Year	Australia[2] (37%-53%)	Brazil (37%)	China (20%-30%)	Gabon (45%-53%)	Ghana (32%-34%)	India (10%-54%)	Kazakh-stan[5] (29%-30%)	Malaysia (32%-45%)	Mexico (27%-50%)	South Africa (30%-48%+)	Ukraine[5] (30%-35%)	Other	World Total
2004	3,431	3,143	5,500	2,460	1,597	1,776	2,318	----	377	4,282	2,362	656	27,900
2005	3,136	3,200	7,500	2,859	1,715	2,386	2,208	----	369	4,612	2,260	745	31,000
2006	4,556	3,390	8,000	3,000	1,659	2,084	2,531	----	346	5,213	1,606	752	33,100
2007	5,289	1,570	10,000	3,300	1,854	2,016	1,003	57	423	5,996	1,720	1,270	34,500
2008	4,812	3,200	11,000	3,248	914	2,293	1,117	537	472	6,807	1,447	1,700	37,900
2009	4,451	2,575	12,000	1,992	882	2,347	982	469	330	4,579	932	1,660	33,800
2010	6,474	3,125	13,000	3,201	1,529	2,858	1,094	900	485	7,172	1,589	1,850	44,000
2011	6,963	3,483	14,000	4,070	1,729	2,542	1,096	598	468	8,652	972	1,820	47,000
2012	7,172	3,571	14,500	3,637	1,244	2,225	1,071	1,100	515	8,943	1,189	1,740	47,200
2013[1]	7,448	3,600	15,000	4,297	1,912	2,264	1,112	1,100	572	10,988	983	1,640	51,300

[1] Preliminary.   [2] Metallurgical Ore.   [3] Concentrate.   [4] Ranges of percentage of manganese.   *Source: U.S. Geological Survey (USGS)*

Salient Statistics of Manganese in the United States   In Thousands of Metric Tons (Gross Weight)

Year	Net Import Reliance As a % of Apparent Consump	Manganese Ore (35% or More Manganese) Imports for Consumption	Exports	Consumption	Stocks Dec. 31[3]	Ferromanganese Imports for Consumption	Exports	Consumption	Avg Price Mn. Metallurgical Ore $/Lg. Ton Unit[4]	Silicomanganese Exports	Imports
2006	100	572	2	365	153	358	22	297	3.22	0.9	400.0
2007	100	602	29	351	190	315	29	272	3.10	3.3	414.0
2008	100	571	48	464	255	448	23	304	12.15	7.1	365.0
2009	100	269	15	422	115	153	24	242	7.95	18.8	130.0
2010	100	489	14	450	168	326	19	292	9.64	9.4	297.0
2011	100	552	1	532	250	348	5	303	7.88	8.5	348.0
2012	100	506	2	538	203	401	5	382	6.04	5.9	348.0
2013	100	549	1	523	217	331	2	368	6.00	6.0	329.0
2014[1]	100	396	1	551	158	364	2	360		3.0	444.0
2015[2]	100	430	1	530	200	330	3	330		1.0	340.0

[1] Preliminary.   [2] Estimate.   [3] Including bonded warehouses; excludes Gov't stocks; also excludes small tonnages of dealers' stocks.
[4] 46-48% Mn, C.I.F. U.S. Ports.   *Source: U.S. Geological Survey (USGS)*

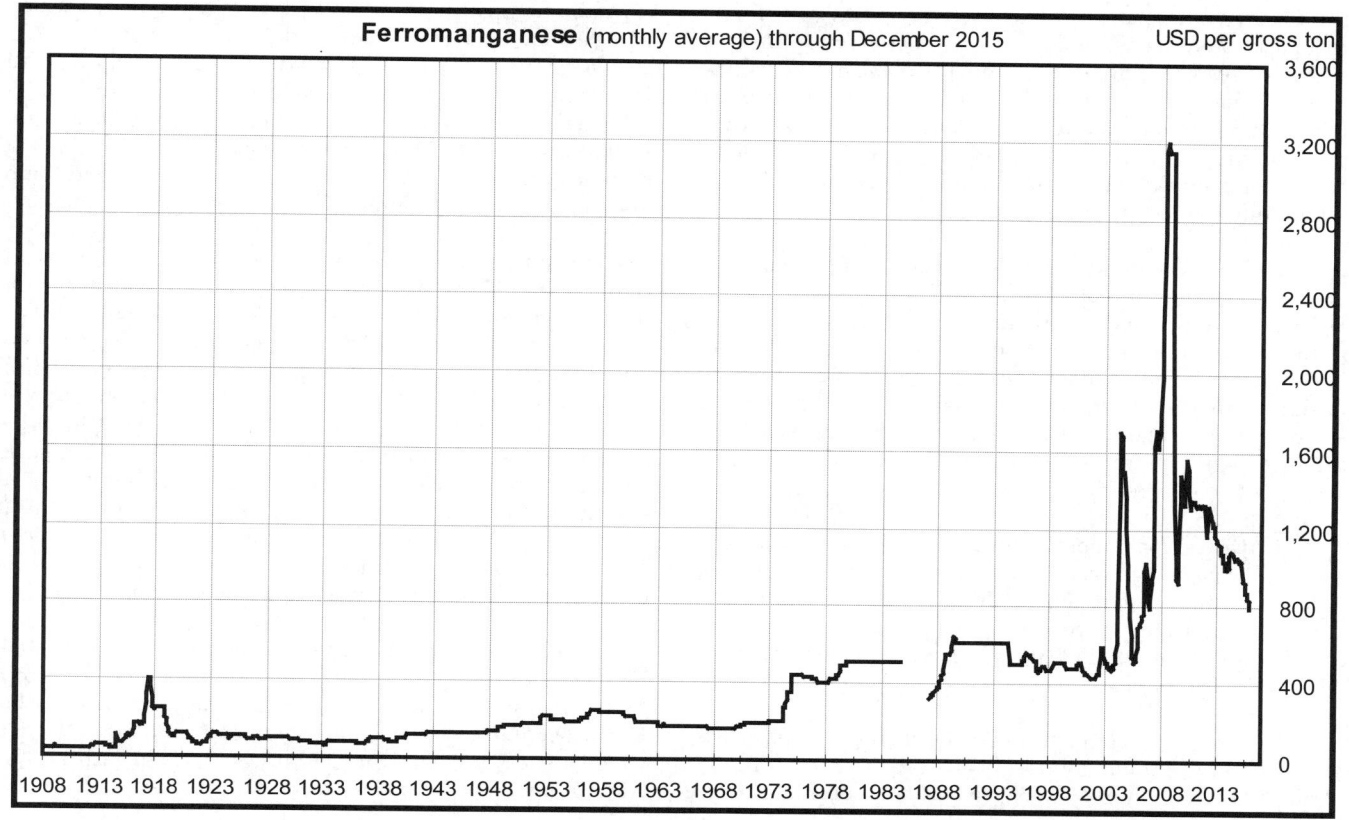

Ferromanganese (monthly average) through December 2015 — USD per gross ton

Imports[3] of Manganese Ore (20% or More Mn) in the United States   In Metric Tons (Mn Content)

Year	Australia	Brazil	Gabon	Mexico	Morocco	South Africa	Total	Customs Value ($1,000)
2004	27,700	----	188,000	1,640	----	13,200	234,000	37,700
2005	21,300	7,020	252,000	4,320	----	33,100	334,000	58,200
2006	12,800	5,800	120,000	1,320	----	91,200	270,000	53,900
2007	34,900	20,000	170,000	3,670	----	53,600	298,000	57,600
2008	51,900	34,400	181,000	----	----	14,600	289,000	154,000
2009	15,400	1,540	96,500	671	9	----	154,000	82,600
2010	65,200	3,440	125,000	1,050	791	40,100	255,000	133,000
2011	70,500	4,750	183,000	1,640	454	5,530	266,000	145,000
2012[1]	15,000	3,970	152,000	2,200	2,670	46,400	226,000	101,000
2013[2]	29,200	3,850	192,000	4,810	3,800	12,900	263,000	126,000

[1] Preliminary.   [2] Estimate.   [3] Imports for consumption.   *Source: U.S. Geological Survey (USGS)*

Average Price of Ferromanganese[1]   In Dollars Per Gross Ton -- Carloads

Year	Jan.	Feb.	Mar.	Apr.	May	June	July	Aug.	Sept.	Oct.	Nov.	Dec.	Average
2006	707.25	712.50	737.50	759.00	764.55	870.23	987.50	1,025.00	1,021.25	946.25	836.25	790.00	846.44
2007	834.29	930.00	949.55	1,000.00	1,074.43	1,633.33	1,705.00	1,620.00	1,656.96	1,700.00	1,785.53		1,375.76
2008	1,978.57	2,262.75	2,734.29	3,145.45	3,200.00	3,200.00	3,175.00	3,150.00	3,150.00	3,150.00	3,150.00	3,150.00	2,953.84
2009	2,225.00	1,300.00	1,300.00	1,038.10	950.00	928.18	955.45	1,071.43	1,344.52	1,481.67	1,431.84	1,365.26	1,282.62
2010	1,326.58	1,387.50	1,530.43	1,559.09	1,507.00	1,389.09	1,310.00	1,320.45	1,327.38	1,345.00	1,345.00	1,345.00	1,391.04
2011	1,336.25	1,320.00	1,320.00	1,327.62	1,321.43	1,315.00	1,315.00	1,327.39	1,330.00	1,330.00	1,330.00	1,303.95	1,323.05
2012	1,171.50	1,179.38	1,285.23	1,317.86	1,280.68	1,263.34	1,238.45	1,220.33	1,214.48	1,202.39	1,171.25	1,144.58	1,224.12
2013	1,140.00	1,128.16	1,128.81	1,121.14	1,076.94	1,071.25	1,037.50	1,037.50	1,031.88	1,000.00	1,000.00	1,000.00	1,064.43
2014	1,006.19	1,066.50	1,088.58	1,090.00	1,080.00	1,078.22	1,041.25	1,060.00	1,053.34	1,055.22	1,060.00	1,039.53	1,064.43
2015	1,042.00	1,036.06	1,029.09	944.66	939.75	929.77	876.82	875.00	841.67	836.36	825.00	797.73	914.49

[1] Domestic standard, high carbon, FOB plant, carloads.   *Source: American Metal Market (AMM)*

Meats

U.S. commercial red meat includes beef, veal, lamb, and pork. Red meat is a good source of iron, vitamin B12, and protein, and eliminating it from the diet can lead to iron and zinc deficiencies. Today, red meat is far leaner than it was 30 years ago due to newer breeds of livestock that carry less fat. The leanest cuts of beef include tenderloin, sirloin, and flank. The leanest cuts of pork include pork tenderloin, loin chops, and rib chops.

The USDA (United States Department of Agriculture) grades various cuts of meat. "Prime" is the highest USDA grade for beef, veal, and lamb. "Choice" is the grade designation below Prime for beef, veal, and lamb. "Commercial" and "Cutter" grades are two of the lower designations for beef, usually sold as ground meat, sausage, and canned meat. "Canner" is the lowest USDA grade designation for beef and is used primarily in canned meats not sold at retail.

Supply – World meat production in 2015 (most recent data) is expected to rise +0.2% to a new record high of 170.584 million metric tons. China is projected to be the world's largest meat producer in 2015 with 63.750 million metric tons of production (up +1.2% yr/yr), accounting for 37.2% of world production.

U.S. production of meat in 2014 (latest data) fell -2.3% yr/yr to 48.135 billion pounds, below the 2008 record high of 50.362 billion pounds. U.S. production of beef in 2015 is

expected to fall -1.7% yr/yr to 23.830 billion pounds, which will be just moderately below the record high of 27.192 billion pounds in 2002. Beef accounted for 50.4% of all U.S. meat production. U.S. production of pork in 2015 is expected to rise +4.6% yr/yr to 23.895, a new record high. Pork accounts for 47.5% of U.S. meat production. Veal accounts for only 0.3% of U.S. meat production, and lamb and mutton account for only 0.4% of U.S. meat production.

Demand – U.S. per capita meat consumption in 2014 (latest data) fell by -2.8% yr/yr to 101.5 pounds per person per year, below the 2006-07 record low of 117.5 pounds per person reflecting the trend towards eating more chicken and fish and the availability of meat substitutes. Per capita beef consumption in 2015 is expected to fall -3.0% yr/yr to 52.7 pounds per person per year, which was about half the record high of 127.5 pounds seen in 1976. Per capita pork consumption in 2015 is expected to rise +1.3% yr/yr to 47.1 pounds per person per year, and remain above the 2011 record low of 45.7 pounds. Per capita consumption of veal is negligible at 0.4 pounds per person and lamb/mutton consumption is also negligible at 0.8 pound per person.

Trade – World red meat exports in 2015 are expected to rise +2.6% to 17.139 million metric tons, a new record high. The world's largest red meat exporters will be the U.S. with 20.6% of world exports expected in 2015, Brazil with 17.1%, European Union with 14.3%, India with 11.4%, Australia with 9.5%, and Canada with 9.0%.

World Total Meat Production[4]   In Thousands of Metric Tons

Year	Argentina	Australia	Brazil	Canada	China[4]	European Union	India	Mexico	New Zealand	Russia	South Africa	United States	World Total
2007	3,576	2,554	12,293	3,024	49,012	31,233	2,490	2,752	658	3,070	867	22,059	152,865
2008	3,424	2,483	12,039	3,090	52,337	30,852	2,700	2,828	694	3,226	859	22,762	156,744
2009	3,669	2,430	12,065	3,033	55,263	29,933	2,950	2,867	669	3,304	876	22,333	158,523
2010	2,899	2,468	12,310	3,059	57,243	30,728	3,125	2,920	690	3,416	1,042	22,232	161,573
2011	2,831	2,473	12,257	2,958	57,079	31,067	3,308	3,006	651	3,424	1,028	22,314	161,805
2012	2,951	2,504	12,637	2,904	60,050	30,234	3,491	3,060	673	3,555	1,037	22,402	165,460
2013	3,266	2,719	13,010	2,871	61,660	29,747	3,800	3,091	667	3,780	1,079	22,276	168,355
2014	3,142	2,957	13,123	2,904	63,600	29,976	4,100	3,117	701	3,880	1,101	21,446	170,312
2015[1]	3,215	2,920	12,876	2,865	63,125	30,540	4,200	3,180	704	3,985	1,115	22,019	169,901
2016[2]	3,190	2,670	13,110	2,855	63,285	30,460	4,500	3,250	720	4,080	1,130	22,703	171,158

[1] Preliminary.   [2] Forecast.   [3] Data through 2000, includes beef, veal, pork, sheep and goat meat. Beginning 2001, excludes sheep and goat.
[4] Predominately pork production.   *Source: Foreign Agricultural Service, U.S. Department of Agriculture (FAS-USDA)*

Production and Consumption of Red Meats in The United States

	Beef			Veal			Lamb & Mutton			Pork (Excluding Lard)			All Meats		
	Commercial Production	- Consumption -		Commercial Production	- Consumption -		Commercial Production	- Consumption -		Commercial Production	- Consumption -		Commercial Production	- Consumption -	
		Total	Per Capita		Total	Per Capita		Total	Per Capita		Total	Per Capita		Total	Per Capita
Year	- Million Pounds -		Lbs.	- Million Pounds -		Lbs.	- Million Pounds -		Lbs.	- Million Pounds -		Lbs.	- Million Pounds -		Lbs.
2006	26,256	28,137	65.9	156	155	0.4	190	356	1.1	21,074	19,055	49.4	47,675	47,703	116.8
2007	26,523	28,141	65.2	146	145	0.4	189	385	1.1	21,962	19,763	50.8	48,820	48,434	117.5
2008	26,664	27,194	62.5	152	150	0.4	180	343	1.0	23,367	19,431	49.5	50,362	47,118	113.3
2009	26,068	26,836	61.1	147	147	0.4	177	338	1.0	23,020	19,870	50.1	49,412	47,191	112.6
2010	26,304	26,390	59.6	145	150	0.4	168	317	0.9	22,437	19,077	47.8	49,183	45,935	108.6
2011	26,195	25,538	57.3	130	137	0.4	149	295	0.8	22,758	18,382	45.7	49,232	44,351	104.2
2012	25,913	25,755	57.3	118	123	0.3	156	299	0.8	23,253	18,607	45.9	49,439	44,784	104.4
2013[1]	25,720	25,476	56.3	111	119	0.3	156	324	0.9	23,187	19,104	46.8	49,174	45,022	104.3
2014[2]	24,252	24,687	54.1	94	97	0.3	156	340	0.9	22,843	19,071	46.4	47,345	44,195	101.7
2015[3]	23,690	24,767	53.9	82	88	0.2	150	357	1.0	24,499	20,656	49.9	48,422	45,868	105.0

[1] Preliminary.   [2] Estimate.   [3] Forecast.   *Source: Economic Research Service, U.S. Department of Agriculture (ERS-USDA)*

MEATS

Total Red Meat Imports[3] (Carcass Weight Equivalent) of Principal Countries   In Thousands of Metric Tons

Year	Brazil	Canada	European Union	Egypt	Hong Kong	Japan	Korea, South	Mexico	Philip-pines	Russia	Taiwan	United States	World Total
2007	30	412	293	683	391	1,896	755	854	196	2,032	120	1,823	12,238
2008	29	424	166	528	464	1,926	725	943	238	2,334	141	1,528	13,067
2009	35	427	180	547	523	1,835	705	1,000	233	1,929	182	1,569	12,132
2010	36	426	260	467	501	1,919	748	983	292	1,974	188	1,432	12,551
2011	41	486	217	384	584	1,999	1,071	859	284	1,965	188	1,297	13,072
2012	63	541	250	369	655	1,996	872	921	273	2,104	148	1,371	13,608
2013	60	516	195	391	872	1,983	763	1,015	317	1,891	170	1,419	14,151
2014	84	498	270	386	993	2,071	872	1,024	365	1,444	201	1,794	14,258
2015[1]	71	510	270	382	830	2,010	1,000	1,085	360	1,000	255	2,061	13,997
2016[2]	66	495	285	382	900	1,977	1,079	1,125	380	935	253	1,835	14,177

[1] Preliminary.   [2] Forecast.   [3] Data through 2000, includes beef, veal, pork, sheep and goat meat. Beginning 2001, excludes sheep and goat.
Source: Foreign Agricultural Service, U.S. Department of Agriculture (FAS-USDA)

Total Red Meat Exports[3] (Carcass Weight Equivalent) of Principal Countries   In Thousands of Metric Tons

Year	Argentina	Australia	Brazil	Canada	China	Denmark	France	India	Ireland	Nether-lands	New Zealand	United States	World Total
2007	506	1,454	2,919	1,490	431	1,381	678	496	8	52	2,075	386	12,780
2008	398	1,455	2,426	1,623	281	1,878	672	533	11	24	3,015	361	13,764
2009	623	1,404	2,303	1,603	270	1,506	609	514	9	27	2,735	376	13,066
2010	278	1,409	2,177	1,682	329	2,042	917	530	6	20	2,958	347	13,826
2011	214	1,451	1,924	1,623	299	2,595	1,268	503	8	35	3,620	320	15,030
2012	165	1,443	2,185	1,578	277	2,461	1,411	517	22	52	3,552	360	15,410
2013	187	1,629	2,434	1,578	274	2,471	1,765	529	11	41	3,436	340	16,157
2014	198	1,888	2,465	1,596	307	2,466	2,082	579	11	43	3,370	350	16,863
2015[1]	231	1,853	2,190	1,585	270	2,650	2,000	590	9	80	3,303	360	16,746
2016[2]	266	1,665	2,355	1,580	275	2,640	2,175	598	11	20	3,470	395	17,185

[1] Preliminary.   [2] Forecast.   [3] Data through 2000, includes beef, veal, pork, sheep and goat meat. Beginning 2001, excludes sheep and goat.
Source: Foreign Agricultural Service, U.S. Department of Agriculture (FAS-USDA)

Exports and Imports of Meats in the United States (Carcass Weight Equivalent)[3]

	Exports				Imports			
Year	Beef and Veal	Lamb and Mutton	Pork[3]	All Meat	Beef and Veal	Lamb and Mutton	Pork[3]	All Meat
2007	1,434	9	3,141	4,585	3,052	203	968	4,223
2008	1,996	12	4,667	6,660	2,538	183	832	3,553
2009	1,935	16	4,126	6,045	2,626	171	834	3,631
2010	2,299	16	4,223	6,539	2,297	166	859	3,322
2011	2,785	----	5,196	7,981	2,057	162	803	3,022
2012	2,452	----	5,379	7,831	2,220	154	802	3,176
2013	2,589	----	4,988	7,577	2,250	173	880	3,303
2014	2,573	----	4,857	7,430	2,947	195	1,008	4,150
2015[1]	2,266	----	4,941	7,207	3,370	213	1,111	4,694
2016[2]	2,475	----	5,100	7,575	2,845	195	1,100	4,140

[1] Preliminary.   [2] Estimate.   [3] Includes meat content of minor meats and of mixed products.
Source: Economic Research Service, U.S. Department of Agriculture (FAS-USDA)

Average Wholesale Prices of Meats in the United States   In Cent Per Pound

Year	Composite Retail Price of Beef, Choice, Grade 3	of Pork[3]	Wholesale Value[4] Beef	Wholesale Value[4] Pork	Net Farm Value[5] of Pork Central US	Cow Beef Canner & Cutter, Central US	Boxed Beef Cut-out, Choice 1-3, Central US 550-700 Lb.	Pork Carcass Cut-out, U.S., No. 2	Lamb Carcass, Choice-Prime, E. Coast 55-65 lbs.	Pork[6] Loins, Central US 14-18 lbs.	Skinned Ham, Central US 17-20 lbs.	Pork Bellies, Central US 12-14 lbs.
2006	397.02	280.72	228.17	121.38	83.27	NA	146.82	67.62	199.10	104.46	64.04	82.81
2007	415.85	287.03	231.08	121.44	81.98	NA	149.80	67.54	215.96	104.17	57.96	88.97
2008	432.58	293.65	235.04	124.73	82.48	NA	153.17	69.24	226.63	106.63	63.52	69.86
2009	425.81	291.97	217.18	111.19	71.56	NA	140.77	58.13	225.45	92.81	51.34	60.91
2010	438.40	311.36	241.08	141.16	95.68	NA	156.91	81.25	263.02	115.96	76.41	93.63
2011	480.73	343.35	275.82	158.89	113.93	NA	181.29	93.69	364.95	129.51	82.19	123.60
2012	498.59	346.67	290.59	147.10	104.88	NA	190.36	84.65	329.48	119.85	73.04	107.20
2013	528.93	364.39	298.48	157.58	110.07	NA	195.64	91.69	281.52	116.53	79.12	152.15
2014[1]	597.03	401.88	364.71	187.66	131.80	NA	238.94	110.10	339.65	141.93	107.00	144.90
2015[2]	628.89	385.25	362.78	145.72	87.39	NA	237.48	78.96	342.99	103.77	65.11	119.90

[1] Preliminary.   [2] Estimate.   [3] Sold as retail cuts (ham, bacon, loin, etc.).   [4] Quantity equivalent to 1 pound of retail cuts.
[5] Portion of gross farm value minus farm by-product allowance.   *Source: Economic Research Service, U.S. Department of Agriculture (ERS-USDA)*

177

MEATS

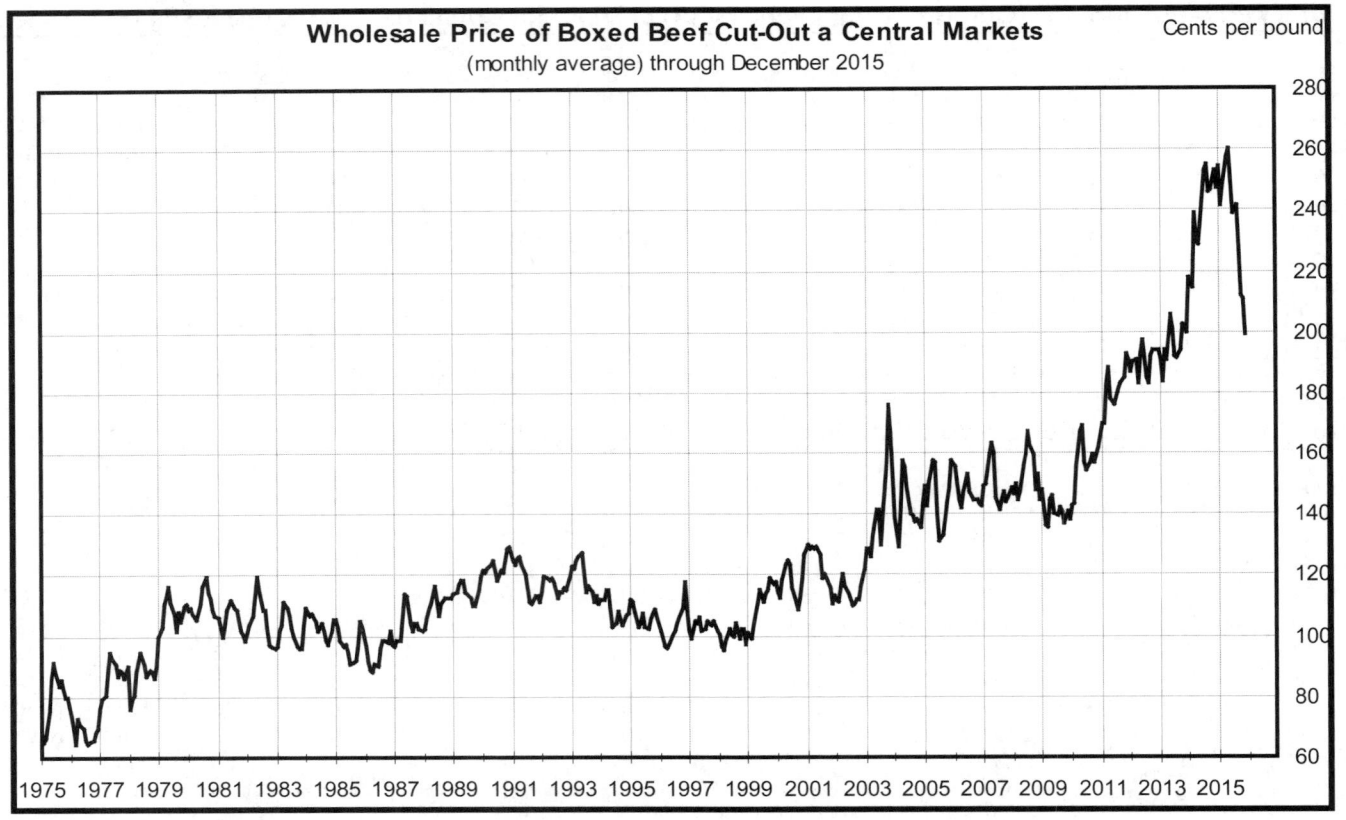

Wholesale Price of Boxed Beef Cut-Out a Central Markets
(monthly average) through December 2015

Cents per pound

Average Wholesale Price of Boxed Beef Cut-Out[2], Choice 1-3, at Central US   In Cents Per Pound

Year	Jan.	Feb.	Mar.	Apr.	May	June	July	Aug.	Sept.	Oct.	Nov.	Dec.	Average
2006	155.60	149.71	144.94	141.83	147.45	153.09	147.01	146.22	144.69	144.79	143.64	142.92	146.82
2007	149.15	149.54	159.23	163.23	160.20	145.59	141.47	144.51	146.99	144.09	145.39	148.25	149.80
2008	146.41	149.63	144.42	147.47	156.07	159.10	167.33	162.31	159.56	148.03	153.29	144.42	153.17
2009	147.68	136.03	135.91	144.42	146.22	140.22	139.59	142.13	140.94	137.15	140.60	138.35	140.77
2010	142.87	143.22	155.73	167.37	168.80	156.54	154.53	156.67	159.20	156.58	159.25	162.20	156.91
2011	169.96	169.82	182.52	188.05	177.96	176.02	178.44	181.12	183.05	185.34	192.51	190.72	181.29
2012	186.77	190.46	190.54	183.43	192.84	197.24	185.25	183.00	192.09	194.19	194.22	194.25	190.36
2013	191.12	183.60	193.79	191.01	205.64	200.83	191.87	191.66	194.01	202.33	202.01	199.77	195.64
2014	218.00	214.43	239.03	229.14	228.96	236.60	252.87	254.83	246.14	246.80	253.18	247.35	238.94
2015[1]	254.45	241.30	247.62	257.44	260.25	250.06	238.91	241.81	227.68	212.10	210.63	207.46	237.48

[1] Preliminary.   [2] Data through 2004: 550-750 pounds; beginning 2005: 600-900 pounds.   *Source: Economic Research Service, U.S. Department of Agriculture (ERS-USDA)*

Production (Commercial) of All Red Meats in the United States   In Millions of Pounds (Carcass Weight)

Year	Jan.	Feb.	Mar.	Apr.	May	June	July	Aug.	Sept.	Oct.	Nov.	Dec.	Total
2006	3,899.6	3,489.9	4,112.2	3,614.8	4,063.8	4,136.2	3,790.6	4,257.6	3,950.0	4,197.3	4,151.3	3,874.5	47,538
2007	4,093.8	3,615.3	4,012.3	3,753.4	4,075.5	4,027.5	3,940.4	4,325.7	3,863.7	4,615.6	4,300.2	4,059.9	48,683
2008	4,417.7	3,967.3	4,089.8	4,298.2	4,222.1	4,050.0	4,250.1	4,095.2	4,273.0	4,529.3	3,869.5	4,162.8	50,225
2009	4,170.2	3,827.0	4,141.8	4,085.1	3,919.5	4,162.0	4,124.5	4,077.0	4,262.7	4,391.2	3,963.8	4,148.7	49,274
2010	3,915.9	3,735.8	4,281.2	4,012.3	3,731.2	4,176.5	3,955.5	4,125.9	4,160.1	4,262.1	4,329.2	4,352.9	49,039
2011	4,041.1	3,809.9	4,346.8	3,867.8	3,914.8	4,218.8	3,792.2	4,303.5	4,192.1	4,270.6	4,258.9	4,215.2	49,232
2012	4,122.9	3,914.0	4,171.4	3,855.3	4,182.7	4,022.5	3,945.3	4,391.0	3,948.0	4,580.1	4,309.3	3,996.9	49,439
2013	4,348.4	3,673.2	3,994.3	4,091.6	4,151.4	3,859.7	4,158.0	4,203.2	3,937.9	4,509.5	4,119.5	4,136.0	49,183
2014	4,248.9	3,653.1	3,814.8	3,976.9	3,952.8	3,824.0	3,906.9	3,795.3	3,958.8	4,319.3	3,759.3	4,136.2	47,346
2015[1]	4,087.0	3,731.8	4,064.3	4,015.5	3,805.3	4,017.4	4,038.5	3,901.4	4,140.2	4,313.4	4,033.2	4,274.0	48,422

[1] Preliminary.   *Source: Economic Research Service, U.S. Department of Agriculture (ERS-USDA)*

Production (Commercial) of Beef in the United States   In Millions of Pounds (Carcass Weight)

Year	Jan.	Feb.	Mar.	Apr.	May	June	July	Aug.	Sept.	Oct.	Nov.	Dec.	Total
2006	2,051.0	1,826.9	2,203.7	1,969.2	2,309.0	2,446.1	2,213.6	2,450.0	2,169.9	2,236.4	2,226.6	2,049.6	26,152
2007	2,166.0	1,952.5	2,118.2	2,015.0	2,285.1	2,348.5	2,256.7	2,450.6	2,094.7	2,443.0	2,228.8	2,061.4	26,421
2008	2,232.7	2,038.6	2,100.5	2,255.4	2,380.1	2,263.4	2,371.6	2,266.8	2,269.9	2,340.9	1,959.3	2,082.0	26,561
2009	2,117.9	1,986.0	2,144.0	2,133.4	2,179.4	2,289.0	2,271.2	2,184.2	2,234.1	2,275.7	2,016.1	2,134.4	25,965
2010	2,081.8	1,955.2	2,211.2	2,139.2	2,087.2	2,320.0	2,229.6	2,286.6	2,252.2	2,234.9	2,235.5	2,270.9	26,304
2011	2,122.9	2,020.4	2,266.2	2,052.5	2,131.9	2,375.0	2,134.1	2,386.9	2,215.2	2,215.1	2,148.8	2,126.3	26,195
2012	2,113.1	2,008.9	2,159.5	1,990.6	2,231.9	2,250.7	2,201.4	2,368.6	2,015.5	2,344.8	2,207.5	2,020.1	25,913
2013	2,260.0	1,873.7	2,038.6	2,127.3	2,228.0	2,161.4	2,293.5	2,241.6	2,073.6	2,316.5	2,057.3	2,046.5	25,718
2014	2,141.1	1,788.9	1,938.4	2,042.8	2,071.6	2,068.7	2,085.9	2,024.4	2,067.4	2,171.5	1,850.6	2,000.7	24,252
2015[1]	1,963.8	1,768.7	1,931.6	1,928.5	1,924.9	2,001.2	2,046.1	1,934.1	2,085.7	2,125.3	1,934.1	2,045.9	23,690

[1] Preliminary.   Source: Economic Research Service, U.S. Department of Agriculture (ERS-USDA)

Production (Commercial) of Pork in the United States   In Millions of Pounds (Carcass Weight)

Year	Jan.	Feb.	Mar.	Apr.	May	June	July	Aug.	Sept.	Oct.	Nov.	Dec.	Total
2006	1,820.5	1,637.0	1,877.5	1,618.3	1,726.0	1,663.3	1,552.6	1,780.2	1,753.7	1,932.0	1,896.4	1,796.4	21,054
2007	1,898.5	1,636.3	1,861.0	1,711.5	1,762.6	1,654.1	1,659.5	1,850.0	1,746.0	2,145.1	2,045.2	1,972.7	21,943
2008	2,159.0	1,902.7	1,962.0	2,015.6	1,815.5	1,761.8	1,852.5	1,803.9	1,975.8	2,159.9	1,886.1	2,052.1	23,347
2009	2,027.0	1,817.3	1,969.7	1,925.0	1,716.8	1,847.7	1,828.5	1,868.9	2,002.1	2,089.0	1,921.7	1,985.3	22,999
2010	1,809.7	1,757.5	2,040.1	1,849.1	1,621.3	1,831.7	1,702.2	1,815.3	1,883.5	2,002.7	2,068.0	2,055.4	22,437
2011	1,896.2	1,768.1	2,054.4	1,790.7	1,759.7	1,820.0	1,637.1	1,892.1	1,954.4	2,033.2	2,086.7	2,065.6	22,758
2012	1,987.3	1,883.0	1,987.7	1,841.9	1,926.8	1,750.5	1,721.9	1,998.1	1,911.2	2,210.7	2,079.2	1,954.2	23,253
2013	2,065.5	1,779.0	1,932.7	1,941.8	1,900.0	1,677.1	1,840.8	1,938.7	1,844.1	2,169.9	2,041.3	2,066.5	23,197
2014	2,086.1	1,844.4	1,854.5	1,910.5	1,859.5	1,734.3	1,799.3	1,752.1	1,871.9	2,126.7	1,890.7	2,114.5	22,845
2015[1]	2,104.7	1,945.2	2,111.5	2,066.8	1,861.9	1,995.8	1,972.6	1,949.1	2,035.5	2,168.9	2,080.2	2,207.1	24,499

[1] Preliminary.   Source: Economic Research Service, U.S. Department of Agriculture (ERS-USDA)

Cold Storage Holdings of All[2] Meats in the United States, on First of Month   In Millions of Pounds

Year	Jan.	Feb.	Mar.	Apr.	May	June	July	Aug.	Sept.	Oct.	Nov.	Dec.
2006	877.2	1,012.4	987.3	959.8	979.1	940.8	880.9	915.5	918.2	969.4	994.0	1,009.9
2007	946.6	977.3	963.4	943.5	970.3	925.7	919.7	943.5	958.7	991.8	1,003.2	968.4
2008	961.6	1,047.5	1,072.6	1,106.9	1,103.9	1,024.5	983.8	960.5	970.9	1,009.4	1,027.8	1,037.8
2009	1,078.5	1,096.2	1,084.9	1,045.3	1,050.6	1,030.1	1,043.1	1,014.7	980.2	984.0	968.4	936.8
2010	924.9	938.4	941.9	921.8	876.3	837.8	816.1	808.6	803.4	844.7	918.6	925.3
2011	939.9	1,017.4	1,050.6	1,036.6	1,009.5	1,014.9	949.4	894.2	896.7	944.9	929.3	961.1
2012	961.5	1,092.6	1,118.7	1,139.8	1,201.0	1,157.7	1,087.6	1,039.1	1,047.7	1,082.8	1,060.9	1,023.4
2013	1,043.8	1,114.8	1,148.1	1,182.4	1,238.0	1,166.3	1,071.3	1,035.5	1,005.0	1,041.0	1,033.0	1,021.9
2014	1,022.2	1,077.0	1,093.6	1,012.3	1,015.9	981.4	930.1	939.1	934.0	970.8	956.5	930.3
2015[1]	988.5	1,131.2	1,224.3	1,196.3	1,229.0	1,174.1	1,147.5	1,135.6	1,172.8	1,201.7	1,156.2	1,122.8

[1] Preliminary.   [2] Includes beef and veal, mutton and lamb, pork and products, rendered pork fat, and miscellaneous meats. Excludes lard.
Source: Economic Research Service, U.S. Department of Agriculture (ERS-USDA)

Cold Storage Holdings of Frozen Beef in the United States, on First of Month   In Millions of Pounds

Year	Jan.	Feb.	Mar.	Apr.	May	June	July	Aug.	Sept.	Oct.	Nov.	Dec.
2006	434.4	465.9	440.6	436.2	441.3	446.3	449.1	479.2	484.5	491.9	485.7	520.3
2007	482.1	470.6	458.9	427.2	417.3	411.5	430.3	467.7	480.9	486.7	488.0	475.3
2008	482.5	450.8	436.5	426.7	416.4	420.4	428.1	430.8	441.2	454.5	471.0	481.6
2009	492.6	462.5	435.5	425.9	410.7	417.9	434.8	444.8	420.1	428.9	427.7	430.9
2010	430.3	426.3	404.5	384.6	369.5	362.8	374.2	388.8	387.4	396.8	414.6	435.2
2011	445.0	461.7	459.8	445.5	443.2	447.6	432.8	415.2	428.6	427.6	417.0	443.8
2012	457.2	485.1	470.8	503.2	517.9	497.9	468.7	461.1	432.8	424.9	430.3	441.8
2013	465.7	484.6	490.0	511.2	510.1	482.6	481.2	462.6	430.2	445.2	440.1	450.8
2014	439.4	429.3	409.5	405.8	402.3	377.6	358.2	367.9	346.6	378.2	380.9	400.8
2015[1]	444.4	492.0	491.9	481.5	484.3	476.3	474.2	459.5	470.5	498.3	505.9	510.6

[1] Preliminary.   Source: Economic Research Service, U.S. Department of Agriculture (ERS-USDA)

Mercury

Mercury (atomic symbol Hg) was known to the ancient Hindus and Chinese, and was also found in Egyptian tombs dating back to 1500 BC. The ancient Greeks used mercury in ointments, and the Romans used it in cosmetics. Alchemists thought mercury turned into gold when it hardened.

Mercury, also called quicksilver, is a heavy, silvery, toxic, transitional metal. Mercury is the only common metal that is liquid at room temperatures. When subjected to a pressure of 7,640 atmospheres (7.7 million millibars), mercury becomes a solid. Mercury dissolves in nitric or concentrated sulfuric acid, but is resistant to alkalis. It is a poor conductor of heat. Mercury has superconductivity when cooled to sufficiently low temperatures. It has a freezing point of about −39 degrees Celsius and a boiling point of about 357 degrees Celsius.

Mercury is found in its pure form or combined in small amounts with silvers, but is found most often in the ore cinnabar, a mineral consisting of mercuric sulfide. By heating the cinnabar ore in air until the mercuric sulfide breaks down, pure mercury metal is produced. Mercury forms alloys called amalgams with all common metals except iron and platinum. Most mercury is used for the manufacture of industrial chemicals and for electrical and electronic applications. Other uses for mercury include its use in gold recovery from ores, barometers, diffusion pumps, laboratory instruments, mercury-vapor lamps, pesticides, batteries, and catalysts. A decline in mercury production and usage since the 1970s reflects a trend for using mercury substitutes due to its toxicity.

Prices – The average monthly price of mercury in 2015 fell by -12.3% yr/yr to $2.388.95 per flask (34.5 kilograms), further below the record high of $3.438.59 posted in 2013.

Supply – World mine production of mercury in 2015 fell by -0.4% yr/yr to 2,360 metric tons, down from the 18-year high of 2,400 metric tons in 2013. The record low of 1,150 metric tons was posted in 2006. The world's largest miners of mercury are China with 67.8% of world production, Mexico with 21.2%, and Kyrgyzstan with 3.0%. China's production in every year since 2013 has been at the record high of 1,600 metric tons. China's record low of 190 metric tons was posted in 2001.

Demand – The breakdown of domestic consumption of mercury by particular categories is no longer available. However, as of 1997 records showed that chlorine and caustic soda accounted for 46% of U.S. mercury consumption, followed by wiring devices and switches (17%), dental equipment (12%), electrical lighting (8%), and measuring control instruments (7%). Substitutes for mercury include lithium and composite ceramic materials.

Trade – U.S. foreign trade in mercury has been relatively small and U.S. imports of mercury in 2015 fell -69.4% yr/yr to 15 metric tons, far below the 2010 20-year high of 294 metric tons. By contrast the U.S.'s record high imports were in 1974 at 1,799 metric tons. U.S. imports were mostly from Chile and Peru. U.S. exports of mercury in 2012 (latest data) fell by -22.6% to 103 metric tons, but still above 2007's 13-year low of 84 metric tons.

World Mine Production of Mercury   In Metric Tons (1 tonne = 29.008216 flasks)

Year	Chile (byproduct)	China	Finland	Kyrgyzstan	Mexico (Exports)	Morocco	Peru (Exports)	Russia	Tajikistan	United States	World Total
2006	----	760	20	250	8	10	22	50	30	NA	1,150
2007	----	800	20	250	8	10	34	50	30	NA	1,200
2008	----	1,300	20	250	21	10	136	50	30	NA	1,820
2009	88	1,430	6	140	15	10	107	50	30	NA	1,960
2010	176	1,600	9	99	15	10	159	50	15	NA	2,180
2011	89	1,500	----	112	120	9	53	50	15	NA	1,980
2012	49	1,350	----	74	235	8	17	50	103	NA	1,930
2013	19	1,600	----	75	532	8	45	50	30	NA	2,400
2014[1]	10	1,600	----	75	500	8	40	50	30	NA	2,370
2015[2]		1,600	----	70	500		40	50	30	NA	2,360

[1] Preliminary.   [2] Estimate.   NA = Not available.   W = Withheld.   *Source: U.S. Geological Survey (USGS)*

Salient Statistics of Mercury in the United States   In Metric Tons

Year	Producing Mines	Secondary Production Industrial	Secondary Production Government[3]	NDS[4] Shipments	Consumer & Dealer Stocks, Dec. 31	Industrial Demand	Exports	Imports
2007	NA	NA	----	----	18	31	84	67
2008	NA	NA	----	----	24	NA	732	155
2009	NA	NA	----	----	30	NA	753	206
2010	NA	NA	----	----	NA	NA	459	294
2011	NA	NA	----	----	NA	NA	133	110
2012	NA	NA	----	----	NA	NA	103	249
2013	NA	NA	----	----	NA	NA	[5]	38
2014[1]	NA	NA	----	----	NA	NA	----	49
2015[2]	NA	NA	----	----	NA	NA	----	15

[1] Preliminary.   [2] Estimate.   [3] Secondary mercury shipped from the Department of Energy.   [4] National Defense Stockpile.   [5] Less than 1/2 unit.   NA = Not available.   *Source: U.S. Geological Survey (USGS)*

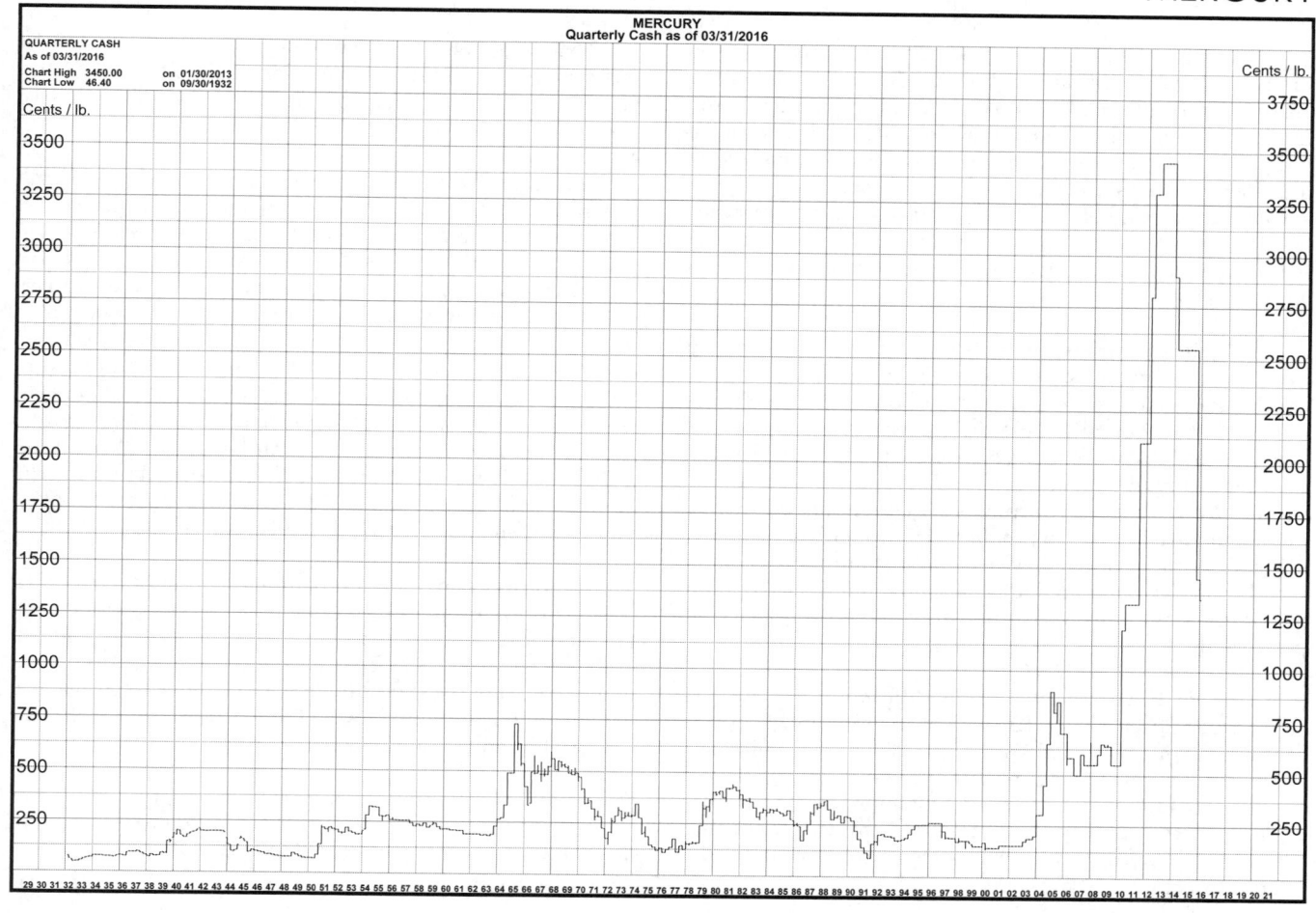

Average Price of Mercury in New York   In Dollars Per Flask of 76 Pounds (34.5 Kilograms)

Year	Jan.	Feb.	Mar.	Apr.	May	June	July	Aug.	Sept.	Oct.	Nov.	Dec.	Average
2006	700.00	700.00	691.30	552.50	574.02	582.50	582.50	582.50	582.50	576.59	513.64	500.00	594.84
2007	500.00	500.00	500.00	500.00	500.00	573.81	600.00	600.00	572.50	550.00	550.00	550.00	541.36
2008	550.00	550.00	550.00	550.00	550.00	550.00	550.00	550.00	590.91	600.00	645.00	650.00	573.83
2009	650.00	647.00	640.00	640.00	642.86	640.00	640.00	640.00	603.18	550.00	550.00	550.00	616.09
2010	550.00	550.00	550.00	550.00	828.57	1,129.55	1,213.64	1,293.18	1,325.00	1,325.00	1,325.00	1,325.00	997.08
2011	1,325.00	1,325.00	1,325.00	1,325.00	1,325.00	1,325.00	1,370.24	2,073.91	2,100.00	2,100.00	2,100.00	2,100.00	1,649.51
2012	2,100.00	2,100.00	2,100.00	2,100.00	2,547.83	2,800.00	2,800.00	2,800.00	3,100.00	3,300.00	3,300.00	3,300.00	2,695.65
2013	3,313.05	3,450.00	3,450.00	3,450.00	3,450.00	3,450.00	3,450.00	3,450.00	3,450.00	3,450.00	3,450.00	3,450.00	3,438.59
2014	3,269.57	3,175.00	2,991.67	2,850.00	2,563.64	2,550.00	2,550.00	2,550.00	2,550.00	2,550.00	2,550.00	2,550.00	2,724.99
2015	2,550.00	2,550.00	2,550.00	2,550.00	2,550.00	2,550.00	2,550.00	2,550.00	2,550.00	2,515.91	1,716.67	1,484.78	2,388.95

Source: American Metal Market (AMM)

Mercury Consumed in the United States   In Metric Tons

Year	Batteries[3]	Chlorine & Caustic Soda	Catalysts, Misc.	Dental Equip.	Electrical Lighting[3]	General Lab Use	Measuring Control Instrument	Paints	Wiring Devices & Switches[3]	Other Uses	Grand Total
1989	250	379	40	39	31	18	87	192	141	32	1,212
1990	106	247	29	44	33	32	108	14	70	38	720
1991	18	184	26	41	39	30	90	6	71	49	554
1992	13	209	20	42	55	28	80	----	82	92	621
1993	10	180	18	35	38	28	65	----	83	103	558
1994	6	135	25	24	27	24	53	----	79	110	483
1995	----	154	----	32	30	----	43	----	84	93	436
1996[1]	----	136	----	31	29	----	43	----	49	86	372
1997[2]	----	160	----	40	29	----	24	----	57	36	346
	Data No Longer Available										

[1] Preliminary.   [2] Estimate.   W = Withheld proprietary data.   *Source: U.S. Geological Survey (USGS)*

Milk

Evidence of man's use of animal milk as food was discovered in a temple in the Euphrates Valley near Babylon, dating back to 3,000 BC. Humans drink the milk produced from a variety of domesticated mammals, including cows, goats, sheep, camels, reindeer, buffaloes, and llama. In India, half of all milk consumed is from water buffalo. Camels' milk spoils slower than other types of milk in the hot desert, but the vast majority of milk used for commercial production and consumption comes from cows.

Milk directly from a cow in its natural form is called raw milk. Raw milk is processed by spinning it in a centrifuge, homogenizing it to create a consistent texture (i.e., by forcing hot milk under high pressure through small nozzles), and then sterilizing it through pasteurization (i.e., heating to a high temperature for a specified length of time to destroy pathogenic bacteria). Condensed, powdered, and evaporated milk are produced by evaporating some or all of the water content. Whole milk contains 3.5% milk fat. Lower-fat milks include 2% low-fat milk, 1% low-fat milk, and skim milk, which has only 1/2 gram of milk fat per serving.

The CME Group has three different milk futures contracts: Milk Class III which is milk used in the manufacturing of cheese, Milk Class IV which is milk used in the production of butter and all dried milk products, and Nonfat Dry Milk which is used in commercial or consumer cooking or to reconstitute nonfat milk by the consumer. The Milk Class III contract has the largest volume and open interest.

Prices – The average monthly price received by farmers for all milk sold to plants in 2015 fell by -28.8% yr/yr to $17.08 per hundred pounds, below last year's record high.

Supply – World milk production in 2016 is expected to rise +1.8% to 591.215 million metric tons. The biggest producers will be the European Union with 25.9% of world production, India with 26.0%, and the U.S. with 16.3%. U.S. 2015 milk production in pounds is expected to rise +1.1% yr/yr to 208.379 billion pounds, setting a new record high. The number of dairy cows on U.S. farms has fallen sharply in the past 3 decades from the 12 million seen in 1970. In 2015, there were 9.313 million dairy cows on U.S. farms, up +0.6% yr/yr. Dairy farmers have been able to increase milk production even with fewer cows because of a dramatic increase in milk yield per cow. In 2015, the average cow produced 22,376 pounds of milk per year, more than double the 9,751 pounds seen in 1970.

Demand – Per capita consumption of milk in the U.S. fell to a new record low of 204 pounds per year in 2008 (latest data), down sharply by -26% from 277 pounds in 1977. The utilization breakdown for 2002 (latest data) shows the largest manufacturing usage categories are cheese (64.504 billion pounds of milk) and creamery butter (30.250 billion pounds).

Trade – U.S. imports of milk in 2015 fell -11.9% yr/yr to 3.800 billion pounds, still well below the record high of 7.500 billion pounds posted in 2005-06.

World Fluid Milk Production (Cow's Milk)   In Thousands of Metric Tons

Year	Argentina	Australia	Brazil	China	European Union	India	Japan	Mexico	New Zealand	Russia	Ukraine	United States	World Total
2008	10,010	9,500	19,864	8,270	35,450	137,848	109,000	11,077	15,580	32,500	11,762	86,173	503,776
2009	10,350	9,326	20,190	8,280	29,625	137,720	112,000	11,036	16,983	32,600	11,610	85,821	502,532
2010	10,600	9,327	21,605	8,350	30,528	139,492	117,000	11,201	17,173	31,847	11,249	87,488	512,697
2011	11,470	9,568	22,449	8,400	31,980	142,920	123,000	11,213	18,965	31,646	11,085	89,020	527,987
2012	11,679	9,811	23,008	8,614	33,960	143,750	129,000	11,434	20,567	31,831	11,378	91,010	542,972
2013	11,519	9,400	24,259	8,443	35,750	144,850	134,500	11,451	20,200	30,529	11,488	91,277	550,333
2014	11,326	9,700	25,489	8,437	38,800	150,850	140,500	11,624	21,893	30,499	11,426	93,461	570,697
2015[1]	11,496	10,000	26,300	8,682	38,800	152,450	147,000	11,910	21,391	30,025	10,950	94,480	580,569
2016[2]	11,650	10,010	27,100	8,685	39,600	153,350	154,000	12,017	20,745	29,980	10,330	96,345	591,215

[1] Preliminary.   [2] Forecast.   *Source: Foreign Agricultural Service, U.S. Department of Agriculture (FAS-USDA)*

Salient Statistics of Milk in the United States   In Millions of Pounds

Year	Number of Milk Cows on Farms[3] (Thousands)	Production Per Cow[4] (Pounds)	Production Total[4]	Beginning Stocks[5]	Imports	Total Supply	Exports[5]	Fed to Calves	Humans	Total Use	All Milk, Wholesale	Milk, Eligible for Fluid Market	Milk, Manufacturing Grade	Per Capita Consumption[6] (Fluid Milk in Lbs)
2009	9,200	20,576	189,320	10,045	5,600	204,965	4,500	901	188,189	193,590	12.84	12.84	12.18	
2010	9,117	21,149	192,819	11,334	4,100	208,253	8,100	873	191,897	200,870	16.27	16.29	14.79	
2011	9,194	21,346	196,245	10,800	3,500	210,545	9,400	867	195,290	205,557	20.14	----	----	
2012	9,232	21,696	200,324	10,904	4,078	215,306	8,810	858	199,687	209,355	18.48	----	----	
2013	9,215	21,413	201,218	12,195	3,722	217,135	12,359	880	200,254	213,493	20.04	----	----	
2014	9,256	22,260	206,046	11,173	4,315	221,534	12,444				23.98	----	----	
2015[1]	9,317	22,394	208,633	13,100	5,900	227,633	11,100				17.08	----	----	
2016[2]	9,311	22,308	207,732	13,900	6,400	228,032					----	----	----	

[1] Preliminary.   [2] Estimate.   [3] Average number on farms during year including dry cows, excluding heifers not yet fresh.   [4] Excludes milk sucked by calves.   [5] Government and commercial.   [6] Product pounds of commercial sales and on farm consumption.
Source: Economic Research Service, U.S. Department of Agriculture (ERS-USDA)

Milk-Feed Price Ratio[1] in the United States   In Pounds

Year	Jan.	Feb.	Mar.	Apr.	May	June	July	Aug.	Sept.	Oct.	Nov.	Dec.	Average
2006	3.17	2.93	2.70	2.48	2.32	2.35	2.33	2.48	2.61	2.53	2.44	2.43	2.56
2007	2.45	2.33	2.39	2.51	2.54	2.88	3.16	3.19	3.19	3.10	3.05	2.85	2.80
2008	2.65	2.24	2.07	1.88	1.81	1.88	1.90	1.81	1.90	2.02	2.01	1.92	2.01
2009	1.60	1.51	1.56	1.59	1.48	1.45	1.57	1.80	2.00	2.11	2.26	2.42	1.78
2010	2.33	2.36	2.18	2.19	2.17	2.26	2.31	2.36	2.36	2.40	2.23	1.98	2.26
2011	1.96	2.01	2.12	1.81	1.73	1.87	1.91	1.83	1.84	1.82	1.89	1.81	1.88
2012	1.72	1.56	1.48	1.41	1.34	1.38	1.34	1.37	1.59	1.74	1.74	1.65	1.53
2013	1.57	1.52	1.48	1.54	1.53	1.52	1.53	1.68	1.88	2.10	2.27	2.30	1.74
2014	2.46	2.59	2.54	2.42	2.24	2.20	2.36	2.63	2.96	2.92	2.75	2.40	2.54
2015[1]	2.11	2.05	2.00	1.95	1.96	2.06	2.01	2.11	2.25	2.29	2.42	2.27	2.12

[1] Pounds of 16% protein mixed dairy feed equal in value to one pound of whole milk.   [2] Preliminary.   *Source: Economic Research Service, U.S. Department of Agriculture (ERS-USDA)*

Milk Production[2] in the United States   In Millions of Pounds

Year	Jan.	Feb.	Mar.	Apr.	May	June	July	Aug.	Sept.	Oct.	Nov.	Dec.	Total
2006	15,343	14,238	15,966	15,538	16,068	15,324	15,168	15,061	14,481	14,857	14,523	15,231	181,798
2007	15,605	14,321	16,132	15,763	16,180	15,476	15,714	15,525	14,871	15,370	15,013	15,632	185,602
2008	15,976	15,176	16,458	16,125	16,707	15,942	15,995	15,757	15,129	15,615	15,212	15,900	189,992
2009	16,135	14,754	16,485	16,148	16,805	15,935	16,018	15,737	15,038	15,420	15,070	15,775	189,320
2010	16,020	14,758	16,614	16,416	17,040	16,353	16,436	16,094	15,540	15,900	15,498	16,150	192,819
2011	16,393	15,077	16,989	16,652	17,278	16,518	16,479	16,422	15,783	16,278	15,820	16,556	196,245
2012	17,016	16,310	17,718	17,232	17,601	16,676	16,585	16,403	15,687	16,267	16,008	16,821	200,324
2013	17,109	15,759	17,677	17,249	17,813	16,935	16,788	16,789	15,831	16,475	16,003	16,790	201,218
2014	17,284	15,907	17,829	17,480	18,094	17,323	17,435	17,224	16,514	17,071	16,551	17,334	206,046
2015[1]	17,685	16,166	18,085	17,788	18,428	17,504	17,665	17,403	16,617	17,130	16,689	17,473	208,633

[1] Preliminary.   [2] Excludes milk sucked by calves.   *Source: Economic Research Service, U.S. Department of Agriculture (ERS-USDA)*

Milk Cows[2] in the United States   In Thousands of Head

Year	Jan.	Feb.	Mar.	Apr.	May	June	July	Aug.	Sept.	Oct.	Nov.	Dec.	Total
2006	9,081	9,088	9,106	9,116	9,129	9,139	9,119	9,114	9,107	9,107	9,111	9,126	9,112
2007	9,135	9,136	9,142	9,132	9,138	9,144	9,153	9,159	9,166	9,181	9,196	9,217	9,158
2008	9,276	9,287	9,295	9,307	9,318	9,321	9,335	9,331	9,323	9,324	9,333	9,334	9,315
2009	9,312	9,289	9,283	9,282	9,270	9,228	9,191	9,162	9,123	9,094	9,085	9,082	9,200
2010	9,089	9,092	9,099	9,108	9,119	9,129	9,135	9,123	9,121	9,123	9,125	9,141	9,117
2011	9,160	9,163	9,180	9,182	9,194	9,196	9,198	9,200	9,201	9,212	9,213	9,223	9,194
2012	9,242	9,257	9,271	9,273	9,263	9,241	9,222	9,217	9,195	9,189	9,201	9,218	9,232
2013	9,222	9,223	NA	NA	NA	NA	9,235	9,229	9,208	9,203	9,198	9,202	9,215
2014	9,212	9,212	9,223	9,240	9,252	9,267	9,268	9,268	9,274	9,277	9,284	9,299	9,256
2015[1]	9,308	9,308	9,311	9,316	9,324	9,323	9,314	9,315	9,317	9,320	9,322	9,320	9,317

[1] Preliminary.   [2] Includes dry cows, excludes heifers not yet fresh.   *Source: Economic Research Service, U.S. Department of Agriculture (ERS-USDA)*

Milk Per Cow[2] in the United States   In Pounds

Year	Jan.	Feb.	Mar.	Apr.	May	June	July	Aug.	Sept.	Oct.	Nov.	Dec.	Total
2006	1,690	1,567	1,753	1,705	1,760	1,676	1,663	1,653	1,590	1,631	1,594	1,669	19,951
2007	1,708	1,567	1,765	1,726	1,771	1,692	1,717	1,695	1,622	1,674	1,633	1,696	20,266
2008	1,722	1,634	1,771	1,733	1,793	1,710	1,713	1,689	1,623	1,675	1,630	1,703	20,396
2009	1,733	1,588	1,776	1,740	1,812	1,726	1,744	1,718	1,649	1,695	1,658	1,737	20,576
2010	1,763	1,623	1,826	1,802	1,869	1,791	1,799	1,764	1,704	1,743	1,698	1,767	21,149
2011	1,790	1,645	1,851	1,814	1,879	1,796	1,792	1,785	1,715	1,767	1,717	1,795	21,346
2012	1,841	1,762	1,911	1,858	1,900	1,805	1,798	1,780	1,706	1,770	1,740	1,825	21,696
2013	1,855	1,709	NA	NA	NA	NA	1,818	1,819	1,719	1,790	1,740	1,825	21,413
2014	1,876	1,727	1,933	1,892	1,956	1,869	1,881	1,858	1,781	1,840	1,783	1,864	22,260
2015[1]	1,900	1,737	1,942	1,909	1,976	1,878	1,897	1,868	1,784	1,838	1,790	1,875	22,394

[1] Preliminary.   [2] Excludes milk sucked by calves.   *Source: Economic Research Service, U.S. Department of Agriculture (ERS-USDA)*

MILK

Average Price Received by Farmers for All Milk (Sold to Plants)   In Dollars Per Hundred Pounds (Cwt.)

Year	Jan.	Feb.	Mar.	Apr.	May	June	July	Aug.	Sept.	Oct.	Nov.	Dec.	Average
2006	14.50	13.50	12.60	12.10	11.90	11.90	11.70	12.00	13.00	13.60	13.90	14.20	12.91
2007	14.50	14.90	15.60	16.60	18.00	20.20	21.60	21.60	21.80	21.40	21.90	21.50	19.13
2008	20.50	19.10	18.10	18.00	18.30	19.30	19.30	18.40	18.20	17.80	17.10	15.50	18.30
2009	13.30	11.60	11.80	11.90	11.60	11.30	11.30	12.10	13.00	14.30	15.40	16.50	12.84
2010	16.10	15.90	14.80	14.60	15.00	15.40	15.90	16.70	17.70	18.50	17.90	16.70	16.27
2011	16.70	19.10	20.40	19.60	19.60	21.10	21.80	22.10	21.10	20.00	20.50	19.70	20.14
2012	19.00	17.70	17.20	16.80	16.20	16.30	16.90	18.20	18.90	21.60	22.10	20.80	18.48
2013	19.90	19.50	19.10	19.50	19.70	19.50	19.10	19.60	20.10	20.90	21.60	22.00	20.04
2014	23.50	24.90	25.10	25.30	24.20	23.20	23.30	24.20	25.70	24.90	23.00	20.40	23.98
2015[1]	17.60	16.80	16.60	16.50	16.70	16.90	16.60	16.70	17.50	17.70	18.20	17.20	17.08

[1] Preliminary.   Source: Economic Research Service, U.S. Department of Agriculture (ERS-USDA)

Production of Nonfat Dry Milk in the United States   In Thousands of Pounds

Year	Jan.	Feb.	Mar.	Apr.	May	June	July	Aug.	Sept.	Oct.	Nov.	Dec.	Total
2006	111,278	117,998	128,867	130,613	132,935	116,846	88,594	73,193	63,278	69,989	76,914	113,567	1,224,072
2007	108,023	96,818	112,867	123,022	115,381	118,173	122,193	102,993	89,844	100,242	99,994	108,930	1,298,480
2008	119,102	118,268	135,244	132,998	128,921	134,386	135,614	115,180	85,516	120,961	134,780	155,237	1,516,207
2009	158,286	125,902	137,301	141,397	150,452	146,065	133,175	107,049	87,808	92,800	102,156	126,720	1,509,111
2010	129,679	118,999	138,305	152,945	154,757	136,990	131,704	119,562	109,286	114,595	116,653	139,043	1,562,518
2011	114,896	106,785	124,065	145,323	147,290	145,125	131,502	113,299	103,115	99,751	119,686	148,640	1,499,477
2012	152,085	171,394	189,227	190,728	193,362	168,394	140,169	106,014	84,498	95,064	115,854	157,660	1,764,449
2013	142,799	137,674	146,576	160,117	150,531	130,901	116,616	106,039	74,026	85,830	101,185	125,570	1,477,864
2014	138,661	141,187	167,853	160,342	162,139	148,648	166,602	116,521	112,338	134,694	151,692	163,833	1,764,510
2015[1]	164,897	150,832	180,004	181,869	180,265	165,078	155,625	124,240	119,695	118,179	125,496	150,732	1,816,912

[1] Preliminary.   Source: Economic Research Service, U.S. Department of Agriculture (ERS-USDA)

Production of Dry Whey in the United States   In Thousands of Pounds

Year	Jan.	Feb.	Mar.	Apr.	May	June	July	Aug.	Sept.	Oct.	Nov.	Dec.	Total
2006	88,391	89,695	100,953	95,662	97,295	89,701	95,226	91,547	86,271	87,434	84,079	91,128	1,097,382
2007	96,757	89,662	98,340	96,812	99,346	94,656	95,549	94,454	88,164	88,895	93,605	97,621	1,133,861
2008	91,772	88,023	97,923	96,747	97,046	92,331	89,821	87,372	82,614	85,248	86,463	91,272	1,086,632
2009	79,395	74,668	82,785	83,218	87,125	92,639	93,640	82,555	79,006	81,709	79,361	85,059	1,001,160
2010	85,766	78,206	92,496	87,728	89,255	86,045	87,529	81,519	77,718	77,888	79,506	89,327	1,012,983
2011	90,192	82,035	94,304	92,037	91,293	83,740	81,752	79,759	76,800	77,517	77,614	83,074	1,010,117
2012	95,588	89,274	88,348	84,014	86,760	83,819	79,807	77,543	74,810	77,195	72,559	89,181	998,898
2013	86,558	77,097	83,248	81,653	75,535	75,425	76,416	73,122	68,692	71,883	74,718	108,633	952,980
2014	70,011	65,603	71,504	71,629	82,480	79,309	73,475	71,031	69,726	68,265	71,490	75,137	869,660
2015[1]	75,580	77,913	86,459	76,535	80,622	85,108	80,716	83,982	78,720	75,619	84,709	94,378	980,341

[1] Preliminary.   Excludes all modified dry whey products.   Source: Economic Research Service, U.S. Department of Agriculture (ERS-USDA)

Production of Whey Protein Concentrate in the United States   In Thousands of Pounds

Year	Jan.	Feb.	Mar.	Apr.	May	June	July	Aug.	Sept.	Oct.	Nov.	Dec.	Total
2006	37,162	34,436	37,766	37,525	37,373	36,190	35,704	35,024	34,581	34,581	33,116	34,266	427,724
2007	33,280	30,166	35,075	33,104	33,460	33,046	33,252	30,970	31,372	32,283	32,252	35,327	393,587
2008	32,825	33,358	35,830	35,170	36,469	34,274	35,813	34,369	33,314	36,624	34,086	35,709	417,841
2009	35,177	32,340	35,259	32,971	34,705	34,572	35,221	35,284	34,810	35,830	34,061	34,785	415,015
2010	34,765	31,417	37,775	36,265	36,811	35,307	36,441	35,142	36,005	35,583	34,952	37,447	427,910
2011	34,871	32,701	36,809	34,668	36,669	36,292	34,683	35,248	35,571	37,323	36,818	39,285	430,938
2012	38,845	35,064	41,433	39,077	38,417	39,942	35,590	36,804	37,469	38,627	37,735	40,471	459,474
2013	39,262	36,941	41,742	40,396	43,391	41,501	40,265	39,461	39,386	45,542	43,194	46,567	497,648
2014	44,325	42,131	45,027	45,979	46,380	43,703	44,569	44,949	41,281	46,167	46,655	46,991	538,157
2015[1]	47,134	38,872	42,024	41,849	44,202	38,454	41,594	39,871	37,275	41,046	41,112	40,907	494,340

[1] Preliminary.   Source: Economic Research Service, U.S. Department of Agriculture (ERS-USDA)

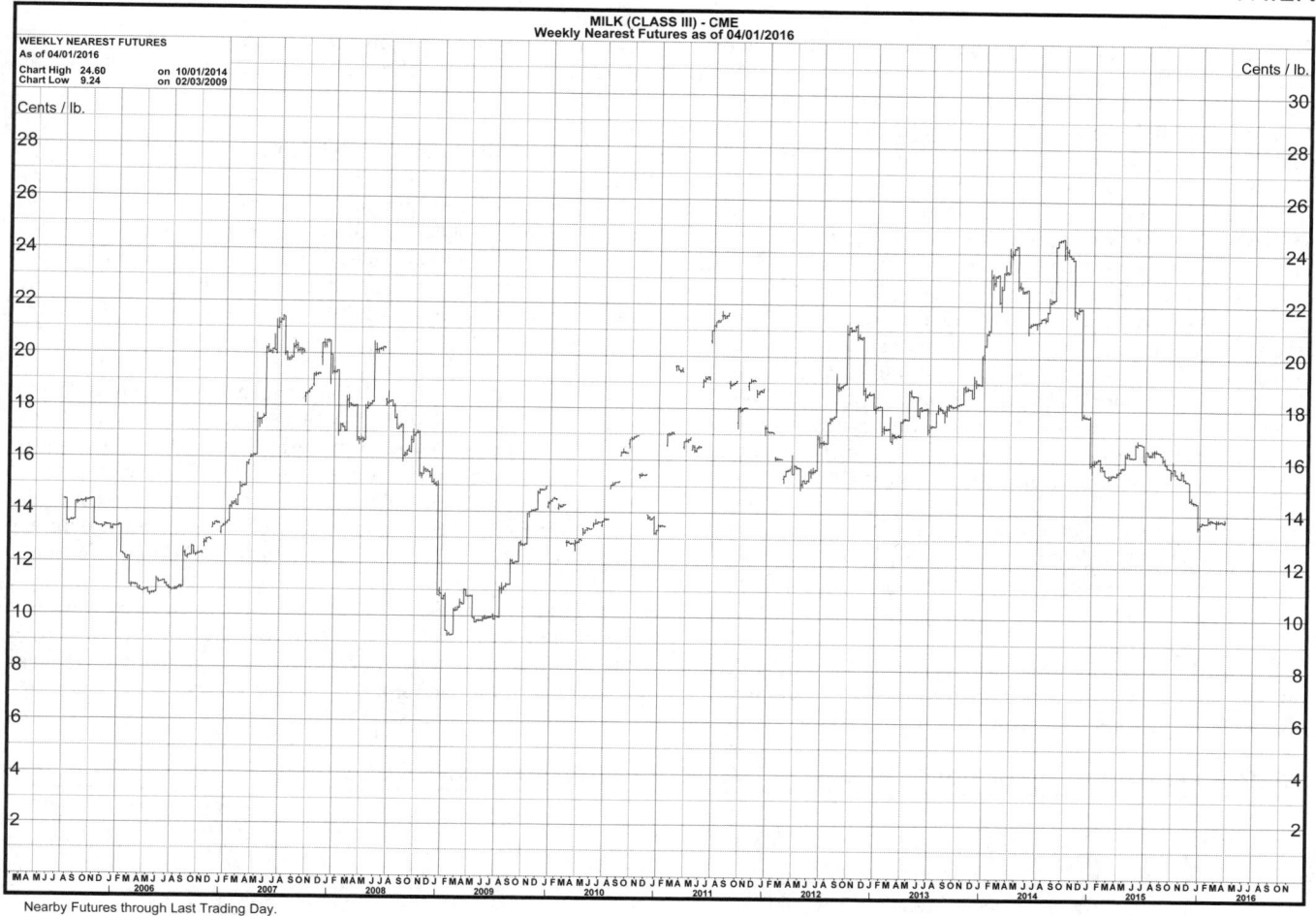

MILK (CLASS III) - CME
Weekly Nearest Futures as of 04/01/2016

WEEKLY NEAREST FUTURES
As of 04/01/2016
Chart High 24.60 on 10/01/2014
Chart Low 9.24 on 02/03/2009

Nearby Futures through Last Trading Day.

Volume of Trading of Class III Milk Futures in Chicago   In Contracts

Year	Jan.	Feb.	Mar.	Apr.	May	June	July	Aug.	Sept.	Oct.	Nov.	Dec.	Total
2006	23,025	26,229	21,112	9,975	19,374	18,328	15,205	18,627	15,148	23,892	20,264	13,958	225,137
2007	26,017	22,343	26,109	33,860	34,154	35,602	19,918	22,058	28,078	20,241	23,638	19,441	311,459
2008	29,875	19,221	19,877	23,359	27,767	28,652	22,218	29,485	24,902	31,238	19,601	28,559	304,754
2009	29,313	21,085	22,708	19,126	21,625	26,902	26,248	21,781	20,214	25,391	17,874	28,369	280,636
2010	28,947	22,118	25,828	22,661	21,808	16,183	19,302	17,900	19,066	25,489	33,175	25,383	277,860
2011	48,169	40,246	37,892	16,713	24,145	30,885	27,495	37,989	29,503	25,880	25,522	24,175	368,614
2012	27,318	27,399	31,079	21,345	22,468	19,617	27,152	28,798	23,819	25,021	22,239	18,242	294,497
2013	22,182	20,654	25,964	29,668	24,403	22,482	23,762	28,680	19,519	24,806	21,210	30,611	293,941
2014	37,317	27,468	31,390	23,084	22,764	21,118	26,702	28,532	38,651	33,233	25,464	42,936	358,659
2015	30,448	29,457	23,844	22,999	21,087	21,649	23,920	16,422	19,958	18,049	22,488	25,218	275,539

Contract size = 200,000 lbs.   Source: CME Group; Chicago Mercantile Exchange (CME)

Average Open Interest of Class III Milk Futures in Chicago   In Contracts

Year	Jan.	Feb.	Mar.	Apr.	May	June	July	Aug.	Sept.	Oct.	Nov.	Dec.
2006	24,077	28,425	30,871	31,894	30,767	30,737	30,795	29,771	27,567	27,523	27,893	27,064
2007	26,542	30,517	32,057	33,766	37,342	39,254	37,426	34,841	34,108	31,402	31,279	30,368
2008	30,376	30,478	29,534	29,651	29,781	33,265	33,597	36,122	37,165	36,678	36,744	36,815
2009	37,081	36,447	33,843	30,337	28,648	28,695	27,551	25,535	24,131	23,388	23,538	24,950
2010	27,126	29,049	30,462	29,520	29,035	28,974	27,487	26,200	26,869	25,722	28,261	30,694
2011	33,741	38,813	38,723	34,509	33,021	35,150	35,730	36,553	33,284	31,322	33,127	33,472
2012	32,511	33,482	31,516	28,476	26,706	24,376	24,511	26,462	26,559	25,497	22,784	20,226
2013	19,320	20,206	21,408	23,180	22,062	21,456	21,802	23,267	23,463	22,153	22,480	24,287
2014	26,264	28,094	29,393	28,695	27,114	26,298	26,128	29,218	32,844	36,731	39,197	43,959
2015	46,134	44,918	42,292	37,710	34,509	31,725	28,890	28,792	26,554	25,839	27,821	29,784

Contract size = 200,000 lbs.   Source: CME Group; Chicago Mercantile Exchange (CME)

Molybdenum

Molybdenum (atomic symbol Mo) is a silvery-white, hard, malleable, metallic element. Molybdenum melts at about 2610 degrees Celsius and boils at about 4640 degrees Celsius. Swedish chemist Carl Wilhelm Scheele discovered molybdenum in 1778.

Molybdenum occurs in nature in the form of molybdenite and wulfenite. Contributing to the growth of plants, it is an important trace element in soils. Approximately 70% of the world supply of molybdenum is obtained as a by-product of copper mining. -Molybdenum is chiefly used as an alloy to strengthen steel and resist corrosion. It is used for structural work, aircraft parts, and forged automobile parts because it withstands high temperatures and pressures and adds strength. Other uses include lubricants, a refractory metal in chemical applications, electron tubing, and as a catalyst.

Prices – The average monthly U.S. merchant price of molybdic oxide in 2015 fell -41.7% yr/yr to $6.83 per pound. That was far below the 2005 record high of $32.70 per pound.

Supply – World production of molybdenum in 2015 fell -5.0% yr/yr to 267,000 metric tons. The 18-year low of 122,000 metric tons was seen in 2002. The world's largest producers of molybdenum are China with 37.8% of world production in 2015, the U.S. with 21.1%, and Chile with 18.4%

U.S. production of molybdenum concentrate in 2015 fell -17.4% yr/yr to 56,300 metric tons, well above the 30-year low of 32,300 metric tons posted in 2002. U.S. net production of molybdic oxide in 2009 (latest data available) rose +1.9% to 32,100 metric tons. U.S. net production of molybdenum metal powder is now being withheld as proprietary data but in 2008 the figure was 1,640 metric tons.

Demand – U.S. consumption of molybdenum concentrate in 2008 (latest data available) rose by +1.4% yr/yr to 44,500 metric tons, remaining well above the 14-year low of 21,200 metric tons posted in 2002. U.S. consumption of molybdenum concentrate has more than doubled over the last 13 years. U.S. consumption of molybdenum primary products in 2015 fell by -2.6% yr/yr to 19,000 metric tons.

Trade – U.S. imports of molybdenum concentrate for consumption in 2014 (latest available data) rose by +20.6% yr/yr to 15,800 metric tons, well above the 16-year low of 4,710 metric tons posted in 2002.

World Mine Production of Molybdenum   In Metric Tons (Contained Molybdenum)

Year	Armenia	Canada[3]	Chile	China	Iran	Kazak-hstan	Mexico	Mongolia	Peru	Russia	United States	Uzbek-isten	World Total
2009	4,365	8,721	34,925	93,500	2,500	----	10,166	2,140	12,297	4,562	47,800	500	221,000
2010	4,335	8,524	37,186	96,600	3,900	----	10,849	2,198	16,963	5,777	59,400	500	246,000
2011	4,817	8,543	40,889	103,000	3,400	----	10,787	1,960	19,141	6,014	63,700	557	266,000
2012	6,500	8,936	35,090	105,000	3,900	----	11,366	1,903	16,790	4,939	61,500	522	256,000
2013	6,700	7,956	38,715	101,000	4,000	----	12,562	1,815	18,140	4,753	61,000	530	258,000
2014[1]	7,100	9,698	48,770	103,000	4,000	----	14,370	1,999	17,018	4,800	68,200	530	281,000
2015[2]	7,300	9,300	49,000	101,000	4,000	----	13,000	2,000	18,100	4,800	56,300	520	267,000

[1] Preliminary.   [2] Estimate.   [3] Shipments.   *Source: U.S. Geological Survey (USGS)*

Salient Statistics of Molybdenum in the United States   In Metric Tons (Contained Molybdenum)

		Concentrate						Primary Products[4]						
			Shipments						Net Production			Shipments		
										Molyb-denum Metal Powder	Avg Price Value	To Oxide for Exports,		
Year	Pro-duction	Total (Including Exports)	Value Million $	For Exports	Con-sumption	Imports For Con-sumption	Stocks Dec. 31[3]	Grand Total	Molybolic Oxide[5]		$ / Kg.[6]	Domestic Dest-inations	Exports, Gross Weight	Con-sumption	Producer Stocks, Dec. 31
2009	47,800	63,700	----	----	W	7,520	2,550	33,700	32,100	W	25.84	43,300	10,600	17,700	3,660
2010	59,400	59,400	----	----	W	12,900	2,200	42,100	W	W	34.83	51,100	6,040	19,200	W
2011	63,700	62,800	----	----	W	14,600	3,520	45,500	W	W	34.34	W	4,840	19,100	W
2012	61,500	61,600	----	----	W	12,000	W	----	----	----	28.09	W	1,590	19,400	W
2013	61,000	68,100	----	----	W	13,100	W	----	----	----	22.85	W	1,320	18,600	W
2014[1]	68,200	71,400	----	----	W	15,800	W	----	----	----	25.84	W		19,500	W
2015[2]	56,300		----	----	W		W	----	----	----	17.80	W		19,000	W

[1] Preliminary.   [2] Estimate.   [3] At mines & at plants making molybdenum products.   [4] Comprises ferromolybdenum, molybdic oxide, & molybdenum salts & metal.   [5] Includes molybdic oxide briquets, molybdic acid, molybdenum trioxide, all other.   [6] U.S. producer price per kilogram of molybdenum oxide contained in technical-grade molybdic oxide.   W = Withheld proprietary data.   E = Net exporter.   *Source: U.S. Geological Survey (USGS)*

US Merchant Price of Molybdic Oxide   In Dollars Per Pound

Year	Jan.	Feb.	Mar.	Apr.	May	June	July	Aug.	Sept.	Oct.	Nov.	Dec.	Average
2009	9.78	9.61	9.03	8.55	9.08	10.34	11.56	17.35	15.24	13.22	10.86	11.15	11.31
2010	14.04	15.91	17.68	17.89	17.34	14.60	14.13	15.57	16.20	15.20	15.65	16.03	15.85
2011	16.73	17.63	17.70	17.36	17.25	16.87	14.95	14.83	14.70	13.80	13.24	13.47	15.71
2012	13.87	14.56	14.38	14.21	14.09	13.53	12.79	11.69	11.68	10.87	10.76	11.06	12.79
2013	11.71	11.44	11.11	11.05	11.10	11.06	9.87	9.29	9.50	9.36	9.67	9.75	10.41
2014	9.92	10.26	10.29	11.60	14.05	14.72	13.55	13.25	12.84	10.59	9.78	9.59	11.70
2015	9.41	8.58	8.17	8.02	7.63	7.32	6.04	6.11	5.88	5.01	4.73	5.02	6.83

Source: American Metal Market (AMM)

Nickel

Nickel (atomic symbol Ni) is a hard, malleable, ductile metal that has a silvery tinge that can take on a high polish. Nickel is somewhat ferromagnetic and is a fair conductor of heat and electricity. Nickel is primarily used in the production of stainless steel and other corrosion-resistant alloys. Nickel is used in coins to replace silver, in rechargeable batteries, and in electronic circuitry. Nickel plating techniques, like electro-less coating or single-slurry coating, are employed in such applications as turbine blades, helicopter rotors, extrusion dies, and rolled steel strip.

Nickel futures and options trade at the London Metal Exchange (LME). The nickel futures contract calls for the delivery of 6 metric tons of primary nickel with at least 99.80% purity in the form of full plate, cut cathodes, pellets or briquettes. The contract is priced in terms of U.S. dollars per metric ton.

Prices – Nickel prices posted a record high of $17.75 per pound in 2007 but have since remained well below that level. The average price of nickel in 2015 fell -26.5% to $6.09 per pound.

Supply – World mine production of nickel in 2015 rose +2.1% yr/yr to 2.450 million metric tons, but still below the 2013 record high of 2.630 million metric tons. The current levels are almost triple the production seen in 1970. The world's largest mine producers of nickel in 2015 were Philippines (with 21.3% of world production), Russia and Canada (9.8%), Australia (9.6%), and Indonesia (7.3%). In 2012 (latest data available) U.S. secondary nickel production rose +3.8% to 89,900 metric tons, still below the 2006 decade-high of 103,630 metric tons.

Demand – U.S. consumption of nickel in 2015 fell -5.4% to 226,000 metric tons. The primary U.S. nickel consumption use is for stainless and heat-resisting steels, which accounted for 56.0% of U.S. consumption in 2012 (latest data). Other consumption uses in 2012 were super alloys (12.1%), nickel alloys (8.2%), electro-plating anodes (3.2%), alloy steels (2.2%), copper base alloys (1.0%), and chemicals (0.8%).

Trade – The U.S. relied on imports for 37% of its nickel consumption in 2015, down from 56% in 2014. U.S. imports of primary and secondary nickel in 2015 fell -16.5% to 162,7001 metric tons, but still well above the 2009 record low of 117,600 metric tons. U.S. exports of primary and secondary nickel in 2015 fell -8.3% to 61,270 metric tons.

World Mine Production of Nickel   In Metric Tons (Contained Nickel)

Year	Australia[3]	Botswana	Brazil	Canada	China	Dominican Republic	Greece	Indonesia	New Caledonia	Philippines	Russia	South Africa	Total
2009	165,000	28,595	41,059	135,037	84,800	500	10,203	202,800	92,500	119,000	261,787	34,605	1,380,000
2010	170,000	23,053	108,983	160,063	80,000	----	16,345	235,800	129,800	190,000	269,272	39,960	1,650,000
2011	212,000	15,675	131,673	219,025	90,000	21,693	21,710	297,000	130,700	319,363	267,393	43,321	2,050,000
2012	246,000	17,948	139,230	204,161	93,300	25,590	22,000	228,000	131,700	317,621	245,295	45,945	2,000,000
2013	234,000		138,000	223,000	95,000	15,800		440,000	164,000	446,000	275,000	51,200	2,630,000
2014[1]	245,000		102,000	235,000	100,000			177,000	165,000	440,000	260,000	51,200	2,630,000
2015[2]	234,000		110,000	240,000	102,000			178,000		523,000	239,000	55,000	2,450,000

[1] Preliminary.   [2] Estimate.   [3] Content of nickel sulfate and concentrates.   *Source: U.S. Geological Survey (USGS)*

Salient Statistics of Nickel in the United States   In Metric Tons (Contained Nickel)

Year	Net Import Reliance As a % of Apparent Consumption	Production Plant[4]	Secondary[5]	Alloy Sheets	Cast Iron	Copper Base Alloys	Electro-plating Anodes	Nickel Alloys	Stainless & Heat Resisting Steels	Super Alloys	Chemicals	Apparent Consumption	Stocks, Dec. 31 At Consumer Plants	Stocks, Dec. 31 At Producer Plants	Primary & Secondary Exports	Primary & Secondary Imports	Avg. Price LME $/Lb.
2008	32	----	86,750	8,680	232	4,930	9,560	22,200	110,400	22,900	844	128,000	15,800	5,860	106,200	149,100	9.57
2009	22	----	79,830	6,330	204	2,870	11,500	20,100	104,000	13,000	1,740	164,000	14,660	5,490	97,030	117,600	6.65
2010	41	----	81,940	1,370	292	3,550	7,200	16,000	117,000	20,700	919	196,000	17,050	6,240	92,900	152,800	9.89
2011	48	----	86,640	6,110	67	2,150	6,910	19,000	118,000	24,400	951	213,000	18,340	6,650	77,200	159,300	10.38
2012	49	----	89,900	4,880	2,130	2,250	6,980	17,800	122,000	26,400	1,670	218,000	16,600	6,550	68,900	155,300	7.95
2013[1]	46	----										200,000	18,600	9,730	71,800	152,300	6.81
2014[2]	56	----										239,000	17,800	9,290	66,800	194,900	7.65

[1] Exclusive of scrap.   [2] Preliminary.   [3] Estimate.   [4] Smelter & refinery.   [5] From purchased scrap (ferrous & nonferrous). W = Withheld proprietary data.   NA = Not available.   *Source: U.S. Geological Survey (USGS)*

Average Price of Nickel[1] in the United States   In Cents Per Pound

Year	Jan.	Feb.	Mar.	Apr.	May	June	July	Aug.	Sept.	Oct.	Nov.	Dec.	Average
2011	1,242.88	1,361.67	1,298.06	1,275.63	1,180.33	1,090.85	1,154.75	1,077.02	1,000.59	933.70	891.56	899.85	1,117.24
2012	977.36	1,000.39	913.14	869.82	828.25	800.53	783.19	763.76	835.67	834.31	787.80	841.55	852.98
2013	846.82	858.29	812.99	765.63	732.69	701.86	676.33	702.50	679.63	692.78	679.12	694.11	736.90
2014	703.14	708.28	774.92	855.13	943.44	906.85	927.94	907.24	883.35	778.75	773.39	784.30	828.89
2015	731.81	722.45	690.11	647.56	676.12	641.79	574.56	572.69	572.69	572.69	461.43	446.04	609.16

[1] Plating material, briquettes.   *Source: American Metal Market (AMM)*

Oats

Oats are seeds or grains of a genus of plants that thrive in cool, moist climates. There are about 25 species of oats that grow worldwide in the cooler temperate regions. The oldest known cultivated oats were found inside caves in Switzerland and are believed to be from the Bronze Age. Oats are usually sown in early spring and harvested in mid to late summer, but in southern regions of the northern hemisphere, they may be sown in the fall. Oats are used in many processed foods such as flour, livestock feed, and furfural, a chemical used as a solvent in various refining industries. The oat crop year begins in June and ends in May. Oat futures and options are traded at the CME Group.

Prices – CME oat futures prices (Barchart.com electronic symbol ZO) on the nearest-futures chart fell sharply in 2015 to post a new 5-1/2 year low and close the year down -28.5% at 217.25 cents per bushel. Regarding cash prices, the average monthly price received by farmers for oats in the U.S. in the first eight months of the 2015-16 marketing year (June/May) fell -24.1% yr/yr to $2.83 per bushel.

Supply – World oat production in 2015-16 fell -0.5% yr/yr to 22.204 million metric tons, moderately above the record low of 19.625 million metric tons posted in 2010-11. World annual oat production in the past three decades has dropped very sharply from levels above 50 million metric tons in the early 1970s. The world's largest oat producers are the European Union with 34.4% of world production in 2015-16, Russia 20.5%, Canada with 15.4%, and Australia with 5.9%.

U.S. oat production in the 2014-15 marketing year rose +7.8% yr/yr to 69.684 million bushels, above the 2011-12 record low of 53.649 million bushels. U.S. oat production has fallen sharply from levels mostly above 1 billion bushels seen from the early 1900s into the early 1960s. U.S. farmers harvested 1.276 million acres of oats in 2015-16, which was up +23.29% from the 2011-12 record low. That is down from the almost 40 million acres harvested back in the 1950s. The oat yield in 2015-16 rose +3.4% to 70.2 bushels per acre. Oat stocks in the U.S. as of September 2015 were up +26.3% yr/yr to a 93.866 million bushels. The largest U.S. oat-producing states in 2015 were the states of Wisconsin (15.7% of U.S. production), Minnesota (13.9%), North Dakota (11.6%), Iowa (4.6%), Pennsylvania (4.0%), and Michigan (3.7%).

Demand – U.S. usage of oats in 2015-16 rose +20.5% yr/yr to 177.000 million bushels, above the 2011-12 record low of 106.360 million bushels. Regarding U.S. usage of oats in 2014-15 (latest data), 56.5% was for feed and residual, 40.0% for food, alcohol and industrial, 4.5% for seed, and 1.1% for exports.

Trade – U.S. exports of oats rose +11.4% yr/yr to 2.000 million bushels in 2015-16. U.S. imports of oats in 2015-16 rose -11.6% yr/yr to 95.000 million bushels, below the 2007 record high of 123.29 million bushels.

World Production of Oats In Thousands of Metric Tons

Crop Year	Argentina	Australia	Belarus	Brazil	Canada	Chile	China	European Union	Kazakstan	Russia	Ukraine	United States	World Total
2006-07	400	748	555	406	3,852	342	400	7,835	183	4,860	690	1,357	22,636
2007-08	472	1,502	580	238	4,618	384	643	8,690	230	5,384	544	1,313	25,536
2008-09	291	1,160	605	239	4,273	344	530	9,000	138	5,835	944	1,307	25,637
2009-10	182	1,162	552	253	2,912	381	580	8,641	204	5,401	731	1,321	23,334
2010-11	660	1,128	442	379	2,451	564	525	7,500	134	3,218	458	1,188	19,645
2011-12	345	1,262	448	354	3,158	451	600	7,927	258	5,332	506	728	22,308
2012-13	496	1,121	422	361	2,830	680	600	7,909	200	4,027	630	892	21,119
2013-14[1]	445	1,255	352	380	3,906	610	580	8,380	305	4,932	467	938	23,502
2014-15[2]	525	1,087	470	300	2,979	421	600	7,845	226	5,267	610	1,019	22,310
2015-16[3]	485	1,300	400	300	3,430	470	600	7,640	244	4,550	490	1,300	22,204

[1] Preliminary. [2] Estimate. [3] Forecast. Source: Foreign Agricultural Service, U.S. Department of Agriculture (FAS-USDA)

Official Oats Crop Production Reports in the United States In Thousands of Bushels

Year	July 1	Aug. 1	Sept. 1	Oct. 1	Dec. 1	Final	Year	July 1	Aug. 1	Sept. 1	Oct. 1	Dec. 1	Final
2004	121,860	127,950	----	----	----	115,695	2010	87,726	87,239	----	----	----	81,190
2005	131,314	127,819	----	----	----	114,878	2011	56,551	57,489	----	----	----	53,649
2006	110,322	107,423	----	----	----	93,522	2012	65,276	66,519	----	----	----	61,486
2007	100,921	98,341	----	----	----	90,430	2013	74,459	75,210	----	----	----	64,642
2008	92,872	89,897	----	----	----	89,135	2014	75,507	77,267	----	----	----	70,232
2009	91,277	91,960	----	----	----	93,081	2015[1]	83,640	85,456	----	----	----	89,535

[1] Preliminary. Source: National Agricultural Statistics Service, U.S. Department of Agriculture (NASS-USDA)

Oat Stocks in the United States   In Thousands of Bushels

	On Farms				Off Farms				Total Stocks			
Year	Mar. 1	June 1	Sept. 1	Dec. 1	Mar. 1	June 1	Sept. 1	Dec. 1	Mar. 1	June 1	Sept. 1	Dec. 1
2006	42,200	25,190	60,800	53,000	32,673	27,376	39,284	45,889	74,873	52,566	100,084	98,889
2007	33,900	18,400	53,650	43,100	37,158	32,198	34,710	51,331	71,058	50,598	88,360	94,431
2008	31,000	16,100	52,800	42,600	47,988	50,674	66,296	72,322	78,988	66,774	119,096	114,922
2009	30,200	17,480	54,500	43,000	65,250	66,619	73,875	67,629	95,450	84,099	128,375	110,629
2010	30,900	17,600	46,250	34,100	67,091	62,716	70,722	66,911	97,991	80,316	116,972	101,011
2011	26,950	14,580	31,000	24,900	59,361	53,049	47,391	54,235	86,311	67,629	78,391	79,135
2012	19,750	11,120	34,100	26,100	55,044	43,869	50,872	47,051	74,794	54,989	84,972	73,151
2013	18,900	11,380	37,150	25,650	33,726	24,957	26,339	22,394	52,626	36,337	63,489	48,044
2014	19,800	9,710	41,400	31,300	15,323	15,029	32,910	35,670	35,123	24,739	74,310	66,970
2015[1]	20,810	15,120	47,800	36,750	38,609	38,625	46,066	46,135	59,419	53,745	93,866	82,885

[1] Preliminary.   Source: National Agricultural Statistics Service, U.S. Department of Agriculture (NASS-USDA)

Supply and Utilization of Oats in the United States   In Millions of Bushels

Crop Year Beginning June 1	Acreage Planted (1,000 Acres)	Harvested (1,000 Acres)	Yield Per Acre (Bushels)	Production	Imports	Total Supply	Feed & Residual	Food, Alcohol & Industrial	Seed	Exports	Total Use	Ending Stocks	Farm Price (Dollars Per Bushel)	Findley Loan Rate	Target Price
2006-07	4,168	1,566	59.8	93.5	106.2	252.3	124.9	64.5	9.7	201.7	2.6	50.6	1.87	1.33	1.44
2007-08	3,763	1,504	60.1	90.4	123.3	264.3	120.2	66.0	8.5	197.5	2.9	66.8	2.63	1.33	1.44
2008-09	3,247	1,400	63.7	89.1	114.6	270.5	108.1	66.1	8.9	186.4	3.3	84.1	3.15	1.33	1.44
2009-10	3,404	1,379	67.5	93.1	94.9	272.1	115.2	66.2	8.2	191.8	2.2	80.3	2.02	1.33	1.44
2010-11	3,138	1,263	64.3	81.2	85.1	247.3	102.9	67.2	6.8	179.7	2.9	67.6	2.52	1.39	1.79
2011-12	2,496	939	57.1	53.6	94.1	211.8	78.5	68.8	7.2	156.9	2.4	54.9	3.49	1.39	1.79
2012-13	2,700	1,005	61.2	61.5	92.9	209.3	95.7	68.1	7.8	171.6	1.4	36.3	3.89	1.39	1.79
2013-14	2,980	1,009	64.1	64.6	97.1	198.1	98.5	66.2	7.1	171.8	1.6	24.7	3.75	1.39	1.79
2014-15[1]	2,753	1,035	67.9	70.2	107.5	202.4	69.9	69.0	8.0	146.9	1.8	53.7	3.21		
2015-16[2]	3,088	1,276	70.2	89.5	95.0	238.3	100.0	69.0	8.0	177.0	2.0	59.3	2.10-2.60		

[1] Preliminary.   [2] Forecast.   [3] Less than 500,000 bushels.   NA = Not available.
Source: Economic Research Service, U.S. Department of Agiculture (ERS-USDA)

Production of Oats in the United States, by States   In Thousands of Bushels

Year	Illinois	Iowa	Michigan	Minnesota	Nebraska	New York	North Dakota	Ohio	Pennsylvania	South Dakota	Texas	Wisconsin	Total
2006	3,080	8,360	4,030	11,200	2,025	4,958	4,920	4,125	7,040	5,415	3,700	14,490	93,522
2007	1,488	4,757	3,080	10,800	2,135	3,480	15,340	3,100	4,480	9,360	4,000	10,720	90,430
2008	2,100	4,875	3,960	11,900	2,450	4,224	6,630	3,500	4,640	8,760	5,000	11,780	89,135
2009	1,625	6,175	3,465	12,070	2,070	4,620	11,220	3,375	4,880	6,570	2,820	13,260	93,081
2010	1,950	4,340	4,080	11,385	1,700	3,886	6,405	3,500	4,720	7,560	4,160	9,860	81,190
2011	1,360	3,250	1,920	5,940	1,300	1,700	4,420	2,052	2,760	4,130	2,100	7,130	53,649
2012	1,140	3,770	2,100	8,370	1,026	3,250	6,510	2,576	3,965	3,060	3,185	7,800	61,486
2013	1,725	3,960	1,860	5,985	1,625	3,082	8,370	1,575	3,100	9,240	1,840	6,825	64,642
2014	2,000	3,520	2,760	7,875	2,400	2,520	7,665	2,205	3,480	9,300	1,710	8,680	70,232
2015[1]	1,925	4,161	3,350	12,480	2,680	2,320	10,360	2,520	3,575	12,615	2,640	14,040	89,535

[1] Preliminary.   Source: National Agricultural Statistics Service, U.S. Department of Agriculture (NASS-USDA)

Average Cash Price of No. 2 Heavy White Oats in Toledo   In Dollars Per Bushel

Year	Jan.	Feb.	Mar.	Apr.	May	June	July	Aug.	Sept.	Oct.	Nov.	Dec.	Average
1996-97	NQ	2.45	2.34	2.19	2.02	1.96	1.96	1.99	2.16	2.26	2.12	2.08	2.14
1997-98	2.12	1.79	1.84	1.80	1.77	NQ	NQ	NQ	NQ	NQ	NQ	NQ	1.86
1998-99	NQ	NQ	NQ	NQ	NQ	NQ	NQ	NQ	NQ	NQ	NQ	NQ	NQ
1999-00	NQ	NQ	NQ	NQ	NQ	NQ	NQ	NQ	NQ	NQ	NQ	NQ	NQ
2000-01	NQ	NQ	NQ	NQ	NQ	NQ	NQ	NQ	NQ	NQ	NQ	NQ	NQ
2001-02	NQ	NQ	NQ	NQ	NQ	NQ	NQ	NQ	NQ	NQ	NQ	NQ	NQ
2002-03	NQ	NQ	NQ	NQ	NQ	NQ	NQ	NQ	NQ	NQ	NQ	NQ	NQ
2003-04	NQ	NQ	NQ	NQ	NQ	NQ	NQ	NQ	NQ	NQ	NQ	NQ	NQ
2004-05	NQ	NQ	NQ	NQ	NQ	NQ	NQ	NQ	NQ	NQ	NQ	NQ	NQ
2005-06[1]	NQ	NQ	NQ										

[1] Preliminary.   NQ = No quotes.   Source: Economic Research Service, U.S. Department of Agriculture (ERS-USDA)

OATS

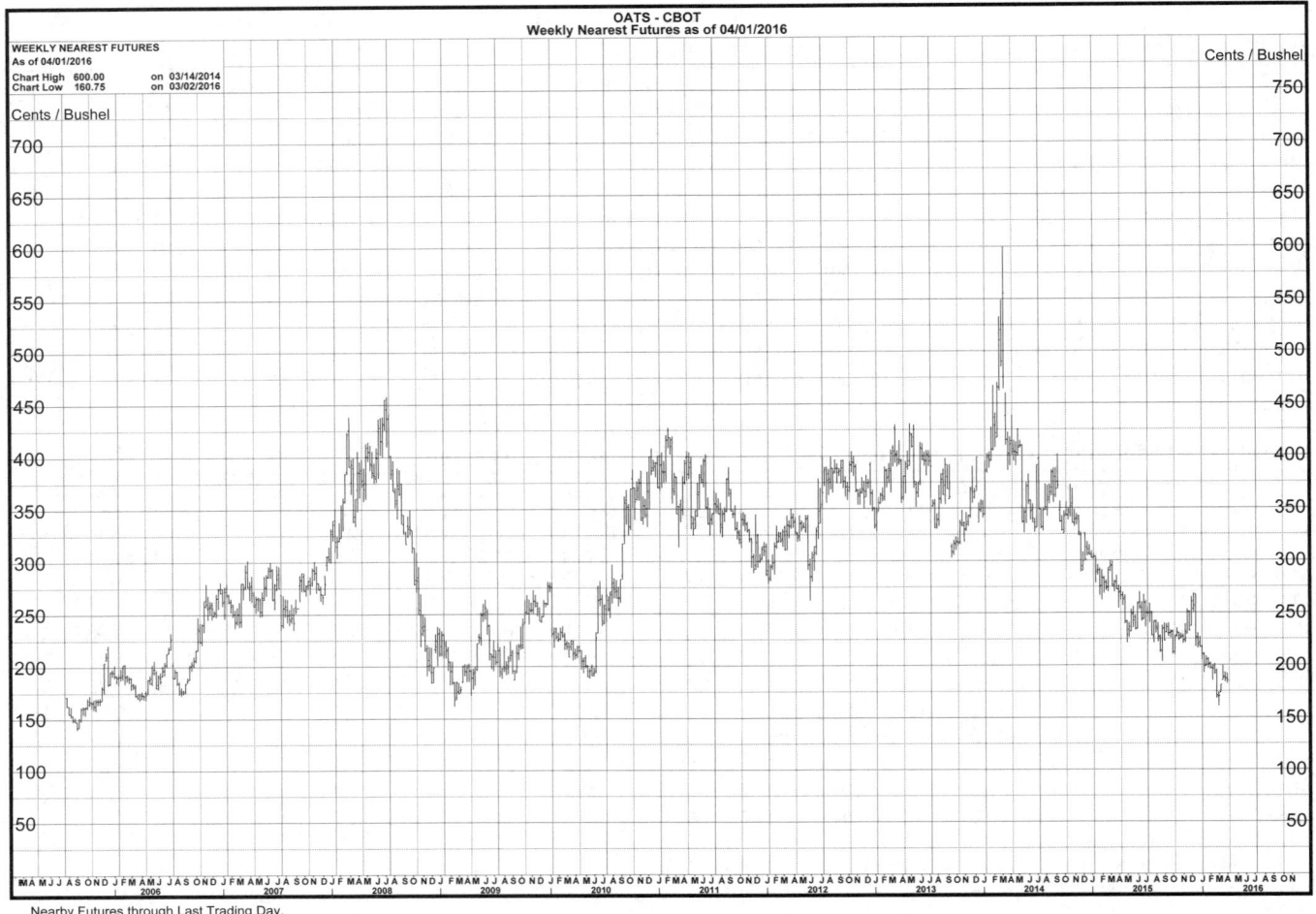

OATS - CBOT
Weekly Nearest Futures as of 04/01/2016

WEEKLY NEAREST FUTURES
As of 04/01/2016
Chart High 600.00   on 03/14/2014
Chart Low   160.75   on 03/02/2016

Cents / Bushel

Nearby Futures through Last Trading Day.

Volume of Trading in Oats Futures in Chicago   In Contracts

Year	Jan.	Feb.	Mar.	Apr.	May	June	July	Aug.	Sept.	Oct.	Nov.	Dec.	Total
2006	25,667	40,534	30,437	35,799	39,362	42,812	35,751	30,790	25,700	43,724	51,304	25,435	427,315
2007	42,231	41,327	41,259	46,054	31,288	43,157	32,977	30,240	24,565	29,484	48,488	21,671	432,741
2008	44,184	61,469	44,478	47,918	37,813	52,116	27,923	32,074	19,009	31,829	23,978	18,797	441,588
2009	17,494	34,259	19,035	34,277	25,365	41,961	19,370	24,801	20,076	29,720	29,328	18,619	314,305
2010	31,060	32,283	23,890	37,409	21,363	54,174	26,097	23,735	22,430	25,743	30,649	15,754	344,587
2011	28,513	41,210	32,798	35,451	25,962	42,810	17,687	26,037	24,613	23,352	41,624	9,259	349,316
2012	19,267	27,361	29,511	22,787	28,013	31,967	16,898	20,154	15,311	22,011	28,859	17,431	279,570
2013	21,246	34,411	16,949	31,035	16,891	28,267	18,156	16,459	17,388	21,863	22,977	9,316	254,958
2014	18,860	30,902	18,786	18,113	11,938	19,491	11,446	13,556	11,300	16,754	21,903	7,482	200,531
2015	14,618	19,923	12,461	25,243	15,152	21,734	11,399	13,953	9,614	13,216	24,979	12,283	194,575

Contract size = 5,000 bu.   *Source: CME Group; Chicago Board of Trade (CBT)*

Average Open Interest of Oats in Chicago   In Contracts

Year	Jan.	Feb.	Mar.	Apr.	May	June	July	Aug.	Sept.	Oct.	Nov.	Dec.
2006	10,200	11,697	10,960	10,961	13,529	14,128	13,965	11,620	11,178	13,483	14,714	13,818
2007	16,176	18,406	19,178	19,255	18,061	17,909	14,824	13,387	14,158	14,251	13,223	10,914
2008	13,696	14,812	14,764	15,097	15,957	16,802	16,667	15,027	14,740	15,495	15,108	16,848
2009	16,519	16,927	14,367	15,142	13,304	14,380	13,805	13,649	13,684	13,526	13,593	11,976
2010	12,601	13,869	15,662	17,612	17,244	16,838	10,329	10,956	11,664	13,477	13,452	11,707
2011	13,104	14,297	13,191	13,677	12,577	12,457	12,287	13,127	14,082	15,902	16,557	12,802
2012	13,363	11,924	10,849	10,879	11,516	11,021	9,959	10,708	11,328	11,802	11,567	10,439
2013	10,568	11,022	10,619	9,356	8,634	10,207	8,659	9,000	9,941	10,805	9,767	8,937
2014	10,414	11,168	9,529	8,350	7,356	7,793	7,292	8,382	8,987	9,787	9,813	8,151
2015	7,684	8,794	8,965	8,729	8,375	8,570	7,926	8,408	8,902	10,129	10,793	8,789

Contract size = 5,000 bu.   *Source: CME Group; Chicago Board of Trade (CBT)*

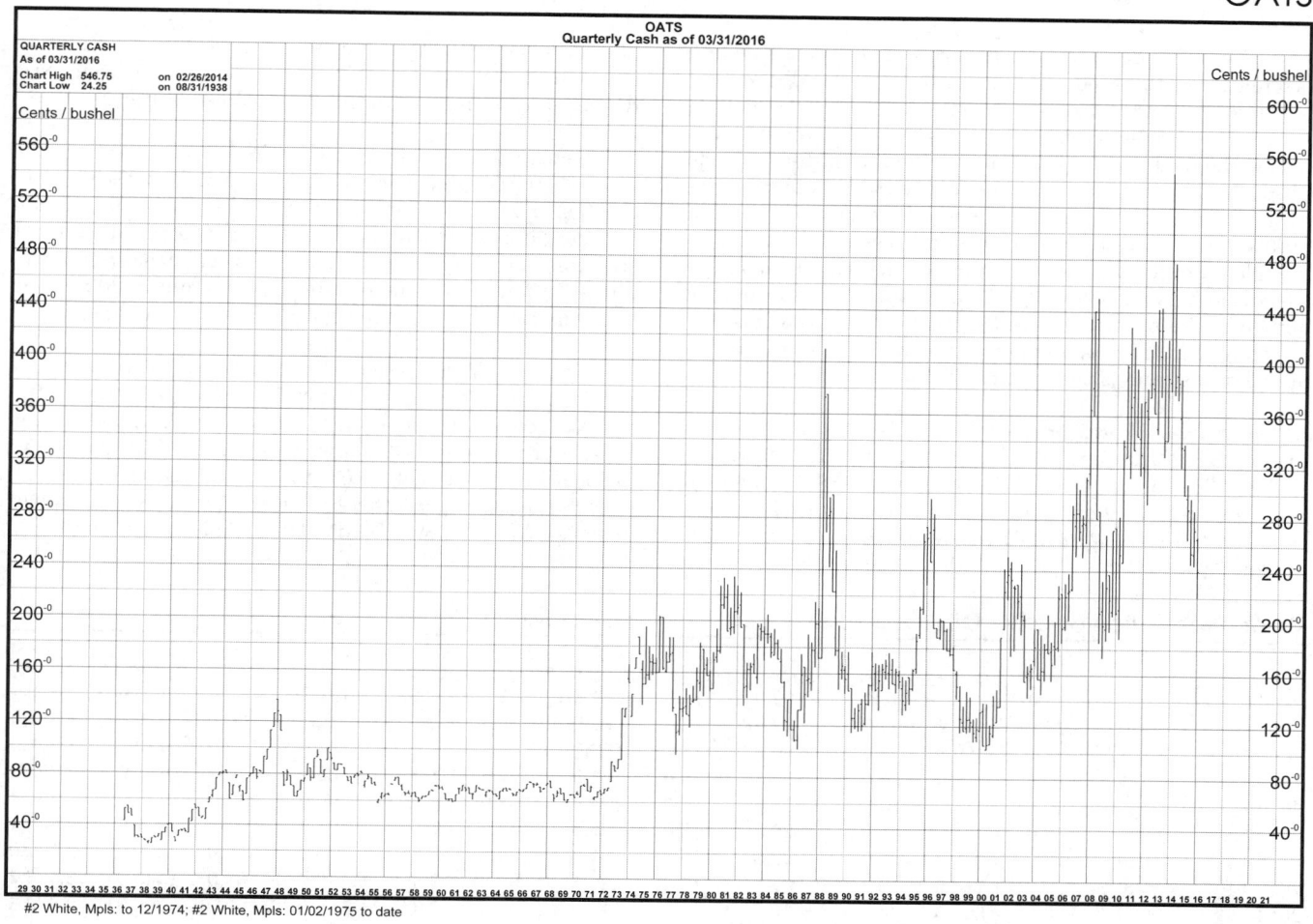

OATS
Quarterly Cash as of 03/31/2016

QUARTERLY CASH
As of 03/31/2016
Chart High   546.75   on 02/26/2014
Chart Low   24.25   on 08/31/1938

Cents / bushel

#2 White, Mpls: to 12/1974; #2 White, Mpls: 01/02/1975 to date

Average Cash Price of No. 2 Heavy White Oats in Minneapolis   In Dollars Per Bushel

Year	June	July	Aug.	Sept.	Oct.	Nov.	Dec.	Jan.	Feb.	Mar.	Apr.	May	Average
2006-07	2.21	2.25	2.06	2.17	2.43	2.70	2.81	2.78	2.65	2.84	2.82	2.76	2.54
2007-08	2.90	2.69	2.61	2.68	2.70	2.79	2.95	3.24	3.66	3.82	3.75	3.96	3.15
2008-09	4.07	4.07	----	----	----	2.14	2.13	2.18	1.89	1.97	2.01	2.33	2.53
2009-10	2.33	2.15	2.12	2.03	2.34	2.56	2.56	2.44	2.30	2.19	2.10	1.98	2.26
2010-11	2.39	2.58	2.69	3.14	3.56	3.54	3.88	3.93	4.08	3.55	3.83	3.55	3.39
2011-12	3.68	3.68	3.69	3.72	3.51	3.36	3.30	3.16	3.46	3.48	3.55	3.48	3.50
2012-13	3.37	3.95	3.99	3.89	3.98	3.85	3.94	3.79	4.07	4.26	4.13	3.99	3.93
2013-14	4.21	3.84	3.78	3.40	3.57	3.79	3.80	4.30	4.64	4.66	4.58	4.03	4.05
2014-15	3.88	3.85	3.83	3.86	3.68	3.53	3.49	3.26	3.11	3.14	2.94	2.75	3.44
2015-16[1]	2.89	2.82	2.63	2.70	2.58	2.67	NQ	2.64					2.70

[1] Preliminary.   NQ = No qoute.   *Source: Economic Research Service, U.S. Department of Agriculture (ERS-USDA)*

Average Price Received by Farmers for Oats in the United States   In Dollars Per Bushel

Year	June	July	Aug.	Sept.	Oct.	Nov.	Dec.	Jan.	Feb.	Mar.	Apr.	May	Average
2006-07	1.90	1.78	1.67	1.70	1.77	2.05	2.01	2.20	2.35	2.40	2.46	2.49	2.07
2007-08	2.54	2.32	2.24	2.47	2.45	2.63	2.69	2.88	3.19	3.43	3.47	3.63	2.83
2008-09	3.56	3.44	3.16	3.29	3.26	3.00	3.12	2.77	2.69	2.77	2.37	2.64	3.01
2009-10	2.37	2.03	1.86	1.82	2.03	2.02	2.22	2.19	2.30	2.29	2.25	2.20	2.13
2010-11	2.11	2.11	2.09	2.30	2.55	3.07	2.94	3.13	3.27	3.28	3.54	3.55	2.83
2011-12	3.43	3.35	3.20	3.67	3.69	3.38	3.57	3.56	3.47	3.77	3.84	4.12	3.59
2012-13	3.80	3.70	3.82	3.76	3.93	3.88	3.90	4.06	4.14	4.20	4.43	4.45	4.01
2013-14	3.93	3.88	3.67	3.57	3.49	3.63	3.59	3.70	3.75	4.13	3.96	3.98	3.77
2014-15	3.73	3.49	3.24	3.20	3.16	2.95	3.21	3.02	3.08	2.91	2.82	2.90	3.14
2015-16[1]	2.83	2.33	2.08	2.03	2.20	2.10	2.11	1.92	2.21				2.20

[1] Preliminary.   *Source: National Agricultural Statistics Service, U.S. Department of Agriculture (NASS-USDA)*

Olive Oil

Olive oil is derived from the fruit of the olive tree and originated in the Mediterranean area. Olives designated for oil are picked before ripening in the fall. Olive picking is usually done by hand. The olives are then weighed and washed in cold water. The olives, along with their oil-rich pits, are then crushed and kneaded until a homogeneous paste is formed. The paste is spread by hand onto metal plates, which are then stacked and pressed hydraulically to yield a liquid. The liquid is then centrifuged to separate the oil. It takes 1,300 to 2,000 olives to produce 1 quart of olive oil. The best olive oil is still produced from the first pressing, which is usually performed within 24 to 72 hours after harvest and is called extra virgin olive oil.

Supply – World production of olive oil (pressed oil) in the marketing year 2014-15 (latest data) fell -24.5% to 2.579 million metric tons, slightly below the 2011-12 record high of 3.630 million metric tons. The world's largest producers of olive oil in 2014-15 were Spain (with 35.3% of world production), Italy (13.6%), Greece (12.6%), Syria

(2.3%), Turkey (6.2%), and Morocco (4.6%). Production levels in the various countries vary considerably from year-to-year depending on weather and crop conditions.

Demand – World consumption of olive oil in the 2014-15 (latest data) marketing year fell -8.2% yr/yr to 2.920 million metric tons, below the 2011-12 record high of 3.351 million metric tons. The U.S. is the world's largest consumer of olive oil with 10.3% of world consumption in 2014-15. The U.S. consumption of olive oil at 300,000 is below last year's record high of 305,000 metric tons.

Trade – World olive oil imports in 2014-15 (latest data) rose +3.8% to 920,000 metric tons. The U.S. was the world's largest importer in 2014-15 with 288,000 metric tons, representing 31.3% of world imports. World olive oil exports in 2014-15 fell -3.0% to 892,000 metric tons. The world's largest exporters were Tunisia (with 28.0% of world exports), Italy (25.8%), Spain (19.6), and Turkey (3.4%).

World Production of Olive Oil (Pressed Oil) In Thousands of Metric Tons

Crop Year	Algeria	Argentina	Greece	Italy	Jordan	Libya	Morocco	Portugal	Spain	Syria	Tunisia	Turkey	World Total
2006-07	21.5	15.0	398.0	532.0	39.0	11.0	81.0	51.3	1,139.0	171.5	172.5	174.5	2,916.7
2007-08	24.0	27.0	353.2	553.0	22.5	13.0	92.0	39.3	1,280.0	111.0	183.0	79.0	2,886.5
2008-09	61.5	23.0	329.0	586.0	20.0	15.0	92.0	57.0	1,125.3	142.0	179.0	140.0	2,888.0
2009-10	26.5	17.0	346.0	557.7	29.5	15.0	151.5	57.5	1,494.5	163.0	170.0	157.0	3,298.2
2010-11	67.0	20.0	334.0	551.8	28.0	15.0	137.0	67.9	1,512.9	196.0	140.0	174.0	3,384.4
2011-12	39.5	32.0	322.6	576.0	20.5	15.0	126.5	82.3	1,701.9	165.0	202.0	205.0	3,630.1
2012-13[1]	66.0	17.0	393.9	440.5	22.5	15.0	107.0	64.6	709.6	155.0	240.0	209.0	2,573.0
2013-14[2]	44.0	20.0	148.5	490.7	31.0	15.0	128.5	97.6	1,913.0	147.0	84.0	145.0	3,416.2
2014-15[3]	44.0	8.0	325.0	352.0	36.0	15.0	118.0	100.0	910.0	60.0	290.0	160.0	2,579.5

[1] Preliminary. [2] Estimate. [3] Forecast. *Source: The Oil World*

World Imports and Exports of Olive Oil (Pressed Oil) In Thousands of Metric Tons

Crop Year	Imports							Exports					
	Australia	Brazil	Italy	Japan	Spain	United States	World Total	Greece	Italy	Spain	Tunisia	Turkey	World Total
2006-07	42.1	36.6	154.1	32.0	71.3	262.5	801.6	17.8	208.6	148.5	220.7	47.2	804.2
2007-08	27.8	42.9	119.4	30.4	41.8	264.5	737.6	12.0	197.9	158.8	187.4	18.3	740.8
2008-09	29.0	41.4	82.6	33.3	12.1	276.5	713.1	13.4	195.9	179.0	152.2	27.9	717.5
2009-10	35.6	51.3	56.8	42.6	17.9	272.0	740.7	13.7	213.8	208.0	115.3	27.2	731.5
2010-11	32.0	65.0	57.5	37.7	16.5	292.0	802.0	14.4	243.3	229.2	109.0	12.9	808.1
2011-12	31.9	71.0	73.9	45.6	21.4	317.4	891.3	18.1	254.9	285.8	149.5	19.4	902.8
2012-13[1]	28.8	74.9	79.8	54.0	61.5	298.8	947.6	20.1	235.3	223.5	178.3	80.7	940.1
2013-14[2]	28.9	73.6	29.1	56.2	20.4	312.4	886.4	17.9	255.6	333.8	84.0	34.9	919.7
2014-15[3]	28.0	70.0	70.0	54.0	85.0	288.0	920.5	24.0	230.0	175.0	250.0	30.0	892.0

[1] Preliminary. [2] Estimate. [3] Forecast. *Source: The Oil World*

World Consumption and Ending Stocks of Olive Oil (Pressed Oil) In Thousands of Metric Tons

Crop Year	Consumption							Ending Stocks					
	Brazil	Morocco	Syria	Tunisia	Turkey	United States	World Total	European Union	Morocco	Syria	Tunisia	Turkey	World Total
2006-07	36.6	71.8	128.3	26.8	90.3	244.2	3,003.8	782.3	14.0	43.0	38.0	45.0	990.2
2007-08	42.9	77.9	105.2	28.1	97.8	258.7	3,038.1	741.0	25.0	5.0	8.0	8.0	842.9
2008-09	41.4	92.8	112.0	29.8	105.2	266.3	3,072.6	541.0	34.0	8.0	9.0	15.0	697.9
2009-10	51.3	89.4	133.0	32.0	116.8	272.0	3,184.2	577.0	85.0	20.4	33.0	28.0	822.8
2010-11	65.0	96.7	138.1	34.5	129.2	284.8	3,294.8	575.4	90.0	45.0	30.0	60.0	906.3
2011-12	71.0	103.3	136.6	38.8	155.7	298.7	3,353.7	751.0	105.0	50.0	44.0	90.0	1,171.2
2012-13[1]	74.9	111.3	139.5	41.0	138.3	303.7	3,111.5	250.0	86.0	40.0	65.0	80.0	640.2
2013-14[2]	73.6	115.0	129.7	32.5	130.2	305.2	3,180.0	481.1	95.0	35.0	35.0	60.0	843.2
2014-15[3]	70.0	110.0	80.0	35.8	126.0	300.0	2,920.5	222.1	81.0	15.0	40.0	65.0	530.7

[1] Preliminary. [2] Estimate. [3] Forecast. *Source: The Oil World*

Onions

Onions are the bulbs of plants in the lily family. Onions can be eaten raw, cooked, pickled, used as a flavoring or seasoning, or dehydrated. Onions rank in the top 10 vegetables produced in the U.S. in terms of dollar value. Since 1629, onions have been cultivated in the U.S., but are believed to be indigenous to Asia.

The two main types of onions produced in the U.S. are yellow and white onions. Yellow varieties comprise approximately 75% of all onions grown for bulb production in the U.S. Onions that are planted as a winter crop in warm areas are milder in taste and odor than onions planted during the summer in cooler regions.

Prices – Onion prices in 2015 averaged $13.60 per hundred pounds, down-9.3% yr/yr.

Supply – U.S. production in 2015 fell -17.9% to 6.503 billion pounds, still below the 2004 record high of 8.307 billion pounds. The farm value of the U.S. production crop in 2015 rose +11.3% to 993,360, well below the 2006 record high of $1.084 billion. U.S. farmers harvested 132.900 acres, down -5.0% yr/yr, a new decade low. The yield in 2015 was 507 pounds per acre.

Demand – U.S. per capita consumption of onions in 2012 (latest data) rose +3.4% yr/yr to 21.3 pounds.

Trade – U.S. exports of fresh onions in 2012 (latest data) totaled 648 million pounds, and imports totaled 849 million pounds.

Salient Statistics of Onions in the United States

Crop Year	Harvested Acres	Yield Per Acre	Pro- duction 1,000 Cwt.	Price Per Cwt.	Farm Value $1,000	Jan. 1 Pack Frozen	Anual Pack Frozen	Imports Canned	Exports (Fresh)	Imports (Fresh)	Per Capita[3] Utilization -- Lbs., Farm Weight -- All	Fresh
							--- In Millions of Pounds ---					
2009	151,060	500	75,599	15.00	1,054,227	36.2	----	18.9	561.2	681.6	21.5	19.6
2010	149,270	493	73,599	15.60	1,049,704	39.0	----	17.7	713.5	869.1	21.1	19.6
2011	147,630	502	74,097	10.90	742,236	37.5	----	18.8	700.9	868.9	20.6	19.1
2012	146,870	487	71,495	14.20	942,340	73.7	----	21.1	648.0	849.4	21.3	19.8
2013	143,340	486	69,654	15.00	969,170	58.0	----					
2014[1]	139,850	499	69,815	13.60	892,325	49.8	----					
2015[2]	132,900	507	67,380	17.60	993,360	45.0	----					

[1] Preliminary. [2] Forecast. [3] Includes fresh and processing. *Source: Economic Research Service, U.S. Department of Agiculture (ERS-USDA)*

Production of Onions in the United States   In Thousands of Hundredweight (Cwt.)

Crop Year	Arizona	Cali- fornia	Texas	Total (All)	Cali- fornia	Colo- rado	Idaho	Mich- igan	Minne- sota	Mexico	New York	Oregon, Malheur	Texas	Total (All)	Grand Total
		Spring						Summer							
2009	576	2,460	3,003	8,523	14,287	2,739	6,512	1,330	----	----	4,275	7,840	----	67,076	75,599
2010	----	2,542	2,666	7,484	13,050	2,880	6,840	880	----	----	3,087	8,588	----	66,115	73,599
2011	----	2,520	3,360	8,845	12,980	2,864	7,176	816	----	----	1,891	8,249	----	65,252	74,097
2012	----	2,480	3,090	8,008	12,354	2,604	6,205	644	----	----	2,480	7,950	----	63,487	71,495
2013	----	2,720	3,492	9,209	11,700	1,700	7,380	810	----	----	2,015	7,848	----	60,445	69,654
2014	----	2,992	2,340	7,917	16,120	1,800	5,658	925	----	----	2,360	7,440	----	64,889	72,806
2015[1]	----	3,015	800	6,503	14,450	1,476	6,048	816	----	----	2,312	6,480	----	62,616	69,119

[1] Preliminary. *Source: Agricultural Statistics Board, U.S. Department of Agiculture (ASB-USDA)*

Cold Storage Stocks of Frozen[2] Onions in the United States, on First of Month   In Thousands of Pounds

Year	Jan.	Feb.	Mar.	Apr.	May	June	July	Aug.	Sept.	Oct.	Nov.	Dec.
2010	38,967	38,348	35,231	29,333	26,484	25,109	25,119	23,805	30,594	32,146	29,197	30,444
2011	37,504	33,942	34,401	43,066	49,076	58,596	53,773	56,913	68,638	74,735	58,288	68,902
2012	73,678	68,208	67,465	71,295	72,894	75,430	75,960	74,299	82,451	62,101	65,917	59,641
2013	58,030	53,882	55,947	52,566	52,835	51,059	50,557	53,048	50,048	50,252	49,506	52,770
2014	49,806	50,425	47,054	46,423	46,175	50,046	55,773	64,252	60,862	52,736	50,282	45,791
2015[1]	45,001	43,865	48,055	48,960	52,702	56,381	56,673	53,472	53,428	48,106	48,935	46,921

[1] Preliminary. *Source: National Agricultural Statistics Service, U.S. Department of Agiculture (NASS-USDA)*

Average Price Received by Growers for Onions in the United States   In Dollars Per Hundred Pounds (Cwt.)

Year	Jan.	Feb.	Mar.	Apr.	May	June	July	Aug.	Sept.	Oct.	Nov.	Dec.	Season Average
2010	11.20	15.00	34.20	29.90	19.30	16.10	16.30	13.10	11.70	9.61	12.10	11.60	15.60
2011	12.40	9.97	8.04	10.80	15.10	22.40	19.00	9.46	8.59	7.82	9.35	9.48	10.90
2012	6.59	4.90	7.07	18.80	26.30	21.30	27.50	30.50	11.10	10.10	12.40	17.50	14.20
2013	32.30	28.80	21.10	NQ	NQ	NQ	NQ	NQ	NQ	NQ	NQ	NQ	15.00
2014	NQ	NQ	NQ	25.10	27.20	17.30	23.50	14.50	11.90	10.30	9.12	9.56	13.60
2015[1]	8.39	7.67	7.89	18.90	19.30	30.20	31.90	15.60	11.80	12.50	12.00	12.20	17.60

[1] Preliminary.   NQ = Not quoted.   *Source: Economic Research Service, U.S. Department of Agiculture (ERS-USDA)*

Oranges and Orange Juice

The orange tree is a semi-tropical, non-deciduous tree, and the fruit is technically a hesperidium, a kind of berry. The three major varieties of oranges include the sweet orange, the sour orange, and the mandarin orange (or tangerine). In the U.S., only sweet oranges are grown commercially. Those include Hamlin, Jaffa, navel, Pineapple, blood orange, and Valencia. Sour oranges are mainly used in marmalade and in liqueurs such as triple sec and curacao.

Frozen Concentrated Orange Juice (FCOJ) was developed in 1945, which led to oranges becoming the main fruit crop in the U.S. The world's largest producer of orange juice is Brazil, followed by Florida. Two to four medium-sized oranges will produce about 1 cup of juice, and modern mechanical extractors can remove the juice from 400 to 700 oranges per minute. Before juice extraction, orange oil is recovered from the peel. Approximately 50% of the orange weight is juice, the remainder is peel, pulp, and seeds, which are dried to produce nutritious cattle feed.

The U.S. marketing year for oranges begins December 1 of the first year shown (e.g., the 2005-06 marketing year extends from December 1, 2005 to November 30, 2006). Orange juice futures prices are subject to upward spikes during the U.S. hurricane season (officially June 1 to November 30), and the Florida freeze season (late-November through March).

Frozen concentrated orange juice future and options are traded on ICE Futures U.S. The ICE orange juice futures contract calls for the delivery of 15,000 pounds of orange solids and is priced in terms of cents per pound.

Prices – ICE orange juice futures prices (Barchart.com symbol OJ) declined into Q3-2015 as the plunge in the Brazilian real to a 12-year low against the dollar gave Brazil's orange producers, the biggest in the world, incentive to boost more-profitable exports with the weak real. FCOJ prices posted a 3-1/2 year low of 103.45 cents in September as the Atlantic hurricane season passed with no damage to Florida's orange groves. However, FCOJ prices rallied sharply in Q4-2015 and in November posted a 1-1/2 year high, and the high for 2015, at 160.70 cents as the persistence of citrus-greening disease decimated Florida's orange crop. The USDA in the December WASDE report cut its Florida 2015/16 orange crop production estimate to 69 million boxes, down -29% y/y and a 52-year low. It was also the fourth consecutive seasonal decline, the longest slump since 1913. The surge in prices, though, curbed demand and FCOJ prices retreated and finished 2015 unchanged y/y at 140.05 cents.

Supply – World production of oranges in the 2014-15 marketing year fell -4.3% yr/yr to 48.797 million metric tons. The world's largest producers of oranges in 2014-15 were Brazil with 33.4% of world production, followed by the U.S. (12.5%), and Mexico (8.8%).

U.S. production of oranges in 2013-14 (latest data) fell -17.7% yr/yr to 156.376 million boxes (1 box equals 90 lbs). Florida's production in 2013-14 fell -21.7% yr/yr to 104.600 million boxes and California's production fell -8.3% to 50.000 million boxes.

World Production of Oranges   In Thousands of Metric Tons

Year	Argen-tina	Australia	Brazil	China	Egypt	European Union	Mexico	Morocco	South Africa	Turkey	United States	Vietnam	World Total
2006-07	990	419	18,482	4,800	2,054	6,486	4,248	721	1,412	1,536	6,917	623	49,520
2007-08	940	403	16,850	5,450	2,138	6,492	4,297	732	1,526	1,427	9,141	655	50,720
2008-09	900	430	17,014	6,000	2,372	6,530	4,193	790	1,445	1,430	8,281	679	50,818
2009-10	770	380	15,830	6,500	2,401	6,244	4,051	823	1,459	1,690	7,478	694	49,151
2010-11	850	300	22,603	5,900	2,430	6,198	4,080	904	1,428	1,710	8,078	730	55,942
2011-12	565	390	20,482	6,900	2,350	6,023	3,666	850	1,466	1,650	8,166	530	53,830
2012-13	550	435	16,361	7,000	2,450	5,890	4,400	784	1,659	1,600	7,501	520	49,871
2013-14[1]	800	430	17,870	7,600	2,570	6,550	4,533	1,001	1,715	1,700	6,140	520	52,136
2014-15[2]	1,000	430	16,320	6,900	2,630	5,959	4,158	868	1,700	1,650	5,786	520	48,644
2015-16[3]	1,000	455	16,728	7,000	2,750	6,107	3,534	920	1,690	1,700	4,758	520	47,904

[1] Preliminary.   [2] Estimate.   [3] Forecast.   NA = Not available.   *Source: Foreign Agricultural Service, U.S. Department of Agriculture (FAS-USDA)*

Salient Statistics of Oranges & Orange Juice in the United States

	Production[4]					Florida Crop Processed				Frozen Concentrated Orange Juice - Florida			
Year	California	Florida	Total U.S.	Farm Price $ Per Box	Farm Value Million $	Frozen Concen-trates	Chilled Products	Total Pro-cessed	Yield Per Box Gallons[5]	Carry-in	Pack	Total Supply	Total Season Movement
	Million Boxes					Million Boxes				In Millions of Gallons (42 Deg. Brix)			
2005-06	61.0	147.7	210.8	8.60	1,829.9	51.9	88.7	141.7	1.6	107.8	85.2	193.0	160.8
2006-07	46.0	129.0	177.3	12.56	2,216.5	48.0	74.5	123.4	1.6	67.2	79.6	146.8	149.2
2007-08	62.0	170.2	234.4	9.36	2,198.8	80.8	84.7	165.5	1.7	52.1	135.6	187.7	137.7
2008-09	46.5	162.5	210.7	9.22	1,970.1	72.5	82.6	156.2	1.7	108.0	153.9	261.9	143.9
2009-10	57.5	133.7	192.8	10.24	1,997.2	52.7	74.9	128.2	1.6	118.0	82.3	200.3	130.2
2010-11	62.5	140.5	204.9	10.90	2,230.4	51.8	82.6	135.2	1.6	95.0	82.1	177.1	148.5
2011-12	58.0	146.7	206.1	12.70	2,621.6	65.4	75.5	141.3	1.6	51.6	175.4	227.0	124.3
2012-13[1]	54.5	133.6	189.9	10.85	2,073.6	48.0	79.2	128.2	1.6	61.1	127.9	189.0	108.4
2013-14[2]	49.5	104.7	156.0	14.29	2,254.3	22.7	76.0	99.5	1.6				
2014-15[3]	49.0	96.8	147.3	13.22	1,960.6				1.5				

[1] Preliminary.   [2] Estimate.   [3] Forecast.   4/ Fruit ripened on trees, but destroyed prior to picking not included.   [5] 42 deg. Brix equivalent.
Source: Economic Research Service, U.S. Department of Agriculture (ERS-USDA); Florida Department of Citrus

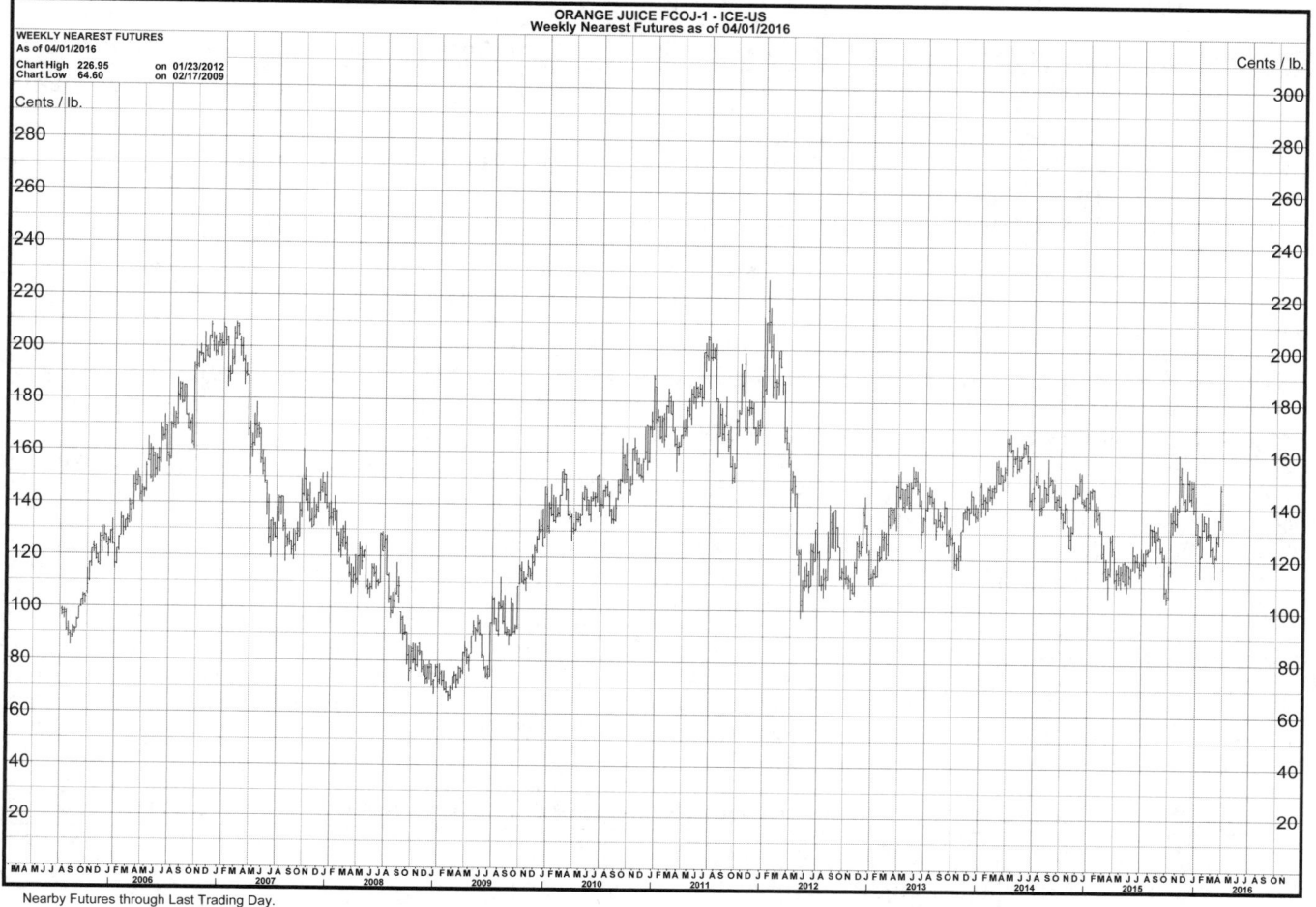

ORANGE JUICE FCOJ-1 - ICE-US
Weekly Nearest Futures as of 04/01/2016

WEEKLY NEAREST FUTURES
As of 04/01/2016

Chart High 226.95 on 01/23/2012
Chart Low 64.60 on 02/17/2009

Nearby Futures through Last Trading Day.

Volume of Trading of Frozen Concentrated Orange Juice Futures in New York   In Contracts

Year	Jan.	Feb.	Mar.	Apr.	May	June	July	Aug.	Sept.	Oct.	Nov.	Dec.	Total
2006	65,978	98,034	82,293	92,312	73,517	87,429	63,429	84,160	50,871	95,955	54,975	74,743	923,696
2007	70,773	84,076	63,417	87,759	59,937	84,150	50,721	78,502	48,392	103,218	45,539	69,308	845,792
2008	57,421	78,860	52,166	80,331	43,942	70,780	51,859	67,402	41,353	78,327	29,013	59,058	710,512
2009	28,514	63,757	31,766	67,156	30,396	81,964	56,197	65,286	40,276	86,071	28,426	77,186	656,995
2010	55,002	62,671	42,726	73,654	36,599	63,734	37,098	64,224	50,953	72,996	34,959	96,967	691,583
2011	39,184	63,134	43,077	63,680	41,142	89,150	28,260	80,733	32,920	59,502	24,493	62,335	627,610
2012	59,578	68,746	29,672	58,405	42,001	56,218	28,654	57,465	31,796	51,993	36,729	65,518	586,775
2013	46,432	54,711	37,532	67,361	31,399	63,622	26,724	43,047	29,937	40,275	24,295	39,684	505,019
2014	27,695	39,560	29,605	51,337	24,033	51,811	21,141	36,438	18,068	35,974	27,182	35,685	398,529
2015	21,377	37,435	34,855	39,065	23,789	42,032	18,914	42,607	24,694	48,774	28,965	36,060	398,567

Contract size = 15,000 lbs.   *Source: ICE Futures U.S. (ICE)*

Average Open Interest of Frozen Concentrated Orange Juice Futures in New York   In Contracts

Year	Jan.	Feb.	Mar.	Apr.	May	June	July	Aug.	Sept.	Oct.	Nov.	Dec.
2006	30,485	35,479	36,603	36,617	34,418	29,180	27,169	29,872	29,515	30,852	29,873	28,342
2007	29,484	28,370	32,312	29,430	28,830	31,917	30,457	29,540	28,335	29,599	26,608	27,412
2008	24,919	26,603	29,806	32,831	32,102	33,136	28,353	31,133	29,112	31,060	28,254	28,802
2009	27,889	28,234	26,905	27,982	29,370	31,608	30,602	31,281	28,806	30,805	29,677	34,210
2010	35,442	34,435	35,991	31,854	29,524	29,143	26,424	27,037	27,400	29,340	28,707	29,996
2011	31,885	31,086	27,618	27,153	31,594	36,039	35,046	28,253	23,967	25,308	27,118	27,105
2012	26,892	23,743	21,892	20,278	22,652	25,461	21,779	23,214	23,078	23,687	22,412	24,458
2013	20,672	20,900	18,819	20,972	20,719	22,432	19,760	19,241	16,646	15,809	14,609	14,636
2014	15,542	15,905	16,793	18,372	18,487	17,605	13,552	13,068	12,175	13,385	13,798	12,089
2015	10,973	12,605	15,506	15,799	14,630	14,192	12,421	13,196	13,358	15,172	14,651	14,759

Contract size = 15,000 lbs.   *Source: ICE Futures U.S. (ICE)*

ORANGES AND ORANGE JUICE

Cold Storage Stocks of Orange Juice Concentrate[2] in the U.S., on First of Month   In Millions of Pounds

Year	Jan.	Feb.	Mar.	Apr.	May	June	July	Aug.	Sept.	Oct.	Nov.	Dec.
2006	1,044.7	1,065.9	1,076.8	1,005.7	1,087.5	1,157.7	1,104.1	1,002.6	888.8	776.0	714.3	650.3
2007	678.2	726.0	751.1	825.1	901.5	960.7	909.7	849.1	761.2	620.4	582.2	563.7
2008	682.5	837.8	942.4	1,031.9	1,210.6	1,442.7	1,514.9	1,424.9	1,319.4	1,199.7	1,086.0	1,034.6
2009	1,088.0	1,193.2	1,261.2	1,291.4	1,415.4	1,497.2	1,519.7	1,404.3	1,316.7	1,252.2	1,150.3	1,127.2
2010	1,185.2	1,289.7	1,300.4	1,305.1	1,377.6	1,434.2	1,353.1	1,235.7	1,133.9	1,036.8	903.6	795.3
2011	809.7	834.7	869.2	842.0	835.2	864.5	797.3	732.0	641.5	588.9	522.3	479.6
2012	632.1	710.1	788.8	889.0	1,006.7	1,057.6	956.6	857.9	773.6	675.6	606.4	598.0
2013	695.4	781.6	875.4	946.8	1,021.3	1,042.3	996.2	915.0	864.6	795.8	785.9	732.6
2014	739.5	750.5	799.3	813.0	877.8	872.9	853.7	815.9	773.0	712.0	721.9	676.8
2015[1]	734.8	720.7	728.4	832.3	857.5	947.9	943.8	868.0	807.8	757.1	695.9	641.7

[1] Preliminary.   [2] Adjusted to 42.0 degrees Brix equivalent (9.896 pounds per gallon).   Source: Agricultural Statistics Board, U.S. Department of Agriculture (ASB-USDA)

Producer Price Index of Frozen Orange Juice Concentrate   1982 = 100

Year	Jan.	Feb.	Mar.	Apr.	May	June	July	Aug.	Sept.	Oct.	Nov.	Dec.	Average
2006	138.3	142.1	150.1	160.9	161.0	164.1	172.3	174.8	185.4	197.6	208.9	208.7	172.0
2007	198.1	191.7	198.5	179.6	187.7	184.1	173.6	171.5	152.9	159.3	162.6	168.2	177.3
2008	168.0	166.6	160.0	159.2	159.3	159.6	126.0	121.8	121.4	116.8	115.2	124.3	141.5
2009	124.6	124.4	124.4	117.6	125.0	118.0	118.0	119.8	119.1	119.0	119.0	128.8	121.5
2010	141.3	141.1	141.5	144.5	144.5	144.5	144.7	145.0	150.0	150.4	150.4	150.6	145.7
2011	164.1	163.9	163.9	169.6	169.8	170.4	170.8	188.8	187.6	181.7	190.5	175.7	174.7
2012	177.5	188.7	184.9	173.4	170.7	133.5	131.6	130.0	127.0	125.5	123.1	132.0	149.8
2013	130.8	122.6	123.0	124.1	145.6	148.6	145.5	149.2	149.2	136.7	140.1	140.9	138.0
2014	138.3	139.0	135.1	184.0	184.4	184.6	184.5	184.0	190.2	183.4	178.3	178.1	172.0
2015[1]	177.8	178.2	178.2	176.5	180.3	178.3	178.8	178.6	178.3	178.6	179.0	180.4	178.6

[1] Preliminary.   Source: Bureau of Labor Statistics, U.S. Department of Labor (BLS)

Average Price Received by Farmers for Oranges (Equivalent On-Tree) in the U.S.   In Dollars Per Box

Year	Jan.	Feb.	Mar.	Apr.	May	June	July	Aug.	Sept.	Oct.	Nov.	Dec.	Average
2006	5.16	5.27	5.78	6.44	7.13	7.05	6.56	12.03	17.96	13.89	6.95	7.28	8.46
2007	8.25	8.11	10.58	10.62	11.12	11.07	8.95	8.81	7.84	9.60	8.14	5.80	9.07
2008	5.77	5.83	6.20	6.40	7.01	6.75	5.79	4.78	5.92	5.57	7.53	5.39	6.08
2009	5.74	6.04	7.08	6.54	6.61	7.04	7.38	8.58	W	W	11.61	6.13	7.28
2010	6.41	6.78	7.97	7.49	8.00	8.85	7.10	7.49	6.88	6.96	11.47	6.66	7.67
2011	6.58	6.50	6.77	7.00	7.53	8.46	7.74	7.53	7.60	8.47	8.86	7.29	7.53
2012	7.65	8.25	8.52	9.53	10.35	12.49	9.60	7.81	9.08	9.57	8.92	6.64	9.03
2013	6.85	7.05	7.84	8.46	9.27	12.85	10.64	10.00	12.24	12.94	13.07	6.93	9.85
2014	8.24	10.71	10.90	9.68	10.27	11.12	14.60	14.78	15.84	13.82	16.26	9.43	12.14
2015[1]	9.35	9.85	10.83	9.85	9.70	10.59	10.79	12.24	14.80	15.28	17.56	9.71	11.71

[1] Preliminary.   Source: Economic Research Service, U.S. Department of Agriculture (ERS-USDA)

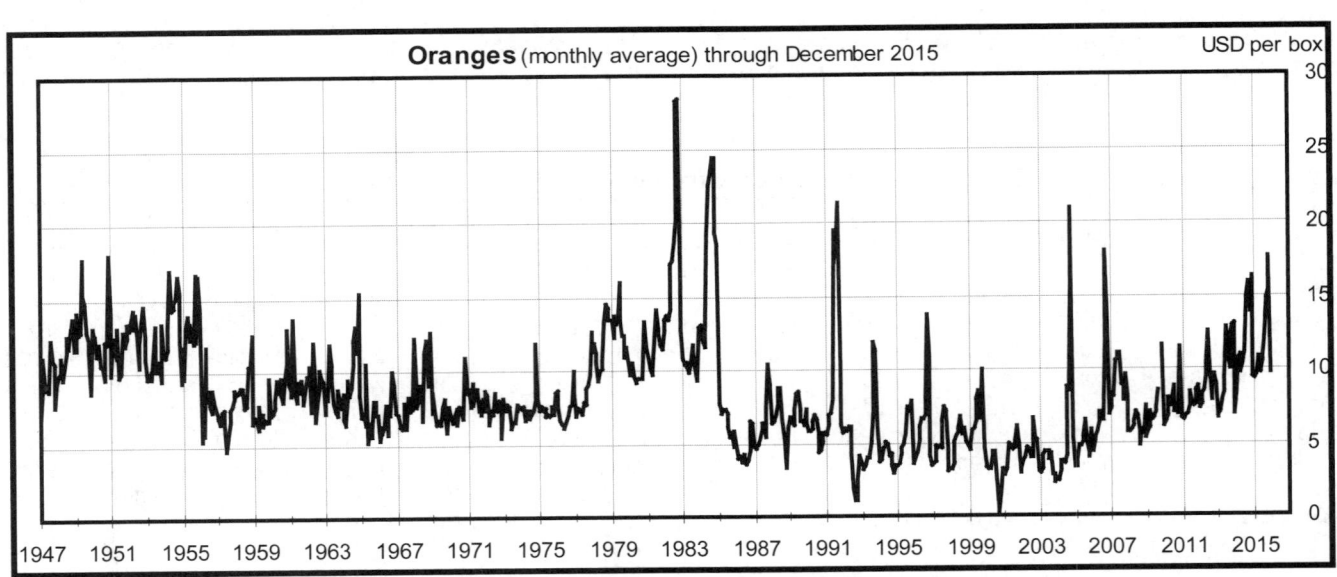

Oranges (monthly average) through December 2015   USD per box

Palm Oil

Palm oil is an edible vegetable oil produced from the flesh of the fruit of the oil palm tree. The oil palm tree is a tropical palm tree that is a native of the west coast of Africa and is different from the coconut palm tree. The fruit of the oil palm tree is reddish, about the size of a large plum, and grows in large bunches. A single seed, the palm kernel, is contained in each fruit. Oil is extracted from both the pulp of the fruit (becoming palm oil) and the kernel (palm kernel oil). About 1 metric ton of palm kernel oil is obtained for every 10 metric tons of palm oil.

Palm oil is commercially used in soap, ointments, cosmetics, detergents, and machinery lubricants. It is also used worldwide as cooking oil, shortening, and margarine. Palm kernel oil is a lighter oil and is used exclusively for food use. Crude palm oil and crude palm kernel oil are traded on the Bursa Malaysia Derivatives Berhad (BMD). Futures are also traded on the Dalian Commodity Exchange (DCE), Indonesia Commodity & Derivatives Exchange (ICDX), and the National Commodity & Derivatives Exchange (NCDEX).

Prices – The monthly average wholesale price of palm oil (CIF, bulk, U.S. ports) in 2014 fell by -3.1% yr/yr to 39.86 cents per pound, below the 2011 record high of 55.98 cents per pound.

Supply – World production of palm oil in the 2015-16 marketing year rose by +1.3% to 62.219 million metric tons. World palm oil production has grown by over twenty times the production level of 1.922 million metric tons seen back in 1970. Indonesia and Malaysia are the world's two major global producers of palm oil. Indonesian production remained unchanged yr/yr at the record high of 33.000 million metric tons in 2015-16 and Indonesian production accounted for 53.0% of world production. Malaysian production in 2015-16 rose +0.6% to a record high of 20.000 million metric tons and Malaysian production accounted for 32.1% of world production. Other smaller global producers include Thailand with 3.5% of world production, Columbia with 1.9% and Nigeria with 1.6%.

Demand – U.S. total disappearance of palm oil in 2015-16 rose +5.1% yr/yr to 1.345 million metric tons which was a new record high.

Trade – World palm oil exports in 2015-16 rose by +0.3% to 46.901 million metric tons, which was a new record high. The world's largest exporters are Indonesia with a 52.2% share of world exports and Malaysia with a share of 38.5%. World palm oil imports in 2015-16 rose +1.8% to 45.441 million metric tons. The world's largest importers are India with a 21.2% share of world imports and European Union with a 15.3% share.

World Production of Palm Oil   In Thousands of Metric Tons

Crop Year	Brazil	Colombia	Costa Rica	Cote d'Ivoire	Ecuador	Guatemala	Honduras	Indonesia	Malaysia	Nigeria	Papua New Guinea	Thailand	World Total
2006-07	190	714	189	281	352	125	195	16,600	15,290	810	422	1,170	37,581
2007-08	205	733	199	289	396	153	278	18,000	17,567	820	447	1,050	41,418
2008-09	230	778	207	345	418	194	280	20,500	17,259	850	501	1,540	44,450
2009-10	250	805	227	330	429	177	275	22,000	17,763	850	510	1,287	46,372
2010-11	270	753	242	360	380	231	320	23,600	18,211	971	488	1,832	49,239
2011-12	310	945	260	371	473	291	395	26,200	18,202	970	580	1,892	52,582
2012-13	340	974	230	418	540	365	425	28,500	19,321	970	520	2,135	56,422
2013-14[1]	340	1,041	210	415	565	434	460	30,500	20,161	970	500	2,000	59,383
2014-15[2]	340	1,110	210	415	485	448	470	33,000	19,879	970	520	1,800	61,432
2015-16[3]	340	1,174	250	415	510	470	490	33,000	20,000	970	580	2,200	62,219

[1] Preliminary.   [2] Estimate.   [3] Forecast.   *Source: The Oil World*

World Trade of Palm Oil   In Thousands of Metric Tons

	Imports						Exports						
Crop Year	China	European Union	India	Pakistan	Other	World Total	Benin	European Union	Indonesia	Malaysia	Papua/New Guinea	United Arab Emirates	World Total
2006-07	5,139	4,339	3,650	1,618	12,389	27,135	269	162	11,419	13,766	449	334	28,542
2007-08	5,223	4,967	5,013	1,958	13,499	30,660	358	134	13,969	15,040	451	336	32,641
2008-09	6,118	5,509	6,867	1,957	13,548	33,999	352	131	15,964	15,990	496	232	35,217
2009-10	5,760	5,442	6,603	1,989	15,617	35,411	466	144	16,573	16,610	520	344	36,565
2010-11	5,711	4,944	6,661	2,064	17,245	36,625	255	200	16,423	17,151	578	400	38,081
2011-12	5,841	5,707	7,473	2,218	17,584	38,823	253	169	18,452	17,586	585	385	39,785
2012-13	6,589	6,812	8,364	2,246	17,853	41,864	430	135	20,373	18,524	564	217	43,136
2013-14[1]	5,573	6,941	7,820	2,758	18,724	41,816	600	162	21,719	17,344	539	250	43,200
2014-15[2]	5,696	6,800	9,129	2,830	20,170	44,625	550	160	25,300	17,378	575	250	46,777
2015-16[3]	5,700	6,950	9,625	3,200	19,966	45,441	580	160	24,500	18,050	590	250	46,901

[1] Preliminary.   [2] Estimate.   [3] Forecast.   *Source: The Oil World*

PALM OIL

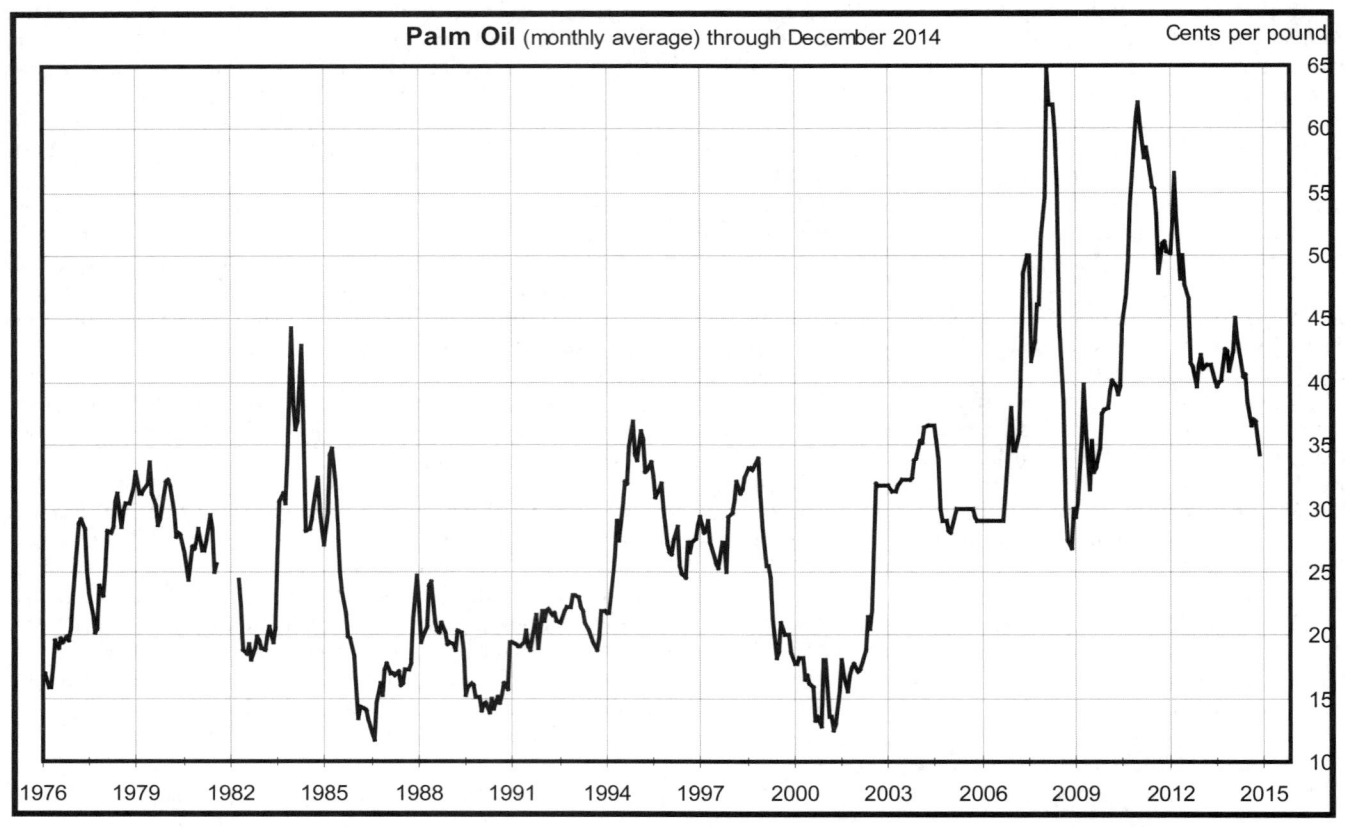

Palm Oil (monthly average) through December 2014 — Cents per pound

Supply and Distribution of Palm Oil in the United States   In Thousands of Metric Tons

Crop Year Beginning Oct. 1	Stocks Oct. 1	Imports	Total Supply	Edible Products	Inedible Products	Total End Products	Total Disappearance	Exports	U.S. Import Value[4]	Malaysia, F.O.B., RBD	Palm Kernel Oil, Malaysia, C.I.F Rotterdam
				------- In Millions of Pounds -------					--------- U.S. $ Per Metric Ton ----------		
2006-07	94.0	692.0	786.0	568.5	W	568.5	635.8	58.7	----	685	768
2007-08	91.5	954.7	1,046.2	789.3	W	789.3	934.7	38.3	----	1053	1248
2008-09	73.2	1,035.5	1,108.7	973.6	W	973.6	917.0	62.1	----	628	662
2009-10	129.6	996.6	1,126.2	1,140.8	W	1,140.8	894.6	80.9	----	807	972
2010-11	150.7	979.7	1,130.4	1,049.7	W	1,049.7	887.6	97.8	----	1146	1741
2011-12	145.0	1,030.1	1,175.1	NA	NA	NA	964.7	84.0	----	1053	1220
2012-13	126.3	1,285.1	1,411.4	----	----	----	1,163.4	103.1	----	835	836
2013-14[1]	145.0	1,227.6	1,372.6	----	----	----	1,189.9	76.7	----	867	1146
2014-15[2]	155.0	1,140.0	1,295.0	----	----	----	1,280.0	88.0	----	694	1000
2015-16[3]	165.0	1,180.0	1,345.0	----	----	----	1,345.0	23.0	----		

[1] Preliminary. [2] Estimate. [3] Forecast. [4] Market value in the foreign country, excluding import duties, ocean freight and marine insurance.
W = Withheld. *Sources: The Oil World; Economic Research Service, U.S. Department of Agriculture (ERS-USDA)*

Average Wholesale Palm Oil Prices, CIF, Bulk, U.S. Ports   In Cents Per Pound

Year	Jan.	Feb.	Mar.	Apr.	May	June	July	Aug.	Sept.	Oct.	Nov.	Dec.	Average
2005	28.20	28.00	28.67	30.00	30.00	30.00	30.00	30.00	30.00	30.00	29.25	29.00	29.43
2006	29.00	29.00	29.00	29.00	29.00	29.00	29.00	29.00	29.00	29.00	31.00	35.75	29.73
2007	38.00	34.50	34.50	36.00	42.38	48.63	50.00	NA	41.67	43.19	46.20	46.20	41.93
2008	51.48	54.66	64.63	61.96	61.90	59.70	55.41	44.43	38.52	30.11	27.41	26.91	48.09
2009	29.98	29.32	30.32	35.46	39.86	36.45	31.40	35.39	32.90	33.24	34.66	37.53	33.88
2010	37.83	37.91	39.35	40.11	39.60	38.97	39.64	44.57	47.00	49.55	54.00	58.60	43.93
2011	60.88	62.06	60.44	57.80	58.44	57.56	55.40	55.25	53.25	48.63	51.00	51.05	55.98
2012	50.25	50.19	52.60	56.56	52.94	48.20	50.06	47.75	46.63	41.44	41.25	39.69	48.13
2013	41.38	42.06	41.00	41.38	41.35	41.31	40.19	39.70	40.00	40.19	42.65	42.38	41.13
2014	40.90	42.50	45.00	43.44	42.40	40.38	40.63	38.35	36.56	37.00	36.94	34.19	39.86

Source: Economic Research Service, U.S. Department of Agriculture (ERS-USDA)

Paper

The earliest known paper that is still in existence was made from cotton rags around 150 AD. Around 800 AD, paper made its appearance in Egypt but was not manufactured there until 900 AD. The Moors introduced the use of paper to Europe, and around 1150, the first papermaking mill was established in Spain, followed by England in 1495, and the U.S. in 1690.

During the 17th and 18th centuries, the increased usage of paper created a shortage of cotton rags, which were the only source for papermaking. The solution to this problem lead to the introduction of the ground-wood process of pulp-making in 1840 and the first chemical pulp process 10 years later.

Today, the paper and paperboard industries, including newsprint, are sensitive to the economic cycle. As the economy strengthens, paper use increases, and vice versa.

Prices – The average monthly index price (1982 = 100) for paperboard in 2015 fell -2.20% yr/yr to 243.1, below last year's record high of 248.6. The average monthly producer price index of standard newsprint paper in 2015 fell by -12.0% to 113.6, well below the 12-year high of 151.8 posted in 2006.

Supply – U.S. production of paper and paperboard in 2014 (latest data) fell -1.3% yr/yr to 71.767 million metric tons. The U.S. is the world's largest producer of paper and paperboard by far, followed by Germany with 22.540 million metric tons and Canada with 11.102 million metric tons.

U.S. production of newsprint fell by −2.4% yr/yr to a record low of 414.6 metric tons per month in 2005 which is the latest data available. U.S. production of newsprint is second in the world, after Canada, which had production of 657.167 metric tons per month in 2005.

Production of Paper and Paperboard by Selected Countries — In Thousands of Metric Tons

Year	Austria	Canada	Finland	France	Germany	Italy	Nether-lands	Norway	Russia/3	Spain	Sweden	United Kingdom	United States
2009	4,606	12,823	10,602	8,332	20,870	8,404	2,609	1,577	7,373	5,700	10,932	4,293	71,355
2010	5,009	12,755	11,758	8,830	23,072	9,087	2,859	1,695	5,606	6,193	11,410	4,300	77,689
2011	4,901	12,057	11,329	8,527	22,706	9,130	2,748	1,496	7,549	6,203	11,298	4,342	76,431
2012	5,004	10,756	10,847	8,354	22,603	8,588	2,761	1,209	7,661	6,177	11,417	4,292	75,423
2013	4,837	11,174	10,592	8,043	22,401	8,652	2,814	1,079	7,740	6,733	10,792	4,561	72,744
2014[1]	4,865	11,102	10,408	8,191	22,540	8,648	2,814	1,023	8,023	6,680	10,419	4,393	71,767

[1] Preliminary.   *Source: Food and Agriculture Organization of the United Nations (FAO)*

Production of Newsprint by Selected Countires (Monthly Average) — In Thousands of Metric Tons

Year	Australia	Brazil	Canada	China	Finland	France	Germany	India	Japan	Rep. of Korea	Russia/3	Sweden	United States
2010	NA	NA	NA	358.9	NA	NA	213.4	80.9	280.1	132.6	162.8	201.2	NA
2011	NA	NA	NA	296.3	NA	NA	213.4	74.4	267.1	130.6	160.8	188.2	NA
2012	NA	NA	NA	326.1	NA	NA	184.3	NA	271.1	126.1	151.7	167.7	NA
2013	NA	NA	NA	305.4	NA	NA	176.4	NA	268.2	124.1	132.1	127.4	NA
2014[1]	NA	NA	NA	282.5	NA	NA	NA	NA	261.1	118.1	136.3	104.0	NA
2015[2]				282.4					252.5	114.1	123.5	101.2	

[1] Preliminary.   [2] Estimate.   NA = Not available.   *Source: Food and Agriculture Organization of the United Nations (FAO)*

Index Price of Paperboard   (1982 = 100)

Year	Jan.	Feb.	Mar.	Apr.	May	June	July	Aug.	Sept.	Oct.	Nov.	Dec.	Average
2009	224.6	221.3	216.7	211.8	205.3	203.0	202.8	202.0	202.4	199.1	198.8	197.9	207.1
2010	198.0	210.3	212.6	214.5	229.2	231.4	232.2	232.3	236.3	234.2	233.7	233.8	224.9
2011	233.6	230.6	230.7	230.6	230.0	232.0	232.6	231.6	231.6	230.0	226.3	226.4	230.5
2012	226.4	226.3	225.9	226.1	226.0	225.9	224.9	226.1	226.6	230.3	235.5	235.7	228.0
2013	235.7	235.8	236.8	236.8	241.1	246.4	247.7	249.3	249.0	249.0	248.8	248.3	243.7
2014	249.0	249.6	249.7	249.2	249.3	249.3	249.2	248.8	247.7	247.3	247.0	246.9	248.6
2015[1]	246.9	245.2	244.5	242.6	243.6	242.6	241.9	241.4	242.2	242.1	242.9	242.0	243.2

[1] Preliminary.   *Source: Bureau of Labor Statistics, U.S. Department of Commerce (BLS) (0914)*

Producer Price Index of Standard Newsprint   (1982 = 100)

Year	Jan.	Feb.	Mar.	Apr.	May	June	July	Aug.	Sept.	Oct.	Nov.	Dec.	Average
2009	162.3	158.9	153.0	141.1	129.6	120.3	107.5	105.3	105.5	107.7	111.0	114.6	126.4
2010	116.5	116.9	118.3	114.8	122.3	124.8	128.6	129.5	132.5	133.5	135.3	134.7	125.6
2011	137.3	137.8	136.2	136.1	136.0	137.5	135.2	137.1	138.2	138.1	138.8	138.4	137.2
2012	138.9	138.6	143.9	144.1	144.1	138.7	138.4	138.2	138.3	138.1	137.9	138.1	139.8
2013	136.3	132.6	130.1	129.7	129.1	127.8	130.8	129.6	129.4	129.9	131.3	130.3	130.6
2014	130.7	130.5	130.2	129.2	128.3	129.2	129.1	129.0	128.7	128.4	128.1	127.2	129.1
2015[1]	126.3	123.3	121.4	119.1	116.1	114.4	112.9	106.5	106.3	105.6	105.4	105.6	113.6

[1] Preliminary.   *Source: Bureau of Labor Statistics, U.S. Department of Commerce (BLS) (0913-02)*

Peanuts and Peanut Oil

Peanuts are the edible seeds of a plant from the pea family. Although called a nut, the peanut is actually a legume. Ancient South American Inca Indians were the first to grind peanuts to make peanut butter. Peanuts originated in Brazil and were later brought to the U.S. via Africa. The first major use of peanuts was as feed for pigs. It wasn't until the Civil War that peanuts were used as human food when both Northern and Southern troops used the peanut as a food source during hard times. In 1903, Dr. George Washington Carver, a talented botanist who is considered the "father of commercial peanuts," introduced peanuts as a rotation crop in cotton-growing areas. Carver discovered over 300 uses for the peanut including shaving cream, leather dye, coffee, ink, cheese, and shampoo.

Peanuts come in many varieties, but there are four basic types grown in the U.S.: Runner, Spanish, Valencia, and Virginia. Over half of Runner peanuts are used to make peanut butter. Spanish peanuts are primarily used to make candies and peanut oil. Valencia peanuts are the sweetest of the four types. Virginia peanuts are mainly roasted and sold in and out of the shell.

Peanut oil is extracted from shelled and crushed peanuts through hydraulic pressing, expelled pressing, or solvent extraction. Crude peanut oil is used as a flavoring agent, salad oil, and cooking oil. Refined, bleached and deodorized peanut oil is used for cooking and in margarines and shortenings. The by-product called press cake is used for cattle feed along with the tops of the plants after the pods are removed. The dry shells can be burned as fuel.

Prices – The average monthly price received by farmers for peanuts (in the shell) in the first six months of the 2015-16 marketing year (Aug/July) fell -12.3% to 19.3 cents per pound. The record high is 34.7 cents posted in 1990-91. The average monthly price of peanut oil in the 2015-16 marketing year (through January 2015) rose +1.3% yr/yr to 58.09 cents per pound, below the 2007-08 record high of 100.91 cents per pound.

Supply – World peanut production in 2015-16 rose+1.6% to 40.066 million metric tons, slightly below the 2012-13 record high of 40.453 million metric tons. The world's largest peanut producers are China with 41.7% of world production, India with 10.2%, Nigeria with 7.5% and U.S. with 7.0%. U.S. peanut production in the 2015-16 marketing year rose by +19.8% to 6.213 billion pounds, below the 2012-13 record high of 6.763 billion pounds.

U.S. farmers harvested 1.568 million acres of peanuts in 2015-16, up +18.6% yr/yr. That was below the 16-year high harvest of 1.629 million acres in 2005-06. U.S. peanut yield in 2015-16 rose +1.0% yr/yr to 3,963 pounds per acre, slightly below the 2012-13 record high of 4,217 pounds per acre. The largest peanut producing states in the U.S.in 2015 are Georgia (with 55.9% of U.S. production), Florida (10.6%), Alabama (10.6%), Texas (9.5%), and North Carolina (4.8%). U.S. crude peanut oil production in 2015 rose +2.0% to 214.041 million pounds, which was only about 40% of the record high level of 358,195 million pounds posted in 1996.

Demand – U.S. disposition of peanuts in 2015-16 rose by +9.5% yr/yr to 5.514 billion pounds. Of that disposition, 54.7% of the peanuts went for food, 20.2% for exports, 14.2% for crushing into peanut oil, and 10.9% for seed, loss and residual. The most popular type of peanut grown in the U.S. is the Runner peanut with 88.0% of U.S. production in 2015-16. This was followed by the Virginia peanut with 10.8% of production and the Spanish peanut far behind with only 1.3% of production. Peanut butter is a primary use for Runner and Virginia peanuts. It accounts for 62.9% of Runner peanut usage and 44.0% of Virginia peanut usage. In lagging third place, only about 5% of Spanish peanuts are used for peanut butter. Snack peanuts is also a key usage category and accounts for 39.5% of Virginia peanut usage, 24.4% of Spanish peanut usage, and 17.4% of Runner peanut usage. Candy accounts for 56.7% of Spanish peanut usage, 18.3% of Runner peanut usage, and 5.2% of Virginia peanut usage.

Trade – U.S. exports of peanuts in 2015-16 rose +3.1% yr/yr to 1.115 billion pounds. U.S. imports of peanuts fell by -5.6% yr/yr in 2014-15 to 85 million pounds.

World Production of Peanuts (in the Shell)   In Thousands of Metric Tons

Crop Year	Argentina	Burma	Cameroon	China	India	Indonesia	Nigeria	Senegal	Sudan	Tanzania	United States	Vietnam	World Total
2006-07	775	1,024	414	12,887	5,385	1,200	3,062	460	555	350	1,571	463	32,625
2007-08	800	1,088	449	13,027	6,800	1,150	2,847	331	564	408	1,666	510	34,048
2008-09	860	1,202	484	14,286	6,250	1,250	2,873	731	716	341	2,342	534	37,263
2009-10	836	1,305	503	14,708	4,900	1,250	2,978	1,033	942	348	1,675	525	36,183
2010-11	1,033	1,362	536	15,644	5,850	1,250	3,799	1,286	763	465	1,886	441	39,901
2011-12	1,020	1,399	564	16,046	5,500	1,165	2,963	528	1,185	651	1,660	471	38,456
2012-13	1,016	1,372	634	16,692	5,000	1,145	3,314	693	1,032	810	3,064	468	40,453
2013-14	997	1,375	636	16,972	5,650	1,160	3,000	677	1,767	900	1,893	455	41,116
2014-15[1]	1,188	1,375	640	16,482	4,900	1,150	3,000	669	963	800	2,354	473	39,419
2015-16[2]	1,070	1,375	550	16,700	4,100	1,130	3,000	725	1,871	800	2,819	485	40,066

[1] Preliminary.   [2] Estimate.   *Source: Foreign Agricultural Service, U.S. Department of Agriculture (FAS-USDA)*

Salient Statistics of Peanuts in the United States

Crop Year Beginning Aug. 1	Acreage Planted	Acreage Harvested for Nuts	Average Yield Per Acre In Lbs.	Production (1,000 Lbs)	Season Farm Price (Cents Lb.)	Farm Value (Million Dollars)	Exports Unshelled	Exports Shelled	Imports Unshelled	Imports Shelled
	------- 1,000 Acres ------						---------- In Thousands of Pounds ----------			
2006-07	1,243.0	1,210.0	2,863	3,464,250	17.7	612.8	603,000	----	60,962	----
2007-08	1,230.0	1,195.0	3,130	3,740,650	20.5	758.6	750,000	----	72,939	----
2008-09	1,534.0	1,507.0	3,426	5,162,400	23.0	1,193.6	727,000	----	85,788	----
2009-10	1,116.0	1,079.0	3,421	3,691,650	21.7	793.1	592,000	----	71,972	----
2010-11	1,288.0	1,255.0	3,312	4,156,840	22.5	938.6	606,000	----	64,592	----
2011-12	1,140.6	1,080.6	3,386	3,658,590	31.8	1,168.6	546,000	----	253,897	----
2012-13	1,638.0	1,604.0	4,211	6,753,880	30.1	2,026.3	1,175,000	----	115,000	----
2013-14	1,067.0	1,043.0	4,001	4,173,170	24.9	1,055.1	650,000	----	65,000	----
2014-15[1]	1,353.5	1,322.5	3,923	5,188,665	22.0	1,122.3				
2015-16[2]	1,625.0	1,567.0	3,963	6,210,590	18.75-21.25					

[1] Preliminary. [2] Estimate. *Source: Economic Research Service, U.S. Department of Agriculture (ERS-USDA)*

Supply and Disposition of Peanuts (Farmer's Stock Basis) & Support Program in the United States

Crop Year Beginning Aug. 1	Production	Imports	Stocks Aug. 1	Total	Exports	Crushed for Oil	Seed, Loss & Residual	Food	Total Disappearance	Support Price	Additional	Quantity (Mil. Lbs.)	% of Production
	------------------ Supply ------------------				--------------------- Disposition ---------------------					------ Government Support Program ------		Amount Put Under Support ---	
	--- In Millions of Pounds ---									--- Cents Per Lb. ---			
2007-08	3,741	73	1,520	5,265	750	496	471	2,517	4,234	355.00	495.0	1,363	74.2
2008-09	5,162	86	1,031	6,280	727	445	407	2,571	4,150	355.00	495.0	2,073	80.5
2009-10	3,692	72	2,130	5,894	592	435	569	2,675	4,271	355.00	495.0	1,674	90.7
2010-11	4,157	65	1,829	6,050	606	587	350	2,840	4,382	355.00	495.0	1,811	87.1
2011-12	3,659	254	1,516	5,428	546	604	470	2,805	4,425	355.00	495.0	1,402	77.1
2012-13	6,754	119	1,003	7,876	1,190	656	524	2,735	5,105	355.00	495.0	2,640	77.8
2013-14	4,173	88	2,771	7,032	1,096	663	530	2,886	5,174				
2014-15[1]	5,189	90	1,858	7,136	1,081	675	334	2,945	5,035				
2015-16[2]	6,211	85	2,101	8,397	1,115	785	599	3,014	5,513				

[1] Preliminary. [2] Estimate. *Source: Economic Research Service, U.S. Department of Agriculture (ERS-USDA)*

Production of Peanuts (Harvested for Nuts) in the United States, by States   In Thousands of Pounds

Crop Year	Alabama	Florida	Georgia	Mississippi	New Mexico	North Carolina	Oklahoma	South Carolina	Texas	Virginia	Total
2006	407,500	300,000	1,598,500	46,400	43,200	268,800	62,700	168,000	514,750	54,400	3,464,250
2007	400,350	321,300	1,622,400	59,400	32,000	261,000	57,800	173,600	691,900	52,500	3,740,650
2008	675,500	448,000	2,329,000	81,900	25,600	358,900	63,000	265,200	834,900	80,400	5,162,400
2009	495,000	336,000	1,797,800	54,000	21,700	244,200	42,900	148,800	506,850	44,400	3,691,650
2010	481,000	472,500	1,959,150	63,000	34,000	232,200	70,350	224,000	586,800	33,840	4,156,840
2011	489,700	549,500	1,645,750	56,000	19,800	291,600	54,600	240,900	249,240	61,500	3,658,590
2012	876,000	760,500	3,343,400	215,600	26,000	427,180	80,300	417,300	525,600	82,000	6,753,880
2013	489,900	517,450	1,887,180	122,100	21,700	315,900	59,200	273,000	423,540	63,200	4,173,170
2014	544,950	668,000	2,435,515	124,000	15,750	401,760	44,000	410,400	459,740	84,550	5,188,665
2015[1]	659,950	657,000	3,473,190	151,200	15,000	299,200	31,500	262,400	588,000	73,150	6,210,590

[1] Preliminary. *Source: Agricultural Statistics Board, U.S. Department of Agriculture (ASB-USDA)*

Supply and Reported Uses of Shelled Peanuts and Products in the United States   In Thousands of Pounds

Crop Year Beginning Aug. 1	Shelled Peanuts Stocks, Aug. 1 Edible	Shelled Peanuts Stocks, Aug. 1 Oil Stock[2]	Shelled Peanuts Production Edible	Shelled Peanuts Production Oil Stock[2]	Candy[3]	Snack[4]	Butter[5]	Other Products	Total	Shelled Peanuts Crushed[6]	Crude Oil Production	Cake & Meal Production
					------------------- Edible Grades Used In -------------------							
2006-07	510,097	21,499	2,415,495	347,243	373,684	415,131	993,445	9,397	1,791,657	385,375	166,450	223,537
2007-08	528,918	33,401	2,291,603	319,186	320,467	425,166	1,012,263	10,676	1,768,572	372,980	158,144	211,733
2008-09	431,593	39,508	2,442,345	253,778	316,275	367,478	1,102,698	9,840	1,796,291	334,296	142,666	190,748
2009-10	554,295	35,498	2,457,434	280,888	315,595	352,963	1,191,821	15,840	1,876,219	326,779	139,903	185,452
2010-11	473,878	43,380	2,450,639	357,130	395,452	395,177	1,213,229	16,890	2,020,748	441,017	190,110	250,043
2011-12	466,310	52,883	2,399,094	345,565	394,678	390,068	1,197,748	19,661	2,002,155	453,835	188,479	250,037
2012-13	547,965	33,883	3,125,786	351,284	381,914	400,429	1,227,859	20,664	2,030,866	493,205	210,702	270,328
2013-14	519,824	25,364	3,098,392	373,008	395,726	429,796	1,218,170	29,103	2,072,795	497,272	209,808	268,554
2014-15[1]	431,674	31,012	2,997,078	391,728	375,856	428,477	1,303,755	53,179	2,161,267	506,677	214,041	278,380

[1] Preliminary. [2] Includes straight run oil stock peanuts. [3] Includes peanut butter made by manufacturers for own use in candy. [4] Formerly titled "Salted Peanuts." [5] Includes peanut butter made by manufacturers for own use in cookies and sandwiches, but excludes peanut butter used in candy. [6] All crushings regardless of grade. *Source: National Agricultural Statistics Service, U.S. Department of Agriculture (NASS-USDA)*

PEANUTS AND PEANUT OIL

Shelled Peanuts (Raw Basis) Used in Primary Products, by Type   In Thousands of Pounds

Crop Year Beginning Aug. 1	Virginia				Runner				Spanish			
	Candy[2]	Peanuts	Butter[3]	Total	Candy[2]	Peanuts	Butter[3]	Total	Candy[2]	Peanuts	Butter[3]	Total
2005-06	25,738	81,617	123,402	231,893	335,748	361,176	849,176	1,557,025	15,291	11,531	W	28,498
2006-07	29,542	75,858	113,689	220,196	329,806	328,167	869,014	1,535,250	14,335	11,104	W	36,211
2007-08	27,909	71,059	125,497	225,445	279,564	344,551	878,026	1,511,807	12,994	9,556	W	31,321
2008-09	26,342	52,925	110,737	191,770	276,212	303,730	981,546	1,569,531	13,721	10,823	W	34,990
2009-10	17,361	50,812	W	198,497	286,277	290,358	1,056,699	1,646,454	11,957	11,793	W	31,269
2010-11	16,070	62,708	W	211,194	365,260	319,529	1,076,521	1,774,346	14,122	12,940	W	35,207
2011-12	17,856	78,333	W	203,958	360,797	303,631	1,091,541	1,770,809	16,025	8,104	W	27,390
2012-13	17,731	83,722	82,981	192,888	347,428	309,860	1,143,108	1,812,591	16,755	6,847	W	25,389
2013-14	17,109	85,298	86,759	202,536	W	337,934	1,128,206	1,844,490	15,996	6,564	W	W
2014-15[1]	12,079	91,909	102,340	232,768	348,367	329,930	1,196,277	1,901,311	15,410	6,638	W	27,188

[1] Preliminary.   [2] Includes peanut butter made by manufacturers for own use in candy.   [3] Includes peanut butter made by manufacturers for own use in cookies and sandwiches, but excludes peanut butter used in candy.
Source: National Agricultural Statistics Service, U.S. Department of Agriculture (NASS-USDA)

Production, Consumption, Stocks and Foreign Trade of Peanut Oil in the United States   In Millions of Pounds

Crop Year Beginning Aug. 1	Production		Consumption		Stocks, Dec. 31		Imports for Consumption	Exports
	Crude	Refined	In Refining	In End Products	Crude	Refined		
2002-03	267.7	166.3	W	277.6	52.9	3.5	----	----
2003-04	180.7	115.8	W	203.8	23.0	1.8	----	----
2004-05	135.7	91.0	W	181.9	40.3	2.4	----	----
2005-06	188.0	119.9	W	152.1	15.4	3.7	----	----
2006-07	173.8	115.1	W	W	35.5	5.6	----	----
2007-08	168.7	111.2	W	W	14.1	1.8	----	----
2008-09	150.8	99.9	W	W	17.6	3.0	----	----
2009-10[1]	146.3	96.6	W	W	18.1	2.1	----	----
2010-11[2]	196.9	132.0	W	W	----	----	----	----
2011-12[2]	NA	NA	NA	NA	NA	NA	----	----

[1] Preliminary.   [2] Forecast.   W = Withheld.   *Source: Bureau of the Census, U.S. Department of Commerce*

Farmer Stock Equivalent Total[2/3] Stocks of Peanuts in the United States at End of Month   In Million Pounds

Crop Year	Aug.	Sept.	Oct.	Nov.	Dec.	Jan.	Feb.	Mar.	Apr.	May.	June	July
2006-07	1,854.5	1,791.2	3,202.6	4,119.5	3,942.2	3,648.0	3,318.9	2,929.0	2,587.4	2,223.1	1,897.7	1,520.1
2007-08	1,173.6	1,073.9	2,752.7	3,401.0	3,199.8	2,898.1	2,622.8	2,322.2	1,967.5	1,625.4	1,331.0	1,031.3
2008-09	718.7	1,042.8	3,212.5	4,301.6	4,367.0	4,074.4	3,818.6	3,448.3	3,085.4	2,763.7	2,447.5	2,130.1
2009-10	1,837.6	1,657.4	2,922.1	3,973.0	3,862.4	3,602.9	3,541.8	3,153.2	2,785.9	2,451.9	2,158.8	1,828.7
2010-11	1,502.4	1,778.9	3,651.7	4,150.9	3,887.3	3,565.5	3,258.3	2,867.1	2,443.1	2,148.3	1,820.9	1,515.9
2011-12	1,171.5	1,252.4	2,888.2	3,389.3	3,237.9	2,938.7	2,652.9	2,333.0	1,966.5	1,553.1	1,261.8	1,003.3
2012-13	669.6	1,623.1	5,050.1	5,758.2	5,570.7	5,184.7	4,792.2	4,382.6	3,953.0	3,559.0	3,202.7	2,770.7
2013-14	2,427.0	2,172.4	3,776.3	4,641.5	4,710.1	4,299.6	3,919.4	3,505.5	3,092.3	2,741.2	2,304.4	1,857.8
2014-15	1,426.7	1,330.5	4,246.1	4,717.3	4,573.2	4,297.1	3,893.3	3,487.2	3,105.8	2,717.9	2,401.4	2,101.0
2015-16[1]	1,729.7	2,054.6	4,173.7	5,077.9	5,372.5	5,270.5						

[1] Preliminary.   [2] Excludes stocks on farms. Includes stocks owned by or held for account of peanut producers and CCC in commercial storage facilities. Farmer stock on net weight basis.   [3] Actual farmer stock, plus roasting stock, plus shelled peanuts.   W = Withheld.   *Source: Agricultural Marketing Service, U.S. Department of Agriculture (AMS-USDA)*

Farmer Stock Peanuts[2], Total All Types, in the United States at End of Month   In Millions of Pounds

Crop Year	Aug.	Sept.	Oct.	Nov.	Dec.	Jan.	Feb.	Mar.	Apr.	May.	June	July
2006-07	1,085.2	994.4	2,383.5	3,269.5	3,109.8	2,770.3	2,436.4	2,064.0	1,728.1	1,378.9	1,080.9	730.1
2007-08	446.6	431.5	2,186.1	2,821.3	2,614.7	2,236.8	1,872.4	1,514.5	1,168.1	855.5	585.4	346.9
2008-09	123.8	606.4	2,693.9	3,692.9	3,698.4	3,345.2	3,019.4	2,643.5	2,316.6	2,013.7	1,652.7	1,360.0
2009-10	1,037.5	859.2	2,113.7	3,143.5	3,035.0	2,783.8	2,656.9	2,258.7	1,903.9	1,595.4	1,286.0	991.4
2010-11	711.4	1,064.9	2,900.3	3,394.2	3,178.3	2,852.9	2,501.4	2,066.1	1,657.1	1,343.8	1,027.3	769.0
2011-12	472.0	613.8	2,300.1	2,780.8	2,581.2	2,239.4	1,888.5	1,514.2	1,145.2	772.3	507.9	272.8
2012-13	98.2	1,164.8	4,442.1	5,098.6	4,865.5	4,447.0	4,032.1	3,548.0	3,073.4	2,629.0	2,266.4	1,925.0
2013-14	1,527.6	1,296.5	2,909.0	3,790.8	3,876.1	3,472.0	3,045.7	2,615.1	2,195.8	1,819.1	1,423.3	1,059.5
2014-15	661.8	573.0	3,517.7	4,046.4	3,947.9	3,622.6	3,224.0	2,789.6	2,394.6	2,056.4	1,697.5	1,445.3
2015-16[1]	1,149.0	1,513.8	3,561.3	4,450.3	4,745.0	4,619.0						

[1] Preliminary.   [2] Excludes stocks on farms. Includes stocks owned by or held for account of peanut producers and CCC in commercial storage facilities. Farmer stock on net weight basis.   *Source: Agricultural Marketing Service, U.S. Department of Agriculture (AMS-USDA)*

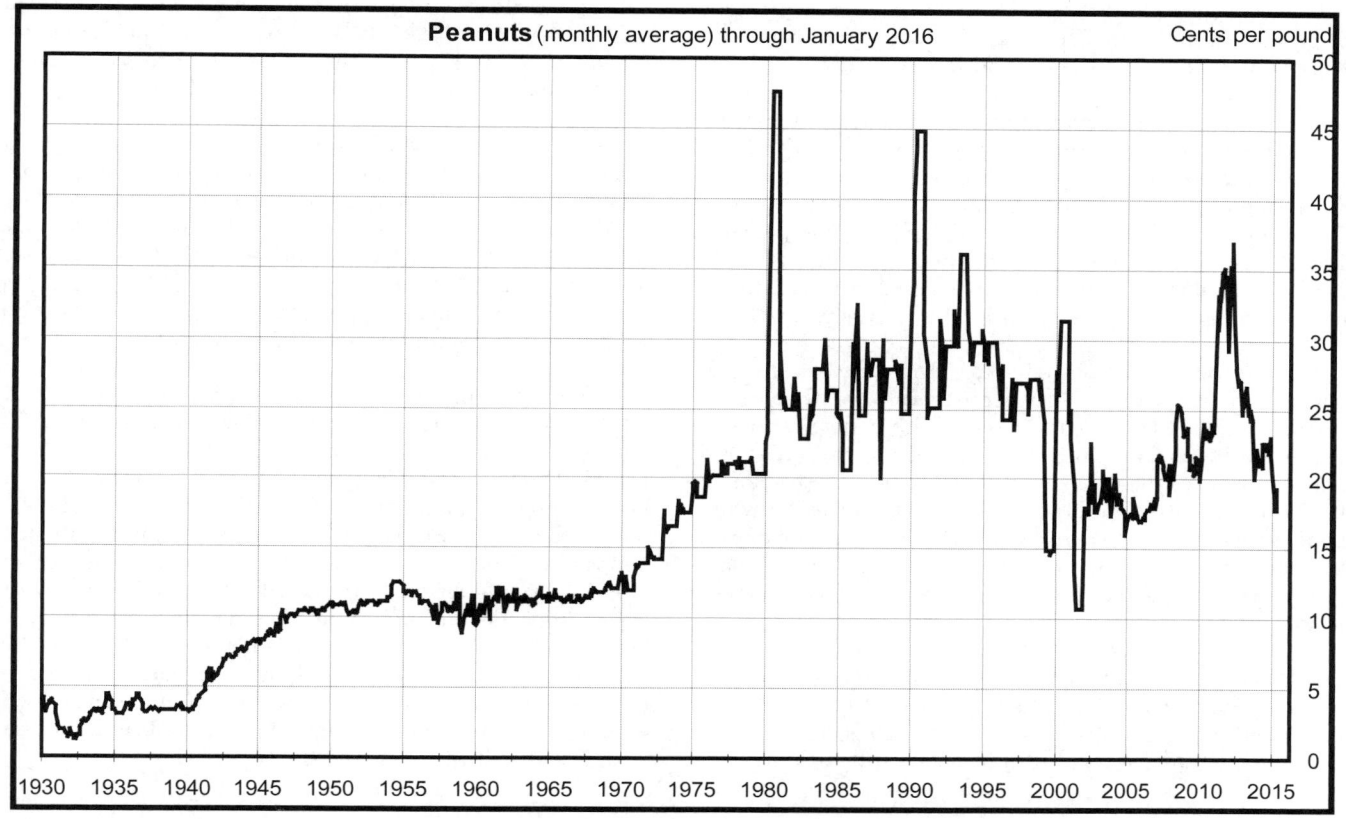

Peanuts (monthly average) through January 2016   Cents per pound

Average Price[2] Received by Farmers for Peanuts (in the Shell) in the United States   In Cents Per Pound

Year	Jan.	Feb.	Mar.	Apr.	May	June	July	Aug.	Sept.	Oct.	Nov.	Dec.	Average[1]
2006-07	17.0	17.3	17.2	17.2	17.6	17.8	17.8	17.8	18.3	17.9	18.1	18.7	17.7
2007-08	18.0	18.6	21.4	21.7	21.3	21.6	21.0	20.7	20.0	20.4	20.1	21.1	20.5
2008-09	18.9	21.0	20.6	20.1	21.7	23.9	25.3	25.4	25.2	24.8	24.7	23.4	22.9
2009-10	23.1	23.3	23.7	21.7	21.7	20.7	21.0	20.6	20.4	20.5	21.6	21.5	21.7
2010-11	20.7	19.9	21.4	22.3	24.0	23.0	23.5	23.4	23.1	22.8	23.3	23.9	22.6
2011-12	23.4	23.5	28.9	33.2	30.8	33.7	32.9	34.8	35.1	33.8	34.4	34.5	31.6
2012-13	29.3	35.2	33.7	32.6	36.9	31.2	28.2	27.8	26.8	27.1	27.0	24.7	30.0
2013-14	25.1	25.3	26.0	26.6	24.6	25.4	24.3	25.0	24.2	23.7	20.0	21.7	24.3
2014-15	22.1	21.5	21.0	21.4	20.9	22.5	22.2	22.5	22.1	22.5	21.8	23.0	22.0
2015-16[1]	21.9	20.1	18.7	17.8	17.8	19.3	19.7						19.3

[1] Preliminarly.   [2] Weighted average by sales.   *Source: National Agricultural Statistics Service, U.S. Department of Agriculture (NASS-USDA)*

Average Price of Domestic Crude Peanut Oil (in Tanks) F.O.B. Southeast Mills   In Cents Per Pound

Year	Jan.	Feb.	Mar.	Apr.	May	June	July	Aug.	Sept.	Oct.	Nov.	Dec.	Average
2006-07	52.67	52.50	50.00	49.25	46.25	48.20	52.63	55.63	62.56	69.63	70.00	73.00	56.86
2007-08	76.75	93.20	98.50	97.33	99.00	100.00	104.38	104.80	107.00	110.00	110.00	110.00	100.91
2008-09	97.00	90.00	85.25	79.10	75.00	62.50	58.75	56.60	57.00	60.70	62.00	54.00	69.83
2009-10	51.20	52.00	52.20	59.00	59.50	58.75	63.60	67.63	67.75	67.80	68.38	68.81	61.39
2010-11	71.40	75.13	77.90	80.06	79.63	77.50	78.70	82.81	78.50	88.05	95.56	97.50	81.90
2011-12	97.00	98.75	96.10	95.81	95.00	96.60	102.38	106.13	111.00	110.00	110.00	104.50	101.94
2012-13	103.00	99.90	98.56	96.75	86.00	79.05	77.50	80.00	82.75	84.00	83.00	82.00	87.71
2013-14	81.00	78.70	75.38	65.70	62.06	59.06	57.75	57.20	58.25	58.63	62.80	61.75	64.86
2014-15	59.95	60.63	60.13	56.15	55.56	54.69	54.81	54.65	56.31	58.15	58.63	58.69	57.36
2015-16[1]	57.70	58.06	58.50	56.19	55.00								57.09

[1] Preliminary.   *Source: Agricultural Marketing Service, U.S. Department of Agriculture (AMS-USDA)*

Pepper

The pepper plant is a perennial climbing shrub that originated in India and Sri Lanka. Pepper is considered the world's most important spice and has been used to flavor foods for over 3,000 years. Pepper was once considered so valuable that it was used to ransom Rome from Attila the Hun. Black pepper alone accounts for nearly 35% of the world's spice trade. Unlike many other popular herbs and spices, pepper can only be cultivated in tropical climates. The pepper plant produces a berry called a peppercorn. Both black and white pepper are obtained from the same plant. The colors of pepper are determined by the maturity of the berry at harvest and by different processing methods.

Black pepper is picked when the berries are still green and immature. The peppercorns are then dried in the sun until they turn black. White pepper is picked when the berries are fully ripe and bright red. The red peppercorns are then soaked, washed to remove the skin of the berry, and dried to produce a white to yellowish-white peppercorn. Black pepper has a slightly hotter flavor and stronger aroma than white pepper. Piperine, an alkaloid of pyridine, is the active ingredient in pepper that makes it hot.

Black pepper oil is obtained from crushed berries using solvent extraction. Black pepper oil is used in the treatment of pain, chills, flu, muscular aches, and in some perfumes. It is also helpful in promoting digestion in the colon.

The world's key pepper varieties are known by their place of origin. Popular types of pepper include Lampong Black and Muntok White from Indonesia, Brazilian Black, and Malabar Black and Tellicherry from India.

Production – World production of pepper in 2013 (latest data) rose by +4.6% yr/yr to 472,526 metric tons. The world's largest pepper producer is Vietnam with a 34.5% share of world production, followed by Indonesia with a 18.8% share and India with a 11.2% share. Pepper production in 2013 in Vietnam rose by +4.5% yr/yr to 163,000 metric tons. Pepper production in 2013 rose by +1.0% yr/yr in Indonesia to 88,700 metric tons.

Trade – The world's largest exporters of pepper in 2011 (latest data available) were Vietnam (with 123,800 metric tons of exports), India (37,419), Indonesia (36,487), Brazil (32,696), and Malaysia (14,237). U.S. imports of black pepper in 2008 (latest data) fell -2.6% yr/yr to 49,625 metric tons. The primary source of U.S. imports of black pepper in 2008 was Indonesia which accounted for 41% of U.S. imports, followed by India with 20%, and Brazil with 17%. Imports from Malaysia have dropped by over 95% since 2003. U.S. imports of white pepper in 2008 rose by +25.1% yr/yr to 6,960 metric tons. The primary source of U.S. imports of white pepper was Indonesia, which accounted for 69% of U.S. imports, followed by Malaysia with 5%, Brazil with 1%, and China with 1%.

World Production of Pepper   In Metric Tons

Year	Brazil	Cambodia	China	India	Indonesia	Madagascar	Malaysia	Mexico	Philippines	Sri Lanka	Thailand	Vietnam	World Total
2006	80,316	2,278	24,000	92,900	77,534	5,443	19,092	4,915	3,678	18,600	12,156	102,570	466,456
2007	77,770	2,373	26,000	69,000	80,420	5,200	20,145	6,854	3,270	19,390	10,419	116,090	461,825
2008	69,600	2,557	27,000	47,010	80,420	4,264	22,218	6,653	3,426	22,870	5,852	128,000	444,207
2009	65,398	2,375	28,262	47,400	82,834	5,010	23,210	6,269	3,432	25,300	6,730	140,000	457,972
2010	52,137	2,356	30,210	51,020	83,700	5,018	24,227	3,640	3,348	26,620	6,391	137,000	448,638
2011	44,610	2,304	29,192	52,000	87,100	4,092	25,600	3,453	3,369	25,770	4,395	146,000	450,429
2012¹	43,345	2,400	31,200	41,000	87,841	5,000	26,000	3,025	3,248	24,950	3,504	156,000	451,632
2013²	42,312	2,498	31,410	53,000	88,700	5,000	26,500	3,199	2,716	26,730	2,791	163,000	472,526

¹ Preliminary.   ² Estimate.   Source: Food and Agricultural Organization of the United Nations (FAO-UN)

World Imports of Pepper   In Metric Tons

Year	European Union	France	Germany	India	Japan	Netherlands	Pakistan	Russia	Singapore	United Arab Em.	United Kingdom	United States	World Total
2005	82,669	9,210	22,731	18,858	8,993	13,183	5,165	9,356	12,936	510	6,840	66,895	284,509
2006	93,290	9,439	26,031	16,897	9,208	15,409	6,424	10,099	15,847	3,422	9,105	70,539	304,571
2007	94,694	8,656	31,460	13,301	9,108	14,745	5,332	7,473	13,154	10,071	7,201	63,941	292,133
2008	87,483	8,812	28,084	11,567	7,781	13,090	7,562	9,589	13,144	10,782	8,066	64,789	295,341
2009	88,822	8,357	26,219	17,444	8,785	15,765	6,564	9,358	12,437	10,782	7,761	65,855	311,400
2010	100,359	9,719	28,948	11,913	8,908	19,856	7,267	10,244	10,130	10,782	10,269	70,470	315,162
2011¹	96,875	8,827	25,480	13,548	8,855	18,331	8,893	8,603	11,923	2,572	10,799	68,489	314,091
2012²	95,998	7,882	27,653	16,009	8,130	16,950	5,691	9,705	11,936	6,013	11,944	62,458	308,246

¹ Preliminary.   ² Estimate.   Source: Food and Agricultural Organization of the United Nations (FAO-UN)

World Exports of Pepper   In Metric Tons

Year	Brazil	European Union	Germany	India	Indonesia	Malaysia	Mexico	Netherlands	Singapore	Sri Lanka	United States	Vietnam	World Total
2005	38,424	25,949	8,092	21,470	34,531	18,097	4,485	10,417	12,190	8,131	4,601	109,900	300,987
2006	42,200	29,770	9,802	35,499	36,953	16,610	6,593	11,655	15,231	7,596	3,876	115,000	333,689
2007	38,679	30,212	9,387	47,464	38,447	15,165	4,081	11,342	16,007	6,940	5,310	83,000	309,983
2008	36,728	34,078	14,350	39,645	52,407	13,592	5,376	9,705	12,363	6,237	5,364	90,300	322,688
2009	35,770	31,812	10,850	26,281	50,642	13,153	6,175	9,974	9,570	6,576	5,472	134,300	342,371
2010	30,761	32,982	11,128	25,847	62,599	14,107	6,590	9,153	9,777	12,236	5,605	116,859	343,075
2011¹	32,696	36,163	11,031	37,419	36,487	14,237	5,998	10,848	9,119	5,057	7,110	123,800	330,548
2012²	29,129	40,977	10,915	29,263	62,608	10,613	6,122	13,903	12,504	10,488	9,213	116,826	350,356

¹ Preliminary.   ² Estimate.   Source: Food and Agricultural Organization of the United Nations (FAO-UN)

Petroleum

Crude oil is petroleum that is acquired directly from the ground. Crude oil was formed millions of years ago from the remains of tiny aquatic plants and animals that lived in ancient seas. Ancient societies such as the Persians, 10th century Sumatrans, and pre-Columbian Indians believed that crude oil had medicinal benefits. Around 4,000 BC in Mesopotamia, bitumen, a tarry crude, was used as caulking for ships, as a setting for jewels and mosaics, and as an adhesive to secure weapon handles. The walls of Babylon and the famed pyramids were held together with bitumen, and Egyptians used it for embalming. During the 19th century in America, an oil find was often met with dismay. Pioneers who dug wells to find water or brine, were disappointed when they struck oil. It wasn't until 1854, with the invention of the kerosene lamp, that the first large-scale demand for petroleum emerged. Crude oil is a relatively abundant commodity. The world has produced approximately 650 billion barrels of oil, but another trillion barrels of proved reserves have yet to be extracted. Crude oil was the world's first trillion-dollar industry and accounts for the single largest product in world trade.

Crude Oil futures and options are traded at the CME Group, the ICE Futures Europe, and the JSE Securities Exchange. Futures are also traded at the Dubai Mercantile Exchange (DME), the Multi Commodity Exchange of India (MCX), the Thailand Futures Exchange, and the Tokyo Commodity Exchange (TOCOM). The CME trades two main types of crude oil: light sweet crude oil and Brent crude oil. The light sweet futures contract calls for the delivery of 1,000 barrels of crude oil in Cushing, Oklahoma. Light sweet crude is preferred by refiners because of its low sulfur content and relatively high yield of high-value products such as gasoline, diesel fuel, heating oil, and jet fuel. The Brent blend crude is based on a light, sweet North Sea crude oil. Brent blend crude production is approximately 500,000 barrels per day, and is shipped from Sullom Voe in the Shetland Islands.

Prices – CME West-Texas Intermediate crude oil prices (Barchart.com symbol CL) moved lower in Q1-2015 and posted a 6-year low of $42.03 a barrel in March as the global oil supply glut showed no signs of abating. The IEA projected that the record oil surplus in the U.S. may strain storage capacity and further pressure prices as the oil-storage hub in Cushing, OK, the largest in the U.S., was over 75% filled. In addition, crude fell as the dollar index rallied to an 11-3/4 year high and on concern that the Iranian nuclear deal would allow Iran to boost crude exports into an already-saturated global market. Crude prices recovered and rallied into May when they posted the high for the year at $62.58 a barrel. Crude found support after Saudi Arabian airstrikes against militants in Yemen sparked concern that Middle East oil shipments may be disrupted. Also, the slide in oil prices spurred increased demand from China, the world's second-largest crude consumer, after China April crude imports rose +8.7% y/y to a record 30.29 MMT. Crude prices failed to hold their gains, however, and sold-off the rest of the year and posted a 6-3/4 year low in December at $33.98 a barrel. OPEC June crude production rose to a 7-year high of 32.37 million bpd and in December OPEC raised its production target to 31.5 million bpd from 30 million bpd. U.S. crude production climbed to 9.61 million bpd in June, the highest since EIA data began in 1983, while EIA crude supplies and Cushing stockpiles rose to record highs. Crude prices finished 2015 down -30% at $37.04 a barrel.

Supply – World crude oil production in 2013 (latest data) rose +0.1% yr/yr to 76.047 million barrels per day, which was a new record high. The world's largest oil producers in 2013 were Russia (with 13.2%), Saudi Arabia (12.8%), the United States (9.8%), China (5.5%), and Canada (4.1%). U.S. crude oil production in 2013 rose +15.4% yr/yr to 7.478 million barrels per day. Alaskan production in 2013 fell −2.1% yr/yr to 515,000 barrels per day, the lowest level since 1977 and far below the peak level of 2.017 million barrels per day seen in 1988.

Demand – U.S. demand for crude oil in 2013 rose +2.2% yr/yr to 15.321 million barrels per day, which was well below the 2004 record high of 15.475 million barrels. Most of that demand went for U.S. refinery production of products such as gasoline fuel, diesel fuel, aviation fuel, heating oil, kerosene, asphalt, and lubricants.

Trade – The U.S. is still highly dependent on imports of crude oil to meet its energy needs even though U.S. imports in 2013 fell -9.4% yr/yr to 7.729 million barrels per day, down from the 2005 record high of 10.126 million barrels.

World Production of Crude Petroleum   In Thousands of Barrels Per Day

Year	Canada	China	Iran	Iraq	Kuwait	Mexico	Nigeria	Russia	Saudi Arabia	United Arab Em	United States	Vene- zuela	World Total
2005	2,369	3,609	4,139	1,878	2,529	3,423	2,627	9,043	9,550	2,535	5,182	2,565	73,866
2006	2,525	3,673	4,028	1,996	2,535	3,345	2,440	9,247	9,152	2,636	5,088	2,511	73,478
2007	2,628	3,729	3,912	2,086	2,464	3,143	2,350	9,437	8,722	2,603	5,077	2,490	73,164
2008	2,579	3,790	4,050	2,375	2,586	2,839	2,165	9,357	9,261	2,681	5,000	2,510	74,062
2009	2,579	3,796	4,037	2,391	2,350	2,646	2,208	9,495	8,250	2,413	5,350	2,520	72,871
2010	2,741	4,078	4,080	2,399	2,300	2,621	2,455	9,694	8,900	2,415	5,482	2,410	74,653
2011	2,901	4,059	4,054	2,626	2,530	2,600	2,550	9,774	9,458	2,679	5,645	2,500	74,734
2012	3,138	4,085	3,387	2,983	2,635	2,593	2,520	9,922	9,832	2,804	6,497	2,500	76,160
2013[1]	3,325	4,164	3,113	3,054	2,650	2,562	2,367	10,054	9,693	2,820	7,441	2,500	76,248
2014[2]	3,603	4,189	3,236	3,368	2,619	2,459	2,423	10,107	9,735	2,820	8,653	2,500	77,834

Includes lease condensate.   [1] Preliminary.   [2] Estimate.   *Source: Energy Information Administration, U.S. Department of Energy (EIA-DOE)*

PETROLEUM

World Imports of Crude Petroleum   In Thousands of Barrels Per Day

Year	China	France	Germany	India	Italy	Japan	Korea, South	Nether-lands	Singa-pore	Spain	United Kingdom	United States	World Total
2004	2,449	1,733	2,229	1,912	1,892	4,236	2,305	1,283	881	1,187	1,254	11,118	45,552
2005	2,599	1,714	2,280	1,938	1,942	4,304	2,369	1,320	1,046	1,205	1,165	11,311	46,431
2006	2,905	1,666	2,222	2,156	1,899	4,249	2,439	1,283	1,012	1,209	1,172	11,564	46,820
2007	3,264	1,637	2,163	2,412	1,952	4,192	2,419	1,330	963	1,176	1,151	11,559	47,162
2008	3,578	1,692	2,130	2,557	1,813	4,225	2,359	1,296	1,006	1,213	1,198	11,392	47,112
2009	4,082	1,465	1,980	3,185	1,668	3,724	2,349	1,320	1,078	1,113	1,103	10,436	45,728
2010	4,754	1,307	1,883	3,267	1,736	3,755	2,401	1,347	929	1,127	1,120	10,592	46,040
2011	5,052	1,309	1,827	3,355	1,586	3,644	2,540	1,266	974	1,121	1,180	10,406	45,862
2012[1]	5,421	1,159	1,888	3,696	1,531	3,724	2,574	1,274	976	1,233	1,222	9,812	46,267
2013[2]		1,129	1,830		1,346	3,692	2,479	1,204		1,224	1,221	9,080	

Includes lease condensate.   [1] Preliminary.   [2] Estimate.   *Source: Energy Information Administration, U.S. Department of Energy (EIA-DOE)*

World Exports of Crude Petroleum   In Thousands of Barrels Per Day

Year	Angola	Canada	Iran	Iraq	Kuwait	Mexico	Nigeria	Norway	Russia	Saudi Arabia	United Arab Em	Vene-zuela	World Total
2004	1,011	1,783	2,556	1,600	1,479	2,095	2,176	2,726	5,211	7,143	2,172	1,587	44,053
2005	1,220	1,735	2,497	1,381	1,690	2,038	2,260	2,377	5,222	7,216	2,107	2,418	44,131
2006	1,393	1,904	2,540	1,480	1,760	1,977	2,190	2,211	5,106	7,036	2,324	2,349	44,112
2007	1,659	1,958	2,618	1,618	1,645	1,793	2,120	2,013	5,172	6,969	2,289	2,225	43,699
2008	1,849	1,976	2,475	1,767	1,785	1,499	1,932	1,701	5,120	7,299	2,339	1,861	43,139
2009	1,909	1,980	2,297	1,903	1,495	1,303	2,115	1,801	4,891	6,250	2,181	1,594	43,006
2010	1,934	2,058	2,331	1,948	1,391	1,403	2,341	1,628	4,888	6,944	2,141	1,262	43,596
2011	1,783	2,339	2,207	2,176	1,777	1,365	2,402	1,446	4,892	7,478	2,366	1,253	43,782
2012[1]	1,909	2,470	2,297	1,903	1,495	1,280	2,115	1,324	4,871	6,250	2,181	1,594	42,845
2013[2]		2,733				1,220		1,218					

Includes lease condensate.   [1] Preliminary.   [2] Estimate.   *Source: Energy Information Administration, U.S. Department of Energy (EIA-DOE)*

World Production of Petroleum Products   In Thousands of Barrels Per Day

Year	Brazil	Canada	China	Germany	India	Italy	Japan	Korea, South	Russia	Saudi Arabia	United Kingdom	United States	World Total
2004	2,137	2,163	6,178	2,540	2,700	2,048	4,241	2,395	4,153	1,985	1,897	17,814	80,758
2005	2,180	2,102	6,354	2,617	2,746	2,116	4,360	2,502	4,361	2,087	1,823	17,800	82,556
2006	2,167	2,069	6,495	2,580	2,895	2,050	4,262	2,559	4,549	2,289	1,757	17,975	82,615
2007	2,185	2,117	7,019	2,539	3,121	2,112	4,215	2,552	4,568	2,145	1,719	17,994	81,586
2008	2,008	2,029	7,069	2,484	3,226	1,971	4,136	2,535	4,802	2,103	1,678	18,146	81,774
2009	2,236	1,962	8,209	2,333	3,837	1,823	3,863	2,476	4,934	1,934	1,584	17,882	82,426
2010	2,467	2,016	8,737	2,198	4,219	1,887	3,857	2,537	5,298	1,935	1,549	18,452	84,183
2011	2,473	1,906	9,298	2,184	4,356	1,791	3,658	2,685	5,390	1,901	1,594	18,673	84,715
2012[1]	2,554	1,927	9,879	2,206	4,505	1,692	3,645	2,790	5,517	1,971	1,453	18,564	85,216
2013[2]		1,894		2,150		1,506	3,686	2,697			1,409	19,106	

Includes lease condensate.   [1] Preliminary.   [2] Estimate.   *Source: Energy Information Administration, U.S. Department of Energy (EIA-DOE)*

Supply and Disposition of Crude Oil in the United States   In Thousands of Barrels Per Day

	-- Field Production --		----------- Imports ------------			Unaccounted for Crude Oil	---- Stock Withdrawal[3] ----		---- Disposition ----		-------- Ending Stocks --------		
Year	Total Domestic	Alaskan	Total	SPR[2]	Other		SPR[2]	Other	Refinery Inputs	Exports	Total	SPR[2]	Other Primary
	In Thousands of Barrels Per Day										In Millions of Barrels		
2007	5,077	722	10,031	7	----	----	----	----	15,156	27	983	697	286
2008	5,000	683	9,783	19	----	----	----	----	14,648	29	1,028	702	326
2009	5,350	645	9,013	56	----	----	----	----	14,336	44	1,052	727	325
2010	5,482	600	9,213	----	----	----	----	----	14,724	42	1,060	727	333
2011	5,645	561	8,935	----	----	----	----	----	14,806	47	1,027	696	331
2012	6,497	526	8,527	----	----	----	----	----	14,999	67	1,061	695	365
2013	7,464	515	7,730	----	----	----	----	----	15,312	134	1,053	696	357
2014[1]	8,680	497	7,337	----	----	----	----	----	15,844	346	1,085	691	394

[1] Preliminary.   [2] Strategic Petroleum Reserve.   [3] A negative number indicates a decrease in stocks and a positive number indicates an increase.
Source: Energy Information Administration, U.S. Department of Energy (EIA-DOE)

Crude Petroleum Refinery Operations Ratio[2] in the United States   In Percent of Capacity

Year	Jan.	Feb.	Mar.	Apr.	May	June	July	Aug.	Sept.	Oct.	Nov.	Dec.	Average
2006	87.0	86.5	85.8	88.0	91.2	93.0	92.5	93.2	93.0	87.9	88.0	90.6	89.7
2007	88.2	84.7	87.1	88.1	89.7	88.5	91.2	90.8	88.9	87.4	88.9	88.7	88.5
2008	85.8	85.0	83.2	86.2	88.8	89.5	88.8	87.1	74.6	85.3	85.8	83.9	85.3
2009	82.3	81.5	81.5	82.7	84.0	86.0	84.2	84.1	84.9	81.5	81.1	81.3	82.9
2010	79.9	81.1	83.2	88.7	88.2	90.7	91.2	89.1	86.5	82.5	86.5	88.4	86.3
2011	84.8	80.0	84.4	82.9	85.3	89.0	90.2	90.3	88.7	84.9	87.0	86.5	86.2
2012	85.6	86.5	85.6	86.6	90.6	92.5	92.5	91.1	87.6	87.1	88.6	90.4	88.7
2013	83.8	81.7	84.0	85.8	88.2	91.7	92.6	91.5	90.7	86.9	90.6	92.0	88.3
2014	87.2	86.6	85.8	90.7	90.2	90.3	94.6	93.7	91.8	87.7	92.0	94.2	90.4
2015[1]	88.4	87.6	88.7	92.0	92.5	94.0	95.1	93.9	90.5	86.6	91.8	92.6	91.1

[1] Preliminary.   [2] Based on the ration of the daily average crude runs to stills to the rated capacity of refineries per day.   Source: Energy Information Administration, U.S. Department of Energy (EIA-DOE)

Crude Oil Refinery Inputs in the United States   In Thousands of Barrels Per Day

Year	Jan.	Feb.	Mar.	Apr.	May	June	July	Aug.	Sept.	Oct.	Nov.	Dec.	Average
2006	14,805	14,581	14,582	14,928	15,516	15,843	15,702	15,792	15,739	15,008	15,009	15,354	15,242
2007	14,992	14,435	14,840	15,045	15,380	15,248	15,671	15,685	15,226	14,933	15,151	15,202	15,156
2008	14,804	14,625	14,364	14,799	15,263	15,417	15,255	14,947	12,759	14,552	14,606	14,352	14,648
2009	14,146	14,134	14,118	14,382	14,483	14,850	14,636	14,593	14,710	14,095	13,898	13,983	14,336
2010	13,666	13,950	14,314	15,131	15,215	15,382	15,519	15,110	14,740	14,000	14,637	14,976	14,724
2011	14,423	13,676	14,451	14,231	14,718	15,294	15,589	15,556	15,275	14,570	14,960	14,842	14,799
2012	14,374	14,615	14,476	14,609	15,097	15,637	15,665	15,325	14,910	14,843	15,085	15,330	14,997
2013	14,567	14,230	14,703	14,864	15,305	15,833	16,042	15,793	15,636	14,991	15,633	16,069	15,306
2014	15,311	15,128	15,116	15,864	15,946	15,817	16,534	16,460	16,074	15,361	16,043	16,469	15,844
2015[1]	15,493	15,414	15,657	16,299	16,435	16,695	16,884	16,662	16,174	15,465	16,489	16,765	16,203

[1] Preliminary.   Source: Energy Information Administration, U.S. Department of Energy (EIA-DOE)

Production of Major Refined Petroleum Products in Continental United States   In Millions of Barrels

Year	Asphalt	Aviation Gasoline	Fuel Oil Distillate	Fuel Oil Residual	Gasoline	Jet Fuel	Kero-sene	Natural Gas Plant Liquids	Lubri-cants	Liquified Gasses Total	Liquified Gasses at L.P.G.[2]	Liquified Gasses AT L.P.G.[3]
2005	186.0	6.1	1,441.4	227.9	3,014	561.5	23.6	623.9	60.8	736.9	527.2	209.8
2006	184.8	6.6	1,478.1	231.5	3,036	540.4	17.3	633.4	66.8	757.6	537.8	219.9
2007	166.1	6.0	1,507.7	244.4	3,045	528.6	12.7	648.3	65.1	789.0	552.8	236.2
2008	150.9	5.5	1,569.5	227.1	3,072	539.5	12.0	651.9	63.2	786.1	556.2	229.9
2009	131.0	5.0	1,476.7	218.6	3,199	510.2	6.9	688.5	55.4	821.1	591.3	229.8
2010	132.1	5.4	1,384.7	200.8	3,298	519.7	7.2	730.4	47.6	869.3	631.7	237.6
2011	129.6	5.4	1,405.1	175.3	3,189	520.2	4.4	825.0	45.3	915.5	689.1	226.4
2012	124.5	5.0	1,369.8	126.2	3,185	512.2	1.4	830.7	41.4	992.0	762.6	229.4
2013	117.0	4.2	1,727.0	170.4	3,347	547.8	4.0	809.0	59.8	1,162.2	933.1	229.1
2014[1]	118.7	4.3	1,463.7	93.9	3,257	536.6	3.2	940.7	45.2	1,322.3	1,081.9	240.3

[1] Preliminary.   [2] Gas processing plants.   [3] Refineries.   Source: Energy Information Administration, U.S. Department of Energy (EIA-DOE)

Stocks of Petroleum and Products in the United States on January 1   In Millions of Barrels

Year	Crude Petroleum	Strategic Reserve	Total	Asphalt	Aviation Gasoline	Fuel Oil Distillate	Fuel Oil Residual	Finished Gasoline	Jet Fuel	Kero-sene	Gases[2]	Lubri-cants	Motor Gasoline Total	Motor Gasoline Finished[3]
2006	1,007.8	684.5	403.6	21.0	1.2	136.0	37.3	134.8	41.8	5.1	117.6	9.7	----	135
2007	998.4	688.6	405.9	28.8	1.4	143.7	42.4	118.3	39.1	3.4	125.2	12.4	----	118
2008	982.8	696.9	374.3	22.2	1.2	133.5	38.6	110.0	39.5	2.8	105.5	10.6	----	110
2009	1,026.1	701.8	367.8	20.3	1.2	145.9	36.2	98.2	38.2	2.2	126.9	10.7	----	98
2010	1,051.8	726.6	375.1	17.9	1.0	164.7	37.8	85.9	43.4	2.5	113.2	8.9	----	86
2011	1,058.5	726.5	357.4	19.9	1.1	164.5	41.3	63.4	43.2	2.4	121.3	8.2	----	63
2012	1,026.8	696.0	332.7	19.6	1.1	149.7	34.1	61.4	41.7	2.4	111.1	9.9	----	61
2013	1,060.3	695.3	313.6	22.1	1.0	134.7	33.9	56.8	39.5	1.7	140.9	9.6	----	57
2014	1,053.6	696.0	291.3	21.4	0.9	127.3	37.7	39.7	37.2	1.9	112.7	10.1	----	40
2015[1]	1,084.7	691.0	286.9	21.2	1.1	136.1	33.7	30.6	37.5	2.1	154.8	11.2	----	31

[1] Preliminary.   [2] Includes ethane & ethylene at plants and refineries.   [3] Includes oxygenated.
Source: Energy Information Administration, U.S. Department of Energy (EIA-DOE)

PETROLEUM

Stocks of Crude Petroleum in the United States, on First of Month   In Millions of Barrels

Year	Jan.	Feb.	Mar.	Apr.	May	June	July	Aug.	Sept.	Oct.	Nov.	Dec.
2006	1,006.8	1,027.4	1,028.8	1,035.5	1,029.2	1,024.6	1,019.4	1,020.7	1,020.6	1,027.9	1,023.1	1,000.9
2007	1,013.2	1,006.2	1,019.5	1,031.4	1,043.6	1,044.3	1,027.0	1,011.0	1,003.9	1,001.4	995.0	983.0
2008	994.6	1,001.1	1,015.0	1,021.2	1,007.9	1,001.7	1,002.4	1,009.7	1,006.4	1,014.5	1,023.4	1,027.7
2009	1,055.1	1,063.1	1,079.7	1,089.7	1,081.2	1,071.2	1,069.5	1,059.7	1,060.1	1,057.6	1,063.0	1,051.8
2010	1,063.4	1,069.8	1,085.8	1,089.9	1,088.5	1,092.1	1,084.2	1,085.9	1,089.3	1,094.1	1,079.0	1,060.0
2011	1,071.6	1,075.0	1,086.8	1,093.1	1,094.9	1,082.3	1,064.6	1,043.2	1,026.1	1,032.9	1,032.8	1,026.6
2012	1,039.4	1,044.4	1,069.1	1,078.8	1,083.9	1,083.9	1,068.6	1,058.4	1,064.9	1,071.3	1,074.4	1,060.8
2013	1,073.5	1,080.9	1,088.1	1,091.8	1,088.2	1,071.7	1,062.5	1,059.5	1,067.1	1,079.8	1,072.5	1,053.6
2014	1,059.7	1,069.3	1,079.7	1,086.5	1,085.0	1,074.9	1,059.7	1,051.6	1,051.9	1,073.0	1,078.5	1,084.7
2015[1]	1,112.4	1,139.0	1,165.8	1,174.3	1,171.7	1,163.4	1,150.6	1,152.9	1,155.9	1,181.8	1,182.5	1,176.5

[1] Preliminary.   Source: Energy Information Administration; U.S. Department of Energy

Production of Crude Petroleum in the United States   In Thousands of Barrels Per Day

Year	Jan.	Feb.	Mar.	Apr.	May	June	July	Aug.	Sept.	Oct.	Nov.	Dec.	Average
2006	5,085	5,026	5,025	5,080	5,150	5,160	5,093	5,038	5,030	5,108	5,064	5,187	5,087
2007	5,104	5,129	5,112	5,174	5,205	5,072	5,037	4,986	4,902	5,054	5,041	5,108	5,077
2008	5,111	5,155	5,192	5,154	5,143	5,136	5,177	5,008	3,980	4,736	5,084	5,110	4,999
2009	5,126	5,234	5,211	5,274	5,377	5,272	5,402	5,374	5,561	5,516	5,392	5,451	5,349
2010	5,403	5,548	5,514	5,395	5,400	5,382	5,314	5,444	5,609	5,600	5,577	5,604	5,482
2011	5,497	5,392	5,604	5,555	5,619	5,582	5,344	5,627	5,590	5,875	6,006	6,027	5,643
2012	6,153	6,262	6,297	6,296	6,342	6,252	6,391	6,318	6,574	6,941	7,044	7,081	6,496
2013	7,078	7,095	7,161	7,375	7,301	7,264	7,453	7,502	7,727	7,702	7,897	7,873	7,453
2014	7,998	8,087	8,244	8,568	8,577	8,678	8,754	8,835	8,959	9,129	9,201	9,428	8,705
2015[1]	9,341	9,451	9,648	9,694	9,479	9,315	9,433	9,407	9,452	9,377	9,305	9,262	9,430

[1] Preliminary.   Source: Energy Information Administration, U.S. Department of Energy (EIA-DOE)

U.S. Foreign Trade of Petroleum and Products   In Thousands of Barrels Per Day

	---------------- Exports -----------------		--- Imports ---				
Year	Total[2]	Petroleum Products	Crude	Petroleum Products	Distillate Fuel Oil	Residual Fuel Oil	Net Imports[3]
2005	1,165	1,133	10,126	3,588	329	530	12,549
2006	1,317	1,292	10,118	3,517	365	350	12,390
2007	1,433	1,405	10,031	2,761	304	372	12,035
2008	1,802	1,773	9,783	2,570	213	349	11,113
2009	2,024	1,980	9,013	2,122	225	331	9,667
2010	2,353	2,311	9,213	1,986	228	366	9,440
2011	2,986	2,939	8,935	1,994	179	328	8,450
2012	3,205	3,137	8,527	1,689	126	256	7,393
2013	3,621	3,487	7,730	1,749	155	225	6,238
2014[1]	4,180	3,834	7,337	1,518	194	172	5,041

[1] Preliminary.   [2] Includes crude oil.   [3] Equals imports minus exports.
Source: Energy Information Administration, U.S. Department of Energy (EIA-DOE)

Domestic First Purchase Price of Crude Petroleum at Wells[2]   In Dollars Per Barrel

Year	Jan.	Feb.	Mar.	Apr.	May	June	July	Aug.	Sept.	Oct.	Nov.	Dec.	Average
2006	57.85	55.69	55.59	62.51	64.31	64.36	67.72	67.21	59.36	53.26	52.42	55.03	59.61
2007	49.32	52.94	54.95	58.20	58.90	62.35	69.23	67.78	73.16	79.32	87.16	85.29	66.55
2008	87.06	89.41	98.44	106.64	118.55	127.47	128.08	112.83	98.50	73.22	53.67	36.80	94.22
2009	35.00	34.14	42.46	45.22	52.69	63.08	60.43	65.28	65.27	69.82	71.99	70.42	56.32
2010	72.87	72.74	75.77	78.80	70.91	70.77	71.37	72.07	71.23	76.02	79.20	83.98	74.64
2011	85.66	86.69	99.19	108.80	102.46	97.30	97.82	89.00	90.22	92.28	100.18	98.71	95.69
2012	98.99	102.04	105.42	103.62	95.57	83.59	86.10	92.53	95.98	92.24	89.64	89.81	94.63
2013	95.00	95.01	95.54	94.41	94.75	93.82	101.41	102.96	102.32	96.18	88.70	91.85	96.00
2014	89.57	96.86	96.17	96.49	95.74	98.68	96.70	90.72	86.87	78.84	71.07	54.86	87.71
2015[2]	43.06	44.35	42.66	49.30	54.38	55.88	47.70	39.98	41.60	42.33	38.19	32.26	44.31

[1] Preliminary.   [2] Buyers posted prices.   Source: Energy Information Administration, U.S. Department of Energy (EIA-DOE)

Refiner Sales Prices of Residual Fuel Oil   In Dollars Per Gallon

Year	Jan.	Feb.	Mar.	Apr.	May	June	July	Aug.	Sept.	Oct.	Nov.	Dec.	Average
2008	1.997	1.870	1.956	2.139	2.322	2.578	2.833	2.546	2.175	1.574	1.036	1.010	1.918
2009	1.035	1.011	1.019	1.077	1.205	1.401	1.417	1.584	1.531	1.619	1.743	1.723	1.337
2010	1.767	1.725	1.739	1.827	1.675	1.629	1.686	1.705	1.716	1.793	1.865	2.036	1.756
2011	NA	2.100	2.344	2.555	2.463	2.467	2.547	2.394	2.368	2.512	2.566	2.473	2.389
2012	2.591	2.739	2.921	2.805	2.589	2.275	2.271	2.586	2.558	2.464	2.385	2.341	2.548
2013	2.530	2.571	2.479	2.354	2.316	2.285	2.282	2.331	2.359	2.338	2.296	2.315	2.371
2014	2.337	2.459	2.470	2.401	2.350	2.358	2.287	2.148	2.100	1.893	1.639	1.237	2.140
2015[1]	0.936	1.150	1.093	1.124	1.198	1.175	1.080	0.797	0.819	0.812	0.766	0.552	0.959

Sulfur 1% or less, excluding taxes.   [1] Preliminary.   *Source: Energy Information Administration, U.S. Department of Energy (EIA-DOE)*

Refiner Sales Prices of No. 2 Fuel Oil   In Cents Per Gallon

Year	Jan.	Feb.	Mar.	Apr.	May	June	July	Aug.	Sept.	Oct.	Nov.	Dec.	Average
2008	2.564	2.607	2.977	3.195	3.536	3.762	3.802	3.287	3.003	2.400	1.947	1.579	2.745
2009	1.548	1.427	1.358	1.397	1.468	1.744	1.658	1.804	1.774	1.918	2.004	1.989	1.657
2010	2.075	1.986	2.100	2.214	2.129	2.037	2.001	2.041	2.093	2.221	2.308	2.435	2.147
2011	2.585	2.737	2.996	3.167	3.039	2.956	3.024	2.927	2.927	2.915	3.050	2.928	2.907
2012	3.027	3.166	3.211	3.153	2.976	2.635	2.774	2.988	3.128	3.155	3.049	3.003	3.031
2013	3.069	3.168	2.977	2.793	2.708	2.741	2.894	2.954	2.973	2.955	2.910	3.011	2.966
2014	3.059	3.051	2.979	2.911	2.883	2.878	2.825	2.784	2.701	2.476	2.371	2.050	2.747
2015[1]	1.669	1.850	1.847	1.740	1.852	1.813	1.654	1.461	1.438	1.411	1.356	1.126	1.601

Excluding taxes.   [1] Preliminary.   *Source: Energy Information Administration, U.S. Department of Energy (EIA-DOE)*

Refiner Sales Prices of No. 2 Diesel Fuel   In Cents Per Gallon

Year	Jan.	Feb.	Mar.	Apr.	May	June	July	Aug.	Sept.	Oct.	Nov.	Dec.	Average
2008	2.580	2.738	3.158	3.356	3.712	3.859	3.876	3.338	3.160	2.514	1.955	1.469	2.994
2009	1.480	1.326	1.315	1.456	1.531	1.828	1.745	1.937	1.848	1.978	2.037	1.997	1.713
2010	2.078	2.025	2.163	2.312	2.177	2.120	2.098	2.161	2.190	2.325	2.392	2.486	2.214
2011	2.621	2.820	3.134	3.296	3.116	3.079	3.135	3.032	3.035	3.035	3.157	2.927	3.034
2012	3.018	3.163	3.308	3.252	3.039	2.741	2.907	3.206	3.278	3.265	3.117	3.022	3.109
2013	3.046	3.259	3.082	2.969	2.958	2.923	3.015	3.084	3.095	3.006	2.949	2.998	3.028
2014	2.981	3.091	3.031	3.027	2.987	2.973	2.921	2.900	2.806	2.639	2.558	1.980	2.825
2015[1]	1.616	1.861	1.815	1.805	1.973	1.881	1.729	1.562	1.551	1.572	1.456	1.176	1.666

Excluding taxes.   [1] Preliminary.   *Source: Energy Information Administration, U.S. Department of Energy (EIA-DOE)*

Refiner Sales Prices of Kerosine-Type Jet Fuel   In Cents Per Gallon

Year	Jan.	Feb.	Mar.	Apr.	May	June	July	Aug.	Sept.	Oct.	Nov.	Dec.	Average
2008	2.665	2.674	3.106	3.315	3.642	3.912	3.978	3.393	3.278	2.569	1.974	1.470	3.020
2009	1.472	1.352	1.266	1.425	1.460	1.780	1.759	1.894	1.822	1.917	2.060	2.012	1.719
2010	2.121	1.999	2.129	2.247	2.186	2.094	2.100	2.138	2.131	2.263	2.342	2.459	2.185
2011	2.585	2.783	3.095	3.259	3.188	3.101	3.090	3.040	3.025	2.962	3.089	2.951	3.014
2012	3.059	3.186	3.296	3.255	3.076	2.747	2.850	3.129	3.245	3.182	3.015	2.982	3.080
2013	3.093	3.250	3.036	2.884	2.763	2.784	2.899	2.995	3.017	2.928	2.868	2.978	2.953
2014	2.964	2.981	2.939	2.911	2.932	2.917	2.882	2.882	2.823	2.547	2.410	1.998	2.766
2015[1]	1.612	1.722	1.731	1.709	1.933	1.813	1.655	1.479	1.443	1.451	1.400	1.207	1.596

Excluding taxes.   [1] Preliminary.   *Source: Energy Information Administration, U.S. Department of Energy (EIA-DOE)*

Refiner Sales Prices of Propane[2]   In Cents Per Gallon

Year	Jan.	Feb.	Mar.	Apr.	May	June	July	Aug.	Sept.	Oct.	Nov.	Dec.	Average
2008	1.519	1.469	1.495	1.571	1.675	1.761	1.833	1.667	1.565	1.242	1.005	0.916	1.437
2009	0.974	0.890	0.805	0.719	0.728	0.838	0.760	0.837	0.923	1.004	1.088	1.178	0.921
2010	1.332	1.324	1.179	1.144	1.098	1.049	1.012	1.084	1.151	1.253	1.277	1.322	1.212
2011	1.380	1.401	1.403	1.433	1.515	1.503	1.513	1.522	1.557	1.511	1.498	1.444	1.467
2012	1.341	1.282	1.293	1.163	0.950	0.762	0.809	0.875	0.910	0.979	0.955	0.894	1.033
2013	0.928	0.953	0.952	0.949	0.932	0.861	0.903	1.059	1.114	1.154	1.219	1.342	1.048
2014	1.641	1.654	1.198	1.121	1.057	1.054	1.075	1.055	1.097	1.044	0.966	0.819	1.148
2015[1]	0.713	0.748	0.689	0.566	0.475	0.404	0.405	0.402	0.469	0.524	0.505	0.499	0.533

[1] Preliminary.   [2] Consumer Grade, Excluding taxes.   *Source: Energy Information Administration, U.S. Department of Energy (EIA-DOE)*

PETROLEUM

CRUDE OIL, LIGHT - NYMEX
Weekly Nearest Futures as of 04/01/2016

WEEKLY NEAREST FUTURES
As of 04/01/2016
Chart High 147.27   on 07/11/2008
Chart Low   26.05   on 02/11/2016

Nearby Futures through Last Trading Day.

Volume of Trading of Crude Oil Futures in New York   In Thousands of Contracts

Year	Jan.	Feb.	Mar.	Apr.	May	June	July	Aug.	Sept.	Oct.	Nov.	Dec.	Total
2006	5,482	5,594	5,937	5,285	5,861	5,134	4,500	5,409	6,067	7,492	7,555	6,739	71,053
2007	10,367	9,092	10,069	9,287	9,487	9,862	9,656	10,647	10,670	12,390	11,307	8,692	121,526
2008	10,815	10,100	12,577	11,066	13,497	12,453	11,321	10,589	11,554	11,638	8,662	9,910	134,183
2009	11,369	11,411	11,340	10,106	9,939	11,367	11,924	11,823	11,462	13,179	11,600	11,906	137,428
2010	10,894	12,772	13,298	17,433	17,591	14,458	11,427	14,494	16,018	14,423	13,429	12,416	168,652
2011	17,948	17,757	15,675	12,089	15,126	15,815	11,571	17,178	13,488	14,785	13,609	9,994	175,036
2012	12,557	14,693	13,290	10,627	12,402	12,593	10,870	11,687	10,572	11,660	11,055	8,524	140,532
2013	12,028	11,540	10,515	13,354	13,825	13,111	15,384	12,849	11,139	13,792	10,569	9,586	147,691
2014	11,162	9,862	11,700	11,467	10,283	11,398	13,174	11,016	12,824	15,939	12,204	14,119	145,147
2015	16,514	20,263	17,884	17,638	13,553	13,995	14,863	19,197	16,605	17,484	16,145	18,064	202,202

Contract size = 1,000 bbl.   *Source: CME Group; New York Mercantile Exchange (NYMEX)*

Average Open Interest of Crude Oil Futures in New York   In Thousands of Contracts

Year	Jan.	Feb.	Mar.	Apr.	May	June	July	Aug.	Sept.	Oct.	Nov.	Dec.
2006	903.5	927.5	954.2	1,000.4	1,055.7	1,016.2	1,068.7	1,164.0	1,181.8	1,168.7	1,176.6	1,200.0
2007	1,284.9	1,281.7	1,314.3	1,328.0	1,390.4	1,431.6	1,523.6	1,477.4	1,483.3	1,447.1	1,451.8	1,362.3
2008	1,393.5	1,384.6	1,428.5	1,393.8	1,396.5	1,351.8	1,277.9	1,224.1	1,171.2	1,076.8	1,139.7	1,160.9
2009	1,232.4	1,223.3	1,190.2	1,163.0	1,159.6	1,180.5	1,170.7	1,176.0	1,174.2	1,231.2	1,207.8	1,200.4
2010	1,303.5	1,304.8	1,324.1	1,375.8	1,416.3	1,307.3	1,252.7	1,262.3	1,338.2	1,419.1	1,414.1	1,380.0
2011	1,494.0	1,540.7	1,551.4	1,565.5	1,591.3	1,531.0	1,517.1	1,521.8	1,433.7	1,406.6	1,332.6	1,321.5
2012	1,374.6	1,475.5	1,565.8	1,561.7	1,520.9	1,446.8	1,408.6	1,473.6	1,575.5	1,574.3	1,548.8	1,514.8
2013	1,504.5	1,636.4	1,690.3	1,751.8	1,753.7	1,813.5	1,835.7	1,872.0	1,896.1	1,821.8	1,682.1	1,631.0
2014	1,607.4	1,628.5	1,653.4	1,654.8	1,633.4	1,703.8	1,687.6	1,572.7	1,518.4	1,495.4	1,464.1	1,450.3
2015	1,699.2	1,713.6	1,725.0	1,734.5	1,683.7	1,648.2	1,693.9	1,702.7	1,661.4	1,652.0	1,666.0	1,674.5

Contract size = 1,000 bbl.   *Source: CME Group; New York Mercantile Exchange (NYMEX)*

Plastics

Plastics are moldable, chemically fabricated materials produced mostly from fossil fuels, such as oil, coal, or natural gas. The word plastic is derived from the Greek *plastikos*, meaning "to mold," and the Latin *plasticus*, meaning "capable of molding." Leo Baekeland created the first commercially successful thermosetting synthetic resin in 1909. More than 50 families of plastics have since been produced.

All plastics can be divided into either thermoplastics or thermosetting plastics. The difference is the way in which they respond to heat. Thermoplastics can be repeatedly softened by heat and hardened by cooling. Thermosetting plastics harden permanently after being heated once.

Prices – The average monthly producer price index (1982=100) of plastic resins and materials in the U.S. in 2015 fell -11.0% yr/yr to 228.8, below last year's record high of 257.0. The average monthly producer price index of thermoplastic resins in the U.S. in 2015 fell -12.1% yr/yr to 230.5, below last year's record high of 262.1. The average monthly producer price index of thermosetting resins in the U.S. in 2015 fell -4.9% to 232.6, below last year's record high of 244.4.

Supply – Total U.S. plastics production in 2014 (latest data) rose +0.5% yr/yr to 108.112 billion pounds, which was well below the 2007 record high of 115.793 billion pounds. U.S. plastics production has more than doubled in the past two decades. By sector, the thermoplastics sector is by far the largest, with 2014 production down -0.3% yr/yr to 92.298 billion pounds and accounting for 85.4% of total U.S. plastic production. Production in the thermosetting plastic sector (polyester unsaturated, phenolic, and epoxy) rose +3.7% yr/yr in 2014 to 15.814 billion pounds and accounted for 13.914.6% of total U.S. plastics production. The category of "other plastics" fell -14.7% to 11.952 billion pounds and accounted for 12% of total U.S. plastics production in 2008 (latest data available).

Demand – Total usage of plastic resins by important markets in 2014 (latest data) in the U.S. fell by -0.9% to 75.028 billion pounds. The breakdown by market shows that the largest single consumption category is "Packaging" with 2.608 billion pounds of usage in 2014, accounting for 34.8% of total U.S. consumption. After packaging, the largest categories are "Consumer and Industrial" (19.9% of U.S. consumption), and "Building and Construction" (16.8% of U.S. consumption).

Trade – U.S. exports of plastics in 2014 rose +16.9% yr/yr to 12.666 billion pounds, below the 2011 record high of 14.858 billion pounds. U.S. exports accounted for 16.9% of U.S. supply disappearance in 2014.

Plastics Production by Resin in the United States — In Millions of Pounds

	----------- Thermosets ------------				-------------------------------- Thermoplastics --------------------------------										
Year	Polyester Unsat-urated	Phenolic	Epoxy	Total Thermo-sets	Thermo-plastic Polyester	Polyvinyl Chloride	Poly-styrene	Poly-propy-lene	Nylon	Low Density Polye-thylene[1]	High Density Polye-thylene	Total Thermo-plastics	Total Selected Plastics	Other Plastics	Total Plastics
2005	3,359	4,689	609	8,657	7,749	15,259	6,293	17,965	1,252	19,736	16,155	87,524	96,181	13,595	109,776
2006	3,430	4,809	624	8,863	8,290	14,919	6,269	18,775	1,270	20,926	17,645	91,204	100,067	13,970	114,037
2007	3,471	4,838	642	8,951	8,745	14,606	6,015	19,445	1,295	21,511	18,222	92,835	101,786	14,007	115,793
2008	2,798	4,233	583	15,091	8,159	12,789	5,220	16,768	1,148	19,061	16,247	86,455	89,594	11,952	101,546
2009	NA	NA	535	12,713	NA	12,754	4,865	16,623	943	19,793	16,956	85,983	98,696	NA	98,696
2010	NA	NA	610	13,214	NA	14,017	5,055	17,254	1,027	20,530	16,887	89,592	102,806	NA	102,806
2011	----	----	613	13,800	----	14,434	5,472	16,418	1,106	20,130	17,116	89,408	103,208	----	103,208
2012	----	----	545	14,519	----	15,310	5,452	16,326	1,193	20,328	17,738	91,426	105,945	----	105,945
2013	----	----	499	14,975	----	15,373	5,405	16,427	1,238	20,772	17,899	92,547	107,522	----	107,522
2014	----	----	561	15,814	----	15,038	5,408	16,446	1,299	20,968	17,514	92,298	108,112	----	108,112

[1] Includes LDPE and LLDPE.   *Source: American Plastics Council (APC)*

Total Resin Sales and Captive Use by Important Markets — In Millions of Pounds (Dry Weight Basis)

Year	Adhesive, Inks & Coatings	Building & Con-struction	Consumer & Indust-rial	Electrical & Elect-ronics	Exports	Furniture & Fur-nishings	Industrial & Mach-inary	Pack-aging	Trans-portation	Other	Total
2005	1,160	15,483	17,400	2,917	9,790	3,406	1,087	25,144	4,711	2,133	83,231
2006	1,078	15,486	17,823	2,641	10,244	3,332	1,004	26,280	4,559	2,031	84,478
2007	1,069	14,289	17,193	1,980	12,346	3,091	943	26,527	3,312	1,604	82,354
2008	937	12,313	15,461	1,755	11,962	2,671	834	24,097	2,751	1,375	74,156
2009	798	11,102	14,717	1,519	14,691	1,877	678	23,702	1,971	972	72,025
2010	846	10,914	14,782	1,561	14,488	1,894	774	25,041	2,558	1,200	74,057
2011	801	11,036	14,743	1,618	14,858	1,818	781	25,302	2,649	1,206	74,811
2012	334	11,704	14,613	1,643	14,588	1,471	845	25,828	2,725	1,259	75,010
2013	322	12,287	14,739	1,731	14,232	1,470	852	25,998	2,791	1,293	75,714
2014	327	12,626	14,968	1,770	12,666	1,372	861	26,081	3,005	1,352	75,028

[1] Included in other.   *Source: American Plastics Council (APC)*

PLASTICS

Average Producer Price Index of Plastic Resins and Materials (066) in the United States (1982 = 100)

Year	Jan.	Feb.	Mar.	Apr.	May	June	July	Aug.	Sept.	Oct.	Nov.	Dec.	Average
2006	203.9	200.0	198.9	194.3	195.9	198.5	199.2	202.3	202.4	200.0	196.2	189.1	198.4
2007	187.6	185.5	187.0	192.1	193.8	196.9	198.6	198.7	198.0	199.3	205.9	207.5	195.9
2008	209.7	209.6	210.8	212.1	216.4	219.1	229.2	233.3	227.1	222.3	200.3	190.3	215.0
2009	184.6	190.1	188.6	183.5	185.9	185.9	194.4	194.5	196.4	194.5	194.5	196.8	190.8
2010	195.0	206.4	208.2	222.4	213.1	208.1	212.7	211.1	210.7	215.0	210.3	208.4	210.1
2011	213.2	218.8	223.2	229.1	239.5	238.4	236.7	233.8	235.3	229.2	231.5	227.2	229.7
2012	232.0	234.9	238.0	239.6	238.7	236.3	233.8	234.8	231.8	234.4	234.2	233.9	235.2
2013	239.7	244.1	247.1	245.9	244.6	245.4	244.4	245.1	245.5	245.8	247.9	247.7	245.3
2014	250.6	253.8	256.6	257.5	257.3	255.2	257.1	259.4	261.7	263.0	259.7	252.4	257.0
2015[1]	243.2	237.3	230.2	229.4	230.3	231.5	230.5	227.7	223.1	218.9	220.4	220.1	228.6

[1] Preliminary.   Source: Bureau of Labor Statistics, U.S. Department of Commerce (BLS)

Average Producer Price Index of Thermoplastic Resins (0662) in the United States (1982 = 100)

Year	Jan.	Feb.	Mar.	Apr.	May	June	July	Aug.	Sept.	Oct.	Nov.	Dec.	Average
2006	207.9	202.8	201.5	195.6	197.6	201.1	201.6	205.1	205.0	201.6	196.8	188.1	200.4
2007	186.0	183.4	185.3	190.7	193.0	196.2	198.2	198.4	197.6	199.3	206.6	208.2	195.2
2008	209.9	209.9	211.5	213.2	218.4	221.2	232.4	236.5	229.0	223.5	197.6	187.1	215.9
2009	179.3	187.1	185.9	180.3	183.1	183.2	193.2	192.9	194.5	192.2	192.8	194.9	188.3
2010	193.2	206.8	208.8	225.7	214.9	208.8	214.3	212.6	212.1	217.2	211.7	209.3	211.3
2011	214.7	221.1	226.0	232.6	244.6	242.1	239.9	236.3	238.1	230.9	233.6	228.6	232.4
2012	234.3	237.6	241.1	242.9	241.7	238.8	235.6	236.8	233.2	236.2	236.1	235.4	237.5
2013	242.8	247.4	250.7	249.4	247.7	248.7	246.7	247.7	249.2	249.6	251.8	251.7	248.6
2014	254.9	258.5	261.7	262.8	262.1	260.0	262.3	265.0	267.2	269.0	265.3	255.9	262.1
2015[1]	245.6	239.2	231.3	230.5	233.0	234.3	233.2	229.8	222.1	219.8	221.7	221.3	230.2

[1] Preliminary.   Source: Bureau of Labor Statistics, U.S. Department of Commerce (BLS)

Average Producer Price Index of Thermosetting Resins (0663) in the United States (1982 = 100)

Year	Jan.	Feb.	Mar.	Apr.	May	June	July	Aug.	Sept.	Oct.	Nov.	Dec.	Average
2006	200.0	200.8	200.8	201.7	201.6	200.5	202.1	203.6	204.2	206.3	206.6	206.3	202.9
2007	207.8	208.3	207.8	211.7	210.0	212.6	212.3	212.4	211.9	211.6	214.7	216.8	211.5
2008	221.4	220.7	220.0	219.0	218.5	220.3	224.8	229.3	229.8	229.6	228.3	220.7	223.5
2009	226.7	219.3	216.2	213.5	213.9	213.7	213.5	215.5	219.7	220.0	216.2	220.0	217.4
2010	218.0	216.8	217.1	216.7	216.1	217.2	216.3	215.2	215.3	215.4	215.3	216.1	216.3
2011	218.0	219.4	220.6	223.0	224.8	231.9	233.0	233.7	234.0	233.9	233.8	233.4	228.3
2012	233.2	234.0	235.1	235.9	236.4	236.6	238.1	237.6	238.6	238.6	238.1	239.3	236.8
2013	236.4	240.1	241.8	241.4	241.8	241.8	246.2	245.6	239.7	239.9	240.7	240.2	241.3
2014	241.5	242.6	243.4	243.7	245.9	244.3	243.5	244.2	246.3	245.7	244.6	247.6	244.4
2015[1]	244.6	241.0	237.9	237.2	229.2	230.1	229.5	229.6	230.5	227.7	226.9	226.7	232.6

[1] Preliminary.   Source: Bureau of Labor Statistics, U.S. Department of Commerce (BLS)

Average Producer Price Index of Styrene Plastics Materials (0662-06) in the United States (1982 = 100)

Year	Jan.	Feb.	Mar.	Apr.	May	June	July	Aug.	Sept.	Oct.	Nov.	Dec.	Average
1995	129.0	127.0	132.5	134.7	135.9	137.5	135.1	133.2	132.1	130.1	127.9	126.1	131.8
1996	125.7	123.5	125.0	118.3	120.1	122.7	123.4	123.3	123.6	122.8	122.0	120.9	122.6
1997	120.6	123.1	123.0	121.6	121.6	121.6	122.7	117.7	118.0	116.5	113.5	113.7	119.5
1998	113.3	113.9	115.5	114.9	114.1	112.8	111.3	111.2	107.6	107.9	107.1	106.3	111.3
1999	103.5	102.4	103.5	104.7	103.0	102.3	103.1	101.5	101.4	99.8	99.4	100.5	102.1
2000	103.0	104.3	110.5	113.0	116.2	116.9	118.5	116.5	115.0	114.1	112.1	110.4	112.5
2001	110.5	109.2	107.9	108.0	101.8	99.9	97.6	95.7	87.3	89.4	90.0	85.4	98.6
2002	85.7	85.8	87.9	88.5	90.4	91.7	93.7	100.6	100.5	108.9	108.1	103.9	95.5
2003[1]	102.9	110.2	119.5	127.2	126.7	119.1	118.0	113.3	112.8	113.6	113.7	111.6	115.7
2004[1]	Data no longer available												

[1] Preliminary.   Source: Bureau of Labor Statistics, U.S. Department of Commerce (BLS)

Platinum-Group Metals

Platinum (atomic symbol Pt) is a relatively rare, chemically inert metallic element that is more valuable than gold. Platinum is a grayish-white metal that has a high fusing point, is malleable and ductile, and has a high electrical resistance. Chemically, platinum is relatively inert and resists attack by air, water, single acids, and ordinary reagents. Platinum is the most important of the six-metal group, which also includes ruthenium, rhodium, palladium, osmium, and iridium. The word "platinum" is derived from the Spanish word *platina* meaning silver.

Platinum is one of the world's rarest metals with new mine production totaling only about 5 million troy ounces a year. All the platinum mined to date would fit in the average-size living room. Platinum is mined all over the world with supplies concentrated in South Africa. South Africa accounts for nearly 80% of world supply, followed by Russia, and North America.

Because platinum will never tarnish, lose its rich white luster, or even wear down after many years, it is prized by the jewelry industry. The international jewelry industry is the largest consumer sector for platinum, accounting for 51% of total platinum demand. In Europe and the U.S., the normal purity of platinum is 95%. Ten tons of ore must be mined and a five-month process is needed to produce one ounce of pure platinum.

The second major consumer sector for platinum is for auto catalysts, with 21% of total platinum demand. Catalysts in autos are used to convert most of vehicle emissions into less harmful carbon dioxide, nitrogen, and water vapor. Platinum is also used in the production of hard disk drive coatings, fiber optic cables, infra-red detectors, fertilizers, explosives, petrol additives, platinum-tipped spark plugs, glassmaking equipment, biodegradable elements for household detergents, dental restorations, and in anti-cancer drugs.

Palladium (atomic symbol Pd) is very similar to platinum and is part of the same general metals group. Palladium is mined with platinum, but it is somewhat more common because it is also a by-product of nickel mining. The primary use for palladium is in the use of automotive catalysts, with that sector accounting for about 63% of total palladium demand. Other uses for palladium include electronic equipment (21%), dental alloys (12%), and jewelry (4%).

Rhodium (atomic symbol Rh), another member of the platinum group, is also used in the automotive industry in pollution control devices. To some extent palladium has replaced rhodium. Iridium (atomic symbol Ir) is used to process catalysts and it has also found use in some auto catalysts. Iridium and ruthenium (atomic symbol Ru) are used in the production of polyvinyl chloride. As the prices of these metals change, there is some substitution. Therefore, strength of platinum prices relative to palladium should lead to the substitution of palladium for platinum in catalytic converters.

Platinum futures and options are traded at the CME Group, the JSE Securities Exchange, and the Moscow Exchange. Platinum futures are also traded on the Multi Commodity Exchange of India (MCX), the National Commodity & Derivatives Exchange (NCDEX), and the Tokyo Commodity Exchange (TOCOM). Palladium futures and options are traded at the CME Group. Palladium futures are also traded on the Moscow Exchange and the Tokyo Commodity Exchange (TOCOM). The CME platinum futures contract calls for the delivery of 50 troy ounces of platinum (0.9995 fineness) and the contract trades in terms of dollars and cents per troy ounce. The CME palladium futures contract calls for the delivery of 50 troy ounces of palladium (0.9995 fineness) and the contract is priced in terms of dollars and cents per troy ounce.

Prices – CME platinum futures prices (Barchart.com symbol PL) on the nearest-futures chart sold off steadily during 2015, posting a 7-year low and closing the year down -26.2% at $891.7 per troy ounce.

CME palladium futures prices (Barchart.com symbol PA) on the nearest-futures chart sold off sharply, posting a 5-year low and closing the year down -29.6% at $562.00 per troy ounce.

Supply – World mine production of platinum in 2015 rose +21.1% yr/yr to 178,000 kilograms, but remained below the record high of 218,000 kilograms in 2006. South Africa is the world's largest producer of platinum by far with 70.2% of world production in 2015, followed by Russia (12.9%), Zimbabwe (7.0%), Canada (5.1%) and the U.S. (2.1%). World mine production of palladium in 2015 ROSE +7.8% to 208,000 kilograms, which was still below the record high production level of 224,000 in 2007. The world's largest palladium producers are Russia with 38.5% of world production in 2015, South Africa with 35.1%, Canada with 11.5%, and the U.S. with 6.0%. World production of platinum group metals other than platinum and palladium in 2013 (latest data available) rose by +88.1% yr/yr to 67,700 kilograms, but still below the 2007 record high of 79,600 kilograms.

U.S. mine production of platinum in 2015 was virtually unchanged yr/yr at 3,700 kilograms, and still below the record high of 4,390 kilograms posted in 2002. U.S. mine production of palladium in 2015 was also virtually unchanged yr/yr at 12,500 kilograms, well below the record high of 14,800 kilograms posted in 2002. U.S. refinery secondary production of scrap platinum and palladium in 2013 (latest data available) rose +14.4% to 43,000 kilograms, a new 20-year high.

Demand – The total of platinum-group metals sold to consuming industries in the U.S. in 2004 (latest data available) rose +7.1% to 91,434 kilograms. The two main U.S. industries that use platinum are the auto industry, which accounted for about 74% of U.S. platinum usage in 2004, and the jewelry industry, which accounted for about 26% of U.S. platinum usage.

Trade – U.S. imports of refined platinum and palladium in 2015 for consumption fell -3.5% yr/yr to 248,770 kilograms. U.S. exports of refined platinum and palladium in 2015 rose +2.0% yr/yr to 39,400 kilograms, well below the record high of 103,590 kilograms in 2006. The U.S. relied on imports for 90% of its platinum and palladium consumption in 2015.

PLATINUM-GROUP METALS

World Mine Production of Platinum   In Kilograms

Year	Australia	Canada	Colombia[3]	Finland	Japan	Russia	Serbia/ Montenegro	Africa	United States	Zimbabwe	World Total
2006	209	8,510	1,438	800	760	29,000	2	168,125	4,290	4,998	218,000
2007	142	8,000	1,526	461	1,000	27,000	2	160,940	3,860	5,306	209,000
2008	120	8,500	1,370	214	1,442	25,000	----	146,140	3,580	5,642	193,000
2009	230	4,000	929	265	1,417	24,500	12	140,819	3,830	6,849	185,000
2010	130	3,500	997	500	1,331	25,000	----	147,790	3,450	8,800	193,000
2011	95	8,000	1,231	400	1,765	25,900	----	148,008	3,700	10,826	202,000
2012	90	7,500	1,460	400	1,735	24,600	6	128,590	3,670	10,500	181,000
2013	90	7,000	1,330	400	1,963	25,500	3	131,000	3,720	12,400	184,000
2014[1]		8,500				23,000	3	94,000	3,660	12,500	147,000
2015[2]		9,000				23,000		125,000	3,700	12,500	178,000

[1] Preliminary.   [2] Estimate.   [3] Placer platinum.   W = Withheld.   *Source: U.S. Geological Survey (USGS)*

World Mine Production of Palladium and Other Group Metals   In Kilograms

				Palladium							Other Group Metals		
Year	Australia	Canada	Finland	Japan	Russia	Serbia/ Montenegro	South Africa	United States	Zim-babwe	Total	Russia	South Africa	World Total
2006	750	10,493	----	5,400	98,400	15	86,265	14,400	4,022	222,000	15,600	53,138	74,600
2007	600	14,100	----	6,505	96,800	15	83,643	12,800	4,180	224,000	14,500	59,449	76,500
2008	580	14,700	342	7,526	87,700	70	75,537	11,900	4,386	206,000	12,500	53,999	69,100
2009	800	7,000	560	6,675	83,200	38	75,117	12,700	5,680	195,000	11,900	55,456	69,500
2010	650	11,000	1,493	6,107	84,700	22	82,222	11,600	7,000	208,000	12,000	57,292	71,500
2011	350	17,400	1,058	7,534	84,100	4	82,731	12,400	8,241	216,000	12,000	58,111	72,700
2012	300	17,300	1,100	8,052	82,000	22	74,738	12,300	7,800	206,000	12,000	21,010	36,000
2013	320	16,500	1,100	6,239	80,000	20	75,000	12,600	9,600	203,000	12,000	52,000	67,700
2014[1]		20,000			83,000		58,400	12,400	10,100	193,000			
2015[2]		24,000			80,000		73,000	12,500	10,000	208,000			

[1] Preliminary.   [2] Estimate.   *Source: U.S. Geological Survey (USGS)*

Salient Statistics of Platinum and Allied Metals[3] in the United States   In Kilograms

	Net Import Reliance as a % of Apparent	Mine Production		Refinery Pro- duction (Secon-	Total	Refiner, Importer & Dealer Stocks as of Dec. 31				Imports		Exports		Apparent Con-
Year	Consump	Platinum	Palladium	dary)	Refined	Platinum	Palladium	Other[4]	Total	Refined	Total	Refined	Total	sumptio
2006	90	4,290	14,400	12,530	12,530	261	----	111	372	287,756	----	103,590	----	----
2007	91	3,860	12,800	16,340	16,340	261	----	18	279	362,733	----	81,100	----	----
2008	89	3,580	11,900	15,050	15,050	261	----	18	279	334,961	----	50,430	----	----
2009	95	3,830	12,700	15,030	15,030	261	----	18	279	286,688	----	51,140	----	----
2010	91	3,450	11,600	12,230	12,230	261	----	18	279	253,206	----	61,040	----	----
2011	89	3,700	12,400	33,000	33,000	261	----	18	279	257,138	----	45,820	----	----
2012	90	3,670	12,300	37,600	37,600	261	----	18	279	276,460	----	43,510	----	----
2013	84	3,720	12,600	43,000	43,000	261	----	18	279	227,297	----	39,640	----	----
2014[1]	89	3,660	12,400			----				257,912	----	38,629	----	----
2015[2]	90	3,700	12,500			----				248,770	----	39,400	----	----

[1] Preliminary.   [2] Estimate.   [3] Includes platinum, palladium, iridium, osmium, rhodium, and ruthenium.   [4] Includes iridium, osmium, rhodium, and ruthenium.   W = Withheld.   *Source: U.S. Geological Survey (USGS)*

Average Producer Price of Rhodium in the United States   In Dollars Per Troy Ounce

Year	Jan.	Feb.	Mar.	Apr.	May	June	July	Aug.	Sept.	Oct.	Nov.	Dec.	Average
2006	3,134.29	3,493.68	3,876.74	4,465.53	5,543.41	4,898.86	4,602.11	4,647.83	4,824.75	4,930.00	4,883.75	5,390.00	4,557.58
2007	5,738.64	5,947.50	6,065.91	6,293.75	6,144.55	6,107.62	6,050.48	6,104.78	6,201.32	6,258.70	6,648.75	6,815.00	6,198.08
2008	7,042.27	8,531.25	9,248.75	9,065.91	9,553.57	9,775.00	9,385.23	6,247.62	4,501.19	2,460.87	1,393.06	1,214.29	6,534.92
2009	1,147.62	1,178.95	1,169.32	1,346.90	1,417.50	1,463.64	1,490.91	1,671.43	1,650.00	1,782.95	2,332.89	2,410.71	1,588.57
2010	2,668.75	2,483.75	2,514.57	2,846.43	2,768.75	2,484.09	2,341.67	2,148.86	2,203.57	2,279.76	2,341.25	2,361.98	2,453.62
2011	2,436.90	2,475.00	2,396.74	2,340.00	2,120.24	2,067.05	1,982.50	1,876.09	1,817.86	1,625.00	1,660.00	1,475.00	2,022.70
2012	1,390.00	1,513.75	1,484.09	1,383.25	1,345.91	1,250.00	1,224.52	1,123.26	1,175.00	1,184.78	1,137.50	1,091.50	1,275.30
2013	1,123.64	1,226.00	1,254.00	1,184.32	1,127.95	1,037.00	988.64	1,000.23	1,000.00	987.83	958.50	916.43	1,067.05
2014	1,047.73	1,068.00	1,092.14	1,134.52	1,071.67	1,118.81	1,187.27	1,375.24	1,310.48	1,228.70	1,224.44	1,206.36	1,172.11
2015	1,195.95	1,184.50	1,166.59	1,146.90	1,105.75	976.14	857.05	847.86	772.38	767.95	741.90	678.70	953.47

Source: American Metal Market (AMM)

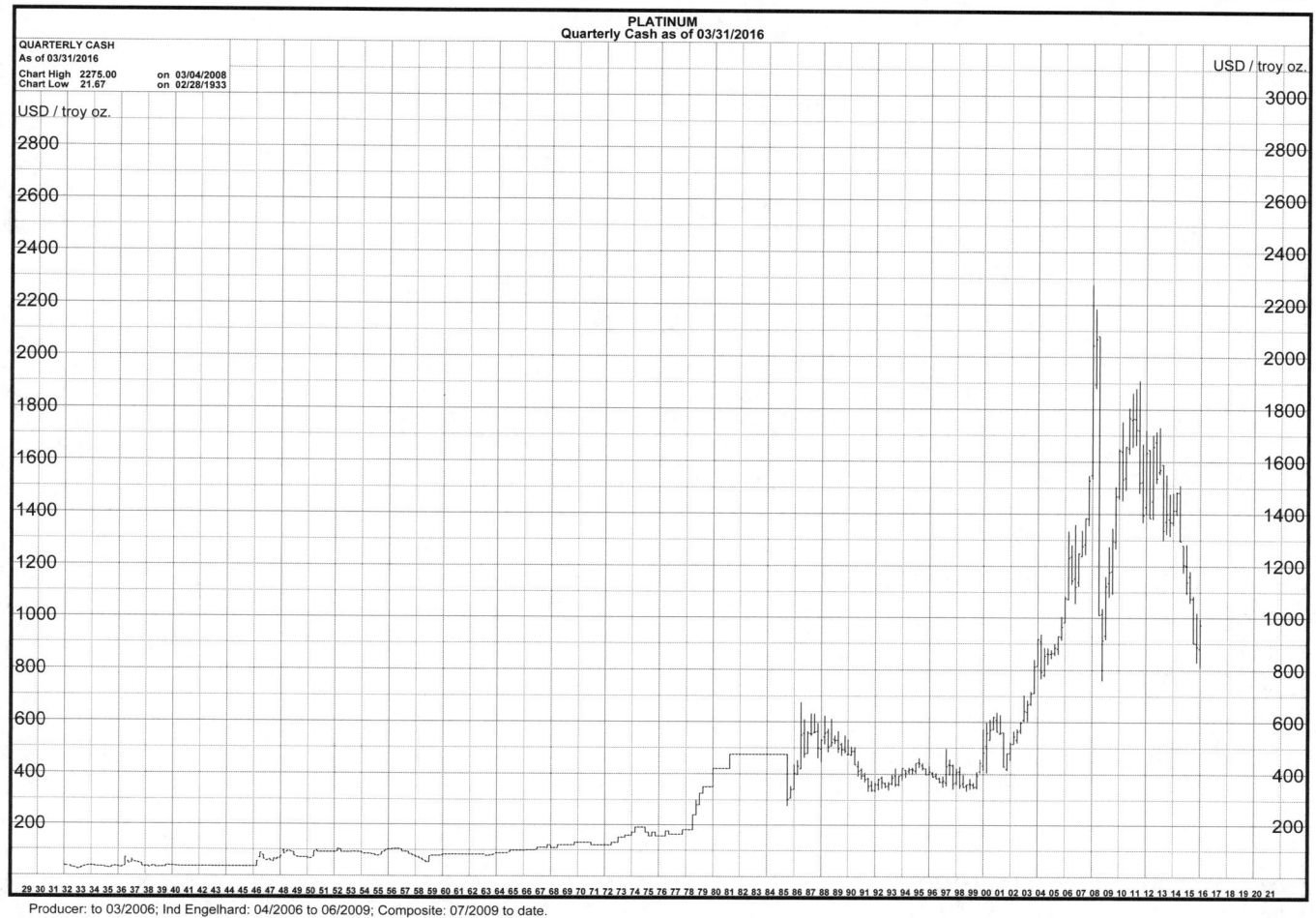

PLATINUM
Quarterly Cash as of 03/31/2016

QUARTERLY CASH
As of 03/31/2016
Chart High 2275.00 on 03/04/2008
Chart Low 21.67 on 02/28/1933

USD / troy oz.

Producer: to 03/2006; Ind Engelhard: 04/2006 to 06/2009; Composite: 07/2009 to date.

Average Merchant's Price of Platinum in the United States   In Dollars Per Troy Ounce

Year	Jan.	Feb.	Mar.	Apr.	May	June	July	Aug.	Sept.	Oct.	Nov.	Dec.	Average
2006	1,032.48	1,045.16	1,044.39	1,105.00	1,264.05	1,192.73	1,233.03	1,236.74	1,183.30	1,085.32	1,183.73	1,124.79	1,144.23
2007	1,151.90	1,206.47	1,222.77	1,280.90	1,306.50	1,289.14	1,307.38	1,267.30	1,313.00	1,413.87	1,449.45	1,492.47	1,308.43
2008	1,585.09	2,002.55	2,043.65	1,991.32	2,053.57	2,042.24	1,904.68	1,492.52	1,221.71	917.13	841.22	842.40	1,578.17
2009	949.76	1,037.26	1,084.59	1,169.57	1,134.45	1,220.41	1,163.82	1,248.24	1,294.71	1,335.86	1,401.26	1,447.20	1,207.26
2010	1,567.15	1,525.63	1,602.65	1,718.33	1,633.45	1,556.77	1,530.57	1,543.82	1,598.57	1,692.29	1,702.35	1,715.05	1,615.55
2011	1,790.62	1,828.68	1,773.26	1,804.00	1,792.24	1,771.45	1,766.65	1,810.52	1,745.43	1,539.81	1,607.65	1,461.81	1,724.34
2012	1,510.85	1,664.50	1,660.05	1,590.85	1,474.45	1,450.05	1,425.86	1,455.70	1,629.89	1,639.26	1,578.85	1,583.00	1,555.28
2013	1,646.43	1,676.95	1,586.30	1,497.23	1,478.95	1,431.20	1,405.14	1,496.50	1,454.05	1,415.52	1,423.85	1,355.25	1,488.95
2014	1,423.73	1,411.30	1,457.52	1,435.38	1,461.07	1,457.81	1,497.05	1,449.90	1,362.10	1,263.61	1,213.00	1,222.48	1,387.91
2015	1,247.38	1,200.79	1,140.00	1,154.33	1,143.25	1,091.77	1,011.23	985.86	966.38	978.95	885.10	863.30	1,055.70

Source: American Metal Market (AMM)

Average Dealer Price[1] of Palladium in the United States   In Dollars Per Troy Ounce

Year	Jan.	Feb.	Mar.	Apr.	May	June	July	Aug.	Sept.	Oct.	Nov.	Dec.	Average
2006	275.95	291.58	312.70	355.74	372.82	319.36	320.21	332.57	324.40	315.18	326.91	328.00	322.95
2007	339.81	344.26	352.27	370.35	369.50	370.76	368.67	344.61	337.63	368.70	366.75	355.42	357.39
2008	376.95	473.65	490.35	449.05	438.29	453.57	428.27	318.29	250.19	193.30	212.61	178.00	355.21
2009	189.81	207.63	203.73	228.29	230.45	247.18	250.64	278.38	295.86	324.45	354.84	376.60	265.66
2010	437.15	429.16	464.48	535.33	495.05	465.18	459.86	493.45	543.24	596.33	687.75	760.05	530.59
2011	797.48	823.47	766.48	777.30	743.38	774.55	794.80	766.57	710.14	620.45	637.70	650.57	738.57
2012	664.28	708.05	689.86	660.65	624.68	617.95	582.95	607.04	664.00	637.78	639.20	694.95	649.28
2013	716.62	755.68	761.20	710.27	723.91	716.70	725.18	746.23	711.75	727.61	737.20	721.45	729.48
2014	738.59	733.90	783.19	804.62	829.67	841.19	880.95	884.10	844.57	784.30	783.78	810.71	809.96
2015	788.29	789.95	789.55	771.86	787.00	729.77	643.64	598.24	612.76	693.82	575.57	555.96	694.70

[1] Based on wholesale quantities, prompt delivery.   Source: American Metal Market (AMM)

PLATINUM-GROUP METALS

PLATINUM - NYMEX
Weekly Selected Futures as of 04/01/2016

WEEKLY SELECTED FUTURES
As of 04/01/2016

Chart High 2308.80 on 03/04/2008
Chart Low 761.80 on 10/27/2008

USD / troy oz.

Nearby Futures through Last Trading Day.

Volume of Trading of Platinum Futures in New York   In Contracts

Year	Jan.	Feb.	Mar.	Apr.	May	June	July	Aug.	Sept.	Oct.	Nov.	Dec.	Total
2006	20,604	27,572	42,804	17,215	34,684	45,985	16,220	21,428	44,000	21,182	46,754	34,671	373,119
2007	20,534	26,975	59,099	26,457	35,525	66,968	35,371	35,975	58,091	34,100	36,126	66,324	501,545
2008	54,479	71,978	84,901	41,283	54,476	66,398	43,127	47,539	74,165	38,107	30,011	69,079	675,543
2009	31,090	35,199	82,949	30,849	34,962	104,413	46,045	48,650	134,462	55,865	63,896	134,504	802,884
2010	85,446	83,630	176,594	91,365	133,781	144,344	71,314	74,099	188,874	99,204	151,998	185,858	1,486,507
2011	123,012	97,150	235,375	105,524	113,655	216,647	95,589	188,066	293,142	156,172	136,109	232,822	1,993,263
2012	150,111	172,872	252,464	136,954	181,216	283,780	138,326	217,759	371,411	211,656	183,154	322,051	2,621,754
2013	280,979	275,013	335,276	277,634	243,442	388,436	188,942	216,194	341,340	222,190	185,380	307,949	3,262,775
2014	217,465	194,296	389,315	182,628	239,397	379,860	210,163	179,938	399,265	271,921	211,151	360,542	3,235,941
2015	243,017	200,204	408,528	217,744	211,710	434,374	262,007	268,391	443,850	281,094	261,514	408,711	3,641,144

Contract size = 50 oz.   *Source: CME Group; New York Mercantile Exchange (NYMEX)*

Average Open Interest of Platinum Futures in New York   In Contracts

Year	Jan.	Feb.	Mar.	Apr.	May	June	July	Aug.	Sept.	Oct.	Nov.	Dec.
2006	10,625	9,995	8,407	9,486	9,681	8,265	8,575	9,889	9,076	7,276	8,332	8,186
2007	8,810	10,752	11,154	13,413	15,173	15,033	16,641	12,347	12,341	15,199	14,427	15,404
2008	17,912	15,770	12,966	12,977	15,869	15,821	14,198	12,325	13,904	15,111	16,530	17,267
2009	18,300	20,041	20,388	20,506	21,045	23,755	21,952	25,303	28,571	31,236	33,730	33,542
2010	34,160	34,637	36,720	37,368	33,840	30,242	28,369	31,026	35,528	38,402	36,959	37,115
2011	40,572	41,823	35,986	35,925	36,214	35,150	32,278	37,063	39,229	37,910	38,779	42,652
2012	43,893	44,519	43,028	40,337	45,372	50,530	50,160	53,902	57,555	63,289	60,641	62,626
2013	64,184	70,544	64,608	63,193	63,406	62,590	61,937	65,515	61,739	59,391	59,092	63,028
2014	59,980	63,324	69,278	65,308	68,150	68,004	71,271	64,416	64,103	59,701	61,768	65,647
2015	66,436	66,642	70,775	69,165	71,645	79,378	79,326	76,953	73,817	72,160	72,938	73,105

Contract size = 50 oz.   *Source: CME Group; New York Mercantile Exchange (NYMEX)*

PALLADIUM - NYMEX
Weekly Selected Futures as of 04/01/2016

WEEKLY SELECTED FUTURES
As of 04/01/2016

Chart High 912.00 on 09/02/2014
Chart Low 160.00 on 12/05/2008

USD / troy oz.

Nearby Futures through Last Trading Day.

Volume of Trading of Palladium Futures in New York   In Contracts

Year	Jan.	Feb.	Mar.	Apr.	May	June	July	Aug.	Sept.	Oct.	Nov.	Dec.	Total
2006	28,447	59,279	32,573	23,135	64,863	25,857	13,464	41,123	16,222	14,351	47,797	11,005	378,116
2007	23,636	62,815	14,987	25,166	69,089	16,322	15,072	65,106	16,975	26,385	52,411	13,029	400,993
2008	26,954	105,845	49,411	24,750	66,939	18,934	26,245	53,692	25,253	28,627	43,879	13,299	483,828
2009	14,284	41,726	14,509	17,332	51,635	23,403	25,689	57,502	25,393	29,401	71,228	28,719	400,821
2010	48,438	90,368	48,314	58,104	134,435	45,840	45,847	87,366	55,399	69,623	156,495	61,355	901,584
2011	72,121	121,271	94,402	85,897	132,608	80,665	66,290	139,208	80,932	72,895	119,732	73,508	1,139,529
2012	74,977	125,721	75,910	61,833	136,033	67,710	59,308	123,731	85,209	84,730	145,835	77,483	1,118,480
2013	126,987	198,821	87,681	122,520	181,016	93,497	77,175	163,892	82,470	99,944	182,133	69,880	1,486,016
2014	87,502	158,760	136,126	111,648	195,880	101,610	97,809	208,474	126,132	115,708	161,947	72,376	1,573,972
2015	99,787	146,928	100,748	78,232	131,105	91,044	102,665	185,094	87,201	92,284	162,382	66,956	1,344,426

Contract size = 100 oz.   *Source: CME Group; New York Mercantile Exchange (NYMEX)*

Average Open Interest of Palladium Futures in New York   In Contracts

Year	Jan.	Feb.	Mar.	Apr.	May	June	July	Aug.	Sept.	Oct.	Nov.	Dec.
2006	14,353	16,632	15,426	17,783	18,002	14,251	14,087	13,166	11,247	11,836	12,511	11,210
2007	13,794	16,132	15,587	18,126	19,682	18,288	18,152	18,035	16,062	16,286	17,194	14,820
2008	18,184	20,999	20,227	19,571	19,197	17,106	15,223	13,821	14,294	14,656	13,435	12,688
2009	12,442	12,596	12,230	14,237	15,594	16,288	17,150	20,669	21,877	21,881	22,650	22,692
2010	23,356	22,566	22,944	23,905	23,152	21,271	19,732	19,808	23,036	24,706	24,747	23,089
2011	22,340	22,939	21,584	21,325	20,376	20,615	21,809	21,576	19,590	19,074	19,368	18,558
2012	18,051	21,035	20,978	21,174	22,931	21,951	22,676	23,304	19,987	20,172	22,005	25,798
2013	31,036	37,519	37,181	37,118	36,554	36,219	35,682	38,564	34,971	37,152	39,264	36,781
2014	39,059	40,226	41,494	42,071	43,466	39,964	43,791	44,286	38,776	33,587	34,170	32,060
2015	33,813	33,807	31,897	32,138	31,396	33,426	36,629	34,717	27,329	25,978	27,440	25,030

Contract size = 100 oz.   *Source: CME Group; New York Mercantile Exchange (NYMEX)*

Potatoes

The potato is a member of the nightshade family. The leaves of the potato plant are poisonous and a potato will begin to turn green if left too long in the light. This green skin contains solanine, a substance that can cause the potato to taste bitter and even cause illness in humans.

In Peru, the Inca Indians were the first to cultivate potatoes around 200 BC. The Indians developed potato crops because their staple diet of corn would not grow above an altitude of 3,350 meters. In 1536, after conquering the Incas, the Spanish Conquistadors brought potatoes back to Europe. At first, Europeans did not accept the potato because it was not mentioned in the Bible and was therefore considered an "evil" food. But after Marie Antoinette wore a crown of potato flowers, it finally became a popular food. In 1897, during the Alaskan Klondike gold rush, potatoes were so valued for their vitamin C content that miners traded gold for potatoes. The potato became the first vegetable to be grown in outer space in October 1995.

The potato is a highly nutritious, fat-free, cholesterol-free and sodium-free food, and is an important dietary staple in over 130 countries. A medium-sized potato contains only 100 calories. Potatoes are an excellent source of vitamin C and provide B vitamins as well as potassium, copper, magnesium, and iron. According to the U.S. Department of Agriculture, "a diet of whole milk and potatoes would supply almost all of the food elements necessary for the maintenance of the human body."

Potatoes are one of the largest vegetable crops grown in the U.S., and are grown in all fifty states. The U.S. ranks about 4th in world potato production. The top three types of potatoes grown extensively in the U.S. are white, red, and Russets (Russets account for about two-thirds the U.S. crop). Potatoes in the U.S. are harvested in all four seasons, but the vast majority of the crop is harvested in fall. Potatoes harvested in the winter, spring and summer are used mainly to supplement fresh supplies of fall-harvested potatoes and are also important to the processing industries. The four principal categories for U.S. potato exports are frozen, potato chips, fresh, and dehydrated. Fries account for approximately 95% of U.S. frozen potato exports.

Prices – The average monthly price received for potatoes by U.S. farmers in 2015 fell -1.4% to $8.75 per hundred pounds, below the 2013 record high of $9.75.

Supply –The total potato U.S. crop in 2015 rose +0.6% to 44.560 billion pounds, well below the record high of 50.936 billion pounds posted in 2000. The fall crop in 2015 rose by +75.5% to 70.863 million pounds and it accounted for 91.7% of the total crop. Stocks of the fall crop (as of Dec 1, 2015) were 26.740 billion pounds. In 2015, the spring crop rose +2.1% to 2.260 billion pounds, the summer crop fell -8.0% to 1.585 billion pounds, and the winter crop (annualized through 2015) rose +2.1% to 403.703 million pounds.

The largest producing states for the fall 2015 crop were Idaho (with 32.9% of the crop), Washington (25.1%), Wisconsin (6.5%), North Dakota (5.9%), and Colorado (5.7%). For the spring crop, the largest producing states were California with 51.6% of the crop and Florida with 31.1% of the crop. Farmers harvested 1.053 million acres in 2015, down -0.2% yr/yr and slightly above the 2010 record low of 1.008 million acres. The yield per harvested acre in 2015 fell -0.7% to 41,800 pounds per acre.

Demand – Total utilization of potatoes in 2014 (latest data) rose +1.7% yr/yr to 44.217 billion pounds, up from the 2010 record low of 40.427 billion pounds. The breakdown shows that the largest consumption category for potatoes is frozen French fries with 34.6% of total consumption, followed closely by table stock (24.3%), chips and shoestrings (16.6%), and dehydration (11.0%). U.S. per capita consumption of potatoes in 2013 (latest data) rose +1.7% to 116.7 pounds, below the record high of 145.0 pounds per capita seen in 1996.

Trade – U.S. exports of potatoes in 2011 (latest data) rose +16.2% to 944,494 thousand pounds, a new record high. U.S. imports in 2011 rose +19.2% to 909,645 thousand pounds, down from the 2008 record high of 1.071 million pounds.

Salient Statistics of Potatoes in the United States

Crop Year	Acreage Planted --- 1,000 Acres ---	Harvested	Yield Per Harvested Acre Cwt.	Total Production	Seed & Feed	Shrinkage & Loss	Sold[2]	Farm Price ($ Cwt.)	Production[3] ---- Million $ ----	Sales	Stocks Jan. 1 (1,000 Cwt)	Exports (Fresh) -- Millions of Lbs. --	Imports	Fresh	Total
2006	1,139	1,120	393	440,698	4,750	29,639	406,309	7.31	3,209	2,970	225,800	600,715	611,229	38.6	123.7
2007	1,142	1,122	396	444,873	4,105	29,561	411,209	7.51	3,340	3,089	232,300	615,784	923,574	38.7	124.4
2008	1,060	1,047	396	415,055	4,138	26,438	384,478	9.09	3,770	3,494	213,200	616,290	1,071,973	37.8	118.3
2009	1,071	1,044	414	432,601	4,535	29,135	398,931	8.25	3,558	3,292	234,300	682,190	794,611	36.7	113.5
2010	1,026	1,008	401	404,273	4,220	24,990	375,063	9.20	3,722	3,449	209,400	812,748	762,876	36.8	113.9
2011	1,099	1,077	399	429,647	4,142	27,755	397,750	9.37	4,041	3,743	NA	944,494	909,645	34.1	110.3
2012	1,155	1,139	408	464,970	4,869	28,356	429,541	8.63	4,017	3,728	NA				
2013	1,064	1,051	414	434,652	4,323	26,211	404,118	9.75	4,237	3,943	NA				
2014[1]	1,063	1,051	421	442,170	4,192	26,762	411,216	8.88	3,928	3,658					
2015[1]	1,065	1,053	418	440,498					3,848						

[1] Preliminary. [2] For all purposes, including food, seed processing & livestock feed. [3] Farm weight basis, excluding canned and frozen potatoes.
[4] Calendar year. Source: Economic Research Service, U.S. Department of Agriculture (ERS-USDA)

Potato Crop Production Estimates, Stocks and Disappearance in the United States   In Millions of Cwt.

| | Crop Production Estimates | | | | | | Total Storage Stocks² — Following Year | | | | | Fall Crop — 1,000 Cwt. | | | | |
| | Total Crop | | | Fall Crop | | | | | | | | Pro-duction | Disap-pearance (Sold) | Stocks Dec. 1 | Average Price ($/Cwt.) | Value of Sales ($1,000) |
Year	Oct. 1	Nov. 1	Dec. 1	Oct. 1	Nov. 1	Dec. 1	Jan. 1	Feb. 1	Mar. 1	Apr. 1	May 1					
2006	----	434.8	----	----	390.9	258.9	225.8	192.2	159.5	120.9	79.1	389,527	365,863	258,900	6.67	2,442,474
2007	----	448.0	----	----	408.3	265.5	232.3	199.3	163.4	125.5	84.0	397,753	374,617	265,500	7.04	2,636,885
2008	----	415.1	----	----	373.5	243.7	213.2	183.9	152.7	115.8	78.1	369,866	349,580	243,700	8.49	2,967,871
2009	----	429.7	----	----	391.5	265.8	234.3	203.5	169.7	128.7	89.6	383,962	361,316	265,800	7.62	2,751,550
2010	----	399.2	----	----	361.4	240.2	209.4	180.3	148.5	111.0	72.0	357,467	339,051	240,200	8.79	2,981,528
2011	----	429.6	----	----	391.2	253.0	NA	187.5	NA	115.7	NA	382,318	360,620	253,000	8.87	3,197,096
2012	----	467.2	----	----	422.0	271.5	NA	204.6	NA	NA	NA	417,963	385,767	271,500	8.05	3,111,362
2013	----	439.7	----	----	401.5	NA	NA	NA	NA	119.1	NA	395,275	404,118	NA	9.05	3,320,712
2014	----	442.8	----	----	406.2	267.4	NA	202.7	NA	129.2	NA	403,703	411,216	267,400	8.35	3,113,990
2015¹	----	445.6	----	----	408.6							708,627				

¹ Preliminary.   ² Held by growers and local dealers in the fall producing areas.
Source: Agricultural Statistics Board, U.S. Department of Agriculture (ASB-USDA)

Production of Potatoes by Seasonal Groups in the United States   In Thousands of Cwt.

| | Spring | | | | Summer | | | Fall | | | | | | | | |
Year	Cali-fornia	Florida	North Carolina	Total	Illinois	Texas	Total	Colo-rado	Idaho	Maine	Minne-sota	North Dakota	Oregan	Washing--ton	Wis-consin	Total
2006	6,044	6,441	3,255	19,766	2,489	4,268	18,166	22,686	128,915	17,980	20,400	25,480	18,533	89,900	29,370	389,527
2007	6,123	7,807	2,700	19,817	2,440	3,781	15,997	20,981	130,010	16,668	21,560	23,660	20,294	100,800	28,160	397,753
2008	6,930	7,952	2,520	20,132	2,094	2,923	13,805	21,907	116,475	14,769	20,400	22,680	18,674	93,000	25,730	369,866
2009	7,175	7,700	3,375	21,321	2,002	3,767	14,321	22,080	132,500	15,263	20,700	19,125	21,460	87,230	28,980	383,962
2010	10,935	7,950	2,925	24,797	2,205	3,192	12,971	21,528	112,970	15,892	17,010	22,000	20,058	88,440	24,293	357,467
2011	10,920	9,112	2,805	25,573	2,244	3,815	12,894	21,291	128,760	14,310	16,685	18,865	23,342	97,600	25,938	382,318
2012	11,600	8,917	3,200	26,736	2,812	5,292	18,204	19,980	141,820	16,088	18,800	25,200	22,935	95,940	30,360	417,963
2013	10,865	7,080	3,240	22,137	2,479	8,142	17,240	20,304	131,131	15,660	17,325	22,620	21,582	96,000	26,040	395,275
2014	11,656	7,032	2,835	22,608	2,656	6,901	15,859	23,196	132,880	14,645	16,400	23,870	22,562	101,475	26,240	403,703
2015¹	9,761	6,808	2,667	20,251	2,622	6,825	15,734	22,677	130,320	16,002	18,480	27,200	21,784	100,300	29,440	708,627

¹ Preliminary.   *Source: Agricultural Statistics Board, U.S. Department of Agriculture (ASB-USDA)*

Utilization of Potatoes in the United States   In Thousands of Cwt.

| | Sales | | | | | | | | Other Sales | | | Non-Sales | | | |
| | | For Processing | | | | | | | | | | Used on | | | |
Crop Year	Table Stock	Chips, Shoe-strings	Dehyd-ration	Frozen French Fries	Other Frozen Products	Canned Potatoes	Other Canned Products²	Starch & Flour	Live-stock Feed	Seed	Total Sales	Farms Where Grown	Shrink-age & Loss	Total Non-Sales	Total
2005	114,123	52,294	43,387	126,429	25,376	2,174	958	1,622	1,999	22,254	390,616	3,595	28,519	33,310	423,926
2006	113,335	64,377	48,809	126,083	24,229	1,957	930	1,369	1,610	23,610	406,309	3,520	29,639	34,389	440,698
2007	110,860	54,343	49,021	139,624	26,571	2,504	800	4,029	1,160	22,297	411,209	2,986	29,561	33,666	444,875
2008	109,351	50,988	40,646	134,123	19,519	2,070	790	5,288	803	20,900	384,478	3,315	26,438	30,576	415,055
2009	116,326	42,548	44,477	138,589	21,004	1,983	748	6,504	6,533	20,219	398,931	3,346	29,135	33,670	432,601
2010	107,407	54,508	34,164	135,703	13,374	1,659	700	6,334	593	20,621	375,063	3,002	24,990	29,210	404,273
2011	102,655	58,703	45,511	144,626	15,188	1,650	716	6,013	825	21,863	397,750	3,012	27,755	31,897	429,647
2012	118,535	59,304	49,894	142,993	20,635	1,741	734	7,919	4,080	23,706	429,541	3,286	28,356	33,225	462,766
2013	106,930	60,485	47,411	134,966	18,451	188	1,089	8,579	1,251	22,431	404,118	3,215	26,211	30,534	434,652
2014¹	107,344	73,364	48,708	152,832	6,190	316	947		768	22,774	411,216	3,343	26,762	30,954	442,170

¹ Preliminary.   ² Hash, stews and soups.   *Source: Agricultural Statistics Board, U.S. Department of Agriculture (ASB-USDA)*

Cold Storage Stocks of All Frozen Potatoes in the United States, on First of Month   In Millions of Pounds

Year	Jan.	Feb.	Mar.	Apr.	May	June	July	Aug.	Sept.	Oct.	Nov.	Dec.
2006	1,051.1	1,076.2	1,147.0	1,158.9	1,176.6	1,104.9	1,108.1	996.4	964.1	1,009.6	1,066.6	1,052.1
2007	954.8	1,041.3	1,063.6	1,116.2	1,102.2	1,070.7	1,078.2	991.8	1,000.4	1,080.0	1,133.8	1,078.4
2008	1,012.4	1,089.1	1,117.5	1,087.7	1,134.4	1,074.9	1,190.0	1,107.5	1,126.7	1,180.8	1,200.5	1,212.1
2009	1,098.6	1,171.0	1,192.1	1,226.8	1,221.4	1,203.2	1,245.1	1,187.5	1,094.8	1,130.2	1,162.9	1,108.1
2010	1,043.8	1,091.3	1,113.6	1,100.5	1,093.7	1,077.3	1,141.9	1,063.9	1,036.3	1,070.1	1,122.9	1,127.5
2011	1,018.9	1,095.0	1,102.9	1,086.1	1,070.3	1,073.8	1,073.8	1,073.8	1,073.8	1,073.8	1,073.8	1,073.8
2012	999.9	1,072.0	1,111.7	1,129.0	1,138.7	1,091.6	1,161.5	1,065.7	1,019.8	1,123.4	1,184.7	1,144.2
2013	1,110.4	1,175.1	1,232.7	1,226.8	1,222.4	1,181.3	1,270.3	1,138.4	1,091.3	1,137.6	1,175.3	1,150.8
2014	1,095.3	1,104.8	1,124.1	1,044.3	1,009.2	983.4	1,012.8	924.2	936.6	1,039.7	1,099.5	1,105.6
2015¹	1,030.4	1,091.7	1,132.9	1,135.6	1,127.2	1,135.7	1,151.7	1,065.5	1,047.0	1,058.0	1,093.0	1,055.6

¹ Preliminary.   *Source: Agricultural Statistics Board, U.S. Department of Agriculture (ASB-USDA)*

POTATOES

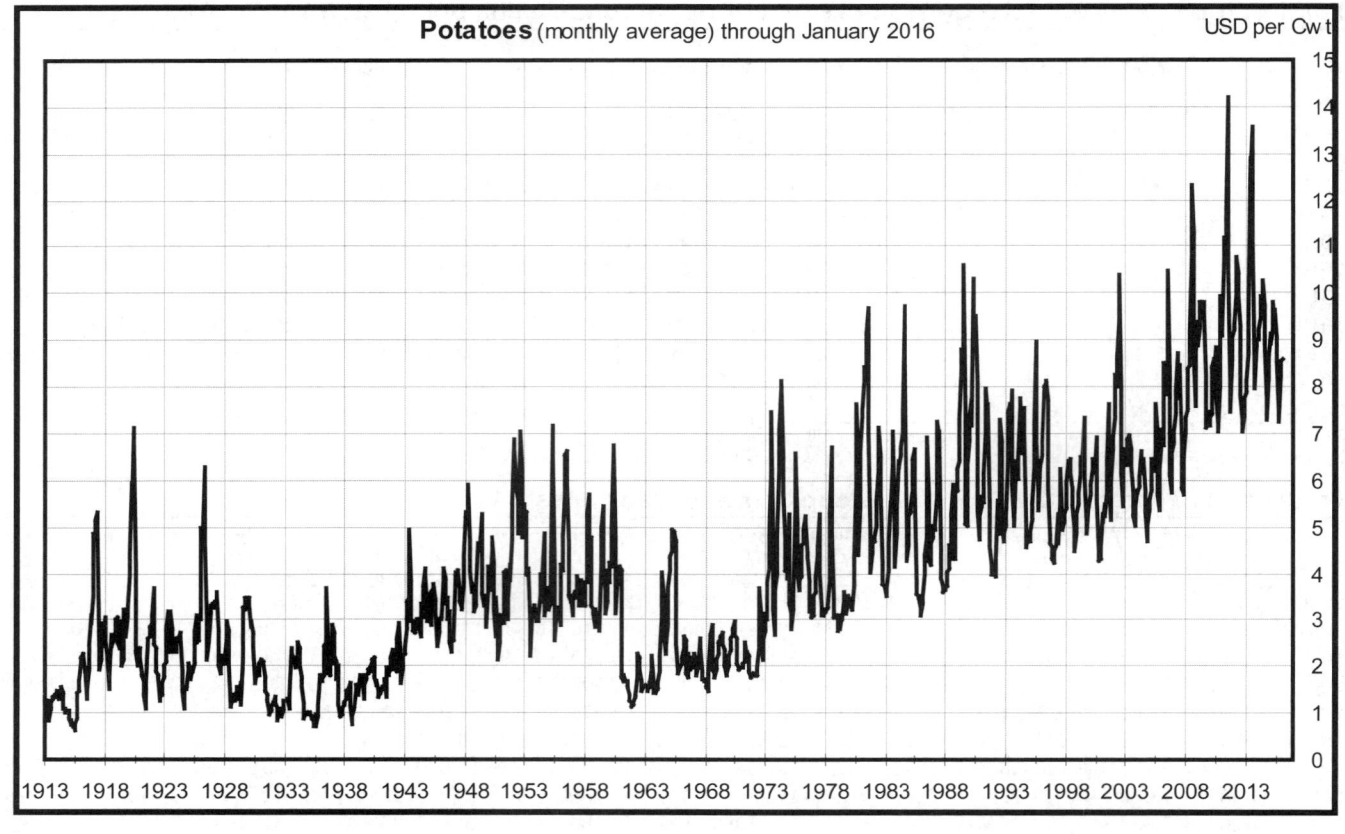

Potatoes (monthly average) through January 2016 — USD per Cwt

Average Price Received by Farmers for Potatoes in the U.S.   In Dollars Per Hundred Pounds (Cwt.)

Year	Jan.	Feb.	Mar.	Apr.	May	June	July	Aug.	Sept.	Oct.	Nov.	Dec.	Season Average
2006	7.07	6.76	8.50	8.35	7.83	8.41	10.46	8.23	6.12	5.76	6.59	6.79	7.31
2007	7.06	7.42	7.93	8.71	7.95	7.75	8.48	6.85	5.81	5.68	6.47	7.02	7.51
2008	7.33	7.51	8.37	8.45	9.16	10.78	12.33	11.33	8.65	7.60	8.77	9.30	9.09
2009	9.40	8.87	9.27	9.81	9.62	9.48	9.81	9.61	8.27	7.11	7.22	7.47	8.25
2010	7.17	7.34	7.42	8.42	8.57	8.25	8.83	7.78	7.22	7.03	8.01	9.94	9.20
2011	9.08	9.26	10.74	11.17	11.17	11.59	14.19	10.47	8.05	7.46	8.58	9.06	9.37
2012	9.23	9.31	9.98	10.75	10.44	9.93	9.29	7.80	7.31	7.02	7.39	7.74	8.63
2013	7.87	8.12	8.72	9.63	12.89	12.57	13.56	11.15	8.48	7.96	8.87	9.02	9.75
2014	9.02	9.22	9.47	9.92	9.53	10.28	9.72	8.88	7.76	7.30	8.19	8.63	8.88
2015[1]	9.12	9.14	9.21	9.82	9.40	9.63	9.04	8.54	7.45	7.23	8.20	8.54	

[1] Preliminary.   *Source: Agricultural Statistics Board, U.S. Department of Agriculture (ASB-USDA)*

Per Capita Utilization of Potatoes in the United States   In Pounds (Farm Weight)

Year	Total	Fresh	Freezing	Chips & Shoe-string	Dehy-drating	Canning	Total Processing
2004	134.5	45.8	57.3	16.4	13.8	1.2	88.7
2005	125.4	41.3	54.3	16.1	12.8	0.9	84.1
2006	123.6	38.6	53.2	18.6	12.4	0.8	85.0
2007	124.4	38.7	53.2	18.6	13.0	0.9	85.6
2008	118.3	37.8	51.5	15.7	12.4	0.9	80.5
2009	113.5	36.7	50.4	13.7	11.8	0.8	76.8
2010	114.0	36.8	50.2	15.0	11.2	0.7	77.2
2011	110.3	34.1	48.2	16.8	10.6	0.7	76.3
2012[1]	114.8	34.4	48.8	17.0	13.9	0.8	80.4
2013[2]	116.7	36.1	50.3	16.7	12.9	0.8	80.6

[1] Preliminary.   [2] Forecast.   *Source: Agricultural Statistics Board, U.S. Department of Agriculture (ASB-USDA)*

Potatoes Processed[1] in the United States, Eight States   In Thousands of Cwt.

States	Storage Season	to Dec. 1	to Jan. 1	to Feb. 1	to Mar. 1	to Apr. 1	to May 1	to June 1	Entire Season
Idaho and Oregon-Malheur Co.	2006-07	27,090	34,070	41,350	49,840	56,650	63,680	71,220	85,630
	2007-08	26,230	33,250	40,310	48,660	55,460	63,000	70,700	88,030
	2008-09	22,380	28,980	35,430	42,150	49,030	55,570	62,940	77,340
	2009-10	23,110	29,180	35,170	42,050	49,200	56,100	62,930	79,400
	2010-11	21,040	26,840	32,700	39,240	46,180	52,830	59,440	70,050
	2011-12	28,060	34,800	41,800	49,460	56,680	63,800	71,510	84,780
	2012-13	27,900	34,740	41,890	49,980	57,750	65,430	73,430	89,780
	2013-14	25,770	32,060	39,090	46,320	53,755	61,780	70,425	85,280
	2014-15	27,685	33,995	40,850	47,985	54,665	63,025	70,600	86,870
Maine[2]	2006-07	1,755	2,360	2,910	3,465	4,185	4,810	5,470	7,560
	2007-08	1,700	2,170	2,815	3,440	3,990	4,670	5,240	7,550
	2008-09	1,635	2,240	2,895	3,515	4,005	4,795	5,540	7,545
	2009-10	1,575	2,060	2,680	3,265	3,915	4,550	5,260	7,160
	2010-11	1,860	2,390	3,000	3,620	4,320	4,980	5,645	7,490
	2011-12	1,860	2,380	3,095	3,695	4,360	4,940	5,345	6,790
	2012-13	1,890	2,380	3,005	3,600	4,290	5,075	5,740	7,720
	2013-14	1,570	1,990	2,510	3,060	3,680	4,240	4,800	6,315
	2014-15	1,410	1,845	2,415	2,930	3,475	3,980	4,445	5,622
Washington & Oregon-Other	2006-07	30,980	37,060	41,290	49,930	56,690	63,170	70,410	77,355
	2007-08	30,595	36,940	42,350	50,165	57,160	67,690	72,380	82,770
	2008-09	32,560	38,050	42,795	49,865	56,350	62,635	70,625	81,260
	2009-10	25,395	31,245	36,530	43,780	50,130	56,700	64,805	75,690
	2010-11	27,670	33,570	38,815	46,700	53,660	60,145	67,655	77,940
	2011-12	31,750	38,165	44,475	51,630	58,515	65,320	73,040	84,105
	2012-13	31,295	37,730	43,820	51,765	57,915	64,500	70,470	80,400
	2013-14	31,575	37,990	45,420	52,690	59,025	64,905	72,325	80,655
	2014-15	31,870	37,190	42,715	50,380	57,340	64,525	72,365	88,615
Other States[3]	2006-07	14,355	17,800	21,415	24,690	28,205	31,560	35,040	43,565
	2007-08	15,040	17,535	20,755	23,900	26,650	29,710	32,600	39,430
	2008-09	12,480	15,120	18,165	21,030	24,025	26,515	29,590	37,285
	2009-10	10,865	13,565	16,305	18,995	21,600	24,355	27,375	34,240
	2010-11	11,820	14,785	17,435	20,370	23,215	25,775	28,690	35,430
	2011-12	14,205	16,770	19,525	21,930	24,910	27,230	29,960	36,200
	2012-13	14,270	16,765	19,785	22,520	25,170	28,320	31,100	40,395
	2013-14	11,365	14,280	17,470	20,475	23,695	26,990	30,195	37,425
	2014-15	13,705	17,295	20,865	24,685	28,550	32,080	35,415	40,456
Total	2006-07	74,210	91,320	107,895	127,050	145,760	163,250	182,170	214,225
	2007-08	73,565	89,895	106,230	126,165	143,260	165,070	180,920	217,780
	2008-09	68,975	84,280	99,155	116,400	133,220	149,285	168,420	203,005
	2009-10	60,945	76,050	90,685	108,090	124,845	141,705	160,370	196,490
	2010-11	62,390	77,585	91,950	109,930	127,375	143,730	161,430	190,910
	2011-12	75,875	92,115	108,895	126,715	144,465	161,290	179,855	211,875
	2012-13	75,355	91,615	108,500	127,865	145,125	163,325	180,740	218,295
	2013-14	70,280	86,320	104,490	122,545	140,155	157,915	177,745	209,675
	2014-15	74,670	90,325	106,845	125,980	144,030	163,610	182,825	221,563
Dehydrated[4]	2006-07	14,590	19,250	23,635	27,885	32,210	36,480	40,915	49,375
	2007-08	12,815	16,785	21,040	25,350	29,500	33,650	37,975	46,660
	2008-09	10,675	14,490	18,335	21,465	24,875	28,195	31,870	39,345
	2009-10	10,985	14,035	17,150	19,895	23,155	26,630	30,045	38,915
	2010-11	7,960	10,795	13,645	16,485	19,415	22,740	25,855	32,700
	2011-12	13,375	16,845	20,875	24,410	28,070	31,533	35,310	42,585
	2012-13	13,965	17,640	22,000	26,105	30,135	34,610	38,945	47,305
	2013-14	12,065	15,875	19,835	23,380	27,140	31,095	34,895	44,385
	2014-15	13,045	16,325	19,965	23,645	26,345	31,515	35,490	46,340

[1] Total quantity received and used for processing regardless of the State in which the potatoes were produced. Amount excludes quantities used for potato chips in Maine, Michigan and Wisconsin.   [2] Includes Maine grown potatoes only.   [3] Colorado, Minnesota, , Nevada, North Dakota and Wisconsin.
[4] Dehydrated products except starch and flour. Included in above totals. Includes CO, ID, NV, ND, OR, WA, and WI.
Source: National Agricultural Statistics Service, U.S. Department of Agriculture (NASS-USDA)

Rice

Rice is a grain that is cultivated on every continent except Antarctica and is the primary food for half the people in the world. Rice cultivation probably originated as early as 10,000 BC in Asia. Rice is grown at varying altitudes (sea level to about 3,000 meters), in varying climates (tropical to temperate), and on dry to flooded land. The growth duration of rice plants is 3-6 months, depending on variety and growing conditions. Rice is harvested by hand in developing countries or by combines in industrialized countries. Asian countries produce about 90% of rice grown worldwide.

Rough rice futures and options are traded at the CME Group. Rice futures are also traded on the Kansai Commodities Exchange, the Moscow Exchange, the Tokyo Grain Exchange (TGE), and the Zhengzhou Commodity Exchange.

Prices – CME rough rice prices (Barchart.com electronic symbol ZR) on the nearest-futures chart in early 2015 extended the 2014 sell-off to post a new 9-year low in May but then rebounded to close 2015 up +0.7% at $11.565 per hundred pounds (cwt). Regarding cash prices, the average monthly price of rice received by farmers in the U.S. in the first six months of the 2014-15 marketing year (i.e., August 2015 through January 2016) fell by -9.0% yr/yr to $12.12 per hundred pounds (cwt.).

Supply – World rice production in the 2015-16 marketing year fell -1.8% to 699.882 million metric tons, below last year's record high of 711.183 million metric tons. The world's largest rice producers were China with 29.8% of world production in 2015-16, India with 21.4%, Indonesia with 8.2%, Bangladesh with 7.4%, Vietnam with 6.4%, and Thailand with 3.4%. U.S. production of rice in 2015-16 fell -13.4 % yr/yr to 192.343 million cwt (hundred pounds), below the 2010-11 record high of 243.104 million cwt (hundred pounds).

Demand – World utilization of rice in 2015-16 rose +0.6% to a record high of 481.715 million metric tons. U.S. rice consumption in 2015-16 fell-2.9% yr/yr to 125.0 million cwt (hundred pounds), below the 2010-11 record high of 136.5 million cwt (hundred pounds).

Trade – World exports of rice in 2015-16 fell -4.8% yr/yr to 41.621 million metric tons, below last year's record high. The world's largest rice exporters are Thailand with 24.0% of world exports, India with 20.4%, Vietnam 16.8%, Pakistan with 11.1%, the U.S. with 7.8%, and Burma with 4.3%. U.S. rice imports in 2015-16 rose +3.4% yr/yr to 25.5 million cwt (hundred pounds), but still below the 2007-08 record high of 23.9 million cwt. U.S. rice exports in 2015-16 fell -3.3% yr/yr to 97.0 million cwt.

World Production of Rough Rice   In Thousands of Metric Tons

Year	Bangla-desh	Brazil	Burma	China	India	Indo-nesia	Japan	Pakistan	Philip-pines	Thailand	United States	Vietnam	World Total
2009-10	46,505	11,660	18,191	195,100	133,648	57,276	10,622	10,326	15,511	30,697	9,972	39,989	656,201
2010-11	47,555	13,676	17,281	195,714	143,984	56,349	10,705	7,235	16,729	30,700	11,027	42,194	672,087
2011-12	50,555	11,600	17,927	201,000	157,981	57,480	10,731	9,241	17,000	31,000	8,388	43,443	697,189
2012-13	50,735	11,819	18,305	204,286	157,876	57,559	10,883	8,305	18,140	30,606	9,069	44,059	704,538
2013-14[1]	51,590	12,206	18,683	203,614	159,985	57,165	10,902	10,198	18,822	31,000	8,615	45,058	713,427
2014-15[2]	51,755	12,449	19,688	206,514	157,216	56,000	10,772	10,509	18,913	28,409	10,079	45,174	712,835
2015-16[3]	51,905	11,625	19,063	208,243	150,015	57,165	10,852	10,351	18,254	24,091	8,724	45,120	699,882

[1] Preliminary.   [2] Estimate.   [3] Forecast.   *Source: Foreign Agricultural Service, U.S. Department of Agriculture (FAS-USDA)*

World Rice Supply and Distribution   In Thousands of Metric Tons

Crop Year	Imports China	European Union	Indo-nesia	Nigeria	Philip-pines	Saudi Arabia	Total	Utilization China	India	Total	Ending Stocks China	India	Total
2009-10	388	1,336	1,150	1,750	2,200	1,069	28,182	134,320	85,508	435,196	40,534	20,500	94,972
2010-11	540	1,408	3,098	2,400	1,300	1,059	33,007	135,000	90,206	443,273	42,574	23,500	100,035
2011-12	1,790	1,301	1,960	3,200	1,200	1,193	35,418	139,600	93,334	456,363	45,023	25,100	106,776
2012-13	3,144	1,395	650	2,800	1,400	1,326	36,660	144,000	94,031	466,076	46,826	25,440	110,514
2013-14[1]	4,015	1,530	1,225	2,800	1,200	1,410	38,377	146,300	99,180	478,178	46,811	22,757	107,384
2014-15[2]	4,315	1,703	1,186	3,500	1,800	1,420	40,534	147,600	98,000	478,885	47,660	17,686	103,460
2015-16[3]	4,700	1,500	1,900	2,500	2,000	1,450	39,659	150,000	98,000	481,715	47,680	11,186	89,284

[1] Preliminary.   [2] Estimate.   [3] Forecast.   *Source: Foreign Agricultural Service, U.S. Department of Agriculture (FAS-USDA)*

World Exports of Rice (Milled Basis)   In Thousands of Metric Tons

Year	Argen-tina	Brazil	Burma	Cam-bodia	Guyana	India	Pakistan	Para-guay	Thailand	United States	Uruguay	Vietnam	World Total
2009-10	488	502	700	750	241	2,082	4,000	151	9,047	3,516	711	6,734	31,344
2010-11	700	1,479	1,075	860	298	2,774	3,385	152	10,647	3,516	966	7,000	35,080
2011-12	593	953	1,357	900	260	10,376	3,456	293	6,945	3,200	971	7,717	39,945
2012-13	533	840	1,163	1,075	265	10,869	3,578	363	6,722	3,385	1,012	6,700	39,350
2013-14[1]	465	819	1,688	1,000	346	10,149	3,200	378	10,969	3,005	890	6,325	41,758
2014-15[2]	400	1,000	1,750	1,100	502	11,871	4,000	410	9,779	3,207	800	6,605	43,711
2015-16[3]	520	830	1,800	800	536	8,500	4,600	500	10,000	3,239	950	7,000	41,621

[1] Preliminary.   [2] Estimate.   [3] Forecast.   *Source: Foreign Agricultural Service, U.S. Department of Agriculture (FAS-USDA)*

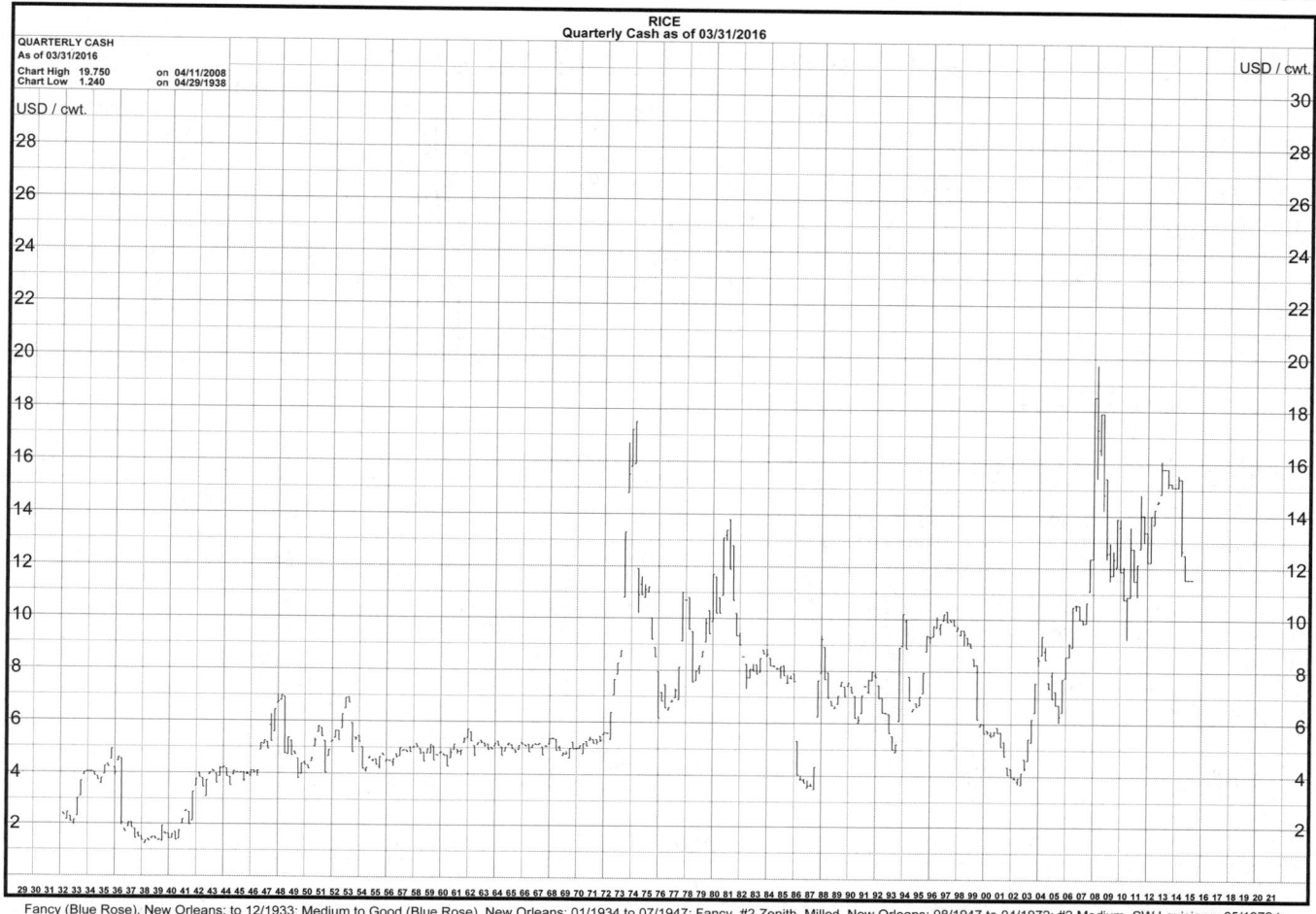

Fancy (Blue Rose), New Orleans: to 12/1933; Medium to Good (Blue Rose), New Orleans: 01/1934 to 07/1947; Fancy, #2 Zenith, Milled, New Orleans: 08/1947 to 04/1972; #2 Medium, SW Louisiana: 05/1972 to 12/2004; Milled, #2 Long grain, Louisiana: 01/2005 to date.

Average Wholesale Price of Rice No. 2 (Medium)[2] Southwest Louisiana   In Dollars Per Cwt. Bagged

Year	Jan.	Feb.	Mar.	Apr.	May	June	July	Aug.	Sept.	Oct.	Nov.	Dec.	Average
2005-06	17.00	17.50	18.45	20.13	21.38	22.50	22.50	22.50	22.50	22.50	22.50	22.35	20.98
2006-07	21.94	22.00	22.00	23.50	23.50	23.50	23.50	23.50	23.50	23.50	23.50	23.50	23.12
2007-08	23.50	23.50	23.30	23.25	23.25	23.25	24.31	27.45	34.00	39.00	40.00	40.00	28.73
2008-09	40.63	43.10	43.25	43.06	42.88	43.25	43.25	42.15	42.25	42.25	42.25	42.25	42.55
2009-10	41.05	35.75	33.25	33.05	32.75	32.75	32.63	32.15	31.56	30.35	29.25	28.88	32.79
2010-11	28.35	28.16	29.69	32.70	33.75	34.15	34.75	34.75	34.00	33.75	33.75	33.75	32.63
2011-12	33.75	33.75	32.55	32.06	31.50	30.70	30.31	29.75	29.75	29.75	29.75	29.75	31.11
2012-13	29.75	29.75	29.75	29.75	29.75	29.75	30.19	30.38	30.38	30.38	30.38	30.38	30.05
2013-14	30.44	30.50	32.00	32.00	32.00	32.00	32.00	32.00	32.00	30.25	32.00	32.00	31.60
2014-15[1]	30.50	29.00	29.00	29.00	29.00	28.75	28.00						29.04

[1] Preliminary.   [2] U.S. No. 2 -- broken not to exceed 4%.   *Source: Economic Research Service, U.S. Department of Agriculture (ERS-USDA)*

Average Price Received by Farmers for Rice (Rough) in the United States   In Dollars Per Hundred Pounds (Cwt.)

Year	Jan.	Feb.	Mar.	Apr.	May	June	July	Aug.	Sept.	Oct.	Nov.	Dec.	Average[2]
2006-07	8.81	9.03	9.65	10.10	9.91	10.40	10.10	10.00	10.20	10.00	10.00	10.10	9.86
2007-08	10.10	10.30	10.70	11.40	11.50	12.40	12.60	13.60	14.60	15.90	16.50	16.80	13.03
2008-09	18.10	16.90	18.10	19.40	18.60	18.20	16.00	15.60	15.00	14.60	14.70	14.20	16.62
2009-10	14.70	14.60	14.30	14.00	14.40	15.00	14.80	14.30	14.30	13.80	13.20	12.60	14.17
2010-11	11.60	11.10	11.50	12.50	13.80	14.00	13.40	13.00	13.10	12.70	12.10	12.90	12.64
2011-12	13.60	14.40	14.70	15.00	14.70	15.20	14.10	14.10	14.40	14.10	14.20	14.40	14.41
2012-13	14.60	14.30	14.40	14.60	14.80	15.30	15.00	15.20	15.40	15.50	15.50	15.60	15.02
2013-14	15.80	15.60	15.80	16.20	16.50	17.10	16.70	16.40	16.20	16.20	16.30	16.10	16.24
2014-15	15.60	14.40	14.00	14.30	13.60	15.10	12.80	12.40	12.50	12.50	11.80	11.20	13.35
2015-16[1]	11.60	11.60	12.30	12.30	12.80	13.60	12.30						12.36

[1] Preliminary.   [2] Weighted average by sales.   *Source: Economic Research Service, U.S. Department of Agriculture (ERS-USDA)*

RICE

Salient Statistics of Rice, Rough & Milled (Rough Equivalent) in the United States   In Millions of Cwt.

Crop Year Beginning Aug. 1	Stocks Aug. 1	Pro-duction	Imports	Total Supply	Food	Brewers	Seed	Total	Resi-dual	United Exports	Total Disap-pearance	CCC Stocks July 31	Put Under Price Support	Long	Med-ium	All Classes	Milled Long
														\-\-\-\-\-\-\- Rough[3] \-\-\-\-\-\-\-\-			
2010-11	36.5	243.1	18.3	297.9	133.6	4	3.3	136.9	4	112.6	249.5	0	86.5	6.50	6.50	6.50	9.91
2011-12	48.5	184.9	19.4	252.8	107.5	4	3.3	110.8	4	100.9	211.7	0	65.8	6.50	6.50	6.50	9.93
2012-13	41.1	199.9	21.1	262.1	116.0	4	3.1	119.0	4	106.6	225.7	0	65.9	6.50	6.50	6.50	10.13
2013-14	36.4	190.0	23.1	249.5	120.7	4	3.6	124.4	4	93.3	217.7	0	36.0	6.50	6.50	6.50	10.34
2014-15/1	31.8	222.2	24.7	277.5	125.5	4	3.2	128.7	4	100.3	229.0			6.50	6.50	6.50	
2015-16/2	48.5	192.3	25.5	263.5	NA	4	NA	125.0	4	97.0	222.0						

[1] Preliminary.   [2] Forecast.   [3] Loan rate for each class of rice is the sum of the whole kernels' loan rate weighted by its milling yield (average 56%) and the broken kernels' loan rate weighted by its milling yield (average 12%).   [4] Included in Food.
Source: Economic Research Service, U.S. Department of Agriculture (ERS-USDA)

Acreage, Yield, Production and Prices of Rice in the United States

Crop Year Beginning Aug. 1	Southern States	Cali-fornia	United States	Cali-fornia	United States	Southern States	Cali-fornia	United States	Value of Pro-duction ($1,000)	Arkan-sas[2]	Hous-ton[2]	No. 2[4]	Thai "A"[5]	Thai "B"[5]
	Acreage Harvested 1,000 Acres			Yield Per Harvested Acre (In Lbs.)		Production 1,000 Cwt.				Wholesale Prices $ Per Cwt.		Milled Rice, Average C.I.F. Rotterdam U.S. $ Per Metric Ton		
2010-11	3,062	553	3,615	8,020	6,725	198,778	44,326	243,104	3,183,213	33.21	27.52	\-\-\-\-	\-\-\-\-	\-\-\-\-
2011-12	2,037	580	2,617	8,350	7,067	136,539	48,402	184,941	2,737,423	30.64	28.47	\-\-\-\-	\-\-\-\-	\-\-\-\-
2012-13	2,122	557	2,679	8,150	7,463	154,526	45,413	199,939	3,067,365	28.27	28.46	\-\-\-\-	\-\-\-\-	\-\-\-\-
2013-14	1,907	562	2,469	8,480	7,694	142,312	47,641	189,953	3,181,993	30.39	30.17	\-\-\-\-	\-\-\-\-	\-\-\-\-
2014-15	2,491	442	2,933	8,580	7,576	184,279	37,936	222,215	3,075,618	30.96	27.38	\-\-\-\-	\-\-\-\-	\-\-\-\-
2015-16[1]	2,154	421	2,575	8,890	7,470	154,902	37,441	192,343	2,579,001			\-\-\-\-	\-\-\-\-	\-\-\-\-

[1] Preliminary.   [2] F.O.B. mills, Arkansas, medium.   [3] Houston, Texas (long grain).   [4] Milled, 4%, container, FAS.
[5] SWR, 100%, bulk.   NA = Not available.   *Source: Economic Research Service, U.S. Department of Agriculture (ERS-USDA)*

U.S. Exports of Milled Rice, by Country of Destination   In Thousands of Metric Tons

Trade Year Beginning October	Canada	Haiti	Iran	Ivory Coast	Jamaica	Mexico	Nether-lands	Peru	Saudi Arabia	South Africa	Switzer-land	United Kingdom	Total
2009-10	220.0	327.5	.0	.4	28.3	827.0	4.4	3.2	116.1	1.2	.3	65.5	4,260
2010-11	229.1	324.1		1.9	23.3	942.0	5.1	1.5	120.3	1.7	.6	47.4	3,920
2011-12	219.9	287.3	3.1	.3	9.1	804.2	5.6	.7	133.4	2.1	.3	36.2	3,578
2012-13	231.6	365.0	125.7	14.9	2.7	885.8	4.6	.3	126.2	2.6	.6	21.4	3,848
2013-14	242.6	346.0	.2	13.5	2.3	741.2	5.4	6.8	106.1	2.3	.6	23.4	3,355
2014-15[1]	219.2	392.1		.1	2.6	820.9	5.3	8.8	112.4	1.6	.6	30.7	4,129

[1] Preliminary.   *Source: Economic Research Service, U.S. Department of Agriculture (ERS-USDA)*

U.S. Rice Exports by Export Program   In Thousands of Metric Tons

Year	PL 480	Section 416	CCC Credit Pro-grams[2]	CCC African Relief Exports	EEP[3]	Export Pro-grams[4]	Exports Outside Specified Export Programs	Total U.S. Rice Exports	% Export Programs as a Share of Total Exports
2005	128	0	\-\-\-\-	0	0	159	4,099	4,258	4
2006	59	0	\-\-\-\-	0	0	107	3,917	4,024	3
2007	103	0	\-\-\-\-	0	0	142	3,174	3,316	4
2008	65	0	\-\-\-\-	0	0	91	3,818	3,909	2
2009[1]	44	0	\-\-\-\-	0	0	54	3,358	3,411	2
2010[1]	\-\-\-\-	\-\-\-\-	\-\-\-\-	\-\-\-\-	\-\-\-\-	\-\-\-\-	\-\-\-\-	\-\-\-\-	\-\-\-\-

[1] Preliminary.   [2] May not completely reflect exports made under these programs.   [3] Sales not shipments.   [4] Adjusted for estimated overlap between CCC export credit and EEP shipments.   *Source: Economice Research Service, U.S. Department of Agriculture (ERS-USDA)*

Production of Rice (Rough) in the United States, by Type and Variety   In Thousands of Cwt.

Year	Long Grain	Medium Grain	Short Grain	Total	Year	Long Grain	Medium Grain	Short Grain	Total
2006	146,214	43,802	3,720	193,736	2011	116,352	65,562	3,027	184,941
2007	143,235	51,063	4,090	198,388	2012	144,280	51,819	3,840	199,939
2008	153,257	47,166	3,310	203,733	2013	131,896	54,915	3,142	189,953
2009	152,725	63,291	3,834	219,850	2014	162,665	57,222	2,328	222,215
2010	183,296	57,144	2,664	243,104	2015[1]	133,032	56,677	2,634	192,343

[1] Preliminary.   *Source: National Agricultural Statistics Service, U.S. Department of Agriculture (NASS-USDA)*

Rubber

Rubber is a natural or synthetic substance characterized by elasticity, water repellence, and electrical resistance. Pre-Columbian Native South Americans discovered many uses for rubber such as containers, balls, shoes, and waterproofing for fabrics such as coats and capes. The Spaniards tried to duplicate these products for many years but were unsuccessful. The first commercial application of rubber began in 1791 when Samuel Peal patented a method of waterproofing cloth by treating it with a solution of rubber and turpentine. In 1839, Charles Goodyear revolutionized the rubber industry with his discovery of a process called vulcanization, which involves combining rubber and sulfur and heating the mixture.

Natural rubber is obtained from latex, a milky white fluid, from the Hevea Brasiliensis tree. The latex is gathered by cutting a chevron shape through the bark of the rubber tree. The latex is collected in a small cup, with approximately 1 fluid ounce per cutting. The cuttings are usually done every other day until the cuttings reach the ground. The tree is then allowed to renew itself before a new tapping is started. The collected latex is strained, diluted with water, and treated with acid to bind the rubber particles together. The rubber is then pressed between rollers to consolidate the rubber into slabs or thin sheets and is air-dried or smoke-dried for shipment.

During World War II, natural rubber supplies from the Far East were cut off, and the rubber shortage accelerated the development of synthetic rubber in the U.S. Synthetic rubber is produced by chemical reactions, condensation or polymerization, of certain unsaturated hydrocarbons. Synthetic rubber is made of raw material derived from petroleum, coal, oil, natural gas, and acetylene and is almost identical to natural rubber in chemical and physical properties.

Rubber futures are traded on the National Commodity & Derivatives Exchange (NCDEX), the Shanghai Futures Exchange (SHFE) and the Tokyo Commodity Exchange (TOCOM).

Prices – Singapore SGX Rubber futures prices (Barchart.com symbol U6) on the nearest-futures chart showed a mild recovery in early 2015 but then resumed the 2011-2014 decline and closed 2015 down -31.3% at $117.50 per metric ton.

Supply – World production of natural rubber in 2013 (latest data) rose +3.4% to 11.965 million metric tons. The world's largest producers of natural rubber in 2013 were Thailand with 32.3% of world production, Indonesia (26.0%), Vietnam (7.9%), India (7.5%), China (7.2%), and Malaysia (6.9%).

Trade – World exports of natural rubber in 2011 (latest data) fell -1.8% yr/yr to 1,037,161 million metric tons. The world's largest exporter of natural rubber in 2011 was Thailand with 84.5% of world exports. U.S. imports of natural dry rubber in 2011 rose by +12.1% yr/yr to 99,373 metric tons.

World Production of Natural Rubber   In Thousands of Metric Tons

Year	Brazil	China	Côte d'Ivoire	India	Indonesia	Liberia	Malaysia	Nigeria	Philip-pines	Sri Lanka	Thailand	Vietnam	Total
2004	98.8	574.7	136.8	749.7	2,065.8	114.5	1,168.7	142.0	102.7	94.7	3,006.7	419.0	8,942.1
2005	103.7	513.6	170.1	802.6	2,270.9	111.0	1,126.0	158.6	104.2	104.4	2,979.7	481.6	9,219.7
2006	105.4	538.0	178.3	852.9	2,637.2	93.5	1,283.6	142.5	116.0	109.1	3,070.5	555.4	9,989.2
2007	111.4	588.4	188.5	825.3	2,755.2	120.8	1,199.6	143.0	133.3	117.6	3,024.2	605.8	10,141.6
2008	120.9	547.9	203.0	864.5	2,751.3	84.8	1,072.4	110.4	135.6	129.2	3,166.9	660.0	10,228.7
2009	127.0	618.9	209.5	831.4	2,440.4	59.5	857.0	145.0	129.0	136.0	3,090.3	711.3	9,758.0
2010	134.0	690.8	235.0	862.0	2,734.9	62.1	939.2	143.5	130.4	153.0	3,051.8	751.7	10,326.2
2011	164.5	750.9	238.7	800.0	2,990.2	63.0	996.2	143.5	140.5	158.2	3,348.9	789.6	11,098.9
2012¹	177.1	802.3	256.6	900.0	3,012.3	63.0	922.8	143.5	110.8	150.6	3,625.0	877.1	11,570.1
2013²	185.7	864.8	289.6	900.0	3,107.5	63.0	826.4	143.5	111.2	130.4	3,863.0	949.1	11,965.8

¹ Preliminary.   ² Estimate.   *Source: Food and Agricultural Organization of the United Nations (FAO-UN)*

World Imports of Natural Rubber   In Metric Tons

Year	Brazil	Canada	China	European Union	Germany	Italy	Malaysia	Mexico	Pakistan	Rep of Korea	United Kingdom	United States	Total
2004	12,345	18,959	211,127	201,100	60,530	34,402	303,345	23,483	26,860	24,189	20,042	112,514	1,056,492
2005	12,358	17,657	201,498	205,401	56,039	34,518	303,852	22,469	24,235	23,636	24,348	97,156	1,002,099
2006	12,100	19,771	280,618	231,829	81,842	35,949	330,408	22,937	29,645	22,964	22,818	68,215	1,124,669
2007	13,024	20,366	256,643	294,455	114,432	38,012	361,713	22,527	22,497	23,399	22,635	89,160	1,204,584
2008	13,649	20,552	257,702	249,299	75,878	34,597	341,173	22,928	22,293	21,342	22,772	93,714	1,145,247
2009	14,003	14,233	312,771	194,890	67,388	24,955	357,254	18,918	16,634	21,036	15,620	69,930	1,104,422
2010	17,180	22,241	262,089	152,269	40,107	24,604	348,487	20,323	17,218	21,316	19,031	53,222	1,027,962
2011	17,752	23,058	280,663	138,609	31,817	24,123	306,561	19,433	14,819	19,252	20,376	49,264	975,316
2012¹	17,397	23,315	327,683	133,535	29,621	20,253	330,910	19,963	14,021	19,306	20,337	44,887	1,032,232
2013²	17,849	22,309	345,330	160,483	32,169	20,894	344,581	19,318	14,023	20,130	28,656	45,939	1,094,304

¹ Preliminary.   ² Estimate.   *Source: Food and Agricultural Organization of the United Nations (FAO-UN)*

RUBBER

World Exports of Natural Rubber   In Metric Tons

Year	Belgium	Came-roon	Hong Kong	Germany	Guate-mala	India	Indonesia	Malaysia	Myanmar	Nether-lands	Thailand	United States	Total
2004	8,193	9,115	10,230	13,560	12,870	5,403	11,755	73,331	31,500	600	853,403	8,624	1,051,981
2005	11,138	9,482	9,627	9,255	20,096	11,125	4,014	55,602	34,000	1,449	814,613	4,094	1,001,822
2006	22,047	9,553	10,262	7,178	17,234	6,763	8,334	58,211	407	16,952	947,755	1,987	1,130,351
2007	42,653	9,173	8,487	10,563	22,800	13,069	7,610	56,704	947	16,650	887,544	5,365	1,118,072
2008	31,402	6,396	5,723	6,732	20,355	13,141	8,547	44,599	1,388	22,650	836,404	5,888	1,031,926
2009	13,266	6,614	3,813	5,076	19,821	7,690	9,147	38,752	1,170	5,857	1,007,957	3,386	1,149,035
2010	14,255	8,160	3,224	6,039	20,603	7,407	12,929	47,773	1,886	694	898,454	5,369	1,056,340
2011	26,934	6,627	2,031	6,273	22,742	9,943	9,502	41,586	1,378	3,127	876,382	7,279	1,037,161
2012[1]	37,031	4,826	1,675	7,332	23,301	4,499	7,620	31,748	50	2,288	949,103	7,909	1,151,861
2013[2]	54,754	9,866	1,414	8,209	24,068	4,635	5,907	33,538	80	3,328	1,038,421	5,398	1,253,098

[1] Preliminary.   [2] Estimate.   *Source: Food and Agricultural Organization of the United Nations (FAO-UN)*

World Imports of Natural Dry Rubber   In Metric Tons

Year	Brazil	Canada	China	European Union	France	Germany	Italy	Japan	Malaysia	Rep of Korea	Spain	United States	Total
2004	171,015	133,676	1,224,415	1,250,441	239,751	210,307	137,872	795,542	148,800	328,117	187,364	1,045,540	5,751,954
2005	183,329	142,460	1,347,662	1,301,640	240,984	248,544	137,884	842,766	173,950	346,866	185,521	1,071,864	6,107,819
2006	166,448	129,971	1,465,027	1,289,884	230,784	246,444	139,991	879,987	190,200	341,772	175,035	943,348	6,210,335
2007	208,453	123,287	1,490,358	1,379,825	233,711	261,495	136,895	842,246	245,317	354,553	199,911	939,367	6,359,097
2008	220,959	121,907	1,506,462	1,211,480	208,921	234,608	123,850	839,170	219,637	337,790	181,472	958,558	6,180,191
2009	138,010	91,646	1,500,896	882,331	131,546	189,322	80,071	584,577	381,483	311,067	126,787	634,888	5,314,528
2010	232,161	128,087	1,724,502	1,304,121	171,252	367,791	103,302	731,498	329,683	366,255	177,182	891,688	6,512,249
2011	205,351	124,911	1,935,738	1,560,294	192,644	392,475	117,765	770,804	360,872	382,908	171,838	999,373	7,179,882
2012[1]	163,742	120,209	1,962,901	1,341,258	162,806	338,306	93,204	685,966	541,519	378,016	141,411	923,981	7,126,938
2013[2]	205,903	109,375	2,241,937	1,314,459	159,935	342,548	97,455	711,490	660,136	376,217	143,491	881,396	7,494,686

[1] Preliminary.   [2] Estimate.   *Source: Food and Agricultural Organization of the United Nations (FAO-UN)*

World Exports of Natural Dry Rubber   In Metric Tons

Year	Côte d'Ivoire	Germany	Guate-mala	India	Indonesia	Liberia	Malaysia	Nigeria	Philip-pines	Sri Lanka	Thailand	Vietnam	Total
2004	137,539	18,995	32,106	31,999	1,862,506	114,500	1,360,977	29,000	43,305	38,460	2,167,961	513,300	6,545,316
2005	155,981	13,634	36,304	48,197	2,019,768	111,000	1,091,505	25,000	41,088	30,595	2,137,538	249,423	6,125,611
2006	172,437	22,006	33,059	41,014	2,277,663	93,500	1,073,193	24,000	33,833	46,022	2,109,080	246,081	6,342,028
2007	182,397	40,572	45,474	39,294	2,399,146	120,800	960,241	33,792	30,417	46,083	2,077,771	247,331	6,425,892
2008	199,721	28,113	53,008	26,031	2,286,910	84,800	870,997	25,900	36,323	42,476	1,995,524	212,850	6,077,168
2009	218,555	56,089	57,770	12,787	1,982,116	59,500	664,306	31,700	24,899	50,246	1,731,787	239,580	5,378,189
2010	238,701	96,979	55,695	8,601	2,338,986	70,620	853,108	42,435	36,355	46,924	1,834,828	782,213	6,824,352
2011	259,459	130,568	65,351	28,154	2,546,237	70,339	904,494	58,088	42,209	41,052	2,120,597	817,502	7,499,757
2012[1]	267,368	112,745	64,267	8,893	2,436,819	70,606	739,426	56,847	38,614	35,313	2,049,683	799,489	7,055,019
2013[2]	259,860	110,488	64,182	22,134	2,696,087	58,946	813,714	51,332	66,930	23,007	2,398,556	674,342	7,648,372

[1] Preliminary.   [2] Estimate.   *Source: Food and Agricultural Organization of the United Nations (FAO-UN)*

Rye

Rye is a cereal grain and a member of the grass family. Hardy varieties of rye have been developed for winter planting. Rye is most widely grown in northern Europe and Asia. In the U.S., rye is used as an animal feed and as an ingredient in bread and some whiskeys. Bread using rye was developed in northern Europe in the Middle Ages where bakers developed dark, hearty bread consisting of rye, oat and barley flours. Those were crops that grew more readily in the wet and damp climate of northern Europe, as opposed to wheat which fares better in the warmer and drier climates in central Europe. Modern rye bread is made with a mixture of white and rye flours. Coarsely ground rye flour is also used in pumpernickel bread and helps provide the dark color and course texture, along with molasses. The major producing states are North and South Dakota, Oklahoma, and Georgia. The crop year runs from June to May.

Supply – World rye production in 2015-16 marketing year fell by -15.5% yr/yr to 12.294 million metric tons, a new record low. The world's largest producers of rye are the European Union with 64.7% of world production in 2015-16, followed by Russia with 17.1%, Belarus with 6.5%, and the Ukraine with 3.2%. U.S. production of rye accounted for only 2.4% of world production.

U.S. production of rye in 2015 rose +59.9% to 11.496 million bushels, far below the production levels of over 20 million bushels seen from the late 1800s through the 1960s. U.S. production of rye fell off in the 1970s, and fell to a record low of 6.311 million bushels in 2007.

U.S. acreage harvested with rye in 2015-16 rose +39.5% yr/yr to 360,000 acres. U.S. farmers in the late 1800s through the 1960s typically harvested more than 1 million acres of rye, showing how domestic planting of rye has dropped off sharply in the past several decades. Rye yield in 2015-16 rose +14.3% to 31.9 bushels per acre, well below the record high of 33.1 bushels per acre posted in 1984-85. Modern rye production yields are, however, more than double the levels seen prior to the 1960s.

Demand – Total U.S. domestic usage of rye in 2015-16 rose +15.0% yr/yr to 18.635 million bushels. The breakdown of domestic usage shows that 46.7% of rye in 2015-16 was used for feed and residual, 19.5% for food, 16.4% for seed, and 16.1% for industry.

Trade – World exports of rye in the 2015-16 marketing year fell -13.4% yr/yr to 361,000 metric tons, still above the record low of 270,000 metric tons in 2008-09. The largest exporters were the European Union with 150,000 metric tons and Canada with 100,000 metric tons of exports. World imports of rye fell -12.1% to 364,000 metric tons. U.S. imports of rye in 2015-16 fell -3.4% yr/yr to 229,000 metric tons.

World Production of Rye   In Thousands of Metric Tons

Crop Year	Argentina	Australia	Belarus	Canada	Chile	European Union	Kazakhstan	Norway	Russia	Turkey	Ukraine	United States	World Total
2006-07	55	20	1,072	383	7	6,546	30	26	2,959	271	584	183	12,188
2007-08	77	20	1,305	252	5	7,683	68	40	3,909	241	562	160	14,370
2008-09	55	35	1,492	297	8	9,266	40	48	4,505	247	1,051	211	17,314
2009-10	55	34	1,227	281	5	9,955	75	27	4,333	343	954	172	17,521
2010-11	40	33	735	237	1	7,576	42	34	1,642	365	464	190	11,407
2011-12	45	40	801	241	1	6,900	28	16	2,967	366	579	154	12,190
2012-13	40	40	1,082	337	4	8,763	50	5	2,132	370	676	166	13,712
2013-14[1]	52	20	648	223	4	10,151	43	11	3,360	350	638	194	15,742
2014-15[2]	97	20	950	218	5	8,858	61	12	3,279	350	638	183	14,554
2015-16[3]	56	22	800	225	5	7,960	37	12	2,100	350	390	292	12,294

[1] Preliminary.   [2] Estimate.   [3] Forecast.   *Source: Foreign Agricultural Service, U.S. Department of Agriculture (FAS-USDA)*

World Imports and Exports of Rye   In Thousands of Metric Tons

Year	European Union	Japan	Korea, South	Norway	Russia	United States	World Total	Belarus	Canada	European Union	Russia	United States	World Total
	----- Imports -----							----- Exports -----					
2006-07	25	258	8	16	32	150	582	50	208	418	26	2	706
2007-08	98	83	6	21	----	179	413	75	191	74	119	6	468
2008-09	9	57	7	11	----	100	209	50	76	111	16	8	267
2009-10	----	103	7	13	----	108	246	25	124	97	12	2	316
2010-11	21	101	11	11	150	141	458	150	189	108	----	4	492
2011-12	291	46	11	11	----	152	533	25	166	57	238	4	504
2012-13	98	27	12	21	25	228	456	25	189	113	133	8	486
2013-14[1]	77	37	8	17	5	234	418	5	118	169	73	7	423
2014-15[2]	102	22	4	8	5	237	414	5	86	184	114	6	417
2015-16[3]	50	25	10	15	5	229	364	5	100	150	80	6	361

[1] Preliminary.   [2] Estimate.   [3] Forecast.   *Source: Foreign Agricultural Service, U.S. Department of Agriculture (FAS-USDA)*

RYE

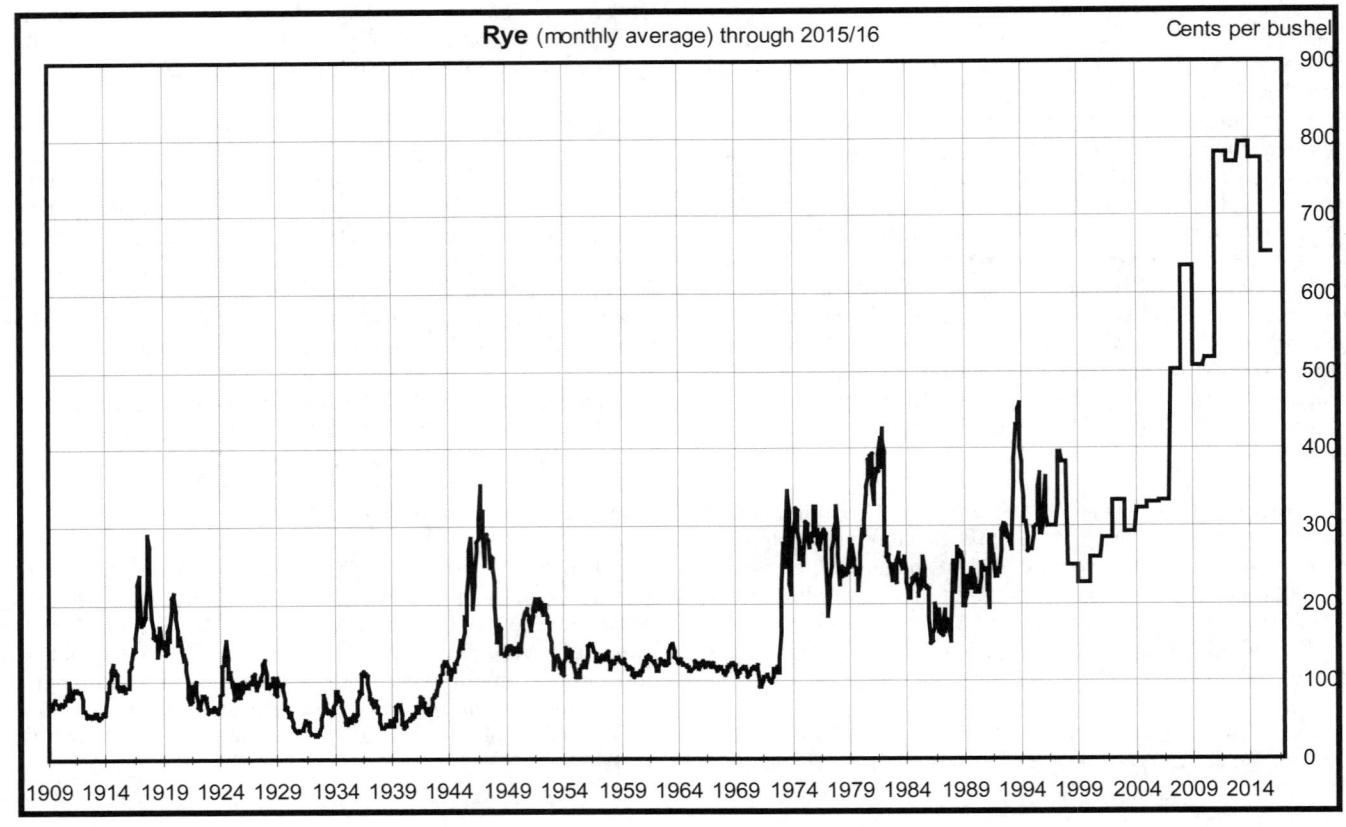

Rye (monthly average) through 2015/16 — Cents per bushel

Production of Rye in the United States   In Thousands of Bushels

Year	Georgia	Kansas	Mich-igan	Minne-sota	Neb-raska	Dakota	Okla-homa	Penn-ylvania	Carolina	Dakota	Texas	Other States	Total
2006	650	2	2	2	2	2	1,040	2	2	2	2	5,503	7,193
2007	800	2	2	2	2	2	1,080	2	2	2	2	4,431	6,311
2008	1,200	2	2	2	2	2	1,045	2	2	2	2	5,734	7,979
2009	525	2	2	2	2	2	560	2	2	2	2	5,908	6,993
2010	960	2	2	2	2	2	1,500	2	2	2	2	4,971	7,431
2011	945	2	2	2	2	2	825	2	2	2	2	4,556	6,326
2012	575	2	2	2	2	2	1,680	2	2	2	2	4,287	6,542
2013	1,080	2	2	2	2	2	1,600	2	2	2	2	4,946	7,626
2014	540	2	2	2	2	2	495	2	2	2	2	6,154	7,626
2015/1	420	2	2	2	2	2	1,920	2	2	2	2	9,156	7,189

[1] Preliminary.   [2] Estimates not published beginning in 2000.   *Source: Agricultural Statistics Board, U.S. Department of Agriculture (ASB-USDA)*

Salient Statistics of Rye in the United States   In Thousands of Bushels

Crop Year Beginning June 1	Supply — Stocks June 1	Supply — Pro-duction	Supply — Imports	Supply — Total Supply	Domestic Use — Food	Domestic Use — Industry	Domestic Use — Seed	Domestic Use — Feed & Residual	Domestic Use — Total	Exports	Total Disap-pearance	Acreage — Planted 1,000 Acres	Acreage — Harvested for Grain 1,000 Acres	Yield Per Harvested Acre (Bushels)
2006-07	706	7,193	5,899	13,798	3,300	3,000	3,000	3,947	13,247	70	13,317	1,396	274	26.3
2007-08	481	6,311	7,064	13,856	3,300	3,000	3,000	3,909	13,209	251	13,460	1,334	252	25.0
2008-09	396	7,979	3,953	12,328	3,300	3,000	3,000	2,539	11,839	316	12,155	1,260	269	29.7
2009-10	509	6,993	4,251	11,753	3,300	3,000	3,000	1,246	10,546	73	10,619	1,241	252	27.8
2010-11	932	7,431	5,552	13,915	3,300	3,000	3,000	3,714	13,014	149	13,163	1,211	265	28.0
2011-12	801	6,326	5,994	13,121	3,310	3,000	3,010	2,917	12,237	157	12,394	1,266	242	26.1
2012-13	452	6,542	8,966	15,960	3,400	3,000	3,020	5,829	15,249	310	15,559	1,300	248	28.0
2013-14[1]	401	7,626	9,227	17,254	3,430	3,000	3,030	7,241	16,701	268	16,969	1,451	278	27.4
2014-15[2]	285	7,189	9,321	16,795	3,460	3,000	3,040	6,466	15,966	240	16,206	1,434	258	27.9
2015-16[3]	589	11,496	8,500	20,585	3,630	3,000	3,050	8,705	18,385	250	18,635	1,569	360	31.9

[1] Preliminary.   [2] Estimate.   [3] Forecast   *Source: Economic Research Service, U.S. Department of Agriculture (ERS-USDA)*

Salt

Salt, also known as sodium chloride, is a chemical compound that is an essential element in the diet of humans, animals, and even many plants. Since prehistoric times, salt has been used to preserve foods and was commonly used in the religious rites of the Greeks, Romans, Hebrews, and Christians. Salt, in the form of salt cakes, served as money in ancient Ethiopia and Tibet. As long ago as 1450 BC, Egyptian art shows records of salt production.

The simplest method of obtaining salt is through the evaporation of salt water from areas near oceans or seas. In most regions, rock salt is obtained from underground mining or by wells sunk into deposits. Salt is soluble in water, is slightly soluble in alcohol, but is insoluble in concentrated hydrochloric acid. In its crystalline form, salt is transparent and colorless, shining with an ice-like luster.

Prices – Salt prices in 2015 (FOB mine, vacuum and open pan) rose +0.8% yr/yr to $182.00 per ton, which was a record high.

Supply – World production of salt in 2015 rose +2.6% yr/yr to 273.000 million metric tons. The world's largest salt producers were China with 25.6% and the U.S. with 17.6% of world production in 2015. U.S. salt production in 2015 rose +6.0% yr/yr to 48.000 million metric tons.

Demand – U.S. consumption of salt in 2015 rose +6.6% to 69.500 million metric tons, a new record high.

Trade – The U.S. relied on imports for 32% of its salt consumption in 2015, a new record high. U.S. imports of salt for consumption in 2015 rose +15.4% yr/yr to 23.200 million metric tons, a new record high. U.S. exports of salt in 2015 fell by -10.0% to 846,000 metric tons, with the bulk of those exports going to Canada.

World Production of All Salt   In Thousands of Metric Tons

Year	Australia	Canada	China	France	Germany	India	Italy	Mexico	Poland	Spain	United Kingdom	United States	World Total
2008	11,160	14,386	66,640	6,240	15,833	16,000	2,200	8,809	4,023	4,303	5,565	48,000	276,000
2009	10,316	14,615	66,630	6,200	18,939	16,500	3,471	7,445	3,831	4,289	6,166	46,000	279,000
2010	11,968	10,537	70,380	5,867	19,676	17,000	4,006	8,431	4,097	4,350	6,666	43,300	280,000
2011	11,744	12,625	67,420	5,430	17,443	16,000	2,912	8,812	4,282	4,371	6,700	45,000	286,000
2012	10,821	10,845	69,120	5,457	14,446	17,000	3,098	10,800	3,926	4,385	6,700	37,200	259,000
2013	11,000	12,210	70,000	6,100	11,900	16,000	2,200	10,800	4,430	4,440	6,700	40,300	262,000
2014[1]	11,000	13,000	68,000	6,000	12,200	16,000		10,700	4,300	4,380	6,700	45,300	266,000
2015[2]	11,000	12,500	70,000	6,000	12,500	17,000		10,500	4,200	4,300	6,700	48,000	273,000

[1] Preliminary.   [2] Estimate.   *Source: U.S. Geological Survey (USGS)*

Salient Statistics of the Salt Industry in the United States   In Thousands of Metric Tons

Year	Net Import Reliance As a % of Apparent Consumption	Average Value FOB Mine Vacuum & Open Pan ($ Per Ton)	Production Total	Production Open & Vacuum Pan	Production Solar	Production Rock	Production Brine	Sold or Used Open & Vacuum Pan	Sold Rock	Sold Brine	Total Salt	Imports Value[3] Million $	Imports for Consumption	Exports Total	Exports To Canada	Apparent Consumption
2008	21	158.59	48,000	4,200	4,070	20,900	18,900	4,120	21,100	18,800	47,400	1,690.0	13,900	1,030	896	60,200
2009	24	178.67	46,000	4,030	3,880	20,300	17,800	3,960	18,200	17,800	43,100	1,750.0	14,700	1,450	1,360	56,400
2010	24	180.08	43,300	4,100	3,120	17,600	18,500	4,020	17,900	18,500	43,500	1,690.0	12,900	595	451	55,800
2011	24	174.00	45,000	4,080	3,230	18,500	19,200	4,000	18,500	19,200	45,500	1,770.0	13,800	846	754	58,500
2012	22	169.93	37,200	4,240	2,760	13,300	16,900	4,200	11,300	16,900	34,900	1,460.0	9,880	809	728	44,000
2013	22	172.09	39,900	4,440	3,560	14,900	17,400	4,380	18,300	17,400	43,100	2,090.0	11,900	525	434	54,500
2014[1]	29	180.61	45,300								46,000		20,100	940		65,200
2015[2]	32	182.00	48,000								47,200		23,200	846		69,500

[1] Preliminary.   [2] Estimate.   [3] Values are f.o.b. mine or refinery & do not include cost of cooperage or containers.   *Source: U.S. Geological Survey (USGS)*

Salt Sold or Used by Producers in the U.S. by Classes & Consumers or Uses   In Thousands of Metric Tons

Year	Chemical[2]	Tanning Leather	Textile & Dyeing	Meat Packers[3]	Canning	Baking	Agricultural Distribution	Feed Dealers	Feed Manufacturers	Rubber	Oil	Paper & Pulp	Metal Processing	Water Treatment	Grocery Stores	Water Conditioning Distrib.	Ice Control and/or Stabilization
2006	18,400	50	121	380	208	203	211	1,090	502	66	2,150	72	49	952	770	489	12,400
2007	21,500	41	98	305	198	149	385	1,160	457	6	211	61	36	1,030	943	522	20,800
2008	18,600	37	78	283	190	144	436	1,260	405	6	286	77	42	1,330	992	464	22,600
2009	17,900	32	48	271	215	324	357	1,310	377	5	314	58	24	1,010	812	469	16,900
2010	20,200	39	59	275	258	364	359	1,330	425	5	325	59	26	913	761	461	18,700
2011	18,500	42	49	260	195	162	375	1,170	438	5	322	67	44	311	706	493	19,600
2012	16,800	36	41	248	182	160	253	1,010	392	7	441	61	53	446	591	472	11,100
2013[1]	18,000	38	38	259	179	162	351	912	516	6	409	66	42	473	665	626	20,400

[1] Preliminary.   [2] Chloralkali producers and other chemical.   *Source: U.S. Geological Survey (USGS)*

Sheep and Lambs

Sheep and lambs are raised for both their wool and meat. In countries that have high wool production, there is also demand for sheep and lamb meat due to the easy availability. Production levels have declined in New Zealand and Australia, but that has been counteracted by a substantial increase in China.

Prices – The average monthly wholesale price of slaughter lambs (choice) at San Angelo, Texas in 2015 fell by -5.5% to 148.91 cents per pound, which was below the record high of 160.75 cents per pound posted in 2011.

Supply – World sheep and goat numbers in 2013 (latest data) rose by +0.1% to 2.138 billion head, a new record high. The world's largest producers of sheep and goats are China with 16.7% of world production in 2013, India (9.3%), Turkey with (1.7%), and United Kingdom (1.5%). The number of sheep and lambs on U.S. farms in 2015 (Jan 1) is projected to rise +0.7% to 5.280 million head. The U.S. states with the most sheep and lambs are Texas (with 13.6% of the U.S. total), California (11.4%), Colorado (8.0%), Wyoming (6.5%), and Utah (5.5%).

World Sheep and Goat Numbers in Specified Countries on January 1   In Thousands of Head

Year	Argentina	Australia	China	India	Kazakhstan	New Zealand	Romania	Russia	South Africa	Spain	Turkey	United Kingdom	World Total
2005	19,697	104,525	366,665	198,507	13,409	40,024	8,086	17,771	31,690	25,654	31,811	35,345	1,999,970
2006	20,038	94,328	372,927	205,171	14,335	40,227	8,298	18,213	31,383	25,408	31,822	34,820	2,016,796
2007	20,430	88,211	369,216	212,098	15,350	38,572	8,405	19,675	31,347	25,086	32,260	34,041	2,065,465
2008	20,238	82,638	368,126	209,732	16,080	34,184	9,334	21,503	31,623	22,912	31,749	33,223	2,070,301
2009	19,528	76,140	369,744	207,387	16,770	32,466	9,780	21,770	31,347	22,652	29,568	31,533	2,070,524
2010	19,062	71,585	372,757	205,065	17,370	32,658	10,059	21,986	30,776	21,455	26,923	31,177	2,073,520
2011	19,011	76,599	363,011	202,766	17,810	31,218	9,658	21,820	30,468	19,696	29,383	31,728	2,108,319
2012	18,650	78,272	366,487	200,242	18,092	31,353	9,770	22,858	30,533	18,977	35,783	32,313	2,137,079
2013[1]	18,950	79,098	373,784	197,800	17,633	30,867	10,100	24,180	31,200	18,729	38,510	32,954	2,138,683
2014[2]	19,100	76,182	390,186	196,000	17,561	29,901	10,449	24,337	26,125	18,136	41,462	33,833	

[1] Preliminary.   [2] Forecast.   *Source: Food and Agricultural Organization of the United Nations (FAO-UN)*

Salient Statistics of Sheep & Lambs in the United States (Average Live Weight)   In Thousands of Head

Year	Inventory, Jan. 1 — Without New Crop Lambs	Inventory, Jan. 1 — With New Crop Lambs	Lamb Crop	Total Supply	Marketings[3] — Sheep	Marketings[3] — Lambs	Slaughter — Farm	Slaughter — Commercial	Slaughter — Total[4]	Net Exports	Total Disappearance	Production (Live Weight) (Mil. Lbs.)	Farm Value Jan. 1	Farm Value Total
2006	6,230	6,230	3,950	10,180	692	4,196	69	2,699	2,768	----	----	463.1	872.4	141.0
2007	6,165	6,273	3,895	10,168	780	3,927	85	2,694	2,778	----	----	473.1	818.5	134.0
2008	5,950	6,055	3,710	9,765	737	3,652	92	2,556	2,647	----	----	417.0	823.4	138.0
2009	5,747	5,855	3,690	9,545	625	3,532	95	2,516	2,611	----	----	421.6	765.2	133.0
2010	5,620	5,727	3,570	9,297	645	3,429	95	2,458	2,553	----	----	405.3	761.1	135.0
2011	5,470	5,579	3,490	9,069	----	----	93	2,164	2,258	----	----	----	938.4	170.0
2012	5,375	5,484	3,445	8,929	----	----	93	2,183	2,275	----	----	----	----	----
2013	5,360	5,467	3,370	8,837	----	----	94	2,319	2,412	----	----	----	----	----
2014[1]	5,245	5,356	3,440	8,796	----	----	95	2,104	2,199	----	----	----	----	----
2015[2]	5,280	5,391	3,440	8,831	----	----	95	1,998	2,093	----	----	----	----	----

[1] Preliminary.   [2] Estimate.   [3] Excludes interfarm sales.   [4] Includes all commercial and farm.
Source: Economic Research Service, U.S. Department of Agriculture (ERS-USDA)

Sheep and Lambs[3] on Farms in the United States on January 1   In Thousands of Head

Year	California	Colorado	Idaho	Iowa	Minnesota	Montana	Mexico	Ohio	Dakota	Texas	Utah	Wyoming	Total
2008	620	420	235	225	145	270	130	125	340	960	280	425	5,950
2009	660	410	210	200	140	255	120	130	305	870	290	420	5,747
2010	610	370	220	210	130	245	120	128	325	830	290	375	5,620
2011	600	370	235	200	130	230	110	129	265	850	280	365	5,470
2012	570	460	240	195	150	225	100	126	285	650	305	370	5,375
2013	570	435	235	175	135	235	100	121	275	700	295	375	5,360
2014	590	365	250	155	135	220	81	117	270	730	280	355	5,245
2015	600	420	260	175	130	215	90	121	255	720	290	345	5,280
2016[1]	575	435	255	175	125	230	90	120	255	735	285	355	5,320

[1] Preliminary.   [2] Includes sheep & lambs on feed for market and stock sheep & lambs.   *Source: Economic Research Service, U.S. Department of Agriculture (ERS-USDA)*

Average Wholesale Price of Slaughter Lambs (Choice[2]) at San Angelo Texas In Dollars Per Hundred Pounds (Cwt.)

Year	Jan.	Feb.	Mar.	Apr.	May	June	July	Aug.	Sept.	Oct.	Nov.	Dec.	Average
2007	81.00	82.27	84.50	85.25	84.20	77.40	86.38	86.19	89.44	84.90	84.83	92.92	84.94
2008	86.63	88.82	83.25	74.70	77.75	86.75	88.81	88.13	89.54	85.55	85.46	95.83	85.94
2009	88.74	89.25	92.75	89.38	95.23	93.91	88.00	88.88	88.17	89.50	89.66	92.25	90.48
2010	95.04	106.63	109.95	112.00	104.47	102.05	109.17	112.15	125.38	129.69	138.50	156.67	116.81
2011	164.19	182.63	177.15	152.88	160.20	160.88	169.47	162.13	152.80	154.00	156.80	135.83	160.75
2012	147.40	148.13	141.94	136.75	128.50	116.00	116.00	75.00	80.88	96.20	84.67	88.67	113.35
2013	114.25	109.57	109.57	88.90	92.50	93.76	90.85	86.50	104.38	146.50	143.09	163.33	111.93
2014	165.00	168.38	154.88	150.97	135.17	160.83	150.23	152.94	164.90	159.25	162.00	166.83	157.62
2015[1]	155.25	166.83	137.75	137.88	134.50	147.13	144.00	148.00	186.40	139.00	148.67	141.50	148.91

[1] Preliminary.   *Source: Economic Research Service, U.S. Department of Agriculture (ERS-USDA)*

Federally Inspected Slaughter of Sheep & Lambs in the United States   In Thousands of Head

Year	Jan.	Feb.	Mar.	Apr.	May	June	July	Aug.	Sept.	Oct.	Nov.	Dec.	Total
2007	204	194	267	203	205	188	191	212	197	232	223	212	2,529
2008	202	202	219	207	195	181	193	186	207	209	180	213	2,393
2009	179	169	210	213	167	185	189	187	207	201	200	217	2,323
2010	173	167	249	175	167	194	178	185	186	185	200	217	2,261
2011	151	146	184	192	166	168	150	183	186	185	201	200	2,261
2012	154	155	180	166	164	155	165	186	163	161	172	167	2,000
2013	165	150	184	175	188	168	193	190	161	190	166	173	2,012
2014	167	155	177	204	177	175	189	190	167	187	170	185	2,120
2015[1]	153	150	190	179	153	173	167	156	167	166	163	182	1,998

[1] Preliminary.   *Source: Economic Research Service, U.S. Department of Agriculture (ERS-USDA)*

Average Live Weight of Sheep & Lambs Slaughtered in the United States   In Pounds per Head

Year	Jan.	Feb.	Mar.	Apr.	May	June	July	Aug.	Sept.	Oct.	Nov.	Dec.	Average
2007	141	143	142	141	145	139	133	130	130	134	138	137	138
2008	141	144	141	141	148	139	134	134	131	135	136	137	138
2009	143	145	143	138	147	140	139	135	134	133	134	139	139
2010	141	143	137	141	142	138	134	129	130	134	134	140	137
2011	142	144	148	142	148	141	136	135	137	138	138	142	141
2012	151	153	152	147	157	152	144	145	148	140	140	138	147
2013	143	145	142	143	142	142	136	134	128	127	130	133	137
2014	140	140	142	140	147	141	135	131	130	132	135	137	138
2015[1]	144	144	142	142	145	142	141	137	132	131	134	135	139

[1] Preliminary.   *Source: Economic Research Service, U.S. Department of Agriculture (ERS-USDA)*

Federally Inspected Slaughter of Goats in the United States   In Thousands of Head

Year	Jan.	Feb.	Mar.	Apr.	May	June	July	Aug.	Sept.	Oct.	Nov.	Dec.	Total
2007	46	41	51	52	55	53	53	56	54	61	56	62	639
2008	49	45	59	52	53	54	57	58	63	57	54	71	671
2009	48	44	56	55	50	57	57	61	60	54	59	58	659
2010	43	39	58	47	46	53	50	59	57	51	58	53	612
2011	41	38	43	47	45	50	50	60	51	52	59	55	589
2012	43	38	44	46	46	45	52	54	44	53	45	48	558
2013	40	34	45	42	45	41	53	49	44	50	42	45	528
2014	35	32	36	42	40	44	45	41	43	44	37	47	486
2015/1	35	28	38	36	34	40	39	37	40	37	36	42	441

[1] Preliminary.   *Source: Economic Research Service, U.S. Department of Agriculture (ERS-USDA)*

Cold Storage Holdings of Lamb and Mutton in the United States, on First of Month   In Thousands of Pounds

Year	Jan.	Feb.	Mar.	Apr.	May	June	July	Aug.	Sept.	Oct.	Nov.	Dec.
2007	15,769	15,640	15,570	15,996	18,206	16,644	15,410	13,811	15,692	14,734	13,944	13,096
2008	12,918	15,177	18,157	17,118	17,783	18,411	19,598	19,723	21,147	20,796	21,331	21,659
2009	21,001	19,469	18,279	19,274	19,801	19,694	21,568	20,062	19,045	17,426	15,301	15,052
2010	14,519	11,759	12,922	16,313	16,453	20,448	22,972	22,059	19,859	18,046	16,189	16,500
2011	15,206	13,278	12,582	12,874	13,279	15,062	18,097	21,034	21,209	22,218	20,021	19,014
2012	16,857	19,275	20,851	21,846	19,711	19,680	22,460	24,291	24,233	23,453	23,210	18,978
2013	21,379	18,768	19,833	17,624	21,463	19,793	19,307	23,324	21,988	23,444	23,967	21,697
2014	24,508	25,658	26,191	28,076	26,536	25,208	31,119	33,968	40,157	23,444	23,967	31,366
2015[1]	33,942	35,206	36,771	34,250	37,004	38,363	35,470	39,064	41,883	41,921	40,742	44,693

[1] Preliminary.   *Source: Economic Research Service, U.S. Department of Agriculture (ERS-USDA)*

Silk

Silk is a fine, tough, elastic fiber produced by caterpillars, commonly called silkworms. Silk is one of the oldest known textile fibers. Chinese tradition credits Lady Hsi-Ling-Shih, wife of the Emperor Huang Ti, with the discovery of the silkworm and the invention of the first silk reel. Dating to around 3000 BC, a group of ribbons, threads, and woven fragments was found in China. Also found, along the lower Yangzi River, were 7,000 year-old spinning tools, silk thread, and fabric fragments.

Silk filament was first woven into cloth in Ancient China. The Chinese successfully guarded this secret until 300AD, when Japan, and later India, learned the secret. In 550 AD, two Nestorian monks were sent to China to steal mulberry seeds and silkworm eggs, which they hid in their walking staffs, and then brought them back to Rome. By the 17th century, France was the silk center of the West. Unfortunately, the silkworm did not flourish in the English climate, nor has it ever flourished in the U.S.

Sericulture is the term for the raising of silkworms. The blind, flightless moth, Bombyx mori, lays more than 500 tiny eggs. After hatching, the tiny worms eat chopped mulberry leaves continuously until they are ready to spin their cocoons. After gathering the complete cocoons, the first step in silk manufacturing is to kill the insects inside the cocoons with heat. The cocoons are then placed in boiling water to loosen the gummy substance, sericin,

holding the filament together. The filament is unwound, and then rewound in a process called reeling. Each cocoon's silk filament is between 600 and 900 meters long. Four different types of silk thread may be produced: organzine, crepe, tram, and thrown singles. During the last 30 years, in spite of the use of man-made fibers, world silk production has doubled.

Raw silk is traded on the Kansai Agricultural Commodities Exchange (KANEX) in Japan. Dried cocoons are traded on the Chuba Commodity Exchange (CCE). Raw silk and dried cocoons are traded on the Yokohama Commodity Exchange.

Supply – World production of silk in 2013 (latest data), fell -0.4% yr/yr to 167,913 metric tons, below last year's record high of 168,511 metric tons. China is the world's largest producer of silk by far with a 75.0% share of world production in 2013. Other key producers include India with 14.1% of world production, Vietnam (3.8%), and Thailand (1.0%).

Trade – In 2011 (latest data), the world's largest exporters of silk were China with 82.7 % of world exports, North Korea with 0.7%, and Japan with 0.4%. In 2011, the world's largest importers of silk were India (with 48.8% of world imports), Japan (5.0%), Italy (6.2%), and Japan (4.9%).

World Production of Raw Silk   In Metric Tons

Year	Brazil	China	India	Iran	Japan	North Korea	Rep. of Korea	Kyrgy-zstan	Thailand	Turkmen-istan	Uzbek-istan	Viet Nam	World Total
2004	1,750	104,800	15,742	900	263	350	3	17	1,600	4,500	1,200	12,323	145,943
2005	1,200	111,950	16,500	900	150	350	3	50	1,600	4,500	1,200	11,475	152,448
2006	1,250	123,491	17,305	900	117	350	3	50	1,600	4,500	1,200	10,413	163,774
2007	1,300	125,001	18,475	900	105	350	3	50	1,600	4,500	1,200	10,110	166,189
2008	1,000	126,001	18,320	900	120	350	3	50	1,600	4,500	1,200	7,746	164,385
2009	800	126,001	18,370	900	150	400	3	50	1,600	4,500	1,200	7,367	163,941
2010	600	126,001	19,690	900	130	400	3	50	1,600	4,500	1,200	7,107	164,779
2011	500	126,001	20,410	900	280	400	3	50	1,600	4,500	1,200	7,057	165,500
2012[1]	400	126,001	23,060	900	280	400	3	50	1,600	4,500	1,200	7,517	168,511
2013[2]	400	126,001	23,679	900	280	400		50	1,600	4,500	1,200	6,300	167,913

[1] Preliminary.   [2] Estimate.   NA = Not avaliable.   *Source: Food and Agricultural Organization of the United Nations (FAO-UN)*

World Trade of Silk by Selected Countries   In Metric Tons

	------------------------------- Imports -------------------------------						------------------------------- Exports -------------------------------					
Year	France	Hong Kong	India	Italy	Japan	Korea, South	World Total	Brazil	China	Hong Kong	Japan	Korea, South	World Total
2004	181	3	7,948	1,983	1,581	1,338	16,607	7	11,308	20	688	227	14,321
2005	262	14	8,383	1,974	1,406	1,359	18,114	36	10,983	11	202	219	13,699
2006	212	3	5,565	2,146	1,295	1,095	15,215	4	6,716	4	11	223	10,008
2007	150	2	7,922	1,463	791	989	15,931	18	13,758	2	10	277	15,696
2008	191	----	8,392	1,040	932	724	16,371	13	13,431	----	16	137	14,903
2009	111	17	7,338	501	733	656	12,552	8	9,243	16	8	100	10,860
2010	109	34	4,525	698	737	645	9,992	6	8,543	34	36	57	10,406
2011	110	9	5,597	711	563	533	16,803	----	7,122	----	35	59	8,608
2012	135	----	5,235	692	607	503	21,161	----	7,676	2	25	245	9,158
2013[1]	248	----	3,609	676	570	410	24,917	----	6,690	----	18	118	8,454

[1] Preliminary.   *Source: Food and Agricultural Organization of the United Nations (FAO-UN)*

Silver

Silver is a white, lustrous metallic element that conducts heat and electricity better than any other metal. In ancient times, many silver deposits were on or near the earth's surface. Before 2,500 BC, silver mines were worked in Asia Minor. Around 700 BC, ancient Greeks stamped a turtle on their first silver coins. Silver assumed a key role in the U.S. monetary system in 1792 when Congress based the currency on the silver dollar. However, the U.S. discontinued the use of silver in coinage in 1965. Today Mexico is the only country that uses silver in its circulating coinage.

Silver is the most malleable and ductile of all metals, with the exception of gold. Silver melts at about 962 degrees Celsius and boils at about 2212 degrees Celsius. Silver is not very chemically active, although tarnishing occurs when sulfur and sulfides attack silver, forming silver sulfide on the surface of the metal. Because silver is too soft in its pure form, a hardening agent, usually copper, is mixed into the silver. Copper is usually used as the hardening agent because it does not discolor the silver. The term "sterling silver" refers to silver that contains at least 925 parts of silver per thousand (92.5%) to 75 parts of copper (7.5%).

Silver is usually found combined with other elements in minerals and ores. In the U.S., silver is mined in conjunction with lead, copper, and zinc. In the U.S., Nevada, Idaho, Alaska, and Arizona are the leading silver-producing states. For industrial purposes, silver is used for photography, electrical appliances, glass, and as an antibacterial agent for the health industry.

Silver futures and options are traded at the CME Group, the NYSE-LIFFE U.S., the EUREX, and the Moscow Exchange. Silver futures are also traded on the Hong Kong Mercantile Exchange (HKMEx), the JSE Securities Exchange, the Multi Commodity Exchange of India (MCX), the National Commodity & Derivatives Exchange (NCDEX), the Shanghai Futures Exchange, and the Tokyo Commodity Exchange (TOCOM). The CME silver futures contract calls for the delivery of 5,000 troy ounces of silver (0.999 fineness) and is priced in terms of dollars and cents per troy ounce.

Prices – CME silver futures prices (Barchart.com symbol SI) began 2015 on a strong note as they rallied up to a 1-1/2 year high of $18.36 an ounce in January 2015. Concern that Greece may leave the Eurozone after the anti-austerity Syriza party won elections there fueled safe-haven demand for precious metals. Holdings of silver in ETFs rose to a record 70.651 million ounces in January 2015. Silver traded sideways into Q3-2015 and then ground lower the rest of the year and posted a 6-1/2 year low in December of $13.64 an ounce. The action by the Fed to raise interest rates in December for the first time in 6 years fueled a rally in the dollar index to a 12-1/2 year high, which undercut silver prices. Also, a lack of global inflation prompted fund liquidation of silver as long silver positions in ETF's fell to a 1-year low in December. Silver prices finished 2015 down -11.5% at $14.78 an ounce.

Supply – World mine production of silver in 2014 rose +0.4% yr/yr to a new record high of 26,100 metric tons, continuing to show some improvement after flat production figures in 2000-03. The world's largest silver producers in 2014 were Mexico with 18.0% of world production, China (16.1%), Peru (14.2%), Australia (7.3%), Russia (6.5%), and Bolivia (5.0%). U.S. production of refined silver in 2014 (through August, annualized) rose by +2.6% to 5,008 metric tons, down from the 2011 record high of 6,375 metric tons.

Demand – U.S. consumption of silver in 2009 (latest data) fell −11.8% yr/yr to 164.4 million troy ounces. The largest consumption of silver is for electrical contacts and conductors with 31.9% of total usage, followed by coinage (20.6%), photographic materials (13.4%), jewelry (7.1%), and brazing alloys and solders (3.2%). The world's largest consuming nation of silver for industrial purposes is the U.S. with 20% of world consumption in 2004 (latest data), followed by Japan (16%), India (10%), and Italy (7%).

Trade – U.S. exports of refined silver in 2011 (latest data) rose +27.5% yr/yr to 29.064 million troy ounces, which is about half of the record high of 99.022 million troy ounces seen in 1997. The major destinations for U.S. silver exports are Japan (17.3%), South Korea (14.3%), and Canada (11.0%). U.S. imports of silver ore and concentrates in 2011 rose from 104,000 troy ounces to 2.707 million troy ounces. U.S. imports of refined silver bullion in 2011 rose +2.2% yr/yr to 168.788 million troy ounces. The bulk of those imports came from Mexico (67.515 million troy ounces), Canada (40.509 million troy ounces), and Chile (3.122 million troy ounces).

World Mine Production of Silver   In Thousands of Kilograms (Metric Ton)

Year	Australia	Bolivia	Canada[3]	Chile	China	Kazakhstan	Mexico	Peru	Poland	Russia	Sweden	United States	World Total[2]
2006	1,727	472	995	1,607	2,600	806	2,970	3,471	1,266	974	268	1,160	20,100
2007	1,879	525	860	1,936	2,700	723	3,135	3,494	1,199	911	270	1,280	20,800
2008	1,926	1,114	709	1,405	2,800	646	3,236	3,686	1,161	1,132	293	1,250	21,300
2009	1,635	1,326	617	1,301	2,900	618	3,554	3,923	1,207	1,590	289	1,250	22,600
2010	1,864	1,259	591	1,287	3,500	552	4,411	3,640	1,181	1,545	302	1,280	24,100
2011	1,725	1,214	661	1,291	3,700	651	4,778	3,419	1,167	1,543	302	1,120	24,300
2012	1,728	1,206	705	1,195	3,900	963	5,358	3,479	1,149	1,679	305	1,060	25,500
2013	1,840	1,287	627	1,174	4,100	1,000	4,861	3,674	1,199	1,720	305	1,040	25,900
2014[1]	1,720	1,340	493	1,570	4,060		5,000	3,780	1,260	1,330		1,180	26,800
2015[2]	1,700	1,300	500	1,600	4,100		5,400	3,800	1,300	1,500		1,100	27,300

[1] Preliminary.   [2] Estimate.   [3] Shipments.   *Source: U.S. Geological Survey (USGS)*

SILVER

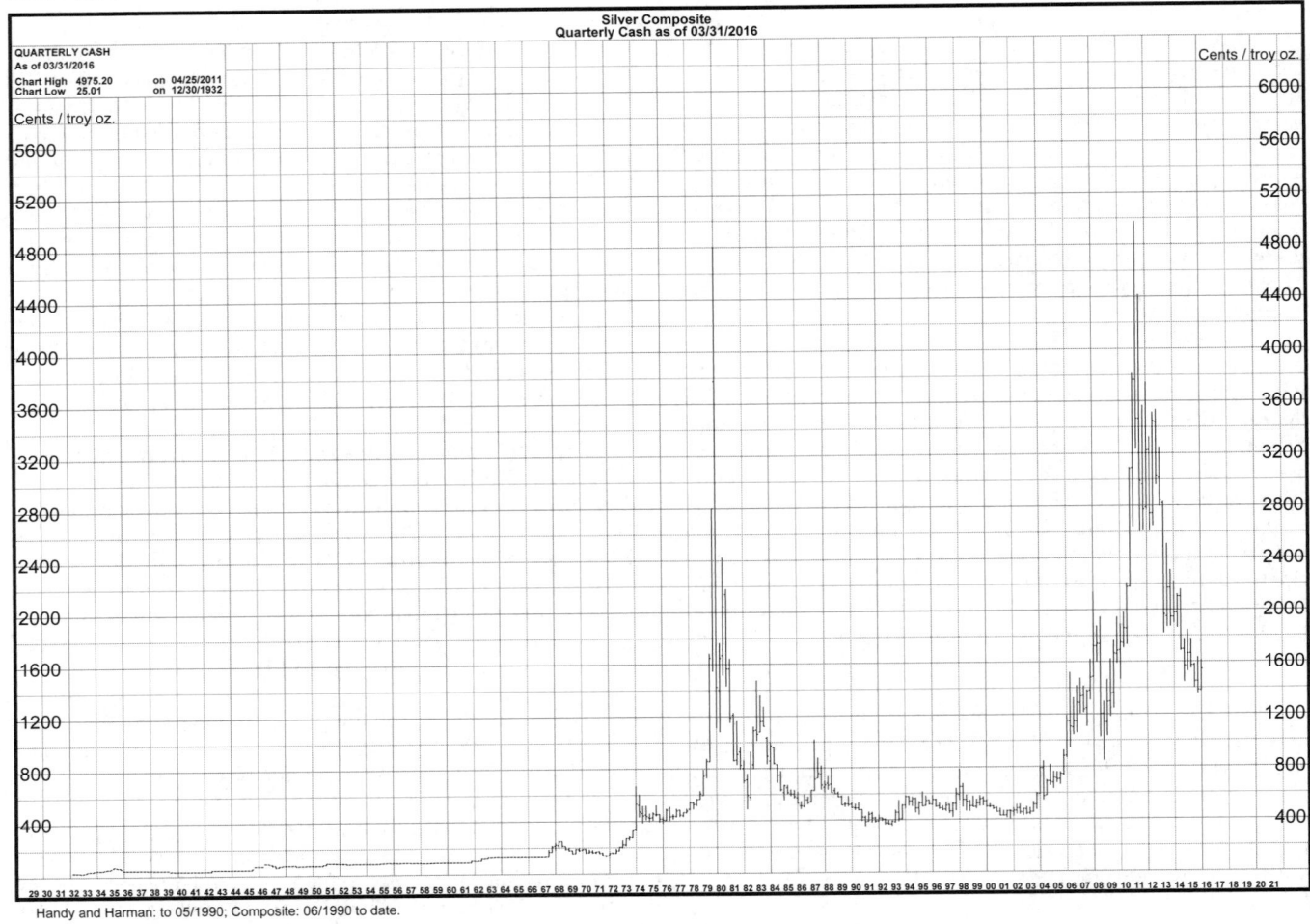

Silver Composite
Quarterly Cash as of 03/31/2016

QUARTERLY CASH
As of 03/31/2016
Chart High 4975.20 on 04/25/2011
Chart Low 25.01 on 12/30/1932

Cents / troy oz.

Handy and Harman: to 05/1990; Composite: 06/1990 to date.

Average Price of Silver in New York (Handy & Harman)   In Cents Per Troy Ounce (.999 Fine)

Year	Jan.	Feb.	Mar.	Apr.	May	June	July	Aug.	Sept.	Oct.	Nov.	Dec.	Average
2006	918.48	952.13	1,037.52	1,263.71	1,337.84	1,077.41	1,121.24	1,225.39	1,159.93	1,161.55	1,298.45	1,329.83	1,156.96
2007	1,286.63	1,394.58	1,316.27	1,373.23	1,319.27	1,315.48	1,295.21	1,233.22	1,292.92	1,372.17	1,467.15	1,431.24	1,341.45
2008	1,605.90	1,766.63	1,921.60	1,751.57	1,704.90	1,703.95	1,806.41	1,457.81	1,219.33	1,042.72	986.78	1,031.66	1,499.94
2009	1,139.90	1,343.68	1,311.50	1,252.02	1,411.30	1,465.93	1,338.64	1,443.05	1,648.74	1,726.34	1,787.68	1,765.68	1,469.54
2010	1,775.05	1,587.21	1,717.11	1,816.83	1,841.90	1,853.43	1,793.98	1,849.25	2,061.12	2,346.86	2,657.20	2,933.00	2,019.41
2011	2,855.15	3,085.61	3,594.61	4,264.45	3,702.67	3,584.09	3,832.95	4,035.17	3,802.10	3,206.33	3,336.08	3,028.07	3,527.27
2012	3,095.25	3,421.95	3,296.32	3,154.65	2,882.00	2,810.29	2,739.74	2,891.35	3,379.18	3,328.57	3,271.00	3,177.13	3,120.62
2013	3,112.05	3,027.53	2,878.90	2,525.25	2,301.95	2,111.53	1,968.66	2,208.02	2,249.40	2,201.43	2,072.35	1,962.29	2,384.95
2014	1,987.52	2,086.53	2,071.60	1,973.64	1,934.19	1,989.24	2,092.25	1,973.56	1,837.10	1,716.33	1,596.61	1,629.48	1,907.34
2015	1,723.55	1,678.71	1,624.00	1,634.00	1,683.28	1,607.45	1,505.32	1,494.12	1,475.02	1,581.25	1,445.22	1,408.55	1,571.71

Source: American Metal Market (AMM)

Average Price of Silver in London (Spot Fix)   In Pence Per Troy Ounce (.999 Fine)

Year	Jan.	Feb.	Mar.	Apr.	May	June	July	Aug.	Sept.	Oct.	Nov.	Dec.	Average
2006	519.94	544.76	594.70	714.36	715.69	584.44	607.69	647.19	615.09	618.97	678.96	677.31	626.59
2007	656.95	712.03	675.74	690.95	665.15	662.06	636.65	613.19	639.99	670.90	708.45	709.65	670.14
2008	815.50	899.50	960.24	883.98	867.12	866.05	907.89	772.57	677.51	617.03	645.37	693.86	800.55
2009	787.02	931.98	923.81	850.16	912.88	894.99	816.90	872.89	1,010.76	1,065.91	1,076.27	1,087.91	935.96
2010	1,098.45	1,016.07	1,140.22	1,184.58	1,256.63	1,255.90	1,172.41	1,181.47	1,323.37	1,479.95	1,665.70	1,880.21	1,304.58
2011	1,808.34	1,912.09	2,224.65	2,602.69	2,266.24	2,209.81	2,373.37	2,466.59	2,410.10	2,032.85	2,111.63	1,942.66	2,196.75
2012	1,994.05	2,164.96	2,082.42	1,970.51	1,811.54	1,806.56	1,756.42	1,839.55	2,097.22	2,070.91	2,049.00	1,967.97	1,967.59
2013	1,949.80	1,957.31	1,908.68	1,649.50	1,505.82	1,362.47	1,296.54	1,424.04	1,416.94	1,368.26	1,286.22	1,197.73	1,526.94
2014	1,206.90	1,259.53	1,246.67	1,178.50	1,148.47	1,175.94	1,225.31	1,181.77	1,126.82	1,067.60	1,012.22	1,042.49	1,156.02
2015	1,138.45	1,094.75	1,084.93	1,092.25	1,089.22	1,031.34	967.53	958.94	961.93	1,031.14	951.23	940.07	1,028.48

Source: American Metal Market (AMM)

234

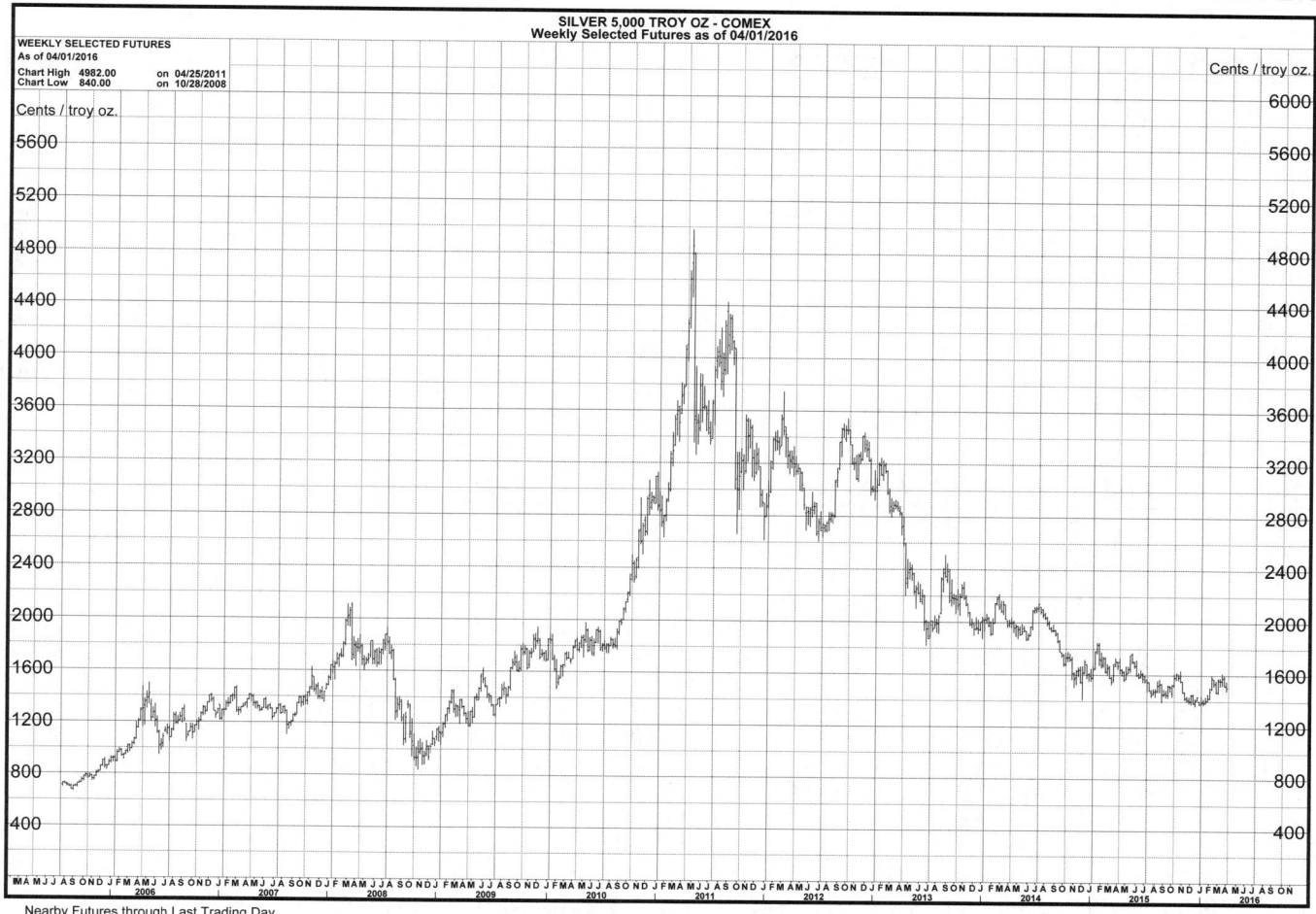

SILVER 5,000 TROY OZ - COMEX
Weekly Selected Futures as of 04/01/2016

WEEKLY SELECTED FUTURES
As of 04/01/2016

| Chart High | 4982.00 | on 04/25/2011 |
| Chart Low | 840.00 | on 10/28/2008 |

Cents / troy oz.

Nearby Futures through Last Trading Day.

Volume of Trading of Silver Futures in New York (COMEX) — In Thousands of Contracts

Year	Jan.	Feb.	Mar.	Apr.	May	June	July	Aug.	Sept.	Oct.	Nov.	Dec.	Total
2006	495.6	624.5	562.3	807.3	513.8	508.7	255.8	452.6	268.4	244.2	424.8	275.1	5,433.1
2007	364.6	589.3	479.9	635.0	417.3	680.6	404.1	784.0	469.5	581.1	1,018.5	393.2	6,817.1
2008	719.3	989.6	881.8	913.0	581.0	860.0	722.7	953.1	792.1	594.3	578.0	332.4	8,917.2
2009	415.6	652.2	433.8	575.7	418.4	869.1	476.6	842.9	657.0	809.6	1,159.3	680.3	7,990.5
2010	755.9	1,065.2	750.2	994.8	936.9	1,079.3	642.8	978.6	757.1	1,314.2	2,282.2	1,269.6	12,826.7
2011	1,429.7	1,674.7	1,685.7	3,014.6	2,461.1	1,768.9	1,325.0	1,982.8	1,220.4	952.6	1,327.4	765.6	19,608.6
2012	826.9	1,478.7	1,120.1	1,224.1	1,028.2	1,416.8	804.5	1,231.9	1,068.8	874.2	1,437.3	804.2	13,315.7
2013	1,021.7	1,346.4	780.3	1,980.5	1,172.0	1,555.4	932.3	1,652.5	958.1	948.4	1,270.3	857.7	14,475.6
2014	915.0	1,498.8	973.7	1,388.9	883.1	1,459.4	957.2	1,216.7	990.8	1,013.7	1,435.1	964.7	13,697.2
2015	979.5	1,196.0	875.8	1,431.4	886.3	1,499.6	988.4	1,511.0	822.3	1,107.5	1,291.7	864.9	13,454.4

Contract size = 5,000 oz.   Source: CME Group; New York Mercantile Exchange (NYMEX), COMEX Division

Average Open Interest of Silver Futures in New York (COMEX) — In Contracts

Year	Jan.	Feb.	Mar.	Apr.	May	June	July	Aug.	Sept.	Oct.	Nov.	Dec.
2006	131,767	129,928	132,140	137,121	110,400	110,631	98,733	110,635	102,159	105,167	114,132	105,741
2007	105,692	122,515	113,749	118,275	109,070	120,179	117,817	118,292	110,958	123,781	144,897	146,891
2008	174,969	182,076	157,971	143,333	123,649	128,645	136,866	131,931	110,333	97,927	91,983	84,986
2009	87,525	96,902	92,756	93,855	95,420	106,283	99,018	103,076	122,052	133,409	137,261	124,797
2010	126,921	118,619	112,234	123,849	122,547	129,561	118,619	126,117	145,022	153,013	148,547	133,596
2011	133,030	138,901	135,793	143,245	124,278	118,740	115,246	117,217	109,908	103,939	107,600	100,220
2012	103,766	108,478	110,777	117,254	113,514	122,240	122,555	124,907	125,957	140,254	145,146	141,906
2013	143,032	141,751	149,900	156,813	145,964	147,042	133,417	130,278	113,116	116,266	130,050	133,668
2014	137,682	145,743	141,847	157,064	152,154	161,079	161,447	161,613	168,883	172,012	169,706	148,854
2015	158,200	167,554	171,411	177,026	176,403	190,678	190,121	173,457	155,598	164,457	167,660	164,215

Contract size = 5,000 oz.   Source: CME Group; New York Mercantile Exchange (NYMEX), COMEX Division

SILVER

Mine Production of Recoverable Silver in the United States   In Metric Tons

Year	Arizona	Cali-fornia	Colo-rado	Idaho	Missouri	Montana	Nevada	New Mexico	South Dakota	Wash-ington	Other States	Total
2005	W	W	W	W	W	W	276	W	W	W	949	1,230
2006	W	W	W	W	W	W	260	W	W	W	895	1,160
2007	W	W	W	W	W	W	243	W	W	W	1,040	1,280
2008	W	W	W	W	W	W	235	W	W	W	1,020	1,250
2009	W	W	W	W	W	W	203	W	W	W	1,040	1,250
2010	W	W	W	W	W	W	224	W	W	W	1,050	1,280
2011	W	W	W	W	W	W	209	W	W	W	913	1,120
2012	W	W	W	W	W	W	250	W	W	W	805	1,060
2013	W	W	W	W	W	W	255	W	W	W	791	1,050
2014[1]	W	W	W	W	W	W	272	W	W	W	694	966

[1] Preliminary.   W = Withheld proprietary data; included in "Other States".   *Source: U.S. Geological Survey (USGS)*

Commodity Exchange, Inc. (COMEX) Warehouse of Stocks of Silver   In Thousands of Troy Ounces

Year	Jan.	Feb.	Mar.	Apr.	May	June	July	Aug.	Sept.	Oct.	Nov.	Dec.
2006	119,974	124,793	127,898	125,763	123,627	108,443	102,268	102,086	103,634	105,451	105,313	107,770
2007	111,071	113,970	117,637	126,433	131,343	130,497	139,935	132,106	133,057	133,474	133,891	134,533
2008	130,072	135,414	135,037	135,881	133,512	134,896	135,959	138,061	137,821	135,719	130,204	127,170
2009	125,536	123,902	124,121	123,615	119,910	120,879	118,519	117,818	117,796	116,159	116,159	112,494
2010	110,588	110,588	110,588	115,786	116,178	119,452	114,015	110,244	110,765	111,075	107,785	107,393
2011	104,548	103,594	102,549	105,495	102,014	100,968	101,720	104,176	104,085	106,012	107,096	110,415
2012	126,218	129,403	130,318	137,073	142,125	143,150	145,933	139,218	140,678	142,047	142,362	145,284
2013	148,205	154,577	162,830	164,163	166,050	165,749	166,746	164,711	163,771	165,329	169,012	169,985
2014	173,927	179,297	182,831	179,791	174,483	175,267	175,517	175,317	179,292	182,194	181,185	177,008
2015	174,359	178,053	177,163	176,650	176,310	179,287	182,384	175,671	170,562	165,009	162,813	158,954

Source: CME Group; New York Mercantile Exchange (NYMEX), COMEX Division

Production[2] of Refined Silver in the United States, from All Sources   In Metric Tons

Year	Jan.	Feb.	Mar.	Apr.	May	June	July	Aug.	Sept.	Oct.	Nov.	Dec.	Total
2006	506	434	500	445	381	554	489	431	349	387	209	305	4,990
2007	401	405	445	436	476	452	335	438	290	388	267	339	4,671
2008	325	360	394	460	401	417	420	428	460	445	422	393	4,925
2009	456	182	270	326	337	394	363	495	535	676	530	778	5,342
2010	553	504	794	503	510	356	383	534	439	460	547	441	6,024
2011	626	512	748	477	485	462	493	491	499	522	426	634	6,375
2012	559	443	443	419	457	426	423	375	344	385	407	393	5,073
2013	505	438	421	486	376	337	415	365	364	450	292	431	4,880
2014	431	334	348	399	450	418	458	386	506	456	430	474	5,080
2015[1]	515	508	473	505	434	479	467	498	452	471	384		5,659

[1] Preliminary.   [2] Includes U.S. mine production of recoverable silver plus imports of refined silver.   *Source: U.S. Geological Survey (USGS)*

U.S. Exports of Refined Silver to Selected Countries   In Thousands of Troy Ounces

Year	Canada	France	Germany	Hong Kong	Japan	Korea, South	Singa-pore	Switzer-land	United Arab Emirates	United Kingdom	Uruguay	Other Countries	Total
2004	7,009	1	3	24	585	1	166	2,321	----	3	108	2,125	12,346
2005	3,729	----	25	3	1	18	95	2,829	----	1,145	563	1,302	9,709
2006	5,433	----	874	----	547	----	120	1,218	2	37,937	----	----	50,797
2007	3,762	3	1,537	1,804	801	25	103	990	----	1,061	498	----	23,373
2008	4,051	----	1,283	5	2,115	1,424	131	527	----	1,929	437	10	20,512
2009	395	1	1,399	159	2	1,816	113	823	----	1,765	----	3	12,989
2010	3,376	----	2,247	139	1,241	1,974	1,010	733	----	1,331	----	28	22,794
2011	3,189	----	389	284	5,015	4,147	566	1,270	----	1,813	----	55	29,064
2012	2,546	----	1,550	208	2,771	170	240	434	----	11,574	----	45	30,414
2013[1]	2,485	----	350	191	601	95	521	93	----	250	----	60	13,149

[1] Preliminary.   [2] Included in "Other Countries", if any.   NA = Not available.   *Source: American Bureau of Metal Statistics, Inc. (ABMS)*

U.S. Imports of Silver From Selected Countries   In Thousands of Troy Ounces

	Ores and Concentrates				Refined Bullion						
Year	Canada	Mexico	Other Countries	Total	Canada	Chile	Mexico	Peru	Uruguay	Other Countries	Total
2004	71	----	----	71	37,616	2,042	59,156	17,297	----	4,774	120,884
2005	14	----	----	14	41,474	2,514	65,908	20,319	----	4,173	134,387
2006	----	----	----	----	47,261	1,106	73,945	13,214	----	2,077	137,602
2007	----	----	12	12	34,722	1,206	78,125	18,358	----	2,942	135,352
2008	----	----	1	1	25,109	2,234	76,196	16,075	----	4,485	124,099
2009	----	----	----	3	24,016	4,019	52,405	6,559	----	3,022	90,020
2010	104	----	----	104	51,119	2,578	82,947	9,999	----	26,003	172,646
2011	2,707	----	----	2,707	40,509	3,122	67,515	952	----	56,690	168,788
2012	2,373	250	----	2,659	42,760	2,350	76,839	1,418	----	6,199	129,565
2013[1]	1	344	----	344	51,440	268	64,622	1,231	----	5,573	123,135

[1] Preliminary.   [2] Included in "Other Countries", if any.   NA = Not available.   Source: American Bureau of Metal Statistics, Inc. (ABMS)

World Silver Consumption   In Millions of Troy Ounces

	Industrial Uses										Coinage							
Year	Canada	France	Germany	India	Italy	Japan	Mexico	United Kingdom	United States	World Total	Austria	Canada	France	Germany	Mexico	United States	Total Coinage	World Total
1995	2.0	30.0	43.6	101.3	49.5	112.7	16.9	31.6	148.7	752.7	.5	.7	1.2	2.4	.6	9.0	24.7	777.4
1996	2.0	26.9	41.0	122.2	51.7	112.1	20.3	33.8	155.0	785.8	.5	.7	.3	4.6	.5	7.1	23.3	809.1
1997	2.2	28.3	42.3	122.9	56.1	119.9	23.3	34.9	166.3	828.2	.4	.6	.3	3.7	.4	6.5	28.5	856.7
1998	2.3	28.4	38.4	114.7	55.9	112.8	21.7	38.6	162.6	801.2	.3	1.1	.3	10.0	.2	7.0	27.8	829.0
1999	2.1	26.6	35.1	121.5	61.8	122.5	21.3	39.3	175.2	838.7	.3	1.4	.3	7.0	.4	10.7	29.2	867.8
2000	2.0	28.8	31.8	131.0	65.1	135.0	16.6	42.7	179.1	871.8	.3	1.0	.4	8.8	.6	13.4	32.1	904.0
2001	2.0	28.7	32.4	154.0	58.2	119.3	15.9	45.9	157.3	836.5	.3	.9	.4	8.1	1.1	12.3	30.5	867.0
2002	2.1	27.1	29.4	122.5	56.0	118.7	17.0	43.1	161.6	807.0	.4	1.0	.5	6.0	1.1	15.3	31.6	838.6
2003	2.2	25.6	29.4	122.5	55.0	115.9	18.7	44.1	160.8	817.5	.4	.3	.5	10.3	1.1	14.5	35.8	853.4
2004[2]	2.1	12.0	30.7	79.2	54.8	125.1	18.6	52.2	164.8	807.0	.5	1.3	.5	10.3	.9	15.5	41.1	836.6

[2] Preliminary.   NA = Not available.   *Source: The Silver Institute*

Consumption of Silver in the United States, by End Use   In Millions of Troy Ounces

Year	Brazing Alloys & Solders	Catalysts	Batteries	Mirrors	Electrical Contacts & Conductors	Photographic Materials	Silverplate	Jewelry	Sterling Ware	Total Net Industrial Consumption	Coinage	Total Consumption
2000	8.7	6.3	5.2	2.6	51.5	70.2	4.5	6.1	5.6	178.8	13.4	192.2
2001	8.3	6.1	5.3	2.5	34.1	65.5	4.0	4.9	4.6	157.3	12.3	169.6
2002	8.4	NA	NA	NA	37.6	64.8	[3]	13.7	[3]	161.7	15.3	177.0
2003	7.9	NA	NA	NA	39.5	58.9	[3]	15.1	[3]	160.8	14.5	175.3
2004	7.3	NA	NA	NA	47.4	55.2	[3]	15.4	[3]	164.8	15.5	180.3
2005	7.7	NA	NA	NA	52.1	56.4	[3]	15.7	[3]	172.8	16.6	189.4
2006	7.2	NA	NA	NA	55.0	46.4	[3]	15.0	[3]	168.2	17.6	185.8
2007	7.7	NA	NA	NA	57.7	35.9	[3]	14.2	[3]	164.2	16.0	180.2
2008	7.2	NA	NA	NA	61.4	29.3	[3]	13.0	[3]	161.0	25.4	186.4
2009[1]	5.2	NA	NA	NA	52.4	22.0	[3]	11.6	[3]	130.5	33.9	164.4

[1] Preliminary.   [3] Included in Jewelry beginning 2002.   NA = Not available.   *Source: American Metal Market*

Soybean Meal

Soybean meal is produced through processing and separating soybeans into oil and meal components. If the soybeans are of particularly good quality, then the processor can get more meal weight by including more hulls in the meal while still meeting a 48% protein minimum. Soybean meal can be further processed into soy flour and isolated soy protein, but the bulk of soybean meal is used as animal feed for poultry, hogs and cattle. Soybean meal accounts for about two-thirds of the world's high-protein animal feed, followed by cottonseed and rapeseed meal, which together account for less than 20%. Soybean meal consumption has been moving to record highs in recent years. The soybean meal marketing year begins in October and ends in September.

Soybean meal futures and options are traded at the CME Group. The CME soybean meal futures contract calls for the delivery of 100 tons of soybean meal produced by conditioning ground soybeans and reducing the oil content of the conditioned product and having a minimum of 48.0% protein, minimum of 0.5% fat, maximum of 3.5% fiber, and maximum of 12.0% moisture.

Soybean crush – The term soybean "crush" refers to both the physical processing of soybeans and also to the dollar-value premium received for processing soybeans into their component products of meal and oil. The conventional model says that processing 60 pounds (one bushel) of soybeans produces 11 pounds of soybean oil, 44 pounds of 48% protein soybean meal, 3 pounds of hulls, and 1 pound of waste. The Gross Processing Margin (GPM) or crush equals (0.22 times Soybean Meal Prices in dollars per ton) + (11 times Soybean Oil prices in cents/pound) – Soybean prices in $/bushel. A higher crush value will occur when the price of the meal and oil products are strong relative to soybeans, e.g., because of supply disruptions or because of an increase in demand for the products. When the crush value is high, companies will have a strong incentive to buy raw soybeans and boost the output of the products. That supply increase should eventually bring the crush value back into line with the long-term equilibrium.

Prices – CME soybean meal futures prices (Barchart.com electronic symbol ZM) sold off in early 2015, showed a temporary recovery rally during mid-year, but then sold off sharply during the remainder of the year to post a new 6-year low and close the year down -27.5% at $264.3 per short ton.

Supply – World soybean meal production in 2015-16 rose +4.8% yr/yr to a new record high of 217.019 million metric tons. The world's largest soybean meal producers are China with 29.4% of world production in 2015-16, the U.S. with 18.6%, Argentina with 15.5%, and Brazil with 14.3%. U.S. production of soybean meal in 2015-16 fell -0.8% yr/yr to 44.715 million short tons, below the 2006-07 record high of 43.054. U.S. soybean meal stocks in 2015-16 (Oct 1) rose +4.0% yr/yr to 260,000 short tons, below the decade high of 383,000 short tons in 2001-02.

Demand – World consumption of soybean meal in 2015-16 rose +6.8% yr/yr to 215.626 million metric tons, a new record high. The European Union accounted for 14.7% of that consumption and the U.S. accounted for 14.1%. U.S. consumption of soybean meal in 2015-16 rose +12.7% yr/yr to 30.391 million metric tons.

Trade – World exports of soybean meal in 2015-16 rose +4.1% to 66.214 million metric tons. Argentina accounted for 48.0% of world exports and the U.S. accounted for 15.3%. World imports of soybean meal in 2015-16 rose +6.3% yr/yr to 63.894 million metric tons. U.S. exports of soybean meal in 2015-16 fell -11.0% yr/yr to 11.700 million short tons. U.S. imports of soybean meal in 2015-16 fell -2.4% yr/yr to 325,000 short tons, below the 2013-14 record high of 383,000 short tons.

Supply and Distribution of Soybean Meal in the United States   In Thousands of Short Tons

Crop Year Beginning Oct. 1	Supply			Distribution			Dollars Per Metric Ton			
	For Stocks Oct. 1	Pro-duction	Total Supply	Domestic	Exports	Total	Decatur 48% Protein Solvent	Decatur 44% Protein Solvent	Brazil FOB 45-46% Protein	Rotter-dam CIF
2006-07	314	43,054	43,524	34,374	8,804	43,178	205.44	226	199	276
2007-08	343	42,284	42,768	33,232	9,242	42,474	335.94	370	337	469
2008-09	294	39,102	39,484	30,752	8,497	39,249	331.17	365	333	401
2009-10	235	41,707	42,101	30,640	11,159	41,800	311.27	343	327	391
2010-11	302	39,251	39,731	30,278	9,104	39,381	345.52	381	383	418
2011-12	350	41,025	41,591	31,548	9,743	41,291	393.53	434	442	461
2012-13	300	39,875	40,420	29,031	11,114	40,145	468.11	516	489	538
2013-14[1]	275	40,685	41,343	29,547	11,546	41,093	489.94	517	524	546
2014-15[2]	250	45,062	45,645	32,235	13,150	45,384	368.49			
2015-16[3]	260	44,165	44,800	33,300	11,200	44,500	270-310			

[1] Preliminary.   [2] Estimate.   [3] Forecast.   *Source: Economic Research Service, U.S. Department of Agriculture (ERS-USDA)*

World Production of Soybean Meal   In Thousands of Metric Tons

Crop Year	Brazil	China	Egypt	European Union	India	Indo-nesia	Iran	Japan	Mexico	Thailand	United States	Vietnam	World Total
2006-07	11,118	27,630	1,169	33,525	1,095	2,236	1,567	3,941	4,674	3,298	31,166	2,191	150,979
2007-08	12,257	30,849	1,291	35,432	1,450	2,370	1,837	3,955	4,450	3,300	30,148	2,345	157,417
2008-09	12,418	31,673	1,450	31,836	2,000	2,383	2,186	3,840	4,350	3,250	27,898	2,500	153,243
2009-10	13,000	37,546	1,725	30,359	2,960	2,527	2,417	3,900	4,160	3,613	27,795	2,800	161,484
2010-11	13,950	43,382	1,900	30,952	2,880	2,784	2,525	3,844	4,340	3,701	27,489	3,100	170,861
2011-12	14,100	47,435	2,100	29,670	3,300	3,218	2,500	3,840	4,370	4,153	28,614	3,300	177,995
2012-13	14,200	50,091	2,220	27,042	3,520	3,430	2,460	3,332	4,250	4,152	26,308	3,700	177,449
2013-14	14,650	52,534	2,400	28,392	3,940	3,825	2,948	3,376	4,575	3,980	26,804	4,250	186,270
2014-15[1]	15,250	57,471	2,630	30,142	4,610	4,100	3,050	3,380	5,035	4,350	29,243	5,100	201,982
2015-16[2]	15,550	62,080	2,830	31,642	5,080	4,450	3,290	3,358	5,200	4,650	30,391	5,750	215,626

Crop year beginning October 1.   [1] Preliminary.   [2] Forecast.   *Source: Foreign Agricultural Service, U.S. Department of Agriculture (FAS-USDA)*

World Exports of Soybean Meal   In Thousands of Metric Tons

Crop Year	Argen-tina	Bolivia	Brazil	Canada	China	European Union	India	Korea, South	Norway	Para-guay	Russia	United States	World Total
2006-07	25,625	1,178	12,715	137	867	544	4,143		144	1,096	2	7,987	54,699
2007-08	26,816	763	12,138	120	634	422	5,285	9	148	1,072	50	8,384	56,063
2008-09	24,025	1,103	13,109	82	1,017	464	3,808	116	153	1,076	14	7,708	52,844
2009-10	24,914	1,114	12,985	126	1,181	471	3,117	75	165	1,124	3	10,125	55,609
2010-11	27,615	1,097	13,987	210	472	609	4,800	72	152	1,043	28	8,238	58,543
2011-12	26,043	1,208	14,678	173	966	884	4,391	38	165	523	10	8,845	58,270
2012-13	23,667	1,528	13,242	245	1,365	536	4,354	115	148	2,149	92	10,111	57,866
2013-14	24,972	1,608	13,948	241	2,017	296	2,742	179	153	2,504	507	10,474	60,158
2014-15[1]	28,545	1,625	14,390	212	1,595	362	1,072	112	175	2,450	505	11,929	63,580
2015-16[2]	31,750	1,650	15,600	275	1,850	400	150	150	150	2,980	450	10,160	66,214

Crop year beginning October 1.   [1] Preliminary.   [2] Forecast.   *Source: Foreign Agricultural Service, U.S. Department of Agriculture (FAS-USDA)*

World Imports of Soybean Meal   In Thousands of Metric Tons

Crop Year	Algeria	European Union	Indo-nesia	Iran	Japan	Korea, South	Malaysia	Mexico	Peru	Philip-pines	Thailand	Vietnam	World Total
2006-07	622	22,362	2,237	817	1,737	1,870	907	1,780	853	1,743	2,275	2,291	52,812
2007-08	724	24,619	2,429	900	1,747	1,761	917	1,401	787	1,627	1,935	2,296	54,860
2008-09	727	21,153	2,339	1,311	1,812	1,813	933	1,518	902	1,575	2,160	2,526	51,686
2009-10	850	20,879	2,507	1,524	2,106	1,737	1,076	1,209	1,072	1,719	2,513	2,879	53,480
2010-11	1,074	21,877	3,069	1,742	2,208	1,658	1,028	1,500	1,059	1,972	2,318	2,719	56,903
2011-12	892	20,872	3,278	2,192	2,282	1,571	1,078	1,548	1,113	1,833	2,928	2,276	56,994
2012-13	1,333	16,941	3,367	2,099	1,765	1,654	1,276	1,295	1,099	1,969	2,874	2,980	53,863
2013-14	1,441	18,135	3,983	2,683	1,976	1,825	1,397	1,410	1,173	2,337	2,665	3,342	57,925
2014-15[1]	1,100	19,260	3,850	1,948	1,699	1,751	1,465	1,795	1,175	2,200	3,017	4,200	60,121
2015-16[2]	1,350	20,300	4,500	2,100	1,850	1,800	1,500	1,850	1,275	2,400	3,050	4,600	63,894

Crop year beginning October 1.   [1] Preliminary.   [2] Forecast.   *Source: Foreign Agricultural Service, U.S. Department of Agriculture (FAS-USDA)*

U.S. Exports of Soybean Cake & Meal by Country of Destination   In Thousands of Metric Tons

Year	Algeria	Australia	Canada	Dominican Republic	Italy	Japan	Mexico	Nether-lands	Philip-pines	Russia	Spain	Vene-zuela	Total
2005	63.0	74.9	1,155.9	264.2	0.2	523.4	1,356.3	10.1	442.0	16.8	5.0	112.5	6,352
2006	18.4	54.3	1,390.4	423.6	1.3	481.1	1,705.7	6.5	519.4	31.1	----	27.9	7,479
2007	39.5	1.2	1,467.4	448.7	0.1	451.3	1,638.4	8.2	626.9	31.8	0.6	49.3	7,922
2008	50.1	45.3	1,365.0	368.5	58.5	385.8	1,447.3	36.8	551.2	27.3	0.0	545.0	7,996
2009	----	121.9	1,154.3	362.4	48.5	366.3	1,323.0	0.2	803.4	20.0	90.0	487.1	8,791
2010	----	208.0	1,069.3	384.4	28.1	389.2	1,382.3	0.8	860.3	22.0	50.6	571.0	9,318
2011	17.4	0.5	1,048.5	358.4	33.7	338.6	1,423.7	0.4	869.5	22.6	0.2	636.1	7,821
2012	16.5	41.8	1,073.0	393.9	63.2	211.6	1,343.0	0.2	1,305.9	25.1	50.5	705.8	9,691
2013	17.3	69.0	895.1	331.6	229.6	180.2	1,269.5	0.9	1,120.6	0.1	198.4	755.1	10,161
2014[1]	3.0	0.1	971.0	352.2	277.0	212.0	1,592.9	1.6	1,107.1	15.0	267.2	842.6	10,245

[1] Preliminary.   *Source: Foreign Agricultural Service, U.S. Department of Agriculture (FAS-USDA)*

SOYBEAN MEAL

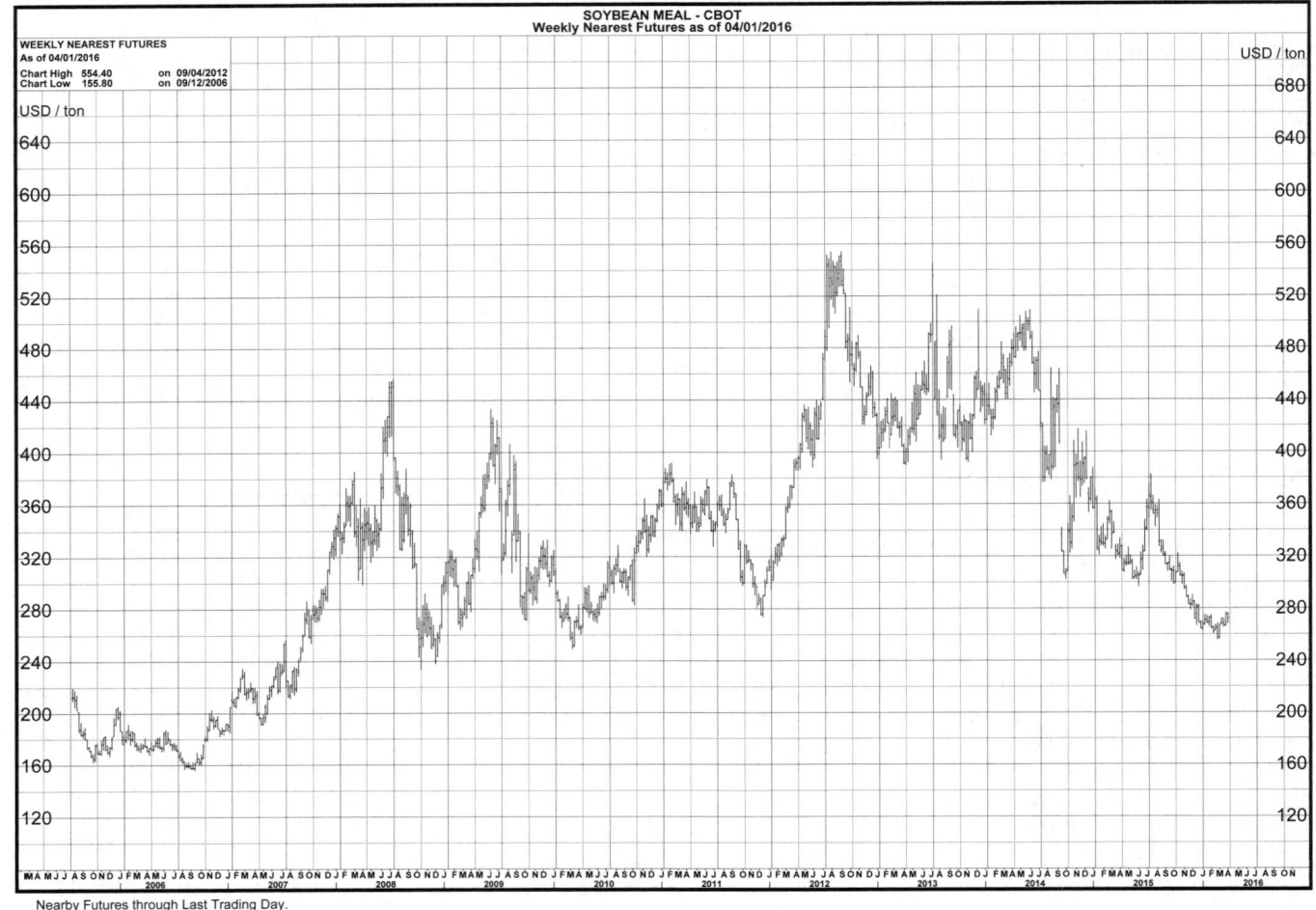

SOYBEAN MEAL - CBOT
Weekly Nearest Futures as of 04/01/2016

WEEKLY NEAREST FUTURES
As of 04/01/2016
Chart High 554.40 on 09/04/2012
Chart Low 155.80 on 09/12/2006

Nearby Futures through Last Trading Day.

Volume of Trading of Soybean Meal Futures in Chicago   In Thousands of Contracts

Year	Jan.	Feb.	Mar.	Apr.	May	June	July	Aug.	Sept.	Oct.	Nov.	Dec.	Total
2006	506.9	605.0	575.3	785.6	716.8	976.1	801.5	819.1	807.7	906.1	1,064.2	785.7	9,350.0
2007	768.9	1,018.8	822.1	985.7	798.9	1,217.3	1,107.9	1,025.1	1,028.6	1,016.4	1,218.8	1,204.7	12,213.3
2008	1,260.6	1,235.1	1,240.4	1,257.7	922.5	1,359.0	1,258.6	1,074.5	1,069.3	1,020.3	837.1	818.9	13,354.2
2009	909.2	988.7	841.7	1,195.1	1,071.4	1,390.1	1,146.6	1,071.8	974.6	1,012.1	1,222.7	1,056.6	12,880.8
2010	994.1	1,134.5	1,330.1	1,264.3	850.7	1,349.0	1,134.2	1,057.8	1,136.4	1,054.7	1,590.7	1,156.3	14,052.8
2011	1,115.7	1,437.9	1,475.1	1,546.9	1,141.0	1,642.3	1,211.5	1,485.3	1,726.2	1,329.8	1,511.7	1,296.8	16,920.2
2012	1,182.2	1,484.7	1,545.3	1,914.5	1,481.2	1,812.1	1,848.1	1,594.8	1,389.8	1,263.9	1,436.3	1,234.5	18,187.4
2013	1,520.3	1,758.3	1,277.9	1,985.6	1,558.3	1,839.5	1,919.1	1,797.3	1,433.2	1,632.4	1,881.6	1,633.7	20,237.2
2014	1,519.1	1,918.1	1,409.7	1,711.2	1,138.3	1,811.9	1,703.3	1,664.5	1,613.9	2,456.8	2,070.8	1,619.9	20,637.4
2015	1,558.6	1,863.0	1,627.7	2,118.1	1,655.7	2,861.9	2,181.3	2,145.4	1,942.1	2,106.6	2,147.4	2,107.4	24,315.3

Contract size = 100 tons.   *Source: CME Group; Chicago Board of Trade (CBT)*

Average Open Interest of Soybean Meal Futures in Chicago   In Contracts

Year	Jan.	Feb.	Mar.	Apr.	May	June	July	Aug.	Sept.	Oct.	Nov.	Dec.
2006	127,922	132,833	147,837	172,905	181,823	182,940	196,236	230,082	236,351	206,002	216,854	206,762
2007	201,214	227,905	213,708	216,258	212,398	217,576	210,612	201,339	219,046	225,683	248,277	251,133
2008	234,286	234,695	225,607	218,126	199,422	216,039	208,444	178,191	163,511	152,968	138,111	124,898
2009	118,930	121,722	110,580	123,445	160,515	190,481	174,733	167,301	155,388	150,639	159,393	165,141
2010	170,924	198,651	200,438	196,464	177,726	187,838	197,981	200,131	208,773	195,256	201,589	194,033
2011	203,340	215,886	213,717	226,365	228,210	223,375	180,790	176,598	187,326	186,973	204,468	206,053
2012	193,344	187,100	226,979	261,896	251,386	253,037	263,064	255,541	235,650	211,525	217,752	222,206
2013	248,644	287,037	281,914	262,103	264,520	305,549	285,970	266,192	267,963	272,131	279,717	274,139
2014	272,424	307,186	312,283	321,497	310,358	320,237	309,536	319,263	340,910	362,209	382,227	353,605
2015	347,095	363,919	341,479	342,428	352,507	402,421	400,309	385,239	379,936	401,497	422,294	415,217

Contract size = 100 tons.   *Source: CME Group; Chicago Board of Trade (CBT)*

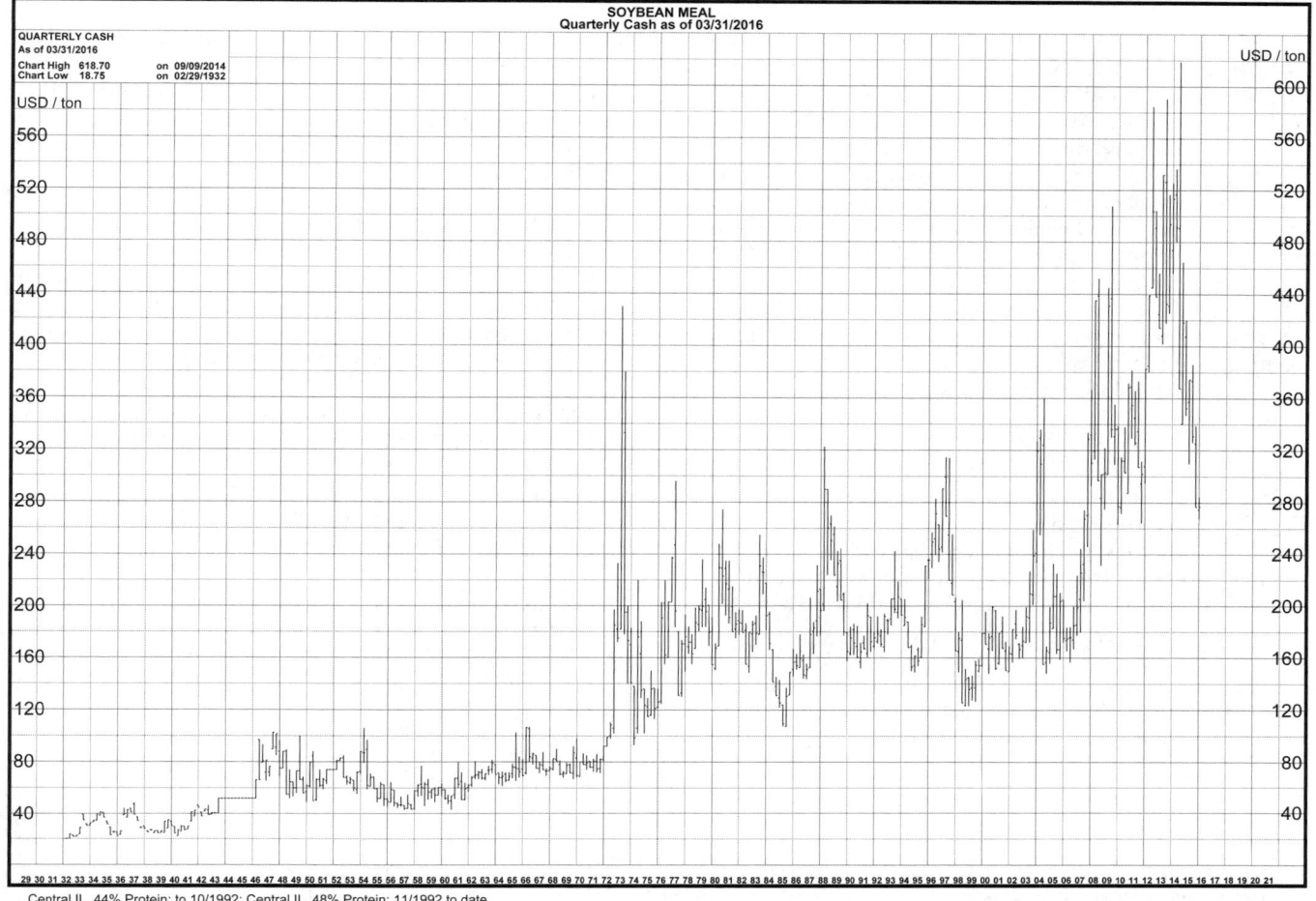

SOYBEAN MEAL
Quarterly Cash as of 03/31/2016

QUARTERLY CASH
As of 03/31/2016

Chart High 618.70 on 09/09/2014
Chart Low 18.75 on 02/29/1932

USD / ton

Central IL, 44% Protein: to 10/1992; Central IL, 48% Protein: 11/1992 to date.

Average Price of Soybean Meal (48% Solvent) in Decatur Illinois   In Dollars Per Short Ton -- Bulk

Year	Jan.	Feb.	Mar.	Apr.	May	June	July	Aug.	Sept.	Oct.	Nov.	Dec.	Average
2006-07	177.71	190.67	180.63	190.36	208.81	205.26	189.37	198.66	229.70	222.05	217.63	254.41	205.44
2007-08	260.55	280.76	314.78	331.28	345.87	331.57	329.94	325.48	390.72	412.25	355.35	352.70	335.94
2008-09	260.66	267.37	268.24	306.85	297.42	292.22	324.27	380.37	418.47	373.18	405.27	379.68	331.17
2009-10	325.69	328.18	333.93	314.23	295.79	277.61	291.21	287.85	305.78	325.56	331.76	317.65	311.27
2010-11	321.92	341.78	351.93	368.54	358.59	345.43	335.87	342.30	347.45	346.52	349.60	336.32	345.52
2011-12	301.45	290.37	281.65	310.65	330.37	365.95	394.29	415.17	422.59	515.82	564.69	529.37	393.53
2012-13	488.46	465.64	459.40	431.39	440.66	437.33	422.07	465.72	496.78	544.59	464.90	500.39	468.11
2013-14	443.63	451.13	498.10	479.54	509.25	495.71	514.01	519.38	501.72	450.79	490.32	525.72	489.94
2014-15	381.50	441.39	431.73	380.03	370.38	357.83	336.61	320.23	335.03	375.71	357.85	333.62	368.49
2015-16	327.97	308.60	289.78	279.56	273.61								295.90

Source: Economic Research Service, U.S. Department of Agriculture (ERS-USDA)

Average Price of Soybean Meal (44% Solvent) in Decatur Illinois   In Dollars Per Short Ton -- Bulk

Year	Jan.	Feb.	Mar.	Apr.	May	June	July	Aug.	Sept.	Oct.	Nov.	Dec.	Average
1992-93	168.6	170.9	176.4	175.6	167.5	172.4	175.6	181.7	181.3	217.6	206.9	186.5	181.8
1993-94	180.6	195.7	192.5	185.9	184.4	182.0	176.4	191.1	183.0	168.1	165.6	162.5	180.7
1994-95	156.4	150.9	145.4	145.1	149.4	145.7	151.0	148.1	149.1	160.1	157.5	171.8	152.5
1995-96	183.4	194.1	213.6	220.5	216.7	215.7	237.9	232.3	227.9	242.3	251.1	265.5	225.1
1996-97	238.0	242.7	240.9	240.7	253.6	270.4	277.7	296.0	275.9	261.5	261.6	265.7	260.4
1997-98	216.0	231.6	214.9	193.1	182.1	165.3	152.8	150.3	157.8	173.3	135.7	126.9	175.0
1998-99	129.4	139.3	139.6	131.0	124.4	127.2	128.6	127.0	131.7	125.7	135.9	144.1	132.0
1999-00	147.2	148.1	145.4	155.0	163.6	166.6	168.1	180.1	170.2	156.8	151.4	166.9	160.0
2000-01	166.0	173.7	187.9	175.6	158.3	149.1	149.7	155.6	163.1	183.9	170.6	163.5	166.4
2001-02	157.7	157.2	146.6	Disc.	Disc.	Disc.	Disc.	Disc.	Disc.	Disc.	Disc.	Disc.	153.8

Source: Economic Research Service, U.S. Department of Agriculture (ERS-USDA)

Soybean Oil

Soybean oil is the natural oil extracted from whole soybeans. Typically, about 19% of a soybean's weight can be extracted as crude soybean oil. The oil content of U.S. soybeans correlates directly with the temperatures and amount of sunshine during the soybean pod-filling stages. Edible products produced with soybean oil include cooking and salad oils, shortening, and margarine. Soybean oil is the most widely used cooking oil in the U.S. It accounts for 80% of margarine production and for more than 75% of total U.S. consumer vegetable fat and oil consumption. Soy oil is cholesterol-free and high in polyunsaturated fat. Soy oil is also used to produce inedible products such as paints, varnish, resins, and plastics. Of the edible vegetable oils, soy oil is the world's largest at about 32%, followed by palm oil and rapeseed oil.

Soybean oil futures and options are traded at the CME Group. Soybean Oil futures are also traded at ICE Futures U.S., the Dalian Commodity Exchange (DCE), the JSE Securities Exchange, the Mercado a Termino de Buenos Aires (MTBA), the Multi Commodity Exchange of India (MCX), and the National Commodity & Derivatives Exchange (NCDEX).

Prices – CME soybean oil futures prices (Barchart.com electronic symbol ZL) on the nearest-futures chart showed a modest recovery rally in the first half of 2015, fell sharply during mid-year, but then rallied late in the year to close 2015 down -4.4% yr/yr at 30.55 cents per pound. Regarding cash prices for the year 2015-16 (through January 2016), the average monthly price of crude domestic soybean oil (in tank cars) in Decatur (F.O.B.) fell by -12.2% yr/yr to 27.76 cents per pound.

Supply – World production of soybean oil in 2015-16 rose +5.3% yr/yr to a new record high of 51.583 million metric tons. China accounts for 28.0% of world soybean oil production, while the U.S. accounts for 19.2%, and Argentina accounts for 16.1%. U.S. production of soybean oil in 2015-16 rose +2.5% yr/yr to 21.925 billion pounds.

Demand – World consumption of soybean oil in 2015-16 rose +5.8% yr/yr to a new record high of 50.741 million metric tons. China accounted for 30.0% of world consumption, while the U.S. accounted for 17.5%, Brazil for 12.5%, and India for 9.5%. U.S. consumption of soybean oil in 2015-16 rose +3.2% yr/yr to 19.600 billion pounds.

Trade – World exports of soybean oil in 2015-16 rose +7.9% yr/yr to 11.872 million metric tons. U.S. exports of soybean oil in 2015-16 rose +14.2% yr/yr to 2.300 billion pounds, well below 2009-10 record high of 3.359 billion pounds.

World Production of Soybean Oil   In Thousands of Metric Tons

Crop Year	Argentina	Bolivia	Brazil	China	European Union	India	Japan	Mexico	Paraguay	Russia	Taiwan	United States	World Total
2006-07	6,424	303	5,970	6,410	2,694	1,175	576	680	248	143	375	9,294	36,429
2007-08	6,627	211	6,160	7,045	2,720	1,499	563	661	264	179	363	9,335	37,737
2008-09	5,914	261	6,120	7,325	2,350	1,319	479	643	275	267	359	8,503	35,942
2009-10	6,476	277	6,470	8,726	2,290	1,381	480	643	296	349	376	8,897	38,848
2010-11	7,181	320	6,970	9,840	2,362	1,646	416	648	300	389	385	8,568	41,350
2011-12	6,839	355	7,310	10,914	2,359	1,708	380	657	172	412	376	8,954	42,743
2012-13	6,364	390	6,760	11,626	2,501	1,752	371	653	564	430	355	8,990	43,100
2013-14	6,785	400	7,070	12,335	2,553	1,478	389	720	640	627	355	9,131	45,022
2014-15[1]	7,687	445	7,660	13,347	2,698	1,245	420	745	697	690	393	9,706	48,994
2015-16[2]	8,290	475	7,680	14,458	2,810	1,150	394	780	783	717	402	9,909	51,583

Crop year beginning October 1.   [1] Preliminary.   [2] Forecast.   *Source: Foreign Agricultural Service, U.S. Department of Agriculture (FAS-USDA)*

World Consumption of Soybean Oil   In Thousands of Metric Tons

Crop Year	Algeria	Argentina	Bangladesh	Brazil	China	Egypt	European Union	India	Iran	Korea, South	Mexico	United States	World Total
2006-07	300	459	342	3,395	8,670	350	3,412	2,700	783	436	845	8,426	35,710
2007-08	355	1,026	360	3,955	9,693	621	3,205	2,330	725	444	877	8,317	37,514
2008-09	384	1,420	373	4,275	9,486	563	2,797	2,320	655	447	895	7,378	36,374
2009-10	395	1,915	371	4,980	10,035	560	2,760	2,820	575	445	875	7,173	38,187
2010-11	475	2,520	388	5,205	11,409	669	2,530	2,610	620	443	840	7,506	40,591
2011-12	490	3,020	465	5,390	12,044	440	2,109	2,750	600	445	845	8,396	42,284
2012-13	540	2,275	475	5,534	12,545	582	1,908	2,950	600	445	860	8,522	42,624
2013-14	610	2,729	540	5,705	13,657	497	1,970	3,300	630	440	890	8,576	45,176
2014-15[1]	640	2,601	625	6,275	14,126	762	2,000	4,050	720	435	1,001	8,616	47,977
2015-16[2]	650	2,500	705	6,365	15,228	682	2,000	4,800	800	455	1,020	8,890	50,741

Crop year beginning October 1.   [1] Preliminary.   [2] Forecast.   *Source: Foreign Agricultural Service, U.S. Department of Agriculture (FAS-USDA)*

World Exports of Soybean Oil   In Thousands of Metric Tons

Crop Year	Argentina	Bolivia	Brazil	Canada	European Union	Malaysia	Paraguay	Russia	South Africa	Ukraine	United States	Vietnam	World Total
2006-07	5,970	210	2,462	24	244	143	260	5	1	9	851	8	10,531
2007-08	5,789	143	2,388	50	335	123	260	10	3	8	1,320	----	10,841
2008-09	4,704	218	1,909	38	398	109	229	127	12	28	995	----	9,183
2009-10	4,453	230	1,449	47	386	126	243	170	30	44	1,524	----	9,160
2010-11	4,561	232	1,668	66	463	134	255	136	62	43	1,466	28	9,643
2011-12	3,794	224	1,885	72	742	146	127	142	68	49	664	73	8,452
2012-13	4,244	285	1,251	102	1,011	127	558	129	76	70	982	44	9,334
2013-14	4,087	371	1,378	92	766	157	650	332	94	118	851	91	9,424
2014-15[1]	5,093	350	1,510	118	1,010	170	660	423	90	136	914	95	11,005
2015-16[2]	5,760	370	1,390	170	1,000	176	735	445	75	160	1,043	100	11,872

Crop year beginning October 1.   [1] Preliminary.   [2] Forecast.   Source: Foreign Agricultural Service, U.S. Department of Agriculture (FAS-USDA)

World Imports of Soybean Oil   In Thousands of Metric Tons

Crop Year	Algeria	Bangladesh	China	Colombia	Egypt	European Union	India	Iran	Korea, South	Peru	Morocco	Venezuela	World Total
2006-07	295	327	2,404	170	124	978	1,447	606	302	360	300	375	9,973
2007-08	383	401	2,727	184	482	1,038	733	545	296	421	292	400	10,397
2008-09	365	258	2,494	164	320	795	1,060	376	266	350	272	388	9,170
2009-10	402	354	1,514	184	243	547	1,598	275	318	379	352	388	8,722
2010-11	516	377	1,319	238	644	906	945	704	300	397	315	302	9,508
2011-12	438	439	1,502	257	----	386	1,174	411	343	367	344	366	7,976
2012-13	575	400	1,409	216	324	322	1,086	543	300	364	363	415	8,493
2013-14	629	443	1,353	288	230	329	1,830	551	278	444	355	374	9,266
2014-15[1]	620	508	773	315	480	252	2,799	421	257	430	355	473	10,060
2015-16[2]	640	520	850	330	400	150	3,650	450	300	460	380	440	11,055

Crop year beginning October 1.   [1] Preliminary.   [2] Forecast.   Source: Foreign Agricultural Service, U.S. Department of Agriculture (FAS-USDA)

Supply and Distribution of Soybean Oil in the United States   In Millions of Pounds

					Domestic Disappearance — Food						Non-Food			
Crop Year	Production	Imports	Stocks Oct. 1	Exports	Total Domestic	Shortening	Margarine	Cooking & Salad Oils	Other Edible	Total Food	Paint & Varnish	Resins & Plastics	Total Non-Food	Total Disappearance
2006-07	20,489	37	3,010	1,877	18,574	6,225	961	8,708	NA	15,894	63	98	3,445	20,451
2007-08	20,580	65	3,085	2,911	18,335	5,271	902	9,612	NA	15,785	33	108	3,466	21,246
2008-09	18,745	90	2,485	2,193	16,265	4,445	W	10,321	NA	14,766	W	106	2,182	18,459
2009-10	19,615	103	2,861	3,359	15,814	3,895	W	9,595	NA	13,490	W	W	3,166	19,173
2010-11	18,888	159	3,406	3,233	16,794	3,670	W	9,541	NA	13,211	NA	NA	NA	20,027
2011-12	19,740	149	2,425	1,464	18,311	NA	NA	NA	NA	NA	NA	NA	NA	19,775
2012-13	19,820	196	2,540	2,164	18,686	----	----	----	----	----	----	----	----	20,851
2013-14	20,130	165	1,655	1,877	18,908	----	----	----	----	----	----	----	----	20,785
2014-15[1]	21,399	264	1,165	2,014	18,959	----	----	----	----	----	----	----	----	20,973
2015-16[2]	21,730	300	1,855	2,100	19,600	----	----	----	----	----	----	----	----	21,700

Crop year beginning October 1.   [1] Preliminary.   [2] Forecast.   Source: Economic Research Service, U.S. Department of Agriculture (ERS-USDA)

U.S. Exports of Soybean Oil[2], by Country of Destination   In Metric Tons

Crop Year	Canada	Ecuador	Ethiopia	Haiti	India	Mexico	Morocco	Pakistan	Panama	Peru	Turkey	Venezuela	Total
2005-06	76,342	2	3,270	3,972	23,031	108,515	21,951	12,000	1,546	19,588	4,032	38	523,153
2006-07	80,068	3	550	1,962	14,301	151,641	60,347	2	3,409	5,940	16	26,806	851,221
2007-08	90,361	3,009	2,141	14,138	11	269,249	107,323	----	6,817	183	73	82,035	1,320,430
2008-09	41,500	----	840	19,127	146,086	173,041	110,249	----	1,715	37,061	2,598	54,438	994,927
2009-10	41,390	----	720	24,616	162,342	211,456	231,996	6,795	5,151	92,004	54	52,702	1,523,384
2010-11	35,001	8,722	700	13,314	49	167,760	291,890	20,900	6,123	44,999	1,120	57,707	1,466,468
2011-12	25,417	15	890	3,156	12	151,224	159,917	----	2,307	7	1,092	22,942	664,111
2012-13	30,867	28	----	2,230	113,104	187,117	23,248	0	6,374	193	76	51,377	981,358
2013-14	31,755	13	390	1,576	22	190,419	29,702	0	4,139	42,121	----	18,988	851,430
2014-15[1]	28,804	11	450	649	39	245,771	64,658	9,190	5,434	104,743	----	61,920	913,572

Crop year beginning October 1.   [1] Preliminary.   [2] Crude & Refined oil combined as such.   Source: Foreign Agricultural Service, U.S. Department of Agriculture (FAS-USDA)

SOYBEAN OIL

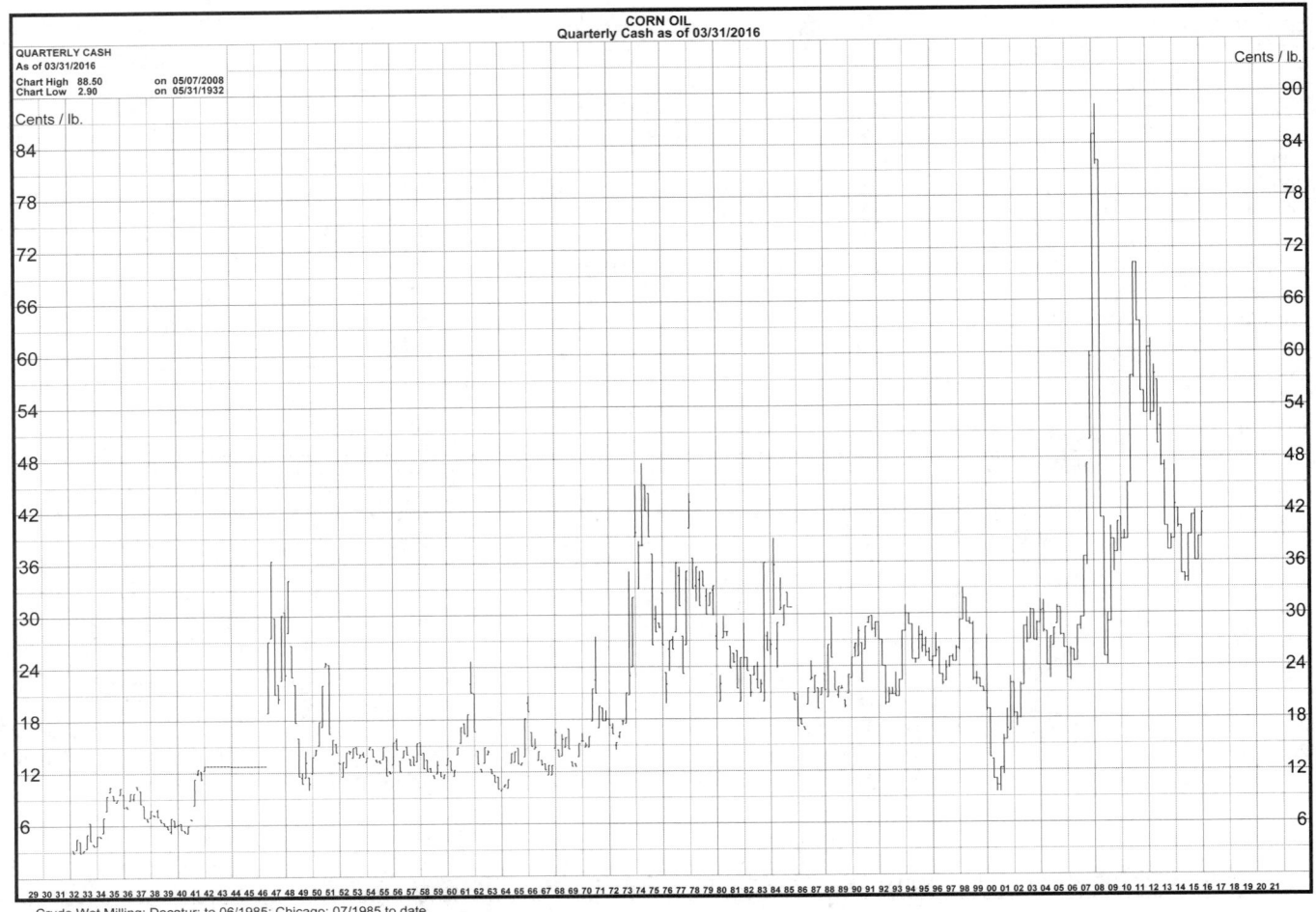

CORN OIL
Quarterly Cash as of 03/31/2016

QUARTERLY CASH
As of 03/31/2016

Chart High 88.50   on 05/07/2008
Chart Low 2.90   on 05/31/1932

Cents / lb.

Crude Wet Milling: Decatur: to 06/1985; Chicago: 07/1985 to date.

Consumption of Soybean Oil in End Products in the United States   In Millions of Pounds

Year	Jan.	Feb.	Mar.	Apr.	May	June	July	Aug.	Sept.	Oct.	Nov.	Dec.	Total
2002	1,461.5	1,395.3	1,568.0	1,505.1	1,549.7	1,492.4	1,490.5	1,545.5	1,543.7	1,710.2	1,587.2	1,458.8	18,308
2003	1,418.1	1,347.4	1,490.0	1,494.9	1,552.6	1,493.1	1,509.5	1,483.5	1,577.7	1,660.7	1,544.2	1,451.4	18,023
2004	1,388.1	1,417.6	1,555.2	1,468.0	1,506.7	1,421.1	1,429.2	1,473.6	1,483.2	1,558.3	1,533.7	1,368.9	17,604
2005	1,365.4	1,609.2	1,609.2	1,587.2	1,589.5	1,496.2	1,523.3	1,570.4	1,527.2	1,589.6	1,546.9	1,416.2	18,430
2006	1,505.2	1,368.8	1,661.4	1,561.1	1,634.9	1,653.2	1,575.5	1,746.2	1,727.9	1,775.6	1,638.6	1,571.5	19,420
2007	1,547.3	1,357.8	1,624.8	1,586.7	1,728.6	1,640.3	1,812.9	1,793.1	1,699.5	1,757.8	1,618.9	1,548.4	19,716
2008	1,623.6	1,476.9	1,625.3	1,580.9	1,510.8	1,528.4	1,589.8	1,624.2	1,559.2	1,662.7	1,500.3	1,348.5	18,630
2009	1,251.8	1,245.9	1,346.9	1,282.5	1,275.3	1,283.6	1,357.4	1,374.8	1,397.9	1,606.5	1,468.2	1,377.4	16,268
2010	1,231.8	1,227.6	1,350.0	1,215.6	1,183.4	1,232.8	1,229.6	1,274.4	1,262.6	1,342.1	1,293.8	1,192.1	15,036
2011[1]	1,222.6	1,190.1	1,458.3	1,413.2	1,421.6	1,500.8	1,508.7	NA	NA	NA	NA	NA	16,655

[1] Preliminary.   Source: Bureau of the Census, U.S. Department of Commerce

U.S. Exports of Soybean Oil (Crude and Refined)   In Millions of Pounds

Year	Jan.	Feb.	Mar.	Apr.	May	June	July	Aug.	Sept.	Oct.	Nov.	Dec.	Total
2006	71.3	67.0	178.2	96.8	53.8	82.0	89.4	64.7	111.8	167.1	120.3	276.7	1,379
2007	176.4	118.2	75.2	102.7	121.3	123.5	202.0	202.3	190.8	132.9	198.0	391.3	2,035
2008	157.7	509.9	385.5	427.1	163.4	171.7	125.5	183.8	64.2	138.1	102.3	119.9	2,549
2009	96.4	145.9	161.3	350.3	277.9	86.5	247.6	302.9	164.2	332.1	241.1	390.3	2,797
2010	513.9	399.5	408.0	148.0	77.2	129.1	179.1	365.7	174.5	440.3	432.5	394.5	3,662
2011	466.3	301.2	330.1	188.6	91.7	129.7	120.0	114.6	223.6	78.0	107.8	59.6	2,211
2012	91.4	142.5	69.8	121.2	193.6	123.8	198.1	206.7	71.6	253.1	274.6	358.6	2,105
2013	258.9	339.7	136.7	135.9	79.3	75.1	70.7	92.8	87.9	71.4	135.9	320.2	1,805
2014	267.2	276.7	195.5	93.0	45.8	78.7	198.0	119.0	75.6	158.1	231.5	235.5	1,975
2015[1]	256.1	221.1	234.8	124.4	72.3	157.4	64.6	153.6	104.7	179.3	233.0	319.4	2,121

[1] Preliminary.   Source: Bureau of the Census, U.S. Department of Commerce

244

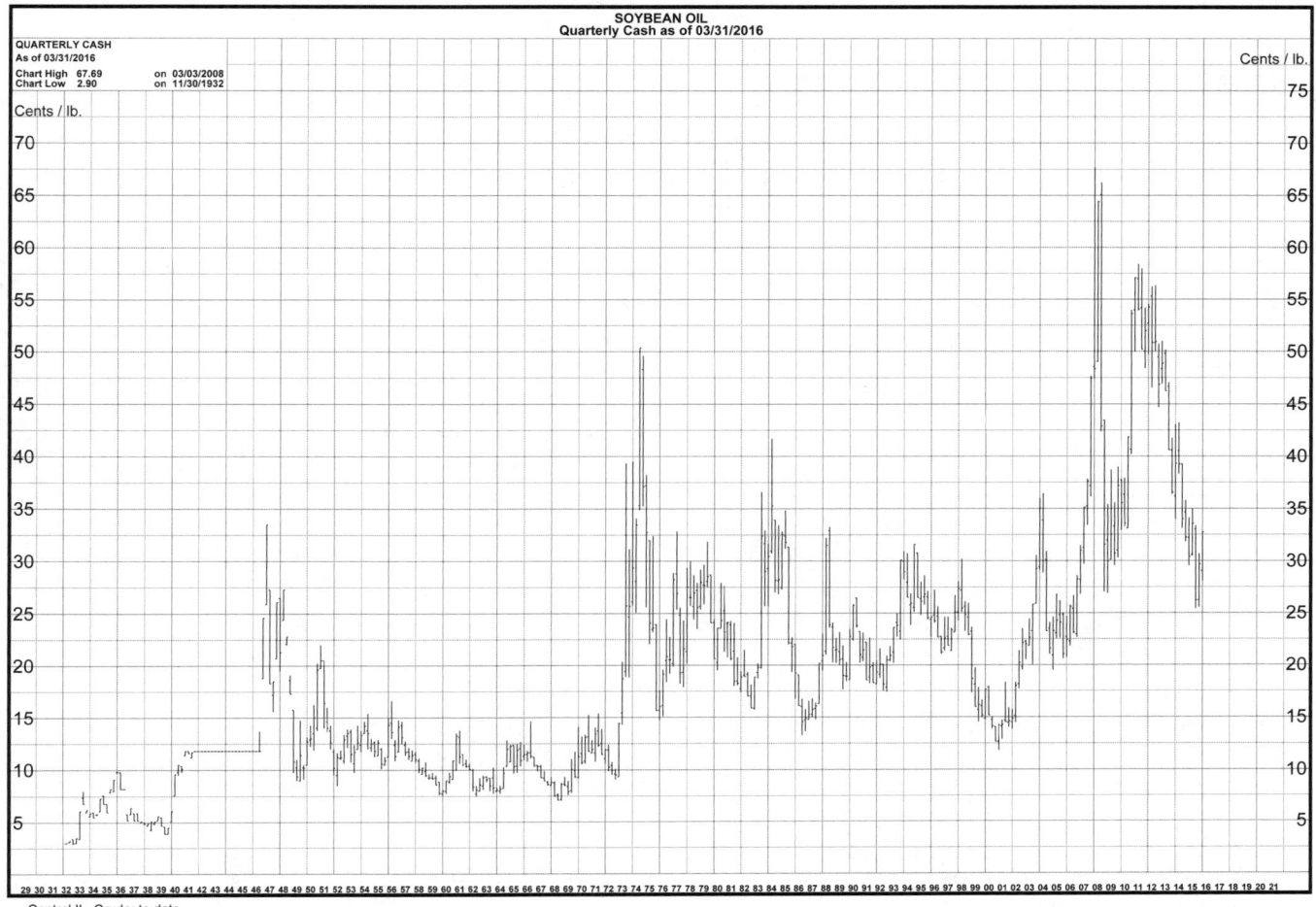

SOYBEAN OIL
Quarterly Cash as of 03/31/2016

QUARTERLY CASH
As of 03/31/2016

Chart High 67.69 on 03/03/2008
Chart Low   2.90   on 11/30/1932

Cents / lb.

Central IL, Crude: to date.

Stocks of Soybean Oil (Crude and Refined) at Factories and Warehouses in the U.S.   In Millions of Pounds

Year	Oct.	Nov.	Dec.	Jan.	Feb.	Mar.	Apr.	May	June	July	Aug.	Sept.
2001-02	2,877.2	2,724.9	2,787.4	2,868.1	3,038.5	2,896.4	2,952.7	2,856.8	2,943.2	2,735.9	2,529.7	2,521.7
2002-03	2,358.6	2,280.1	2,326.1	2,398.0	2,395.7	2,271.9	2,244.6	2,120.2	2,053.9	1,928.5	1,794.2	1,654.4
2003-04	1,490.6	1,411.8	1,530.4	1,579.9	1,945.6	1,988.0	1,855.9	1,644.1	1,651.6	1,514.0	1,412.0	1,180.6
2004-05	1,075.6	1,269.4	1,191.2	1,311.1	1,560.1	1,646.8	1,812.7	1,797.1	1,888.7	1,838.0	1,988.8	1,727.0
2005-06	1,699.0	1,883.5	1,851.8	2,190.5	2,498.7	2,673.4	2,718.1	2,755.4	2,885.0	2,919.2	3,106.1	3,061.2
2006-07	3,009.8	3,012.3	3,081.9	3,090.6	3,356.7	3,477.7	3,558.4	3,500.0	3,468.7	3,549.8	3,399.6	3,200.4
2007-08	3,085.2	3,224.9	3,235.2	3,277.0	3,408.0	3,278.3	3,083.5	2,925.8	2,989.0	2,906.0	2,793.2	2,567.4
2008-09	2,484.6	2,388.5	2,519.0	2,629.6	2,992.3	3,124.1	3,191.6	3,279.4	3,338.8	3,530.3	3,448.9	3,134.0
2009-10	2,860.5	2,809.4	2,990.5	3,150.5	3,221.7	3,295.7	3,317.6	3,152.1	3,521.9	3,597.5	3,594.1	3,337.8
2010-11[1]	3,405.8	3,285.0	3,349.5	3,531.9	3,415.4	3,375.5	3,409.8	3,342.1	3,177.3	3,153.1	3,128.9	2,868.1

On First of Month.   [1] Preliminary.   *Source: Economic Research Service, U.S. Department of Agriculture (ERS-USDA)*

Average Price of Crude Domestic Soybean Oil (in Tank Cars) F.O.B. Decatur   In Cents Per Pound

Year	Oct.	Nov.	Dec.	Jan.	Feb.	Mar.	Apr.	May	June	July	Aug.	Sept.	Average
2006-07	24.80	27.64	27.63	28.00	28.94	29.74	31.06	32.90	34.01	35.74	34.87	36.89	31.02
2007-08	38.10	42.68	45.16	49.77	56.68	57.27	56.58	58.27	62.43	60.54	50.78	46.09	52.03
2008-09	35.50	31.55	29.30	32.16	28.93	28.23	32.76	36.06	35.66	31.08	33.69	30.96	32.16
2009-10	33.15	36.59	36.81	34.88	34.69	36.39	37.11	35.41	34.47	35.07	37.57	39.21	35.95
2010-11	44.02	47.62	51.51	53.84	54.21	54.07	56.65	56.09	55.68	55.16	54.39	55.13	53.20
2011-12	51.73	51.44	50.17	50.99	52.36	53.43	54.96	50.69	48.65	51.96	52.65	53.81	51.90
2012-13	49.31	46.27	47.16	48.85	49.33	48.62	49.28	49.31	47.84	45.19	42.33	42.12	47.13
2013-14	39.66	39.58	37.63	34.95	37.11	40.82	41.87	40.68	39.84	37.60	35.04	33.99	38.23
2014-15	34.10	33.45	32.56	32.33	31.57	30.89	31.13	32.65	33.73	31.54	28.87	26.43	31.60
2015-16[1]	27.14	26.42	29.72	28.89	29.79								28.39

[1] Preliminary.   *Source: Economic Research Service, U.S. Department of Agriculture (ERS-USDA)*

SOYBEAN OIL

SOYBEAN OIL - CBOT
Weekly Nearest Futures as of 04/01/2016

WEEKLY NEAREST FUTURES
As of 04/01/2016

Chart High 71.26 on 03/04/2008
Chart Low 21.00 on 01/18/2006

Cents / lb.

Nearby Futures through Last Trading Day.

Volume of Trading of Soybean Oil Futures in Chicago   In Thousands of Contracts

Year	Jan.	Feb.	Mar.	Apr.	May	June	July	Aug.	Sept.	Oct.	Nov.	Dec.	Total
2006	531.9	611.2	597.6	866.4	688.6	1,024.5	801.2	816.7	729.0	939.3	1,003.3	878.8	9,489
2007	784.1	1,091.9	765.0	1,218.3	805.3	1,476.9	1,113.7	1,092.0	947.7	1,213.6	1,324.4	1,337.9	13,171
2008	1,294.7	1,541.4	1,291.0	1,551.1	1,107.0	1,467.6	1,624.2	1,386.9	1,441.7	1,414.4	1,252.4	1,455.9	16,828
2009	1,211.9	1,518.5	1,189.8	1,429.7	1,202.9	1,993.4	1,543.9	1,400.4	1,217.9	1,342.1	1,527.1	1,554.4	17,132
2010	1,184.3	1,787.0	1,414.2	1,924.2	1,224.4	2,198.2	1,721.4	1,646.8	1,561.7	1,588.9	2,297.3	2,242.9	20,791
2011	1,660.1	2,427.9	2,153.7	2,276.7	1,613.1	2,427.4	1,616.1	1,924.0	2,027.5	1,866.4	2,296.1	1,867.6	24,157
2012	1,649.0	2,155.3	2,107.2	2,732.0	2,333.5	2,846.1	2,394.5	2,206.0	1,958.3	2,392.5	2,683.3	2,169.7	27,628
2013	2,043.6	2,403.6	1,465.9	2,453.7	1,831.6	2,213.7	1,918.7	1,850.1	1,560.5	1,908.5	2,263.2	1,892.7	23,806
2014	1,752.1	2,531.9	1,657.5	2,058.5	1,450.2	2,199.9	1,869.4	1,775.4	1,768.9	2,199.9	2,386.3	2,119.2	23,769
2015	1,985.3	2,348.9	1,683.5	2,527.2	2,042.6	3,236.5	2,358.9	2,412.7	2,190.7	2,519.5	2,667.4	2,924.0	28,897

Contract size = 60,000 lbs.   *Source: CME Group; Chicago Board of Trade (CBT)*

Average Open Interest of Soybean Oil Futures in Chicago   In Contracts

Year	Jan.	Feb.	Mar.	Apr.	May	June	July	Aug.	Sept.	Oct.	Nov.	Dec.
2006	171,317	183,717	192,643	204,132	244,580	241,962	276,251	269,208	259,464	256,153	279,091	273,375
2007	256,800	283,761	285,436	312,454	301,566	309,109	294,005	285,255	277,219	276,874	306,390	298,906
2008	289,892	292,918	287,995	275,016	253,974	259,416	258,412	254,496	256,621	257,226	252,077	220,725
2009	204,502	211,632	206,299	208,101	217,198	246,451	245,978	239,386	217,068	229,387	248,176	229,970
2010	219,042	283,115	282,973	290,577	299,379	319,098	284,484	292,426	290,685	325,697	358,850	347,185
2011	375,563	391,930	358,625	357,657	313,673	322,642	287,408	278,784	287,250	297,663	305,955	305,279
2012	296,889	314,752	340,827	380,916	386,924	377,817	329,673	332,182	314,359	322,262	347,898	310,982
2013	313,467	327,562	329,956	353,044	351,425	357,052	340,600	308,032	291,005	314,235	333,607	344,607
2014	364,056	339,211	302,398	326,545	313,757	333,690	325,337	347,395	373,086	391,486	395,330	365,382
2015	370,576	385,819	367,203	383,502	394,773	410,233	372,932	390,494	413,151	420,227	448,872	412,621

Contract size = 60,000 lbs.   *Source: CME Group; Chicago Board of Trade (CBT)*

Soybeans

Soybean is the common name for the annual leguminous plant and its seed. The soybean is a member of the oilseed family and is not considered a grain. The soybean seeds are contained in pods and are nearly spherical in shape. The seeds are usually light yellow in color. The seeds contain 20% oil and 40% protein. Soybeans were an ancient food crop in China, Japan, and Korea and were only introduced to the U.S. in the early 1800s. Today, soybeans are the second largest crop produced in the U.S. behind corn. Soybean production in the U.S. is concentrated in the Midwest and the lower Mississippi Valley. Soybean crops in the U.S. are planted in May or June and are harvested in autumn. Soybean plants usually reach maturity 100-150 days after planting depending on growing conditions.

Soybeans are used to produce a wide variety of food products. The key value of soybeans lies in the relatively high protein content, which makes it an excellent source of protein without many of the negative factors of animal meat. Popular soy-based food products include whole soybeans (roasted for snacks or used in sauces, stews and soups), soy oil for cooking and baking, soy flour, protein concentrates, isolated soy protein (which contains up to 92% protein), soy milk and baby formula (as an alternative to dairy products), soy yogurt, soy cheese, soy nut butter, soy sprouts, tofu and tofu products (soybean curd), soy sauce (which is produced by a fermentation process), and meat alternatives (hamburgers, breakfast sausage, etc).

The primary market for soybean futures is at the CME Group. The CME's soybean contract calls for the delivery of 5,000 bushels of No. 2 yellow soybeans (at contract par), No. 1 yellow soybeans (at 6 cents per bushel above the contract price), or No. 3 yellow soybeans (at a 6 cents under the contract price). Soybean futures are also traded at exchanges in Brazil, Argentina, China, and Tokyo.

Prices – CME soybean futures prices (Barchart.com electronic symbol ZS) moved sideways to lower in the first half of 2015 as robust supplies limited the upside for soybean prices. The USDA in the May 2015 WASDE report raised its 2014/15 global soybean production estimate to a record 317.25 MMT and projected 2015/16 global soybean production at a record 317.3 MMT. The USDA also projected 2015/16 U.S. soybeans stocks at a 9-year high of 500 million bushels and estimated 2015/16 global soybean ending stocks at a record 96.22 MMT. Soybean prices perked up in June and rallied into July when they posted the high for the year at $10.60 a bushel. Heavy late-spring rains in the Midwest kept farmers out of fields and delayed U.S. soybean plantings. In fact, the USDA reported in a mid-June Crop Progress report that U.S. soybean plantings as of June 21, 2015 were at the slowest pace in 19 years. Soybean prices turned down in August and sold off into November when they posted a 7-year low of $8.44 a bushel. Bumper soybean crops in South America pressured prices after Conab raised its 2015/16 Brazil soybean production estimate to a record 102.5 MMT. Also, the plunge in the Brazilian real to a record low against the dollar provided impetus for Brazil's soybean producers to boost more-profitable exports. That prompted Conab in December to hike their 2015/16 Brazil soybean export forecast to a record 57.5 MMT. Meanwhile, the USDA in the December WASDE report forecast 2015/16 U.S. soybean production at a record 3.98 billion bushels and projected 2015/16 global soybean output at a record 320.11 MMT with record ending stocks of 82.58 MMT. Robust Chinese demand for soybeans was supportive for prices as China 2015 soybean import rose +14% y/y to a record 81.69 MMT. Also, the action by the EPA in November to raise its 2015 and 2016 biofuel mandate was positive for domestic soybean demand and helped to contain the downside in prices. Soybean prices finished 2015 down -14.5% at $8.71 a bushel.

Supply – World soybean production during the 2014-15 marketing year (Sep-Aug) rose by +10.8% yr/yr to 314.369 million metric tons. World soybean production has risen sharply from the 62 million metric ton level seen in 1980. The world's largest soybean producers were the U.S. with 34.5% of world production in 2014-15, Brazil (30.4%), Argentina (17.5%), China (3.8%), and India (3.3%). China's soybean production has roughly doubled since 1980. Brazil's production has risen just over four times since 1980.

U.S. soybean production in 2014-15 rose by +18.2% yr/yr to 3.968 billion bushels, a new record high. U.S. farmers harvested 83.061 million acres of soybeans in 2014-15, which rose +8.9% yr/yr, a new record high. The average yield in 2014-15 was up +8.6% yr/yr to 47.8 bushels per acre, a new record high. U.S. ending stocks for the 2014-15 marketing year fell by -34.6% to 92.0 million bushels.

Demand – Total U.S. distribution in 2014-15 rose +5.1% to 3.655 billion bushels. The distribution tables for U.S. soybeans for the 2014-15 marketing year show that 48.7% of U.S. soybean usage went for crushing into soybean oil and meal, 48.2% for exports, and 3.2% for seed and residual. The quantity of U.S. soybeans that went for crushing rose +2.7% yr/yr in 2014-15 to 1.780 billion bushels. The world soybean crush rose +5.1% yr/yr in 2014-15 to a new record high of 252.528 million metric tons, which was about double the level seen in 1993-94.

Trade – World exports of soybeans in 2014-15 rose +3.2% yr/yr to a new record high of 116.487 million metric tons. The world's largest soybean exporters in 2014-15 were the U.S. with 41.4% of world exports, Brazil with 39.5% of world exports, and Argentina with 6.9% of world exports. U.S. soybean exports in 2014-15 rose +7.5% yr/yr to a 48.172 million metric tons, a new record high. Brazil's soybean exports have more than doubled in the past decade and Canada's exports have almost tripled.

World imports in 2014-15 rose +2.2% yr/yr to a new record high of 112.988 million metric tons. The world's largest importers of soybeans in 2014-15 were China with 65.5% of world imports, the European Union with 11.3%, Mexico with 3.5%, and Japan with 2.6%. China's imports in 2014-15 rose +5.2% yr/yr to a record level of 74.000 million metric tons, which is far from negligible levels prior to 1994.

SOYBEANS

World Production of Soybeans   In Thousands of Metric Tons

Crop Year[4]	Argen-tina	Bolivia	Brazil	Canada	China	European Union	India	Para-guay	Russia	Ukraine	United States	Uruguay	World Total
2006-07	48,800	1,650	59,000	3,466	15,080	1,402	7,690	5,581	807	890	87,001	865	236,300
2007-08	46,200	1,050	61,000	2,686	12,725	814	9,470	5,969	652	723	72,859	843	219,011
2008-09	32,000	1,600	57,800	3,336	15,540	747	9,300	3,647	744	813	80,749	1,170	212,081
2009-10	54,500	1,665	69,000	3,581	14,980	951	9,700	6,462	942	1,044	91,470	1,987	260,555
2010-11	49,000	2,300	75,300	4,445	15,080	1,198	10,100	7,128	1,222	1,680	90,663	1,855	264,345
2011-12	40,100	2,320	66,500	4,467	14,485	1,220	11,700	4,043	1,749	2,264	84,291	2,726	240,427
2012-13	49,300	2,634	82,000	5,086	13,050	948	12,200	8,202	1,880	2,410	82,791	3,650	268,824
2013-14[1]	53,500	2,400	86,700	5,359	11,950	1,211	9,500	8,190	1,636	2,774	91,389	3,300	282,864
2014-15[2]	61,400	2,650	96,200	6,049	12,150	1,810	8,700	8,100	2,595	3,900	106,878	3,109	318,798
2015-16[3]	58,500	3,100	100,000	6,235	12,000	2,050	8,000	8,800	2,850	3,925	106,954	3,110	320,508

[1] Preliminary.   [2] Estimate.   [3] Forecast.   [4] Spilt year includes Northern Hemisphere crops harvested in the late months of the first year shown combined with Southern Hemisphere crops harvested in the early months of the following year.   Sources: Foreign Agricultural Service, U.S. Department of Agriculture (FAS-USDA)

World Crushings of Soybeans   In Thousands of Metric Tons

Crop Year	Argen-tina	Bolivia	Brazil	China	European Union	India	Japan	Mexico	Para-guay	Russia	Taiwan	United States	World Total
2006-07	33,586	1,670	31,109	35,970	14,801	6,585	3,033	3,800	1,305	800	2,040	49,198	195,573
2007-08	34,607	1,160	32,117	39,518	14,947	8,400	2,919	3,700	1,390	1,000	1,940	49,081	202,246
2008-09	31,243	1,435	31,869	41,035	12,940	7,450	2,497	3,600	1,450	1,490	1,920	45,230	193,621
2009-10	34,127	1,520	33,700	48,830	12,595	7,800	2,535	3,600	1,558	1,950	2,010	47,673	209,605
2010-11	37,614	1,800	36,330	55,000	12,430	9,300	2,149	3,625	1,570	2,170	2,060	44,851	221,215
2011-12	35,886	2,000	38,083	60,970	12,414	9,650	1,960	3,675	900	2,300	2,020	46,348	228,390
2012-13	33,611	2,175	35,235	64,950	13,162	9,900	1,915	3,650	2,950	2,400	1,920	45,967	230,138
2013-14[1]	36,173	2,250	36,861	68,850	13,436	8,300	1,969	4,030	3,350	3,500	1,925	47,192	241,309
2014-15[2]	40,235	2,500	39,925	74,500	14,200	7,000	2,150	4,175	3,650	3,850	2,100	50,975	262,669
2015-16[3]	43,500	2,650	40,000	80,700	14,800	6,450	2,020	4,350	4,100	4,000	2,150	51,165	275,855

[1] Preliminary.   [2] Estimate.   [3] Forecast.   Sources: Foreign Agricultural Service, U.S. Department of Agriculture (FAS-USDA)

World Exports of Soybeans   In Thousands of Metric Tons

Crop Year	Argen-tina	Bolivia	Brazil	Canada	China	India	Para-guay	Russia	Serbia	Ukraine	United States	Uruguay	World Total
2006-07	9,560	80	23,485	1,683	446	1	4,136	16	4	420	30,386	813	71,137
2007-08	13,839	79	25,364	1,753	453	12	4,100	5	1	190	31,538	818	78,321
2008-09	5,590	123	29,987	2,017	400	55	2,620	2	2	277	34,817	1,097	77,212
2009-10	13,088	50	28,578	2,247	184	15	4,070		5	263	40,798	1,940	91,440
2010-11	9,205	24	29,951	2,943	190	18	5,226	1	82	989	40,959	1,820	91,702
2011-12	7,368	322	36,257	2,933	275	39	3,574	90	17	1,338	37,186	2,607	92,186
2012-13	7,738	523	41,904	3,470	266	115	5,518	102	6	1,323	36,129	3,532	100,802
2013-14[1]	7,842	141	46,829	3,469	215	183	4,800	24	23	1,261	44,574	3,195	112,701
2014-15[2]	10,573	25	50,612	3,853	143	234	4,375	312	136	2,422	50,169	2,850	125,879
2015-16[3]	11,800	150	57,000	4,200	200	200	4,600	350	150	2,200	45,994	2,850	129,845

[1] Preliminary.   [2] Estimate.   [3] Forecast.   Sources: Foreign Agricultural Service, U.S. Department of Agriculture (FAS-USDA)

World Imports of Soybeans   In Thousands of Metric Tons

Crop Year	China	Egypt	European Union	Indo-nesia	Japan	Korea, South	Mexico	Russia	Taiwan	Thailand	Turkey	Vietnam	World Total
2006-07	28,726	1,328	15,181	1,309	4,094	1,231	3,844	34	2,436	1,532	1,217	74	68,906
2007-08	37,816	1,061	15,139	1,147	4,014	1,232	3,614	442	2,148	1,753	1,339	120	78,395
2008-09	41,098	1,575	13,213	1,393	3,396	1,167	3,327	837	2,216	1,510	1,076	184	77,450
2009-10	50,338	1,638	12,683	1,620	3,401	1,197	3,523	1,037	2,469	1,660	1,648	231	86,863
2010-11	52,339	1,644	12,472	1,898	2,917	1,239	3,498	1,000	2,454	2,139	1,351	932	88,781
2011-12	59,231	1,661	12,070	1,922	2,758	1,139	3,606	741	2,285	1,907	1,057	1,290	93,490
2012-13	59,865	1,730	12,538	1,795	2,830	1,115	3,409	717	2,286	1,867	1,249	1,291	95,941
2013-14[1]	70,364	1,694	13,293	2,241	2,894	1,271	3,842	2,048	2,335	1,798	1,608	1,415	111,781
2014-15[2]	78,350	1,947	13,388	2,000	3,004	1,121	3,819	1,986	2,520	2,411	2,197	1,600	122,234
2015-16[3]	80,500	2,050	13,700	2,300	2,900	1,300	4,050	2,050	2,550	2,350	2,400	1,800	127,193

[1] Preliminary.   [2] Estimate.   [3] Forecast.   Sources: Foreign Agricultural Service, U.S. Department of Agriculture (FAS-USDA)

World Ending Stocks of Soybeans   In Thousands of Metric Tons

Crop Year	Argen-tina	Bolivia	Brazil	Canada	China	European Union	India	Japan	Para-guay	Turkey	Ukraine	United States	World Total
2006-07	21,897	311	19,377	655	1,807	1,007	218	185	148	261	20	15,617	63,013
2007-08	20,945	111	20,246	174	2,472	707	146	262	522	382	30	5,580	52,621
2008-09	15,633	91	13,434	220	7,455	454	561	263	20	407	28	3,761	43,163
2009-10	21,039	121	17,480	305	13,209	541	1,076	239	746	701	150	4,106	60,657
2010-11	21,403	505	23,636	297	14,538	820	438	160	978	644	103	5,852	70,834
2011-12	15,949	413	13,024	231	15,909	800	800	128	466	338	----	4,610	53,912
2012-13	20,962	259	15,355	158	12,378	302	1,135	184	127	206	99	3,825	56,215
2013-14[1]	26,050	175	16,020	246	13,877	533	606	228	74	287	265	2,504	62,427
2014-15[2]	31,655	207	19,013	466	17,034	575	453	218	55	359	176	5,188	77,081
2015-16[3]	29,800	407	19,313	221	15,184	555	193	241	62	389	225	12,233	80,418

[1] Preliminary. [2] Estimate. [3] Forecast.   *Sources: Foreign Agricultural Service, U.S. Department of Agriculture (FAS-USDA)*

Supply and Distribution of Soybeans in the United States   In Millions of Bushels

	Supply					Distribution			
	Stocks, Sept. 1							Seed, Feed &	Total
Crop Year Beginning Sept. 1	Farms	Mills, Elevators[3]	Total	Production	Total Supply	Crushings	Exports	Residual Use	Distri-bution
2006-07	176.3	273.0	449.3	3,188	3,655	1,808	1,116	157	3,081
2007-08	143.0	430.8	573.8	2,676	3,261	1,803	1,159	94	3,056
2008-09	47.0	158.0	205.0	2,967	3,185	1,662	1,279	106	3,047
2009-10	35.1	103.1	138.2	3,359	3,512	1,752	1,499	110	3,361
2010-11	35.4	115.5	150.9	3,329	3,495	1,648	1,501	130	3,280
2011-12	48.5	166.5	215.0	3,094	3,325	1,703	1,365	87	3,155
2012-13	38.3	131.1	169.4	3,042	3,252	1,689	1,317	105	3,111
2013-14	39.6	101.0	140.6	3,358	3,570	1,734	1,638	106	3,478
2014-15[1]	21.3	70.7	92.0	3,927	4,052	1,873	1,843	145	3,862
2015-16[2]	49.7	140.9	190.6	3,929	4,150	1,870	1,690	130	3,690

[1] Preliminary. [2] Estimate. [3] Also warehouses.   *Source: Economic Research Service, U.S. Department of Agriculture (ERS-USDA)*

Salient Statistics & Official Crop Production Reports of Soybeans in the United States   In Millions of Bushels

	Planted	Acreage Har-vested	Yield Per Acre (Bu.)	Farm Price ($/Bu.)	Farm Value (Million Dollars)	Yield of Oil (Lbs. Per Bushel Crushed)	Yield of Meal (Lbs. Per Bushel Crushed)	Crop Production Reports In Thousands of Bushels					
Year	1,000 Acres							Aug. 1	Sept. 1	Oct. 1	Nov. 1	Dec. 1	Final
2006-07	75,522	74,602	42.9	6.67	20,468	11.34	44.03	2,927,634	3,092,970	3,188,576	3,203,908	----	3,188,247
2007-08	64,741	64,146	41.7	11.02	26,974	11.54	43.95	2,625,274	2,618,796	2,598,046	2,594,275	----	2,675,822
2008-09	75,718	74,681	39.7	10.13	29,458	11.36	43.93	2,972,577	2,933,888	2,983,023	2,920,589	----	2,967,007
2009-10	77,451	76,372	44.0	9.61	32,145	11.10	43.82	3,199,172	3,245,292	3,250,113	3,319,270	----	3,359,011
2010-11	77,404	76,610	43.5	12.17	37,547	11.54	44.39	3,433,370	3,482,899	3,408,211	3,375,067	----	3,329,181
2011-12	75,046	73,776	41.9	13.13	38,498	----	----	3,055,882	3,085,340	3,059,987	3,045,558	----	3,093,524
2012-13	77,198	76,144	40.0	14.53	43,723	----	----	2,692,014	2,634,310	2,860,290	2,971,022	----	3,042,044
2013-14	76,840	76,253	44.0	13.32	43,583	----	----	3,255,444	3,149,166	NA	3,257,746	----	3,357,984
2014-15[1]	83,276	82,591	47.5	10.00	40,289	----	----	3,815,679	3,913,079	3,926,812	3,958,272	----	3,927,090
2015-16[2]	82,650	81,814	48.0	8.75		----	----	3,916,448	3,935,277	3,887,721	3,981,337	----	3,929,160

[1] Preliminary. [2] Forecast. NA = Not available.   *Source: National Agricultural Statistics Service, U.S. Department of Agriculture (NASS-USDA)*

Stocks of Soybeans in the United States   In Thousands of Bushels

	On Farms				Off Farms				Total Stocks			
Year	Mar. 1	June 1	Sept. 1	Dec. 1	Mar. 1	June 1	Sept. 1	Dec. 1	Mar. 1	June 1	Sept. 1	Dec. 1
2006	872,000	495,500	176,300	1,461,000	797,206	495,199	273,026	1,240,366	1,669,206	990,699	449,326	2,701,366
2007	910,000	500,000	143,000	1,100,000	876,887	592,185	430,810	1,231,860	1,786,887	1,092,185	573,810	2,331,860
2008	593,000	226,600	47,000	1,189,000	840,982	449,543	158,034	1,086,432	1,433,982	676,143	205,034	2,275,432
2009	656,500	226,300	35,100	1,229,500	645,289	369,859	103,098	1,109,050	1,301,789	596,159	138,198	2,338,550
2010	609,200	232,600	35,400	1,091,000	660,868	338,523	115,485	1,187,084	1,270,068	571,123	150,885	2,278,084
2011	505,000	217,700	48,500	1,139,000	743,800	401,583	166,513	1,230,885	1,248,800	619,283	215,013	2,369,885
2012	555,000	179,000	38,250	910,000	819,488	488,465	131,120	1,056,161	1,374,488	667,465	169,370	1,966,161
2013	456,700	171,100	39,550	955,000	541,320	263,564	101,007	1,198,621	998,020	434,664	140,557	2,153,621
2014	381,900	109,100	21,325	1,218,000	611,928	295,945	70,666	1,309,744	993,828	405,045	91,991	2,527,744
2015[1]	609,200	246,300	49,700	1,309,500	717,399	380,768	140,910	1,405,317	1,326,599	627,068	190,610	2,714,817

[1] Preliminary.   *Source: National Agricultural Statistics Service, U.S. Department of Agriculture (NASS-USDA)*

SOYBEANS

Commercial Stocks of Soybeans in the United States, on First of Month   In Millions of Bushels

Year	Jan.	Feb.	Mar.	Apr.	May	June	July	Aug.	Sept.	Oct.	Nov.	Dec.
2005	26.5	21.5	19.5	16.0	14.8	12.1	11.5	8.8	5.4	17.0	36.7	36.1
2006	36.8	30.2	26.1	25.7	17.6	20.5	14.6	14.5	14.5	19.0	40.1	43.7
2007	42.0	36.5	37.3	34.3	29.7	27.4	26.6	24.6	25.5	32.0	54.0	61.3
2008	51.1	45.5	41.8	36.3	28.2	25.6	19.2	14.8	11.4	19.6	40.5	46.1
2009	44.6	36.8	27.0	15.6	13.9	11.8	10.0	5.8	5.9	24.7	40.5	44.3
2010	30.0	28.5	20.1	22.3	10.8	8.0	8.2	4.5	3.3	19.2	45.0	32.0
2011	32.6	23.2	16.0	11.3	10.2	5.9	6.2	5.7	4.6	9.8	49.4	50.7
2012	42.7	34.8	29.9	28.5	27.1	23.8	16.6	10.4	5.2	18.8	41.6	33.8
2013	25.2	20.3	16.1	10.0	6.4	6.6	4.1	2.9	2.1	27.2	36.9	35.5
2014	30.7	20.4	15.5	12.2	7.0	5.1	5.2	2.3	----	----	----	----

This report was discontinued as of August 26, 2014.   *Source: Livestock Division, U.S. Department of Agriculture (LD-USDA)*

Production of Soybeans for Beans in the United States, by State   In Millions of Bushels

Year	Arkansas	Illinois	Indiana	Iowa	Kentucky	Michigan	Minnesota	Mississippi	Missouri	Nebraska	Ohio	Tennessee	Total
2006-07	107.5	482.4	284.0	510.1	60.3	89.6	319.0	42.9	191.2	250.5	217.1	44.1	3,188.2
2007-08	101.5	360.2	220.3	448.8	30.3	70.7	267.3	58.3	175.1	196.4	199.3	19.2	2,675.8
2008-09	123.5	428.6	244.4	449.7	47.6	69.9	264.9	78.4	191.1	226.0	161.3	49.6	2,967.0
2009-10	122.6	430.1	266.6	486.0	68.2	79.6	284.8	77.1	230.6	259.4	222.0	68.9	3,359.0
2010-11	110.3	466.1	258.5	496.2	47.3	88.7	329.0	76.2	210.4	267.8	220.3	43.7	3,329.2
2011-12	126.3	423.2	240.7	475.3	57.7	85.4	274.6	70.2	190.2	261.4	217.9	40.3	3,093.5
2012-13	137.0	384.0	225.3	419.0	58.8	85.6	304.5	87.8	158.1	207.1	206.6	46.7	3,042.0
2013-14	140.9	474.0	267.3	420.9	83.0	85.4	278.0	91.5	202.0	255.2	222.3	72.1	3,358.0
2014-15	158.4	547.1	301.9	498.3	83.1	86.7	301.7	113.9	259.9	287.8	246.2	74.1	3,927.1
2015-16[1]	155.3	544.3	275.0	553.7	88.7	99.0	377.5	104.4	181.4	305.7	237.0	79.1	3,929.2

[1] Preliminary.   *Source: Agricultural Statistics Board, U.S. Department of Agriculture (ASB-USDA)*

U. S. Exports of Soybeans   In Millions of Bushels

Year	Sept.	Oct.	Nov.	Dec.	Jan.	Feb.	Mar.	Apr.	May	June	July	Aug.	Total
2006-07	64.9	182.7	126.4	122.7	147.3	126.5	97.0	71.2	42.0	48.9	37.9	49.6	1,117.1
2007-08	62.1	138.7	127.5	146.1	146.2	139.3	114.9	72.7	56.3	58.8	51.2	45.9	1,159.5
2008-09	34.3	179.4	173.4	171.0	153.0	159.2	101.7	82.0	60.1	60.6	49.9	55.4	1,280.0
2009-10	39.1	198.1	299.0	226.1	226.5	170.0	131.6	55.5	32.0	28.2	37.4	56.3	1,499.9
2010-11	68.2	296.4	257.8	195.9	185.5	169.5	125.9	66.4	34.7	31.6	30.4	43.6	1,505.8
2011-12	47.6	193.3	184.2	151.2	175.0	153.5	116.0	74.8	67.5	53.9	73.8	76.5	1,367.1
2012-13	96.8	274.3	255.4	186.4	194.5	141.6	72.1	34.6	22.1	19.5	13.7	17.4	1,328.3
2013-14	55.3	290.1	331.5	255.0	258.0	198.7	117.0	43.2	32.2	22.2	19.2	16.4	1,638.8
2014-15	77.9	329.9	404.3	302.6	257.9	169.5	91.3	50.0	44.0	34.8	39.7	42.6	1,844.4
2015-16[1]	86.4	363.1	342.6	249.2									3,123.9

[1] Preliminary.   *Source: Economic Research Service, U.S. Department of Agriculture (ERS-USDA)*

Soybean Crushed (Factory Consumption) in the United States   In Millions of Bushels

Year	Jan.	Feb.	Mar.	Apr.	May	June	July	Aug.	Sept.	Oct.	Nov.	Dec.	Total
2006-07	142.4	161.7	155.1	157.4	155.5	136.9	156.1	145.0	152.1	148.9	150.4	146.2	1,807.7
2007-08	147.3	163.7	156.3	164.1	160.5	146.5	156.0	147.5	152.6	141.0	139.3	128.6	1,803.4
2008-09	125.7	150.0	144.7	141.3	145.2	135.4	144.4	140.3	146.2	140.1	128.8	119.8	1,661.9
2009-10	113.3	163.5	168.7	173.1	167.2	153.9	156.1	136.5	133.0	129.2	129.4	128.1	1,752.0
2010-11	130.4	157.2	155.1	153.0	149.2	129.4	140.3	128.0	128.0	123.6	129.6	125.0	1,648.8
2011-12	----	516.6	----	----	524.0	----	----	453.9	----	----	299.0	----	1,793.5
2012-13	----	631.2	----	----	453.5	----	----	442.3	----	----	267.3	----	1,794.3
2013-14	----	675.8	----	----	457.0	----	----	422.0	----	----	285.6	----	1,840.4
2014-15	----	687.3	----	----	480.2	----	----	522.7	----	----	452.0	----	2,142.2
2015-16[1]	----	470.5	----	----	----	----	----	----	----	----	----	----	1,882.0

[1] Preliminary.   *Source: Economic Research Service, U.S. Department of Agriculture (ERS-USDA)*

SOYBEANS - CBOT
Weekly Nearest Futures as of 04/01/2016

WEEKLY NEAREST FUTURES
As of 04/01/2016

Chart High 1794.75 on 09/04/2012
Chart Low 526.50 on 09/12/2006

Cents / Bushel

Cents / Bushel

Nearby Futures through Last Trading Day.

Volume of Trading of Soybean Futures in Chicago   In Thousands of Contracts

Year	Jan.	Feb.	Mar.	Apr.	May	June	July	Aug.	Sept.	Oct.	Nov.	Dec.	Total
2006	1,503.4	1,889.1	1,501.2	1,916.6	1,682.6	2,443.2	1,798.2	1,638.5	1,420.2	2,884.7	2,017.4	1,952.6	22,648
2007	1,976.3	2,620.6	2,251.0	2,641.2	2,107.2	3,461.3	2,734.6	2,323.7	2,315.2	3,680.4	2,521.3	3,093.5	31,726
2008	3,528.7	3,746.2	2,895.0	3,786.1	2,272.2	3,731.2	3,134.9	2,454.4	2,615.1	3,719.0	1,910.5	2,579.7	36,373
2009	2,773.7	2,892.5	2,576.2	3,638.9	2,635.5	3,439.7	2,845.7	2,417.6	2,348.2	3,996.4	2,820.8	3,373.7	35,759
2010	2,659.0	3,392.5	2,932.8	3,414.4	2,078.2	2,946.5	2,546.1	2,266.1	2,553.0	4,660.2	3,455.9	4,029.3	36,934
2011	3,572.5	4,577.6	3,906.0	4,143.1	2,790.6	3,822.9	2,708.7	3,332.7	4,053.1	5,309.5	3,004.7	3,922.4	45,144
2012	3,342.4	4,370.8	4,388.0	5,314.9	4,556.2	4,887.6	5,195.8	3,879.3	3,925.5	5,272.1	3,027.3	3,881.7	52,042
2013	3,628.0	4,568.4	3,193.0	4,516.5	3,522.9	3,644.1	3,328.3	4,132.9	3,442.2	5,288.6	3,401.3	4,054.9	46,721
2014	3,692.7	5,090.5	3,613.9	4,191.9	2,914.6	3,929.4	3,765.7	2,967.5	3,672.1	7,261.6	3,661.2	4,408.2	49,169
2015	3,570.3	4,867.3	4,011.2	5,029.8	3,422.5	6,284.1	4,425.8	4,256.8	3,693.6	6,251.6	3,314.6	4,967.4	54,095

Contract size = 5,000 bu.   *Source: CME Group; Chicago Board of Trade (CBT)*

Average Open Interest of Soybean Futures in Chicago   In Contracts

Year	Jan.	Feb.	Mar.	Apr.	May	June	July	Aug.	Sept.	Oct.	Nov.	Dec.
2006	315,640	359,379	354,211	374,507	375,124	371,155	336,000	348,321	361,643	384,069	394,259	414,374
2007	416,459	478,579	474,466	470,517	465,303	549,655	536,595	495,302	526,913	580,446	586,635	582,502
2008	563,927	598,278	543,451	506,423	458,047	489,069	446,006	388,939	364,679	348,438	312,905	304,252
2009	297,316	313,704	292,160	358,857	415,599	454,846	410,718	401,752	428,320	461,463	438,531	464,281
2010	446,212	465,666	434,272	477,138	459,342	462,796	470,087	514,703	553,196	633,086	624,213	643,091
2011	643,422	673,796	618,157	624,350	559,493	582,529	529,949	524,547	590,297	567,081	521,277	525,510
2012	474,050	532,738	623,973	793,781	787,884	769,806	805,353	748,382	732,388	704,191	609,007	588,185
2013	549,767	615,897	589,572	565,212	565,761	596,479	517,022	535,645	615,389	626,484	582,859	625,222
2014	589,906	675,981	649,898	645,604	601,103	616,406	622,020	642,043	724,924	766,218	664,485	668,492
2015	644,320	698,627	708,314	746,322	698,151	722,449	663,522	653,707	675,762	701,419	673,127	681,902

Contract size = 5,000 bu.   *Source: CME Group; Chicago Board of Trade (CBT)*

SOYBEANS

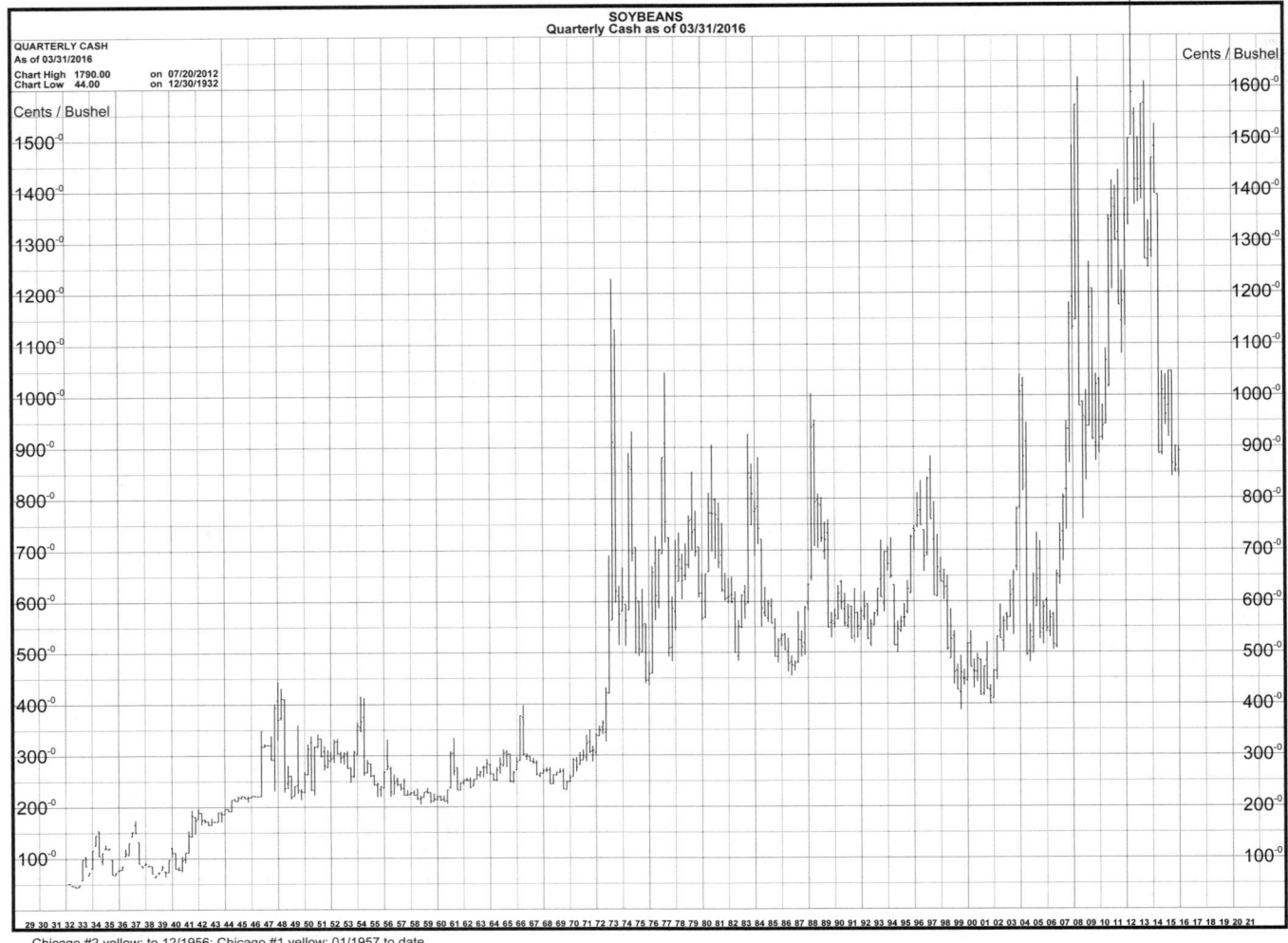

SOYBEANS
Quarterly Cash as of 03/31/2016

QUARTERLY CASH
As of 03/31/2016
Chart High 1790.00 on 07/20/2012
Chart Low   44.00   on 12/30/1932

Cents / Bushel

Chicago #2 yellow: to 12/1956; Chicago #1 yellow: 01/1957 to date.

Average Cash Price of No. 1 Yellow Soybeans at Illinois Processor   In Cents Per Bushel

Year	Jan.	Feb.	Mar.	Apr.	May	June	July	Aug.	Sept.	Oct.	Nov.	Dec.	Average
2001-02	469	430	441	438	437	440	464	471	492	519	575	567	479
2002-03	579	541	575	566	570	590	580	611	640	635	601	589	590
2003-04	639	729	763	772	823	872	975	992	958	890	809	641	822
2004-05	562	519	534	545	539	544	628	622	644	701	703	639	598
2005-06	565	553	574	592	576	575	569	562	581	576	577	542	570
2006-07	535	580	661	657	683	735	730	718	749	792	801	804	704
2007-08	907	944	1,032	1,123	1,216	1,335	1,312	1,292	1,324	1,499	1,516	1,288	1,232
2008-09	1,140	903	893	868	991	938	917	1,025	1,166	1,237	1,096	1,136	1,026
2009-10	1,012	978	1,009	1,033	984	944	949	975	955	955	1,030	1,066	991
2010-11[1]	1,065	1,148	1,252	1,311	1,378	1,386	1,350	1,364	1,368	1,382	1,384	1,381	1,314

[1] Preliminary.   Source: Economic Research Service, U.S. Department of Agriculture (ERS-USDA)

Average Price Received by Farmers for Soybeans in the United States   In Dollars Per Bushel

Year	Jan.	Feb.	Mar.	Apr.	May	June	July	Aug.	Sept.	Oct.	Nov.	Dec.	Average
2006-07	5.23	5.52	6.08	6.18	6.37	6.87	6.95	6.88	7.12	7.51	7.56	7.72	6.67
2007-08	8.15	8.36	9.42	10.00	9.95	11.70	11.40	12.00	12.10	13.10	13.30	12.80	11.02
2008-09	10.80	9.95	9.39	9.24	9.97	9.54	9.12	9.79	10.70	11.40	10.80	10.80	10.13
2009-10	9.75	9.43	9.53	9.80	9.79	9.41	9.39	9.47	9.41	9.45	9.79	10.10	9.61
2010-11	9.98	10.20	11.10	11.60	11.60	12.70	12.70	13.10	13.20	13.20	13.20	13.40	12.17
2011-12	12.20	11.80	11.70	11.50	11.90	12.20	13.00	13.80	14.00	13.90	15.40	16.20	13.13
2012-13	14.30	14.20	14.30	14.30	14.30	14.60	14.60	14.40	14.90	15.10	15.30	14.10	14.53
2013-14	13.30	12.50	12.70	13.00	12.90	13.20	13.70	14.30	14.40	14.30	13.10	12.40	13.32
2014-15	10.90	9.97	10.20	10.30	10.30	9.91	9.84	9.70	9.60	9.58	9.95	9.71	10.00
2015-16[1]	9.05	8.81	8.68	8.76	8.71	8.51							8.75

[1] Preliminary.   Source: Economic Research Service, U.S. Department of Agriculture (ERS-USDA)

Stock Index Futures - U.S.

A stock index simply represents a basket of underlying stocks. Indexes can be either price-weighted or capitalization-weighted. In a price-weighted index, such as the Dow Jones Industrial Average, the individual stock prices are simply added up and then divided by a divisor, meaning that stocks with higher prices have a higher weighting in the index value. In a capitalization-weighted index, such as the Standard and Poor's 500 index, the weighting of each stock corresponds to the size of the company as determined by its capitalization (i.e., the total dollar value of its stock). Stock indexes cover a variety of different sectors. For example, the Dow Jones Industrial Average contains 30 blue-chip stocks that represent the industrial sector. The S&P 500 index includes 500 of the largest blue-chip U.S. companies. The NYSE index includes all the stocks that are traded at the New York Stock Exchange. The Nasdaq 100 includes the largest 100 companies that are traded on the Nasdaq Exchange. The most popular U.S. stock index futures contract is the E-mini S&P 500 futures contract, which is traded at the CME Group.

Prices – The S&P 500 index (Barchart.com symbol $SPX) in early 2015 rallied to a new record high of 2134.72 in May 2015, bringing the overall bull market rally to a total of +220% from the March 2009 low of 666.79. The S&P 500 index in August 2015 then saw a sharp downdraft caused in part by a sharp sell-off in the Chinese stock market. However, the S&P 500 index recovered through year-end and was able to close the year just slightly lower by -0.7% at 2043.94. The S&P 500 index in early 2016 then saw a -15% downward correction due to renewed turmoil in China, fresh weakness in oil prices, and some carry-over effects from the Fed's first rate hike in December 2015.

The long bull market seen since 2009 stalled in 2015 due to (1) a tighter Fed policy as the Fed ended its QE3 program in late 2014 and implemented its first rate hike in December 2015, (2) concern about the slowdown in China's GDP growth to a 25-year low of +6.9% in 2015 and concern about weak world economic growth in general, (3) the plunge in oil prices which caused near-term credit worries tied to oil company defaults and junk bond weakness, (4) negative earnings growth in the second half of 2015, and (5) mildly high valuation levels.

The U.S. stock market in the latter part of 2015 and early 2016 saw weakness as S&P 500 earnings growth turned negative, indicating that companies in 2015 ran out of ways to boost earnings. Earnings growth for the S&P 500 companies was negative at -0.8% y/y in Q3-2015 and -3.4% in Q4-2015, leading to nearly flat earnings growth for all of 2015 of +0.2%, the weakest earnings growth rate since 2009. In addition, the markets as of early 2016 were expecting negative earnings growth to continue with a -5.7% decline in Q1-2016 and -1.2% in Q2-2016. The earnings recession that started in the second half of 2015 helped cause the -15% downside correction in early 2016, particularly since S&P 500 valuation levels remained above long-term averages.

Looking ahead, the U.S. stock market in 2016 will continue to face headwinds from (1) expectations for the Fed to slowly raise interest rates in coming years, (2) uncertainty about whether China may yet experience a hard landing, and (3) concern about the fact that U.S. corporations have at least temporarily run out of ways to boost earnings.

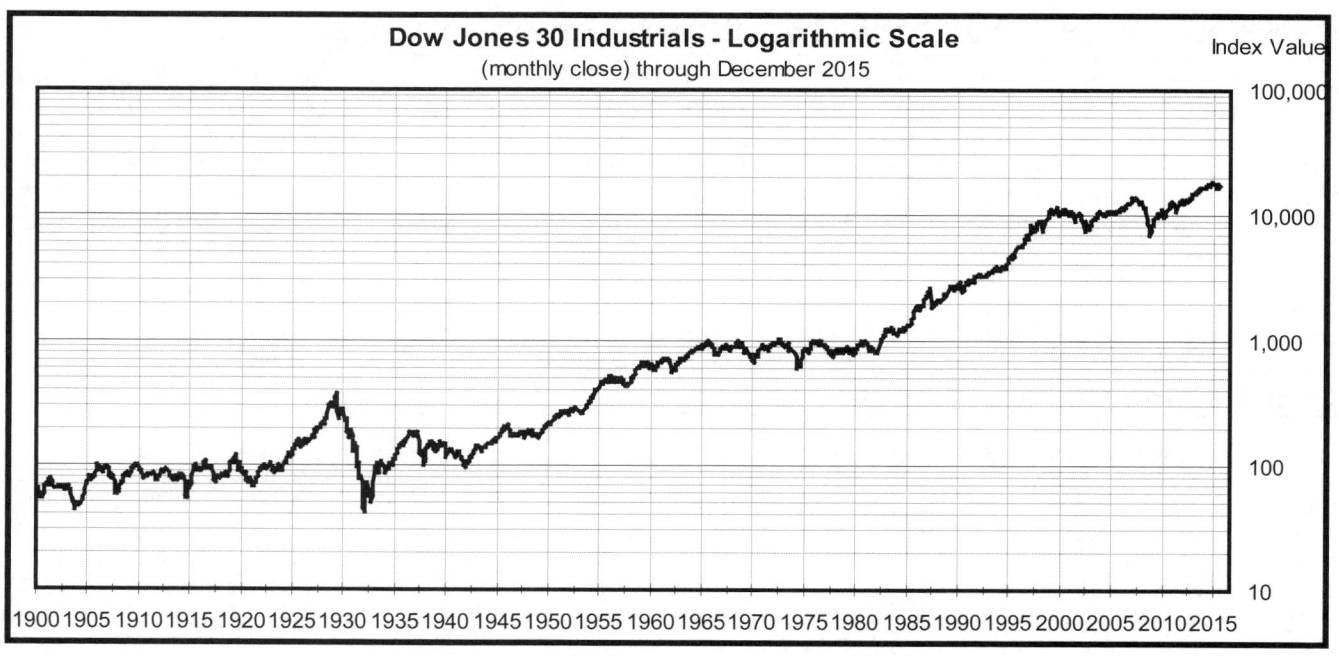

Dow Jones 30 Industrials - Logarithmic Scale
(monthly close) through December 2015

STOCK INDEX FUTURES - U.S.

Composite Index of Leading Indicators   (1992 = 100)

Year	Jan.	Feb.	Mar.	Apr.	May	June	July	Aug.	Sept.	Oct.	Nov.	Dec.	Average
2006	104.7	104.4	104.6	104.4	103.7	103.9	103.7	103.3	103.7	103.9	103.8	104.4	104.0
2007	104.0	103.7	104.1	103.9	104.0	103.9	104.6	103.6	103.7	103.2	102.8	102.6	103.7
2008	102.1	101.9	101.9	102.0	101.9	101.9	101.2	100.3	100.3	99.4	99.0	98.8	100.9
2009	98.8	98.3	98.1	99.2	100.6	101.3	102.5	103.1	104.2	104.7	105.8	106.2	101.9
2010	106.7	107.2	108.6	108.6	109.0	108.8	109.0	109.1	109.9	110.1	111.4	112.3	109.2
2011	91.8	92.7	93.7	93.7	94.2	94.2	94.4	93.7	93.2	93.8	94.1	92.2	93.5
2012	92.2	92.9	93.1	92.9	93.3	92.7	93.1	92.7	93.2	93.4	93.4	94.3	93.1
2013	94.8	95.3	95.1	95.8	96.0	96.1	96.5	97.2	98.2	98.5	99.4	113.8	98.1
2014	113.7	114.3	115.4	115.8	116.5	117.2	118.4	118.5	119.2	119.9	120.5	121.0	117.5
2015[1]	121.2	120.9	121.2	121.9	122.9	123.6							122.0

[1] Preliminary.   Source: The Conference Board

Consumer Confidence, The Conference Board   (2004 = 100)

Year	Jan.	Feb.	Mar.	Apr.	May	June	July	Aug.	Sept.	Oct.	Nov.	Dec.	Average
2006	106.8	102.7	107.5	109.8	104.7	105.4	107.0	100.2	105.9	105.1	105.3	110.0	105.9
2007	110.2	111.2	108.2	106.3	108.5	105.3	111.9	105.6	99.5	95.2	87.8	90.6	103.4
2008	87.3	76.4	65.9	62.8	58.1	51.0	51.9	58.5	61.4	38.8	44.7	38.6	58.0
2009	37.4	25.3	26.9	40.8	54.8	49.3	47.4	54.5	53.4	48.7	50.6	53.6	45.2
2010	56.5	46.4	52.3	57.7	62.7	54.3	51.0	53.2	48.6	49.9	57.8	63.4	54.5
2011	64.8	72.0	63.8	66.0	61.7	57.6	59.2	45.2	46.4	40.9	55.2	64.8	58.1
2012	61.5	71.6	69.5	68.7	64.4	62.7	65.4	61.3	68.4	73.1	71.5	66.7	67.1
2013	58.4	68.0	61.9	69.0	74.3	82.1	81.0	81.8	80.2	72.4	72.0	77.5	73.2
2014	79.4	78.3	83.9	81.7	82.2	86.4	90.3	93.4	89.0	94.1	91.0	93.1	86.9
2015[1]	103.8	98.8	101.4	94.3	94.6	101.4							99.1

[1] Preliminary.   Source: The Conference Board (TCB) Copyrighted.

Capacity Utilization Rates (Total Industry)   In Percent

Year	Jan.	Feb.	Mar.	Apr.	May	June	July	Aug.	Sept.	Oct.	Nov.	Dec.	Average
2006	80.4	80.3	80.4	80.6	80.4	80.6	80.4	80.5	80.3	80.1	79.8	80.5	80.4
2007	79.9	80.6	80.5	81.0	80.9	80.7	80.6	80.7	80.9	80.4	80.9	80.9	80.7
2008	80.7	80.6	80.4	79.9	79.6	79.4	79.0	77.8	74.5	75.1	74.1	71.9	77.8
2009	70.1	69.6	68.5	67.9	67.2	66.9	67.6	68.4	69.0	69.4	69.7	70.0	68.7
2010	71.0	71.4	72.0	72.4	73.6	73.9	74.4	74.8	75.1	75.0	75.1	75.8	73.7
2011	75.8	75.5	76.1	75.7	75.9	76.0	76.2	76.6	76.4	76.8	76.5	76.8	76.2
2012	77.2	77.2	76.5	77.0	76.9	76.7	76.8	76.3	76.2	76.3	76.5	76.6	76.7
2013	76.5	76.7	76.8	76.7	76.6	76.6	76.2	76.7	77.0	76.9	77.0	77.1	76.7
2014	76.8	77.3	77.8	77.8	78.0	78.2	78.3	78.2	78.5	78.5	79.0	79.0	78.1
2015[1]	78.7	78.4	78.2	78.0	77.6	77.5	78.0	77.9	77.9	77.7	77.0	76.4	77.8

[1] Preliminary.   Source: Bureau of Economic Analysis, U.S. Department of Commerce (BEA)

Manufacturers New Orders, Durable Goods   In Billions of Constant Dollars

Year	Jan.	Feb.	Mar.	Apr.	May	June	July	Aug.	Sept.	Oct.	Nov.	Dec.	Average
2006	207.77	217.52	227.78	214.22	215.79	221.02	212.24	210.71	236.17	217.03	225.70	229.24	219.60
2007	218.76	221.08	228.69	233.53	227.31	229.69	239.28	233.95	226.00	229.27	232.49	242.57	230.22
2008	237.10	233.57	230.49	229.64	230.07	229.26	224.26	217.06	211.10	192.05	183.92	173.40	215.99
2009	152.95	145.06	144.84	143.80	150.32	145.40	156.29	157.92	156.90	162.35	161.45	158.42	152.97
2010	181.93	175.89	179.49	187.17	186.16	185.86	189.99	192.13	199.81	194.47	196.29	193.72	188.58
2011	204.16	193.47	210.60	200.25	205.80	198.95	208.72	215.18	207.65	208.10	216.77	226.17	207.98
2012	226.24	225.02	222.52	221.31	218.60	221.63	227.82	203.69	216.36	220.87	219.35	229.72	221.09
2013	219.31	230.45	212.09	221.26	230.34	239.96	218.28	219.76	228.99	224.74	237.39	228.49	225.92
2014	226.16	232.80	238.35	241.14	234.84	242.13	299.87	241.79	238.19	237.75	235.94	226.74	241.31
2015[1]	233.37	225.26	236.67	232.57	227.28	236.61	241.04	233.96	232.02	238.62	237.38	226.39	233.43

[1] Preliminary.   Source: Bureau of Economic Analysis, U.S. Department of Commerce (BEA)

Corporate Profits After Tax -- Quarterly   In Billions of Dollars

Year	First Quarter	Second Quarter	Third Quarter	Fourth Quarter	Total	Year	First Quarter	Second Quarter	Third Quarter	Fourth Quarter	Total
2004	961.1	968.6	1,005.3	974.1	977.3	2010	1,313.7	1,314.8	1,426.6	1,448.4	1,375.9
2005	1,022.7	1,050.4	1,071.2	1,117.2	1,065.4	2011	1,279.9	1,406.6	1,475.6	1,588.0	1,437.5
2006	1,166.7	1,174.0	1,196.8	1,155.0	1,173.1	2012	1,573.3	1,543.7	1,548.1	1,537.1	1,550.6
2007	1,056.8	1,128.8	1,087.1	1,061.2	1,083.5	2013	1,542.4	1,584.1	1,566.5	1,580.9	1,568.5
2008	1,028.1	1,023.5	1,058.7	793.5	976.0	2014	1,427.4	1,543.1	1,642.7	1,623.2	1,559.1
2009	1,044.0	1,060.6	1,178.3	1,227.3	1,127.6	2015[1]	1,494.7	1,533.9	1,507.7		1,512.1

[1] Preliminary.   Source: Bureau of Economic Analysis, U.S. Department of Commerce (BEA)

Change in Manufacturing and Trade Inventories   In Billions of Dollars

Year	Jan.	Feb.	Mar.	Apr.	May	June	July	Aug.	Sept.	Oct.	Nov.	Dec.	Average
2006	85.9	-49.7	129.5	82.7	169.3	169.3	92.2	93.2	65.9	22.9	28.3	4.2	85.2
2007	37.8	43.6	-17.0	59.5	68.1	55.0	75.6	62.7	87.7	23.8	53.3	96.3	53.4
2008	169.4	78.5	35.6	81.4	66.2	133.3	202.6	34.8	-64.9	-99.6		-250.0	35.2
2009	-170.2	-188.5	-232.1	-197.4	-196.7	-218.1	-159.1	-232.5	-46.8	59.8	75.6	-14.9	-126.7
2010	27.9	104.4	95.5	95.3	54.9	136.3	173.2	139.3	179.6	190.5	63.3	173.4	119.5
2011	167.1	129.1	226.8	154.7	184.1	50.0	75.1	114.0	-26.5	158.7	69.4	79.7	115.2
2012	139.9	118.4	47.8	46.5	56.8	27.0	128.1	85.0	118.2	60.8	37.4	33.6	75.0
2013	205.4	30.2	-18.8	66.4	-1.8	17.5	62.3	71.5	117.8	137.2	95.7	82.0	72.1
2014	65.6	74.8	82.9	124.5	104.5	64.6	70.8	32.9	54.1	52.7	20.9	15.3	63.6
2015[1]	-29.5	57.0	25.4	83.8	59.8								39.3

[1] Preliminary.   *Source: Bureau of Economic Analysis, U.S. Department of Commerce (BEA)*

Productivity: Index of Output per Hour, All Persons, Nonfarm Business -- Quarterly   (1992 = 100)

Year	First Quarter	Second Quarter	Third Quarter	Fourth Quarter	Total	Year	First Quarter	Second Quarter	Third Quarter	Fourth Quarter	Total
2004	91.0	91.9	92.2	92.5	91.9	2010	102.7	103.0	103.6	104.0	103.3
2005	93.5	93.4	94.1	94.2	93.8	2011	103.1	103.5	103.3	104.0	103.5
2006	94.8	94.7	94.2	95.0	94.7	2012	104.2	104.9	104.6	104.1	104.4
2007	95.1	95.7	96.8	97.2	96.2	2013	104.0	104.0	104.4	105.3	104.4
2008	96.2	97.2	97.4	96.8	96.9	2014	104.4	105.1	105.9	105.3	105.2
2009	97.6	99.5	100.9	102.1	100.0	2015[1]	105.0	105.9	106.5	105.7	105.8

[1] Preliminary.   *Source: Bureau of Economic Analysis, U.S. Department of Commerce (BEA)*

Civilian Unemployment Rate - U3

Year	Jan.	Feb.	Mar.	Apr.	May	June	July	Aug.	Sept.	Oct.	Nov.	Dec.	Average
2006	4.7	4.8	4.7	4.7	4.6	4.6	4.8	4.7	4.6	4.4	4.5	4.5	4.6
2007	4.6	4.5	4.4	4.5	4.5	4.6	4.7	4.7	4.7	4.8	4.7	5.0	4.6
2008	5.0	4.8	5.1	5.0	5.4	5.5	5.8	6.1	6.2	6.6	6.9	7.4	5.8
2009	7.7	8.2	8.6	8.9	9.4	9.5	9.4	9.7	9.8	10.1	10.0	10.0	9.3
2010	9.7	9.8	9.9	9.9	9.6	9.4	9.5	9.5	9.5	9.5	9.8	9.4	9.6
2011	9.1	9.0	9.0	9.1	9.0	9.1	9.0	9.0	9.0	8.8	8.6	8.5	8.9
2012	8.2	8.3	8.2	8.2	8.2	8.2	8.2	8.1	7.8	7.8	7.8	7.9	8.1
2013	7.9	7.7	7.5	7.5	7.5	7.5	7.3	7.2	7.2	7.2	7.0	6.7	7.4
2014	6.6	6.7	6.6	6.2	6.3	6.1	6.2	6.1	5.9	5.7	5.8	5.6	6.2
2015[1]	5.7	5.5	5.5	5.4	5.5	5.3	5.3	5.1	5.1	5.0	5.0	5.0	5.3

[1] Preliminary.   *Source: Bureau of Economic Analysis, U.S. Department of Commerce (BEA)*

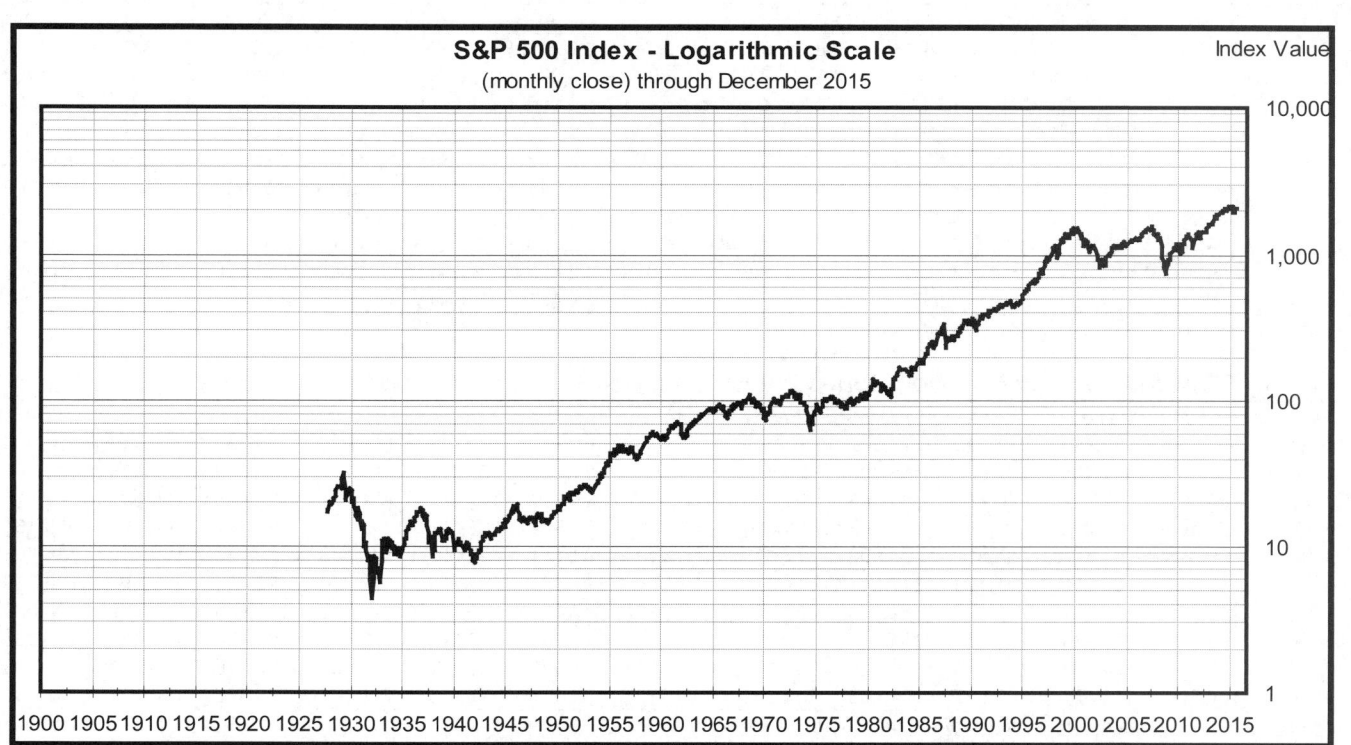

S&P 500 Index - Logarithmic Scale
(monthly close) through December 2015

STOCK INDEX FUTURES - U.S.

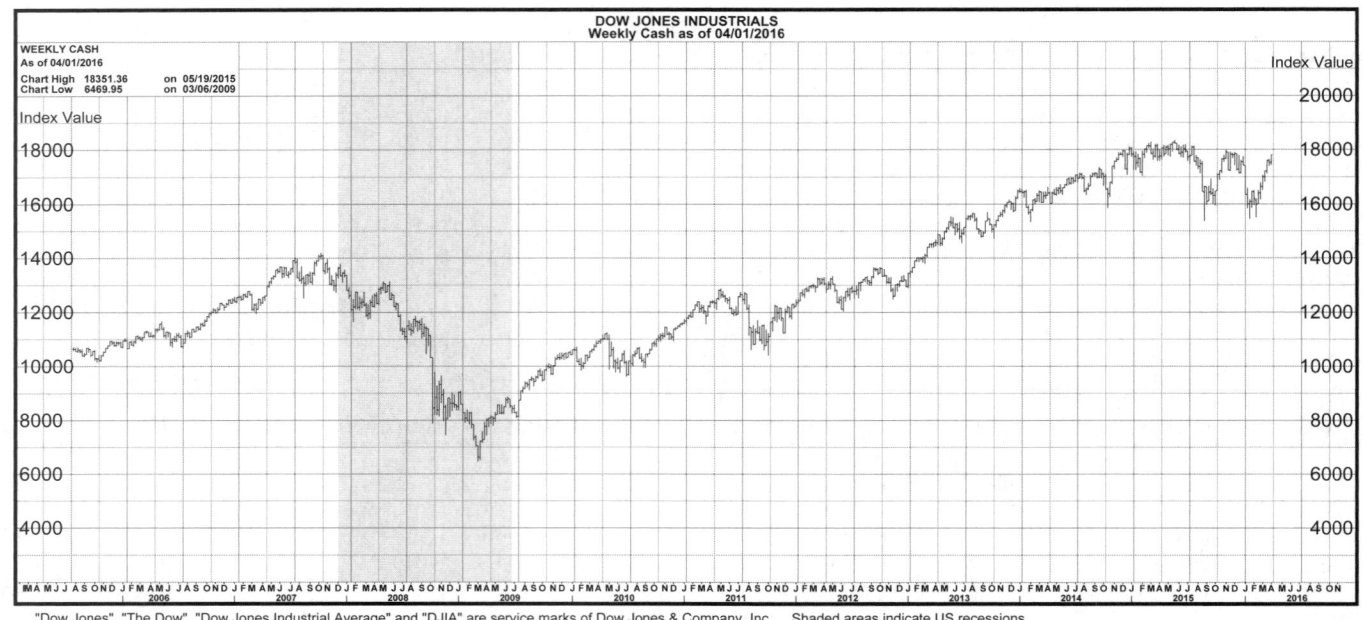

"Dow Jones", "The Dow", "Dow Jones Industrial Average" and "DJIA" are service marks of Dow Jones & Company, Inc.   Shaded areas indicate US recessions.

Average Value of Dow Jones Industrials Index (30 Stocks)

Year	Jan.	Feb.	Mar.	Apr.	May	June	July	Aug.	Sept.	Oct.	Nov.	Dec.	Average
2006	10,872.5	10,971.2	11,144.5	11,234.7	11,333.9	10,998.0	11,032.5	11,257.4	11,533.6	11,963.1	12,185.2	12,377.6	11,408.7
2007	12,512.9	12,631.5	12,268.5	12,754.8	13,407.8	13,480.2	13,677.9	13,239.7	13,557.7	13,901.3	13,200.5	13,406.9	13,170.0
2008	12,537.4	12,419.6	12,193.9	12,656.6	12,812.5	12,056.7	11,322.4	11,530.8	11,114.1	9,176.7	8,614.6	8,595.6	11,252.6
2009	8,396.2	7,690.5	7,235.5	7,992.1	8,398.4	8,593.0	8,679.8	9,375.1	9,635.0	9,857.3	10,227.6	10,433.4	8,876.1
2010	10,471.2	1,021.5	10,677.5	11,052.2	10,500.2	10,159.3	10,222.2	10,350.4	10,598.1	11,044.5	11,198.6	11,465.3	9,896.7
2011	11,802.4	12,190.0	12,081.5	12,434.9	12,580.0	12,097.3	12,512.3	11,326.6	11,175.5	11,515.9	11,804.2	12,075.7	11,966.4
2012	12,550.9	12,889.1	13,079.5	13,030.8	12,721.1	12,544.9	12,814.1	13,134.9	13,418.5	13,380.7	12,896.4	13,144.2	12,967.1
2013	13,615.3	13,967.3	14,418.3	14,675.9	15,172.2	15,035.8	15,390.2	15,195.3	15,269.8	15,289.8	15,870.8	16,095.8	14,999.7
2014	16,243.6	15,958.4	16,308.6	16,399.5	16,567.3	16,843.8	16,988.3	16,775.2	17,098.1	16,701.9	17,649.0	17,754.2	16,774.0
2015	17,542.3	17,945.4	17,931.7	17,970.5	18,124.7	17,927.2	17,795.0	17,061.6	16,340.0	17,182.3	17,723.8	17,542.9	17,590.6

Source: New York Stock Exchange (NYSE)

Volume of Trading of Mini Dow Jones Industrials Index Futures in Chicago   In Thousands of Contracts

Year	Jan.	Feb.	Mar.	Apr.	May	June	July	Aug.	Sept.	Oct.	Nov.	Dec.	Total
2006	2,172.3	1,884.6	2,374.7	2,047.4	2,569.4	2,903.4	2,348.8	1,913.9	2,102.1	2,114.1	2,323.0	2,038.6	26,792.4
2007	2,261.7	2,114.9	3,641.7	2,223.4	2,955.9	3,609.0	3,480.8	5,343.3	3,008.5	3,805.0	4,839.2	2,815.3	40,098.9
2008	4,710.3	3,599.7	4,481.0	3,133.3	3,072.1	4,292.3	4,923.9	4,085.3	6,184.0	7,327.8	5,124.1	4,414.4	55,348.3
2009	3,707.9	4,164.2	4,915.8	3,595.5	3,161.6	3,052.0	2,830.5	2,795.0	3,249.1	3,434.2	2,724.1	2,260.0	39,889.8
2010	2,610.4	2,565.0	2,664.0	2,684.3	4,019.8	3,688.7	3,090.0	2,758.4	2,958.0	2,668.3	2,490.3	1,862.3	34,059.5
2011	2,086.5	2,020.2	3,177.6	1,830.8	2,475.5	2,990.4	2,367.0	4,344.6	3,249.6	2,790.5	2,769.2	2,395.0	32,496.9
2012	1,873.4	2,057.1	2,582.9	2,398.8	3,488.5	3,359.7	2,570.8	2,236.0	2,406.3	2,623.1	2,745.3	2,560.3	30,902.0
2013	2,143.3	2,525.2	3,044.9	3,417.8	3,212.1	4,386.6	2,492.1	2,820.5	2,934.8	3,480.8	2,494.0	2,496.7	35,448.8
2014	3,180.8	3,115.6	3,965.0	3,351.6	2,637.7	2,641.1	3,028.9	2,683.7	3,476.0	5,444.0	1,954.8	3,574.5	39,053.7
2015	4,146.7	2,343.8	3,126.0	2,988.1	2,558.3	3,546.6	3,063.7	4,651.2	4,649.7	3,226.2	2,566.1	3,734.5	40,601.1

Contract value = $5.   *Source: Chicago Board of Trade (CBT)*

Average Open Interest of Mini Dow Jones Industrials Index Futures in Chicago   In Contracts

Year	Jan.	Feb.	Mar.	Apr.	May	June	July	Aug.	Sept.	Oct.	Nov.	Dec.
2006	75,474	89,714	81,712	75,272	87,079	90,968	91,358	100,914	111,938	129,731	126,719	117,905
2007	114,184	131,409	104,909	88,432	129,891	104,429	88,716	99,186	93,797	99,868	104,973	92,308
2008	83,212	92,273	90,482	89,548	104,500	108,579	108,726	115,087	109,257	101,468	109,584	82,817
2009	65,403	75,276	65,501	52,362	53,660	55,979	59,860	68,575	75,719	64,854	66,490	69,164
2010	66,488	66,853	85,812	85,906	77,273	81,840	82,146	91,334	88,463	92,636	100,170	86,604
2011	89,055	94,278	97,112	117,217	113,517	94,274	113,353	86,802	77,776	77,465	86,666	106,153
2012	102,192	109,321	116,358	102,473	103,582	100,349	87,422	109,011	128,525	115,960	99,172	105,089
2013	104,630	122,311	131,290	114,419	118,633	113,230	113,658	115,707	119,479	106,434	131,168	134,255
2014	127,534	114,491	134,383	119,028	127,150	131,818	124,601	115,822	140,265	119,716	139,521	135,980
2015	106,993	111,350	109,677	104,565	112,992	110,880	92,351	93,151	77,209	75,595	100,777	98,535

Contract value = $5.   *Source: Chicago Board of Trade (CBT)*

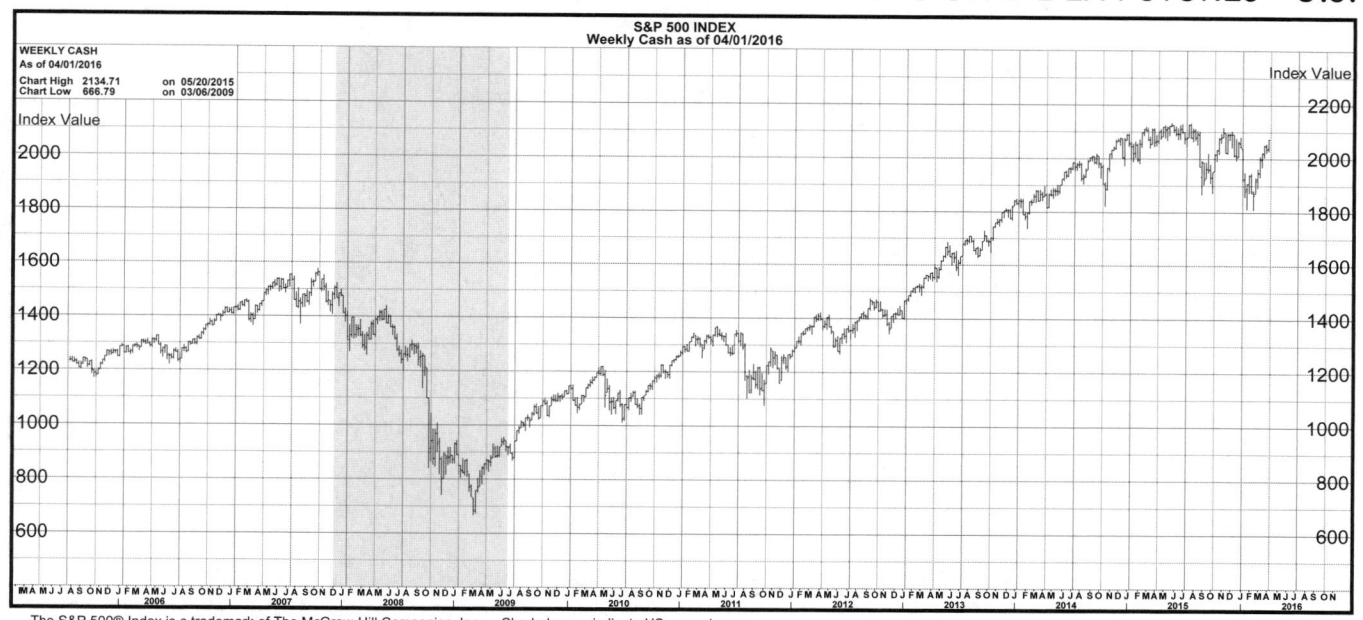

The S&P 500® Index is a trademark of The McGraw-Hill Companies, Inc.   Shaded areas indicate US recessions.

Average Value of Standard & Poor's 500 Index

Year	Jan.	Feb.	Mar.	Apr.	May	June	July	Aug.	Sept.	Oct.	Nov.	Dec.	Average
2006	1,278.7	1,276.7	1,293.7	1,302.2	1,290.0	1,253.1	1,260.2	1,287.2	1,317.8	1,363.3	1,388.6	1,416.4	1,310.7
2007	1,424.2	1,444.8	1,407.0	1,463.7	1,511.1	1,514.5	1,520.7	1,454.6	1,497.1	1,539.7	1,463.4	1,479.2	1,476.7
2008	1,378.8	1,354.9	1,316.9	1,370.5	1,403.2	1,341.3	1,257.3	1,281.5	1,217.0	968.8	883.0	877.4	1,220.9
2009	865.6	805.2	757.1	848.2	902.4	926.1	935.8	1,009.7	1,044.6	1,067.7	1,088.1	1,110.4	946.7
2010	1,123.6	1,089.2	1,152.1	1,197.3	1,125.1	1,083.4	1,079.8	1,087.3	1,122.1	1,171.6	1,198.9	1,241.5	1,139.3
2011	1,282.6	1,321.1	1,304.5	1,331.5	1,338.3	1,287.3	1,325.2	1,185.3	1,173.9	1,207.2	1,226.4	1,243.3	1,268.9
2012	1,300.6	1,352.5	1,389.2	1,386.4	1,341.3	1,323.5	1,359.8	1,403.5	1,443.4	1,437.8	1,394.5	1,422.3	1,379.6
2013	1,480.4	1,512.3	1,550.8	1,570.7	1,639.8	1,618.8	1,668.7	1,670.1	1,687.2	1,720.1	1,783.5	1,807.8	1,642.5
2014	1,822.4	1,817.0	1,863.5	1,864.3	1,889.8	1,947.1	1,973.1	1,961.5	1,993.2	1,937.3	2,044.6	2,054.3	1,930.7
2015	2,028.2	2,082.2	2,080.0	2,094.9	2,111.9	2,099.3	2,094.1	2,039.9	1,944.4	2,024.8	2,080.6	2,054.1	2,061.2

Source: Index and Option Market (IOM), division of the Chicago Mercantile Exchange (CME)

Volume of Trading of E-mini S&P 500 Stock Index Futures in Chicago   In Thousands of Contracts

Year	Jan.	Feb.	Mar.	Apr.	May	June	July	Aug.	Sept.	Oct.	Nov.	Dec.	Total
2006	18,716	16,095	21,357	18,174	24,750	30,359	21,629	19,107	21,986	22,377	23,616	19,760	257,927
2007	21,632	22,507	37,944	20,399	26,266	39,351	35,295	55,547	37,578	38,649	46,727	33,454	415,348
2008	55,257	40,368	56,108	38,472	36,217	49,724	53,375	36,400	76,696	84,259	56,426	50,587	633,889
2009	45,814	49,498	69,321	49,293	46,060	48,779	42,273	38,448	46,864	46,352	36,951	36,662	556,314
2010	40,765	42,986	46,644	43,563	64,388	61,258	44,454	42,196	46,366	41,921	45,468	35,320	555,329
2011	38,684	36,326	60,446	32,705	43,114	59,186	43,083	82,693	71,646	55,044	51,593	45,850	620,369
2012	34,720	32,505	44,161	35,956	47,447	54,942	38,614	33,377	38,685	36,912	39,528	37,433	474,279
2013	30,743	35,953	43,787	41,242	41,901	52,896	29,323	34,906	39,752	39,069	28,689	34,028	452,291
2014	33,770	33,265	43,038	34,460	27,653	33,330	33,263	28,020	40,843	54,465	22,223	40,690	425,020
2015	38,362	25,643	38,949	26,801	24,516	39,037	32,990	46,325	48,962	36,264	28,643	43,312	429,803

Contract value = $50.   *Source: Index and Option Market (IOM), division of the Chicago Mercantile Exchange (CME)*

Average Open Interest of E-mini S&P 500 Stock Index Futures in Chicago   In Thousands of Contracts

Year	Jan.	Feb.	Mar.	Apr.	May	June	July	Aug.	Sept.	Oct.	Nov.	Dec.
2006	1,149.2	1,194.6	1,334.1	1,211.3	1,402.5	1,525.3	1,371.2	1,512.3	1,582.4	1,549.5	1,754.4	1,810.9
2007	1,625.6	1,825.1	2,037.4	1,943.7	2,088.7	2,060.5	1,735.6	2,105.4	2,151.5	1,972.4	2,095.4	2,172.5
2008	2,208.2	2,418.8	2,442.6	2,076.5	2,180.8	2,311.5	2,405.0	2,467.2	2,566.1	2,987.6	3,114.1	2,942.0
2009	2,512.9	2,896.4	3,123.3	2,489.2	2,680.4	2,690.2	2,429.6	2,622.9	2,582.3	2,397.1	2,593.6	2,688.5
2010	2,510.1	2,808.4	2,866.0	2,468.7	2,680.5	2,937.2	2,797.2	2,839.5	2,872.0	2,668.2	2,810.5	2,826.7
2011	2,581.7	2,829.5	2,960.3	2,704.1	2,762.3	2,887.0	2,578.6	3,318.6	3,424.6	3,008.7	2,955.1	2,903.6
2012	2,651.8	2,769.8	2,904.4	2,797.2	2,949.5	2,964.8	2,799.8	2,945.7	3,182.3	2,951.7	3,088.0	3,116.6
2013	2,872.7	3,117.0	3,199.6	3,038.9	3,279.6	3,245.5	2,778.0	2,910.8	2,954.2	2,717.7	2,848.0	2,973.0
2014	2,865.8	3,123.2	3,283.5	2,800.4	2,949.6	3,160.0	2,946.3	2,985.7	3,153.2	2,821.8	2,990.2	3,025.6
2015	2,724.4	2,820.5	3,000.4	2,707.2	2,776.2	2,863.5	2,672.8	2,893.6	3,179.8	2,921.9	2,889.2	2,801.6

Contract value = $50.   *Source: Index and Option Market (IOM), division of the Chicago Mercantile Exchange (CME)*

STOCK INDEX FUTURES - U.S.

NASDAQ 100 Index
Weekly Cash as of 04/01/2016

WEEKLY CASH
As of 04/01/2016

Chart High 4739.75 on 12/02/2015
Chart Low 1018.86 on 11/21/2008

The NASDAQ 100® Index is a trademark of The Nasdaq Stock Market, Inc.   Shaded areas indicate US recessions.

Average Value of NASDAQ 100 Index

Year	Jan.	Feb.	Mar.	Apr.	May	June	July	Aug.	Sept.	Oct.	Nov.	Dec.	Average
2006	1,714.0	1,671.3	1,678.7	1,714.7	1,637.7	1,560.1	1,501.5	1,534.3	1,621.2	1,704.2	1,770.3	1,780.7	1,657.4
2007	1,796.4	1,806.0	1,759.3	1,732.8	1,895.7	1,922.0	1,999.1	1,931.3	2,024.3	2,164.6	2,081.0	2,089.8	1,933.5
2008	1,886.4	1,784.9	1,748.2	1,868.3	1,991.0	1,950.3	1,831.0	1,905.0	1,710.0	1,328.6	1,199.1	1,188.2	1,699.2
2009	1,206.5	1,199.4	1,167.3	1,332.2	1,393.5	1,472.2	1,515.8	1,618.0	1,688.0	1,722.1	1,761.8	1,816.5	1,491.1
2010	1,850.2	1,784.7	1,920.6	2,011.0	1,892.7	1,847.2	1,827.2	1,839.1	1,939.9	2,066.0	2,148.4	2,211.4	1,944.9
2011	2,291.2	2,353.4	2,298.7	2,344.1	2,364.6	2,255.1	2,379.5	2,173.8	2,224.5	2,298.7	2,291.8	2,279.2	2,296.2
2012	2,404.3	2,567.0	2,699.0	2,716.1	2,589.0	2,549.9	2,605.7	2,739.1	2,820.9	2,735.9	2,616.6	2,658.8	2,641.9
2013	2,736.9	2,748.2	2,795.3	2,818.6	2,981.2	2,937.3	3,033.0	3,105.5	3,187.5	3,292.0	3,399.5	3,513.8	3,045.7
2014	3,557.9	3,615.0	3,661.1	3,554.5	3,621.1	3,792.1	3,926.7	3,979.4	4,070.3	3,964.6	4,221.1	4,260.8	3,852.0
2015	4,182.6	4,343.5	4,389.2	4,418.9	4,476.4	4,481.7	4,528.3	4,422.3	4,261.6	4,445.5	4,653.2	4,628.0	4,435.9

Source: Index and Option Market (IOM), division of the Chicago Mercantile Exchange (CME)

Volume of Trading of E-mini NASDAQ 100 Index Futures in Chicago   In Thousands of Contracts

Year	Jan.	Feb.	Mar.	Apr.	May	June	July	Aug.	Sept.	Oct.	Nov.	Dec.	Total
2006	6,627.6	5,802.7	7,479.2	5,458.6	7,386.0	8,257.5	6,741.3	6,315.2	7,074.3	6,768.8	6,333.1	5,695.9	79,940.2
2007	7,121.6	6,685.3	8,699.8	4,975.8	7,068.7	8,426.3	8,122.3	10,558.3	6,855.6	8,915.9	11,146.8	6,732.6	95,309.1
2008	11,604.4	8,072.1	9,676.6	6,987.8	7,042.3	9,911.9	10,151.1	7,606.9	11,522.7	12,287.3	7,300.0	6,571.3	108,734.5
2009	5,713.2	6,789.4	8,800.1	6,383.4	6,240.6	6,721.8	6,243.3	5,958.8	6,808.0	7,048.1	5,686.2	5,579.4	77,972.1
2010	6,711.7	6,179.6	6,447.8	5,937.9	8,666.0	8,054.5	6,905.1	6,619.3	7,365.6	6,249.0	5,996.6	4,504.7	79,637.7
2011	4,986.1	4,764.0	8,138.5	4,912.7	5,944.0	6,778.1	5,276.4	8,884.3	8,034.8	6,813.7	5,807.2	4,825.6	75,165.3
2012	3,623.4	4,274.5	6,068.6	5,655.0	6,428.6	6,100.5	4,852.6	4,448.9	5,148.7	5,578.6	5,845.3	5,506.0	63,530.8
2013	4,420.0	4,365.7	4,911.6	5,226.0	4,549.5	6,411.2	4,222.9	4,686.9	5,210.9	6,077.2	4,280.9	5,030.3	59,393.1
2014	5,641.0	5,236.1	7,514.0	7,765.8	5,541.1	5,252.7	5,305.9	4,774.4	7,103.7	10,105.5	4,013.9	7,229.6	75,483.7
2015	6,833.3	3,985.2	6,094.0	4,617.1	3,880.7	5,542.4	5,100.7	7,432.1	7,310.1	5,782.1	4,431.2	6,301.3	67,310.3

Contract value = $20.   *Source: Index and Option Market (IOM), division of the Chicago Mercantile Exchange (CME)*

Average Open Interest of NASDAQ 100 Index Futures in Chicago   In Contracts

Year	Jan.	Feb.	Mar.	Apr.	May	June	July	Aug.	Sept.	Oct.	Nov.	Dec.
2006	351,240	361,807	345,533	309,746	381,178	427,387	386,930	421,179	437,975	457,275	498,584	433,456
2007	360,663	354,765	423,270	396,080	463,422	454,010	418,512	429,654	451,180	415,073	439,054	408,021
2008	347,374	410,404	424,513	320,046	377,029	358,774	316,037	333,976	336,525	379,643	359,028	302,534
2009	245,830	281,273	302,750	256,064	286,754	284,962	272,424	332,576	341,802	321,653	329,991	338,692
2010	338,217	402,622	362,520	329,709	353,999	353,720	316,651	349,380	397,910	441,782	442,146	401,214
2011	367,204	361,772	350,534	351,601	370,994	321,623	346,518	350,282	369,902	321,427	325,938	308,063
2012	335,164	435,422	484,224	435,734	402,222	376,770	354,698	422,296	480,174	390,199	382,542	380,507
2013	313,000	337,571	376,894	365,878	419,450	381,375	361,111	391,874	393,462	380,763	406,143	439,961
2014	427,403	428,404	452,936	352,802	355,239	383,300	365,320	359,978	399,636	349,013	357,410	376,694
2015	314,070	325,766	352,413	335,425	322,640	342,629	327,815	337,292	287,155	285,539	348,170	334,859

Contract value = $20.   *Source: Index and Option Market (IOM), division of the Chicago Mercantile Exchange (CME)*

Average Value of Dow Jones Transportation Index (20 Stocks)

Year	Jan.	Feb.	Mar.	Apr.	May	June	July	Aug.	Sept.	Oct.	Nov.	Dec.	Average
2006	4,224.5	4,362.5	4,519.5	4,679.6	4,761.4	4,663.1	4,636.1	4,291.1	4,363.3	4,654.7	4,761.6	4,660.0	4,548.1
2007	4,752.2	5,024.6	4,817.3	5,059.2	5,174.8	5,137.2	5,258.8	4,889.0	4,812.7	4,891.2	4,605.9	4,686.4	4,925.8
2008	4,348.7	4,720.0	4,641.9	4,996.9	5,304.5	5,166.7	4,899.2	5,057.0	4,889.3	3,815.4	3,518.5	3,369.2	4,560.6
2009	3,238.3	2,857.3	2,499.9	2,986.8	3,163.7	3,266.6	3,321.5	3,697.2	3,863.1	3,844.4	3,915.2	4,117.2	3,397.6
2010	4,119.6	3,971.7	4,308.5	4,597.7	4,427.6	4,259.5	4,217.9	4,280.6	4,439.9	4,670.6	4,846.8	5,067.4	4,434.0
2011	5,135.4	5,130.2	5,110.7	5,319.1	5,431.5	5,212.9	5,395.0	4,569.8	4,420.8	4,628.8	4,820.8	4,943.3	5,009.8
2012	5,206.5	5,245.1	5,225.4	5,239.7	5,121.6	5,050.9	5,117.2	5,088.7	5,038.1	5,041.0	5,056.3	5,218.7	5,137.4
2013	5,665.7	5,908.1	6,167.2	6,073.4	6,370.3	6,225.1	6,420.2	6,438.7	6,555.1	6,767.9	7,131.0	7,220.9	6,412.0
2014	7,361.9	7,235.3	7,512.0	7,587.8	7,854.6	8,135.4	8,308.7	8,272.8	8,534.2	8,308.9	9,033.8	9,025.7	8,097.6
2015	8,853.6	9,005.2	8,942.9	8,725.1	8,592.8	8,361.0	8,214.8	8,134.2	7,929.8	8,117.2	8,174.0	7,658.2	8,392.4

Source: New York Stock Exchange (NYSE)

Average Value of Dow Jones Utilities Index (15 Stocks)

Year	Jan.	Feb.	Mar.	Apr.	May	June	July	Aug.	Sept.	Oct.	Nov.	Dec.	Average
2006	416.7	408.2	401.7	392.1	401.0	409.2	424.1	436.9	430.1	439.8	449.1	458.5	422.3
2007	449.9	474.1	486.1	516.9	526.2	498.2	502.3	489.0	499.5	514.0	523.5	540.9	501.7
2008	518.8	499.0	480.3	506.2	516.7	519.1	500.8	472.4	446.3	370.1	368.1	362.7	463.4
2009	371.3	356.3	315.8	331.6	339.3	350.6	361.4	373.3	376.0	375.6	373.4	398.9	360.3
2010	393.8	371.9	378.1	384.3	372.7	366.9	379.8	389.8	396.6	404.8	400.5	400.8	386.7
2011	410.1	411.9	409.9	416.5	434.8	427.0	435.3	419.9	431.7	439.9	443.0	451.5	427.6
2012	451.0	451.3	454.8	459.4	467.9	475.6	485.0	479.3	471.5	479.2	449.7	453.9	464.9
2013	463.6	474.7	493.1	522.2	511.0	481.1	496.7	490.3	480.7	492.3	499.5	485.4	490.9
2014	491.9	513.0	519.8	540.7	540.0	556.0	557.5	547.2	555.3	569.2	596.5	609.7	549.7
2015	634.5	610.4	582.6	589.7	584.5	564.1	570.8	587.1	558.1	588.0	566.9	567.7	583.7

Source: New York Stock Exchange (NYSE)

Average Value of Standard & Poor's MidCap 400 Index

Year	Jan.	Feb.	Mar.	Apr.	May	June	July	Aug.	Sept.	Oct.	Nov.	Dec.	Average
2006	1,714.0	1,671.3	1,678.7	1,714.7	1,637.7	1,560.1	1,501.5	1,534.3	1,621.2	1,704.2	1,770.3	1,780.7	1,657.4
2007	1,796.4	1,806.0	1,759.3	1,732.8	1,895.7	1,922.0	1,999.1	1,931.3	2,024.3	2,164.6	2,081.0	2,089.8	1,933.5
2008	1,886.4	1,784.9	1,748.2	1,868.3	1,991.0	1,950.3	1,831.0	1,905.0	1,710.0	1,328.6	1,199.1	1,188.2	1,699.2
2009	1,206.5	1,199.4	1,167.3	1,332.2	1,393.5	1,472.2	1,515.8	1,618.0	1,688.0	1,722.1	1,761.8	1,816.5	1,491.1
2010	1,850.2	1,784.7	1,920.6	2,011.0	1,892.7	1,847.2	1,827.2	1,839.1	1,939.9	2,066.0	2,148.4	2,211.4	1,944.9
2011	2,291.2	2,353.4	2,298.7	2,344.1	2,364.6	2,255.1	2,379.5	2,173.8	2,224.5	2,298.7	2,291.8	2,279.2	2,296.2
2012	2,404.3	2,567.0	2,699.0	2,716.1	2,589.0	2,549.9	2,605.7	2,739.1	2,820.9	2,735.9	2,616.6	2,658.8	2,641.9
2013	2,736.9	2,748.2	2,795.3	2,818.6	2,981.2	2,937.3	3,033.0	3,105.5	3,187.5	3,292.0	3,399.5	3,513.8	3,045.7
2014	3,557.9	3,615.0	3,661.1	3,554.5	3,621.1	3,792.1	3,926.7	3,979.4	4,070.3	3,964.6	4,221.1	4,260.8	3,852.0
2015	4,182.6	4,343.5	4,389.2	4,418.9	4,476.4	4,481.7	4,528.3	4,422.3	4,261.6	4,445.5	4,653.2	4,628.0	4,435.9

Source: Index and Option Market (IOM), division of the Chicago Mercantile Exchange (CME)

Civilian Unemployment Rate - U6

Year	Jan.	Feb.	Mar.	Apr.	May	June	July	Aug.	Sept.	Oct.	Nov.	Dec.	Average
2006	8.4	8.4	8.2	8.1	8.2	8.4	8.5	8.4	8.0	8.2	8.1	8.0	8.2
2007	8.3	8.1	8.0	8.2	8.2	8.2	8.3	8.5	8.4	8.4	8.5	8.8	8.3
2008	9.1	8.9	9.0	9.3	9.7	10.0	10.5	10.9	11.2	11.9	12.8	13.7	10.6
2009	14.0	15.0	15.6	15.8	16.4	16.5	16.4	16.8	17.0	17.4	17.2	17.3	16.3
2010	16.5	16.8	16.9	17.1	16.6	16.5	16.5	16.7	17.1	17.0	17.0	16.7	16.8
2011	16.1	15.9	15.7	15.9	15.8	16.2	16.1	16.2	16.5	16.2	15.6	15.2	16.0
2012	15.1	15.0	14.5	14.5	14.8	14.8	14.9	14.7	14.7	14.5	14.4	14.4	14.7
2013	14.4	14.3	13.8	13.9	13.8	14.3	14.0	13.6	13.6	13.7	13.1	13.1	13.8
2014	12.7	12.6	12.7	12.3	12.2	12.1	12.2	12.0	11.7	11.5	11.4	11.2	12.1
2015[1]	11.3	11.0	10.9	10.8	10.8	10.5	10.4						10.8

The U6 unemployment rate counts not only people without work seeking full-time employment (the more familiar U-3 rate), but also counts "marginally attached workers and those working part-time for economic reasons." Note that some of these part-time workers counted as employed by U-3 could be working as little as an hour a week. And the "marginally attached workers" include those who have gotten discouraged and stopped looking, but still want to work. The age considered for this calculation is 16 years and over.

[1] Preliminary.   *Source: Bureau of Economic Analysis, U.S. Department of Commerce (BEA)*

STOCK INDEX FUTURES - U.S.

Volume of Trading of S&P 500 Index Futures in Chicago   In Thousands of Contracts

Year	Jan.	Feb.	Mar.	Apr.	May	June	July	Aug.	Sept.	Oct.	Nov.	Dec.	Total
2006	711.3	772.9	2,198.8	607.5	1,122.0	2,321.6	726.3	890.8	1,883.1	686.3	935.6	1,988.6	14,845
2007	696.3	765.0	2,341.9	614.6	937.9	2,237.8	803.4	1,546.1	1,941.4	854.5	1,130.8	1,967.9	15,838
2008	1,187.3	907.8	2,374.7	761.0	768.2	1,978.9	921.9	729.7	2,491.2	1,588.1	942.0	2,112.2	16,763
2009	674.4	744.3	2,026.3	555.3	534.7	1,637.5	453.5	427.3	1,338.3	473.3	384.6	1,186.4	10,436
2010	403.6	432.0	1,084.5	363.5	650.7	1,195.3	412.7	433.1	1,027.9	296.8	415.8	974.1	7,690
2011	321.2	330.8	1,162.0	306.6	309.8	1,027.3	283.4	713.6	1,124.3	389.1	394.8	857.8	7,221
2012	228.2	222.9	812.5	233.0	301.8	818.9	243.5	247.9	729.7	192.4	257.1	744.9	5,033
2013	263.4	248.8	699.6	203.8	232.6	693.8	151.4	190.4	584.4	186.8	136.4	565.0	4,156
2014	200.5	193.0	525.4	137.2	145.7	500.1	136.0	118.4	518.8	229.3	152.7	530.7	3,388
2015	200.3	110.0	521.7	132.4	134.5	455.4	131.1	218.8	469.1	147.3	136.3	386.2	3,043

Contract value = $250.   *Source: Index and Option Market (IOM), division of the Chicago Mercantile Exchange (CME)*

Average Open Interest of S&P 500 Index Futures in Chicago   In Contracts

Year	Jan.	Feb.	Mar.	Apr.	May	June	July	Aug.	Sept.	Oct.	Nov.	Dec.
2006	655,483	668,113	682,218	653,044	664,790	670,449	625,142	634,579	634,817	609,410	640,481	679,221
2007	634,075	639,584	654,891	634,576	662,438	652,951	602,222	643,716	663,165	595,908	623,469	623,631
2008	566,839	602,738	607,396	560,088	559,320	558,810	551,609	565,810	578,027	627,531	633,531	603,664
2009	518,589	583,132	566,284	439,705	467,060	456,209	391,596	393,499	400,489	386,593	398,242	379,761
2010	334,063	379,277	384,532	320,130	323,367	354,304	308,220	320,409	327,551	314,245	352,215	341,358
2011	295,221	328,406	351,308	312,007	326,135	314,542	277,586	351,944	367,322	292,018	295,609	285,435
2012	247,547	249,536	248,980	234,595	260,383	266,290	236,315	235,725	225,849	199,981	217,709	215,589
2013	193,514	217,014	202,882	169,581	189,144	203,898	162,175	170,134	196,824	159,233	167,647	168,253
2014	150,125	197,844	198,079	126,277	142,806	163,129	144,257	161,528	165,415	142,572	149,630	146,618
2015	130,204	146,778	154,302	112,920	126,006	132,006	106,046	127,294	149,564	104,817	103,028	97,764

Contract value = $250.   *Source: Index and Option Market (IOM), division of the Chicago Mercantile Exchange (CME)*

Volume of Trading of E-mini S&P 400 Index Futures in Chicago   In Contracts

Year	Jan.	Feb.	Mar.	Apr.	May	June	July	Aug.	Sept.	Oct.	Nov.	Dec.	Total
2006	442,685	370,144	563,420	379,728	468,817	734,165	411,800	389,098	504,454	369,844	368,196	525,912	5,528,263
2007	394,643	334,329	728,851	319,057	475,658	779,491	622,936	977,370	702,416	637,503	709,136	671,037	7,352,427
2008	727,738	513,089	882,372	419,404	468,414	859,153	707,373	437,257	990,434	842,795	694,665	1,037,773	8,580,467
2009	638,571	639,126	1,040,605	715,017	672,835	855,038	609,479	654,219	963,292	921,161	691,942	731,938	9,133,223
2010	575,430	529,499	749,214	556,649	771,715	870,496	612,694	575,424	829,573	526,247	476,898	583,533	7,657,372
2011	421,293	362,478	797,744	427,817	519,082	768,346	407,619	937,031	976,312	687,489	628,695	755,400	7,689,306
2012	408,514	411,301	751,336	513,459	613,049	820,825	494,705	410,688	615,845	453,404	431,072	612,709	6,536,907
2013	309,335	334,867	582,358	434,406	403,614	726,068	369,807	400,705	622,836	478,458	338,633	600,460	5,601,547
2014	369,537	360,548	604,474	385,135	334,222	500,963	343,309	283,606	618,774	648,830	242,848	593,469	5,285,715
2015	414,909	332,866	599,168	325,498	293,658	554,697	369,498	498,662	649,465	402,087	332,728	607,797	5,381,033

Contract value = $20.   *Source: Index and Option Market (IOM), division of the Chicago Mercantile Exchange (CME)*

Stock Index Futures - WorldWide

World stocks – World stock markets in 2015 closed mostly lower. The MSCI World Index, a benchmark for large companies based in 23 developed countries, closed down -2.7% in 2015, snapping a 3-year winning streak of +13.2% in 2012, +24.1% in 2013, and +2.9% in 2014. World stocks in 2015 were undercut by weak global economic growth, a 25-year low in Chinese 2015 GDP of +6.9%, the beginning of what is likely to be a multi-year rate hike regime by the Federal Reserve, and an earnings recession in the U.S. that began in the second half of 2015 and is expected to continue into the second half of 2016. On the supportive side, world stocks saw support from continued positive economic growth in most industrialized nations and highly stimulative monetary policies from central banks in the industrialized world.

Small-Capitalization Stocks – The MSCI World Small-Cap Index, which tracks companies with market caps between $200 million and $1.5 billion, fell by -1.8% in 2015, showing little change for the second straight year after a small +0.4% gain in 2014. The -1.8% decline in the MSCI World Small-Cap Index in 2015 was 0.9 percentage points better than -2.7% decline in the large-cap MSCI World Index. The out-performance by small-caps was a bit surprising given that small-cap stocks usually fall faster than large-cap stocks in a down market. Small-caps under-performed large-cap stocks by -2.5 points in 2014 but outperformed large-caps in the two previous years.

World Industry Groups – The MSCI industry sectors in 2015 produced the following ranked annual returns: Health Care +5.2%, Consumer Staples +4.2%, Consumer Discretionary +4.0%, Information Technology +3.6%, Telecom -0.6%, Industrials -3.8%, Financials -5.6%, Utilities -9.3%, Materials -17.2%, and Energy -25.0%.

Only 4 of the 9 industry groups showed gains in 2015 as the world stock markets were generally weak. Two defensive sectors fared well again in 2015 as they did in 2014 with Health Care up +5.2% and Consumer Staples up +4.2%. Consumer Discretionary (+4.0%) and Information Technology (+3.6%) were the other two sectors that showed gains. Sectors showing declines including Telecom (-0.6%), Industrials (-3.8%), Financials (-5.6%), and Utilities (-9.3%). The worst-performing sectors were Materials (-17.2%) and Energy (-25.0%) which suffered from the weakness in metals and petroleum prices in 2015.

Emerging markets – The MSCI Emerging Markets Free Index, which tracks companies based in 26 emerging countries, fell by -17.0% in 2015, adding to the declines of -5.0% in 2013 and -4.6% in 2014. The emerging markets saw weakness for the third straight year as they battled high inflation and were negatively impacted by (1) weak commodity and energy prices, (2) the strong dollar, and (2) reduced global liquidity as the U.S. Federal Reserve started raising interest rates.

G7 – The G7 stock markets in 2015 saw mixed results with four of the seven countries showing gains. Continental European stocks did well in 2015 as the Eurozone got past the Eurozone financial crisis and showed +1.6% GDP growth in 2015, up from +0.9% in 2014 and negative growth in 2012-2013. Italy's stock market rose by +12.7% in 2015, followed by Germany at +9.6% and France at +8.5%. The UK stock market, by contrast, fell by -4.9%. Japan's stock market did well and rose by +9.1% in 2015. The U.S. S&P 500 index fell slightly by -0.7% in 2015. Canada's stock market fell by -11.1%, weighed down by the sharp decline in crude oil and commodity prices.

North America – In North America, Mexico's Bolsa index did the best by falling by only -0.4%. The U.S. S&P 500 index (-0.7%) in 2015 outperformed Canada's Toronto Composite (-11.1%). The Toronto Composite index has now underperformed the S&P 500 index for five consecutive years after the 7-year winning streak in 2004-2010.

Latin America – The Latin America stock markets in 2015 showed mixed results. The ranked returns are as follows: Venezuela's Stock Market Index +278%, Jamaica's Stock Exchange Index +97%, Argentina's Merval Index +36.1%, Ecuador's Guayaqui Bolsa Index -3.7%, Chile's Stock Market Select Index -4.4%, Costa Rica's Stock Market Index -9.3%, Brazil's Bovespa Index -13.3%, Columbia's General Index -26.5%, and Peru's Lima General Index -33.4%.

Europe – European stocks in 2015 performed better as the Eurozone economy recovered to a GDP growth rate of +1.6% and as the Eurozone sovereign debt crisis further receded. The Euro Stoxx 50 index rose by +3.2%, adding to the gains of +2.9% in 2014, +13.3% in 2013 and +8.8% in 2012. The ranked returns in 2015 were as follows: Italian MIB index +12.7%, German DAX index +9.6%, French CAC 40 index +8.5%, UK FTSE 100 index -4.9%, and Spanish IBEX 35 index -7.2%.

Asia – The Asian stock markets in 2015 closed mixed. The MSCI Far East Index in 2015 rose by +7.0%, more than reversing the small decline of -2.3% seen in 2014. The ranked closes for the Asian stock markets in 2015 were as follows: New Zealand's Exchange 50 Index +13.6%, China's Shanghai Composite Index +9.4%, Japan's Nikkei 225 Index +9.1%, Vietnam's Stock Index +6.1%, South Korea's Composite Index +2.4%, Pakistan's 100 Index +2.1%, Australia's All-Ordinaries Index -0.8%, Philippines' Composite index -3.9%, Malaysia's Kuala Lumpur Composite index -3.9%, India's Mumbai Sensex 30 index -5.0%, Hong Kong's Hang Seng -7.2%, Taiwan's TAIEX Index -10.4%, Indonesia's Jakarta Composite Index -12.1%, Thailand's Stock Exchange index -14.0%, and Singapore's Straights Times Index -14.3%.

STOCK INDEX FUTURES - WORLDWIDE

Comparison of International Indices   (2010=100)

Year	Jan.	Feb.	Mar.	Apr.	May	June	July	Aug.	Sept.	Oct.	Nov.	Dec.	Average
United States													
2009	84.8	77.7	73.1	80.8	84.9	86.8	87.7	94.7	97.4	99.6	103.3	105.4	89.7
2010	105.8	10.3	107.9	111.7	106.1	102.7	103.3	104.6	107.1	111.6	113.2	115.8	100.0
2011	119.3	123.2	122.1	125.6	127.1	122.2	126.4	114.4	112.9	116.4	119.3	122.0	120.9
2012	126.8	130.2	132.2	131.7	128.5	126.8	129.5	132.7	135.6	135.2	130.3	132.8	131.0
2013	137.6	141.1	145.7	148.3	153.3	151.9	155.5	153.5	154.3	154.5	160.4	162.6	151.6
2014	164.1	161.2	164.8	165.7	167.4	170.2	171.7	169.5	172.8	168.8	178.3	179.4	169.5
2015	177.3	181.3	181.2	181.6	183.1	181.1	179.8	172.4	165.1	173.6	179.1	177.3	177.7
Canada													
2009	73.6	69.9	68.9	76.4	83.1	85.9	85.3	89.6	93.2	93.5	94.5	95.9	84.2
2010	96.5	94.9	99.1	100.7	97.9	96.8	95.7	97.2	100.8	104.1	106.4	110.0	100.0
2011	110.9	115.2	115.4	115.7	112.8	108.7	110.1	102.6	100.5	98.8	99.7	98.2	107.4
2012	102.2	104.0	103.2	100.5	96.5	95.2	96.3	98.7	101.8	102.2	100.8	101.8	100.3
2013	104.9	105.5	105.8	101.9	104.3	101.2	103.4	104.6	106.2	108.2	111.0	110.5	105.6
2014	113.7	115.7	118.3	119.6	121.2	123.9	126.5	127.5	127.2	119.8	122.8	118.7	121.2
2015	119.8	125.5	123.6	126.7	125.3	122.9	119.6	116.1	111.6	113.9	111.2	108.6	118.7
France													
2009	82.7	77.7	72.7	80.2	86.6	86.5	85.7	94.5	99.6	100.9	100.1	102.8	89.2
2010	104.7	98.4	104.7	106.0	95.0	94.9	94.4	96.5	99.4	101.4	101.9	102.7	100.0
2011	105.7	109.0	105.2	107.3	106.7	102.8	101.9	85.4	79.6	84.0	80.9	82.5	95.9
2012	86.7	91.3	93.1	86.7	82.3	81.5	85.4	91.5	93.1	91.7	92.4	96.9	89.4
2013	99.6	98.2	101.0	99.7	105.9	101.2	103.4	108.0	109.9	112.8	114.2	111.0	105.4
2014	113.4	114.8	115.8	118.4	119.7	120.7	116.4	113.4	118.1	110.2	113.7	113.7	115.7
2015	117.0	127.2	133.4	138.0	135.0	131.5	132.2	130.4	120.8	125.8	131.0	124.5	128.9
Germany													
2009	73.3	68.9	64.2	73.0	79.0	79.7	80.0	87.2	90.2	91.8	91.2	94.3	81.1
2010	94.8	90.3	96.4	100.5	96.4	98.3	98.0	99.0	100.4	104.0	109.0	113.0	100.0
2011	113.8	117.9	112.4	116.8	118.5	115.7	117.9	95.7	87.3	94.9	94.2	94.8	106.7
2012	101.5	109.7	112.6	108.8	103.8	99.9	105.9	112.3	117.6	117.8	117.0	122.4	110.8
2013	125.2	123.9	127.9	124.8	134.4	130.7	131.9	134.7	137.3	142.2	148.2	149.3	134.2
2014	153.8	153.7	151.0	153.4	156.9	160.5	157.6	149.9	155.8	145.0	153.4	158.6	154.1
2015	163.8	177.4	190.5	193.2	187.5	181.6	182.4	174.8	160.9	165.2	177.6	172.5	177.3
Italy													
2009	89.5	80.6	69.2	84.3	94.8	93.1	91.6	102.7	108.7	111.4	107.9	107.9	95.1
2010	109.7	101.4	106.8	108.2	94.4	93.8	96.3	97.2	97.8	99.8	98.0	96.6	100.0
2011	101.2	107.1	103.6	104.3	101.8	95.3	90.3	73.9	68.2	75.3	71.2	71.4	88.6
2012	73.0	78.1	78.9	69.8	63.9	63.0	64.6	69.8	75.3	74.3	73.2	75.8	71.6
2013	82.6	77.9	75.1	75.3	81.8	76.1	75.5	80.8	83.1	89.4	89.9	86.9	81.2
2014	92.8	95.1	98.9	102.8	100.4	103.9	99.4	94.4	99.1	91.7	92.1	91.2	96.8
2015	92.0	101.1	107.9	111.5	110.8	109.1	109.2	108.3	102.2	105.3	105.6	10.2	97.8
Japan													
2009	83.2	76.9	77.6	87.6	93.0	98.0	96.8	104.2	102.9	100.6	96.3	101.6	93.2
2010	106.5	101.7	106.6	111.3	100.9	97.8	94.5	92.6	93.4	94.5	97.9	102.4	100.0
2011	104.4	106.1	98.4	96.4	96.4	95.3	99.9	90.6	86.9	87.3	85.0	85.0	94.3
2012	86.1	92.3	99.5	96.2	88.3	86.3	87.5	89.4	89.4	88.2	90.5	98.0	91.0
2013	107.4	113.2	122.4	132.1	144.8	130.9	143.0	137.1	143.6	143.2	149.2	156.4	135.3
2014	155.6	146.0	146.8	144.6	143.3	151.2	153.6	153.4	159.3	153.8	171.6	175.2	154.6
2015	172.6	180.4	191.8	197.5	199.5	203.8	203.5	199.0	179.3	183.6	195.6	191.8	191.5
United Kingdom													
2009	78.3	74.5	68.8	74.0	80.4	79.5	80.0	87.0	92.1	94.4	95.9	97.1	83.5
2010	99.0	95.7	102.8	104.6	95.8	94.0	94.3	96.5	100.9	104.0	104.9	107.5	100.0
2011	109.2	110.1	107.1	109.9	108.6	105.9	108.1	96.4	95.6	98.9	98.8	100.2	104.1
2012	104.2	107.8	107.5	104.7	99.9	100.2	103.1	106.0	106.2	106.7	105.9	108.3	105.0
2013	112.7	115.5	117.7	116.3	121.6	115.2	119.2	119.3	119.8	120.2	122.4	120.2	118.4
2014	122.8	122.4	121.3	121.7	125.0	124.4	123.9	122.8	124.0	117.2	121.5	119.7	122.2
2015	120.9	125.8	125.9	128.3	127.7	124.1	121.6	118.1	111.3	116.0	115.4	112.7	120.6

Not Seasonally Adjusted.   *Source: Economic and Statistics Administration, U.S. Department of Commerce (ESA)*

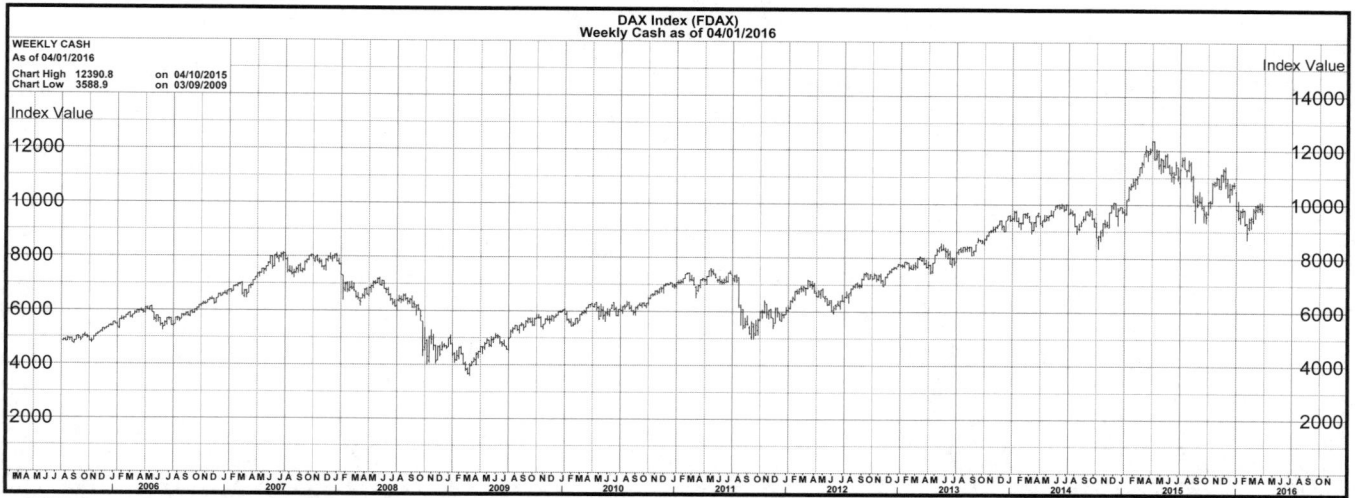

DAX® is Deutsche Börse's blue chip index for the German stock market. It comprises the 30 largest and most actively traded German companies.   Shaded areas indicate German recessions.

Average Value of Deutscher Aktienindex (DAX)

Year	Jan.	Feb.	Mar.	Apr.	May	June	July	Aug.	Sept.	Oct.	Nov.	Dec.	Average
2006	5,494.0	5,762.5	5,861.7	6,010.0	5,845.8	5,495.3	5,594.2	5,750.3	5,901.0	6,161.3	6,368.7	6,492.6	5,894.8
2007	6,692.5	6,913.1	6,706.0	7,237.3	7,582.0	7,874.5	7,888.9	7,463.6	7,638.5	7,950.7	7,715.2	7,945.3	7,467.3
2008	7,323.7	6,886.7	6,499.6	6,762.7	7,056.1	6,716.8	6,341.5	6,421.5	6,137.0	4,946.8	4,692.0	4,657.9	6,203.5
2009	4,534.2	4,265.0	3,969.2	4,519.1	4,886.4	4,930.8	4,949.6	5,395.2	5,584.0	5,680.0	5,642.2	5,836.6	5,016.0
2010	5,863.2	5,584.7	5,965.1	6,215.3	5,966.6	6,080.8	6,061.3	6,122.4	6,214.9	6,436.3	6,744.4	6,991.9	6,187.2
2011	7,039.7	7,294.2	6,952.0	7,227.1	7,330.6	7,158.7	7,292.8	5,923.8	5,402.3	5,871.8	5,826.5	5,867.8	6,598.9
2012	6,278.3	6,789.6	6,966.5	6,731.9	6,424.8	6,184.0	6,549.6	6,949.8	7,274.4	7,288.2	7,238.6	7,576.2	6,854.3
2013	7,747.6	7,666.7	7,913.9	7,723.1	8,317.4	8,089.2	8,161.8	8,332.5	8,497.8	8,800.5	9,170.6	9,235.0	8,304.7
2014	9,516.8	9,509.5	9,339.9	9,490.0	9,709.5	9,927.4	9,751.8	9,273.1	9,638.7	8,971.9	9,490.3	9,812.3	9,535.9
2015	10,133.6	10,977.1	11,784.9	11,956.3	11,599.1	11,236.3	11,288.1	10,818.0	9,953.3	10,222.3	10,986.3	10,673.0	10,969.0

Source: EUREX

The FTSE 100 Index covers 100 of the largest companies traded on the LSE.   Shaded areas indicate United Kingdom recessions.

Average Value of FTSE 100 Stock Index

Year	Jan.	Feb.	Mar.	Apr.	May	June	July	Aug.	Sept.	Oct.	Nov.	Dec.	Average
2006	5,711.15	5,806.74	5,938.81	6,054.41	5,846.00	5,668.05	5,833.67	5,877.73	5,896.10	6,100.49	6,167.75	6,171.56	5,922.71
2007	6,237.79	6,362.53	6,204.92	6,433.93	6,569.76	6,597.96	6,561.87	6,177.22	6,345.11	6,599.27	6,326.71	6,433.54	6,404.22
2008	6,033.15	5,910.13	5,676.27	5,993.33	6,187.20	5,778.27	5,375.22	5,465.71	5,233.92	4,288.83	4,224.87	4,270.73	5,369.80
2009	4,281.85	4,074.38	3,760.23	4,046.33	4,393.78	4,349.25	4,374.50	4,755.63	5,033.13	5,161.18	5,242.29	5,309.54	4,565.17
2010	5,411.65	5,231.92	5,621.03	5,720.73	5,238.81	5,139.26	5,158.39	5,276.00	5,514.67	5,687.17	5,735.84	5,874.87	5,467.53
2011	5,971.31	6,021.12	5,858.24	6,007.85	5,937.95	5,792.18	5,909.81	5,271.31	5,228.50	5,408.62	5,402.52	5,480.08	5,690.79
2012	5,694.45	5,893.35	5,875.40	5,725.58	5,461.45	5,480.44	5,636.47	5,796.96	5,805.45	5,831.81	5,787.52	5,922.72	5,742.63
2013	6,161.87	6,316.35	6,435.58	6,361.01	6,647.35	6,299.43	6,517.86	6,521.48	6,552.36	6,571.95	6,694.32	6,572.98	6,471.05
2014	6,714.51	6,690.79	6,631.69	6,651.96	6,834.80	6,804.31	6,772.02	6,712.21	6,777.75	6,408.63	6,644.12	6,542.62	6,682.12
2015	6,612.63	6,878.54	6,884.51	7,012.39	6,981.68	6,783.17	6,646.60	6,455.96	6,087.34	6,340.81	6,306.91	6,162.31	6,596.07

Source: Euronext LIFFE

Average Value of S&P TSX Index

Year	Jan.	Feb.	Mar.	Apr.	May	June	July	Aug.	Sept.	Oct.	Nov.	Dec.	Average
2006	11,661.8	11,770.3	11,971.7	12,291.1	11,923.0	11,341.1	11,659.3	12,035.2	11,769.6	11,970.2	12,422.3	12,853.5	11,972.4
2007	12,746.7	13,206.7	13,026.1	13,535.0	13,929.3	13,934.9	14,196.8	13,411.1	13,863.9	14,215.4	13,744.9	13,670.6	13,623.5
2008	13,215.5	13,352.5	13,245.4	13,891.3	14,612.9	14,718.8	13,623.0	13,364.1	12,450.5	9,774.1	9,023.7	8,472.7	12,478.7
2009	8,886.5	8,437.6	8,314.1	9,224.7	10,031.3	10,372.3	10,292.8	10,816.4	11,255.1	11,291.5	11,413.6	11,580.1	10,159.7
2010	11,654.3	11,453.7	11,966.8	12,154.2	11,816.5	11,680.2	11,558.6	11,728.5	12,163.8	12,569.5	12,843.2	13,275.4	12,072.1
2011	13,392.8	13,908.2	13,932.9	13,962.4	13,621.2	13,126.1	13,294.7	12,380.7	12,130.8	11,922.8	12,038.1	11,860.7	12,964.3
2012	12,331.8	12,552.7	12,464.0	12,135.4	11,644.1	11,495.7	11,626.9	11,921.0	12,285.6	12,337.7	12,163.2	12,290.3	12,104.0
2013	12,668.8	12,737.0	12,777.3	12,299.2	12,585.1	12,221.4	12,479.7	12,622.7	12,818.9	13,057.7	13,396.1	13,339.2	12,750.3
2014	13,728.1	13,964.5	14,281.4	14,440.5	14,635.7	14,960.5	15,268.3	15,389.4	15,353.5	14,460.8	14,824.8	14,330.5	14,636.5
2015	14,460.9	15,155.0	14,921.6	15,299.3	15,127.2	14,835.9	14,436.4	14,010.4	13,477.6	13,751.9	13,424.2	13,115.1	14,334.6

Source: Toronto Stock Exchange

The CAC 40® is a free float market capitalization weighted index that reflects the performance of the 40 largest and most actively traded shares listed on Euronext Paris, and is the most widely used indicator of the Paris stock market.   Shaded areas indicate French recessions.

Average Value of CAC 40 Index

Year	Jan.	Feb.	Mar.	Apr.	May	June	July	Aug.	Sept.	Oct.	Nov.	Dec.	Average
2006	4,839.7	4,976.6	5,111.9	5,188.6	5,073.2	4,789.2	4,910.6	5,073.3	5,157.9	5,338.8	5,414.5	5,448.1	5,110.2
2007	5,587.0	5,684.2	5,495.4	5,831.8	6,053.9	6,014.9	5,973.5	5,534.8	5,597.2	5,793.7	5,565.3	5,619.1	5,729.2
2008	5,153.6	4,845.2	4,641.1	4,900.2	5,020.2	4,664.6	4,287.2	4,409.9	4,220.5	3,474.7	3,287.2	3,192.2	4,341.4
2009	3,099.7	2,911.5	2,725.3	3,007.2	3,244.0	3,242.9	3,212.0	3,539.9	3,732.7	3,780.0	3,752.7	3,851.9	3,341.6
2010	3,925.2	3,687.1	3,922.2	3,973.7	3,561.5	3,558.0	3,539.3	3,616.9	3,723.6	3,799.4	3,818.4	3,848.5	3,747.8
2011	3,960.7	4,086.4	3,941.7	4,020.3	3,998.6	3,853.3	3,818.0	3,201.9	2,983.1	3,148.4	3,033.0	3,091.9	3,594.8
2012	3,250.6	3,420.4	3,490.0	3,248.8	3,084.4	3,055.9	3,199.6	3,427.4	3,490.9	3,435.7	3,461.5	3,631.8	3,349.7
2013	3,734.0	3,679.4	3,786.4	3,735.1	3,968.7	3,792.5	3,876.6	4,046.3	4,117.7	4,228.0	4,279.9	4,161.4	3,950.5
2014	4,248.4	4,301.1	4,338.1	4,437.3	4,484.8	4,522.0	4,362.0	4,249.6	4,425.3	4,129.8	4,261.0	4,262.2	4,335.1
2015	4,384.2	4,768.5	5,000.7	5,173.4	5,058.2	4,927.9	4,956.2	4,887.1	4,526.6	4,715.6	4,910.3	4,665.7	4,831.2

Source: Euronext Paris

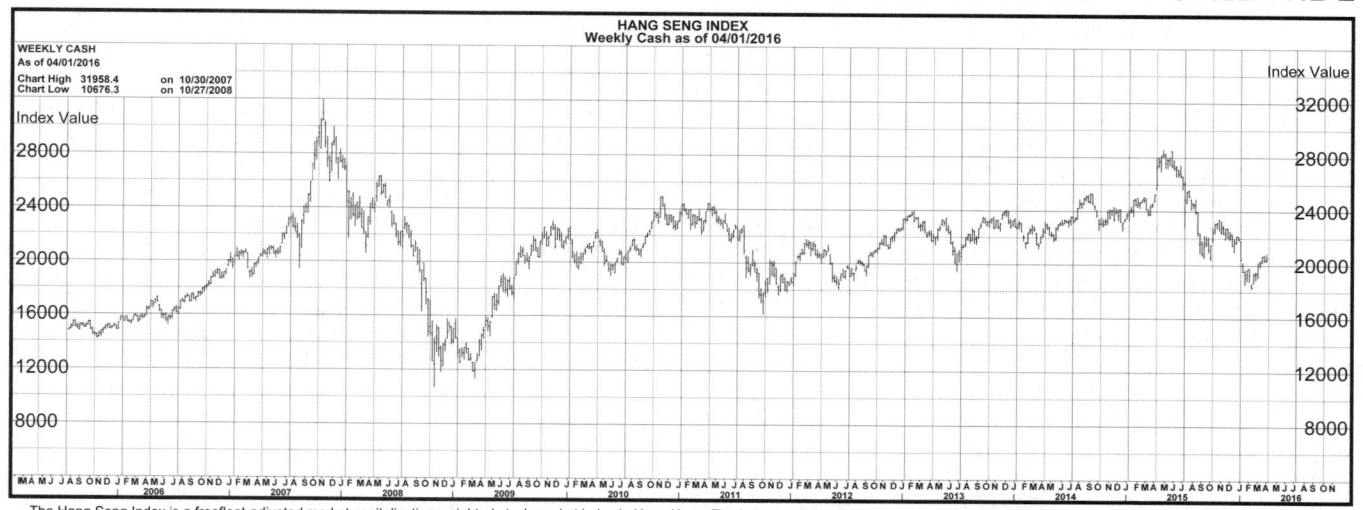

The Hang Seng Index is a freefloat-adjusted market capitalization-weighted stock market index in Hong Kong. The Index was created by Hong Kong banker Stanley Kwan in 1969.

Average Value of Hang Seng Index

Year	Jan.	Feb.	Mar.	Apr.	May	June	July	Aug.	Sept.	Oct.	Nov.	Dec.	Average
2006	15,526	15,581	15,729	16,557	16,473	15,725	16,457	17,139	17,355	17,991	18,952	19,114	16,883
2007	20,197	20,484	19,339	20,439	20,727	21,214	22,878	22,321	24,997	29,153	28,287	28,053	23,174
2008	25,401	23,848	22,561	24,597	25,237	23,184	22,079	21,435	19,370	14,925	13,573	14,593	20,900
2009	13,794	13,167	12,795	15,029	17,124	18,342	18,904	20,475	20,920	21,654	22,219	21,748	18,014
2010	21,409	20,244	21,089	21,624	19,945	20,104	20,446	21,109	21,658	23,301	23,805	23,057	21,483
2011	23,865	23,197	23,110	24,009	23,133	22,342	22,280	20,334	19,007	18,352	18,865	18,586	21,423
2012	19,456	21,128	21,013	20,666	19,615	18,940	19,372	19,946	20,227	21,293	21,650	22,406	20,476
2013	23,471	23,148	22,518	22,054	22,933	21,064	21,299	22,009	22,933	23,102	23,305	23,371	22,601
2014	22,725	22,188	21,981	22,598	22,585	23,145	23,760	24,812	24,342	23,301	23,779	23,386	23,217
2015	24,210	24,670	24,307	27,452	27,656	27,009	25,032	23,223	21,365	22,649	22,510	21,910	24,333

Source: Hong Kong Futures Exchange

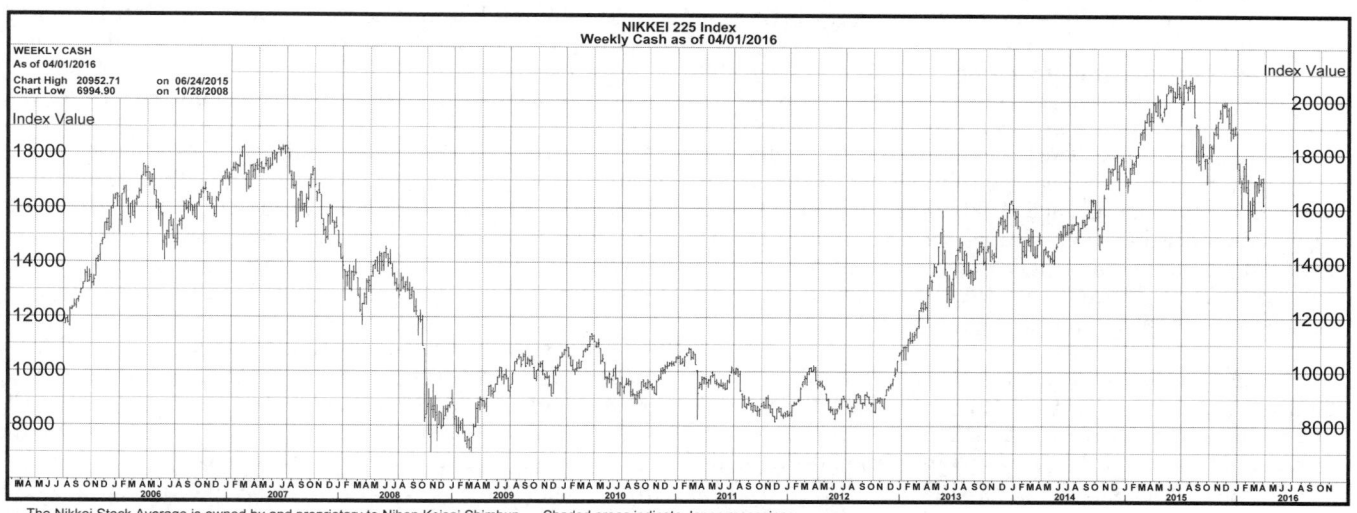

The Nikkei Stock Average is owned by and proprietary to Nihon Keisai Shimbun.   Shaded areas indicate Japan recessions.

Average Value of Nikkei 225 Index

Year	Jan.	Feb.	Mar.	Apr.	May	June	July	Aug.	Sept.	Oct.	Nov.	Dec.	Average
2006	16,085.5	16,187.6	16,311.5	17,233.0	16,322.2	14,990.3	15,147.6	15,786.8	15,934.1	16,519.4	16,101.1	16,790.8	16,117.5
2007	17,286.3	17,741.2	17,128.4	17,469.8	17,595.1	18,001.4	17,974.8	16,461.0	16,235.4	16,903.4	15,543.8	15,545.1	16,990.5
2008	13,731.3	13,547.8	12,602.9	13,357.7	13,995.3	14,084.6	13,168.9	12,989.4	12,123.5	9,117.0	8,531.5	8,463.6	12,142.8
2009	8,331.5	7,694.8	7,764.6	8,768.0	9,304.4	9,810.3	9,691.1	10,430.4	10,302.9	10,066.2	9,641.0	10,169.0	9,331.2
2010	10,661.6	10,175.1	10,671.5	11,139.8	10,104.0	9,786.1	9,456.8	9,268.2	9,346.7	9,455.1	9,797.2	10,254.5	10,009.7
2011	10,449.5	10,622.3	9,852.5	9,644.6	9,650.8	9,541.5	9,996.7	9,072.9	8,695.4	8,733.6	8,506.1	8,506.0	9,439.3
2012	8,616.7	9,242.3	9,962.4	9,627.4	8,842.5	8,638.1	8,760.7	8,949.9	8,948.6	8,827.4	9,059.9	9,814.4	9,107.5
2013	10,750.9	11,327.3	12,254.7	13,224.1	14,494.3	13,106.6	14,317.5	13,726.7	14,372.1	14,329.0	14,931.7	15,655.2	13,540.8
2014	15,578.3	14,617.6	14,694.8	14,475.3	14,343.2	15,131.8	15,379.3	15,358.7	15,948.5	15,394.1	17,179.0	17,541.7	15,470.2
2015	17,274.4	18,053.2	19,197.6	19,767.9	19,974.2	20,403.8	20,372.6	19,919.1	17,944.2	18,374.1	19,581.8	19,202.6	19,172.1

Source: Singapore Exchange

Sugar

The white crystalline substance called "sugar" is the organic chemical compound sucrose, one of several related compounds all known as sugars. These include glucose, dextrose, fructose, and lactose. All sugars are members of the larger group of compounds called carbohydrates and are characterized by a sweet taste. Sucrose is considered a double sugar because it is composed of one molecule of glucose and one molecule of fructose. While sucrose is common in many plants, it occurs in the highest concentration in sugarcane (Saccharum officinarum) and sugar beets (Beta vulgaris). Sugarcane is about 7 to 18 percent sugar by weight while sugar beets are 8 to 22 percent.

Sugarcane is a member of the grass family and is a perennial. Sugarcane is cultivated in tropical and subtropical regions around the world roughly between the Tropics of Cancer and Capricorn. It grows best in hot, wet climates where there is heavy rainfall followed by a dry season. The largest cane producers are Florida, Louisiana, Texas, and Hawaii. On a commercial basis, sugarcane is not grown from seeds but from cuttings or pieces of the stalk.

Sugar beets, which are produced in temperate or colder climates, are annuals grown from seeds. Sugar beets do best with moderate temperatures and evenly distributed rainfall. The beets are planted in the spring and harvested in the fall. The sugar is contained in the root of the beet, but the sugars from beets and cane are identical. Sugar beet production takes place mostly in Europe, the U.S., China, and Japan. The largest sugar beet producing states are Minnesota, Idaho, North Dakota, and Michigan. Sugar beets are refined to yield white sugar and very little raw sugar is produced.

Sugar beets and sugarcane are produced in over 100 countries around the world. Of all the sugar produced, about 25% is processed from sugar beets and the remaining 75% is from sugar cane. The trend has been that production of sugar from cane is increasing relative to that produced from beets. The significance of this in that sugarcane is a perennial plant while the sugar beet is an annual, and due to the longer production cycle, sugarcane production and the sugar processed from that cane, may not be quite as responsive to changes in price.

Sugar futures are traded at the ICE Futures U.S., the Bolsa de Mercadorias & Futuros (BM&F), Kansai Commodities Exchange (KANEX), the Tokyo Grain Exchange (TGE), and the London International Financial Futures and Options Exchange (LIFFE).

Raw sugar is traded on the ICE exchange while white sugar is traded on the London International Financial Futures Exchange (LIFFE). The most actively traded contract is the No. 11 (World) sugar contract at the ICE exchange. The No. 11 contract calls for the delivery of 112,000 pounds (50 long tons) of raw cane centrifugal sugar from any of 28 foreign countries of origin and the United States. The ICE exchange also trades the No. 14 sugar contract (Domestic), which calls for the delivery of raw centrifugal cane sugar in the United States. Futures on white sugar are traded on the London International Financial Futures Exchange and call for the delivery of 50 metric tons of white beet sugar, cane crystal sugar, or refined sugar of any origin from the crop current at the time of delivery.

Prices – ICE World No. 11 Sugar prices on the nearest-futures chart (Barchart.com symbol SB) posted their high for 2015 in January at 16.16 cents per pound. Sugar prices rallied in January after Brazil, the world's biggest sugar producer, raised taxes on gasoline and diesel fuel, which fueled speculation that Brazil's sugar producers would divert more of their sugar-cane crop to ethanol production. Gains in sugar were fleeting, though, as prices trended lower into Q3-2015 when they sank to a 7-1/2 year low in August at 10.13 cents per pound. Sugar prices were hammered by weakness in the Brazilian real which plunged to a record low against the dollar and gave incentive to Brazil's sugar producers to boost more profitable sugar exports. Also, the sell-off in crude oil in 2015 to a 6-3/4 year low undercut ethanol prices, which may curb ethanol production and boost sugar supplies. The International Sugar Organization (ISO) projected 2014/15 global sugar production a record 173.634 MMT with a 2014/15 global sugar surplus of 2.215 MMT. Sugar prices rallied in Q4-2015 and recovered the year's losses after India, the world's second-biggest sugar producer, said a lack of monsoon rains may curb its 2015/16 sugar production by -14.5% y/y to a 6-year low of 23.08 MMT. The ISO then said a projected 2015/16 global sugar deficit of -3.53 MMT, the first deficit in 5 years, may expand to a deficit of -6.2 MMT in 2016/17. Sugar prices finished 2015 up +5% at 15.24 cents per pound.

Supply – World production of centrifugal (raw) sugar in the 2014-15 marketing year (Oct 1 to Sep 30) fell -1.5% to 172.458 million metric tons, below the 2012-13 record high of 177.557 million metric tons. The world's largest sugar producers in 2014-15 were Brazil with 20.8% of world production, India with 15.8%, and the European Union with 9.5%. U.S. centrifugal sugar production in 2014-15 rose +0.1% to 7.677 million metric tons. World ending stocks in 2014-15 fell -3.2% to 42.215 million metric tons. The stocks/consumption ratio fell -5.3% in 2014-15 to 24,700 metric tons. U.S. production of cane sugar in 2014-15 rose +2.1% to 3.740 million short tons and beet sugar production rose +1.6% yr/yr to 4.870 million short tons.

Demand – World domestic consumption of centrifugal (raw) sugar in 2014-15 rose by +2.2% yr/yr to a new record high of 170.996 million metric tons. U.S. domestic disappearance (consumption) of sugar in 2014-15 rose by +2.5% yr/yr to 12.244 million short tons. U.S. per capita sugar consumption in 2013-14 (latest data) rose +2.0% to 67.90 pounds per year, which was only about two-thirds of the levels seen in the early 1970s.

Trade – World exports of centrifugal sugar in 2014-15 fell -6.5% yr/yr to 53.697 million metric tons, below last year's record high of 57.437. The world's largest sugar exporter was Brazil, where exports in 2014-15 fell -8.4% yr/yr to 24.000 million metric tons, which accounted for 44.7% of total world exports. The next largest exporters are Thailand with 15.8% of world exports and Australia with 6.5%. U.S. sugar exports in 2014-15 fell -18.4% yr/yr to 250,000 short tons, which is down from the 15-year high of 422,000 seen in 2006-07. U.S. sugar imports in 2014-15 fell -6.3% yr/yr to 3.149 million short tons, down from the decade high of 3.355 in 2010-11.

World Production, Supply & Stocks/Consumption Ratio of Sugar   In 1000's of Metric Tons (Raw Value)

Marketing Year	Beginning Stocks	Production	Imports	Total Supply	Exports	Domestic Consumption	Ending Stocks	Stocks As a % of Consumption
2006-07	30,474	164,278	44,142	238,894	50,759	149,367	36,736	24.6
2007-08	36,736	163,257	44,959	244,952	50,625	150,876	43,080	28.6
2008-09	43,080	143,833	42,333	229,246	44,962	153,847	29,836	19.4
2009-10	29,836	153,184	48,261	231,276	48,327	154,142	28,028	18.2
2010-11	28,028	162,221	49,119	239,384	53,939	155,403	29,526	19.0
2011-12	29,491	172,371	48,568	250,211	55,026	159,365	35,288	22.1
2012-13	35,183	177,624	51,990	263,848	55,525	164,920	42,631	25.8
2013-14[1]	42,492	175,558	51,178	269,495	57,650	166,724	44,031	26.4
2014-15[2]	43,845	175,103	50,410	269,890	54,126	170,600	44,281	26.0
2015-16[3]	43,558	172,146	52,161	270,553	54,695	173,413	40,529	23.4

[1] Preliminary.   [2] Estimate.   [3] Forecast.   *Source: Foreign Agricultural Service, U.S. Department of Agriculture (FAS-USDA)*

World Production of Sugar (Centrifugal Sugar-Raw Value)   In Thousands of Metric Tons

Year	Australia	Brazil	China	Cuba	European Union	India	Indonesia	Mexico	Pakistan	Thailand	United States	Ukraine	World Total
2006-07	5,212	31,450	12,855	1,200	17,987	30,780	1,900	5,633	3,615	6,720	2,850	7,662	164,278
2007-08	4,939	31,600	15,898	1,420	15,834	28,630	2,000	5,852	4,163	7,820	2,020	7,396	163,257
2008-09	4,814	31,850	13,317	1,340	14,290	15,950	2,053	5,260	3,512	7,200	1,710	6,833	143,833
2009-10	4,700	36,400	11,429	1,250	16,897	20,637	1,910	5,115	3,420	6,930	1,382	7,224	153,184
2010-11	3,700	38,350	11,199	1,150	15,939	26,574	1,770	5,495	3,920	9,663	1,540	7,104	162,221
2011-12	3,683	36,150	12,341	1,400	18,320	28,620	1,830	5,351	4,520	10,235	2,300	7,700	172,371
2012-13	4,250	38,600	14,001	1,600	16,655	27,337	2,300	7,393	5,000	10,024	2,400	8,148	177,624
2013-14[1]	4,380	37,800	14,263	1,650	16,020	26,605	2,300	6,382	5,630	11,333	1,196	7,676	175,558
2014-15[2]	4,700	35,950	11,000	1,850	16,750	30,240	2,100	6,344	5,230	10,790	2,135	7,845	175,103
2015-16[3]	5,000	35,000	10,580	1,850	16,100	28,530	2,250	6,419	5,430	10,800	1,445	7,992	172,146

[1] Preliminary.   [2] Estimate.   [3] Forecast.   *Source: Foreign Agricultural Service, U.S. Department of Agriculture (FAS-USDA)*

World Stocks of Centrifugal Sugar at Beginning of Marketing Year   In Thousands of Metric Tons (Raw Value)

Year	Australia	Brazil	China	Cuba	European Union	India	Indonesia	Iran	Mexico	Philippines	Russia	United States	World Total
2006-07	291	-285	703	225	5,088	4,000	1,170	932	1,294	253	470	1,540	30,474
2007-08	402	-485	1,401	155	2,720	11,701	570	1,292	1,718	262	440	1,632	36,736
2008-09	400	215	3,965	135	3,130	12,296	590	1,362	1,975	547	550	1,510	43,080
2009-10	487	-1,135	3,784	102	2,232	5,880	340	475	623	581	481	1,392	29,836
2010-11	413	-835	2,355	114	1,433	6,223	750	475	973	730	399	1,359	28,028
2011-12	193	260	1,621	59	1,974	6,299	602	650	806	934	350	1,250	29,491
2012-13	64	260	4,140	109	3,303	7,163	409	640	1,024	932	390	1,795	35,183
2013-14[1]	83	10	6,793	170	3,836	9,373	879	700	1,548	942	395	1,958	42,492
2014-15[2]	111	350	8,832	150	3,066	8,227	1,299	750	881	1,032	370	1,642	43,845
2015-16[3]	140	850	7,287	200	2,106	9,947	949	400	860	1,017	100	1,603	43,558

[1] Preliminary.   [2] Estimate.   [3] Forecast.   *Source: Foreign Agricultural Service, U.S. Department of Agriculture (FAS-USDA)*

Centrifugal Sugar (Raw Value) Imported into Selected Countries   In Thousands of Metric Tons

Year	Algeria	Canada	China	European Union	Indonesia	Iran	Japan	Korea, South	Malaysia	Nigeria	Russia	United States	World Total
2006-07	1,110	1,161	1,465	3,530	1,800	1,600	1,432	1,475	1,670	1,240	2,950	1,887	44,142
2007-08	1,105	1,445	972	2,948	2,420	1,200	1,477	1,805	1,425	1,485	3,100	2,377	44,959
2008-09	1,159	1,255	1,077	3,180	2,197	973	1,279	1,687	1,504	1,175	2,150	2,796	42,333
2009-10	1,260	1,114	1,535	2,561	3,200	1,643	1,199	1,617	1,537	1,431	2,223	3,010	48,261
2010-11	1,193	1,135	2,143	3,755	3,082	1,292	1,199	1,688	1,813	1,495	2,510	3,391	49,119
2011-12	1,594	1,103	4,430	3,552	3,027	1,079	1,301	1,668	1,721	1,399	510	3,294	48,568
2012-13	2,014	1,156	3,802	3,790	3,570	1,553	1,246	1,806	1,966	1,450	735	2,925	51,990
2013-14[1]	1,854	1,031	4,275	3,262	3,570	1,629	1,369	1,909	1,897	1,470	1,020	3,395	51,178
2014-15[2]	1,844	1,162	5,058	2,600	3,050	264	1,368	1,881	2,063	1,465	1,100	3,238	50,410
2015-16[3]	1,850	1,130	5,500	2,800	3,200	1,425	1,250	1,890	2,100	1,470	1,150	3,083	52,161

[1] Preliminary.   [2] Estimate.   [3] Forecast.   *Source: Foreign Agricultural Service, U.S. Department of Agriculture (FAS-USDA)*

SUGAR

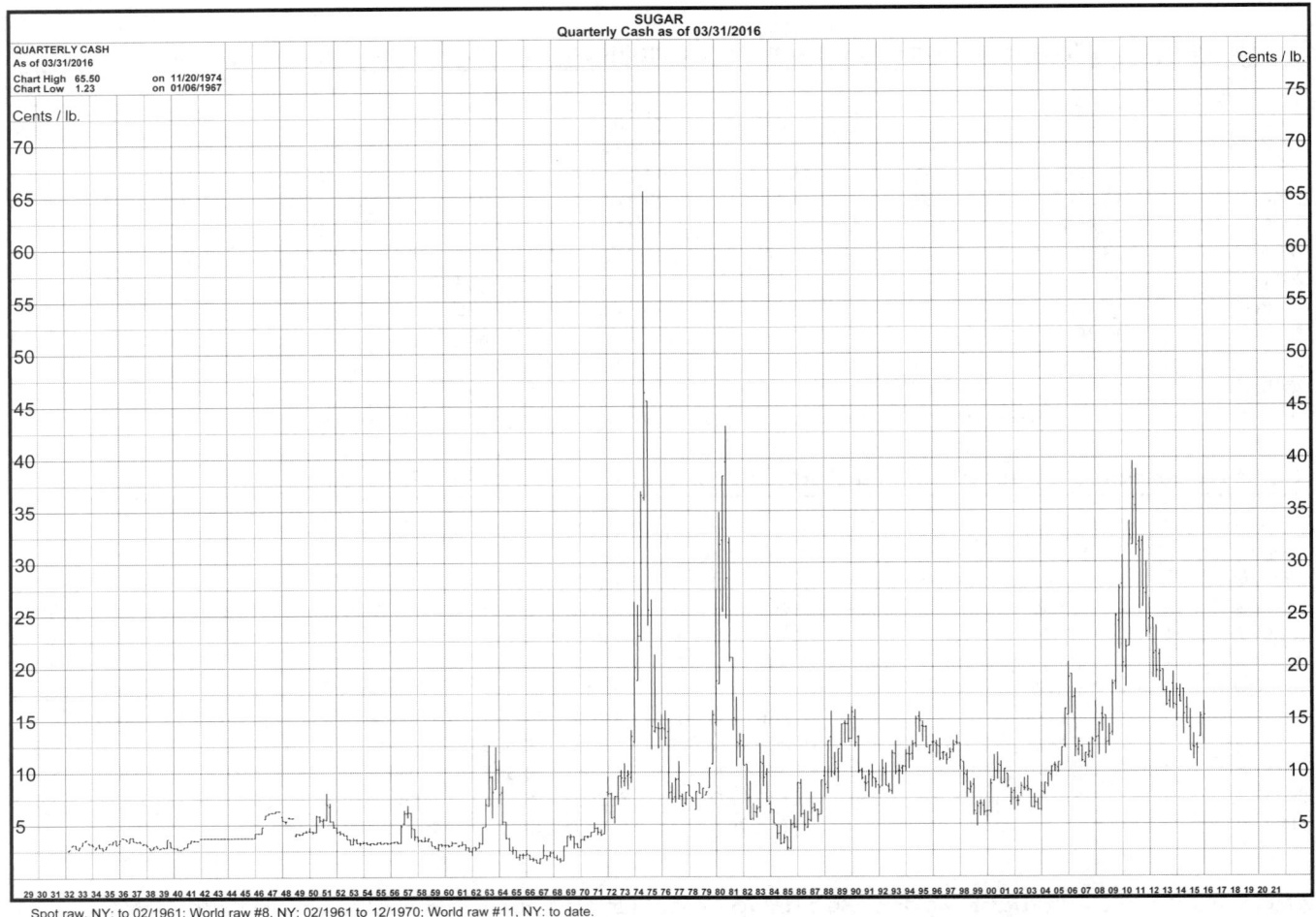

SUGAR
Quarterly Cash as of 03/31/2016

QUARTERLY CASH
As of 03/31/2016

Chart High 65.50 on 11/20/1974
Chart Low   1.23   on 01/06/1967

Cents / lb.

Spot raw, NY: to 02/1961; World raw #8, NY: 02/1961 to 12/1970; World raw #11, NY: to date.

Centrifugal Sugar (Raw Value) Exported From Selected Countries   In Thousands of Metric Tons

Year	Australia	Brazil	Colom-bia	Cuba	Dominican Republic	European Union	Guate-mala	India	Mauritius	South Africa	Swazi-land	Thailand	World Total
2006-07	3,860	20,850	942	795	225	2,439	1,500	2,680	510	1,267	358	4,705	50,759
2007-08	3,700	19,500	661	960	217	1,656	1,333	6,014	443	1,154	350	4,914	50,625
2008-09	3,522	21,550	585	727	239	1,332	1,654	224	455	1,230	350	5,295	44,962
2009-10	3,600	24,300	870	538	261	2,647	1,815	225	271	754	350	4,930	48,327
2010-11	2,750	25,800	830	577	204	1,113	1,544	3,903	338	400	320	6,642	53,939
2011-12	2,800	24,650	876	830	211	2,343	1,619	3,764	370	271	315	7,898	55,026
2012-13	3,100	27,650	542	775	165	1,662	1,911	1,261	384	356	353	6,693	55,525
2013-14[1]	3,242	26,200	900	992	208	1,552	2,100	2,806	406	868	412	7,200	57,650
2014-15[2]	3,561	23,950	845	880	185	1,610	2,200	2,425	416	772	493	8,000	54,126
2015-16[3]	3,650	23,750	790	900	185	1,500	2,350	2,500	420	490	500	8,800	54,695

[1] Preliminary.   [2] Estimate.   [3] Forecast.   Source: Foreign Agricultural Service, U.S. Department of Agriculture (FAS-USDA)

Average Wholesale Price of Refined Beet Sugar[2]--Midwest Market   In Cents Per Pound

Year	Jan.	Feb.	Mar.	Apr.	May	June	July	Aug.	Sept.	Oct.	Nov.	Dec.	Average
2006	34.50	36.50	37.10	36.38	35.00	35.00	35.00	34.50	31.20	28.75	27.19	26.10	33.10
2007	25.50	25.00	24.90	25.00	25.00	25.00	25.38	25.60	25.38	25.00	24.50	24.50	25.06
2008	24.13	26.40	28.00	28.00	29.60	33.25	38.00	38.40	38.50	36.20	35.00	35.00	32.54
2009	35.00	35.00	35.00	34.25	34.40	35.50	35.40	38.00	42.00	42.60	45.00	45.00	38.10
2010	50.50	53.00	52.25	48.20	45.00	50.00	53.40	59.50	59.00	54.40	56.50	57.00	53.23
2011	54.50	54.00	56.50	56.80	54.00	55.00	55.40	57.00	58.60	59.00	58.75	55.10	56.22
2012	51.75	51.00	51.00	50.25	47.81	45.00	42.00	41.20	38.25	36.00	34.60	31.75	43.38
2013	30.50	28.50	27.60	26.63	26.30	26.50	26.00	25.50	26.25	27.38	28.00	27.50	27.22
2014	26.50	26.25	26.50	29.75	31.60	35.00	36.00	36.60	37.50	36.60	36.00	36.00	32.86
2015[1]	36.00	35.25	35.13	35.50	34.30	34.00	33.80	33.13	33.00	32.40	32.00	32.00	33.88

[1] Preliminary.   [2] These are f.o.b. basis prices in bulk, not delivered prices.   Source: Economic Research Service, U.S. Department of Agriculture (ERS-)

Average Price of World Raw Sugar[1]   In Cents Per Pound

Year	Jan.	Feb.	Mar.	Apr.	May	June	July	Aug.	Sept.	Oct.	Nov.	Dec.	Average
2006	17.27	18.93	18.01	18.21	17.83	16.19	16.61	13.58	12.42	12.09	12.38	12.47	15.50
2007	11.85	11.63	11.44	10.85	10.78	11.05	12.18	11.66	11.61	11.86	11.83	12.47	11.60
2008	13.75	15.16	14.60	13.68	12.23	13.29	14.90	15.58	14.74	12.99	12.87	12.31	13.84
2009	13.09	13.90	13.83	14.43	16.89	16.94	18.57	22.37	23.11	23.22	22.96	25.28	18.72
2010	28.94	27.29	21.36	19.87	19.59	21.24	23.42	25.09	31.19	34.80	35.44	36.10	27.03
2011	36.11	35.01	33.22	29.35	26.64	29.75	30.51	28.87	27.71	26.30	24.52	23.42	29.28
2012	24.05	25.81	24.73	22.98	20.25	20.44	22.76	20.53	19.47	20.39	19.31	19.50	21.69
2013	18.37	18.28	18.33	17.71	17.08	16.79	16.38	16.44	17.33	18.81	17.58	16.41	17.46
2014	15.42	16.28	17.58	17.01	17.50	17.22	17.18	15.89	14.60	16.48	15.89	14.99	16.34
2015[1]	15.06	14.52	12.84	12.93	12.70	11.75	11.88	10.67	11.32	14.14	14.89	15.00	13.14

[1] Contract No. 11, f.o.b. stowed Caribbean port, including Brazil, bulk spot price.   [2] Preliminary.   *Source: Economic Research Service, U.S. Department of Agriculture (ERS-USDA)*

Average Price of Raw Sugar in New York (C.I.F., Duty/Free Paid, Contract #12 & #14)   In Cents Per Pound

Year	Jan.	Feb.	Mar.	Apr.	May	June	July	Aug.	Sept.	Oct.	Nov.	Dec.	Average
2006	23.61	24.05	23.10	23.56	23.48	23.32	22.44	21.38	21.27	20.22	19.66	19.59	22.14
2007	20.03	20.59	20.85	20.91	21.27	21.33	22.72	21.80	21.42	20.56	20.25	20.12	20.99
2008	20.24	20.21	20.65	20.54	20.83	21.80	23.76	23.15	23.10	21.46	19.83	20.00	21.30
2009	20.15	19.83	19.75	21.58	21.64	22.47	23.02	26.18	28.91	30.48	31.86	33.30	24.93
2010	39.36	40.13	35.11	30.86	30.89	32.73	33.66	34.24	38.17	39.30	38.84	38.35	35.97
2011	38.46	39.69	39.65	38.32	35.04	35.65	37.93	40.16	40.15	38.19	37.92	36.32	38.12
2012	34.69	33.57	34.94	31.87	30.20	28.89	28.68	28.84	26.27	23.89	22.52	22.41	28.90
2013	21.20	20.72	20.82	20.38	19.51	19.31	19.22	20.97	21.05	21.82	20.61	19.95	20.46
2014	20.27	21.65	22.03	24.33	24.66	25.65	24.78	25.64	25.36	26.41	24.26	24.81	24.15
2015[1]	25.24	24.62	24.07	24.39	24.61	24.76	24.67	24.50	24.21	25.04	26.63	25.83	24.88

[1] Preliminary.   *Source: Economic Research Service, U.S. Department of Agriculture (ERS-USDA)*

Supply and Utilization of Sugar (Cane and Beet) in the United States   In Thousands of Short Tons (Raw Value)

Year	Production Cane	Production Beet	Production Total	Offshore Receipts Foreign	Offshore Receipts Territories	Offshore Receipts Total	Beginning Stocks	Total Supply	Total Use	Exports	Net Changes in Invisible Stocks	Refining Loss Adjustment	Domestic Disappearance In Polyhydric Alcohol[4]	Domestic Disappearance Total	Per Capita Pounds
2006-07	3,438	5,008	8,445	2,080	0	2,080	1,698	12,223	10,424	422	-132	0	53	10,135	62.2
2007-08	3,431	4,721	8,152	2,620	0	2,620	1,799	12,571	10,907	203	0	0	61	10,704	61.2
2008-09	3,317	4,214	7,531	3,082	0	3,082	1,664	12,277	10,743	136	0	0	46	10,607	65.1
2009-10	3,387	4,575	7,963	3,320	0	3,320	1,534	12,817	11,319	211	-45	0	35	11,152	63.4
2010-11	3,172	4,659	7,831	3,738	0	3,738	1,498	13,067	11,689	248	19	0	33	11,422	66.0
2011-12	3,588	4,900	8,488	3,632	0	3,632	1,378	13,498	11,519	269	-64	0	33	11,313	65.9
2012-13	3,905	5,076	8,981	3,224	0	3,224	1,979	14,185	12,027	274	-23	0	185	11,776	66.6
2013-14[1]	3,667	4,794	8,462	3,742	0	3,742	2,158	14,362	12,552	306	0	0	346	12,246	68.0
2014-15[2]	3,763	4,825	8,588	3,544	0	3,544	1,810	13,941	12,244	180	0	0	29	12,064	68.4
2015-16[3]	3,685	5,075	8,760	3,398	0	3,398	1,697	13,856	12,120	200	0	0	35	11,920	

[1] Preliminary.   [2] Estimate.   [3] Forecast.   [4] Includes feed use.   *Source: Economic Research Service, U.S. Department of Agriculture (ERS-USDA)*

Sugar Cane for Sugar & Seed and Production of Cane Sugar and Molasses in the United States

Year	Acreage Harvested (1,000 Acres)	Yield of Cane Per Harvested Acre Net Tons	Production for Sugar (1,000 Tons)	Production for Seed (1,000 Tons)	Production Total (1,000 Tons)	Sugar Yield Per Acre (Short Tons)	Farm Price ($ Per Ton)	Farm Value of Cane Used for Sugar (1,000 Dollars)	Farm Value of Cane Used for Sugar & Seed (1,000 Dollars)	Sugar Production Raw Value Total (1,000 Tons)	Sugar Production Raw Value Per Ton of Cane (In Lbs.)	Refined Basis (1,000 Tons)	Molasses Made Edible (1,000 Gallons)	Molasses Made Total[3] (1,000 Gallons)
2006	897.7	32.9	27,962	1,602	29,564	4.05	30.4	849,157	897,601	3,429	----	----	----	----
2007	879.6	34.1	28,273	1,696	29,969	4.17	29.4	831,218	880,616	3,454	----	----	----	----
2008	868.0	31.8	26,131	1,472	27,603	4.03	29.5	771,134	814,479	3,311	----	----	----	----
2009	873.9	34.8	28,484	1,938	30,432	4.16	34.8	991,424	1,056,613	3,395	----	----	----	----
2010	877.5	31.2	25,663	1,697	27,360	3.83	41.7	1,069,537	1,140,636	3,161	----	----	----	----
2011	872.6	33.5	27,738	1,486	29,224	4.35	47.2	1,308,951	1,379,498	3,599	----	----	----	----
2012	902.4	35.7	30,500	1,727	32,227	4.56	41.9	1,276,631	1,348,361	3,898	----	----	----	----
2013	910.8	33.8	29,023	1,738	30,761	4.50	31.4	910,377	962,807	3,853	----	----	----	----
2014[1]	868.5	35.0	28,895	1,529	30,424		35.7		1,054,657		----	----	----	----
2015[2]	891.7	37.3	31,663	1,581	33,244						----	----	----	----

[1] Preliminary.   [2] Estimate.   [3] Excludes edible molasses.   *Source: Economic Research Service, U.S. Department of Agriculture (ERS-USDA)*

SUGAR

U.S. Sugar Beets, Beet Sugar, Pulp & Molasses Produced from Sugar Beets and Raw Sugar Spot Prices

Year of Harvest	Acreage Planted (1,000 Acres)	Acreage Harvested (1,000 Acres)	Yield Per Harvested Acre (Sh. Tons)	Pro-duction (1,000 Tons)	Sugar Yield Per Acre (Sh. Tons)	Price[3] (Dollars)	Farm Value (1,000 $)	Sugar Production Equiv-alent Raw Value[4] (1,000 Short Tons)	Refined Basis (1,000 Short Tons)	Raw Sugar Prices World[5] Refined #5 (Cents Per Pound)	CSCE #11 World (Cents Per Pound)	N.Y. Duty Paid (Cents Per Pound)	Wholesale List Price HFCS (42%) Midwest
2006	1,366	1,304	26.1	34,064	3.84	44.20	1,506,985	5,008	----	19.01	15.50	22.14	19.35
2007	1,269	1,247	25.5	31,834	3.79	42.00	1,337,173	4,721	----	14.00	11.60	20.99	23.41
2008	1,091	1,005	26.8	26,881	4.15	48.00	1,294,144	4,166	----	15.96	13.84	21.30	27.57
2009	1,186	1,149	25.9	29,783	3.98	51.50	1,532,634	4,575	----	22.13	18.72	24.93	31.51
2010	1,172	1,156	27.7	32,034	4.03	66.90	2,142,162	4,659	----	27.78	27.03	35.97	26.56
2011	1,233	1,213	23.8	28,896	4.04	69.40	2,004,116	4,900	----	31.68	29.28	38.12	30.11
2012	1,230	1,204	29.3	35,224	4.22	66.40	2,338,789	5,076	----	26.50	21.69	28.90	32.92
2013	1,198	1,154	28.4	32,789	4.15	46.90	1,526,821	4,794	----	22.17	17.46	20.46	35.86
2014	1,163	1,146	27.3	31,285	4.27	43.30	1,437,575	4,893	----	20.05	16.34	24.15	29.96
2015[2]	1,159	1,144	30.8	35,278	4.38			5,016	----	16.94	13.14	24.88	32.75

[1] Preliminary. [2] Estimate. [3] Includes support payments, but excludes Gov't. sugar beet payments. [4] Refined sugar multiplied by factor of 1.07.
[5] F.O.B. Europe. *Source: Economic Research Service, U.S. Department of Agriculture (ERS-USDA)*

Sugar Deliveries and Stocks in the United States   In Thousands of Short Tons (Raw Value)

Year	Quota Allocation	Actual Imports	Deliveries by Primary Distributors Cane Sugar Refineries Deliveries	Beet Sugar Factories Deliveries	Importers of Direct Con-sumption Sugar	Mainland Cane Sugar Mills[3]	Total Deliveries	Total Domestic Con-sumption	Stocks, Jan. 1 Cane Sugar Re-fineries	Beet Sugar Factories	CCC	Refiners' Raw	Mainland Cane Mills	Total
2006	----	----	5,230	4,195	577	----	10,002	10,162	328	1,429	0	217	1,382	3,357
2007	----	----	5,123	4,707	116	----	9,946	10,173	452	1,792	0	358	1,437	4,039
2008	----	----	5,075	4,867	773	----	10,715	10,900	400	1,806	0	304	1,500	4,009
2009	----	----	5,493	4,324	667	----	10,485	10,657	440	1,464	0	468	1,612	3,984
2010	----	----	5,635	4,514	843	----	10,992	11,231	484	1,456	0	346	1,274	3,559
2011	----	----	5,572	4,552	995	----	11,118	11,370	466	1,691	0	257	1,455	3,869
2012	----	----	5,648	4,633	977	----	11,257	11,405	315	1,597	0	498	1,370	3,780
2013	----	----	5,849	4,777	949	----	11,575	12,124	388	2,013	0	574	1,646	4,621
2014[1]	----	----	6,069	4,875	760	----	11,704	11,831	572	1,603	0	592	1,714	4,481
2015[2]	----	----	6,285	4,617	1,033	----	11,935		351	1,589	0	556	1,634	4,130

[1] Preliminary. [2] Estimate. [3] Sugar for direct consumption only. [4] Refined. *Source: Economic Research Service,*
U.S. Department of Agriculture (ERS-USDA)

Sugar, Refined--Deliveries to End User in the United States   In Thousands of Short Tons

Year	Bakery & Cereal Products	Bev-erages	Confec-tionery[2]	Hotels, Restar. & Insti-tutions	Ice Cream & Dairy Products	Canned, Bottled & Frozen Foods	All Other Food Uses	Retail Grocers[3]	Wholesale Grocers[4]	Non-food Uses	Non-Industrial Uses	Industrial Uses	Total Deliveries
2006	2,231	228	1,069	88	553	335	535	1,204	2,389	107	3,864	5,057	8,922
2007	2,399	312	1,110	74	609	360	569	1,211	2,411	102	3,888	5,460	9,348
2008	2,312	341	1,108	115	612	427	676	1,212	2,317	97	3,835	5,572	9,407
2009	2,286	351	1,085	127	587	427	573	1,241	2,360	84	3,907	5,393	9,300
2010	2,400	422	1,070	124	583	391	609	1,270	2,471	111	4,079	5,587	9,666
2011	2,324	404	1,048	120	622	411	625	1,239	2,511	128	4,104	5,562	9,665
2012	2,330	486	1,044	130	674	412	687	1,172	2,374	123	3,959	5,755	9,715
2013	2,296	547	1,149	112	678	399	760	1,109	2,427	117	4,040	5,947	9,987
2014	2,435	598	1,142	118	756	434	853	1,193	2,151	118	3,965	6,336	10,300
2015[1]	2,391	755	1,172	103	764	473	791	1,230	2,086	162	3,818	6,509	10,189

[1] Preliminary. [2] And related products. [3] Chain stores, supermarkets. [4] Jobbers, sugar dealers.
Source: Economic Research Service, U.S. Department of Agriculture (ERS-USDA)

Deliveries[1] of All Sugar by Primary Distributors in the United States, by Quarters   In Thousands of Short Tons

Year	First Quarter	Second Quarter	Third Quarter	Fourth Quarter	Total	Year	First Quarter	Second Quarter	Third Quarter	Fourth Quarter	Total
2004	2,324	2,419	2,572	2,586	9,901	2010	2,565	2,759	3,074	2,833	11,231
2005	2,370	2,521	2,711	2,609	10,212	2011	2,649	2,809	3,131	2,781	11,370
2006	2,474	2,522	2,734	2,432	10,162	2012	2,663	2,915	2,954	2,873	11,405
2007	2,364	2,604	2,735	2,471	10,173	2013	2,720	2,954	3,014	3,229	11,916
2008	2,532	2,728	2,865	2,775	10,900	2014	2,742	3,053	3,189	2,847	11,831
2009	2,431	2,649	2,823	2,754	10,657	2015[2]	2,861	3,070	3,274	2,863	12,068

[1] Includes for domestic consumption and for export. [2] Preliminary. *Source: Economic Research Service, U.S. Department of Agriculture (ERS-USDA)*

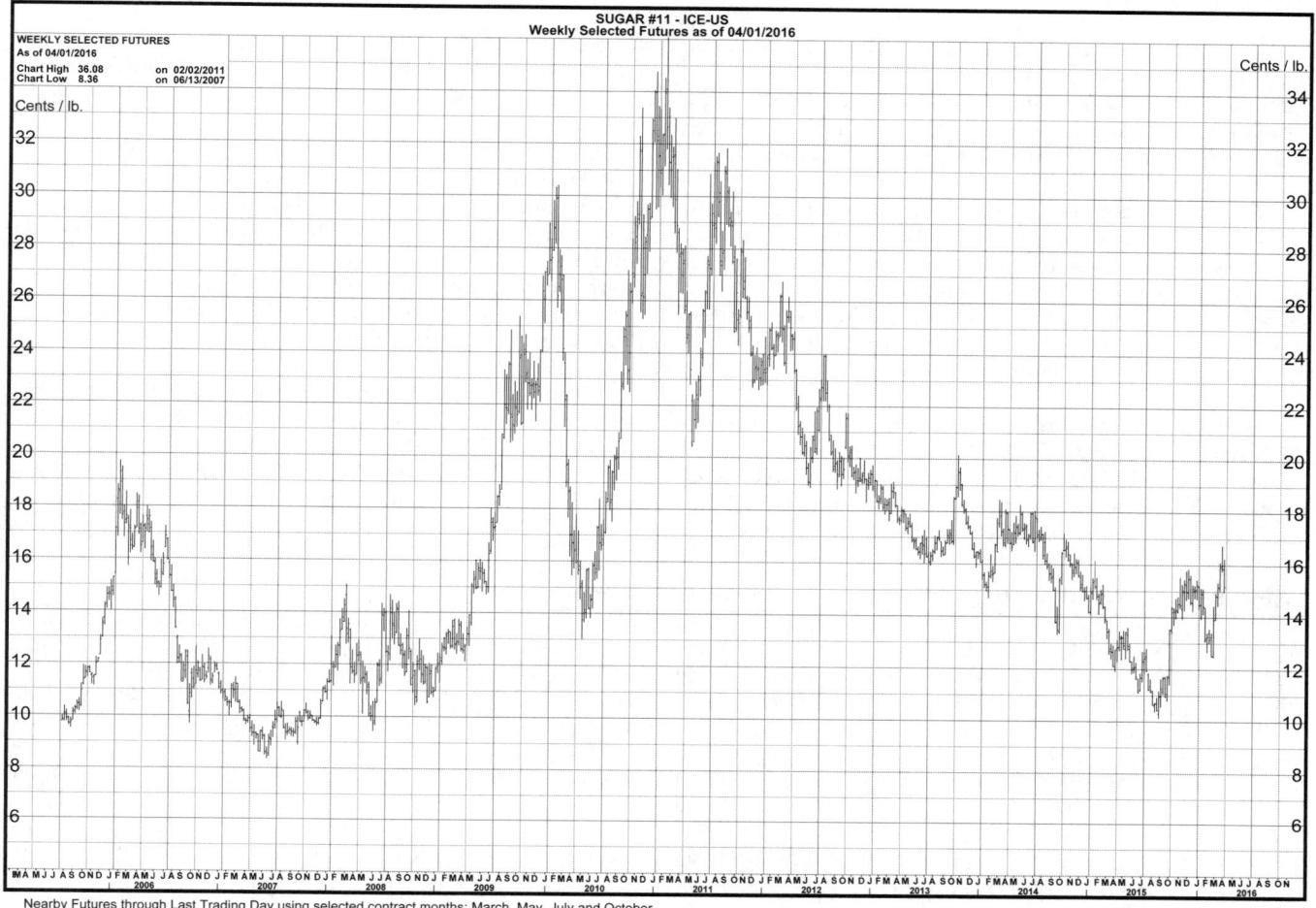

SUGAR #11 - ICE-US
Weekly Selected Futures as of 04/01/2016

WEEKLY SELECTED FUTURES
As of 04/01/2016
Chart High 36.08 on 02/02/2011
Chart Low 8.36 on 06/13/2007

Nearby Futures through Last Trading Day using selected contract months: March, May, July and October.

Volume of Trading of World Sugar #11 Futures in New York   In Thousands of Contracts

Year	Jan.	Feb.	Mar.	Apr.	May	June	July	Aug.	Sept.	Oct.	Nov.	Dec.	Total
2006	1,444.2	1,601.2	1,092.2	1,467.4	1,147.7	1,459.1	825.0	1,278.6	1,746.7	1,095.7	918.7	1,024.0	15,101
2007	1,322.9	2,189.7	1,659.6	2,023.2	1,819.5	2,679.8	1,559.7	1,326.6	2,175.7	1,565.3	1,452.1	1,489.7	21,264
2008	3,566.7	3,280.8	2,237.7	2,889.5	1,941.8	3,067.4	1,820.2	1,721.4	2,540.9	1,629.9	1,085.5	1,238.1	27,020
2009	1,624.6	2,040.3	1,867.0	2,995.5	2,229.3	3,359.1	1,741.5	2,833.2	3,219.5	1,824.3	1,576.4	1,989.5	27,300
2010	2,348.9	2,986.5	2,772.9	2,754.5	1,730.0	2,936.0	1,840.3	2,184.6	3,366.7	1,978.1	2,629.3	1,524.7	29,053
2011	2,180.8	3,341.9	1,774.8	2,338.8	1,832.4	3,266.1	1,702.0	1,986.6	2,555.9	1,258.7	1,286.7	1,104.7	24,629
2012	1,999.3	2,765.1	2,316.0	2,765.4	1,941.5	3,460.7	2,251.7	2,049.8	2,736.2	1,781.4	1,633.1	1,426.4	27,127
2013	2,368.0	3,038.0	2,039.9	3,086.2	1,908.9	3,974.1	2,037.0	2,117.1	3,791.9	2,279.9	1,559.9	1,612.7	29,814
2014	2,461.6	4,157.3	2,477.4	2,857.3	1,906.5	3,370.3	1,981.4	1,853.3	3,657.9	1,651.3	1,574.3	1,448.0	29,397
2015	2,547.7	3,635.6	2,790.0	3,850.9	2,274.2	3,789.2	2,260.8	2,315.0	4,329.7	2,600.5	2,303.8	1,697.0	34,394

Contract size = 112,000 lbs.   Source: ICE Futures U.S. (ICE)

Average Open Interest of World Sugar #11 Futures in New York   In Contracts

Year	Jan.	Feb.	Mar.	Apr.	May	June	July	Aug.	Sept.	Oct.	Nov.	Dec.
2006	526,575	501,074	462,871	474,241	490,201	453,021	457,301	479,420	493,931	447,817	503,364	563,844
2007	632,783	695,426	652,346	686,648	738,708	695,249	674,318	667,523	656,128	681,403	763,910	835,526
2008	1,035,301	1,013,324	973,541	939,615	915,325	885,082	809,433	804,956	774,839	664,164	636,078	644,852
2009	664,303	656,033	644,829	681,177	703,355	764,799	735,556	838,638	821,646	770,085	772,808	813,238
2010	842,463	830,888	745,170	667,291	656,182	635,744	587,509	627,022	651,093	585,353	584,909	592,044
2011	619,904	648,027	597,384	613,301	583,047	627,566	630,027	598,737	544,893	489,135	495,699	533,588
2012	612,932	699,780	729,307	728,645	728,515	744,254	669,730	688,099	705,221	697,064	726,541	756,324
2013	796,708	824,203	804,682	852,113	846,873	901,021	848,276	878,813	870,124	818,823	803,346	810,753
2014	834,655	838,471	787,473	792,420	809,219	870,191	842,551	885,193	851,724	766,320	811,959	828,791
2015	824,778	848,192	862,965	876,247	853,458	885,602	805,457	837,922	790,609	766,704	838,992	861,944

Contract size = 112,000 lbs.   Source: ICE Futures U.S. (ICE)

Sulfur

Sulfur (atomic symbol S) is an odorless, tasteless, light yellow, nonmetallic element. As early as 2000 BC, Egyptians used sulfur compounds to bleach fabric. The Chinese used sulfur as an essential component when they developed gunpowder in the 13th century.

Sulfur is widely found in both its free and combined states. Free sulfur is found mixed with gypsum and pumice stone in volcanic regions. Sulfur dioxide is an air pollutant released from the combustion of fossil fuels. The most important use of sulfur is the production of sulfur compounds. Sulfur is used in skin ointments, matches, dyes, gunpowder, and phosphoric acid.

Supply – World production of all forms of sulfur in 2015 rose +0.1% yr/yr to 70.100 million metric tons, just below the record high of 70.500 million metric tons posted in 2011. The world's largest producers of sulfur are China with 15.7% of world production, the U.S. with 13.3%,

Russia with 10.4%, and Canada with 8.6%. U.S. production of sulfur in 2015 fell by -3.4% yr/yr to 9.300 million metric tons, still above the 2009 record low of 8.940 million metric tons.

Demand – U.S. consumption of all forms of sulfur was unchanged in 2015 at 11.000 million metric tons, well above the 4-decade low of 9.460 million metric tons seen in 2009. U.S. consumption of elemental sulfur in 2013 (latest data) rose +3.3% to 9.830 million metric tons. U.S. consumption of sulfuric acid in 2013 (latest data) rose by +7.8% yr/yr to 7.990 million metric tons.

Trade – U.S. exports of recovered sulfur in 2015 fell -20.0% yr/yr to 1.600 million metric tons, but still above the 25-year low of 635,000 metric tons in 2006. U.S. imports of recovered sulfur in 2015 fell by -7.2% yr/yr to 2.200 million metric tons, down from the 2011 record high of 3.270.

World Production of Sulfur (All Forms)   In Thousands of Metric Tons

Year	Canada	China	France	Germany	Kazakh-stan	Japan	Mexico	Poland	Russia	Saudi Arabia	Spain	United States	World Total
2008	8,156	8,610	650	4,167	3,334	2,030	1,740	1,280	6,450	3,163	637	9,300	68,800
2009	7,467	9,370	650	3,760	3,214	2,500	1,810	735	6,950	3,214	672	8,940	67,900
2010	7,260	9,600	650	3,713	3,292	2,700	1,790	1,020	6,950	3,200	675	9,110	68,100
2011	6,523	9,700	650	3,908	3,205	2,700	1,760	1,189	7,050	4,579	675	8,950	70,500
2012	6,183	9,900	650	3,818	3,247	2,700	1,810	1,229	7,250	4,092	257	9,000	68,100
2013	6,365	10,500	650	3,880	3,300	2,850	1,810	1,080	7,250	3,900	270	9,210	70,400
2014[1]	5,910	10,500	650	3,800	3,250	2,740	1,840	1,070	7,300	3,300	270	9,630	70,000
2015[2]	6,000	11,000		3,800	3,300	2,700	1,800	1,100	7,300	3,300		9,300	70,100

[1] Preliminary.   [2] Estimate.   *Source: U.S. Geological Survey (USGS)*

Salient Statistics of Sulfur in the United States   In Thousands of Metric Tons (Sulfur Content)

	Production of					By-product Sulfuric Acid[4]	Other Sulf. Acid Com-pounds	Imports Sulfuric Acid[4]	Exports Sulfuric Acid[4]	Producer Stocks, Dec. 31[5]	Apparent Con-sumption (All Forms)	Sales Value of Shipments F.O.B. Mine/Plant		
	Elemental Sulfur													
	Native - Sulfur[3]	Recovered			Total Elemental Sulfur							Frasch	Recovered	Average Total
Year	Frasch	Petroleum & Cole	Natural Gas	Total										
2008	----	7,240	1,300	8,550	753	----	9,300	3,440	261	208	12,900	----	----	264.04
2009	----	6,970	1,220	8,190	749	----	8,940	1,270	254	231	9,460	----	----	1.73
2010	----	7,140	1,170	8,320	791	----	9,110	2,110	215	166	11,300	----	----	70.16
2011	----	7,080	1,130	8,230	720	----	8,950	2,670	332	175	11,700	----	----	159.88
2012	----	7,370	1,040	8,410	586	----	9,000	2,850	161	132	11,000	----	----	123.54
2013	----	7,580	1,020	8,600	616	----	9,210	2,980	165	161	11,300	----	----	68.83
2014[1]	----	8,040	1,000	9,040	587	----	9,630	3,240	145	142	11,000	----	----	95.00
2015[2]	----	7,712	977	8,690	575	----	9,300			140	11,000	----	----	

[1] Preliminary.   [2] Estimate.   [3] Or sulfur ore; Withheld included in natural gas.   [4] Basis 100% H2SO4, sulfur equivalent.   [5] Frasch & recovered.
W = Withheld proprietary data.   Source: U.S. Geological Survey (USGS)

Sulfur Consumption & Foreign Trade of the United States   In Thousands of Metric Tons (Sulfur Content)

	Consumption			Sulfuric Acid Sold or Used, by End Use[2]						Foreign Trade				
										Exports			Imports	
Year	Native Sulfur (Frasch)	Rec-overed Sulfur	Total Elemental Form	Pulpmills & Paper Products	Inorganic Chem-icals[3]	Synthetic Rubber & Plastic	Phosph-atic Fertilizers	Petro-leum Refining[4]	Frasch	Re-covered	Value $1,000	Frasch	Re-covered	Value $1,000
2006	W	10,600	10,600	8,750	246	426	250	6,220	262	----	635	43,800	----	2,950	70,400
2007	W	10,300	10,300	8,330	245	245	117	6,280	264	----	922	84,800	----	2,930	79,400
2008	----	----	10,600	7,680	187	293	69	5,690	244	----	952	272,000	----	3,000	753,000
2009	----	----	8,380	7,740	188	286	64	5,430	283	----	1,430	82,200	----	1,700	54,100
2010	----	----	9,870	6,980	79	31	6	5,700	368	----	1,450	171,000	----	2,950	214,000
2011	----	----	10,200	7,650	168	118	70	5,740	422	----	1,310	266,000	----	3,270	301,000
2012	----	----	9,520	7,410	168	107	70	5,420	423	----	1,860	366,000	----	2,930	238,000
2013[1]	----	----	9,830	7,990	168	101	70	5,270	1,270	----	1,770	234,000	----	2,990	202,000

[1] Preliminary.   [2] Sulfur equivalent.   [3] Including inorganic pigments, paints & allied products, and other inorganic chemicals & products.
[4] Including other petroleum and coal products.   W = Withheld proprietary data.   NA = Not available.   *Source: U.S. Geological Survey (USGS)*

Sunflowerseed, Meal and Oil

Sunflowers are native to South and North America, but are now grown almost worldwide. Sunflower-seed oil accounts for approximately 14% of the world production of seed oils. Sunflower varieties that are commercially grown contain from 39% to 49% oil in the seed. Sunflower crops produce about 50 bushels of seed per acre on average, which yields approximately 50 gallons of oil.

Sunflower-seed oil accounts for around 80% of the value of the sunflower crop. Refined sunflower-seed oil is edible and used primarily as a salad and cooking oil and in margarine. Crude sunflower-seed oil is used industrially for making soaps, candles, varnishes, and detergents. Sunflower-seed oil contains 93% of the energy of U.S. No. 2 diesel fuel and is being explored as a potential alternate fuel source in diesel engines. Sunflower meal is used in livestock feed and when fed to poultry, increases the yield of eggs. Sunflower seeds are also used for birdfeed and as a snack for humans.

Prices – The average monthly price received by U.S. farmers for sunflower seeds in the first five months of the 2015-16 marketing year (Sep/Aug) fell -9.2% to $20.40 per hundred pounds, well below the 2011-12 record high of $28.96 per hundred pounds.

Supply – World sunflower-seed production in the 2015-16 fell -0.5% yr/yr to 39.363 million metric tons. The world's largest sunflower-seed producers are Ukraine with 28.7% of world production, the European Union with 19.7%, Russia with 23.1%, Argentina with 6.6%, China with 5.8%, Turkey with 2.5%, and the U.S. with 3.4%.

U.S. production of sunflower seeds in 2015-16 rose by +31.7% yr/yr to 1.326 million metric tons, far below the record production level of 3.309 million metric tons posted in 1979-80. U.S. farmers harvested 1.799 million acres of sunflowers in 2015-16, up +19.2% yr/yr, well below the 9-year high of 2.610 million acres posted in 2005-06. U.S sunflower yield in 2015-16 was 16.25 hundred pounds per acre, a new record high.

Demand – Total U.S. disappearance of sunflower seeds in 2015-16 rose +28.6% yr/yr to 1.509 million metric tons, of which 36.8% went to non-oil and seed use, 31.5% went to crushing for oil and meal, and 8.2% went to exports.

Trade – World sunflower-seed exports in 2015-16 fell -20.0% yr/yr to 1.332 million metric tons. The world's largest exporters are the European Union which accounted for 30.0% of world exports in 2015-16 and Moldova which accounted for 10.5% of world exports. World sunflower-seed imports in 2015-16 fell -16.0% yr/yr to 1.187 million metric tons. The world's largest importers are Turkey which accounted for 33.7% of world exports and European Union with 19.4% of world imports.

World Production of Sunflowerseed   In Thousands of Metric Tons

Crop Year	Argen-tina	China	European Union	India	Kazakh-stan	Pakistan	Russia	Serbia	South Africa	Turkey	Ukraine	United States	World Total
2008-09	2,483	1,792	7,241	1,000	186	420	6,881	490	801	830	7,000	1,553	32,824
2009-10	2,232	1,956	6,985	820	368	325	6,015	400	490	800	7,600	1,377	31,374
2010-11	3,672	2,298	6,959	655	329	404	4,979	400	860	1,000	8,100	1,241	32,713
2011-12	3,341	2,313	8,455	620	409	283	9,062	415	522	925	9,800	925	38,648
2012-13	3,100	2,323	7,088	700	400	243	7,495	350	557	1,125	9,000	1,241	35,060
2013-14	2,000	2,424	9,052	670	573	200	9,842	425	832	1,400	11,600	917	41,622
2014-15[1]	3,160	2,492	8,932	420	513	200	8,374	525	661	1,200	10,200	1,007	39,566
2015-16[2]	2,600	2,300	7,750	420	534	190	9,095	450	625	1,000	11,300	1,326	39,363

[1] Preliminary. [2] Forecast. *Source: Economic Research Service, U.S. Department of Agriculture (ERS-USDA)*

World Exports of Sunflowerseed   In Thousands of Metric Tons

Crop Year	Argen-tina	Canada	China	European Union	Israel	Kazakh-stan	Moldova	Russia	Serbia	Turkey	Ukraine	United States	World Total
2008-09	74	88	109	494	6	1	128	160	10	13	767	184	2,143
2009-10	70	49	132	567	5	21	99	20	2	20	353	179	1,550
2010-11	75	46	175	597	6	1	218	10	10	26	444	160	1,779
2011-12	80	33	186	596	6	36	194	332	15	38	282	106	1,926
2012-13	84	44	158	521	5	31	196	39	50	38	127	136	1,447
2013-14	74	49	173	712	3	145	322	135	106	33	70	120	1,952
2014-15[1]	68	34	244	519	2	116	341	61	77	28	45	116	1,665
2015-16[2]	75	40	175	400	5	120	140	50	100	20	70	127	1,332

[1] Preliminary. [2] Forecast. *Source: Economic Research Service, U.S. Department of Agriculture (ERS-USDA)*

World Imports of Sunflowerseed   In Thousands of Metric Tons

Crop Year	Belarus	Canada	Egypt	European Union	Iran	Mexico	Moldova	Morocco	Pakistan	Russia	Turkey	United States	World Total
2008-09	10	20	11	635	42	14	1	80	190	12	446	70	1,863
2009-10	14	26	30	269	31	14	5	72	92	23	736	46	1,483
2010-11	35	33	49	379	26	15	1	89	37	42	705	41	1,565
2011-12	35	33	75	280	27	15	1	18	159	28	834	44	1,639
2012-13	12	27	59	214	30	14	1	37	2	29	628	54	1,312
2013-14	13	25	43	319	42	18	2	1	197	35	581	65	1,508
2014-15[1]	19	30	57	266	45	18	3	40	178	88	470	75	1,413
2015-16[2]	15	25	55	230	45	20	1	15	140	50	400	75	1,187

[1] Preliminary. [2] Forecast. *Source: Economic Research Service, U.S. Department of Agriculture (ERS-USDA)*

SUNFLOWERSEED, MEAL AND OIL

World Production of Sunflowerseed Oil   In Thousands of Metric Tons

Crop Year	Argentina	Burma	China	European Union	India	Pakistan	Russia	Serbia	South Africa	Turkey	Ukraine	United States	World Total
2008-09	1,345	195	315	2,488	319	234	2,395	180	318	515	2,631	293	11,830
2009-10	1,146	205	324	2,613	255	170	2,354	170	241	626	2,975	327	11,989
2010-11	1,551	202	340	2,493	195	168	1,900	170	284	671	3,330	221	12,029
2011-12	1,565	140	348	2,800	205	153	3,304	170	272	718	3,967	149	14,335
2012-13	980	110	476	2,560	220	97	2,891	131	289	769	3,635	196	12,870
2013-14	934	110	481	3,170	210	148	3,593	123	347	845	4,750	197	15,516
2014-15[1]	1,135	150	466	3,180	120	144	3,366	161	285	725	4,325	166	14,849
2015-16[2]	1,140	150	420	2,980	120	124	3,530	161	258	595	4,663	258	15,054

[1] Preliminary.   [2] Forecast.   *Source: Economic Research Service, U.S. Department of Agriculture (ERS-USDA)*

World Production of Sunflowerseed Meal   In Thousands of Metric Tons

Crop Year	Argentina	Burma	China	European Union	India	Kazakhstan	Pakistan	Russia	South Africa	Turkey	Ukraine	United States	World Total
2008-09	1,390	188	484	3,238	426	86	244	2,320	342	460	2,600	342	12,797
2009-10	1,218	200	495	3,395	341	113	178	2,337	243	559	2,947	382	13,043
2010-11	1,632	198	519	3,231	260	100	176	1,886	287	597	3,296	258	13,002
2011-12	1,621	140	532	3,629	255	127	160	3,280	275	640	3,930	174	15,345
2012-13	1,021	110	726	3,318	294	125	101	2,870	293	685	3,599	229	13,890
2013-14	962	110	732	4,108	280	140	155	3,570	356	753	4,703	230	16,688
2014-15[1]	1,140	150	709	4,119	161	132	150	3,345	290	647	4,285	191	15,963
2015-16[2]	1,200	150	640	3,840	161	140	130	3,510	262	535	4,620	299	16,156

[1] Preliminary.   [2] Forecast.   *Source: Economic Research Service, U.S. Department of Agriculture (ERS-USDA)*

Sunflowerseed Statistics in the United States   In Thousands of Metric Tons

Crop Year Beginning Sept. 1	Acres Harvested (1,000)	Harvested Yield Per CWT	Farm Price ($/Metric Ton)	Value of Production (Million $)	Stocks, Sept. 1	Supply Production	Imports	Total Supply	Crush	Exports	Non-Oil Use & Seed	Total Disappearance
2008-09	2,396	14.29	481	704.1	120	1,553	70	1,743	661	184	675	1,743
2009-10	1,954	15.54	333	459.0	223	1,377	46	1,646	776	179	514	1,646
2010-11	1,874	14.60	514	633.8	177	1,241	41	1,459	588	160	594	1,459
2011-12	1,458	13.98	642	589.3	117	925	44	1,086	349	106	544	1,086
2012-13	1,840	14.87	560	700.0	87	1,241	54	1,382	451	136	641	1,382
2013-14	1,465	13.80	472	443.3	154	917	65	1,136	463	120	462	1,136
2014-15[1]	1,510	14.69	474	504.6	91	1,007	75	1,173	415	120	553	1,173
2015-16[2]	1,799	16.25			108	1,326	75	1,509	476	123	555	1,509

[1] Preliminary.   [2] Forecast.   *Source: Economic Research Service, U.S. Department of Agriculture (ERS-USDA)*

Sunflower Oil Statistics in the United States   In Thousands of Metric Tons

Crop Year Beginning Sept. 1	Supply Stocks, Oct. 1	Production	Imports	Total Supply	Exports	Domestic Use	Total Disappearance	Price $ Per Metric Ton (Crude Mpls.)
2008-09	12	293	30	335	91	194	285	1,170
2009-10	50	327	22	399	98	264	362	1,163
2010-11	37	221	47	305	38	240	278	1,824
2011-12	27	149	74	250	19	208	227	1,871
2012-13	23	196	32	251	28	200	228	1,473
2013-14	23	197	35	255	37	195	232	1,305
2014-15[1]	23	166	80	269	29	217	246	1,449
2015-16[2]	23	258	34	315	32	256	288	1,417

[1] Preliminary.   [2] Forecast.   *Source: Economic Research Service, U.S. Department of Agriculture (ERS-USDA)*

Sunflower Meal Statistics in the United States   In Thousands of Metric Tons

Crop Year Beginning Sept. 1	Supply Stocks, Oct. 1	Production	Imports	Total Supply	Exports	Domestic Use	Total Disappearance	Price USD Per Metric Ton 28% Protein
2008-09	5	342	----	347	7	335	347	172
2009-10	5	382	----	387	6	376	387	164
2010-11	5	258	----	263	3	255	263	233
2011-12	5	174	----	179	3	171	179	264
2012-13	5	229	----	234	19	210	234	279
2013-14	5	230	11	246	8	233	246	270
2014-15[1]	5	191	20	216	7	204	216	224
2015-16[2]	5	299	14	318	9	304	318	196

[1] Preliminary.   [2] Forecast.   *Source: Economic Research Service, U.S. Department of Agriculture (ERS-USDA)*

Average Price Received by Farmers for Sunflower[2] in the United States   In Dollars Per Hundred Pounds (Cwt.)

Year	Sept.	Oct.	Nov.	Dec.	Jan.	Feb.	Mar.	Apr.	May	June	July	Aug.	Average
2008-09	28.20	25.30	23.10	22.80	22.10	22.60	22.10	20.20	21.50	18.40	17.70	20.60	22.05
2009-10	13.90	16.20	14.20	14.80	15.50	16.70	15.80	15.80	14.90	15.10	15.40	14.50	15.23
2010-11	17.30	20.80	18.70	20.60	21.90	27.40	28.30	28.80	30.00	29.00	30.40	32.20	25.45
2011-12	32.90	29.60	29.00	29.60	28.90	29.50	28.80	28.40	27.80	27.20	27.00	28.80	28.96
2012-13	28.80	25.90	26.70	24.80	26.00	26.10	24.60	24.80	24.00	24.40	23.70	23.70	25.29
2013-14	22.60	23.00	20.70	18.80	19.60	22.80	21.60	22.30	24.10	22.80	22.10	22.40	21.90
2014-15	20.20	21.70	20.30	19.70	19.10	21.50	22.20	23.20	26.40	25.60	26.40	24.10	22.53
2015-16[1]	25.20	18.60	18.40	19.40	20.00	20.50							20.35

[1] Preliminary.   [2] KS, MN, ND and SD average.   *Source: Economic Research Service, U.S. Department of Agriculture (ERS-USDA)*

Average Price of Crude Sunflower Oil at Minneapolis   In Cents Per Pound

Year	Sept.	Oct.	Nov.	Dec.	Jan.	Feb.	Mar.	Apr.	May	June	July	Aug.	Average
2008-09	87.50	74.40	53.75	42.50	41.60	40.00	42.50	45.00	49.20	53.75	53.40	53.50	53.09
2009-10	53.25	52.20	53.00	52.00	52.00	52.00	51.25	51.60	52.50	55.75	53.60	53.75	52.74
2010-11	54.00	56.00	63.00	62.90	74.13	85.63	96.75	101.20	103.75	103.25	97.00	95.00	82.72
2011-12	94.80	92.50	91.00	91.00	88.75	86.00	82.00	79.00	80.00	80.20	78.00	75.00	84.85
2012-13	75.00	74.00	70.30	67.50	65.25	65.00	64.60	64.00	64.00	64.00	64.00	64.00	66.80
2013-14	63.75	60.50	57.40	57.00	57.00	57.00	58.00	59.00	59.00	57.50	61.00	63.00	59.18
2014-15	63.00	63.00	61.75	58.00	63.00	65.63	65.56	65.50	65.00	69.75	73.40	75.00	65.72
2015-16[1]	75.00	72.00	64.50	62.00	58.00	54.25							64.29

[1] Preliminary.   *Source: Economic Research Service, U.S. Department of Agriculture (ERS-USDA)*

Average Price of Sunflower Meal (26% protein) in the United States   In Cents Per Pound

Year	Sept.	Oct.	Nov.	Dec.	Jan.	Feb.	Mar.	Apr.	May	June	July	Aug.	Average
2008-09	179.40	161.10	146.90	150.00	164.40	161.90	134.40	130.00	141.30	187.50	170.60	147.50	156.25
2009-10	134.00	151.90	189.40	197.50	181.88	165.63	137.50	132.50	120.50	109.50	120.00	141.20	148.46
2010-11	165.00	190.63	211.50	217.50	205.63	209.38	210.00	196.25	203.13	240.63	241.25	247.00	211.49
2011-12	263.75	232.50	224.00	225.63	223.50	191.88	191.88	211.25	230.50	226.88	300.50	348.13	239.20
2012-13	354.38	287.00	269.38	266.67	252.00	237.50	231.25	222.00	215.00	233.13	245.50	221.25	252.92
2013-14	218.13	236.25	246.88	277.50	283.75	285.00	271.25	267.50	265.00	250.00	192.50	151.25	245.42
2014-15	139.50	162.50	208.13	245.00	247.50	225.63	202.50	202.50	192.50	180.50	214.38	222.50	203.60
2015-16[1]	216.00	212.50	187.50	163.13	156.88	131.88							177.98

[1] Preliminary.   *Source: Economic Research Service, U.S. Department of Agriculture (ERS-USDA)*

Production of Sunflower in the United States   In Thousands of Pounds

Crop Year	California	Colorado	Kansas	Minnesota	Nebraska	North Dakota	Oklahoma	South Dakota	Texas	Total
2008	----	153,400	278,900	163,850	82,900	1,511,400	----	1,049,300	92,400	3,422,840
2009	51,000	122,060	245,200	86,600	62,700	1,317,200	17,500	1,004,400	129,800	3,036,460
2010	40,500	167,950	186,060	116,800	83,400	1,254,980	17,180	772,750	95,950	2,735,570
2011	44,300	124,200	149,400	46,100	75,900	766,250	5,275	776,950	49,900	2,038,275
2012	68,575	52,720	97,950	93,925	26,460	1,430,460	4,720	859,250	102,000	2,736,060
2013	75,150	45,600	82,000	69,250	32,975	600,560	5,180	996,800	114,250	2,021,765
2014	61,925	95,700	91,540	87,870	47,375	847,420	3,200	876,620	137,400	2,219,050
2015[1]	44,720	85,200	135,560	166,050	79,410	1,068,800	6,600	1,230,040	107,350	2,923,730

[1] Preliminary.   *Source: Economic Research Service, U.S. Department of Agriculture (ERS-USDA)*

Production of Sunflower Oil in the United States   In Thousands of Pounds

Crop Year	California	Colorado	Kansas	Minnesota	Nebraska	North Dakota	Oklahoma	South Dakota	Texas	Total
2008	----	128,700	254,200	113,150	55,900	1,329,900	----	970,100	59,400	2,993,510
2009	40,200	89,760	221,200	61,600	31,200	1,155,200	13,750	918,000	53,100	2,584,010
2010	31,050	124,200	144,900	76,500	23,400	1,000,100	15,750	616,000	33,600	2,074,500
2011	39,500	97,000	123,900	35,100	45,500	690,000	4,875	664,950	21,850	1,722,675
2012	65,075	40,120	74,750	70,300	20,650	1,283,500	4,180	761,600	39,600	2,359,775
2013	72,150	29,600	58,000	51,200	19,975	504,000	3,480	820,800	78,000	1,637,205
2014	57,200	44,800	57,540	65,250	29,000	683,400	2,100	668,000	56,800	1,664,090
2015[1]	42,900	68,400	80,560	123,750	42,660	889,350	4,800	1,048,000	82,650	2,383,870

[1] Preliminary.   *Source: Economic Research Service, U.S. Department of Agriculture (ERS-USDA)*

Tallow and Greases

Tallow and grease are derived from processing (rendering) the fat of cattle. Tallow is used to produce both edible and inedible products. Edible tallow products include margarine, cooking oil, and baking products. Inedible tallow products include soap, candles, and lubricants. Production of tallow and greases is directly related to the number of cattle produced. Those countries that are the leading cattle producers are also the largest producers of tallow. The American Fats and Oils Association provides specifications for a variety of different types of tallow and grease, including edible tallow, lard (edible), top white tallow, all beef packer tallow, extra fancy tallow, fancy tallow, bleachable fancy tallow, prime tallow, choice white grease, and yellow grease. The specifications include such characteristics as the melting point, color, density, moisture content, insoluble impurities, and others.

Prices – The monthly average price of tallow (inedible, No. 1 Packers-Prime, delivered Chicago) in 2015 fell -26.7% yr/yr to 26.87 cents per pound. The wholesale price of inedible tallow in 2015 fell -26.6% yr/yr to 28.42 cents per pound.

Supply – World production of tallow and greases (edible and inedible) in 2014 (latest data), fell by -0.9% yr/yr to 8.482 million metric tons, which was below the 2007 record high of 8.530 million metric tons. The world's largest producer of tallow and greases by far is the U.S. with 40.1% of world production, followed by Brazil with 8.0%, Australia with 6.9%, and Canada with 3.2%.

U.S. production of edible tallow in 2014 (latest data) fell -5.6% yr/yr to 2.004 billion pounds, below last year's record high of 2.136 billion pounds. U.S. production of inedible tallow and greases in 2011 (latest data) fell -37.9% yr/yr to 3.653 billion pounds, well below the record high of 7.156 billion pounds posted in 2002.

Demand – U.S. consumption of inedible tallow and greases in 2011 (latest data) fell 0.9% yr/yr to 1.559 billion pounds, of which virtually all went for animal feed. U.S. consumption of edible tallow in 2013 (latest data) fell -0.3% yr/yr to 1.935 billion pounds, down from 2011 record high of 1.954 billion pounds. U.S. per capita consumption of edible tallow in 2010 (latest data) rose from 0.7 pounds per person to 3.3 pounds per person yr/yr, down from the 2000 and 2004 record high of 4.0 pounds.

Trade – U.S. exports of inedible tallow and grease in 2011 (latest data) fell -3.2% yr/yr to 341.551 million pounds, and accounted for 8.7% of total U.S. supply. U.S. exports of edible tallow in 2014 fell -42.7% yr/yr to 90 million pounds, and accounted for 4.8% of U.S. supply.

World Production of Tallow and Greases (Edible and Inedible)   In Thousands of Metric Tons

Year	Argentina	Australia	Brazil	Canada	France	Germany	Korea	Nether-lands	New Zealand	Russia	United Kingdom	United States	World Total
2005	184	493	554	339	171	121	15	106	168	175	128	3,797	8,389
2006	181	503	574	285	195	124	16	107	187	179	135	3,808	8,474
2007	195	501	589	276	192	128	16	116	184	184	140	3,818	8,522
2008	189	499	564	261	196	131	16	122	189	189	138	3,695	8,389
2009	204	483	547	252	188	131	16	123	168	195	134	3,655	8,304
2010	160	488	566	262	200	134	16	131	169	200	141	3,575	8,331
2011	153	493	551	266	209	134	15	121	167	198	144	3,678	8,455
2012	160	494	587	267	198	131	18	106	166	200	139	3,553	8,374
2013[1]	175	548	656	266	191	130	21	103	169	206	138	3,575	8,555
2014[2]	167	586	678	268	192	131	20	101	167	209	142	3,405	8,482

[1] Preliminary.   [2] Forecast.   *Source: Foreign Agricultural Service, U.S. Department of Agriculture (FAS-USDA)*

Salient Statistics of Tallow and Greases (Inedible) in the United States   In Millions of Pounds

	-------------------- Supply ---------------------			---------------- Consumption ----------------				Wholesale Prices, Cents Per Lb. ------	
Year	Production	Stocks, Jan. 1	Total	Exports	Soap	Feed	Total	Edible, (Loose) Chicago	Inedible, Chicago No. 1
2006	6,460	309	6,769	730	W	2,585	2,585	18.6	16.9
2007	6,369	291	6,661	795	W	2,385	2,385	30.7	27.8
2008	6,224	350	6,573	703	W	2,095	2,095	38.0	34.2
2009	5,878	315	6,193	727	W	1,770	1,770	27.5	25.2
2010	5,887	286	6,174	778	W	1,574	1,574	35.1	33.3
2011	3,654	281	3,934	753	W	1,560	1,560	53.2	49.6
2012[1]	NA	NA	NA	NA	NA	NA	NA	47.8	43.8
2013[2]	NA	NA	NA	NA	NA	NA	NA	42.6	40.4
2014[2]	----	----	----	----	----	----	----	38.7	36.7
2015[2]	----	----	----	----	----	----	----	28.4	26.9

[1] Preliminary.   [2] Forecast.   *Source: Foreign Agricultural Service, U.S. Department of Agriculture (FAS-USDA)*

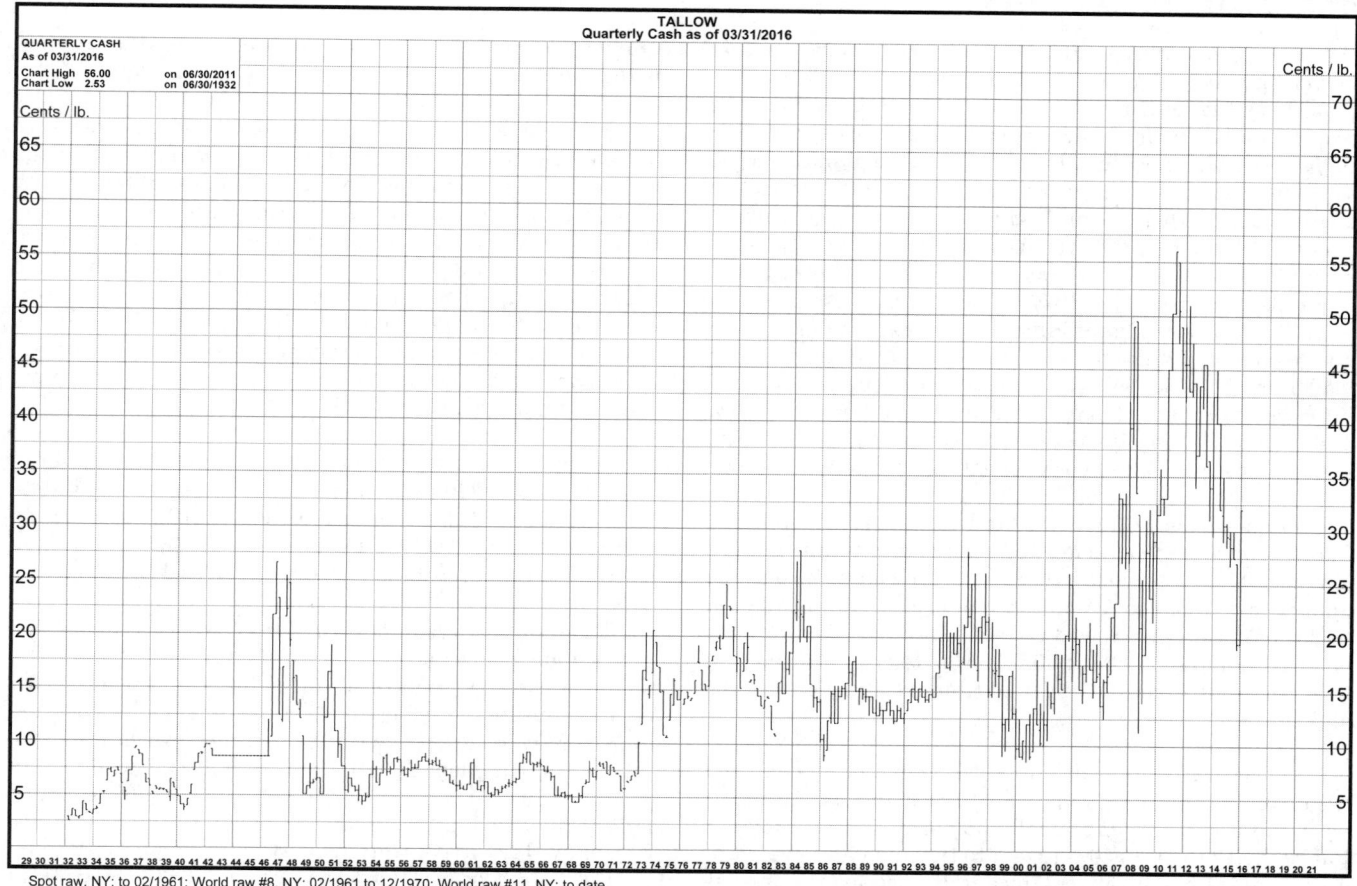

TALLOW
Quarterly Cash as of 03/31/2016

QUARTERLY CASH
As of 03/31/2016

Chart High 56.00   on 06/30/2011
Chart Low   2.53   on 06/30/1932

Cents / lb.

Spot raw, NY: to 02/1961; World raw #8, NY: 02/1961 to 12/1970; World raw #11, NY: to date.

Supply and Disappearance of Edible Tallow in the United States   In Millions of Pounds, Rendered Basis

	-------------------- Supply --------------------			--- Disappearance ---					
Year	Stocks, Jan. 1	Production	Total Supply	Domestic Disap-pearance	Exports	Total Disap-pearance	Direct Use	Baking or Frying Fats	Per Capita (Lbs.)
2005	22	1,813	1,836	1,518	293	1,811	1,116	W	3.8
2006	25	1,861	1,893	1,583	275	1,858	1,160	W	3.9
2007	35	1,789	1,831	1,404	388	1,792	889	W	2.9
2008	39	1,794	1,863	1,648	185	1,833	896	W	2.9
2009	30	1,837	1,903	1,710	162	1,872	212	W	0.7
2010	31	1,859	1,913	1,693	183	1,876	1,050	W	3.4
2011	38	2,050	2,116	1,954	132	2,086	NA	NA	NA
2012	30	2,055	2,136	1,940	166	2,106	NA	NA	NA
2013[1]	30	2,043	2,122	1,935	157	2,092	----	----	----
2014[2]	30	1,922	2,004	1,884	90	1,974	----	----	----

[1] Preliminary.   [2] Forecast.   W = Withheld.   *Sources: Economic Research Service, U.S. Department of Agriculture (ERS-USDA);
Bureau of the Census, U.S. Department of Commerce*

Average Wholesale Price of Tallow, Inedible, No. 1 Packers (Prime), Delivered, Chicago   In Cents Per Pound

Year	Jan.	Feb.	Mar.	Apr.	May	June	July	Aug.	Sept.	Oct.	Nov.	Dec.	Average
2006	17.52	17.05	14.98	13.47	14.77	15.27	17.05	17.35	15.59	17.71	20.42	21.46	16.89
2007	22.02	20.78	21.74	25.04	29.16	33.08	32.58	27.67	30.14	31.29	32.87	27.64	27.83
2008	32.19	36.08	40.03	39.66	40.02	45.36	47.55	40.14	36.17	24.39	14.29	14.23	34.18
2009	22.86	19.57	16.72	21.83	25.80	29.53	26.17	31.75	30.44	22.27	25.89	29.09	25.16
2010	28.37	27.42	31.57	32.74	33.08	32.73	32.15	32.28	32.93	33.88	40.52	42.50	33.35
2011	47.83	47.61	49.49	51.59	52.33	54.52	53.69	49.36	50.02	47.36	44.35	47.21	49.61
2012	44.17	45.67	48.16	47.33	48.98	45.39	45.38	44.59	45.72	40.07	34.05	36.20	43.81
2013	40.00	40.00	42.42	43.06	41.67	45.00	45.39	42.74	40.53	33.37	35.14	35.14	40.37
2014	31.95	31.61	38.52	42.60	44.57	42.04	39.96	39.85	34.90	29.51	32.47	32.09	36.67
2015[1]	28.77	28.84	30.42	28.22	28.64	29.72	28.50	29.21	28.71	22.41	19.48	19.50	26.87

[1] Preliminary.   *Sources: Economic Research Service, U.S. Department of Agriculture (ERS-USDA)*

Tea

Tea is the common name for a family of mostly woody flowering plants. The tea family contains about 600 species placed in 28 genera and they are distributed throughout the tropical and subtropical areas, with most species occurring in eastern Asia and South America. The tea plant is native to Southeast Asia. There are more than 3,000 varieties of tea, each with its own distinct character, and each is generally named for the area in which it is grown. Tea may have been consumed in China as long ago as 2700 BC and certainly since 1000 BC. In 2737 BC, the Chinese Emperor Shen Nung, according to Chinese mythology, was a scholar and herbalist. While his servant boiled drinking water, a leaf from the wild tea tree he was sitting under dropped into the water and Shen Nung decided to try the brew. Today, half the world's population drinks tea. Tea is the world's most popular beverage next to water.

Tea is a healthful drink and contains antioxidants, fluoride, niacin, folic acid, and as much vitamin C as a lemon. The average 5 oz. cup of brewed tea contains approximately 40 to 60 milligrams of caffeine (compared to 80 to 115 mg in brewed coffee). Decaffeinated tea has been available since the 1980s. Herbal tea contains no true tea leaves but is actually brewed from a collection of herbs and spices.

Tea grows mainly between the tropic of Cancer and the tropic of Capricorn, requiring 40 to 50 inches of rain per year and a temperature ideally between 50 to 86 degrees Fahrenheit. In order to rejuvenate the bush and keep it at a convenient height for the pickers to access, the bushes must be pruned every four to five years. A tea bush can produce tea for 50 to 70 years, but after 50 years, the yield is reduced.

The two key factors in determining different varieties of tea are the production process (sorting, withering, rolling, fermentation, and drying methods) and the growing conditions (geographical region, growing altitude, and soil type). Black tea, often referred to as fully fermented tea, is produced by allowing picked tea leaves to wither and ferment for up to 24 hours. After fermenting, the leaves are fired, which stops oxidation. Green tea, or unfermented tea, is produced by immediately and completely drying the leaves and omitting the oxidization process, thus allowing the tea to remain green in color.

Supply – World production of tea in 2013 (latest data) rose +6.2% to 5.345 million metric tons, a new record high. The world's largest producers of tea in 2013 were China (with 36.3% of world production), India (22.6%), Kenya (8.1%), Sri Lanka (6.4%), Turkey (4.0%), and Iran (3.0%).

Trade – U.S. tea imports in 2015 rose +1.3% to 214,035 metric tons, below last year's record high of 216,844 metric tons. World tea imports in 2013 (latest data) fell -2.2% to 1.893 million metric tons. The world's largest tea importers were Russia (with 9.1% of total world imports), the United Kingdom (7.3%), the U.S. (6.9%), and Pakistan (6.4%). World exports of tea in 2013 rose +13.6% to 2.051 million metric tons. The world's largest exporters were Kenya (with 21.9% of world exports), China (16.2%), India (12.4%), Sri Lanka (15.5%), Vietnam (4.4%), Argentina (3.8%), and Indonesia (3.5%).

World Tea Production, in Major Producing Countries   In Metric Tons

Year	Argentina	Bangladesh	China	India	Indonesia	Iran	Japan	Kenya	Malawi	Sri Lanka	Turkey	Ex-USSR[2]	World Total
2007	76,000	58,500	1,165,500	973,000	150,623	49,680	94,100	369,600	48,140	305,220	206,160	16,028	3,978,842
2008	80,142	59,000	1,274,980	987,000	153,971	165,717	96,500	345,800	41,637	318,700	198,046	13,354	4,232,490
2009	71,715	59,500	1,375,780	972,700	156,901	165,717	86,000	314,198	52,555	290,000	198,601	17,157	4,286,820
2010	92,417	60,000	1,467,470	991,182	150,342	165,717	85,000	399,006	51,589	331,400	235,000	14,766	4,606,070
2011	92,892	60,500	1,640,310	1,095,460	150,200	103,890	82,100	377,912	52,000	327,500	221,600	3,704	4,771,210
2012	82,813	60,000	1,804,660	1,135,070	143,400	158,000	85,900	369,400	53,500	330,000	225,000	3,258	5,034,970
2013[1]	105,000	64,000	1,939,460	1,208,780	148,100	160,000	84,800	432,400	54,000	340,230	212,400	3,958	5,345,520

[1] Preliminary. [2] Mostly Georgia and Azerbaijan. *Sources: Foreign Agricultural Service, U.S. Department of Agriculture (FAS-USDA); Food and Agriculture Organization of the United Nations (FAO-UN)*

World Exports of Tea from Producing Countries   In Metric Tons

Year	Argentina	Bangladesh	Brazil	China	India	Indonesia	Kenya	Malawi	Papua New Guinea	Sri Lanka	Vietnam	Zimbabwe	Total
2007	75,767	5,269	3,298	294,329	193,459	83,659	374,329	54,397	6,400	190,203	114,000	6,840	1,787,030
2008	77,498	8,259	3,034	302,020	203,207	96,210	396,641	30,435	5,937	318,329	104,700	5,979	1,908,802
2009	69,816	5,339	2,326	307,434	203,863	92,304	331,594	47,356	6,250	288,528	133,000	7,874	1,822,227
2010	85,695	1,981	2,542	307,777	234,560	87,101	417,661	49,999	4,581	312,908	136,515	10,023	2,022,762
2011	86,650	945	1,965	327,650	322,548	75,450	306,678	46,007	4,224	321,074	133,900	11,221	1,983,292
2012[1]	78,056	838	1,643	319,357	225,082	70,071	234,181	34,679	3,737	318,396	146,898	11,540	1,805,977
2013[2]	77,291	665	623	332,172	254,841	70,842	448,809	43,245	2,943	317,710	90,296	11,863	2,051,373

[1] Preliminary. [2] Estimate. *Source: Food and Agriculture Organization of the United Nations (FAO-UN)*

Imports of Tea in the United States   In Metric Tons

Year	Jan.	Feb.	Mar.	Apr.	May	June	July	Aug.	Sept.	Oct.	Nov.	Dec.	Total
2010	14,752	15,682	18,907	20,421	20,967	19,845	19,856	19,150	18,747	15,722	14,465	13,815	212,329
2011	13,923	15,355	18,580	18,052	21,794	19,831	19,085	19,257	21,617	13,852	15,173	15,055	211,575
2012	15,091	15,277	16,211	16,716	21,047	20,510	21,292	19,525	22,502	15,871	13,926	13,306	211,272
2013	14,558	13,532	15,848	22,563	22,281	20,306	21,342	21,595	22,288	14,234	15,381	12,918	216,844
2014	13,570	13,945	16,047	20,629	19,669	18,546	17,249	18,987	21,626	18,281	17,544	15,138	211,230
2015[1]	13,395	12,987	19,797	18,829	19,762	20,862	19,577	20,090	23,668	15,643	15,727	13,698	214,035

[1] Preliminary. *Source: Foreign Agricultural Service, U.S. Department of Agriculture (FAS-USDA)*

Tin

Tin (atomic symbol Sn) is a silvery-white, lustrous gray metallic element. Tin is soft, pliable and has a highly crystalline structure. When a tin bar is bent or broken, a crackling sound called a "tin cry" is produced due to the breaking of the tin crystals. People have been using tin for at least 5,500 years. Tin has been found in the tombs of ancient Egyptians. In ancient times, tin and lead were considered different forms of the same metal. Tin was exported to Europe in large quantities from Cornwall, England, during the Roman period, from approximately 2100 BC to 1500 BC. Cornwall was one of the world's leading sources of tin for much of its known history and into the late 1800s.

The principal ore of tin is the mineral cassiterite, which is found in Malaya, Bolivia, Indonesia, Thailand, and Nigeria. About 80% of the world's tin deposits occur in unconsolidated placer deposits in riverbeds and valleys, or on the sea floor, with only about 20% occurring as primary hard-rock lodes. Tin deposits are generally small and are almost always found closely allied to the granite from which it originates. Tin is also recovered as a by-product of mining tungsten, tantalum, and lead. After extraction, tin ore is ground and washed to remove impurities, roasted to oxidize the sulfides of iron and copper, washed a second time, and then reduced by carbon in a reverberatory furnace. Electrolysis may also be used to purify tin.

Pure tin, rarely used by itself, was used as currency in the form of tin blocks and was considered legal tender for taxes in Phuket, Thailand, until 1932. Tin is used in the manufacture of coatings for steel containers used to preserve food and beverages. Tin is also used in solder alloys, electroplating, ceramics, and in plastic. The world's major tin research and development laboratory, ITRI Ltd, is funded by companies that produce and consume tin. The focus of the research efforts have been on possible new uses for tin that would take advantage of tin's relative non-toxicity to replace other metals in various products. Some of the replacements could be lead-free solders, antimony-free flame-retardant chemicals, and lead-free shotgun pellets. No tin is currently mined in the U.S.

Tin futures and options trade on the London Metal Exchange (LME). Tin has traded on the LME since 1877 and the standard tin contract began in 1912. The futures contract calls for the delivery of 5 metric tons of tin ingots of at least 99.85% purity. The contract trades in terms of U.S. dollars per metric ton. Futures are also traded on the Multi Commodity Exchange of India (MCX).

Prices – The average monthly price of tin (straights) in New York in 2015 fell by -25.9% yr/yr to $9.91 per pound, further below the 2011 record high of $15.86 per pound. The 2015 price was far above the 3-decade low of $2.83 per pound seen in 2002. The average monthly price of ex-dock tin in New York in 2015 fell -24.5% yr/yr to $7.70 per pound.

Supply – World mine production of tin in 2015 fell by -5.6% yr/yr to 270,000 metric tons, remaining below the 2004 record high of 302,000 metric tons. The world's largest mine producers of tin are China with 37.0% of world production in 2015, Indonesia with 18.5%, and Peru with 8.3%. World smelter production of tin in 2013 (latest data) fell -1.6% yr/yr to 300,000 metric tons, below the 2005 record high of 324,000 metric tons. The world's largest producers of smelted tin are China with 50.0% of world production in 2013, Indonesia with 13.7%, and Malaysia with 10.9%.

The U.S. does not mine tin, and therefore its supply consists only of scrap and imports. U.S. tin recovery in 2014 (latest data) fell -5.4% to 5,680 metric tons, a new record low.

Demand – U.S. consumption of tin (pig) in 2015 rose +7.2% to 26,761 metric tons (annualized through September), up from the 2014 record low of 24,963. The breakdown of U.S. consumption of tin by finished products in 2012 (latest data) shows that the largest consuming industry of tin is chemicals (with 22.3% of consumption), tinplate (19.8%), followed by solder (19.5%), and bronze and brass (7.8%).

Trade – The U.S. relied on imports for 75% of its tin consumption in 2015. U.S. imports of unwrought tin metal in 2014 (latest data) rose +2.0% to 35,600 metric tons, up from the 18-year low of 33,000 in 2009. The largest sources of U.S. imports in 2014 were Indonesia (22.9%), Malaysia (17.0%), Bolivia (12.0%), and China (9.7%). U.S. exports of tin in 2015 rose +1.8% yr/yr to 5,800 metric tons.

World Mine Production of Tin   In Metric Tons (Contained Tin)

Year	Australia	Bolivia	Brazil	China	Indo-nesia	Malaysia	Nigeria	Peru	Portugal	Russia	Thailand	Vietnam	World Total
2006	1,478	18,444	9,528	126,000	80,933	2,398	1,400	38,470	25	3,000	190	5,400	293,000
2007	2,071	15,972	11,835	146,000	66,137	2,263	180	39,019	41	2,500	122	5,400	301,000
2008	1,783	17,320	13,899	110,000	53,228	2,605	185	39,037	29	400	215	5,400	260,000
2009	13,268	19,575	9,500	97,200	46,078	2,412	400	37,503	34	127	166	5,400	246,000
2010	18,263	20,190	10,400	115,000	43,258	2,668	520	33,848	22	144	291	5,400	267,000
2011	14,014	20,373	10,725	120,000	42,000	3,346	570	28,882	39	75	282	5,400	265,000
2012	6,158	19,702	13,667	110,000	41,000	3,726	570	26,105	30	100	124	5,400	243,000
2013	6,474	19,300	12,000	110,000	95,200	3,700	570	23,668	40	420	200	5,400	294,000
2014[1]	7,210	19,900	14,700	96,000	76,000	3,780	2,800	23,100		240	200	5,400	286,000
2015[2]	7,000	20,000	17,000	100,000	50,000	3,800	2,800	22,500		100	200	5,400	270,000

[1] Preliminary.   [2] Estimate.   *Source: U.S. Geological Survey (USGS)*

World Smelter Production of Primary Tin   In Metric Tons

Year	Australia	Bolivia	Brazil	China	Indo-nesia	Japan	Malaysia	Mexico	Russia	South Africa	Spain	Thailand	World Total
2004	467	13,627	11,512	115,000	49,872	707	33,914	25	4,570	----	----	20,800	295,000
2005	594	13,941	8,986	122,000	65,300	754	36,924	17	5,000	----	----	31,600	324,000
2006	572	14,089	8,780	132,000	65,357	854	22,850	25	4,980	----	----	27,540	320,000
2007	118	12,251	9,384	149,000	64,127	879	25,263	25	3,800	----	----	23,104	178,000
2008	170	12,667	11,020	140,000	53,417	956	31,691	15	1,425	----	----	21,860	316,000
2009	----	14,995	8,311	140,000	51,418	757	36,407	15	1,129	----	----	19,423	310,000
2010	----	14,975	9,098	150,000	43,832	841	38,737	----	1,081	----	----	20,000	318,000
2011	----	14,518	9,382	156,000	43,000	947	40,267	----	526	----	----	20,000	321,000
2012	----	14,280	11,955	148,000	42,000	1,133	37,792	----	500	----	----	20,000	305,000
2013[1]	----	14,000	12,250	150,000	41,000	1,000	32,668	----	400	----	----	20,000	300,000

[1] Preliminary.   Source: U.S. Geological Survey (USGS)

United States Foreign Trade of Tin   In Metric Tons

| | | Concentrates[2] (Ore) | | | Imports for Consumption | | | | | | | | |
| | Exports (Metal) | Total All Ore | Bolivia | Peru | Total All Metal (Unwrought Tin Metal) | Bolivia | Brazil | China | Indo-nesia | Malaysia | Singa-pore | Thailand | United Kingdom |
Year													
2005	4,330	----	----	----	37,500	5,400	2,150	4,510	5,220	1,530	194	45	67
2006	5,490	----	----	----	43,300	8,160	1,300	4,440	4,600	245	1,090	210	1,370
2007	6,410	----	----	----	34,600	4,340	2,600	4,230	1,680	14	1,730	15	881
2008	9,800	----	----	----	36,300	4,980	1,570	2,380	2,000	1,740	706	1,670	225
2009	3,170	----	----	----	33,000	6,300	1,050	1,210	3,220	169	451	15	4
2010	5,630	----	----	----	35,300	6,060	75	887	3,970	4,500	996	1,310	4
2011	5,450	----	----	----	34,200	5,680	676	1,490	4,930	3,980	645	2,310	18
2012	5,560	----	----	----	36,900	5,100	2,930	174	6,180	4,590	424	1,750	1
2013	5,870	----	----	----	34,900	6,510	3,100	1,610	5,560	4,190	101	2,380	----
2014[1]	5,700	----	----	----	35,600	4,550	3,030	3,470	8,140	6,050	375	291	----

[1] Preliminary.   [2] Tin content.   [4] Less than 1/2 unit.   Source: U.S. Geological Survey (USGS)

Consumption (Total) of Tin (Pig) in the United States   In Metric Tons

Year	Jan.	Feb.	Mar.	Apr.	May	June	July	Aug.	Sept.	Oct.	Nov.	Dec.	Total
2006	3,877	3,694	3,508	3,439	3,447	3,580	3,475	3,420	3,456	3,442	3,407	3,356	42,101
2007	3,381	3,342	3,601	3,365	3,716	3,811	3,585	4,070	3,910	3,734	3,586	3,628	43,729
2008	2,653	2,626	2,630	2,693	2,639	2,641	2,665	2,697	2,687	2,607	2,662	2,653	31,853
2009	2,642	2,546	2,610	2,573	2,525	2,521	2,630	2,552	2,626	2,646	2,675	2,564	31,110
2010	2,678	2,673	2,689	2,698	2,666	2,655	2,706	2,740	2,724	2,730	2,599	2,951	32,509
2011	2,782	2,769	2,833	2,831	2,862	2,983	2,961	2,823	3,064	3,061	2,973	2,750	34,692
2012	2,718	2,748	2,868	2,829	2,908	2,775	2,735	2,745	2,696	2,724	2,684	2,725	33,155
2013	2,959	2,970	3,009	2,989	2,970	2,949	2,099	2,140	2,079	2,069	2,026	2,047	30,306
2014	1,819	1,818	1,878	1,938	2,164	2,212	2,202	2,202	2,212	2,182	2,193	2,143	24,963
2015[1]	2,183	2,181	2,211	2,241	2,211	2,271	2,251	2,261	2,261				26,761

[1] Preliminary.   Source: U.S. Geological Survey (USGS)

Tin Stocks (Pig-Industrial) in the United States, on First of Month   In Metric Tons

Year	Jan.	Feb.	Mar.	Apr.	May	June	July	Aug.	Sept.	Oct.	Nov.	Dec.
2006	5,400	5,380	5,330	5,350	5,400	5,380	5,420	5,400	5,740	5,650	5,650	5,830
2007	5,700	5,970	6,030	6,030	5,860	5,570	5,270	5,270	5,260	5,310	5,920	6,000
2008	6,140	8,070	8,280	8,020	8,000	7,970	7,930	7,960	7,980	7,960	7,990	7,940
2009	7,970	7,890	7,660	7,640	7,620	7,640	7,570	7,630	7,590	7,540	7,520	7,470
2010	7,450	7,030	7,080	7,060	7,080	7,180	7,270	7,220	7,130	7,060	7,090	7,090
2011	6,920	6,660	6,710	6,740	6,750	6,820	6,860	6,880	6,860	6,860	6,800	6,700
2012	5,230	6,810	6,860	6,780	6,710	6,750	6,790	7,290	7,280	7,340	7,310	6,360
2013	6,470	6,670	6,640	6,590	6,640	7,110	6,660	6,670	6,680	6,580	6,570	6,480
2014	6,520	6,540	6,560	6,570	6,490	6,800	6,800	6,770	6,740	7,360	7,060	6,970
2015[1]	7,010	6,860	6,910	6,960	6,910	6,910	7,360	6,970	6,900			

[1] Preliminary.   Source: U.S. Geological Survey (USGS)

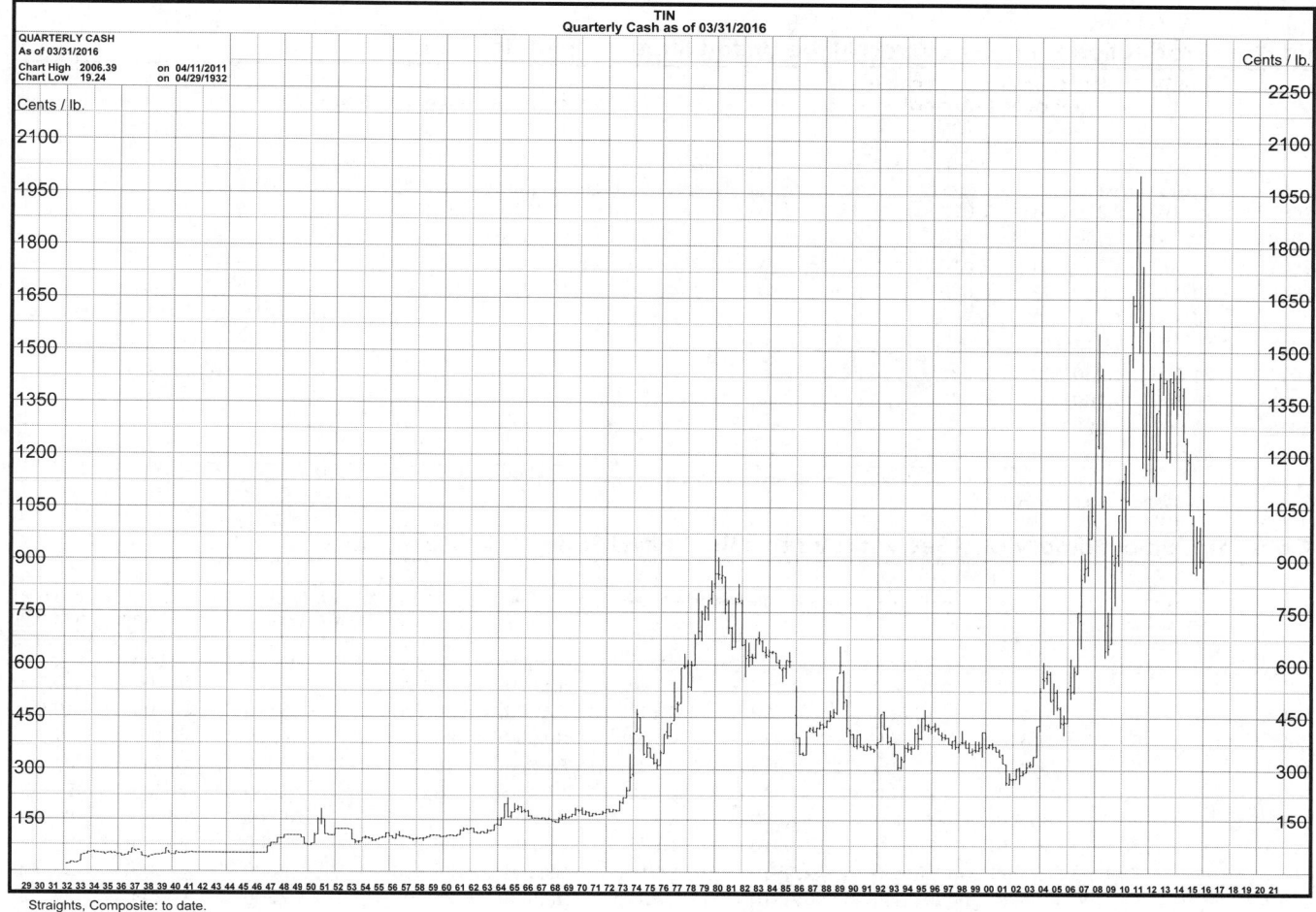

TIN
Quarterly Cash as of 03/31/2016

QUARTERLY CASH
As of 03/31/2016
Chart High 2006.39   on 04/11/2011
Chart Low   19.24   on 04/29/1932

Straights, Composite: to date.

Average Price of Ex-Dock Tin in New York[1]   In Cents Per Pound

Year	Jan.	Feb.	Mar.	Apr.	May	June	July	Aug.	Sept.	Oct.	Nov.	Dec.	Average
2006	338.27	373.87	378.76	420.35	420.53	376.76	400.64	404.26	428.83	461.66	475.57	524.69	417.02
2007	535.46	604.14	648.82	656.53	661.04	659.63	689.99	705.01	700.45	748.39	777.74	756.89	678.67
2008	760.82	800.60	917.15	1,001.99	1,108.30	1,027.62	1,070.50	930.65	850.83	672.97	646.77	532.54	860.06
2009	539.32	523.68	508.12	554.44	646.09	702.56	657.47	694.15	695.88	701.13	698.44	721.79	636.92
2010	823.31	764.25	818.62	870.50	821.34	809.88	851.80	967.17	1,057.81	1,223.59	1,191.80	1,211.71	950.98
2011	1,274.29	1,456.60	1,422.69	1,501.64	1,339.50	1,188.91	1,271.42	1,137.37	1,055.80	1,019.31	998.78	913.27	1,214.96
2012	1,005.52	1,136.74	1,074.53	1,034.47	958.73	905.04	874.07	879.88	972.20	998.11	969.71	1,065.21	989.52
2013	1,147.61	1,132.62	1,088.32	1,016.82	968.64	946.60	914.64	1,008.50	1,062.18	1,076.08	1,064.68	1,061.89	1,040.71
2014	1,026.81	1,061.00	1,074.64	1,088.65	1,083.18	1,059.89	1,041.12	1,037.98	983.57	929.95	931.02	925.65	1,020.29
2015	910.45	857.51	818.81	754.37	745.34	721.70	NQ	NQ	NQ	733.84	694.41	693.59	770.00

Source: American Metal Market (AMM)

Average Price of Tin (Straights) in New York   In Cents Per Pound

Year	Jan.	Feb.	Mar.	Apr.	May	June	July	Aug.	Sept.	Oct.	Nov.	Dec.	Average
2006	464.54	509.45	519.31	574.53	575.57	517.52	548.29	552.06	583.57	623.07	644.19	705.62	568.14
2007	719.05	811.07	873.03	883.74	886.54	884.67	931.50	954.26	949.21	1,012.46	1,049.78	1,025.36	915.06
2008	1,025.05	1,071.97	1,224.20	1,325.79	1,461.85	1,357.22	1,410.60	1,229.27	1,124.02	887.70	841.86	694.41	1,137.83
2009	711.20	686.02	664.21	724.55	841.83	920.39	862.04	902.14	899.35	911.42	922.75	964.64	834.21
2010	1,090.89	1,011.26	1,082.71	1,149.23	1,084.11	1,067.12	1,117.84	1,268.74	1,386.44	1,597.89	1,552.75	1,588.29	1,249.77
2011	1,661.33	1,906.31	1,857.97	1,958.08	1,750.23	1,555.57	1,663.54	1,486.24	1,378.26	1,330.78	1,298.42	1,191.48	1,586.52
2012	1,312.08	1,481.62	1,404.14	1,351.56	1,251.34	1,180.70	1,142.08	1,148.33	1,269.91	1,300.73	1,264.64	1,393.41	1,291.71
2013	1,502.64	1,480.17	1,422.82	1,328.61	1,265.73	1,252.58	1,200.86	1,321.68	1,391.23	1,413.19	1,392.13	1,391.85	1,363.62
2014	1,345.40	1,388.75	1,406.24	1,423.40	1,416.15	1,388.17	1,365.31	1,362.21	1,289.78	1,219.57	1,223.03	1,211.06	1,336.59
2015	1,193.00	1,125.26	1,076.19	989.76	978.73	930.77	924.68	933.28	945.21	973.65	908.21	909.01	990.65

Source: U.S. Geological Survey (USGS)

TIN

Tin Plate Production & Tin Recovered in the United States   In Metric Tons

Year	Tinplate Waste ----- Gross Weight -----	Tinplate (All Forms) Gross Weight	Tin Content (Met. Ton)	Tin per Tonne of Plate (Kilograms)	Tin Metal	Bronze & Brass	Solder	Type Metal	Babbitt	Anti- monial Lead	Chemical Com- pounds	Misc.[2]	Grand Total
2005	W	2,270,000	7,670	3.4	----	----	----	----	----	----	----	----	----
2006	56,400	2,130,000	6,810	3.2	----	----	----	----	----	----	----	----	----
2007	58,900	1,780,000	7,010	3.9	----	----	----	----	----	----	----	----	----
2008	30,900	2,280,000	6,690	2.9	----	----	----	----	----	----	----	----	----
2009	14,500	1,150,000	6,200	5.4	----	----	----	----	----	----	----	----	----
2010	18,163	1,416,758	6,920	4.9	----	----	----	----	----	----	----	----	----
2011	21,500	1,230,000	6,330	5.2	----	----	----	----	----	----	----	----	----
2012	16,300	1,160,000	6,090	5.2	----	----	----	----	----	----	----	----	----
2013	20,800	1,090,000	6,030	5.5	----	----	----	----	----	----	----	----	----
2014[1]	32,900	1,030,000	5,680	5.5	----	----	----	----	----	----	----	----	----

[1] Preliminary.   [2] Includes foil, terne metal, cable lead, and items indicated by symbol "W".   W = Withheld.   NA = Not available.
Source: U.S. Geological Survey (USGS)

Consumption of Primary and Secondary Tin in the United States   In Metric Tons

Year	Net Import Reliance as a % of Apparent Consump	Stocks, Jan. 1[2]	Primary	Secondary	Scrap	Total	Available Supply	Stocks, Dec. 31 (Total Available Less Total Processed)	Total Pro- cessed	Consumed in Manu- facturing Products
2004	92	7,680	40,800	4,160	4,350	49,300	57,000	11,800	45,200	44,700
2005	78	8,060	32,500	5,790	3,840	42,200	50,200	9,120	41,000	40,600
2006	80	7,640	29,900	5,040	4,100	39,000	46,600	8,520	38,100	37,700
2007	72	7,230	25,600	4,950	3,030	33,600	40,800	8,980	31,700	31,100
2008	70	8,760	22,700	4,300	2,410	29,400	38,200	8,460	29,800	29,400
2009	74	8,940	26,200	5,930	2,170	34,300	43,200	10,300	32,900	32,600
2010	73	6,210	25,100	2,910	1,920	29,900	36,100	6,000	30,100	30,100
2011	73	5,830	25,200	2,840	916	29,000	34,800	5,880	28,900	28,500
2012	74	5,800	24,900	2,810	892	28,600	34,400	6,200	28,200	27,800
2013[1]	72	7,110	25,600	2,620	1,970	30,200	37,300	6,850	30,400	30,400

[1] Preliminary.   [2] Includes tin in transit in the U.S.   NA = Not available.   *Source: U.S. Geological Survey (USGS)*

Consumption of Tin in the United States, by Finished Products   In Metric Tons (Contained Tin)

Year	Tin- plate[2]	Solder	Babbitt	Bronze & Brass	Tinning	Chem- icals[3]	Tin Powder	Bar Tin & Anodes	White Metal	Other	Total	Total Primary	Total Secondary
2004	7,700	19,000	728	3,070	798	9,120	W	680	937	2,630	44,700	36,700	7,990
2005	7,250	16,700	554	3,200	790	8,360	W	709	W	3,030	40,600	31,400	9,170
2006	7,110	12,800	484	3,300	696	9,290	W	698	W	1,040	37,700	29,200	8,480
2007	7,010	10,400	604	2,800	451	6,070	W	788	W	1,120	31,100	23,700	7,490
2008	6,840	5,110	604	2,460	395	5,440	227	767	W	5,370	29,200	23,100	6,250
2009	6,130	5,110	322	2,200	340	9,290	193	245	W	7,000	32,600	24,800	7,750
2010	6,920	7,340	288	2,460	387	9,470	192	W	W	811	30,100	25,300	4,820
2011	6,230	4,100	315	3,810	552	9,990	W	W	W	757	28,500	25,200	3,280
2012	6,090	4,930	281	2,460	467	9,860	W	W	W	726	27,800	24,500	3,240
2013[1]	6,030	5,940	820	2,380	511	6,790	W	W	W	807	30,400	25,700	4,730

[1] Preliminary.   [2] Includes small quantity of secondary pig tin and tin acquired in chemicals.   [3] Including tin oxide.
W = Withheld proprietary data.   *Source: U.S. Geological Survey (USGS)*

Salient Statistics of Recycling Tin in the United States

Year	New Scrap[1] In Thousands of Metric Tons	Old Scrap[2]	Recycled Metal[3]	Apparent Supply	Percent Recycled	New Scrap[1] Value in Millions of Dollars	Old Scrap[2]	Recycled Metal[3]	Apparent Supply
2006	2.3	11.6	13.9	51.6	27	29.1	145	174	642
2007	2.9	12.2	15.1	44.5	31	56.7	242	298	882
2008	2.1	11.7	13.8	40.9	34	52.2	291	343	1,020
2009	2.3	11.1	13.4	44.7	30	42.5	204	247	825
2010	2.7	11.1	13.8	44.1	31	73.4	303	376	1,200
2011	2.5	11.0	13.6	42.8	32	87.9	383	470	1,490
2012	2.4	11.2	13.5	43.1	31	67.3	316	383	1,220
2013	2.4	11.1	13.5	39.8	34	71.1	330	401	1,190

[1] Scrap that results from the manufacturing process.   [2] Scrap that results from consumer products.   [3] Metal recovered from new plus old scrap.
Source: U.S. Geological Survey (USGS)

Titanium

Titanium (atomic symbol Ti) is a silver-white, metallic element used primarily to make light, strong alloys. It ranks ninth in abundance among the elements in the crust of the earth but is never found in the pure state. It occurs as an oxide in various minerals. It was first discovered in 1791 by Rev. William Gregor and was first isolated as a basic element in 1910. Titanium was named after the mythological Greek god Titan for its strength.

Titanium is extremely brittle when cold, but is malleable and ductile at a low red heat, and thus easily fabricated. Due to its strength, low weight, and resistance to corrosion, titanium is used in metallic alloys and as a substitute for aluminum. It is used extensively in the aerospace industry, in desalinization plants, construction, medical implants, paints, pigments, and lacquers.

Supply – World production of titanium ilmenite concentrates in 2014 (latest data) fell -15.3% yr/yr to 6.680 million metric tons, down from the 2013 record high of 7,890 million metric tons. The world's largest producers of titanium ilmenite concentrates are Australia with 16.5% of world production in 2014, China (15.0%), Norway (6.0%), Vietnam (7.5%), and India (5.1%). World production of titanium rutile concentrates in 2014 (latest data) rose +15.4% yr/yr to 770,000 metric tons, which is a new record high. The world's largest producers are Australia with 62.3% of world production in 2014 followed by Sierra Leone with 15.6% and South Africa with 8.4%.

Demand – U.S. consumption of titanium dioxide pigment in 2013 (latest data) rose +14.4% yr/yr to 826,000 metric tons, but remained well below 2004's record high of 1.170 million metric tons. U.S. consumption of ilmenite in 2005 (latest data available) fell -12.8% to 1.290 million metric tons, down from 2004's 8-year high of 1.480 million metric tons. U.S. consumption of rutile in 2005 (latest data) fell 4.7% yr/yr to a 7-year low of 424,000 metric tons.

Trade – U.S. imports of titanium dioxide pigment in 2013 (latest data) rose by +4.9% yr/yr to 213,000 metric tons, still below the 2005 record high of 341,000 metric tons. U.S. imports of ilmenite in 2013 rose +4.5% yr/yr to 389,000 metric tons.

World Produciton of Titanium Illmenite Concentrates In Thousands of Metric Tons

Year	Australia[2]	Brazil	China	Egypt	India	Malaysia	Norway	Ukraine	United States	Vietnam	World Total	-- Titaniferous Slag[4] --- Canada	Africa
2005	2,080	82	900	----	686	38	810	375	500	523	6,050	860	1,020
2006	2,508	95	1,000	----	690	46	850	470	500	605	6,860	930	1,230
2007	2,503	100	1,100	----	700	60	882	500	400	643	7,140	960	1,270
2008	2,230	130	1,100	----	610	37	915	520	400	710	7,010	1,000	1,252
2009	1,611	53	900	----	700	16	671	500	300	699	6,260	765	1,084
2010	1,651	166	1,400	----	540	19	864	500	400	912	7,530	1,090	1,252
2011	1,501	166	1,700	----	550	29	870	261	400	841	7,570	878	1,346
2012	1,572	166	1,600	----	560	22	831	247	300	1,144	7,800	900	1,400
2013	960	100	1,020	----	340		498	150	200	720	6,730	770	1,190
2014[1]	1,100	70	1,000	----	340		400	210	100	500	6,680	900	1,100

[1] Preliminary. [2] Includes leucoxene. [3] Approximately 10% of total production is ilmenite. Beginning in 1988, 25% of Norway's ilmenite production was used to produce slag containing 75% TiO2. NA = Not available. *Source: U.S. Geological Survey (USGS)*

Salient Statistics of Titanium in the United States In Metric Tons

Year	--- Titanium Dioxide Pigment --- Production	Imports[3]	Apparent Consumption	------ Ilmenite ------ Imports[3]	Consumption	-- Titanium Slag --- Imports[3]	Consumption	------- Rutile[4] ------- Imports[3]	Consumption	------ Exports of Titanium Products ------ Ores & Concentrates	Scrap	Dioxide & Pigments	Ingots, Billets, Etc.
2004	1,540,000	264,000	1,170,000	701,000	1,480,000	457,000	----	360,000	445,000	8,690	9,760	576,000	4,990
2005	1,310,000	341,000	1,130,000	822,000	1,290,000	667,000	----	366,000	424,000	20,900	20,600	486,000	6,350
2006	1,370,000	288,000	1,080,000	187,000	----	693,000	----	355,000	----	32,800	10,800	513,000	7,900
2007	1,440,000	221,000	979,000	246,000	----	749,000	----	463,800	----	9,730	9,510	564,000	8,670
2008	1,350,000	183,000	800,000	433,000	----	461,000	----	487,000	----	14,900	8,180	668,000	10,500
2009	1,230,000	175,000	757,000	250,000	----	414,000	----	279,600	----	14,800	4,200	617,000	7,240
2010	1,320,000	204,000	767,000	377,000	----	475,000	----	351,000	----	18,900	3,480	717,000	8,450
2011	1,290,000	200,000	706,000	377,000	----	513,000	----	381,000	----	26,600	5,150	741,000	15,600
2012[1]	1,140,000	203,000	722,000	374,000	----	618,000	----	389,000	----	43,000	8,760	587,000	13,800
2013[2]	1,280,000	213,000	826,000	389,000	----	682,000	----	406,000	----	11,500	4,700	624,000	12,500

[1] Preliminary. [2] Estimate. [3] For consumption. [4] Natural and synthetic. W = Withheld. *Source: U.S. Geological Survey (USGS)*

TITANIUM

World Production of Titanium Rutile Concentrates   In Metric Tons

Year	Australia	Brazil	India	Mada-gascar	Malaysia	Mozam-bique	Sierra Leone	South Africa	Sri Lanka	Thailand	Ukraine[2]	United States	World Total
2007	312,000	3,000	21,000	----	1,450	8,782	82,527	114,000	4,607	----	60,000	W	607,000
2008	325,000	2,309	21,000	----	1,834	6,552	78,908	134,000	11,335	----	60,000	W	641,000
2009	285,000	2,737	21,000	3,200	1,502	1,800	63,864	136,000	2,276	----	60,000	W	577,000
2010	429,000	2,331	24,000	5,700	7,567	4,700	68,198	130,000	2,568	----	60,000	W	734,000
2011	474,000	2,350	25,000	9,400	10,810	6,455	67,916	149,000	2,700	----	60,000	W	808,000
2012	439,000	1,881	26,000	13,000	20,008	3,713	94,493	150,000	2,800	----	58,000	W	809,000
2013	423,000	2,000	24,000	8,000	14,000	9,000	81,000	59,000		----	50,000	W	667,000
2014[1]	480,000		26,000	7,000	14,000		120,000	65,000		----	50,000	W	770,000

[1] Preliminary.   NA = Not available.   *Source: U.S. Geological Survey (USGS)*

World Production of Titanium Sponge Metal & U.S. Consumption of Titanium Concentrates

| | Production of Titanium (In Metric Tons) Sponge Metal[2] | | | | | | U.S. Consumption of Titanium Concentrates, by Products (In Metric Tons) Ilmenite (TiO$_2$ Content) | | | Rutile (TiO$_2$ Content) | | | |
Year	China	Japan	Russia	United Kingdom	United States	Total	Pigments	Misc.	Total	Welding Rod Coatings	Pigments	Misc.	Total
2006	18,000	37,800	32,000	----	W	121,000	----	----	1,510,000	----	----	----	----
2007	45,200	38,900	34,200	----	W	153,000	----	----	1,600,000	----	----	----	----
2008	49,600	40,900	29,500	----	W	155,000	----	----	1,440,000	----	----	----	----
2009	61,500	25,000	26,600	----	W	136,000	----	----	1,360,000	----	----	----	----
2010	57,800	31,600	25,800	----	W	137,000	----	----	1,520,000	----	----	----	----
2011	60,000	40,000	25,800	----	W	156,000	----	----	1,500,000	----	----	----	----
2012	80,000	40,000	44,000	----	W	200,000	----	----		----	----	----	----
2013[1]	100,000	40,000	45,000	----	W	222,000	----	----		----	----	----	----

[1] Preliminary.   [2] Unconsolidated metal in various forms.   [4] Included in Pigments.   NA = Not available.   W = Withheld.
Source: U.S. Geological Survey (USGS)

Average Prices of Titanium in the United States

Year	Ilmenite FOB Australian Ports[2]	Slag, 85% TiO2 FOB Richards Bay, South Africa	Rutile Large Lots Bulk, FOB U.S. East Coast[3]	Rutile Bagged FOB Australian Ports	Avg. Price of Grade A Titanium Sponge, FOB Shipping Point	Titanium Metal Sponge	Titanium Dioxide Pigments FOB US Plants Anatase	Titanium Dioxide Pigments FOB US Plants Rutile
	Dollars Per Metric Ton				Dollars Per Pound			
2006	$75 - $85	$402 - $454	$450 - $500	$570 - $700	----	$5.87 - $12.84	----	----
2007	$75 - $85	$418 - $457	$475 - $500	$650 - $700	----	$6.33 - $7.06	----	----
2008	$84 - $137	$393 - $407	$500 - $550	$675 - $725	----	$6.16 - $8.02	----	----
2009	$60 - $85	$401 - $439	$525 - $540	$700 - $800	----	$4.50 - $7.07	----	----
2010	$65 - $85	$367 - $433	$530 - $550	$760 - $805	----	$3.50 - $6.24	----	----
2011	$140 - $250	$468 - $494	$1,300-$1,400	$1,348-$1,600	----	$3.27 - $6.74	----	----
2012	$250 - $350	$512 - $763	$2,050-$2,400	$2,500-$2,800	----	$3.53 - $6.95	----	----
2013[1]	$250 - $350	$450 - $455	$1,400-$1,700	$1,500-$1,700	----	$3.20 - $6.23	----	----

[1] Preliminary.   NA = Not available.   *Source: U.S. Geological Survey (USGS)*

Average Price of Titanium[1] in United States   In Dollars Per Pound

Year	Jan.	Feb.	Mar.	Apr.	May	June	July	Aug.	Sept.	Oct.	Nov.	Dec.	Average
2010	8.75	8.75	8.92	9.13	10.10	10.70	11.00	11.00	11.00	11.00	11.43	11.50	10.27
2011	11.50	11.76	12.00	12.00	12.00	12.00	12.00	12.00	12.23	12.25	12.25	12.25	12.02
2012	12.25	11.95	11.75	11.75	11.72	11.00	11.00	11.00	11.00	11.00	11.00	10.61	11.34
2013	10.40	10.25	10.25	10.25	10.25	10.25	10.25	9.80	9.55	9.09	8.76	8.59	9.81
2014	8.26	8.07	8.13	8.13	8.26	8.38	8.38	8.66	8.75	8.75	8.63	8.50	8.41
2015	8.50	8.50	8.50	8.38	8.38	8.38	8.56	8.62	8.62	8.62	8.62	8.62	8.53

[1] Ingot, 6Al - 4V.   *Source: American Metal Market (AMM)*

Average Price of Titanium[1] in United States   In Dollars Per Pound

Year	Jan.	Feb.	Mar.	Apr.	May	June	July	Aug.	Sept.	Oct.	Nov.	Dec.	Average
2010	26.50	25.55	24.50	25.50	26.50	26.50	28.50	28.50	28.50	28.50	30.20	30.50	27.48
2011	30.50	30.50	30.50	30.50	30.50	30.50	30.50	30.50	30.50	30.50	30.50	30.50	30.50
2012	30.50	29.90	29.50	30.36	30.50	30.50	30.50	30.50	30.50	30.50	30.50	30.31	30.34
2013	29.07	27.50	27.50	27.50	27.50	27.50	27.50	26.77	25.90	25.50	25.50	25.50	26.94
2014	25.50	25.50	25.50	25.50	25.76	26.00	26.00	26.00	26.00	26.00	25.75	25.50	25.75
2015	25.50	25.50	25.50	25.50	25.50	25.50	25.50	25.50	25.50	25.50	25.50	25.50	25.50

[1] Plate, Alloy.   *Source: American Metal Market (AMM)*

Tobacco

Tobacco is a member of the nightshade family. It is commercially grown for its leaves and stems, which are rolled into cigars, shredded for use in cigarettes and pipes, processed for chewing, or ground into snuff. Christopher Columbus introduced tobacco cultivation and use to Spain after observing natives from the Americas smoking loosely rolled tobacco-stuffed tobacco leaves.

Tobacco is cured, or dried, after harvesting and then aged to improve its flavor. The four common methods of curing are: air cured, fire cured, sun cured, and flue cured. Flue curing is the fastest method of curing and requires only about a week compared with up to 10 weeks for other methods. Cured tobacco is tied into small bundles of about 20 leaves and aged one to three years.

Virginia tobacco is by far the most popular type used in pipe tobacco since it is the mildest of all blending tobaccos. Approximately 60% of the U.S. tobacco crop is Virginia-type tobacco. Burley tobacco is the next most popular tobacco. It is air-cured, burns slowly and provides a relatively cool smoke. Other tobacco varieties include Perique, Kentucky, Oriental, and Latakia.

Prices – U.S. tobacco farm prices in 2014 (latest data) fell -3.8% to 209.4 cents per pound, below last year's record high.

Supply – World production of tobacco in 2013 (latest data) rose +2.6% yr/yr to 7.435 million metric tons, a new record high. The world's largest producers of tobacco are China with 42.4% of world production, followed at a distance by Brazil (with 11.4% of world production), India (11.2%), and the U.S. (4.7%). U.S. production in 2013 remained unchanged yr/yr at 345,837 metric tons, where it was down by more than half from the 2-decade high of 810,750 metric tons posted in 1997. Tobacco in the U.S. is grown primarily in the Mid-Atlantic States and they account for the vast majority of U.S. production. Specifically, the largest tobacco producing states in the U.S. are North Carolina (with 52.8% of U.S. production in 2015), Kentucky (21.1%), Virginia (7.4%), Tennessee (6.8%), Georgia (4.6%), and South Carolina with (3.7%).

U.S. production of flue-cured tobacco (type 11-14), the most popular tobacco type grown in the U.S., fell by -15.9% yr/yr to 481.850 million pounds in 2015. The second most popular type is burley tobacco (type 31), which saw U.S. production in 2015 fell -32.0% to 148.195 million pounds.

Total U.S. production of tobacco in 2015 fell -18.8% yr/yr to 711.236 million pounds, which is less than half of the 2-decade high of 1.787 billion pounds posted in 1997. U.S. farmers have sharply reduced the planting acreage for tobacco. In 2015, harvested tobacco acreage fell -13.7% yr/yr to 326,550 acres, which is up from the 2005 record low of 297,080 but still far below the 25-year high of 836,230 posted in 1997. Yield in 2015 fell -6.0% to 2,178 down from a 15-year high of 2,325 pounds per acre in 2009. The farm value of the U.S. tobacco crop in 2014 (latest data) rose +16.5% yr/yr to $1.835 billion.

U.S. marketings of flue-cured tobacco (Types 11-14) in the 2006-07 (latest data) marketing year rose by +18.5% yr/yr to 454.7 million pounds. U.S. marketings of burley tobacco (Type 31) in the 2006-07 marketing year rose by +6.9% yr/yr to 224.6 million pounds.

U.S. production of cigarettes in 2009 (latest data) fell -14.6% to 338.1 billion cigarettes, which was far below the record high of 754.5 million posted in 1996. U.S. production of cigars rose by +65.2% yr/yr to 8.231 billion in 2009. U.S. production of chewing tobacco in 2009 fell by 9.8% to 29.3 million pounds, which was a record low.

Demand – U.S. per capita consumption of tobacco products in 2006 (latest data) was unchanged at 3.69 pounds per person but there appears to be a shifting from cigarettes to cigars. The 3.69 pounds per capita consumption of tobacco in 2006 is less than half the record high of 9.68 pounds per person that occurred at the beginning of the series in 1970. Per capita cigarette consumption in 2006 fell 1.5% yr/yr to 1,691 cigarettes per person, which was a record low. Per capita consumption of cigars in 2006 rose +1.9% yr/yr to a record high of 47.80 cigars per person. Per capita consumption of loose smoking tobacco in 2006 fell –6.3% yr/yr to 0.15 pounds.

Trade – U.S. tobacco exports in 2014 (latest data) fell -5.5% yr/yr to 330.3 million pounds but remained above the record low of 325.8 million pounds seen in 2002. Meanwhile, U.S. tobacco imports in 2004 (latest data) fell –10.9% yr/yr to 561.7 million pounds from the 11-year high of 630.1 million pounds see in 2003. The U.S. exported 111.3 billion cigarettes and 180 million cigars in 2006.

World Production of Leaf Tobacco   In Metric Tons

Year	Brazil	Canada	China	Greece	India	Indo-nesia	Italy	Japan	Pakistan	Turkey	United States	Zim-babwe	World Total
2004	921,281	42,430	2,406,000	133,937	549,900	165,108	117,882	52,659	86,200	133,913	400,012	78,312	6,590,379
2005	889,426	43,000	2,683,000	124,351	549,100	153,470	115,983	46,800	100,500	135,247	292,574	83,230	6,757,733
2006	900,381	48,525	2,744,000	37,405	552,200	146,265	96,600	37,700	112,592	98,137	330,169	44,451	6,598,165
2007	908,679	44,000	2,395,480	29,370	520,000	164,851	110,000	37,800	103,240	74,584	357,273	79,000	6,186,873
2008	851,058	44,718	2,839,950	20,500	490,000	168,037	92,560	38,500	107,765	93,403	363,103	81,952	6,594,880
2009	863,079	45,951	3,067,930	27,098	622,830	176,510	97,860	36,600	104,996	85,000	373,117	85,085	7,056,890
2010	787,817	40,120	3,005,930	22,000	690,000	135,700	89,112	29,300	119,323	55,000	325,766	109,737	6,889,920
2011	951,933	33,575	3,158,740	23,900	830,000	214,600	70,130	23,600	102,834	45,000	271,363	111,570	7,448,830
2012[1]	810,550	34,500	3,127,870	24,000	820,000	260,800	50,620	19,700	97,878	75,000	345,837	115,000	7,248,320
2013[2]	850,673	34,500	3,150,200	24,000	830,000	260,200	49,770	19,700	108,307	90,000	345,837	150,000	7,435,070

[1] Preliminary.   [2] Estimate.   *Source: Food and Agriculture Organization of the United Nations (FAO-UN)*

TOBACCO

Production and Consumption of Tobacco Products in the United States

Year	Cigar-ettes - Billions -	Cigars[3] - Millions -	Plug	Twist	Chewing Tobacco Loose-leaf	Total	Smoking Tobacco	Snuff[4]	Cigar-ettes	Cigars[3]	Cigar-ettes	Cigars[3]	Smoking Tobacco	Chewing Tobacco	Total Products
					In Millions of Pounds				Number		In Pounds				
2000	593.2	2,825	2.6	0.8	46.0	49.4	13.6	69.5	2,049	38.0	3.40	.62	.13	.48	4.10
2001	562.8	3,741	2.4	0.8	43.9	47.1	12.8	70.9	2,051	41.2	3.50	.68	.15	.47	4.30
2002	484.3	3,816	2.2	0.8	41.5	44.5	15.5	72.7	1,982	41.8	3.40	.68	.16	.43	4.16
2003	499.4	4,017	1.7	0.7	39.2	41.6	17.8	73.8	1,890	44.5	3.20	.73	.16	.40	3.97
2004	492.7	4,342	1.7	0.7	37.0	39.3	16.1	79.3	1,814	47.9	3.10	.79	.15	.37	3.87
2005	498.7	3,674	1.4	0.6	37.2	39.2	17.4	86.7	1,716	46.9	2.90	.77	.16	.36	3.69
2006	483.7	4,256	1.3	0.6	36.4	38.3	16.5	81.8	1,691	47.8	2.90	.78	.15	.37	3.69
2007	449.7	4,797	1.2	0.5	35.1	36.8	NA	NA	NA	NA	NA	NA	NA	NA	NA
2008[1]	396.1	4,984	1.1	0.5	30.9	32.5	----	----	----	----	----	----	----	----	----
2009[2]	338.1	8,232	0.9	0.5	28.0	29.3	----	----	----	----	----	----	----	----	----

[1] Preliminary.   [2] Estimate.   [3] Large cigars and cigarillos.   [4] Includes loose-leaf.   [5] Consumption of tax-paid tobacco products. Unstemmed rocessing weight.   [6] 18 years and older.   NA = Not available.   *Source: Economic Research Service, U.S. Department of Agriculture (ERS-USDA)*

Production of Tobacco in the United States, by States   In Thousands of Pounds

Year	Georgia	Kentucky	North Carolina	Ohio	Pennsyl-vania	South Carolina	Tennessee	Virginia	Total
2006	30,090	186,780	330,580	7,000	16,790	48,300	49,135	47,322	727,897
2007	39,775	197,040	383,420	7,175	18,310	46,125	38,636	46,142	787,653
2008	33,600	205,850	390,360	6,970	17,630	39,900	52,380	45,970	800,504
2009	28,014	206,900	423,856	6,800	18,660	38,850	49,960	46,530	822,581
2010	26,790	181,760	352,625	5,125	19,965	36,000	45,740	44,299	718,190
2011	26,775	172,140	251,565	3,360	20,655	26,350	45,363	48,125	598,252
2012	22,500	195,800	381,190	3,990	22,985	25,200	53,000	53,599	762,709
2013	22,400	187,240	362,660	4,620	21,260	24,650	44,570	52,613	723,579
2014	34,500	214,280	453,860	4,300	22,250	33,180	52,155	57,651	876,415
2015[1]	32,400	149,830	375,850	3,610	18,090	26,000	48,460	52,430	711,236

[1] Preliminary.   *Source: Agricultural Statistics Board, U.S. Department of Agriculture (ASB-USDA)*

Salient Statistics of Tobacco in the United States

Year	Acres Harvested 1,000 Acres	Yield Per Acre Pounds	Pro-duction Million Pounds	Farm Price cents Lb.	Farm Value Million $	Tobacco (June - July) Exports[2]	Imports[3]	Cigar-ettes	U.S. Exports of Cigars & Cheroots Tobacco	All Tobacco	Smoking Tobacco[4]	Stocks of Tobacco[5] Various Types All Tobacco	Fire Cured[6]	Cigar Filler[7]	Mary-land
						Million Pounds		In Millions				In Millions of Pounds			
2006	339.0	2,144	728	166.5	1,211	----	----	111,317	180	----	----	1,167	----	10.8	0.8
2007	356.0	2,213	788	169.3	1,329	----	----	----	-----	----	----	----	----	----	----
2008	354.5	2,258	801	185.9	1,488	----	----	----	-----	----	----	----	----	----	----
2009	354.0	2,323	823	183.7	1,511	----	----	----	-----	----	----	----	----	----	----
2010	337.5	2,128	718	178.2	1,280	----	----	----	-----	----	----	----	----	----	----
2011	325.0	1,841	598	184.7	1,105	----	----	----	-----	----	----	----	----	----	----
2012	336.2	2,268	763	207.2	1,580	----	----	----	-----	----	----	----	----	----	----
2013	355.7	2,034	724	217.7	1,575	----	----	----	-----	----	----	----	----	----	----
2014	378.4	2,316	876	209.4	1,835	----	----	----	-----	----	----	----	----	----	----
2015[1]	326.6	2,178	711	201.6	1,434	----	----	----	-----	----	----	----	----	----	----

[1] Preliminary.   [2] Domestic.   [3] For consumption.   [4] In bulk.   [5] Flue-cured and cigar wrapper, year beginning July 1; for all other types, October 1.   [6] Kentucky-Tennessee types 22-23.   [7] Types 41-46.   *Source: Economic Research Service, U.S. Department of Agriculture (ERS-USDA)*

Tobacco Production in the United States, by Types   In Thousands of Pounds (Farm-Sale Weight)

Year	Class 1, Flue-cured (11-14)	Class 2, Fire-cured (21-23)	Class 3A, Light air-cured (31-32)	Class 3B, Dark air-cured (35-37)	Total Cigar types (41-61)	US Total
2006	447,190	39,392	219,895	13,155	8,265	727,897
2007	503,760	40,888	218,507	13,056	11,442	787,653
2008	499,220	62,190	205,310	25,340	8,444	800,504
2009	525,414	52,990	219,726	17,040	7,411	822,581
2010	451,290	48,379	192,520	15,180	10,821	718,190
2011	344,610	51,721	178,265	16,082	7,574	598,252
2012	472,900	53,764	211,550	15,250	9,245	762,709
2013	454,350	50,388	197,165	13,790	7,886	723,579
2014	572,880	59,146	217,860	17,490	9,039	876,415
2015[1]	481,850	55,815	148,195	17,050	8,326	711,236

[1] Preliminary.   *Source: Agricultural Statistics Board, U.S. Department of Agriculture (ASB-USDA)*

U.S. Exports of Unmanufactured Tobacco   In Millions of Pounds (Declared Weight)

Year	Australia	Belgium-Luxem.	Denmark	France	Germany	Italy	Japan	Nether-lands	Sweden	Switzer-land	Thailand	United Kingdom	Total U.S. Exports
2006	4.9	16.8	8.4	7.5	81.2	3.2	3.9	37.0	.7	38.5	3.0	1.1	397.6
2007	3.5	18.0	9.7	13.2	63.1	.7	4.0	24.0	.3	41.7	1.8	.0	411.5
2008	1.3	3.9	6.5	7.0	39.2	.0	.0	46.3	.3	69.3	3.0	.1	372.3
2009	6.4	3.6	6.4	7.7	23.9	.4	.0	37.7	.3	59.1	2.8	.1	380.3
2010	5.2	44.6	4.5	8.3	20.8	.6	.0	44.7	.4	34.7	3.0	1.1	394.0
2011	.8	10.0	.7	8.9	25.9	.8	.0	27.2	.5	65.6	3.7	6.0	406.5
2012	.7	10.3	.8	11.8	20.2	.5	.2	29.6	.2	46.2	3.6	2.9	353.4
2013	.3	3.8	.7	6.5	20.1	1.5	.0	25.0	.5	62.2	2.7	1.4	349.9
2014	.1	9.8	1.2	9.8	14.4	.5	.0	14.3	.4	63.5	3.2	3.2	330.3
2015[1]	.1	10.9	1.1	5.2	15.2	.6	.0	7.9	.4	89.7	1.8	1.0	344.1

[1] Preliminary.   *Source: Economic Research Service, U.S. Department of Agriculture (ERS-USDA)*

U.S. Salient Statistics for Flue-Cured Tobacco (Types 11-14) in the United States   In Millions of Pounds

Year	Acres Harvested 1,000	Yield Per Acre Pounds	Mar-ketings	Stocks Oct. 1	Total Supply	Exports	Domestic Disap-pearance	Total Disap-pearance	Farm Price cents/Lb.	Placed Under Gov't Loan (Mil. Lb.)	Price Support Level (cents/) Lb.	Loan Stocks Nov. 30	Uncom-mitted
2006-07	213.1	2,095	455	604	1,058	270	248	518	149.6	----	----	----	----
2007-08	223.0	2,259	----	----	----	----	----	----	152.7	----	----	----	----
2008-09	223.0	2,239	----	----	----	----	----	----	175.7	----	----	----	----
2009-10	223.8	2,348	----	----	----	----	----	----	175.4	----	----	----	----
2010-11	210.9	2,140	----	----	----	----	----	----	----	----	----	----	----
2011-12	206.9	1,666	----	----	----	----	----	----	----	----	----	----	----
2012-13	206.0	2,296	----	----	----	----	----	----	----	----	----	----	----
2013-14	228.8	1,986	----	----	----	----	----	----	----	----	----	----	----
2014-15[1]	245.3	2,335	----	----	----	----	----	----	----	----	----	----	----
2015-16[2]	218.0	2,210	----	----	----	----	----	----	----	----	----	----	----

[1] Preliminary.   [2] Estimate.   NA = Not available.   *Source: Economic Research Service, U.S. Department of Agriculture (ERS-USDA)*

Salient Statistics for Burley Tobacco (Type 31) in the United States   In Millions of Pounds

Year	Acres Harvested 1,000	Yield Per Acre Pounds	Mar-ketings	Stocks Oct. 1	Total Supply	Exports	Domestic Disap-pearance	Total Disap-pearance	Farm Price cents/Lb.	Gross Sales[3]	Price Support Level cents/Lb.	Loan Stocks Nov. 30	Uncom-mitted
2006-07	103.6	2,095	225	403	628	190	56	246	163.8	----	----	----	----
2007-08	106.3	2,033	----	----	----	----	----	----	160.1	----	----	----	----
2008-09	97.5	2,067	----	----	----	----	----	----	166.9	----	----	----	----
2009-10	101.9	2,109	----	----	----	----	----	----	170.9	----	----	----	----
2010-11	97.6	1,922	----	----	----	----	----	----	----	----	----	----	----
2011-12	88.9	1,938	----	----	----	----	----	----	----	----	----	----	----
2012-13	101.4	2,021	----	----	----	----	----	----	----	----	----	----	----
2013-14	99.0	1,944	----	----	----	----	----	----	----	----	----	----	----
2014-15[1]	101.5	2,100	----	----	----	----	----	----	----	----	----	----	----
2015-16[2]	78.9	1,834	----	----	----	----	----	----	----	----	----	----	----

[1] Preliminary.   [2] Estimate.   [3] Before Christmas holidays.   NA = Not available.
Source: Economic Research Service, U.S. Department of Agriculture (ERS-USDA)

Exports of Tobacco from the United States (Quantity and Value)   In Metric Tons

Year	Unmanufactured Flue-Cured	Value 1,000 USD	Burley	Value 1,000 USD	Total	Value 1,000 USD	Manu-factured	Value 1,000 USD
2006	88,020	569,431	63,214	409,272	180,368	1,141,374	22,261	1,320,283
2007	82,093	541,816	75,905	498,168	186,643	1,207,945	17,552	1,122,176
2008	100,848	730,677	44,506	342,732	168,885	1,238,047	25,474	824,638
2009	86,429	659,772	37,395	300,744	172,504	1,158,970	4,654	489,480
2010	85,789	662,648	32,687	265,927	178,726	1,167,644	4,981	454,459
2011	88,876	643,946	33,385	256,006	184,369	1,148,991	7,472	489,454
2012	77,073	607,725	32,051	243,411	160,308	1,101,214	18,405	482,614
2013	78,079	650,887	32,124	265,809	158,728	1,137,947	21,930	485,412
2014[1]	76,239	645,462	25,441	217,329	149,834	1,086,013	18,095	426,879
2015[2]	77,942	657,193	26,157	227,153	156,101	1,109,329	21,769	422,498

[1] Preliminary.   [2] Forecast.   *Source: Foreign Agricultural Service, U.S. Department of Agriculture (FAS-USDA)*

Tungsten

Tungsten (atomic symbol W) is a grayish-white, lustrous, metallic element. The atomic symbol for tungsten is W because of its former name of Wolfram. Tungsten has the highest melting point of any metal at about 3410 degrees Celsius and boils at about 5660 degrees Celsius. In 1781, the Swedish chemist Carl Wilhelm Scheele discovered tungsten.

Tungsten is never found in nature but is instead found in the minerals wolframite, scheelite, huebnertite, and ferberite. Tungsten has excellent corrosion resistance qualities and is resistant to most mineral acids. Tungsten is used as filaments in incandescent lamps, electron and television tubes, alloys of steel, spark plugs, electrical contact points, cutting tools, and in the chemical and tanning industries.

Prices – The average monthly price of tungsten at U.S. ports in 2015 fell by -36.4% yr/yr to $227.32 per short ton, moving farther below the 2012 record high of $375.16.

Supply – World concentrate production of tungsten in 2015 rose by +0.2% yr/yr to 87,000 metric tons, which is a new record high. The world's largest producer of tungsten by far is China with 71,000 metric tons of production in 2015, which was 81.6% of total world production. Russia is the next largest producer at 2.9% with miniscule production of only 2,500 metric tons.

Trade – The U.S. in 2015 relied on imports for 49% of its tungsten consumption. U.S. imports for consumption in 2015 fell by -4.4% yr/yr to 3,900 metric tons. U.S. exports in 2015 fell by -75.6% yr/yr to only 300 metric tons.

World Concentrate Production of Tungsten   In Metric Tons (Contained Tungsten[3])

Year	Austria	Bolivia	Brazil	Burma	Canada	China	Korea, North	Mongolia	Portugal	Russia	Rwanda	Thailand	Total
2008	1,122	1,148	408	136	2,277	50,000	270	142	982	3,163	670	420	61,900
2009	887	1,023	192	87	1,964	51,000	100	39	823	2,665	380	190	61,200
2010	977	1,204	166	163	420	59,000	110	20	799	2,785	330	300	68,400
2011	861	1,124	244	140	1,966	61,800	110	13	819	3,314	520	160	73,900
2012	706	1,247	381	140	2,194	64,000	100	66	763	3,537	700	80	76,400
2013	850	1,253	380	140	2,128	68,000	65	----	692	3,600	730	100	81,400
2014[1]	870	1,250			2,340	71,000			671	2,800	1,000		86,800
2015[2]	870	1,200			1,700	71,000			630	2,500	1,000		87,000

[1] Preliminary.   [2] Estimate.   [3] Conversion Factors: WO$_3$ to W, multiply by 0.7931; 60% WO$_3$ to W, multiply by 0.4758.
Source: U.S. Geological Survey (USGS)

Salient Statistics of Tungsten in the United States   In Metric Tons (Contained Tungsten)

Year	Net Import Reliance as a % Apparent Consump	Total Con-sumption	Steel Tool	Stainless & Heat Assisting	Alloy Steel[3]	Super-alloys	Cutting & Wear Resistant Materials	Products Made From Metal Powder	Miscel-laneous	Chemical and Ceramic	Exports	Imports for Con-sumption	Stocks, Dec. 31 Concentrates Con-sumers	Pro-ducers
2008	60	W	W	283	W	W	6,650	W	----	80	496	3,990	W	W
2009	68	W	W	244	W	386	4,070	W	----	84	38	3,590	W	W
2010	63	4,820	W	71	W	W	5,990	W	----	99	276	2,740	W	W
2011	40	W	W	96	W	W	6,760	W	----	88	169	3,640	W	W
2012	39	W	W	123	W	W	6,800	W	----	90	203	3,650	W	W
2013	41	W	W	86	W	W	6,260	W	----	88	1,060	3,690	W	W
2014[1]	43	W									1,230	4,080	W	W
2015[2]	49	W									300	3,900	W	W

[1] Preliminary.   [2] Estimate.   [3] Other than tool.   [4] Included with stainless & heat assisting.   W = Withheld.
Source: U.S. Geological Survey (USGS)

Average Price of Tungsten at U.S. Ports (Including Duty)   In Dollars Per Short Ton

Year	Jan.	Feb.	Mar.	Apr.	May	June	July	Aug.	Sept.	Oct.	Nov.	Dec.	Average
2008	252.50	252.50	252.50	252.50	252.50	252.50	252.50	252.50	252.50	252.50	252.50	252.50	252.50
2009	252.50	215.00	205.00	205.00	165.00	165.00	165.00	165.00	165.00	165.00	166.58	180.00	184.51
2010	173.95	175.00	175.65	177.50	177.50	177.50	175.12	169.46	217.50	238.21	240.00	240.00	194.78
2011	263.45	307.00	307.00	307.00	307.00	307.00	307.00	307.00	307.00	385.67	425.00	425.00	329.59
2012	420.50	395.00	393.64	389.64	382.84	402.50	402.50	390.00	360.00	346.96	320.50	297.78	375.16
2013	297.74	329.45	351.29	351.50	356.73	382.55	406.86	417.28	407.13	392.50	387.29	378.50	371.57
2014	374.39	368.18	367.12	363.64	368.81	376.00	369.60	363.57	353.81	345.00	329.31	309.19	357.39
2015	293.18	281.80	272.64	254.20	243.45	228.50	222.95	207.90	188.81	184.77	173.33	176.28	227.32

U.S. Spot Quotations, 65% WO$_3$, Basis C.I.F.   *Source: U.S. Geological Survey (USGS)*

Turkeys

During the past three decades, the turkey industry has experienced tremendous growth in the U.S. Turkey production has more than tripled since 1970, with a current value of over $7 billion. Turkey was not a popular dish in Europe until a roast turkey was eaten on June 27, 1570, at the wedding feast of Charles XI of France and Elizabeth of Austria. The King was so impressed with the birds that the turkey subsequently became a popular dish at banquets held by French nobility.

The most popular turkey product continues to be the whole bird, with heavy demand at Thanksgiving and Christmas. The primary breeders maintain and develop the quality stock, concentrating on growth and conformation in males and fecundity in females, as well as characteristics important to general health and welfare. Turkey producers include large companies that produce turkeys all year-round and relatively small companies and farmers who produce turkeys primarily for the seasonal Thanksgiving market.

Prices – The average monthly price received by farmers for turkeys in the U.S. in 2015 rose +10.9% yr/yr to 81.1 cents per pound, a new record high. The monthly average retail price of turkeys (whole frozen) in the U.S. in 2015 fell -5.7% yr/yr to 151.1 cents per pound, below last year's record high of 164.9 cents per pound. Turkey prices have more than tripled from the low 40-cent area seen in the early 1970s.

Supply – World production of turkeys in 2014 (latest data) fell -1.4% yr/yr to 5.288 million metric tons. World production of turkeys has grown by more than two and one-half times since 1980 when production was 2.090 million metric tons. The U.S. was the largest producer of turkeys by far with 2.600 million metric tons of production in 2014, which is 49.2% of world production. The value of U.S. turkey production in the U.S. in 2013 (latest data) was $4.839 billion.

Demand – World consumption of turkeys in 2014 (latest data) fell -2.5% to 4.937 million metric tons. U.S. turkey consumption was 2.253 million metric tons in 2014, which accounts for 45.6% of world consumption. U.S. per capita consumption of turkeys in 2016 is forecasted to rise +3.2% yr/yr to 16.2 pounds per person per year. U.S. per capital consumption of turkeys has been in the range of 16-18 pounds since 1990, but the USDA is projecting that per capita consumption will drop somewhat.

Production of Turkey Meat, by Selected Countries   In Thousands of Metric Tons (RTC)

| | | | Production | | | | | | | | Consumption | | | | |
Year	Brazil	Canada	European Union	Mexico	Russia	United States	World Total	Brazil	Canada	European Union	Mexico	Russia	United States	World Total
2005	360	155	1,919	14	11	2,464	4,936	199	143	1,888	194	118	2,247	4,857
2006	353	163	1,858	14	16	2,543	4,960	197	144	1,841	197	107	2,297	4,866
2007	458	170	1,790	15	30	2,664	5,143	281	150	1,770	211	105	2,404	5,026
2008	465	180	1,830	15	39	2,796	5,337	261	163	1,836	212	107	2,434	5,101
2009	466	167	1,795	11	31	2,535	5,018	302	151	1,802	155	72	2,363	4,911
2010	485	159	1,946	11	70	2,527	5,212	327	143	1,913	163	105	2,306	5,023
2011	489	160	1,950	13	90	2,592	5,308	348	150	1,886	164	117	2,273	5,010
2012	510	161	2,010	14	100	2,671	5,480	340	142	1,953	173	120	2,282	5,105
2013[1]	520	168	1,950	10	100	2,599	5,361	359	150	1,893	166	112	2,291	5,063
2014[2]	470	170	1,920	9	105	2,600	5,288	350	152	1,848	158	115	2,253	4,937

[1] Preliminary.   [2] Forecast.   Source: Foreign Agricultural Service, U.S. Department of Agriculture (FAS-USDA)

Salient Statistics of Turkeys in the United States

| | | | Liveweight | | Value | | Ready-to-Cook Basis | | | | Production | | Wholesale Ready-to-Cook | |
| | | | | | | | Be-ginning | | Consumption | | Costs | | | |
Year	Poults Placed[3] In Thousands	Number Raised[4] In Thousands	Pro-duced Mil Lbs	Price cents Per Lb.	of Pro-duction Million $	Pro-duction In Millions of Pounds	ginning Stocks In Millions of Pounds	Exports In Millions of Pounds	Total In Millions of Pounds	Per Capita Lbs.	Feed Liveweight Basis	Total Liveweight Basis	Pro-duction Costs	3-Region Weighted Avg Price[5]
2005	293,683	252,053	7,096.0	44.9	3,182.8	5,432	288,357	570	4,952	16.7	----	----	----	----
2006	293,137	262,460	7,463.9	47.9	3,573.7	5,607	206,166	547	5,060	16.9	----	----	----	----
2007	308,402	266,828	7,566.3	52.3	3,954.5	5,873	218,356	547	5,294	17.5	----	----	----	----
2008	295,584	273,088	7,911.8	56.4	4,471.0	6,165	260,594	676	5,361	17.6	----	----	----	----
2009	273,992	247,359	7,149.3	49.9	3,573.3	5,588	396,144	535	5,201	16.9	----	----	----	----
2010	275,384	244,188	7,108.2	61.2	4,372.4	5,644	261,838	583	5,081	16.4	----	----	----	----
2011	277,931	248,500	7,313.2	68.0	4,987.6	5,791	191,560	703	5,014	16.1	----	----	----	----
2012	283,550	253,500	7,561.9	71.9	5,452.1	5,967	210,787	800	5,027	16.0	----	----	----	----
2013[1]	260,571	240,000	7,277.5	66.4	4,839.6	5,959	296,479	758	5,052	15.9	----	----	----	----
2014[2]	267,142	237,500	7,217.1	73.2	5,304.5	5,756	237,407	804	5,024	15.7	----	----	----	----

[1] Preliminary.   [2] Estimate.   [3] Poults placed for slaughter by hatcheries.   [4] Turkeys place August 1-July 31.   [5] Regions include central, eastern and western. Central region receives twice the weight of the other regions in calculating the average.
Source: Economic Research Service, U.S. Department of Agriculture (ERS-USDA)

TURKEYS

Turkey-Feed Price Ratio in the United States In Pounds[2]

Year	Jan.	Feb.	Mar.	Apr.	May	June	July	Aug.	Sept.	Oct.	Nov.	Dec.	Average
2006	7.0	6.9	6.9	7.3	7.1	7.6	7.7	8.5	9.1	9.6	9.4	5.9	7.8
2007	5.6	5.3	5.5	5.8	5.9	6.1	6.6	6.7	6.6	6.4	6.1	4.9	6.0
2008	4.1	3.6	4.0	4.0	4.3	4.3	4.5	4.7	5.4	5.9	5.6	4.4	4.6
2009	4.1	4.6	4.8	4.7	4.7	4.8	5.1	5.2	5.3	5.6	5.7	5.6	5.0
2010	4.8	5.3	5.6	5.9	6.2	6.9	6.9	6.7	6.6	6.8	6.4	5.6	6.1
2011	4.6	4.2	4.4	4.5	4.6	4.8	4.7	4.7	5.2	5.8	5.9	5.4	4.9
2012	4.8	4.7	4.8	5.0	5.0	5.1	4.4	4.3	4.8	4.9	4.7	4.3	4.7
2013	4.0	3.9	4.1	4.2	4.1	4.1	4.3	4.6	5.0	5.8	5.3	5.5	4.6
2014	5.2	5.4	5.3	5.1	5.4	5.6	6.2	6.8	7.6	8.3	8.1	7.1	6.3
2015[1]	6.3	6.6	6.8	7.1	7.9	8.4	8.5	9.4	10.0	10.6	10.2	9.8	8.5

[1] Preliminary.   [2] Pounds of feed equal in value to one pound of turkey, liveweight.   *Source: Economic Research Service, U.S. Department of Agriculture (ERS-USDA)*

Average Price Received by Farmers for Turkeys in the United States (Liveweight) In Cents Per Pound

Year	Jan.	Feb.	Mar.	Apr.	May	June	July	Aug.	Sept.	Oct.	Nov.	Dec.	Average
2006	40.8	39.6	40.3	42.5	43.3	45.4	45.9	48.6	53.3	62.7	66.3	42.7	47.6
2007	40.8	42.4	44.3	46.8	48.3	52.0	55.5	57.2	60.4	61.5	61.6	52.6	52.0
2008	44.8	47.5	52.9	55.1	58.1	59.8	60.9	63.2	66.4	64.6	58.6	44.5	56.4
2009	43.8	46.5	47.1	47.6	50.1	52.5	52.0	51.1	48.5	52.1	54.1	53.7	49.9
2010	46.5	49.1	52.2	53.7	56.1	61.7	64.7	66.8	69.0	73.4	73.6	67.7	61.2
2011	56.4	57.8	59.9	65.7	67.9	69.5	67.5	70.7	73.1	77.3	78.1	71.5	68.0
2012	65.7	65.0	69.0	73.7	72.7	73.9	72.9	74.4	76.2	76.9	75.1	67.4	71.9
2013	62.9	62.7	65.0	66.2	64.9	65.7	67.7	67.4	67.9	72.4	65.6	68.7	66.4
2014	64.5	66.4	68.3	68.7	72.6	72.8	74.0	75.6	77.5	82.2	82.1	73.4	73.2
2015[1]	66.2	66.9	68.3	70.2	75.9	81.2	84.8	89.7	92.5	97.2	92.2	88.6	81.1

[1] Preliminary.   *Source: Economic Research Service, U.S. Department of Agriculture (ERS-USDA)*

Average Wholesale Price of Turkeys[1] (Hens, 8-16 Lbs.) in New York In Cents Per Pound

Year	Jan.	Feb.	Mar.	Apr.	May	June	July	Aug.	Sept.	Oct.	Nov.	Dec.	Average
2006	68.29	65.84	67.67	69.75	71.27	72.95	74.95	78.70	84.40	95.83	99.51	74.20	76.95
2007	67.63	69.84	71.66	74.45	76.98	82.12	86.89	89.70	93.12	95.20	94.71	82.47	82.06
2008	73.74	76.40	82.20	85.99	89.19	91.45	92.91	96.85	99.62	97.27	87.44	74.88	87.33
2009	71.20	74.32	75.22	76.59	78.71	82.00	82.68	81.33	80.26	82.52	84.96	83.95	79.48
2010	76.50	78.72	82.64	83.90	86.45	93.38	98.68	102.45	105.81	111.03	109.29	101.16	94.17
2011	88.14	89.97	92.38	96.68	99.75	103.14	104.00	105.39	109.79	114.83	113.57	106.54	102.02
2012	98.35	100.15	103.70	106.89	107.77	106.00	106.43	108.90	110.54	110.27	108.86	99.08	105.58
2013	96.27	95.00	96.58	97.30	97.59	98.18	100.40	NA	101.22	106.75	105.64	103.83	99.89
2014	99.78	99.88	102.34	103.52	106.15	107.18	108.56	109.15	112.79	116.20	118.78	106.79	107.59
2015[2]	99.12	99.12	100.57	104.06	108.82	112.53	120.86	126.62	131.65	135.68	130.63	123.96	116.14

[1] Ready-to-cook.   [2] Preliminary.   *Source: Economic Research Service, U.S. Department of Agriculture (ERS-USDA)*

Certified Federally Inspected Turkey Slaughter in the U.S. (Ready-to-Cook Weights) In Millions of Pounds

Year	Jan.	Feb.	Mar.	Apr.	May	June	July	Aug.	Sept.	Oct.	Nov.	Dec.	Total
2006	443.0	412.4	487.9	430.3	492.8	504.4	453.5	493.6	456.5	535.8	499.7	423.5	5,633
2007	479.0	442.7	478.8	459.6	507.5	495.7	502.0	517.3	456.4	577.8	520.3	457.3	5,894
2008	544.6	504.0	484.5	515.9	517.9	519.7	544.1	503.8	511.5	570.1	507.9	488.2	6,212
2009	465.5	441.6	467.7	472.2	448.8	490.7	482.3	460.7	463.8	504.4	475.3	453.2	5,626
2010	421.1	423.3	488.0	452.8	437.5	487.0	463.9	478.2	464.1	521.7	518.0	458.6	5,614
2011	460.9	432.8	500.4	453.8	494.6	516.3	445.7	499.1	470.8	521.5	509.3	456.9	5,762
2012	474.5	464.8	499.9	475.2	516.9	504.1	494.9	526.3	450.7	576.3	512.9	438.5	5,935
2013	522.1	458.8	470.1	502.3	505.8	471.5	512.1	482.4	438.1	514.2	477.0	420.4	5,775
2014	451.3	419.6	455.0	468.5	469.3	484.2	498.0	480.6	490.4	558.2	478.4	472.1	5,726
2015[1]	489.6	431.5	499.0	493.9	432.4	455.9	446.2	447.3	450.1	522.4	466.9	458.3	5,594

[1] Preliminary.   *Source: Economic Research Service, U.S. Department of Agriculture (ERS-USDA)*

Per Capita Consumption of Turkeys in the United States   In Pounds

Year	First Quarter	Second Quarter	Third Quarter	Fourth Quarter	Total	Year	First Quarter	Second Quarter	Third Quarter	Fourth Quarter	Total
2005	3.6	3.9	4.2	5.1	16.7	2011	3.5	3.5	4.0	5.0	16.1
2006	3.5	3.9	4.3	5.2	16.9	2012	3.5	3.6	4.1	4.9	16.0
2007	3.8	4.1	4.2	5.5	17.5	2013	3.7	3.6	4.0	4.7	15.9
2008	4.0	4.1	4.3	5.3	17.6	2014	3.4	3.5	3.9	5.0	15.7
2009	3.7	3.9	4.0	5.3	16.9	2015[1]	3.5	3.6	3.9	4.9	16.0
2010	3.5	3.6	4.1	5.2	16.4	2016[2]	3.4	3.5	4.3	5.0	16.2

[1] Preliminary.   [2] Estimate.   *Source: Economic Research Service, U.S. Department of Agriculture (ERS-USDA)*

Storage Stocks of Turkeys (Frozen) in the United States on First of Month   In Millions of Pounds

Year	Jan.	Feb.	Mar.	Apr.	May	June	July	Aug.	Sept.	Oct.	Nov.	Dec.
2006	206,166	260,469	315,679	377,747	423,732	466,482	507,466	512,223	500,258	464,219	404,171	214,526
2007	218,356	293,379	312,878	346,784	360,220	397,984	448,410	503,547	524,386	504,913	416,971	206,862
2008	260,594	327,590	416,694	428,133	491,283	522,421	562,693	620,692	629,236	621,475	577,984	360,379
2009	396,144	446,197	462,395	513,384	571,708	585,745	594,742	641,060	653,546	613,891	517,463	244,480
2010	261,838	302,058	342,418	379,720	422,064	461,805	507,174	501,511	502,175	473,745	410,161	174,110
2011	191,560	253,527	288,976	325,688	364,503	447,895	508,657	524,846	528,396	509,650	406,864	194,227
2012	210,787	297,736	349,577	375,268	438,384	498,419	547,091	547,465	547,766	521,810	453,378	255,191
2013	296,479	360,018	394,755	401,246	457,575	521,556	566,475	581,357	580,069	541,183	434,493	221,221
2014	237,407	275,787	310,756	336,383	375,013	422,502	462,586	489,758	494,786	484,547	390,654	187,563
2015[1]	193,429	280,400	321,337	345,578	394,415	439,156	462,020	494,037	475,966	449,782	351,828	190,268

[1] Preliminary.   *Source: Economic Research Service, U.S. Department of Agriculture (ERS-USDA)*

Average Retail Price of Turkeys (Whole frozen) in the United States   In Cents Per Pound

Year	Jan.	Feb.	Mar.	Apr.	May	June	July	Aug.	Sept.	Oct.	Nov.	Dec.	Average
2006	1.069	1.197	1.209	1.111	1.084	1.128	1.130	1.106	1.151	1.149	0.973	0.991	1.108
2007	1.103	1.136	1.079	1.081	1.146	1.223	1.222	1.229	1.216	1.241	1.113	1.010	1.150
2008	1.207	1.230	1.151	1.170	1.258	1.238	1.270	1.288	1.320	1.222	1.309	1.332	1.250
2009	1.365	1.369	1.347	1.354	1.366	1.410	1.445	1.461	1.454	1.480	1.336	1.365	1.396
2010	1.398	1.375	1.425	1.479	1.464	1.474	1.554	1.521	1.566	1.677	1.407	1.380	1.477
2011	1.459	1.526	1.572	1.562	1.596	1.581	1.603	1.641	1.676	1.673	1.541	1.574	1.584
2012	1.671	1.671	1.812	1.791	1.608	1.557	1.561	1.586	1.621	1.661	1.488	1.433	1.622
2013	1.579	1.591	1.593	1.649	1.654	1.595	1.624	1.663	1.819	NA	1.721	1.650	1.649
2014	1.713	1.699	1.733	1.610	1.602	1.606	1.641	1.604	1.584	1.667	1.425	1.331	1.601
2015[1]	1.445	1.480	1.503	1.487	1.527	1.541	1.568	1.546	1.538	1.558	1.424	1.448	1.505

[1] Preliminary.   *Source: Economic Research Service, U.S. Department of Agriculture (ERS-USDA)*

Average Retail-to-Consumer Price Spread of Turkeys (Whole) in the United States   In Cents Per Pound

Year	Jan.	Feb.	Mar.	Apr.	May	June	July	Aug.	Sept.	Oct.	Nov.	Dec.	Average
2006	29.4	44.5	44.8	32.8	28.6	30.8	29.6	22.9	21.5	9.3	-11.3	15.9	24.9
2007	33.7	34.3	27.2	25.2	28.7	30.9	26.5	24.6	19.7	20.0	7.4	9.8	24.0
2008	38.0	37.5	23.7	21.6	27.3	23.4	25.1	23.0	23.4	18.0	33.9	48.8	28.6
2009	NA	NA	NA	NA	NA	51.0	53.9	56.0	56.2	56.3	39.4	43.7	50.9
2010	55.6	50.6	51.9	55.5	52.2	NA	NA	42.8	42.9	49.3	22.7	28.8	45.2
2011	48.8	NA	NA	NA	NA	NA	NA	49.7	48.8	43.5	31.5	41.9	44.0
2012	59.8	58.0	68.5	63.2	44.0	40.7	40.7	41.1	42.6	46.8	30.9	35.2	47.6
2013	52.6	55.1	53.7	58.6	58.8	52.3	54.3	58.0	71.7	NA	57.5	52.2	56.8
2014	62.5	61.0	62.0	48.5	45.1	44.4	46.5	42.3	36.6	41.5	14.7	17.3	43.5
2015[1]	36.4	39.9	40.7	35.6	34.9	32.6	26.9	19.0					33.3

[1] Preliminary.   *Source: Economic Research Service, U.S. Department of Agriculture (ERS-USDA)*

291

Uranium

Uranium (atomic symbol U) is a chemically reactive, radioactive, steel-gray, metallic element and is the main fuel used in nuclear reactors. Uranium is the heaviest of all the natural elements. Traces of uranium have been found in archeological artifacts dating back to 79 AD. Uranium was discovered in pitchblende by German chemist Martin Heinrich Klaproth in 1789. Klaproth named it uranium after the recently discovered planet Uranus. French physicist Antoine Henri Becquerel discovered the radioactive properties of uranium in 1896 when he produced an image on a photographic plate covered with a light-absorbing substance. Following Becquerel's experiments, investigations of radioactivity led to the discovery of radium (atomic symbol Ra) and to new concepts of atomic organization.

The principal use for uranium is fuel in nuclear power plants. Demand for uranium concentrates is directly linked to the level of electricity generated by nuclear power plants. Uranium ores are widely distributed throughout the world and are primarily found in Canada, DRC (formerly Zaire), and the U.S. Uranium is obtained from primary mine production and secondary sources. Two Canadian companies, Cameco and Cogema Resources, are the primary producers of uranium from deposits in the Athabasca Basin of northern Saskatchewan. Secondary sources of uranium include excess inventories from utilities and other fuel cycle participants, used reactor fuel, and dismantled Russian nuclear weapons.

Prices – CME uranium swap futures prices (Barchart. com symbol UX) during 2015 traded sideways with a slight downward trend and finally closed the year down -2.4% at $34.40 per pound. Uranium prices have fallen sharply from levels above $100 per pound seen in 2007.

Supply – World production of uranium oxide (U308) concentrate in 2003 (latest data available) rose +7.3% yr/yr to a 13-year high of 56,552 short tons; up from 2002's production of 52,709 short tons. The world's largest uranium producers in 2003 were Canada with 17,050 short tons of production in 2003 (30% of world production), the U.S. with 10,200 short tons of production (18% of world production), and Australia with 9,326 short tons of production (16% of world production).

Trade – U.S. imports of uranium in 2013 (latest data) rose +2.0% yr/yr to 57.300 million pounds. The record high of 66.100 million pounds was posted in 2004. The U.S. has generally been forced to import more uranium as domestic production steadily declined. U.S. exports of uranium in 2013 rose +5.0% yr/yr to 18.900 million pounds, which is below the record high of 23.500 million pounds posted in 2009.

Uranium Industry Statistics in the United States   In Millions of Pounds U_3O_8

	----- Production -----		Concent-rate Ship-ments	-------------- Employment - Person Years ----------					Deliveries to U.S. Utilities[2]	Avg Price Delivered Uranium $/lb U_3O_8	Imports	Avg Price Delivered Uranium Imports $/lb U_3O_8	Exports
Year	Mine	Concent-rate		Explor-ation	Mining	Milling	Pro-cessing	Total[1]					
2008	75.16	39.62	W	48.49	59.55	43.47	66.95	41.59	51.0	32.78	54.1	34.18	14.8
2009	W	41.88	W	46.68	48.92	45.35	46.45	45.74	53.4	45.88	57.1	41.30	17.2
2010	47.13	44.98	42.24	51.30	45.25	49.64	43.99	50.43	49.8	45.86	58.9	41.23	23.5
2011	58.12	53.29	52.50	56.60	52.12	55.98	54.69	55.90	46.6	49.29	55.3	47.01	23.1
2012	W	54.44	W	54.40	59.44	54.07	51.04	55.65	54.8	55.64	54.4	54.00	16.7
2013	W	50.44	W	51.93	56.37	51.13	43.83	54.00	57.5	54.99	56.2	51.44	18.0
2014	W	42.90	W	47.62	48.11	46.03	36.64	49.73	57.4	51.99	57.3	48.24	18.9

[1] From suppliers under domestic purchases.   *Source: Energy Information Administration, U.S. Department of Energy (EIA-DOE)*

Commercial and U.S. Government Stocks of Uranium, End of Year   In Millions of Pounds U_3O_8 Equivalent

	----------------- Utility -----------------		----------- Domestic Supplier ------------		Total Commercial Stocks	DOE Owned & USEC Held	
Year	Natural Uranium	Enriched Uranium[1]	Natural Uranium	Enriched Uranium[1]		Natural Uranium	Enriched Uranium[1]
2005	45.3	19.4	[2]	29.1	93.8	W	W
2006	54.3	23.2	[2]	29.1	106.6	W	W
2007	55.9	25.3	[2]	31.2	112.4	W	W
2008	58.8	24.2	[2]	27.0	110.0	W	W
2009	53.6	31.2	[2]	26.8	111.5	W	W
2010	48.8	37.7	W	24.7	111.3	W	W
2011	50.6	39.2	W	22.3	112.1	W	W
2012	45.0	52.6	W	23.3	120.9	W	W
2013	56.5	56.6	W	21.3	134.4	W	W
2014	61.5	54.6	W	18.6	134.6	W	W

[1] Includes amount reported as UF_6 at enrichment suppliers.   DOE = Department of Energy   USEC = U.S. Energy Commission
Source: Energy Information Administration, U.S. Department of Energy (EIA-DOE)

World Production of Uranium Oxide (U3O8) Concentrate   In Metric Tons (Uranium Content)

Year	Australia	Canada	China	Czech Republic	Kazakh-stan	Namibia	Niger	Russia	South Africa	United States	Ukraine	Uzbeki-stan	World Total
2006	7,593	9,862	750	375	5,281	3,076	3,434	3,190	534	1,805	810	2,260	37,377
2007	8,602	9,476	710	307	6,633	2,832	3,153	3,413	540	1,747	800	2,270	38,989
2008	8,433	9,000	770	275	8,512	4,365	2,993	3,521	566	1,492	830	2,283	41,535
2009	7,934	10,174	1,200	258	14,020	4,626	3,245	3,565	563	1,594	815	2,657	51,513
2010	5,900	9,775	1,350	254	17,803	4,503	4,199	3,562	582	1,630	837	2,874	54,680
2011	5,967	9,145	1,400	229	19,450	3,954	4,264	2,993	556	1,582	873	2,500	54,766
2012[1]	7,009	8,998	1,450	228	21,240	5,026	4,773	2,862	467	1,667	1,012	2,400	59,197
2013[2]	6,700	9,000	1,450	213	22,500	5,627	4,277	3,133	540	1,700	1,075	2,400	60,797

[1] Preliminary.   [2] Estimate.   *Source: Food and Agriculture Organization of the United Nations (FAO-UN)*

Total Production of Uranium Concentrate in the United States, by Quarters   In Pounds U_3O_8

Year	First Quarter	Second Quarter	Third Quarter	Fourth Quarter	Total	Year	First Quarter	Second Quarter	Third Quarter	Fourth Quarter	Total
2004	600,000	400,000	588,738	600,000	2,188,738	2010	876,084	1,055,102	1,150,725	1,153,104	4,235,015
2005	709,600	630,053	663,068	686,456	2,689,177	2011	1,063,047	1,189,083	846,624	892,013	3,990,767
2006	931,065	894,268	1,083,808	1,196,485	4,105,626	2012	1,078,404	1,061,289	1,048,018	957,936	4,145,647
2007	1,162,737	1,119,536	1,075,460	1,175,845	4,533,578	2013	1,147,031	1,394,232	1,171,278	946,301	4,658,842
2008	810,189	1,073,315	980,933	1,037,946	3,902,383	2014[1]	1,242,179	1,095,011	1,468,608	1,085,534	4,891,332
2009	880,036	982,760	956,657	888,905	3,708,358	2015[2]	1,154,408	789,980	774,541	585,048	3,303,977

[1] Preliminary.   [2] Estimate.   *Source: Energy Information Administration, U.S. Department of Energy (EIA-DOE)*

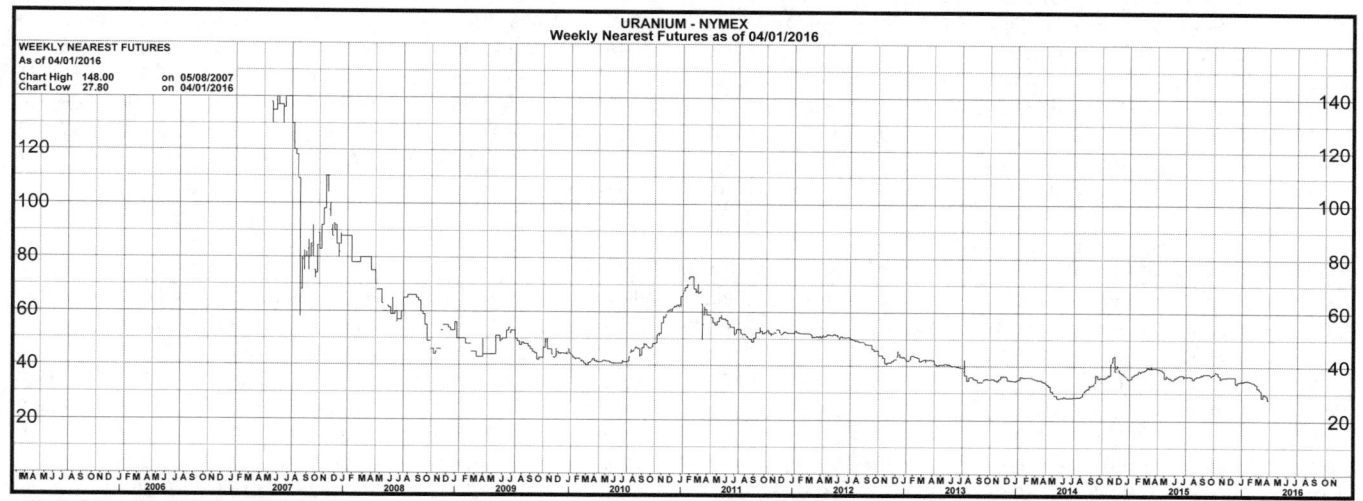

Nearby Futures through Last Trading Day.

Volume of Trading of Uranium Futures   In Contracts

Year	Jan.	Feb.	Mar.	Apr.	May	June	July	Aug.	Sept.	Oct.	Nov.	Dec.	Total
2009	408	40	1,400	16	1	600	1,300	400	403	0	1,581	0	6,149
2010	152	2	101	2,031	4,024	1,743	4,728	330	750	2,933	7,619	1,684	26,097
2011	537	2,483	2,996	845	2,049	10,438	436	1,026	466	906	211	205	22,598
2012	421	1,109	400	817	306	12	1,000	202	965	976	400	1,505	8,113
2013	1,203	201	155	268	432	58	1,751	1,207	34	201	----	1,005	6,515
2014	564	7	181	77	----	200	825	----	224	821	186	368	3,453
2015	186	706	300	----	1	1,154	----	1	600	402	----	1,198	4,548

Contract size = 250 pounds of U_3O_8.   *Source: CME Group; New York Mercantile Exchange (NYMEX)*

Month-End Open Interest of Uranium Futures   In Contracts

Year	Jan.	Feb.	Mar.	Apr.	May	June	July	Aug.	Sept.	Oct.	Nov.	Dec.
2009	2,135	1,951	2,524	2,656	2,665	2,847	3,220	3,751	3,837	3,504	3,229	3,364
2010	3,327	3,173	2,953	3,612	6,541	8,312	11,271	11,643	11,843	13,215	15,014	15,174
2011	14,512	14,833	15,312	14,922	15,078	11,203	7,682	7,230	6,467	6,566	6,298	5,568
2012	5,159	5,045	4,567	4,407	3,676	3,278	3,604	3,938	4,484	5,019	5,223	5,028
2013	5,171	5,615	5,456	5,705	5,368	5,300	5,973	7,186	7,714	7,789	7,310	7,177
2014	6,733	6,477	6,456	6,540	6,215	6,237	5,973	6,452	6,233	5,994	5,318	4,870
2015	4,202	4,368	4,614	4,529	4,439	4,816	4,605	4,549	4,492	4,537	4,242	4,193

Contract size = 250 pounds of U_3O_8.   *Source: CME Group; New York Mercantile Exchange (NYMEX)*

URANIUM

Uranium Industry Statistics in the United States   In Millions of Pounds U_3O_8

Year	Total Operable Units[2/3] Number	Net Summer Capacity of Operable Units[3/4] Million Kilowatts	Nuclear Electricity Net Generation Million Kilowatthours	Nuclear Share of Electricity Net Gen. Percent	Capacity Factor Percent	Year	Total Operable Units[2/3] Number	Net Summer Capacity of Operable Units[3/4] Million Kilowatts	Nuclear Electricity Net Generation Million Kilowatthours	Nuclear Share of Electricity Net Gen. Percent	Capacity Factor Percent
2002	104.0	98.7	780,064	20.2	90.3	2009	104.0	101.0	798,855	20.2	90.3
2003	104.0	99.2	763,733	19.7	87.9	2010	104.0	101.2	806,968	19.6	91.1
2004	104.0	99.6	788,528	19.9	90.1	2011	104.0	101.4	790,204	19.3	89.1
2005	104.0	100.0	781,986	19.3	89.3	2012	104.0	101.9	769,331	19.0	86.1
2006	104.0	100.3	787,219	19.4	89.6	2013	100.0	99.2	789,016	19.4	89.9
2007	104.0	100.3	806,425	19.4	91.8	2014	99.0	99.1	797,167	19.5	91.7
2008	104.0	100.8	806,208	19.6	91.1	2015[1]	99.0	98.7	797,177	19.6	92.2

[1] Preliminary.   [2] Total of nuclear generating units holding full-power licenses, or equivalent permission to operate, at end of period.
[3] At end of period.   [4] Beginning in 2011, monthly capacity values are estimated in two steps: 1) uprates and derates reported on Form EIA-860M are added to specific months; and 2) the difference between the resulting year-end capacity and final capacity is allocated to the month of January. purchases.   Source: Energy Information Administration, U.S. Department of Energy (EIA-DOE)

Nuclear Electricity Net Generation   In Million Kilowatthours

Year	Jan.	Feb.	Mar.	Apr.	May	June	July	Aug.	Sept.	Oct.	Nov.	Dec.	Total
2006	71,912	62,616	63,721	57,567	62,776	68,391	72,186	72,016	66,642	57,509	61,392	70,490	787,219
2007	74,006	65,225	64,305	57,301	65,025	68,923	72,739	72,751	67,579	61,690	64,899	71,983	806,425
2008	70,735	65,130	64,716	57,333	64,826	70,319	74,318	72,617	67,054	62,820	63,408	72,931	806,208
2009	74,102	64,227	67,241	59,408	65,395	69,735	72,949	72,245	65,752	58,021	59,069	70,710	798,855
2010	72,569	65,245	64,635	57,611	66,658	68,301	71,913	71,574	69,371	62,751	62,655	73,683	806,968
2011	72,743	64,789	65,662	54,547	57,013	65,270	72,345	71,339	66,849	63,337	64,474	71,837	790,204
2012	72,381	63,847	61,729	55,871	62,081	65,140	69,129	69,602	64,511	59,743	56,713	68,584	769,331
2013	71,406	61,483	62,947	56,767	62,848	66,430	70,539	71,344	65,799	63,184	64,975	71,294	789,016
2014	73,163	62,639	62,397	56,385	62,947	68,138	71,940	71,129	67,535	62,391	65,140	73,363	797,167
2015[1]	74,270	63,462	64,547	59,757	65,833	68,546	71,412	72,415	66,466	60,571	60,264	69,634	797,177

[1] Preliminary.   Source: Energy Information Administration, U.S. Department of Energy (EIA-DOE)

Nuclear Share of Electricity Net Generation   In Percent

Year	Jan.	Feb.	Mar.	Apr.	May	June	July	Aug.	Sept.	Oct.	Nov.	Dec.	Average
2006	21.9	20.4	20.0	19.3	19.0	18.8	17.6	17.7	20.1	17.9	19.9	21.0	19.4
2007	20.9	20.2	20.1	18.9	19.7	19.0	18.5	17.2	19.0	18.5	20.7	20.8	19.4
2008	19.5	20.0	19.9	18.7	19.9	18.8	18.4	18.7	19.8	19.7	20.5	21.2	19.6
2009	20.9	21.3	21.6	20.5	21.0	20.1	19.6	19.0	20.1	18.9	19.9	20.2	20.2
2010	20.1	20.4	20.7	20.0	20.3	18.2	17.6	17.5	20.0	20.4	20.5	20.3	19.6
2011	20.0	20.7	20.6	18.0	17.6	17.7	17.3	17.5	19.8	20.5	21.2	21.4	19.3
2012	21.3	20.6	20.0	18.9	18.4	18.1	16.7	17.6	19.3	19.2	18.5	20.5	19.0
2013	20.5	19.9	19.3	19.0	19.5	18.6	17.9	18.5	19.3	20.1	20.7	20.2	19.4
2014	19.4	19.3	18.8	18.9	19.4	19.0	18.6	18.5	19.9	19.8	20.5	21.7	19.5
2015[1]	20.5	18.9	19.9	20.3	20.4	18.9	17.8	18.4	18.9	19.4	20.0	21.5	19.6

[1] Preliminary.   Source: Energy Information Administration, U.S. Department of Energy (EIA-DOE)

Capacity Factor   In Percent

Year	Jan.	Feb.	Mar.	Apr.	May	June	July	Aug.	Sept.	Oct.	Nov.	Dec.	Average
2006	96.3	92.9	85.4	79.7	84.1	94.7	96.7	96.5	92.3	77.0	85.0	94.4	89.6
2007	99.2	96.8	86.2	79.4	87.2	95.5	97.5	97.5	93.6	82.7	89.9	96.5	91.8
2008	94.4	92.9	86.3	79.0	86.5	96.9	99.1	96.9	92.4	83.8	87.4	97.3	91.1
2009	98.6	94.6	89.5	81.7	87.0	95.9	97.1	96.1	90.4	77.2	81.2	94.1	90.3
2010	96.4	96.0	85.9	79.1	88.6	93.8	95.5	95.1	95.2	83.4	86.0	97.9	91.1
2011	96.6	95.3	87.2	74.9	75.7	89.5	96.0	94.6	91.6	84.0	88.4	95.2	89.1
2012	95.8	90.3	81.7	76.4	82.1	89.0	91.3	91.8	88.0	78.8	77.3	90.5	86.1
2013	93.9	90.3	83.4	77.6	83.3	93.1	95.6	96.7	92.2	85.7	91.0	96.6	89.9
2014	99.1	94.0	84.5	78.8	85.2	95.4	97.5	96.4	94.6	84.5	91.3	99.6	91.7
2015[1]	101.3	95.8	88.0	84.2	89.7	96.4	97.2	98.6	93.5	82.5	84.8	94.8	92.2

[1] Preliminary.   [2] Beginning in 2008, capacity factor data are calculated using a new methodology.   Source: Energy Information Administration, U.S. Department of Energy (EIA-DOE)

Vanadium

Vanadium (atomic symbol V) is a silvery-white, soft, ductile, metallic element. Discovered in 1801, but mistaken for chromium, vanadium was rediscovered in 1830 by Swedish chemist Nils Sefstrom, who named the element in honor of the Scandinavian goddess Vanadis.

Never found in the pure state, vanadium is found in about 65 different minerals such as carnotite, roscoelite, vanadinite, and patronite, as well as in phosphate rock, certain iron ores, some crude oils, and meteorites. Vanadium is one of the hardest of all metals. It melts at about 1890 degrees Celsius and boils at about 3380 degrees Celsius.

Vanadium has good structural strength and is used as an alloying agent with iron, steel, and titanium. It is used in aerospace applications, transmission gears, photography, as a reducing agent, and as a drying agent in various paints.

Prices – The price of vanadium in 2015 fell by -21.6% to $4.40 per pound, remaining well below the record high of $16.28 per pound in 2005.

Supply – Virtually all (99%) of vanadium is produced from ores, concentrates, and slag, with the remainder coming from petroleum residues, ash, and spent catalysts.

World production in 2015 from ore, concentrates and slag fell -4.1% yr/yr to 78,800 metric tons. World production of all vanadium in 2015 fell -4.0% yr/yr to 79,400 metric tons.

The world's largest producer of vanadium from ores, concentrates and slag is China with 42,000 metric tons of production in 2015 which was 53.3% of total world production. The two other major producers are South Africa with 19,000 metric tons of production in 2015, which was 24.1% of world production, and Russia with 15,000 metric tons of production which was 19.0% of world production. Production in Russia and South Africa has been relatively stable in recent years, while China's production grew sharply in the late 1990s. China's production level of 45,000 metric tons in 2014 was a new record high and more than four times the levels seen in the early 1990s.

Trade – U.S. exports of vanadium in 2015 were in the forms of vanadium pent-oxide, anhydride (105 metric tons, -47.8%yr/yr); ferro-vanadium (120 metric tons, -52.6%yr/yr); and oxides & hydroxides (200 metric tons, -42.9% yr/yr). U.S. imports of vanadium in 2015 were in the forms of ferro-vanadium (3,300 metric tons, +2.2% yr/yr); vanadium pent-oxide (3,500 metric tons, +2.6% yr/yr); ore, slag and residues (200 metric tons, -96.8% yr/yr); and oxides & hydroxides (35 metric tons, -66.3% yr/yr).

World Production of Vanadium   In Metric Tons (Contained Vanadium)

| | From Ores, Concentrates and Slag | | | | | | From Petroleum Residues Ash, Spent Catalysts | | | |
Year	Australia	China[3]	Kazak-hstan	Russia	South Africa	Total[4]	Japan[5]	United States[6]	Total	World Total
2010	----	32,480	----	15,000	22,606	71,100	560	----	560	71,700
2011	----	36,400	----	12,860	21,652	71,500	560	----	560	72,100
2012	----	40,000	----	14,856	19,957	74,900	580	----	580	75,500
2013	400	44,000	----	14,403	21,397	80,400	580	----	580	81,000
2014[1]	----	45,000	----	15,100	21,000	82,200	580	----	580	82,700
2015[2]	----	42,000	----	15,000	19,000	78,800	600	----	600	79,400

[1] Preliminary.   [2] Estimate.   [3] In vanadiferous slag product.   [4] Excludes U.S. production.   [5] In vanadium pentoxide product.
[6] In vanadium pentoxide and ferrovanadium products.   Source: U.S. Geological Survey (USGS)

Salient Statistics of Vanadium in the United States   In Metric Tons (Contained Vanadium)

| | Con-sumer & Producer Stocks, | Vanadium Consumption by Uses in the U.S. | | | | | | | | | Average $ Per Lb. | Exports | | | Imports | | | |
Year	Dec. 31	Tool Steel	Cast Irons	High Strength, Low Alloy	Stainless & Heat Resisting	Super-alloys	Carbon	Full Alloy	Total		V2O5	Vanadium Pent-oxide, & Anhydride	Oxides & Hydr-oxides	Ferro-Vana-dium	Ores, Slag, Residues	Vanadium Pent-oxide, & Anhydride	Oxides & Hydr-oxides	Ferro-Vana-dium
2010	248	W	W	W	120	9	843	2,030	5,030		6.46	140	1,120	610	1,010	4,000	167	1,340
2011	193	W	W	W	62	16	815	1,530	4,140		6.76	89	264	316	1,510	2,800	886	2,220
2012	219	165	----	W	62	9	759	1,510	3,960		6.49	62	305	337	2,210	1,640	905	4,190
2013	220	161	W	W	61	9	671	1,510	3,980		6.04	90	427	299	4,190	2,040	205	3,710
2014[1]	225	W	W	W	61	8	710	1,540	4,070		5.61	201	350	253	6,160	3,410	104	3,230
2015[2]	180	W	W	W	59	2	532	1,470	3,600		4.40	105	200	120	200	3,500	35	3,300

[1] Preliminary.   [2] Estimate.   W = Withheld.   *Source: U.S. Geological Survey (USGS)*

Average Price of Vanadium Pentoxide   In Dollars Per Pound

Year	Jan.	Feb.	Mar.	Apr.	May	June	July	Aug.	Sept.	Oct.	Nov.	Dec.	Average
2010	6.97	7.25	7.72	8.00	7.85	6.96	6.23	6.41	6.75	6.63	6.63	6.63	7.00
2011	6.63	6.63	6.63	6.63	6.63	6.63	6.63	6.63	6.63	6.63	6.63	6.63	6.63
2012	6.65	6.75	6.75	6.75	6.39	5.87	5.69	5.53	5.37	5.30	5.30	5.63	6.00
2013	6.37	6.64	6.75	6.35	5.78	5.68	5.68	5.46	5.78	5.80	5.80	5.82	5.99
2014	5.83	5.82	5.80	5.79	5.39	5.54	5.31	5.30	5.27	5.25	5.24	5.10	5.47
2015	4.97	4.55	3.94	3.80	3.97	4.25	3.83	3.44	3.09	2.72	2.51	2.38	3.62

Source: American Metal Market (AMM)

Vegetables

Vegetables are the edible products of herbaceous plants, which are plants with soft stems. Vegetables are grouped according to the edible part of each plant including leaves (e.g., lettuce), stalks (celery), roots (carrot), tubers (potato), bulbs (onion), fruits (tomato), seeds (pea), and flowers (broccoli). Each of these groups contributes to the human diet in its own way. Fleshy roots are high in energy value and good sources of the vitamin B group, seeds are relatively high in carbohydrates and proteins, while leaves, stalks, and fruits are excellent sources of minerals, vitamins, water, and roughage. Vegetables are an important food for the maintenance of health and prevention of disease. Higher intakes of vegetables have been shown to lower the risks of cancer and coronary heart disease.

Vegetables are best consumed fresh in their raw state in order to derive the maximum benefits from their nutrients. While canned and frozen vegetables are often thought to be inferior to fresh vegetables, they are sometimes nutritionally superior to fresh produce because they are usually processed immediately after harvest when nutrient content is at its peak. When cooking vegetables, aluminum utensils should not be used, because aluminum is a soft metal that is affected by food acids and alkalis. Scientific evidence shows that tiny particles of aluminum from foods cooked in aluminum utensils enter the stomach and can injure the sensitive lining of the stomach.

Prices – The monthly average index of fresh vegetable prices received by growers in the U.S. in 2015 rose +9.3% to 224.9, slightly below last year's new record high of 206.6.

Demand – The leading vegetable in terms of U.S. per capita consumption in 2013 (latest data) was the potato with 116.7 pounds of consumption. Runner-up vegetables were tomatoes (87.2 pounds), sweet corn (22.0 pounds), lettuce (23.8 pounds), and onions (18.7 pounds). Total U.S. per capita vegetable consumption in 2013 fell -2.0% to 385.7 pounds.

Index of Prices Received by Growers for Fresh Vegetables in the United States   (1990-92=100)

Year	Jan.	Feb.	Mar.	Apr.	May	June	July	Aug.	Sept.	Oct.	Nov.	Dec.	Average
2006	207.6	138.8	137.6	174.4	147.9	128.7	134.1	179.5	193.1	167.7	138.3	178.4	160.5
2007	175.3	190.3	222.4	222.5	142.1	145.4	146.0	137.8	162.7	218.3	177.4	204.5	178.7
2008	200.2	158.3	194.1	179.3	170.7	191.7	168.3	146.1	158.7	185.1	200.3	155.9	175.7
2009	179.8	163.6	167.4	182.3	134.1	182.5	149.8	144.3	140.4	180.6	197.8	210.4	169.4
2010	178.6	190.6	310.4	274.1	215.4	158.6	177.1	157.3	171.2	153.7	156.0	186.7	194.1
2011	211.2	341.1	267.7	184.7	156.9	174.2	148.7	146.6	174.1	171.4	199.1	169.7	195.5
2012	146.9	129.5	150.2	133.7	144.2	156.2	147.1	159.4	163.7	143.2	164.7	154.0	149.4
2013	240.8	182.0	236.8	201.0	211.6	195.8	175.1	229.1	188.8	222.2	218.5	177.0	206.6
2014	197.0	193.3	197.1	200.2	195.9	214.6	197.3	184.7	191.0	219.6	249.1	229.0	205.7
2015[1]	253.2	197.1	200.5	211.0	230.2	213.5	209.9	206.2	235.1	229.4	228.3	284.0	224.9

[1] Preliminary.   Not seasonally adjusted.   *Source: National Agricultural Statistics Service, U.S. Department of Agriculture (NASS-USDA)*

Producer Price Index of Canned[2] Processed Vegetables in the United States   (1982 = 100)

Year	Jan.	Feb.	Mar.	Apr.	May	June	July	Aug.	Sept.	Oct.	Nov.	Dec.	Average
2006	138.0	136.8	137.1	137.3	138.8	140.2	140.0	140.5	141.4	141.5	142.2	142.2	139.7
2007	142.8	142.9	143.1	143.3	143.5	143.6	143.1	143.1	144.0	143.9	144.2	144.6	143.5
2008	147.8	148.4	149.6	151.2	150.2	151.3	153.3	158.6	162.5	163.0	164.2	167.8	155.7
2009	168.9	169.0	170.5	170.7	171.0	171.1	171.3	170.9	170.6	170.7	169.9	169.2	170.3
2010	169.8	167.3	167.2	167.0	166.7	166.0	164.1	164.6	161.6	161.1	162.0	161.7	164.9
2011	162.2	162.0	162.7	164.4	164.4	164.9	166.9	168.1	169.8	169.7	170.3	170.3	166.3
2012	171.3	171.1	171.7	171.5	170.7	172.9	172.4	175.6	175.0	175.3	174.2	174.3	173.0
2013	173.9	174.1	173.9	174.6	174.0	173.7	173.9	174.1	174.0	173.9	173.6	173.6	173.9
2014	173.2	173.4	173.0	172.4	172.3	172.9	173.0	173.7	174.2	174.6	174.7	174.8	173.5
2015[1]	175.7	176.3	179.4	175.0	174.9	177.0	176.2	172.6	172.1	172.3	172.3	170.7	174.5

[1] Preliminary.   [2] Includes canned vegetables and juices, including hominy and mushrooms.   Not seasonally adjusted.   *Source: Bureau of Labor Statistics, U.S. Department of Labor (BLS)*

Producer Price Index of Frozen Processed Vegetables in the United States   (1982 = 100)

Year	Jan.	Feb.	Mar.	Apr.	May	June	July	Aug.	Sept.	Oct.	Nov.	Dec.	Average
2006	137.3	137.7	138.7	138.6	138.8	139.5	139.4	139.3	139.9	142.0	142.7	142.6	139.7
2007	144.0	144.0	144.0	145.2	145.9	146.7	148.2	149.3	149.9	151.5	152.5	153.2	147.9
2008	153.3	153.8	155.6	156.5	156.7	157.1	158.8	161.1	163.9	170.6	172.7	177.9	161.5
2009	176.5	178.1	178.5	178.1	178.1	178.5	178.1	177.4	179.3	180.3	180.4	180.1	178.6
2010	179.9	180.3	180.8	180.2	180.5	180.3	179.6	179.8	179.0	174.9	175.5	175.9	178.9
2011	174.8	175.2	175.3	176.0	176.1	177.7	183.9	185.1	186.0	186.5	191.4	193.3	181.8
2012	193.8	193.7	193.7	194.1	194.1	194.5	194.5	194.1	193.6	193.6	193.9	193.9	194.0
2013	194.0	194.5	194.4	194.4	194.6	194.6	194.6	192.4	192.5	192.3	192.4	192.3	193.6
2014	192.2	192.3	192.3	192.4	192.4	192.3	192.3	192.9	193.2	193.5	193.5	193.5	192.7
2015[1]	193.8	193.1	193.2	193.3	193.5	193.3	193.3	193.1	195.9	195.8	195.2	195.3	194.1

[1] Preliminary.   Not seasonally adjusted.   *Source: Bureau of Labor Statistics, U.S. Department of Labor (BLS)*

Per Capita Use of Selected Commercially Produced Fresh and Processing Vegetables and Melons in the United States   In Pounds, farm weight basis

Crop	2006	2007	2008	2009	2010	2011	2012	2013	2014[10]	2015[11]
Asparagus, All	1.4	1.4	1.5	1.5	1.6	1.6	1.7	1.6	1.8	1.7
Fresh	1.1	1.2	1.2	1.3	1.4	1.4	1.4	1.4	1.6	1.5
Canning	0.2	0.1	0.2	0.2	0.1	0.1	0.1	0.1	0.1	0.1
Freezing	0.1	0.1	0.1	0.1	0.1	0.1	0.1	0.1	0.1	0.1
Snap beans, All	7.9	7.8	7.4	7.2	7.5	6.4	6.5	6.6	6.0	6.4
Fresh	2.1	2.2	2.0	1.8	1.9	1.7	1.6	1.6	1.5	1.6
Canning	3.9	3.5	3.3	3.6	3.7	3.2	2.9	2.9	2.8	2.9
Freezing	1.9	2.1	2.1	1.9	2.0	1.5	1.9	2.1	1.8	1.9
Broccoli, All [1]	8.0	8.3	8.7	8.7	8.1	8.6	8.9	9.4	9.2	9.2
Fresh	5.8	5.6	6.0	6.2	5.6	5.9	6.3	6.9	6.6	6.6
Freezing	2.3	2.7	2.7	2.5	2.5	2.7	2.6	2.5	2.6	2.6
Cabbage, All	9.0	9.0	9.0	8.1	8.5	7.6	7.4	7.9	7.7	7.3
Fresh	7.8	8.0	8.1	7.3	7.5	6.6	6.3	6.9	6.7	6.3
Canning (kraut)	1.2	1.0	0.9	0.9	1.0	1.0	1.2	1.0	1.0	1.0
Carrots, All [2]	11.2	10.5	10.6	9.7	10.0	9.9	9.9	10.5	10.4	10.4
Fresh	8.1	8.1	8.1	7.4	7.8	7.5	7.9	8.0	8.5	8.3
Canning	1.0	0.9	1.0	0.9	0.7	0.8	0.8	0.8	0.7	0.7
Freezing	2.1	1.5	1.5	1.5	1.5	1.6	1.2	1.7	1.2	1.4
Cauliflower, All [1]	2.1	2.0	2.0	2.1	1.7	1.7	1.5	1.7	1.6	1.7
Fresh	1.7	1.7	1.6	1.7	1.3	1.2	1.2	1.3	1.3	1.4
Freezing	0.4	0.4	0.4	0.4	0.4	0.4	0.3	0.3	0.4	0.3
Celery	6.1	6.3	6.2	6.2	6.1	6.0	6.0	5.5	5.5	5.4
Sweet Corn, All [3]	26.1	26.1	25.1	25.8	24.6	23.7	24.3	21.6	21.1	21.6
Fresh	8.3	9.2	9.1	9.2	9.2	8.2	8.7	8.9	7.6	8.6
Canning	8.4	6.9	6.7	7.6	6.9	5.8	5.9	5.8	5.8	5.3
Freezing	9.4	10.0	9.3	9.1	8.5	9.8	9.8	7.0	7.7	7.7
Cucumbers, All	9.1	10.2	9.9	11.9	10.5	9.2	10.1	10.5	11.3	10.9
Fresh	6.2	6.4	6.4	6.8	6.7	6.4	7.1	7.3	7.4	7.5
Pickling	3.0	3.7	3.5	5.1	3.7	2.8	3.0	3.2	3.9	3.4
Melons	26.9	26.4	26.7	26.2	26.4	25.5	----	----	----	----
Watermelon	15.1	14.4	15.6	14.9	15.7	14.8	----	----	----	----
Cantaloupe	9.3	9.6	8.9	9.1	8.6	8.7	----	----	----	----
Honeydew	1.9	1.8	1.7	1.6	1.5	1.5	----	----	----	----
Other	0.6	0.6	0.5	0.6	0.6	0.5	----	----	----	----
Lettuce, All	32.0	29.9	27.3	26.1	27.9	27.5	27.9	25.5	25.2	24.5
Head lettuce	20.1	18.4	16.9	16.1	15.9	15.8	15.9	14.1	14.5	13.5
Romaine & Leaf	12.0	11.5	10.4	10.0	12.0	11.7	11.9	11.4	10.8	11.0
Onions, All	21.7	22.6	21.7	21.5	20.9	20.4	20.8	19.4	19.7	20.0
Fresh	19.9	21.6	20.2	19.6	19.6	19.1	19.5	18.5	18.3	18.6
Dehydrating	1.8	1.0	1.5	1.9	1.3	1.3	1.3	0.9	1.4	1.4
Green Peas, All [4]	2.8	3.0	2.9	3.0	2.6	2.4	2.7	2.4	2.3	2.3
Canning	1.2	1.2	1.1	1.3	1.1	0.8	0.8	0.9	0.7	0.8
Freezing	1.6	1.8	1.8	1.7	1.5	1.6	1.9	1.5	1.6	1.5
Peppers, All	15.8	15.2	15.8	16.4	16.9	17.2	17.9	17.0	17.9	18.3
Bell Peppers, All	9.5	9.4	9.6	9.8	10.3	10.6	10.7	10.0	10.7	11.1
Chile Peppers, All	6.4	5.9	6.2	6.6	6.6	6.6	7.2	7.0	7.2	7.2
Tomatoes, All	84.3	87.9	85.6	89.9	91.6	86.7	87.3	86.1	87.7	76.8
Fresh	19.8	19.2	18.5	19.6	20.6	21.0	20.8	20.2	20.5	20.6
Canning	64.5	68.7	67.1	70.3	71.1	65.7	66.5	65.9	67.2	56.2
Other, Fresh [5]	20.1	19.4	19.1	18.5	18.4	18.9	19.3	18.6	20.3	17.7
Other, Canning [6]	2.6	2.6	2.5	2.3	2.5	2.5	2.6	2.6	2.5	2.4
Other, Freezing [7]	4.1	4.1	4.0	4.3	4.5	4.3	4.5	4.3	4.6	4.7
Subtotal, All [8]	291.1	292.7	286.0	263.3	264.0	254.5	259.2	251.2	254.8	241.3
Fresh	175.2	174.5	170.0	141.4	144.3	141.9	144.7	140.6	141.7	139.7
Canning	92.3	94.5	92.6	98.7	97.4	89.4	90.9	90.1	91.8	80.1
Freezing	21.8	22.6	21.9	21.4	20.9	21.9	22.3	19.5	19.8	20.1
Potatoes, All	123.6	124.4	118.3	113.5	113.9	110.3	114.7	113.3	112.1	113.7
Fresh	38.6	38.7	37.8	36.7	36.8	34.1	34.5	34.5	33.5	34.0
Processing	85.0	85.7	80.5	76.8	77.1	76.2	80.2	78.8	78.5	79.7
Sweet Potatoes	4.6	5.1	5.1	5.3	6.3	7.1	6.9	6.3	7.5	7.5
Mushrooms	4.0	3.9	3.6	3.6	3.6	3.8	4.0	3.8	3.8	4.0
Dry Peas & Lentils [9]	1.2	0.7	0.4	0.9	1.6	0.8	0.6	1.3	1.3	1.3
Dry Edible Beans	6.5	6.4	6.5	6.1	7.0	5.7	6.1	5.9	5.7	7.2
Total, All Items	430.9	433.2	419.9	392.7	396.4	382.3	391.5	381.9	385.1	375.0

[1] All production for processing broccoli and cauliflower is for freezing.   [2] Industry allocation suggests that 27 percent of processing carrot production is for canning and 73 percent is for freezing.   [3] On-cob basis.   [4] In-shell basis.   [5] Includes artichokes, brussels sprouts, eggplant, endive/escarole, garlic, radishes, green limas, squash, and spinach. In 2000, okra, pumpkins, kale, collards, turnip greens and mustard greens added.   [6] Includes beets, green limas (1992-2003), spinach, and miscellaneous imports (1990-2001).   [7] Includes green limas, spinach, and miscellaneous freezing vegetables.   [8] Fresh, canning, and freezing data do not sum to the total because onions for dehydrating are included in the total.   [9] Production from new areas in upper midwest added in 1998. A portion of this is likely for feed use.   [10] Preliminary.   [11] Forecast.   NA = Not available.   *Source: Economic Research Service, U.S. Department of Agriculture (ERS-USDA)*

VEGETABLES

Average Price Received by Growers for Broccoli in the United States   In Dollars Per Cwt

Year	Jan.	Feb.	Mar.	Apr.	May	June	July	Aug.	Sept.	Oct.	Nov.	Dec.	Season Average
2008	47.90	24.40	30.80	52.10	25.20	29.60	26.70	26.60	41.10	57.50	41.20	33.70	36.20
2009	44.60	29.50	46.90	41.90	32.80	31.00	26.50	29.70	31.60	64.60	57.10	53.50	37.80
2010	26.50	26.70	48.30	35.40	43.50	34.50	29.30	25.70	33.30	30.40	55.30	66.60	37.60
2011	57.10	45.40	40.80	33.90	40.20	55.70	28.70	35.60	33.60	33.10	42.90	51.60	35.40
2012	28.80	23.70	33.70	24.10	31.40	49.20	30.00	30.20	40.40	30.30	35.40	28.20	33.80
2013	80.40	38.10	30.60	NA	NA	NA	NA	NA	NA	NA	NA	NA	43.20
2014	NA	NA	NA	40.10	48.00	49.60	31.80	47.10	53.40	34.60	45.00	33.10	40.60
2015[1]	67.30	29.90	47.80	50.60	54.50	34.70	38.20	49.90	57.10	58.10	65.10	84.70	

[1]Preliminary.   NA = Not available.   *Source: National Agricultural Statistics Service, U.S. Department of Agriculture (NASS-USDA)*

Average Price Received by Growers for Carrots in the United States   In Dollars Per Cwt

Year	Jan.	Feb.	Mar.	Apr.	May	June	July	Aug.	Sept.	Oct.	Nov.	Dec.	Season Average
2008	16.20	25.90	25.90	25.50	32.00	25.60	25.60	25.60	25.30	25.20	24.70	25.20	24.50
2009	25.20	25.20	25.20	25.20	25.50	25.80	25.60	24.00	25.20	25.30	27.20	27.80	25.20
2010	28.50	23.90	27.50	27.40	27.40	26.20	27.10	27.10	26.80	26.90	27.60	33.00	26.60
2011	38.00	40.70	44.60	46.20	44.80	35.10	28.40	20.40	17.30	14.80	14.10	25.50	32.50
2012	26.30	26.30	26.80	27.60	27.40	27.50	28.10	24.20	21.70	26.00	26.70	27.40	26.60
2013	28.20	28.50	30.80	NA	NA	NA	NA	NA	NA	NA	NA	NA	28.60
2014	NA	NA	NA	28.20	27.20	25.50	25.10	23.00	21.50	26.90	28.00	33.40	26.50
2015[1]	33.80	33.00	32.20	31.80	31.40	30.60	29.90	30.20	30.40	31.30	31.00	32.90	

[1]Preliminary.   NA = Not available.   *Source: National Agricultural Statistics Service, U.S. Department of Agriculture (NASS-USDA)*

Average Price Received by Growers for Cauliflower in the United States   In Dollars Per Cwt

Year	Jan.	Feb.	Mar.	Apr.	May	June	July	Aug.	Sept.	Oct.	Nov.	Dec.	Season Average
2008	51.80	30.00	41.70	63.80	24.90	53.90	38.20	43.20	29.50	48.50	29.50	43.90	40.70
2009	68.20	30.00	51.30	41.40	46.60	43.50	41.70	31.90	26.90	58.10	54.40	47.10	44.30
2010	33.20	36.70	50.40	58.00	68.60	32.90	31.20	26.30	27.70	31.50	52.60	66.40	41.80
2011	41.10	55.90	51.30	43.10	56.80	52.80	38.40	30.90	29.70	30.30	67.30	66.20	46.80
2012	31.90	32.10	39.00	28.50	35.40	38.90	27.90	29.60	39.20	29.40	47.70	40.00	35.90
2013	69.90	43.30	46.00	NA	NA	NA	NA	NA	NA	NA	NA	NA	44.50
2014	NA	NA	NA	65.80	79.10	66.30	43.10	31.80	64.70	43.20	67.60	84.80	50.00
2015[1]	58.40	40.10	85.10	87.80	108.00	49.60	31.10	42.80	55.50	68.60	121.00	184.00	

[1]Preliminary.   NA = Not available.   *Source: National Agricultural Statistics Service, U.S. Department of Agriculture (NASS-USDA)*

Average Price Received by Growers for Celery in the United States   In Dollars Per Cwt

Year	Jan.	Feb.	Mar.	Apr.	May	June	July	Aug.	Sept.	Oct.	Nov.	Dec.	Season Average
2008	16.20	13.20	13.40	14.00	37.40	30.10	22.10	12.40	11.90	17.10	16.90	20.30	18.50
2009	35.10	29.70	15.00	17.40	17.40	11.70	11.30	11.40	12.00	20.90	21.10	38.80	20.10
2010	37.40	21.60	25.70	17.10	20.00	15.80	16.00	13.90	15.10	15.00	14.30	20.20	18.60
2011	25.10	46.50	29.50	19.30	33.10	17.10	20.00	16.70	16.30	16.30	15.00	14.90	19.70
2012	20.10	12.60	12.50	12.70	15.80	13.50	23.60	22.10	24.80	19.10	20.30	21.20	18.20
2013	39.70	47.00	29.20	NA	NA	NA	NA	NA	NA	NA	NA	NA	25.40
2014	NA	NA	NA	15.50	15.80	14.50	20.60	18.70	17.90	16.90	26.60	28.70	16.70
2015[1]	19.40	14.60	14.00	18.60	26.80	17.60	17.10	23.50	22.70	28.00	40.60	59.80	

[1]Preliminary.   NA = Not available.   *Source: National Agricultural Statistics Service, U.S. Department of Agriculture (NASS-USDA)*

Average Price Received by Growers for Sweet Corn in the United States   In Dollars Per Cwt

Year	Jan.	Feb.	Mar.	Apr.	May	June	July	Aug.	Sept.	Oct.	Nov.	Dec.	Season Average
2008	30.80	23.00	28.60	20.50	21.90	19.90	28.50	27.20	27.10	23.70	30.80	22.20	25.90
2009	24.90	46.40	59.30	32.50	20.80	25.40	34.60	26.40	23.70	23.30	19.80	19.40	29.30
2010	37.80	58.50	62.70	40.10	25.10	16.00	20.20	23.10	24.00	28.00	20.60	31.60	25.90
2011	62.20	51.80	42.40	21.50	19.90	24.30	32.90	20.70	24.40	26.40	26.60	14.90	26.70
2012	37.30	31.00	33.70	22.90	21.10	22.80	25.60	16.60	22.70	25.60	26.60	27.80	26.30
2013	30.40	36.70	33.30	NA	NA	NA	NA	NA	NA	NA	NA	NA	28.20
2014	NA	NA	NA	26.00	25.40	32.00	37.70	29.00	23.10	42.20	40.70	41.40	28.90
2015[1]	39.80	40.00	31.70	29.60	26.80	27.70	33.70	29.50	32.30	47.90	24.40	26.00	

[1]Preliminary.   NA = Not available.   *Source: National Agricultural Statistics Service, U.S. Department of Agriculture (NASS-USDA)*

Average Price Received by Growers for Head Lettuce in the United States   In Dollars Per Cwt

Year	Jan.	Feb.	Mar.	Apr.	May	June	July	Aug.	Sept.	Oct.	Nov.	Dec.	Season Average
2006	10.50	12.00	19.10	22.40	33.70	11.80	12.20	20.70	16.30	11.80	12.50	22.40	16.90
2007	20.80	15.50	29.70	17.80	13.60	17.80	17.30	23.10	29.20	44.40	17.40	16.00	21.70
2008	17.60	13.40	14.70	21.60	15.50	17.70	17.30	17.20	31.90	32.90	18.80	23.50	20.10
2009	28.50	17.80	19.40	27.70	18.20	18.90	16.90	16.70	16.60	27.20	49.60	38.70	22.40
2010	17.30	14.10	20.80	19.00	24.30	25.70	26.00	23.30	17.20	20.20	35.40	17.50	21.10
2011	27.20	54.40	35.20	17.80	26.40	17.10	19.40	14.70	14.80	17.00	30.50	17.40	23.00
2012	13.40	12.60	12.00	17.90	19.00	19.00	19.10	19.20	20.50	17.70	20.10	12.80	17.70
2013	44.80	31.70	46.90	NA	NA	NA	NA	NA	NA	NA	NA	NA	26.70
2014	NA	NA	NA	18.20	26.10	35.30	29.00	29.60	32.90	33.40	49.10	15.90	25.20
2015[1]	38.20	15.20	19.10	23.10	25.10	30.30	18.80	35.70	48.90	34.40	60.10	51.90	

[1]Preliminary.   NA = Not available.   *Source: National Agricultural Statistics Service, U.S. Department of Agriculture (NASS-USDA)*

Average Price Received by Growers for Tomatoes in the United States   In Dollars Per Cwt

Year	Jan.	Feb.	Mar.	Apr.	May	June	July	Aug.	Sept.	Oct.	Nov.	Dec.	Season Average
2006	79.20	46.50	24.80	34.40	23.30	30.90	25.10	27.80	79.80	53.20	28.10	24.80	43.70
2007	35.60	31.20	26.30	52.60	35.60	29.60	26.70	28.60	33.10	41.60	58.70	81.20	34.80
2008	58.20	45.50	66.10	47.40	48.20	56.80	40.90	29.40	25.60	33.80	64.90	37.90	45.30
2009	29.30	32.70	41.50	45.40	33.20	67.20	31.70	35.90	34.40	40.20	73.70	65.00	40.40
2010	58.90	84.60	109.00	103.00	65.20	37.30	33.60	35.50	38.40	32.00	38.10	37.30	48.20
2011	51.90	108.00	98.70	67.60	49.10	44.60	33.10	30.30	35.50	26.60	42.40	26.50	36.10
2012	28.90	30.60	36.60	26.70	34.10	45.10	24.70	23.70	26.20	20.90	45.30	49.40	30.50
2013	34.10	37.70	53.50	NA	NA	NA	NA	NA	NA	NA	NA	NA	44.60
2014	NA	NA	NA	45.20	39.10	57.60	27.00	33.20	34.70	54.60	71.80	66.70	41.60
2015[1]	34.80	49.40	44.20	45.20	24.00	33.50	41.30	36.30	35.80	41.80	39.30	42.50	

[1]Preliminary.   NA = Not available.   *Source: National Agricultural Statistics Service, U.S. Department of Agriculture (NASS-USDA)*

Frozen Vegetables: January 1 and July 1 Cold Storage Holdings in the United States   In Thousands of Pounds

Crop	2011 July 1	2012 Jan. 1	July 1	2013 Jan. 1	July 1	2014 Jan. 1	July 1	2015 Jan. 1	July 1	2016[1] Jan. 1
Asparagus	10,018	6,615	11,376	8,304	9,900	9,758	15,185	13,603	14,457	11,926
Limas, Fordhook	----	----	----	----	----	----	----	----	----	----
Limas, Baby	34,313	54,711	18,192	57,819	29,717	60,262	34,333	54,530	41,133	57,841
Green Beans, Reg. Cut	61,436	192,235	91,790	252,309	143,931	181,073	96,376	182,136	113,449	199,994
Green Beans, Fr. Style	8,220	22,509	11,019	15,761	8,749	14,248	8,194	14,754	8,025	15,279
Broccoli, Spears	32,338	25,164	39,251	27,652	27,359	21,705	34,093	27,108	27,821	25,023
Broccoli, Chopped & Cut	37,149	44,822	60,293	52,022	41,353	34,836	33,394	36,143	42,211	39,398
Brussels sprouts	10,510	11,135	10,466	13,663	10,675	13,612	12,480	15,960	14,691	19,843
Carrots, Diced	91,040	158,524	83,281	170,186	109,846	157,220	97,279	168,289	99,334	161,755
Carrots, Other	79,677	145,066	87,419	173,980	108,905	160,585	102,942	180,493	88,645	166,317
Cauliflower	16,707	23,433	21,877	26,249	21,738	23,139	16,497	20,567	18,203	26,448
Corn, Cut	216,687	458,788	189,031	465,827	249,147	550,708	250,726	529,586	262,028	520,804
Corn, Cob	101,891	249,459	85,464	235,766	100,019	238,575	101,087	223,053	88,817	220,295
Mixed vegetables	45,834	49,143	45,576	43,340	46,674	50,977	49,422	53,082	58,099	55,067
Okra	24,921	34,611	16,789	23,643	17,750	21,405	14,800	39,375	16,337	56,080
Onion Rings	5,611	4,435	7,197	8,214	12,287	9,889	11,141	9,057	13,135	12,004
Onions, Other	48,162	69,243	68,763	49,816	38,270	39,917	44,632	35,944	43,538	33,020
Blackeye Peas	2,447	1,756	1,818	1,597	1,693	1,386	1,655	1,565	2,869	2,434
Green Peas	234,439	238,909	288,133	219,559	240,208	228,586	284,293	243,251	314,155	274,778
Peas and Carrots Mixed	6,294	5,082	6,146	7,178	6,951	6,250	7,274	7,671	7,580	7,052
Spinach	84,296	49,062	75,117	48,781	55,678	39,053	52,579	38,024	60,413	42,629
Squash, Summer/Zucchini	39,010	73,109	49,364	64,510	49,657	61,133	42,958	62,828	39,517	65,550
Southern greens	20,022	15,084	17,194	12,432	17,240	11,043	14,873	11,253	19,717	18,405
Other Vegetables	264,367	372,890	294,654	387,366	298,588	425,010	281,639	381,070	302,891	391,886
Total	1,475,389	2,305,785	1,580,209	2,365,974	1,646,335	2,360,370	1,607,852	2,359,342	1,697,065	2,423,828
Potatoes, French Fries	866,965	802,278	924,433	905,662	1,009,457	902,139	807,376	842,464	916,294	809,569
Potatoes, Other Frozen	220,707	197,635	237,070	204,726	260,865	193,161	205,458	187,967	235,411	197,327
Potatoes, Total	1,087,672	999,913	1,161,503	1,110,388	1,270,322	1,095,300	1,012,834	1,030,431	1,151,705	1,006,896
Grand Total	2,563,061	3,305,698	2,741,712	3,476,362	2,916,657	3,455,670	2,620,686	3,389,773	2,848,770	3,430,724

VEGETABLES

Cold Storage Stocks of Frozen Green Beans[2] in the United States, on First of Month   In Thousands of Pounds

Year	Jan.	Feb.	Mar.	Apr.	May	June	July	Aug.	Sept.	Oct.	Nov.	Dec.
2010	176,371	159,532	142,137	123,047	92,954	80,754	70,842	109,413	164,357	223,928	198,883	182,202
2011	166,011	139,152	124,368	105,607	86,575	76,704	61,436	94,272	168,094	233,617	208,185	195,833
2012	192,235	172,413	150,764	125,018	104,127	96,182	91,790	149,376	252,740	288,757	301,782	273,657
2013	252,309	203,122	201,608	179,446	164,526	152,338	143,931	166,636	237,400	252,315	224,385	200,790
2014	181,073	162,305	149,444	139,195	125,882	109,855	96,376	147,470	225,135	253,066	235,830	205,861
2015[1]	182,136	161,510	153,916	135,211	123,221	119,266	113,449	155,386	225,251	255,661	243,986	225,001

[1] Preliminary.   [2] Regular cut.   *Source: Economic Research Service, U.S. Department of Agriculture (ERS-USDA)*

Cold Storage Stocks of Frozen Corn[2] in the United States, on First of Month   In Thousands of Pounds

Year	Jan.	Feb.	Mar.	Apr.	May	June	July	Aug.	Sept.	Oct.	Nov.	Dec.
2010	584,048	547,232	497,712	448,133	401,942	343,136	305,686	291,404	472,963	629,274	676,527	617,660
2011	571,012	521,993	467,481	405,714	340,257	283,392	216,687	181,404	302,134	506,672	541,733	505,252
2012	458,788	440,071	390,574	334,802	293,211	242,158	189,031	195,078	349,927	478,194	529,202	490,123
2013	465,827	450,464	410,588	369,771	330,335	282,126	249,147	226,862	397,483	585,455	630,849	581,072
2014	550,708	492,643	460,752	397,092	345,504	296,765	250,726	273,738	462,352	596,616	631,669	576,419
2015[1]	529,586	464,026	431,593	389,943	345,672	312,941	262,028	287,718	446,215	621,237	640,668	582,672

[1] Preliminary.   [2] Cut.   *Source: Economic Research Service, U.S. Department of Agriculture (ERS-USDA)*

Cold Storage Stocks of Frozen Corn[2] in the United States, on First of Month   In Thousands of Pounds

Year	Jan.	Feb.	Mar.	Apr.	May	June	July	Aug.	Sept.	Oct.	Nov.	Dec.
2010	252,108	236,435	214,708	188,317	164,144	132,229	102,824	100,184	203,300	259,187	260,414	254,363
2011	249,387	230,771	210,381	180,463	156,146	132,393	101,891	89,845	181,470	270,417	261,853	254,979
2012	249,459	225,895	194,851	173,112	148,582	118,460	85,464	87,499	166,073	233,153	257,504	245,195
2013	235,766	219,301	202,672	173,684	150,267	123,501	100,019	83,647	151,447	244,077	271,819	251,382
2014	238,575	225,426	200,562	174,569	156,311	121,262	101,087	108,477	175,199	258,604	268,087	240,784
2015[1]	223,053	206,000	175,910	156,425	132,387	110,643	88,817	112,873	165,657	239,922	244,687	229,113

[1] Preliminary.   [2] Cob.   *Source: Economic Research Service, U.S. Department of Agriculture (ERS-USDA)*

Cold Storage Stocks of Frozen Green Peas in the United States, on First of Month   In Thousands of Pounds

Year	Jan.	Feb.	Mar.	Apr.	May	June	July	Aug.	Sept.	Oct.	Nov.	Dec.
2010	275,625	255,309	236,609	203,325	172,781	149,428	298,995	456,725	437,177	384,187	348,511	311,507
2011	276,587	234,314	209,119	178,577	147,077	126,467	234,439	440,127	392,908	345,682	321,545	275,665
2012	238,909	209,567	170,753	143,400	118,689	102,379	288,133	404,734	364,629	323,968	278,459	241,233
2013	219,559	195,388	165,683	138,449	112,263	99,542	240,208	392,588	349,572	305,131	285,313	256,457
2014	228,586	192,134	168,608	136,081	111,179	95,529	284,293	427,634	395,401	354,716	314,577	285,406
2015[1]	243,251	205,887	189,997	154,385	127,621	127,798	314,155	414,693	397,020	372,987	335,536	308,934

[1] Preliminary.   *Source: Economic Research Service, U.S. Department of Agriculture (ERS-USDA)*

Cold Storage Stocks of Other Frozen Vegetables in the United States, on First of Month   In Thousands of lbs

Year	Jan.	Feb.	Mar.	Apr.	May	June	July	Aug.	Sept.	Oct.	Nov.	Dec.
2010	408,829	374,017	357,202	326,698	327,483	302,126	280,686	313,144	387,885	395,523	417,899	385,495
2011	360,009	322,773	293,177	278,745	268,754	264,758	264,367	268,594	325,000	354,130	398,891	383,782
2012	372,890	329,313	314,884	319,645	308,607	308,273	294,654	325,156	396,862	428,486	445,035	426,539
2013	387,366	363,899	352,909	350,651	349,274	301,871	298,588	310,171	369,266	436,882	455,362	433,678
2014	425,010	371,053	366,772	359,294	311,776	285,450	281,639	310,021	348,093	402,271	415,446	392,454
2015[1]	381,070	357,718	335,823	327,915	319,475	307,628	302,891	321,779	364,047	397,496	407,400	391,876

[1] Preliminary.   *Source: Economic Research Service, U.S. Department of Agriculture (ERS-USDA)*

Cold Storage Stocks of Total Frozen Vegetables in the United States, on First of Month   In Millions of Pounds

Year	Jan.	Feb.	Mar.	Apr.	May	June	July	Aug.	Sept.	Oct.	Nov.	Dec.
2010	2,471.8	2,315.0	2,151.8	1,959.8	1,808.8	1,621.6	1,664.9	1,859.8	2,263.4	2,529.3	2,619.7	2,517.1
2011	2,354.1	2,117.0	1,934.9	1,751.2	1,602.4	1,503.7	1,475.4	1,654.6	1,984.8	2,372.8	2,493.6	2,422.9
2012	2,305.8	2,125.1	1,935.6	1,769.1	1,637.8	1,521.6	1,580.2	1,779.1	2,164.7	2,416.1	2,584.1	2,494.7
2013	2,366.0	2,203.9	2,046.3	1,874.4	1,760.8	1,581.4	1,646.3	1,763.7	2,090.0	2,431.0	2,578.5	2,480.2
2014	2,360.4	2,157.4	2,025.0	1,842.1	1,660.2	1,519.9	1,607.9	1,863.8	2,232.8	2,530.6	2,663.6	2,546.8
2015[1]	2,359.3	2,144.9	1,995.5	1,844.7	1,711.2	1,619.7	1,697.1	1,889.2	2,221.2	2,570.1	2,688.7	2,580.2

[1] Preliminary.   *Source: Economic Research Service, U.S. Department of Agriculture (ERS-USDA)*

Wheat

Wheat is a cereal grass, but before cultivation it was a wild grass. It has been grown in temperate regions and cultivated for food since prehistoric times. Wheat is believed to have originated in southwestern Asia. Archeological research indicates that wheat was grown as a crop in the Nile Valley about 5,000 BC. Wheat is not native to the U.S. and was first grown here in 1602 near the Massachusetts coast. The common types of wheat grown in the U.S. are spring and winter wheat. Wheat planted in the spring for summer or autumn harvest is mostly red wheat. Wheat planted in the fall or winter for spring harvest is mostly white wheat. Winter wheat accounts for nearly three-fourths of total U.S. production. Wheat is used mainly as a human food and supplies about 20% of the food calories for the world's population. The primary use for wheat is flour, but it is also used for brewing and distilling, and for making oil, gluten, straw for livestock bedding, livestock feed, hay or silage, newsprint, and other products.

Wheat futures and options are traded at the CME Group, ICE Futures U.S., the Minneapolis Grain Exchange (MGEX), the Budapest Stock Exchange (BSE), the JSE Securities Exchange , the Mercado a Termino de Buenos Aires (MTBA), the NYSE LIFFE European Derivatives Market, and the Sydney Futures Exchange (SFE). The CME's wheat futures contract calls for the delivery of soft red wheat (No. 1 and 2), hard red winter wheat (No. 1 and 2), dark northern spring wheat (No. 1 and 2), No.1 northern spring at 3 cents/bushel premium, or No. 2 northern spring at par. Futures are also traded at ICE Futures Canada, the Moscow Exchange, the Multi Commodity Exchange of India (MCX), the National Commodity & Derivatives Exchange (NCDEX), the Rosario Futures Exchange, the Turkish Derivatives Exchange, and the Zhengzhou Commodity Exchange (ZCE).

Prices – CME wheat futures prices (Barchart.com electronic symbol ZW) drifted lower into Q2-2015 and in April posted then 4-3/4 year low of $4.60 a bushel on ample global supplies. The USDA in the May 2015 WASDE report projected that 2015/16 global wheat ending stocks would climb +1.2% y/y to a 16-year high of 203.32 MMT. Also, Russia said it would ease restrictions that it had implemented on its wheat exports in Q4-2014, which would increase global wheat supplies. Wheat prices turned higher in June, however, and in July posted the high for 2015 at $6.16 a bushel as drought in Europe and Canada reduced the yield prospects for their wheat crops, while excessive rains in the Great Plains hurt U.S. wheat yield prospects. The rally was short-lived, though, as wheat prices tumbled the second-half of 2015 and slid to a 5-1/2 year low in December of $4.51 a bushel. The surge in the dollar index to a 12-1/2 year high in 2015 hurt U.S. wheat export prospects which already weak as U.S. wheat remained expensive relative to cheaper foreign supplies. The USDA in the December WASDE report projected 2015/16 U.S. wheat exports of 800 million bushels, the lowest since 1972. The USDA also projected that Russia, the world's soon-to-be largest wheat

exporter, will export a record 23.5 MMT of wheat as the slump in the ruble to a record low against the dollar spurs Russian wheat exports. In addition, Argentina eliminated its corn and wheat export taxes, which boosted Argentina's wheat exports at the expense of U.S. exports. Finally, the USDA raised its 2015/16 global wheat production forecast to a record 734.93 MMT and hiked its 2015/16 global wheat ending stocks estimate to a record 229.86 MMT. Wheat prices finished 2015 down -20% at $4.70 a bushel.

Supply – World wheat production in the 2014-15 marketing year rose +1.1% to 723.384 million metric tons, a new record high. The world's largest wheat producers were the European Union with 21.5% of world production in 2014-15, China (17.4%), India (13.3%), Russia (8.2%), the U.S. (7.6%), and Pakistan (3.5%). China's wheat production in 2014-15 rose +3.3% yr/yr to 126.000 million metric tons, but is still below its record high of 123.289 million metric tons seen in 1997-98. India's wheat production rose +2.6% yr/yr to 95.910 million metric tons in 2014-15, a new record high. The world land area harvested with wheat in 2014-15 rose +0.5% yr/yr to 221.8 million hectares (1 hectare equals 10,000 square meters or 2.471 acres). World wheat yield in 2014-15 rose +3.1% to 3.30 metric tons per acre, a new record high.

U.S. wheat production in 2014-15 fell -5.1% yr/yr to 2.025 billion bushels, which was below the record crop of 2.785 billion bushels seen in 1981-82. Ending stocks for U.S. wheat for 2014-15 rose 17% to 691 million bushels. The U.S. winter wheat crop in 2014 fell -10.7% yr/yr to 1.377 billion bushels, which was well below the record winter wheat crop of 2.097 billion bushels seen in 1981. U.S. production of durum wheat in 2014 fell -8.4% yr/yr to 53.087 million bushels. U.S. production of other spring wheat in 2014 rose +11.4% yr/yr to 595.038 million bushels. The largest U.S. producing states of winter wheat in 2014 were Kansas with 17.9% of U.S. production, Montana with 6.7%, Colorado with 6.5%, and Washington with 6.2%. U.S. farmers planted 56.822 million acres of wheat in 2014, which was up +1.0% yr/yr. U.S. wheat yield in 2014-15 was 43.7 bushels per acre, a new record high.

Demand – World wheat utilization in 2014-15 rose +1.4% yr/yr to 714.1 million metric tons. U.S. consumption of wheat in 2014-15 fell -5.7% yr/yr to 1.183 billion bushels, below 2012-13 record high of 1.387 billion bushels. The consumption breakdown shows that 81.1% of U.S. wheat consumption in 2014-15 went for food, 12.7% for feed and residuals, and 6.2% for seed.

Trade – World trade in wheat in 2014-15 fell -3.4% yr/yr to 156.600 million metric tons, below last year's record high of 162.1 million metric tons. U.S. exports of wheat in 2014-15 fell -21.4% yr/yr to 925.000 million bushels, and remained below the record of 1.771 billion bushels of exports seen in 1981-82. U.S. imports of wheat in 2014-15 rose +6.8% to 180.0 million bushels, a new record high.

WHEAT

World Production of Wheat   In Thousands of Metric Tons

Crop Year	Australia	Canada	China	European Union	India	Iran	Kazakh-stan	Pakistan	Russia	Turkey	Ukraine	United States	World Total
2006-07	10,822	25,265	108,466	125,670	69,355	14,664	13,460	21,277	44,927	17,500	13,947	49,217	596,663
2007-08	13,569	20,090	109,298	120,833	75,807	15,887	16,466	23,295	49,368	15,500	13,938	55,821	612,602
2008-09	21,420	28,619	112,464	151,922	78,570	7,957	12,538	20,959	63,765	16,800	25,885	68,363	683,649
2009-10	21,834	26,950	115,120	139,720	80,679	13,485	17,051	24,033	61,770	18,450	20,866	60,117	687,052
2010-11	27,410	23,300	115,180	136,667	80,804	13,500	9,638	23,311	41,508	17,000	16,844	58,868	649,321
2011-12	29,905	25,288	117,400	138,182	86,874	12,400	22,732	25,214	56,240	18,800	22,324	54,244	696,636
2012-13	22,856	27,205	121,023	133,949	94,882	13,800	9,841	23,473	37,720	16,000	15,761	61,298	658,282
2013-14[1]	25,303	37,530	121,930	144,583	93,506	14,500	13,941	24,211	52,091	18,750	22,278	58,105	715,354
2014-15[2]	23,666	29,420	126,208	156,525	95,850	13,000	12,996	25,979	59,080	15,250	24,750	55,147	725,911
2015-16[3]	26,000	27,600	130,190	157,977	88,940	14,000	13,748	25,478	61,000	19,500	27,250	55,840	735,766

[1] Preliminary.   [2] Estimate.   [3] Forecast.   Source: Foreign Agricultural Service, U.S. Department of Agriculture (FAS-USDA)

World Supply and Demand of Wheat   In Millions of Metric Tons/Hectares

Year	Area Harvested	Yield	Production	World Trade	Utilization Total	Ending Stocks	Stocks as a % of Utilization
2006-07	212.3	2.81	596.5	111.7	616.5	134.1	21.8
2007-08	217.1	2.82	612.7	116.7	617.7	129.0	20.9
2008-09	224.1	3.05	683.9	144.2	644.3	168.6	26.2
2009-10	225.6	3.05	686.8	137.1	654.2	201.2	30.8
2010-11	216.9	2.99	649.6	132.8	653.4	197.4	30.2
2011-12	220.9	3.15	695.8	158.3	697.0	196.1	28.1
2012-13	215.8	3.05	658.3	138.2	679.0	137.4	20.2
2013-14[1]	219.8	3.25	715.4	126.7	698.3	165.9	23.8
2014-15[2]	220.9	3.28	725.5	131.8	704.9	164.1	23.3
2015-16[3]	224.3	3.27	732.3	133.5	709.4	162.7	22.9

[1] Preliminary.   [2] Estimate.   [3] Forecast.   Source: Foreign Agricultural Service, U.S. Department of Agriculture (FAS-USDA)

Salient Statistics of Wheat in the United States

Year	Planting Intentions	Acreage Harvested Winter (1,000 Acres)	Spring	All	Average All Yield Per Acre in Bushels	Value of Production $1,000	Foreign Trade[5] Domestic Exports[2] (In Millions of Bushels)	Imports[3]	Per Capita[4] Consumption Flour (In Pounds)	Cereal
2006-07	57,344	31,117	16,769	46,810	38.7	7,694,734	908.5	121.9	135.7	----
2007-08	60,460	35,938	15,061	50,999	40.5	13,289,326	1,262.6	112.6	138.1	----
2008-09	63,193	39,608	16,091	55,699	44.9	16,625,759	1,015.4	127.0	136.5	----
2009-10	59,168	34,510	15,383	49,893	44.5	10,654,115	879.3	118.6	134.7	----
2010-11	53,593	31,741	15,878	47,619	46.3	12,827,254	1,291.4	96.9	135.0	----
2011-12	54,409	32,314	13,391	45,705	43.7	14,322,909	1,051.1	113.1	133.0	----
2012-13	55,294	34,609	14,149	48,758	46.2	17,383,149	1,012.1	124.3	134.0	----
2013-14	56,236	32,650	12,672	45,332	47.1	14,604,442	1,175.8	173.1		
2014-15	56,841	32,299	14,086	46,385	43.7	11,914,954	854.3	149.5		
2015-16[1]	54,644	32,257	14,837	47,094	43.6	10,203,360	775.0	120.0		

[1] Preliminary.   [2] Includes flour milled from imported wheat.   [3] Total wheat, flour & other products.   [4] Civilian only.   [5] Year beginning June.
Source: Economic Research Service, U.S. Department of Agriculture (ERS-USDA)

Supply and Distribution of Wheat in the United States   In Millions of Bushels

Crop Year Beginning June 1	Supply Stocks, June 1 On Farms	Mills, Elevators[3]	Total Stocks	Pro-duction	Imports[4]	Total Supply	Domestic Disappearance Food	Seed	Feed & Residual[5]	Total	Exports[4]	Total Disap-pearance
2006-07	111.0	460.2	571.2	1,812.0	121.9	2,501.5	937.9	81.9	117.1	1,136.8	908.5	2,045.3
2007-08	73.2	383.0	456.2	2,051.1	112.6	2,619.9	947.9	87.6	16.0	1,051.4	1,262.6	2,314.1
2008-09	25.6	280.2	305.8	2,499.2	127.0	2,932.0	926.8	77.7	268.3	1,272.8	1,015.4	2,288.2
2009-10	140.7	515.8	656.5	2,218.1	118.6	2,993.2	918.9	68.0	142.2	1,129.1	879.3	2,008.4
2010-11	209.9	765.7	975.6	2,206.9	96.9	3,235.6	925.6	70.7	84.8	1,081.1	1,291.4	2,372.6
2011-12	130.9	731.3	862.2	1,999.3	113.1	2,969.2	941.4	75.6	158.5	1,175.5	1,051.1	2,226.6
2012-13	112.0	630.6	742.6	2,252.3	124.3	3,119.2	950.8	73.1	365.3	1,389.3	1,012.1	2,401.4
2013-14	120.2	597.7	717.9	2,135.0	173.1	3,025.9	955.1	77.0	227.7	1,259.8	1,175.8	2,435.6
2014-15[1]	97.0	493.3	590.3	2,026.3	149.5	2,766.1	958.2	78.9	122.2	1,159.4	854.3	2,013.7
2015-16[2]	155.2	597.2	752.4	2,051.8	120.0	2,924.1	967.0	66.0	150.0	1,183.0	775.0	1,958.0

[1] Preliminary.   [2] Estimate.   [3] Also warehouses and all off-farm storage not otherwise designated, including flour mills.   [4] Imports & exports are for wheat, including flour & other products in terms of wheat.   [5] Mostly feed use.
Source: Economic Research Service, U.S. Department of Agriculture (ERS-USDA)

Stocks, Production and Exports of Wheat in the United States, by Class   In Millions of Bushels

Year	Hard Spring Stocks June 1	Hard Spring Pro-duction	Hard Spring Exports[3]	Durum[2] Stocks June 1	Durum[2] Pro-duction	Durum[2] Exports[3]	Hard Winter Stocks June 1	Hard Winter Pro-duction	Hard Winter Exports[3]	Soft Red Winter Stocks June 1	Soft Red Winter Pro-duction	Soft Red Winter Exports[3]	White Stocks June 1	White Pro-duction	White Exports[3]
2006-07	132	432	250	40	53	35	215	682	281	106	390	146	78	254	197
2007-08	117	450	305	21	72	42	165	956	538	109	352	209	44	221	170
2008-09	68	512	210	8	84	24	138	1,035	447	55	614	199	37	255	136
2009-10	142	548	214	25	109	44	254	920	370	171	404	109	64	237	143
2010-11	234	570	339	35	106	43	385	1,018	616	242	237	109	80	275	182
2011-12	185	398	242	35	50	27	386	780	397	171	458	165	85	314	218
2012-13	151	505	232	25	83	29	317	1,000	380	185	420	193	64	259	174
2013-14	165	490	246	23	58	31	343	747	446	124	568	283	63	271	171
2014-15	169	556	270	22	54	37	237	739	269	113	455	133	50	224	146
2015-16[1]	212	564	245	26	82	35	294	827	230	154	359	125	67	219	140

[1] Preliminary.   [2] Includes "Red Durum."   [3] Includes four made from U.S. wheat & shipments to territories.
Source: Economic Research Service, U.S. Department of Agriculture (ERS-USDA)

Seeded Acreage, Yield and Production of all Wheat in the United States

Year	Seed Acreage - 1,000 Acres Winter	Other Spring	Durum	All	Yield Per Harvested Acre (Bushels) Winter	Other Spring	Durum	All	Production (Million Bushels) Winter	Other Spring	Durum	All
2006	40,575	14,899	1,870	57,344	41.7	33.2	29.5	38.7	1,298.1	460.5	53.5	1,812.0
2007	45,012	13,292	2,156	60,460	41.7	37.1	34.1	40.2	1,499.2	479.6	72.2	2,051.1
2008	46,307	14,165	2,721	63,193	47.1	40.5	32.6	44.9	1,867.3	548.0	83.8	2,499.2
2009	43,346	13,268	2,554	59,168	44.2	45.1	44.9	44.5	1,524.6	584.4	109.0	2,218.1
2010	37,335	13,698	2,560	53,593	46.8	46.1	42.1	46.3	1,484.9	616.0	106.1	2,206.9
2011	40,646	12,394	1,369	54,409	46.2	37.7	38.5	43.7	1,493.7	455.2	50.5	1,999.3
2012	40,897	12,259	2,138	55,294	47.1	44.9	38.4	46.2	1,630.4	540.4	81.5	2,252.3
2013	43,230	11,606	1,400	56,236	47.3	47.1	43.3	47.1	1,542.9	534.1	58.0	2,135.0
2014	42,409	13,025	1,407	56,841	42.6	46.7	40.2	43.7	1,377.2	595.0	54.1	2,026.3
2015[1]	39,461	13,247	1,936	54,644	42.5	46.3	43.5	43.6	1,370.2	599.1	82.5	2,051.8

[1] Preliminary.   *Source: Economic Research Service, U.S. Department of Agriculture (ERS-USDA)*

Production of Winter Wheat in the United States, by State   In Thousands of Bushels

Year	Colorado	Idaho	Illinois	Kansas	Missouri	Montana	Nebraska	Ohio	Okla-homa	Oregon	Texas	Wash-ington	US Total
2006	39,900	54,670	60,970	291,200	49,140	82,560	61,200	65,280	81,600	38,690	33,600	118,800	1,298,081
2007	91,650	51,830	48,950	283,800	37,840	83,220	84,280	44,530	98,000	38,160	140,600	104,780	1,499,241
2008	57,000	60,000	73,600	356,000	55,680	94,380	73,480	74,120	166,500	44,950	99,000	96,320	1,867,333
2009	98,000	56,700	45,920	369,600	34,310	89,540	76,800	70,560	77,000	42,000	61,250	96,760	1,524,608
2010	105,750	58,220	16,520	360,000	12,600	93,600	64,070	45,750	120,900	54,270	127,500	117,990	1,484,861
2011	78,000	63,140	46,665	276,500	34,000	89,790	65,250	49,300	70,400	63,525	49,400	129,750	1,493,677
2012	68,200	59,200	40,960	382,200	39,440	84,630	53,300	30,600	154,800	51,810	95,700	116,900	1,630,387
2013	40,750	63,640	56,280	321,100	56,145	81,700	39,900	44,800	105,400	48,360	68,150	115,230	1,542,902
2014	89,300	58,400	44,890	246,400	42,920	91,840	71,050	40,330	47,600	40,700	67,500	85,280	1,377,216
2015[1]	79,180	57,400	33,800	321,900	32,330	91,020	45,980	32,160	98,800	34,545	106,500	89,040	1,370,188

[1] Preliminary.   *Source: Crop Reporting Board, U.S. Department of Agriculture (CRB-USDA)*

Official Winter Wheat Crop Production Reports in the United States   In Thousands of Bushels

Crop Year	May 1	June 1	July 1	August 1	September 1	Current December	Final
2006-07	1,322,831	1,263,766	1,280,005	1,283,134	----	----	1,298,081
2007-08	1,615,613	1,609,679	1,561,907	1,537,262	----	----	1,499,241
2008-09	1,777,532	1,817,364	1,864,245	1,874,857	----	----	1,867,333
2009-10	1,502,074	1,491,769	1,524,771	1,537,348	----	----	1,524,608
2010-11	1,458,350	1,482,364	1,505,493	1,522,902	----	----	1,484,861
2011-12	1,424,357	1,450,115	1,491,739	1,497,429	----	----	1,493,677
2012-13	1,693,710	1,683,667	1,670,346	1,682,726	----	----	1,630,387
2013-14	1,485,757	1,509,142	1,543,095	1,542,605	----	----	1,542,902
2014-15	1,402,505	1,381,060	1,367,432	1,396,742	----	----	1,377,216
2015-16[1]	1,471,802	1,505,072	1,455,516	1,438,278	----	----	1,370,188

[1] Preliminary.   *Source: Crop Reporting Board, U.S. Department of Agriculture (CRB-USDA)*

WHEAT

Production of All Spring Wheat in the United States, by State   In Thousands of Bushels

	Durum Wheat						Other Spring Wheat							
Year	Arizona	California	Montana	North Dakota	South Dakota	Total	Idaho	Minnesota	Montana	North Dakota	Oregon	South Dakota	Washington	Total
2006	7,400	6,435	6,715	31,500	90	53,475	34,310	77,550	63,800	212,350	5,750	42,600	21,250	460,480
2007	8,364	8,000	11,400	43,070	175	72,224	30,600	79,200	55,200	234,000	5,520	52,260	20,562	479,623
2008	14,602	15,225	10,830	42,250	190	83,827	37,440	100,800	59,520	246,400	7,650	68,400	22,470	548,004
2009	12,400	17,000	16,585	61,230	207	109,042	40,810	82,150	70,500	289,800	6,858	64,680	26,325	584,411
2010	9,085	10,450	18,020	66,750	555	106,080	47,970	85,250	103,740	277,200	9,316	59,220	29,900	615,975
2011	7,979	12,535	10,780	18,233	196	50,482	52,080	69,000	74,400	167,750	10,990	37,820	38,130	455,188
2012	9,880	12,720	15,260	42,720	115	81,501	37,240	74,670	95,700	256,500	5,766	41,410	27,775	540,419
2013	7,548	4,900	15,225	29,453	168	57,976	39,270	66,120	104,710	235,290	5,544	51,260	30,300	534,101
2014	8,436	3,150	13,330	28,223	180	54,056	34,580	64,900	104,300	291,650	3,744	71,680	23,180	595,038
2015/1	14,140	6,180	18,755	42,463	246	82,484	29,750	85,800	75,640	319,200	4,650	60,480	22,500	599,080

[1] Preliminary.   *Source: Crop Reporting Board, U.S. Department of Agriculture (CRB-USDA)*

Stocks of All Wheat in the United States   In Millions of Bushels

	On Farms				Off Farms				Total Stocks			
Year	Mar. 1	June 1	Sept. 1	Dec. 1	Mar. 1	June 1	Sept. 1	Dec. 1	Mar. 1	June 1	Sept. 1	Dec. 1
2006	256.0	111.0	572.0	403.3	716.2	460.2	1,178.5	911.4	972.2	571.2	1,750.5	1,314.7
2007	192.5	73.2	495.0	289.5	664.3	383.0	1,221.9	842.4	856.7	456.2	1,716.9	1,131.9
2008	92.0	25.6	635.7	454.0	617.3	280.2	1,222.2	968.1	709.3	305.8	1,857.9	1,422.1
2009	280.4	140.7	836.0	558.8	759.7	515.8	1,373.3	1,222.9	1,040.1	656.5	2,209.3	1,781.7
2010	348.3	209.9	812.1	550.0	1,008.1	765.7	1,637.5	1,382.9	1,356.4	975.6	2,449.6	1,932.9
2011	288.0	130.9	633.0	405.4	1,137.3	731.3	1,513.7	1,257.3	1,425.3	862.2	2,146.7	1,662.7
2012	217.1	112.0	572.9	399.5	982.2	630.6	1,531.8	1,271.1	1,199.3	742.6	2,104.7	1,670.6
2013	237.0	120.2	555.0	398.4	997.9	597.7	1,314.6	1,076.5	1,234.8	717.9	1,869.6	1,474.9
2014	237.5	97.0	713.5	472.8	819.4	493.3	1,193.8	1,056.8	1,057.0	590.3	1,907.2	1,529.6
2015[1]	278.7	155.2	650.2	503.5	861.7	597.2	1,446.9	1,234.9	1,140.4	752.4	2,097.1	1,738.4

[1] Preliminary.   *Source: National Agricultural Statistics Service, U.S. Department of Agriculture (NASS-USDA)*

Stocks of Durum Wheat in the United States   In Millions of Bushels

	On Farms				Off Farms				Total Stocks			
Year	Mar. 1	June 1	Sept. 1	Dec. 1	Mar. 1	June 1	Sept. 1	Dec. 1	Mar. 1	June 1	Sept. 1	Dec. 1
2006	39.7	23.1	31.5	25.9	25.8	17.3	31.5	25.4	65.5	40.4	63.0	51.3
2007	17.1	9.0	34.7	17.6	21.7	12.4	35.8	22.2	38.8	21.4	70.5	39.8
2008	8.1	2.4	36.2	26.1	17.1	5.9	22.6	18.4	25.2	8.3	58.8	44.5
2009	18.7	13.3	74.1	50.6	13.6	11.8	27.7	25.2	32.3	25.1	101.8	75.8
2010	34.3	23.9	71.2	46.6	21.2	10.7	28.9	21.7	55.5	34.6	100.1	68.3
2011	35.7	22.1	34.9	24.5	20.7	13.4	28.8	24.0	56.4	35.5	63.7	48.5
2012	17.9	15.2	43.6	36.7	17.9	10.3	24.8	24.3	35.8	25.5	68.4	61.0
2013	21.4	13.6	42.9	32.8	21.1	9.5	23.5	21.2	42.5	23.1	66.4	54.0
2014	20.7	12.8	38.7	23.9	17.4	8.7	19.1	20.1	38.1	21.5	57.8	44.0
2015[1]	16.2	10.3	44.9	35.7	21.5	15.4	29.1	24.8	37.7	25.7	74.0	60.5

[1] Preliminary.   *Source: National Agricultural Statistics Service, U.S. Department of Agriculture (NASS-USDA)*

Wheat Supply and Distribution in Canada, Australia and Argentina   In Millions of Metric Tons

	Canada (Year Beginning Aug. 1)					Australia (Year Beginning Oct. 1)					Argentina (Year Beginning Dec. 1)				
	Supply			Disappearance		Supply			Disappearance		Supply			Disappearance	
Crop Year	Stocks Aug. 1	New Crop	Total Supply	Domestic	Exports[3]	Stocks Oct. 1	New Crop	Total Supply	Domestic	Exports[3]	Stocks Dec. 1	New Crop	Total Supply	Domestic	Exports[3]
2006-07	9.7	25.3	35.0	9.0	19.4	9.4	10.8	20.2	7.4	8.7	0.4	16.3	16.7	5.4	10.7
2007-08	6.9	20.1	27.0	6.9	16.1	4.2	13.6	17.8	6.6	7.5	0.6	18.6	19.2	5.7	11.2
2008-09	4.4	28.6	33.0	7.8	18.9	3.7	21.4	25.1	7.4	14.7	2.4	11.0	13.4	5.3	6.8
2009-10	6.6	27.0	33.6	7.2	19.0	3.1	21.8	24.9	5.2	14.8	1.3	12.0	13.3	5.8	5.1
2010-11	7.7	23.3	31.0	7.6	16.6	5.1	27.4	32.5	5.8	18.6	2.3	17.2	19.5	6.0	9.5
2011-12	7.4	25.3	32.7	9.9	17.4	8.2	29.9	38.1	6.5	24.7	4.1	15.5	19.6	6.0	12.9
2012-13	5.9	27.2	33.1	9.5	19.0	7.1	22.9	30.0	6.7	18.6	0.7	9.3	10.0	6.2	3.6
2013-14	5.1	37.5	42.6	9.4	23.3	4.7	25.3	30.0	7.0	18.6	0.3	10.5	10.8	6.1	2.3
2014-15[1]	10.4	29.4	39.8	9.1	24.1	4.6	23.7	28.3	7.5	16.6	2.5	12.5	15.0	6.4	5.5
2015-16[2]	7.1	27.6	34.7	8.8	22.0	4.3	26.0	30.3	7.4	18.0	3.2	11.0	14.2	6.4	6.5

[1] Preliminary.   [2] Forecast.   [3] Including flour.   *Source: Foreign Agricultural Service, U.S. Department of Agriculture (FAS-USDA)*

Quarterly Supply and Disappearance of Wheat in the United States   In Millions of Bushels

Crop Year Beginning June 1	Supply				Disappearance						Ending Stocks		
					Domestic Use								
	Beginning Stocks	Pro-duction	Imports[3]	Total Supply	Food	Seed	Feed & Residual	Total	Exports[3]	Total Disap-pearance	Gov't Owned[4]	Privately Owned[5]	Total Stocks
2005-06	2,105.0	2,104.7	81.0	4,290.7	914.0	78.0	154.0	1,146.0	1,009.0	2,155.0			571.0
June-Aug.	540.1	2,104.7	19.0	2,663.0	231.0	2.0	263.0	496.0	244.0	740.0	48.3	1,875.0	1,923.0
Sept.-Nov.	1,923.0	----	20.0	1,944.0	238.0	51.0	-61.0	228.0	286.0	514.0	44.1	1,385.4	1,429.0
Dec.-Feb.	1,429.0	----	20.0	1,450.0	219.0	1.0	1.0	221.0	257.0	478.0	----	----	972.0
Mar.-May	972.0	----	22.0	995.0	226.0	24.0	-49.0	201.0	222.0	423.0	----	----	571.0
2006-07	571.0	1,808.0	121.0	2,500.0	937.0	81.0	117.0	1,135.0	908.0	2,043.0	----	----	456.0
June-Aug.	571.0	1,808.0	26.0	2,406.0	235.0	2.0	205.0	442.0	214.0	656.0	----	----	1,751.0
Sept.-Nov.	1,751.0	----	29.0	1,780.0	243.0	56.0	-47.0	252.0	212.0	464.0	----	----	1,315.0
Dec.-Feb.	1,315.0	----	32.0	1,346.0	225.0	1.0	28.0	254.0	235.0	489.0	----	----	857.0
Mar.-May	857.0	----	34.0	891.0	234.0	22.0	-69.0	187.0	247.0	434.0	----	----	456.0
2007-08	456.0	2,051.0	112.0	2,619.0	947.0	88.0	16.0	1,051.0	1,262.0	2,313.0	----	----	306.0
June-Aug.	456.0	2,051.0	30.0	2,538.0	240.0	1.0	257.0	498.0	323.0	821.0	----	----	1,717.0
Sept.-Nov.	1,717.0	----	21.0	1,738.0	245.0	60.0	-120.0	185.0	421.0	606.0	----	----	1,132.0
Dec.-Feb.	1,132.0	----	24.0	1,156.0	227.0	2.0	-42.0	187.0	261.0	448.0	----	----	709.0
Mar.-May	709.0	----	37.0	746.0	235.0	25.0	-79.0	181.0	257.0	438.0	----	----	306.0
2008-09	306.0	2,499.0	127.0	2,932.0	924.0	75.0	256.0	1,255.0	1,016.0	2,271.0	----	----	657.0
June-Aug.	306.0	2,499.0	28.0	2,833.0	236.0	2.0	393.0	631.0	345.0	976.0	----	----	1,858.0
Sept.-Nov.	1,858.0	----	28.0	1,886.0	238.0	54.0	-124.0	168.0	295.0	463.0	----	----	1,422.0
Dec.-Feb.	1,422.0	----	36.0	1,459.0	219.0	1.0	28.0	248.0	170.0	418.0	----	----	1,040.0
Mar.-May	1,040.0	----	35.0	1,075.0	231.0	18.0	-41.0	208.0	206.0	414.0	----	----	657.0
2009-10	657.0	2,218.0	119.0	2,994.0	917.0	69.0	150.0	1,136.0	881.0	2,017.0	----	----	976.0
June-Aug.	657.0	2,218.0	28.0	2,902.0	231.0	1.0	261.0	493.0	200.0	693.0	----	----	2,209.0
Sept.-Nov.	2,209.0	----	24.0	2,234.0	237.0	46.0	-83.0	200.0	252.0	452.0	----	----	1,782.0
Dec.-Feb.	1,782.0	----	30.0	1,812.0	221.0	1.0	31.0	253.0	202.0	455.0	----	----	1,356.0
Mar.-May	1,356.0	----	37.0	1,393.0	228.0	21.0	-59.0	190.0	227.0	417.0	----	----	976.0
2010-11	976.0	2,207.0	96.0	3,279.0	930.0	80.0	170.0	1,180.0	1,288.0	2,468.0	----	----	862.0
June-Aug.	976.0	2,207.0	27.0	3,212.0	235.0	2.0	262.0	499.0	266.0	765.0	----	----	2,450.0
Sept.-Nov.	2,450.0	----	24.0	2,473.0	242.0	52.0	-63.0	231.0	310.0	541.0	----	----	1,933.0
Dec.-Feb.	1,933.0	----	23.0	1,956.0	221.0	1.0	-2.0	220.0	311.0	531.0	----	----	1,425.0
Mar.-May	1,425.0	----	22.0	1,448.0	233.0	73.0	-65.0	241.0	401.0	642.0	----	----	862.0
2011-12	862.0	1,993.1	112.1	2,968.2	941.4	75.6	157.4	1,174.4	1,051.2	2,225.6	----	----	742.6
June-Aug.	862.0	1,993.1	20.8	2,876.9	230.0	4.7	200.8	435.5	294.8	730.3	----	----	2,146.7
Sept.-Nov.	2,146.7	----	32.3	2,178.9	244.0	51.0	-16.4	278.5	237.9	516.4	----	----	1,662.5
Dec.-Feb.	1,662.5	----	30.1	1,692.6	230.9	1.4	43.5	275.9	217.4	493.3	----	----	1,199.3
Mar.-May	1,199.3	----	28.9	1,228.2	236.5	18.5	-70.5	184.5	301.1	485.6	----	----	742.6
2012-13	742.6	2,252.3	124.3	3,119.2	950.8	73.1	365.3	1,389.3	1,012.1	2,401.4	----	----	717.9
June-Aug.	742.6	2,252.3	25.5	3,020.4	237.6	1.4	402.7	641.7	263.7	905.3	----	----	2,115.1
Sept.-Nov.	2,115.1	----	32.9	2,148.0	246.6	55.4	-22.4	279.6	197.9	477.5	----	----	1,670.6
Dec.-Feb.	1,670.6	----	34.7	1,705.3	229.0	1.4	4.9	235.3	235.2	470.4	----	----	1,234.8
Mar.-May	1,234.8	----	31.2	1,266.0	237.6	15.0	-19.9	232.8	315.4	548.1	----	----	717.9
2013-14	717.9	2,135.0	173.1	3,025.9	955.1	77.0	227.7	1,259.8	1,175.8	2,435.6	----	----	590.3
June-Aug.	717.9	2,135.0	35.7	2,888.5	234.8	4.1	422.4	661.4	357.5	1,018.9	----	----	1,869.6
Sept.-Nov.	1,869.6	----	48.0	1,917.7	249.3	52.7	-168.0	134.0	308.8	442.8	----	----	1,474.9
Dec.-Feb.	1,474.9	----	42.0	1,516.9	231.1	1.9	-0.4	232.6	227.4	459.9	----	----	1,057.0
Mar.-May	1,057.0	----	47.3	1,104.3	239.9	18.3	-26.3	231.9	282.1	514.0	----	----	590.3
2014-15[1]	590.3	2,026.3	149.5	2,766.1	958.2	78.9	122.2	1,159.4	854.3	2,013.7	----	----	752.4
June-Aug.	590.3	2,026.3	44.2	2,660.8	238.9	6.4	255.8	501.1	252.5	753.6	----	----	1,907.2
Sept.-Nov.	1,907.2	----	33.9	1,941.1	248.2	48.5	-93.0	203.7	207.7	411.5	----	----	1,529.6
Dec.-Feb.	1,529.6	----	36.1	1,565.7	230.8	2.1	8.2	241.1	184.3	425.3	----	----	1,140.4
Mar.-May	1,140.4	----	35.2	1,175.6	240.3	22.0	-48.8	213.5	209.8	423.2	----	----	752.4
2015-16[2]	752.4	2,051.8	120.0	2,924.1	967.0	66.0	150.0	1,183.0	775.0	1,958.0	----	----	966.1
June-Aug.	752.4	2,051.8	28.2	2,832.4	240.1	1.7	289.9	531.7	203.5	735.3	----	----	2,097.1
Sept.-Nov.	2,097.1	----	27.0	2,124.1	248.7	43.8	-101.2	191.3	194.4	385.7	----	----	1,738.4

[1] Preliminary.   [2] Forecast.   [3] Imports & exports include flour and other products expressed in wheat equivalent.   [4] Uncommitted, Government only.
[5] Includes total loans.   [6] Includes alcoholic beverages.   *Source: Economic Research Service, U.S. Department of Agriculture (ERS-USDA)*

WHEAT

Exports of Wheat (Only)[2] from the United States   In Thousands of Bushels

Year	June	July	Aug.	Sept.	Oct.	Nov.	Dec.	Jan.	Feb.	Mar.	Apr.	May	Total
2006-07	63,115	67,846	78,225	76,431	70,752	60,595	72,226	84,629	75,412	76,512	75,130	85,565	886,438
2007-08	73,088	80,285	153,223	149,168	158,064	116,504	82,343	87,539	84,414	92,251	82,781	79,725	1,239,385
2008-09	77,176	119,492	141,173	117,332	93,462	75,311	54,389	56,634	55,825	75,580	61,048	65,884	993,306
2009-10	63,851	58,627	68,321	100,213	77,627	68,117	54,438	65,060	76,522	73,780	76,958	68,473	851,987
2010-11	74,400	80,546	104,145	130,529	86,525	92,159	85,582	108,741	105,409	120,873	146,979	126,991	1,262,879
2011-12	107,349	83,260	100,294	99,523	71,073	61,287	72,639	71,447	68,957	86,770	103,778	102,576	1,028,953
2012-13	89,731	70,378	97,249	92,915	51,751	46,512	62,763	76,874	91,025	101,785	108,878	96,400	986,261
2013-14	98,174	113,731	141,038	151,309	94,466	63,040	74,469	77,203	70,973	78,911	103,942	93,715	1,160,971
2014-15	76,739	72,407	100,573	94,279	59,095	47,047	59,842	54,751	64,226	72,310	65,986	65,699	832,954
2015-16[1]	59,459	63,616	74,775	92,452	44,717	50,962	63,981	54,747					757,063

[1] Preliminary.   [2] Grains.   *Source: Economic Research Service, U.S. Department of Agriculture (ERS-USDA)*

Wheat Government Loan Program Data in the United States   Loan Rates--Cents Per Bushel

Crop Year Beginning June 1	National Average[3]	Target Rate[4]	Corn Belt (Soft Red Winter)	Central & Southern Plains (Hard Winter)	Northern Plains (Spring & Durum)	Pacific Northwest (White)	Placed Under Loan	% of Pro- duction	Acquired by CCC Under Program	Total Stocks May 31	CCC Stocks May 31	CCC Loans	Farmer- Owned Reserve	"Free"
										In Millions of Bushels				
2004-05	275	392	----	----	----	----	178	8.3	10	540	55	58	0	486
2005-06	275	392	----	----	----	----	170	8.1	1	571	43	NA	0	528
2006-07	275	392	----	----	----	----	94	5.2	0	456	41	NA	0	437
2007-08	275	392	----	----	----	----	36	1.8	0	306	0	NA	NA	NA
2008-09	275	392	----	----	----	----	84	3.4	0	657	0	----	----	----
2009-10	275	392	----	----	----	----	103	4.6	0	976	0	----	----	----
2010-11	294	417	----	----	----	----	67	3.0	0	862	0	----	----	----
2011-12	294	417	----	----	----	----	36	1.8	0	743	0	----	----	----
2012-13[1]	294	417	----	----	----	----	28	1.2	0	718	0	----	----	----
2013-14[2]	294	417	----	----	----	----	25	1.1	0	590	0	----	----	----

[1] Preliminary.   [2] Estimate.   [3] The national average loan rate at the farm as a percentage of the parity-priced wheat at the beginning of the marketing year.   [4] 1996-97 through 2001-02 marketing year, target prices not applicable.   NA = Not avaliable.
Source: Agricultural Marketing Service, U.S. Department of Agriculture (AMS-USDA)

United States Wheat and Wheat Flour Imports and Exports   In Thousands of Bushels

Crop Year Beginning June 1	Suitable for Milling	Wheat Unfit for Human Consump.	Grain	Flour & Products[2]	Total	P.L. 480	Foreign Donations Sec. 416	Aid[3]	Total con- cessional	CCC Export Credit	Export Enhance- ment Program	Total U.S. Wheat
	Wheat		-- Wheat Equivalent --			In Thousands of Metric Tons						
2006-07	92,928	----	92,928	28,942	121,870	767	0	----	961	1,008	0	29,636
2007-08	85,806	----	85,806	26,825	112,631	734	12	----	841	1,360	0	32,847
2008-09	101,964	----	101,964	25,006	126,970	722	12	----	965	2,691	0	22,545
2009-10	93,003	----	93,003	25,588	118,591	793	16	----	901	2,078	0	25,698
2010-11	69,053	----	69,053	27,866	96,918	521	0	----	673	2,785	0	34,583
2011-12	83,336	----	83,336	28,733	112,069	595	13	----	661	2,388	0	----
2012-13[1]	94,548	----	94,548	28,208	122,756							

[1] Preliminary.   [2] Includes macaroni, semolina & similar products.   [3] Shipment mostly under the Commodity Import Program, financed with foreign aid funds.   NA = Not available.   *Source: Economic Research Service, U.S. Department of Agriculture (ERS-USDA)*

Comparative Average Cash Wheat Prices   In Dollars Per Bushel

Crop Year June to May	Received by U.S. Farmers	No. 2 Soft Red Winter, Chicago	No 1 Hard Red Ordinary Protein, Kansas City	No 2 Soft Red Winter, St. Louis	No 1 Dark Northern Spring 14%	No 1 Hard Amber Durum	No 1 Soft White, Portland	No 2 Western White Pacific Northwest	No 2 Soft White, Toledo	Aust- ralian Standard White	Canada Vancouver No 1 CWRS 13 1/2%	Argen- tina F.O.B. B.A.	U.S. Gulf No. 2 Hard Winter	Rotterdam C.I.F. U.S. No 2 Hard Winter
2008-09	6.78	5.04	7.03	4.86	8.53	----	6.25	6.62	4.98	217	350	244	292	----
2009-10	4.87	4.39	5.24	3.88	6.96	----	4.91	5.00	4.31	209	280	227	205	----
2010-11	5.70	6.60	7.55	7.01	9.93	----	6.77	4.63	6.62	273	394	302	284	----
2011-12	7.24	6.36	7.81	6.59	10.13	----	6.69	----	6.50	249	416	271	290	----
2012-13	7.77	7.82	8.95	7.91	9.61	----	8.34	----	7.71	324	359	330	332	----
2013-14	6.87	6.52	8.34	6.71	8.85	----	7.26	----	6.38	281	331	327	309	----
2014-15	5.99	5.31	7.04	5.32	8.08	----	6.65	----	5.13	253	285	270	252	----
2015-16[1]	4.90-5.10	4.97	5.69	4.56	6.46	----	5.40	----	5.12	225	236	212	188	----

[1] Preliminary.   [2] Calendar year.   NA = Not available.   *Source: Economic Research Service, U.S. Department of Agriculture (ERS-USDA)*

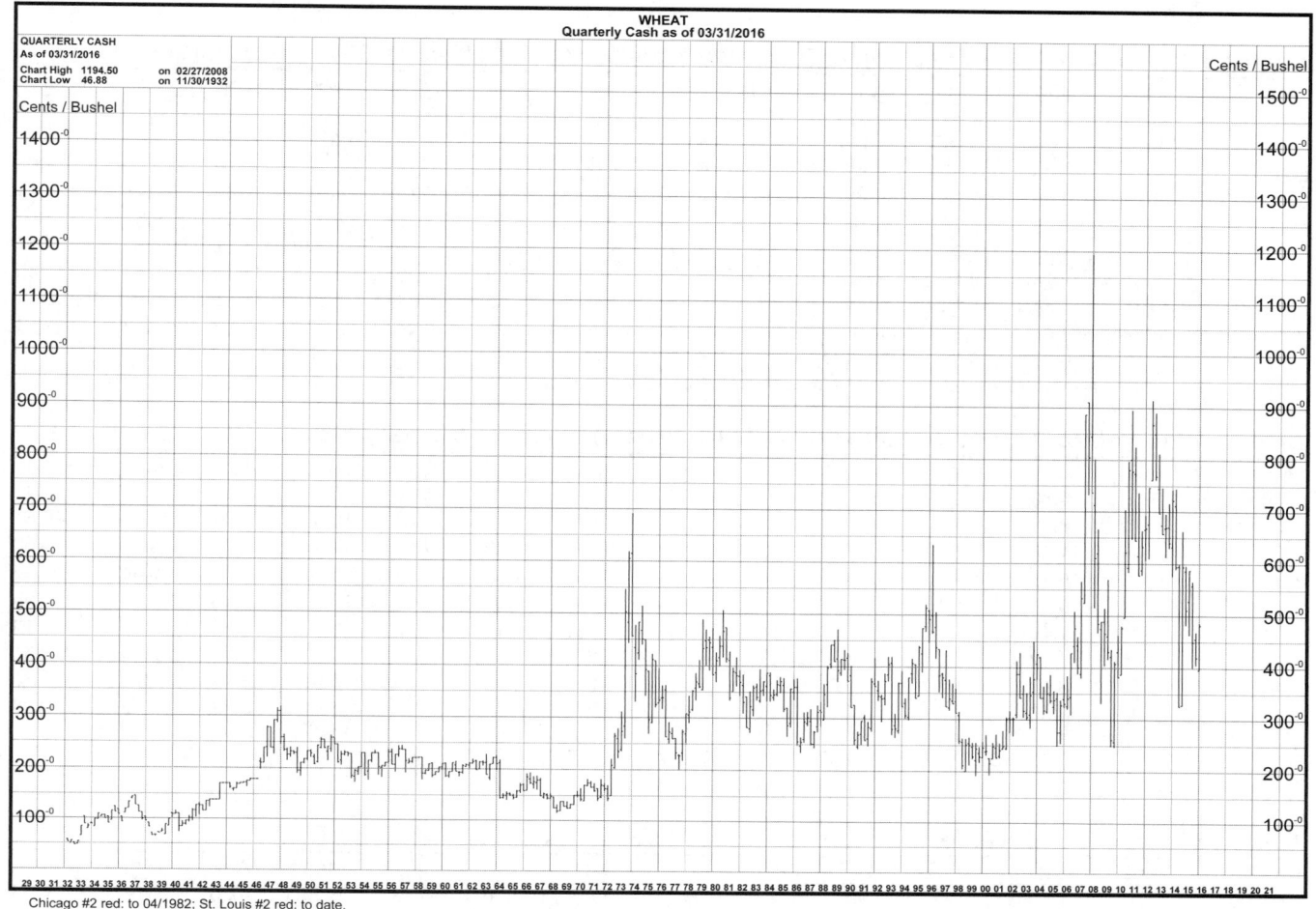

WHEAT
Quarterly Cash as of 03/31/2016

QUARTERLY CASH
As of 03/31/2016
Chart High 1194.50 on 02/27/2008
Chart Low 46.88 on 11/30/1932

Chicago #2 red: to 04/1982; St. Louis #2 red: to date.

Average Price of No. 2 Soft Red Winter (30 Days) Wheat in Chicago   In Dollars Per Bushel

Year	June	July	Aug.	Sept.	Oct.	Nov.	Dec.	Jan.	Feb.	Mar.	Apr.	May	Average
2006-07	3.26	3.43	3.20	3.39	4.40	4.35	4.49	4.19	4.20	4.07	4.25	4.50	3.98
2007-08	5.25	5.52	6.24	7.98	7.89	7.57	8.69	8.55	10.12	10.40	7.72	6.59	7.71
2008-09	7.20	6.87	6.77	5.45	3.76	3.68	4.01	4.62	4.28	4.40	4.43	4.96	5.04
2009-10	4.96	4.45	4.18	3.70	4.01	4.53	4.67	4.55	4.37	4.38	4.43	4.49	4.39
2010-11	4.26	5.38	6.29	6.43	5.97	6.20	7.20	7.55	7.99	6.95	7.56	7.44	6.60
2011-12	6.71	6.54	7.03	6.40	5.96	6.09	5.94	6.23	6.44	6.44	6.24	6.29	6.36
2012-13	6.56	8.57	8.70	8.62	8.49	8.58	8.03	7.69	7.40	7.18	6.97	7.01	7.82
2013-14	6.94	6.60	6.26	6.41	6.77	6.46	6.23	5.86	6.08	6.91	6.91	6.86	6.52
2014-15	5.87	5.30	5.34	4.82	5.04	5.43	6.21	5.56	5.19	5.07	5.02	4.87	5.31
2015-16[1]	5.17	5.40	5.00	4.86	5.02	4.98	4.83	4.75	4.69				4.97

[1] Preliminary.   *Source: Economic Research Service, U.S. Department of Agriculture (ERS-USDA)*

Average Price Received by Farmers for All Wheat in the United States   In Dollars Per Bushel

Year	June	July	Aug.	Sept.	Oct.	Nov.	Dec.	Jan.	Feb.	Mar.	Apr.	May	Average
2006-07	3.98	3.88	3.91	4.06	4.59	4.59	4.52	4.53	4.71	4.75	4.89	4.88	4.44
2007-08	5.03	5.17	5.64	6.76	7.65	7.39	7.71	7.96	10.10	10.50	10.10	8.87	7.74
2008-09	7.62	7.15	7.61	7.43	6.65	6.29	5.95	6.20	5.79	5.71	5.75	5.84	6.50
2009-10	5.72	5.17	4.85	4.48	4.47	4.79	4.87	4.90	4.73	4.70	4.41	4.33	4.79
2010-11	4.16	4.49	5.44	5.79	5.88	6.10	6.44	6.69	7.42	7.55	8.01	8.16	6.34
2011-12	7.41	7.10	7.59	7.54	7.27	7.30	7.20	7.05	7.10	7.20	7.11	6.67	7.21
2012-13	6.70	7.89	8.04	8.27	8.38	8.47	8.30	8.12	7.97	7.79	7.71	7.68	7.94
2013-14	7.37	6.95	6.88	6.80	6.94	6.85	6.73	6.65	6.50	6.74	6.82	7.08	6.86
2014-15	6.49	6.15	5.97	5.71	5.71	6.04	6.14	6.15	5.89	5.70	5.56	5.33	5.90
2015-16[1]	5.43	5.23	4.85	4.72	4.87	4.86	4.71	4.82	4.61				4.90

[1] Preliminary.   *Source: Economic Research Service, U.S. Department of Agriculture (ERS-USDA)*

WHEAT

Average Price of No. 1 Hard Red Winter (Ordinary Protein) Wheat in Kansas City — In Dollars Per Bushel

Year	June	July	Aug.	Sept.	Oct.	Nov.	Dec.	Jan.	Feb.	Mar.	Apr.	May	Average
2006-07	5.25	5.27	5.00	5.16	5.62	5.61	5.49	5.29	5.39	5.40	5.52	5.54	5.38
2007-08	6.22	6.28	6.84	8.52	8.89	8.62	9.80	9.97	12.28	12.29	10.29	9.33	9.11
2008-09	9.19	8.68	8.64	7.52	6.17	6.21	6.06	6.59	6.21	6.23	6.10	6.70	7.03
2009-10	6.63	5.58	5.15	4.56	5.06	5.58	5.37	5.24	5.10	4.99	4.86	4.78	5.24
2010-11	4.50	5.26	6.76	7.01	7.04	7.13	8.04	8.54	9.23	8.44	9.28	9.38	7.55
2011-12	8.61	8.03	8.63	8.30	7.77	7.74	7.46	7.69	7.59	7.52	7.11	7.24	7.81
2012-13	7.61	9.13	9.43	9.56	9.62	9.73	9.36	9.09	8.70	8.35	8.30	8.53	8.95
2013-14	8.32	8.14	8.12	8.00	8.70	8.44	8.03	7.56	8.04	8.87	8.81	9.01	8.34
2014-15	8.23	7.61	7.33	7.11	7.35	7.20	7.54	6.75	6.44	6.46	6.22	6.18	7.04
2015-16[1]	6.40	6.27	5.70	5.44	5.62	5.55	5.60	5.46	5.20				5.69

[1] Preliminary.   Source: Economic Research Service, U.S. Department of Agriculture (ERS-USDA)

Average Price of No. 1 Dark Northern Spring (14% Protein) Wheat in Minneapolis — In Dollars Per Bushel

Year	June	July	Aug.	Sept.	Oct.	Nov.	Dec.	Jan.	Feb.	Mar.	Apr.	May	Average
2006-07	5.59	5.65	4.94	4.86	5.36	5.55	5.44	5.27	5.40	5.55	5.65	5.64	5.41
2007-08	6.19	6.60	6.88	8.20	9.27	9.39	11.06	12.59	19.00	15.60	12.93	12.06	10.81
2008-09	11.46	11.46	9.87	8.51	7.37	6.80	7.78	8.02	7.64	7.57	7.72	8.13	8.53
2009-10	7.96	6.82	6.17	6.30	6.36	7.29	6.79	7.39	7.57	7.48	6.88	6.55	6.96
2010-11	6.90	6.89	7.92	8.35	8.61	8.67	10.14	11.24	12.22	12.36	12.76	13.04	9.93
2011-12	12.97	11.16	10.21	9.80	9.80	10.61	9.69	9.43	9.53	9.62	9.63	9.11	10.13
2012-13	9.31	10.12	9.71	9.82	10.17	10.15	9.83	9.43	9.33	9.17	9.11	9.15	9.61
2013-14	9.18	8.57	8.37	8.21	8.78	8.39	8.64	9.32	9.03	9.64	8.73	9.32	8.85
2014-15	9.00	8.66	8.17	8.47	8.11	8.50	8.22	7.37	7.51	7.91	7.39	7.62	8.08
2015-16[1]	7.56	7.12	6.16	6.15	6.44	6.49	6.25	6.05	5.93				6.46

[1] Preliminary.   Source: Economic Research Service, U.S. Department of Agriculture (ERS-USDA)

Average Farm Prices of Winter Wheat in the United States — In Dollars Per Bushel

Year	June	July	Aug.	Sept.	Oct.	Nov.	Dec.	Jan.	Feb.	Mar.	Apr.	May	Average
2008-09	7.51	7.10	7.30	6.99	6.03	5.65	5.40	5.70	5.26	5.27	5.26	5.52	6.08
2009-10	5.47	5.02	4.67	4.20	4.27	4.60	4.68	4.57	4.53	4.45	4.19	4.21	4.57
2010-11	4.05	4.47	5.47	5.76	5.83	6.02	6.40	6.35	7.03	7.02	7.37	7.80	6.13
2011-12	7.13	6.77	7.27	7.00	6.53	6.44	6.41	6.57	6.68	6.70	6.47	6.42	6.70
2012-13	6.55	7.76	7.92	8.25	8.33	8.38	8.15	8.01	7.85	7.63	7.52	7.49	7.82
2013-14	7.18	6.85	6.81	6.80	7.07	6.96	6.84	6.72	6.58	6.92	7.07	7.26	6.92
2014-15	6.34	5.99	5.90	5.69	5.65	5.87	6.14	6.02	5.70	5.55	5.50	5.19	5.80
2015-16[1]	5.20	5.15	4.82	4.64	4.79	4.66	4.49	4.63	4.47				4.76

[1] Preliminary.   Source: Economic Research Service, U.S. Department of Agriculture (ERS-USDA)

Average Farm Prices of Durum Wheat in the United States — In Dollars Per Bushel

Year	June	July	Aug.	Sept.	Oct.	Nov.	Dec.	Jan.	Feb.	Mar.	Apr.	May	Average
2008-09	8.48	11.70	12.60	11.90	11.50	8.93	8.40	8.26	7.53	7.40	7.18	7.05	9.24
2009-10	6.83	7.57	4.95	4.86	4.59	4.91	4.94	4.94	4.61	4.57	4.17	4.28	5.10
2010-11	4.58	4.44	4.45	4.89	5.07	5.55	5.71	7.09	8.45	8.09	8.60	7.86	6.23
2011-12	9.18	10.20	10.20	10.80	9.60	10.30	10.30	8.84	8.98	8.39	9.22	8.95	9.58
2012-13	8.31	8.67	7.76	7.77	7.61	8.11	8.31	8.24	8.19	8.12	8.01	8.06	8.10
2013-14	8.51	8.32	7.73	7.84	7.03	6.72	6.90	7.01	6.43	6.69	6.80	7.21	7.27
2014-15	7.96	8.13	8.03	8.25	8.48	11.00	10.70	9.89	10.10	9.54	7.79	8.02	8.99
2015-16[1]	9.16	8.74	7.30	6.36	6.56	6.99	6.93	6.60	5.97				7.18

[1] Preliminary.   Source: Economic Research Service, U.S. Department of Agriculture (ERS-USDA)

Average Farm Prices of Other Spring Wheat in the United States — In Dollars Per Bushel

Year	June	July	Aug.	Sept.	Oct.	Nov.	Dec.	Jan.	Feb.	Mar.	Apr.	May	Average
2008-09	10.10	9.52	8.18	7.76	7.20	7.10	6.89	7.02	6.61	6.50	6.49	6.76	7.51
2009-10	6.66	5.96	5.54	4.85	5.00	5.19	5.18	5.30	5.04	5.04	4.89	4.61	5.27
2010-11	4.58	4.71	5.47	5.97	6.14	6.35	6.60	7.14	7.68	8.07	8.67	8.85	6.69
2011-12	9.26	8.45	8.28	8.09	8.19	8.43	8.25	8.09	8.01	8.04	7.96	7.93	8.25
2012-13	7.78	8.39	8.27	8.38	8.56	8.65	8.48	8.34	8.11	7.95	7.90	7.84	8.22
2013-14	7.72	7.30	6.97	6.71	6.66	6.70	6.55	6.48	6.40	6.56	6.61	6.85	6.79
2014-15	6.60	6.23	5.93	5.51	5.57	5.73	5.80	5.84	5.55	5.53	5.51	5.29	5.76
2015-16[1]	5.20	5.15	4.72	4.68	4.80	4.91	4.77	4.80	4.56				4.84

[1] Preliminary.   Source: Economic Research Service, U.S. Department of Agriculture (ERS-USDA)

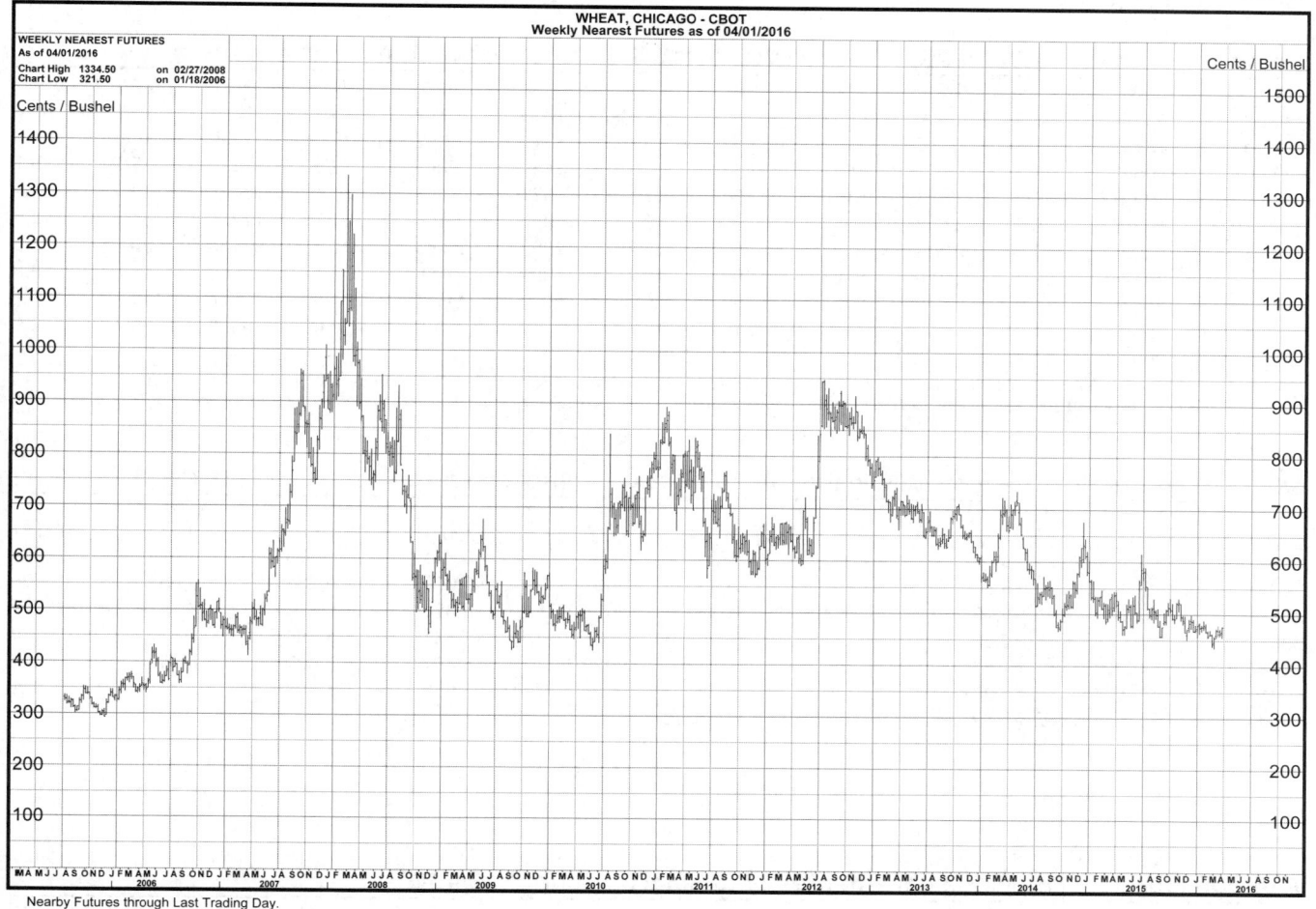

WHEAT, CHICAGO - CBOT
Weekly Nearest Futures as of 04/01/2016

WEEKLY NEAREST FUTURES
As of 04/01/2016

Chart High 1334.50 on 02/27/2008
Chart Low   321.50   on 01/18/2006

Nearby Futures through Last Trading Day.

Volume of Trading of Wheat Futures in Chicago   In Thousands of Contracts

Year	Jan.	Feb.	Mar.	Apr.	May	June	July	Aug.	Sept.	Oct.	Nov.	Dec.	Total
2006	889.2	1,421.3	1,059.6	1,300.0	1,511.6	1,617.1	1,067.4	1,659.9	1,365.9	1,938.1	1,613.7	781.2	16,224.9
2007	1,346.2	1,506.0	1,148.0	2,082.5	1,170.5	2,343.7	1,514.4	2,111.3	1,320.3	1,648.4	2,109.7	1,281.8	19,582.7
2008	1,861.3	2,527.7	1,398.7	1,558.6	1,121.6	2,185.7	1,314.2	2,093.6	1,228.1	1,139.0	1,644.5	939.0	19,011.9
2009	986.9	1,505.7	1,213.8	1,747.8	1,300.1	2,350.9	1,298.1	1,926.4	1,040.0	1,451.2	1,952.5	904.2	17,677.5
2010	1,297.9	1,936.2	1,289.8	2,029.8	1,392.3	2,547.3	2,394.8	3,386.6	1,501.6	1,527.8	2,383.2	1,402.9	23,090.3
2011	1,651.7	2,601.4	2,131.8	2,475.9	2,095.9	2,857.2	1,699.9	2,301.0	1,470.5	1,594.4	2,217.0	1,186.8	24,283.3
2012	2,014.0	2,433.7	2,088.5	2,563.3	2,670.7	3,244.9	2,404.1	2,433.4	1,541.6	1,776.4	2,769.4	1,439.5	27,379.4
2013	2,006.5	2,679.0	1,937.3	2,888.9	1,872.7	2,488.8	1,872.6	2,487.0	1,323.5	1,741.4	2,312.0	1,235.7	24,845.5
2014	1,888.8	2,681.9	2,375.1	2,605.2	2,389.1	3,028.9	2,210.8	3,064.6	1,804.6	1,793.2	2,387.5	1,962.5	28,192.3
2015	1,787.2	2,610.9	2,394.8	3,074.8	3,832.7	4,970.3	3,314.0	2,961.6	1,919.4	2,322.0	3,144.4	1,611.0	33,943.0

Contract size = 5,000 bu.   Source: CME Group; Chicago Board of Trade (CBT)

Average Open Interest of Wheat Futures in Chicago   In Contracts

Year	Jan.	Feb.	Mar.	Apr.	May	June	July	Aug.	Sept.	Oct.	Nov.	Dec.
2006	320,974	380,405	389,284	385,698	466,013	491,343	473,749	459,650	455,755	476,906	435,059	426,976
2007	453,140	441,924	405,383	377,162	363,297	401,509	411,971	404,940	379,871	407,669	414,509	423,198
2008	443,193	440,137	400,426	375,845	362,835	359,429	332,360	331,301	294,696	279,041	283,832	250,914
2009	268,513	297,116	291,831	309,503	302,088	335,407	317,024	327,977	320,607	331,678	355,414	353,774
2010	388,660	431,434	427,821	457,548	469,103	490,351	477,461	504,547	487,184	516,982	507,512	480,059
2011	515,137	538,874	482,060	482,702	457,289	451,965	428,043	427,516	411,468	426,188	411,485	376,671
2012	435,379	458,289	446,242	462,078	431,133	425,379	450,423	456,537	450,653	462,690	478,767	444,929
2013	463,359	470,154	457,785	436,052	410,871	414,728	404,821	399,943	358,054	366,743	394,264	396,016
2014	429,507	413,808	350,290	371,767	371,689	389,610	407,989	417,932	400,815	419,886	403,348	372,284
2015	382,618	415,559	426,147	453,404	444,906	432,352	402,961	406,381	372,538	377,775	381,822	351,546

Contract size = 5,000 bu.   Source: CME Group; Chicago Board of Trade (CBT)

WHEAT

Commercial Stocks of Domestic Wheat[1] in the United States, on First of Month   In Millions of Bushels

Year	July	Aug.	Sept.	Oct.	Nov.	Dec.	Jan.	Feb.	Mar.	Apr.	May	June
2005-06	127.5	138.6	159.9	163.5	158.5	147.8	137.9	130.9	128.8	122.9	116.7	126.2
2006-07	154.3	172.5	190.3	170.9	166.8	159.5	154.7	146.7	136.3	129.3	116.6	99.2
2007-08	108.6	155.9	173.1	185.7	164.8	151.2	148.3	138.9	123.5	112.3	87.1	78.7
2008-09	98.2	150.4	176.4	214.5	212.9	179.7	167.8	135.9	126.1	124.9	119.5	115.0
2009-10	152.4	198.2	221.3	224.5	219.8	208.8	199.8	192.9	184.1	177.1	181.2	174.8
2010-11	229.8	237.4	247.3	242.3	235.4	229.5	222.6	234.4	223.0	201.9	190.8	178.1
2011-12	202.9	220.3	232.6	236.2	219.9	203.8	193.4	184.6	172.1	160.4	154.3	159.5
2012-13	202.0	211.9	225.2	219.2	212.6	206.3	206.3	195.1	181.5	169.9	144.9	128.1
2013-14	136.1	159.5	168.3	167.9	157.0	145.3	136.3	121.6	106.0	95.9	89.4	84.9
2014-15	89.2	113.5	----	----	----	----	----	----	----	----	----	----

This report was discontinued as of August 26, 2014.   [1] Domestic wheat in storage in public and private elevators in 39 markets and wheat afloat in vessels or barges at lake and seaboard ports, the first Saturday of the month.   *Source: Livestock Division, U.S. Department of Agriculture (LD-USDA)*

Stocks of Wheat Flour Held by Mills in the United States   In Thousands of Sacks--100 Pounds

Year	Jan. 1	April 1	July 1	Oct. 1	Year	Jan. 1	April 1	July 1	Oct. 1
2000	5,099	5,217	5,062	5,244	2006	5,211	5,775	5,576	5,587
2001	5,241	5,506	5,178	5,393	2007	5,919	5,884	5,587	6,188
2002	5,377	5,164	4,632	4,184	2008	6,374	6,219	6,157	6,719
2003	4,265	4,707	4,622	4,554	2009	5,831	5,561	5,607	5,430
2004	4,764	4,666	4,700	4,868	2010	5,407	5,637	5,596	5,517
2005	5,085	4,268	4,637	4,781	2011[1]	5,660	5,680	NA	NA

[1] Preliminary.   *Source: Bureau of the Census, U.S. Department of Commerce*

Average Producer Price Index of Wheat Flour (Spring[2])   June 1983 = 100

Year	Jan.	Feb.	Mar.	Apr.	May	June	July	Aug.	Sept.	Oct.	Nov.	Dec.	Average
2006	130.2	134.2	132.8	139.4	142.2	144.2	148.5	141.6	144.2	151.9	151.8	147.5	142.4
2007	144.8	144.6	148.2	153.2	154.3	161.9	167.4	174.0	196.2	209.4	207.1	229.5	174.2
2008	239.6	278.9	293.6	262.8	248.1	246.5	228.5	229.5	214.6	194.8	190.8	181.5	234.1
2009	187.4	185.3	186.5	183.4	185.0	196.2	176.4	171.1	165.2	168.0	169.2	168.5	178.5
2010	167.2	168.1	163.7	162.5	167.1	161.7	169.7	190.5	190.6	190.1	200.5	204.9	178.1
2011	212.0	228.4	211.8	226.5	225.2	219.5	217.0	224.1	224.8	216.1	216.5	207.8	219.1
2012	206.8	216.4	219.2	219.7	214.3	214.4	231.2	226.5	232.0	232.4	236.4	233.8	223.6
2013	231.0	223.5	219.6	220.6	229.1	230.2	226.0	219.8	218.4	225.5	220.1	218.4	223.5
2014	223.3	224.9	235.6	229.5	234.8	225.5	225.7	218.8	231.5	225.3	225.6	230.5	227.6
2015[1]	213.4	214.5	214.5	210.5	212.2	216.1	214.3	193.5	189.1	192.6	191.2	196.8	204.9

[1] Preliminary.   [2] Standard patent.   *Source: Bureau of Labor Statistics, U.S. Department of Commerce (BLS) (0212-0301)*

World Wheat Flour Production (Monthly Average)   In Thousands of Metric Tons

Year	Australia	France	Germany	Hungary	India	Japan	Kazak-hstan	Korea, South	Mexico	Poland	Russia	Turkey	United Kingdom
2006	NA	472.3	444.2	62.2	180.3	384.6	207.9	154.2	243.8	211.9	776.1	290.4	366.0
2007	NA	478.2	437.7	59.7	181.1	387.8	224.6	146.7	243.8	124.3	547.7	309.8	NA
2008	NA	477.8	453.0	57.6	178.6	387.3	242.0	140.1	244.1	109.8	762.4	327.8	NA
2009	NA	449.5	429.1	59.2	195.1	379.9	255.0	150.7	249.3	143.2	774.1	349.7	NA
2010	NA	461.9	458.0	NA	212.5	401.0	NA	160.5	257.5	122.6	746.7	371.4	NA
2011	NA	443.8	446.7	NA	215.0	408.9	NA	159.9	266.8	118.3	753.5	399.1	NA
2012	NA	NA	453.5	NA	NA	404.8	NA	161.9	266.5	124.5	735.1	374.6	NA
2013	NA	NA	465.3	NA	NA	403.1	NA	156.9	277.2	125.4	759.4	407.5	NA
2014[1]	NA	NA	487.3	NA	NA	403.0	NA	163.6	277.6	125.4	738.0	455.6	NA
2015[2]			487.0			396.1		171.1	262.2	127.1	711.9	522.3	

[1] Preliminary.   [2] Estimate.   NA = Not available.   *Source: United Nations (UN)*

Production of Wheat Flour in the United States — In Millions of Sacks--100 Pounds Each

Year	July	Aug.	Sept.	Oct.	Nov.	Dec.	Jan.	Feb.	Mar.	Apr.	May	June	Total
2002-03	-----	102.1	-----	-----	100.3	-----	-----	95.9	-----	-----	96.8	-----	395.0
2003-04	-----	103.1	-----	-----	100.5	-----	-----	96.6	-----	-----	96.8	-----	396.9
2004-05	-----	100.9	-----	-----	99.7	-----	-----	95.9	-----	-----	96.2	-----	392.7
2005-06	-----	102.5	-----	-----	100.3	-----	-----	98.1	-----	-----	98.0	-----	398.9
2006-07	-----	104.9	-----	-----	102.5	-----	-----	100.3	-----	-----	102.5	-----	410.1
2007-08	-----	109.0	-----	-----	107.1	-----	-----	101.4	-----	-----	102.5	-----	420.0
2008-09	-----	108.2	-----	-----	104.2	-----	-----	100.7	-----	-----	102.9	-----	416.0
2009-10	-----	107.4	-----	-----	103.7	-----	-----	102.5	-----	-----	101.5	-----	415.1
2010-11	-----	108.6	-----	-----	104.8	-----	-----	100.0	-----	-----	100.3	-----	413.7
2011-12[1]	-----	NA	-----	-----	NA	-----	-----		-----	-----		-----	

[1] Preliminary.   Source: Bureau of the Census, U.S. Department of Commerce

United States Wheat Flour Exports (Grain Equivalent[2]) — In Thousands of Bushels

Year	June	July	Aug.	Sept.	Oct.	Nov.	Dec.	Jan.	Feb.	Mar.	Apr.	May	Total
2006-07	720	488	780	610	532	754	756	786	999	941	1,425	2,711	11,502
2007-08	1,467	1,220	1,277	1,135	1,758	2,515	1,960	1,224	1,544	1,328	1,114	1,126	17,668
2008-09	1,417	1,052	1,093	1,053	856	1,055	958	969	858	750	687	793	11,541
2009-10	865	1,515	1,704	1,473	2,255	1,609	1,194	1,231	1,722	2,525	1,652	1,993	19,738
2010-11	1,158	915	898	1,005	1,727	988	1,130	1,638	1,641	1,239	1,982	1,116	15,437
2011-12	1,078	874	1,774	1,101	1,002	1,182	725	766	727	1,152	780	1,528	12,689
2012-13	1,264	1,883	1,616	1,790	1,236	1,021	1,023	1,077	1,112	928	785	1,506	15,241
2013-14	1,623	986	846	1,014	1,219	987	1,164	953	803	953	1,143	1,138	12,829
2014-15	955	1,213	1,035	1,299	1,404	1,436	1,094	1,088	1,297	1,515	1,049	1,314	14,699
2015-16[1]	1,386	1,233	1,187	1,427	1,453	1,549	1,459	1,455					16,721

[1] Preliminary.   [2] Includes meal, groats and durum.   Source: Economic Research Service, U.S. Department of Agriculture (ERS-USDA)

Supply and Distribution of Wheat Flour in the United States

Year	Wheat Ground -- 1,000 Bu. --	Milfeed Production - 1,000 Tons -	Flour Production[3]	Flour & Product Imports[2]	Total Supply	Exports Flour	Exports Products	Domestic Disappearance	Total Population July 1 -- Millions --	Per Capita Disappearance -- Pounds --
2004	876,047	6,764	393,925	10,726	404,651	5,152	4,662	394,837	293.3	134.6
2005	884,101	6,826	394,973	11,262	406,235	3,747	4,741	397,748	296.0	134.4
2006	894,527	6,916	403,391	11,740	415,131	3,412	5,867	405,852	298.8	135.8
2007	923,756	7,103	418,836	11,511	430,347	6,707	6,486	417,155	301.7	138.3
2008	907,979	6,753	416,283	10,822	427,105	4,925	6,179	416,001	304.5	136.6
2009	896,060	6,460	414,658	10,313	424,971	5,911	5,338	413,722	307.2	134.7
2010	901,843	6,480	417,396	11,206	428,602	7,004	3,930	417,667	309.8	134.8
2011	895,255	6,402	411,745	11,698	423,443	6,309	3,615	413,519	312.0	132.5
2012	921,853	6,637	420,365	11,991	432,356	5,997	3,894	422,465	314.3	134.4
2013[1]	678,351	4,679	423,214	12,276	435,490	5,276	3,755	426,459	316.5	134.7

[1] Preliminary.   [2] Commercial production of wheat flour, whole wheat, industrial and durum flour and farina reported by Bureau of Census.
Source: Economic Research Service, U.S. Department of Agriculture (ERS-USDA)

Wheat and Flour Price Relationships at Milling Centers in the United States — In Dollars

	At Kansas City					At Minneapolis				
	Cost of Wheat to Produce 100 lb. Flour[1]	Wholesale Price of Bakery Flour 100 lb. Flour[2]	Wholesale Price of By-Products Obtained 100 lb. Flour[3]	Total Products Actual	Total Products Over Cost of Wheat	Cost of Wheat to Produce 100 lb. Flour[1]	Wholesale Price of Bakery Flour 100 lb. Flour[2]	Wholesale Price of By-Products Obtained 100 lb. Flour[3]	Total Products Actual	Total Products Over Cost of Wheat
Year										
2008-09	17.14	17.60	2.18	19.77	2.63	19.44	19.18	2.15	21.33	1.89
2009-10	13.29	14.13	1.51	15.64	2.35	16.16	15.90	1.55	17.45	1.29
2010-11	18.97	18.78	2.35	21.13	2.16	22.97	21.56	2.40	23.96	.99
2011-12	19.21	18.76	2.96	21.71	2.51	23.10	21.87	3.11	24.98	1.88
2012-13	21.29	19.92	3.62	23.53	2.25	21.91	19.46	4.06	24.98	1.61
2013-14	19.20	19.23	2.70	21.93	2.73	20.17	19.17	2.79	21.96	1.78
2014-15	16.16	17.24	1.91	19.15	2.99	19.35	18.75	1.86	20.61	1.37
2015-16	13.39	14.12	1.75	15.87	2.47	14.46	18.75	1.49	15.96	
June-Aug.	14.33	15.37	1.42	16.78	2.45	----	15.35	1.60	16.95	----
Sept.-Nov.	12.95	13.52	1.99	15.51	2.56	14.50	14.20	1.86	16.06	1.56

[1] Based on 73% extraction rate, cost of 2.28 bushels: At Kansas City, No. 1 hard winter 13% protein; and at Minneapolis, No. 1 dark northern spring, 14% protein.   [2] quoted as mid-month bakers' standard patent at Kansas City and spring standard patent at Minneapolis, bulk basis.   [3] Assumed 50-50 millfeed distribution between bran and shorts or middlings, bulk basis.   Source: Agricultural Marketing Service, U.S. Department of Agriculture

311

Wool

Wool is light, warm, absorbs moisture, and is resistant to fire. Wool is also used for insulation in houses, for carpets and furnishing, and for bedding. Sheep are sheared once a year and produce about 4.3 kg of "greasy" wool per year.

Greasy wool is wool that has not been washed or cleaned. Wool fineness is determined by fiber diameter, which is measured in microns (one millionth of a meter). Fine wool is softer, lightweight, and produces fine clothing. Merino sheep produce the finest wool.

Greasy Wool futures are traded on the Sydney Futures Exchange (SFE). The SFE futures contract calls for the delivery of merino combing wool.

Prices – Average monthly wool prices at U.S. mills in 2015 (through November) fell by -15.0% yr/yr to $3.59 per pound, below the 2011 record high of $5.16 per pound. The value of U.S. wool production in 2015 rose +1.0% to $39.298 million, below the 2011 record high of $48.925 million.

Supply – World production of wool has been falling in the past decade due to the increased use of polyester fabrics. Greasy wool world production in 2013, the latest reporting year for the data series, rose +1.6% yr/yr to 2.126 million metric tons. The world's largest producers of greasy wool in 2013 were China with 22.2% of world production, followed by Australia (17.0%), and New Zealand (7.8%).

U.S. wool production of 14,000 metric tons in 2013 (latest data) accounted for only 0.7% of world production.

Trade – U.S. exports of domestic wool in 2015 rose +1.3% yr/yr to 8.000 million pounds. U.S. imports in 2014 (latest data) rose +1.5% to 3.917 million pounds.

World Production of Wool, Greasy   In Metric Tons

Year	Argen-tina	Australia	China	Kazak-hstan	New Zealand	Pakistan	Romania	Russia	South Africa	United Kingdom	United States	Uruguay	World Total
2004	60,000	467,580	373,902	28,499	217,700	39,900	17,505	47,111	44,000	60,000	17,046	37,271	2,158,877
2005	63,696	465,700	393,172	30,444	215,500	40,000	17,600	48,033	44,000	60,000	16,865	42,009	2,209,767
2006	67,794	472,530	388,777	32,389	224,700	40,100	19,378	50,276	44,000	57,552	16,284	46,709	2,213,761
2007	68,743	450,220	363,470	34,200	217,900	40,600	21,025	52,022	42,000	62,000	15,750	46,709	2,192,715
2008	65,000	407,880	367,687	35,200	157,500	41,000	22,051	53,491	41,583	63,290	14,952	45,085	2,091,810
2009	65,000	370,600	364,002	36,400	185,800	41,540	22,352	54,658	43,320	65,393	13,770	41,057	2,065,570
2010	54,000	352,740	386,768	37,600	176,300	42,000	20,457	53,521	41,091	67,000	13,776	34,700	2,020,030
2011	48,000	368,330	443,981	38,500	163,700	42,500	19,026	52,575	41,197	67,500	13,286	34,700	2,089,520
2012[1]	45,000	362,100	437,119	38,437	165,000	43,000	18,600	55,253	39,904	68,000	14,000	36,000	2,093,600
2013[2]	45,000	360,520	471,111	37,638	165,000	43,600	18,600	54,651	39,904	68,000	14,000	36,000	2,126,900

[1] Preliminary. [2] Estimate. NA = Not avaliable. *Source: Food and Agriculture Organization of the United Nations (FAO-UN)*

Average Wool Prices[1] --Australian-- 64's, Type 62, Duty Paid--U.S. Mills   In Dollars Per Pound

Year	Jan.	Feb.	Mar.	Apr.	May	June	July	Aug.	Sept.	Oct.	Nov.	Dec.	Average
2006	2.43	2.56	2.59	2.51	2.58	2.54	2.60	2.60	2.58	2.60	3.08	3.15	2.65
2007	3.52	3.44	3.55	3.67	3.81	3.80	3.78	3.59	3.64	3.93	4.05	4.00	3.73
2008	4.16	4.11	4.07	4.04	3.78	3.76	3.86	3.46	3.17	2.57	2.26	2.39	3.47
2009	2.29	2.23	2.30	2.50	2.87	2.95	2.95	3.18	3.39	3.79	3.86	3.92	3.02
2010	4.23	4.04	4.12	4.04	3.81	3.79	3.81	3.81	3.90	4.19	4.50	4.79	4.09
2011	5.17	5.44	5.86	6.37	6.43	7.42	7.13	6.49	6.10	5.62	4.50	6.24	6.06
2012	6.35	6.67	6.68	6.35	6.07	5.76	5.78	5.36	5.17	5.33	5.42	5.89	5.90
2013	5.87	5.95	5.84	5.38	5.17	5.09	4.71	4.67	4.79	5.45	5.37	4.89	5.27
2014	5.18	5.06	4.86	4.92	5.04	4.98	5.02	4.86	4.79	4.71	4.68	4.56	4.89
2015	4.34	4.27	4.21	4.34	4.90	5.17	4.64	4.62	4.30	4.28	4.43	4.55	4.50

[1] Raw, clean basis. *Source: Economic Research Service, U.S. Department of Agriculture (ERS-USDA)*

United States Imports[2] of Unmanufactured Wool (Clean Yield)   In Thousands of Pounds

Year	Jan.	Feb.	Mar.	Apr.	May	June	July	Aug.	Sept.	Oct.	Nov.	Dec.	Total
2006	1,886.2	975.3	1,755.7	1,451.4	1,254.9	1,592.2	880.8	1,536.9	1,178.3	1,524.9	1,612.6	1,604.2	17,253.4
2007	1,250.1	1,097.3	1,429.4	1,417.0	1,356.5	1,302.7	1,141.2	892.5	846.7	1,252.0	1,328.0	956.3	14,269.7
2008	1,753.3	888.8	1,405.6	1,090.1	1,269.2	1,100.0	1,259.0	825.6	1,231.3	980.6	706.8	671.5	13,181.8
2009	1,061.7	982.9	1,043.0	803.5	536.2	745.1	833.8	847.4	447.4	798.8	626.0	627.0	9,352.8
2010	705.5	340.8	663.7	757.1	424.3	576.4	1,183.0	702.2	652.4	607.1	594.8	385.4	7,592.7
2011	857.1	451.2	564.5	681.2	698.5	503.3	1,046.5	1,306.0	1,590.9	1,168.2	635.5	404.2	9,907.1
2012	711.7	968.1	1,018.9	880.7	919.9	944.7	715.9	536.0	779.2	693.8	610.2	416.4	9,195.5
2013	457.3	251.4	358.7	819.7	909.1	891.0	796.5	889.8	437.1	919.6	458.2	430.8	7,619.2
2014	597.6	379.1	348.3	583.8	868.5	553.2	707.7	718.8	544.0	967.5	403.5	420.5	7,092.5
2015[1]	504.8	800.1	420.0	657.0	765.2	585.8	677.2	619.8	349.3	664.2	527.1	662.1	7,232.6

[1] Preliminary.   [2] Data are imports for consumption. *Source: Economic Research Service, U.S. Department of Agriculture (ERS-USDA)*

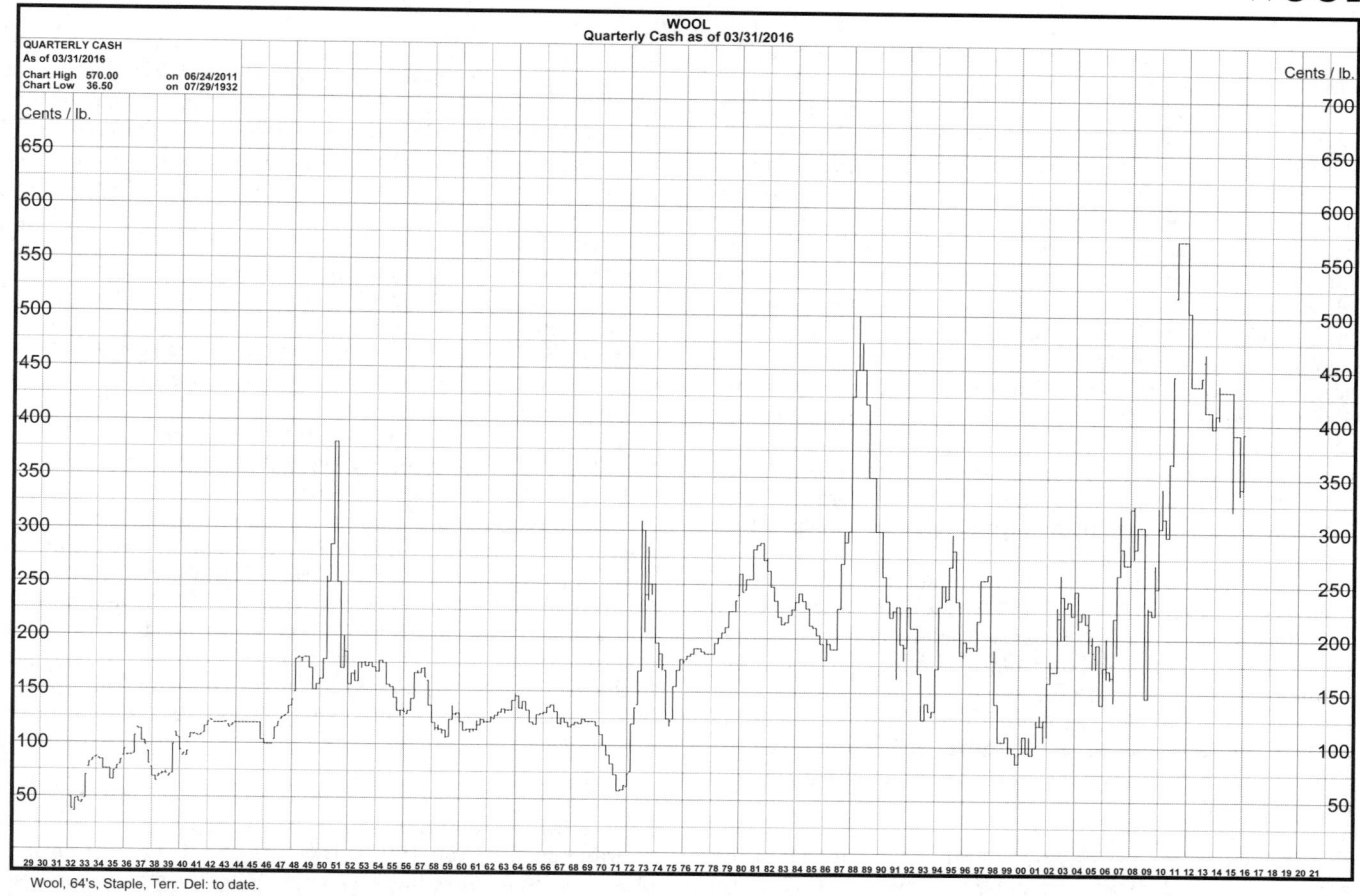

WOOL
Quarterly Cash as of 03/31/2016

QUARTERLY CASH
As of 03/31/2016
Chart High 570.00 on 06/24/2011
Chart Low 36.50 on 07/29/1932

Wool, 64's, Staple, Terr. Del: to date.

Salient Statistics of Wool in the United States

Year	Sheep & Lambs Shorn[4] -1,000's-	Weight per Fleece -In Lbs.-	Shorn Wool Pro- duction 1,000 Lbs.	Price per Lb.	Value of Pro- duction -$1,000-	Shorn Wool Support	Shorn Wool Payment Rate -- Cents Per Lb. --	Total Wool Pro- duction	Domestic Pro- duction	Domestic Wool Exports	Dutiable Imports for Consump- tion[3] (48's & Finer)	Total New Supply[2]	Duty Free Raw Imports (Not Finer than 46's)	Mill - Consumption - Apparel	Carpet
2008	4,434	7.43	32,963	99.0	32,486	100	40.0	32,963	17,404	10,307	4,551	20,279	8,631	----	----
2009	4,195	7.40	38,060	79.0	24,337	100	40.0	30,860	16,294	10,207	3,306	15,439	6,046	----	----
2010	4,180	7.30	30,370	115.0	35,018	115	40.0	30,360	16,035	9,973	3,108	14,098	4,928	----	----
2011	4,030	7.30	29,290	167.0	48,925	115	40.0	29,280	15,465	9,586	3,791	14,364	4,694	----	----
2012	3,750	7.30	27,400	152.0	41,595	115	40.0	27,630	14,467	7,741	4,564	15,841	4,551	----	----
2013	3,700	7.30	26,990	145.0	39,209	115	40.0	26,990	14,256	9,997	3,858	11,863	3,746	----	----
2014	3,680	7.30	26,680	146.0	38,909				14,200	7,900	3,917		3,159	----	----
2015[1]	3,680	7.40	27,050	145.0	39,298				14,200	8,000				----	----

[1] Preliminary.   [2] Production minus exports plus imports; stocks not taken into consideration.   [3] Apparel wool includes all dutiable wool; carpet wool includes all duty-free wool.   [4] Includes sheep shorn at commercial feeding yards.
Source: Economic Research Service, U.S. Department of Agriculture (ERS-USDA)

Shorn Wool Prices   In Dollars Per Pound

Year	US Farm Price Shorn Wool Greasy Basis[1] -- cents/Lb --	Australian Offering Price, Clean[2] Grade 70's type 61	Grade 64's type 63	Grade 62's type 64	Grade 60/62's type 64A	Grade 58's-56's 433-34	Market Indicator[3] - Cents/Kg. -	Graded Territory Shorn Wool, Clean Basis[4] 62's Staple 3"& up	60's Staple 3"& up	58's Staple 3 1/4"& up	56's Staple 3 1/4"& up	54's Staple 3 1/2"& up
2007	87.0	4.41	3.73	3.90	3.31	2.77	NA	2.65	2.24	1.82	1.32	1.04
2008	99.0	4.35	3.47	3.59	3.19	2.71	NA	3.09	2.45	2.25	1.82	1.20
2009	79.0	3.48	3.02	3.08	2.86	2.46	NA	2.27	1.89	1.73	1.36	1.34
2010	115.0	5.34	4.10	4.24	3.78	2.78	NA	3.27	2.54	2.15	1.89	1.48
2011	167.0	7.61	6.30	6.55	6.02	5.62	NA	4.25	4.36	4.07	3.40	NA
2012	152.0	5.77	5.90	5.98	5.78	5.66	NA	2.81	1.65	3.46	NA	NA
2013	145.0	5.59	5.34	5.39	5.24	3.69	1,073	4.23	3.36	3.01	2.17	NA
2014	146.0	5.03	4.89	4.91	4.80	3.39	1,046	4.17	3.44	3.00	2.47	2.21

[1] Annual weighted average.   [2] F.O.B. Australian Wool Corporation South Carolina warehouse in bond.   [3] Index of prices of all wool sold in Australia for the crop year July-June.   [4] Wool principally produced in Texas and the Rocky Mountain States.
Source: Economic Research Service, U.S. Department of Agriculture (ERS-USDA)

Zinc

Zinc (atomic symbol Zn) is a bluish-while metallic element that is the 24th most abundant element in the earth's crust. Zinc is never found in its pure state but rather in zinc oxide, zinc silicate, zinc carbonate, zinc sulfide, and in minerals such as zincite, hemimorphite, smithsonite, franklinite, and sphalerite. Zinc is utilized as a protective coating for other metals, such as iron and steel, in a process known as galvanizing. Zinc is used as an alloy with copper to make brass and also as an alloy with aluminum and magnesium. There are, however, a number of substitutes for zinc in chemicals, electronics, and pigments. For example, with aluminum, steel and plastics can substitute for galvanized sheets. Aluminum alloys can also replace brass. Zinc is used as the negative electrode in dry cell (flashlight) batteries and also in the zinc-mercuric-oxide battery cell, which is the round, flat battery typically used in watches, cameras, and other electronic devices. Zinc is also used in medicine as an antiseptic ointment.

Zinc futures and options are traded on the London Metals Exchange (LME). The LME zinc futures contract calls for the delivery of 25 metric tons of at least 99.995% purity zinc ingots (slabs and plates). The contract trades in terms of U.S. dollars per metric ton. Zinc first started trading on the LME in 1915. Futures are also traded on the Multi Commodity Exchange of India (MCX), the Shanghai Futures Exchange (SHFE), and the Singapore Exchange (SGX).

Prices – Zinc prices in 2015 fell -10.8% to a monthly average of 95.51 cents per pound, remaining below the 2006 record high of 158.44 cents per pound.

Supply – World smelter production of zinc in 2013 (latest data) rose +3.2% to 13.000 million metric tons, just slightly below the 2011 record high of 13.100 million metric tons. The world's largest producer of zinc in 2013 (latest data) was China with 40.8% of world smelter production, followed by Canada with 5.0%, Japan with 4.5%, Spain with 4.0%, and Australia with 3.9%. China's production of 5.300 million metric tons in 2013 was almost ten times its production level of 550,000 metric tons seen in 1990.

U.S. smelter production in 2013 fell by -10.7% to 233,000 metric tons. U.S. mine production of recoverable zinc in 2015 fell -1.8% yr/yr to 788,618 metric tons. U.S. production in 2015 of slab zinc on a primary basis rose +13.6% yr/yr to 120,000 metric tons, while secondary production fell -28.6% yr/yr to 50,000 metric tons.

Demand – U.S. consumption of slab zinc in 2015 fell by -3.0% yr/yr to 960,000 metric tons, but still up from the 34-year low of 891,000 metric tons seen in 2012. U.S. consumption of all classes of zinc fell by -16.4% yr/yr in 2007 (latest data) to 1.170 million metric tons, which was a new 16-year low. U.S. consumption of slab zinc by fabricators in 2015 fell by -2.7% yr/yr to 938,509 metric tons, down from the 2014 record high of 965,000.

The breakdown of consumption by industries for 2013 (latest data) showed that 86.2% of slab zinc consumption was for galvanizers, 5.8% for brass products, and the rest for other miscellaneous industries. The consumption breakdown by grades for 2013 showed that 48.6% for re-melt and other, 19.9% for high grade, 24.5% was for special high grade, and 7.1% for prime western. Within that grade breakdown, Prime Western consumption has fallen by over 80% since 2000.

Trade – The U.S. in 2015 relied on imports for 82% of its consumption of zinc, up sharply from the 35% average seen in the 1990s. U.S. imports for consumption of slab zinc fell by -0.6% yr/yr to 800,000 metric tons in 2015, while imports of zinc ore in 2013 (latest data) fell -51.1% yr/yr to 3,000 metric tons. The dollar value of U.S. zinc imports in 2014 (latest data) rose by +26.0% yr/yr to $2.252 billion, well below the 2007 record high $3.091 billion. The breakdown of imports in 2013 shows that most zinc is imported as blocks, pigs and slabs (655,000 metric tons); followed by dust, powder and flakes (31,700 metric tons); waste and scrap (24,900 metric tons); dross, ashes and fume (8,590 metric tons); sheets, plates, other (4,090 metric tons), and ores (2.0 metric tons).

Salient Statistics of Zinc in the United States   In Metric Tons

Year	Slab Zinc Production Primary	Slab Zinc Production Secondary	Mine Production Recovered	Imports for Consumption Slab Zinc	Imports for Consumption Ore (Zinc Content)	Exports Slab Zinc	Exports Ore (Zinc Content)	Consumption Slab Zinc	Consumption Consumed as Ore	Consumption All Classes[3]	Net Import Reliance As a % of Apparent Consump	High-Grade, Price -Cents/Lb.-
2006	113,000	156,000	727,000	895,000	383,000	2,530	825,000	1,190,000	----	1,400,000	78	158.89
2007	121,000	157,000	803,000	758,000	271,000	8,070	816,000	1,040,000	----	1,170,000	73	154.40
2008	125,000	161,000	778,000	725,000	63,200	3,250	725,000	1,010,000	----	----	72	88.93
2009	94,000	109,000	736,000	686,000	74,200	2,960	785,000	893,000	----	----	77	77.91
2010	120,000	129,000	748,000	671,000	32,200	4,200	752,000	907,000	----	----	73	101.98
2011	110,000	138,000	769,000	716,000	26,700	19,000	653,000	939,000	----	----	74	106.24
2012	114,000	147,000	738,000	655,000	6,140	14,100	591,000	891,000	----	----	71	95.80
2013	106,000	127,000	784,000	713,000	3,000	12,000	669,000	940,000	----	----	75	95.60
2014[1]	110,000	70,000	832,000	805,000	----	20,000	644,000	990,000	----	----	81	107.50
2015[2]	125,000	50,000	850,000	800,000	----	15,000	740,000	960,000	----	----	82	95.00

[1] Preliminary. [2] Estimate. [3] Based on apparent consumption of slab zinc plus zinc content of ores and concentrates and secondary materials used to make zinc dust and chemicals. *Source: U.S. Geological Survey (USGS)*

World Smelter Production of Zinc[3]   In Thousands of Metric Tons

Year	Australia	Belgium	Canada	China	France	Germany	Italy	Japan	Kazakhstan	Mexico	Spain	United States	World Total
2004	538.0	263.0	805.4	2,720.0	268.4	382.0	118.0	667.2	357.1	316.9	524.8	350.0	10,600
2005	463.3	257.0	724.0	2,780.0	267.5	344.9	121.0	675.2	364.8	327.2	506.2	351.0	10,300
2006	469.0	251.0	824.5	3,170.0	127.8	342.6	109.0	654.2	364.8	279.7	507.4	269.0	10,800
2007	508.0	241.3	802.1	3,740.0	129.1	294.7	109.0	638.7	358.2	321.9	494.1	278.0	11,400
2008	505.0	239.0	764.3	4,000.0	117.9	292.3	100.0	615.5	365.6	305.4	456.1	286.0	11,700
2009	531.0	14.0	685.5	4,290.0	161.0	153.0	100.0	540.6	327.9	385.4	515.0	203.0	11,400
2010	505.0	260.0	691.2	5,210.0	163.0	165.0	105.0	574.0	318.9	328.1	515.0	249.0	12,800
2011	513.0	282.0	662.2	5,210.0	164.0	170.0	100.0	544.7	319.8	322.1	524.0	248.0	13,100
2012[1]	504.0	250.0	648.6	4,890.0	161.0	169.0	100.0	571.3	319.8	322.1	524.0	261.0	12,600
2013[2]	504.0	252.0	651.6	5,300.0	152.0	162.0	110.0	587.3	320.2	322.8	521.0	233.0	13,000

[1] Preliminary.   [2] Estimate.   [3] Secondary metal included.   *Source: U.S. Geological Survey (USGS)*

Consumption (Reported) of Slab Zinc in the United States, by Industries and Grades   In Metric Tons

| | ---- By Industries ---- | | | | | | ---- By Grades ---- | | | |
Year	Total	Galvanizers	Brass Products	Zinc-Base Alloy[3]	Zinc Oxide	Other	Special High Grade	High Grade	Remelt and Other	Prime Western
2004	510,000	248,000	96,700	W	[4]	NA	321,000	58,800	33,600	96,200
2005	486,000	238,000	83,900	W	[4]	NA	316,000	62,100	40,300	68,000
2006	504,000	259,000	42,300	W	[4]	203,000	315,000	69,100	73,900	75,400
2007	484,000	304,000	39,700	W	[4]	141,000	242,000	80,700	92,700	69,000
2008	433,000	262,000	107,000	23,200	[4]	40,600	195,000	60,400	75,800	102,000
2009	306,000	226,000	45,500	17,900	[4]	17,200	170,000	46,600	55,000	34,600
2010	475,000	369,000	45,800	35,000	[4]	25,100	205,000	91,900	121,684	56,500
2011	604,000	496,000	40,400	40,400	[4]	27,600	177,000	111,000	237,233	78,000
2012[1]	806,000	685,000	49,700	44,700	[4]	26,500	255,000	138,000	357,455	55,300
2013[2]	428,000	369,000	24,900	24,200	[4]	9,660	105,000	85,200	208,038	30,300

[1] Preliminary.   [2] Estimated.   [3] Die casters.   [4] Included in other.   W = Withheld.   NA = Not applicable.   *Source: U.S. Geological Survey (USGS)*

United States Foreign Trade of Zinc   In Metric Tons

| | ---- Imports for Consumption ---- | | | | | | ---- Zinc Ore & Manufactures Exported ---- | | | | | | |
| | | | | | | | Blocks, Pigs, Anodes, etc. | | Wrought & Alloys | | | | | |
Year	Ores[3]	Blocks, Pigs, Slabs	Sheets, Plates, Other	Waste & Scrap	Dross, Ashes, Fume	Dust, Powder & Flakes	Total Value $1,000	Unwrought	Unwrought Alloys	Sheets, Plates & Strips	Angles, Bars, Rods, etc.	Waste & Scrap	Dust (Blue Powder)	Zinc Ore & Concentrates
2005	156,000	700,000	3,630	9,580	15,800	23,400	1,198,040	----	----	----	----	56,000	9,310	786,000
2006	383,000	895,000	2,050	14,200	31,100	30,100	2,771,580	2,530	19,900	3,780	11,200	83,800	16,400	825,000
2007	271,000	758,000	2,160	21,800	18,600	31,300	3,090,910	8,070	22,500	4,310	26,700	102,000	19,400	816,000
2008	63,200	725,000	3,330	17,000	13,200	28,500	1,919,030	3,250	8,550	4,970	28,100	91,000	13,000	725,000
2009	74,200	686,000	3,010	9,100	8,610	20,400	1,336,134	2,960	6,280	6,160	16,600	47,100	12,100	785,000
2010	32,200	671,000	3,440	15,600	17,900	31,600	1,846,320	4,200	11,400	7,380	27,800	77,900	14,900	752,000
2011	26,600	716,000	3,650	18,500	14,400	30,100	2,023,910	19,000	13,500	8,730	25,700	85,600	15,600	660,000
2012	6,140	655,000	2,920	20,000	23,200	28,200	1,684,190	14,100	17,900	6,040	17,700	90,500	14,200	592,000
2013[1]	2,550	713,000	3,570	21,000	13,000	24,500	1,787,320	11,500	23,200	6,500	8,580	87,500	10,700	670,000
2014[2]	2	655,000	4,090	24,900	8,590	31,700	2,252,374	19,800	27,100	6,710	10,000	71,400	10,400	644,000

[1] Preliminary.   [2] Estimate.   [3] Zinc content.   *Source: U.S. Geological Survey (USGS)*

Mine Production of Recoverable Zinc in the United States   In Thousands of Metric Tons

Year	Jan.	Feb.	Mar.	Apr.	May	June	July	Aug.	Sept.	Oct.	Nov.	Dec.	Total
2006	58.1	51.4	61.5	54.2	54.3	59.8	64.7	62.3	65.8	65.1	51.5	47.4	699.0
2007	60.3	55.8	63.5	56.6	61.2	64.1	63.1	69.5	61.3	64.6	53.9	69.6	769.0
2008	72.4	67.3	72.1	65.6	68.7	72.5	72.4	61.6	58.7	52.2	52.8	64.7	748.0
2009	69.3	54.0	55.2	58.4	56.1	58.6	57.0	62.1	60.5	65.2	49.9	62.1	710.0
2010	59.4	56.5	63.5	61.6	62.6	57.4	64.8	60.3	60.0	66.0	50.0	63.2	723.0
2011	69.5	54.9	62.1	59.3	66.2	57.9	70.0	63.6	60.0	55.4	58.5	67.8	743.0
2012	58.0	57.5	58.4	60.4	60.2	54.7	58.4	56.8	60.2	55.8	65.1	68.2	713.0
2013	64.1	54.5	56.0	63.2	65.8	61.3	61.7	67.2	66.7	68.0	68.8	68.7	761.0
2014	67.9	67.8	70.6	69.5	63.3	61.2	64.6	65.6	66.4	63.2	71.3	75.0	803.0
2015[1]	67.3	63.6	72.4	68.5	74.5	70.4	62.5	65.9	58.4	58.9	60.5		788.6

[1] Preliminary.   *Source: U.S. Geological Survey (USGS)*

ZINC

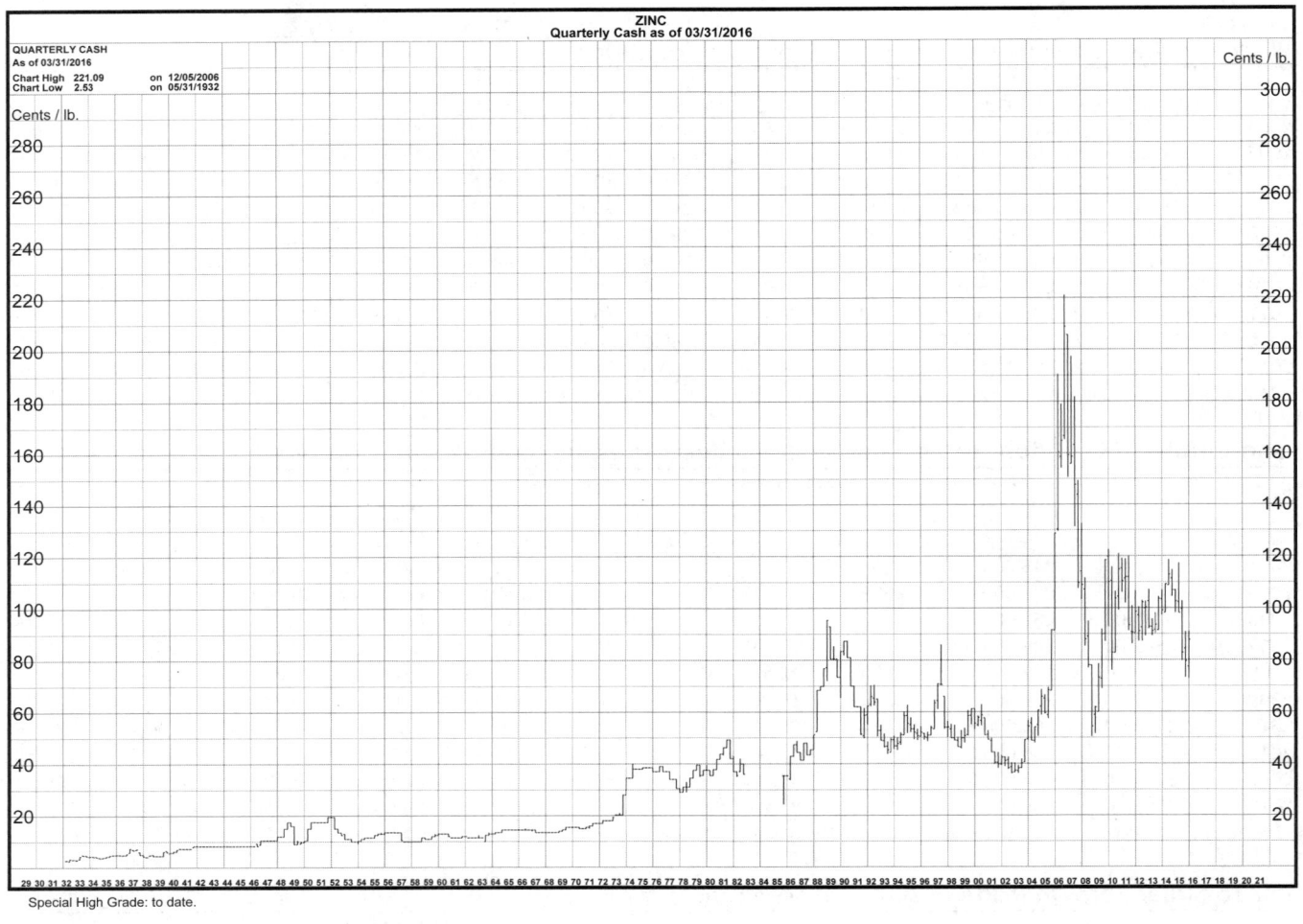

ZINC
Quarterly Cash as of 03/31/2016

QUARTERLY CASH
As of 03/31/2016
Chart High 221.09 on 12/05/2006
Chart Low 2.53 on 05/31/1932

Special High Grade: to date.

Average Price of Zinc, Prime Western Slab (Delivered U.S. Basis)   In Cents Per Pound

Year	Jan.	Feb.	Mar.	Apr.	May	June	July	Aug.	Sept.	Oct.	Nov.	Dec.	Average
2006	100.02	106.57	116.10	147.28	170.57	158.11	163.89	164.23	166.56	185.80	210.32	211.82	158.44
2007	183.91	161.21	158.81	171.08	184.68	173.23	169.81	155.93	139.28	140.84	122.63	112.65	156.17
2008	111.49	115.37	117.27	107.07	102.59	89.16	87.44	81.53	81.83	62.25	55.26	53.22	88.71
2009	57.28	53.96	57.96	65.19	69.91	73.34	74.38	85.30	88.25	97.11	102.32	109.97	77.91
2010	113.30	100.72	106.15	110.33	93.02	83.34	88.25	97.11	102.16	112.55	109.67	108.04	102.05
2011	112.47	116.61	111.76	112.83	104.86	108.12	115.41	107.26	101.03	91.28	94.18	94.73	105.88
2012	97.62	101.31	99.99	98.01	95.19	91.62	91.32	89.77	98.67	94.43	94.32	100.33	96.05
2013	100.21	104.53	95.62	92.04	91.25	91.88	92.18	95.47	93.11	93.86	93.40	98.17	95.14
2014	101.35	101.41	100.58	101.54	102.75	105.78	113.91	114.56	112.82	112.02	111.17	107.09	107.08
2015	104.08	103.48	100.33	108.09	112.42	102.59	98.49	89.77	85.54	86.07	79.26	76.02	95.51

Source: American Metal Market (AMM)

Consumption of Refined Zinc in the United States   In Thousands of Metric Tons

Year	Jan.	Feb.	Mar.	Apr.	May	June	July	Aug.	Sept.	Oct.	Nov.	Dec.	Total
2006	92.7	74.7	93.2	85.1	89.2	95.7	95.8	93.0	117.0	117.0	83.7	74.8	1,150.0
2007	95.9	78.8	84.4	74.3	76.7	80.2	70.8	84.5	89.8	103.0	78.4	82.8	1,050.0
2008	78.2	88.0	90.4	85.6	83.6	85.2	93.8	77.0	87.1	74.0	76.2	82.6	1,000.0
2009	78.9	69.6	85.5	67.2	78.6	70.8	80.0	72.6	76.9	68.7	75.5	80.0	891.0
2010	79.1	72.7	84.3	76.1	76.5	71.9	66.9	98.5	66.7	73.2	75.8	76.0	919.0
2011	76.3	67.1	83.2	72.1	67.4	87.2	61.8	74.2	73.4	95.0	69.0	87.2	939.0
2012	73.1	71.4	72.9	77.0	77.4	85.2	71.7	74.6	71.7	77.1	71.5	78.6	904.0
2013	77.6	77.1	77.3	98.4	78.9	76.7	75.2	138.0	85.1	78.9	68.5	80.7	934.0
2014	106.0	62.4	69.2	86.7	116.0	69.3	70.6	92.3	72.2	62.4	79.3	79.2	965.0
2015[1]	73.2	60.9	73.8	73.9	116.0	92.5	66.2	98.2	69.5	66.3	69.8		938.5

[1] Preliminary.   *Source: U.S. Geological Survey (USGS)*